Lecture Notes in Computer Science 6426

Commenced Publication in 1973
Founding and Former Series Editors:
Gerhard Goos, Juris Hartmanis, and Jan van Leeuwen

Robert Meersman Tharam Dillon
Pilar Herrero (Eds.)

On the Move to Meaningful Internet Systems: OTM 2010

Confederated International Conferences:
CoopIS, IS, DOA and ODBASE
Hersonissos, Crete, Greece, October 25-29, 2010
Proceedings, Part I

Springer

Volume Editors

Robert Meersman
Vrije Universiteit Brussel (VUB), STAR Lab
Bldg G/10, Pleinlaan 2, 1050 Brussel, Belgium
E-mail: meersman@vub.ac.be

Tharam Dillon
Curtin University, Digital Ecosystems and Business Intelligence
Institute (DEBII), EU4, De Laeter Way, Bentley, 6102 Australia
E-mail: t.dillon@curtin.edu.au

Pilar Herrero
Universidad Politécnica de Madrid, Facultad de Informática
Campus de Montegancedo S/N
28660 Boadilla del Monte, Madrid, Spain
E-mail: pherrero@fi.upm.es

Library of Congress Control Number: 2010938246

CR Subject Classification (1998): C.2, D.2, H.4, I.2, H.3, K.6.5

LNCS Sublibrary: SL 3 – Information Systems and Application, incl. Internet/Web and HCI

ISSN 0302-9743
ISBN-10 3-642-16933-3 Springer Berlin Heidelberg New York
ISBN-13 978-3-642-16933-5 Springer Berlin Heidelberg New York

springer.com

Printed in Germany

Typesetting: Camera-ready by author, data conversion by Scientific Publishing Services, Chennai, India
Printed on acid-free paper 06/3180

General Co-chairs' Message for OnTheMove 2010

The OnTheMove 2010 event in Hersonissos, Crete, during October 24–29, further consolidated the growth of the conference series that was started in Irvine, California, in 2002, and held in Catania, Sicily, in 2003, in Cyprus in 2004 and 2005, in Montpellier in 2006, in Vilamoura in 2007 and 2009, and in Monterrey, Mexico, in 2008. The event continues to attract a diversified and representative selection of today's worldwide research on the scientific concepts underlying new computing paradigms, which, of necessity, must be distributed, heterogeneous and autonomous yet meaningfully collaborative. Indeed, as such large, complex and networked intelligent information systems become the focus and norm for computing, there continues to be an acute and ever increasing need to address and discuss face to face in an integrated forum the implied software, system and enterprise issues as well as methodological, semantic, theoretical and application issues. As we all realize, e-mail, the Internet and even video conferences are not by themselves sufficient for effective and efficient scientific exchange.

The OnTheMove (OTM) Federated Conferences series has been created to cover the scientific exchange needs of the community/ies that work in the broad yet closely connected fundamental technological spectrum of Web-based distributed computing. The OTM program every year covers data and Web semantics, distributed objects, Web services, databases, information systems, enterprise workflow and collaboration, ubiquity, interoperability, mobility, grid and high-performance computing.

OTM does not consider itself a so-called multi-conference but instead is proud to give meaning to the "federated" aspect in its full title: it aspires to be a primary scientific meeting place where all aspects of research and development of Internet- and intranet-based systems in organizations and for e-business are discussed in a scientifically motivated way, in a forum of (loosely) interconnected workshops and conferences. This ninth edition of the OTM Federated Conferences event therefore once more provided an opportunity for researchers and practitioners to understand and publish these developments within their individual as well as within their broader contexts. To further promote synergy and coherence, the main conferences of OTM 2010 were conceived against a background of three interlocking global themes, namely, "Cloud Computing Infrastructures," "The Internet of Things, or Cyberphysical Systems," "(Semantic) Web 2.0 and Social Computing for the Enterprise."

Originally the federative structure of OTM was formed by the co-location of three related, complementary and successful main conference series: DOA (Distributed Objects and Applications, since 1999), covering the relevant infrastructure-enabling technologies, ODBASE (Ontologies, DataBases and Applications of SEmantics, since 2002), covering Web semantics, XML databases and ontologies, and CoopIS (Cooperative Information Systems, since 1993), covering the application of these technologies in an enterprise context through, for example, workflow systems and knowledge management. In 2007 the IS workshop (Information Security) was added to try cover also the specific issues of security in complex Internet-based information systems. Each of the main conferences specifically seeks high-quality contributions and encourages researchers to treat their respective topics within a framework that incorporates jointly (a) theory, (b) conceptual design and development, and (c) applications, in particular case studies and industrial solutions.

Following and expanding the model created in 2003, we again solicited and selected quality workshop proposals to complement the more "archival" nature of the main conferences with research results in a number of selected and more "avant-garde" areas related to the general topic of Web-based distributed computing. For instance, the so-called Semantic Web has given rise to several novel research areas combining linguistics, information systems technology and artificial intelligence, such as the modeling of (legal) regulatory systems and the ubiquitous nature of their usage. We were glad to see that seven of our successful earlier workshops (ADI, EI2N, SWWS, ORM, OnToContent, MONET, ISDE) re-appeared in 2010 with, in some cases, a fourth or even fifth edition, often in alliance with other older or newly emerging workshops, and that no fewer than four brand-new independent workshops could be selected from proposals and hosted: AVYTAT, DATAVIEW, P2PCDVE, SeDeS. Our OTM registration format ("one workshop buys all") actively intends to stimulate workshop audiences to productively mingle with each other and, optionally, with those of the main conferences.

We were also most happy to see that once more in 2010 the number of quality submissions for the OnTheMove Academy (OTMA, formerly called Doctoral Consortium Workshop), our "vision for the future" in research in the areas covered by OTM, took off again and with increasing success. We must thank the team of collaborators led by Peter Spyns and Anja Schanzenberger, and of course the OTMA Dean, Erich Neuhold, for their continued commitment and efforts in implementing our unique interactive formula to bring PhD students together. In OTMA, research proposals are submitted for evaluation; selected submissions and their approaches are (eventually) presented by the students in front of a wider audience at the conference, and are intended to be independently and are extensively analyzed and discussed in public by a panel of senior professors.

As said, all four main conferences and the associated workshops shared the distributed aspects of modern computing systems, and the resulting application pull created by the Internet and the so-called Semantic Web. For DOA 2010, the primary emphasis stayed on the distributed object infrastructure; for ODBASE 2010, it became the knowledge bases and methods required for enabling the use of formal semantics; for CoopIS 2010, the focus as usual was on the interaction of such technologies and methods with management issues, such as occur in networked organizations, and for IS 2010 the emphasis was on information security in the networked society. These subject areas overlap in a scientifically natural fashion and many submissions in fact also treated an envisaged mutual impact among them. As for the earlier editions, the organizers wanted to stimulate this cross-pollination by a "shared" program of famous keynote speakers around the chosen themes: we were quite proud to announce Wil van der Aalst, T.U. Eindhoven, The Netherlands, Beng Chin Ooi, National University of Singapore, Michael Brodie, Chief Scientist, Verizon, USA, and Michael Sobolewski, Polish-Japanese Institute of IT, Poland.

We received a total of 223 submissions for the four main conferences and 127 submissions in total for the workshops. The numbers are about 5% lower than for 2009. Not only may we indeed again claim success in attracting an increasingly representative volume of scientific papers, many from the USA and Asia, but these numbers of course allow the Program Committees to compose a high-quality cross-section of current research in the areas covered by OTM. In fact, the Program Chairs of the CoopIS 2010 conferences decided to accept only approximately one paper from every five submissions, while ODBASE 2010 and DOA 2010 accepted about the same number of papers for presentation and publication as in 2008 and 2009 (i.e., average one paper out of three to four submitted, not counting posters). For the workshops and IS 2010 the acceptance rate varied but the aim was to stay consistently at about one accepted paper for two to three submitted, and subordinated of course to scientific quality assessment. As usual we have separated the proceedings into three volumes with their own titles, two for the main conferences and one for the workshops, and we are most grateful to the Springer LNCS team in Heidelberg for their professional suggestions and meticulous collaboration in producing the files for downloading on the USB sticks.

The reviewing process by the respective Program Committees was again performed very professionally, and each paper in the main conferences was reviewed by at least three referees, with arbitrated e-mail discussions in the case of strongly diverging evaluations. It may be worthwhile to emphasize that it is an explicit OTM policy that all conference Program Committees and Chairs make their selections completely autonomously from the OTM organization itself. Like last year, paper proceedings were on separate request and order this year, and incurred an extra charge.

The General Chairs are once more especially grateful to the many people directly or indirectly involved in the set-up of these federated conferences. Few people realize what a large number of individuals have to be involved, and what a huge amount of work, and in 2010 certainly also financial risk, the organization of an event like OTM entails. Apart from the persons in their roles mentioned above, we therefore wish to thank in particular our eight main conference PC Co-chairs: CoopIS 2010: Herve Panetto, Jorge Cardoso, M. Brian Blake; ODBASE 2010: Alejandro Buchmann, Panos Chrysanthis, York Sure; DOA 2010: Ernesto Damiani, Kai Hwang. And similarly the 2010 IS, OTMA and Workshops PC (Co-)chairs: Javier Cámara, Carlos E. Cuesta, Howard Foster, Miguel Angel Pérez-Toledano, Stefan Jablonski, Olivier Curé, David Thau, Sara Comai, Moira Norrie, Alessandro Bozzon, Giuseppe Berio, Qing Li, Kemafor Anyanwu,

Hervé Panetto (again), Alok Mishra, Jürgen Münch, Deepti Mishra, Patrizia Grifoni, Fernando Ferri, Irina Kondratova, Arianna D'Ulizia, Paolo Ceravolo, Majed Ayyad, Terry Halpin, Herman Balsters, Laura Ricci, Yan Tang, Jan Vanthienen, Yannis Charalabidis, Ernesto Damiani (again), Elizabeth Chang, Gritzalis Stefanos, Giles Hogben, Peter Spyns, Erich J. Neuhold and Anja Schanzenberger. Most of them, together with their many PC members, performed a superb and professional job in selecting the best papers from the harvest of submissions. We are all grateful to our supremely competent and experienced Conference Secretariat and technical support staff in Antwerp, Daniel Meersman, Ana-Cecilia, and Jan Demey, and last but certainly not least to our editorial team in Perth (DEBII-Curtin University) chaired by Houwayda El Fawal Mansour. The General Co-chairs acknowledge with gratitude the academic freedom, logistic support and facilities they enjoy from their respective institutions, Vrije Universiteit Brussel (VUB), Curtin University, Perth, Australia, and Universitad Politécnica de Madrid (UPM), without which such an enterprise would not be feasible. We do hope that the results of this federated scientific enterprise contribute to your research and your place in the scientific network... We look forward to seeing you again at next year's event!

August 2010

Robert Meersman
Tharam Dillon
Pilar Herrero

Organization

OTM (On The Move) is a federated event involving a series of major international conferences and workshops. These proceedings contain the papers presented at the OTM 2010 Federated conferences, consisting of four conferences, namely, CoopIS 2010 (Cooperative Information Systems), IS 2010 (Information Security), DOA 2010 (Distributed Objects and Applications) and ODBASE 2010 (Ontologies, Databases and Applications of Semantics).

Executive Commitee

General Co-chairs

Robert Meersman	VU Brussels, Belgium
Tharam Dillon	Curtin University of Technology, Australia
Pilar Herrero	Universidad Politécnica de Madrid, Spain

CoopIS 2010 PC Co-chairs

Hervé Panetto	Nancy University, France
Jorge Cardoso	Universidade de Coimbra, Portugal
Brian Blake	University of Notre Dame, USA

IS 2010 PC Co-chairs

Giles Hogben	European Network and Information Security Agency, Greece
Stefanos Gritzalis	University of the Aegean, Greece

DOA 2010 PC Co-chairs

Ernesto Damiani	Università degli Studi di Milano, Italy
Kai Hwang	University of Southern California, USA

ODBASE 2010 PC Co-chairs

Alejandro Buchmann	Technische Universität Darmstadt, Germany
Panos Chrysanthis	University of Pittsburgh, USA
York Sure	GESIS, Germany

Publication Chair

Houwayda Elfawal Mansour	DEBII, Australia

Publicity-Sponsorship Chair

Ana-Cecilia Martinez Barbosa	DOA Institute, Belgium

Logistics Team

Daniel Meersman	Head of Operations
Ana-Cecilia Martinez Barbosa	
Jan Demey	

CoopIS 2010 Program Committee

Marco Aiello
Antonia Albani
Antonio Ruiz Cortés
Kemafor Anyanwu
Joonsoo Bae
Zohra Bellahsene
Salima Benbernou
M. Brian Blake
Nacer Boudjlida
Christoph Bussler
James Caverlee
Francisco Curbera
Vincenzo D'Andrea
Xiaoyong Du
Schahram Dustdar
Johann Eder
Rik Eshuis
Opher Etzion
Renato Fileto
Ted Goranson
Paul Grefen
Michael Grossniklaus
Amarnath Gupta
Mohand-Said Hacid
Geert-Jan Houben
Zhixing Huang
Stefan Jablonski
Paul Johannesson
Epaminondas Kapetanios
Dimka Karastoyanova
Rania Khalaf
Hiroyuki Kitagawa
Akhil Kumar
Frank Leymann
ZongWei Luo
Sanjay K. Madria
Tiziana Margaria
Leo Mark
Maristella Matera
Massimo Mecella
Ingo Melzer
Jan Mendling
John Miller
Arturo Molina
Jörg Müller
Nirmal Mukhi
Miyuki Nakano
Moira C. Norrie
Werner Nutt
Andreas Oberweis
Gerald Oster
Jin Woo Park
Cesare Pautasso
Barbara Pernici
Li Qing
Lakshmish Ramaswamy
Manfred Reichert
Stefanie Rinderle-Ma
Duncan Ruiz
Paulo Rupino
Kai-Uwe Sattler
Ralf Schenkel
Jialie Shen
Aameek Singh
Michael W. Sobolewski
Xiaoping Sun
Susan Urban
Willem-Jan Van den Heuvel
Irene Vanderfeesten
François B. Vernadat
Maria Esther Vidal
Mathias Weske
Jian Yang
Aoying Zhou

IS 2010 Program Committee

Alessandro Acquisti
Vijay Atluri
Daniele Catteddu
Bruno Crispo
Gwenael Doerr
Josep Domingo Ferrer
Simone Fischer-Huebner
Clemente Galdi
Janusz Gorski
Jiankun Hu
Hai Jin
Maria Karyda
Stefan Katzenbeisser
Spyros Kokolakis
Wei-Shinn Ku
Evangelos Markatos
Sjouke Mauw
Chris Mitchell
Yi Mu
Nuno Ferreira Neves
Siani Pearson
Milan Petkovic
Andreas Pfitzmann
Frank Piessens
Norbert Pohlmann
Rodrigo Roman
Pierangela Samarati
Biplab K. Sarker
Aggeliki Tsochou
Luis Javier Garcia Villalba
Roman Yampolskiy
Alec Yasinsac
Andre Zuquete

DOA 2010 Program Committee

Subbu Allamaraju
Mark Baker
Boualem Benatallah
Elisa Bertino
Lionel Brunie
Athman Bouguettaya
Judith Bishop
Gordon Blair
Harold Carr
Geoffrey Coulson
Schahram Dustdar
Frank Eliassen
Pascal Felber
Benoit Garbinato
Niels Gruschka
Medhi Jazayeri
Eric Jul
Nick Kavantzas
Deyi Li
Ling Liu
Joe Loyall
Frank Manola
Gero Mühl
Nikola Milanovic
Graham Morgan
Lionel Ni
Rui Oliveira
Francois Pacull
Arno Puder
Michel Riveill
Luis Rodrigues
George Spanoudakis
Joerg Schwenk
Cyrus Shahabi
Azzel Taleb-Bendiab
Gaogang Xie
Kokou Yentongon
Albert Zomaya

ODBASE 2010 Program Committee

Karl Aberer
Harith Alani
María Auxilio Medina
Sonia Bergamaschi
Leopoldo Bertossi
Alex Borgida
Christof Bornhoevd
Mohand Boughanem
Paolo Bouquet
Silvana Castano
Tiziana Catarci
Paolo Ceravolo
Catherine Chronaki
Oscar Corcho
Ernesto Damiani
Irini Fundulaki
Aldo Gangemi
Benjamin Habegger
Mounira Harzallah
Manfred Hauswirth
Bin He
Prateek Jain
Vana Kalogeraki
Uladzimir Kharkevich
Manolis Koubarakis
Werner Kuhn
Maurizio Lenzerini
Li Ma
Vincenzo Maltese
Riichiro Mizoguchi
Peter Mork
Anne Ngu
Olga Papaemmanouil
Adrian Paschke
Ilia Petrov
Peter R. Pietzuch
Evaggelia Pitoura
Demetris Plexousakis
Wenny Rahayu
Rajugan Rajagopalapillai
Satya Sahoo
Pavel Shvaiko
Sergej Sizov
Veda C. Storey
Umberto Straccia
Heiner Stuckenschmidt
York Sure
Robert Tolksdorf
Susan Urban
Guido Vetere
Kevin Wilkinson
Baoshi Yan
Benjamin Zapilko
Demetris Zeinalipour

Supporting and Sponsoring Institutions

OTM 2010 was proudly supported or sponsored by Vrije Universiteit Brussel in Belgium, Curtin University of Technology in Australia, Universidad Politecnica de Madrid in Spain, Object Management Group, and Collibra.

Table of Contents – Part I

On the Move 2010 Keynotes

Cooperative Information Systems (CoopIS) International Conference 2010

Coopis Keynote Paper

Process Models and Management

Modeling of Cooperation

Services Computing

Information Processing and Management

Human-Based Cooperative Systems

Ontology and Workflow Challenges

International Symposium on Information Security (IS) International Conference 2010

Access Control, Authentication and Policies

Secure Architectures

Cryptography

Table of Contents – Part II

On the Move 2010 Keynotes

Distributed Objects and Applications (DOA) International Conference 2010

Data Storage and Processing

Transaction and Event Management

Virtualization Performance, Risk and Scalability

Cloud and Distributed System Security

Ontologies, DataBases, and Applications of Semantics (ODBASE) International Conference 2010

Invited Talks

Annotations

Inconsistencies

Reactivity and Semantic Data

Ontology Mapping and Semantic Similarity

Domain Specific Ontologies

OTM'10 Keynote

Beng Chin Ooi

National University of Singapore (NUS)

Short Bio

Beng Chin is Professor of Computer Science at School of Computing, at the National University of Singapore (NUS). He obtained his BSc (1st Class Honors) and PhD from Monash University, Australia, in 1985 and 1989 respectively. His research interests include database performance issues, indexing techniques, multimedia and spatio-temporal databases, P2P systems and advanced applications, and cloud computing. His current system projects include BestPeer, P2P based data management system, and epiC, a data-intensive cloud computing platform.

He has served as a PC member for international conferences including ACM SIGMOD, VLDB, IEEE ICDE, WWW, SIGKDD and Vice PC Chair for ICDE'00, 04,06, co-PC Chair for SSD'93 and DASFAA'05, PC Chair for ACM SIGMOD'07, and Core DB track PC chair for VLDB'08. He is the Editor-in-Chief of IEEE Transactions on Knowledge and Data Engineering (TKDE), and a trustee member of VLDB Endowment Board. He is the recipient of ACM SIGMOD 2009 Contributions award.

Talk

"Supporting OLTP and OLAP Queries on Cloud Platforms"

MapReduce-based systems have been widely used for large-scale data analysis. Although these systems achieve storage-system independence, high scalability, and fine-grained fault tolerance, their performance have been shown to be unsatisfactory.It has also been shown that MapReduce-based systems are significantly slower than Parallel Database systems in performing a variety of analytic tasks. Some attribute the performance gap between MapReduce-based and Parallel Database systems to architectural design. This speculation yields an interesting question: Must a system sacrifice performance to achieve flexibility and scalability? Consequently, we conducted an in-depth performance study of MapReduce in its open source implementation, Hadoop. We identified various factors that have significant performance effect on the system. Subsequently, based on what we have learned, we propose a new architectural design as an attempt to support both OLTP and OLAP queries on Cloud platforms. I shall describe some of our ongoing work in this talk.

R. Meersman et al. (Eds.): OTM 2010, Part I, LNCS 6426, p. 1, 2010.

OTM'10 Keynote

Michael Brodie

Chief Scientist, Verizon, USA

Short Bio

Dr Michael Brodie is Chief Scientist of Verizon Services Operations in Verizon Communications, one of the world's leading providers of communications services. Dr Brodie works on large-scale strategic Information Technology opportunities and challenges to deliver business value from advanced and emerging technologies and practices. He is concerned with the Big Picture, core technologies and integration within a large scale, operational telecommunications environment.

Dr Brodie holds a PhD in Databases from the University of Toronto and has active interests in the Semantic Web, SOA, and other advanced technologies to address secure, interoperable web-scale information systems, databases, infrastructure and application architectures. Dr Brodie has authored over 150 books, chapters and articles and has presented over 100 keynotes or invited lectures in over 30 countries.

Dr Brodie is a member of the USA National Academies Committee on Technical and Privacy Dimensions of Information for Terrorism Prevention and other National Goals. He is an Adjunct Professor, National University of Ireland, Galway (2006-present) and Visiting Professor, Curtin University of Technology, Perth, Australia (2009). He chairs three Advisory Boards Semantic Technology Institutes International, Vienna, Austria (January 2007 present); Digital Enterprise Research Institute, National University of Ireland (2003-present); Semantic Technology Institute, Innsbrck, Austria (2003-present); and is a member of several advisory boards - The European Research Consortium for Informatics and Mathematics (2007 present); School of Computer and Communication Sciences, cole Polytechnique Fdrale de Lausanne, Switzerland (2001 present); European Unions Information Society Technologies 5th, 6th and 7th Framework Programmes (2003-present); several European and Asian research projects; editorial board of several research journals; past Board member of research foundations including the VLDB Endowment (Very Large Data Bases, 1992 - 2004), and of the Advisory Board of Forrester Research, Inc. (2006-2008). He is on the Advisory Board of Chamberlain Studios (2006-present).

Talk

"Over The Moon: Data Integration's Essential Challenges"

R. Meersman et al. (Eds.): OTM 2010, Part I, LNCS 6426, pp. 2–3, 2010.

To understand and communicate reality, man simplifies his perception of reality by creating models that are necessarily simpler than reality. For an Information System and its supporting databases to fulfill their requirements, the databases are modeled by radical simplification of reality by identifying those aspects of reality that are essential to the intended perception, i.e., those that are relevant to the requirements, and eliminating all other aspects; and representing the essential properties of those aspects in terms that meet the requirements within the perceptual and modelling limits of the human modeler.

Data modelling involves human designers using a database design methodology together with data modelling tools, e.g., Entity-Relational (ER) and Relational, based on data models, e.g., ER and Relational, and implemented using a relational DBMS. To be more precise, data modelling is an integral component with Information Systems design and development that involves additional methodologies, models, e.g., workflow, and implementation information, e.g., workflow engines, application servers, and web servers. The design, development, and operation of an Information Systems and its databases in dependent on all of the methodologies, models, and tools. For simplicity, we limit this discussion to the design, development, and operation of databases; even though the requirements, loosely referred as the semantics, of the intended perception can be represented anywhere in the Information System - in the databases, the processes, or the application code.

Just as two or more human perceptions of the same or overlapping aspects of reality are unlikely to be identical, so are two or more databases representing overlapping aspects of reality unlikely to be identical. Different databases are designed and developed at different times, to meet different requirements, by different people with different understandings of reality, using different tools, and different methodologies. Hence, two or more different perceptions or databases are typically distinct and are relatively incomplete, inconsistent, and potentially conflicting.

Over time, business, legal, and other requirements have led to the need to represent the real world more precisely in Information Systems. Large-scale integration beyond the scale of most applications necessarily brings in real requirements that prevent the application of simplifying assumptions normally used to solve theses problems (as lower scale). It is likely that as modelling requirements become increasingly complex and as scale of integration grows, this complexity will arise for future Information Ecosystems and the conventional techniques will no longer work.

COOPIS'10 Keynote

Wil van der Aalst

Eindhoven University of Technology, The Netherlands

Short Bio

Prof. Dr. Wil van der Aalst is a full professor of Information Systems at the Technische Universiteit Eindhoven (TU/e. Currently he is also an adjunct professor at Queensland University of Technology (QUT) working within the BPM group there. His research interests include workflow management, process mining, Petri nets, business process management, process modeling, and process analysis. Wil van der Aalst has published more than 115 journal papers, 15 books (as author or editor), 230 refereed conference/workshop publications, and 40 book chapters. Many of his papers are highly cited (he has an H-index of more than 70 according to Google Scholar, making him the Dutch computer scientist with the highest H-index) and his ideas have influenced researchers, software developers, and standardization committees working on process support. He has been a co-chair of many conferences including the Business Process Management conference, the International Conference on Cooperative Information Systems, the International conference on the Application and Theory of Petri Nets, and the IEEE International Conference on Services Computing. He is also editor/member of the editorial board of several journals, including the Distributed and Parallel Databases, the International Journal of Business Process Integration and Management, the International Journal on Enterprise Modelling and Information Systems Architectures, Computers in Industry, Business and Information Systems Engineering, IEEE Transactions on Services Computing, Lecture Notes in Business Information Processing, and Transactions on Petri Nets and Other Models of Concurrency. He is also a member of the Royal Holland Society of Sciences and Humanities (Koninklijke Hollandsche Maatschappij der Wetenschappen).

Talk

"Configurable Services in the Cloud: Supporting Variability While Enabling Cross-Organizational Process Mining"

The Software as a Service (SaaS) paradigm is particularly interesting for situations where many organizations need to support similar processes. For example, municipalities, courts, rental agencies, etc. support highly similar processes. However, despite these similarities, there is also the need to allow for local variations in a controlled manner. Therefore, cloud infrastructures should provide

R. Meersman et al. (Eds.): OTM 2010, Part I, LNCS 6426, pp. 4–5, 2010.

configurable services such that products and processes can be customized while sharing commonalities. Configurable and executable process models are essential to realize such infrastructures. This will finally transform reference models from "paper tigers" (reference modeling a la SAP, ARIS, etc.) into an "executable reality". Moreover, "configurable services in the cloud" enable cross-organizational process mining. This way, organizations can learn from each other and improve their processes.

COOPIS'10 - PC Co-chairs Message

Welcome to the 18th International Conference on Cooperative Information Systems (CoopIS 2010). This year CoopIS was held in Crete, Greece, during October 27-29, 2010.

Cooperative Information Systems (CIS) provide enterprises and communities of users with flexible, scalable and intelligent services in large-scale networking environments. Building a scalable cooperative information system requires technical breakthroughs to overcome tough challenges that traditional rigid distributed systems did not face. The new grand challenge in the modern enterprise is now dealing with assessing and benchmarking the realistic benefits of social- and community-based collaborative computing against the traditional integrated approaches. The CIS paradigm has traditionally encompassed distributed systems technologies such as middleware, business process management (BPM) and Web technologies. In recent years, several innovative technologies are emerging: SaaS, cloud computing, Internet of Service, Internet of Things, Service Oriented Computing, mash-ups, Web Services, Semantic Web and Knowledge Grid. These new technologies enable us to consider more aggressive solutions for building scalable cooperative information systems. The CoopIS conference series has established itself as a major international forum for exchanging ideas and results on scientific research for practitioners in fields such as computer supported cooperative work (CSCW), middleware, Internet/Web data management, electronic commerce, workflow management, knowledge flow, agent technologies, and software architectures, to name a few. In addition, the 2010 edition of CoopIS aims to highlight the impact of social and community networks, cloud computing, semantic computing and the future internet enterprise systems collaborative issues for collaborative information systems. We are very pleased to share the proceedings comprising the exciting technical program with you. This year's conference included eight full-paper research sessions, three short-paper research sessions, and one industry panel. The industry panel entitled Cooperative Information Systems for Highly Configurable Infrastructures will feature 3 industry-oriented speakers. The program covered a broad range of topics in the areas of design and development of cooperative information systems: business process technologies, process modelling and management, services computing, information processing and management, workflow, ontology, and business applications. We were very pleased to have Wil van der Aalst keynote speaker that has given a talk with the title "Configurable Services in the Cloud: Supporting variability while enabling cross-organizational process mining". This high-quality program would not have been possible without the authors who chose CoopIS as a venue to submit their publications to, and the Program Committee members who dedicated their efforts and time to the review and the online PC meeting discussions. We received about 143 submissions from 30 countries and 5 continents. Every paper received

R. Meersman et al. (Eds.): OTM 2010, Part I, LNCS 6426, pp. 6–7, 2010.

at least three independent reviews. Through a careful two-phase review process, consisting of PC members' independent reviews and online PC meeting discussions, 28 full papers and 11 short papers were selected and included in this year's technical program. We are grateful for the dedication and excellent job of the CoopIS 2010 PC members, who are experts in the field. We would also like to thank the General Chairs of OTM, Robert Meersman, Tharam Dillon and Pilar Herrero, for their constant support. They provided leadership, organization and infrastructure for the consolidated conferences and workshops. CoopIS benefits greatly from the larger mature structure of OTM. We would like to take this opening to express our sincere thanks to Daniel Meersman for his hard work, passion, and almost constant availability. Daniel was critical in customizing the paper management systems to our needs and making sure that the review process stayed on track. Our thanks also go to the OTM support team Ana-Cecilia Martinez Barbosa and Jan Demey who worked behind the scenes performing the many tasks that move things along. The Publication chair, Houwayda Elfawal Mansour, has our appreciation for her efforts on having all the material publish on time. Our deepest thanks go to the members of the PC, who worked tight deadlines, providing the technical guidance that can be clearly seen in the quality of the papers. And finally, we wish to thank the authors. We hope that all participants will enjoy this program and find it worthwhile. Your work is appreciated.

August 2010

Hervé Panetto
Jorge Cardoso
Brian Blake
COOPIS'10

Configurable Services in the Cloud: Supporting Variability While Enabling Cross-Organizational Process Mining

Wil M.P. van der Aalst

Eindhoven University of Technology, The Netherlands
w.m.p.v.d.aalst@tue.nl

Abstract. The *Software as a Service* (SaaS) paradigm is particularly interesting in situations where many organizations need to support similar processes. For example, municipalities, courts, rental agencies, etc. all need to support highly similar processes. However, despite these similarities, there is also the need to allow for local variations in a controlled manner. Therefore, cloud infrastructures should provide configurable services such that products and processes can be customized while sharing commonalities. Configurable and executable process models are essential for realizing such infrastructures. This will finally transform reference models from "paper tigers" (reference modeling à la SAP, ARIS, etc.) into an "executable reality". Moreover, "configurable services in the cloud" enable *cross-organizational process mining*. This way, organizations can learn from each other and improve their processes.

Keywords: Configurable process models, Process Mining, Business Process Management, YAWL, ProM.

1 Motivation

Cloud computing is not a new idea. In 1961, in a speech given to celebrate MIT's centennial, John McCarthy stated "If computers of the kind I have advocated become the computers of the future, then computing may someday be organized as a public utility just as the telephone system is a public utility. The computer utility could become the basis of a new and important industry." In 1961, even ARPANET, the predecessor Internet, did not exist and it is remarkable that people like John McCarthy, who received the Turing Award in 1971 for his work on AI, could predict that computing would become a utility as is signified today by Gmail, Google Apps. Salesforce.com, Amazon EC2/S3, etc. *Cloud computing* is typically defined as Internet-based computing, whereby shared resources, software, and information are provided on demand, like the electricity grid. The term is closely related to the notion of *Software as a Service* (SaaS). SaaS refers to a software distribution model in which applications are hosted by a vendor or service provider and made available to customers over a network, typically the Internet. The terms SaaS and cloud computing are strongly related. People talking about cloud computing tend to emphasize the computing infrastructure and

R. Meersman et al. (Eds.): OTM 2010, Part I, LNCS 6426, pp. 8–25, 2010.

combine this with a broad vision on computing as a utility. The term SaaS tends to emphasize the role of services that are provided and consumed. SaaS service providers typically offer a subscription model where service consumers do not pay for software but only pay for the actual use of software. A well-known example of a SaaS provider that is using a cloud infrastructure is SalesForce.com. This company allows organizations to outsource the IT support of standard functionality such as sales, customer relationship management, etc. without worrying about scalability and maintenance. Another example is the conference management system EasyChair that is currently probably the most commonly used system to host conferences and to manage the reviewing of scientific papers. To organize a conference, there is no need to install any software as everything is hosted and managed centrally.

Cloud computing and SaaS have in common that multiple organizations, often called *tenants*, are sharing the same infrastructure/software. This provides many advantages: lower costs (only pay for actual use), reduced setup times, reduced maintenance and management efforts, etc. However, it also creates the *challenge of dealing with variability across organizations*. It is not realistic to enforce "one size fits all" as tenants may have different needs and preferences. In this paper, we focus on the process perspective and suggest using so-called *configurable process models* to support variability [1,3,14,15,16,17,23,24]. The basic idea of configurable process models is that one model does not represent a single process, but a family of processes. By configuring a configurable process model one obtains a concrete process model that can be executed within an organization. Configurability is essential for the success of SaaS software. Ideally, tenants are provided with a multitude of options and variations using a single code base, such that it is possible for each tenant to have a unique software configuration. Related to variability, there are other concerns raised by multi-tenancy. For example, how to ensure correctness of all possible configurations? It is not sufficient to guarantee the correct operation of a single process. Instead one needs to ensure the correctness of a process family and all of its configurations. Another concern is security; How to make sure that data and processes of different tenants are isolated while using the same code base and infrastructure?

Besides these challenges, there are also many opportunities. Besides the obvious "economies of scale" achievable from consolidating IT resources, there is the possibility to carefully analyze software usage and process executions across different organizations. In the situation where customized enterprise information systems are running inside organizations, the software vendor has little insight into the actual use of its software. Moreover, it is impossible to analyze differences between organizations. In this paper, we suggest using *cross-organizational process mining* using multi-tenancy environments provided through SaaS and cloud computing. The goal of process mining is to use event data to extract process-related information, e.g., to automatically discover a process model by observing events recorded by some enterprise system [5,4,6,9,11,12,18,26]. Where data mining focuses on relatively simple tasks such as classification (e.g., decision trees), clustering, and regression that aim at analyzing *data*, process mining focuses

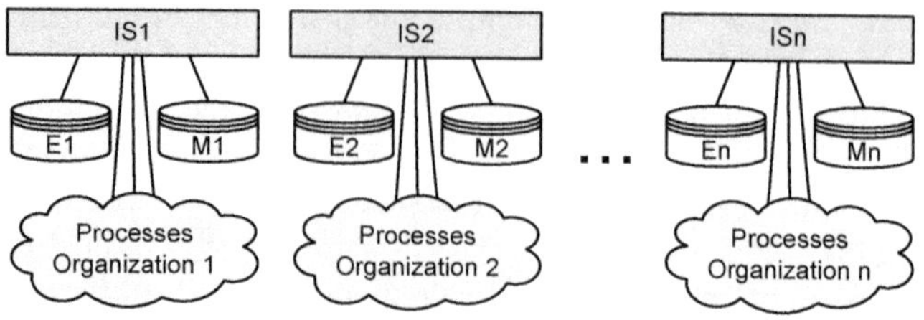

(a) Traditional situation with, per process, one model, and a dedicated system and database for each organization

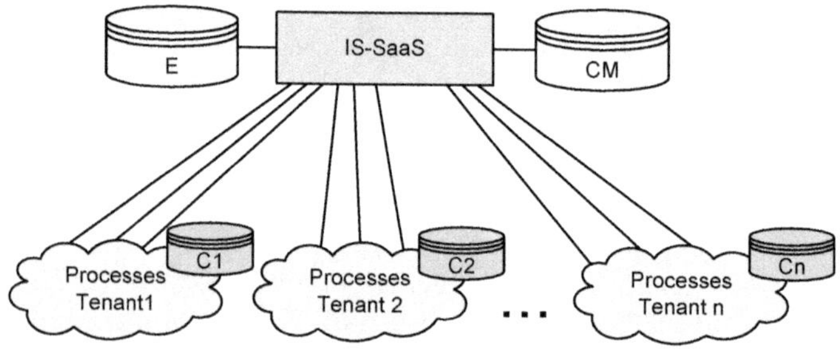

(b) New situation using SaaS technology based on configurable services

Fig. 1. The traditional situation where each organization has it's own IT infrastructure (a) and the situation where each organization is a tenant of a "shared configurable cloud" (b). (IS = Information System, M = Process Model, CM = Configurable Process Model, E = Event Log, and C = Configuration.)

on *operational processes*, i.e., identifying causal dependencies between activities, visualizing bottlenecks inside the discovered process, measuring conformance, detecting deviations, predicting cycle times, etc.

We will use Figure 1 to illustrate the above. Figure 1(a) shows the traditional situation where each organization uses its own infrastructure, process models ($M_1, M_2, \ldots M_n$), event logs ($E_1, E_2, \ldots E_n$), and information system ($IS_1, IS_2, \ldots IS_n$). Note that we assume that organizations are using a *Process-Aware Information System* (PAIS) [10], i.e., a system that is driven by some process model and that is recording events. Note that Workflow Management (WfM) systems, Business Process Management (BPM) systems, Enterprise Resource Planning (ERP) systems, Customer Relationship Management (CRM) systems, etc. are all examples of such systems. Some of these systems are driven by explicit graphical process models and record events in a structured manner, while others are supporting processes in a more implicit manner and some efforts are needed to extract event logs suitable for analysis. In any case, processes are being supported and it is possible to extract the information required for process mining. Each organization has complete freedom to change processes provided that they have the resources needed to re-configure or replace parts of the information system.

Figure 1(b) shows the situation where the n organizations have become tenants of a shared SaaS system. In this paper, we propose using *one configurable model* (CM) per service and each tenant uses a particular configuration for this service ($C_1, C_2, \ldots C_n$).[1] The configurable model needs to be able to support meaningful variations of the same process required by the different organizations. In the new situation events are recorded in a unified manner. This allows for comparing processes within different organizations. We have identified two possible use cases for *cross-organizational process mining.*

- The *service provider* can use the event logs of all tenants to *improve its services* and *provide guidance* to tenants when configuring their processes. Note that the focus can be on the software or on the processes supported by the software. For example, the service provider may note that there are situations where the system has poor response times or even fails. Using process mining it is possible to identify possible causes for such problems. Moreover, the usability of the system can be analyzed, e.g., measuring the time to complete a task or the number of retries. However, the service provider can also analyze differences in the processes supported by these systems, e.g., comparing flow times of different organizations. These can be used to give advice to individual organizations. Note that data privacy is an important factor. However, the service provider can do many types of analysis without looking into sensitive data, e.g., the identities of individual workers or customers are irrelevant for most analysis questions and no information about one tenant is shared with other tenants.
- Another use case is where multiple comparable *organizations wish to share information.* In this case, cross-organizational process mining is used to benchmark different organizations and differences in performance are analyzed. This is of course only possible in a non-competitive environment, e.g., different branches of some multinational organization, franchises, municipalities, courts, etc. The goal is to let organizations learn from each other and establish proven best practices. Of course privacy issues may again complicate such analysis, however, it may be sufficient to compare things at an aggregate level or to anonymize the results.

The goal of this paper is to discuss the opportunities and challenges provided by cloud computing and SaaS. In particular, we focus on the need for process configuration and the opportunities provided by cross-organizational process mining. This will be illustrated by a short description of the *CoSeLoG* (Configurable Services for Local Governments) project. Ten municipalities and two software organizations are involved in this project. The goal of CoSeLoG is to develop and analyze configurable services for local municipalities while using the SaaS paradigm, process configuration, and process mining.

[1] We assume that any service is characterized by an interface that describes the information exchanged. However, in this paper we focus on the process-related aspects of a service. Therefore, we will use the terms "service" and "process" interchangeably.

Before introducing the CoSeLoG project in Section 4, we first present our ideas related to process configuration in the cloud (Section 2) followed by an introduction to cross-organizational process mining (Section 3).

2 Turning "Paper Tigers" into an "Executable Reality"

In this section we focus on configurable process models in a SaaS setting. These enable service providers to support variability among different organizations in a structured manner.

2.1 The Need for Configurable Process Models

Although large organizations support their processes using a wide variety of Process-Aware Information Systems (PAISs) [10], the majority of business processes are still not directly driven by explicit process models. Despite the success of Business Process Management (BPM) thinking in organizations, Workflow Management (WfM) systems — today often referred to as *BPM systems* — are not widely used. One of the main problems of BPM technology is the "lack of content", that is, providing just a generic infrastructure to build process-aware information systems is insufficient as organizations need to support specific processes. Organizations want to have "out-of-the-box" support for standard processes and are only willing to design and develop system support for organization-specific processes. Yet most BPM systems expect users to model basic processes from scratch. Enterprise Resource Planning (ERP) systems such as SAP and Oracle, on the other hand, focus on the support of these common processes. Although all main ERP systems have workflow engines comparable to the engines of BPM systems, the majority of processes are not supported by software that is directly driven by process models. For example, most of SAP's functionality is not grounded in their workflow component, but hard-coded in application software. ERP vendors try to capture "best practices" in dedicated applications designed for a particular purpose. Such systems can be configured by setting parameters. System configuration can be a time consuming and complex process. Moreover, configuration parameters are exposed as "switches in the application software", thus making it difficult to see the intricate dependencies among certain settings.

A model-driven process-oriented approach toward supporting business processes has all kinds of benefits ranging from improved analysis possibilities (verification, simulation, etc.) and better insights, to maintainability and ability to rapidly develop organization-specific solutions. Although obvious, this approach has not been widely adopted thus far, probably because BPM vendors have failed to provide content and ERP vendors suffer from the "Law of the handicap of a head start". ERP vendors manage to effectively build data-centric solutions to support particular tasks. However, the complexity and large installed base of their products makes it impossible to refactor their software and make it truly process-centric.

Based on the limitations of existing BPM and ERP systems, we propose to use *configurable process models*. A configurable process model represents a *family of process models*, that is, a model that through configuration can be customized for a particular setting. Configuration is achieved by *hiding* (i. e., bypassing) or *blocking* (i. e., inhibiting) certain fragments of the configurable process model [14]. In this way, the desired behavior is selected. From the viewpoint of generic BPM software, configurable process models can be seen as a mechanism to add content to these systems. By developing comprehensive collections of configurable models, particular domains can be supported. From the viewpoint of ERP software, configurable process models can be seen as a means to make these systems more process-centric, although in the latter case quite some refactoring is needed as processes are hidden in table structures and application code.

Various configurable languages have been proposed as extensions of existing languages (e. g., C-EPCs [24], C-iEPCs, C-WF-nets [1], C-SAP, C-BPEL) but few are actually supported by enactment software (e. g., C-YAWL [16]). In this paper, we are interested in the latter class of languages, which, unlike traditional reference models [8,7,13], are executable after they have been configured. In this paper, we focus on configurable services offered over the Internet. Therefore, the models need to be executable to be of any use.

2.2 An Example: C-YAWL

As an example of a configurable language we briefly describe C-YAWL [16,17]. YAWL is a process modeling notation and workflow environment based on Petri nets but extended with powerful features for cancelation, OR-joins, etc. It has been developed with the aim to provide a notation with formal semantics that supports all desired workflow patterns [19]. The YAWL system is open-source and supports the execution and work distribution of workflows depicted in such models even in production environments. Thus, although originally developed as a proof of concept, the YAWL system can be used for practical applications [19].

Figure 2 depicts a simple YAWL model for the process executed by municipalities when a man registers that he will become the father of a not-yet-born child although he is not married to the mother [17]. In this model tasks are depicted as rectangles while circles represent conditions like the initial and final condition in this example. Conditions mark the states between tasks but can be omitted for simplicity (like in the example). Composite tasks enable the hierarchical specification of sub-processes while split and join types of tasks allow the specification of how the process should proceed in case a task splits or joins the process's control flow. For this, YAWL distinguishes an XOR-split (as in the example in Figure 2) allowing the triggering of only one of the subsequent paths, an AND-split requiring the triggering of all subsequent paths, and an OR-split requiring the triggering of at least one subsequent path but allowing also for path combinations. Similarly, a task with an XOR-join can be executed as soon as one of its incoming paths is triggered, an AND-join requires that all incoming arcs are triggered, and a task with an OR-join allows for the execution of the task as soon as no further incoming paths can potentially be triggered at any future point in time (see [19] for further details).

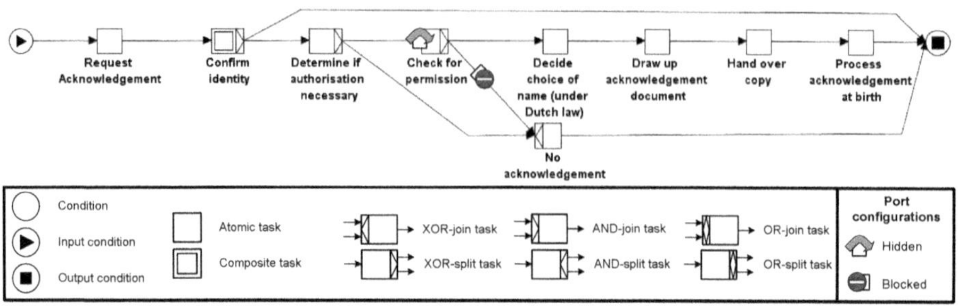

Fig. 2. A YAWL process model for acknowledging an unborn child [17]. The input port of *check permission* is configured as hidden and one output port is blocked.

This routing behavior can be restricted by *process configuration*. For this purpose, *input ports* are assigned to each task depicting how the task can be triggered and *output ports* are assigned to depict which paths can be triggered after the completion of the task. A task with an XOR-join can be triggered via each of its incoming paths. Thus, it has a dedicated input port for each of these paths. Tasks with AND-joins and OR-joins can only be executed if all paths (that can potentially be triggered) are triggered, i.e. there is only one way these tasks can be triggered and thus there is only one input port. A task with an XOR-split has an output port for each subsequent path as each of these paths can be triggered individually while a task with an AND-split has only one output port as all subsequent tasks must always be triggered. A task with an OR-split can trigger a subset of the outgoing paths, i.e. in this case a separate output port exists for each of these combinations.

The process flow can be restricted at these ports. A *blocked* port prevents the process flows through it, i.e. a blocked input port prevents the triggering of the task through the port while a blocked output port prevents that the corresponding output paths can be triggered. In the model in Figure 2, we blocked the output port from *Check for permission* to *No acknowledgement*. Thus, the task *Check for permission* must always be followed by the task *Decide choice of name (under Dutch law)* as the path to the task *No acknowledgement* can no longer be triggered. Input ports can not only be blocked but also be configured as *hidden*. Similarly, the subsequent task can then not be triggered through this port anymore. However, in this case the process flow is not completely blocked, but only the execution of the corresponding task is skipped. The process execution continues afterwards. In Figure 2 the input port of the task *Check for permission* is hidden. Thus, the execution of this task is skipped which also explains why we blocked one of the task's output ports: the configuration results in skipping the check. Hence, it can no longer fail and the process must continue normally. Further details on configurable YAWL can be found in [16,19].

As we can observe from this example, the configurations of ports are often not independent from each other and require extensive domain knowledge.

In [23] it is shown how domain knowledge can be taken into account and used to drive the configuration process. In [1,3] different techniques are provided for ensuring the correctness of the resulting models.

2.3 Challenges

There are many challenges related to process configuration. First of all, there is a need to develop *complete collections of high-quality configurable models*. Often the ideas and the technology are in place, but the actual "content" is missing or of very low quality (see for example the many errors in SAP's well-known reference model [21]). It is important to develop a *sound methodology* to extract best practise models. Process mining can help to find out what the actual processes are and how they perform. A second challenge is how to *extract a manageable configurable process from a set of concrete models*. As shown in [17] techniques from process mining can be adapted for this purpose. However, the resulting models are rather spaghetti-like. In [20] another approach, more related to ad-hoc change, is used. Here a reference model is chosen that requires the least number of edit operations. Unfortunately, one needs to manually modify the reference model to create a selected variant. Finally, there are many issues related to multi-tenancy, flexibility and change. How to change a configurable model used by many tenants? How to ensure privacy and isolation? How to accommodate exceptional requests that do not fit the configurable model?

3 Cross-Organizational Process Mining

This section first provides a high-level overview of process mining techniques. Subsequently, we introduce the concept of cross-organizational process mining and discuss the corresponding challenges.

3.1 Process Mining in One Organization

More and more information about (business) processes is recorded by information systems in the form of so-called "event logs" (e.g., transaction logs, audit trails, databases, message logs). IT systems are becoming more and more intertwined with the processes they support, resulting in an "explosion" of available data that can be used for analysis purposes. Cloud computing and SaaS will fuel this development even more.

To illustrate the role that event logs can play, let us first explain Figure 3. We assume the existence of a collection of information systems that are supporting a "world" composed of business processes, people, organizations, etc. The *event data* extracted from such systems are the starting point for *process mining*. Note that Figure 3 distinguishes between *current data* and *historic data*. The former refers to events of cases (i.e., process instances) that are still actively worked on ("pre mortem"). The latter refers to events of completed cases, i.e., process instances that cannot be influenced anymore ("post mortem"). The historic data

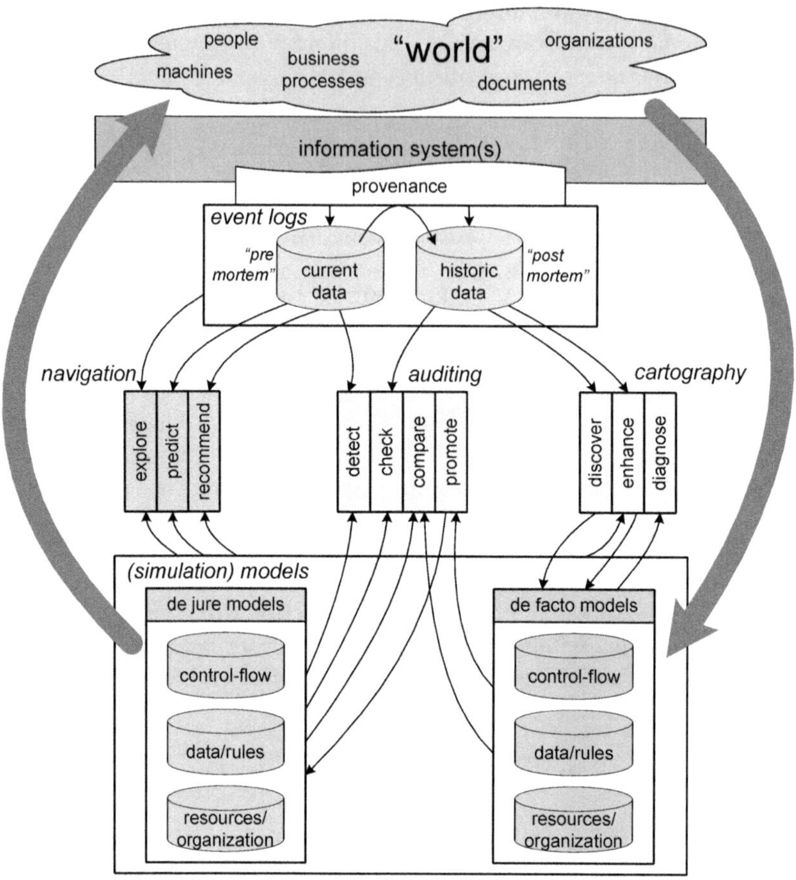

Fig. 3. Overview of various process mining activities

("post mortem") can be any collection of events where each event refers to an instance (i.e., case), has a name (e.g., activity name), and has a timestamp.

The collection of event data is becoming more important. One the one hand, more and more event data are available. On the other hand, organizations depend on such data; not only for performance measurement, but also for auditing. We use the term *business process provenance* to refer to the systematic collection of the information needed to reconstruct what has actually happened. The term signifies that for most organizations it is vital that "history cannot be rewritten or obscured". From an auditing point of view the systematic, reliable, and trustworthy recording of events is essential. Fortunately, cloud computing and SaaS can assist in the systematic and unified collection of event data.

The lower part of Figure 3 shows two types of models: *de jure models* are normative models that describe a desired or required way of working while *de facto models* aim to describe the actual reality with all of its intricacies (policy violations, inefficiencies, fraud, etc.). Both types of models may cover one or more perspectives and thus describe control-flow, time, data, organization, resource, and/or cost aspects. For process mining one can focus on a particular perspective. However, when the goal is to build simulation models, all factors influencing performance need to be taken into account (e.g., when measuring utilization and response times, it is not possible to abstract from resources and focus on control-flow only). Models can also be based on a mixture of "de jure" and "de facto" information. The key idea of process mining is to not simply rely on de jure models that may have little to do with reality. Therefore, the goal is to shift more to "de facto models"; this will save time and increase the quality of analysis results.

In Figure 3 three main categories of activities have been identified: *cartography*, *auditing*, and *navigation*. The individual activities are briefly described below.

1. **Discover.** The discovery of good process models from events logs - comparable to geographic maps - remains challenging. Process discovery techniques can be used to discover process models (e.g., Petri nets) from event logs [4,5].
2. **Enhance.** Existing process models (either discovered or hand-made) need to be related to events logs such that these models can be enhanced by making them more faithful or by adding new perspectives based on event data. By combining historic data and pre-existing models, these models can be repaired (e.g., a path that is never taken is removed) or extended (e.g., adding time information extracted from logs).
3. **Diagnose.** Models (either de jure or de facto) need to be analyzed using existing model-based analysis techniques, e.g., process models can be checked for the absence of deadlocks or simulated to estimate cycle times. Probably the most widely used model-based analysis technique is simulation.
4. **Detect.** For on-line auditing, de jure models need to be compared with current data (events of running process instances) and deviations of such partial cases should to be detected at runtime. By replaying the observed events on a model, it is possible to do conformance checking while the process is unfolding.
5. **Check.** Similarly, historic "post mortem" data can be cross-checked with de jure models. For this conformance checking techniques are used that can pinpoint deviations and quantify the level of compliance [25].
6. **Compare.** De facto models can be compared with de jure models to see in what way reality deviates from what was planned or expected.
7. **Promote.** Based on an analysis of the differences between a de facto model and a de jure model, it is possible to promote parts of the de facto model to a new de jure model. By promoting proven "best practises" to the de jure model, existing processes can be improved. For example, a simulation model may be improved and calibrated based on elements of a de facto model.
8. **Explore.** The combination of event data and models can be used to explore business processes. Here new forms of interactive process visualization can be used (visual analytics).

9. **Predict.** By combining information about running cases with models (discovered or hand-made), it is possible to make predictions about the future, e.g., the remaining flow time and the probability of success. Here techniques such as simulation and regression analysis can be used.
10. **Recommend.** The information used for predicting the future can also be used to recommend suitable actions (e.g. to minimize costs or time). The goal is to enable functionality similar to the guidance given by navigation systems like TomTom, but now in the context of BPM.

3.2 Example: Control-Flow Discovery

It is impossible to give concrete examples for all process mining techniques referred to in Figure 3. Therefore, we only illustrate the first activity, i.e., process discovery. Input for process discovery and any other process mining technique is an event log. The event log typically contains information about events referring to an *activity* and a *case*. The case (also named *process instance*) is the "thing" which is being handled, e.g., a customer order, a job application, an insurance claim, a building permit, etc. The activity (also named task, operation, action, or work-item) is some operation on the case. Typically, events have a *timestamp* indicating the time of occurrence. Moreover, when people are involved, event logs will characteristically contain information on the person executing or initiating the event, i.e., the *performer*. Also any other data can be attached to events. Various process mining techniques depend on subsets of this information. For example, techniques focusing on performance take timestamps into account, techniques focusing on decision points take data attributes into account, techniques focusing on the organizational perspective take performers into account. Figure 4 shows the minimal input required for applying the so-called α algorithm [5]. The left-hand side represents cases as sequences of activities, also referred to a traces. Every sequence corresponds to a case. For example for the first case, A, B, C, and D are executed. For the second case, the same activities are executed but B and C are reversed. Etc. The traces in Figure 4 suggest that the process always starts with A and always ends with D. In-between A and D either E or B and C are executed. The α algorithm analyzes the log for particular patterns and deduces the Petri net model shown on the right-hand side of Figure 4. Note that the Petri net indicates that after A either just E or both B and C are executed. Activities B and C are put in parallel. Activity D either waits for the completion of E or needs to wait until both B and C complete.

The α algorithm is able to identify all of the common control-flow patterns (AND/XOR-split/join, loops, etc.) [5]. However, it has many limitations when applied to real-life logs. Fortunately, many more mature techniques exist [4,18,26]. The α algorithm also only uses a subset of the information available and is restricted to the control-flow perspective.

Figure 5 shows an example of a real life process discovered through process mining. It is the invoice payment process of one of the twelve provincial offices of "Rijkswaterstaat", the Dutch national public works department, often abbreviated as "RWS". The process was discovered based on the event logs of RWS's

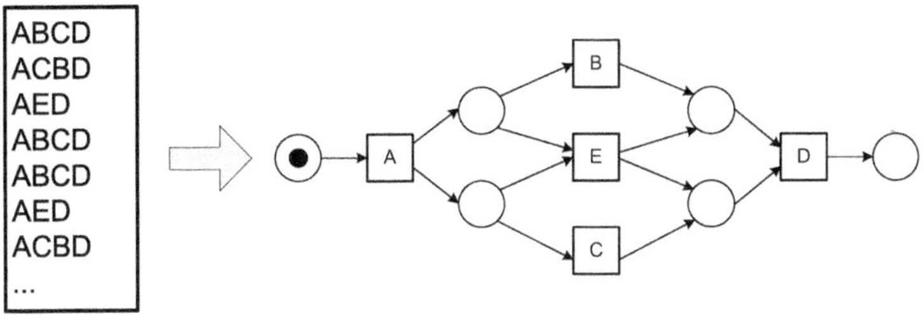

Fig. 4. Process discovered using the α algorithm [5]

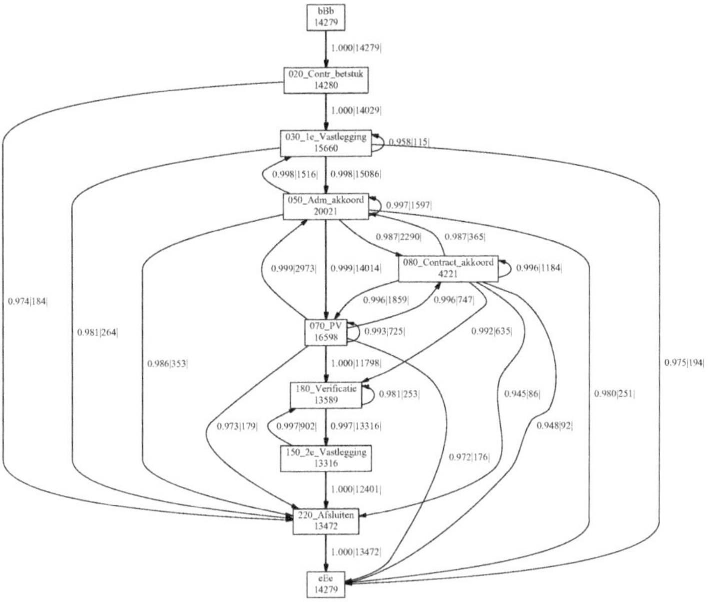

Fig. 5. Discovered process for invoice payments in RWS [4]

information system. The goal was to find out what the real process was and use this information to improve and streamline it. Figure 5 shows a particular view on the control-flow of the RWS process. We also discovered models for other perspectives such as the organizational perspective, the time perspective, etc. See [4] for a detailed analysis. We have been applying process mining in over 100 organizations. Typically, we see that processes are less structured than people think. Moreover, conformance checking typically reveals many deviations and inefficiencies.

3.3 Process Mining in Multi-Tenancy Environments

Thus far process mining research mainly focused on the analysis of a single process typically residing in one organization. Some authors have investigated interactions between web services [2,11,22], however, the focus is always on a single process. In a multi-tenancy environment provided by a cloud or SaaS infrastructure, there will be *many variants of the same process* running in parallel. This creates many interesting challenges.

Assume that there are n configured processes $P_1, P_2, \ldots, P_n$ that are all variants of some configurable model CM. Each of these processes has a configuration C_k and a set of process instances (cases) I_k (with $k \in \{1, 2, \ldots n\}$). Using conventional techniques, one can derive a model for every variant, e.g., model M_k is derived from I_k using some process discovery algorithm. It is also possible to derive a model based on all instances; model M^* is derived from $I^* = \bigcup_k I_k$. M^* can be seen as the "least common multiple" of all variants. If no configurable model is given and only the variants are given, then M^* can serve as a starting point for constructing CM.

The challenge is to compare the different process variants and their performance. Note that different processes may share the same configuration but operate under different circumstances. For example, two tenants may use the same configuration, but one has a only a few customers while the other has many. Each of the configured processes has a set of *features*. These features are based on properties of the process model M_k, properties of the configuration C_k, and performance related properties such as average flow times, average response times, service levels, frequencies, etc. Using *clustering* one can group process variants into coherent clusters. Cluster analysis or clustering is "the assignment of a set of observations into subsets (called clusters) so that observations in the same cluster are similar in some sense". Using *classification* one tries to explain one feature in terms of other features, e.g., processes with a particular configuration tend to have a better performance. A common technique is decision tree learning. Clustering is sometimes referred to as unsupervised learning while classification is referred to as supervised learning. The large scale adoption of multi-tenancy environments will enable machine learning techniques such as clustering and classification. This way cross-organizational process mining comes into reach.

Cross-organizational process mining is an unexplored area. One of the reasons is that this requires comparable event logs, i.e., events need to be recorded in a consistent manner across multiple organizations. Fortunately, this can easily be achieved in SaaS and cloud infrastructures. Even if data is collected in a unified manner across different organizations, there are still several challenges. First of all, there is the concern that enough variants of the same process should be available to enable learning. Second, there is the problem of *concept drift.*[2] The same process variant may operate under different circumstances. For example, there may be seasonal effects affecting the features of a process. The same process may have long flow times in December and short flow times in January due

[2] In machine learning, concept drift means that the statistical properties of the target variable, which the model is trying to predict, change over time in unforeseen ways. This causes problems because the predictions become less accurate as time passes. In the context of process mining one is not investigating a single variable but a complete process model. This makes it more difficult to properly define this notion.

to differences in workload. This should be taken into account when comparing variants. In fact, the analysis of concept drift in processes is related to cross-organizational process mining. Instead of comparing different processes operating in the same time period, one can also compare different episodes of the same process.

4 CoSeLoG Project

In this section, we briefly introduce the CoSeLoG project and present an example showing that municipalities form an interesting application domain for the ideas presented in this paper.

4.1 Overview

Since there are 430 municipalities in the Netherlands and they are all providing similar services and are executing similar processes, the use of SaaS technology could potentially be very beneficial for these local governments. The CoSeLoG project was established to exploit this observation. The goal of the project is to create a *cloud infrastructure for municipalities*. More precisely: we want to transition from situation depicted in Figure 1(a) to the situation depicted in Figure 1(b) in a prototypical setting involving several municipalities. Such a cloud infrastructure for municipalities would offer services for handling various types of permits, taxes, certificates, and licences. Although municipalities are similar, their internal processes are typically different. Within the constraints of national laws and regulations, municipalities can differentiate because of differences in size, demographics, problems, and policies. Therefore, the cloud should provide *configurable services* such that products and processes can be customized while sharing a common infrastructure. The CoSeLoG project aims at the development and analysis of such services using the results described in sections 2 and 3.

The following (end-)user organizations are participating in the CoSeLoG proposal: Pallas Athena, D!MPACT, and 10 Dutch municipalities (Bergeijk, Bladel, Coevorden, Eersel, Emmen, Gemert-Bakel, Hellendoorn, Noordoostpolder, Reusel de Mierden, and Zwolle). The project started in May 2010 and is supported by the Jacquard program `www.jacquard.nl` which aims to promote SaaS research.

Municipalities provide an *ideal setting for SaaS, configurable models, and cross-organizational mining*. In principle all 430 municipalities need to offer the same services to their citizens, and need to manage similar collections of processes. However, due to demographics and political choices, municipalities are handling things differently. Sometimes these differences are unintentional, however, often these differences can be easily justified by the desired "Couleur Locale". Hence, it is important to support variability. Interestingly, municipalities are *not* in direct competition with one another. Therefore, cross-organizational process mining is not a threat and municipalities are eager to share information and experiences and learn from each other. Therefore, a widely used cloud infrastructure for municipalities can help to establish best practices based on evidence obtained through cross-organizational process mining.

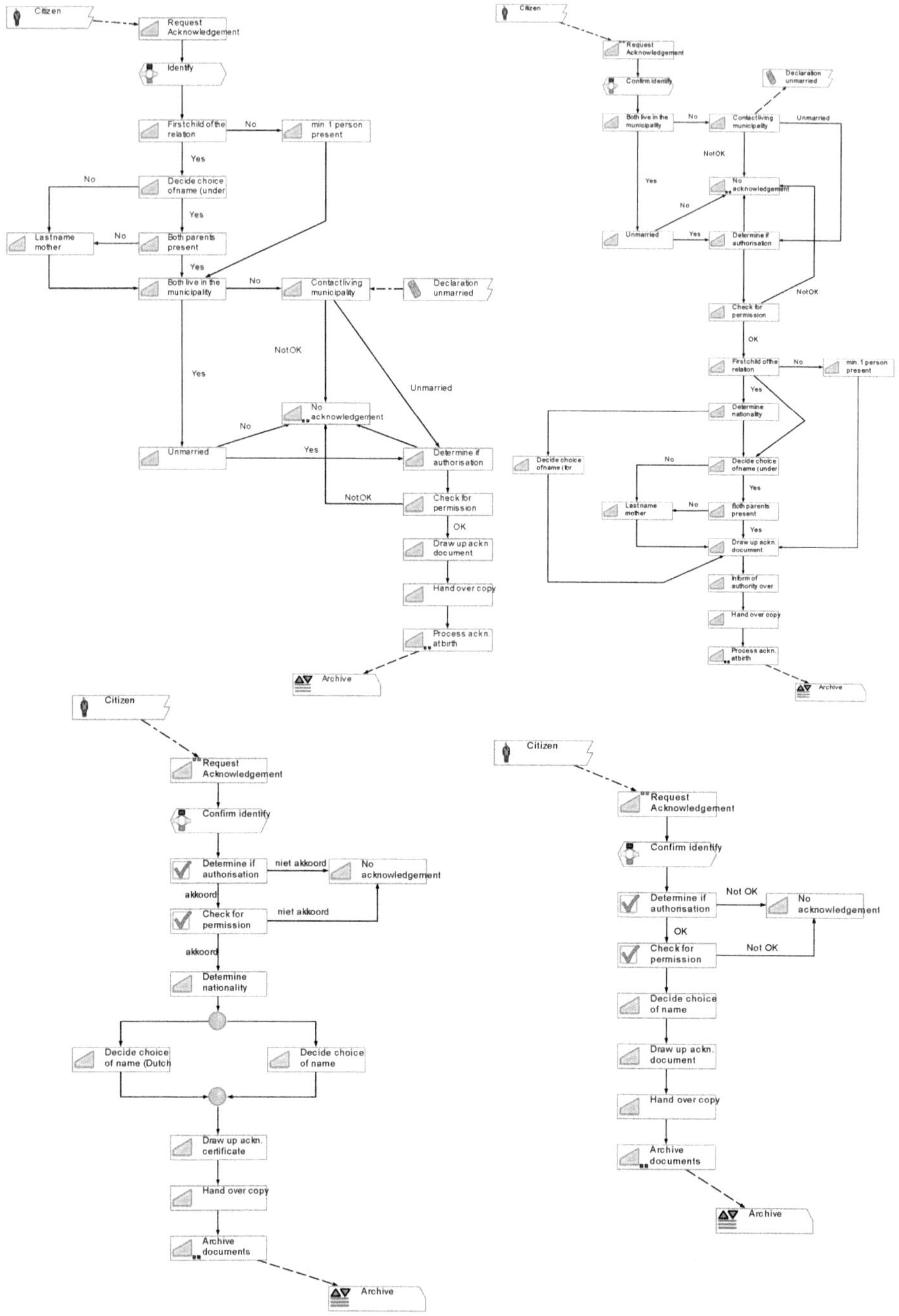

Fig. 6. The process "acknowledgement of an unborn child" in four municipalities [17]

4.2 Example

In [17] we analyzed four of the most frequently executed processes in municipalities: (a) acknowledging an unborn child, (b) registering a newborn child, (c) marriage, and (d) issuing a death certificate. Any municipality has these processes, however, as we found out, these processes are implemented and executed differently among municipalities. In [17] we compared the processes of four municipalities and the reference model provided by the NVVB (Nederlandse Vereniging Voor Burgerzaken). For example, Figure 6 shows four variants of the process related to "acknowledging an unborn child". Each of the four municipalities is using a specific variant of the processes. Moreover, the NVVB reference model (not shown in Figure 6) is yet another variant of the same process. Based on a detailed analysis of the differences we derived a *configurable process model*, i.e., a model that captures all variants observed. By setting the configuration parameters, one can reconstruct each of the original process models (and many more). The study reported in [17] revealed that: (a) it is possible to construct (or even generate) configurable process models for the core processes in municipalities, (b) municipalities use similar, but at the same time really different, processes, and (c) the comparison of the same process in multiple municipalities provides interesting insights and triggers valuable discussions.

Figure 6 illustrates that it is a challenge to merge different models into one configurable model. As shown in [17] the resulting configurable model tends to be rather complex and difficult to manage. Moreover, it is questionable whether the models shown in Figure 6 adequately reflect the real processes. Using process mining, more realistic models can be discovered and compared across municipalities. The CoSeLoG project will research these problems and, hopefully, provide solutions.

5 Conclusions

In this paper, we discussed configurable services that run in a cloud/SaaS infrastructure where multiple organizations need support for variants of the same process. We showed that supporting variability is one of the main challenges. Moreover, we discussed the potential of process mining techniques in such environments. We believe that "configurable services in the cloud" enable a new kind of process mining, coined "cross-organizational process mining" in this paper. The CoSeLoG project, presented in Section 4, aims to address the challenges presented in this paper.

Acknowledgments. The author would like to thank all the people that contributed to the development of ProM and (C-)YAWL. Special thanks go to Florian Gottschalk and Marcello La Rosa for their seminal work on process configuration and Boudewijn van Dongen and Eric Verbeek for driving the process mining work at TU/e. We thank the Jacquard program for their support and Joos Buijs and Jan Vogelaar for their efforts within the CoSeLoG project.

References

1. van der Aalst, W.M.P., Dumas, M., Gottschalk, F., ter Hofstede, A.H.M., La Rosa, M., Mendling, J.: Preserving Correctness During Business Process Model Configuration. Formal Aspects of Computing 22(3), 459–482 (2010)
2. van der Aalst, W.M.P., Dumas, M., Ouyang, C., Rozinat, A., Verbeek, H.M.W.: Conformance Checking of Service Behavior. ACM Transactions on Internet Technology 8(3), 29–59 (2008)
3. van der Aalst, W.M.P., Lohmann, N., La Rosa, M., Xu, J.: Correctness Ensuring Process Configuration: An Approach Based on Partner Synthesis. In: Hull, R., Mendling, J., Tai, S. (eds.) BPM 2010. LNCS, vol. 6336, pp. 95–111. Springer, Heidelberg (2010)
4. van der Aalst, W.M.P., Reijers, H.A., Weijters, A.J.M.M., van Dongen, B.F., Alves de Medeiros, A.K., Song, M., Verbeek, H.M.W.: Business Process Mining: An Industrial Application. Information Systems 32(5), 713–732 (2007)
5. van der Aalst, W.M.P., Weijters, A.J.M.M., Maruster, L.: Workflow Mining: Discovering Process Models from Event Logs. IEEE Transactions on Knowledge and Data Engineering 16(9), 1128–1142 (2004)
6. Agrawal, R., Gunopulos, D., Leymann, F.: Mining Process Models from Workflow Logs. In: Schek, H.-J., Saltor, F., Ramos, I., Alonso, G. (eds.) EDBT 1998. LNCS, vol. 1377, pp. 469–483. Springer, Heidelberg (1998)
7. Becker, J., Delfmann, P., Knackstedt, R.: Adaptive Reference Modeling: Integrating Configurative and Generic Adaptation Techniques for Information Models. In: Becker, J., Delfmann, P. (eds.) Reference Modeling: Efficient Information Systems Design Through Reuse of Information Models, pp. 27–58. Springer, Heidelberg (2007)
8. Curran, T., Keller, G.: SAP R/3 Business Blueprint: Understanding the Business Process Reference Model, Upper Saddle River (1997)
9. Datta, A.: Automating the Discovery of As-Is Business Process Models: Probabilistic and Algorithmic Approaches. Information Systems Research 9(3), 275–301 (1998)
10. Dumas, M., van der Aalst, W.M.P., ter Hofstede, A.H.M.: Process-Aware Information Systems: Bridging People and Software through Process Technology. Wiley & Sons, Chichester (2005)
11. Dustdar, S., Gombotz, R.: Discovering Web Service Workflows Using Web Services Interaction Mining. International Journal of Business Process Integration and Management 1(4), 256–266 (2006)
12. Ferreira, D.R., Gillblad, D.: Discovering Process Models from Unlabelled Event Logs. In: Dayal, U., Eder, J., Koehler, J., Reijers, H.A. (eds.) Business Process Management. LNCS, vol. 5701, pp. 143–158. Springer, Heidelberg (2009)
13. Fettke, P., Loos, P.: Classification of Reference Models - A Methodology and its Application. Information Systems and e-Business Management 1(1), 35–53 (2003)
14. Gottschalk, F., van der Aalst, W.M.P., Jansen-Vullers, H.M.: Configurable Process Models: A Foundational Approach. In: Becker, J., Delfmann, P. (eds.) Reference Modeling: Efficient Information Systems Design Through Reuse of Information Models, pp. 59–78. Springer, Heidelberg (2007)
15. Gottschalk, F., van der Aalst, W.M.P., Jansen-Vullers, M.H.: SAP WebFlow Made Configurable: Unifying Workflow Templates into a Configurable Model. In: Alonso, G., Dadam, P., Rosemann, M. (eds.) BPM 2007. LNCS, vol. 4714, pp. 262–270. Springer, Heidelberg (2007)

16. Gottschalk, F., van der Aalst, W.M.P., Jansen-Vullers, M.H., La Rosa, M.: Configurable Workflow Models. International Journal of Cooperative Information Systems 17(2), 177–221 (2008)
17. Gottschalk, F., Wagemakers, T., Jansen-Vullers, M.H., van der Aalst, W.M.P., La Rosa, M.: Configurable Process Models: Experiences From a Municipality Case Study. In: van Eck, P., Gordijn, J., Wieringa, R. (eds.) CAiSE 2009. LNCS, vol. 5565, pp. 486–500. Springer, Heidelberg (2009)
18. Günther, C.W., van der Aalst, W.M.P.: Fuzzy Mining: Adaptive Process Simplification Based on Multi-perspective Metrics. In: Alonso, G., Dadam, P., Rosemann, M. (eds.) BPM 2007. LNCS, vol. 4714, pp. 328–343. Springer, Heidelberg (2007)
19. ter Hofstede, A., van der Aalst, W., Adams, M., Russell, N.: Modern Business Process Automation: YAWL and its Support Environment. Springer, Heidelberg (2010)
20. Li, C., Reichert, M., Wombacher, A.: Discovering Reference Models by Mining Process Variants Using a Heuristic Approach. In: Dayal, U., Eder, J., Koehler, J., Reijers, H.A. (eds.) BPM 2009. LNCS, vol. 5701, pp. 344–362. Springer, Heidelberg (2009)
21. Mendling, J., Verbeek, H.M.W., van Dongen, B.F., van der Aalst, W.M.P., Neumann, G.: Detection and Prediction of Errors in EPCs of the SAP Reference Model. Data and Knowledge Engineering 64(1), 312–329 (2008)
22. Motahari Nezhad, H.R., Saint-Paul, R., Benatallah, B., Casati, F.: Deriving Protocol Models from Imperfect Service Conversation Logs. IEEE Transactions on Knowledge and Data Engineering 20(12), 1683–1698 (2008)
23. La Rosa, M., van der Aalst, W.M.P., Dumas, M., ter Hofstede, A.H.M.: Questionnaire-based Variability Modeling for System Configuration. Software and Systems Modeling 8(2), 251–274 (2009)
24. Rosemann, M., van der Aalst, W.M.P.: A Configurable Reference Modelling Language. Information Systems 32(1), 1–23 (2007)
25. Rozinat, A., van der Aalst, W.M.P.: Conformance Checking of Processes Based on Monitoring Real Behavior. Information Systems 33(1), 64–95 (2008)
26. Weijters, A.J.M.M., van der Aalst, W.M.P.: Rediscovering Workflow Models from Event-Based Data using Little Thumb. Integrated Computer-Aided Engineering 10(2), 151–162 (2003)

A Process View Framework for Artifact-Centric Business Processes

Sira Yongchareon and Chengfei Liu

Faculty of Information and Communication Technologies
Swinburne University of Technology
Melbourne, Victoria, Australia
{syongchareon,cliu}@swin.edu.au

Abstract. Over the past several years, the artifact-centric approach to workflow has emerged as a new paradigm of business process modelling. It provides a robust structure of workflow and supports the flexibility of workflow enactment and evolution especially in a collaborative environment. To facilitate and foster business collaborations, the customisation, privacy protection, and authority control of business processes are essential. Given the diverse requirements of different roles involved in business processes, providing various views with adequate process information is critical to effective business process management. Several approaches have been proposed to construct views for traditional process-centric business processes; however, no approach has been developed for artifact-centric processes. The declarative manner of process modelling in artifact-centric approaches makes view construction challenging. In this paper, we propose a novel process view framework for artifact-centric business processes. The framework consists of artifact-centric process models, view models, and a mechanism to derive views from underlying process models. Consistency rules are also defined to preserve the consistency between a constructed view and its base process model.

1 Introduction

The artifact-centric business process model has emerged as a new promising approach for modeling business processes, as it provides a highly flexible solution to capture operational specifications of business processes. It particularly focuses on describing the data of business processes, known as "*artifacts*", by characterizing business-relevant data objects, their lifecycles, and related services. The artifact-centric process modelling approach fosters the automation of the business operations and supports the flexibility of the workflow enactment and evolution [1, 7, 10, 11]. Further, it also effectively enables collaboration of the business processes as the lifecycle of an artifact may span multiple business units when it evolves through the process. Each time the artifact moves from one state to another state, its relevant information/data is updated. Services that update on the artifact can be performed by various roles of participants, which may belong to a single organization or different organizations. Given the diversity of the participants involved in business processes, providing various views with adequate information of artifacts and business processes to participants according to

R. Meersman et al. (Eds.): OTM 2010, Part I, LNCS 6426, pp. 26–43, 2010.

their roles is considered as a critical requirement to enable the effective business process modelling and management [5].

For example, top-level executives may need high level information about all important artifacts, while operational level employees may need to know the detailed information of some artifacts and their progresses. Based on these requirements, there is a need of a flexible and customizable process model to support appropriate artifact-centric process abstractions that encapsulate sensitive information for different roles of participants.

The process view approaches have been proposed in several works [2, 3, 5, 6] to provide various levels of visibility to process information which enable organizations to maintain appropriate levels of privacy and security. These works are based on the traditional process-centric business processes. To the best of our knowledge, the problem of constructing views for the artifact-centric processes has not yet been well studied. We observed that the approaches to process view construction of those two paradigms of business process modelling are different. (1) The approach to view construction of the process-centric processes is task-based abstraction, while for the artifact-centric processes is object-based. The former is more explicit while the latter is more implicit. (2) The process logic of process-centric processes is described in a procedural manner using control flows, while the logic of artifact-centric processes is captured and maintained in a declarative manner using business rules and services to define the interaction of artifacts, tasks and their flow. As such, this brings in a new challenge on how views can be defined and derived for different roles for such declaratively defined specifications of business processes.

To address the above requirements, we propose a novel artifact-centric process view framework which consists of an artifact-centric business process model, a process view model with the construction approach, and a comprehensive set of view consistency rules to preserve the structural and behavioural consistency between process views. Our proposed framework enhances the artifact-centric business process model as it can provide various roles of participants with different views of a process to meet their requirements and to support different levels of authority when accessing artifacts of collaborative business processes.

The remainder of this paper is organized as follows. Section 2 introduces process view framework with our motivating example. Section 3 introduces the artifact-centric process model, definitions, and syntaxes for both business processes and views. Section 4 provides a process view construction framework based on role-based view configurations and consistency constraints. Section 5 reviews the related works. Finally, the conclusion and future work are given in Section 6.

2 Motivating Example

In the artifact-centric approach, business processes are structured around business artifacts. An artifact holds its data and its current state. The move of one state to another state of an artifact is triggered by a pre-defined business rule of the processes, i.e., a business rule describes how state changes. This rule also induces a service invocation which will modify data of related artifacts. The detail of artifact-centric process model is described in Section 3.

In this section, we introduce an example of business processes to illustrate and motivate the process views that can be constructed based on the underlying business process with role-based view requirements. Our example of business processes is adapted from a general buyer-seller business and its supply chain process. It consists of two business processes: product ordering and shipping. The ordering process starts when a customer places an order to the retailer for a particular product and ends when the customer pays the invoice. The shipping process starts when the retailer creates a shipment and ends when the item arrives to the customer. Now, we start with introducing artifacts used in the processes. Figure 1 shows the cross-boundary view of five main artifacts that involve in our collaborative business processes. The shaded boundary of each artifact indicates that the state/data of artifact is changed or updated by some participants in the collaboration. The boundary of an artifact may cover multiple departments in the organization or even span to other organizations. Here, we do not detail how data/state of each artifact can be changed; however, some artifacts are described when we run through Section 3.

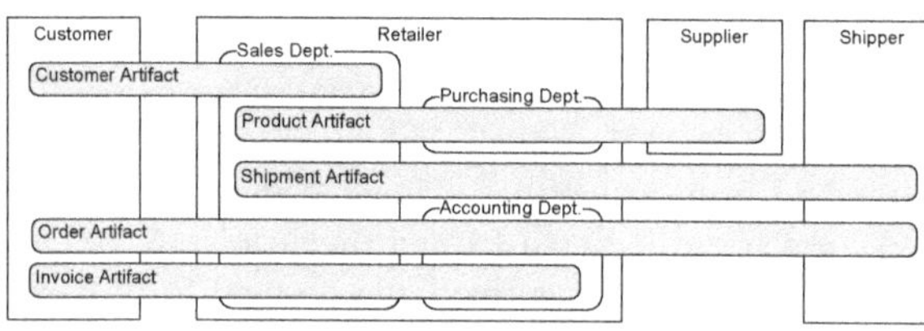

Fig. 1. Business artifacts in collaborative business processes

Now, we can see that an artifact which spans multiple departments or organizations is an interest of some participants that belong to those organizational units, e.g., the *Order* artifact involved in the Sale and Accounting departments is of course interesting to sale clerks, sale managers, accounting clerks, and accounting managers, etc. Each role of stakeholders who are interested in the artifact may have different requirements or restrictions of how much details of the artifact they want to see or are able to see depending on the authority of the role together with the privacy and security concerns for the artifact in the processes. When process modelers discover artifacts and model processes, they may not need to concern with these requirements of the stakeholders. The artifact then is defined at the most detailed level that is adequate enough to be used for the operation of processes. Later, they define/customize different views of the artifact for different roles depending on user's requirements, e.g., customization, privacy protection, and authority control. The view requirement for users of a particular role specifies a structure of artifact's states and their visibility.

Figure 2 shows different views of the *Order* artifact in our business processes. Figure 2 (a) presents the original (or operational) view of the *Order* artifact. Figure 2 (b) illustrates the views of the *Order* artifact for the *Sale* and *Accounting* roles, respectively, according to the view requirements specified in Figure 2 (c). In this example, the requirement for the *Sale* role specifies that: (1) the *delivering* and *billed* states are nested under the *in_processing* state and *delivering* nests the *in_shipping* and *shipped*; (2) the *init, open_for_item, in_shipping,* and *shipped* states are hidden. We use a white rectangle to represent a visible state while a gray shaded rectangle represents a hidden state.

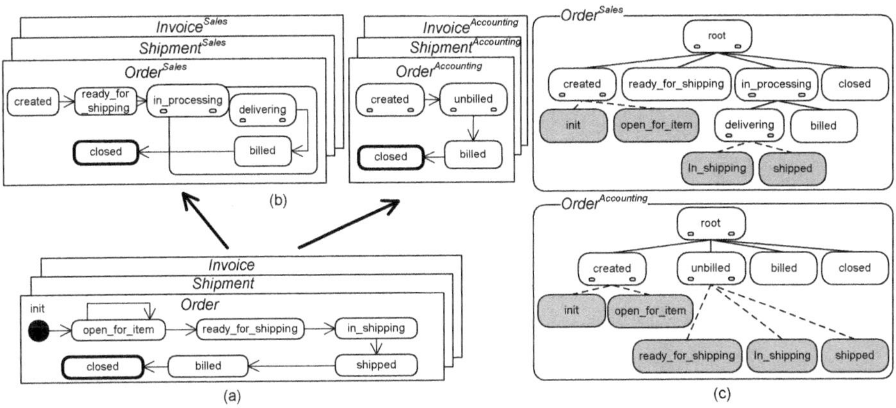

Fig. 2. Operational view vs. Role-based view

It is understandable that the view requirements can be specified at the artifact level in the artifact-centric approach, i.e., each artifact in business processes will have its corresponding requirement for each role. However, when constructing process views, we do not only consider individual artifacts, but we need to take into account business rules as well. For example, if a business rule makes a change of two states of different artifacts, then hiding a state of one artifact will have an impact on the another artifact. In order to maintain the integrity of business rules for constructed process views, a well-defined set of rules for the view construction is required. Technically, this brings in the challenge to develop a mechanism to generate a process view that correctly preserves the consistency between itself and its underlying business processes.

3 Artifact-Centric Process Model for Business Processes and Views

The concept of modelling artifact-centric processes has been established under the framework proposed in [10] and its formal model can be found in [11]. We extend their artifact-centric business process model to *process views*. The artifact-centric process (ACP) model consists of three core constructs: *artifacts*, *services*, and *business rules*. An *artifact* is a business entity or an object involved in business process(es). Each artifact contains a set of attributes and states. For each artifact, the evolution of states from the initial to the final states describes its lifecycle. A *service* is a task that requires input data from artifact(s) or users, and produces an output by performing an update on artifact(s). We use a *business rule* to associate service(s) with artifact(s) in a *Condition-Action* style. Each rule describes which service is invoked and which state of artifact is changed under what pre-condition and post-condition. We describe the behavior of each artifact in the ACP model by adopting the state machine, and formally define a view of artifact and a view of ACP which is derived from the ACP model.

3.1 Syntax of Artifact-Centric Process Model

In this section, components and syntaxes of artifact-centric process model for business processes are introduced and defined.

Definition 1: (Artifact class). An *artifact class* abstracts a group of artifacts with their data attribute and states. An artifact class C is a tuple (A, S) where,

- $A = \{a_1, a_2, \ldots, a_x\}$, $a_i \in A (1 \le i \le x)$ is an attribute of a scalar-typed value (string and real number) or an undefined value
- $S = \{s_1, s_2 \ldots, s_y\} \cup \{s^{init}\}$, $s_i \in S (1 \le i \le y)$ is a state and s^{init} denotes initial state.

Definition 2: (Artifact schema). An *artifact schema* Z contains a set of artifact classes, i.e., $Z = \{C_1, C_2, \ldots, C_n\}$ where $C_i \in Z$ $(1 \le i \le n)$ is an *artifact class.*

From our business scenario, we define a primary set of original artifact classes used for the product ordering and shipping processes.

- *Order* = ({*orderID*, *customerID*, *grandTotal*}, {*open_for_item*, *ready_for_shipping*, *in_shipping*, *shipped*, *billed*, *closed*})
- *Shipment* = ({*shipID*, *customerID*, *shipDate*, *shipCost*}, {*open_for_shipitem*, *ready_to_dispatch*, *in_shipping*, *completed*})
- *OrderItem* = ({*orderID*, *productID*, *shipID*, *qty*, *price*}, {*newly_added*, *on_hold*, *ready_to_ship*, *added_to_shipment*, *in_shipping*, *shipped*})
- *Invoice* = ({*invoiceID*, *ordereID*, *invoiceDate*, *amountPaid*}, {*unpaid*, *paid*})

We also define some basic predicates over schema Z:

- *defined*(C, a) if the value of attribute $a \in C.A$ in artifact of class C is defined
- *instate*(C, s) if the current (active) state of artifact of class C is s. Initially, *instate*(C, *init*) implies $\forall x \in C.A$, $\neg$*defined*(C, x). If *instate*(C, s) then every state in *ancestor*(s) is also active.

Definition 3: (Business Rule). A business rule regulates which service can be invoked under what pre-condition. The conditional effect is also defined to restrict the post-condition after performing such service. Business rule r can be defined as tuple (λ, β, v) where,

- λ and β are a *pre-condition* and *post-condition*, respectively. Both are defined by a quantifier-free first-order logic formula. For the simplification, it allows only AND logical connective ($\wedge$) and variables. The formula contains two types of proposition over schema Z: (1) *state proposition* (the *instate* predicate) and (2) *attribute proposition* (the *defined* and scalar comparison operators), e.g., *defined*(*Order*, *orderID*) $\wedge$ *instate*(*Order*, *in_shipping*) $\wedge$ *Order*.*grandTotal* > 10.
- $v \in V$ is a service to be performed. A service may involve with several artifacts of classes $C_1, C_2, \ldots, C_y$, where $C_i \in Z (1 \le i \le y)$.

In order to maintain the existence of valid state changes of an artifact in business rule r, we require that there exists a couple of *instate* predicates of that artifact in both pre-condition and post-condition of r, i.e., we have states $s_x, s_y \in C.S$ such that *instate*(C, s_x) exists in $r.\lambda$ and *instate*(C, s_y) exists in $r.\beta$. The state change refers to either a transition from one state to another state, or to itself. Due to page limitation, we only list some business rules in Table 1 which are used for the ordering process in our business scenario.

Table 1. Example of business rules

r1 : *Customer c* requests to make an *Order o*	
Pre-condition	*instate(o, init)* ∧ ¬*defined(o.orderID)* ∧ ¬*defined(o.customerID)* ∧ *defined(c.customerID)*
Service	*createOrder(c, o)*
Post-condition	*instate(o, open_for_item)* ∧ *defined(o.orderID)* ∧ *defined(o.customerID)* ∧ *defined(c.customerID)* ∧ *o.customerID* = *c.customerID*
r2: Add *OrderItem oi* of *Product p* with a quantity *qty* to *Order o*	
Pre-condition	*instate(o, open_for_item)* ∧ *instate(oi, init)* ∧ *defined(p.productID)* ∧ *defined(oi.productID)* ∧ ¬*defined(oi.orderID)* ∧ *defined(oi.qty)* ∧ ¬ *defined(oi.price)*
Service	*addItem(o, p, oi)*
Post-condition	*instate(o, open_for_item)* ∧ *instate(oi, newly_added)* ∧ *defined(oi.orderID)* ∧ *defined(oi.price)*
r3: Complete *Order o*	
Pre-condition	*instate(o, open_for_item)* ∧ *o.grandTotal* > 0
Service	*completeOrder(o)*
Post-condition	*instate(o, ready_for_shipping)*
r4: Ship *Shipment s* which contains *OrderItem oi* of *Order o*	
Pre-condition	*instate(o, ready_for_shipping)* ∧ *instate(oi, added_to_shipment)* ∧ *instate(s, ready_to_dispatch)* ∧ *defined(oi.shipID)* ∧ *defined(s.shipID)* ∧ *oi.shipID* = *s.shipID*
Service	*startShipping(s, o, oi)*
Post-condition	*instate(s, in_shipping)* ∧ *instate(oi, in_shipping)* ∧ *instate(o, in_shipping)*
r5: Clear *Invoice v* for *Order o*	
Pre-condition	*instate(o, billed)* ∧ *instate(v, unpaid)* ∧ *defined(v.orderID)* ∧ *o.orderID* = *v.orderID* ∧ *o.grandTotal* = *v.amountPaid*
Service	*payInvoice(v, o)*
Post-condition	*instate(o, closed)* ∧ *instate(v, paid)*

As we can see that pre- and post- conditions of each business rule contain two groups of conditioning: *attribute* (attribute's value evaluation) and *state*. We also classify state conditioning into two types by determining the existence of *instate* predicate in the pre- and post- conditions of a business rule. The first type is classified by the case that a change of state occurs for only one artifact, e.g., rules *r1* and *r3*. The second type refers to changes of states of multiple artifacts, i.e., more than one pair of *instate* predicates appears in pre- and post-conditions of a single business rule for different artifacts. This type indicates that a single business rule is used to induce multiple state changes such that each change occurs once on each artifact, e.g. rule r_5 changes for the *Order* artifact from the *billed* state to the *closed* state, and simultaneously changes from the *unpaid* state to the *paid* state for the *Invoice* artifact.

Definition 4: (Artifact-Centric Process Model or ACP model). Let ∏ denote an artifact-centric process model, and it is tuple (*Z*, *V*, *R*) where *Z* is an artifact schema, *V* and *R* are sets of services and business rules over *Z*, respectively.

In this paper, we assume that the ACP model is correct and valid, so we do not consider the verification of the model. Actually, the verification can be adopted from the work presented in [11]. Our focus is on the model of views and their construction.

3.2 View Definitions

As discussed earlier, process views for artifact-centric business processes are defined and constructed according to view requirements for particular roles of the organizations. The view requirement of a particular view specifies a hierarchal structure of states of an artifact and their visibility. As such, we introduce composite states to define and represent a view of an artifact.

Definition 5: (Role). A role defines the capability of a group of users. Different roles may have different views/accesses to artifacts. The role can be used to differentiate an external organization from a home organization, inter-organizational units, or different groups within an organizational unit. We denote role domain $L = \{l_1, l_2, \ldots, l_x\}$, where $l_i \in L (1 \leq i \leq x)$ is a role of users who involve in the business processes.

Definition 6: (Artifact view). Given artifact class *C*, we denote C^l for a *view* of *C* for role $l \in L$, and it is tuple (A^l, S^l, pc) where $A^l = C.A$, S^l is a set of states that are defined as nodes in a hierarchal tree structure (state tree), and $pc \subseteq S^l \times S^l$ is a finite set of parent-child relations.

We define predicate $child(s_x, s_y)$ to mean that state s_y is a child of state s_x, and function $children$: $S \rightarrow 2^S$ to define for each state its set of child states. In addition, we define function *descendant* as the reflexive transitive closure of *children*. We can say that state s_y is an *ancestor* of state s_x in the state tree if $s_x \in descendant(s_y)$. Correspondingly, let $ancestor$: $S \rightarrow 2^S$ be the function that defines for each state its set of ancestors, i.e., $ancestor(s_x)$ returns a set of all ancestors of s_x.

As we are required to ensure the hierarchal structure of the state tree, we add the root state to a set of states for each artifact class. The root state is ancestor of every state in *S*. For simplicity, we do not show the root state in a class.

Note that for *artifact view* C^l, we write s_y: $\{s_1, s_2, .., s_x\}$ where s_y and $s_i \in C^l.S (1 \leq i \leq x)$ to denote composite state s_y together with its nested states $\{s_1, s_2, .., s_x\}$, e.g., a set of states of the *Order* artifact for the *Sale* role in Figure 2 (c) can be defined as {*created*: {*init*, *open_for_item*}, *ready_for_shipping*, *in_processing*: {*delivering*: {*in_shipping*, *shipped*}, *billed*}, *closed*}.

Definition 7: (ACP view). Given role $l \in L$ and ACP model $\Pi = (Z, V, R)$, we denote Π^l for the ACP view of Π for role *l*, and it is tuple (Z^l, V^l, R^l), where Z^l, V^l, and R^l is a set of *views* of artifact classes for role *l*, the services, and business rules over Z^l, respectively, such that for every view $C^l \in Z^l$ of artifact class *C* then $C \in Z$.

An ACP view is an abstract process model derived from its corresponding business ACP model which represents the original (base) process, namely *operational view*, or an existing view. We also use the term *operational view* of an artifact for the most detailed view of the artifact. In order to generate ACP views, we propose the so called *state condensation* technique that constructs a view of an artifact by abstraction of states of the artifact, and it is described in Section 4. One artifact may have different views depending on different view requirements specified by different roles. In short, an ACP view for a particular role will have for each artifact its view for that role.

Without loss of generality, we assume the uniqueness of artifact's state in a schema, i.e., a state belongs to only one artifact class. Given ACP model $\prod = (Z, V, R)$, we can simply use the abbreviated notation $\prod.s_x$ instead of using $\prod.Z.C.s_x$ as well as the state set $\prod.S$ is denoted for $\bigcup_i^{|Z|} \prod.Z.C_i.S$. It also has the implication that when referring a state in $\prod$, it will match with only one corresponding artifact class in $\prod.Z$. This abbreviated uses of notation are also applied for ACP views.

3.3 Artifact Lifecycle Model

Each artifact has its own life-cycle showing how its states are changed through the business processes. We adopt the state machine to capture a lifecycle of each individual artifact, namely *Artifact lifecycle model* (*ALM*). Each artifact has its corresponding ALM. Given an ACP model, a lifecycle model of an artifact can be generated by deriving from corresponding business rules that are used to induce state transitions of the artifact.

Definition 8: (Artifact Lifecycle Model). An *Artifact Lifecycle Model* defines the state transition of an artifact class. Given ACP model $\prod = (Z, V, R)$ and artifact class $C_i = (A_i, S_i)$ where $C_i \in Z$, an artifact lifecycle model for C_i, denoted as LM_{C_i}, can be defined as tuple (C_i, T), where

- $T \subseteq C_i.S \times R \times C_i.S$ is a 3-ary transition relation where R is a set of business rules. A transition $t = (s_s, r_i, s_t) \in T$ means that the state of the artifact will change from source state s_s to target state s_t where $s_s, s_t \in C_i.S$, if the pre-condition λ of business rule r_i holds.
- T^* is reflexive transitive closure of T. We write $s_i T^* s_j$ if there exists sequence of transitions from s_i to s_j, i.e., state s_j can be reached from state s_i by some business rules in R.

Figure 3 depicts the artifact lifecycle diagram for each artifact class of our business scenario. A label on a transition (arrow) denotes a business rule that corresponds to a transition, and it is one-to-one correspondence. We can see that rule r_4 induces three transitions of *Order*, *Shipment*, and *OrderItem* artifact lifecycles.

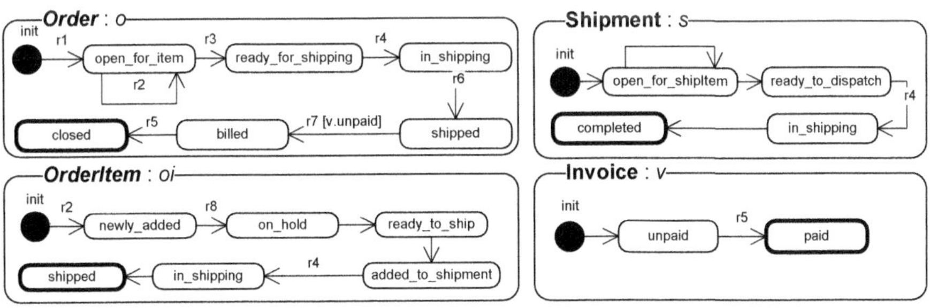

Fig. 3. Artifact Lifecycle Diagrams

Note that ALM is also used for describing the lifecycle of an artifact view in ACP views. We define an artifact lifecycle model for *view* $C_i^{\,l}$ of artifact class C_i, denoted as $LM_{C_i^{\,l}}$, and it is tuple ($C_i^{\,l}$, *T*).

Definition 9: (Ordering relation). Given artifact lifecycle model LM_{C_i} = (C_i, *T*) for artifact class (or *view*) C_i, state $s_x \in C_i.S$ is *before* state $s_y \in C_i.S$ if there is a sequence from state s_x to state s_y, i.e., $s_x T^* s_y$. We denote $s_x < s_y$ for their ordering relation. If $s_x T^* s_y$ and $s_y T^* s_x$, i.e., $s_x < s_y$ and $s_y < s_x$, then every state in sequences from s_x to s_y and s_y to s_x is in a loop. If $\neg(s_x < s_y) \wedge \neg(s_y < s_x)$, then state s_x and s_y are independent and we denote it as $s_x \parallel s_y$ for their ordering relation.

4 View Construction Framework for Artifact-Centric Business Processes

In this section, we propose a framework for constructing process views for artifact-centric business processes. The framework consists of operational business process model and its constructed views. We formally introduce definitions, syntaxes, rules, and related functions that will be used in the framework, and present a *condensation technique* to construct views based on its underlying process models with role-based view configurations. The details of this technique are described along with related cases regarding our motivating example. In addition, *process view consistency rules* are also defined for preserving the consistency between a constructed process view and its underlying process.

The condensation process is divided into two steps: (1) *State composition* and (2) *State hiding*. The *state composition* step is straightforward by nesting specified states in a composite state. The *state hiding* hides a specified set of states. The process of hiding states is more complex than composing states as business rules that has any reference to the hidden states will be affected. We also define *view consistency rules* to preserve the structural and behavioral consistencies between constructed view and its underlying view when applying those two steps.

The relation between a constructed view and its underlying view is defined by a *view transformation* function which provides the mapping between them. Here, we assume the existence of ACP view set $\Sigma = \{\Pi, \Pi^{l_1}, \Pi^{l_2}, \ldots, \Pi^{l_x}\}$, where Π is the *operational view* of ACP model and Π^{l_i} is an ACP View for role $l_i \in L (1 \leq i \leq x)$, and Σ forms a hierarchal structure having Π as its root, such that for any two ACP views in Σ, the state ordering of them must be consistent.

Consistency Rule 1: (State ordering relation preservation). Let Π^{l_1} and Π^{l_2} be ACP view for role l_1 and role l_2, respectively. For any two states that belong to two views of the same artifact class C_i in both Π^{l_1} and Π^{l_2}, the ordering relation between them must be consistent, i.e.,

If $s_x, s_y \in \Pi^{l_1}.S \cap \Pi^{l_2}.S$ such that $s_x < s_y$ in Π^{l_1}, then $s_x < s_y$ in Π^{l_2}, or if s_x, $s_y \in \Pi^{l_1}.S \cap \Pi^{l_2}.S$ such that $s_x \parallel s_y$ in Π^{l_1}, then $s_x \parallel s_y$ in Π^{l_2}.

This consistency rule ensures that the transitions corresponding to business rules of two ACP views are consistent.

Definition 10: (View transformation). Given ACP view set Σ for ACP model $\prod = (Z, V, R)$, the *view transformation* $vt = sh \circ sc$: $\Sigma \times SR^{+} \times SR^{-} \rightarrow \Sigma$ is a composite function where state composition function *sc* and state hiding function *sh* are composed, i.e., the result ACP view after applying state composition function is then applied with the state hiding function. Function $vt(\prod, sr_l^{+}, sr_l^{-})$ returns a role-based view, i.e., $\prod^{l}$, of ACP model$\prod$ that constructed based on *state composition requirement* $sr_l^{+}$and *state hiding requirement* sr_l^{-} for role *l*.

We use the term *view configuration* for the combined set of state composition and state hiding requirements. To limit the scope of the paper, we also assume that the view configuration that is used to transformed from ACP view $\prod^{i}$ to ACP view $\prod^{j}$ contains non-conflict set of state composition and hiding requirements, i.e., the view shall be constructed by satisfying every requirement and preserving every view consistency rule.

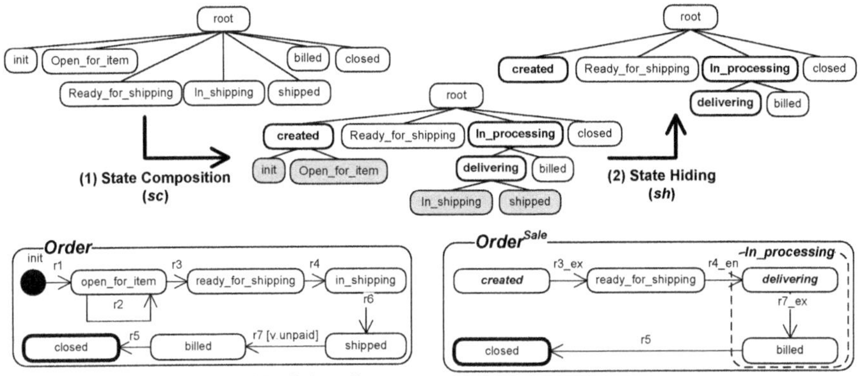

(a) the *operational view* of the *Order* artifact
(b) the *Sale* view of the *Order* artifact

Fig. 4. Two views of the *Order* artifact

Figure 4 illustrates an example of two different views of the *Order* artifact regarding our motivating example. Figure 4 (b) shows an abstraction of the *Order* artifact for the *Sale* role that is transformed from its operational view in Figure 4 (a) based on two specified view configuration requirements: (1) *composition requirement* for nesting the *in_shipping* and *shipped* states under the *deliverying* composite state and then nesting the *in_shipping* and *billed* states under the *in_processing* composite state, (2) *hiding requirement* for hiding the *in_shipping* and *shipped* states under the *delivering* state. Here, we also name an *intermediate ACP view* for a view of an artifact that is generated by state composition function (*sc*), and will be further used as an input of state hiding function (*sh*).

In order to preserve the structural and behavioral consistencies of the operational ACP, the condensation process may incur a rearrangement of state transition of an artifact. The rearrangement of a transition is achieved by a modification of corresponding business rule that induces such transition. The detail of modification is described in Section 4.3.

4.1 State Composition

State composition refers to the process of nesting states at same level under the new defined *composite state*. The composition of states will amend the structure of the state tree by inserting the new composite state into the hierarchy. Generally, defining a new composite state and inserting it into the tree hierarchy can be done iteratively in bottom-up manner.

Definition 11: (State composition). Given ACP view set Σ for ACP model $\prod = (Z, V, R)$, the state composition *sc*: $\Sigma \times SR^{+} \rightarrow \Sigma$ is a bijective function that maps one ACP view onto another ACP view in which the state trees of views of artifact classes are restructured and corresponding business rules are rewritten according to the state composition requirement set $SR^{+}=\{sr_n^{+}\}$, and a single *state composition requirement* $sr_n^{+} = \{\oplus_{C_1}, \oplus_{C_2}, \ldots, \oplus_{C_x}\}$, where $\oplus_{C_i}(1 \leq i \leq x) = \{(s_{j1}, S_{k1}), (s_{j2}, S_{k2}), \ldots (s_{jx}, S_{kx})\}$ is a set of *atomic composition requirements* for artifact $C_i \in \prod.Z (1 \leq i \leq x)$. The atomic requirement $(s_j, S_k) \in \oplus_{C_i} (1 \leq j \leq y, 1 \leq k \leq z)$ defines the state composition s_j for all states in S_k ($|S_k| > 1$) of artifact class C_i. Composite state s_j is inserted into the state tree as a parent of all nested states in S_k in the constructed ACP view.

An *atomic composition requirement* (s_j, S_k) is said to be *valid* if every state to be composed in S_k, belonging to the same artifact class, is at the same height of the state tree and owns the same parent. For example, we assume that ACP model $\prod$ contains the original *Order* artifact in Figure 4 (a) and let a single composition requirement sr^{+} be $\{\oplus_{Order}\}$, where $\oplus_{Order} = \{$(*delivering*, {*in_shipping*, *shipped*}), (*in_processing*, {*delivering*, *billed*}), (*created*, {*init*, *open_for_item*})$\}$. Then, we will have an intermediate ACP view $\prod^{Sale'}$ for role *Sale* after applying the state composition function *sc* to $\prod$ with requirement sr^{+}.

4.2 State Hiding

The process of hiding states is an important step of the condensation process. Unlike the state composition which mainly focuses on the state tree structure of artifact, hiding states deals with behavior of the artifact. The hidden state must be invisible in (or removed from) the tree structure and the business rule that such state is referenced.

Definition 12: (State hiding). Given ACP view set Σ for ACP model $\prod = (Z, V, R)$, the state hiding *sh*: $\Sigma \times SR^{-} \rightarrow \Sigma$ is a bijective function that maps one ACP view onto another ACP view in which the state tree and transitions of views of artifact classes are restructured and corresponding business rules are modified according to the state hiding requirement set $SR^{-}= \{sr_n^{-}\}$, and a single *state hiding requirement* $sr_n^{-} = \{\ominus_{C_1}, \ominus_{C_2}, \ldots, \ominus_{C_x}\}$, where $\ominus_{C_i}(1 \leq i \leq x) \subseteq C_i.S$ is a set of states to be hidden for artifact $C_i \in \prod.Z(1 \leq i \leq x)$.

The set of states $\ominus_{C_i}$ to be hidden is said to be *valid* if every state in $\ominus_{C_i}$ has its own parent and the parent is not the *root* of the state tree. This restriction is used to ensure that every state to be hidden is under some composite state, which is not the *root*, in the tree. For example in Figure 4, after the state composition step, states *init*, *open_for_item*, *in_shipping*, and *shipped* of the *Order* artifact can be hidden in the *Saleís* view. This implies that if we want to hide such states, we must first compose them and then we can hide them, e.g., the *delivering* composite state is created for the purpose of allowing the *in_shipping* and the *shipped* states to be hidden. If any composite state is to be hidden, all of its descendant states must be also hidden to ensure that a constructed view preserves the hierarchical structure.

Consistency Rule 2: (Hierarchy preservation). Let $\prod^{l_1}$ be ACP view for role l_1 and $\prod^{l_2}$ be ACP view for role l_2 that is constructed based on $\prod^{l_1}$. For any state s_x that belongs to the same artifact class C_i in both $\prod^{l_1}$ and $\prod^{l_2}$, the set of ancestors S_1 of $s_x$in $\prod^{l_1}$ is a subset of the set of ancestors S_2 of s_x in $\prod^{l_2}$, and the states in S_1 but not in S_2 do not exist in $\prod^{l_1}$, i.e.,

If $s_x \in \prod^{l_1}.S \cap \prod^{l_2}.S$ then $ancestor(\prod^{l_1}.s_x) \subseteq ancestor(\prod^{l_2}.s_x)$ and $tor(\prod^{l_2}.s_x) \setminus ancestor(\prod^{l_1}.s_x)) \rightarrow s_y \notin \prod^{l_1}.S$.

We take ACP view for role *Sale* from Figure 4 (b) as an example, and choose the *billed* state to be validated for the hierarchy consistency between the original state tree and the state tree after state composition for role *Sale*. The set of *ancestors* of the *billed* state for the view in Figure 4 (b) is {*in_processing*, *root*}, while for the view in Figure 4 (a) is {*root*}. As {*root*} ⊆ {*in_processing*, *root*}, and the *in_processing* state does not appear in the original state tree, we say that the *billed* state preserves the hierarchy consistency between the *Sale*'s view and its underlying original view. If every state that exists in both ACP views preserves the hierarchy consistency, then the state tree of a constructed view is consistent with its base view. This rule is also used to ensure that if any composite state is created, e.g., states *created*, *delivering*, and *in_processing*, then it must be correctly structured in the state tree.

4.3 Modification of Business Rules

We classify the modification of business rules into two categories regarding two types of conditionings which can be defined in business rules: (1) *state conditioning modification* and (2) *attribute conditioning modification*. The *state conditioning modification* is the process of hiding specified states and rearranging all effected transitions by considering *instate* predicates in pre- and post-conditions of the business rule that is related to the hidden state. The *attribute conditioning modification* updates every attribute condition of the business rule that is affected by hidden states. A business rule may be removed if it is no longer used in the constructed view.

Definition 13: (Modified business rule). Let $\prod^{l_y'} = sc(\prod^{l_x}, s\tau_{l_y}^{+})$ be an intermediate ACP view for role l_y constructed based on ACP view $\prod^{l_x}$ with state composition requirement $sr_{l_y}^{+}$, and $sh(\prod^{l_y'}, sr_y^{-})$ be the function that returns ACP view $\prod^{l_y} = (Z^{u_y}, V^{l_y}, R^{l_y})$ for role l_y that is constructed based on $\prod^{l_y'}$ with state hiding requirement $sr_{l_y}^{-}$, we have a *modified business rule set*, denoted as $R_{mod}^{l_y}$, such that each rule $r \in R_{mod}^{l_y}$ is the modified version of its original business rule in R^{l_y} according to the effect of state hiding requirement $sr_{l_y}^{-}$.

The modification of business rules must preserve the behavioral consistency between the constructed process view and its underlying base view. We define and describe related consistency rules to be used within the modification processes.

4.3.1 State Conditioning Modification

It is the fact that hiding any state of an artifact will break up the transition relation between such hidden state and other state, i.e., some paths or ordering relations in a lifecycle of the artifact are broken. To preserve such relations for maintaining the consistent behavior of the artifact lifecycles between ACP views, we consider the rearrangement of transitions that are affected by a hidden state, i.e., modifying state conditions of business rules that correspond to those transitions.

In order to explain the modification processes, we combine state tree with the lifecycle diagram of an artifact. Figure 5 (a) illustrates an example of combined diagram of the *Order* artifact. The dotted arrow indicates the hidden state transition and its corresponding hidden business rule, while the normal arrow indicates a rearranged transition with its modified business rule.

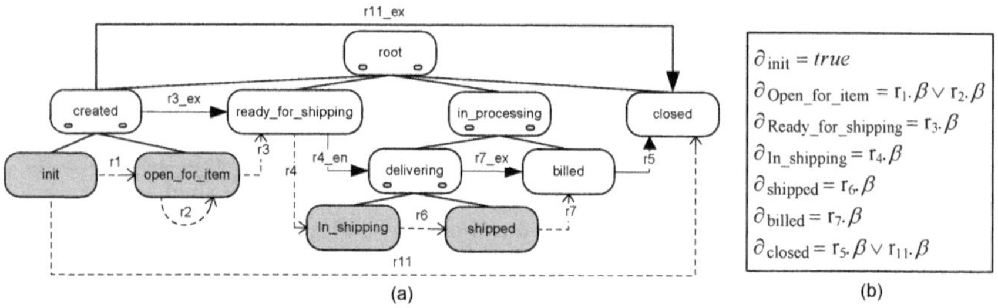

Fig. 5. (a) combined diagram for the *Order* artifact (b) compensating conditions

The modification process starts with finding *entry* and *exit* transitions of every hidden state and their parent composite state. If any transition is connected from/to a hidden state that is nested under the composite state to/from a non-hidden state, then that transition is rearranged to replace the hidden state with the composite state. If the transition is used to connect between nested hidden states, then that transition is hidden. We define two auxiliary functions for finding the entry and exit transitions of the composite state. Function $entry(s_c)$ returns a set of entry transitions T_{en} of composite state s_c, such that every transition in T_{en} has the source state which is not a descendant of s_c and the target state which is a descendant of s_c. Function $it(s_c)$ returns a set of exit transitions $T_{ex}$of composite state s_c, such that every transition in T_{en} has the source state which is a descendant of s_c and the target state which is not a descendant of s_c. For example in Figure 5 (a), *entry*(*delivering*) returns {{*ready_for_shipping*, r_4, *in_shipping*}} and *exit*(*delivering*) returns {{*shipped*, r_7, *billed*}}.

Once we obtain entry and exit transitions from the *entry* and *exit* functions, respectively, then we rearrange them to the composite state by modifying business rules that corresponds to them, e.g., r_4 is modified to r_{4-en} and r_7 is modified to r_{7-ex}. The state propositions in their pre- and post- conditions are changed accordingly, e.g., for rule r_{4-en}, the *in_shipping* state is substituted by the *delivering* state for *instate* predicate in the post-condition of r_4, and for rule r_{7-ex}, the *shipped* state is substituted by the *delivering* state for *instate* predicate in the pre-condition of r_7. However, transitions for business rules r_1 and r_2 are hidden as they do not exist in the result set of either *entry* or *exit* function. We can say that those hidden states and hidden transitions are encapsulated in the *created* composite state. Note that hiding a business rule may have a propagate modification effect to other artifact if such rule is used to induce any transition of the other artifact, e.g., r_2 also induces the transition from its *init* state to *newly_added* state of the *OrderItem* artifact, so such transition must be hidden as well as those two states.

Due to the limitation of our scope discussed earlier, we consider only non-conflict set of state composition and hiding requirements, i.e., the view configuration must be self-completed, e.g., those two *init* and *newly_added* states must be predefined in the requirement in order to be hidden. Here, we also define another two consistency rules that the modification process must conform to.

Consistency Rule 3: (Atomicity of composite state preservation). Let $\prod^{l_2'} = sc(\prod^{l_1}, sr_{l_2}^{\ +})$ be an intermediate ACP view for role l_2 constructed based on ACP view $\prod^{l_1}$ with state composition requirement $sr_{l_2}^{\ +}$, and let $\prod^{l_2} = sh(\prod^{l_2'}, sr_{l_2}^{\ -})$ be an ACP view for role l_2 that is constructed based on $\prod^{l_2'}$ with state hiding requirement $sr_{l_2}^{\ -}$. For any composite state that belongs to the view of artifact class C_i in $\prod^{l_2'}$ and every of its descendant that is hidden in $\prod^{l_2}$, the *entry transitions* and *exit transitions* to/from the composite state must be consistent if such composite state exists in both $\prod^{l_2}$ and $\prod^{l_2'}$, i.e.,

Given artifact lifecycle models $LM_{C_i^{l_2'}} = (C_i^{l_2'}, T)$ for a view of artifact class C_i in $\prod^{l_2'}$, and $LM_{C_i^{l_2}} = (C_i^{l_2}, T)$ for a view of artifact class C_i in $\prod^{l_2}$, if $s_x \in \prod^{l_2'}.S \cap \prod^{l_2}.S$ such that $|\,children(\prod^{l_2'}.s_x)\,| > 1 \wedge |\,children(\prod^{l_2}.s_x)\,| = 0$, then

(1) $\exists s_m \in \prod^{l_2'}.S \cap \prod^{l_2}.S$, $\exists s_n \in descendant(\prod^{l_2'}.s_x)$, $\exists r_p \in \prod^{l_2'}.R$, $\exists r_q \in \prod^{l_2}.R$, $(s_m, r_p, s_n) \in LM_{C_i^{l_2'}}.T$, $(s_m, r_q, \prod^{l_2}.s_x) \in LM_{C_i^{l_2}}.T$, $s_n \notin \prod^{l_2}.S$, and

(2) $\exists s_m \in descendant(\prod^{l_2'}.s_x)$, $\exists s_n \in \prod^{l_2'}.S \cap \prod^{l_2}.S$, $\exists r_p \in \prod^{l_2'}.R$, $\exists r_q \in \prod^{l_2}.R$, $(s_m, r_p, s_n) \in LM_{C_i^{l_2'}}.T$, $(\prod^{l_2}.s_x, r_q, s_n) \in LM_{C_i^{l_2}}.T$, $s_m \notin \prod^{l_2}.S$, and

(3) $\forall s_n (s_n \in descendant(\prod^{l_2'}.s_x) \rightarrow s_n \notin \prod^{l_2}.s_x)$

Condition (1) preserves the consistency of every *entry transition* that is changed from other non-hidden state to any nested hidden states under the composite state. Correspondingly, Condition (2) preserves *exit transitions*. Condition (3) ensures that every nested hidden state is removed and it also implies that every transition between those states is hidden. This ensures that the atomicity of the composite state is preserved in the constructed ACP view as well as the integrity of business rules of the ACP view is maintained.

Consistency Rule 4: (Business rule – transitions of multiple artifacts preservation). Let $\prod^{l_1}$ be ACP view for role l_1 and $\prod^{l_2}$ be ACP view for role l_2 that is constructed based on $\prod^{l_1}$. If a business rule induces transitions of multiple artifacts and any of these transitions in one artifact is hidden in $\prod^{l_2}$ then such rule and its induced transitions in the other artifacts must be hidden in $\prod^{l_2}$, i.e.,

Given artifact lifecycle models $LM_{C_i^{l_1}} = (C_i^{l_1}, T)$ for a view of one artifact class C_i in $\prod^{l_1}$, and $LM_{C_i^{l_2}} = (C_i^{l_2}, T)$ for a view of artifact class C_i in $\prod^{l_2}$, if $\exists r \in \prod^{l_1}.R$, $\exists s_x, s_y \in \prod^{l_1}.S$, $(s_x, r, s_y) \in LM^{l_1}{}_{C_i}.T$, $s_x, s_y \notin \prod^{l_2}.S$ then $\forall C_m \in \prod^{l_1}.Z \cap \prod^{l_2}.Z$, $\forall s_j, s_k \in \prod^{l_1}.S$, $(s_j, r, s_k) \in LM^{l_1}{}_{C_m}.T \rightarrow s_j, s_k \notin \prod^{l_2}.S \wedge r \notin \prod^{l_2}.R$

Revisiting the lifecycles of the *Order* and *OrderItem* artifacts in Figure 3, if we hide the *open_for_item* state of the *Order* artifact, then business rule r_2 is hidden, and consequently, the *init* state, the *newly_added* state, and their transition of the *OrderItem* artifact must also be hidden.

4.3.2 Attribute Conditioning Modification

Before we explain the detail of the *attribute conditioning modification*, we would like to explain the reason why this kind of modification is needed. As already discussed, when any state is hidden and *entry/exit* transition is rearranged to its composite state, the source state of the rearranged transition is changed from the concrete state to the composite state. In order to compromise the loss of the details about specific states when composing and hiding states, we attempt to maintain the condition of each business rule that corresponds to the rearranged transition as most specific as possible. As such, we propose to *strengthen* the attribute condition of the business rule.

Revisiting Figure 5, when the *init* and *open_for_item* states are hidden, business rule r_3 and r_{11} are modified to r_{3-ex} and r_{11-ex}, respectively. Both r_{3-ex} and r_{11-ex} will have the more abstract state condition in their pre-conditions, i.e., *instate*(*created*) instead of *instate*(*open_for_item*) in r_3 and *instate*(*init*) in r_{11}. So, we will need to strengthen their attribute condition in both r_{3-ex} and r_{11-ex}. Informally, strengthening an attribute condition of business rule for a particular transition is done by extracting other attribute condition in a post-condition of business rule that is used to move artifact into the source state of that transition.

Referring to the artifact lifecycle, we can see that when the artifact is in a particular state, it holds a post-condition of one of the transitions that bring it into that state, e.g., in Figure 5, if the *Order* artifact is in the *open_for_item* state, there will be an implication that either post-condition of the business rules r_1 or r_2 holds as they induce the transition into the *open_for_item* state.

Here, we define *compensating condition* for a group of attribute propositions of such post-condition that holds for each state.

Definition 14: (Compensating condition). Given ACP $\prod = (Z, V, R)$ and artifact lifecycle model $LM_{C_i} = (C_i, T)$ for artifact $C_i \in Z$, a *compensating condition* on state $s_j \in C_i.S$, denoted as ∂_{s_j}, is the logical disjunction of every attribute proposition of C_i in post-condition β of every business rule $r \in R$ that triggers a transition from any state in $C_i.S$ to state s_j.

Figure 5 (b) lists the set of compensating conditions for every state of the *Order* artifact. These conditions are extracted from the business rules defined in Table 1, e.g., for the *open_for_item* state, we have compensating condition $\partial_{open\_for\_item} = (r_1.\beta \vee r_2.\beta)$ = ((*defined(o.orderID)* ∧ *defined(o.customerID)* ∧ *equal(o.customerID, c.customerID)*) ∨ *false*). As the post-condition of business rule r_2 contains no attribute propositions of the *Order* artifact, so Boolean *false* is substituted for $r_2.\beta$. As discussed, at least one of the attribute post-condition of business rule $r_1$or business rule $r_2$must hold when the artifact is in the *open_for_item* state.

In order to strengthen the pre-condition of such rule, we add the compensating condition to its pre-condition. Now, we define a *modified condition* on transition $t_k \in T$, denoted as $\partial_{s_j}^{t_k}$, with state s_j as its source state, such that $\partial_{s_j}^{t_k}$ holds compensating condition ∂_{s_j} and pre-condition λ of corresponding business rule r_y for t_k, i.e., $\partial_{s_j}^{t_k}$ holds $(r_y.\lambda \wedge \partial_{s_j})$. Thus, we can see that the pre-condition of modified business rule for transition t_k is stronger than its original rule.

Revisiting the example in Figure 5, the pre-condition of a modified business rule for each rearranged transition of the *Order* artifact is: $\partial_{created}^{(created,\ r_{3\_ex},\ ready\_for\_shipping)}$ holds (r_3 .λ ∧ $\partial_{open\_for\_item}$), $\partial_{delivering}^{(delivering,\ r_{7\_ex},\ billed)}$ holds $(r_7.\lambda \wedge \partial_{shipped})$, $\partial_{created}^{(created,\ r_{11\_ex},\ closed)}$ holds $(r_{11}.\lambda \wedge \partial_{init})$, while $\partial_{ready\_for\_shipping}^{(ready\_for\_shipping,\ r_{4\_en},\ delivering)}$ holds the original pre-condition of r_4 as the source state of its transition is not changed. By adding compensating conditions, at least two transitions in the *Order* artifact for business rules r_{11-ex} and r_{3-ex} are different even they both have the same source state.

Note that if a business rule induces multiple state transitions of different artifacts, then every compensating condition on each transition in each artifact is added to the pre-condition of the modified business rule. This modification process conforms to consistency *Rule 5*.

Consistency Rule 5: (Attribute condition preservation). Let $\prod^{l_2'} = sc(\prod^{l_1}, sr_{l_2}{}^{+})$ be an intermediate ACP view for role l_2 constructed based on ACP view $\prod^{l_1}$ with state composition requirement $sr_{l_2}{}^{+}$, and let $\prod^{l_2} = sh(\prod^{l_2'}, sr_{l_2}{}^{-})$ be an ACP view for role l_2 that is constructed based on $\prod^{l_2'}$ with state hiding requirement $r_{l_2}{}^{-}$. For any rearranged *entry* or *exit* transition of a composite state in $\prod^{l_2}$, the attribute condition of the pre-condition of a business rule for such transition must hold a *modified condition* on that transition: (1) an attribute condition of the pre-condition of its original business rule in $\prod^{l_2'}$ and (2) a compensating condition on the source state of that transition. However, the post-conditions of them must be identical, i.e.,

(1) $\exists s_i \in \prod^{l_2'}.S \cap \prod^{l_2}.S,\ \exists s_j \in \prod^{l_2'}.S,\ \exists s_m \in ancestor(s_j),\ \exists r_p \in \prod^{l_2'}.R,$ $\exists r_q \in \prod^{l_2}.R,\ (s_i, r_p, s_j) \in LM^{l_2'}{}_{c_i}.T,\ (s_i, r_q, s_m) \in LM^{l_2}{}_{c_i}.T,\ s_j \notin \prod^{l_2}.S \rightarrow$ $(attr(r_q.\lambda) = attr(r_p.\lambda)) \wedge (attr(r_q.\beta) = attr(r_p.\beta))$, or

(2) $\exists s_i \in \prod^{l_2'}.S \cap \prod^{l_2}.S, \exists s_j \in \prod^{l_2'}.S, \exists s_m \in ancestor(s_j), \exists r_p \in \prod^{l_2'}.R, \exists r_q \in \prod^{l_2}.R,$ $(s_j, r_p, s_i) \in LM^{l_2'}{}_{c_i}.T,\ (s_m, r_q, s_i) \in LM^{l_2}{}_{c_i}.T,\ s_j \notin \prod^{l_2}.S \rightarrow (attr(r_q.\lambda) =$ $attr(r_p.\lambda \wedge \partial_{s_j})) \wedge (attr(r_q.\beta) = attr(r_p.\beta))$, where *attr(r.y)* is the function that

returns the attribute propositions in a conditional statement $y \in \{\lambda, \beta\}$ of business rule r, and λ, β is the pre-condition and post-condition of r, respectively.

Condition (1) is used to preserve the consistency of an *entry transition* in which a set of attribute conditions in the pre-conditions of them must be identical, as well as for the post-condition. Condition (2) is for an *exit transition* where a set of attribute conditions in the post-conditions of them must be identical, but stronger condition is allowed for the pre-conditions by adding the *compensating condition* on the source state of the transition.

5 Related Work and Discussion

The concept of business artifacts was firstly introduced in [7] with the modelling concept of artifact lifecycles. Gerede and Su [9] presented a formal model for artifact-centric business process specifications. Artifact classes are represented by adding object oriented classes with states, and guarded finite state automata is used to capture the logic of entities that carry out the work in a business model. Similarly, [11] focuses on the evolution of the business process logic by using services to model activities and a set of business rules to declaratively capture and represent a business model. Their work is in accordance with the four-dimensional framework laid in [10] for the specification of processes where business artifacts, artifact lifecycles, services, and associations between services and artifacts are constructed for describing business processes. The artifact-centric process model presented in our work is adapted based on their work with an additional specification to capture nesting states for constructing views of an artifact.

In the area of business process views, Zhao, Liu, Sadiq, and Kowalkiewicz [3] proposed the process view approach based on the perspective of role-based perception control. A set of rules on consistency and validity between the constructed process views and their underlying process view is defined. Many other closely-related works [2, 3, 5, 6] also presented approaches for defining and constructing process views, i.e., abstracted process, based on the consistency rules and constraints to support security/privacy requirements and to facilitate intra/inter organizational collaboration of business processes. Compared with our work, their work aims at process view construction for traditional activity-centric business processes while we propose the view framework for artifact-centric business processes.

Küster, Ryndina, and Gall [12] proposed a technique for generating a compliant business process model from a set of given reference object life cycles. Compared with our work, they transform the object-oriented process into the activity-centric process, while our work generates artifact-centric process views. Hull, Narendra, and Nigam [1] proposed a new approach to interoperation of organizations hubs based on business artifacts. It provides a centralized, computerized rendezvous point, where stakeholders can access data of common interest and check the current status of an aggregate process. They proposed three types of access restriction for stakeholders, namely *window*, *view*, and CRUD. *Window* provides a mechanism to restrict which artifacts a stakeholder can see. *View* provides a mechanism to restrict what parts of an artifact a stakeholder can see. CRUD is used to restrict the ways that stakeholders can read and modify artifacts. As far as process views are concerned, they did preliminary work on individual artifacts and did not consider business rules. No technique on view construction of business processes is proposed in their work. In contrast, we take business rules of business processes into account and propose a view condensation technique. We also define a comprehensive set of consistency rules to preserve the structural and behavioural correctness between constructed view and its base model.

6 Conclusion and Future Work

This paper presents a novel view framework for artifact-centric business processes. It consists of a process view model, a set of consistency rules, and the construction approach for building process views. The formal model of artifact-centric business processes and views, namely ACP, is defined and used to describe artifacts, services, business rules that control the processes, as well as views. We develop a mechanism of process view construction to derive views from underlying process models according to view requirements. Consistency rules are also defined to preserve the consistency between constructed view and its underlying process. Our future work will apply the framework for tracking and monitoring artifact instances in the context of process views.

References

1. Hull, R., Narendra, N.C., Nigam, A.: Facilitating Workflow Inter-operation Using Artifact-Centric Hubs. In: Baresi, L., Chi, C.-H., Suzuki, J. (eds.) ICSOC-ServiceWave 2009. LNCS, vol. 5900, pp. 1–18. Springer, Heidelberg (2009)
2. Eshuis, R., Grefen, P.: Constructing customized process views. Data & Knowledge Engineering 64, 419–438 (2008)
3. Zhao, X., Liu, C., Sadiq, W., Kowalkiewicz, M.: Process View Derivation and Composition in a Dynamic Collaboration Environment. In: CoopIS 2008, pp. 82–99 (2008)
4. Liu, C., Li, Q., Zhao, X.: Challenges and opportunities in collaborative business process management. Information System Frontiers (May 21, 2008)
5. Liu, D., Shen, M.: Workflow modeling for virtual processes: an order-preserving process-view approach. Information Systems (28), 505–532 (April 2003)
6. Chebbi, I., Dustdar, S., Tata, S.: The view-based approach to dynamic inter-organizational workflow cooperation. Data & Knowledge Engineering 56, 139–173 (2006)
7. Nigam, A., Caswell, N.S.: Business artifacts: An approach to operational specification. IBM Systems Journal 42(3), 428–445 (2003)
8. Liu, R., Bhattacharya, K., Wu, F.Y.: Modeling business contexture and behavior using business artifacts. In: Krogstie, J., Opdahl, A.L., Sindre, G. (eds.) CAiSE 2007 and WES 2007. LNCS, vol. 4495, pp. 324–339. Springer, Heidelberg (2007)
9. Gerede, C.E., Su, J.: Specification and Verification of Artifact Behaviours in Business Process Models. In: Krämer, B.J., Lin, K.-J., Narasimhan, P. (eds.) ICSOC 2007. LNCS, vol. 4749, pp. 181–192. Springer, Heidelberg (2007)
10. Hull, R.: Artifact-Centric Business Process Models: Brief Survey of Research Results and Challenges. In: Meersman, R., Tari, Z. (eds.) OTM 2008, Part II. LNCS, vol. 5332, pp. 1152–1163. Springer, Heidelberg (2008)
11. Bhattacharya, K., Gerede, C., Hull, R.: Towards Formal Analysis of Artifact-Centric Business Process Models. In: Alonso, G., Dadam, P., Rosemann, M. (eds.) BPM 2007. LNCS, vol. 4714, pp. 288–304. Springer, Heidelberg (2007)
12. Küster, J., Ryndina, K., Gall, H.: Generation of Business Process Models for Object Life Cycle Compliance. In: Alonso, G., Dadam, P., Rosemann, M. (eds.) BPM 2007. LNCS, vol. 4714, pp. 165–181. Springer, Heidelberg (2007)

Monitoring Unmanaged Business Processes

Nirmal K. Mukhi

IBM T J Watson Research Center
P.O. Box 704, Yorktown Heights, NY 10598
nmukhi@us.ibm.com

Abstract. Unmanaged business processes are an inevitable part of the operation of enterprises of all kinds. At the same time, monitoring such processes and measuring compliance against business policies is particularly difficult due to the effort needed to manually piece together information. A major challenge here is the presumption of incomplete or missing information and the uncertainty in making inferences about what actually occured.

This work proposes the use of a probabilistic provenance model to track the history of various process artifacts and reconstruct process traces. The major contribution of the work is the method of modeling the uncertainty associated with raw information as well as inferred relationships in a first class manner within the provenance model. We apply the techniques described here to a real world problem and compare results obtained in previous work where such uncertainties were ignored. The techniques described here are widely applicable to unmanaged business processes.

Keywords: Unmanaged processes, process compliance, probabilistic data.

1 Introduction

Unmanaged business processes are a vital part of a modern enterprise - they encompass a large number of human driven unmanaged workflows, the use of collaborative platforms to accomplish shared tasks, handling of exceptional situations that arise in the context of an automated workflow and so on. While they follow some notion of a business process, they are characterized by the free rein provided to actors to complete the necessary procedures. As a result these processes can be efficient as human actors flexibly adapt to various situations; however this also leads to such processes being a nightmare to monitor and audit. Records typically consist of information fragmented across various systems, often including unstructured documents and communications such as emails. Automation of such processes is certainly one way to alleviate these issues, but for various reasons such as cost or the inherent variability of the process, this is not always an option. Additionally, automation does not produce a fully-integrated end-to-end process; there are always gaps between systems and exceptional situations that have to be flexibly dealt with by humans. Thus, given the inevitability that such processes will always be around, it is prudent to study

R. Meersman et al. (Eds.): OTM 2010, Part I, LNCS 6426, pp. 44–59, 2010.

how we can monitor them. Monitoring generally is performed for two reasons: for measuring performance (perhaps feeding back into process improvement) or for the purposes of keeping records for audit. In this paper we address the latter application of monitoring, but the methodology could just as well be used for performance monitoring.

Provenance tracking is an important part of the methodology described. In general, provenance systems track artifacts from various systems and correlate these to create a provenance graph. Using the provenance graph, it is possible to recover process traces, data lineage, or maintain a record of user activity for various purposes. Provenance tracking has been used to assist in reproducibility of scientific experiments [17],[8],[16], monitoring complex processes that span multiple systems [7] and even measure compliance of unmanaged processes[9]. However existing literature has not sufficiently dealt with the issue of uncertainty in provenance data in a first class manner.

In this paper we first classify the uncertainties involved in creating provenance traces for unmanaged processes. Next, we propose a provenance data model for representing uncertain provenance traces. We describe the semantics of a provenance graph described following this model. A realization of this data model using a probabilistic database is described. We describe how we leverage facilities provided by probabilistic databases to perform queries over provenance graphs and thus efficiently answer questions about these process traces. We then describe a real world unmanaged process to which these techniques have been applied. We compare our results versus those obtained through a different approach that ignored uncertainties in the data[9].

2 Inaccuracies in Reconstructing Process Traces

2.1 Provenance Graphs

Provenance graphs are graphs that generally speaking have a fixed set of node and edge types and can be interpreted as a correlated network of events that occurred in one or many systems. One use of provenance graphs is to represent events that took place in the context of a workflow. In this particular application, nodes are used to represent instances of data, tasks, processes and so on at a particular moment in time. Edges connect nodes in order to represent semantic ties; common edge types include those that signify the temporal order of events, connect data to the corresponding task where it was processed, connect task instances to corresponding actors and so on. In the rest of this section, we will discuss how such graphs are created, and the issues around dealing with inaccurate reconstruction of process traces.

2.2 Trace Reconstruction

The process of reconstructing process traces from provenance data involves three distinct phases.

- Collection: This phase involves gathering provenance data from various source systems. Adapters are built to extract events or log information from the source system, perform appropriate transformations to produce provenance items and then record these provenance items into a centralized provenance store. For reconstructing unmanaged processes, a provenance solution would involve deploying adapters to all systems where any process activity occurs, such as document repositories, web servers, email servers and so on.
- Correlation: This phase involves correlation of provenance items within the provenance store. Correlation for the purpose of reconstructing a process trace will involve using an opaque process identifier if available, or a set of application data that collectively serves as the identifier for a process, and then using the identifier to stitch together the tasks, data and actors involved in the correct temporal sequence.
- Enrichment: When reconstructing process traces, provenance items recorded as multiple tasks by adapters may together correspond to a single business process activity from the user's perspective. Creation of this higher level abstraction would be done at this time.

It is important to note that these phases need to operate concurrently; data that is being recorded has to be correlated and enriched at the same time other data is coming in; i.e. development of the provenance information and its use to reconstruct the process trace is a continuous process. The outcome of this continuous process is a process trace represented as a provenance graph.

2.3 Uncertainties in Process Trace Reconstruction

Let us consider a simple unmanaged process. This is derived from actual customer experience and has also been used in an earlier work[9]. An e-hosting company manages applications for various clients. To comply with standard IT policies, the company is required to secure the client applications using a firewall. A set of firewall rules governs the operation of the firewall, and controls the IT security of the application being hosted. As a part of its process, the company is required to periodically evaluate the firewall rules and ensure that the client agrees to the current set of rules. The objective of this activity is to ensure that both the e-hosting account representatives and the customers understand what rules exist in the customer environment and ensure customer is aware of existing deviations from best practices defined by the e-hosting security policy. If such a process is not implemented, the customer may be at risk due to no longer needed protocols being available for transit traffic, or not being made aware of what protocols are in place and required for support of their environment. The e-hosting company may be held liable for insecure activities if the customer is not informed of risks involved or does not agree to them.

In this process, the information security architect (U_{isa}) initiates firewall rules revalidation periodically. The set of firewall rules is communicated to the account team (U_{at}) who has to then pass these on to the customer (U_{cust}). Once the customer has verified the rules, he will respond to the account team who then has to comunicate this to the U_{isa}. Communications between these parties take place

Fig. 1. The Firewall Rule Revalidation Process

via email. U_{isa} and U_{at} are responsible for storing these emails into a document repository for recording and auditing purposes. This process is illustrated in figure 1. Note that such processes are typically documented informally using textual documentation or Visio diagrams. Auditors are concerned about ensuring compliance with business policies that are for the most part concerned with timeliness of various activities. While there are many policies, we will concern ourselves with one particular one: the account team must receive a response from the customer within ten days. To check for compliance, in the current system auditors randomly select a few firewall rule revalidation processes that have been undertaken, and examine the recorded email artifacts. They have to then manually compare dates that the emails were sent and make their decision. The quality of the data records is extremely poor: in the process of uploading emails, users often skip headers or other email fragments that might be needed in order to ascertain the context of the email within the overall process. While in most cases email text contents are stored, sometimes users scan emails as images and upload these for recording purposes. Additionally, there may be missing or superfluous emails within the repository. Reconstructing a trace of what occurred is therefore non-trivial.

For this particular process, a provenance solution would involve deploying an adapter to the document repository to extract emails when they are uploaded and record relevant details to the provenance system. Correlation of emails to classify them into the particular process instance they belong would be performed through comparison of document metadata: this is fairly trivial and accurate in this example since emails are stored in appropriate document folder in the repository, and this is done with high accuracy by users. Next, emails need to be ordered by time and then classified based on the type of email. This would entail enriching the graph with additional edges to represent the relationships between items, and creating higher level abstractions to label emails after classification. In this example, even though the provenance data is trusted and correlation is accurate, the enrichment of the graph is bound to introduce uncertainty. The sample graph shown in figure 2 is a subgraph of the provenance graph obtained following this methodology.

The ultimate goal, for the purposes of checking compliance against the policy of interest, is to identify the first relevant communication between the account team and the customer, and the first relevant customer response following this communication. There may be multiple emails between the account team and the customer. Identifying the first *relevant* communication is the problem: deciphering the semantics of the email is difficult; given the limited scope of the problem various text analytics methods can be applied with some success, but ultimately we can classify the email with less than 100% confidence. The poor quality of data and the possibility of missing or superfluous data being present compound these difficulties.

Current provenance data models do not allow for the expression of uncertainty. In these systems, an event occurred or did not, and a relation exists or does not. In this process we describe, we would persist what would essentially be best guesses of what occurred. Now if we queried the graph for processes wherein account teams did not receive customer responses within ten days, we would retrieve a set of process traces that exhibited this feature. However the query results would not reflect the fact that for at least some of those traces the evidence to support the conclusion would be uncertain.

This discussion motivates us to classify uncertainties in provenance traces as follows:

1. Node versus Edge uncertainty: All the nodes in the provenance graph can be grouped into two categories, nodes recorded by adapters (*Type A* nodes) and nodes created through derivation from those (*Type B* nodes). Nodes recorded by adapters are accurate since they exactly represent something that occurred in a source system. Derived nodes, added through feature extraction or enrichment may however be inaccurate, and may therefore have uncertainty associated with them.

   Edges are recorded based on correlations or shared features between nodes. When edges are recorded between Type A nodes that were recorded from the same source system, they are guaranteed to be accurate (since they are based on correlations of consistent and accurate data). All other edges may be imprecise. For example, an edge showing time ordering between Type A nodes from different source systems may be inaccurate if the clocks are not synchornized. Additionally, edges beween Type B nodes may be imprecise since the node uncertainty is propagated to the edge, i.e. the edge may be created based on imprecise data.
2. Simple versus Complex Uncertainty: Uncertainty associated with a provenance item may be entirely a function of features of that provenance item itself. We call such uncertainty *simple*. Sometimes the uncertainty is a function of a set of provenance data; in such cases it is said to be *complex*.
3. Static versus Dynamic uncertainty: When the uncertainty associated with a given provenance item is fixed, it is said to be *static* uncertainty. Sometimes

the uncertainty associated with a piece of information varies over time. This is *dynamic* uncertainty.

In figure 2, all edges have *simple* and *static* uncertainty except for the *accessed* edges. These are still *static* since the uncertainty values do not change over time; however they are *complex* since they are not independent of each other.

3 An Uncertain Provenance Data Model

The provenance data model defines nodes and edges, the standard metadata associated with them and semantics of various types of nodes and edges. Applications share a data model and associated API and can then use the provenance system for adding, enriching or querying provenance data. The data model is thus crucial, and is akin to a standardized database schema or RDF model. The Open Provenance Model[13] is one proposed standard interchange format, but typically each provenance system has its own.

In our data model, node as well as edge uncertainty is captured in a first class manner. This data model extends the one defined in [7]. Provenance items belong to one of five distinct classes: data, tasks, processes, resources and relations. The *resources* class stands for provenance items meant to represent human actors, systems or applications and physical objects, while *relations* are a kind of provenance item that relate other items; the first three are self-explanatory. The essential properties of each of these provenance type are:

- Process: {ID,Timestamp,ProcessInstanceID,ProcessModelID,Confidence}
- Task: {ID,Timestamp,TaskID,TaskName,Confidence}
- Data: {ID,Timestamp,DataID,DataName,DataLink,Confidence}
- Resource: {ID,ResourceName,Timestamp,Name,Confidence}
- Relation: {ID,Timestamp,SourceID,TargetID,Confidence}

All provenance nodes have a unique identifier and thus all the types possess an *ID* attribute. The *Timestamp* attribute denotes the time when the provenance record was created and is also standard, as is the *Confidence* attribute which we will describe later.

Provenance data of the *Process* type represents an instance of a business process. The *ProcessInstanceID* identifies the process instance uniquely: this may be an opaque identifier such as process instance ID generated by a BPM engine, or it might be derived from application data: in the context of the Firewall Rule Revalidation process, the customer identifier and time the process was initiated could together be used as the *ProcessInstanceID*. The *ProcessModelID* references the process model that this particular process is an instance of. As with all provenance types, this is only the mandatory set of attributes; applications can extend these types and add additional attributes as needed.

Tasks associated with the process would be represented by *Task* nodes. *Data* nodes represent a piece of data at a point in time. The *DataLink* attribute is a URL that references the actual data on a repository or other location, which is to say that the data value itself is not maintained in provenance, just a reference to it is. Applications would define different subtypes of *Data* (for example *Document*) and add additional attributes as needed. For our scenario, all emails would be appropriate extensions of *Data* provenance items, and would include additional attributes such as *from*, *to*, etc. *Resource* items correspond to human actors or automated systems that are capable of performing tasks, accessing data and so on.

The interesting part of this model of course is the addition of the `Confidence` property to each provenance item. Confidence values reside in the set [0..1] and represent the confidence in the accuracy of that provenance item. If at the time of reconstructing the process we are unsure about the accuracy of a piece of data (for example whether the timestamp associated with it should be t_1 or t_2) we will record two separate provenance items for each of these possibilities, and associated appropriate confidences with each.

3.1 Semantics of the Model

Possible worlds semantics can be applied to the interpretation of a provenance graph created from these items. Following these semantics, each provenance item may be present or absent based on the confidence associated with its accuracy.

Given a set S of n provenance items $S = \{p_1, p_2, p_3 \dots p_n\}$, the power set $P(S) = \{\{\}, \{p_1\}, \{p_1, p_2\} \dots\}$ lists the set of possible worlds. Each member of $P(S)$ represents one possible reality of what actually occurred. According to the Bayesian interpretation, one of these possible worlds is a reflection of what actually occurred. The likelihood of a possible world being the correct one can be calculated based on the confidences associated with each of the provenance

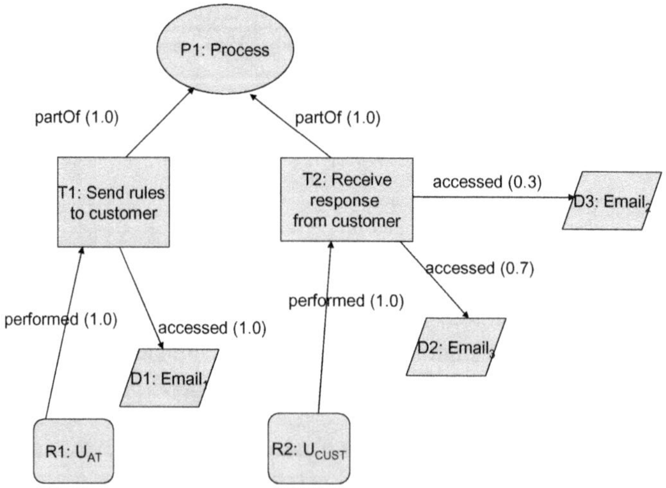

Fig. 2. A Probabilistic Provenance Graph

items within that world. If the confidence associated with each provenance item is assumed to be independent (a major assumption we will address further later), this is merely the product of the confidence of each of the items, that is for the possible world $S_k = \{p_1, p_2, p_4\}$, $Prob(S_k) = \prod p_1.c, p_2c, p_4c$ where $p_i.c$ denotes the value of the `Confidence` property associated with p_i. As an example, consider the sample provenance graph shown in figure 2. This is a fragment of a sample reconstruction of a process trace for the firewall rules revalidation process we introduced earlier. Node labels in the figure represent the type of node; $P1$ refers to a process node, $D1$ to a data node and so on. The numbers within parenthesis denote the confidences associated with the provenance data; confidences for all nodes are 1.0 (i.e. these are all known for certain and are thus not shown). As is evident, the part of the trace that is uncertain here is which of $Email_2$ and $Email_3$ correspond to the actual response from the customer to the account team. This is crucial knowledge since it may possibly determine if the process followed policy or not. This is a simple example; in practice there are many candidate emails, and most often a single email is a candidate email for multiple steps within the process.

3.2 A Probabilistic Database Realization

Probabilistic databases[2] extend traditional relational database systems with the goal of storing imprecise information and providing responses to traditional relational queries over this data. This has been an active field of research since the late 1980s; it has become more relevant as large sets of imprecise data such as that from sensors, unstructured data sources including the World Wide Web etc. are more available and vital to enterprises.

Probabilistic databases offer levels of scalability comparable to relational database systems, but suffer from two main drawbacks: they make simplistic assumptions about data in order to be able to perform queries efficiently (for example, the assumption that all tuples are independent, i.e. the uncertainty of one is not a function of any other) and they do not support the full range of queries defined in SQL. However for our purposes this is a reasonable first realization of the provenance data model; in the future work section we ouline other possible approaches.

For our work we used the MayBMS([2],[3]) system to store our probabilistic provenance graphs. The provenance probabilistic database consists of tables for each base provenance type, i.e. we have tables for processes, tasks, data, resources and relations. The table storing relations stores all edges and thus references data stored in the other tables. Each tuple has a column to store the probability associated with it.

Initially the probabilities associated with each tuple are just numbers to the database; the system has to be directed to, in effect, create the probabilistic variant of a given table. In this process, the probability distribution of the various tuples has to be specified. This can be done fairly simply: we merely need to identify, for each table, a key against which we can distribute the tuples in the table. This is well known for each kind of provenance item. For example, for data, the key is completely identified by the column *DataID*. Multiple provenance items with the same *DataID* correspond to the same piece of data. The total of the confidences associated with each of these items should total to exactly 1.0. We can direct the database system to distribute tuples in the *Data* table using the *DataID* column as the key, and the *Confidence* column for the actual probability.

Queries on probabilitic tables work as they do on relational tables for the most part; of particular interest is the `conf` operator provided by MayBMS. This operator returns the confidence that the associate query will return a result.

4 Firewall Rule Revalidation Revisited

We revisit the problem of recording provenance traces for the Firewall Rule Revalidation process discussed earlier, and show how we can efficiently compute compliance rates for the policy of interest. We reuse provenance collection, correlation and enrichment from earlier work; however this time we use our new provenance store implementation and redesigned compliance queries.

4.1 Solution Outline

We will focus our discussion on a subset of the process relevant to our compliance goal. The provenance collection and correlation will produce a partial trace consisting of emails correlated with process instances. We introduce our changes to deal with uncertainty in the enrichment process. During enrichment for this process, emails are connected to tasks in the process based on our assessment of which task the email corresponds to. In our earlier approach we combined feature extraction and scoring to evaluate candidate emails for this classification. However, only the best (highest scoring) candidates were selected and others ignored. With the luxury of being able to represent multiple possibilities, we now record each email as a possible candidate for each classification, with a confidence associated with it. The difficulty though is in deciding what the confidence should be.

For this purpose, we need to first go through a training phase where we determine how to assign a confidence level with each email classification. Next, we design our compliance queries for the scenario. Finally, we present our results and compare with the earlier approach.

4.2 Determining Uncertainty

We possess records for 55 process instances for the Firewall Rule Revalidation process. We randomly select 28 of these instances for the training phase. We go through the feature extraction and scoring process for each email. We now need to determine how well the score actually predicts the email.

For this purpose, we use the technique of logistic regression[12]. This regression analysis approach maps a set of predictor variables to a logistic function. These functions are constrained to have values in the range [0..1] and represent the

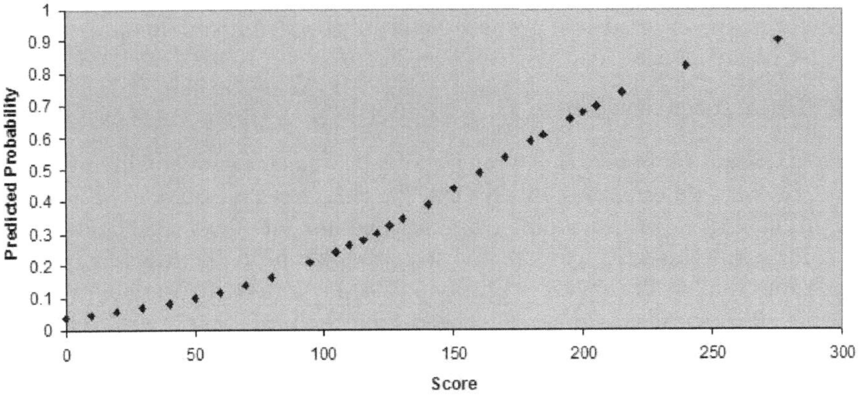

Fig. 3. Developing a Predictor Function for *Account Team To Customer* Email Classifier

probability of a particular outcome. In our case, we have one predictor variable (the score computed from the extracted features). For each process in the training set, we first manually determine what the correct email classification would be. Then, for each email in these processes, we run the scoring function to find how we would have scored the email. Given the set of scores and outcomes, we can run it through the logistic regression to produce our predictor function. We need one such function for each of the two classifications we are attempting to determine.

Figure 3 shows the results of applying this method to develop the function for classifying the first email (from the account team to the customer) of relevance to us. The regression method involves first carrying out a simle weighted linear regression of the observed $log[odds]$, where $odds$ refers to the odds that the email is classified correctly, given the score. For this we use our training data set. Once this regression is plotted, we can calculate the y-intercept (referred to as R_{int} in the equation below) and the slope (R_{coeff} below) of the regression function. From this, we can calculate the actual probability for an email outside the training set as follows.

$$log[odds] = R_{int} + R_{coeff}.score \tag{1}$$

$$odds = e^{log[odds]} \tag{2}$$

$$prob = \frac{odds}{1 + odds} \tag{3}$$

Here $score$ is the value of the scoring function used to classify emails. R_{int} for the first classification is calculated from the regression method as -3.2124. R_{coeff} is determined to be 0.0197. Following the same procedure to find these values for our second classification (the classification of emails as the first relevant email from the customer to the account team), R_{int} is determined to be -2.5393 and R_{coeff} 0.0085.

Emails may also be classified as having been sent by the information security architect to the account team; this is determined in similar fashion.

4.3 Data Integrity Issues

Once we assign probabilities for the possible classification of emails, we are still not done with determining uncertainty for our provenance nodes. The sum of the probabilities of the possible classifications for an email must add up to 1. To enforce this integrity constraint, we normalize probabilities over the range of possible values. The predicted probabilities for a particular email over all its possible classifications is summed up and then the probabilities are recalculated in the same proportion so that they add up to 1.

At this point we can record the classification information into the provenance graph. Each possible classification is recorded as an edge from the email node to the process instance node and has the calculated uncertainty associated with it. The classification itself is an annotation on the edge (we could also model this as an annotation on the email node itself). We now have a provenance graph as in figure 4 consisting of multiple instances of the Firewall Rule Revalidation process; each process instance is connected to multiple emails through one or more labeled edges that have confidence associated with them.

We now need to confront a second integrity issue: our scoring function naively assumes that each email can be independently classified. For our scenario, this is simply not true: one particular email can never in actuality be both the one sent from the account team to the customer and the response from the customer to the account team. For this purpose, we go through a filtering process to extract valid possibilities from the provenance graph. Each valid process instance consists of at least three emails: an email classified as having been sent from the information

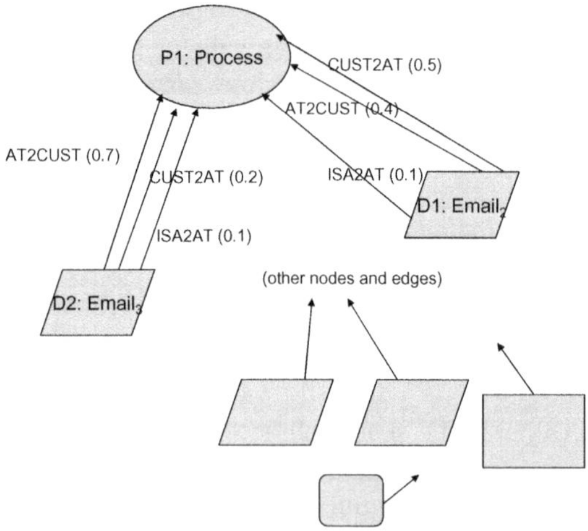

Fig. 4. Provenance Graph After Determining Uncertainty

security architect to the account team (U_{isa} to U_{at}), an email classified as being sent by the account team to the customer (U_{at} to U_{cust}) and finally an email from U_{cust} to U_{at}. Additionally, these emails have to be in the correct temporal sequence. This will give us a subset of the provenance graph we had previously constructed, this time consisting of valid instances.

4.4 Compliance Query Results

To measure the compliance rates against our policy of interest, we run a SQL query against the table containing valid processes (queried from the provenance graph as described above). Table 1 presents a sample of the data in our table. In this table, we represent the node IDs and timestamps for the three kinds of email classifications (U_{isa} to U_{at} referred to as `isa2at`, U_{at} to U_{cust} referred to as `at2cust` and U_{cust} to U_{at}, referred to as `cust2at`. Note that for a given process ID, there will be multiple rows representing the various possible worlds for that process. Additionally, since this table has been derived from the probabilistic table, each of the rows within this table would have the necessary metadata to support probabilistic queries (these columns have not been shown).

Table 1. Valid Process Instances

Process ID	ISA2AT ID	ISA2AT Time	AT2CUST ID	AT2CUST TIME	CUST2AT ID	CUST2AT TIME
1	dxl339-100301	1208878080000	dxl339-100283	1209044520000	dxl339-100270	1209044640000
2	dxl339-100717	1167769560000	dxl339-100741	1169138160000	dxl339-100711	1201202040000
2	dxl339-100717	1167769560000	dxl339-100741	1169138160000	dxl339-100705	1202481900000
2	dxl339-100717	1167769560000	dxl339-100711	1201202040000	dxl339-100705	1202481900000
2	dxl339-100726	1167765240000	dxl339-100741	1169138160000	dxl339-100711	1201202040000
2	dxl339-100726	1167765240000	dxl339-100741	1169138160000	dxl339-100705	1202481900000
2	dxl339-100726	1167765240000	dxl339-100711	1201202040000	dxl339-100705	1202481900000
2	dxl339-100726	1167765240000	dxl339-100717	1167769560000	dxl339-100741	1169138160000
2	dxl339-100726	1167765240000	dxl339-100717	1167769560000	dxl339-100711	1201202040000
2	dxl339-100726	1167765240000	dxl339-100717	1167769560000	dxl339-100705	1202481900000
3	dxl339-100741	1169138160000	dxl339-100711	1201202040000	dxl339-100705	1202481900000

The *conf* operator, as explained earlier, in a useful aggregate operator offered by the MayBMS system to measure confidence that a particular query returns a result. Our query thus takes the following form:

```
select processid,conf() as compliance from processes
where
   cust2at_time-at2cust_time<864000000
group by
   processid
```

Table 2 presents our query results. Given the estimate of compliance for a given process, this data can be used by auditors to select appropriate candidates for manual audit. Another possible use of this data is to use it to estimate an overall compliance percentage for this policy. One way to do this is to use an appropriate

Table 2. Query Results

Process ID	Compliance
1	0.674965
2	1
3	0.201406
4	0.276889226
5	0.07782871
6	0.453703
7	1
8	1
9	1
10	1
11	0.473442732
12	0.573093579
13	0.704026257
14	0.626483
15	0.983581
16	0.305146789
17	0.781029
18	0.698236
19	0.528497
20	1
21	0.252042688
22	0.504016644
23	0.609562552
24	0.63259198

threshold and estimate that process instances over the threshold must have been actually compliant, while those below the threshold were not.

Using the conservative value of 0.9, it turns out that 13 of our processes are marked as being compliant (all of which were in fact compliant when checked), while 11 are marked as non-compliant (of which, in reality, only 7 are non compliant). This means that we have a total of 4 false positives and overall accuracy of 83.33%. When the threshold is reduced slightly, we get more false negatives and fewer false positives, but poorer overall accuracy.

4.5 Comparison with Earlier Approach

As stated earlier, the earlier approach classified emails on the basis of the same feature extraction and scoring functions we used, with the major difference that only the email that scored highest for a particular classification (for example U_{at} to U_{cust}) and crossed a minimum threshold were classified as such. Let us consider a particular process instance.

The process instance with ID 6 has 8 emails correlated with it. As a result, there were many candidates for the three classifications needed. Our feature extraction and scoring functions were not able to confidently classify the U_{cust}

to U_{at} email (none of emails had scores that crossed the threshold). As a result, compliance with our policy could not be computed by the earlier method (in those results, such process instances would be marked as requiring human intervention).

By contrast, our current approach will consider all emails, even if they have poor scores - they will just be low probability classifications. For this particular process, we actually have 22 possible valid process instances. It turns out that many of these are non-compliant, and the overall probability that this process instance is compliant is only 45.3703%. Thus following our approach, this process is marked as non-compliant. Our method is thus shown to be more accurate when dealing with poor quality data.

Overall, the previous approach demonstrated accuracy of 75%, compared to the slightly higher 83.33% accuracy demonstrated using the probabilistic provenance graph approach. Notably, the new approach preserved all the conclusions of the earlier method that were correct (i.e. it did not result in any degradation), and provided additional correct conclusions for a few more process instances.

5 Conclusions

We have articulated how unmanaged processes are difficult to monitor and hence present challenges when it comes to checking for compliance. Traditional BPM research has focused on compliance from different angles: static analysis of business process models against stated compliance goals([10],[15],[4]), the prevention of non-compliant behavior through rules or business controls that are embedded into the process, the use of process mining to discover observed process behaviors and infer models that can be checked for conformance ([1]) and various commercial solutions, provided by most large BPM vendors, based on a combination of industry-specific rules and business rule engines. All these approaches are designed to work against formal processes that run in BPM systems and cannot be applied effectively to unmanaged processes. Process mining is the most similar to what we do in that it is focused on after-the-fact analysis of what actually happened. However, it is focused on discovering aggregate behavior, not on tracking individual process instances; additionally current techniques work off well-correlated process logs, not uncertain data sources.

In this work, we have shown how our probabilistic data model can represent events occurring in various data sources associated with unmanaged processes, and illustrated how these can be correlated and enriched to reconstruct process traces. Our MayBMS-based database was a first serious attempt at implementing a probabilistic provenance store and using it to run compliance queries against such processes. Our results for checking compliance of an actual unmanaged business process against one stated policy were encouraging in that we demonstrated improvement over a previous approach that disregarded uncertainty by considering only a single version of events.

There are many open questions we plan to consider in future work. The most important of these are how to best represent our data: probabilistic databases are one option, but graphical models such as Bayesian Belief Networks (BBNs) also offer support for representing such information; additionally they can also support representation of correlations between data (thus allowing easier expression of the kinds of data integrity constraints we discussed in section 4.3). Answering a query about the provenance graph would be recast to an inference problem over the appropriately constructed graphical model. Another issue concerns queries: queries over unmanaged process traces operate over structures that are logically graphs. A natural expression of queries over such structures would require us to look beyond relational query languages. Connectivity queries expressed using path logic ([5],[6]), datalog-like languages such as SPARQL ([14]) or specialized graph query languages ([11]) all represent possible options. We would also like to design a simple language for expressing queries over our probabilistic provenance model and use this to encode a standard set of process monitoring queries to capture common patterns. Finally, the set of possible worlds associated with even a small set of provenance data is huge: a set of n provenance items will have 2^n possible worlds. This exponential order implies that we have to be more selective in what is recorded, and develop more sophisticated algorithms for querying this data.

References

1. van der Aalst, W.M.P., van Dongen, B.F., Günther, C.W., Mans, R.S., de Medeiros, A.K.A., Rozinat, A., Rubin, V., Song, M., Verbeek, H.M.W.E., Weijters, A.J.M.M.: Prom 4.0: Comprehensive support for *eal* process analysis. In: Kleijn, J., Yakovlev, A. (eds.) ICATPN 2007. LNCS, vol. 4546, pp. 484–494. Springer, Heidelberg (2007)
2. Antova, L., Koch, C., Olteanu, D.: Maybms: Managing incomplete information with probabilistic world-set decompositions. In: ICDE, pp. 1479–1480 (2007)
3. Antova, L., Koch, C., Olteanu, D.: $10^{(10^6)}$ worlds and beyond: efficient representation and processing of incomplete information. VLDB J. 18(5), 1021–1040 (2009)
4. Awad, A., Decker, G., Weske, M.: Efficient compliance checking using bpmn-q and temporal logic. In: Dumas, M., Reichert, M., Shan, M.-C. (eds.) BPM 2008. LNCS, vol. 5240, pp. 326–341. Springer, Heidelberg (2008)
5. Benedikt, M., Grohe, M., Libkin, L., Segoufin, L.: Reachability and connectivity queries in constraint databases. J. Comput. Syst. Sci. 66(1), 169–206 (2003)
6. Benedikt, M., Reps, T.W., Sagiv, S.: A decidable logic for describing linked data structures. In: Swierstra, S.D. (ed.) ESOP 1999. LNCS, vol. 1576, pp. 2–19. Springer, Heidelberg (1999)
7. Curbera, F., Doganata, Y.N., Martens, A., Mukhi, N., Slominski, A.: Business provenance - a technology to increase traceability of end-to-end operations. In: Meersman, R., Tari, Z. (eds.) OTM 2008, Part I. LNCS, vol. 5331, pp. 100–119. Springer, Heidelberg (2008)
8. Davidson, S.B., Freire, J.: Provenance and scientific workflows: challenges and opportunities. In: Proceedings of ACM SIGMOD, pp. 1345–1350 (2008)
9. Doganata, Y.N., Curbera, F.: Effect of using automated auditing tools on detecting compliance failures in unmanaged processes. In: Dayal, U., Eder, J., Koehler, J., Reijers, H.A. (eds.) Business Process Management. LNCS, vol. 5701, pp. 310–326. Springer, Heidelberg (2009)

10. Ghose, A., Koliadis, G.: Auditing business process compliance. In: Krämer, B.J., Lin, K.-J., Narasimhan, P. (eds.) ICSOC 2007. LNCS, vol. 4749, pp. 169–180. Springer, Heidelberg (2007)
11. Giugno, R., Shasha, D.: Graphgrep: A fast and universal method for querying graphs. In: ICPR, vol. (2), pp. 112–115 (2002)
12. Hosmer, D.W., Lemeshow, S.: Applied logistic regression, 2nd edn. Wiley Series in probability and statistics. Wiley-Interscience Publication, Hoboken (2000)
13. Moreau, L., Freire, J., Futrelle, J., McGrath, R.E., Myers, J., Paulson, P.: The open provenance model: An overview. In: Freire, J., Koop, D., Moreau, L. (eds.) IPAW 2008. LNCS, vol. 5272, pp. 323–326. Springer, Heidelberg (2008)
14. Pérez, J., Arenas, M., Gutierrez, C.: Semantics and complexity of sparql. ACM Trans. Database Syst. 34(3) (2009)
15. Sadiq, S.W., Governatori, G., Namiri, K.: Modeling control objectives for business process compliance. In: Alonso, G., Dadam, P., Rosemann, M. (eds.) BPM 2007. LNCS, vol. 4714, pp. 149–164. Springer, Heidelberg (2007)
16. Simmhan, Y.L., Plale, B., Gannon, D.: Karma2: Provenance management for data driven workflows. International Journal of Web Services Research 5 (2008)
17. System, W., Altintas, I., Barney, O., Jaeger-frank, E.: Provenance collection support in the kepler scientific workflow system. In: Moreau, L., Foster, I. (eds.) IPAW 2006. LNCS, vol. 4145, pp. 118–132. Springer, Heidelberg (2006)

Fast Business Process Similarity Search with Feature-Based Similarity Estimation

Zhiqiang Yan, Remco Dijkman, and Paul Grefen

Eindhoven University of Technology
P.O. Box 513, NL-5600 MB Eindhoven, The Netherlands
{z.yan,r.m.dijkman,p.w.p.j.grefen}@tue.nl

Abstract. Nowadays, business process management plays an important role in the management of organizations. More and more organizations describe their operations as business processes, and the intra- and inter-organizational interactions between operations as services. It is common for organizations to have collections of hundreds or even thousands of business processes. Consequently, techniques are required to quickly find relevant business process models in such a collection. Currently, techniques exist that can rank all business process models in a collection based on their similarity to a query business process model. However, those techniques compare the query model with each model in the collection in terms of graph structure, which is inefficient and computationally complex. Therefore, this paper presents a technique to make this more efficient. The technique selects small characteristic model fragments, called features, which are used to efficiently estimate model similarities and classify them as *relevant, irrelevant or potentially relevant* to a query model. Only *potentially relevant* models must be compared using the existing techniques. Experiments show that this helps to retrieve similar models at least 3.5 times faster without impacting the quality of the results; and 5.5 times faster if a quality reduction of 1% is acceptable.

1 Introduction

Nowadays, service and business process management technologies develop quickly in both academic and industrial fields. To increase the flexibility and controllability of the management of organizations, business processes are used to describe functions organization provides and services are used to describe the both intra- and inter-organizational cooperations. As a result, it is common to see collections of hundreds or even thousands of business process models. For example, the SAP reference model consists of more than 600 business process models [16], and the reference model for Dutch Local Governments contains a similar number of models [9]. As business process model collections increase in size, tools and techniques are required to manage them. This includes tools and techniques for quickly searching a collection for business process models that meet certain criteria. These criteria can be specified by means of a search query [2,5], but also by means of (a part of) a business process model for which similar models must be retrieved [6,7].

R. Meersman et al. (Eds.): OTM 2010, Part I, LNCS 6426, pp. 60–77, 2010.

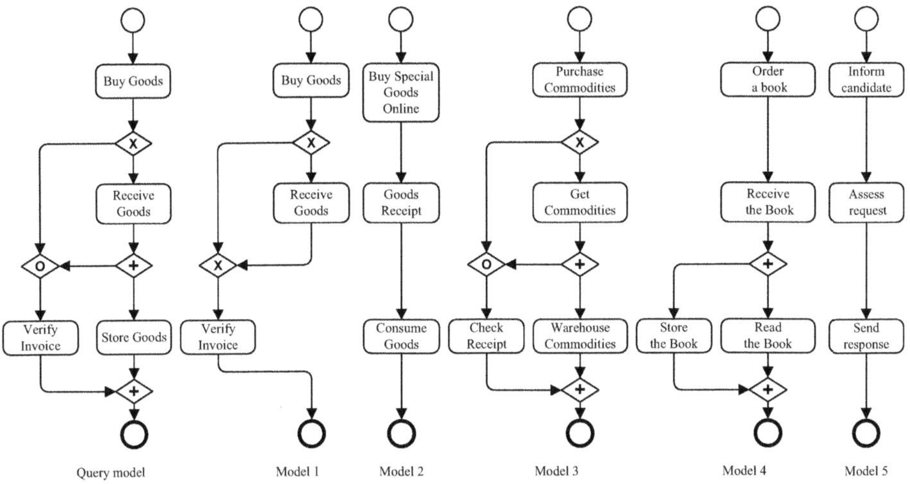

Fig. 1. Searching a collection of business process models

This paper focuses on the second class of search techniques, which are also called *similarity search* techniques. Similarity search can, for example, be applied to search a collection of reference process models for the model that best matches a process model from a specific organization; or in case of merger between two organizations to search which business process model from one organization matches which business process model of the other. Figure 1 shows an example of a business process similarity search. It shows one *query model* and five *process models* in the BPMN notation. Given a search query model, a similarity search technique should only return those process models that are similar to the search query model and it should return those similar process models in order of their similarity to the search query model. In the example, the technique could return models 1, 2 and 3.

There currently exist similarity search techniques [6,7]. However, these techniques focus on defining a metric to compute the similarity between two process models. To rank the business process models in a collection, the similarity of each of the process models to the query model must be computed. Subsequently, the process models are ordered according to their similarity. This is time consuming and can cause a similarity search operation to take multiple seconds or even minutes, depending on the metric and algorithm that is used, while a search query should be performed within milliseconds by a search engine, e.g., Google.

Therefore, the goal of this paper is to develop a similarity search technique that is both accurate *and* fast. The technique works by quickly classifying process models as 'relevant', 'irrelevant' or 'potentially relevant' to a search query model, based on an estimation of their similarity to the search model. Existing similarity search techniques then only have to be used to rank the process models in the 'potentially relevant' category, which typically contains much fewer models than the collection as a whole (in our evaluation set only 10% of the number of models in the collection), therewith significantly reducing the search time.

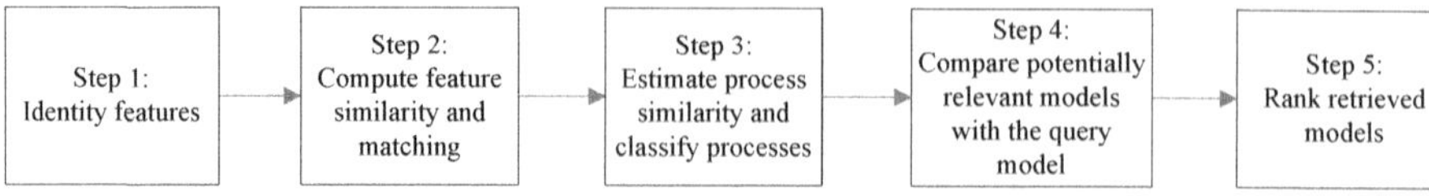

Fig. 2. Steps of the technique in this paper

The technique classifies process models based on the number of *features* that they have that match with the search model. The technique consists of five steps, as shown in Figure 2. First, features are identified in the process models that have to be searched. Features are simple but representative abstractions of a business process model, e.g., tasks and task succession. Second, the search model and the process models are compared based by looking at the features that they have in common, i.e.: that are similar enough such that we say that they are 'matched'. For example, suppose that we use tasks and task succession as features in figure 1. We can observe that model 1 has six matching features with the search model: the task features 'Buy Goods', 'Receive Goods' and 'Verify Invoice'; and the succession features ('Buy Goods','Receive Goods'), ('Buy Goods','Verify Invoice') and ('Receive Goods','Verify Invoice'). Models 2 and 3 have fewer matches or have weaker similarity with respect to their matches (e.g.: 'Buy Goods', 'Buy Special Goods Online' and 'Purchase Commodities' are similar but not identical labels). Models 4 and 5 have an even weaker match or no match at all with respect to the features that they have in common with the search model. Third, an estimation of the similarity of process models to the search model is made, based on the ratio of matching features, and models are classified based on their estimated similarity. For example, depending on the exact metrics that are used, model 1 could be considered as relevant based on matching features, models 2 and 3 considered as potentially relevant, and models 4 and 5 as irrelevant. Fourth, using existing technologies [6], process model similarities are computed for potentially relevant models, e.g., models 2 and 3. Fifth, retrieved models are ranked. Relevant models, which are ranked by their *estimated* similarity, (e.g., model 1), are followed by potentially relevant models, which are ranked by the similarities computed in step 4 (e.g., model 2 and 3). This finally leads to a ranked list of search results.

Experiments show that the technology helps to retrieve similar models at least 3.5 times faster without impacting the quality of the results; and 5.5 times faster if a quality reduction of 1% as a tradeoff is acceptable.

The rest of the paper is organized as follows. Section 2 defines the concept of feature and presents features that can be used for business process similarity estimation. Section 3 defines metrics for measuring the similarity of features and checking whether features match. Section 4 presents metrics to determine whether a model is relevant, irrelevant or potentially relevant to a search query, based on the features that match with features from the query model. Section 5 presents the experiments to determine the search time and quality of the similarity search technique. Section 6 presents related work and section 7 concludes.

2 Business Process Model Features

In this paper features are defined as simple but representative abstractions of business process models. Their simplicity allows similarity computation based on them to be fast and their representativeness ensures that their similarity is strongly related to similarity of the business process models themselves. This makes features very suitable as means to quickly estimate the similarity of business process models.

Provided that we choose business process model features carefully, we can further speed up similarity search by building an index of business process models based on those features. In this section, we present the business process model features that we explore in this paper.

In previous work [6,7] we have shown that the most representative features of business process models are their task labels and their structure. This means that if two business processes have similar labels for their activities, it is also likely that the processes themselves are similar. Similarly, if two business processes have a similar structure, it is also likely that the processes themselves are similar.

Labels can be conveniently used as features, because they are simple strings and therefore qualify as simple abstractions. In addition, indexing mechanisms for strings are well-known, which enables indexing of label features. However, it is harder to use the structure of a business process model as a feature. In fact, considering the structure of a graph when computing the similarity between business process models in our previous work is what makes the problem computationally hard. Therefore, we consider the structure of a business process model in terms the more simple structural features: start, stop, sequence, split and join. We define these features on the abstraction of a business process graph.

Definition 1 (Business Process Graph, Pre-set, Post-set). *Let $\mathcal{L}$ be a set of labels. A business process graph is a tuple (N, E, λ), in which:*

- *N is the set of nodes;*
- *$E \subseteq N \times N$ is the set of edges; and*
- *$\lambda : N \rightarrow \mathcal{L}$ is a function that maps nodes to labels.*

Let $G = (N, E, \lambda)$ be a business process graph and $n \in N$ be a node: $\bullet n = \{m|(m, n) \in E\}$ is the pre-set of n, while $n\bullet = \{m|(n, m) \in E\}$ is the post-set of n.

A business process graph is a graph representation of a business process model. As such, it is an abstraction of a business process model that focuses purely on the structure of that model, while abstracting from other aspects, e.g., different types of process modeling notations (BPMN, EPC, Petri net, etc.). However, because our measure of similarity is defined on the structure of a business process model, abstracting from these aspects is acceptable. Optionally, certain types of nodes can be disregarded in a business process graph. For example, figure 3 shows the business process graphs for the models from figure 1. Only tasks are considered in these graphs. Events and gateways are disregarded. We define our

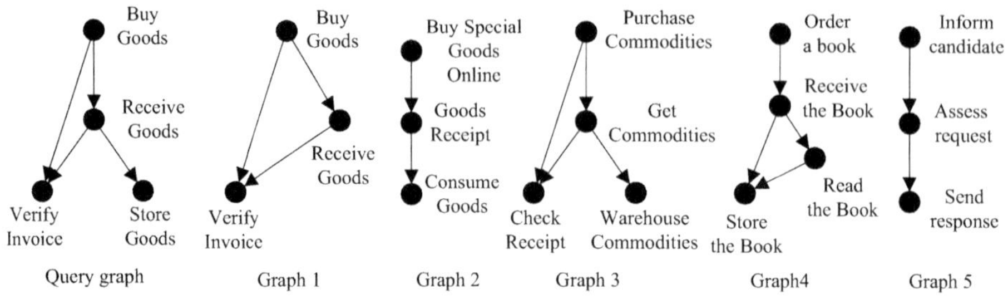

Fig. 3. Business process graphs

similarity search techniques on business process graphs to be independent of a specific notation.

Based on this the structural features are defined in Definition 2.

Definition 2 (Structural Business Process Model Features). *Let $G = (N, E, \lambda)$ be a business process graph.*

- *A start feature is a node $n \in N$ that has an empty pre-set;*
- *A stop feature is a node $n \in N$ that has an empty post-set;*
- *A sequence feature of size s is a list of nodes $[n_1, n_2, n_3, \ldots, n_s] \subseteq N$, such that $(n_1, n_2) \in E, (n_2, n_3) \in E, \ldots, (n_{s-1}, n_s) \in E$, for $s \geq 2$;*
- *A split feature of size s is a split node n and a set of nodes $\{n_1, n_2, \ldots, n_{s-1}\} \subseteq N$, such that $(n, n_1) \in E, (n, n_2) \in E, \ldots, (n, n_{s-1}) \in E$, for $s \geq 3$;*
- *A join feature of size s is a join node n and a set of nodes $\{n_1, n_2, \ldots, n_{s-1}\} \subseteq N$, such that $(n_1, n) \in E, (n_2, n) \in E, \ldots, (n_{s-1}, n) \in E$, for $s \geq 3$;*

For example, for graph 1 in figure 3, the label feature set is {Buy Goods, Receive Goods, Verify Invoice}, the start feature set is {Buy Goods} (using node labels to identify nodes), the stop feature set is {Verify Invoice}, the sequence feature set is {(Buy Goods, Receive Goods), (Buy Goods, Verify Invoice), (Receive Goods, Verify Invoice)}, the split feature set is {(Buy Goods,{Receive Goods, Verify Invoice})}, and the join feature set is {({Buy Goods, Receive Goods},Verify Invoice)}.

Many more possible features can be considered in business process models, depending on the business process model aspects that are taken into account (e.g. the organizational aspect or the data aspect), the desired performance of the algorithm (adding more features decreases performance) and the desired quality of the results (adding more features is expected to increase the quality of the search results). In this paper we focus on the most basic process model features. Extensions are possible and are a topic for future work.

Structural features can be considered in two fundamentally different ways:

1. by focusing on a single node and the interconnections that it has; or
2. by focusing on a small number of connected nodes.

More explanation will be given in Section 3.

3 Feature Similarity, Matching and Indexing

It is possible to use the similarity of the features of two business process models as an estimator of the similarity of the business process models themselves. To this end, metrics must be defined that quantify the similarity of the business process model features. We say that two features that are sufficiently similar are *matching features* and we show how we can determine feature matching based on their similarity. The ratio of matching features will be used in the next section as an estimator of the similarity of business process models. To be able to quickly identify matching features, and therewith similar business process models, feature indices must be defined.

This section first presents metrics to quantify feature similarity. Second, it explains how a feature match can be determined based on feature similarity and, third, it presents feature-based indices.

3.1 Feature Similarity

Label feature similarity can be measured in a number of different ways [7]. For illustration purposes we will use a syntactic similarity metric, which is based on string edit-distance, in this paper. However, in realistic cases more advanced metrics should be used that take synonyms and stemming [7] and, if possible, domain ontologies into account [10]. The label feature similarity is defined in the former work [6].

Definition 3 (Label Feature Similarity). *Let $G = (N, E, \lambda)$ be a business process graph and $n, m \in N$ be two nodes and let $|x|$ represent the number of characters in a label x. The string edit distance of the labels $\lambda(n)$ and $\lambda(m)$ of the nodes, denoted* $\mathrm{ed}(\lambda(n), \lambda(m))$ *is the minimal number of atomic string operations needed to transform $\lambda(n)$ into $\lambda(m)$ or vice versa. The atomic string operations are: inserting a character, deleting a character or substituting a character for another. The label feature similarity of $\lambda(n)$ and $\lambda(m)$, denoted* $\mathrm{lsim}(n, m)$ *is:*

$$\mathrm{lsim}(n, m) = 1.0 - \frac{\mathrm{ed}(\lambda(n), \lambda(m))}{\max(|\lambda(n)|, |\lambda(m)|)}$$

For example, the string edit distance between 'Transportation planning and processing' and 'Transporting' is 26: delete 'ion planning and process'. Consequently, the label feature similarity is $1.0 - \frac{26}{38} \approx 0.32$. Optional pre-processing steps, such as lower-casing and removing special characters, can improve the results of feature similarity measurements.

The drawback of measuring feature similarities only by labels is that related tasks can be labeled differently. For example, in figure 3, 'Buy Special Goods Online' of Graph 2 and 'Purchase Commodities' of Graph 3 are related to 'Buy Goods' of Query graph. However, compared with 'Buy Goods', the former one is more verbose and the later one uses synonyms. They may not match based on the label similarity. To deal with this situation, we use structural information together with the labels.

We can measure the structural similarity of two nodes, by determining the similarity of the (structural) roles that they have in their business process graphs. We distinguish five different roles that nodes can have: start, stop, sequence, split or join. We do not distinguish the type of splits or joins (e.g.: XOR or AND), because we established in previous work [6] that the similarity of the types of two splits or two joins is a bad indication for whether they are similar. Although we ackowledge that the disctinction between different types of splits or joins is of utmost importance when determining behavioral equivalence, we point out that measuring similarity is different from determining equivalence.

Definition 4 (Role Feature). *Let* $n \in N$ *be a node and* $\mathcal{R} = \{\text{start}, \text{stop}, \text{split}, \text{join}, \text{regular}\}$ *be a set of roles that a node can have. The roles of* n *are determined by the function* $\text{roles} : N \rightarrow I\!P(\mathcal{R})$*, such that*

$$\begin{array}{ll} \text{start} \in \text{roles}(n) & \Leftrightarrow |\bullet n| = 0 \\ \text{stop} \in \text{roles}(n) & \Leftrightarrow |n \bullet| = 0 \\ \text{split} \in \text{roles}(n) & \Leftrightarrow |n \bullet| \geq 2 \\ \text{join} \in \text{roles}(n) & \Leftrightarrow |\bullet n| \geq 2 \\ \text{regular} \in \text{roles}(n) & \Leftrightarrow |\bullet n| = 1 \wedge |n \bullet| = 1 \end{array}$$

Roles of nodes are considered to be similar or not with respect to the input and output paths of the nodes. The definition of role feature similarity is inspired by string edit-distance, i.e., mainly considering the differences between numbers of input (output) paths of two nodes. Formally, role feature similarity is defined as follows:

Definition 5 (Role Feature Similarity). *Let* $n, m \in N$ *be two nodes. The role feature similarity of these two nodes, denoted* $\text{rsim}(n, m)$*, is defined as:*[1]

$$\text{rsim}(n,m) = \begin{cases} 1 & \text{if start} \in \text{croles} \wedge \text{stop} \in \text{croles} \\ \text{avg}(1 - \frac{\text{abs}(|n\bullet| - |m\bullet|)}{|n\bullet| + |m\bullet|}, 1) & \text{if start} \in \text{croles} \wedge \text{stop} \notin \text{croles} \\ \text{avg}(1, 1 - \frac{\text{abs}(|\bullet n| - |\bullet m|)}{|\bullet n| + |\bullet m|}) & \text{if start} \notin \text{croles} \wedge \text{stop} \in \text{croles} \\ \text{avg}(1 - \frac{\text{abs}(|n\bullet| - |m\bullet|)}{|n\bullet| + |m\bullet|}, & \\ \quad 1 - \frac{\text{abs}(|\bullet n| - |\bullet m|)}{|\bullet n| + |\bullet m|}) & \text{otherwise} \end{cases}$$

Where $\text{croles} = \text{roles}(n) \cap \text{roles}(m)$.

This formula covers all possible combinations of roles that nodes can have. For example, the situation in which both nodes are split nodes as well as join nodes is covered by the case 'otherwise' ($\text{start} \notin \text{croles} \wedge \text{stop} \notin \text{croles}$). The situation in which both nodes are sequence nodes is covered by the same case and leads to a role feature similarity score of 1.

The drawback of measuring role similarity in this way is that it does not discount for the fact that there is a large difference between the frequency of the occurrence of the different role features. Therefore, using the role similarity

[1] *avg* returns the average value; *abs* returns the absolute value.

metric in this way is ineffective. Since, if we give a bonus for matching role features, most nodes would receive that bonus. Therewith, the effect of the bonus would be minimal.

For that reason we refine the role similarity metric to take this effect into account. We do that by not considering features that appear too frequently in the dataset; we say that those features lack 'discriminative power'.

Definition 6 (Discriminative Role Features). *Let $\mathcal{N}$ be the set of nodes of all business process models in a collection. We say that a role feature $r \in \mathcal{R}$ is discriminative, denoted* discriminative(r) *if and only if the fraction of the nodes that have the feature is sufficiently small:*

$$\frac{|\{n|n \in \mathcal{N}, \mathrm{r} \in roles(n)\}|}{|\mathcal{N}|} \leq \mathrm{dcutoff}$$

Where dcutoff *is a cutoff value that determines when the fraction of nodes that have the feature is sufficiently small. This cutoff value is a parameter that can be set as desired, to produce the best results.*

In general a good setting for dcutoff is easy to determine, because there is a large difference between the frequency of features with a low frequency of occurrence and features with a high frequency of occurrence. For example, in the set of business process models that we use for evaluation in this paper, there are 374 nodes in total and 178 the 'stop' role, 153 have the 'start' role, 58 the 'seq' role, 52 the 'split' role, 36 the 'join' role. Here, we have far more nodes with the 'start' and 'stop' roles than other nodes. Hence, if we set the dcutoff anywhere between 0.16 and 0.40, 'start' and 'stop' role features are not considered discriminative, while other role features *are* considered discriminative. We incorporate the discriminative power of role features into their similarity using the following formula.

Definition 7 (Role Feature Similarity with Discriminative Power). *Let $n, m \in N$ be two nodes. Their role feature similarity with discriminative power, denoted* rdsim(n, m)*, is defined as:*

$$\mathrm{rdsim}(n,m) = \begin{cases} \mathrm{rsim}(n,m) & \textit{if } \forall \mathrm{r} \in \mathrm{roles}(n) \cap \mathrm{roles}(m) : \mathrm{discriminative(r)} \\ 0 & \textit{otherwise} \end{cases}$$

3.2 Feature Matching

We say that two features are matched if they are sufficiently similar. What is considered to be sufficient is determined by cutoff parameters that can be set accordingly. If two business process models have sufficiently many matching features, we consider them similar. This is explained in the next section.

We consider two node features to be matched, if their component features (label features and role features) are matched. Strong label feature similarity is a strong indication that two nodes are matched, while a combination of role feature similarity and (less strong) label feature similarity is also an indication that two nodes are matched. We distinguish between these two cases when determining a node feature match, such that we can set different thresholds for label similarity in case there is also role similarity and in case there is no role similarity.

Definition 8 (Node Feature Match). *Let $n, m \in N$ be two node features with their respective label features and role features. The node features are matched if they satisfy one of the following two rules:*

- *their label features are similar to a high degree, i.e.,* $\text{lsim}(n, m) \geq \text{lcutoff}_{\text{high}}$*;*
- *their role features are similar, and their label features are similar to a medium degree, i.e.,* $\text{rdsim}(n, m) \geq \text{rcutoff}$ *and* $\text{lsim}(n, m) \geq \text{lcutoff}_{\text{med}}$.

Where $\text{lcutoff}_{\text{high}}$, rcutoff *and* $\text{lcutoff}_{\text{med}}$ *are parameters that determine what is considered to be a similar to what degree. The parameters can be set as desired, to produce the best results.*

We consider two structural features to be matched, if their component features (node features) are matched.

Definition 9 (Structural Feature Match). *Two start features with nodes n and m are matched if and only if their node features are matched. A stop feature match is defined similarly.*

Two sequence features of size s with lists of nodes $Ln = [n_1, n_2, n_3, \ldots, n_s]$ and $Lm = [m_1, m_2, m_3, \ldots, m_s]$ are matched if and only if for each $1 \geq i \geq s$: the node features of n_i and m_i are matched.

Two split features of size s with split nodes n and m and sets of nodes $Sn = \{n_1, n_2, \ldots, n_{s-1}\}$ and $Sm = \{m_1, m_2, \ldots, m_{s-1}\}$ are matched if and only if the node features of nodes n and m are matched and there exists a mapping $\text{Map} : Sn \rightarrow Sm$ *holds that for each* $(\text{sn}, \text{sm}) \in \text{Map}$*: the node features of sn and sm are matched. A join feature match is defined similarly.*

Features of different types or sizes are never matched with each other. We can use these two definition to define general feature matching.

Definition 10 (Feature Match). *Let f_1 and f_2 be two features. f_1 and f_2 are matched, denoted* $\text{match}(f_1, f_2)$*, if and only if they are of the same type and they are matched according to definition 8 in case they are node features or definition 9 in case they are structural features.*

3.3 Index Construction

Node feature matching is mainly based on label similarity and structural feature matching is as well, because it is based on node feature matching. Therefore, if we can speed up finding similar labels, we can speed up feature matching. We use two index techniques to speed up finding similar labels.

First, we use an M-Tree index [3] on node labels. An M-Tree index is specifically meant for quickly finding items that are similar to a given item to a given degree. In our case, we can use it to quickly find node labels that have a label feature similarity (definition 3) with a given node label that is higher than a specified cutoff ($lcutoff_{high}$ or $lcutoff_{med}$ in definition 8).

Second we use an inverted index [14] that maps node labels to nodes, to obtain the set of similar nodes from the set of similar labels. We use the inverted index, because multiple nodes with the same label may exist in a collection of business process models. For example, in the set of business process models that we use for evaluation in this paper, there are 374 labels, but only 190 distinct ones. The inverted index can prevent comparing identical labels repeatedly.

For other features, we also build inverted indices to prevent comparing identical ones repeatedly. Furthermore, we can build another index, if we exploit the fact that, to match a sequence of two nodes, we always need to match a node feature and, to match a sequence of three nodes, we always need to match a sequence of two nodes. In other words to match a 'larger' feature, we always need to match a 'smaller' feature. Using this observation we can build a parent/child index. This index functions like a cache that stores the similarity between smaller 'parent features' as well as the relation between larger 'child features' and their smaller 'parent features'. Using this cache, to match two 'child features' we can look up the corresponding 'parent features' and their similarity.

Definition 11 (Parent Feature, Child Feature). *If feature A can generate feature B by adding some node(s), feature A is a parent feature of feature B, and feature B is a child feature of feature A. If feature A can generate feature B by adding only one node, feature A is a direct parent feature of feature B, and feature B is a direct child feature of feature A.*

For example, node feature 'Buy Goods' is a direct parent feature of sequence feature ('Buy Goods', 'Receive Goods'), and sequence feature ('Buy Goods', 'Receive Goods') is a direct child feature of node feature 'Buy Goods'. An example of the parent/child feature index is shown in figure 4, which is an example of for graph 2 in figure 3. The index has different feature size levels, and the features of the same size are at the same level. Between levels features connect to their direct parent and child features. By doing this, we can start comparing features from node feature level and only need to compare larger features whose parent features are matched.

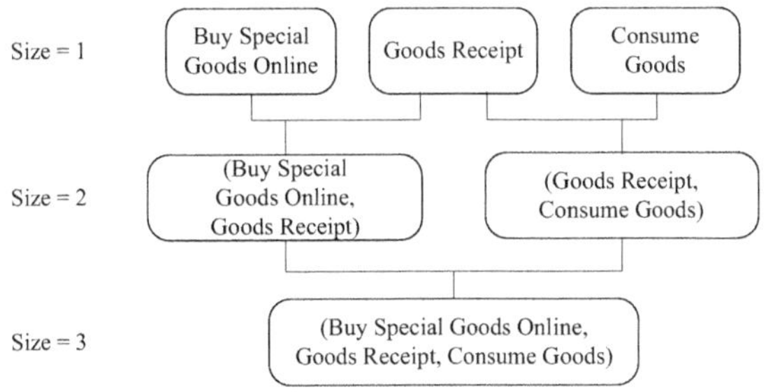

Fig. 4. Feature Index

4 Feature-Based Similarity Estimation

We use the fraction of features that match between two business process models to estimate their similarity, as shown in Definition 12.

Definition 12 (Estimated Business Process Model Similarity). *Given a query process graph G_q and another process graph G, with feature sets F_q and F derived automatically from G_q and G. The estimated business process similarity, denoted* $\mathrm{GSim}(G_q, G)$ *is the number of features in G_q or G that are matched by a feature in the other process graph, divided by the number of all features in G_q and G:*

$$\frac{|\{f_q \in F_q | \exists f \in F : \mathrm{match}(f_q, f)\}| + |\{f \in F | \exists f_q \in F_q : \mathrm{match}(f_q, f)\}|}{|F_q| + |F|}$$

Note that we count the number of features in G_q that match a feature in G separately from the number of features in G that match a feature in G_q, because the match is not necessarily one-to-one. For example, a label feature 'Fill-out Request Forms' can match with label features 'Fill-out Requester's Detail' and 'Fill-out Request Details' in the other process graph.

Based on the estimated graph similarity, we can classify graphs as relevant, irrelevant or potentially relevant to a search graph. We do that by defining the minimal estimated similarity that a graph must have to the search query graph to be considered relevant and the minimal estimated similarity that a graph must have to be considered potentially relevant. We retrieve relevant one directly, check the potentially relevant ones with expensive similarity search algorithms [6,7], and discard irrelevant ones.

Definition 13 (Graph Relevance Classification). *Given a query process graph G_q and another process graph G, we classify G as:*

- *relevant to G_q if and only if* $\mathrm{GSim}(G_q, G) \geq \mathrm{ratio_r}$
- *potentially relevant to G_q if and only if* $\mathrm{ratio_r} > \mathrm{GSim}(G_q, G) > \mathrm{ratio_p}$
- *irrelevant to G_q if and only if* $\mathrm{ratio_p} \geq \mathrm{GSim}(G_q, G)$

Where $\mathrm{ratio_r}$ *and* $\mathrm{ratio_p}$ *are parameters that determine when a process graph is considered to be relevant, potentially relevant or irrelevant and can be set as desired, to produce the best results.*

After determining the sets of process graphs that are relevant and potentially relevant to a query graph, we can rank them. We rank the process graphs in the 'relevant' set according to their estimated similarities (GSim) with respect to the query graph. We rank the process graphs in the 'potentially relevant' set by computing their similarity to the query graph, using an existing process similarity metric (e.g. one from [6,7]). The complete ranked list is formed by the ranked relevant process models followed by the ranked potentially relevant process models.

5 Evaluation

This section shows how the estimation step affects process similarity search in terms of the quality of the retrieved results and the execution time. It first explains the setup of the evaluation and second the results. We implemented a tool for the technique in this paper (including transferring process models to process graphs automatically).[2]

5.1 Evaluation Setup

We have two experimental setups one for evaluating the quality of retrieved results and one for evaluating the execution time, respectively. We use 10 search models for both of the evaluations, which are derived from the SAP reference model. We made some adaption to these 10 models to better evaluate the technique in this paper, e.g., rephrasing labels (synonyms) and using sub-models.

To evaluate the quality of retrieved results, we use the same evaluation dataset as in [6]. This dataset consists of 100 process models that are derived from the SAP reference model. This is a collection of 604 business process models (described as EPCs) capturing business processes supported by the SAP enterprise system. On average the process models contain 21.6 nodes with a minimum of 3 and a maximum 130 nodes. The average size of node labels is 3.8 words. For each of the 1000 combinations of a search model and a process model a human observer judged whether the process model was relevant to the search model. The R-Precision [4] of the search results returned by a particular similarity search algorithm can then be computed to indicate the quality of those results.

Definition 14 (R-Precision). *Let* $\mathcal{D}$ *be the set of process models,* $\mathcal{Q}$ *be the set of query models and* relevant : $\mathcal{Q} \rightarrow \mathbb{P}(\mathcal{D})$ *be the function that returns the set of relevant process models for each query model (as determined by the human observer).*

Given the list of search results $D = [d_1, d_2, ..., d_n]$ *for a query* q *with* $\forall d_i \in \mathcal{D}$, *the R-Precision is the precision of the first* R *results, where* $R = |\text{relevant}(q)|$ *is the total number of process models that is relevant to the query:*

$$\text{R-Precision} = \frac{|[d_i \in D | i \leq n, i \leq R, d_i \in \text{relevant}(q)]|}{R}$$

To evaluate the quality of the retrieved results, we compare the R-Precision of the greedy graph similarity search algorithm that we developed in previous work [6] to the R-Precision of the same algorithm with feature-based similarity estimation applied first. We use the greedy graph similarity search algorithm, because it is the fastest algorithm of the ones we studied [6] and, therefore, provides a lower-bound for improvements in execution time.

To evaluate the execution time, we compare the 10 queries with all 604 business process models in the SAP reference model, instead of just the 100 process models. We can do this, because to compute the execution time we do not need the relevance scores.

[2] http://is.tm.tue.nl/research/apromore.html

5.2 Evaluation Results

Table 1 shows the quality of the results that are retrieved by the original greedy similarity search algorithm and those returned by the algorithm in combination with similarity estimation, based on various feature types.

Table 1. Quality of retrieved results

Feature(n)	Occurrences	Matches	Relevant	Potential	Irrelevant	R-Precision
Former Work [6]	-	-	0	100	0	0.84
1:Node(1)	374	581	5.5	10.9	83.6	0.84
2:1+Seq(2)	+267	+197	8.1	8	83.9	0.83
3:2+Seq(3)	+175	+96	7.8	10.1	82.1	0.83
4:2+Split(3)	+87	+93	7.8	10.1	82.1	0.83
5:4+Split(4)	+23	+11	7.8	10.1	82.1	0.83
6:2+Join(3)	+58	+18	7.8	10.1	82.1	0.83
7:6+Join(4)	+14	+1	7.8	10.1	82.1	0.83

The rows in the table show the features that are used to do the feature-based similarity estimation. In the first row no feature-based similarity estimation is done, so this row lists the performance of the original algorithm. In the second row similarity estimation is done based only on node features (of size 1). In the third row similarity estimation is done based on node features plus sequence features of size 2 and so on and so forth (when a feature, whose size is bigger than 1, is evaluated, its parent features are always included).

The columns in the table show the properties of the features and similarity estimation based on the features. First, they show the number of times features of a given type occur in the set of process models and the number of times features of a certain type match in the set of process models. For example, in the set of process models, there could be four nodes labeled 'A'. These nodes count as four occurrences of the node feature type. Because of their high label feature similarity, these nodes can be considered to match. This leads to six matches, because each of the four nodes can be matches to each of the others. Second, the columns show the average number of process models that is estimated as being relevant, potentially relevant and irrelevant over the ten queries. Third, the columns show the average R-Precision over the ten queries.

The table shows that when similarity estimation is done based only on node features on average 5.5 models are estimated to be relevant, 10.9 models to be potentially relevant and 83.6 models as irrelevant. Therefore, in this situation, the original algorithm only has to be used to measure the similarity of about 11% of the total number of process models. In this case the R-Precision remains the same. If sequences of size two are also used to perform the similarity estimation, only 8% of the process models has to be compared using the original algorithm. However, this does lead to a slightly lower R-Precision. Inclusion of other types of features does not improve the similarity estimation any further.

Table 2. Execution time of similarity search

Features(n)	Relevant	Potential	Irrelevant	$T_{estimate}$	$T_{compute}$	T^{avg}_{total}	T^{min}_{total}	T^{max}_{total}
Former Work [6]	0	604	0	0.00s	0.60s	0.60s	0.16s	1.45s
1:Node(1)	7	73	524	0.05s	0.12s	0.17s	0.03s	0.40s
2:1+Seq(2)	13.7	44.9	554.4	0.05s	0.06s	0.11s	0.03s	0.24s
3:2+Seq(3)	9.5	73.2	521.3	0.05s	0.16s	0.21s	0.03s	0.43s
4:2+Split(3)	9.5	73.2	521.3	0.05s	0.16s	0.21s	0.03s	0.43s
5:4+Split(4)	9.5	73.2	521.3	0.05s	0.16s	0.21s	0.03s	0.43s
6:2+Join(3)	9.5	73.2	521.3	0.05s	0.16s	0.21s	0.03s	0.43s
7:6+Join(4)	9.5	73.2	521.3	0.05s	0.16s	0.21s	0.03s	0.43s

Table 2 shows the execution time of the similarity search both when only using the original algorithm and when using certain feature types for similarity estimation. All the experiment are run on a laptop with the Intel Core2 Duo processor T7500 CPU (2.2GHz, 800MHz FSB, 4MB L2 cache), 4 GB DDR2 memory, the Windows Vista operating system and the SUN Java Virtual Machine version 1.6.

The execution time consists of two parts: the total time it takes to estimate the similarity and classify process models as relevant, potentially relevant or irrelevant, denoted $T_{estimate}$; and the time it takes to compute the similarity for the models classified as potentially relevant, denoted $T_{compute}$. Table 2 shows the average estimation and computation times over the ten search queries. In addition to that it shows the average total time over the ten queries and the (minimum) time of processing the query that takes the least time and the (maximum) time of processing the query that takes the most time.

The table shows that if we, on average, estimating similarity based on node features helps to retrieve similar models 3.5 times faster and from table 1 we know that this does not impact the quality of the search results. Also involving the sequence of size two feature type even helps retrieve similar models 5.5 times faster, but from table 1 we know that this reduces the quality of the results by about 1% as a tradeoff.

The table also shows that, on average, the total search time for the original algorithm is quite acceptable and takes only 0.60 seconds. However, in the worst case the total search time for the original algorithm is already 1.45 seconds and this time is linear over the number of models in the collection, meaning that if we were to search a collection of 2000 models (the size of the collection of business process of a large telecom provider in the Netherlands) the search time would already be around 5 seconds in the worst case. This is still much slower than common search engines, e.g., Google.

The technique depends on several parameters:

- dcutoff, which is a parameter that determines whether a role feature is considered to be discriminative (Definition 6).
- $lcutoff_{high}$, rcutoff and $lcutoff_{med}$, which are parameters that determine what is considered to be a sufficiently similar for a feature to match (Definition 10).

- ratio_r and ratio_p, which are parameters that determine which class a process model belongs to based on the fraction of features that match with the search query model (Definition 13).

We vary each of these parameters from 0 to 1 in increments of 0.1 and ran the experiments with all possible combinations of parameter values within this range. We use the parameters that, on average, gives the highest R-Precision or the fewest potentially relevant models with respect to the queries to show attractive tradeoffs. The values that we use are $dcutoff = 0.3$, $lcutoff_{high} = 0.8$, $rcutoff = 1.0$ and $lcutoff_{med} = 0.2$. The other two parameters also depend on the type of features we use. For the node feature (the second row in Table 1 or 2), $ratio_r = 0.5$; otherwise, $ratio_r = 0.2$. For the node and sequence (with two nodes) features (the second and third rows in Table 1 or 2), $ratio_p = 0.1$; otherwise, $ratio_p = 0.0$. The values of the parameters are specific to this dataset. More general values for should be obtained by doing more experiments.

6 Related Work

The work presented in this paper is related to business process similarity search techniques and to general graph similarity search techniques, which we use as a basis for the work in this paper.

Business process similarity search techniques have been developed from different angles [1,10,11,12,13,15,19]. These techniques mainly vary with respect to the information, incorporated in the business process models, that they use to determine similarity [6] and the underlying formalism that they use to determine similarity [8]. The work described in this paper complements existing business process similarity search techniques, because it focuses on estimating business process similarity, rather than measuring it exactly, and using that estimate to improve the time performance of existing techniques. As such it can be combined with any of the existing techniques to improve their performance. Lu and Sadiq [12] also use features to determine similarity, but because their goal differs from the goal of this paper (they want to measure similarity exactly), their features are larger than ours, potentially consisting of a complete process model. This makes their features suitable for measuring similarity exactly, but not for estimating it quickly.

General graph similarity search has been applied in various application domains, including fingerprint search, DNA search and chemical compound search. In these domains feature-based methods have been used for similarity estimation and measurement. Willett et al. [18] describe feature-based similarity search in a chemical compound databases. For the structure-based method, ShaSha et al. [17] propose a path-based approach; Yan et al. [20] use discriminative frequent structures to index graphs; Zhao et al. [22] prove that using tree structures and a small number of discriminative graph structures to index graphs is a good choice. Furthermore, Yan et al. [21] also investigate the relationship between feature-based and structure-based methods and built an connection between the two. The main difference between the work that has been done in this area and the work in this paper, is the different nature of business process graphs as compared to graphs in other domains. In particular, there is practically no restriction to the number of possible node labels in a business process graphs and matching nodes do not necessarily have the identical labels. In comparison dna nodes have four possible labels, chemical compound nodes have 117 possible labels, and in both cases matching nodes have identical labels. Also, business process graphs have different structural properties and patterns. These characteristics require that feature types are defined specifically for business process graphs. In addition to that processing feature similarity is different, because business process graphs do not require features to match exactly for graphs to be similar, while graphs in other domains do require features to match exactly.

7 Conclusion

This paper presents a technique for improving the speed of business process similarity search. The evaluation shows that the search time of the fastest algorithm for business process similarity search that exists today can be reduced by a factor 3.5 on average, without impacting the quality of the results. The execution time can even be reduced by a factor 5.5, if a reduction of the quality of the results of 1% is acceptable. These reductions are computed as the average reduction over ten queries. The reduction for the most complex query is a factor 16.5 and the reduction for the least complex query is a factor 2.5.

The technique works by quickly classifying models in a collection as either relevant, irrelevant or potentially relevant to a search query. The original algorithm then only has to be used to classify the potentially relevant models in the collection. The classification is done based on simple, but representative, parts of business process models, also called features. The evaluation shows that the factor 3.5 reduction of processing time is achieved, if the labels and the interconnections of individual nodes from a business process model are used as features to estimate the similarity. The factor 5.5 reduction of processing time with a reduction of 1% on the quality of the search results is achieved, if individual nodes, their interconnections and sequences of two nodes are used as features to estimate the similarity. Other features that have been used are sequences of three nodes and splits and joins. However, these features do not further improve the quality of the search results or reduce the search time.

Let k be the number of process models in the collection and n be the maximum number of nodes in a single process model. To determine similarity of process models based on node features, for each node in the search graph, similar nodes need to be selected from all the nodes in the M-Tree. There are at most $k \cdot n$ nodes in the M-Tree when all the nodes are distinct from each other. Therefore, the time complexity of node feature similarity has an upper bound of $O(n \cdot log(k \cdot n))$, while the time complexity of the, currently fastest, greedy algorithm for process similarity search is $O(k \cdot n^3)$ [6]. The complexity of similarity with respect to other features is linear, because it depends on node feature similarity of which the results can be stored.

There are some drawbacks to the technique in this paper. First, the estimation is mainly based on label similarity. However, similar tasks can be labeled differently, e.g., synonyms, different levels of verbosity. The paper uses discriminative role features to deal with this issue, which have proven to be effective in the context of our evaluation data set. However, in our evaluation data set process models were constructed by the same people, leading to models that have similar labels for similar tasks. This may not always be the case. Therefore, we applied more advanced metrics for label similarity that consider synonyms [7] and domain ontologies [10]. The integration of these advanced metrics into the technique described in this paper is left for future work. Second, the technique in this paper mainly focuses on tasks and connections between them. However, process models often contain more information that may be exploited when determining their similarity, e.g., resources and data used. Using this information when determining process similarity is left for future work.

Acknowledgement

The research is supported by the China Scholarship Council (CSC).

References

1. van der Aalst, W.M.P., de Medeiros, A.K.A., Weijters, A.J.M.M.T.: Process Equivalence: Comparing Two Process Models based on Observed Behavior. In: Dustdar, S., Fiadeiro, J.L., Sheth, A.P. (eds.) BPM 2006. LNCS, vol. 4102, pp. 129–144. Springer, Heidelberg (2006)
2. Awad, A.: BPMN-Q: A language to query business processes. In: Proceedings of EMISA 2007, Nanjing, China, pp. 115–128 (2007)
3. Bartolini, I., Ciaccia, P., Patella, M.: String Matching with Metric Trees Using an Approximate Distance. In: Laender, A.H.F., Oliveira, A.L. (eds.) SPIRE 2002. LNCS, vol. 2476, p. 271. Springer, Heidelberg (2002)
4. Buckley, C., Voorhees, E.M.: Evaluating Evaluation Measure Stability. In: Proceedings of the ACM SIGIR Conference, pp. 33–40 (2000)
5. Choi, I., Kim, K., Jang, M.: An xml-based process repository and process query language for integrated process management. Knowledge and Process Management 14(4), 303–316 (2007)
6. Dijkman, R.M., Dumas, M., García-Bañuelos, L.: Graph Matching Algorithms for Business Process Model Similarity Search. In: Dayal, U., Eder, J., Koehler, J., Reijers, H.A. (eds.) Business Process Management. LNCS, vol. 5701, pp. 48–63. Springer, Heidelberg (2009)
7. van Dongen, B.F., Dijkman, R.M., Mendling, J.: Measuring Similarity between Business Process Models. In: Bellahsène, Z., Léonard, M. (eds.) CAiSE 2008. LNCS, vol. 5074, pp. 450–464. Springer, Heidelberg (2008)
8. Dumas, M., García-Bañuelos, L., Dijkman, R.M.: Similarity Search of Business Process Models. Technical Committee on Data Engineering 32(3), 23–28 (2009)
9. Documentair structuurplan, `http://www.model-dsp.nl`
10. Ehrig, M., Koschmider, A., Oberweis, A.: Measuring similarity between semantic business process models. In: Proceedings of the 4th Asia-Pacific Conference on Conceptual Modelling, Ballarat, Victoria, Australia, pp. 71–80 (2007)

11. Li, C., Reichert, M.U., Wombacher, A.: On Measuring Process Model Similarity based on High-level Change Operations. In: Li, Q., Spaccapietra, S., Yu, E., Olivé, A. (eds.) ER 2008. LNCS, vol. 5231, pp. 248–264. Springer, Heidelberg (2008)
12. Lu, R., Sadiq, S.K.: On the Discovery of Preferred Work Practice through Business Process Variants. In: Parent, C., Schewe, K.-D., Storey, V.C., Thalheim, B. (eds.) ER 2007. LNCS, vol. 4801, pp. 165–180. Springer, Heidelberg (2007)
13. Madhusudan, T., Zhao, L., Marshall, B.: A Case-based Reasoning Framework for Workflow Model Management. Data Knowledge Engineering 50(1), 87–115 (2004)
14. Manning, C.D., Raghavan, P., Schütze, H.: Introduction to Information Retrieval. Cambridge University Press, Cambridge (2008)
15. Minor, M., Tartakovski, A., Bergmann, R.: Representation and structure-based similarity assessment for agile workflows. In: Weber, R.O., Richter, M.M. (eds.) ICCBR 2007. LNCS (LNAI), vol. 4626, pp. 224–238. Springer, Heidelberg (2007)
16. Curran, T.A., Keller, G.: SAP R/3 Business Blueprint - Business Engineering mit den R/3-Referenzprozessen. Addison-Wesley, Bonn (1999)
17. ShaSha, D., Wang, J., Giugno, R.: Algorithmics and applications of tree and graph searching. In: Proceedings of the 21th ACM International Symposium on Principles of Database Systems, pp. 39–53 (2002)
18. Willett, P., Barnard, J., Downs, G.: Chemical similarity searching. J. Chem. Inf. Comput. Sci. 38, 983–996 (1998)
19. Wombacher, A.: Evaluation of technical measures for workflow similarity based on a pilot study. In: Meersman, R., Tari, Z. (eds.) OTM 2006. LNCS, vol. 4275, pp. 255–272. Springer, Heidelberg (2006)
20. Yan, X., Yu, P.S., Han, J.: Graph Indexing: A Frequent Structure-based Approach. In: Proceedings of the 2004 ACM SIGMOD, pp. 335–346 (2004)
21. Yan, X., Yu, P.S., Han, J.: Substructure Similarity Search in Graph Databases. In: Proceedings of the 2005 ACM SIGMOD, pp. 766–777 (2005)
22. Zhao, P., Yu, J.X., Yu, P.S.: Graph Indexing: Tree + Delta >= Graph. In: Proceedings of the 2007 ACM VLDB, pp. 938–949 (2007)

Quality Assessment of Business Process Models Based on Thresholds

Laura Sánchez-González[1], Félix García[1], Jan Mendling[2], and Francisco Ruiz[1]

[1] Grupo Alarcos, Universidad de Castilla La Mancha, Paseo de la Universidad, nº4, 13071 Ciudad Real, España
{laura.sanchez,felix.garcia,francisco.ruizg}@uclm.es
[2] Humboldt-Universität zu Berlin, Unter den Linden 6, D-10099 Berlin, Germany,
jan.mendling@wiwi.hu-berlin.de

Abstract. Process improvement is recognized as the main benefit of process modelling initiatives. Quality considerations are important when conducting a process modelling project. While the early stage of business process design might not be the most expensive ones, they tend to have the highest impact on the benefits and costs of the implemented business processes. In this context, quality assurance of the models has become a significant objective. In particular, understandability and modifiability are quality attributes of special interest in order to facilitate the evolution of business models in a highly dynamic environment. These attributes can only be assessed a posteriori, so it is of central importance for quality management to identify significant predictors for them. A variety of structural metrics have recently been proposed, which are tailored to approximate these usage characteristics. The aim of this paper is to verify how understandable and modifiable BPMN models relate to these metrics by means of correlation and regression analyses. Based on the results we determine threshold values to distinguish different levels of process model quality. As such threshold values are missing in prior research, we expect to see strong implications of our approach on the design of modelling guidelines.

Keywords: Business process, measurement, correlation analysis, regression analysis, BPMN.

1 Introduction

Organizations are increasingly concerned about business process improvement, since organizational excellence is recognized as a determination of business efficiency [1]. A business process is a complex entity, therefore improvement initiatives require a prior study of them at each of its lifecycle stages. The early phases of business process design might not be the most expensive ones, but they tend to have the highest impact on the benefits and costs of the implemented business processes [2]. However, process modeling on a large, company-wide scale require substantial efforts in terms of investments in tools, methodologies, training and the actual conduct of process modeling [3], resulting in several thousand models and involving a significant number

R. Meersman et al. (Eds.): OTM 2010, Part I, LNCS 6426, pp. 78–95, 2010.

of non-expert modellers. It is well known that poor quality of conceptual models can increase development efforts or results in a software system that does not satisfy user needs [4]. It is therefore vitally important to understand the factors of process model quality and to identify guidelines and mechanisms to guarantee a high level of quality from the outset. As Mylopoulos [5] suggests,''Conceptual modeling is the activity of formally describing some aspects of the physical and social world around us for the purposes of understanding and communication''. Therefore, understanding the process is a crucial task in any process analysis technique, and the process model itself should be intuitive and easy to comprehend [6].

An important step towards improved quality assurance is a precise assessment of quality. In this context, quality can be understood as "the totally of features and characteristics of a conceptual model that bear on its ability to satisfy stated or implied needs" [7]. We analyze quality from the perspective of understandability and modifiability, which are both sub-characteristics of usability and maintainability, respectively [8]. Several initiatives about business process metrics were published [9]. Most of these metrics focus on structural aspects including size, complexity, coupling and cohesion. The significance of these metrics relies on a thorough empirical validation of their connection with quality attributes [10]. There are, to date, still rather few initiatives to investigate the connection between structural process model metrics and quality characteristics, so we detect a gap in this area which needs more empirical research.

In accordance with the previously identified issues, the purpose of this paper is to contribute to the maturity of measuring business process models. The aim of our empirical research approach is to validate the connections between an extensive set of metrics and the ease with which business process models can be understood (understandability) and modified (modifiability). This was achieved by adapting the measures defined in [11] to BPMN business process models [12]. The empirical data of six experiments that had been defined for previous works were used. A correlation analysis and a regression estimation were applied in order to test the connection between the metrics and both the understandability and modifiability of the models. After the selection of the most suitable metrics for understandability and modifiability, we extracted threshold values in order to evaluate the measurement results. Such thresholds are an important aid to support the modeller of a business process.

The remainder of the paper is as follows. In Section 2 we describe the theoretical background of our research and the set of metrics considered. Section 3 describes the series of experiments that were used, and presents the results (correlation and regression analysis). This Section also discusses the findings in the light of related work. Section 4 described threshold values of measures and different levels of understandability and modifiability, and, finally, Section 5 draws conclusions and presents topics for future research.

2 Theoretical Background

This section presents the background of our research. Section 2.1 discusses theories that are relevant when considering structural metrics for process models. Section 2.2 describes the set of process model metrics that we consider for this research.

2.1 Theoretical Considerations on Process Model Usability

The usability of process models can be approached from the perspective of the ISO 9126 standard on software engineering product quality [8]. This specification identifies several dimensions of usability and maintainability, of which understandability and modifiability are among the most important. The significance of these two dimensions relates to several observations.

The subject of understanding is well-suited to the role of a pillar in the quest for theories of process modelling quality. Insights from cognitive research on programming languages point to the fact that `design is redesign' [13]: a computer program is not written sequentially; a programmer typically works on different chunks of the problem in an opportunistic order. Therefore, the designer has to constantly reinterpret the current work context. There are some indications that process modelling involves this kind of re-inspection activities [14]. This fact points to understanding as an important quality factor. There are also indications that process models have to be constantly reworked and modified, and that a lack of maintenance procedures can have a detrimental effect on process modelling initiatives [15]. In other words, the process model should be constructed in such a way that it reveals its content in the best possible manner. Both understandability and modifiability can, therefore, be leveraged.

A set of different factors for process model understanding has been discussed in literature, including personal factors, modelling purpose, domain knowledge, and modelling notation [16]. Several works have identified structural parameters as significant factors in understanding [12-15]. The importance of structural aspects stems from cognitive considerations. Research into the cognitive dimensions framework defines flow charting languages as being abstraction hating [17]. This signifies that languages for process modelling do not provide a direct mechanism for grouping activities. Another characteristic is that there are so-called hidden dependencies in process models. This entails that attainable states and potential transitions have to be inferred by the reader of a process model. These points imply that even small changes to the structural level can make a process model much more difficult to understand. This raises the question of how structure can be effectively measured.

2.2 Structural Metrics for Process Models

There is a wide range of structural metrics for process models. Their advantage is that they can be objectively measured by considering the formal graph structure of a process model. These metrics are, therefore, also called internal attributes of a process model. In our discussion on usability and maintainability we are interested in how far these internal attributes can approximate understandability and modifiability. As these aspects cannot be directly measured for the process model at hand, they are referred to as external attributes. They need to be determined by empirical evaluation through, for example, the help of experiments. Figure 1 shows how this experimental data can then be used to correlate internal and external attributes. Once clear correlations have been identified, the data can be used to statistically estimate prediction models. Such a prediction model is typically derived through the use of regression analysis.

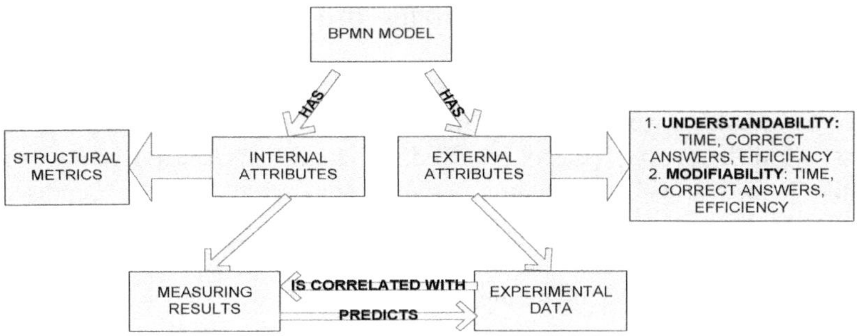

Fig. 1. Internal and external attributes of BPMN models

In this paper we consider a set of metrics defined in [9] for a series of experiments on process model understanding and modifiability. The hypothetical correlation with understandability and modifiability is annotated in brackets as (+) for positive correlation or (-) for negative correlation. The metrics include:

- Number of nodes (-): This variable is related to the number of activities and routing elements in a process model;
- Diameter (-): The length of the longest path from a start node to an end node in the process model;
- Density (-) relates to the ratio of the total number of arcs in a process model to the theoretically maximum number of arcs;
- The Coefficient of Connectivity (-) relates to the ratio of the total number of arcs in a process model to its total number of nodes;
- The Average Gateway Degree (-) expresses the average of the number of both incoming and outgoing arcs of the gateway nodes in the process model;
- The Maximum Gateway Degree (-) captures the maximum sum of incoming and outgoing arcs of these gateway nodes;
- Separability (+) is the ratio of the number of cut-vertices on the one hand, i.e. nodes that serve as bridges between otherwise disconnected components, to the total number of nodes in the process model on the other;
- Sequentiality (+) is the degree to which the model is constructed out of pure sequences of tasks.
- Depth (-) defines maximum nesting of structured blocks in a process model;
- Gateway Mismatch (-) is the sum of gateway pairs that do not match with each other, e.g. when an AND-split is followed by an OR-join;
- Gateway Heterogeneity (-) is the extent to which different types of gateways are used in a process model;
- Cyclicity (-) relates the number of nodes in a cycle to the sum of all nodes;
- Concurrency(-) captures the maximum number of paths in a process model that may be concurrently activate due to AND-splits and OR-splits.

The series of experiments and their results are described in the following section.

3 Correlational Analysis on Metrics and Performance

In this section we describe the series of experiments used in this research, which were defined for previous works. Section 3.1 defines the research design. Among other aspects, we describe the subjects involved, the treatments and questions used, the variation of factors, and the response variables considered. Section 3.2 presents the results of the correlation analysis and Section 3.3 presents the results of the regression analysis. Section 3.4 discusses these results and their corresponding implications, while Section 3.5 compares the findings to related work.

3.1 Research Design

This section describes the empirical analysis performed to test which structural metrics can be used as predictors of understandability and modifiability for BPMN models. Figure 2 shows the chronology of the experiments whose empirical data were used for the analysis. A total of six experiments were conducted: three (one experiment and two replicas) to evaluate understandability and three (one experiment and two replicas) to evaluate modifiability. Altogether, 127 students from four different universities took part in the experiments.

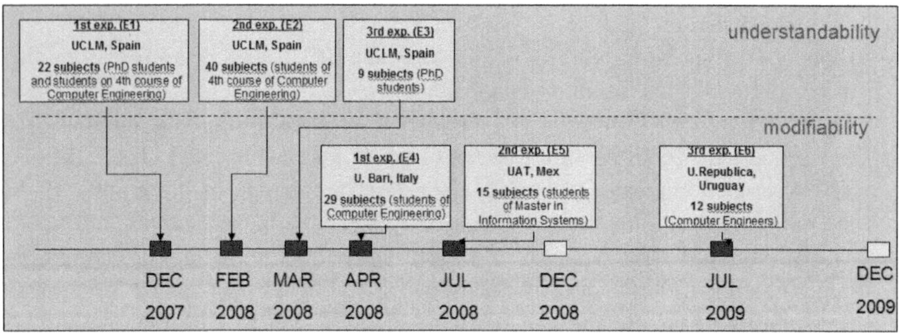

Fig. 2. Chronology of the family of experiments

The experimental material for the first three experiments consisted of 15 BPMN models with different structural complexity. Each model included a questionnaire related to its understandability. The experiments on modifiability included 12 BPMN models (selected from the 15 models concerning understandability) and each model was related to a particular modification task. A more detailed description of the material used in the family of experiments can be found in [18].

It was possible to collect the following objective data for each model and each task: time of understandability or modifiability for each subject, number of correct answers in understandability or modifiability, and efficiency defined as the number of correct answers divided by time.

The first step in validating the error probability measures was to calculate their values in each of the 15 BPMN models designed for the family of experiments. The results are shown in Table 1:

Table 1. Mean and Standard Deviation of the sample models

Measures	Average	Standard deviation
N° nodes	43.60	24.28
Diameter	12.20	5.185
Density	.038	.041
Coefficient of Connectivity	.944	.243
Average gateway degree	2.789	1.263
Maximum gateway degree	3.333	1.914
Separability	.384	.239
Sequentiality	.492	.271
Depth	1.733	1.279
Gateway mismatch	11.60	11.08
Gateway heterogeneity	-.689	.481
Cyclicity	.053	.124
Concurrency	.200	.414

Once the values had been obtained, the variability of the values was analyzed to ascertain whether the measures varied sufficiently to be considered in the study. Two measures were excluded as a result of this, namely Cyclicity and Concurrency, because the results they offered had little variability (80% of the models had the same value for both measures, the mean value was near to 0, as was their standard deviation). The remaining measures were included in the correlation analysis.

The experimental data was accordingly used to test the following null hypotheses for the current empirical analysis, which are:

- For the experiments on understandability,
  H0,1: There is no correlation between structural metrics and understandability
- For the experiments on modifiability,
  H0,2: there is no correlation between structural metrics and modifiability

The following sub-sections show the results obtained for the correlation and regression analysis of the empirical data.

3.2 Correlation Analysis

We first discuss the results for understandability and then turn to modifiability.

Understandability: Understanding time is strongly correlated with most of the probability error measures (number of nodes, diameter, density, average gateway degree, depth, gateway mismatch, and gateway heterogeneity in all three experiments). There is no significant correlation with the connectivity coefficient, and the separability ratio was only correlated in the first experiment.

With regards to correct answers, size measures, number of nodes (-.704 with p-value of .003), diameter (-.699, .004), and gateway heterogeneity (.620, .014) have a significant and strong correlation. With regard to efficiency, we obtained evidence of the correlation of all the measures with the exception of separability.

The correlation analysis results indicate that there is a significant relationship between structural metrics and the time and efficiency of understandability. The results for correct answers are not as conclusive, since there is only a correlation of 3 of the 11 analyzed measures. In conclusion, measures with a significant correlation value (n° nodes, diameter, density, average gateway degree, maximum gateway degree, depth, gateway mismatch and gateway heterogeneity) can be traced back to particular BPMN elements, such as number of nodes (task, decision nodes, events, subprocesses, and data objects), decision nodes and sequence flow. We have therefore found evidence to reject the null hypothesis **H0,1.** The alternative hypothesis suggests that these BPMN elements affect the level of understandability of conceptual models in the following way:

- If there are more nodes, it is more difficult to understand models.
- If the path from a start node to the end is longer, it is more difficult to understand models.
- If there are more nodes connected to decision nodes, it is more difficult to understand models.
- If there is higher gateway heterogeneity, it is more difficult to understand models.

Modifiability: The correlation analysis results of the experiments concerning modifiability are described as follows. We observed a strong correlation between structural metrics and time and efficiency. For correct answers there is no significant connection in general, while there are significant results for diameter, but these are not conclusive since there is a positive relation in one case and a negative correlation in another. For efficiency we find significant correlations with average (.745, .005) and maximum gateway degree (.763, .004), depth (-.751, .005), gateway mismatch (-.812, .001) and gateway heterogeneity (.853, .000). We have therefore found some evidence to reject the null hypothesis **H0,2.** The usage of decision nodes in conceptual models apparently implies a significant reduction in efficiency in modifiability tasks. In short:

- If more nodes are connected to decision nodes, it is more difficult to modify the model.
- If there is higher gateway heterogeneity, it is more difficult to modify models.

3.3 Regression Analysis

The correlation analysis presented above suggests that it is necessary to investigate the quantitative impact of structural metrics on the respective time, accuracy and efficiency dependent variables of both understandability and modifiability. This goal was achieved through the statistical estimation of a linear regression. The regression equations were obtained by performing a regression analysis with 80% of the experimental data (obtained from the family of experiments). The remaining 20% were used for the validation of the regression models.

a) Selection of models

Table 2 and Table 3 show the prediction models obtained for each experiment. All of the regression models obtained were significant with p-values below 0.05.

b) Validation of regression models

One of the threats to the validity of the findings of a study is that of not satisfying the statistical model assumptions. In the case of a linear regression model we must determine whether the observed data complies with the theoretical model. We verified the distribution of residuals, which is the difference between the predicted value with the regression equation and the actual value obtained in experiments. The residuals were analyzed for normality (Kolmogorov-Smirnov) and independence of the residuals (Durbin-Watson). The normality of the data is confirmed, since in all cases the p-value of Kolmogorov-Smirnov test is below 0.05. If the value of the second test (which typically ranges between 0 and 4) is 2, the residue is completely independent. Values between 1.5 and 2.5 are considered to be satisfactory. Values of residues for understandability and modifiability followed a normal distribution, with the exception of efficiency in E1. In the other cases, we can affirm the normality of the residuals obtained after regression analysis. For the verification of the independence of the residues we can verify compliance with the exception of the efficiency of E2 in understandability. As is true in most cases, we can state that the regression analysis is applicable to the data of the experiments.

c) Precision of models

The accuracy of the models was studied by using the Mean Magnitude Relative Error (MMRE) [19] and the prediction level Pred(25) and Pred(30) on the remaining 20% of the data, which were not used in the estimation of the regression equation. These levels indicate the percentage of model estimations that do not differ from the observed data by more than 25% and 30%. A model can therefore be considered to be accurate when it satisfies any of the following cases:

- $MMRE \leq 0{,}25$ *or*
- $Pred\ (0{,}25) \geq 0{,}75$ *or*
- $Pred\ (0{,}30) \geq 0{,}70$

Understandability: The corresponding results are shown in Table 2 and Table 3. The best model for predicting the understandability time is obtained with the second replica E3, which has the lowest MMRE value of all the models. The best models with which to predict correct understandability answers originate from the first replication E2, and this also satisfies all the assumptions. For efficiency, no model was found that satisfied all the assumptions. The model with the lowest value of MMRE is obtained in the second replica E3. In general, the results further support the rejection of the null hypothesis **H0,1.**

Table 2. Prediction models of understandability

Undestandability	Exp	Prediction model	p-value	MMRE	p(0.25)	p(0,30)
Time	E1	T1 = 19.11 + 2 nºnodes + 3.2 gateway mismatch - 25.64 depth + 64.63 coeff. of connectivity -3.2 diameter	.000	.36	.12	.51
	E2	T2 = 95.91 + 1.51 nºnodes + 3.04 gateway mismatch- 17.35 depth - 55.98 sequentiality + 34.45 gateway heterogeneity	.000	.33	.47	.54
	E3	T3 = 47.04 + 2.46 nºnodes	.000	**.32**	**.51**	**.58**
Correct Answers	E1	CA1 = 3.125 - 0.004 nºnodes - 0.251 separability	.000	.21	.71	.71
	E2	CA2 = 3.17 - 0.005 nºnodes - 0.38 coeff. of connectivity + 0.17 depth - 0.015 gateway mismatch	.000	**.18**	**.79**	**.79**
	E3	No variable has been selected		---	---	---
Efficiency	E1	EF1 = 0.040 - 0.0004 nºnodes + 0.019 sequentiality + 0.014 density	.000	1.58	.17	.23
	E2	EF2 = -0.065 + 0.005 gateway mismatch + 0.114 sequentiality - 0.001 nºnodes	.000	4.14	.03	.03
	E3	EF3 = 0.042 - 0.0005 nºnodes + 0.026 sequentiality	.000	**0.84**	**.22**	**.25**

Table 3. Prediction models of modifiability

Modifiability	Exp	Prediction model	p-value	MMRE	p(0.25)	p(0,30)
Time	E4	E4 = 50.08 + 3.77 gateway mismatch + 422.95 density	.000	**.37**	**.31**	**.38**
	E5	E5 = 143.53 + 16.44 MaxGatewaysDegree	.010	.65	.45	.54
	E6	E6 = 175.97 + 3.88 gateway mismatch	.000	.54	.41	.50
Correct Answers	E4	CA4 = 1.85 - 3.569 density	.000	**.23**	**.82**	**.83**
	E5	CA5 = 0.62 + 0.684 sequentiality + 0.471 connectivity	.005	.28	.33	.51
	E6	No variable has been selected		---	---	---
Efficiency	E4	EF4 = 0.006 + 0.008 sequentiality	.000	**.62**	**.32**	**.42**
	E5	EF5 = 0.009 + 0.008 separability - 0.029 density	.030	.98	.45	.51
	E6	EF6 = 0.013 - 0.0002 gateway mismatch	.001	.72	.29	.37

Modifiability: We did not obtain any models which satisfy all of the assumptions for the prediction of modifiability time, but we have highlighted the prediction model obtained in E4 since it has the best values. However, the model to predict the number of correct answers may be considered to be a precise model as it satisfies all the assumptions. The best results for predicting efficiency of modifiability are also provided by E4, with the lowest value of MMRE. In general, we find some further support for rejecting the null hypothesis **H0,2.** The best indicators for modifiability are gateway mismatch, density and sequentiality ratio. Two of these metrics are related to decision nodes. Decision nodes apparently have a negative effect on time and the number of correct answers in modifiability tasks.

3.4 Discussion of Regression Results

The statistical analyses suggest rejecting the null hypotheses, since the structural metrics apparently seem to be closely connected with understandability and modifiability. There are certain metrics that may be considered to be the best owing to their significance in different experiments. For understandability these include Number of Nodes, Gateway Mismatch, Depth, Coefficient of Connectivity and Sequentiality. For modifiability Gateway Mismatch, Density and Sequentiality showed the best results. The regression analysis also provides us with some hints with regard to the interplay of different metrics. Some metrics are not therefore investigated in greater depth owing to their correlations with other metrics. For example, average gateways degree was found to correlate with depth (.810, p-value=.000) and gateway mismatch (.863, p-value=.000), signifying that information provided by these measures may be redundant. The contribution of this work is the evaluation of structural metrics by considering their relative importance in the regression analysis. We conclude that the understandability and modifiability of models is related to decision nodes and connections with others elements, which are represented in the selected measures. In the Section 5, we turn to threshold values. Thresholds are an important communication tool in order to state towards modellers when a process model might be considered to be of bad quality. We will focus on those metrics that are significant in the correlation and regression analysis.

3.5 Related Metrics for Business Process Models

The interest in the measurement of business processes has grown in recent years. It is consequently possible to find a considerable amount of measurement proposals in literature. In previous works [9] we conducted a systematic review by following the Kitchenham and Charters protocol [20], as a result of which various relevant measurement proposals were selected, which could be grouped according to the lifecycle stage they have to be applied to. The most important stages are those of design and execution, and we therefore grouped the measures into "design measures" and "execution measures". Design measures are more numerous, specifically 80% of the proposals found. A summary of the proposed measures in selected publications (updated version of the systematic review until 2010) is shown in Table 4.

Some validated measures more directly related to this work are those of Cardoso [21] and Rolón [22]. Cardoso proposes a Control Flow Complexity metric (CFC). This measure takes into account the quantity and characteristics of the gateways that the business process presents, in order to provide a numerical indication of the complexity of the business process flow. This measure has been empirically validated through experiments, and a correlation analysis was carried out in [23], in which the specific measure was applied to BPMN models. On the other hand, Rolón [24] defined other measures that can be applied to BPMN models in order to quantify the understandability and modifiability of conceptual models. These measures have been validated through a correlation and regression analysis, which was published in [25]. We therefore extracted measures from this analysis, which are the most useful to measure understandability and modifiability (Table 5).

Table 4. Measures for Business Process Models

Source	Measurable Concept	Notation
Vanderfeesten et al [26], [27]	Coupling, cohesion, connectivity level	Petri net
Rolón et al. [22]	Understandability and modifiability	BPMN
Mendling [28]	Error probability	EPC
Cardoso [29] [30]	complexity	Graph
Jung [31]	Entropy	Petri net
Latva-koivisto [32]	complexity	Graph
Gruhn and Laue [33], [34]	complexity	UML, BPMN, EPC
Rozinat and van der Aalst [35]	compliance model-logs	Simulation Logs
Laue and Mendling [36]	Structuredness	EPC
Meimandi and Abdul Azim [37]	Activity complexity, control-flow complexity, data-flow complexity and resource complexity	BPEL
Bisgaard and van der Aalst [38]	Extended Control Flow Complexity, extended cyclomatic metric and structuredness	WF-net
Huan and Kumar [39]	Goodness of models respect generated logs in execution	Simulation logs

Table 5. Others validated understandability and modifiability measures

Measure	Description	U*	M*
	Measures of Rolón		
TNSF	Total Number of sequence flows	X	
TNE	Total Number of events	X	
TNG	Total Number of gateways	X	
NSFE	Number of sequence flows from events	X	
NMF	Number of message flows	X	
NSFG	Number of sequence flows from gateways	X	X
CLP	Connectivity level between participants	X	
NDOOut	Number of data objects which are outputs of activities	X	
NDOIn	number of data objects which are inputs of activities	X	
CLA	Connectivity level between activities		X
	Measures of Cardoso		
CFC	Control flow complexity. Sum over all gateways weighted by their potential combinations of states after the split	X	X

U*: Underttandability, M*: modifiability

A comparison of the correlation values of Cardoso and Rolón measures with respect to structural measures correlations presented in this work in each of the conducted experiments show that: CFC for understandability has a correlation value about 0.5, specifically CFC-efficiency (.503, .590, .515) and for modifiability it does not exceed 0.5: CFC-efficiency (-.412,-.126, -.252). Correlation values of Rolón measures are close to 0.6 for understandability, for example, between efficiency and NSFE (-.668, -.621, -.563) or CLA (-.676, -.635, -.600), and 0.4 for modifiability, TNG-efficiency (-.381, -.126, -.270) or NSFG-efficiency (-.413, -.130, -.250)). On the other hand, structural measures have correlation values for understandability around 0.8 as correlation values of efficiency and number of nodes are (-.835, -.796, -.943) or gateway mismatch are (-.761, -.768, -.737). Modifiability has also higher correlation values, for example (.814, .392, .273) for separability-efficiency or (-.573, -.655, -.751) for depth- efficiency. As a result, the validated metrics seem to be good indicators of understandability and modifiability.

4 Acceptable Risk Levels for Process Model Metrics

This section derives threshold values for process model metrics. We also discuss the merit of this research for quality management of process models in Section 4.2.

4.1 Deriving Thresholds for Process Model Metrics

After analyzing which measures are most useful, it is interesting to know what values of these measures indicate poor quality in models. That means, thresholds values could be used as an alarm of detecting low-quality structures in conceptual models. Henderson-Sellers emphasizes the practical utility of thresholds by stating that "an alarm would occur whenever the value of a specific internal measure exceeded some predetermined value"[40]. The idea of extracting thresholds is to use them to identify unsound design structures, thus enabling engineers to gauge the threshold values to avoid obtaining hazardous structures [41]. The problem of determining appropriate threshold values is made even more difficult by many factors that may vary from experiment to experiment [42]. The identification of such threshold values, therefore, requires methods for quantitative risk assessment [43].

The statistical method used to extract threshold values is the method proposed by Bender [43]. It obtains thresholds values through a univariate logistic regression analysis. In this particular case, we use as a dependent variable the efficiency of understandability and modifiability. As a first step it is required to dichotomized the variable, signifying that it would be 1 when it was higher than the median and 0 when it was lower [44].

The method defines a "value of an acceptable risk level (VARL)". This value is given by a probability $p0$. This means that when measuring measures values below VARL, the risk of the model being non-understandable and non-modifiable is lower than $p0$. This value is calculated as follows:

$$VARL = p^{-1}(p0) = \frac{1}{beta}\left(\log\left(\frac{p0}{1-p0}\right) - alpha\right)$$

We consider these *p0* values to constitute different levels of understandability and modifiability, which is described as follows:

- **Level 1:** there is a 10% of probability of considering the model efficient
- **Level 2:** there is a 30% of probability of considering the model efficient
- **Level 3**: there is a 50% of probability of considering the model efficient
- **Level 4:** there is a 70% of probability of considering the model efficient

For each experiment, we obtain different threshold values. They are stated in Table 6 and Table 7.

Table 6. Thresholds for error probability metrics related to understandability

level	Nº nodes			Gateway mismatch			Depth			Connectivity coefficient			Sequentiality		
	E1	E2	E3	E1	E2	E3	E1	E2	E3	E1	E2	E3	E1	E2	E3
1	63	67	65	27	30	29	4	4	4	1,7	1,7	1,6	0,1	0,1	0
2	49	50	50	16	17	16	2	2	2	1,1	1,1	1,1	0,36	0,37	0,32
3	38	37	37	7	6	6	2	1	1	0,6	0,6	0,6	0,58	0,58	0,64
4	32	29	30	2	0	0	1	1	1	0,4	0,4	0,4	0,7	0,7	0,84

Table 7. Thresholds for error probability metrics related to modifiability

level	Gateway mismatch			Density			Sequentiality		
	E4	E5	E6	E4	E5	E6	E4	E5	E6
1	31	75	32	0,2	0,5	1,1	0	0	0
2	18	31	18	0,1	0,2	0,36	0,3	0,05	0,2
3	7	0	6	0,004	0	0	0,5	0,8	0,6
4	1	0	0	0	0	0	0,6	1,2	0,8

The values described in Table 6 and Table 7 could be interpreted as follows: if number of nodes of a model is between 30 and 32, gateway mismatch is between 0 an 2, depth is 1, connectivity coefficient is 0,4 and sequentially is between 0,7 and 0,84 the probability of considering the model efficient in understandability tasks is about 70%, which means model has an acceptable level of quality. It is interesting to note that many of the threshold values are rather close to each other. This is a good indication that the thresholds can be considered to be rather stable.

Following the same steps, we extracted threshold values for the whole selected group of metrics, and organized them in different levels of understandability and modifiability. These levels classify business process models according to their quality (see Table 8). The values reported in the different rows are the median values drawn from the different experiments reported above.

The information contained in Table 6 can be interpreted as the following: if number of nodes is less or equal to 31, gateway mismatch is 1 or depth is 1, the model is considered as "very efficient" in understandability tasks, while if gateway is 1, density 0 or sequentiality is 0,86, the model is considered as "very efficient" in modifiability tasks.

In the same way, if a model has more than 65 nodes, gateway mismatch is more than 29 or CFCxor is more than 30, the model is considered as very inefficient in understandability tasks and if gateway mismatch is about 46 or density is 0,6, the models is considered as very inefficient in modifiability tasks.

Table 8. Threshold values for conceptual model metrics

	1: very inefficient	2: rather inefficient	3: rather efficient	4: very efficient
		Understandability		
Nºnodes	65	50	37	31
GatewayMismatch	29	16	6	1
Depth	4	2	1	1
Coefficient of connectivity	1,7	1,1	0,6	0,4
Sequentiality	0,1	0,35	0,6	0,7
TNSF	72	49	34	20
TNE	20	12	7	2
TNG	17	10	5	0
NSFE	28	13	4	0
NMF	27	15	7	1
NSFG	40	22	11	0
CLP	7,5	4,23	2,2	0,2
NDOIN	31	44	4	0
NDOOUT	23	11	3	0
CFCxor	30	17	8	1
CFCor	9	4	1	0
CFCand	4	2	0	0
		Modifiability		
GatewayMismatch	46	22	4	1
Denstiy	0,6	0,22	0,0013	0
Sequentiality	0	0,18	0,6	0,86
NSFG	25	13	9	0
CLA	0,53	0,875	1,1	1,3
CFCxor	27	16	8	1
CFCor	9	4	1	0
CFCand	6	2,3	0	0

4.2 The Contribution of Thresholds for Process Model Quality Research

Our research on thresholds is informative to research on process modeling guidelines. Quality of conceptual process models is discussed by different frameworks such as SEQUAL or the Guidelines of Modeling [41, 42]. Many operational guidelines on process modeling can be found in practitioner's books such as the one by Sharp and McDermott [43]. Up until now, we are only aware of the Seven Process Modeling Guidelines [44] as a guideline set that tries to define simple rules with empirical foundation. This paper extends this stream of research by applying a threshold derivation approach from biometrics for the process model metrics. We deem this approach to be an important step towards translating statistical insights on correlations between metrics and quality attributes into operational design rules.

5 Conclusions and Future Work

In this paper we have investigated structural metrics and their connection with the quality of process models, namely understandability and modifiability. We have analyzed performance measures including time, correct answers and efficiency from a family of experiments for correlations with an extensive set of structural process model metrics. Our findings demonstrate the potential of these metrics to serve as validated predictors of process model quality. This research contributes to the area of process model measurement and its still limited degree of empirical validation. Beyond that, we have adapted an approach for threshold derivation for process model quality assessment. The threshold approach can be regarded as an important step towards translating statistical insights into operational design rules.

This work has implications both for research and practice. The strength of the correlation of structural metrics with different quality aspects (up to 0.85 for gateway heterogeneity with modifiability) clearly shows the potential of these metrics to accurately capture aspects closely connected with actual usage. Moreover, we demonstrated how threshold values for selected measures can be found, and related these values to different levels of quality related to understandability and modifiability for business process models. From a practical perspective, these structural metrics can provide valuable guidance for the design of process models, in particular for selecting semantically equivalent alternatives that differ structurally. A first attempt into this direction is made in [35].

In future research we aim to contribute to the further validation and applicability of process model metrics. First, there is a need for more cross validation of regression models. In particular, we will investigate in how far regression models derived from this family of experiments provide good predictions on data that is currently collected in Berlin. Second, there is a need for more formal work on making metrics applicable in modelling tools. Structural metrics provide condensed information such that non-expert modellers will hardly be able to modify a model to improve the metrics. Therefore, we see a huge potential for automatically using behaviour-preserving change operations for generating a model of higher quality.

Acknowledgments. This work was partially funded by projects INGENIO (Junta de Comunidades de Castilla-La Mancha, Consejería de Educación y Ciencia, PAC 08-0154-9262); ALTAMIRA (Junta de Comunidades de Castilla-La Mancha, Fondo Social Europeo, PII2I09-0106-2463), ESFINGE (Ministerio de Educación y Ciencia, Dirección General de Investigación/Fondos Europeos de Desarrollo Regional (FEDER), TIN2006-15175-C05-05) and PEGASO/MAGO (Ministerio de Ciencia e Innovación MICINN and Fondo Europeo de Desarrollo Regional FEDER, TIN2009-13718-C02-01).

References

1. Pfleeger, S.L.: Integrating Process and Measurement. In: Melton, A. (ed.) Software Measurement, pp. 53–74. International Thomson Computer Press (1996)
2. Rosemann, M.: Potential pitfalls of process modeling: part A. Business Process Management Journal 12(2), 249–254 (2006)

3. Indulska, M., Green, P., Recker, J., Rosemann, M.: Business Process Modeling: Perceived Benefits. In: Laender, A.H.F. (ed.) ER 2009. LNCS, vol. 5829, pp. 458–471. Springer, Heidelberg (2009)
4. Moody, D.: Theoretical and practical issues in evaluating the quality of conceptual models: current state and future directions. Data and Knowledge Engineering, 55, 243–276 (2005)
5. Mylopoulos, J.: Conceptual modeling and telos. In: Conceptual Modeling, Databases, and Case: an Integrated View of Information Systems Development, ch. 2, pp. 49–68 (1992)
6. Dandekar, A., Perry, D.E., Votta, L.G.: Studies in Process Simplification. In: Proceedings of the Fourth International Conference on the Software Process, pp. 27–35 (1996)
7. ISO/IEC, ISO Standard 9000-2000: Quality Management Systems: Fundamentals and Vocabulary (2000)
8. ISO/IEC, 9126-1, Software engineering - product quality - Part 1: Quality Model (2001)
9. Sánchez González, L., García, F., Ruiz, F., Piattini, M.: Measurement in Business Processes: a Systematic Review. Business Process Management Journal 16(1), 114–134 (2010)
10. Zelkowitz, M., Wallace, D.: Esperimental models for validating technology. IEEE Computer, Computing practices (1998)
11. Mendling, J.: Metrics for Process Models: Empirical Foundations of Verification, Error Prediction, and Guidelines for Correctness. Springer Publishing Company, Incorporated, Heidelberg (2008)
12. OMG. Business Process Modeling Notation (BPMN), Final Adopted Specification (2006), http://www.omg.org/bpm
13. Gilmore, D., Green, T.: Comprehension and Recall of miniature programs. International Jounal of Man-Machine Studies archive 21(1), 31–48 (1984)
14. Rittgen, P.: Negotiating Models. In: Krogstie, J., Opdahl, A.L., Sindre, G. (eds.) CAiSE 2007 and WES 2007. LNCS, vol. 4495, pp. 561–573. Springer, Heidelberg (2007)
15. Rosemann, M.: Potential pitfalls of process modeling: part B. Business Process Management Journal 12(3), 377–384 (2006)
16. Mendling, J., Reijers, H.A., Cardoso, J.: What makes process models understandable? In: Alonso, G., Dadam, P., Rosemann, M. (eds.) BPM 2007. LNCS, vol. 4714, pp. 48–63. Springer, Heidelberg (2007)
17. Green, T.R.G., Petre, M.: Usability analysis of visual programming environments: a cognitive dimensions framework. J. Visual Languages and Computing 7, 131–174 (1996)
18. Experiments (2009), http://alarcos.inf-cr.uclm.es/bpmnexperiments/
19. Foss, T., Stensrud, E., Kitchenham, B., Myrtveit, I.: A Simulation Study of the Model Evaluation Criterion MMRE. IEEE Transactions on Software Engineering 29, 985–995 (2003)
20. Kitchenham, B., Charters, S.: Guidelines for performing systematic literature reviews in software engineering, T. report, Editor, Keele University and University of Durham (2007)
21. Cardoso, J.: Process control-flow complexity metric: An empirical validation. In: SCC 2006: Proceedings of the IEEE International Conference on Services Computing, pp. 167–173 (2006)

22. Rolón, E., García, F., Ruiz, F.: Evaluation Measures for Business Process Models. In: Symposium in Applied Computing SAC 2006 (2006)
23. Rolón, E., Cardoso, J., García, F., Ruiz, F., Piattini, M.: Analysis and Validation of Control-Flow Complexity Measures with BPMN Process Models. In: The 10th Workshop on Business Process Modeling, Development, and Support (2009)
24. Rolón, E., Ruiz, F., García, F., Piattini, M.: Applying Software Process Metrics in Business Process. Procesos y Métricas, Asociación Española de Métricas del Software 3(2) (2006)
25. Rolon, E., Sanchez, L., Garcia, F., Ruiz, F., Piattini, M., Caivano, D., Visaggio, G.: Prediction Models for BPMN Usability and Maintainability. In: BPMN 2009 - 1st International Workshop on BPMN, pp. 383–390 (2009)
26. Vanderfeesten, I., Reijers, H.A., van der Aalst, W.M.P.: Evaluating Workflow Process Designs using Cohesion and Coupling Metrics. In: Computer in Industry (2008)
27. Vanderfeesten, I., Reijers, H.A., Mendling, J., van der Aalst, W.M.P., Cardoso, J.: On a Quest for Good Process models: the Cross Conectivity Metric. In: Bellahsène, Z., Léonard, M. (eds.) CAiSE 2008. LNCS, vol. 5074, pp. 480–494. Springer, Heidelberg (2008)
28. Mendling, J.: Testing Density as a complexity Metric for EPCs, in Technical Report JM-2006-11-15 (2006)
29. Cardoso, J.: How to Measure the Control-Flow Complexity of Web Processes and Workflows. In: Workflow Handbook 2005 (2005)
30. Cardoso, J.: Business Process Quality Metrics: Log-based Complexity of Workflow Patterns. In: Meersman, R., Tari, Z. (eds.) OTM 2007, Part I. LNCS, vol. 4803, pp. 427–434. Springer, Heidelberg (2007)
31. Jung, J.Y.: Measuring entropy in business process models. In: International Conference on Innovative Computing, Information and Control, pp. 246–252 (2008)
32. Latva-Koivisto, A.M.: Finding a Complexity Measure for Business Process Models. Individual Research Projects in Applied Mathematics (2001)
33. Gruhn, V., Laue, R.: Complexity Metrics for business Process Models. In: International Conference on Business Information Systems (2006)
34. Gruhn, V., Laue, R.: Adopting the Cognitive Complexity Measure for Business Process Models. In: 5th IEEE International Conference on Cognitive Informatics, ICCI 2006, vol. 1, pp. 236–241 (2006)
35. Rozinat, A., van der Aalst, W.M.P.: Conformance checking of processes based on monitoring real behavior. Information Systems 33, 64–95 (2008)
36. Laue, R., Mendling, J.: Structuredness and its Significance for Correctness of Process Models. In: Information Systems and E-Business Management (2009)
37. Meimandi Parizi, R., Ghani, A.A.A.: An Ensemble of Complexity Metrics for BPEL Web Processes. In: Ninth ACIS International Conference on Software Engineering, Artificial Intelligence, Networking, and Parallel/Distributed Computing, pp. 753–758 (2008)
38. Bisgaard Lassen, K., Van der Aalst, W.: Complexity Metrics for Workflow Nets. In: Information and Software Technology, pp. 610–626 (2008)
39. Huan, Z., Kumar, A.: New quality metrics for evaluating process models. In: Business Process Intelligence Workshop (2008)
40. Henderson-Sellers, B.: Object-Oriented Metrics: Measures of Complexity. Prentice-Hall, Englewood Cliffs (1996)

41. Shatnawi, R., Li, W., Swain, J., Newman, T.: Finding Software Metrics Threshold values using ROC Curves. In: Sofware Maintenance and Evolution: Research and Practice (2009)
42. Churchill, G.A., Doerge, R.W.: Empirical Threshold Values for Quantitative Trait Mapping. Genetics Society of America 138, 963–971 (1995)
43. Bender, R.: Quantitative Risk Assessment in Epidemiological Studies Investigatin Threshold Effects. Biometrical Journal 41(3), 305–319 (1999)
44. Royston, P., Douglas, G.A., Sauerbrei, W.: Dichotomizing continuous predictors in multiple regression: a bad idea. Statistics in Medicine 25, 127–141 (2005)

Merging Business Process Models

Marcello La Rosa[1], Marlon Dumas[2], Reina Uba[2], and Remco Dijkman[3]

[1] Queensland University of Technology, Australia
m.larosa@qut.edu.au
[2] University of Tartu, Estonia
{marlon.dumas,reinak}@ut.ee
[3] Eindhoven University of Technology, The Netherlands
r.m.dijkman@tue.nl

Abstract. This paper addresses the following problem: given two business process models, create a process model that is the union of the process models given as input. In other words, the behavior of the produced process model should encompass that of the input models. The paper describes an algorithm that produces a single configurable process model from a pair of process models. The algorithm works by extracting the common parts of the input process models, creating a single copy of them, and appending the differences as branches of configurable connectors. This way, the merged process model is kept as small as possible, while still capturing all the behavior of the input models. Moreover, analysts are able to trace back which model(s) a given element in the merged model originates from. The algorithm has been prototyped and tested against process models taken from several application domains.

1 Introduction

In the context of company mergers and restructurings, it often occurs that multiple alternative processes, previously belonging to different companies or units, need to be consolidated into a single one in order to eliminate redundancies and create synergies. To this end, teams of business analysts need to compare similar process models so as to identify commonalities and differences, and to create integrated process models that can be used to drive the process consolidation effort. This process model merging effort is tedious, time-consuming and error-prone. In one instance reported in this paper, it took a team of three analysts 130 man-hours to merge 25% of two variants of an end-to-end process model.

In this paper, we consider the problem of (semi-)automatically merging process models under the following requirements:

1. The behavior of the merged model should subsume that of the input models.
2. Given an element in the merged process model, analysts should be able to trace back from which process model(s) the element in question originates.
3. One should be able to derive the input process models from the merged one.

The main contribution of the paper is an algorithm that takes as input a collection of process models and generates a *configurable process model* [15]. A

R. Meersman et al. (Eds.): OTM 2010, Part I, LNCS 6426, pp. 96–113, 2010.

configurable process model is a modeling artifact that captures a family of process models in an integrated manner and that allows analysts to understand what these process models share, what their differences are, and why and how these differences occur. Given a configurable process model, analysts can derive individual members of the underlying process family by means of a procedure known as *individualization*. We contend that configurable process models are a suitable output for a process merging algorithm, because they provide a mechanism to fulfill the second and third requirements outlined above. Moreover, they can be used to derive new process models that were not available in the originating process family, e.g. when the need to capture new business procedures arises. In this respect, the merged model can be seen as a reference model [4] for the given process family.

The algorithm requires as input a mapping that defines which elements from one process model correspond to which elements from another process model. To assist in the construction of this mapping, a mapping is suggested to the user who can then adapt the mapping if necessary.The algorithm has been tested on process models sourced from different domains. The tests show that the process merging algorithm produces compact models and scales up to process models containing hundreds of nodes.

The paper is structured as follows. Section 2 introduces the notion of configurable process model as well as a technique for proposing an initial mapping between similar process model elements. Section 3 presents the process merging algorithm. Section 4 reports on the implementation and evaluation of the algorithm. Finally, Section 5 discusses related work and Section 6 draws conclusions.

2 Background

This section introduces two basic ingredients of the proposed process merging technique: a notation for configurable process models and a technique to match the elements of a given pair of process models. This latter technique is used to assist users in determining which pairs of process model elements should be considered as equivalent when merging.

2.1 Configurable Business Processes

There exist many notations to represent business processes, such as Event-driven Process Chains (EPC), UML Activity Diagrams (UML ADs) and the Business Process Modeling Notation (BPMN). In this paper we abstract from any specific notation and represent a business process model as a directed graph with labeled nodes as per the following definition. This process abstraction allows us to merge process models defined in different notations.

Definition 1 (Business Process Graph). *A business process graph G is a set of pairs of process model nodes—each pair denoting a directed edge. A node n of G is a tuple $(id_G(n), \lambda_G(n), \tau_G(n))$ consisting of a unique identifier $id_G(n)$ (of type string), a label $\lambda_G(n)$ (of type string), and a type $\tau_G(n)$. In situations where there is no ambiguity, we will drop the subscript G from id_G, λ_G and τ_G.*

For a business process graph G, its set of nodes, denoted N_G, is $\bigcup\{\{n_1, n_2\}|(n_1, n_2) \in G\}$. Each node has a type. The available types of nodes depend on the language that is used. For example, BPMN has nodes of type 'activity', 'event' and 'gateway'. In the rest of this paper we will show examples using the EPC notation, which has three types of nodes: i) 'function' nodes, representing tasks that can be performed in an organization; ii) 'event' nodes, representing pre-conditions that must be satisfied before a function can be performed, or post-conditions that are satisfied after a function has been performed; and iii) 'connector' nodes, which determine the flow of execution of the process. Thus, $\tau_G \in \{$"f", "e", "c"$\}$ where the letters represent the (f)unction, (e)vent and (c)onnector type. The label of a node of type "c" indicates the kind of connector. EPCs have three kinds of connectors: AND, XOR and OR. AND connectors either represent that after the connector, the process can continue along multiple parallel paths (AND-split), or that it has to wait for multiple parallel paths in order to be able to continue (AND-join). XOR connectors either represent that after the connector, a choice has to be made about which path to continue on (XOR-split), or that the process has to wait for a single path to be completed in order to be allowed to continue (XOR-join). OR connectors start or wait for multiple paths. Models G_1 and G_2 in Fig. 1 are two example EPCs.

A Configurable EPC (C-EPC) [15] is an EPC where some connectors are marked as configurable. A configurable connector can be configured by removing one or more of its incoming branches (in the case of a join) or one or more of its outgoing branches (in the case of a split). The result is a regular connector with a possibly reduced number of incoming or outgoing branches. In addition, a configurable OR connector can be mutated into a regular XOR or a regular AND. After all nodes in a C-EPC are configured, a C-EPC needs to be individualized by removing those branches that have been excluded during the configuration of each configurable connector. Model CG in Fig. 1 is an example of C-EPC featuring a configurable XOR-split, a configurable XOR-join and a configurable OR-join, while the two models G_1 and G_2 are two possible individualizations of CG. G_1 can be obtained by configuring the three configurable connectors in order to keep all branches labeled "1", and restricting the OR-join to an AND-join; G_2 can be obtained by configuring the three configurable connectors in order to keep all branches labeled "2" and restricting the OR-join to an XOR-join. Since in both cases only one branch is kept for the two configurable XOR connectors (either the one labeled "1" or the one labeled "2"), these connectors are removed during individualization. For more details on the individualization algorithm, we refer to [15].

According to requirement (2) in Section 1, we need a mechanism to trace back from which variant a given element in the merged model originates. Coming back to the example in Fig. 1, the C-EPC model (CG) can also be seen as the result of merging the two EPCs (G_1 and G_2). The configurable XOR-split immediately below function "Shipment Processing" in CG has two outgoing edges. One of them originates from G_1 (and we thus label it with identifier "1") while the second originates from G_2 (identifier "2"). In some cases, an edge in the merged

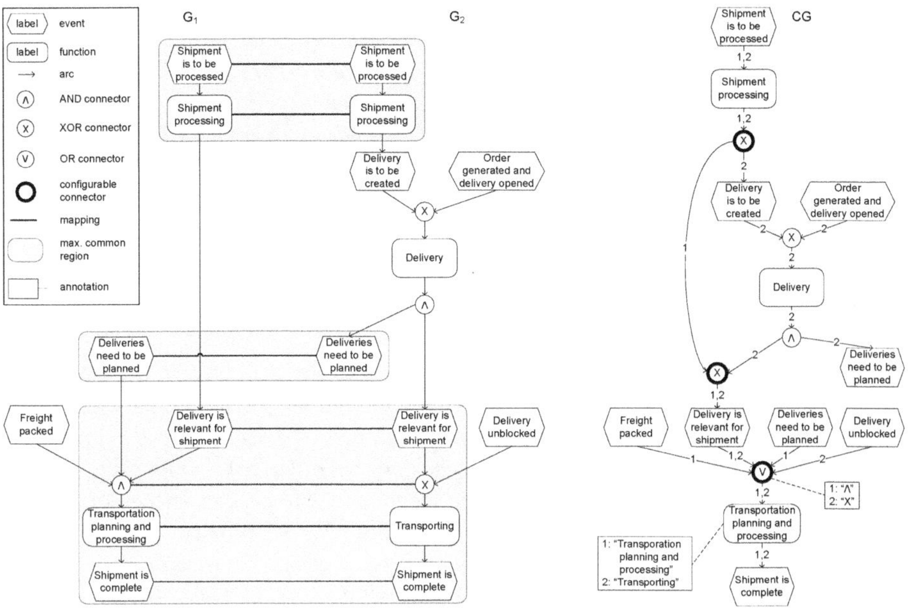

Fig. 1. Two business process models with a mapping, and their merged model

model originates from multiple variants. For example, the edge that emanates from event "Delivery is relevant for shipment" is labeled with both variants ("1" and "2") since this edge can be found in both original models.

Also, since nodes in the merged model are obtained by combining nodes from different variants, we need to capture the label of the node in each of its variants. For example, function "Transportation planning and processing" in CG stems from the merger of the function with the same name in G_1, and function "Transporting" in G_2. Accordingly, this function in CG will have an annotation (as shown in the figure), stating that its label in variant 1 is "Transportation planning and processing", while its label in variant 2 is "Transporting". Similarly, the configurable OR connector just above "Transportation planning and processing" in CG stems from two connectors: an AND connector in variant 1 and an XOR connector in variant 2. Thus an annotation will be attached to this node (as shown in the figure) which will record the fact that the label of this connector is "and" in variant 1, and "xor" in variant 2. In addition to providing traceability, these annotations enable us to derive the original process models by configuring the merged one, as per requirement (3) in Section 1. Thus, we define the concept of *Configurable Process Graph*, which attaches additional configuration metadata to each edge and node in a business process graph.

Definition 2 (Configurable Business Process Graph). *Let $\mathcal{I}$ be a set of identifiers of business process models, and $\mathcal{L}$ the set of all labels that process* *model nodes can take. A Configurable Business Process graph is a tuple* $(G, \alpha_G, \gamma_G, \eta_G)$ *where* G *is a business process graph,* $\alpha_G : G \rightarrow \wp(\mathcal{I})$ *is a function that maps each edge in* G *to a set of process graph identifiers,* $\gamma_G : N_G \rightarrow \wp(\mathcal{I} \times \mathcal{L})$ *is a function that maps each node* $n \in N_G$ *to a set of pairs* (pid, l) *where pid is a process graph identifier and* l *is the label of node* n *in process graph pid, and* $\eta_G : N_G \rightarrow \{true, false\}$ *is a boolean indicating whether a node is configurable or not.*

Because we attach annotations to graph elements, our concept of configurable process graph slightly differs from the one defined in [15].

Below, we define some auxiliary notations which we will use when matching pairs of process graphs.

Definition 3 (Preset, Postset, Transitive Preset, Transitive Postset). *Let* G *be a business process graph. For a node* $n \in N_G$ *we define the preset as* $\bullet n = \{m|(m, n) \in G\}$ *and the postset as* $n\bullet = \{m|(n, m) \in G\}$. *We call an element of the preset* predecessor *and an element of the postset* successor. *There is a* path *between two nodes* $n \in N_G$ *and* $m \in N_G$, *denoted* $n \hookrightarrow m$, *if and only if (iff) there exists a sequence of nodes* $n_1, \ldots, n_k \in N_G$ *with* $n = n_1$ *and* $m = n_k$ *such that for all* $i \in 1, \ldots, k-1$ *holds* $(n_i, n_{i+1}) \in G$. *If* $n \neq m$ *and for all* $i \in 2, \ldots, k-1$ *holds* $\tau(n_i) =$ "c", *the path* $n \overset{c}{\hookrightarrow} m$ *is called a* connector chain. *The set of nodes from which a node* $n \in N_G$ *is reachable via a connector chain is defined as* $\overset{c}{\bullet} n = \{m \in N_G | m \overset{c}{\hookrightarrow} n\}$ *and is called the* transitive preset *of* n *via connector chains. Similarly,* $n \overset{c}{\bullet} = \{m \in N_G | n \overset{c}{\hookrightarrow} m\}$ *is the* transitive postset *of* n *via connector chains.*

For example, the transitive preset of event "Delivery is relevant for shipment" in Figure 1, includes functions "Delivery" and "Shipment Processing", since these two latter functions can be reached from the event by traversing backward edges and skipping any connectors encountered in the backward path.

2.2 Matching Business Processes

The aim of matching two process models is to establish the best mapping between their nodes. Here, a mapping is a function from the nodes in the first graph to those in the second graph. What is considered to be the best mapping depends on a scoring function, called the *matching score*. The matching score we employ is related to the notion of graph edit distance [1]. We use this matching score as it performed well in several empirical studies [17,2,3]. Given two graphs and a mapping between their nodes, we compute the matching score in three steps.

First, we compute the matching score between each pair of nodes as follows. Nodes of different types must not be mapped, and splits must not be matched with joins. Thus, a mapping between nodes of different types, or between a split and a join, has a matching score of 0. The matching score of a mapping between two functions or between two events is measured by the *similarity* of their labels. To determine this similarity, we use a combination of a syntactic similarity measure, based on *string edit distance* [10], and a linguistic similarity measure, based on the Wordnet::Similarity package [13] (if specific ontologies for a domain are available, such ontologies can be used instead of Wordnet). We apply these measures on pairs of words from the two labels, after removing stop-words (e.g. articles and conjunctions) and stemming the remaining words (to remove word endings such as "-ing"). The similarity between two words is the maximum between their syntactic similarity and their linguistic similarity. The total similarity between two labels is the average of the similarities between each pair of words (w_1, w_2) such that w_1 belongs to the first label and w_2 belongs to the second label. With reference to the example in Fig. 1, the similarity score between nodes 'Transportation planning and processing' in G_1 and node 'Transporting' in G_2 is around 0.35. After removing the stop-word "and", we have three pairs of terms. The similarity between 'Transportation" and "'Transporting" after stemming is 1.0, while the similarity between "plan" and "process" or between "plan" and "transport" is close to 0. The average similarity between these three pairs is thus around 0.35. This approach is directly inspired from established techniques for matching pairs of elements in the context of schema matching [14].

The above approach to compute similarities between functions/events cannot be used to compute the similarity between pairs of splits or pairs of joins, as connectors' labels are restricted to a small set (e.g. 'OR', 'XOR' and 'AND') and they each have a specific semantics. Instead, we use a notion of *context similarity*. Given two mapped nodes, context similarity is the fraction of nodes in their transitive presets and their transitive postsets that are mapped (i.e. the contexts of the nodes), provided at least one mapping of transitive preset nodes and one mapping of transitive postset nodes exists.

Definition 4 (Context similarity). *Let G_1 and G_2 be two process graphs. Let $M : N_{G_1} \nrightarrow N_{G_2}$ be a partial injective mapping that maps nodes in G_1 to nodes in G_2. The context similarity of two mapped nodes $n \in N_{G_1}$ and $m \in N_{G_2}$ is:*

$$\frac{|M(\overset{c}{\bullet} n) \cap \overset{c}{\bullet} m| + |M(n \overset{c}{\bullet}) \cap m \overset{c}{\bullet}|}{max(|\overset{c}{\bullet} n|, |\overset{c}{\bullet} m|) + max(|n \overset{c}{\bullet}|, |m \overset{c}{\bullet}|)}$$

where M applied to a set yields the set in which M is applied to each element.

For example, the event 'Delivery is relevant for shipment' preceding the AND-join (via a connector chain of size 0) in model G_1 from Fig. 1 is mapped to the event 'Delivery is relevant for shipment' preceding the XOR-join in G_2. Also, the function succeeding the AND-join (via a connector chain of size 0) in G_1 is mapped to the function succeeding the XOR-join in G_2. Therefore, the context similarity of the two joins is: $\frac{1+1}{3+1} = 0.5$.

Second, we derive from the mapping the number of: *Node substitutions* (a node in one graph is substituted for a node in the other graph iff they appear in the mapping); *Node insertions/deletions* (a node is inserted into or deleted from one graph iff it does not appear in the mapping); *Edge substitutions* (an edge from node a to node b in one graph is substituted for an edge in the other graph iff node a is matched to node a', node b is matched to node b' and there exists an edge from node a' to node b'); and *Edge insertions/deletions* (an edge is inserted into or deleted from one graph iff it is not substituted).

Third, we use the matching scores from step one and the information about substituted, inserted and deleted nodes and edges from step two, to compute the matching score for the mapping as a whole. We define the matching score of a mapping as the weighted average of the fraction of inserted/deleted nodes, the fraction of inserted/deleted edges and the average score for node substitutions. Specifically, the matching score of a pair of process graphs and a mapping between them is defined as follows.

Definition 5 (Matching score). *Let G_1 and G_2 be two process graphs and let M be their mapping function, where* $\mathrm{dom}(M)$ *denotes the domain of M and* $\mathrm{cod}(M)$ *denotes the codomain of M. Let also* $0 \leq \mathrm{wsubn} \leq 1$, $0 \leq \mathrm{wskipn} \leq 1$ *and* $0 \leq \mathrm{wskipe} \leq 1$ *be the weights that we assign to substituted nodes, inserted or deleted nodes and inserted or deleted edges, respectively, and let $Sim(n, m)$ be the function that returns the similarity score for a pair of mapped nodes, as computed in step one.*

The set of substituted nodes, denoted subn, inserted or deleted nodes, denoted skipn, substituted edges, denoted sube, and inserted or deleted edges, denoted skipe, are defined as follows:

$$\mathrm{subn} = \mathrm{dom}(M) \cup \mathrm{cod}(M) \qquad \mathrm{skipn} = (N_{G_1} \cup N_{G_2}) - \mathrm{subn}$$
$$\mathrm{sube} = \{(a, b) \in E_1 | (M(a), M(b)) \in E_2\} \cup \{(a', b') \in E_2 | (M^{-1}(a'), M^{-1}(b')) \in E_1\} \qquad \mathrm{skipe} = (E_1 \cup E_2) \setminus \mathrm{sube}$$

The fraction of inserted or deleted nodes, denoted fskipn, *the fraction of inserted or deleted edges, denoted* fskipe, *and the average distance of substituted nodes, denoted* fsubsn, *are defined as follows.*

$$\mathrm{fskipn} = \frac{|\mathrm{skipn}|}{|N_1|+|N_2|} \quad \mathrm{fskipe} = \frac{|\mathrm{skipe}|}{|E_1|+|E_2|} \quad \mathrm{fsubn} = \frac{2.0 \cdot \Sigma_{(n,m) \in M} 1.0 - \mathrm{Sim}(n,m)}{|\mathrm{subn}|}$$

Finally, the matching score of a mapping is defined as:

$$1.0 - \frac{\mathrm{wskipn} \cdot \mathrm{fskipn} + \mathrm{wskipe} \cdot \mathrm{fskipe} + \mathrm{wsubn} \cdot \mathrm{fsubn}}{\mathrm{wskipn} + \mathrm{wskipe} + \mathrm{wsubn}}$$

For example, in Fig. 1 the node 'Freight packed' and its edge to the AND-join in G_1 are inserted, and so are the node 'Delivery unblocked' and its edge to the XOR-join in G_2. The AND-join in G_1 is substituted by the second XOR-join in G_2 with a matching score of 0.5, while the node 'Transportation planning and processing' in G_1 is substituted by the node 'Transporting' in G_2 with a matching score of 0.35 as discussed above. Thus, the edge between 'Transportation planning and processing' and the AND-join in G_1 is substituted by the edge between 'Transporting' and the XOR-join in G_2, as both edges are between two substituted nodes. All the other substituted nodes have a matching score of 1.0. If all weights are set to 1.0, the total matching score for this mapping is $1.0 - \frac{\frac{7}{21} + \frac{11}{19} + \frac{2 \cdot 0.5 + 2 \cdot 0.65}{14}}{3} = 0.64$.

Definition 5 gives the matching score of a given mapping. To determine the matching score of two business process graphs, we must exhaustively try all possible mappings and find the one with the highest matching score. Various algorithms exist to find the mapping with the highest matching score. In the experiments reported in paper, we use a greedy algorithm from [2], since its computational complexity is much lower than that of an exhaustive algorithm, while having a high precision.

3 Merging Algorithm

The merging algorithm is defined over pairs of configurable process graphs. In order to merge two or more (non-configurable) process graphs, we first need to convert each process graph into a configurable process graph. This is trivially achieved by annotating every edge of a process graph with the identifier of the process graph, and every node in the process graph with a pair indicating the process graph identifier and the label for that node. We then obtain a configurable process graph representing only one possible variant.

Given two configurable process graphs G_1 and G_2 and their mapping M, the merging algorithm (Algorithm 1) starts by creating an initial version of the merged graph CG by doing the union of the edges of G_1 and G_2, excluding the edges of G_2 that are substituted. In this way for each matched node we keep the copy in G_1 only. Next, we set the annotation of each edge in CG that originates from a substituted edge, with the union of the annotations of the two substituted edges in G_1 and G_2. For example, this produces all edges with label "1,2" in model CG in Fig. 1. Similarly, we set the annotation of each node in CG that originates from a matched node, with the union of the annotations of the two matched nodes in G_1 and G_2. In Fig. 1, this produces the annotations of the last two nodes of CG—the only two nodes originating from matched nodes with different labels (the other annotations are not shown in the figure).

Next, we use function *MaximumCommonRegions* to partition the mapping between G_1 and G_2 into maximum common regions (Algorithm 2). A maximum common region (mcr) is a maximum connected subgraph consisting only of matched nodes and substituted edges. For example, given models G_1 and G_2 in Fig. 1, *MaximumCommonRegions* returns the three mcrs highlighted by rounded boxes in the figure. To find all mcrs, we first randomly pick a matched node that has not yet been included in any mcr. We then compute the mcr of that node using a breadth-first search. After this, we choose another mapped node that is not yet in an mcr, and we construct the next mcr. We then postprocess the set of maximum common regions to remove from each mcr those nodes that are at the beginning or at the end of one model, but not of the other (this step is not shown in Algorithm 2). Such nodes cannot be merged, otherwise it would not be possible to trace back which model they come from. For example, we do not merge event "Deliveries need to be planned" in Fig. 1 as this node is at the beginning of G_1 and at the end of G_2. In this case, since the mcr contains this node only, we remove the mcr altogether.

Algorithm 1. Merge

```
function Merge(Graph G1, Graph G2, Mapping M)
init
  Mapping mcr, Graph CG
begin
  CG ⇐ G1 ∪ G2 \ (G2 ∩ sube)
  foreach (x, y) ∈ CG ∩ sube do
    α_CG(x, y) ⇐ α_G1(x, y) ∪ α_G2(M(x), M(y))
  end
  foreach n ∈ N_CG ∩ subn do
    γ_CG(n) ⇐ γ_G1(n) ∪ γ_G2(M(n))
  end
  foreach mcr ∈ MaximumCommonRegions(G1, G2, M) do
    FG1 ⇐ {x ∈ dom(mcr) | •x ∩ dom(mcr) = ∅ ∨ •M(x) ∩ cod(mcr) = ∅}
    foreach fG1 ∈ FG1 such that |•fG1| = 1 and |•M(fG1)| = 1 do
      pfG1 ⇐ Any(•fG1), pfG2 ⇐ Any(•M(fG1))
      xj ⇐ new Node("c","xor",true)
      CG ⇐ (CG \ ({(pfG1, fG1), (pfG2, fG2)})) ∪ {(pfG1, xj), (pfG2, xj), (xj, fG1)}
      α_CG(pfG1, xj) ⇐ α_G1(pfG1, fG1), α_CG(pfG2, xj) ⇐ α_G2(pfG2, fG2)
      α_CG(xj, fG1) ⇐ α_G1(pfG1, fG1) ∪ α_G2(pfG2, fG2)
    end
    LG1 ⇐ {x ∈ dom(mcr) | x• ∩ dom(mcr) = ∅ ∨ M(x)• ∩ cod(mcr) = ∅}
    foreach lG1 ∈ LG1 such that |lG1•| = 1 and |M(lG1)•| = 1 do
      slG1 ⇐ Any(lG1•), slG2 ⇐ Any(M(lG1)•)
      xs ⇐ new Node("c","xor",true)
      CG ⇐ (CG \ ({(lG1, slG1), (lG2, slG2)})) ∪ {(xs, slG1), (xs, slG2), (lG1, xs)}
      α_CG(xs, slG1) ⇐ α_G1(lG1, slG1), α_CG(xs, slG2) ⇐ α_G2(lG2, slG2)
      α_CG(lG1, xs) ⇐ α_G1(lG1, slG1) ∪ α_G2(lG2, slG2)
    end
  end
  CG ⇐ MergeConnectors(M, CG)
  return CG
end
```

Once we have identified all mcrs, we need to reconnect them with the remaining nodes from G_1 and G_2 that are not matched. The way a region is reconnected depends on the position of its sources and sinks in G_1 and G_2. A region's source is a node whose preset is empty (the source is a start node) or at least one of its predecessors is not in the region; a region's sink is a node whose postset is empty (the sink is an end node) or at least one of its successors is not in the region. We observe that this condition may be satisfied by a node in one graph but not by its matched node in the other graph. For example, a node may be a source of a region for G_2 but not for G_1.

If a node fG_1 is a source in G_1 or its matched node $M(fG_1)$ is a source in G_2 and both fG_1 and $M(fG_1)$ have exactly one predecessor each, we insert a configurable XOR-join xj in CG to reconnect the two predecessors to the copy of fG_1 in CG. Similarly, if a node lG_1 is a sink in G_1 or its matched node $M(lG_1)$ is a sink in G_2 and both nodes have exactly one successor each, we insert a

Algorithm 2. Maximum Common Regions

```
function MaximumCommonRegions(Graph G1, Graph G2, Mapping M)
init
  {Node} visited ⇐ ∅, {Mapping} MCRs ⇐ ∅
begin
  while exists c ∈ dom(M) such that c ∉ visited do
    {Node} mcr ⇐ ∅
    {Node} tovisit ⇐ {c}
    while tovisit ≠ ∅ do
      c ⇐ dequeue(tovisit)
      mcr ⇐ mcr ∪ {c}
      visited ⇐ visited ∪ {c}
      foreach n ∈ dom(M) such that ((c, n) ∈ G1 and (M(c), M(n)) ∈ G2) or
      ((n, c) ∈ G1 and (M(n), M(c)) ∈ G2) and n ∉ visited do
        enqueue(tovisit, n)
      end
    end
    MCRs ⇐ MCRs ∪ {mcr}
  end
  return MCRs
end
```

configurable XOR-split xs in CG to reconnect the two successors to the copy of lG_1 in CG. We also set the labels of the new edges in CG to track back the edges in the original models. This is illustrated in Fig. 2 where we use symbols pfG_1 to indicate the only predecessor of node fG_1 in G_1, slG_1 to indicate the only successor of node lG_1 in G_1 and so on. Moreover, in Algorithm 1 we use function *Node* to create the configurable XOR joins and splits that we need to add, and function *Any* to extract the element of a singleton set.

In Fig. 1, node "Shipment processing" in G_1 and its matched node in G_2 are both sink nodes and have exactly one successor each ("Delivery is relevant for shipment" in G_1 and "Delivery is to be created" in G_2). Thus, we reconnect this node in CG to the two successors via a configurable XOR-join and set the labels of the incoming and outgoing edges of this join accordingly. The same operation applies when a node is source (sink) in a graph but not in the other.

By removing from $MCRs$ all the nodes that are at the beginning or at the end of one model but not of the other, we guarantee that either both a source and its matched node have predecessors or none has, and similarly, that either both a sink and its matched node have successors or none has. In Fig. 1, the region containing node "Deliveries need to be planned" is removed after postprocessing $MCRs$ since this node is a start node for G_1 and an end node for G_2.

If a source has multiple predecessors (i.e. it is a join) or a sink has multiple successors (i.e. it is a split), we do not need to add a configurable XOR-join before the source, or a configurable XOR-split after the sink. Instead, we can simply reconnect these nodes with the remaining nodes in their preset (if a join) or postset (if a split) which are not matched. This case is covered by

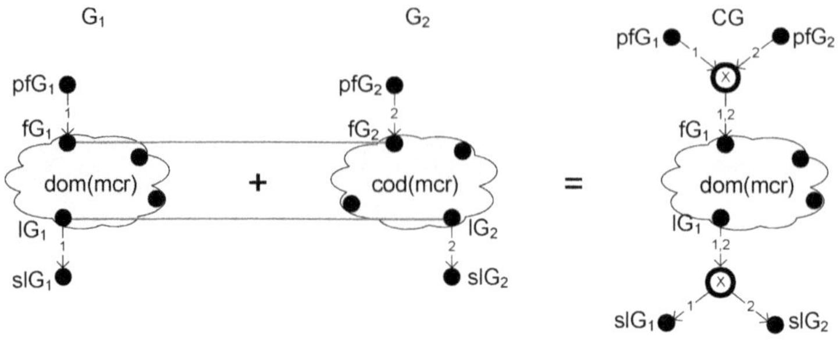

Fig. 2. Reconnecting a maximum common region to the nodes that are not matched

function *MergeConnectors* (Algorithm 3). This function is invoked in the last step of Algorithm 1 to merge the preset and postset of all matched connectors, including those that are source or sink of a region, as well as any matched connector inside a region. In fact the operation that we need to perform is the same in both cases. Since every matched connector c in CG is copied from G_1, we need to reconnect to c the predecessors and successors of $M(c)$ that are not matched. We do so by adding a new edge between each predecessor or successor of $M(c)$ and c. If at least one such predecessor or successor exists, we make c configurable, and if there is a mismatch between the labels of the two matched connectors (e.g. one is "xor" and the other is "and") we also change the label of c to "or". For example, the AND-join in G_1 of Fig. 1 is matched with the XOR-join that precedes function "Transporting" in G_2. Since both nodes are source of the region in their respective graphs, we do not need to add a further configurable XOR-join. The only non-matched predecessor of the XOR-join in G_2 is node "Delivery unblocked". Thus, we reconnect the latter to the copy of the AND-join in CG via a new edge labeled "2". Also, we make this connector configurable and we change its label to "or", obtaining graph CG in Fig. 1.

After merging two process graphs, we can simplify the resulting graph by applying a set of reduction rules. These rules are used to reduce connector chains that may have been generated after inserting configurable XOR connectors. This reduces the size of the merged process graph while preserving its behavior and its configuration options. The reduction rules are: 1) merge consecutive splits/joins, 2) remove redundant transitive edges between connectors, and 3) remove trivial connectors (i.e. those connectors with one input edge and one output edge), and are applied until a process graph cannot be further reduced. For space reasons, we cannot provide full details of the reduction rules. Detailed explanations and formal descriptions of the rules are given in a technical report [9].

The worst-case complexity of the process merging procedure is $O(|N_G|^3)$ where $|N_G|$ is the number of nodes of the largest graph. This is the complexity of the process mapping step when using a greedy algorithm [2], which dominates the complexity of the other steps of the procedure. The complexity of the algorithm for merging connectors is linear on the number of connectors. The algorithm for calculating the maximum common regions is a breadth-first search, thus linear on the number of edges. The algorithm for calculating the merged

Algorithm 3. Merge Connectors

function MergeConnectors(Mapping M, {Edge} CG)
init
{Node} $\mathsf{S} \Leftarrow \emptyset$, {Node} $\mathsf{J} \Leftarrow \emptyset$
begin
foreach $\mathsf{c} \in \mathrm{dom}(\mathsf{M})$ *such that* $\tau(\mathsf{c}) = \text{“}\mathsf{c}\text{”}$ **do**
$\mathsf{S} \Leftarrow \{\mathsf{x} \in \mathsf{M}(\mathsf{c})\bullet \mid \mathsf{x} \notin \mathrm{cod}(\mathsf{M})\}$
$\mathsf{J} \Leftarrow \{\mathsf{x} \in \bullet\mathsf{M}(\mathsf{c}) \mid \mathsf{x} \notin \mathrm{cod}(\mathsf{M})\}$
$\mathsf{CG} \Leftarrow (\mathsf{CG} \setminus \bigcup_{\mathsf{x}\in\mathsf{S}}\{(\mathsf{M}(\mathsf{c}),\mathsf{x})\} \cup \bigcup_{\mathsf{x}\in\mathsf{J}}\{(\mathsf{x},\mathsf{M}(\mathsf{c}))\}) \cup \bigcup_{\mathsf{x}\in\mathsf{S}}\{(\mathsf{c},\mathsf{x})\} \cup \bigcup_{\mathsf{x}\in\mathsf{J}}\{(\mathsf{x},\mathsf{c})\}$
foreach $\mathsf{x} \in \mathsf{S}$ **do**
$\alpha_{\mathsf{CG}}(\mathsf{c},\mathsf{x}) \Leftarrow \alpha_{\mathsf{G}_2}(\mathsf{M}(\mathsf{c}),\mathsf{x})$
end
foreach $\mathsf{x} \in \mathsf{J}$ **do**
$\alpha_{\mathsf{CG}}(\mathsf{x},\mathsf{c}) \Leftarrow \alpha_{\mathsf{G}_2}(\mathsf{x},\mathsf{M}(\mathsf{c}))$
end
if $|\mathsf{S}| > 0$ *or* $|\mathsf{J}| > 0$ **then**
$\eta_{\mathsf{CG}}(\mathsf{c}) \Leftarrow$ true
end
if $\lambda_{\mathsf{G}_1}(\mathsf{c}) \neq \lambda_{\mathsf{G}_2}(\mathsf{M}(\mathsf{c}))$ **then**
$\lambda_{\mathsf{CG}}(\mathsf{c}) \Leftarrow$“or”
end
end
return CG
end

model calls the algorithm for calculating the maximum common regions, then visits at most all nodes of each maximum common region, and finally calls the algorithm for merging connectors. Since the number of nodes in a maximum common region and the number of maximum common regions are both bounded by the number of edges, and given that different regions do not share edges, the complexity of the merging algorithm is also linear on the number of edges.

The merged graph subsumes the input graphs in the sense that the set of traces induced by the merged graph includes the union of the traces of the two input graphs. The reason is that every node in an input graph has a corresponding node in the merged graph, and every edge in any of the original graphs has a corresponding edge (or pair of edges) in the merged graph. Hence, for any *run* of the input graph (represented as a sequence of traversed edges) there is a corresponding run in the merged graph. The run in the merged graph has additional edges which correspond to edges that have a configurable xor connector either as source or target. From a behavioral perspective, these configurable xor connectors are “silent” steps which do not alter the execution semantics. If we abstract from these connectors, the run in the input graph is equivalent to the corresponding run in the merged graph. Furthermore, each reduction rule is behavior-preserving. A detailed proof is outside the scope of this paper.

We observe that the merging algorithm accepts both configurable and non-configurable process graphs as input. Thus, the merging operator can be used for multi-way merging. Given a collection of process graphs to be merged, we can start by merging the first two graphs in the collection, then merge the resulting configurable process graph with the third graph in the collection and so on.

4 Evaluation

The algorithm for process merging has been implemented as a tool which is freely available as part of the Synergia toolset (see: `http://www.processconfiguration.com`). The tool takes as input two EPCs represented in the EPML format and suggests a mapping between the two models. Once this mapping has been validated by the user, the tool produces a configurable EPC in EPML by merging the two input models. Using this tool, we conducted tests in order to evaluate (i) the size of the models produced by the merging operator, and (ii) the scalability of the merging operator.

Size of merged models. Size is a key factor affecting the understandability of process models and it is thus desirable that merged models are as compact as possible. Of course, if we merge very different models, we can expect that the size of the merged model will almost equal to the sum of the sizes of the two input models, since we need to keep all the information in the original models. However, if we merge very similar models, we expect to obtain a model whose size is close to the size of the largest of the two models.

We conducted tests aimed at comparing the sizes of the models produced by the merging operator relative to the sizes of the input models. For these tests, we took the SAP reference model, consisting of 604 EPCs, and constructed every pair of EPCs from among them. We then filtered out pairs in which a model was paired with itself and pairs for which the matching score of the models was less than 0.5. As a result of the filtering step, we were left with 489 pairs of similar but non-identical EPCs. Next, we merged each of these model pairs and calculated the ratio between the size of the merged model and the size of the input models. This ratio is called the *compression factor* and is defined as $CF(G_1, G_2) = |CG|/(|G_1| + |G_2|)$, where $CG = Merge(G_1, G_2)$. A compression factor of 1 means that the input models are totally different and thus the size of the merged model is equal to the sum of the sizes of the input models (the merging operator merely juxtaposes the two input models side-by-side). A compression factor close to 0.5 (but still greater than 0.5) means that the input models are very similar and thus the merged model is very close to one of the input models. Finally, if the matching score of the input models is

Table 1. Size statistics of merged SAP reference models

	Size 1	Size 2	Size merged	Compression	Merged after reduction	Compression after reduction
Min	3	3	3	0.5	3	0.5
Max	130	130	194	1.17	186	1.05
Average	22.07	24.31	33.90	0.75	31.52	0.68
Std dev	20.95	22.98	30.35	0.15	28.96	0.13

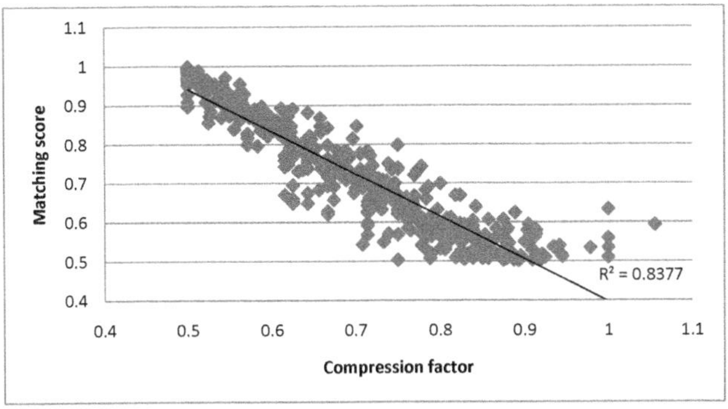

Fig. 3. Correlation between matching score of input models and compression factor

very low (e.g. only a few isolated nodes are similar), the addition of configurable connectors may induce an overhead explaining a compression factor above 1.[1]

Table 1 summarizes the test results. The first two columns show the size of the initial models. The third and fourth column show the size of the merged model and the compression factor before applying any reduction rule, while the last two columns show the size of the merged model and the compression factor after applying the reduction rules. The table shows that the reduction rules improve the compression factor (average of 68% vs. 75%), but the merging algorithm itself yields the bulk of the compression. This can be explained by the fact that the merging algorithm factors out common regions when merging. In light of this, we can expect that the more similar two process models are, the more they share common regions and thus the smaller the compression factor is. This hypothesis is confirmed by the scatter plot in Figure 3 which shows the compression factors (X axis) obtained for different matching scores of the input models (Y axis). The solid line is the linear regression of the points.

Scalability. We also conducted tests with large process models in order to assess the scalability of the proposed merging operator. We considered four model pairs. The first three pairs capture a process for handling motor incident and personal injury claims at an Australian insurer. The first pair corresponds to the claim initiation phase (one model for motor incident and one for personal injury), the second pair corresponds to claim processing and the third pair corresponds to payment of invoices associated to a claim. Each pair of models has a high similarity, but they diverge due to differences in the object of the claim.

A fourth pair of models was obtained from an agency specialized in handling applications for developing parcels of land. One model captures how land development applications are handled in South Australia while the other captures the same process in Western Australia. The similarity between these models was

[1] In file compression, the compression factor is defined as $1 - |CG|/(|G_1| + |G_2|)$, but here we use the reverse in order to compare this factor with the matching score.

Table 2. Results of merging insurance and land development models

Pair #	Size 1	Size 2	Merge time (msec.)	Size merged	Compression	Merged after reduction	Compression after reduction
1	339	357	79	486	0.7	474	0.68
2	22	78	0	88	0.88	87	0.87
3	469	213	85	641	0.95	624	0.92
4	200	191	20	290	0.75	279	0.72

high since they cover the same process and were designed by the same analysts. However, due to regulatory differences, the models diverge in certain points.

Table 2 shows the sizes of the input models, the execution time of the merging operator and statistics related to the size of the merged models. The tests were conducted on a laptop with a dual core Intel processor, 2.53 GHz, 3 GB memory, running Microsoft Vista and SUN Java Virtual Machine version 1.6 (with 512MB of allocated memory). The execution times include both the matching step and the merging step, but they exclude the time taken to read the models from disk.

The results show that the merging operator can handle pairs of models with around 350 nodes each in a matter of milliseconds—an observation supported by the execution times we observed when merging the pairs from the SAP reference model. Table 2 also shows the compression factors. Pairs 2 and 3 have a poor compression factor (lower is better). This is in great part due to differences in the size of these two models, which yields a low matching score. For example, in the case of pair 2 (matching score of 0.56) it can be seen that the merged model is only slightly larger than the larger of the two input models.

When the insurance process models were given to us, a team of three analysts at the insurance company had tried to manually merge these models. It took them 130 man-hours to merge about 25% of the end-to-end process models. The most time-consuming part of the work was to identify common regions manually. Later, we compared the common regions identified by our algorithm and those found manually. Often, the regions identified automatically were smaller than those identified manually. Closer inspection showed that during the manual merge, analysts had determined that some minor differences between the models being merged were due to omissions. Figure 4 shows a typical case (full node names are not shown for confidentiality reasons). Function C appears in one model but not in the other, and so the algorithm identifies two separate common regions. However, the analysts determined that the absence of C in the motor insurance model was an omission and created a common region with all four nodes. This scenario

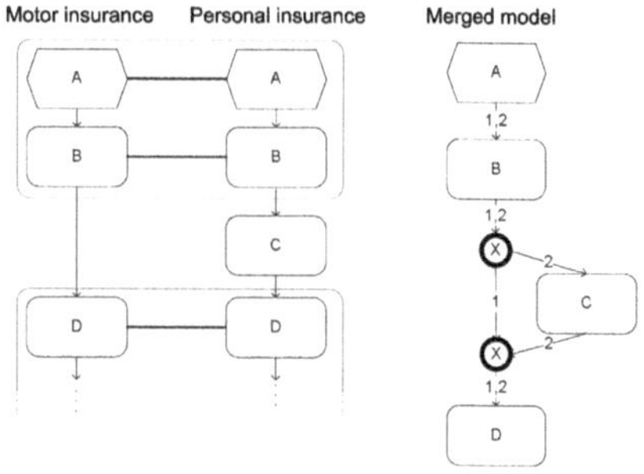

Fig. 4. Fragment of insurance models

suggests that when two regions are separated only by one or few elements, this may be due to omissions or minor differences in modeling granularity. Such patterns could be useful in pinpointing opportunities for process model homogenization.

5 Related Work

The problem of merging process models has been posed in [16], [7], [5] and [11]. Sun et al. [16] address the problem of merging block-structured Workflow nets. Their approach starts from a mapping between tasks of the input process models. Mapped tasks are copied into the merged model and regions where the two process models differ, are merged by applying a set of "merge patterns" (sequential, parallel, conditional and iterative). Their proposal does not fulfill the criteria in Section 1: the merged model does not subsume the initial variants and does not provide traceability. Also, their method is not fully automated.

Küster et al. [7] outline requirements for a process merging tool targeted towards version conflict resolution. Their envisaged merge procedure is not automated. Instead the aim is to assist modelers in resolving differences manually, by pinpointing and classifying changes using a technique outlined in [6].

Gottschalk et al. [5] merge pairs of EPCs by constructing an abstraction of each EPC, namely a *function graph*, in which connectors are replaced with edge annotations. Function graphs are merged using set union. Connectors are then restituted by inspecting the annotations in the merged function graph. This approach does not address criteria 2 and 3 in Section 1: the origin of each element cannot be traced, nor can the original models be derived from the merged one. Also, they only merge two nodes if they have identical labels, whereas our approach supports approximate matching. Finally, they assume that the input models have a single start and a single end event and no connector chains.

Li et al. [11] propose another approach to merging process models. Given a set of similar process models (the *variants*), their technique constructs a single model (the *generic* model) such that the sum of the *change distances* between each variant and the generic model is minimal. The change distance is the minimal number of change operations needed to transform one model into another. This work does not fulfill the criteria in Section 1. The generic model does not subsume the initial variants and no traceability is provided. Moreover, the approach only works for block-structured process models with AND and XOR blocks.

The problem of process model merging is related to that of integrating multiple views of a process model [12,8]. A process model view is the instantiation of a process model for a specific stakeholder or business object involved in the process. Mendling and Simon [12] propose, but do not implement, a merging operator that taken to different EPCs each representing a process view, and a mapping of their correspondences, produces a merged EPC. Correspondences can only be defined in terms of events, functions or sequences thereof (connectors and more complex graph topologies are not taken into account). Moreover, a method for identifying such correspondences is not provided. Since the models to be merged represent partial views of a same process, the resulting merged model allows the various views to be executed in parallel. In other words, common elements are taken only once and reconnected to view-specific elements by a preceding AND-join and a subsequent AND-split. However, the use of AND connectors may introduce deadlocks in the merged model. In addition, the origin of the various elements in the merged model cannot be traced.

Ryndina et al. [8] propose a method for merging state machines describing the lifecycle of independent objects involved in a business process, into a single UML AD capturing the overall process. Since the aim is to integrate partial views of a process model, their technique significantly differs from ours. Moreover, the problem of merging tasks that are similar but not identical is not posed. Similarly, the lifecycles to be merged are assumed to be disjoint and consistent, which eases the merge procedure.

For a comparison of our algorithm with work outside the business process management discipline, e.g. software merging and database schema integration, we refer to the technical report [9].

6 Conclusion

The main contribution of this paper is a merging operator that takes as input a pair of process models and produces a (configurable) process model. The operator ensures that the merged model subsumes the original model and that the original models can be derived back by individualizing the merged model. Additionally, the merged model is kept as compact as possible in order to enhance its understandability. Since the merging algorithm accepts both configurable and non-configurable process models as input, it can be used for multi-way merging. In the case of more than two input process models, we can start by merging two process models, then merge the resulting model with a third model and so on.

We extensively tested the merging operator using process models from practice. The tests showed that the operator can deal with models with hundreds of nodes and that the size of the merged model is, in general, significantly smaller than the sum of the sizes of the original models.

The merging operator essentially performs a union of the input models. In some scenarios, we do not seek the union of the input models, but rather a "digest" showing the most frequently observed behavior in the input models. In future, we plan to define a variant of the merging operator addressing this requirement. We also plan to extend the merging operator in order to deal with process models containing modeling constructs not considered in this paper. For example, BPMN offers constructs such as error handlers and non-interrupting events that are not taken into account by the current merging operator and that would require non-trivial extensions.

Finally, the merging operator relies on a mapping between the nodes of the input models. In this paper we focused on 1:1 mappings. Recent work has addressed the problem of automatically identifying complex 1:n or n:m mappings between process models [18]. Integrating the output of such matching techniques into the merging operator is another avenue for future work.

References

1. Bunke, H.: On a relation between graph edit distance and maximum common subgraph. Pattern Recognition Letters 18(8), 689–694 (1997)
2. Dijkman, R.M., Dumas, M., García-Bañuelos, L.: Graph matching algorithms for business process model similarity search. In: Dayal, U., Eder, J., Koehler, J., Reijers, H.A. (eds.) BPM 2009. LNCS, vol. 5701, pp. 48–63. Springer, Heidelberg (2009)
3. Dijkman, R.M., Dumas, M., García-Banuelos, L., Käärik, R.: Aligning business process models. In: Proc. of EDOC. IEEE, Los Alamitos (2009)
4. Fettke, P., Loos, P.: Classification of Reference Models – A Methodology and its Application. In: Information Systems and e-Business Management, vol. 1, pp. 35–53 (2003)
5. Gottschalk, F., van der Aalst, W.M.P., Jansen-Vullers, M.H.: Merging event-driven process chains. In: Meersman, R., Tari, Z. (eds.) OTM 2008, Part I. LNCS, vol. 5331, pp. 418–426. Springer, Heidelberg (2008)
6. Küster, J.M., Gerth, C., Förster, A., Engels, G.: Detecting and resolving process model differences in the absence of a change log. In: Dumas, M., Reichert, M., Shan, M.-C. (eds.) BPM 2008. LNCS, vol. 5240, pp. 244–260. Springer, Heidelberg (2008)
7. Küster, J.M., Gerth, C., Förster, A., Engels, G.: A tool for process merging in business-driven development. CEUR Workshop Proceedings, vol. 344, pp. 89–92. CEUR (2008)
8. Küster, J.M., Ryndina, K., Gall, H.: Generation of business process models for object life cycle compliance. In: Alonso, G., Dadam, P., Rosemann, M. (eds.) BPM 2007. LNCS, vol. 4714, pp. 165–181. Springer, Heidelberg (2007)
9. La Rosa, M., Dumas, M., Käärik, R., Dijkman, R.: Merging business process models (extended version). Technical report, Queensland University of Technology (2009), `http://eprints.qut.edu.au/29120`
10. Levenshtein, I.: Binary code capable of correcting deletions, insertions and reversals. Cybernetics and Control Theory 10(8), 707–710 (1966)
11. Li, C., Reichert, M., Wombacher, A.: Discovering reference models by mining process variants using a heuristic approach. In: Dayal, U., Eder, J., Koehler, J., Reijers, H.A. (eds.) Business Process Management. LNCS, vol. 5701, pp. 344–362. Springer, Heidelberg (2009)
12. Mendling, J., Simon, C.: Business process design by view integration. In: Eder, J., Dustdar, S. (eds.) BPM Workshops 2006. LNCS, vol. 4103, pp. 55–64. Springer, Heidelberg (2006)
13. Pedersen, T., Patwardhan, S., Michelizzi, J.: WordNet: Similarity - Measuring the Relatedness of Concepts. In: Proc. of AAAI, pp. 1024–1025. AAAI, Menlo Park (2004)
14. Rahm, E., Bernstein, P.A.: A survey of approaches to automatic schema matching. VLDB Journal 10(4), 334–350 (2001)
15. Rosemann, M., van der Aalst, W.M.P.: A configurable reference modelling language. Information Systems 32(1), 1–23 (2007)
16. Sun, S., Kumar, A., Yen, J.: Merging workflows: A new perspective on connecting business processes. Decision Support Systems 42(2), 844–858 (2006)
17. van Dongen, B.F., Dijkman, R.M., Mendling, J.: Measuring similarity between business process models. In: Bellahsène, Z., Léonard, M. (eds.) CAiSE 2008. LNCS, vol. 5074, pp. 450–464. Springer, Heidelberg (2008)
18. Weidlich, M., Dijkman, R.M., Mendling, J.: The icop framework: Identification of correspondences between process models. In: Pernici, B. (ed.) Advanced Information Systems Engineering. LNCS, vol. 6051, pp. 483–498. Springer, Heidelberg (2010)

Compliant Business Process Design Using Refinement Layers

Daniel Schleicher, Tobias Anstett, Frank Leymann, and David Schumm

Institute of Architecture of Application Systems,
University of Stuttgart
Universitätsstraße 38, 70569 Stuttgart, Germany
{schleicher,anstett,leymann,schumm}@iaas.uni-stuttgart.de

Abstract. In recent years compliance has emerged as one of the big IT challenges enterprises are faced with. The management of a multitude of regulations and the complexity of current business processes are problems that need to be addressed.

In this paper we present an approach based on so-called *compliance templates* to develop and manage compliant business processes involving different stakeholders.

We introduce the concept of a *refinement process*. In the refinement process each compliance template is refined in a layered way to get an executable business process. The refinement steps are executed on *refinement layers* by different stakeholders. Compliance constraints are used to restrict the way a compliance template can be refined. Introduced in a certain refinement layer of the refinement process, compliance constraints are propagated to higher refinement layers.

1 Introduction

In the last years compliance has become one of the most important business-requirements for companies. Due to financial and other scandals, institutions responsible for controlling certain aspects of the market decided to define huge bodies of laws and regulations to protect the economy. Recent crises, such as the subprime crisis, clarify that existing regulations like the Sarbanes-Oxley Act [2], which regulates financial transactions, need to be adapted. New regulations are required to prevent new financial disasters from happening. Furthermore regulations may also be imposed by company-internal policies and social expectations such as realising a *green IT*.

From a company's point of view the requirement of being compliant introduces new challenges on both organisational as well as on a technical level. People have to be sensitised to compliance and new jobs or departments dealing with compliance have to be established. For example the Siemens AG increased the amount of compliance officers in the business years 2006 to 2008 by factor seven [5]. Business process development tools have to be adapted to meet new requirements. Examples for these requirements are the increasing complexity of real world business processes and the growing number of compliance constraints coming from new laws or enterprise-internal regulations.

R. Meersman et al. (Eds.): OTM 2010, Part I, LNCS 6426, pp. 114–131, 2010.

In this paper we focus on compliance by design, meaning that design-tools support the process designer in developing compliant processes. To accomplish this, we are proposing a technique to design compliant business processes based on incremental refinements of *compliance templates* introduced in [14]. Therefore we depict a concept called to model compliant business processes in a layered way. The layers of this concept are mapped to different stakeholders with different areas of expertise. With this approach external consultants can for example be involved into the modelling process. These consultants may have only partial access to the process model. Thus, companies do not have to disclose the internal logic of their business processes. They only give access to the details necessary to complete certain constraint regions.

The approach of incremental refinement today is used to build cars, houses, and software. It is a divide and conquer approach that reduces complexity of the single decisions to make during the design phase of a business process. Thus, it is a logical way to design business processes with this approach in contrast to the brute force approach where the process is developed without preparations to improve the eventual design. Incremental refinement is no new approach but we want to introduce it in the field of business process design to develop solutions dealing with compliance. Thus, the contribution of this paper is the introduction of a refinement approach in business process design to conquer the manageability of complex processes that have to be compliant to a growing number of regulations. Along with that we present solutions on how to forward constraints between layers of refinement and show how constraints are merged.

Requirements engineering is the field of research, our work on regulatory compliance is based on. Requirements to a business process are desirable or undesirable. Analogous to that, requirements to a business process are compliant or non compliant to relevant law. Compliance of a requirement refers to its relationship to relevant law. Thus, compliance introduces law as a new dimension to be handled during the development of business processes. The question if a set of requirements is compliant or not is becoming the central question of requirements engineering in the future. A software project that fails to consider regulatory compliance when collecting requirements will not be realisable [7].

This paper is structured as follows: In Section 2 we present a motivational example. Section 3 provides a short overview of the concepts of a compliance template and process fragments. Section 4 presents the main contribution of this paper by describing the concept of a layered refinement process. Section 5 explains how compliance constraints are passed on between the layers of the refinement process. The satisfiability of these constraints is examined in Section 6. Section 7 describes a prototype implementing the concepts of this paper. Related work is presented in Section 8. And finally, conclusion and future work are provided in Section 9.

2 Motivating Example

When designing a business process, typically different stakeholders are involved. As discussed by Sadiq, et al. [13], there might be a clash between the business objectives and control objectives of a process. Control objectives are imposed by compliance requirements shown in Section 1. We illustrate the concepts introduced in this section by means of an fictive company named ACME.

In the department for business process design of ACME the employees have two roles. There are process owners and compliance officers, like shown in Figure 1. The process owners are aware of the actual work that is performed on a business process. While the compliance officers have to manage compliance requirements imposed on the business processes. This can easily result in conflicts, inconsistencies and redundancies that need to be resolved.

Let us assume the ACME company has been ordered to develop a back office solution based on business process technology. The customer provided a set of compliance requirements to be obeyed. In the following we introduce a high level methodology to be used with the concept of a refinement process. The refinement process is a human-driven, non-IT process it is run by humans during the design phase of a business process.

The first step for ACME is to develop so-called compliance templates for the business processes that later form the back office application. These compliance templates are the basis for the new business processes that to be used in the back office application. The compliance templates for these processes are stored in a repository shown in Figure 1. The process owner checks out a suitable compliance template from the repository and does a first refinement. This compliance template is used as a starting point for the refinement process. Compliance-aware process design tools are needed to support the process designers to build compliant processes.

The process owner acts on layer one of the refinement process. Then, other stakeholders (e.g. compliance officers) are assigned for refinement and completion of the compliance template. One of these stakeholders can for example be the legal department of the ACME company. The legal department acts on layer two of the refinement process. It does some further refinements. Afterwards it passes the compliance template on to another department of the ACME company opening another layer of the refinement process. After several refinements are done the completed business process is returned to the process owner. The process owner verifies the collaboratively created business process and deploys it for execution. The refinement process is explained in detail in Section 4. In this section we provide answers to questions, that arise when passing a compliance template around, like: How are new constraints introduced on each layer of the refinement process passed on between the layers? And, how are constraints of different layers merged?

3 Compliance Template

In [14] concepts and corresponding algorithms, which support the process designer in modelling compliant business processes, have been introduced. As a core concept we introduced *compliance templates*. Compliance templates consist of an *abstract business process*, *compliance descriptors* and *variability descriptors*.

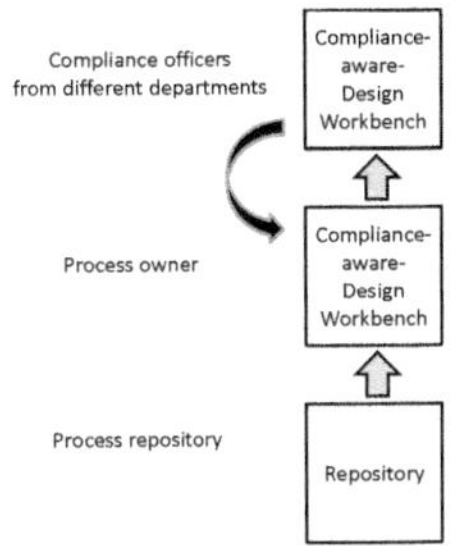

Fig. 1. The refinement process: Concrete View

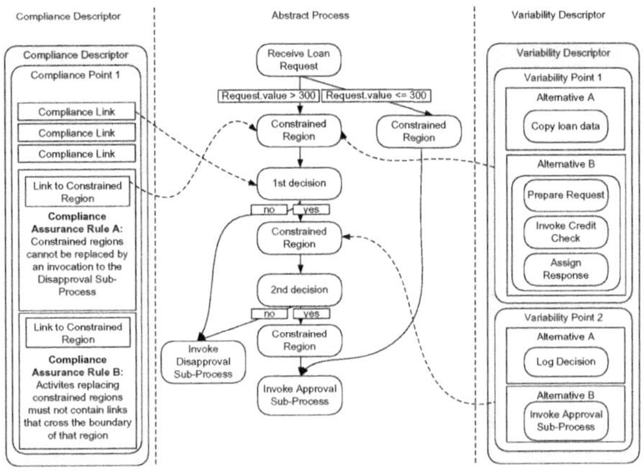

Fig. 2. Compliance Template: Basis for compliant process

Figure 2 shows the abstract business process in the middle, the compliance descriptor to the left, and the variability descriptor to the right. These constituent parts of a compliance template are explained in the following.

3.1 Abstract Process

The abstract business process is the basis for the process designer to start modelling a new business process. It is called abstract, because it does not contain all information required to be automatically executed by a business process execution engine. The abstract process roughly defines how the eventual business process should behave to be compliant. It contains so-called constrained regions which need to be completed (filled with activities) in order to get an executable process. It is not allowed to change the abstract process in any other way, as this could violate compliance rules implicitly contained within the abstract process. Take a look at Figure 2 for an example. The abstract process starts with an activity receiving a loan request. Afterwards a decision is made if the value of the loan request is above or below \$300. It depends on the result of this decision if the control flow of the process takes the right path or the left path. The abstract process of this compliance template implicitly implements a number of compliance requirements. One requirement is that the activities labelled 1st decision and 2nd decision must have been executed when the process is finished compliantly and the request value is above \$300. If a process instance is finished not having executed these two activities the instance is considered as non-compliant. Another requirement is that the disapproval sub-process can only be invoked after these activities have ended. Thus, it should not be possible to delete these activities from the abstract process.

A constrained region can be filled with a single activity, with further compliance templates, or with *process fragments*. Process fragments are an approach to facilitate the reuse of certain areas of a business process as described in [15]. In this work process fragments have been introduced as connected sub graph of a process graph, whereas some parts of a fragment may be subject to parametrisation and regions may be explicitly stated as variable in order to increase the freedom for reuse.

The fact, that only the constrained regions of the abstract process can be filled with activities, preserves the compliance of the process. The basic structure of the process cannot be changed and thus implicit compliance rules cannot be violated. One example for an implicit compliance rule is, activity A should always be executed before activity B.

3.2 Variability Descriptor

Variability descriptors [11] are used to describe variability of applications. For example a GUI written in HTML or in our case a business process can contain such points of variability. During the design-phase of a business process, variability descriptors provide the process designer with a choice of activities for each constrained region which can be used to fill the abstract process in order to get an executable process. Variability descriptors consist of *variability points* containing *locators* and *alternatives* (see Figure 3). Locators are used to point to artifacts of applications that are variable. The alternatives within a variability point describe the values that can be inserted at this point. Variability points can be dependent on each other. This means for example when a certain activity is used to fill a constrained region another activity from another variability point must be inserted, too. These dependencies describe the order in which variability points must be used.

Figure 3 shows a variability descriptor along with an application template. This template contains a BPEL process [12] and two corresponding WSDL-files. The locators of the variability descriptor point to the places where the BPEL process and the WSDL-files can be customised. Dependencies between the variability points A, B, and C are expressed by the arrows between them. Thus, variability point B depends on variability point A for example. That means, if variability point B is used then variability point A must be used, too.

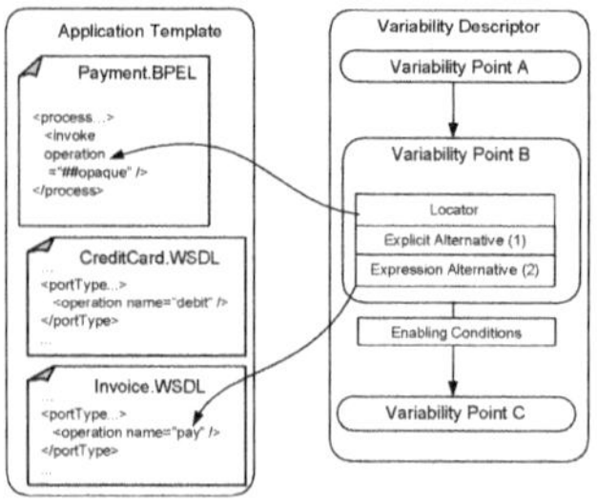

Fig. 3. Variability Descriptor

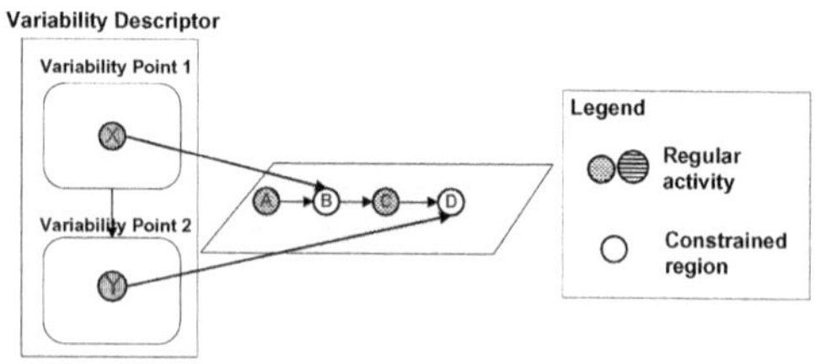

Fig. 4. Dependencies of variability points

As an example see Figure 4. Here variability point 2 is dependent on variability point 1. That means, if activity X is inserted into a constrained region, activity Y also has to be used in the process model. It depends on the constraints of the different constrained regions if activity Y can be inserted in the same constrained region as activity X.

3.3 Compliance Descriptor

Compliance descriptors (see left side of Figure 2) are defined following the design of variability descriptors. They consist of *compliance points* containing *compliance links* and *compliance assurance rules.* Compliance links point to certain activities in a business process where the corresponding compliance assurance rule should be applied. A formal representation of these rules can then be used to verify a certain replacement for a constrained region. An example for a compliance assurance rule is: "Constrained regions must not be replaced with exit activities." That means, the process designer is not allowed to insert an activity that immediately ends a process when it is executed. Without this rule a process designer could stop the execution of a process at a certain point, preventing the execution of activities important for compliant execution.

4 Refinement Layers

The abstract process contained in a compliance template provides the fundamentals to develop a compliant business process. In many cases different human process designers with different areas of expertise are involved in the design of a business process. These process designers need to be able to refine the process model according to their compliance and business requirements. For instance, dealing with quality assurance is handled differently from business to business. Some companies might have a single activity for a quality check, while others might have a multi-stage approval chain that spans over different departments.

In the following we describe a multilayer process design approach which allows such refinements, called *the refinement process.* The refinement layers of the refinement process are a concept being introduced to distinguish the work of the different process designers involved in the refinement process.

The purpose of the refinement process is to complete the abstract process of a compliance template to be executable. Many process designers of different departments of the enterprise can be involved into this process. The refinement process is started by a process designer on the layer of the abstract process. Figure 5 shows tree layers of the refinement process. The process designer takes a compliance template from the repository of the enterprise and begins to fill the constrained regions with sets of activities provided in the variability descriptor. It is not mandatory on any layer of the refinement process that all constrained regions are filled with a set of activities. It can also happen that a compliance template is further constrained by activities which are inserted. This comes from the fact, that constrained regions can be filled with a set of activities containing one ore more constrained regions. See refinement layer 2 of Figure 5 for an example. Here activity B is a constrained region.

This refinement process has the following steps:

1. A set of activities is inserted into constrained regions of the current layer. If this set of activities again contains one or more constrained regions a new refinement layer is created.
2. The inserted activities are validated against the constraints of the constrained region in which they were inserted.
3. All constraints of the constrained regions of the current layer are added to the constraints of possible new constrained regions of the higher layer.
4. Move one layer up.
5. Proceed from step one.

Each constrained region of an abstract process can be expanded into another modelling layer for refinement (see Figure 5). Within this layer, the person performing the refinement is free to place activities, as long as the result of the refinement complies with the given constraints. In Figure 5 the constrained region in the abstract process of refinement layer 1 are again refined with a process fragment.

The introduction of refinement layers is useful in many scenarios, for example when numerous departments in the management hierarchy of an enterprise have to cope with compliance in their business processes. These departments can then be mapped to corresponding refinement layers of the overall modelling process. Thus, every department has the ability to implement individual compliance requirements independently from the other departments, retaining the lower layer constraints. When changes on the process are performed on a lower layer, the persons responsible for the upper layers have to be informed to adjust their refinement layers accordingly. With the approach of refinement layers also external experts can be involved into the design phase of a business process. Enterprises typically do not want to disclose the internals of a business process. Thus, it is possible to give away parts of the business process and restrict the external expert. This is done by attaching constraints to the constrained regions that do not allow the expert to build a non-functional process.

4.1 Example

The multilayer process design approach described in this section can be applied recursively on each refinement layer. This facilitates the collaboration of independent process designers which are allowed to implement new compliance requirements on each layer of process refinement. The abstract process is refined until all constrained regions are filled and all constraints are successfully validated. Figure 5 shows an example spanning three layers.

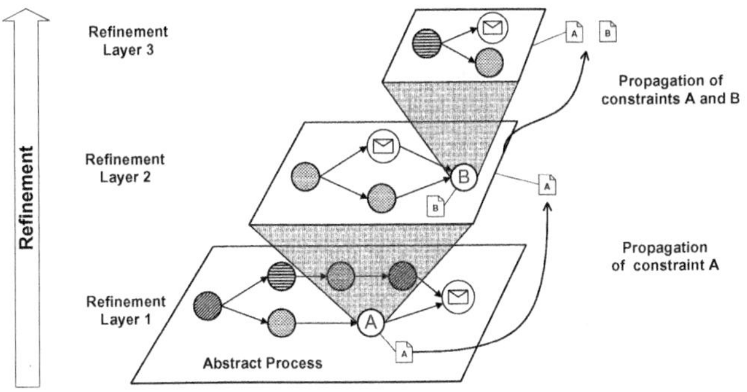

Fig. 5. Constraint-propagation over refinement layers

In the following we want to describe our intentions of compliant process modelling with a more detailed example than in Section 2. We look at a process designer working at the head office of an international bank, let us name it *InterBank*. This process designer defines a compliance template to be used to design credit-application processes. It is used on layer one of the refinement process like shown in Figure 5. The business processes that implements a credit application of the branch offices of InterBank may slightly vary in the way they handle their customer data. Thus, the process designer of layer 1 defined a constrained region where each branch office has to fill in its business logic. To ensure that the refinement of a branch office can not alter the process logic of the abstract process of layer 1, the constrained region contained in the abstract process of layer 1 is annotated with a constraint A. This constraint prevents the insertion of activities that terminate the process and modify existing variables of layer 1. After the process designer has completed the refinements, the compliance template is published to be refined in the next layer.

In layer 2 another process designer located in the head office of InterBank in Germany has to refine this abstract process to be compliant to the local customer data protection regulations. These regulations state that all data being sent away must be encrypted. Thus a process fragment is defined, adding the required business logic by using message-layer security and encryption techniques (denoted with an envelope symbol in the activity).

To allow further refinements by the local branch offices located e.g. in Hanover, the process designer integrates a constrained region within his compliance template at layer 2. To prevent further potential disclosure of information by the process designers working on the third layer, the constrained region of layer two is annotated with a constraint B which prevents the insertion of activities sending unencrypted messages. Constraints defined on lower layers must also hold on higher layers. To accomplish this we show how to propagate constraints between the layers of the refinement process in the next section.

5 Propagation of Constraints

In Figure 5 constraint A annotated to the constrained region A must hold for all activities inserted. Thus, constraint A must also hold for all activities being inserted in refinement layer 2. To meet this requirement we propose an approach called *constraint propagation*.

We assume, compliance templates always contain constrained regions. Otherwise they loose the property of being a template. Templates in a technical view are for example models for a piece of software to be built. Thus, a compliance template is a model for an eventual business process. In Figure 5, a new compliance template is inserted into constrained region A. All constraints of activity A are thus propagated to the next refinement layer. The two sets of constraints A and B are merged in refinement layer 2. Thus, constrained region B on refinement layer 2 now is annotated with the constraints A and B. This is done recursively for all further refinement layers.

A problem for the process of constraint propagation is that blind merging of two sets of constraints can lead to a set of constraints not being satisfiable anymore in a logical sense. Mutual exclusive constraints can be the cause for this. An example for a set of constraints obviously not being satisfiable is the following:

- Activities of type invoke are allowed to be placed in this activity
- Activities of all other types but the invoke-type are allowed to be placed in this activity

In the following section we take a detailed look at the satisfiability of such constraints.

6 Satisfiability of Sets of Constraints

The satisfiability problem (SAT) deals with the question whether a boolean expression is satisfiable. A boolean expression is satisfiable if there is at least one assignment making the expression true. In order to use algorithms to verify if a set of constraints is satisfiable we have to map the constraints from the representation in natural language to a representation in classical logic. To automatically verify the satisfiability of a boolean expression a number of algorithms are presented in the literature. We want to keep the discussion of what algorithm fits best for the purpose of this paper out of scope.

In the following we show examples of how constraints written in natural language can be mapped to constraints written in classical logic to clarify how constraints in classical logic should be understood. We do not intent to provide a full formal mapping from natural language to classical logic. In the future we will extend our approach to more powerful languages like linear temporal logic (LTL) or deontic logic. These languages on the one hand enable constraint designers to design more complex constraints but on the other hand the more complex structure of these languages makes it harder to validate them automatically.

6.1 Mapping of Constraints in Natural Language to Formulas in Classical Logic

The following set contains two mutual exclusive constraints. With these constraints we want to show the mapping of constraints expressed in natural language to constraints expressed in classical logic and the need for the verification of satisfiability of a set of constraints. The mapping from natural language constraints to constraints in classical logic is presented to clarify how constraints in classical logic should be read. We do not intent to provide a full formal mapping from natural language to classical logic.

1. "This constrained region must not be replaced with an exit activity".
2. "This constrained region must be replaced with an exit activity".

The first constraint can be mapped to a term in conjunctive normal form (CNF) in the following way:

1. **Identify the subject the constraint has to be applied to.** In the example of the first constraint we have one subject, the constrained region. Thus, the constraint is added to this particular constrained region.
2. **Identify the objects of the constraint.** In the example of the first constraint the object is the exit activity. We map this object to a logical variable called e. If there is more than one object present in the constraint, we map each object to a separate logical variable and put it into a separate clause. The formula would now look like this:

$$(e) \tag{1}$$

   For a number of objects (e, a, and b) in a constraint the formula would look like this:

$$(e) \wedge (a) \wedge (b) \tag{2}$$

3. **Identify if a negation is applied to certain objects.** In case of the first constraint the completed formula for this constraint would now look like this:

$$(\neg e) \tag{3}$$

The formula for the second constraint would look like this:

$$(e) \tag{4}$$

We assume that the first constraint is passed on to a higher layer of the refinement process where the second constraint applies to another constrained region. We want to merge formula 4 to formula 3. This is done by appending formula 4 with an $\wedge$ operator at the end of formula 3. The new formula would now look like this:

$$(\neg e) \wedge (e) \tag{5}$$

This formula is in CNF and it is not satisfiable. The outcome of the validation of formula 5 is always false for values of e of true or false.

Mutual exclusive constraints can also be expressed with classical logic. Let us assume the following constraint in natural language: "This constrained region can be replaced by either an invoke activity or an empty activity."

If we map the invoke activity to variable i and the empty activity to variable e the corresponding logical formula in CNF would look like this:

$$(i \vee e) \tag{6}$$

Another constraint can look like this: "This constrained region can be replaced by either an invoke activity and an assign activity or an invoke activity and an empty activity." We map this constraint to classical logic in the following way. We keep the mapping of the invoke activity and the empty activity to i and e respectively. And we add a mapping of the assign activity to a. The resulting logical formula in conjunctive normal form would look like this:

$$(a \vee e) \wedge (i) \tag{7}$$

6.2 Deletion of Constraints

It is worthwhile to keep the number of constraints that are annotated to constrained regions low. One reason for a low number of constraints is the polynomial complexity of the algorithms to compute the satisfiability of logical terms [6].

We address this requirement by deleting constraints that have been satisfied. An example is shown in Figure 6. Here the constrained region in refinement layer 1 is annotated with the constraints X and Y. In refinement layer 2 a compliance template is inserted. The activity labelled X satisfies constraint X. Thus, constraint X is deleted from the set of constraints of the constrained region in refinement layer 1. Constraint X is also not propagated to refinement layer 2 in

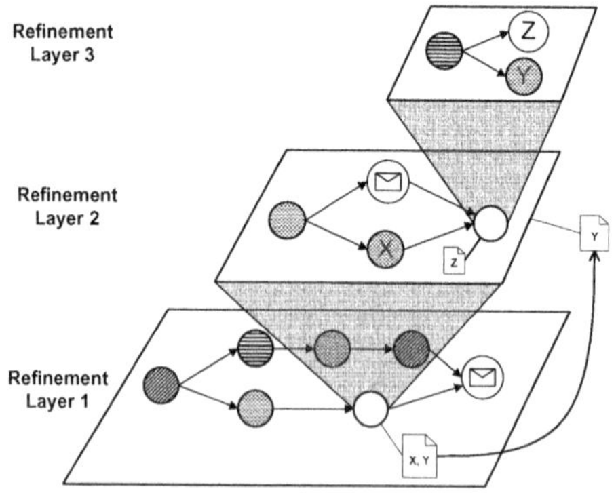

Fig. 6. Deletion of satisfied constraints

contrast to constraint Y. Further, a new constraint Z is introduced in refinement layer 2. It is merged with constraint Y of refinement layer 1. The set of activities inserted in refinement layer 3 satisfies the constraints Y and Z. Thus, they are deleted from the set of constraints. The process is now executable because there is no constrained region left to be filled. In our example no constraints are left after all constrained regions are filled with activities. But there can also be the case that not all constraints are deleted. This is the case for constraints that never can be satisfied. Like the constraint: "This constrained region must not be filled with an activity of type invoke". This constraint will never be satisfied during the refinement process because the eventual business process would become non compliant.

6.3 Direct and Indirect Conflicts

With the approach of deletion of constraints we solve another problem that we want to describe in the following. To do this we introduce the terms *direct* and *indirect* conflict in the refinement process.

Definition 1. *During the merge of two sets of constraints in the refinement process a direct conflict occurs when a negated literal of a lower layer clashes with a positive literal with the same name of a higher layer or vice versa.*

Figure 7 shows an example for a direct conflict. Let us assume that the constraint on refinement layer 1 states: "No activities of type A should be inserted into this constrained region". Whereas the constraint on refinement layer 2 states:"Only activities of type A can be inserted into this constrained region". In this situation the rule set of refinement layer 1 is in direct conflict with the rule set of refinement layer 2. If these sets of constraints are merged the resulting set of constraints is not satisfiable. Let us now take a look at the definition of an indirect conflict.

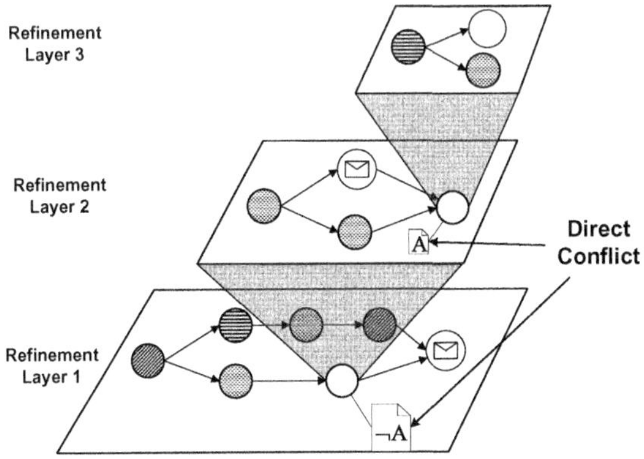

Fig. 7. Direct conflict of constraints in two refinement layers

Definition 2. *During the merge of two sets of constraints in the refinement process an indirect conflict occurs when a positive literal of a lower layer clashes with a negative literal of a higher layer.*

Let us assume in Figure 7 the constraints of refinement layer 1 and refinement layer 2 have switched. When we merge these two sets of constraints, the resulting set of constraints obviously is not satisfiable. However, the constraint from refinement layer 1 could have been satisfied before the two sets of constraints are merged. This is the case when in refinement layer 2 an activity of type A has been inserted in the new constrained region. After the insertion of an activity of type A, the now satisfied constraint of refinement layer 1 is deleted. Thus, the indirect conflict is resolved.

7 Prototypical Implementation

We have extended the web based BPMN editor Oryx[1] with a number of concepts shown in this paper. Oryx does not require to install any third party software and runs in a web browser. With this editor it is possible to share process models over the Internet. Different stakeholders can use Oryx for modelling business processes in a collaborative way. It is platform independent and thus facilitates the integration of people with special skills into the process of business process modelling. Oryx has been adjusted to be run in google wave. This provides further possibilities to collaboratively design business processes. With the google wave integration two remote human process designers can see live changes of each other while modelling a business process[2].

Oryx consists of two architectural components, the front end and the back end. The front end component comprises the elements being visible in the browser window. The back end component comprises a number of Java servlets providing functionality like a process model database.

Figure 8 shows the front end of the Oryx process editor. It mainly consists of three parts. The modelling canvas in the middle, the shape repository (labelled 1), and the properties pane (labelled 2). The shape repository contains all elements of the currently loaded process modelling language. This set of modelling elements is called a stencil set. Modelling elements can be used by dragging them from the shape repository to the canvas.

To provide the process designer with a means to develop process models containing constrained regions a new stencil has been added. We used the extension mechanism of Oryx to add the new stencil to the BPMN2.0 stencil set. This new stencil is called *Constrained Region*. The constrained region is labelled 3 in Figure 8. This stencil is capable of containing any kind of BPMN2.0 elements or group of BPMN2.0 elements up to a whole process model including other constrained regions. The stencil has a property called *compliance descriptor* used to store the

[1] http://code.google.com/p/oryx-editor/
[2] http://www.processwave.org/

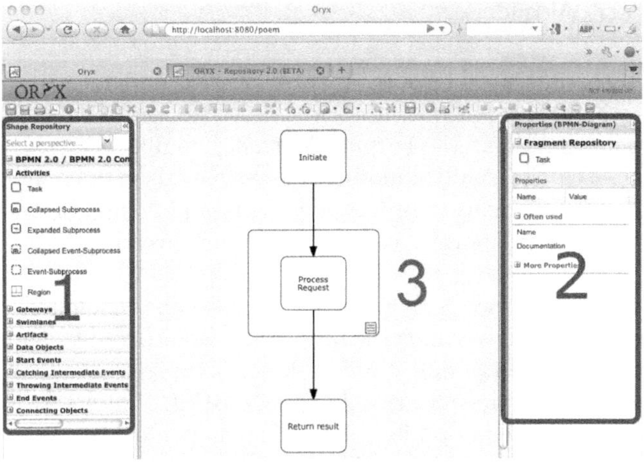

Fig. 8. Surface of Oryx BPMN modelling tool

constraints of the constrained region. This property is now shown on the properties pane on the right when a constrained region is selected on the canvas. The logical terms in a compliance descriptor have to be in conjunctive normal form.

Besides the new stencil we added three new functionalities to the Oryx editor, a fragment repository, a compliance checker, and a satisfiability checker for logical formulas.

The fragment repository is a frontend plugin. On the Oryx surface it is located on the right side above the properties pane in Figure 8. The fragment repository implements the concepts of the variability descriptor described in Section 3.2. It contains a list of process fragments that can be used to complete an abstract process to become an executable process.

The compliance checker is a backend plugin. It is responsible to check whether a set of activities being inserted into a constrained region does not violate any constraints. If an activity violates a constraint, red markers will be visible around the corners of the constrained region. Then it is not possible to insert the activity.

The satisfiability checker is a backend plugin. It is used to check the satisfiability of the merged sets of constraints of two constrained regions. These constraints are taken from the compliance descriptor property of a constrained region. We chose the SAT4J[3] framework to perform the check for satisfiability. If a set of constraints is not satisfiable the corresponding constrained region is marked with red corners.

With our additions the Oryx editor can now be used for two intended purposes. It can be used to design compliance templates and to complete a compliance template. Compliance templates can be created by modelling a process and inserting constrained regions into this process model. By adding compliance constraints to the compliance descriptor property, the user can restrict what kinds of activities can be inserted into specific constrained regions.

[3] http://www.sat4j.org

8 Related Work

An approach to annotate business processes with compliance rules is shown by Sadiq, et al. [13]. In this paper compliance objectives are modelled independently from the process models in the Formal Contract Language FCL [4]. These objectives are then used to visually annotate process models with compliance requirements. With this information process designers and compliance officers have a discussion basis to collaborate and eventually achieve the goal of a compliant process model.

An orthogonal approach is shown in [9]. In this paper compliance of a process model is checked by transforming the process model into a Pi-Calculus model and then subsequently into an finite state machine. Compliance rules are modelled in the Business Property Specification Language BPSL. The BPSL model is then translated into linear temporal logic LTL. The finite state machine and the LTL model are used to check, if the original process model is compliant to the rules defined in LTL. This is done with model checking techniques as shown by Clarke, et al. [1].

Our approach differs from the approaches above by the fact that in our approach the original process model implicitly contains the rules it should be compliant with. During the design process the software used to design the process model automatically checks the compliance of the process model.

In [16] Yi et al. show how constraints in real time systems can be verified. Here constraints like *process P will never reach state S* are verified by a backward analysis of the process graph. The analysis starts at the final state of the process and searches back to the start. Either the algorithm reaches the start of the process or not. Depending on that a constraint can be verified. Our approach differs drastically. We do not consider the whole process model to verify constraints. Instead, we consider important parts of the process when a new activity is inserted at design time. This can reduce verification time.

Eberle et al. [3] understand process fragments as building blocks for the creation of process-based applications. They discuss an algebraic foundation in order to enable the representation of small pieces of process knowledge and to allow the composition of fragments into more complex structures. Ma [10] proposes process fragments as a concept for flexible and modularised reuse. In this approach a formal definition of a process fragment for the business process execution language BPEL [12] is presented. Khalaf [8] presents a static approach for distributed process execution, including the identification, creation and execution of BPEL process fragments while keeping the original execution semantics of the original process. Those approaches are relevant for our overall approach, however those approaches do not address compliance aspects.

9 Conclusion and Future Work

Building on the work presented in [14] we introduced the concept of a refinement process. The refinement process starts with an abstract business process that is refined in a layered way. The refinement can be made at different levels of granularity: either single activities can be included, higher level structures (i.e. process fragments) can be reused, or new compliance templates can be integrated in a layer. This refinement approach can be executed in enterprises facilitating the involvement of different departments in the development process. To be able to develop compliance constraints coming with constrained regions, we showed how to map constraints in natural language to logical formulas in conjunctive normal form. Furthermore we brought up concepts on how constraints on different layers of the refinement process are handled and propagated. The propagation of constraints lead us to the problem of satisfiability of boolean expressions. We addressed this problem by discussing approaches to delete satisfied constraints from these boolean expressions. Furthermore we discussed the notion of direct versus indirect conflicts of constraints and showed that only direct conflicts always lead to not satisfiable boolean expressions.

With an eye to process fragments, we will investigate how process fragments can be split up and integrated into more than one constrained region of an abstract process. In Figure 9 two process fragments are merged. We consider the process fragment containing the activity A as the abstract process from the compliance template. Now the process fragment containing the activities E, F, and G is inserted into this process. To do this, a suitable place has to be found. Requirements for this place are defined by the structure of the process fragment to be inserted. In our case the abstract process has to have two constrained regions with at least one activity in between them. Note, there could be an arbitrary set of activities between these two constrained regions. One possibility to insert the new process fragment is to place activity E in constrained region B, and activity C in constrained region F.

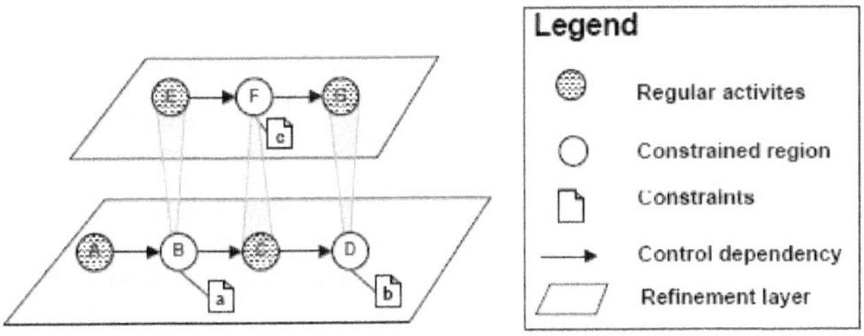

Fig. 9. Composition of process fragments

There is a need to support a variety of constraint languages in the refinement process. This requirement arises from the nature of the refinement process presented in this paper. As there could be separate parties developing parts of the eventual business process it is necessary to support the introduction of separate constraint languages for each refinement layer. E.g. to check properties of activities used within a XML-based workflow language such as BPEL [12], XPath might be used. Also, graphical notations, like UML or BPMN, will be examined to determine if they are suitable to express compliance requirements.

We will further examine how semantics of activities can be integrated into constraints. There is a need to be able to express e.g. if a BPEL invoke activity invokes Web service A or Web service B. There is also a need to create a universal mapping from BPMN constructs to literals of logical formulas. One problem here is that a task in BPMN is a generic construct to execute something. The naming of the task tells the process developer what the task is really doing. Thus, if we want to provide a mapping from tasks to literals we need to introduce semantics in the naming of tasks.

The current prototype based on the Oryx BPMN editor should be further extended. We want to integrate two design modes. The first mode is the compliance template design mode. In this mode compliance templates can be created. This means in this mode abstract business processes can be built, compliance descriptors defined, and variability descriptors can be added to the compliance template. In the second mode only the variability descriptor is shown to the process designer. With the activities provided in the variability descriptor the process designer can complete the process.

To use the tools in enterprises we want to come up with a methodology describing what stakeholders are needed to be part of a refinement process and how tools can support this process.

Acknowledgements

The work published in this article was partially funded by the MASTER project[4] (contract no. FP7-216917) and the COMPAS project[5] (contract no. FP7-215175) of the EU 7th Research Framework Programme Information and Communication Technologies Objective.

References

1. Clarke, E.M., Grumberg, O., Peled, D.A.: Model Checking. MIT Press, Cambridge (2000)
2. U.S. Code. Sarbanes-Oxley Act of 2002, PL 107-204, 116 Stat 745 (2002)
3. Eberle, H., Unger, T., Leymann, F.: Process Fragments. In: Meersman, R., Dillon, T., Herrero, P. (eds.) OTM 2009. LNCS, vol. 5870, pp. 398–405. Springer, Heidelberg (2009)
4. Governatori, G., Milosevic, Z.: A formal analysis of a business contract language. Int. J. Cooperative Inf. Syst. 15(4), 659–685 (2006)
5. Halfmann, A.: Siemens versiebenfacht Zahl der Compliance-Mitarbeiter (January 2009)
6. Hopcroft, J.E., Motwani, R., Ullman, J.D.: Introduction to Automata Theory, Languages and Computation, 3rd edn. Pearson Addison-Wesley, Upper Saddle River (2007)

---

[4] http://www.master-fp7.eu

[5] http://www.compas-ict.eu

7. Jureta, I., Siena, A., Mylopoulos, J., Perini, A., Susi, A.: Theory of regulatory compliance for requirements engineering. CoRR, abs/1002.3711, informal publication (2010)
8. Khalaf, R.: Supporting business process fragmentation while maintaining operational semantics: a BPEL perspective. Doctoral thesis, University of Stuttgart, Faculty of Computer Science, Electrical Engineering, and Information Technology, Germany (March 2008)
9. Liu, Y., Müller, S., Xu, K.: A static compliance-checking framework for business process models. IBM Syst. J. 46(2), 335–361 (2007)
10. Ma, Z., Leymann, F.: Bpel fragments for modularized reuse in modeling bpel processes. In: ICNS 2009: Proceedings of the 2009 Fifth International Conference on Networking and Services, Washington, DC, USA, pp. 63–68. IEEE Computer Society, Los Alamitos (2009)
11. Mietzner, R., Leymann, F.: Generation of BPEL Customization Processes for SaaS Applications from Variability Descriptors. In: Proceedings of the International Conference on Services Computing, Industry Track, SCC 2008. IEEE, Los Alamitos (Juli 2008)
12. OASIS. Web Services Business Process Execution Language Version 2.0 – OASIS Standard (2007)
13. Sadiq, S.W., Governatori, G., Namiri, K.: Modeling control objectives for business process compliance. In: Alonso, G., Dadam, P., Rosemann, M. (eds.) BPM 2007. LNCS, vol. 4714, pp. 149–164. Springer, Heidelberg (2007)
14. Schleicher, D., Anstett, T., Leymann, F., Mietzner, R.: Maintaining Compliance in Customizable Process Models. In: Meersman, R., Dillon, T., Herrero, P. (eds.) OTM 2009. LNCS, vol. 5870, pp. 1–16. Springer, Heidelberg (2009)
15. Schumm, D., Leymann, F., Ma, Z., Scheibler, T., Strauch, S.: Integrating Compliance into Business Processes: Process Fragments as Reusable Compliance Controls. In: Proceedings of the Multikonferenz Wirtschaftsinformatik (MKWI 2010), Universitaetsverlag Goettingen (2010)
16. Yi, W., Pettersson, P., Daniels, M.: Automatic verification of real-time communicating systems by constraint-solving. In: Proc. of the 7th International Conference on Formal Description Techniques, pp. 223–238 (1994)

COMPRO: A Methodological Approach for Business Process Contextualisation

Jose Luis de la Vara[1], Raian Ali[2], Fabiano Dalpiaz[2], Juan Sánchez[1], and Paolo Giorgini[2]

[1] Centro de Investigación en Métodos de Producción de Software
Universidad Politécnica de Valencia, Spain
{jdelavara,jsanchez}@pros.upv.es
[2] Department of Information Engineering and Computer Science
University of Trento, Italy
{raian.ali,fabiano.dalpiaz,paolo.giorgini}@disi.unitn.it

Abstract. Context-awareness has emerged as a new perspective for business process modelling. Business processes are strongly influenced by context, the environment where they are executed, and thus context should not be ignored when modelling them. This calls for new approaches that facilitate contextualisation, i.e. identification and representation of the way context influences a business process. In addition, detailed methodological guidance for correct business process contextualisation should be provided. However, existing works on context-aware business process modelling do not deal with these challenges. This paper addresses them by presenting COMPRO, a methodological approach for business process contextualisation. Starting from an initial business process model, context is analysed in order to discover its relevant variations and specify their effect on a business process. Our approach helps process designers to adequately specify context variants and business process variants that accommodate them. Our ultimate goal is to guarantee the correct design of business processes that fit their context. In addition, we report initial results about COMPRO application and evaluation.

Keywords: business process modelling, context-awareness, business process contextualisation, correctness of business process models, context analysis.

1 Introduction

The importance of business process modelling is undeniable. It plays a major role in many fields such as business process management and information system development both in industry and in academia [10]. Traditional approaches for business process modelling have not paid much attention to the dynamism of the environment in which a business process is executed. However, organizations and their software systems currently operate in an environment where changes happen frequently, so they need to adapt their behaviour in order to effectively operate in the new situation. The research community has acknowledged the importance of considering flexibility and variability in business processes modelling [10, 21]. Since business processes are

R. Meersman et al. (Eds.): OTM 2010, Part I, LNCS 6426, pp. 132–149, 2010.

influenced by their environment, business process modelling inevitably has to consider such factor and its variable nature.

Context-awareness has emerged as a new perspective for business process modelling in order to meet these needs [19]. It has already been applied in software-related fields such as human computer interaction [5] and pervasive computing [9], and it is expected to improve business process modelling by explicitly addressing fitness between business processes and their context. Context should be analysed when modelling a business process to identify its variations (relevant states of the world in which the business process is executed) and how they influence the business process, and to determine how the business process has to adapt to them.

Although several works have contributed to the advance of context-aware business process modelling, e.g. [8, 19, 22], research on this topic is still at an initial stage. An important unexplored challenge is provision of techniques to identify those context properties that influence a business process. Process designers need to understand business process context, reason about it, analyse context variations (changes) and discover the relevant context properties [7, 16]. These properties are necessary to be able to check if a given context variant holds.

Creation of contextualised business process models, which explicitly depict and support a set of context variants, should also be facilitated. Methodology is a top issue for business process modelling [10], and mechanisms and guidance for business process contextualisation must be provided in order to help process designers to properly represent and support context variants in business process models.

Furthermore, several properties should hold in contextualised business process models to guarantee its quality [26]. For example, a contextualised business process model should be correct. Correctness properties and their verification are important concerns for the research community [11], and they should always be taken into account when modelling business processes. As explained below, adding the context dimension to a business process involves new threats to its correctness, and this issue shall be addressed when defining a contextualisation approach.

This paper aims to advance in research on context-aware business process modelling by dealing with the aforementioned challenges. The objectives of the paper are to determine how business process context can be analysed, how it can influence business processes, how to create contextualised business process models, and how to guarantee their correctness.

We achieve these objectives by defining COMPRO (COntextualisation Method for business PROcesses), a methodological approach for business process contextualization. The baseline for our approach is context analysis [1, 2], a technique that aims to support reasoning about context and discovery of context properties. We adapt it to business process modelling. COMPRO provides mechanisms and detailed guidance that help process designers to reason about business process context and to model business processes that fit their context and are correct. Context properties and variants are analysed in order to determine how they influence a business process, to guarantee that a business process is properly executed in all its context variants, and to correctly model contextualised business processes.

In addition, we report on preliminary evaluation of COMPRO. The approach has been applied and initially evaluated in organizations of several sectors, and this evaluation has allowed us to get important feedback from industry, to identify benefits and limitations of the approach and to determine future research directions.

The paper is organised as follows. Section 2 reviews related work. Section 3 describes COMPRO. Section 4 presents its application and the lessons learnt from it. Finally, Section 5 summarises our conclusions and future work.

2 Related Work

The notion of context plays an important role in fields such as pragmatics, natural language semantics, linguistics, cognitive psychology and artificial intelligence [4]. For business processes, context can be defined as the set of environmental properties that have an impact on process design and/or execution [19], i.e. properties that can influence and change business process execution and that should be analysed when designing a business process.

We review related work to business process contextualisation according to three categories: context-aware workflows, principles for context-aware business process modelling and modelling of context effect on business processes.

Smanchat et al. [22] provide a survey of works about context-aware workflows. For example, they deal with context-aware exception handling, management of context-aware workflow systems and context-aware execution languages. These works focus on provision of technological solutions for context-aware execution of business processes, but do not provide guidance to analyse business process context and to contextualise business processes.

Works on principles for context-aware business process modelling have addressed context-awareness from a more general and conceptual point of view. These works have analysed the different kinds of business process contexts [20] and the importance of external factors for contextualisation [19], and have defined models for context discovery from existing process instances [7], frameworks for context variations [16] and context-aware process management cycles [17]. Explicitly or implicitly, they all have acknowledged the need of analysis of business process context. Their main weakness is that they are too general and abstract. More detailed and systematic guidance is necessary to facilitate application of their ideas for business process contextualisation from a methodological perspective.

Other works provide mechanisms for modelling of context effect on business processes. Some examples are labelling of transitions [3], variant-specific adaptations [8] and context sensitive regions [14]. Although these works can help process designers to model contextualised business processes, their guidance is insufficient. They explain how to specify context effect in a business process model, but do not explain how to analyse business process context and discover its effect. Furthermore, just [8] addresses correctness of contextualised business process models, but only for its mechanism for modelling of context effect instead of from a general point of view.

Finally, we have presented initial work on and ideas about business process contextualisation in [6]. Their application, evaluation, extension and improvement have resulted in COMPRO.

3 COMPRO Description

The main objective of COMPRO is to provide mechanisms and detailed guidance for correct modelling of business processes that fit their context and thus are properly executed in all the context variants of their business environment. Fig. 1 outlines COMPRO.

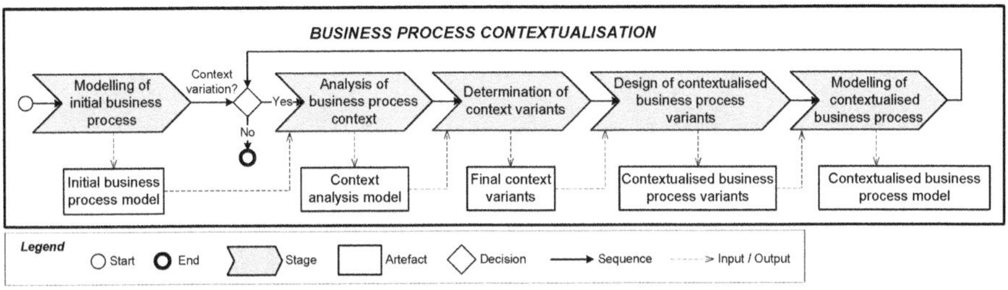

Fig. 1. Business process contextualisation through COMPRO

First, an initial version of a business process is modelled. Then, the following stages are iterated while relevant context variations are found and they are not represented and properly supported in the business process model. Relevant context variations can influence the business process and imply that business process execution has to change, i.e. tasks of the business process have to be either executed or not depending on context variations.

If a context variation is found, then business process context is analysed to find the context properties that allow business process participants to know if a given context variant holds. A context analysis model is created, and context variants of the business process have to be analysed in order to adequately specify them. Afterwards, contextualised business process variants are designed on the basis of the final context variants and their effect on the business process. Finally, a contextualised business process model is created from contextualised business process variants.

Our approach identifies relevant context variations and addresses flexibility and variability of business processes at design time [21]. As a result, it can increase process flexibility, decrease reaction time to context variations and improve risk management [19].

Throughout this section we use product promotion in a department store as a running example. Such scenario is an adaptation of a real business process of a Spanish company with which we applied COMPRO. Although it is relatively small, the example allows us to clearly show all the mechanisms and guidance of the approach.

After performing product promotion as a strategy for income increase for one year, company managers have realised that return on investment is negative and that product promotion resulted effective only in some sections. Company managers wonder why product sales did not sufficiently increase during promotion periods so that they covered the associated expenses, especially given the fact that product promotion works and is a common practice in competitors.

Managers of the company need to make a decision about whether cancel the strategy or not. After discussing product promotion, they have decided to give it a new chance. They have also decided to analyse how products were promoted the previous year and how they should be promoted in future before launching any new product promotion. It is evident that the business process that was enacted failed, and a possible cause is that it did not properly fit the context in which it was executed. Analysis of the business process and of its context can help managers to find previous problems and to define new solutions so that product promotion does not fail again.

The following subsections describe each stage of COMPRO and present the mechanisms and guidance that are necessary to carry them out.

3.1 Modelling of Initial Business Process

In the first stage of COMPRO, an initial version of the business process that needs to fit its context is modelled. This model defines the context scope that has to be analysed, is the starting point for understanding of an organization and its context, and is used as basis for subsequent analysis of business process context.

The initial business process model can be created in different ways. For example, it could correspond to a reference model that will be adapted to the context of an organization, to a model that depicts the current behaviour of an organization and that needs to be contextualised for proper execution, or to a model that is created for a new scenario in an organization that was not previously needed. These situations may correspond to ERP implementation, business process reengineering and need of a new business process for new regulations compliance, respectively.

Fig. 2 shows the initial business process model for the running example and represents how product promotion has been executed. Although Fig. 2 has been modelled with BPMN (http://www.bpmn.org), COMPRO is not targeted to be only used with this notation.

When a product is promoted, section managers notify assistants of the promotion. Assistants have to find potential buyers for the product and to explain the promotion to them. If a customer is interested in and thus wants the promotion, then assistants give him the product to buy it. Assistants repeat this process until shift change.

The business process model does not reflect some relevant context variations and thus does not fit its context. For example, most of customers prefer not being addressed for product promotion unless they have addressed an assistant, especially when they are in a hurry. If an assistant addresses a customer that probably does not correspond to a potential buyer, then the customer can have a negative reaction about product promotion and the department store and may refuse product promotion in future. In addition, the assistant is missing the chance to address a real potential buyer, and addressing this customer may not be possible later. Consequently, assistants must be careful when looking for (finding) potential buyers. If context variations like these are disregarded, then product promotion may fail. They should be explicitly modelled so that assistants are aware of them and behave adequately.

Although all tasks (and thus the entire business process) of Fig. 2 could be a subject of contextualization, in the rest of Section 3 we focus on contextualization of the task “Find Potential Buyer”.

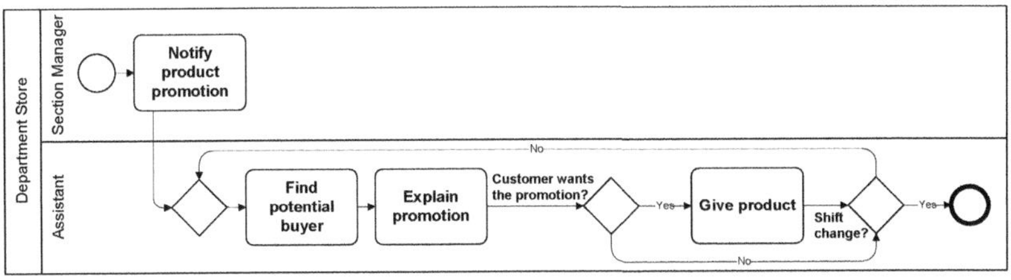

Fig. 2. Initial business process model

3.2 Analysis of Business Process Context

The second stage aims to understand context, to reason about it and to discover the context properties that influence a business process. For these purposes, we adopt context analysis proposed in [1, 2] and adapt it for analysis of business process context. This technique has been presented in the requirements engineering field, and is redefined from a business process perspective in COMPRO.

Context is specified as a world predicates formula. The EBNF of such formula is shown in Fig.3. World predicates are classified on the basis of their verifiability by a business process participant into two kinds: facts and statements.

Definition 1 (Fact). A world predicate *F* is a fact for a business process participant *P* iff *F* can be verified by *P*.

A business process participant has a clear way to verify a fact. He possesses or can obtain the necessary data to objectively judge the truth value of a fact. For example, a world predicate such as "Customer asks for the product" can be verified by an assistant and its truth value will be the same for any person at a given moment.

Definition 2 (Statement). A world predicate *S* is a statement for a business process participant *P* iff *S* cannot be verified by *P*.

Unlike facts, some world predicates are not objectively verifiable by a participant because of reasons such as lack of information and their subjective nature. For example, the world predicate "Customer is willing to buy the product" is a statement. An assistant may guess that it is true, but he cannot guarantee it. However, the truth value of a statement can be assumed or supposed if there are evidences that support it.

Definition 3 (Support). A statement *S* is supported by a formula of world predicates *Fm* iff *Fm* gives enough evidence to the truth of *S*.

A statement can be supported both by facts and by other statements, which can also be supported by other formulas. The support relationship is transitive, thus statements can be iteratively refined to facts that provide enough evidence. For example, if a formula Fm1 supports a statement S1 and 'S1 AND Fm2' supports S2, then 'Fm1 AND Fm2' supports S2.

```
Formula ::= World_Predicate | (Formula) | Formula AND Formula | Formula OR Formula
```

Fig. 3. EBNF grammar for context specification formula

Nonetheless, refinement of statements to formulas of facts is not always possible. For example, facts that support the statement "Customer is willing to buy a present" may not be found. Our analysis of business process context only deals with statements and thus contexts that can be refined to facts, i.e. they are judgeable.

Definition 4 (Judgeable Statement). A statement *S* is judgeable iff there exist a formula of facts *Fm* that supports *S*.

Definition 5 (Judgeable Context). A context *C* is judgeable iff *C* can be specified as a formula of facts and judgeable statements *Fm*.

Obtaining a judgeable context and discovering the formula that implies it can be considered the main purposes of analysis of business process context. The facts of the formula correspond to the context properties that characterise the context and its variants, and their truth values determine how a business process should be executed.

Facts that allow a context to be judgeable are discovered by analysing the formula that specifies the context. In this analysis, world predicates that correspond to statements have to be further analysed and refined until they are judgeable. If a non-judgeable statement was found when analysing the formula of a context, then the statement would have to be discarded. This statement would not allow relevant context properties (facts) to be found, and the resulting context would not be judgeable.

A context analysis model is created to facilitate reasoning about business process context and discovery of the facts of the formula that implies it. An example is shown in Fig. 4, which corresponds to context analysis for the task "Find potential buyer" of Fig. 2.

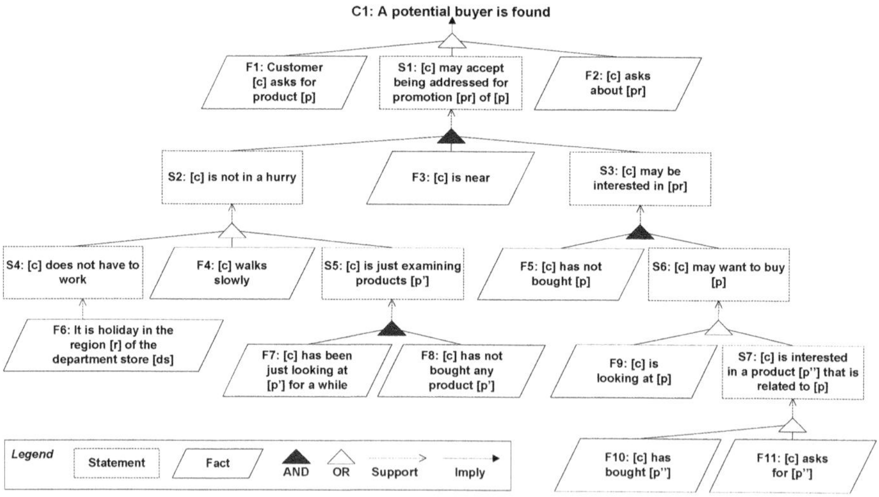

Fig. 4. Context analysis model

A context analysis model is created by following these steps:

1. Determine the desired general context of the business process or fragment for which analysis is carried out.
2. Decompose the context to define the formula that specifies it.
3. Refine the statements of the formula until all of them are judgeable. If a statement is not judgeable, then it has to be removed from the model.

For Fig. 4, the desired context (C1) is "A potential buyer is found", the formula that implies it is 'F1 OR F2 OR (F3 AND (F4 OR F6 OR (F7 AND F8)) AND F5 AND (F9 OR F10 OR F11))', and all statements are judgeable. If the statement "Customer wants to buy a present" had refined S6, then it would have been removed.

Differently from other approaches for context modelling (see survey in [23]), context analysis does not provide an ontology or a modelling language for representing context, but modelling constructs to hierarchically analyse context. Nonetheless, a data conceptual model can be derived from facts of a context analysis model [1]. This model represents the information that has to be checked to verify the facts of the formula that implies a context.

3.3 Determination of Context Variants

Once a judgeable context has been found for a business process, context variants are determined in the third stage of COMPRO.

Definition 6 (Context variant) A context variant *CV* is a set of facts whose conjunction implies a context *C*.

The main purposes of this stage are to adequately specify the (final) context variants in which the business process can be executed and that the context variants allow correct business process contextualisation and thus correct execution.

A context variant represents a state of the world in which a business process can be executed and (successfully) finished. For C1, a context variant corresponds to the set of facts '{F3, F4, F5, F9}' (the formula 'F3 AND F4 AND F5 AND F9' implies the context). Fig. 5 (a) shows the eleven initial context variants for C1, which are derived from the formula that implies it.

As explained in the next subsection, contextualised business process variants have to be determined for each context variant of a business process and must allow the business process to be correct. Correctness of business processes is usually related to its soundness [26]. Soundness implies that, for a business process that is executed on the basis of a business process model, any business process instance can reach the final state, can only terminate in this state, and there are no dead transitions. If so, a business process is sound and all its business process executions will be correct.

Two situations can impede soundness of contextualised business process variants. The first one is that context variants contain conflicting facts, i.e. facts that cannot be true in a same business process instance. This situation is addressed in this stage. The second one is to follow a sequence of fact verifications that will not allow a business process instance to be finished, i.e. facts need to be verified in a given order so that verification of all of them is possible. This situation is addressed in the next stage.

Initial Context Variants
{F1}
{F2}
{F3, F4, F5, F9}
{F3, F4, F5, F10}
{F3, F4, F5, F11}
{F3, F5, F6, F9}
{F3, F5, F6, F10}
{F3, F5, F6, F11}
{F3, F5, F7, F8, F9}
{F3, F5, F7, F8, F10}
{F3, F5, F7, F8, F11}

(a)

→

Final Context Variants
CV1: {F1}
CV2: {F2}
CV3: {F3, F4, F5, F9}
CV4: {F3, F4, F5, F10}
CV5:{F4, F5, F11}
CV6: {F6, F3, F5, F9}
CV7: {F6, F3, F5, F10}
CV8:{F6, F11, F5}
CV9:{F3, F7, F8, F9}
CV10: {F11, F7, F8}

(b)

Fig. 5. Context variants

The first situation is avoided by analysing the context variants of a business process in order to detect conflicts between facts. For this purpose, a table is created to specify the relationships between facts. The table also aims to obtain context variants whose set of facts are the minimum ones, i.e. no more facts are necessary (and thus do not need to be verified) to imply a context.

A table of relationships between facts of the running example is shown in Table 1, in which the relevant relationships (they affect context variants) are in bold and italics. For each cell of the table, the relationship between two facts is specified as follows:

Given a pair of facts Fr (fact of a row) and Fc (fact of a column),

- 'X': no context variant contains Fr and Fc together, thus analysis is not necessary (this relationship can be automatically detected from initial context variants).
- 'Ur': Fr is always true when Fc is true, thus Fr verification will be unnecessary when Fc is true.
- 'Uc' (opposite to 'Ur'): Fc verification will be unnecessary when Fr is true.
- 'C': Fr and Fc are conflicting.
- '-': no relationship exists between Fr and Fc.

For the running example, no analysis is necessary between F1 and other facts, F3 verification will be unnecessary if F11 is true, F8 and F10 are conflicting, and no relationship exists between F7 and F8.

As a result of the specification of the relationships between facts, the set of initial context variants is refined by removing conflicting variants and unnecessary facts. Refinement can be automated from a set of initial context variants and a table of relationships between facts, and is based on these two rules:

1) If two facts are conflicting, then the context variants that contain both facts are removed.
2) If the truth value of fact implies that verification of another is unnecessary, then the latter fact is removed from the context variants to which the first one belongs.

For the running example, the initial context variant '{F3, F5, F7, F8, F10}' is removed because F8 and F10 are conflicting, and F3 is removed from the initial context variant '{F3, F4, F5, F11}' because its verification is unnecessary when F11 is true. Fig. 5 (b) shows the final context variants.

Table 1. Relationships between facts

	F11	F10	F9	F8	F7	F6	F5	F4	F3	F2
F1	X	X	X	X	X	X	X	X	X	X
F2	X	X	X	X	X	X	X	X	X	
F3	*Ur*	-	-	-	-	-	-	-		
F4	-	-	-	X	X	X	-			
F5	-	-	-	*Ur*	-	-				
F6	-	-	-	X	X					
F7	-	-	-	-						
F8	-	*C*	-							
F9	X	X								
F10	X									

3.4 Design of Contextualised Business Process Variants

Contextualised business process variants of a business process are designed from the set of final context variants in the fourth stage of COMPRO.

Definition 7 (Contextualised business process variant). A contextualised business process variant *CBPV* is an ordered set of fact verifications and task executions that specifies a correct execution of a business process for a context variant *CV*.

A contextualised business process variant corresponds to a possible execution of a business process that fits business process context and can be finished successfully. In addition, contextualised business process variants must allow a business process to be sound.

More specifically, the second situation in which a contextualised business process is not correct (sequence of fact verifications, which has been described in the previous subsection) is addressed in this stage. This situation is avoided by analysing the final context variants of a business process in order to determine the order of fact verification. For this purpose, a new table is created to specify the precedence between fact verifications. The table also aims to obtain efficient contextualised business process variants, i.e. no unnecessary actions are executed in them.

A table of precedence between fact verifications for the running example is shown in Table 2, in which the relevant precedence that is discovered (it affects contextualised business process variants) is in bold and italics. For each cell of the table, the precedence between two facts is specified as follows:

Given a pair of facts Fr (fact of a row) and Fc (fact of a column),

- 'X': no context variant contains Fr and Fc together, thus analysis is not necessary (this relationship can be automatically detected from final context variants).
- 'Pr': Fc verification is only possible if Fr is true, thus Fr verification will precede Fc verification.
- 'Pc' (opposite to 'Pr'): Fc verification will precede Fr verification.
- 'Kr': Fr truth value will be known before Fc verification.
- 'Kc' (opposite to 'Kr'): Fc truth value will be known before Fr verification.
- '-': no relationship exists between Fr and Fc.

Table 2. Precedence between fact verifications

	F11	F10	F9	F8	F7	F6	F5	F4	F3	F2
F1	X	X	X	X	X	X	X	X	X	X
F2	X	X	X	X	X	X	X	X	X	
F3	X	***Pr***	***Pr***	***Pr***	***Pr***	***Kc***	***Pr***	***Pr***		
F4	-	-	-	X	X	X	-			
F5	***Pc***	-	-	X	-	***Kc***				
F6	***Kr***	***Kr***	***Kr***	X	X					
F7	-	-	-	-						
F8	***Pc***	X	-							
F9	X	X								
F10	X									

For the running example, no analysis is necessary between F1 and other facts, F3 verification will precede F10 verification, F6 truth value will be known before F11 verification, and no relationship exists between F7 and F8.

As a result of specification of relationships between facts, the order in which facts have to be verified for a given final context variant is specified. Specification of sequences of fact verification can be automated from a set of final context variants and a table of precedence between fact verifications, and is based on these two rules:

1) If verifications of several facts succeed or the truth values of the facts are known after verification of another, then the succeeding facts are put in brackets.
2) If verification of a fact precedes or the truth value of the fact is known before verification of another (or of a set of facts), then and arrow ('→') is introduced in the specification of the final context variant. The arrow precedes the first fact and succeeds the second one.

For the running example, the context variant '{F3, F4, F5, F9}' turns into '{F3 → (F4, F5, F9)}' because F3 verification precedes F4, F5 and F9 verification. Fig. 6 shows the set of sequences of fact verifications.

Final Context Variants	→	Sequences of Fact Verification
CV1: {F1}		{F1}
CV2: {F2}		{F2}
CV3: {F3, F4, F5, F9}		{F3 → (F4, F5, F9)}
CV4: {F3, F4, F5, F10}		{F3 → (F4, F5, F10)}
CV5:{F4, F5, F11}		{F4, F11 → F5}
CV6: {F6, F3, F5, F9}		{F6 → F3 → (F5, F9)}
CV7: {F6, F3, F5, F10}		{F6 → F3 → (F5, F10)}
CV8:{F6, F11, F5}		{F6 → F11→ F5}
CV9:{F3, F7, F8, F9}		{F3 → (F7, F8, F9)}
CV10: {F11, F7, F8}		{F7, F11 → F8}

Fig. 6. Sequences of fact verification

The next step for design of contextualised business process variants is to determine the tasks that will be part of them. The tasks can correspond to three types: 1) tasks of the initial business process model; 2) tasks that are defined from refinement of the tasks of the initial business process model, and; 3) tasks that make facts true.

The first type corresponds to those tasks whose execution will not be influenced by context. The task "Give product" of Fig. 2 is of this type. The second type corresponds to tasks that were not initially modelled but that are considered necessary for proper execution of a business process and whose execution depends on context. For the running example, a task of this type is "Address customer", which refines "Find potential buyer". The third type corresponds to tasks that make facts true. If a task of this type is executed when a given fact is false, then the fact turns into true. These facts are called manageable.

Definition 8 (Manageable fact). A fact *F* is manageable iff execution of a task *T* makes *F* true.

For the running example, F3 ("[c] is near") is manageable. If this fact is false, then an assistant can approach a customer (execute the task "Approach customer") so that the fact becomes true. Therefore, the task allows F3 to be manageable.

Once tasks are determined, a table is created to specify their relationships with the facts of the final context variants. An example is shown in Table 3 for the running example, in which the relevant relationships that are discovered (they affect contextualised business process variants) are in bold and italics. Tasks of the first type have not been included. For each cell of the table, the relationship between a fact and a task is specified as follows:

Given a fact F, a set of facts φ and a task T:

- 'M': T allows F to be manageable.
- 'U': T execution will be unnecessary if F is true.
- 'Sc': T cannot be executed unless F is true, thus T execution will succeed F verification.
- 'ScX' (where 'X' is a number that identifies different instances of this relationship): T should only be executed if some fact of φ is true, thus T execution will succeed verification of the facts of φ.
- '-': no relationship exists between F and T.

For the running example, T1 allows F3 to be manageable, T1 execution will be unnecessary if F1 is true, T2 execution will succeed F3 verification, T2 execution will succeed F4, F5, F6, F7, F8, F9, F9 and F11 verification, and no relationship exists between T1 and F8.

Table 3. Relationships between tasks and facts

	F1	F2	F3	F4	F5	F6	F7	F8	F9	F10	F11
T1: Approach customer	***U***	***U***	***M***	-	-	-	-	-	-	-	***U***
T2: Address customer	***U***	***U***	***Sc***	***Sc1***	***Sc1***	***Sc1***	***Sc1***	***Sc1***	***Sc1***	***Sc1***	***U***

The final step of this stage is to specify the contextualised business process variants. It is carried by extending the sequences of fact verification of a business process with tasks. Specification of contextualised business process variants can be automated from a set of sequences of fact verifications and a table of relationships between tasks and facts, and is based on these three rules:

1) If execution of a task T is unnecessary if a fact F is true, then T is not introduced in any sequence of fact verifications to which F belongs.
2) If verification of a fact F or a set of facts φ precedes execution of a task T, then T and an arrow ('→') are introduced in the sequences of fact verifications to which F or φ belong. The arrow precedes T and succeeds F or φ.
3) If a task T allows a fact F to be manageable, then a new contextualised business process variant is specified for each sequence of facts to which F belongs. The new contextualised business process variants are specified from the sequences of fact verifications by turning F into '¬F' and introducing T and an arrow ('→'). The arrow succeeds '¬F' and precedes T.

For the running example, T1 is not introduced in the sequence of fact verifications {F4, F11 → F5}' because its execution is unnecessary if F11 is true. The sequence of fact verifications '{F3 → (F4, F5, F9)}' produces the contextualised business process variants '{F3 → (F4, F5, F9) → T2}' and '{¬F3 →T1 → (F4, F5, F9) → T2}' because verification of F4, F5 and F9 precedes T2 execution and T1 allows F3 to be manageable. Fig. 7 shows all the contextualised business process variants.

CBPV1: {F1}	CBPV8: {F6 → ¬F3 → T1 → (F5, F9) → T2}
CBPV2: {F2}	CBPV9: {F6 → F3 → (F5, F10) → T2}
CBPV3: {F3 → (F4, F5, F9) → T2}	CBPV10: {F6 → ¬F3 → T1 → (F5, F10) → T2}
CBPV4: {¬F3 → T1 → (F4, F5, F9) → T2}	CBPV11: {F4, F11 → F5}
CBPV5: {F3 → (F4, F5, F10) → T2}	CBPV12: {F6 → F11→ F5}
CBPV6: {¬F3 → T1 → (F4, F5, F10) → T2}	CBPV13: {F3 → (F7, F8, F9) → T2}
CBPV7: {F6 → F3 → (F5, F9) → T2}	CBPV14: {¬F3 → T1 → (F7, F8, F9) → T2}
CBPV15: {F7, F11 → F8}	

Fig. 7. Contextualised business process variants

3.5 Modelling of Contextualised Business Process

The purpose of the last stage is to correctly model a contextualised business process so that it supports and can be properly executed in all its context variants. Since the procedure to specify contextualised business process variants guarantees that they fit the analysed context and are correct, the contextualised business process model that is obtained also fits its context and is correct.

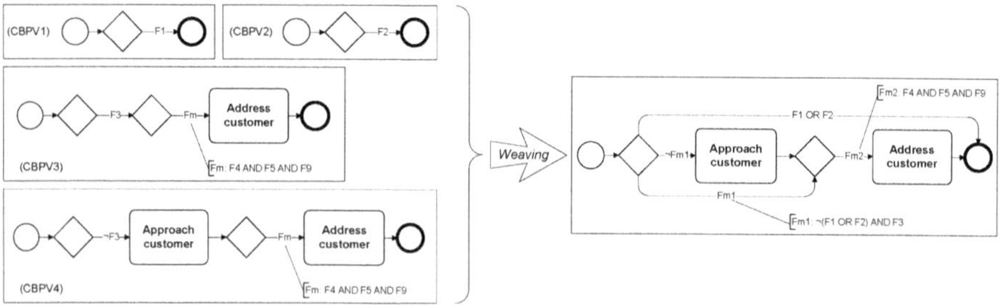

Fig. 8. Weaving of contextualised business process variants

The contextualised business process model is created on the basis of the fact verification and task execution sequences of the contextualised business process variants. First, the contextualised business process variants are graphically represented (e.g. CBPV1 to 4 in Fig. 8). BPMN has been extended by labelling sequence flows for specification of conditions (formulas) that have to hold so that a sequence flow is executed. Fact and formula verification is represented by means of gateways (exclusive decisions), and tasks by means of BPMN tasks.

Second, the contextualised business process model is obtained by weaving together the graphical representations of the contextualised business process variants. An example of weaving is shown in Fig. 8, and Fig. 9 shows the result of contextualisation of the task "Find potential buyer" for the running example. The task has turned into a looping sub-process and has been divided into two sub-processes and four possible (groups of) paths execution: 'F1 OR F2', 'Fm1', '¬Fm AND ¬F11' and '¬Fm1 AND F11'. The sub-processes include the tasks "Approach customer" and "Address customer". "Find potential customer" has to be executed until C1 is true.

Some parts of a contextualised business process model can be automatically derived from contextualised business process variants (e.g. modelling of a sequence of gateways and tasks), but human intervention and decisions may also be necessary (e.g. looping and sub-process modelling). This issue has to be further studied, and use of existing techniques for management of business process variants [12] have to be analysed (e.g. for their weaving). We also assume that soundness of a contextualised business process model still holds after human intervention.

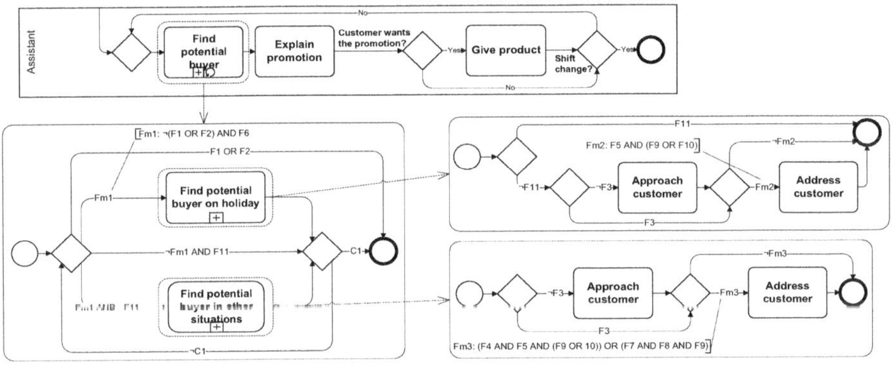

Fig. 9. Contextualised business process model

4 COMPRO Application and Lessons Learnt

This section presents and discusses COMPRO application (and thus its current evaluation), the considerations that arose from our experience and the lessons learnt.

By following an action research strategy [18], COMPRO has been applied and evaluated with business processes and stakeholders (managers, decision makers on business process execution and process designers) from eight organizations[1] of

[1] Many details of the organizations and thus of COMPRO application and evaluation are not presented for confidentiality reasons.

different sectors (automobile manufacture, construction, food and goods distribution and sale, public transport and software development). As a result, the approach has been defined and refined iteratively from needs and improvements that have been identified in its application. In this sense, applying COMPRO in industry examples has allowed us to identify its benefits and limitations.

For evaluation, first we explained context-awareness for business process modelling to stakeholders. Second, we discussed the influence of context in their business processes. Third, we presented COMPRO and applied it collaboratively on at least one business process of the organization. Finally, we discussed with stakeholders about the approach. Evaluation was qualitative and data were collected through semi-structured interviews.

The evaluation showed that context can have a substantial influence on business processes. A clear example of context influence that we encountered concerns piece manufacture and delivery in a provider of the automotive sector. The company manufactures pieces for an important carmaker, and have to meet very strict requirements. For example, the carmaker's plants follow a just-in-time strategy, which implies that pieces are not stored and that providers have to deliver them the day in which they are going to be assembled. If a provider fails to deliver the pieces and thus a plant has to stop manufacture, then the provider has to pay for the expenses that are derived from the stop. These expenses are very high, and have led some providers to bankruptcy. As a result, company managers have to check and control several context properties (related to, for instance, providers, production, weather and transport) in order to adapt the business processes of the company. Otherwise, pieces may not be delivered timely.

The main results, feedback and lessons learnt through COMPRO application with stakeholders are the following ones.

1) Good support for specification of indicators and for decision making
In general, most of the stakeholders regarded COMPRO as a means for discovery and specification of indicators that determine how a business process should be executed. The approach can help an organization to make decisions on business processes execution.

2) Help for discovery of new context variants
Although most of the context properties (facts) that were specified in the context analysis models were already known by the stakeholders, new context variants (both facts and their combination) were discovered in all organizations.

3) Better fit between business processes and context
All stakeholders stated that COMPRO could help their organizations to discover context variants and fit their business process to context. Systematic analysis of business process context and subsequent modelling of contextualised business process was considered very effective: organizations usually define responses to context variations in an ad-hoc way and do not try to discover new context variations (they have not happened yet).

4) New expected advantages from business process contextualisation
Although many works on business process contextualisation regard it as a problem of performance improvement (e.g. [19]), many stakeholders regarded it as a problem of exception discovery and definition of responses to them. This means that performance improvement is not the only and main expected advantage from business process contextualisation.

5) Limitations in creation of context analysis model
Creating a context analysis model is a slightly subjective activity. Statements are refined until stakeholders state that facts have been found, thus a context analysis model is considered to be finished on the basis of stakeholders perception. Furthermore, it is not possible to guarantee that a unique context analysis model exists for a given business process. In this sense, it is also not possible to guarantee that a context analysis model is complete (i.e. no more facts exist). This decision is based on stakeholders' validation.
6) Difficulty in modelling of contextualised business processes
If contextualised business process variants are woven together into a single contextualised business process model, then the model may get too tangled. We have used BPMN and labelling of sequence flows as mechanisms for modelling of contextualised business processes, but other approaches and mechanisms may be used. For example, declarative approaches for business process modelling (e.g. [15]) and/or mechanisms of related work that addresses modelling of context effect. We plan to analyse them in future.
7) Need of COMPRO automation
One of the main concerns of stakeholders was the availability of tool support for the approach in order to automate and facilitate its application. This is an essential point for future work. Integration of tool support for COMPRO with existing tools for business process modelling and management must also be addressed.
8) Other suggestions from stakeholders
Some stakeholders made comments about possible extensions of and improvements on COMPRO. All of them are not presented for the sake of brevity. For example, they asked about the definition of procedures for mitigation of the impact of context variations (before a context variant holds) in addition to definition of responses, and about specification of happening probability of facts and context variants. They have to be addressed in future.

We consider that the results from evaluation have been positive. Evaluation has not only allowed us to obtain very valuable feedback about the expected benefits of COMPRO, but also to identify relevant future work from a industry perspective. Nonetheless, the approach has to be further evaluated. We plan to execute case studies to check how practitioners use COMPRO on their own and benefit from it.

Last but not least, we are aware that COMPRO application and evaluation has not been presented as formally, systematically and in depth as it should be. For example, the interview instrument is not presented and threats to validity are not discussed due to page limitations.

5 Conclusions and Future Work

Context-aware business process modelling is an emerging topic and different benefits are expected from it. Nonetheless, further research has to be carried out to facilitate business process contextualisation. Approaches that address analysis of business process context and provide mechanisms and guidance for correct modelling of contextualised business process are necessary.

This paper has presented COMPRO, a methodological approach that addresses these challenges. The approach helps process designers to analyse business process context, to discover its relevant properties and variants, to determine their effect on a business process and to correctly contextualise it.

COMPRO adopts context analysis and adapts it from a business process perspective. The approach also provides mechanisms and detailed guidance for analysis of business process context, context variants and business process variants and for modelling of contextualised business processes. They facilitate discovery and adequate specification of context properties (facts) and context variants, as well as of the relationships between facts and between facts and tasks of a business process. These relationships determine and constrain business process execution. Furthermore, the mechanisms and guidance aim to guarantee that a contextualised business process fits its context, is properly executed in all its context variants and is sound.

COMPRO application and current evaluation has shown its benefits and limitations. Since it facilitates identification of context variants and definition of responses to them, practitioners consider the approach to be useful. Nonetheless, some issues need to be addressed in order to meet some industry needs and to improve support for business process contextualisation.

As future work, we have mentioned several points of COMPRO that need more study or that may be carried out differently (Sections 4.4 and 5). Further work is especially important to maximize the industrial acceptance of business process contextualisation. In addition, we want to study the use of business process mining techniques (e.g. [25]) at analysis of business process context stage, of workflow patterns [24] and best practices for business process reengineering [13] at design of contextualised business process variants stage, and of layers of business process context (immediate, internal, external and environmental layers) [19] throughout COMPRO.

Acknowledgements. This work has been developed with the support of the Spanish Government under the projects SESAMO TIN2007-62894 and HI2008-0190 and the program FPU AP2006-02324, partially funded by the EU Commission through the projects COMPAS, NESSOS and ANIKETOS, and co-financed by FEDER. The authors would also like to thank all the people that participated in COMPRO application, and Amit K. Chopra and Richard Bertnsson Svensson for their useful comments on the paper.

References

1. Ali, R., Dalpiaz, F., Giorgini, P.: A Goal Modelling Framework for Self-Contextualizable Software. In: Halpin, T., et al. (eds.) BPMDS 2009 and EMMSAD 2009. LNBIP, vol. 29, pp. 326–338. Springer, Heidelberg (2009)
2. Ali, R., Dalpiaz, F., Giorgini, P.: A Goal-based Framework for Contextual Requirements Modeling and Analysis. Requirements Engineering Journal (to appear, 2010)
3. Born, M., Kirchner, J., Mueller, J.P.: Context-driven Business Process Modeling. In: TCoB 2009 (2009)
4. Bouquet, P., et al.: Theories and uses of context in knowledge representation and reasoning. Journal of Pragmatics 35(3), 455–484 (2003)

5. Calvary, G., et al.: A Unifying Reference Framework for multi-target user interfaces. Interacting with Computers 15(3), 289–308 (2003)
6. de la Vara, J.L., et al.: Business Process Contextualisation via Context Analysis. In: ER 2010 (to appear, 2010)
7. Ghattas, J., Soffer, P., Peleg, M.: A Formal Model for Process Context Learning. In: Rinderle-Ma, S., et al. (eds.) BPM 2009 Workshops. LNBIP, vol. 43, pp. 140–157. Springer, Heidelberg (2010)
8. Hallerbach, A., Bauer, T., Reichert, M.: Capturing Variability in Business Process Models: The Provop Approach. Journal of Software Maintenance and Evolution: Research and Practice (in press, 2010)
9. Henricksen, K., Indulska, J.: A software engineering framework for context-aware pervasive computing. In: PerCom 2004, pp. 74–86 (2004)
10. Indulska, M., et al.: Business Process Modeling: Current Issues and Future Challenges. In: van Eck, P., Gordijn, J., Wieringa, R. (eds.) CAiSE 2009. LNCS, vol. 5565, pp. 501–514. Springer, Heidelberg (2009)
11. Indulska, M., et al.: Business Process Modeling: Perceived Benefits. In: Laender, A.H.F. (ed.) ER 2009. LNCS, vol. 5829, pp. 458–471. Springer, Heidelberg (2009)
12. la Rosa, M., Dumas, M., ter Hofstede, A.H.M.: Modelling Business Process Variability for Design-Time Configuration. In: Cardoso, J., van der Aalst, W. (eds.) Handbook of Research on Business Process Modeling, pp. 204–228. IGI Global (2009)
13. Mansar, S.L., Reijers, H.A.: Best practices in business process redesign: validation of a redesign framework. Computers in Industry 56(5), 457–471 (2005)
14. Moddaferi, S., et al.: A Methodology for Designing and Managing Context-Aware Workflows. In: Krogstie, J., Kautz, K., Allen, D. (eds.) Mobile Information Systems II, pp. 91–106. Springer, Heidelberg (2005)
15. Pesic, M., et al.: Constraint-Based Workflow Models: Change Made Easy. In: Meersman, R., Tari, Z. (eds.) OTM 2007, Part I. LNCS, vol. 4803, pp. 77–94. Springer, Heidelberg (2007)
16. Ploesser, K., et al.: Context Change Archetypes: Understanding the Impact of Context Change on Business Processes. In: ACIS 2009, pp. 225–234 (2009)
17. Ploesser, K., et al.: Learning from Context to Improve Business Process. BPTrends 2009(1), 1–9 (2009)
18. Robson, C.: Real World Research. Blackwell, Oxford (2002)
19. Rosemann, M., Recker, J., Flender, C.: Contextualisation of business processes. International Journal of Business Process Integration and Management 3(1), 47–60 (2008)
20. Saidani, O., Nurcan, S.: Towards Context Aware Business Process Modelling. In: BPMDS 2007 (2007)
21. Schonenberg, H., et al.: Process Flexibility: a Survey of Contemporary Approaches. In: Dietz, J.L.G., et al. (eds.) CIAO! 2008 and EOMAS 2008. LNBIP, vol. 10, pp. 16–30. Springer, Heidelberg (2008)
22. Smanchat, S., Ling, S., Indrawan, M.: A Survey on Context-Aware Workflow Adaptations. In: MoMM 2008, pp. 414–417 (2008)
23. Strang, T., Linnhoff-Poppien, C.: A Context Modeling Survey. In: Workshop on Advanced Context Modelling, Reasoning and Management, UbiComp 2004 (2004)
24. van der Aalst, W.M.P., et al.: Workflow Patterns. Distributed and Parallel Databases 14(1), 5–51 (2003)
25. van der Aalst, W.M.P., et al.: Business process mining: An industrial application. Information Systems 32(5), 713–732 (2007)
26. Weske, M.: Business Process Management: Concepts, Languages, Architectures. Springer, Heidelberg (2007)

Reducing Exception Handling Complexity in Business Process Modeling and Implementation: The WED-Flow Approach

João E. Ferreira[1], Osvaldo K. Takai[1], Simon Malkowski[2], and Calton Pu[2]

[1] Institute of Mathematics and Statistics,
University of São Paulo
{jef,otakai}@ime.usp.br
[2] Center for Experimental Research in Computer Systems,
Georgia Institute of Technology
{zmon,calton}@cc.gatech.edu

Abstract. Today's enterprises reevaluate and adjust their business processes at a very high frequency, which presents a non-trivial challenge to classic BPM methodology. In particular, the dynamic nature of exception handling may generate highly significant costs when business processes are modeled and implemented statically based on formal frameworks (e.g., process algebra and Petri nets). In this work we introduce the WED-flow (Workflow, Event processing, and Data-flow) approach, a novel concept for modeling and implementation of business processes that significantly reduces the complexity of exception handling—quantitatively, as compared to current approaches. WED-flows explicitly integrate events, data, conditions, and transitions by capturing data instances (future, current, and historical) as data states, which enables incremental business process development. More generally, this paper provides a conceptual basis and guidelines for capturing, processing, and storing event-handling environments. Consequently, information systems that implement business processes as WED-flows are truly dynamic and no longer time-invariant by design.

Keywords: business process modeling and implementation, exception handling complexity, events, critical paths, data states.

1 Introduction

Several formal approaches (e.g., Petri nets [1], graphs, and process algebras [2]) have been successful in supporting Business Process Management (BPM) with automated execution and provable properties. One limitation of these techniques is that they provide support only for business processes specified *a priori* using the appropriate language (Petri Net or process algebra as examples). When a business process is changed or revised, it is the developer's responsibility to rewrite the revised business process. On the other hand, programming-oriented languages such as BPEL [3] provide more flexibility to support incremental system changes, but their expressive power present serious challenges to formal

R. Meersman et al. (Eds.): OTM 2010, Part I, LNCS 6426, pp. 150–167, 2010.

verification and model checking. Instead of trying to bridge this gap directly (e.g., translating BPEL into process algebra), we describe the WED-flow approach (Workflow, Event processing, and Data-flow). WED-flow supports flexible adaptations in business processes, and offers the hope of easier property verification than general programming languages.

The WED-flow approach consists of three main phases. First, a business process is separated into two parts: the critical path and the exception handling. Intuitively, the critical path is the "money-making" part of business, and exception handling is the "overhead part", where errors are detected and recovered, difficult rare cases are handled, and consistent system state is restored. Second, both the critical path and the exception handling are modeled by a composition of the four fundamental concepts (events, data, conditions, and transitions, to be elaborated in Section 2). Third, the WED-flow model is translated into a concrete specification language, which is in turn translated into executable programs through automated software tools.

This paper primarily focuses on the first two phases of WED-flow approach. We briefly motivate the separation of a business process into the critical path and exception handling. This separation follows from the observation that most business processes have a well-defined business objective, and a clear path to achieve it through a sequence of state transitions. In an e-commerce purchase example, the customer chooses the merchandise and delivery options, and provides payment, which is followed by order fulfillment and delivery. Along the critical path, problems may arise in several states, e.g., cancellation of the purchase. Exception handling routines need to recover from these problems and restore the system (and databases) to a consistent state. Due to the many possibilities of errors, exception handling code tends to grow much bigger than the critical path. Consequently, many business processes leave many exception conditions undefined, relying on human operators (e.g., in call centers). WED-flow is able to reduce the complexity of exception handling through an explicit representation of data instances and state transitions, which are linked by events and conditions. In WED-flow, a business process is triggered by an event, which initiates data state capture, pre-condition verification, and state transition if appropriate. The explicit representation of data and state transitions facilitates both condition verification and translation of WED-flow specifications to executable code.

The first and more conceptual contribution of this paper is a description of WED-flows first two phases, including the capturing, processing, and storing of business processes. This is illustrated by a concrete example (purchase from an online book store). The second and more technical contribution of the paper is a demonstration of the advantages of WED-flow through the reduction in exception handling complexity. This is achieved by a detailed calculation of the number of states (in a transition graph) of the bookstore example. For completeness, we include a mapping of WED-flow specifications to an abstract implementation based on two systems: continual queries [4] and multiversion databases [5].

Although business processes consists of four equally important elements—events, data, conditions, and transitions—current modeling approaches rarely treat all four elements equally. In fact, none of the popular modeling approaches such as essential analysis [6], event-driven modeling [7], data-driven modeling [8], business artifacts [9], and Event-Condition-Action (ECA) rules [10] actually represent all four building blocks explicitly with a uniform degree of importance. As a consequence, contemporary business process modeling is not able to fully integrate and exhaustively explore temporal and causal dependence structures for exception handling. In contrast, our approach takes a historical perspective on events, data, conditions, and transitions and enables the treatment of exceptions as new aspects (analogous to Aspect Oriented Programing (AOP) [11]) of business processes. The WED-flow concept is an evolution of preliminary results in the RiverFish architecture [12,13] and a practical system implementation project (DECA system [14]) for the Brazilian Government.

This paper is organized as follows. Definitions, guidelines for modeling and implementation, and the exception handling complexity of the WED-flow approach are described in Section 2. Section 3 details a bookstore ordering example to illustrate our approach. Section 4 discusses related work, and Section 5 concludes this paper.

2 WED-Flow Approach

Events, conditions, transitions, and data are elements of the same object under study, the business process, from different perspectives. Consequently, the integration of events, data, conditions, and transitions in the WED-flow approach is based on three important rules: 1) a distinct set of transitions that modifies the current data state has to be described for each event; 2) any data state that is queried, modified, or generated by a transition must be representable explicitly and stored permanently; 3) all transitions from one data state to another must be triggered by an event and may only be executed when a distinct set of conditions is satisfied.

The actual WED-flow definitions are included in the next subsection. Conceptually, the definition and capturing of events through triggers is the starting point of the WED-flow methodology. These events initiate the validation of a set of conditions on attribute values that have to be satisfied in order for a transition to be executed. Attribute values have to be defined in form of data states before and after the treatment of each event.

2.1 WED-Flow Definitions

The WED-flow approach is based on the following definitions, which have previously appeared in a preliminary version of this work [15]. Definitions 1, 2, 3, and 4 introduce the elements of the WED-flow approach: data states, conditions, transitions, and triggers, respectively. Definition 5 defines a WED-flow as a set of data states, conditions, events (captured by triggers), and transitions. Definition 6 links the initial data states, their respective conditions, and transitions to the final data states, forming an elementary WED-flow unit. Definition 7 ensures the proper storage of the business process execution history.

Definition 1. *WED-state. A WED state, denoted by WED-state, is a set of attribute values captured from some database applications.*

Definition 2. *WED-condition. A WED condition, denoted by WED-cond, is a set of predicates defined over a specific set of WED-states.*

Definition 3. *WED-transition. A work/event/data-flow transition, denoted by WED-transition, transforms a set of WED-states (input) into another set of WED-states (output). This transformation is done using a set of atomic actions. Each transition nowadays is implemented using a classical transaction concept.*

Definition 4. *WED-trigger. A WED trigger, denoted by WED-trigger, starts a WED-transition on the satisfaction of a WED-condition.*

Definition 5. *WED-flow. A work/event/data-flow, denoted by WED-flow, is a set of WED-states, WED-conditions, WED-triggers, and WED-transitions.*

Definition 6. *eo. An elementary objective, denoted by eo is described by a 4-tuple. Each tuple combines a WED-trigger with its corresponding WED-state domains and conditions. This 4-tuple takes the form:*
$eo =< D(\textit{WED-state}_{i-1}), \textit{WED-cond}_i, \textit{WED-transition}_i, D(\textit{WED-state}_i) >$

Definition 7. *history(WF). An execution history of a WED-flow WF is a sequence of each eo execution, denoted by history (WF). The history (WF) starts from WED-state*$_0$*, and contains WED-condition*$_1$*, WED-transition*$_1$*, WED-state*$_1$*, ..., WED-condition*$_n$*, WED -transition*$_n$*, WED-state*$_n$*, the final state of WF.*

2.2 Capturing Events and Storing Data-States

To capture and implement internal and external events, the WED-flow approach uses the concept of continual queries [4]. The results of each event processing action on each data state are stored through the concept of multiversion databases [5]. Liu et al. define continual queries through a triple $(Q, T_{cq}, Stop)$. Q is a normal query (usually written in SQL); T_{cq} is a trigger condition; and $Stop$ is a termination condition [4]. For example, the continual query "Report to the bookstore manager, every day at 4:00 p.m., all order books and their respective customers above 3,000" can be expressed as follows.

```
Create CQ order_book_management as
Query:
     SELECT order_book_id, customer_id, amount_money
     FROM  OrderBook
     WHERE amount_money > 3,000
     Trigger: 4:00 pm every day
     Stop:  end of current year
```

Any historical snapshot can be explored and the data history is searchable through maintaining all historical (multi)versions of each data attribute [16].

The Immortal DB [5] is an example of such a multiversion database. The main goal of the Immortal DB project is to provide the infrastructure for saving and indexing all states of a database. Versions are stamped with the times of their updating transactions. The timestamp order agrees with the transaction serialization order. All versions are kept in an integrated storage structure, and historical versions are stored with their respective data—in our case their WED-states.

Concretely, WED-triggers and WED-conditions are expressed using continual queries in the WED-flow approach. WED-states are represented using the concept of multiversion databases. The definitions of elementary objectives (eo) and WED-triggers are illustrated in Figure 1.

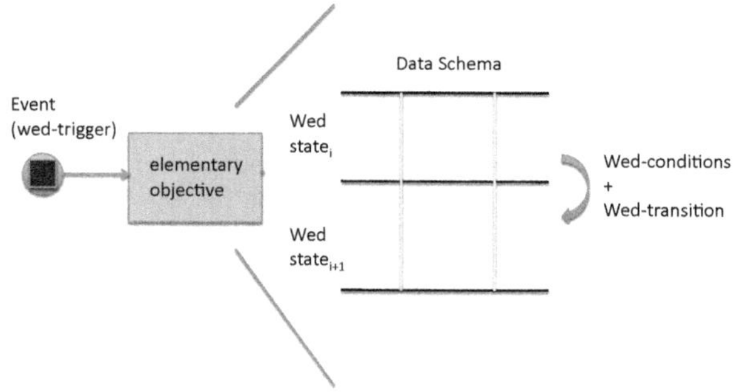

Fig. 1. WED-flow representation

2.3 Guidelines for Business Process Modeling and Implementation

After defining the main concepts of WED-flows, we describe guidelines for *three-phase* business process modeling and implementation. As previously described, events are phenomenological manifestations of business processes. Then events have to be the initial and final goal of the BPM modeling and implementation. In phase I, the first step identifies and describes main events. After, these events are separated into critical events (i.e., minimum set of events to achieve the main goal of a business process) that generate the critical path (i.e., a time ordered sequence of critical events required to make money); and exception events (i.e., unexpected events that happen at some point in the critical path generating a specific overhead).

In phase II for each event belonging to a critical path and exception handling, valid WED-states, WED-conditions, and WED-transitions need to be described. First, each data entity or data class belonging to critical events has its specific sequence of valid states with different durations. In order to create the corresponding WED-state all entity sequences need to be normalized (refers to the pattern recognition concept and not the database concept) creating the link of valid WED-states based on their time ordering (see Figures 3b and 3c). Second, after creating a critical path, conditions, and transitions for each valid WED-state, the latter need to be described and implemented using the WED-flow definitions. Third step defines WED-triggers to capture the WED-state of each exception. Next, the last valid WED-state related to each exception event needs to be localized. At the end of phase II, all WED-conditions and WED-transitions are described between initial and final states. Phase III, the WED-flow model is translated into a concrete specification language, which is in turn translated into executable programs through automated software tools. This phase III is out scope of this paper.

As a pseudo-algorithmic representation for business process modeling and implementation the WED-flow approach can be summarized in the following steps:

Phase I

1. Identify events belonging to BPM;
2. Separate these events into two parts: critical path and exception handling.

Phase II

1. For each event belonging to the critical path:
   (a) Model WED-states sequence (time-line) for each entity/data class;
   (b) Normalize WED-states according to time;
   (c) Chain all "canonic" WED-states creating the critical path;
   (d) Describe conditions belonging to each event;
   (e) Describe transitions related to conditions for each event.
2. For each event belonging to the exception handling:
   (a) Create a WED-trigger to capture each exception;
   (b) Localize WED-states related to this event in critical path;
   (c) Describe conditions belong to events;
   (d) Describe transitions related to conditions;
   (e) Insert the conditions and transitions for each respective WED-state.

Phase III

1. Translate all event-data-condition transitions belong to critical path into a concrete specification language;
2. Translate all event-data-condition-transitions belong to exception handling into a concrete specification language.

2.4 Numbers of Additional States for Exception Events

Of course the final implementation code (if implemented correctly) is equivalent for both classical approaches and the WED-flow approach; nonetheless, there is a significant difference in the generation of additional (exception event) states between classical methodology and WED-flow. In classical approaches all exception events are treated (and therefore implemented) identically to critical events (same semantic value). In the WED-flow approach, on the other hand, exception events are treated as templates for the entire critical path. The WED-flow code for exception events is included in the final code (execution code) dynamically, on demand. In other words, the WED-flow approach concept describes exception events and states at a higher (meta) level, and in classical approaches, the exception events have to be fully implemented.

To calculate the number of additional states that can occur for each expectation event in a sequential critical path, one can define:

$CPstates$ = the number of states in the critical path generated by critical events;
$EEvents$ = the number of exception events (each $EEvent_j$ can occur in any state of critical path);
t_j = the number of states for each transition to treat $EEvent_j$.

The number of additional states in classical approach ($addclassicSTATES$) is calculated for each $EEvent_j$ that can occur in the critical path. Considering a sequential critical path, the exception event $EEvent_j$, can occur in all state positions in a set of states $\{s_1, s_2, s_3, \ldots, s_{CPstates}\}$. In other words, our assumption is an upper bound calculation where each exception event $EEvent_j$ can occur after the execution of the first activity and stop the process.The same exception event can occur after the first and second activity execution and then stop the process. This reasoning can be continued analogously. To calculate the number of states that can happen, $CanHappenSt(EEvent_j)$ is defined as a function that counts the number of possible states for each $EEvent_j$ in a set of states $\{s_1, s_2, s_3, \ldots, s_{CPstates}\}$ that belong to the critical path.

$addclassicSTATES =$
$CanHappenSt(EEvent_1)\{s_1, s_2, s_3, \ldots, s_{CPstates}\} * t_1 +$
$CanHappenSt(EEvent_2)\{s_1, s_2, s_3, \ldots, s_{CPstates}\} * t_2 +$
$CanHappenSt(EEvent_3)\{s_1, s_2, s_3, \ldots, s_{CPstates}\} * t_3 + \ldots$
$CanHappenSt(EEvent_{EEvents})\{s_1, s_2, s_3, \ldots, s_{CPstates}\} * t_{EEvents}$
$addclassicSTATES = (\sum_{j=1,EEvents} CanHappenSt(EEvent_j) * t_j * CPstates)$

To facilitate the visualization of this number, let us suppose that $t_j = 1$ for any $j = 1, 2, \ldots, EEvents$. Then:

$addclassicalSTATES = EEvents * CPstates$

In WED-flow approach, for each exception $EEvent_j$, we have only one new wed-state with t_j states. When an exception event occurs, we need a WED-trigger to capture this event and localize the last valid state. Then all new events in the WED-flow imply in the same task: define a WED-trigger to capture this event, wed-conditions, and wed-transition to create another wed-state. The number of additional states in the WED-flow approach ($addwedflowSTATES$) is calculated as each exception event times its respective t_j states. Thus, the $addwedflowSTATES$ are given by:

$addwedflowSTATES = \sum_{j=1,EEvents} t_j$. Using the same consideration for $t_j = 1$ for any $j = 1, 2, \ldots, EEvents$. Then:
$addwedflowSTATES = EEvents$
ω is defined as the number of additional states for classical approach in relation to WED-flow approach.

$$\omega = addclassicalSTATES - addwedflowSTATES$$
$$\omega = (EEvents * CPstates) - (EEvents)$$
$$\omega = EEvents * (CPstates - 1)$$

The ω number is significant because of the increasing complexity of control-flows generated through the use of classical models that require details in the low level of implementation. This implementation approach is faced with a dilemma: a high expressivity and the decidability of behavioral property checking generates a lot of code. In the WED-flow approach the control-flow is a result and not a cause of business processing. Our main goal is to get the system back (either directly or indirectly) to a state belonging to the critical path. Another important observation is that all exception events are difficult to be identified in the first version of the business process model. Considering that all remote possibilities of all exception events have to be captured, the representation and implementation task in classical approaches may be arduous and thankless.

3 Bookstore Example

To illustrate business process modeling and implementation using the WED-flow approach, consider a bookstore that sells books through orders over the Internet. An important event that a bookstore needs to manage is the ordering of books made by its customers. For this purpose our sample bookstore has created a business process called order book. Whenever a customer makes a book order, an instance of this business process commences execution. The most important common events and their respective activities are represented for such a book order process illustrated in Figure 2 (using the classical BPMN modeling). In the figure, a clear dependency relation between events is observable—except in first event that initiates the process.

The main lifecycle is represented by events and activities that belong to the critical path (customer orders books, bookstore validates the order, customer pays the order, bookstore sends a book, and customer receives books) and the events and activities that belong to the exception events (customer cancel order, customers reclaim, customer does not pay orders, bookstore abort orders, bookstore does not send books, and customer returns books).

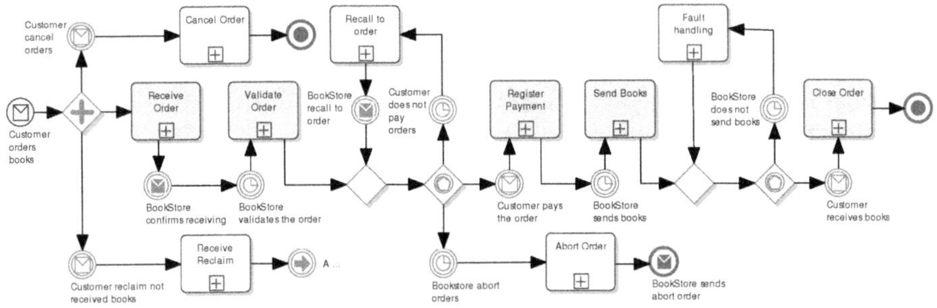

Fig. 2. BPMN modeling of bookstore example

3.1 Bookstore Example Using WED-Flow Guidelines

Following the guidelines for modeling and implementation of business processes through the WED-flow approach, all events have to first be listed, time-ordered, and separated into critical path and exception handling parts. Critical path is shown separately in Figure 3a. For each data entity participants of these events the sequence of data states is shown in Figure 3b. With the normalization of data states by determining the earliest change time, the sequence of valid data states for the critical path can be created. For each valid data state the appropriate conditions and transitions are associated, as shown in Figure 3c. Figure 4 illustrates, in summary, the representation of each WED-state and its respective transitions. The attributes belonging to the data schema can be more than one. However, we use only one attribute status and identification (id) for each data class (Customer, Book, and Order) to simplify the example illustration.

The complexity of the control-flow can grow significantly according to each new event. In this book order example, $CPstates = 6$ and $EEvents = 5$ (customer cancel orders, customer reclaims, customer does not pay orders, bookstore abort orders, and bookstore does not send books). The additional states can be calculated using the specific count for this example ($additionalSTATES\text{-}book$) for each $EEvent_j$ that can actually occur in the critical path of the bookstore process. According to Subsection 2.4 each $EEvent_j$, its position state for occurrence, and the number of states generated for each event can be calculated using $CanHappenSt(EEvent_j)$.

1. $EEvent_1$: Cancel order
   $CanHappenSt(EEvent_1)\{s_1, s_2, s_3, s_4, s_5, s_6\} = 6$
2. $EEvent_2$: Receive reclaim
   $CanHappenSt(EEvent_2)\{s_1, s_2, s_3, s_4, s_5, s_6\} = 6$
3. $EEvent_3$: Customer does not pay order
   (Assumptions: recursive activity r_1 times $= 1$, and $EEvent_3$ must occurs after s_2)
   $CanHappenSt(EEvent_3)\{s_3, s_4, s_5, s_6\} = 4$
4. $EEvent_4$: Abort order
   $CanHappenSt(EEvent_4)\{s_1, s_2, s_3, s_4, s_5, s_6\} = 6$
5. $EEvent_5$: Bookstore does not send book
   Assumptions: (recursive activity r_2 times $= 1$, and $EEvent_5$ must occurs after s_3)
   $CanHappenSt(EEvent_2)\{s_1, s_2, s_3, s_4, s_5, s_6\} = 3$

$addclassicSTATES\text{-}book = CanHappenSt(EEvent_1) + CanHappenSt(EEvent_2) + CanHappenSt(EEvent_3) + CanHappenSt(EEvent_4) + CanHappenSt(EEvent_5)$
$addclassicSTATES\text{-}book = 6 + 6 + 4 + 6 + 3 = 25$

Using the expressions to calculate the number of additional classic states in face of exception events ($addclassicSTATES$) according to Subsection 2.4:

$addclassicSTATES = EEvents * CPstates = 6 * 5 = 30$

The difference of 5 states between $additionalSTATES$ and $additionalSTATES\text{-}book$ is explicable by the real limits of the $EEvent_3$

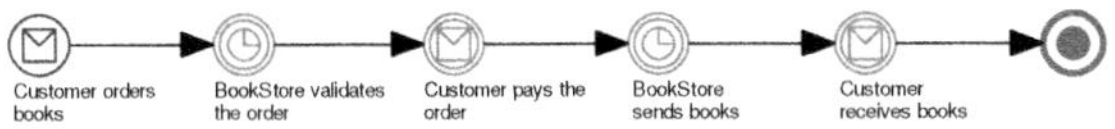

Figure 3a

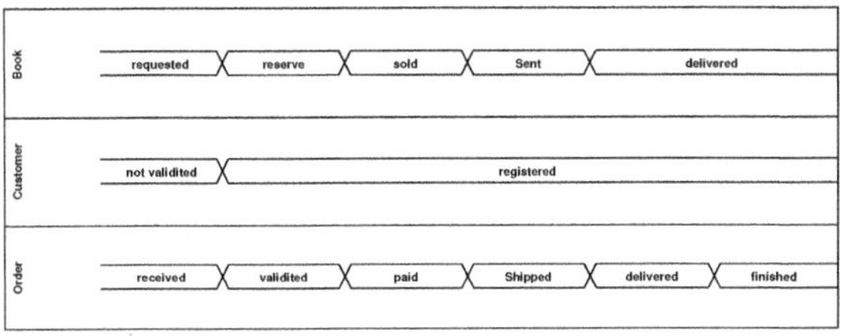

Figure 3b

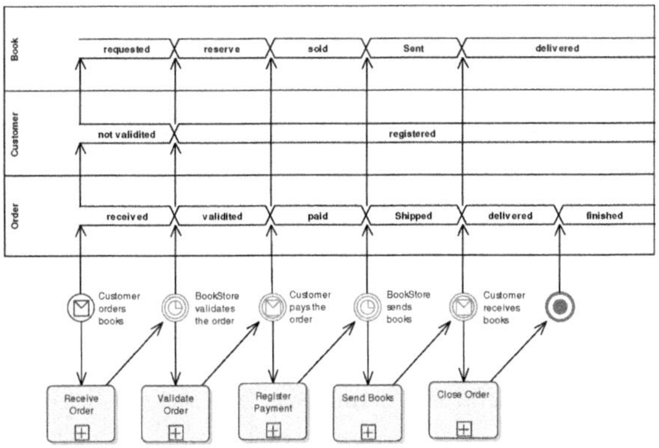

Figure 3c

Fig. 3. a) critical path for bookstore example; b) time line for each WED-sates; c) normalization-WEDstates

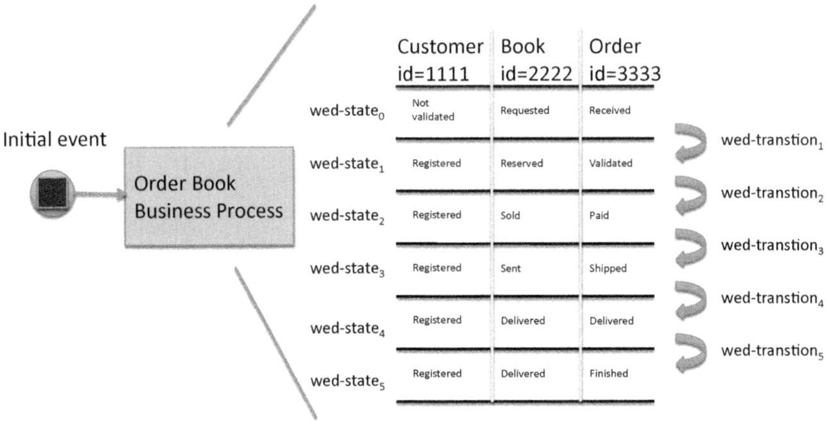

Fig. 4. WED-states for bookstore example

and $EEvent_5$ exception events. This specific state calculation for the bookstore example illustrates the expression for the upper bound of exception events in a sequential critical path as described in Subsection 2.4.

Now, calculating the $addwedflowSTATES$ and ω given by Subsection 2.4:

$addwedflowSTATES = EEvents = 6$
$\omega = addclassicalSTATES - addwedflowSTATES = 30 - 6 = 24$ or
$\omega = 19$ in case of $addclassicSTATES$-*book*

A BPEL code example is implemented to show details of WED-flow approach for critical path and exception handling belonging to the order book. Details of this BPEL code example is available at:
`www.ime.usp.br/~jef/appendix-CoopIS2010.pdf`.

3.2 Order Bookstore and New Exception Events

In this subsection we use two exception events (customer cancels the order and customer pays the order with a "bad check") to illustrate the WED-flow approach further.

Customer Cancels the Order. To handle this event, a WED-trigger that captures the event of a customer canceling an order needs to be defined. After localizing the last valid WED-state when this event occurs, the corresponding conditions and transitions have to be defined. Going back to Figure 4, suppose that the event "customer cancels order" occurs after WED-state 1. The new WED-trigger and the localization are expressed by the continual queries shown below in pseudo SQL code. Figure 5 illustrates this scenario. The WED-state concurrency control is provided through database algorithms (e.g., two-phase locking and multiversion timestamp) to guarantee ACID proprieties. Further discussion of this issue is beyond the scope of this paper.

```
Create WED-trigger cancel_order as
Query:
      SELECT order_id,
    FROM  Order
    WHERE Order.status = "request to cancel"
Trigger: every minute
Stop:  order.status = canceled

Create WED-condition cancel_order as
Query:
  For each order_id select in WED-trigger cancel-order
    If Order.status = "validated" and
       Customer.status = "registered" and
       Book.status = "reserved"
       CALL WED-transition cancel_order_validation (&order_id)
       Endif
       ...
```

```
Create WED-transition cancel_order_validation (&order_id) as
Query:
    SELECT Order.id = &order_id
    UPDATE Order.status = "canceled"
    UPDATE Book.status = "available"
```

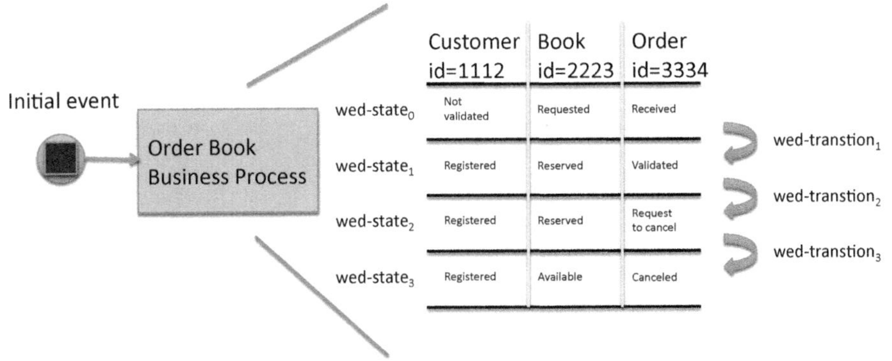

Fig. 5. WED-states for cancel exception event

Customer Pays the Order with "Bad-Check". The second example is the event "customer pays the order" to illustrate another important difference between the WED-flow approach and other related works. Suppose that the customer pays the book order using a check. However, this "bad check" bounces. It is unclear how to treat this new event. Assume that in this case the business rule is optimistic and friendly (i.e., the operation to treat "payment returned" does not introduce any additional fee or penalty for the customer). From the database side, the compensate transaction only goes back to the WED-state where the book was reserved, the customer was registered, and the order validated. In the classical approach, the lifecycle needs to be redefined following the new terms. Sometimes, this redefinition is not a trivial task because even a small change may imply significant redesigning of the control-flow including new recursions and many execution lines. In this case, the classical approach requires another split point after the registration payment activity, a new transition to treat returned payments, and a recursion point to recall order activities. On the contrary, the treatment of the event "check has returned" in the WED-flow approach only requires the definition of a WED-trigger that captures the WED-state "payment returned" and its WED-conditions and WED-transitions. The following pseudo SQL code and Figure 6 illustrate this situation.

```
Create WED-trigger payment_returned as
Query:
      SELECT order_id,
    FROM  Order
    WHERE Order.status = "payment returned"
Trigger: every minute
Stop:  order.status = "finished"

Create WED-condition payment_returned as
Query:
  For each order_id select in WED-trigger payment_ returned
    If Customer.status = "registered" and
       Book.status = "sold"
       CALL WED-transition payment_returned (&order_id)
       Endif
    ...

Create WED-transition payment_returned (&order_id) as
Query:
   SELECT Order.id = &order_id
   UPDATE Order.status = "validated"
   UPDATE Book.status = "reserved"
End
```

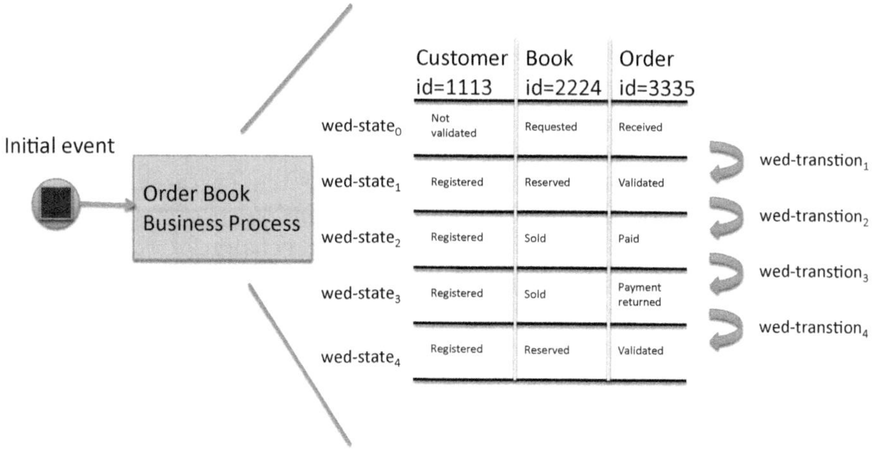

Fig. 6. WED-states for customer pays the order with "bad-check"

4 Related Work

Business process management in the cooperative information systems are commonly constructed around workflow engines that enact either control-flow or data-flow specifications. In the following overview of related work, we follow the axes of modeling and implementation to highlight the important differences among the variety of approaches. We examine event-driven modeling, data-driven modeling, control-flow-modeling, ECA-rule modeling, and the history of workflow implementation.

From the system modeling perspective an older but, nonetheless, very important reference that treats events and data repositories is Essential System Analysis [6]. According to this reference, the main step in modeling of information systems for business processes is the capturing and ordering of all events. These events are ordered through temporal dependencies [17], and the data repository is modeled using classical database design methodology [18]. This approach, and/or its variations, has often been applied in the development of information systems to this date. This is mainly due to its strong modeling emphasis and the intuitive linking of events and data. Current state-of-the-art in event-driven methodology [7] and event modeling [17], even if not directly, can be regarded as dependent of Essential System Analysis concepts. Consequently, modeling of events is a well-known strategy to identify and represent business processes. The main idea behind this strategy is that companies do not create business processes on a whim. Business processes are created because companies have to treat events that are central components of their business. However, capturing and representing events is not sufficient to satisfy the complex task of modeling business processes completely. Events are only phenomena in the context of the evolution of a data set. In real processes this evolution is curbed by conditions and transitions that are applied to the data set.

Following the notion of data-flow, several previous works [8, 19, 20] introduced approaches to treating complex products and coordination of thousand of processes in management systems such as car assembly lines. The data-driven paradigm has four important requirements: enabling the creation of objects (data structures), association of a set of sub-processes (activities) with these objects, setting activity dependencies to create a life cycle coordination structure, and enabling the automated creation of a data-driven process structure. Activities are applied to instances of structured data based on a labeled transition system with only one initial and one end state. Capturing of activity dependencies and their representation is enabled through object lifecycles. Closely related to the data-driven approach is the concept of business artifacts [9, 21, 22], which combine data and processes as a unit that is identifiable, self-describing, and indivisible. These data structures and their lifecycle models are the expected results of this approach. However, both approaches (data-driven and business artifacts) do not explicitly represent data attributes for each transition under specific conditions. More concretely, in the data-driven approach the data drives the processes based on data tests (e.g.,"if car is tested proceed to release") using object lifecycles to control the flow. Therefore, in reality the data does not drive the process because it is actually driven by the object lifecycle's flow of the data.

In 1999 Wil van der Aalst and Arthur ter Hofstede worked together on an initiative to identify, document, and evaluate control-flow patterns (Workflow Patterns Initiative [23]), which may be regarded as major milestone in control-flow modeling. The objective of this effort was to unify the development of control-flow technologies and establish criteria for the comparison of heterogeneous workflow tools. Similar as in other areas, the various tasks within a workflow can be viewed as patterns, reflecting common characteristics of various scientific and business scenarios. In order to address the majority of such scenarios, Aalst et al. [23] proposed four categories of workflow patterns. Categorized by the nature of the operations to be performed the authors identified four perspectives: Workflow Control-Flow Patterns (WCP) [24], Workflow Resource Patterns (WRP) [25], Workflow Data Patterns (WDP) [26], and Exception Handling Patterns [27]. Aalst et al. [24] subsequently published workflow patterns that have been cited in various academic and application papers. All of these patterns are based on the lifecycle concept and therefore do not represent events, conditions, and data attributes for each transition.

In ECA rules [10, 28] the execution of the action of an active rule is matched with the event by triggers. In other words, the verification of conditions is initiated after the occurrence of an event. In some cases, actions may also be calls to external programs or remote procedures. It is important to note that events are regarded as internal database operations (e.g., insert, delete, or update). This approach is characterized by the important link between events, conditions, and actions. However, the notion of events is restricted by the limits of internal database operations and data attributes. Therefore, not every generic transition can be represented, and this approach also does not represent data states.

The first initiative for workflow implementation (e.g., the logic associated to the ordering of activity execution) was identified in the 1970's as an alternative for office process automation [24]. Before that, both the flow and the activities were "mixed" in the Information Technology Systems (IT-Systems). The workflow concept attracted the attention of several large companies, which formed in 1993 the Workflow Management Coalition (WfMC) [29] together with universities and research groups. Some workflow languages based on formal representation (e.g., graph-oriented models [29], Petri nets [1], or process algebras [2]) have been proposed to support such workflow implementations. In workflow composition, BPEL can be regarded as de-facto standard for implementing system workflows in service-oriented software environments. This standard has spawn research on modeling and verifying BPEL [3] through mapping the language to formal frameworks [30]. Popular works employ finite state machines [31], process algebra [32, 33, 34], abstract state machines [35], and Petri nets [36]. In all these implementation initiatives events and data attributes for each transition are not explicitly represented for all potential scenarios.

In summary, all of these approaches to workflow engines are characterized by the fact that their central focus lays either control-flow or data-flow. In case of control-flow, the main focus is the process itself (i.e., "process A is executed before or in parallel to process B"). In data-flow (or data-driven modeling), the focus is workflow activities which are data transformations ("transform data object A into data object B"). In order to represent control-flow and/or data-flow all of these approaches use some form of a lifecycle concept. These lifecycles are implemented through classical frameworks such as Petri nets, process algebra, or graph representation. However, all of them rely on defining object lifecycles to drive the next step. In other words, for every single one of these approaches the question of what the next step will be has to be answered during modeling and implementation. In contrast, our WED-flow approach does not require that this question is addressed explicitly. The next step in a flow is automatically determined by means of transition from any data-state that satisfied certain conditions.

5 Conclusion

In this paper we presented the WED-flow approach, a novel unified approach to modeling and implementation of business process with dynamic changes. We provided WED-flow definitions, guidelines for business process modeling and implementation, a calculation of additional states for exception events; and a bookstore example to illustrate our approach. We showed that WED-flows are based on an integrated perspective on events, data, conditions, and transition, reducing quantitatively the complexity of exception handling as compared to current approaches.

The WED-flow approach considers that events are phenomenological manifestations of business processes and have to be the initial and final goal of the BPM modeling and implementation. We also showed that events are identified and separated into critical events (minimum set of events to achieve the main goal of a business process) generating a critical path (a time ordered sequence of critical events to make money) or exception events (unexpected events that happen at some point in the critical path generating a specific overhead).

All events in WED-flows are captured through WED-triggers, and for each of them, valid WED-states, WED-conditions, and WED-transitions need to be described. This way to capture events and create data states using conditions and transitions are the main contribution to reduction of exception handling complexity. We also showed that the additional number of states (ω) that have to implemented in classical approaches is significant. The classical approach has to implement a high expressivity and the decidability of behavioral property checking, which naturally generates a lot of code. In contrast, the conceptual level of WED-flows is higher, which allows the reduction of code that must be implement by programmers.

Our ongoing research includes the development of a WED-flow engine, modeling of control-flow and data-flow patterns using WED-flow guidelines, and the reduction of overhead messages in web services.

Acknowledgments. This work has been supported by CNPq (Brazilian National Research Council) grant number 201557/2009-6. Additional support is provided by FAPESP (São Paulo State Research Foundation).

References

1. Murata, T.: Petri nets: Properties, analysis and applications. Proceedings of the IEEE 77(4), 541–580 (1989)
2. Bergstra, J., Ponse, A., Smolka, S.: Handbook of Process Algebra. Elsevier Science Publishers B. V., Amsterdam (2001)

3. Jordan, D., Evdemon, J.: Web services business process execution language version 2.0. Public Review Draft OASIS WS-BPEL Technical Committee (2007)
4. Liu, L., Pu, C., Tang, W.: Continual queries for internet scale event-driven information delivery. IEEE Trans. on Knowl. and Data Eng. 11, 610–628 (1999)
5. Lomet, D., Barga, R., Mokbel, M.F., Shegalov, G., Wang, R., Zhu, Y.: Immortal db: transaction time support for sql server. In: SIGMOD 2005: Proceedings of the 2005 ACM SIGMOD International Conference on Management of Data, pp. 939–941. ACM, New York (2005)
6. Menamin, S.M.M., Palmer, J.F.: Essential Systems Analysis. Yourdon, New York (1984)
7. Alexopoulou, N., Nikolaidou, M., Anagnostopoulos, D., Martakos, D.: An event-driven modeling approach for dynamic human-intensive business. In: BPM 2009 International Workshops. LNBIP, vol. 43, pp. 393–404. Springer, Heidelberg (2010)
8. Müller, D., Reichert, M., Herbst, J.: Data-driven modeling and coordination of large process structures. In: Meersman, R., Tari, Z. (eds.) OTM 2007, Part I. LNCS, vol. 4803, pp. 131–149. Springer, Heidelberg (2007)
9. Nigam, A., Caswell, N.S.: Business artifacts: an approach to operation specificaiton. IBM Journal 42, 428–445 (2003)
10. Dittrich, K.R., Gatziu, S., Geppert, A.: The active database management system manifesto: A rulebase of adbms features. In: Sellis, T.K. (ed.) RIDS 1995. LNCS, vol. 985, pp. 3–20. Springer, Heidelberg (1995)
11. Laddad, R.: Practical Aspect-Oriented Programming: AspectJ in Action. Manning Publications Co. (2003)
12. Ferreira, J.E., Takai, O.K., Pu, C.: Integration of collaborative information system in internet applications using riverfish architecture. In: CollaborateCom, p. 8. IEEE, Los Alamitos (2005)
13. Zuliane, D., Oikawa, M.K., Malkowski, S., Alcazar, J.P., Ferreira, J.E.: The riverfish approach to business process modeling: Linking business steps to control-flow patterns. In: Collaborative Computing: Networking, Applications and Worksharing, pp. 179–193 (2008) ISBN 978-3-642-03353-7
14. Ferreira, J.E., Takai, O.K., Pu, C.: Integration of business processes with autonomous information systems: A case study in government services. In: IEEE International Conference on E-Commerce Technology, pp. 471–474 (2005)
15. Ferreira, J.E., Wu, Q., Malkowski, S., Pu., C.: Towards flexible event-handling in workflows through data states (accepted). In: IEEE Services 2010, IEEE 2010 Fourth International Workshop on Scientific Workflows, SWF (2010)
16. Plattner, C., Wapf, A., Alonso, G.: Searching in time. In: SIGMOD Conference, pp. 754–756 (2006)
17. Luckham, D.: The Power of Events: An Introduction to Complex Event Processing in Distributed Enterprise Systems. Addison-Wesley Professional, Reading (2001)
18. Elmasri, R., Navathe, S.B.: Fundamentals of Database Systems. Addison-Wesley, Reading (2010)
19. Müller, D., Reichert, M., Herbst, J., Köntges, D., Neubert, A.: Corepro sim: A tool for modeling, simulating and adapting data-driven process structures. In: Dumas, M., Reichert, M., Shan, M.-C. (eds.) BPM 2008. LNCS, vol. 5240, pp. 394–397. Springer, Heidelberg (2008)
20. Müller, D., Reichert, M., Herbst, J.: A new paradigm for the enactment and dynamic adaptation of data-driven process. In: Bellahsène, Z., Léonard, M. (eds.) CAiSE 2008. LNCS, vol. 5074, pp. 48–63. Springer, Heidelberg (2008)

21. Bhattacharya, K., Caswell, N.S., Kumaran, S., Nigam, A., Wu, F.Y.: Artifact-centered operational modeling: Lessons from artifact-centered operational modeling: Lessons from customer engagements. IBM Journal 46, 703–721 (2007)
22. Gerede, C.E., Bhattacharya, K., Su, J.: Static analysis of business artifact-centric operational models. In: IEEE International Conference on Service-Oriented Computing and Applications, pp. 133–140 (2007)
23. van der Aalst, W.M.P., ter Hofstede, A.H.M., Kiepuszewski, B., Barros, A.P.: Workflow patterns. Distributed and Parallel Databases 14, 5–51 (2003)
24. van der Aalst, W., van Hee, K.: Workflow Management: Models, Methods, and Systems. The MIT Press, Cambridge (2002) ISBN-10: 0-262-01189-1
25. Russell, N., ter Hofstede, A.H., Edmond, D., van der Aalst, W.M.: Workflow Resource Patterns: Identification, Representation and Tool Support. In: Pastor, Ó., Falcão e Cunha, J. (eds.) CAiSE 2005. LNCS, vol. 3520, pp. 216–232. Springer, Heidelberg (2005) ISBN 978-3-540-26095-0
26. Russell, N., ter Hofstede, A.H., Edmond, D., van der Aalst, W.M.: Workflow Data Patterns: Identification, Representation and Tool Support. In: Delcambre, L.M.L., Kop, C., Mayr, H.C., Mylopoulos, J., Pastor, Ó. (eds.) ER 2005. LNCS, vol. 3716, pp. 353–368. Springer, Heidelberg (2005) ISBN 978-3-540-29389-7
27. Russell, N., van der Aalst, W.M., ter Hofstede, A.H.: Exception handling patterns in process-aware information systems. In: BPM centerreport, BPM (2006)
28. Bry, F., Eckert, M., Pătrânjan, P.-L., Romanenko, I.: Realizing business processes with eca rules: Benefits, challenges, limits. In: Alferes, J.J., Bailey, J., May, W., Schwertel, U. (eds.) PPSWR 2006. LNCS, vol. 4187, pp. 48–62. Springer, Heidelberg (2006)
29. WfMC: Workflow management coalition (2008), `http://www.wfmc.org`
30. Hull, R., Su, J.: Tools for design of composite web services. In: Weikum, G., König, A.C., Deßloch, S. (eds.) SIGMOD Conference, pp. 958–961. ACM, New York (2004)
31. Fisteus, J.A., Fernández, L.S., Kloos, C.D.: Formal verification of BPEL4WS business collaborations. In: Bauknecht, K., Bichler, M., Pröll, B. (eds.) EC-Web 2004. LNCS, vol. 3182, pp. 76–85. Springer, Heidelberg (2004)
32. Turner, K.J.: Representing and analysing composed web services using CRESS. J. Network and Computer Applications 30, 541–562 (2007)
33. Ferreira, J.E., Takai, O.K., Braghetto, K.R., Pu, C.: Large scale order processing through navigation plan concept. In: I.I.C (ed.) IEEE on Services Computing Conference, SCC 2006, Chicago, Illinois, USA, pp. 297–300 (2006)
34. Braghetto, K.R., Ferreira, J.E., Pu, C.: NPTool: Towards Scalability and Reliability of Business Process Management. In: van der Aalst, W.M.P., Benatallah, B., Casati, F., Curbera, F. (eds.) BPM 2005. LNCS, vol. 3649, pp. 99–112. Springer, Heidelberg (2005)
35. Fahland, D., Reisig, W.: ASM-based semantics for BPEL: The negative control flow. In: Abstract State Machines, pp. 131–152 (2005)
36. Ouyang, C., Verbeek, E., van der Aalst, W.M.P., Breutel, S., Dumas, M., ter Hofstede, A.H.M.: WofBPEL: A tool for automated analysis of BPEL processes. In: Benatallah, B., Casati, F., Traverso, P. (eds.) ICSOC 2005. LNCS, vol. 3826, pp. 484–489. Springer, Heidelberg (2005)

Continuous Monitoring in Evolving Business Networks

Marco Comuzzi, Jochem Vonk, and Paul Grefen

Eindhoven University of Technology, Eindhoven, The Netherlands
{m.comuzzi,j.vonk,p.w.p.j.grefen}@tue.nl

Abstract. The literature on continuous monitoring of cross-organizational processes, executed within virtual enterprises or business networks, considers monitoring as an issue regarding the network formation, since what can be monitored during process execution is fixed when the network is established. In particular, the impact of evolving agreements in such networks on continuous monitoring is not considered. Also, monitoring is limited to process execution progress and simple process data. In this paper, we extend the possible monitoring options by linking monitoring requirements to generic clauses in agreements established across a network and focus on the problem of preserving the continuous monitorability of these clauses when the agreements evolve, i.e. they are introduced, dropped, or updated. We discuss mechanisms to preserve continuous monitorability in a business network for different types of agreement evolution and we design a conceptual and technical architecture for a continuous monitoring IT infrastructure that implements the requirements derived from such mechanisms.

Keywords: Monitoring, Business Network, Agreement Evolution.

1 Introduction

In collaborative settings, where autonomous parties perform part(s) of a business process governed by an established agreement/contract, continuous assurance of a process can be defined as the set of methodology and tools for issuing audit reports and assessing compliance to agreements simultaneously with, or within a reasonably short period after, the occurrence of relevant events in the process. Compared to ex-post assurance, which relies on ex-post audit trails, continuous assurance enables providers and consumers to achieve unprecedented benefits, in terms of reduced costs for information collection, search, and retrieval, and more timely and complete detection of deviations from contracts. Moreover, continuous assurance allows the application of recovery actions on-the-fly, further reducing the risks associated with deviations occurrence [1],[2].

Faster market dynamics and fiercer competition have pushed organizations to engage in complex, Internet-enabled, highly dynamic collaborations, referred to as virtual enterprises (organizations) or collaborative business networks [3],[4],[5]. Such collaborations entail the enactment of cross-organizational business processes, which are regulated by agreements established between the participants constituting the business network. Because of the high variability of the environment in which they

R. Meersman et al. (Eds.): OTM 2010, Part I, LNCS 6426, pp. 168–185, 2010.

are situated, however, agreements in a network may evolve during the network lifetime. We argue that the evolving nature of business networks poses additional challenges for continuous assurance of cross-organizational business processes, since the IT infrastructure supporting assurance should adapt to enable and preserve continuous assurance in reaction to evolution.

Assurance is constituted by two phases, namely the *monitoring* and the *auditing* phases [2]. From an individual actor's perspective, monitoring concerns the collection of relevant information regarding the agreements established with other actors in the network. Examples of monitoring information are: the process execution progress and exceptions, data produced during the process execution, response times of invoking services, choices made and process paths taken in the process execution (and the argumentation leading to those choices), etc. Proper monitoring represents a prerequisite for correct and complete auditing, i.e. checking the compliance of process execution with constraints set by agreements. In this paper we focus on the monitoring phase, and, therefore, on continuous monitoring of cross-organizational business processes. Our objective is to study how to guarantee continuous monitoring in a business network in which agreements evolve during the network operation.

Research on continuous monitoring in cross-organizational processes shows three main limitations. First, monitoring is usually limited to the reporting of the status (progress and simple process-level variables) of a process execution to interested parties [4], [6]. Second, monitoring and the setup of the IT monitoring infrastructure is always considered in 1:1 settings, i.e. the monitoring by one consumer of the processes outsourced to one specific provider [6]. Third, the setup of the monitoring infrastructure is considered only in the network formation phase [3], [4], i.e., at the time an agreement is established and fixed (it cannot change anymore). In our approach, continuous monitoring is not limited to the status of processes, but it rather concerns monitoring requirements of a consumer derived from any clause that may be included in an agreement. In addition, we consider the possibility for agreements in the network, and, consequently, the monitoring requirements of participants, to evolve, extending the scope of monitoring beyond the 1:1 setting. Eventually, because of evolving agreements, we consider the need for the IT monitoring infrastructure to be constantly updated to be able to facilitate the continuous monitoring in such evolving business networks.

In this paper, after having introduced a running example and the main concepts related to collaborations in business networks (in Section 2), we classify the types of evolution of business networks (Section 3) and discuss mechanisms to preserve the continuous monitorability of agreements in reaction to their evolution (Section 4). Then, we design the conceptual and technical architecture of the continuous monitorability IT infrastructure of one actor in a business network (Section 5). A prototype implementation of the architecture and mechanisms is presented next (Section 6) and the paper ends with related work (Section 7), conclusions and an outline of future work (Section 8).

2 Business Networks

To introduce the concepts related to business networks, we first consider a running example of a Business Network (BN) in the healthcare domain. The example is a simplification of a real-world teleradiology process extensively described in [7]. A representation of the BN at a given moment in time is shown in Fig. 1. A set of business actors participate in the BN (GP, PC, HOS, and SIS in the example). In their internal processes, general practitioners (GPs) and private clinics (PCs) rely on a hospital (HOS) to provide a radiology service. Each process comprises a sequence of blocks, i.e. structured set of activities. A block may be either executed internally by a business actor or outsourced to another business actor in the BN. In the example, HOS runs internally the scan acquisition (sa) and the result transfer (rt) blocks, and outsources the scan interpretation (si) to a scan interpretation service provider (SIS).

The cross-organizational collaboration among actors in the BN is regulated by established contracts, e.g. on service levels, and by internal or industry-level policies. We use the generic term *agreement* to identify the artifacts regulating the provisioning of processes among business actors in the BN. Agreements are constituted by a set of *clauses*, which capture the individual cross-organizational constraints on the BN operation.

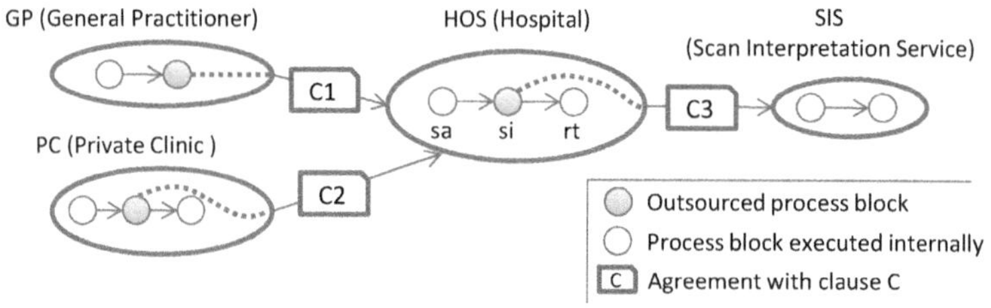

Fig. 1. Example BN in healthcare industry

As a sample, we consider the following three types of clauses that may appear in agreements between actors in the BN of Fig. 1:

- C1: HOS allows GP to get information about the quality of acquired scans;
- C2: HOS must guarantee that scan interpretation is performed by two different scan interpreters, and their identity should be traceable by PC;
- C3: SIS must guarantee that scan interpretation is performed by two different scan interpreters, and their identity should be traceable by HOS.

For continuous monitorability, C1 requires HOS to make available information regarding the quality of scan acquisitions to GP. C3 requires SIS to disclose information on the identity of the interpreters of the scan to HOS. Similarly, C2 requires HOS to disclose information on the identity of the scan interpreters to PC. The continuous monitoring of the clauses defined for the BN in Fig. 1, therefore, can be guaranteed if service providers, i.e. HOS and SIS, expose suitable monitoring capabilities to match the monitoring information requirements of their consumers, i.e. GP, PC, and HOS, respectively. We define a monitoring capability of a provider in the network as the ability to provide the specific monitoring information required by consumers for continuously monitor a given clause. Monitoring capabilities exposed by a business actor are queried by consumers to obtain the information required for checking the compliance of process execution with clauses that apply to it.

Note that in our example, a dependency exists between clauses C3 and C2, since HOS cannot guarantee the continuous monitoring of C2 if it cannot access the information required to monitor C3, i.e., the identity of scan interpreters. The monitoring capabilities to match the information requirements of PC is built by HOS using the information obtained through the monitoring capabilities exposed by SIS to let HOS monitor C2. Hence, monitoring capabilities may be either *native* or *aggregated.* Native capabilities refer to information that can be captured within the business domain of the provider of the monitored clause, e.g. SIS exposes a native monitoring capability to HOS for monitoring C3 and HOS exposes a native capability to GP for monitoring C1. Aggregated monitoring capabilities are built by the provider of a clause through information obtained by the monitoring capabilities of other providers to which it outsources part of its process, e.g. HOS exposes an aggregated capability to PC for monitoring C2.

3 Modeling Evolving Business Networks

In this section we introduce a formal model of business networks and their evolution. The model allows us, in Section 4, to describe algorithmically the mechanisms for the preservation of continuous monitorability in reaction to evolution.

3.1 Modeling Business Networks

Our model of a business network relies on a set of simplifying assumptions. With these assumptions, we limit the complexity of our notation without losing focus on the main principles behind our monitorability preservation mechanisms. We discuss later in Section 4 how such assumptions can be relaxed in more complex scenarios:

1. One actor contributes only one process to the network;
2. Any pair of actors in the network, i.e. a provider and a consumer, can establish at most one agreement;
3. We consider single-entry, single-exit, block-structured processes [8]; blocks are not hierarchically structured, i.e. a process is constituted by a flat set of blocks structured according to common business process patterns, such as sequential, conditional or parallel execution, and loops.
4. For the provider, a clause in an agreement always refers to one specific block in the process contributed to the BN;
5. A block in a process can be outsourced to at most one actor;

A business network *BN* is defined as:

$$BN = \langle ACT, PRO, AGR \rangle$$

where *ACT* is the set of actors, *PRO* the set of processes, and *AGR* the set of agreements. *BN* has *A* actors act_a:

$$ACT = \{act_a\}_{a=1,\dots,A}.$$

Because of assumption 1, we can write:

$$PRO = \{pro_a\}_{a=1,\dots,A}$$

where pro_a is the process contributed by the actor act_a.

For a process pro_a we define the set BLK_a of its K_a blocks:

$$BLK_a = \{blk_{a,k_a}^{bt}\}_{\substack{bt \in \{IN,OUT\} \\ k_a=1,\dots,K_a}}$$

A block *blk* may be either executed internally by act_a (block type $bt = IN$), e.g. the block sa in HOS's process in Fig. 1, or outsourced to another actor act_b ($bt = OUT$), e.g. block si for HOS in Fig. 1. In the remainder, we will make the block type *bt* explicit only when necessary.

We capture the outsourcing relation through the predicate:

$$executedBy(blk_{a,k_a}^{OUT}, act_b)$$

which evaluates to true if the block blk_{a,k_a}^{OUT} is outsourced by act_a to act_b, and to false otherwise.

An agreement always regulates the outsourcing relationship between act_c (consumer) and act_p (provider). Hence, given the set of all possible agreements *P*, we define the set of agreements *AGR* in place in the *BN* as:

$$AGR = \{agr_{c,p} \in P: \exists blk_{c,k_c}^{OUT} \in BLK_c \wedge executedBy(blk_{c,k_c}^{OUT}, act_p) \wedge act_c, act_p \in ACT\}$$

For each actor act_a, we define the provider set $PS(act_a)$ as the set of actors to which act_a outsources part of its process, and the consumer set $CS(act_a)$ as the set of actors that have outsourced part of their processes to act_a:

$$PS(act_a) = \{act_j: \exists agr_{a,j} \in AGR \wedge act_j \in ACT\}$$
$$CS(act_a) = \{act_j: \exists agr_{j,a} \in AGR \wedge act_j \in ACT\}$$

An agreement $agr_{c,p}$ is constituted by $L_{c,p}$ clauses. We define the set of $L_{c,p}$ clauses $CLA_{c,p}$ of the agreement $agr_{c,p}$ as:

$$CLA_{c,p} = \{cla_{c,p,l_{c,p}}\}_{l_{c,p}=1,\dots,L_{c,p}}$$

Note that, because of assumption 4, from the point of view of the provider act_p, a clause $cla_{c,p,l_{c,p}}$ always refers to one specific block blk_{p,k_p}. This association between clauses and blocks is captured by the predicate:

$$refersTo\left(cla_{c,p,l_{c,p}}, blk_{p,k_p}^{bt}\right)$$

which evaluates to true if $cla_{c,p,l_{c,p}}$ refers to blk_{p,k_p}, and to false otherwise. In Fig. 1, for actor HOS, C1 refers to the block sa, whereas C2 refers to the block si outsourced to SIS. Similarly, for SIS, C3 refers to a block executed internally.

From the provider point of view, outsourcing entails also a relation between clauses. Specifically, if a provider act_p has outsourced a block of its process pro_p to another provider act_d, and act_p has also established a clause $cla_{c,p,l_{c,p}}$ with an actor act_c, with

$act_c \in CS(act_p)$, which refers to the outsourced block, then a link exists between the clauses $cla_{c,p,l_{c,p}}$ and the clause $cla_{p,d,l_{p,d}}$ that regulates the provisioning of the process pro_d to act_p by act_d. We say in this case that $cla_{p,d,l_{p,d}}$ is a projection of $cla_{c,p,l_{c,p}}$. The projection relation between clauses is captured by the predicate:

$$projectsTo\left(cla_{c,p,l_{c,p}}, cla_{p,d,l_{p,d}}\right)$$

In Fig. 1, the predicate *projectsTo* can be used to capture the relation between the clauses C2 and C3. Specifically, with an abuse of notation, if we write C2 as $cla_{PC,HOS,2}$ and C3 as $cla_{HOS,SIS,3}$, then the predicate $projectsTo(cla_{PC,HOS,2}, cla_{HOS,SIS,3})$ holds for the shown *BN*. Although not explicitly modeled, we hypothesize that clause projection can only occur between semantically related clauses. In our example, both C2 and C3 refer to the four eyes principle on scan interpretation.

Providers expose monitoring capabilities to match monitoring requirements, derived from the establishment of clauses. The actor act_a exposes a set of M_a monitoring capabilities MCP_a:

$$MCP_a = \{mcp_{a,m_a}^{mt}\}_{\substack{mt \in \{NAT,AGG\} \\ m_a = 1,\ldots,M_a}}$$

A monitoring capability may be either native (monitoring capability type *mt=NAT*) or aggregated (*mt=AGG*). In the remainder, we will make the monitoring capability type *mt* explicit only when necessary.

3.2 Modeling Evolution of Business Networks

Since we aim at designing the continuous monitoring IT infrastructure of one actor in the BN, in modeling evolution of BNs we take the vantage point of an individual actor act_a in the BN. Thus, evolution concerns the modifications of the agreements in which act_a is involved, as either a provider or a consumer. We distinguish between two evolution categories: *clause-* and *agreement-level* evolution; within each category, we identify several evolution types. An evolution type is modeled by listing the changes that it implies on the BN. Specifically, the BN in the *as-is* situation is compared to the BN in the *to-be* situation, i.e. the BN resulting from the application of the evolution type.

Clause-level evolution. This concerns the insertion or deletion of clauses in an existing agreement in which act_a is involved (an update of a clause is a sequential combination of a deletion and insertion). We identify four types of clause-level evolution:

1. *Insert clause in provider-side agreement* (INS_PSC): it occurs when a new clause $cla_{j,a,n}$, with $n=L_{j,a}+1$, is added to an existing agreement with a consumer act_j, with $act_j \in CS(act_a)$:

$$CLA_{j,a}^{to-be} = CLA_{j,a}^{as-is} \cup \{cla_{j,a,n}\}$$

2. *Insert clause in consumer-side agreement* (INS_CSC): it occurs when a new clause $cla_{a,j,n}$, with $n=L_{a,j}+1$, is added to an existing agreement with a provider act_j, with $act_j \in PS(act_a)$:

$$CLA_{a,j}^{to-be} = CLA_{a,j}^{as-is} \cup \{cla_{a,j,n}\}$$

3. *Delete clause in provider-side clause* (DEL_PSC): it occurs when a clause $cla_{j,a,l}$, with $1 \leq l \leq L_{j,a}$, is removed from an existing agreement with a consumer act_j, with $act_j \in CS(act_a)$.

$$CLA_{j,a}^{to-be} = CLA_{j,a}^{as-is} \setminus \{cla_{j,a,l}\}$$

4. *Delete clause in consumer-side agreement* (DEL_CSC): it occurs when a clause $cla_{a,j,l}$, with $1 \leq l \leq L_{a,j}$ is removed from an existing agreement with a provider act_j, with $act_j \in PS(act_a)$.

$$CLA_{a,j}^{to-be} = CLA_{a,j}^{as-is} \setminus \{cla_{a,j,l}\}$$

Clause-level evolution is typical of highly regulated industries, such as the financial or healthcare industries. For what concerns the financial industry, for instance, changes of regulations, such as the introduction of the Sarbanes-Oxley act [9] in the US (and similar regulations in Europe), or the new lending policies for banks following the world economic crisis in 2009, introduce new constraints on BN processes without modifying, in most cases, the structure of the network and, therefore, without introducing new agreements.

Agreement-level evolution. Agreement-level evolution implies changes in the set of agreements *AGR*. In particular, we focus on the insertion and deletion of an empty agreement, i.e. an agreement $agr_{b,a}$ without clauses ($CLA_{b,a} = \varnothing$), in which clauses can be added through clause-level evolution. From the continuous monitorability of act_a perspective, the establishment of a new agreement $agr_{b,a}$ is constituted by the insertion of an empty agreement $agr_{b,a}$ followed by the insertion of a new clauses (i.e., INS_PSC evolution type for each clause to be included). Similarly, the deletion of an established agreement is a sequence of clause deletion for each clause in the agreement, followed by the deletion of the resulting empty agreement.

We identify four types of agreement-level evolution:

1. *Insert empty provider-side agreement* (INS_PSA): it occurs when the actor act_a becomes provider for a new consumer act_b:

$$AGR^{to-be} = AGR^{as-is} \cup \{agr_{b,a}\}$$

2. *Insert empty consumer-side agreement* (INS_CSA): it occurs when the actor act_a outsources a process segment to another actor act_b:

$$AGR^{to-be} = AGR^{as-is} \cup \{agr_{a,b}\}$$

3. *Delete empty provider-side agreement* (DEL_PSA): it occurs when act_a cancels a business relationship with a consumer act_b:

$$AGR^{to-be} = AGR^{as-is} \setminus \{agr_{b,a}\}$$

4. *Delete empty consumer-side agreement* (DEL_CSA): it occurs when act_a cancels a business relationship with a provider act_b:

$$AGR^{to-be} = AGR^{as-is} \setminus \{agr_{a,b}\}$$

Agreement-level evolution occurs in many traditional virtual enterprise scenarios; new consumers may be discovered, or partners in the network can decide, for cost or quality reasons, to outsource part of their processes to an external party [4], [6].

4 Algorithms for Preserving Continuous Monitorability

When evolution occurs, the continuous monitorability of new and existing agreements may be disrupted. Hence, the continuous monitorability IT infrastructure of the actor act_a involved in an evolution type needs to undertake some corrective actions to reestablish the continuous monitorability of the agreements in which act_a is involved. In the following we describe algorithmically and by example such corrective actions for each evolution type.

$PROCEDURE :: INS\_PSC(cla_{b,a,n}, act_b, act_a)$ // $n=L_{b,a}+1$
$mcp_{a,m_a} = BuildCapability(cla_{b,a,n}, act_b, act_a)$
$SetMonitor(mcp_{a,m_a}, cla_{b,a,n}, act_a)$ // link the new capability to the new clause
END PROCEDURE

PROCEDURE:: $BuildCapability(cla_{c,p,l}, act_c, act_p)$
$blk^{bt}_{p,k_p} = \{blk: blk \in BLK_p \wedge refersTo(cla_{c,p,l}, blk)\}$ // identify the block to which clause refers
IF $bt = IN$ // block is executed internally
  $mcp^{NAT}_{p,m_p} = CreateNatMcp(cla_{c,p,l}, act_p)$ //act_p (provider) creates native capability
ELSE // block is outsourced
  $act_o = \{act: act \in ACT \wedge executedBy(blk_{p,k_p}, act)\}$ // identify outsourcer
  $cla_{p,o,M_{p,o}+1} = Project(cla_{c,p,l}, act_p, act_o)$ // project the clause
  $mcp_{o,m_o} = BuildCapability(cla_{p,o,M_{p,o}+1}, act_p, act_o)$ // call to external provider (recursive)
  $mcp^{AGG}_{p,m_p} = CreateAggMcp(cla_{c,p,l}, mcp_{o,m_o}, act_p)$ // aggregate returned monitoring capability
END ELSE
return mcp_{p,m_p} // return the capability
END PROCEDURE

(a) algorithm

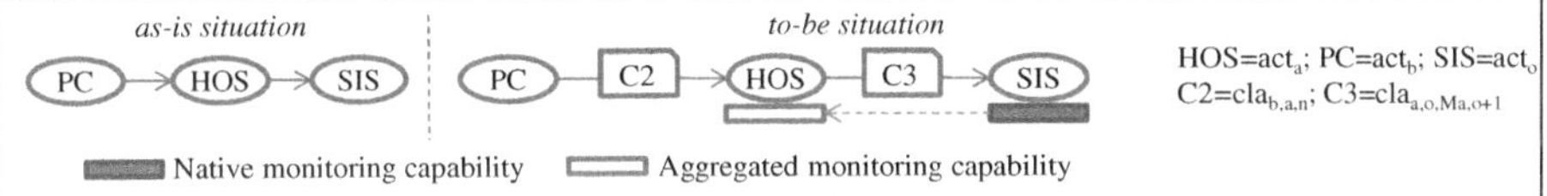

(b) example

Fig. 2. Monitorability preservation algorithm for evolution INS_PSC

Insert clause in provider-side agreement (INS_PSC). When a new clause $cla_{b,a,n}$, with $n=L_{b,a}+1$, is introduced, act_a must check whether the monitoring capability to match act_b's new monitoring requirements can be built on the fly. If the creation of a monitoring capability for a new clause is not successful, the actor can either decide to include the new clause in the agreement (the clause will not be continuously monitorable), or not to include the new clause in the agreement. The decision depends on the risk exposure policy of the actor, which is out of scope in this paper. In this paper, we assume that the creation of monitoring capabilities is always successful.

The steps to be followed by the provider act_a to build a monitoring capability for a new clause $cla_{b,a,n}$ are shown in the procedures in Fig. 2a. These use the four primitives *CreateNatMcp*(), *Project*(), *CreateAggMcp*(), and *SetMonitor*(), which capture the functionality of the continuous monitorability IT infrastructure as follows:

- *CreateNatMcp*(*cla*, *act*) represents the creation by the provider *act* of a new native monitoring capability for the continuous monitoring of the clause *cla* by its consumers. This involves the retrieval of the monitoring information required by consumers, e.g. through a native monitoring API or the instrumentation of the IT infrastructure on which the block to which the clause *cla* refers is executed;
- *Project*(*cla*, *act*, act_c) represents the projection of a clause *cla* towards an actor act_c made by the consumer *act* of a process provided by act_c. The projection triggers the establishment of a new clause cla_p, which is returned by the execution of the primitive. From the modeling perspective, after the execution of this primitive the predicate *projectsTo*(*cla*, cla_p) will evaluate to true;
- *CreateAggMcp*(*cla*, *mcp*, *act*) represents the creation by the provider *act* of a new monitoring capability mcp_n^{AGG} built as the aggregation of information retrieved from the capability *mcp*, exposed by one of the *act*'s providers;
- *SetMonitor*(*mcp*,*cla*,*act*) represents the creation made by the provider *act* of the mechanism that enables the consumer of the clause *cla*, to use the monitoring capability *mcp* to obtain the information required for monitoring the clause *cla*.

In Fig. 2a (line 5 onward), first act_a identifies the block to which the new clause refers. If such block is not outsourced, then the (native) monitoring capability to match the consumer's new monitoring information requirements is built by the provider, using the *CreateNatMcp*() primitive. If the block is outsourced, then act_a must (i) project the new clause towards the provider of the block and (ii) request the creation of the capability, which will be aggregated by act_a for guaranteeing the monitoring of the new clause to act_b. Note that the mechanism is recursively iterated till the outsourcer that can natively provide the information required for monitoring the new clause is found.

In our example (see Fig. 2b) PC and HOS may agree on a new clause, such as C2 (traceability of scan interpreters). PC, for instance, may be required by a new regulation for improving transparency towards patients to provide the identity of two different scan interpreters for every scan request. HOS identifies that the new clause refers to a process block that is outsourced to SIS and, therefore, projects the clause C2 on C3 and forwards the request for the new monitoring capability to SIS. The identity of the scan interpreters can be natively captured and made available by SIS to HOS. Therefore SIS exposes a native monitoring capability to HOS, who may apply a domain specific translation or integrate it with internal information before making it available, as an aggregated monitoring capability, to PC.

Insert clause in consumer-side agreement (INS_CSC). This case is not relevant from the point of view of act_a. The consumer act_a will rely, in fact, on the provider act_j to provide the monitoring capability that matches act_a's monitoring information requirements derived from the insertion of a new clause $cla_{a,j,n}$.

Delete clause in provider-side agreement(DEL_PSC). This case is also not relevant from the point of view of act_a, since the deletion of a clause does not introduce new monitoring information requirements for the actors in *CS*(act_a). In other words, there is no garbage collection made by the provider of the monitoring capabilities that are no longer used by consumers for monitoring established clauses. We argue, in fact, that a monitoring capability may be reused in the future to satisfy the monitoring information requirements of new consumers.

PROCEDURE::$INS\_CSA(act_a, agr_{a,b})$
FORALL j: $act_j \in CS(act_a)$
FORALL c: $cla_{j,a,c} \in CLA_{j,a} \wedge refersTo(cla_{j,a,c}, blk^{bt}_{a,k_a}) \wedge bt = OUT \wedge executedBy(blk^{bt}_{a,k_a}, act_b)$
$l_j = L_{a,b} + 1$
$cla_{a,b,l_j} = Project(cla_{j,a,c}, act_b, act_a)$ // Create projected clause
$CLA^{to-be}_{a,b} = CLA^{as-is}_{a,b} \cup \{cla_{a,b,l_j}\}$ // Add clause to set of existing clauses
$mcp_{b,m_b} = BuildCapability(cla_{a,b,l_j}, act_a, act_b)$ // actb creates and returns new capability
$mcp^{AGG}_{a,m_a} = CreateAggMcp(cla_{j,a,c}, mcp_{b,m_b}, act_a)$ // acta creates new aggregated capability
$SetMonitor(mcp^{AGG}_{a,m_a}, cla_{j,a,c}, act_a)$ // link new capability to new clause
END FORALL
END FORALL
END PROCEDURE

(a) algorithm

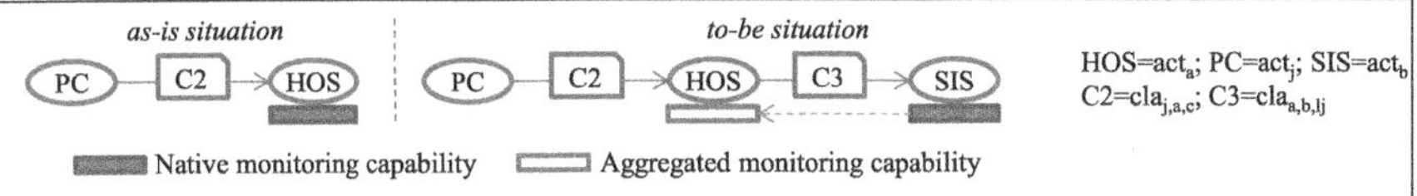

(b) example

Fig. 3. Monitorability preservation algorithm for INS_CSA evolution

Delete clause in consumer-side agreement (DEL_CSC). The deletion of a clause $cla_{a,j,l_{a,j}}$ in which the actor acta appears as a consumer is allowed only if $cla_{a,j,l_{a,j}}$ is not a projection of any already existing clause. In other words, the deletion of $cla_{a,j,l_{a,j}}$ is allowed only if the set $\{cla: cla \in CLA_{a,j} \wedge projectsTo(cla, cla_{a,j,l_{a,j}}) \wedge act_j \in CS(act_a)\}$ is not empty.

In our example of Fig. 1, clause C3 cannot be removed, since it is the projection of C2 and HOS will not be able to let PC monitor C2 without the information obtained by SIS for monitoring C2. Clauses that represent a projection of existing clauses that act_a has with its consumers can only be deleted when the agreement in which they appear is removed afterwards (see evolution type DEL_CSA).

Insert empty consumer-side agreement (INS_CSA). When an actor act_a outsources part of a process to a new provider act_b, then act_a should coherently project the existing clauses in agreements with actors in $CS(act_a)$ towards act_b and modify its monitoring capability accordingly. In Fig. 3b, PC and HOS have agreed in the as-is situation on a clause similar to C2 (four-eyes principle on scan interpretations). Starting from the situation in which HOS executes internally the whole radiology process, HOS outsources part of the process to SIS. HOS needs to project C2 to regulate its relationship with SIS, i.e. creating the clause C3 that guarantees the four-eyes principle on the service provided by SIS. In the to-be situation, HOS has new information requirements for the continuous monitorability of C3, which should be matched by a suitable monitoring capability exposed by SIS, i.e. for the traceability of the scan interpreters. HOS will use such capability to update the capability exposed to GP, which now becomes aggregated.

The monitorability preservation algorithm for evolution type INS_CSA is shown in Fig. 3a. The algorithm uses the procedure *BuildCapability()* already defined for evolution type INS_PSC.

Insert empty provider-side agreement (INS_PSA). From the point of view of preserving continuous monitorability, this type of evolution does not imply any corrective actions by act_a. The creation of suitable monitoring capabilities is required from act_a only when the empty agreement will be filled in with new clauses (see INS_PSC evolution type).

Delete provider-side agreement (DEL_PSA). In this case an agreement between the provider act_a and one of its consumers act_b is cancelled. No specific actions should be taken in this case by act_a to preserve continuous monitorability.

Delete consumer-side agreement (DEL_CSA). In this case an agreement between the provider act_a and one of its providers act_b is cancelled. If the agreement is empty, then no specific actions should be taken by act_a to preserve continuous monitorability.

PROCEDURE::$DEL\_CSA(, agr_{a,b}, act_a, act_b)$
FORALL l: $cla_{a,b,l} \in CLA_{a,b}$ // for every clause still in the agreement $agr_{a,b}$
FORALL j: $act_j \in CS(act_a)$
FORALL c: $projectsTo(cla_{j,a,c}, cla_{a,b,l})$
$mcp^{NAT}_{a,m_a} = CreateNatMcp(cla_{j,a,c})$ // Create new native capability
$SetMonitor(mcp^{NAT}_{a,m_a}, cla_{j,a,c})$ // Link clause to new native capability
END FORALL
END FORALL
$blk^{OUT}_{a,k_a} = \{blk\text{: } blk \in BLK_a \wedge refersTo(cla_{a,b,l}, blk) \wedge executedBy(blk, act_b)\}$ //select outsourced block
$BLK^{to-be}_a = \{BLK^{as-is}_a \setminus blk^{OUT}_{a,k_a}\} \cup \{blk^{IN}_{a,k_a}\}$ // mark originally outsourced block as internal
END FORALL
END PROCEDURE

(a) algorithm

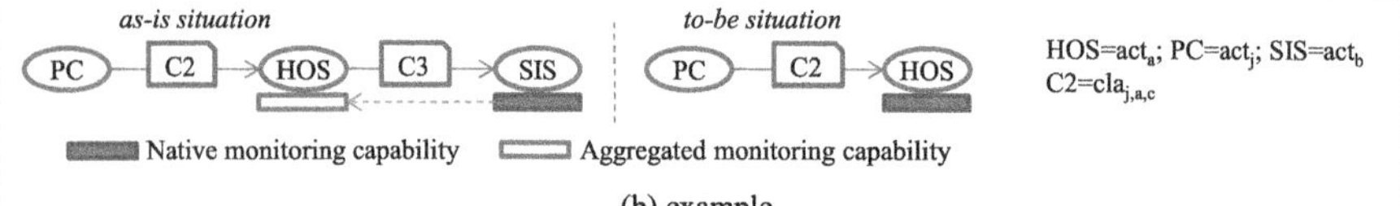

(b) example

Fig. 4. Monitorability preservation algorithm for evolution DEL_CSA

If the agreement is not empty, the it contains clauses that are the projection of one or more clauses established between act_a and its consumers (see evolution type DEL_CSC). For each of this clauses $cla_{a,b,l_{a,b}}$, established by act_a with a provider act_b, the preservation of continuous monitorability is made possible only if act_a re-sources internally the block that was originally outsourced to act_b (and to which $cla_{a,b,l_{a,b}}$ refers). In our example (see Fig. 4b), when the agreement between SIS and HOS is deleted, it will still contain the clause C2, since it represents the projection of C3. HOS will first re-source internally the scan interpretation process. Then, HOS needs to check whether some of the clauses that it has established with its own consumers, e.g. C2 with PC, require information made available by SIS's monitoring capabilities for continuous monitoring. If this is the case, then HOS creates a new native monitoring capability that substitutes the capability originally obtained through the aggregation of SIS's capability. The monitorability preservation algorithm for evolution type DEL_CSA in the generic case is shown in Fig. 4a.

After having discussed the mechanisms for the preservation of monitorability, we can now go back to the simplifying assumptions adopted in the modeling of business networks made in Section 3.1. We argue that the relaxation of assumptions 1 and 2 leads to a more complex notation, but it does not change the rationale behind our monitorability preservation mechanisms. Relaxing assumptions 3, 4, and 5 should result in more complex primitives for the creation of aggregated monitoring capabilities and projections of clauses. As a sample, the relaxation of assumption 4 implies that a block can be outsourced to more than one actor. In our example, in order to maintain the four-eyes principles, the scan interpretation may be outsourced by HOS to two different scan interpretation services, each of which provides a single scan interpretation. The projection of clauses needs to be updated is such a way that every clause of type C2 established by HOS with a consumer triggers the establishment of two different clauses, one for each scan interpretation service. The aggregation of capabilities should be modified in such a way that the capability exposed by HOS to its consumers combines the identity of the scan interpreters retrieved from the capabilities exposed by the scan interpretation services to which the service is outsourced. Improved mechanisms that account for the relaxation of our simplifying assumptions are target of future research.

5 Architecture of Continuous Monitoring Infrastructure

From the definition of the continuous monitoring problem in BNs and the discussion of the mechanisms for preserving continuous monitorability in reaction to evolution, we derive the list of functional requirements for the Continuous Monitoring Infrastructure (CMon-I) of a business actor act_a in a BN (see Table 1). We distinguish between requirements relevant when act_a is a provider in the BN (see PRO in the second column of Table 1), a consumer in the BN (CON), or both. Requirements REQ1-2 derive from the need for act_a to provision monitoring capabilities to consumers and to access the capabilities of providers, whereas REQ3-8 derive from the need to preserve continuous monitorability in reaction to evolution of the agreements that involve act_a.

From the list of requirements, we derive a conceptual architecture for CMon-I. We present a two-level decomposition of such an architecture. The level-1 decomposition of the architecture is shown in Fig. 5. The required functionality to support continuous monitoring is clustered in several modules. Fig. 5 shows the requirements that are implemented by each module. The monitoring client (MC) retrieves the capabilities and monitoring data from the actors in the provider set. Monitoring data are provided by the monitoring service (MS) module. The evolution manager (EM) detects changes in the BN and instructs the monitoring capability builder (MCB) to create a new monitoring capability, using, if necessary, the provider capabilities retrieved through MC. Note that a business actor in a BN, i.e. HOS in Fig. 1, acts at the same time as a provider and a consumer, whereas business actors at the edges of the network, i.e. PC or SIS in Fig. 1, participate only as consumers or providers of business processes. In the latter case, the architecture, shown in Fig. 5, can be simplified to include only those modules, which satisfy the requirement that are relevant for that role (as indicated in Table 1).

Table 1. Functional requirements for CMon-I

REQ1	PRO	CMon-I allows the provisioning of the monitoring capabilities referring to the process that act_a is contributing to the actors in $CS(act_a)$, covered by the primitive *SetMonitor*() of Section 4.
REQ2	CON	CMon-I allows act_a to access the monitoring capabilities of actors in $PS(act_a)$
REQ3	both	CMon-I allows act_a to detect the evolution of the agreements in the BN, either at agreement- or clause-level
REQ4	both	CMon-I has access to the agreements (including process specifications) that act_a has established with other actors in the BN, either as a consumer or a provider
REQ5	PRO	CMon-I allows act_a to build native monitoring capabilities to match the monitoring information requirements of actors in $CS(act_a)$ [see the primitive *CreateNatMcp*() of Section 4]
REQ6	PRO	CMon-I allows act_a to build aggregated monitoring capabilities to match the monitoring information requirements of actors in $CS(act_a)$ as aggregation of monitoring capabilities of actors in $PS(act_a)$ [see the primitive *CreateAggMcp*() of Section 4]
REQ7	both	CMon-I allows act_a to project clauses across the network in reaction to evolution [see the primitive *Project*()of Section 4]
REQ8	both	CMon-I allows act_a to detect if a new monitoring capability needs to be created in reaction to evolution. In this case, CMon-I starts the creation of a new, aggregated or native, monitoring capability

We make the assumption that CMon-I is situated within a generic Business Process Management (BPM) infrastructure, on which the actor runs its processes. Such BPM infrastructure is constituted by a process execution engine, an E-Contracting system, which can be triggered for the projection of clauses, an Agreement Repository, which stores the agreements established by an actor, either as a provider or a consumer, and a Compliance (Auditing) Engine, which checks the satisfaction of clauses during process execution according to the information captured through monitoring capabilities of actors in $PS(act_a)$.

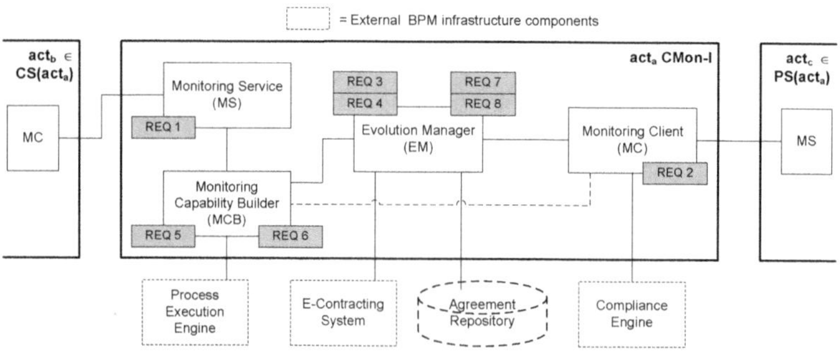

Fig. 5. Level 1 decomposition of CMon-I architecture

Our decomposition of the CMon-I architecture is iterated until we identify only modules that implement at most one of the requirements, so that a clear separation of concerns is reached in which each module provides functionality to satisfy one specific requirement. Hence, the level 2 decomposition, i.e. the internal conceptual architecture of the CMon-I modules, is shown only for those modules that implement two or more requirements in the level 1 decomposition, i.e. MCB and EM (see Fig. 6).

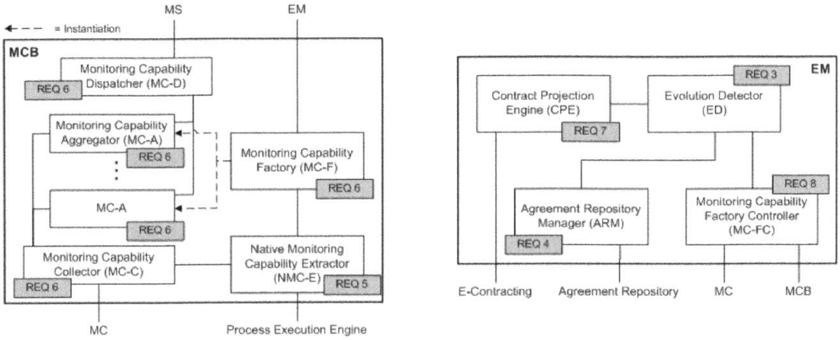

Fig. 6. Conceptual architecture of MCB and EM

Since new monitoring capabilities should be created when evolution occurs in the BN, EM commands the Monitoring Capability Factory (MC-F) to create a new capability when required from a detected evolution. In response to requests from EM, MC-F instantiates a new Monitoring Capability Aggregator (MC-A), which implements the aggregation of native or external, i.e. from actors in $PS(act_a)$, capabilities to provide the monitoring capability required by the actors in $CS(act_a)$. The instantiation of a new MC-A can be seen as the result of the execution of the primitives *CreateNatMcp*() or *CreateAggMcp*() introduced in Section 4.

A separate module (NMC-E) is required to extract native monitoring capabilities from the process engine on which act_a executes the processes contributed to the BN. Most of the commonly used workflow engines provide a native monitoring API for inspecting the execution of process instances. This is the case, for instance, of the BPELMonitor API for the Open-ESB BPEL Open source engine (see http://wiki.open-esb.java.net/Wiki.jsp?page=BPELMonitor), or the YAWL Observer interface for the YAWL engine [10]. Similar native monitoring interfaces are also available in commonly used ERP packages. NMC-E sits on top of such native API to extract the information required for monitor a clause.

For what concerns EM, the ARM provides access to the external Agreement Repository. ED is responsible for analyzing agreements, detecting the evolution of the BN. ED may either poll ARM for retrieving new agreements, or new agreements may be proactively pushed by ARM to ED. ED runs the business logic of the mechanisms discussed in Section 3 and may trigger the projection of contracts, implied by the execution of the *Project*() primitive introduced in Section 3, and the construction of new monitoring capabilities, e.g. in reaction to INS_PSC evolution. CPE is responsible of managing the projection of clauses and interacts, therefore, with the external

E-contracting system. MCF-C controls the MC-F in MCB for requesting new monitoring capabilities. MCF-C is also connected to MC, in order to establish access to the monitoring capabilities provided by providers in $PS(act_a)$.

6 Implementation

As a proof of concept, the continuous monitoring approach has been implemented in the PROXE (PROcesses in a Cross-organizational Environment) system. PROXE is based on the Business Process Web Services (BP-WS) framework, the aim of which is to 'open-up' black-box Web Services. BP-WS services expose the enclosed business processes through a set of standard interfaces, so that service consumers can monitor, control, and synchronize with the service execution progress of the service provider [11].

Fig. 7 shows the implementation architecture of the PROXE system (excluding those components and interfaces that are not relevant for the work presented in this paper). The teleradiology process has been used as a test scenario to validate the continuous monitoring approach implemented in the system. As can be seen in the figure, three parties (GP, HOS, and SIS) are included and their systems are connected through the ACT and MON interfaces. The ACT interface is used to invoke the service and is handled by the invoker module. The MON interface is used to monitor service execution and is backed by the CMon-I modules.

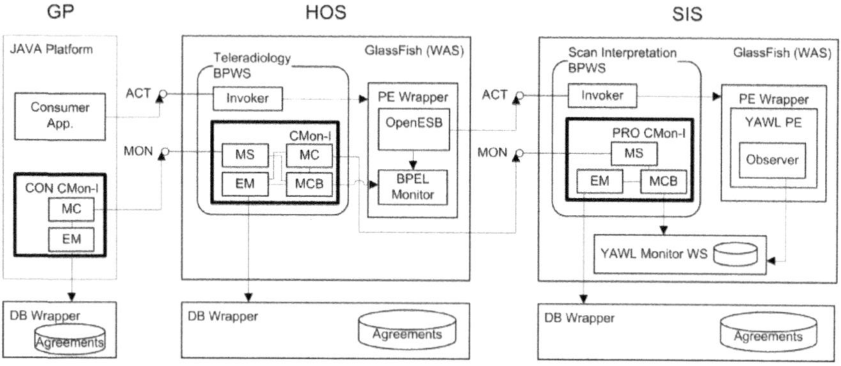

Fig. 7. Implementation Architecture

The process that is performed by HOS, i.e., the teleradiology process as shown in Fig. 1, is executed on a BPEL process engine (OpenESB BPEL Engine on the GlassFish Web Application Server). The scan interpretation part of this process is however outsourced and is executed on the YAWL workflow system [10] by SIS. Both process engines have their own mechanisms to expose monitoring information. The BPEL Monitor is an addition to the BPEL Engine and can be directly accessed through its API. YAWL exposes process events to a, so called, ObserverGateway. This ObserverGateway passes the events to the YAWL Monitor Web Service, which subsequently stores the relevant information contained in an event into a database. On request by the CMon-I, e.g., as a response to a query posed by HOS to retrieve the scan interpreters identity, the YAWL Monitor Web Service retrieves the desired monitoring information from the database.

Each party has its own database, in which the agreements and clauses are stored. Any component within the BPWS, i.e., Teleradiology BPWS and Scan Interpretation BPWS, can access the database. This is required to validate calls to the BPWS against the contract. For the CMon-I component, access is required as explained in the previous section. The process engines and databases are part of the BPM infrastructure, as defined in Section 5. The e-contracting systems and compliance engines, which are also part of the BPM infrastructure, have not been included in the PROXE system as they do not address the core issues of continuous monitoring.

SIS is only a provider in the business network, so SIS has only native monitoring capabilities, indicated through the single connection of CMon-I/MCB to the YAWL Monitoring WS. HOS acts as both a consumer (of SIS) and provider (to GP). The CMon-I/MC of HOS is therefore connected to the MON interface of SIS (and will aggregate the monitoring information retrieved through this interface if required by GP) and CMon-I/MCB is connected to the BPEL Monitor (to provide native monitoring capabilities to GP. GP acts as a consumer only and retrieves the required monitoring information of HOS through the exposed MON interface. The connections to the databases are used to access the stored agreements and clauses.

As an example of agreement evolution, we use the outsourcing by HOS of the scan interpretation to SIS (evolution type INS_CSA, see Figure 3). For the implementation, this type evolution implies that the retrieval of the identities of scan interpreters is moved from the BPEL Monitor of HOS to the YAWL Monitor WS of SIS. YAWL provides two API methods to acquire the required information: getUserWhoIsExecutingThisItem():String and get_whoStartedMe():String. HOS's CMon-I/MCS transforms the returned results into terminology that is expected by GP.

In the current PROXE system, the creation of a monitoring capability related to a clause is done manually. For example, discovering that the four-eyes principle can be supported through the identification of the persons who performed the specific scan interpretation task (and that they should not be the same person) and that this information, in turn, can be retrieved through some specific API calls, is done manually. A (semi-)automatic translation is considered future research.

7 Related Work

Business process monitoring has been largely investigated under the labels of Business Process Intelligence (BPI) [12] and Business Activity Monitoring (BAM) [13]. BPI and BAM, however, are situated in the context of stand-alone organizations and mostly concern process optimization. Auditing for compliance checking has been investigated by research on process mining [14] and normative reasoning applied in the context of business process management [15]. Process mining does not represent a suitable solution for continuous assurance, since it relies on the ex-post analysis of process logs. Normative reasoning is focused on defining languages for the formal definition of compliance. Approaches in this category are usually not focused on cross-organizational processes and they tend to overlook the architectural aspects related to cross-organizational collaboration enactment.

Research on Web service management has also focused on business process monitoring and assurance. Research in this area, however, maintains a technological focus, concerning the definition of XML-based languages for the definition of clear and precise SLAs [16] or the design of monitoring engines compliant with Web service technology [17]. An approach for the controlled evolution of Web service contracts is discussed in [18], but without reference to how such an evolution impacts the monitoring of the service execution. A methodology for auditing Web service-based processes is discussed in [19]. Such a methodology, however, is applied only within the domain of the orchestrator of the collaboration and considers the services invoked by a business process as black boxes.

Monitoring in the CrossFlow project [6] concerns only information on the progress of an outsourced process and basic process variables, which are accessible at specific monitoring points specified in the contract. Moreover, CrossFlow considers 1:1 outsourcing scenario and does not account for the transitivity/aggregation of monitoring information in a business network. Dynamic cross-organizational collaboration is also considered in the CrossWork project [4]. In CrossWork, however, contracts are not considered and monitoring still concerns the progress of outsourced services. Moreover, the impact of the business network evolution on the monitorability of cross-organizational processes is not taken into account. Recursive mechanisms for the definition of goals and processes during the formation of virtual enterprises are considered by the SUDDEN project [20]. Monitoring requirements and evolution of a formed network are, however, not considered. The design of cross-organizational processes with evolving requirements is tackled in [21], but without explicit focus on monitorability requirements.

Similarly to the monitoring capabilities defined in this paper, the E-Adome workflow engine [3] introduces the notion of external information requirement, i.e. information required by a consumer from its providers to enforce and monitor a contract. External information requirements are not directly linked with contract clauses. Moreover, the architectural support for monitoring based on such external information is not specified.

8 Conclusions

This paper analyzes the issue of continuous monitorability of cross-organizational business processes. In particular, we discuss the case of the evolution of agreements in a business network and show how the continuous monitoring IT infrastructure should adapt to preserve the monitorability of agreements. The paper formally describes algorithms for restoring the continuous monitorability of agreements in reaction to their evolution. We also discussed the PROXE system, which implements the requirements for continuous monitorability derived from our modeling of evolving business networks.

Future work will concern the refinement of our model of business networks, relaxing the assumptions made in Section 3, and the analysis of alternative forms of evolution for BNs. We also plan to consider, within the PROXE system, template-based agreement lifecycles and to link monitoring with control actions to be undertaken when the compliance to existing clauses in not verified.

References

1. Alles, M.G., Kogan, A., Vasarhely, M.A.: Feasibility and Economics of Continuous Assurance. Auditing: Journal of Practice and Theory 21(1) (2002)
2. Coderre, D.: Continuous Auditing: Implications for Assurance Monitoring and Risk Assessment (2005)
3. Chiu, D.K.W., Karlapalem, K., Li, Q., Kafeza, E.: Workflow View Based E-Contracts in a Cross-Organizational E-Services Environment. Distrib. Parallel. Dat. 12, 193–216 (2002)
4. Grefen, P., Eshuis, R., Mehandijev, N., Kouvas, G., Weichart, G.: Internet-based support for Process-Oriented Instant Virtual Enterpises. IEEE Internet Comput., 30–38 (November/December 2009)
5. van Heck, E., Vervest, P.: Smart Business Networks: How the network wins. Communications of the ACM 50, 28–37 (2007)
6. Grefen, P., Aberer, K., Hoffner, Y., Ludwig, H.: CrossFlow: cross-organizational workflow management in dynamic virtual enterprises. Comput. Syst. Sci. & Eng. 5, 277–290 (2000)
7. Vonk, J., Wang, T., Grefen, P., Swennenhuis, M.: An Analysis of Contractual and Transactional Aspects of a Teleradiology Process. Beta Technical Report 263, Eindhoven University of Technology, Eindhoven (2008)
8. Mendling, J., Reijers, H., van der Aalst, W.M.P.: Seven Process Modeling Guidelines (7PMG). Information and Software Technology 52(2) (2010)
9. Hall, J.A., Liedtka, S.T.: The Sarbanes-Oxley Act: Implication for large-scale IT outsourcing. Communications of the ACM 50(3), 95–100 (2007)
10. ter Hofstede, A., van der Aalst, W.M.P., Adams, M., Russell, N.: Modern Business Process Automation: YAWL and its support environment. Springer, Heidelberg (2010)
11. Grefen, P., Ludwig, H., Dan, A., Angelov, S.: An analysis of web services support for dynamic business process outsourcing. Informtation and Software Technology 48, 1115–1134 (2006)
12. Grigori, D., Casati, F., Castellanos, M., Dayal, U., Sayal, M., Shan, M.-C.: Business Process Intelligence. Computers in Industry 53, 321–343 (2004)
13. McCoy, D.W.: Business Activity Monitoring, Gartner Group Research Report ID LE-15-9727 (2002)
14. van der Aalst, W.M.P., Dumas, M., Ouyang, C., Rozinat, A., Verbeek, E.: Conformance checking of Service Behavior. ACM TOIT 8(3) (2008)
15. Sadiq, S., Governatori, G., Namiri, K.: Modeling control Objectives for Business Process Compliance. In: Alonso, G., Dadam, P., Rosemann, M. (eds.) BPM 2007. LNCS, vol. 4714, pp. 149–164. Springer, Heidelberg (2007)
16. Skene, J., Raimondi, F., Emmerich, W.: Service-Level Agreements for Electronic Services. IEEE Transactions on Software Engineering (forthcoming, 2010)
17. Moser, O., Rosenberg, F., Dustdar, S.: Non-intrusive monitoring and service adaptation for WS-BPEL. In: Proc. WWW 2008 (2008)
18. Andrikopoulos, V., Benbernou, S., Papazoglou, M.: Evolving Services from a Contractual Perspective. In: van Eck, P., Gordijn, J., Wieringa, R. (eds.) CAiSE 2009. LNCS, vol. 5565, pp. 290–304. Springer, Heidelberg (2009)
19. Orriens, B., van den Heuvel, W.-J., Papazoglou, M.: On The Risk Management and Auditing of SOA Based Business Processes. In: Proc. 3rd Int. ISoLA Symposium, pp. 124–138 (2008)
20. Mehandjiev, N. D., Stalker, I. D., Carpenter, M. R.: Recursive Construction and Evolution of Collaborative Business Processes. In : BPM 2008 Workshops, pp. 573–584 (2008)
21. Desi, N., Chopra, A.K., Singh, M.P.: Amoeba: A methodology for modeling and evolving cross-organizational business processes. ACM TOSEM 19(2), Article 6 (2009)

Collaborative Coordination of Activities with Temporal Dependencies

Jörn Franke[1,2], François Charoy[2], and Paul El Khoury[1]

[1] Public Security, SAP Research Center (Sophia Antipolis), 805 Avenue du Docteur Maurice Donat, BP1216-06254 Mougins, France
{joern.franke,paul.el.khoury}@sap.com
[2] LORIA-INRIA-CNRS, Université de Lorraine, BP 239-54506 Vandoeuvre-lès-Nancy Cedex, France
charoy@loria.fr

Abstract. Business process management and systems have been proven mature and highly beneficial in many domains. Recent surveys by leading market analysts say that the next challenge for BPM are unstructured processes. Based on a domain study in disaster response management, we identify current shortcomings of business process models and management with respect to unstructured processes. We develop a generic model for flexible temporal ad-hoc coordination of activities. Its focus lies on awareness and feedback as well as loosely structuring the process with temporal dependencies. It is implemented as an extension to the open Google Wave collaboration infrastructure. The approach is commented by commanders in the disaster management domain.

1 Introduction

Highly dynamic scenarios challenge existing technologies for managing processes performed in the real world. According to Gartner and McKinsey the management of activities in unstructured processes becomes more and more important for many organizations [1]. Two key characteristics have been identified by them. Firstly, they are predominantly executed by an individual or group in a dynamic fashion. Secondly, they are highly dependent on the interpretation, expertise and judgment of the humans doing the work for their successful completion. It implies that people work collaboratively on single activities and that dependencies between activities are also coordinated by people in a dynamic and ad-hoc fashion. Different participants of different organizations do not have necessarily common goals, but their efforts need to be unified and synchronized by providing awareness and feedback mechanisms. Disaster management is a special case of a domain that requires the management of highly dynamic unstructured processes to coordinate people and teams from multiple organizations distributed between different command centers and the field. Results can be seen as an important contribution to the BPM community [2,3,1]. Our research is grounded in a study of process management within the SoKNOS project in section 2 [4]. This project mainly aims at integrating the systems of different command centers of public

R. Meersman et al. (Eds.): OTM 2010, Part I, LNCS 6426, pp. 186–203, 2010.

safety organizations in a disaster response. Real world studies have shown that a real-time overview of the activities and dependencies between organizations in a disaster is beneficial [5,6]. We have found out that the traditional view of sequential processes is limited with respect to unstructured processes [7]. This led us to the development of a new model for coordinating and executing disaster response activities in section 3. Its emphasis is different from traditional BPM approaches, which control and structure whole processes. It is about awareness and feedback of activities as well as the management of temporal dependencies. The model can be collaboratively defined and executed ad-hoc by integrating shared activities of different stakeholders cross hierarchies and organizations. We describe the formal foundation of the model using Allen's interval algebra and how it can be verified and executed. In section 4 we explain how our model is implemented in the collaboration infrastructure Google Wave. We discuss comments of domain experts about our approach section 5. Finally, we describe future research directions in the last section.

2 Domain Study

We describe the investigation that we have conducted in the field BPM for disaster management in subsection 2.1. Disasters should be differentiated from emergencies by the scale of the considered event, the number of people and organizations involved, the evolving nature of the events and also the inability of existing plans to cope with them [8]. Recent news gave us examples of such events like the earthquakes in Haiti or Chile. In subsection 2.2 we describe the state of art regarding BPM and crisis management. Finally, we provide a scenario in subsection 2.3, which is used as an example throughout the paper.

2.1 BPM for Disaster Management

To conduct this study, we investigated the requirements of the disaster management domain in general, within the SoKNOS project [4] and participated in workshops and interviews with disaster management stakeholders in Germany. We evaluated with them also the use of business process modeling languages for disaster response management using event-driven process chains (EPC) [9]. It is mandatory to model a process in order to support its coordination by a system. Together with a senior police commander, we modeled the response process to a train accident with hazardous material threatening a residential area nearby. Fig. 1 shows the process model immediately after the interview. We show only a few activities in detail due to space restrictions. In the first half a special organizational structure is created for responding to the disaster. The second half describes the actual response at a very high level. The model still did not provide a useful excerpt of the reality. Basically it shows that many activities are running in parallel. The process model does not deal with dynamically evolving situations requiring creation of new activities by anyone involved in the process (even new participants). For example, a fire fighter gets injured and his colleagues

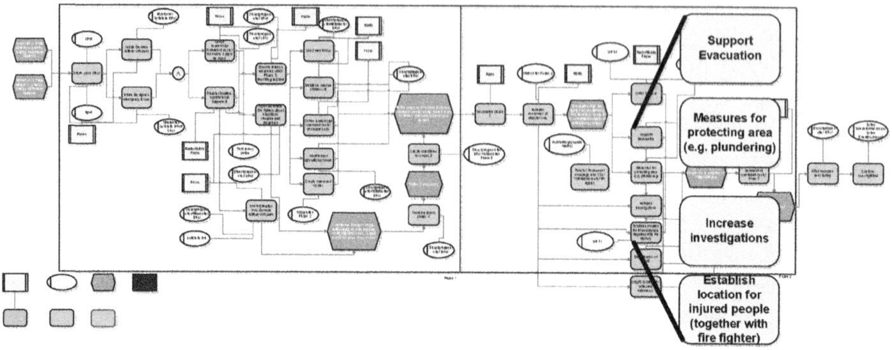

Fig. 1. Results of Modeling Disaster Response Processes using a Business Process Modeling Language

rescue him before continuing fighting the fire. It does not deal with the integration of activities of other hierarchy layers, e.g. teams in the field giving feedback on activities or creating new activities of relevance for the coordination by the command center. It also does not deal properly with the ad-hoc integration of other organizations in the process (illustrated in the first half). Only messages are sent to them with no further explanation (e.g. what they do with it) and feedback. The use of gateways (e.g. XOR-gateway) or other advanced modeling constructs make the model more complex, because many described alternatives are irrelevant in a specific situation. It unnecessarily limits the choices that can be made to the alternatives prescribed in the model and prevents creativity. This is an unrealistic assumptions for dynamic situations involving unstructured processes [6]. In particular, it does not seem to be very useful for supporting the temporal coordination of the activities during the disaster response. Temporal coordination is important to synchronize the execution of different activities of different organizations. Given these results, it is not surprising that the disaster response plans from fire fighters and police from the SoKNOS project do not contain business process models or textual description of activity sequences. They cover mostly available resources, a textual description of generic activities and interfaces with other organizations. However, usually one or more of these things changes during a disaster [5,6] and this requires that the organizations collaboratively coordinate their activities. This way of planning is more adequate for dynamic scenarios where the evolution of the situation cannot be prescribed. This can be seen in current practices of disaster management, but has also be proven by studies (e.g. several studies conducted by the Disaster Research Center of the University of Delaware [8]).

Other modeling attempts with three other public safety organizations showed the same results, even when using other modeling notations, such as the Business Process Modeling Notation (BPMN). This is not surprising, because research has shown that they are used similarly [10].

2.2 Related Research

Georgakopoulos et al. [11] and Fahland et al. [12] propose a scenario based approach for describing and executing processes. Depending on the situation different scenarios can be composed dynamically to represent the process. These are more suitable for managing predictable scenarios, which is not the case of a disaster. De Leoni et al. [13] adapt emergency processes automatically if the context, described in situation calculus, changes. They rely on modeling activity sequences and the context in detail, which makes it more suitable for predictable scenarios. The approach in [14] is similar. Based on our interactions with disaster response stake holders, we consider both approaches as too time and resource intensive for a disaster response. Reijers et al. analyze different resource scheduling mechanisms for workflow systems in emergency management [2]. They assume routine emergencies, standard business process models and no unexpected situations (e.g. failure of activities or unexpected extension of the crisis). Flexible business process management systems have been applied to the emergency management domain (e.g. [15]). They describe predictable routine emergencies. As mentioned before, business process models are not suitable to model a disaster response, which is about collaboration and coordination of activities with temporal dependencies. Our research confirms related research [12,16,13,11].

Ad-hoc or flexible workflow systems (e.g. [17,18,19,20,21,22]) rely on traditional business process models and thus have the same limitations with respect to coordinating disaster response activities mentioned before. Many of these limitations hold also for declarative process management approaches (e.g. [23,24]), but correct modeling requires also a lot of experience and time. They are also still very close to the workflow paradigm by describing a schema and instances. We are more interested in an ad-hoc collaborative approach. We also investigated disaster management software (e.g. the SAP Defense Force & Public Security system [25] or Sahana [26]), but they do not support temporal coordination of disaster response processes explicitly (i.e. by modeling, executing and monitoring them).

All these approaches consider predictable routine scenarios and structured business processes consisting of activity sequences using one centralized system. We argued before and confirmed in our interviews that modeling business processes is not suitable for disaster response processes [7]. This also means existing (flexible) systems using business process models are not suitable for coordinating unstructured processes in the disaster response. There is a need for a model for coordinating activities more closely to reality and not focusing on isolated processes. It should be able to (re-)combine activities in an ad-hoc manner crossing hierarchies and organizations [27], management of temporal dependencies and provide activity awareness for all stakeholders.

2.3 Scenario

The scenario in Fig. 2 is part of a larger case study derived from real flood disasters, established together with end users, such as fire fighter and police, in

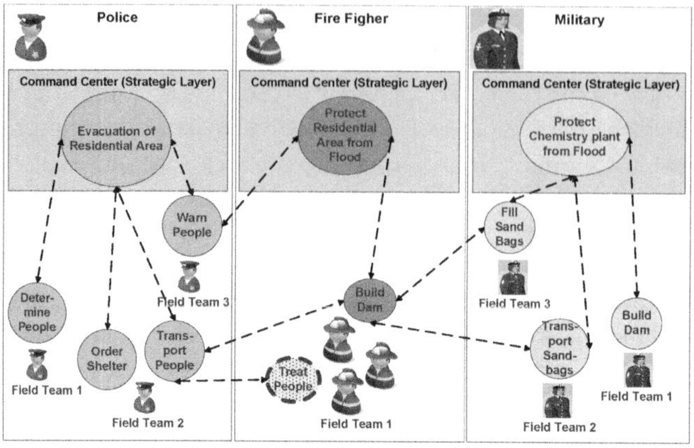

Fig. 2. Scenario

the SoKNOS project [4]. It will be used throughout the paper as an example. A residential area and a chemistry plant are threatened by a flood. Three organizations are responding to the disaster: police, fire fighter and military. Each organization has a command center and one or more teams in the field performing activities. In more complex disasters (cross regions/state/countries) more command centers are established (e.g. command center of the state) supporting the coordination of command centers of other organizations. These command centers do not build a hierarchical structure, but a network of organizations, which need to unify and synchronize their efforts [28]. Command centers communicate with each other by exchanging messages about, for example, the situation, what activities they are aware of or what the status of these activities is. In this use case, the police is responsible for evacuating the residential area. The fire fighters are building a dam to protect the residential area from the flood. The military is filling sandbags and transporting them to the disaster side. These sandbags are used by the fire fighters and the military to build a dam. Different kinds of activities are managed differently. For example, managing logistics activities, such as transporting sandbags, is different from evacuation activities, such as warning people. The relationship between activities can be described using temporal relationships (e.g. overlapping of activities). Some typical problems occurring when there is lack of coordination are, for example, no or too many sandbags arrive at the disaster site, transports fail, double efforts or no efforts etc. New activities can occur to cope with the situation. For example, it might happen that the fire fighters have to treat injured people of an evacuated area. Thus, there is a need for a better support for coordination to distribute and control the activities as well as their temporal relationships. It needs to provide the different stakeholder with enhanced situational awareness and to overcome the typical limitations of message-based exchange of the current situation/status. The proposed solutions from the BPM field do not seem to cope with these requirements. This is why we are proposing a new model that aims to answer this need.

3 A Coordination Model for Activities

We describe in this section the model for ad-hoc coordination of activities with temporal dependencies. The core idea of this model is that it is not imposed by the command center, but that all parts of a hierarchy (e.g. people in the field) and different organizations have influence on it. It has its foundation in Weick's sense-making theory [5] as well as Klein's work on naturalistic decision-making [6]. Both theories are grounded in real disasters and interviews with domain experts in disaster management and other domains, such as military, health care or complex engineering processes. In the sense-making theory people make sense out of what is going on and when they detect inconsistencies or ambiguity they start to interact to create a mutual understanding of the situation. We focus in our model on activities and temporal dependencies between activities as well as their violation during execution. Violation of dependencies needs to be managed by the users and/or the system. The idea for focusing on activities is also motivated by other disaster researcher, who define disasters as social constructions [29]. There, a disaster is defined by the activities humans execute to respond to a disaster. In the first subsection, we provide a description of the model. Then, we describe how this description can be verified to avoid inconsistent models. In the third subsection, we explain how activities are executed and how violation of temporal dependencies can be detected and managed during the execution. Although we describe this in a sequential manner, it is possible to do all this at same time, i.e. there is not a distinguishable modeling, verification and execution phase. There is a continuum of activity creation and execution that may occur all along the disaster. Finally, we show on an example based on our scenario how a system built on this model could actually be used.

3.1 Modeling

We distinguish between three model elements: activity type, activity and temporal dependency. The activity type describes the states of a management lifecycle of an activity and governance roles. For example, a logistic activity has different states in the management lifecycle in comparison to a more simple activity in the field (e.g. fighting fire). The activity, based on an activity type, describes disaster response activities. A temporal dependency can be established between states of different activities. It is qualitative (e.g. when activity "'Protect Area" is executed then the activity "Treat injured People" in this area can be executed). This is easier to define and agree on than providing concrete times (e.g. 5 hours and 5 minutes). Deadlines can still be integrated in our model, but this does not change the general concept. We do not use gateways, because they are difficult to model correctly ad-hoc and introduce unnecessary complexity. Different execution paths can be defined using the activity type instead. Our dependency model is able to reflect the temporal relations in a disaster response more adequately than typical sequential dependencies found in business process models, because it provides a greater variety of dependencies.

Definition 1. An *activity type* $at_d = (S, st, se, f, G)$ represents the management lifecycle of an activity with S is a finite set of activity states, $st \in S$ describes the start state of an activity type, $se \in S$ describes the end state of an activity type (i.e. a state where no further transition is possible), $st \neq se$ a start state is not an end state and $f : S \rightarrow S$ is a transition function defining the possible transitions from one state to another for one activity type. The lifecycle must not contain strongly connected components, because they can lead to confusion (e.g. an activity is re-executed although it has been finished before).

The specification of the activity type can be extended by governance rules G. They describe who can transit from one state to another. For example, an activity can be created by the command center that will be accountable for its execution. The responsibility to execute the activity will be given to someone on the field. Decision for cancellation or failure will be based on these roles. Modeling the activity type allows to intuitively specify deviations and to plan them in advance (e.g. activity "Build Dam" failed and this starts the execution of activity "Evacuate Area") as we will see later. Different kinds of activity types can be used in a given setting. They differ mostly by their life cycle and their governance rules. Some can be very simple (start, execute, terminate), some can be more complex and require more detailed planning and approval phases. Fig. 3 illustrates an example for such an activity type. The white circle describes the start state and the black circle describes an end state. Other states are "Plan", "Execute", "Idle", "Fail", "Cancel" and "Finish".

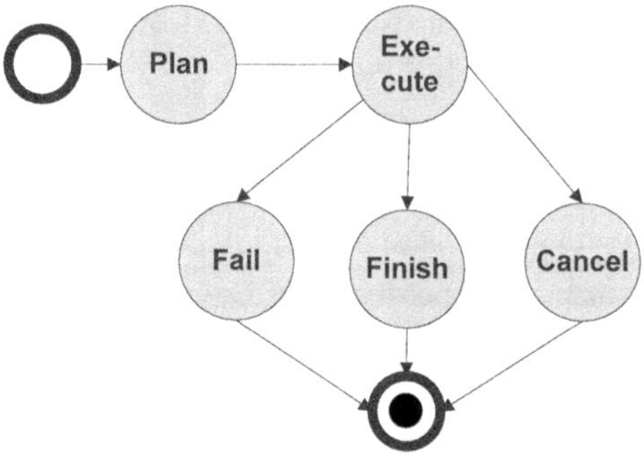

Fig. 3. Example for an activity type without governance rules

Definition 2. An *activity* is defined as $a_i = (uid, name, cs, cat)$ where uid is a unique identifier of the activity, $name$ describes the activity, $cs \in SA$ is the current state of the activity. On creation it must be the start state st of an activity type. $cat \in AT = (at_1, .., at_n)$ one activity type in the set of existing activity types.

An activity is by default independent from other activities. That means they can change their state in parallel without affecting other activities. However, a

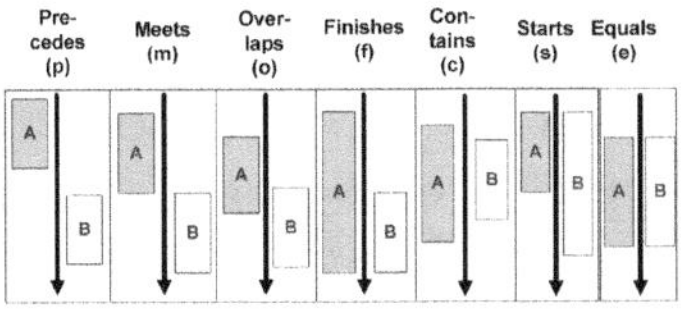

Fig. 4. Temporal dependencies between states of activities

dependency can be established between activities, if it is perceived by the user as important and if the user is aware of this dependency.

Definition 3. A *temporal dependency* is defined as $d_i = (a_s, s_s, a_d, s_d, type)$ with a_s is the source activity, s_s is the state of the source activity, a_d is the destination activity, s_d is the state of the destination activity and *type* is the type of temporal dependency. A temporal dependency can be established between two states of two different activities. Temporal dependencies are the core mechanism used to represent explicitly coordination between activities in our model. It is not necessary to connect every activity directly or indirectly via dependencies, i.e. the users of the system can focus on the most important ones as perceived by him/her. We use Allen's proposed time interval relationships for describing different types of temporal dependencies [30]. This provides a great level of flexibility regarding the kind of relationship that can be established between two states of an activity. A *type* describes the dependency (i.e. describes one or more of Allen's time interval relationships). This will be explained later in the subsection Execution.

Fig. 4 illustrates seven of them, because the other six are just the inverse of the first six. The dependencies have some interesting characteristics: they are qualitative, exhaustive and distinct. Temporal dependencies in highly dynamic scenarios are easier to define when they are qualitative, i.e. we do not need to specify exact times (e.g. 5 hours and 5 minutes). It is not always possible to define exact times, because this information is simply not available or subject to continuous change. As mentioned before, our model does not prevent to specify exact times. In our case, this means a temporal dependency of the state of one activity is relative to the state of another activity. This is different from BPM, where an activity depends only on the output of one or more activities. For instance, a rescue activity can only be executed during the execution of an activity for protecting an area. When we apply the notion of Allen's time interval relationships to the use case then we can describe the temporal dependency between the state "Execute" of the activity "Warn people" and the state "Execute" of the activity "Protect area" as "contains".

Further type of dependencies exist (e.g. resource or data dependencies), but we focus here on temporal dependencies, because they can be applied to all kind of activities and are important. The model can be extended by further dependencies, if there is a need.

3.2 Verification

It must be ensured that all inconsistent specifications of the model, which can be detected before adding a dependency to the model, are forbidden. An example for an inconsistent model, would be a simple model with three activities "A", "B" and "C". A dependency "precedes" is established between "A" and "B". Another dependency "precedes" is established between "B" and "C". Finally a dependency "precedes" is established between "C" and "A". This basically means that activity "A" (or any other activity) precedes itself.

Allen proposed in his work the path consistency algorithm for reasoning about a network of interval relationships [30]. Reasoning means that the algorithm is able to derive all other temporal constraints from a given temporal constraint network. This algorithm can be also used to detect an inconsistent network of temporal constraints. A constraint network can be constructed from our model by representing the transition of the states within one activity using the meets (m) constraint. Temporal dependencies between activity states of different activities can be represented using the corresponding constraints (i.e. all basic time interval relationships). A network is inconsistent if it is not possible to find a temporal constraint between nodes (or states) which fits with the other dependencies in the model. The path consistency algorithm is not complete when considering all possible compositions of time interval relationships between two nodes [30]. However, it is complete for some subsets of them. We restrict our model to the Ord-Horn-Class, which is such a subset of composition of time interval relationships (more details and detailed analysis of this class can be found in [31]). It contains all the basic relationships mentioned before (i.e. it allows verification of our model). The composed constraints it does not support are not seen as relevant for the practice [30] and are not needed for our model since we only rely on the basic dependencies mentioned above. A complete version of the path consistency algorithm for verifying a constraint network is a NP-hard problem [30]. Our model only requires the compositions of time interval relationships defined in the Ord-Horn-Class. This means we can use the path consistency algorithm by Allen and it is complete for this subset [31]. This path consistency algorithm has a computational complexity of $O(N^3)$ assuming a given constraint network, whereby N is the number of connected nodes (states of activities). Adding a new connected node (e.g. by establishing a dependency in our model) and verifying the model leads to a computational complexity of $O(N)$ [30]. This is acceptable for our case. Another interesting aspect of the formalism is that it allows to change (i.e. add activities and dependencies) and verify the model during execution, because it does not depend on a specific execution state. This is very difficult to achieve with other well-known formalisms, such as Petri nets [32].

3.3 Execution

Execution of activities is about changing the state of an activity. This may violates temporal dependencies connected to the activity. We describe how the violation of temporal dependencies can be managed and how it can be detected.

Managing Violation of Dependencies. A dependency can be violated, if one or more activities changes their state contradictory to the dependency (e.g. activity "Build Dam" changes into a state "Execute", although activity "Transport Sandbags" was supposed to change into the state "Execute" before). There are two options to manage this: (1) State changes that violate dependencies can be prevented, (2) violated dependencies can be displayed to the users. Although usually the latter treatment is preferred, when managing disaster response activities, we plan to support also the other case, so that our approach can be applied to more different domains and also work with automated activities. Option (1) can lead to a situation, where the system cannot continue execution, although not all activities are in end states. We ensured in the verification section that this cannot happen by defining all dependencies as conflict-free. Option (2) requires detection and displaying of violated dependencies. If a violated dependency is visualized then user has to deal with it outside the system. After resolving the issue, the user can deactivate the violated dependency.

Sometimes it is the case that dependency violation should be avoided. This means that one or more other activities should change into a desired state. The user might be able to do this or ask other users (or machines in case of automated activities) to do this, because he/she has not the right to do so. For example, if the activity "Build Dam" changes into state "Execute" before the activity "Transport Sandbags" changes into the state "Execute" then the system can trigger itself (if possible) or ask the corresponding role of activity "Transport Sandbags" to do a state change into state "Execute". If this is not possible then the corresponding users are notified that the dependency is violated or if the dependency needs to be enforced then it is not possible to perform the initial state change. This can be supported by a protocol in our system.

Detecting Violation of Dependencies. We describe the detection of violation of dependencies with algorithm 1. The algorithm checks all dependencies associated with all activities performing a state change (described in L). It allows, for example, detecting a violation if two or more activities have to be in the same state at the same time (this corresponds to the dependency

```
input  : List L of state changes of one or more activities
output: A set V of violated dependencies

dependencylist ← GetAllDependencies(L)
for i ← 0 to dependencylist.size - 1 do
    CheckDependency(dependencylist[i],L);
    if GetState(dependencylist[i] == violated) then
        V ← dependencylist[i]
    end
end
```

Algorithm 1. Detect violation of dependencies when executing activities "equals"). Execution has a complexity of $O(M)$ whereby M is the number of dependencies associated with the activities of which the state needs to be changed. This is also acceptable for our use case. Our approach does not rely on specifying quantitative time (e.g. [22]), inflexible enforcement of the constraints (e.g. [33]) or defining fixed workflows (e.g. [21]) to execute the model. The first one contradicts Allen's idea of qualitative constraints and it is very difficult in a disaster with a dynamic evolving situation to define exact times (e.g. activity "Build Dam" will be executed 5 hours and 5 minutes). They would be also subject to continuous change and disagreement between different organizations. The latter ones require defining sequential business process models, which do not work well for disaster response processes as we have shown before.

Detecting violation of dependencies (CheckDependency) works as follows: Different types of dependencies are represented as different finite state machines. State changes are input for the finite state machine. Depending on the input they change into the state "Violate" or "Neutral".

Definition 4. The type of a dependency is defined as $type = (\Upsilon, \Omega, s, t)$ with Υ is the input alphabet (all accepted state changes of the activities involved in the dependency), Ω is the finite set of states of the dependency, s is the current state and $t : \Omega \times \Upsilon \rightarrow \Omega$ is the transition function.

Definition 5. The transition function t supports the following constructs and their combination: $A : Sa$ activity A changes into the state Sa, $\neg(A : Sa)$ activity A changes into any other successor state of Sa, $A : Sa \wedge B : Sb$ activity A changes into the state Sa and activity B changes into the state Sb or $else$ any other state change of activity A or B.

Example. Fig. 5 provides an example for a finite state machine representing the dependency "overlapped by". The dependency is established between an activity "A" in the state "Sa" and an activity "B" in the state "Sb". Initially, the finite state machine is in the state "Neutral". This means the dependency is not violated. If activity "B" changes in the state "Sb" then finite state machine of the dependency changes into the state "Violated". If activity "B" changes now to any other state than "Sb" then the finite state machine of the dependency transits to the state "Neutral".

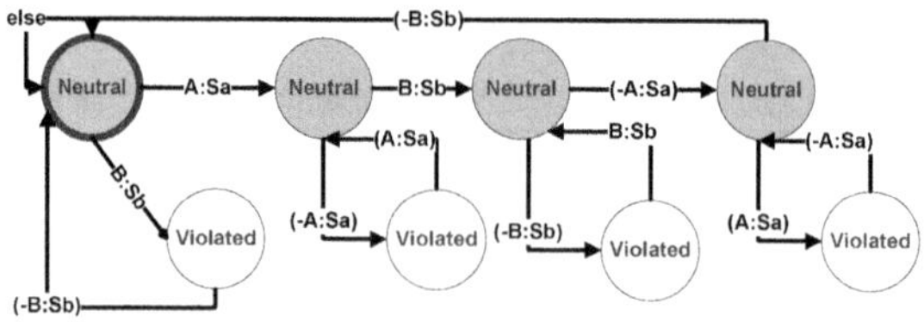

Fig. 5. Finite state machine describing the dependency "overlapped by"

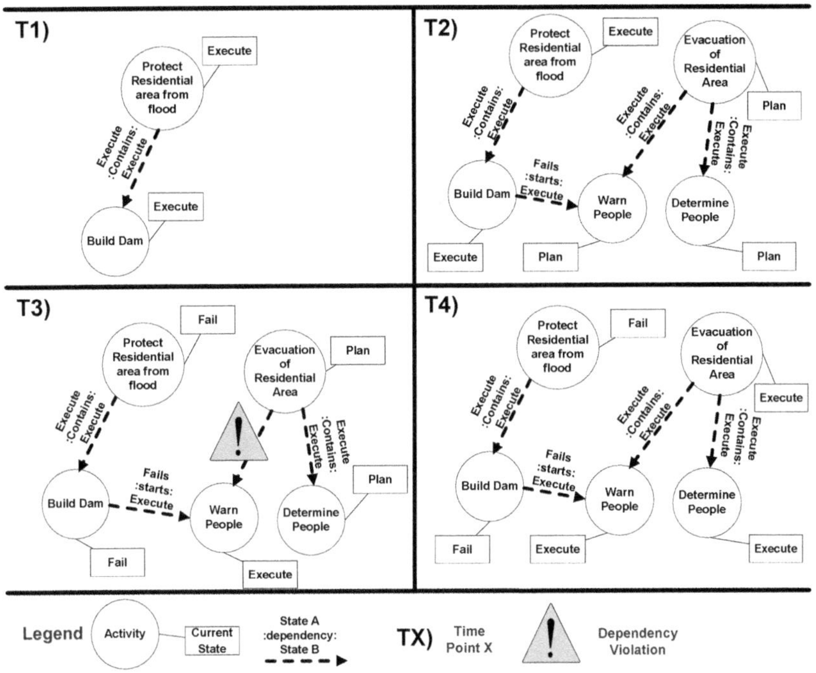

Fig. 6. Example for modeling and executing the scenario

3.4 Example in Context of the Use Case

We demonstrate an example of the evolution of our model in Fig. 6 based on the use case described before (cf. Fig. 2). The evolution of the situation is illustrated in four phases. In phase one, the fire fighters have created the activities "Protect Residential area flood" and "Build Dam". The first activity is on the strategic command center level and the second activity is an activity in the field. Both have a dependency "contains" between them in state "Execute". Both activities are currently in the state "Execute". In the second phase, the activities "Evacuation of Residential Area", "Warn People" and "Determine People" added to the model in the state "Plan" by the police. A dependency "starts" is established between the state "Fail" of activity "Build Dam" and the state "Execute" of the activity "Warn people" of the police. In the third phase, the activity "Build Dam" enters the state "Fail" and "Warn people" enters the state "Execute". This leads to violation of the dependency "contains" between the activity "Warn people" and "Evacuation of Residential Area", because the latter is still in the state "Plan". In the fourth phase, this is corrected by changing the state of activity "Evacuation of Residential Area" to the state "Execute". The modeling is usually not done using one system, but there can be many different systems and models exchanging activities and establishing dependencies in a decentralized manner as illustrated in [7]. This means that different organizations are allowed to define different dependencies to activities and not all dependencies and activities are shared. This is scope of another paper. We do not envision one large model where all organizations model their activities and dependencies. Several models can exist (e.g. one by each organization) and one shared activity can be part of several models [7]. This fits to the requirements of the disaster management domain. There we have several independent organizations and each organization has their own tools, but they need to coordinate with each other in a de-centralized setting.

4 Solution Design in the Open Wave Federation Context

We have implemented our model as an extension to the collaborative infrastructure Google Wave [34]. It allows for a decentralized infrastructure (e.g. every organization can have its own server) and it enables real-time interaction between the participants of different organizations (i.e. servers) based on the OpenWave Federation Protocol [35]. This provides us also a solution for sharing of activities. A web-based interface, which can be accessed by any standard compliant browser, is another important requirement of the end users. Google Wave has been used in previous disasters (e.g. in the Haiti earthquake [36]) and other software is able to inter-operate with it (e.g. SAP Streamwork). In the following subsections, we introduce briefly Google Wave and how it can be extended. Afterwards, we describe how we implemented our model as part of this.

4.1 Preliminaries

The Open Wave Federation Protocol supports communication between different Wave servers. Participants register to one of these servers. Wave servers host documents, which can be collaboratively edited by different participants. A collaborative document is called a "Wave". At any point in time participants can be added to a "Wave". It is replicated to all the servers of the participants. The server, which created the wave, holds the reference copy of the "Wave" and manages the distribution of updates to it using Operational Transformations [35]. A "Wave" can contain one or more "Wavelets". They have similar characteristics like a "Wave", but they can have their own set of participants. The reference copy of the "Wavelet" can be managed by a different server than the one managing the reference copy of the "Wave". Google Wave and the Open Wave Federation Protocol support two extensions: "Gadget" and "Robot". A "Gadget" can be inserted into a "Wavelet" and it is basically a web-based graphical user interface to support new collaborative functionality (e.g. modeling of processes). A "Robot" is added to a "Wave" or "Wavelet" the same way as a participant and they link the outer world (e.g. a stock market feed, social networks or other "Waves") with a "Wave" and/or "Wavelet". It represents automated behavior.

4.2 Implementation

We represent one activity as a "Wave", the so-called "Activity-Wave". Participants can be added to it. For example, if a fire fighter in the field is rescued then an "Activity-Wave" can be created for this activity. People in the command center can be invited to it and they can integrate it in their models (see below). An "Activity-Wave" contains at least two "Gadgets": The "Gadget-Activity-Specification" and the "Gadget-Activity-ParticipantView". The "Gadget-Activity-Specification" allows to specify the activity name, the activity type and governance roles (This is part of the governance concept we did not describe in detail here). Each "Model-Wave", the activity is modeled in, has an own "Wavelet" in the "Activity-Wave" where participants of this "Model-Wave" define the current state of the activity in the model using the "Gadget-Activity-ParticipantView". This allows detection of conflicting perceived states and allows participants continuing to change the state of a shared activity in case of disconnection. This requires special synchronization mechanisms not detailed here.

A "Model-Wave" is a "Wave" containing the "Gadget-CurrentModelView" which allows modeling activities and dependencies. Activities modeled in this "Gadget" are linked to an "Activity-Wave". By clicking on these modeled activities we can switch to the linked "Activity-Wave".

The "Robot-UProMan" is participant in the "Activity-Waves" and the "Model-Waves". It verifies the model using the path consistency algorithm described before. It displays a warning in the "Gadget-CurrentModelView" if the model is inconsistent. It manages violation of dependencies during execution of activities as described above. Logging of the execution of activities is also done by this robot.

Fig. 7 illustrates a "Model-Wave" (left) as well as an "Activity-Wave" (right) of one activity ("Transport Sandbags") in the model. The "Model-Wave" is managed by the commander of the fire fighter. It contains the activities "Protect Area from Flood", "Fill Sandbags", "Build Dam" and "Transport Sandbags". Initially, all activities are in the state "Plan". There are three dependencies "contains" from the state "Execute" of the activity "Protect Area from Flood" to the three other activities in state "Execute". The activity "Transport Sandbags" has been changed into state "Execute", which violates the dependency "contains" to the activity "Protect Area From Flood", because it is still in state "Plan". It turns out that the person responsible for transport already initiated it, although the situation is still assessed. The violation is visualized by a red dependency and a warning sign. For example, the commander can now change the activity "Protect Area from Flood" into the state "Execute" or start a discussion in the "Wave" of the activity "Transport Sandbags". Participants can enrich models or activities by adding text or other gadgets to the "Wave". This is illustrated in the "Model-Wave" where a user inserted a map of the area.

The "Robot-UProMan" also supports further functionality such as execution of activities part of several models (e.g. in an inter-organisational setting) as well as re-synchronization of activities and models after disconnection or conflicting states of an activity, which we did not detail in this paper.

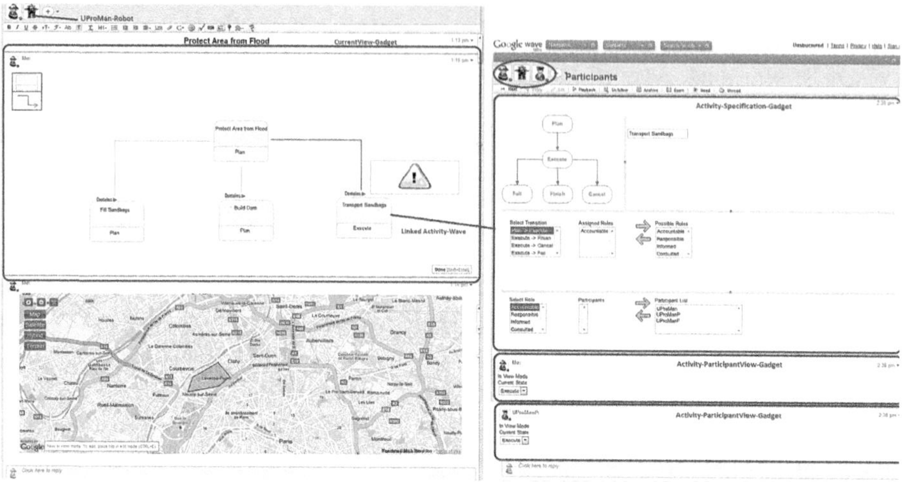

Fig. 7. Screenshot of our Prototype

5 Discussion

We let domain-experts in disaster management comment our approach, by presenting it to them, to find out how our approach is seen in comparison with other systems or concepts currently used for activity management and what the limitations of such an approach are. End users currently use means such as whiteboards, web-based mission diaries or email. The problem is that they can become even in smaller disasters quickly counterproductive (e.g. many mails with different context and not related with each other). We evaluated the model together with commanders of three fire fighter departments in France and in the US as well as with an international humanitarian aid organization in Germany. The interview with the fire fighters in France was a face to face interview of about three hours. The other interviews were one hour phone interviews, but we shared our screen via Internet to illustrate the approach.

The model of activities and temporal dependencies seems to be a concept familiar to the end users: "we use time lines as markers for future action, we have what we call trigger points, when the incident advances to a certain point, it triggers other things, so that would fit into your model as well, using time lines, connecting inter-dependencies" (Fire Fighter Commander Southern California).

It was highlighted that this model can overcome the limitations of web-based mission diaries used at the moment: "we have an incident action plan which each entity utilizes and keeps track of their system and activities, more or less on a manual basis and entering who is command and what actions are taken [..] it outlines future actions and intended actions for the next twelve hours operational period [..] (but it) does not alert you to inter-connection failures [..]" (Fire Fighter Commander Southern California). In a mission diary entries are sequential and not related (e.g. by temporal dependencies). This leads to cases where someone might read outdated information and is not aware of this.

The interviews confirmed that the model and the implementation could be useful in the following situations: complex situation, large geographical area, many organizations involved and long enduring response. Examples given by the end users were low-pacing floods or snow storms. They also described the limitations of information system support for the disaster response. There are situations, such as wildfires, where it is very difficult for teams in the field to use any kind of information technology. In these situations they hardly use any communication devices and communication occurs infrequently. Nevertheless the approach can still be useful for command centers in these situations. These are positive indicators, but a detailed study with a stable version of the prototype including some more usability features is part of future research.

6 Conclusion and Further Research

Unstructured processes introduce new technical challenges for supporting their coordination by a system. However, such support is seen as beneficial to be able to manage them. We analyzed the requirements for process management in the domain of disaster response management to challenge the concept of unstructured processes. In the beginning we invalidated together with end users the use of business process models for disaster response processes. We developed a generic model for coordination of activities with temporal dependencies. We demonstrated how the model can be verified using Allen's interval algebra and managed by a system. The model can be integrated with further views, e.g. resource view or geographical view. The model puts different emphasis on the benefits of BPM than traditional BPM approaches. Structuring of the process is more loosely fitting to the requirements of unstructured processes. Managing dependency violation, activity awareness and feedback are more important than controlling and enforcing a process within the system. Not all possible dependencies need to be modeled, but only the ones perceived as important by the users. The main difference is that it allows collaborative coordination of activities with temporal dependencies. All these features are reflected in the implementation leveraging the Google Wave collaboration infrastructure based on open standards. Although the results of our interviews look promising, we are going to conduct further evaluations. This will help us to identify further human and organizational limitations (e.g. scalability) of the model implemented in the prototype. The literature, describing the underlying human aspects of our model, suggests that results from disaster management can be applied to other domains with similar characteristics [6,5], e.g. military, project management or ad-hoc supply chains. From a technical perspective we want to investigate how our approach can work on the distributed level and how automated activities or coordinators (i.e. systems that create and manage models) can be integrated.

Acknowledgements. The research was partially funded by the German Federal Ministry of Education and Research under the promotional reference 01ISO7009 and by the French Ministry of Research within the RESCUE-IT project [37]. The authors take the responsibility for the content. We thank the domain experts for providing us detailed insights.

References

1. Olding, E., Rozwell, C.: Expand your bpm horizons by exploring unstructured processes. Technical Report G00172387, Gartner (2009)
2. Reijers, H.A., Jansen-Vullers, M.H., zur Muehlen, M., Appl, W.: Workflow management systems + swarm intelligence = dynamic task assignment for emergency management applications. In: Alonso, G., Dadam, P., Rosemann, M. (eds.) BPM 2007. LNCS, vol. 4714, pp. 125–140. Springer, Heidelberg (2007)
3. Bunker, D., Smith, S.: Disaster management and community warning systems: Inter-organsational collaboration and ict innovation. In: Pacific Asia Conference on Information Systems, PACIS (2009)
4. SoKNOS: Soknos (soa zur unterstützung von netzwerken im rahmen oeffentlicher sicherheit) (2009), `http://www.soknos.de` (retrieved 03.06.2009)
5. Weick, K.: Making Sense of the Organization. Blackwell, Malden (2000)
6. Klein, G.: Sources of Power: How People Make Decisions. MIT Press, Cambridge (1999)
7. Franke, J., Charoy, F.: Design of a collaborative disaster response process management system. In: 9th International Conference on the Design of Cooperative Systems (2010)
8. Quarantelli, E.: Emergent behavior at the emergency - time periods of disasters. Technical report, Disaster Research Center, University of Delaware (1983)
9. Scheer, A.W.: ARIS - Business Process Modeling, 3rd edn. Springer, Heidelberg (2000)
10. Recker, J.: Understanding Process Modelling Grammer Continuance - A Study of the Consequences of Representational Capabilities. PhD thesis, School of Information Systems, Queensland University of Technology, Brisbane, Australia (2008)
11. Georgakopoulos, D., Schuster, H., Baker, D., Cichocki, A.: Managing escalation of collaboration processes in crisis mititgation situations. In: 16th International Conference on Data Engineering (2000)
12. Fahland, D., Woith, H.: Towards process models for disaster response. In: Process Management for Highly Dynamic and Pervasive Scenarios (2008)
13. de Leoni, M., Mecella, M., De Giacomo, G.: Highly dynamic adaptation in process management systems through execution monitoring. In: Alonso, G., Dadam, P., Rosemann, M. (eds.) BPM 2007. LNCS, vol. 4714, pp. 182–197. Springer, Heidelberg (2007)
14. Zahoor, E., Perrin, O., Godart, C.: An integrated declarative approach to web services composition and monitoring. In: Vossen, G., Long, D.D.E., Yu, J.X. (eds.) WISE 2009. LNCS, vol. 5802, pp. 247–260. Springer, Heidelberg (2009)
15. Rüppel, U., Wagenknecht, A.: Improving emergency management by formal dynamic process-modelling. In: 24th Conference on Information Technology in Construction (2007)
16. Denning, P.J.: Infoglut. Communications of the ACM 49(7), 15–19 (2006)
17. Huth, C., Erdmann, I., Nastansky, L.: Groupprocess: using process knowledge from the participative design and practical operation of ad hoc processes for the design of structured workflows. In: 34th Annual Hawai International Conference on System Sciences (2001)

18. Grigori, D., Charoy, F., Godart, C.: Anticipation to enhance flexibility of workflow execution. In: Mayr, H.C., Lazanský, J., Quirchmayr, G., Vogel, P. (eds.) DEXA 2001. LNCS, vol. 2113, Springer, Heidelberg (2001)
19. van der Aalst, W., Weske, M., Grünbauer, D.: Case handling: A new paradigm for business process support. Data & Knowledge Engineering 53, 129–162 (2005)
20. Dadam, P., Reichert, M.: The adept project. Computer Science - Research and Development 23(2), 81–97 (2009)
21. Lu, R., Sadiq, S., Padmanabhan, V., Governatori, G.: Using a temporal constraint network for business process execution. In: 17th Australasian Database Conference (2006)
22. Kafeza, E., Karlapalem, K.: Gaining control over time in workflow management applications. In: Ibrahim, M., Küng, J., Revell, N. (eds.) DEXA 2000. LNCS, vol. 1873, Springer, Heidelberg (2000)
23. van der Aalst, W.M.P., Pesic, M.: Decserflow: Towards a truly declarative service flow language. In: Bravetti, M., Núñez, M., Zavattaro, G. (eds.) WS-FM 2006. LNCS, vol. 4184, pp. 1–23. Springer, Heidelberg (2006)
24. Leymann, F., Unger, T., Wagner, S.: On designing a people-oriented constraint-based workflow language. In: 2nd Central-European Workshop on Services and their Composition (2010)
25. SAP: Defense force & public security (dfps) system, `http://help.sap.com/content/documentation/industry/docu_is_ds.htm` (retrieved 03.06.2009)
26. Sahana: Free and open source disaster crisis management system (2009), `http://www.sahana.lk/` (retrieved retrieved 03.06.2009)
27. Franke, J., Charoy, F., Ulmer, C.: A model for temporal coordination of disaster response activities. In: 7th International Conference on Information Systems for Crisis Response and Management (2010)
28. Tierney, K., Trainor, J.: Networks and resilience in the world trade center disaster 2003-2004. In: MCEER: Research progress and accomplisments, Multidisciplinary Center for Earthquake Engineering Research (MCEER), pp. 157–172 (2004)
29. Perry, R.W., Quarantelli, E. (eds.): What is a Disaster? New Answers to Old Questions. Xlibris Corp. (2005)
30. Allen, J.F.: Maintaining knowledge about temporal intervals. Communications of the ACM 26(11), 832–843 (1983)
31. Nebel, B., Bürckert, H.J.: Reasoning about temporal relations: A maximal tractable subclass of allen's interval algebra. Journal of the ACM 42(1), 43–66 (1995)
32. Ellis, C., Keddara, K., Rozenberg, G.: Dynamic change within workflow systems. In: Conference on Organizational Computing Systems (1995)
33. Raposo, A.B., Magalhaes, L.P., Ricarte, I.L.: Petri nets based coordination mechanisms for multi-workflow environments. International Journal of Computer Systems Science & Engineering 15(5), 315–326 (2000)
34. Google: Google wave, `http://www.googlewave.com` (retrieved 27.05.2010)
35. Lassen, S., Thorogood, S.: Google wave federation architecture, `http://www.waveprotocol.org/whitepapers/google-wave-architecture` (retrieved 27.05.2010)
36. gwtips: Wavers collaborating for haiti, `http://gwtips.com/wavers-collaborating-for-haiti/` (retrieved 04.05.2010)
37. Schaad, A., Ulmer, C., Gomez, L.: Rescueit - sécurisation d'une chaine logistique internationale. In: Workshop Interdisciplinaire sur la Sécurité Globale (2010)

Generic Algorithms for Consistency Checking of Mutual-Exclusion and Binding Constraints in a Business Process Context

Mark Strembeck[1] and Jan Mendling[2]

[1] Vienna University of Economics and Business (WU Vienna), Austria
mark.strembeck@wu.ac.at
[2] Humboldt-Universität zu Berlin, Germany
jan.mendling@wiwi.hu-berlin.de

Abstract. In this paper, we present generic algorithms to ensure the consistency of mutual-exclusion and binding constraints in a business process context. We repeatedly identified the need for such generic algorithms in our real-world projects. Thus, the algorithms are a result of the experiences we gained in analyzing, designing, and implementing a number of corresponding software systems and tools. In particular, these algorithms check corresponding consistency requirements to prevent constraint conflicts and to ensure the design-time and runtime compliance of a process-related role-based access control (RBAC) model.

1 Introduction

Security properties such as mutual-exclusion and binding-of-duty play an increasingly important role in process-aware information systems [11]. In the context of business process management, *mutual exclusion* and *binding constraints* are an important means to assist the specification of business processes and to control the execution of workflows. In particular, they are used to enforce process-related separation of duty (SOD) and binding of duty (BOD) policies with respect to a corresponding role-based access control (RBAC) model (see, e.g., [1,3,4,17,18]). A number of approaches exist that allow for the formal specification and analysis of process-related access control policies and constraints (see, e.g., [2,8,17]). However, when building a software system we have to "translate" such formal approaches for the specification of access control policies and constraints to the (programming) language that is used to implement the respective system. With respect to the rapidly increasing importance of process-aware information systems, the correct implementation of corresponding consistency checks in these systems is an important issue.

In this paper, we present a set of algorithms that check and ensure the consistency of mutual-exclusion and binding constraints in a business process context. The definition of these algorithms was inspired by our real-world RBAC and role engineering projects, where we repeatedly identified the need for such generic (i.e. programming language independent) consistency checks. In particular, the algorithms result from the experiences we gained in the analysis, design, and implementation of corresponding software systems and tools (see, e.g., [6,9,10,13,14,15,16]).

R. Meersman et al. (Eds.): OTM 2010, Part I, LNCS 6426, pp. 204–221, 2010.

The remainder of this paper is structured as follows. Section 2 gives an overview of mutual-exclusion and binding constraints. Next, Section 3 defines the essential elements of process-related RBAC models and specifies requirements for design-time and runtime consistency of these models. Sections 4 and 5 present our algorithms for ensuring the consistency of mutual-exclusion and binding constraints in a process-related RBAC model. Section 6 discusses related work and Section 7 concludes the paper.

2 Mutual Exclusion and Binding Constraints

Separation of duty (SOD) constraints enforce conflict of interest policies [1,5,7]. Conflict of interest arises as a result of the simultaneous assignment of two mutual exclusive tasks or roles to the same subject. Thus, the definition of mutual exclusive artifacts is a well-known mechanism to enforce separation of duty. *Mutual exclusive* roles or tasks result from the division of powerful rights or responsibilities to prevent fraud and abuse. An example is the common practice to separate the "controller" role and the "chief buyer" role in medium-sized and large companies. In this context, a *task-based SOD constraint* is a constraint that considers task order and task history in a particular process instance to decide if a certain subject or role is allowed to perform a certain task [3,17,19]. Task-based SOD constraints can be static or dynamic. A *static task-based SOD constraint* can be enforced by defining that two statically mutual exclusive (SME) tasks must never be assigned to the same role and must never be performed by the same subject. This constraint is global with respect to *all process instances* in the corresponding information system. In contrast, a *dynamic task-based SOD constraint* refers to individual process instances and can be enforced by defining that two dynamically mutual exclusive (DME) tasks must never be performed by the same subject in the *same process instance*. In other words: two DME tasks can be assigned to the same role. However, to complete a process instance which includes two DME tasks, one needs at least two different subjects. This means, although a subject might possess a role which includes all permissions to perform two DME tasks, a DME constraint enforces that the same subject does not perform both tasks in the same process instance.

Binding of Duty (BOD) constraints [4,17,18] define a connection between two (or more) tasks so that a subject (or role) who performed one of these tasks must also perform the corresponding related task(s). In other words, in a given process instance two "bound tasks" must always be performed by the same subject/role, e.g. because of specific knowledge the subject/role acquires while performing the first of two bound tasks, for reasons of organization-internal processing standards, or to simplify interaction with other process stakeholders. Moreover, BOD can be subdivided in subject-based and role-based constraints. A *subject-based BOD constraint* then defines that the *same individual* who performed the first task must also perform the bound task(s). In contrast to that, a *role-based BOD constraint* defines that bound tasks must be performed by members of the *same role*, but not necessarily by the same individual. Throughout the paper, we will use the terms *subject-binding* and *role-binding* as synonyms for subject-based BOD constraints and role-based BOD constraints respectively.

3 Basic Definitions for Process-Related RBAC Models

The context of a workflow system is given through process instances and corresponding task instances. In this paper, we therefore focus on mutual-exclusion and binding constraints defined on the task level. Definition 1 specifies the essential elements of process-related RBAC models and their basic interrelations.

Definition 1 (Process-related RBAC Model). *A Process-related RBAC Model* $PRM = (E, Q, D)$ *where* $E = S \cup R \cup P_T \cup P_I \cup T_T \cup T_I$ *refers to pairwise disjoint sets of the model,* $Q = rh \cup rsa \cup tra \cup es \cup er \cup ar \cup pi \cup ti$ *to mappings that establish relationships, and* $D = sb \cup rb \cup sme \cup dme$ *to binding and mutual-exclusion constraints, such that:*

- *For the sets of the meta model:*
  - *An element of* S *is called* Subject. $S \neq \emptyset$.
  - *An element of* R *is called* Role. $R \neq \emptyset$.
  - *An element of* P_T *is called* Process Type. $P_T \neq \emptyset$.
  - *An element of* P_I *is called* Process Instance. $P_I \neq \emptyset$.
  - *An element of* T_T *is called* Task Type. $T_T \neq \emptyset$.
  - *An element of* T_I *is called* Task Instance.
- *For the partial mappings of the meta model (*$\mathcal{P}$ *refers to the power set):*
  1. *The mapping* $rh : R \mapsto \mathcal{P}(R)$ *is called* role hierarchy. *For* $rh(r_s) = R_j$ *we call* r_s senior role *and* R_j *the set of direct* junior roles. *The transitive closure* rh^* *defines the inheritance in the role-hierarchy such that* $rh^*(r_s) = R_{j^*}$ *includes all direct and transitive junior-roles that the senior-role* r_s *inherits from. The role-hierarchy is cycle-free, i.e. for each* $r \in R : rh^*(r) \cap \{r\} = \emptyset$.
  2. *The mapping* $rsa : S \mapsto \mathcal{P}(R)$ *is called* role-to-subject assignment. *For* $rsa(s) = R_s$ *we call* s subject *and* $R_s \subseteq R$ *the set of* roles assigned to this subject *(the set of roles owned by* s*). The mapping* $rsa^{-1} : R \mapsto \mathcal{P}(S)$ *returns all subjects assigned to a role (the set of subjects owning a role).*

     This assignment implies a mapping role ownership $rown : S \mapsto \mathcal{P}(R)$, *such that for each subject* s *all direct and inherited roles are included, i.e.* $rown(s) = \bigcup_{r \in rsa(s)} rh^*(r) \cup rsa(s)$. *The mapping* $rown^{-1} : R \mapsto \mathcal{P}(S)$ *returns all subjects assigned to a role (directy or transitively via a role-hierarchy).*
  3. *The mapping* $es : T_I \mapsto S$ *is called* executing-subject mapping. *For* $es(t) = s$ *we call* s *the* executing subject *and* t *is called* executed task instance.
  4. *The mapping* $er : T_I \mapsto R$ *is called* executing-role mapping. *For* $er(t) = r$ *we call* r *the* executing role *and* t *is called* executed task instance.
  5. *The mapping* $tra : R \mapsto \mathcal{P}(T_T)$ *is called* task-to-role assignment. *For* $tra(r) = T_r$ *we call* r role *and* $T_r \subseteq T_T$ *is called the set of* tasks assigned to r. *The mapping* $tra^{-1} : T_T \mapsto \mathcal{P}(R)$ *returns the set of roles a task is assigned to (the set of roles owning a task).*

     This assignment implies a mapping task ownership $town : R \mapsto \mathcal{P}(T_T)$, *such that for each role* r *the tasks inherited from its junior-roles are included, i.e.* $town(r) = \bigcup_{r_{inh} \in rh^*(r)} tra(r_{inh}) \cup tra(r)$. *The mapping* $town^{-1} : T_T \mapsto \mathcal{P}(R)$ *returns the set of roles a task is assigned to (directly or transitively via a role-hierarchy).*

6. *The mapping* $ti : (T_T \times P_I) \mapsto \mathcal{P}(T_I)$ *is called* task instantiation. *For* $ti(t_T, p_I) = T_i$ *we call* $T_i \subseteq T_I$ *set of* task instances, $t_T \in T_T$ *is called* task type *and* $p_I \in P_I$ *is called* process instance.
7. *The mapping* $pi : P_T \mapsto \mathcal{P}(P_I)$ *is called* process instantiation. *For* $pi(p_T) = P_i$ *we call* p_T *process type and* $P_i \subseteq P_I$ *the set of process instances instantiated from process type* p_T.
8. *The mapping* $ar : S \mapsto R$ *is called* active role mapping. *For* $ar(s) = r$ *we call* s *the subject and* r *the active-role of* s[1].
9. *The mapping* $sb : T_T \mapsto \mathcal{P}(T_T)$ *is called* subject-binding. *For* $sb(t_1) = T_{sb}$ *we call* t_1 *the* subject binding task *and* $T_{sb} \subseteq T_T$ *the set of* subject-bound tasks.
10. *The mapping* $rb : T_T \mapsto \mathcal{P}(T_T)$ *is called* role-binding. *For* $rb(t_1) = T_{rb}$ *we call* t_1 *the* role binding task *and* $T_{rb} \subseteq T_T$ *the set of* role-bound tasks.
11. *The mapping* $sme : T_T \mapsto \mathcal{P}(T_T)$ *is called* static mutual exclusion. *For* $sme(t_1) = T_{sme}$ *with* $T_{sme} \subseteq T_T$ *we call each pair* t_1 *and* $t_x \in T_{sme}$ statically mutual exclusive tasks.
12. *The mapping* $dme : T_T \mapsto \mathcal{P}(T_T)$ *is called* dynamic mutual exclusion. *For* $dme(t_1) = T_{dme}$ *with* $T_{dme} \subseteq T_T$ *we call each pair* t_1 *and* $t_x \in T_{dme}$ dynamically mutual exclusive tasks.

For process-related RBAC Models there are two types of correctness. *Static correctness* refers to the design-time consistency of the elements and relationships in the Process-related RBAC Model. In particular, it refers to process types and task types. *Dynamic correctness* relates to the compliance of runtime process instances with the mutual-exclusion and binding constraints. Definition 2 provides the rules for static correctness.

Definition 2. *Let* $PRM = (E, Q, D)$ *be a Process-related RBAC Model.* PRM *is said to be statically correct if the following requirements hold:*

1. *Tasks cannot be mutual exclusive to themselves:*
   $\forall t_2 \in sme(t_1) : t_1 \neq t_2$ *and* $\forall t_2 \in dme(t_1) : t_1 \neq t_2$
2. *Mutuality of mutual exclusion constraints:*
   $\forall t_2 \in sme(t_1) : t_1 \in sme(t_2)$ *and* $\forall t_2 \in dme(t_1) : t_1 \in dme(t_2)$
3. *Tasks cannot be bound to themselves:*
   $\forall t_2 \in sb(t_1) : t_1 \neq t_2$ *and* $\forall t_2 \in rb(t_1) : t_1 \neq t_2$
4. *Mutuality of binding constraints:*
   $\forall t_2 \in sb(t_1) : t_1 \in sb(t_2)$ *and* $\forall t_2 \in rb(t_1) : t_1 \in rb(t_2)$
5. *Tasks are either statically or dynamically mutual exclusive:*
   $\forall t_2 \in sme(t_1) : t_2 \notin dme(t_1)$
6. *Either SME constraint or binding constraint:*
   $\forall t_2 \in sme(t_1) : t_2 \notin sb(t_1) \wedge t_2 \notin rb(t_1)$
7. *Either DME constraint or subject-binding constraint:*
   $\forall t_2 \in dme(t_1) : t_2 \notin sb(t_1)$
8. *Consistency of task-ownership and SME:*
   $\forall t_2 \in sme(t_1) : town^{-1}(t_2) \cap town^{-1}(t_1) = \emptyset$

[1] We assume that each subject can (at the subject's discretion) activate the roles that are directly assigned to this subject as well as the junior-roles of its directly assigned roles (see, e.g., [5,12]).

9. *Consistency of role-ownership and SME:* $\forall t_2 \in sme(t_1), r_2 \in town^{-1}(t_2), r_1 \in town^{-1}(t_1) : rown^{-1}(r_2) \cap rown^{-1}(r_1) = \emptyset$

Definition 2.6 states that it is *not* possible to have a SME constraint *and* a binding constraint between the same task types t_1 and t_2. In other words: *SME constraints conflict with* all types of *binding constraints* (subject-binding and role-binding). This is because a binding constraint defines that (in the context of the same process instance) the instances of two bound task types *must* be performed by the same subject respectively the same role, while a SME constraint defines that the instances of two statically mutual exclusive task types *must not* be performed by the same subject respectively the same role. Obviously, it is impossible to fulfill both constraints at the same time.

Furthermore, Definition 2.7 states that it is *not* possible to specify a DME constraint *and* a subject-binding constraint between the same two task types t_1 and t_2. This means: *DME constraints and subject-binding constraints conflict.* This is because a subject-binding constraint defines that (in the context of the same process instance) the instances of two bound task types *must* be performed by the same subject (the same individual). In contrast, a DME constraint defines that (in the context of the same process instance) the instances of two task types *must not* be performed by the same subject. Again, it is obvious that we cannot fulfill both constraints at the same time. Note that it *is* possible, however, to simultaneously define a role-binding constraint *and* a DME constraint on two tasks. This is because a DME constraint defines that (in the context of the same process instance) a subject *must not* own the instances of two dynamically mutual exclusive task types (see above). A role-binding constraint yet only defines that (in the context of the same process instance) the instances of two bound task types *must* be performed by the same *role*, not by the same subject/individual. This can be interpreted as a peer review (different subjects owning the same role). Therefore, DME constraints and role-binding constraints do *not* conflict. Definition 2.8 specifies that no role can own two SME tasks, neither directly nor via a role-hierarchy (see also Def. 1.1 and Def. 1.5). Finally, Definition 2.9 specifies that no subject can own two roles that are associated with SME tasks.

Definition 3 provides the rules for dynamic correctness of a process-related RBAC model, i.e. the rules that can only be checked in the context of runtime process *instances*.

Definition 3. *Let* $PRM = (E, Q, D)$ *be a Process-related RBAC Model and* P_I *its set of process instances.* PRM *is said to be dynamically correct if the following requirements hold:*

1. *In the same process instance, the executing subjects of SME tasks must be different:* $\forall t_2 \in sme(t_1), pi \in P_I : \forall t_x \in ti(t_2, pi), t_y \in ti(t_1, pi) : es(t_x) \cap es(t_y) = \emptyset$ *Please note that we include this rule for the sake of completeness only, as the rule must always hold due to the consistency rule for role-ownership and SME (see Def. 2.9).*
2. *In the same process instance, the executing subjects of DME tasks must be different:* $\forall t_2 \in dme(t_1), pi \in P_I : \forall t_x \in ti(t_2, pi), t_y \in ti(t_1, pi) : es(t_x) \cap es(t_y) = \emptyset$
3. *In the same process instance, role-bound tasks must have the same executing-role:* $\forall t_2 \in rb(t_1), pi \in P_I : \forall t_x \in ti(t_2, pi), t_y \in ti(t_1, pi) : er(t_x) = er(t_y)$
4. *In the same process instance, subject-bound tasks must have the same executing-subject:* $\forall t_2 \in sb(t_1), pi \in P_I : \forall t_x \in ti(t_2, pi), t_y \in ti(t_1, pi) : es(t_x) = es(t_y)$.

4 Algorithms for Design-Time Consistency

The algorithms defined in this section check the design-time consistency of a process-related RBAC model. Therefore, these algorithms operate on task *types* defined in the context of a process-related RBAC model (see Section 3). For the purposes of this paper, we distinguish algorithms and procedures. Here, an *algorithm* performs certain checks based on the current configuration of a process-related RBAC model. Algorithms either return true or false. A *procedure* operates on the current configuration of a process-related RBAC model and may include side-effects (i.e. change model elements, relations, or variables). Procedures either return a set or do not return anything (void).

4.1 Checks for Constraint Definition

Algorithm 1. *Check if it is allowed to define a (new) SME constraint on two task types.*

Input: $task_1, task_2 \in T_T$

1: **if** $task_1 == task_2$ **then return** false
2: **if** $task_1 \in dme(task_2)$ **then return** false
3: **if** $task_1 \in rbt(task_2)$ **then return** false
4: **if** $task_1 \in sbt(task_2)$ **then return** false
5: **if** $\exists\, r \in R \mid r \in town(task_1) \wedge r \in town(task_2)$
6:     **then return** false
7: **if** $\exists\, s \in S \mid r_1 \in rown(s) \wedge r_2 \in rown(s) \wedge$
8:     $r_1 \in town(task_1) \wedge r_2 \in town(task_2)$
9:     **then return** false
10: **return** true

A task type must not be mutual exclusive to itself (see Def. 2.1). Thus, line 1 of Algortihm 1 returns false if this consistency requirement is not fulfilled. Next, lines 2-4 check the consistency requirements specified in Def. 2.5 and Def. 2.6. Subsequently, lines 5-6 check if a role exists which already owns the two task types. In case a corresponding role is found, the algorithm returns false because defining a SME constraint on two task types that are owned by the same role would violate the consistency requirement specified in Def. 2.8. For example, the definition of a new SME constraint on the tasks t_1 and t_2 in Figure 1a) must be forbidden. Otherwise, r would subsequently own two SME tasks. Similarily, the definition of a new SME constraint on tasks t_3 and t_4 in Figure 1b) must be forbidden. Otherwise, the senior-role r_s would subsequently

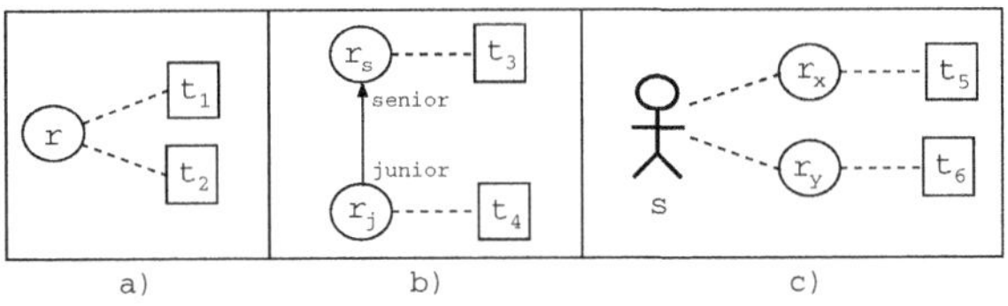

Fig. 1. Examples for Algorithm 1

own two SME tasks (t_3 is directly assigned to r_s and t_4 is inherited from its junior-role r_j). Afterwards, lines 7-9 check if a subject exists that (via its roles) already owns the two task types. In case a corresponding subject is found, the algorithm returns false because defining a SME constraint on two task types that are owned by the same subject would violate the consistency requirements specified in Def. 2.9. Figure 1c) shows an example where the definition of a new SME constraint on the tasks t_5 and t_6 must be forbidden. Otherwise, subject s would subsequently own the right to perform two SME tasks (via its roles r_x and r_y). If none of the above checks returns false, the algorithm finally reaches line 10 and returns true – meaning that it is allowed to define a new SME constraint on the respective task types.

Algorithm 2. *Check if it is allowed to define a (new) DME constraint on two task types.*

```
Input: task_1, task_2 ∈ T_T
1: if task_1 == task_2 then return false
2: if task_1 ∈ sme(task_2) then return false
3: if task_1 ∈ sbt(task_2) then return false
4: return true
```

Because it requires less consistency checks, Algorithm 2 is much more simple compared to Algorithm 1. In Algorithm 2, line 1 first ensures the consistency requirement specified in Def. 2.1. Next, lines 2-3 check if the new DME constraint would violate the consistency requirements specified in Def. 2.5 and Def. 2.7. In case none of the above checks returns false, the algorithm finally reaches line 4 and returns true – meaning that it is allowed to define a new DME constraint on the respective task types.

Procedure 1. *Compile the set of all task types that have a direct or a transitive subject-binding relation to a particular* $task_a$.

```
Name: allSubjectBindings
Input: task_a ∈ T_T
1: task_a set visited = true
2: create_empty_set directbindings
3: create_empty_set transitivebindings
4: for each task_b ∈ sbt(task_a)
5:     if ! task_b visited then
6:         add task_b to directbindings
7:         add allSubjectBindings(task_b) to transitivebindings
8: return directbindings ∪ transitivebindings
```

Procedure 1 traverses a graph consisting of task types (forming the graph's nodes) and subject-binding relations (forming the graph's edges) that are defined on these task types. In particular, the procedure receives a certain task type ($task_a$) as input parameter and compiles the list of all task types that have a direct or a transitive subject-binding relation to $task_a$. In accordance with standard graph traversal algorithms, each node processed by the algorithm is marked as "visited" in order to have a stop criterion (i.e. all reachable nodes have been visited). To find all transitive nodes, the algorithm includes a recursion (see line 7). After all reachable nodes have been visited, the algorithm returns

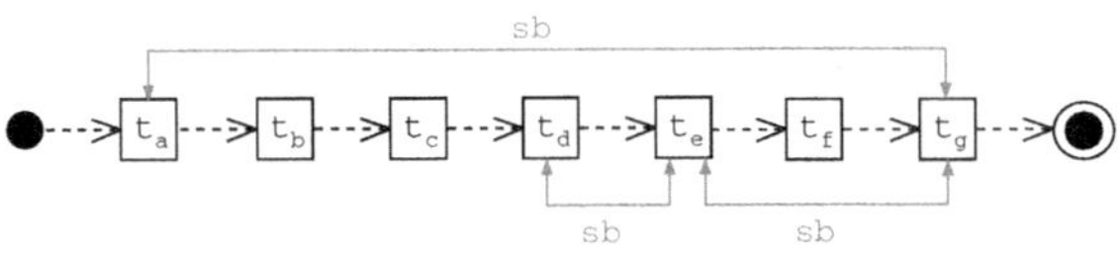

Fig. 2. Example for Procedure 1

the set of all task types having a (direct or transitive) subject-binding to $task_a$. In case no subject-binding for $task_a$ exists, the procedure returns an empty set. The example from Figure 2 shows a process that includes three subject-binding relations between t_a and t_g, t_g and t_e, as well as t_e and t_d respectively. In this example, t_a thus has a direct subject-binding to t_g and transitive subject-bindings to t_e and t_d.

Procedure 2. *Compile the set of all task types that have a direct or a transitive role-binding relation to a particular* $task_a$.

Name: *allRoleBindings*
Input: $task_a \in T_T$
$task_a$ **set** *visited* = true
create_empty_set *directbindings*
create_empty_set *transitivebindings*
for each $task_b \in rbt(task_a)$
    if $!\ task_b$ *visited* **then**
        add $task_b$ to *directbindings*
        add *allRoleBindings*($task_b$) to *transitivebindings*
return *directbindings* $\cup$ *transitivebindings*

Procedure 2 is similar to Procedure 1, only that it compiles and returns the set of all task types that have a (direct or transitive) role-binding to a certain task type $task_a$.

Algorithm 3. *Check if it is allowed to define a (new) subject-binding constraint on two task types* $task_1$ *and* $task_2$.

Input: $task_1, task_2 \in T_T$
if $task_1 == task_2$ **then return** false
if $task_1 \in dme(task_2)$ **then return** false
if $task_1 \in sme(task_2)$ **then return** false
if $\exists\ task_x \in sme(task_1) \mid task_x \in$ *allSubjectBindings*($task_2$)
    then return false
if $\exists\ task_x \in dme(task_1) \mid task_x \in$ *allSubjectBindings*($task_2$)
    then return false
if $\exists\ task_x \in sme(task_2) \mid task_x \in$ *allSubjectBindings*($task_1$)
    then return false
if $\exists\ task_x \in dme(task_2) \mid task_x \in$ *allSubjectBindings*($task_1$)
    then return false
return true

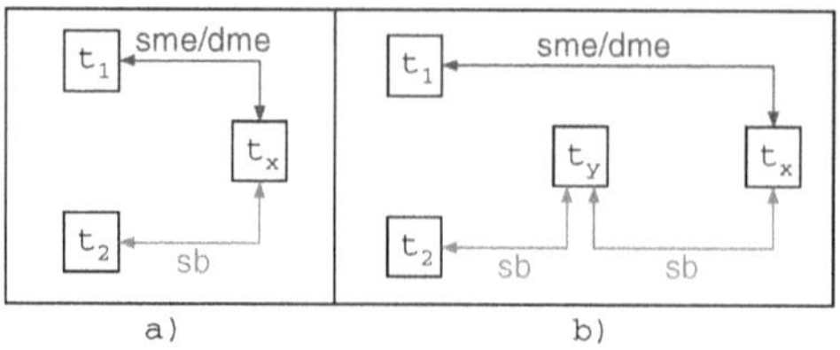

Fig. 3. Examples for Algorithm 3

In Algorithm 3, lines 1-3 ensure that the consistency requirements specified in Def. 2.3, 2.6, and 2.7 hold. Next, lines 4-5 check if some $task_x$ exists that is already defined as SME to $task_1$ while having a subject-binding relation to $task_2$ at the same time. In case such a $task_x$ exists, Algorithm 3 returns false because the definition of a new (direct) subject-binding relation between $task_1$ and $task_2$ would also define a (transitive) subject-binding between $task_1$ and $task_x$. In other words, because SME constraints and binding constraints conflict, such a configuration would violate the consistency requirement specified in Def. 2.6. Lines 6-7 perform a similar check for DME constraints to ensure that the consistency requirement specified in Def. 2.7 holds. Figure 3a) shows an example, where the definition of a new subject-binding between the tasks t_1 and t_2 must be forbidden because t_1 already has a (static or dynamic) mutual-exclusion relation to a third task t_x which, at the same time, has a subject-binding relation to t_2. Figure 3b) shows another example, where a new subject-binding between t_1 and t_2 must be forbidden because t_2 has a transitive subject-binding relation to a task t_x which also has a (static or dynamic) mutual-exclusion relation to t_1 (see also Procedure 1). Note that it is necessary to perform the checks from the perspective of $task_1$ (lines 4-7) *and* from the perspective of $task_2$ (lines 8-11). In case none of the above checks returns false, the Algorithm finally reaches line 12 and returns true – meaning that it is allowed to define a new subject-binding constraint on the respective task types.

Algorithm 4. *Check if it is allowed to define a (new) role-binding constraint on two task types*

Input: $task_1, task_2 \in T_T$
1: **if** $task_1 == task_2$ **then return** false
2: **if** $task_1 \in sme(task_2)$ **then return** false
3: **if** $\exists\, task_x \in sme(task_1) \mid task_x \in allRoleBindings(task_2)$
4:     **then return** false
5: **if** $\exists\, task_x \in sme(task_2) \mid task_x \in allRoleBindings(task_1)$
6:     **then return** false
7: **return** true

In principle, the checks in Algorithm 4 are similar to the checks performed by Algorithm 3. However, because DME constraints do not conflict with role-binding constraints (see Section 3), Algorithm 4 only has to ensure that the consistency requirements specified in Def. 2.3 (line 1) and Def. 2.6 (lines 2-6) hold. If none of the above checks returns false, Algorithm 4 finally reaches line 7 and returns true – meaning that it is allowed to define a new role-binding constraint on the corresponding task types.

4.2 Checks for new Assignment Relations

Procedure 3. *Compile the set of all direct and transitive senior-roles of a* $role_a$.

Name: *allSeniorRoles*
Input: $role_a \in R$
1: create_empty_set *transitiveseniorroles*
2: **for each** $role_x \in directSeniorRoles(role_a)$
3: add *allSeniorRoles*($role_x$) to *transitiveseniorroles*
4: **return** *transitiveseniorroles* ∪ *directSeniorRoles*($role_a$)

First, we define the procedure *allSeniorRoles* because this procedure is needed for the definition of the subsequent algorithms. Procedure 3 traverses the role-hierarchy to compile the set of all (direct and transitive) senior-roles of a particular role. To find all transitive senior-roles the procedure includes a recursion (see line 3).

Algorithm 5. *Check if it is allowed to assign a particular task type* $task_x$ *to a particular* $role_y$ *(also called task-to-role assignment).*

Input: $task_x \in T_T, role_y \in R$
1: **if** $\exists\, task_y \in town(role_y) \mid task_y \in sme(task_x)$
2: **then return** false
3: **if** $\exists\, role_z \in allSeniorRoles(role_y) \mid$
4: $task_z \in town(role_z) \wedge task_z \in sme(task_x)$
5: **then return** false
6: **if** $\exists\, s \in S \mid role_y \in rown(s) \wedge role_z \in rown(s) \wedge$
7: $task_z \in town(role_z) \wedge task_z \in sme(task_x)$
8: **then return** false
9: **return** true

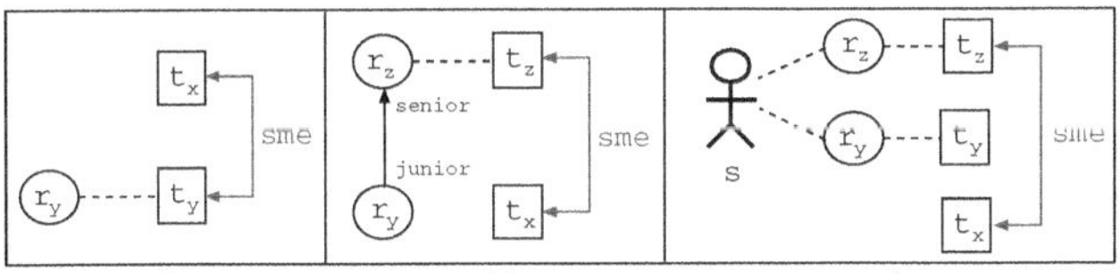

Fig. 4. Examples for Algorithm 5

In Algorithm 5, lines 1-2 check if the role already owns some $task_y$ which has a SME constraint to $task_x$. If such a $task_y$ exists, the algorithm returns false to ensure the consistency requirement specified in Def. 2.8. Figure 4a) shows a corresponding example, where task t_x must not be assigned to role r_y because r_y already owns t_y which is defined as SME to t_x. Next, lines 3-5 check if $role_y$ has a (direct or tranisitive) senior-role $role_z$ which again owns a $task_z$ that has a SME constraint to $task_x$. In case such a $role_z$ exists, the algorithm returns false to ensure the consistency requirement specified in Def. 2.8. Figure 4b) shows an example where a senior-role r_z owns a task t_z which is defined as SME to task t_x. Therefore, t_x must not be assigned to r_y (or any other junior-role of r_z). This is because assigning t_x to r_y would also mean to transitively assign t_x to r_z (and to any other senior-role of r_y). Thus, r_z would inherit t_x from its junior-role r_y and thereby own two SME tasks (see also Def. 1.1 and Def. 1.5). Subsequently, lines 6-8 check if one of the subjects owning $role_y$ does also own another $role_z$ which again has a $task_z$ that is defined as SME to $task_x$. In case such a subject exists, the algorithm returns false to ensure the consistency requirement specified in Def. 2.9. In the example from Figure 4c), subject s owns the right to perform the tasks t_y and t_z (via its roles r_y and r_z). Moreover, t_z has an SME constraint on t_x. Therefore, t_x must not be assigned to r_y. This means, although r_y does not own a task which has a SME constraint on t_x (neither directly nor transitively), the assignment of t_x to r_y must still be forbidden because subject s simultaneously owns r_y and r_z. In case none of the above checks returns false, Algorithm 5 finally reaches line 9 and returns true – meaning that it is allowed to assign $task_x$ to $role_y$.

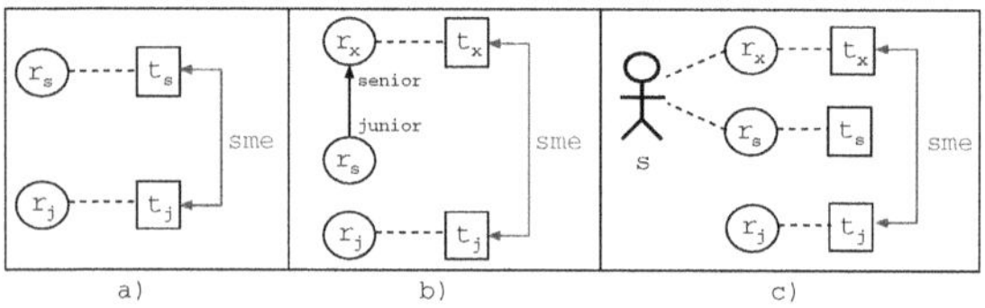

Fig. 5. Examples for Algorithm 6

Algorithm 6. *Check if it is allowed to define a (new) junior-role relation between two roles. In particular, check if it is allowed to define a role $junior$ as junior-role of another role $senior$ (also called role-to-role assignment).*

Input: $junior, senior \in R$

1: **if** $junior == senior$ **then return** false
2: **if** $\exists\, task_j \in town(junior) \wedge task_s \in town(senior) \mid$
3: $\quad task_j \in sme(task_s)$
4: $\quad$ **then return** false
5: **if** $\exists\, role_x \in allSeniorRoles(senior) \mid$
6: $\quad task_x \in town(role_x) \wedge task_j \in town(junior) \wedge$
7: $\quad task_x \in sme(task_j)$
8: $\quad$ **then return** false
9: **if** $\exists\, s \in S \mid senior \in rown(s) \wedge role_x \in rown(s) \wedge$
10: $\quad task_x \in town(role_x) \wedge task_j \in rown(junior) \wedge$
11: $\quad task_x \in sme(task_j)$
12: $\quad$ **then return** false
13: **return** true

Because a role cannot be its own junior-role, line 1 of Algorithm 6 first checks this consistency requirement (see also Def. 1.1). Next, lines 2-4 check if the designated $junior$

role owns a $task_j$ that has a SME constraint to another $task_s$ which is owned by the designated $senior$ role. In case such two a $task_j$ and $task_s$ exist, the algorithm returns false to ensure the consistency requirement specified in Def. 2.8. Figure 5a) shows a corresponding example, where the definition of a new junior-role relation between r_s and r_j must be forbidden, because t_s and t_j are SME tasks. Next, lines 5-8 check if the designated $senior$ role already has a (direct or transitive) senior-role $role_x$ that owns a $task_x$ and has a SME constraint to another $task_j$ that is assigned to the designated $junior$ role. In case such a $role_x$ exists, the algorithm returns false to ensure the consistency requirement specified in Def. 2.8. For example, in Figure 5b) role r_j must not be defined as junior-role of r_s. Otherwise, r_x (senior-role of r_s) would be able to perform the two SME tasks t_x and t_j. Subsequently, lines 9-12 check if one of the subjects already owning the designated $senior$ role, does also own another $role_x$ that grants the right to perform a $task_x$ which has a SME constraint to another $task_j$ assigned to the designated $junior$ role. In case such a $role_x$ exists the algorithm returns false to ensure the consistency requirement specified in Def. 2.9. Figure 5c) shows a corresponding example where role r_j must not be defined as junior-role of r_s. This means, although r_s and r_j do not own two SME tasks, the definition of a new junor-role relation between r_s and r_j must still be forbidden because subject s simultaneously owns r_x and r_s. Otherwise, s would acquire the right to perform two SME tasks (t_x and t_j). In case none of the above checks returns false, Algorithm 6 finally reaches line 13 and returns true – meaning that it is allowed to define a new junior-role/senior-role relation between the corresponding roles. Note, that because role-hierarchies are directed acyclic graphs, it is in fact also necessary to check if a new junior-role relation (a new role-to-role assignment) would create a cycle in the role-hierarchy (see also Def. 1.1). However, because this issue is generic to each DAG and is not related to mutual-exclusion or binding constraints, we decided to omit the cycle check in Algorithm 6.

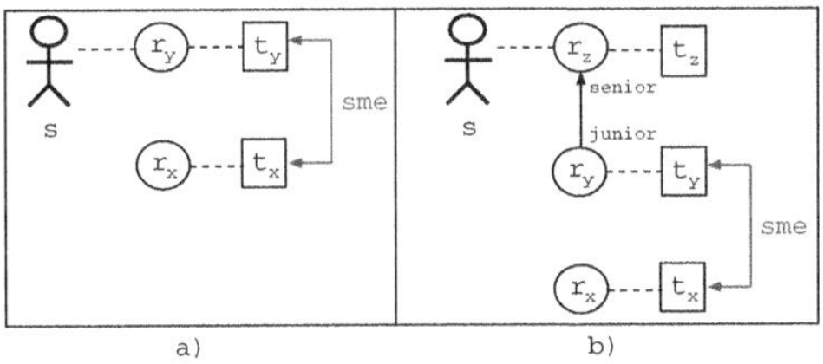

Fig. 6. Examples for Algorithm 7

Algorithm 7. *Check if it is allowed to assign a particular role to a particular subject (role-to-subject assignment).*

Input: $role_x \in R, subject \in S$

if $\exists\ role_y \in rown(subject) \mid task_y \in town(role_y) \wedge$
  $task_x \in town(role_x) \wedge task_y \in sme(task_x)$
  then return *false*
return *true*

In Algorithm 7, lines 1-3 check if the respective subject already owns a $role_y$ which grants the right to perform a $task_y$ that has a SME constraint to one of the tasks assigned to $role_x$. In case such a $role_y$ exists, the algorithm returns false to ensure the consistency requirement specified in Def. 2.9. Figure 6a) shows a respective example, where role r_x must not be assigned to subject s, because s already owns role r_y. Otherwise, s would acquire the right to perform two SME tasks (t_x and t_y). In Figure 6b) we see another example, where r_x must not be assigned to s because s already owns r_z and can thereby (via the role-hierarchy) perform t_y which has an SME constraint on t_x.

5 Algorithms for Runtime Consistency

Runtime consistency refers to the fact that the constraints defined in a process-related RBAC model must not only be enforced at design-time but also when executing actual process instances (see Section 3). In particular, mutual-exclusion and binding constraints directly impact the allocation of tasks to subjects. First, we define the procedure $executableTasks$ because it is needed for the definition of the subsequent algorithm.

Procedure 4. *Compile the set of all tasks a particular subject could currently execute (based on the roles currently assigned to this subject).*

```
Name: executableTasks
Input: s ∈ S
create_empty_set executable
for each role ∈ rown(s)
    add town(role) to executable
return executable
```

Procedure 4 visits all roles assigned to a particular subject to compile the set of all tasks that can (potentially) be executed by this particular subject, i.e. all tasks that are directly or transitively assigned to the respective subject (see also Def. 1.2 and Def. 1.5).

Algorithm 8. *Check if particular task instance (which is part of a particular process instance) can be allocated to a particular subject.*

```
Input: subject ∈ S, task_type ∈ T_T, process_type ∈ P_T,
       process_instance ∈ pi(process_type),
       task_instance ∈ ti(task_type, process_instance)
if task_type ∉ executableTasks(subject) then return false
if es(task_instance) ≠ ∅ then return false
if er(task_instance) ≠ ∅ ∧ er(task_instance) ≠ ar(subject)
    then return false
if ∃ type_x ∈ allSubjectBindings(task_type) |
    type_x ∉ executableTasks(subject)
    then return false
if ∃ instance_y ∈ ti(type_y, process_instance) |
    type_y ∈ dme(task_type) ∧ es(instance_y) == subject
    then return false
return true
```

Algorithm 8 checks if the instance of a certain task type can be allocated to a certain subject. First, line 1 checks if the corresponding $subject$ is allowed to execute the $tasks_{type}$ the corresponding $task_{instance}$ was instantiated from (see also Procedure 4). If the $subject$ is not allowed to execute this particular $task_{type}$ the respective instance must not be allocated to this subject and therefore the algorithm returns false. Next, line 2 checks if the corresponding task instance has already been allocated, i.e. if this task instance already has an executing-subject (see also Def. 1.3). In case the respective task instance is already allocated to another subject, the algorithm returns false. In particular, this means that the $subject$ cannot be allocated to this very $task_{instance}$ but it can still be allocated to other instances of the corresponding $task_{type}$, of course. Afterwards, lines 3-4 check if the $task_{instance}$ already has an executing-role, and if so whether this executing-role is also the currently active role of the respective $subject$. If this is not the case, the algorithm returns false (note that the executing-role of a task instance can be allocated before allocating an executing-subject to this task instance, see also discussion concerning Procedure 5 below). Subsequently, lines 5-7 check if a $type_x$ exists that has a subject-binding relation to $task_{type}$ but cannot be executed by the $subject$. In case such a $type_x$ exists, the algorithm returns false to ensure the consistency requirement specified in Def. 3.4. In other words, a $task_{instance}$ must only be allocated to a certain $subject$ if this subject owns the right to perform the corresponding $task_{type}$ as well as all subject-bound tasks. Next, lines 8-10 check if the $subject$ is already allocated to the $instance_y$ of a $task_y$ which has a DME constraint to $task_{type}$. If the $subject$ already is the executing-subject of such an $instance_y$, the algorithm returns false to ensure the consistency requirement specified in Def. 3.2. In other words, in the same process instance a task instance must not be allocated to a particular subject if this very subject is already allocated to the instance of a DME task type. If none of the above checks returns false, Algorithm 8 finally reaches line 11 and returns true – meaning that the corresponding $subject$ may actually be allocated to the corresponding $task_{instance}$. Algorithm 8 may also be used to compile the set of all subjects who are potentially allocatable to a certain task instance and then randomly allocate the corresponding task instance to one of these subjects (see also [11]). Note that we do not need to check static mutual-exclusion constraints when allocating a task, because in conformance with algorithms 1 to 7 no subject can ever be assigned to two SME tasks.

Procedure 5. *Allocate a certain task instance to a certain subject.*

Name: $allocateTask$
Input: $s \in S, task_{type} \in T_T, process_{instance} \in P_I$
    $task_{instance} \in ti(task_{type}, process_{instance})$
set $es(task_{instance})$ to s
set $er(task_{instance})$ to $ar(s)$
for each $type_x \in allSubjectBindings(task_{type})$
    for each $instance_x \in ti(type_x, process_{instance})$
        set $es(instance_x)$ to s
        set $er(instance_x)$ to $ar(s)$
for each $task_y \in allRoleBindings(task_{type})$
    for each $instance_y \in ti(task_y, process_{instance})$
        set $er(instance_y)$ to $ar(s)$

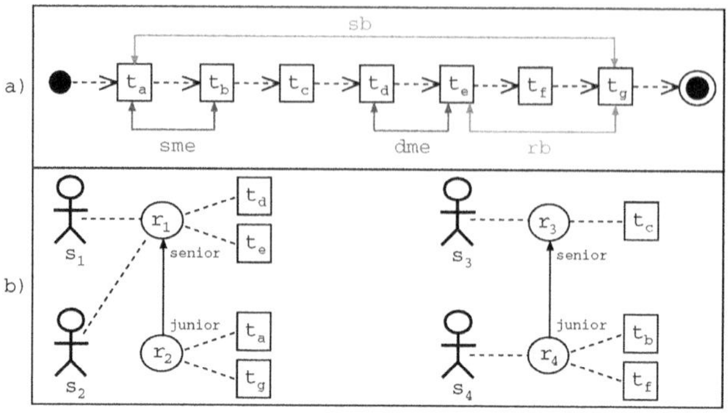

Fig. 7. Example for Procedure 5 (Design level)

After we used Algorithm 8 to check if a certain task instance can (potentially) be allocated to a particular subject, we can actually allocate the task instance. Procedure 5 describes the steps that are performed to allocate a task instance. First, we define the respective subject as the executing-subject of the $task_{instance}$, and the subject's active role as the executing role of the $task_{instance}$ (see lines 1-2). Next, lines 3-6 perform a lookup to find all instances of subject-bound tasks (see also Procedure 1) and define the executing-subject and the executing-role for each of the subject-bound tasks accordingly. In particular, all instances of subject-bound tasks are allocated at the same time to ensure the consistency requirements specified in Def. 3.3 and Def. 3.4. Finally, lines 7-9 perform a lookup to find all role-bound tasks and set the executing-role of all role-bound tasks. In particular, the executing-role of all role-bound tasks is allocated at the same time to ensure the consistency requirement specified in Def. 3.3. This means that the executing-role of a certain task instance may be allocated before allocating an executing subject (see example below).

Figure 7a) shows an example process consisting of seven task types t_a to t_g. For the sake of simplicity, we chose a linear example process. However, the task allocation procedure can be applied to arbitrary process definitions, of course. In addition to the process flow, Figure 7a) also indicates different mutual-exclusion and binding relations between some of the tasks. In particular, it shows a SME constraint between t_a and t_b, a DME constraint between t_d and t_e, a subject-binding between t_a and t_g, and a role-binding between t_e and t_g. Moreover, Figure 7b) shows a corresponding process-related RBAC model that includes four roles (r_1 to r_4) as well as four subjects (s_1 to s_4). Role r_1 is assigned to subjects s_1 and s_2, r_3 is assigned to s_3, and r_4 is assigned to s_4.

Now we give an example that demonstrates the allocation of executing-subjects and executing-roles for a particular instance of the process type from Figure 7a) considering the process-related RBAC model from Figure7b). Figure 8 depicts an instance of the respective process type and the successive allocation of the corresponding task instances (in the example an additional index i is used to indicate task instances t_{a_i} to t_{g_i}). First, we have to allocate t_{a_i}. Using Algorithm 8, we find that t_{a_i} is allocatable to subjects s_1 and s_2. In our example, we choose to allocate t_{a_i} to s_1, see Figure 8a). Moreover, because t_a has a subject-binding to t_g (see Figure 7), we allocate t_{g_i} to s_1

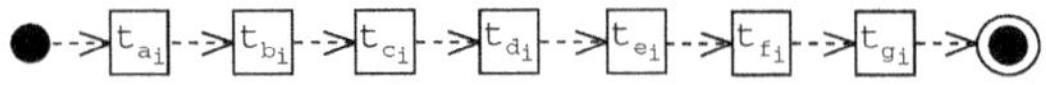

a)

	t_{a_i}	t_{b_i}	t_{c_i}	t_{d_i}	t_{e_i}	t_{f_i}	t_{g_i}
executing subject	s_1						s_1
executing role	r_1				r_1		r_1

b)

	t_{a_i}	t_{b_i}	t_{c_i}	t_{d_i}	t_{e_i}	t_{f_i}	t_{g_i}
executing subject	s_1	s_4					s_1
executing role	r_1	r_4			r_1		r_1

c)

	t_{a_i}	t_{b_i}	t_{c_i}	t_{d_i}	t_{e_i}	t_{f_i}	t_{g_i}
executing subject	s_1	s_4	s_3				s_1
executing role	r_1	r_4	r_3		r_1		r_1

d)

	t_{a_i}	t_{b_i}	t_{c_i}	t_{d_i}	t_{e_i}	t_{f_i}	t_{g_i}
executing subject	s_1	s_4	s_3	s_1			s_1
executing role	r_1	r_4	r_3	r_1	r_1		r_1

e)

	t_{a_i}	t_{b_i}	t_{c_i}	t_{d_i}	t_{e_i}	t_{f_i}	t_{g_i}
executing subject	s_1	s_4	s_3	s_1	s_2		s_1
executing role	r_1	r_4	r_3	r_1	r_1		r_1

f)

	t_{a_i}	t_{b_i}	t_{c_i}	t_{d_i}	t_{e_i}	t_{f_i}	t_{g_i}
executing subject	s_1	s_4	s_3	s_1	s_2	s_4	s_1
executing role	r_1	r_4	r_3	r_1	r_1	r_4	r_1

Fig. 8. Example for Procedure 5 (Runtime task allocation)

in the same step. In addition, because of the role-binding between t_e and t_g we also set the executing-role of t_{e_i} to r_1, see Figure 8a). Thus, in order to ensure the runtime consistency of the binding relations defined at the design-level (see Figure 7), the allocation of t_{a_i} transitively affects t_{g_i} and t_{e_i} (see also Procedure 5, Def. 3.3, and Def. 3.4). Next, we use Algorithm 8 and Procedure 5 to allocate t_{b_i} to s_4, t_{c_i} to s_3, and t_{d_i} to s_1, see Figure 8b) - d). Subsequently, we have to allocate t_{e_i}. In principle, instances of t_e could be allocated to s_1 or s_2 (see Figure 7). However, because of the DME constraint between t_d and t_e, instances of these tasks must be allocated to different subjects (see also Algorithm 8 and Def. 3.2). In our example, we therefore have to allocate t_{e_i} to s_2 because t_{d_i} was allocated to s_1, see Figure 8e). Finally, we allocate t_{f_i} to s_4 and thereby have allocated all task instances, see Figure 8f).

6 Related Work

A number of contributions exist that discuss constraint specification or possible conflicts that may occur when defining SOD or BOD constraints. In [1], Ahn and Sandhu present the RCL 2000 language for the specification of role-based authorization constraints. They also show how separation of duty constraints can be expressed in RCL 2000 and discuss different types of conflicts that may result from constraints specified via RCL 2000. Bertino et al. [2] present a language to express SOD constraints as clauses in logic programs. Moreover, they present corresponding algorithms that check the consistency of such constraints with the users/roles that execute the tasks in a workflow. Thereby they ensure that all tasks within a workflow are performed by predefined users/roles only. In [3], Botha and Eloff present an approach called conflicting entities administration paradigm. In particular, they discuss possible conflicts of static and dynamic SOD constraints in a workflow environment and share a number of lessons learned from the implementation of a prototype system. Tan et al. [17] define a model for constrained workflow systems, including SOD and BOD constraints. They discuss different issues concerning the consistency of such constraints and provide a set of formal consistency rules that guarantee the definition of a sound constrained workflow specification. In [5] Ferraiolo et al. present RBAC/Web, a model and implementation for RBAC in Web servers. They also discuss the inheritance and resulting consistency issues of SOD constraints in role-hierarchies.

While most of these works use declarative formalisms, we provide imperative algorithms for implementing SOD and BOD correctness checks. Our work complements previous contributions by providing generic algorithms and procedures to ensure the design-time and runtime consistency of process-related RBAC models. The algorithms result from our experiences in analyzing, designing, and implementing corresponding software systems (see, e.g., [9,10,13,14,15,16]).

7 Conclusion

In this paper, we presented a set of algorithms that ensure the consistency of mutual-exclusion and binding constraints in a business process context. In particular, the algorithms ensure the design-time and runtime consistency of a process-related RBAC model, with respect to the mutual-exclusion and binding constraints that are included in the respective model. The algorithms are defined in a generic fashion that is independent of a certain software platform or programming language. They were inspired through our real-world RBAC and role engineering projects, where we repeatedly identified the need for such generic consistency checks. Thus, our algorithms complement previous work on mutual-exclusion and binding constraints by providing a practical and implementation-oriented perspective on constraint consistency.

In recent years, we see an increasing interest in process-aware information systems in both research and practice. In this context, an increasing number of existing and future systems will have to be extended with respective consistency checks. Among other things, we already implemented the algorithms in an RBAC service, a general-purpose policy framework (supporting authorization, obligation, and delegation policies), a runtime-engine for business processes, as well as in a role-engineering tool.

References

1. Ahn, G., Sandhu, R.: Role-based Authorization Constraints Specification. ACM Transactions on Information and System Security (TISSEC) 3(4) (November 2000)
2. Bertino, E., Ferrari, E., Atluri, V.: The Specification and Enforcement of Authorization Constraints in Workflow Management Systems. ACM Transactions on Information and System Security (TISSEC) 2(1) (February 1999)

3. Botha, R., Eloff, J.: Separation of duties for access control enforcement in workflow environments. IBM Systems Journal 40(3) (2001)
4. Casati, F., Castano, S., Fugini, M.: Managing Workflow Authorization Constraints through Active Database Technology. Information Systems Frontiers 3(3) (September 2001)
5. Ferraiolo, D., Barkley, J., Kuhn, D.: A Role-Based Access Control Model and Reference Implementation within a Corporate Intranet. ACM Transactions on Information and System Security (TISSEC) 2(1) (February 1999)
6. Kunz, S., Evdokimov, S., Fabian, B., Stieger, B., Strembeck, M.: Role-Based Access Control for Information Federations in the Industrial Service Sector. In: Proc. of the 18th European Conference on Information Systems (ECIS) (June 2010)
7. Li, N., Tripunitara, M., Bizri, Z.: On Mutually Exclusive Roles and Separation-of-Duty. ACM Transactions on Information and System Security (TISSEC) 10(2) (May 2007)
8. Li, N., Wang, Q.: Beyond separation of duty: An algebra for specifying high-level security policies. Journal of the ACM (JACM) 55(3) (July 2008)
9. Mendling, J., Ploesser, K., Strembeck, M.: Specifying Separation of Duty Constraints in BPEL4 People Processes. In: Proc. of the 11th International Conference on Business Information Systems (BIS). LNBIP, vol. 7, Springer, Heidelberg (2008)
10. Neumann, G., Strembeck, M.: Design and Implementation of a Flexible RBAC-Service in an Object-Oriented Scripting Language. In: Proc. of the 8th ACM Conference on Computer and Communications Security (CCS) (November 2001)
11. Russell, N., van der Aalst, W.M.P., ter Hofstede, A.H.M., Edmond, D.: Workflow Resource Patterns: Identification, Representation and Tool Support. In: Pastor, Ó., Falcão e Cunha, J. (eds.) CAiSE 2005. LNCS, vol. 3520, pp. 216–232. Springer, Heidelberg (2005)
12. Sandhu, R., Coyne, E., Feinstein, H., Youman, C.: Role-Based Access Control Models. IEEE Computer 29(2) (February 1996)
13. Strembeck, M.: Conflict Checking of Separation of Duty Constraints in RBAC - Implementation Experiences. In: Proc. of the Conference on Software Engineering, SE 2004 (February 2004)
14. Strembeck, M.: A Role Engineering Tool for Role-Based Access Control. In: Proc. of the 3rd Symposium on Requirements Engineering for Information Security (SREIS) (August 2005)
15. Strembeck, M.: Scenario-Driven Role Engineering. IEEE Security & Privacy 8(1) (January/February 2010)
16. Strembeck, M., Neumann, G.: An Integrated Approach to Engineer and Enforce Context Constraints in RBAC Environments. ACM Transactions on Information and System Security (TISSEC) 7(3) (August 2004)
17. Tan, K., Crampton, J., Gunter, C.: The Consistency of Task-Based Authorization Constraints in Workflow Systems. In: Proc. of the 17th IEEE Workshop on Computer Security Foundations (CSFW) (June 2004)
18. Wainer, J., Barthelmes, P., Kumar, A.: W-RBAC - A Workflow Security Model Incorporating Controlled Overriding of Constraints. International Journal of Cooperative Information Systems (IJCIS) 12(4) (December 2003)
19. Warner, J., Atluri, V.: Inter-Instance Authorization Constraints for Secure Workflow Management. In: Proc. of the 11th ACM Symposium on Access Control Models and Technologies (SACMAT) (June 2006)

Collaborative Filtering Technique for Web Service Recommendation Based on User-Operation Combination

Nguyen Ngoc Chan, Walid Gaaloul, and Samir Tata

Institut TELECOM, TELECOM SudParis
UMR 5157 CNRS Samovar, France

Abstract. The tremendous growth in the amount of available web services impulses many researchers on proposing recommender systems to help users discover services. Most of the proposed solutions analyzed query strings and web service descriptions to generate recommendations. However, these text-based recommendation approaches depend mainly on user's perspective, languages and notations which easily decrease recommendation's efficiency. In this paper, we present our approach in which we take into account historical usage data instead of the text based analysis. We apply collaborative filtering technique on user's interactions. We propose and implement three algorithms based on Vector Space Model to validate our approach. We also provide evaluation methods based on the precision, recall and root mean square error in order to compare and assert the efficiency of our algorithms.

Keywords: Web Service, Recommender System, Vector Space Model.

1 Introduction

Web services (WS) are loosely-coupled software applications supporting interpretable machine-to-machine interactions. They are described by Web Service Description Language (WSDL) files and commonly discovered via the Universal Description Discovery and Integration (UDDI) registries [1]. However, the growing number of web services and the discontinuing of public UDDIs make web services more and more scattered. Some portals such as XMethods, BindingPoint, WebServiceX.NET, WebServiceList, StrikeIron, Woogle, RemoteMethods, or eSynaps assist users by providing interfaces for searching and invoking web services. Meanwhile there is neither collaboration among WS providers nor system checking the WS's availability, accessibility and usability [2]. From user's perspective, the traditional service discovery has the following drawbacks: (1) users get confused on the number of web services returned by search engines or special crawlers and (2) users do not know about the advantage of a web service (i.e. decide which is the best) in comparison with other retrieved ones. This issue opens a new area for researches to find the best solutions for enhancing the efficiency of WS discovery.

R. Meersman et al. (Eds.): OTM 2010, Part I, LNCS 6426, pp. 222–239, 2010.

To overcome the drawbacks described above, intuitively, users need a special system which can understand their interests and suggest them the best usable services. In this case, recommender systems (RS), which can provide users the most suitable items (such as music, films, books, etc.) to their interests, have been considered as one of the best solutions(RS) [3]. Based on their functionality, the recommender systems can be classified in four types: Demographic Filtering, Content-based Filtering, Collaborative Filtering and Association Rules based Recommendation [4]. Since web services are described and discovered by XML artifacts, some approaches [5,6] applied the content-based filtering technique of the RS on WS descriptions and user's query strings to provide users the most suitable services. These approaches can generate good recommendations without asking any efforts from users, such as providing their profiles and comments. However, they have other drawbacks which can decrease the efficiency of their systems: (1) the text-based analysis encounters the synonym and polysenym problems (one word can have many meanings and one meaning can be described by different words); (2) they provide users recommendations from the provider side (based on WS descriptions) which are not close to user's behaviors or interests and (3) they capture only the explicit knowledge which is described in the WSDL files and they ignore the implicit knowledge which can be inferred from past usage (such as used times of each operations, user's common used WS operations, etc.).

[7,8] applied the associated rules based technique and [9] applied collaborative filtering technique on the service's QoS to deploy a WS recommender system, but they did not take into account user's behavior which is a very important parameter for finding the closest WS operations to users' interests. [10,11] analyze the semantic web service descriptions in which each user is able to employ a standard ontology, consisting of a set of basic classes and properties. However, creating and publishing ontology annotated content is time-consuming and error prone task as it needs to be done by domain human experts using questionable editing tools.

In this paper, we propose an approach that aims at solving the problem from the **user side**. We focus on **user's IDs** and their used **WS operations** instead of query strings and services descriptions. We realize that user's interactions, which are recored in historical data, are very important because they reflect user's behaviors and interests. Therefore, we propose a WS recommender system based on user's historical data. We apply the **collaborative filtering based technique** to capture the relationships among users and WS operations. Concretely, we deployed a WS recommender application and implemented three algorithms based on the Vector Space Model (VSM), which are user-based algorithm, operation-based algorithm and combination-based algorithm, to generate recommendations. The efficiency of our approach is validated by precision, recall and root mean square error (RMSE) measures. Our solution can (1) provide users the most suitable WS operations to their needs since we deal with their behaviors which are mined from their historical data; (2) avoid the synonym and polysenym problems; and (3) capture the implicit knowledge which are relationships among users and operations. By tracking **user's interactions**, our system can generate good recommendations without asking additional efforts from the users (such as providing their profiles and comments) or the service providers (such as functional and nonfunctional descriptions of their services).

The rest of this paper is organized as follows: section 2 details our algorithms to generate WS recommendations; section 3 describes our implementation and experimental results done in order to validate our algorithms; the related work is presented in section 4 and finally, we conclude our approach and sketch the future work in section 5.

2 Recommendations Based on User-Operation Data

In this section, we present our algorithms based on the collaborative filtering technique, which is the Vector Space Model (VSM) to generate recommendations for the WS users. The algorithms are processed in three steps:

1. Processing historical data: In the first step (see section 2.1), users' usage data are processed to map to the terms-documents structure.
2. Computing similarities vectors: In the second step (see section 2.2), the weight matrix and the distribution matrix of WS operations which contain similarities vectors are computed based on the historical data.
3. Generating recommendations: In the third step (see section 2.3), based on the similarities vectors, recommendations are provided.

2.1 Processing Historical Data

VSM is firstly introduced by Gerard Salton et al. [12] and became a popular technique in research and industry. It is an algebraic model which represents objects as vectors by which we can infer the similarity between two objects based on the angle between their respective vectors. All objects are presented in the same k-dimensional space and each entry in a vector presents the weight of that vector in a particular dimension. The common weight which is used along with VSM in most of applications is Term Frequency-Inverse Document Frequency (TF-IDF) [13]. In practical, TF-IDF is often used to reflect the importance of a word in a collection of documents but theoretically, it can be used to assess the importance of an object in a particular dimension in a k-dimensional space.

In Information Retrieval (IR), the science of searching for data related to documents, the VSM is applied to find the similarities among documents in a corpus. Each document is represented as a vector and each word inside a document has a weight value. This weight value present the importance of the word in the corpus and it is commonly computed by the TF-IDF measure. Data in the corpus can be denoted by a $m \times n$ term-document matrix where m is the number of terms (or words) and n is the number of documents. The similarity between two documents is inferred by the cosine value of the angle between two respective vectors.

We were inspired by the idea of computing similarities among documents using VSM to propose three algorithms in the web service context. The recommendation in our algorithms is generated based on the similarities among WS operations. We deployed a WS recommender application and store the usage data in term of "user ID" and "operation ID". Hence, the historical data can be represented by an operation-user matrix $A_{m \times n}$, where m is the number of operations and n is the number of users in the system. Each entry $A[i,j]$ in this matrix presents the number of times that the user U_j used the operation O_i. Our operation-user matrix is equivalent to the term-document matrix on which we can apply the VSM to compute the similarities among documents. Based on the similarities among users (and operations) computed by the VSM model, we proposed three algorithms to extract the suitable operations for each user.

To illustrate our techniques, we use a scenario with four users who used a set of service operations as following: U_1 = {getWeather(2), getLocation(2), getNews(1), getHotels(3)}; U_2 = {getLocation(4), getBook(1), getNews(2), getHotelID(4), getPlaces(3), getWeatherByZipCode(2)}; U_3 = {getPlaces(2), getWeatherByDate(5), getWeatherByZipCode(3), getHotelID(5), getCityDescByName(2)} and U_4 = {getHotel(7), getCityDescByName(8)}. For instance, the record "getWeather(2)" in the set U_1 means that the user U_1 has used the WS operation getWeather two times. These historical data is represented in a $m \times n$ matrix given in the Table 1 where $m = 10$ and $n = 4$.

Table 1. Original usage matrix

	U_1	U_2	U_3	U_4
getWeather	2	0	0	0
getLocation	2	4	0	0
getNews	1	2	0	0
getHotels	3	0	0	7
getBook	0	1	0	0
getHotelID	0	4	5	0
getPlaces	0	3	2	0
getWeatherByZipCode	0	2	3	0
getWeatherByDate	0	0	5	0
getCityDescByName	0	0	2	8

2.2 Computing Similarities Vectors

We proposed three algorithms to generate the WS recommendations which are: user-based algorithm, operation-based algorithm, and combination-based algorithm. Following the VSM principle, we use the TF-IDF to compute the weight of each operation (and user) in our algorithms. These weights are the vectors' constituent elements. Details of the similarities vectors computation in our algorithms are presented as following.

User-based. In this algorithm, we target to generate recommendations based on the similarity among users. We considered each user as a "document" and each operation as a "term" in a corpus. Since the original operation-user matrix can be considered as the term-document matrix in IR, we can apply the TF-IDF to compute the weight of each operation in the historical data and use the cosine measure to find the similar users with the current one. Suppose that that $|A_{ij}|$ is the number of times that the user U_j has used the operation O_i, $|O_i|$ is the number of times that O_i was used by all users and $|U_j|$ is the number of operations that were used by the user U_j. Then, the following TF-IDF equation (see (1)) computes the weight of each item A_{ij} in the operation-user matrix:

$$w_{i,j} = TF_{i,j} * IDF_j = \frac{|A_{ij}|}{|O_i|} * log\frac{|m|}{|U_j|} \quad (1)$$

Applying (1) for all $i = \overline{1..m}$ and $j = \overline{1..n}$ we get a new matrix $W_{o(m \times n)}$ which contains the weights of all operations. Each column of the $W_{o(m \times n)}$ matrix can be considered as a "document" vector. Applying the TF-IDF computation on our example's data, we will have the weight matrix shown in Table.2.

Table 2. Operation weights computed by TF-IDF

	U_1	U_2	U_3	U_4
getWeather	0.35	0	0	0
getLocation	0.17	0.17	0	0
getNews	0.09	0.09	0	0
getHotels	0.26	0	0	0.32
getBook	0	0.09	0	0
getHotelID	0	0.17	0.20	0
getPlaces	0	0.13	0.08	0
getWeatherByZipCode	0	0.09	0.12	0
getWeatherByDate	0	0	0.41	0
getCityDescByName	0	0	0.08	0.37

Operation-based. In this algorithm, we inverse the original matrix used in the first algorithm by defining each operation as a "document" and each user as a "term" in the corpus. The weight of each user computed by TF-IDF is given by (2).

$$w_{i,j} = TF_{i,j} * IDF_i = \frac{|A_{ij}|}{|U_j|} * log\frac{|n|}{|O_i|} \quad (2)$$

where $|U_j|$ is the number of times that the user U_j used all WS operations and $|O_i|$ is the number of users who used the operation O_i.

Using our illustrated example, each row in the original operation-user matrix is considered as a "document" and the weight of each "term" (user) is given by the Table 3.

Table 3. User weights computed by TF-IDF

	U_1	U_2	U_3	U_4
getWeather	0.92	0	0	0
getLocation	0.31	0.34	0	0
getNews	0.31	0.34	0	0
getHotels	0.27	0	0	1.13
getBook	0	0.51	0	0
getHotelID	0	0.23	0.39	0
getPlaces	0	0.31	0.28	0
getWeatherByZipCode	0	0.02	0.42	0
getWeatherByDate	0	0	0.69	0
getCityDescByName	0	0	0.14	1.29

Combination-based. Intuitively, the user-based algorithm can return the recommendations based on the historical data with only the user's ID regardless the chosen operation's ID. In contrast, the operation-based does not take into account the user's ID. Hence, the first two algorithms can miss some important operations which can increase the accuracy since they do not utilize all inputs for their computations. To overcome this shortcoming, we propose the third algorithm which is a combination of the two previous algorithms and takes into account both of user's ID and operation's ID as its input. This algorithm is processed in two steps and it reuses weight matrices computed by the previous algorithms. Details of this algorithm is presented in the sub-section 2.3.

2.3 Generating Recommendations

In VSM, the similarities among items are computed based on the weight matrix and the popular metric used for this computation is the cosine measure since it can achieve high accuracy. The cosine value of the angle between two vectors presents their closeness, hence, it presents the similarity between them. The key step of our algorithms is finding the similarity between two users or two operations. The cosine value of two vectors $\overrightarrow{v_i}(i_1, i_2, \ldots, i_k)$ and $\overrightarrow{v_j}(j_1, j_2, \ldots, j_k)$, which present two items I and J respectively in a k-dimensional space, is computed by (3).

$$similarity(I, J) = |cosine(\overrightarrow{v_i}, \overrightarrow{v_j})| = \frac{|\sum_{t=1}^{k} i_t * j_t|}{\sqrt{\sum_{t=1}^{k} i_t^2} \times \sqrt{\sum_{t=1}^{k} j_t^2}} \tag{3}$$

(3) is used in our proposed algorithms. The items I and J are replaced respectively by users or operations depending on the applied algorithm.

User-based. In the weight matrix $W_{o(m \times n)}$ of the user-based algorithm, each user U_j is represented by a m-dimensional vector (column) in which each element's value is an operation's weight. Based on $W_{o(m \times n)}$, we compute the recommended WS operations in three steps: (1) Firstly, we apply the similarity computation given by (3) on $W_{o(m \times n)}$ to compute the similarities among the current user and others; (2) Secondly, we sort the similarities values in descending order and select the k-most similar users with the current user based on these values and (3) Finally, for each selected user, we select the t-most-used operations for the recommendation.

In our example, suppose that we aim at generating the recommendation for the user U_1 based on the historical data of his two closest users ($k = 2$) with the maximum operations is 4 ($t = 2$), the first step of this algorithm computes the U_1's similarities as $\{U_2(0.25), U_3(0.00), U_4(0.36)\}$. Then, in the second steps, the user U_4 and U_2 are selected. Finally, the last step takes from each selected user (U_2 and U_4) the two most used operations for the recommendation. The recommendation list in this case is {getLocation, getHotelID, getHotel, getCityDescByName}.

Since the most-used operations reflect the user's interest and behavior, our algorithm is expected to generate the closest operations to the current user. In our experiments, we validated this algorithm with k={3, 4, 5} and 10 recommended operations, the evaluation showed that the algorithm can archive the best results (see section 3).

Operation-based. Similar to the $W_{o(m \times n)}$, each row in the $W_{u(m \times n)}$ presents an operation's vector in which each element is the weight of the respective user. In this algorithm, we also use the cosine measure in the recommendation process. For a given operation, we apply (3) to find the similar operations to a given one. Then, we sort the similarities in descending order and select the l operations which have the highest similarities values for the recommendation.

In the given example, suppose that that we target to find the 4 most similar operations to *getPlaces*, by applying the similarity computation (3) on the rows of the matrix (Table.3), the similarities of the other operations to the *getPlaces* are {getWeather(0.00), getLocation(0.55), getNews(0.55), getHotels(0.00), getBook(0.74), getHotelID(0.95), getWeatherByZipCode(0.92), getWeatherByDate (0.67), getCityDescByName(0.07)}. In the next step, four operations which have the highest similarity values are selected for recommendation, which are {getHotelID, getWeatherByZipCode, getBook, getWeatherByDate}.

In our experiments, we validated this algorithm with l={5, 10, 15}. The evaluation shows that the algorithm achieved the best results with the smallest l value (see section 3).

Combination-based. In this algorithm, we utilize both user's ID and operation's ID for the recommendation. Suppose that the user U_j currently selects the WS operation O_i, the combination-based algorithm is processed in two steps:

1. Finding the k-most similar users with U_j.
2. Finding the l-most similar WS operations with O_i from the set of WS operations used by the k selected users.

In the first step, we find the k-most similar users with the current one (U_j) using the first algorithm. Then, we eliminate the unselected users' data from the original operation-user matrix to get a smaller matrix $A'_{m \times k}$ with m operations and k selected users. In the second step, we recompute the weight of each user in the selected matrix $A'_{m \times k}$ and apply the second algorithm to find the l most similar operations with the current one (O_i). The selected operations are the ones to be recommended.

In our example, suppose that we target to generate the recommendation for the user U_1, who is using the operation *getPlaces*. And suppose that we apply the combination-based algorithm to find the 4 most suitable operations (l=4) based on the 2 closest users (k=2) to U_1, the algorithm's first step selects the user U_4 and U_2 since they have the highest similarity values to U_1 which are 0.36 and 0.25. Then, we eliminate the unselected users's data (U_3) from the original matrix to have a smaller matrix with three columns. The user's weights computed based on the new matrix are given by the Table 4. In the last step, we apply the operation-based algorithm on the computed user weight matrix to find the most similar operations (l=4) to the given one (*getPlaces*), our recommended operations given by this algorithm are: {getBook, getHotelID, getWeatherByZipCode, getLocation} since they have the highest similarity values, which are {1.00, 1.00, 1.00 0.74} respectively, to *getPlaces*.

Table 4. User weights given by the combination-based algorithm

	U_1	U_2	U_4
getWeather	0.92	0	0
getLocation	0.31	0.34	0
getNews	0.31	0.34	0
getHotels	0.27	0	1.13
getBook	0	0.51	0
getHotelID	0	0.51	0
getPlaces	0	0.51	0
getWeatherByZipCode	0	0.51	0
getWeatherByDate	0	0	0
getCityDescByName	0	0	1.61

In this algorithm, the operations' vectors are represented in a k dimensional space. This space is created by the k most similar users with the current one. Since the historical data is limited to the closest data with the current user, this algorithm is expected to generate good recommendations.

2.4 The k Parameter

In the user-based algorithm and the combination-based algorithm, the k parameter is the number of selected users. In these algorithms, we filter k users from the historical data before selecting the operations. Each operation is represented by a k dimensional vector and the selected operations are retrieved from a $m \times k$ matrix. Hence, in these algorithms, the k can be considered as the number of dimensions of a space which is used to represent the historical data for the next computation step. In our experiments, we will analyze the impact of this k parameter to the results. In the second algorithm, since we select the similar operations from the $m \times n$ weight matrix, the k parameter in this algorithm is alway equal to n.

3 Implementation and Experiments

In this section, we present the implementation efforts we have done to validate our approach. Firstly, we describe the application we have developed to implement our proposed algorithms. Secondly, we specify our evaluation methods and finally, we analyze the experimental results to assert the quality of the produced recommendations.

3.1 Implementation

We have developed a server-client application which allows users to register, set up their profiles and use the WS operations; and providers to upload their WSDL web services files. Besides a simple search engine, our tool provides to the user recommendation lists based on the current invoked WS operation. Our tool can be found at http://www-inf.it-sudparis.eu/SIMBAD/tools/WSRS/ws_recommender.html. The application was deployed in two parts: front-end written in Flex[1] and back-end in Java (see Figure 1). Mechanisms used to exchange data between server and client are the RemoteObject and BlazeDS framework[2]. Tomcat server 5.5 was set up for hosting our application.

Our tool's architecture is given in Fig.2. Concretely, a user can search or invoke a WS operation. His search results are recorded by an "Evaluation Module" for the evaluation steps. A "Data Preparation Module" manipulates the historical data for the recommendation and evaluation. The "DB Management Module" handles and monitors all of the interactions with the database. The "WS Collector & Checker" collects service descriptions from providers, crawlers, search engines, anonymous systems or even users.

3.2 Evaluation Methods

We evaluated the proposed algorithms using the precision and the recall which are commonly used in IR to evaluate the efficiency of a recommender system.

---

1 http://www.adobe.com/devnet/flex/

2 http://opensource.adobe.com/wiki/display/blazeds/BlazeDS

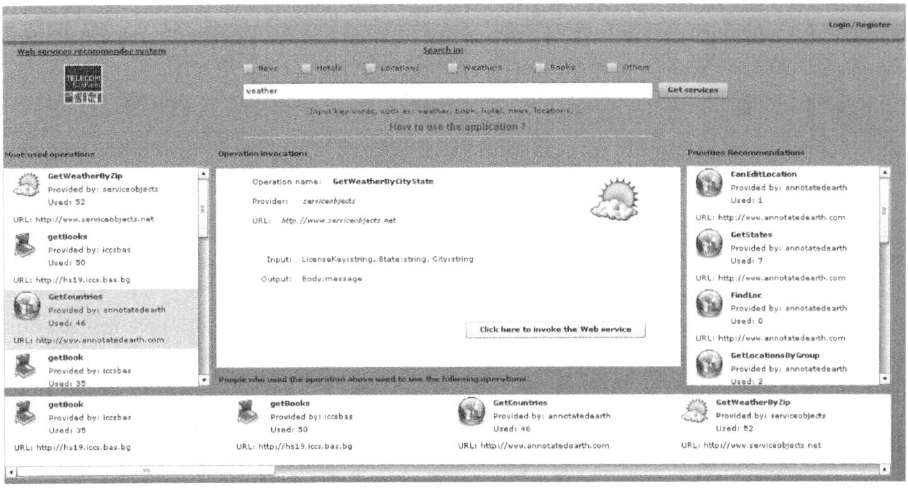

Fig. 1. WS Recommender System Application

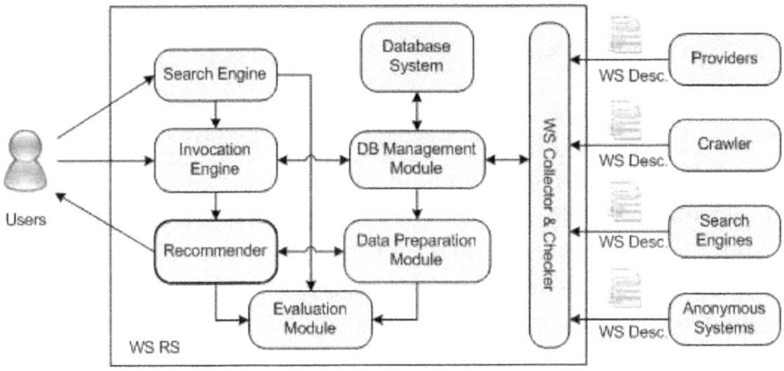

Fig. 2. Architecture of the WS Recommender System

These measures were computed using data set extracted from our application. We also extend our evaluation using the Root Mean Square Error (RMSE) [14] applied on an external and bigger data set.

Precision and the recall. To compute precision and recall, a relevant list of WS operations has to be specified in order to them with the operation lists returned by our algorithms. In our evaluation, we defined the relevant data in two ways: 1. the m most-used operations returned by our application's search engine and 2. the l last-used operations by users.

In the first way, suppose that a user U has typed a query string Q and gets a list of operations S from the system's search engine. The system extracts the m most-used operations from the list S into the list $S^*(m)$. $R_1(r)$, $R_2(r)$ and $R_3(r)$

are the recommendation lists with r WS operations generated by the proposed algorithms respectively when U selects an operation O. $M_1(m_1)$, $M_2(m_2)$ and $M_3(m_3)$ are the lists of operations matched between $S^*(m)$ with $R_1(r)$, $R_2(r)$ and $R_3(r)$ respectively. Then, the precisions and recalls are computed by (4).

$$Precision(i) = \frac{m_i}{r} \quad ; \quad Recall(i) = \frac{m_i}{m} \tag{4}$$

In the second way, we target to detect the behavior of each user and we change the **relevant operations** to *user's last used operations*. Since the recent used WS operations reflect the upcoming user interactions with a slight change if the user's behavior is stable, we consider them as the relevant operations as our proposed recommendation aims to be close to the upcoming user's interactions. We defined the relevant list as the last-r used operations of each user regardless the duplication of operations in the list. We computed the precision and recall based on the matched items between the lists retrieved by our algorithms with this list. Concretely, suppose that l-last used operations of the user U are given by the list L and $L_1(l_1)$, $L_2(l_2)$ and $L_3(l_3)$ are the lists of operations matched between $L(l)$ with $R_1(r)$, $R_2(r)$ and $R_3(r)$ respectively. Then, the precisions and recalls are computed by (5).

$$Precision(i) = \frac{l_i}{r} \quad ; \quad Recall(i) = \frac{l_i}{l} \tag{5}$$

RMSE. We also targeted to get more experiments with our algorithms on another data set, which is equivalent and larger than the data that we collected via our application. We decided to use the AudioScrobbler[3], a huge and richer data set about musical usage. Since each record in this data set includes three elements: a user ID, an artist ID and the number of hits that the user selected songs of the given artist, the AudioScrobbler data set is equivalent to our collected data and suitable to validate our algorithms. However, since the AudioScrobbler data set does not provide the relevant data as search engine's data or last usage data, we decided to get experiments with the RMSE measure.

In common, RMSE measure is used to evaluate the efficiency of a prediction system by comparing the predicted data to an existing ground-truth data set. It is famously used in the Netflix Prize[4] Contest [15]. Small RMSE values indicate good prediction. Basically, suppose that the prediction matrix is $P \in R_{(m \times n)}$ and the ground-truth answer matrix $A \in R_{(m \times n)}$. Let $I \in \{0,1\}_{(m \times n)}$ be the indicator of A. The RMSE between the prediction P and the answer A is defined as:

$$RMSE(P, A) = \sqrt{\frac{\sum_{i=1}^{m}\sum_{j=1}^{n} I_{ij}(A_{ij} - P_{ij})^2}{\sum_{i=1}^{m}\sum_{j=1}^{n} I_{ij}}} \tag{6}$$

[3] http://www.audioscrobbler.net/development/
[4] http://www.netflixprize.com/

Our algorithms aim at generating the most suitable WS operations to user's needs. In other words, our algorithm aim at predicting the operations that users can use based on the historical data. Hence, we extended our evaluation for more experiments by using RMSE. To evaluate our algorithms using this measure, we divided the AudioScrobbler data set, which consists 1033 user's IDs, 3435 artist's IDs, 644.281 records and 12.332.214 hits, into two parts: the training part consists of 4/5 the number of records and the rest (1/5) was used as the test set. We mapped the artist IDs in this data to the WS operation IDs in our application's data and run the algorithms with the k parameter. Due to the space's limitation, we present a short evaluation in section 3.4. Details of the evaluation can be found at http://www-inf.it-sudparis.eu/SIMBAD/tools/WSRS/wsr_evaluation.html.

3.3 Precision and the Recall Results

During two weeks, our application collected 271 interactions including anonymous usage. We run the proposed algorithms and evaluation methods in background. In the first evaluation, we use 10 operations returned from the search engine and set $k = 3$. The results (see Table.5) show that the User-based algorithm has the highest value of precision and recall. This result is impacted by the relevant data which is the results returned from the search engine. Indeed, the historical data is collected from the usage of PhD students who have somehow similar behavior. Hence, the user-based algorithm can return good results and become the suitable algorithm for this context.

Table 5. Experiments with k=3

	Search based (10)		Last-used (10)		Last-used (20)	
	Precision	Recall	Precision	Recall	Precision	Recall
User-based	0.192	0.611	0.248	0.384	0.307	0.404
Operation-based	0.107	0.521	0.351	0.704	0.464	0.689
Combination-based	0.075	0.23	0.216	0.458	0.334	0.415

In the second evaluation with the last usage data, we also set $k = 3$ and validate our algorithms in two cases with 10 and 20 last used operations of each user. The relevant data in this evaluation is more stable than the data returned by the search engine because the result returned by the search engine depends on users' queries and can have different numbers of operations. The algorithm which takes into account the whole set of historical data return the better results (see Table 5). The user-based algorithm and combination-based algorithm limit the original data into the data of k users, hence, they can easily miss the potential items which can make the evaluation more accurate. Meanwhile, the operation-based algorithm computes the similarities based on the relationships of all operations, hence, they are the best choices for this context.

Impact of the *k* parameter. To study the impact of the k parameter, we run the application with three different values of k which are 3, 4 and 5. The results in both evaluation methods (see Fig.3 and Fig.4) show that the precision and recall values of the user-based algorithm and the combination-based algorithm increase when k increases. Since the number of space's dimensions increases, the data is more accurate represented and our algorithms generate more precise recommendations. The operation-based algorithm compute the operation's similarities using the whole data set instead of reducing it to k-dimension. Therefore, its precision and recall are not impacted by the k parameter.

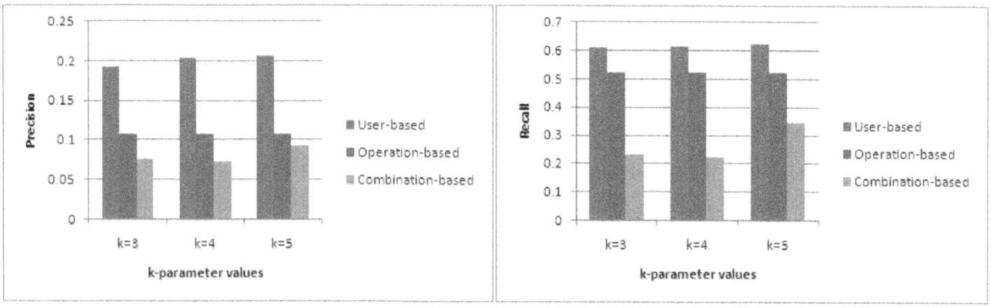

Fig. 3. Impact of k in the search-based evaluation method

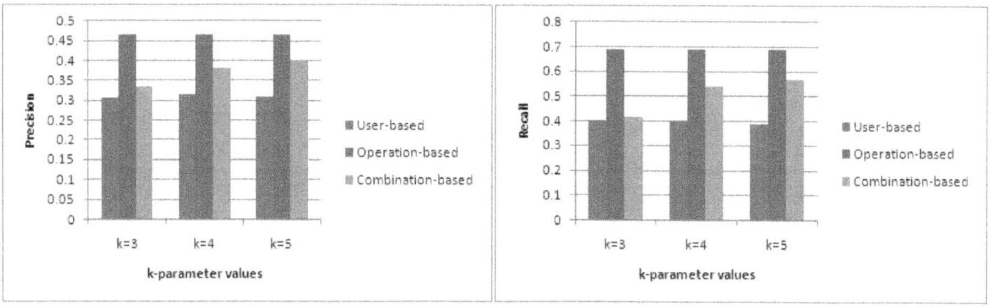

Fig. 4. Impact of k in the last usage-based evaluation method

Impact of the number of retrieved operations. The operation-based algorithm is not impacted by the k parameter since it does not represent the historical data set in a k-dimensional space. However, it is impacted by the number of retrieved operations. We got this experiment by varying the number of retrieved operations from 5 to 15 and re-computing its precision with the first evaluation method. Figure 5 shows that the less retrieved operations, the more accurate the recommendations. Since the accurate recommended operations are at the beginning of the recommendation list and the precision is computed by the fraction of exact items and retrieved items, the precision decreases if the

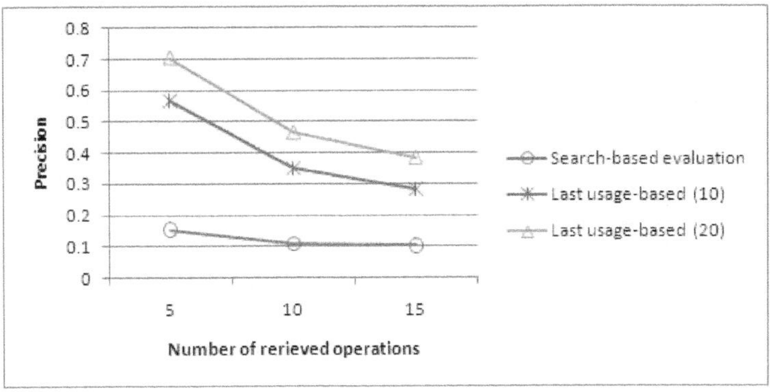

Fig. 5. Impact of the number of retrieved operations

retrieved items increase. In both evaluation methods based on the search data and last usage data, the results show that our best experience is achieved with 5 retrieved items.

The operation-based algorithm computes the similarities without reducing the number of dimensions which are used to present an operation. In our experience, this algorithm achieves the best result with the highest precision values.

3.4 RMSE Results

For RMSE, we run our algorithms on the training set of the AudioScrobller and compared the results with the test set. Due to the lack of space, we present only the result of the combination-based algorithm. We computed the RMSE for each users and validated the proposed algorithms with various k-parameter values from 1 to 100. Fig.6 shows the distribution of RMSE and the average RMSE values computed by the combination-based algorithm.

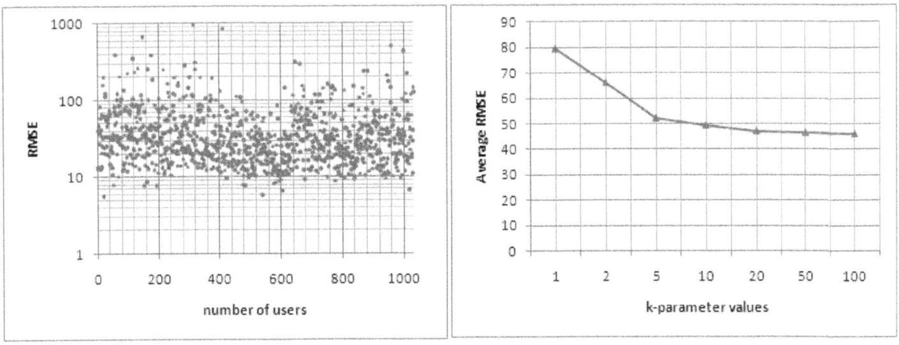

Fig. 6. Evaluation of the combination-based algorithm based on RMSE

As the number of space dimensions increases, the cropped data in the first step of the combination-based algorithm is represented by more-dimensions vectors. Consequently, our algorithm captured more detailed historical data and returned more accurate predictions to the user's usage. In general, our algorithms achieve better results when k increases.

4 Related Work and Discussion

The main goal of building a recommender system for web service discovery is providing the closest services with user's interests. The basic measure which is used to find the expected services is the similarity between request from users (query, profile, historic data, etc) and data stored in the service repository. Previous approaches, which were based on the traditional service descriptions (WSDL documents), could be classified in the categories: clustering [5], rating based [16], words analysis [17] and vector space model [6,7,18]. A recent work built a WS recommender system based on the Pearson Correlation Coefficient (PCC) and collaborative prediction [9]. However they provided the recommendations based on the QoS values which do not reflect the user's interest and expectation.

In semantic web services discovery, the similarity can be computed using the service's elements [10] (such as input, output, pre-condition and effect), service requests [19] or ontologies matches [20,16]. However, the semantic web service descriptions are somewhat the extensions of traditional WSDL files with new elements and annotations which can link them to semantic concepts and defined domains or ontologies. The recommendation processes based on semantic descriptions are also the text based analysis. The advantage of our approach is that we can capture the "semantic" model without using the semantic service descriptions or the web ontology language (OWL).

Some approaches applied Latent Semantic Indexing (LSI) which is a mathematical, statistical technique for extracting and inferring relations of documents and terms. This technique is applied in various fields of study, including IR, synonym testing, semantic priming, information filtering, novel applications and other statistics aspects [21,22] and it can be apply for deploying a good recommender system. A remarkable approach which applied LSI on a set of WSDL documents and terms was proposed by Chen Wu et. al. [23]. They followed the guide of [24] to find the most similar service descriptions with the user's query. However, their prototype supported only single-word queries and the evaluation was done with 10 queries at all.

Another approach applied the Singular Vector Decomposition, which generates a reduced latent space and contains the main latent information among the co-occurrence activities[25,26], on services descriptions to generate services recommendations [27]. They proposed a "divide and conquer" method, using the Bisecting k-means algorithm and Euclidean distance, to handle the poor scalability in the Web environment and the issue of lacking semantics. Their approach was also a text-based solution which is different from us.

In our work, we employed three collaborative filtering algorithms based on VSM using implicit historical data. Our algorithms generate recommendations without asking the users any explicit knowledge such as interesting, ratings, comments, profiles, etc. In practice, our experiments showed that by tracking user's historical data, which reflects the user's behavior, we can infer good recommendations.

5 Conclusion

Collaborative filtering is one of the most powerful techniques in making recommendations. Based on this technique, we proposed three algorithms which can generate good recommendations and avoid the problems of text-based approaches. Our contributions in this work can be summarized in three main points: (1) we provided VSM-based algorithms applied in **new context** which is **web services recommendation** based on **user's behaviors**; (2) we proposed **innovative recommendation methods** in which we represented the usage data as vectors in a k-dimensional space; (3) we brought not only **original evaluation methods** which are based on precision and recall but also an efficient measure which is RMSE to prove the efficiency of our algorithms.

Our proposed algorithms generate recommendations based only on the user's usage data within the discovery process. Thus, our approach is **self-contained** within the web service discovery process, **independent** from any explicit or human centric or error prone knowledge. Whereas other information such as user's rating or service reputation can be hard to be captured, our approach is a good solution as it does not use such kind of explicit knowledge as inputs to propose recommendations.

In our future works, we will build a specific recommender system for web service discovery by taking into account other WS parameters such as services descriptions, relations, compositions, etc. We are also looking on measuring the satisfactory of users. To that end, other parameters such as the implicit relations among users (or WS operations) and the number of times that a user accesses to the system will be considered. We are also working on how to compare our experiments with other approaches as we (our approach and the others) do not use the same input data. To do so, we have already published on the web our results and we are looking for the other approaches' published implementations and experiments.

References

1. Ferris, C., Farrell, J.: What are web services? ACM Commun. 46(6), 31 (2003)
2. Daniel, B., Katharina, S., Holger, L., Fensel, D.: Web service discovery? a reality check. In: Sure, Y., Domingue, J. (eds.) ESWC 2006. LNCS, vol. 4011, Springer, Heidelberg (2006)
3. Resnick, P., Varian, H.R.: Recommender systems. ACM Commun. 40(3), 56–58 (1997)
4. Wu, C.-T., Wang, H.-F.: Recent development of recommender systems. In: IEEE International Conference on Industrial Engineering and Engineering Management, pp. 228–232 (December 2007)

5. Dong, X., Halevy, A., Madhavan, J., Nemes, E., Zhang, J.: Similarity search for web services. In: VLDB 2004: Proceedings of the Thirtieth international conference on Very large data bases, pp. 372–383. VLDB Endowment (2004)
6. Platzer, C., Dustdar, S.: A vector space search engine for web services. In: Third IEEE European Conference on Web Services, ECOWS 2005, p. 9 (November 2005)
7. Birukou, A., Blanzieri, E., D'Andrea, V., Giorgini, P., Kokash, N.: Improving web service discovery with usage data. IEEE Software 24(6), 47–54 (2007)
8. Kokash, N., Birukou, A., D'Andrea, V.: Web Service Discovery Based on Past User Experience. In: Abramowicz, W. (ed.) BIS 2007. LNCS, vol. 4439, pp. 95–107. Springer, Heidelberg (2007)
9. Zheng, Z., Ma, H., Lyu, M.R., King, I.: Wsrec: A collaborative filtering based web service recommender system. In: ICWS 2009: Proceedings of the 2009 IEEE International Conference on Web Services, Washington, DC, USA, pp. 437–444. IEEE Computer Society, Los Alamitos (2009)
10. Wang, Z., Liu, K., Lv, G., Hao, X.: Study of an algorithm of web service matching based on semantic web service. In: ALPIT 2007: Proceedings of the Sixth International Conference on Advanced Language Processing and Web Information Technology (ALPIT 2007), Washington, DC, USA, pp. 429–433. IEEE Computer Society, Los Alamitos (2007)
11. Paolucci, M., Kawamura, T., Payne, T.R., Sycara, K.P.: Semantic matching of web services capabilities. In: Horrocks, I., Hendler, J. (eds.) ISWC 2002. LNCS, vol. 2342, pp. 333–347. Springer, Heidelberg (2002)
12. Salton, G., Wong, A., Yang, C.S.: A vector space model for automatic indexing. ACM Commun. 18(11), 613–620 (1975)
13. Manning, C.D., Raghavan, P., Schutze, H.: Introduction to Information Retrieval. Cambridge University Press, Cambridge (2008)
14. Herlocker, J.L., Konstan, J.A., Terveen, L.G., Riedl, J.T.: Evaluating collaborative filtering recommender systems. ACM Trans. Inf. Syst. 22(1), 5–53 (2004)
15. James, B., Stan, L.: The netflix prize. In: KDDCup 2007 (2007)
16. Manikrao, U.S., Prabhakar, T.V.: Dynamic selection of web services with recommendation system. In: NWESP 2005: Proceedings of the International Conference on Next Generation Web Services Practices, Washington, DC, USA, p. 117. IEEE Computer Society, Los Alamitos (2005)
17. Blake, M.B., Nowlan, M.F.: A web service recommender system using enhanced syntactical matching. In: ICWS, pp. 575–582 (2007)
18. Kokash, N., Birukou, R.: Web service discovery based on past user experience. In: Abramowicz, W. (ed.) BIS 2007. LNCS, vol. 4439, pp. 95–107. Springer, Heidelberg (2007)
19. Paliwal, A.V., Adam, N.R., Bornhovd, C.: Web service discovery: Adding semantics through service request expansion and latent semantic indexing. In: IEEE International Conference on Services Computing, pp. 106–113 (2007)
20. Wu, S.: A new web services matching algorithm. In: IUCE 2009: Proceedings of the 2009 International Symposium on Intelligent Ubiquitous Computing and Education, Washington, DC, USA, pp. 414–416. IEEE Computer Society, Los Alamitos (2009)
21. Landauer, T.K., Foltz, P.W., Laham, D.: An introduction to latent semantic analysis. Discourse Processes (25), 259–284 (1998)
22. Berry, M.W., Dumais, S.T., O'Brien, G.W.: Using linear algebra for intelligent information retrieval. SIAM Rev. 37(4), 573–595 (1995)

23. Wu, C., Potdar, V., Chang, E.: Latent Semantic Analysis — The Dynamics of Semantics Web Services Discovery. In: Dillon, T.S., Chang, E., Meersman, R., Sycara, K. (eds.) Advances in Web Semantics I. LNCS, vol. 4891, pp. 346–373. Springer, Heidelberg (2008)
24. Kontostathis, A., Pottenger, W.M.: A framework for understanding latent semantic indexing (lsi) performance. Inf. Process. Manage. 42(1), 56–73 (2006)
25. Baeza-Yates, R., Ribeiro-Neto, B.: Modern Information Retrieval, 1st edn. Addison-Wesley, Reading (May 1999)
26. Paterek, A.: Improving regularized singular value decomposition for collaborative filtering. In: KDDCup 2007 (2007)
27. Ma, J., Zhang, Y., He, J.: Web services discovery based on latent semantic approach. In: ICWS 2008: Proceedings of the 2008 IEEE International Conference on Web Services, Washington, DC, USA, pp. 740–747. IEEE Computer Society, Los Alamitos (2008)

Policy-Based Attestation of Service Behavior for Establishing Rigorous Trust

Dongxi Liu and John Zic

CSIRO ICT Centre, Australia
firstname.lastname@csiro.au

Abstract. A service is rigorously trusted if it can provide firm evidences to its users about its behavior. The evidences ensure that the service really follows its claimed behavior to process the requests and sensitive input data from users. In this paper, we propose a framework, which can attest the behavior of web services according to the trust policies specified by users. Different users may concern different aspects of service behavior. By using policies, this framework allows user-specific behavior attestation. In addition, this framework also protects service providers. When a user sends a service request, the framework needs the user to show that he has agreed on the service behavior. A case study is used to describe the critical processing steps of the framework to deliver rigorously trusted services.

1 Introduction

Web services or web-based applications are attracting more and more users to engage in sensitive tasks like online shopping, trip planning and medical consultation. Many of these tasks need users to provide their sensitive data like credit card numbers and medication records to services. To be widely accepted, the services need to be rigorously trusted. That is, users need firm evidence to make sure the services always use their sensitive data responsibly. For example, users would only like to use a medical consultation service if they can make sure their health information are not released improperly.

At present, most users select services based on their reputations. Although useful, reputation-based trusted systems [1] do not provide rigorous trust since a good reputation is not a firm evidence of good system behavior. In current trusted computing [2], remote attestation is used to report the state of a system to a remote entity. If the system is in a *desired* state, then the system is trusted. The system state is generally measured as a hash value obtained by hashing software binaries running on the system. An expected hash value ensures the integrity of the remote system, but not its behavior. Hence, the remote attestation simply based on hash values cannot provide rigorous trust. For example, a malicious service (or a service with bad behavior) should not obtain your sensitive data no matter whether it has been tampered or not.

To address the above problem of remote attestation, semantic or property-based remote attestation has been proposed. Terra [3] binds a certificate with a hash value. This certificate maps the hash value to software names and versions. In [4], Haldar et al. propose to use a trusted virtual machine to attest properties of code running on it. However, as commented in the survey [2], Haldar et al. do not specify how the trusted virtual

R. Meersman et al. (Eds.): OTM 2010, Part I, LNCS 6426, pp. 240–255, 2010.

machine decides whether a piece of software provides a given property. Hence, it is not clear whether their approach can let users to check the service behavior. Sadeghi et al. proposes the property-based attestation by mapping the platform configurations (or hash values) to properties [5], but do not describes what properties they will support and how to check properties of a piece of software [2]. On the other hand, these approaches do not support policies for user to choose the interested properties to attest. For example, the approach in [4] attests the property of class hierarchies in a service implementation, which however may not be concerned by users.

In this paper, we propose a framework to deliver rigourously trusted services. This framework includes a trusted third party, called Trust Authority, to attest the behavior of services. Briefly, to deliver a rigorously trusted service, the Trust Authority first requires an abstract model from a service provider that describes service behavior; then, it verifies the behavioral model against trust policies formulated by users who want to invoke this service. A user's desired behavioral properties is satisfied when the model conforms to the trust policies. After a successful verification, the Trust Authority returns to users a certificate, which is used as an evidence of the service behavior conforming to trust policies. By this way, this framework conveys the high level properties of the service to users. Additionally, this certificate is also needed to invoke a service to ensure that users has agreed on the behavior of the service. The Trusted Authority in our framework is easier to deploy than the trusted virtual machine in [4] since it is independent of the platforms used by service providers.

The Trust Authority verifies services by using their behavioral models rather than by using service code directly. This is more efficient since models are generally more compact than code. There might be a large number of user requests for verifying service behavior, so it is important for the Trust Authority to perform verification efficiently. In our framework, the behavioral models are constructed by service providers. The Trust Authority does not have the burden of transforming code into models. In addition to the behavioral models, the service providers also provide a proof which shows the validity of the models against the corresponding service code to the Trust Authority. After simply checking the proof, the Trust Authority can determine whether the models can represent the behavior of service code. This idea is inspired by proof-carrying code (PCC) [6] to improve the scalability of the Trust Authority since checking a proof is much easier than generating a proof.

Users depend on trust policies to express their trust requirements on the service behaviors. In our framework, trust policies are enforced against service behavioral models at the verification time, so the executions of services are not affected by the enforcement of trust policies. Hence, our framework delivers trusted services without causing performance overhead after a service is selected and successfully verified. Our trust policies can express both safety properties and liveness properties. For example, a policy for a safety property could express that a credit card number cannot be released to a bad web service, while a policy for a liveness property can express that a tax report must be sent to the tax office by a tax agency service. In addition, our trust policies can describe information flow [7]. An information flow policy concerns whether a value is implicitly or explicitly dependent on another value. For example, a client can use an information flow policy to express that any information derived from a credit card number cannot be released improperly.

The details of our framework are described in Section 2. We then describe how to construct service behavior from service code in Section 3. The trust policies are defined in Section 4. A case study is described in Section 5. The paper closes with a review of related work and conclusion in Sections 6 and 7, respectively.

2 The Framework for Attesting Service Behavior

As shown in Figure 1, the framework consists of three kinds of components: Trust Authorities, Service Providers and Clients (or Users). Trust Authorities are the critical components of our framework. Service Providers and Clients are also found in existing SOA systems [8]. Other components of the existing SOA systems like Service Registries are not shown in this framework since they are independent of our purpose of behavior attestation and we do not need to change them. Our framework is an incremental extension of the existing SOA systems.

Our framework is distinguished from the existing SOA systems by the protocol that is used to build a rigorous, mutual trust relationship between clients and service providers. The protocol consists in three phases, which are described and discussed below. At the end of these phases, the behavioral information of services is conveyed from service providers to clients.

Phase 1: Service Certification. In the framework, all services that want to be rigorously trusted must be certified by Trust Authorities. For each service offered by a provider, the provider needs to send a message (M_1 in Figure 1) containing three pieces of information to a Trust Authority: (1) the service implementation code, (2) the service's behavioral model and (3) a proof showing that the service conforming to the behavioral model. Upon receiving such a request, the Trust Authority checks

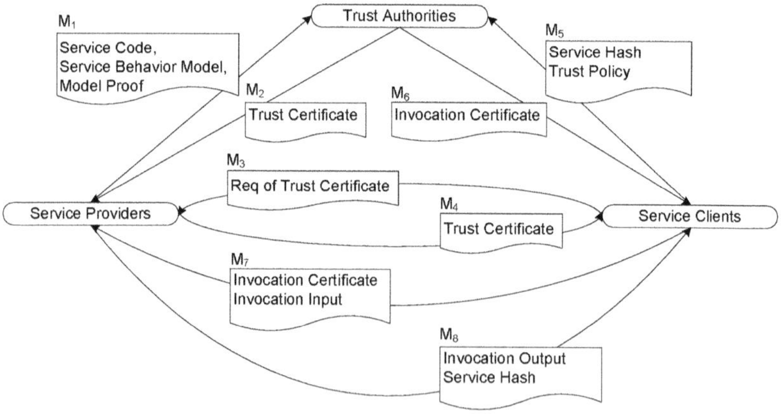

Fig. 1. The Framework of Behavior Attestation

the proof and determines whether the model can represent the behavior of the service. Since checking a proof is much easier than generating a proof, we use the proof-carrying mechanism [6] to improve the scalability of the Trust Authority.

If the check is successful, the Trust Authority sends message M_2 to the provider. This message consists of a trust certificate, which contains a hash value of the service and location of the Trust Authority to the provider. The trust certificate indicates that the service is now certified by a Trust Authority and that the claimed behavior model is correct against the service code. The hash value of the service simply allows it to be identified, and also allows any changes to be detected that may be made to the certified service. The hash value and the behavioral model of a service are kept by the Trust Authority and are used to check whether a certified service satisfies the trust requirements of clients. Note that the Trust Authority does not restrict where to deploy and how to invoke any certified services.

Phase 2: Verifying Service Behavior. In this phase, we assume a client has discovered the service that matches their service requirements from some service registry. How to query a service is beyond the purpose of our framework. After discovering a service, the client sends a request M_3 to the service provider to ask whether it has certified the service. If the service provider is providing a trusted service, it can send back the trust certificate for this service in message M_4.

At this point, the client then sends message M_5 to the Trust Authority specified in the trust certificate to verify the behavior of the candidate service against the client's trust requirements. The message itself contains the client's trust requirements and a hash value that is used to index or identify the service behavioral model to be verified. If the behavioral model satisfies the trust requirements, the Trust Authority returns an invocation certificate in message M_6, otherwise the clients have to check other candidate services. An invocation certificate includes the trust requirements and the service hash value. That is, a service is bound to the trust requirements of client in an invocation certificate. The reception of the invocation certificate by the client is an evidence that the candidate service satisfies their trust requirements, and is used to invoke the candidate service.

Phase 3: Mutual Trustworthiness of Service Invocation. When a client receives the invocation certificate, he gains the confidence that the candidate service is trustworthy in terms of their trust requirements. At this point, however, it would be a mistake to follow standard SOA techniques and allow the client to invoke the service by constructing input messages and then receive the result from the provider. This is because the client and provider (at this stage) have still not established a trust relationship. As examples, consider the following situations. First, from the point of view of the provider: if a client complains that its input data has been misused despite being run on a faithful service, the provider does not have evidence to show that the client has agreed on the service behavior before invoking it. From the client's perspective, suppose that the client received an invocation result from a provider. Using the protocol elaborated so far still leaves the client unable to be sure whether the invocation result was really generated by the service with its behavioral model verified by the Trust Authority at the last step. In other words, a dishonest service provider may send to clients a trust certificate for a service (call it S_A) which satisfies their trust requirements. However, the service provider actually executes another service S_B to deal with the sensitive inputs from clients.

Establishing trust between the client and provider requires two final steps in the protocol. In the first step, we insist that each client include an invocation certificate together with any input data when invoking a service before constructing message M_7 that is sent to the provider. The invocation certificate is an evidence for the provider that clients have agreed that the invoked service satisfies their trust requirements. That is, the invocation certificate is used as an agreement on the service behavior and trust requirements between the service provider and clients, and hence can be used to eliminate the first fault condition.

In the second step of this phase, the service provider not only returns the invocation output (the service result) in message M_8, but also returns the hash value of the executed service. If this hash value matches the hash value return in the trust certificate in message M_4, then the executed service is really the one whose behavioral model is certified by the Trust Authority and satisfies the trust requirements.

The hash value of an executed service could be generated by the service engine when it launches the service. For example, if the service is deployed as Java bytecode files, the service engines like Axis2 can generate the service hash at the time of loading these files to execute. In the next section, we will describe how to construct service behavioral models automatically for the services implemented in Java. To trust the hash value of an executed service, we need to trust the service engine. The existing integrity measurement techniques and protocols [9] can be used for this purpose. For example, if the hash values of widely-used service engines and operating systems are already known by clients, the integrity of the platforms of service providers can be checked by clients by using the exiting remote attestation protocols. That is, our framework attests the behavior of the service code, which encodes the logic of dealing with the clients' request, rather than the whole platforms. Hence, the behavioral attestation provided by our framework is complementary to the existing hash-value based remote attestation.

3 Certifying Service Behaviors

There are many programming and process description languages for implementing services. Our initial prototype is implemented in one of the most popular languages: Java, and we hope to support other languages in future. In the following section, we introduce an overview of a Java Virtual Machine (JVM) bytecode that is used to implement services and can be executed on a service engine (e.g., Axis2), before moving on to describe our model of service behavior, and finally the section closes with a discussion of the behavioral model construction and how to certify these models.

3.1 JVM Bytecode for Coding Services

Figure 2 shows a subset of JVM bytecode used to implement services. Note that programmers do not directly write services in bytecode. They write Java programs, compile

$$
\begin{aligned}
M &::= (C, m, \Delta \rightarrow \delta) \mapsto B \\
\delta &::= \texttt{int} \mid C \mid \delta[] \\
\Delta &::= \epsilon \mid \delta \cdot \Delta \\
B &::= \epsilon \mid in \cdot B \\
in &::= \texttt{new}\ C \mid \texttt{iconst}\ n \mid \texttt{store}\ x \mid \texttt{load}\ x \\
&\quad \mid \texttt{newarray}\ \delta \mid \texttt{astore} \mid \texttt{aload} \mid \texttt{alength} \\
&\quad \mid \texttt{putfield}\ f \mid \texttt{getfield}\ f \mid \texttt{add} \\
&\quad \mid \texttt{ifne}\ l \mid \texttt{goto}\ l \mid \texttt{return} \mid \texttt{invoke}\ (C, m)
\end{aligned}
$$

Fig. 2. JVM Bytecode Syntax

them into bytecode, and then deploy them into some service engine like Axis2. Since our behavioral model is designed for service bytecode, the Java compiler is not needed to be a part of trusted computing base in our framework.

Figure 2 gives the syntax for methods. The definition of class C is ignored for compactness. A method M is described by the class C in which it is defined, its name m, type $\Delta \rightarrow \delta$ and body B that is a sequence of instructions. In the type $\Delta \rightarrow \delta$, Δ is a sequence of types, corresponding to a sequence of input arguments for a method and δ is the type for output. An empty sequence is represented by ϵ. The bytecode is a stack-based language, with instruction operands and results passed through a stack. The operational semantics of instructions in Figure 2 is explained informally below and the mechanism of constructing behavioral models is based on the bytecode semantics.

The instruction `new` C creates an uninitialized object of class C and pushes its reference onto the top of the operand stack. `iconst` n pushes onto the stack the integer n. `store` x and `load` x manipulates the local variable x by assigning it the top value of the stack or pushing its value back to the stack. There are four instructions for dealing with arrays. An array of type δ is created by `newarray` δ and its size is determined by the top value of the stack; `astore` and `aload` set or get the array elements; the instruction `arraylength` returns the length of array at the top of the operand stack.

An object field f can be updated by the instruction `putfield` f with the top value of the stack and accessed by `getfield` f, which pushes the value of f back onto the stack. The instruction add adds the two values at the top of the stack and pushes the result back. The conditional instruction `ifne` l transfers execution control to the instruction at l if the top two values of the stack are not equal, otherwise the control is transferred to the next instruction. For `goto` l, the control is transferred to the instruction at l unconditionally. The instruction `return` terminates the current execution and returns the top value on the stack. The method m in class C is invoked by `invoke` (C, m) with the arguments pushed onto the stack.

3.2 The Service Behavioral Model

A service behavioral model is more compact than the service bytecode, hence more efficient for a Trust Authority to check the service behavior based on the behavioral model. Various software models have been proposed for model-checking software reliability and security [10,11,12]. These models are usually designed for their specific model-checking purposes. For example, the model in [12] concerns only the order of system calls, which is not suitable for checking how client data are processed by service bytecode. Because of the wide variety of applications of models, there is no universal software behavior models.

The model we design for abstracting service bytecode is called the *ordered relational behavioral model.* This model reflects all data relationships built by the service bytecode, while removing the operational details like moving data between the operand stack and the local store. An ordered relational behavioral model is represented as a tree (R, E), where R is a set of tree nodes and E is a set of tree edges. A node $r \in R$ is a data relation and an edge $r_1 \rightarrow r_2$ means that the relation r_1 is built before the relation r_2 when executing the modeled service. By traversing the model from the root node, we can see how data relations are being built and where data is flowing.

Table 1 gives a set of relations that is able to represent the behavior of services implemented in the JVM bytecode defined in Figure 2. Though we take Java as an example language of implementing services, the relations could in principle also be used to model services implemented in other object-oriented language such as $C\sharp$. Note that the relations in Table 1 can be extended if needed.

Table 1. Relations for Behavioral Model

Relations	Description
$\texttt{entry}(v_1, ..., v_n)$	$v_1, ..., v_n$ are method inputs.
$\texttt{exit}(v)$	v is a return value.
$\texttt{newv}(v, n)$	v is a new value initialized as integer n.
$\texttt{newa}(v_1, v_2)$	v_1 is a new array with length v_2.
$\texttt{newo}(v)$	v is a new object.
$\texttt{cmpne}(v_1, v_2, 0)$	v_1 and v_2 is not unequal.
$\texttt{cmpne}(v_1, v_2, 1)$	v_1 and v_2 is unequal.
$\texttt{sum}(v_1, v_2, v_3)$	The addition of v_1 and v_2 is v_3.
$\texttt{fput}(v_1, f, v_2)$	The value of field f in object v_1 is updated to v_2.
$\texttt{fget}(v_1, f, v_2)$	v_2 is assigned the value of field f in object v_1.
$\texttt{aput}(v_1, i, v_2)$	v_1 is an array, and the value of its entry i is changed to v_2.
$\texttt{aget}(v_1, i, v_2)$	v_1 is an array, and v_2 is changed to the value of its entry i.
$\texttt{alen}(v_1, v_2)$	v_1 is an array, and v_2 is its length.
$\texttt{call}(C, m, V, v)$	A call to method m in class C with argument list V returns v.

When implemented in Java, a *service operation* corresponds to a *method.* The model of a method always takes the $\texttt{entry}(v_1, ..., v_n)$ relation as its root node, with v_i corresponding to the ith parameter of the method. A leaf node of the model takes the $\texttt{exit}(v)$, meaning that the operation returns v. These two relations are only used in the root and leaf nodes in a model. The other relations in Table 1 corresponds to some instructions in Figure 2. For example, the `add` instruction has a corresponding relation $\texttt{sum}(v_1, v_2, v_3)$, which explicitly represents the relation between arguments and result that are passed through the operand stack operationally by the `add` instruction; the `ifne` l has two corresponding relations $\texttt{cmpne}(v_1, v_2, 0)$ and $\texttt{cmpne}(v_1, v_2, 1)$, which are to express the path conditions [13]. The chidren node of the $\texttt{cmpne}(v_1, v_2, 0)$ relation models the code following the `ifne` l instruction, while the children node of the $\texttt{cmpne}(v_1, v_2, 1)$ relation models the code at label l.

3.3 Model Construction and Proof

Automatic construction of the ordered relational models is crucial for the applicability of the behavior attestation framework. An automatic model construction mechanism is expected to produce a model that should: (1) match the service semantics, (2) capture all data flows within a service and (3) be finite.

We have developed a natural deductive system for automatically constructing service behavioral models. The system consists of a set of inference rules, with each Java bytecode instruction having one or two rules to construct the corresponding relation. The system is used by service providers to construct behavioral models and their proofs, and used by Trust Authorities to check proofs.

Given a piece of bytecode by a service provider, the deduction system infers the constituent instructions in order and constructs the service behavioral model. The system also outputs a derivation tree of inference rules, which is then used as the proof of the behavioral model. When a Trust Authority receives a certifying request, it checks the validity of the proof by checking whether each derivation step in the proof is valid, that is, whether it corresponds to a valid inference rule. In particular, each proof step can be checked independently, and so it is suitable for parallel processing.

The details of these rules are not described in this paper due to space limitation. Basically, the rules have a similar format as the rules used in type-checking bytecode programs [14,15]. The difference is that in the type-checking system, the result is the types of the bytecode programs, while in our system, the result is a behavioral model. In addition, our system uses the derivation tree as a proof to convey the trust of constructed models, while in the type-checking system, the derivation tree is not used any more after a bytecode program is checked.

4 Trust Requirements and Policies

Service clients describe their trust requirements in trust policies, which express how their data must be processed by remotely-executed services. Services are trusted if their behavioral models satisfy the trust policies.

4.1 Data Processing Actions

Trust policies depend on a set of actions to describe data processing. Since clients do not have the knowledge of service implementation, the actions here focus on the data flow channels, including the channels between services and clients, the channels between services and the platforms running them, and the channels between services and network applications (e.g., web services or servers).

- `input`$(v_1, ..., v_n)$: $v_1,...,v_n$ are n service inputs.
- `output`(v): v is a service output to clients.
- `read`(v): v is read from a local location(i.e., the storage on the machine running the service). This action reflects the integrity of service outputs. For example, by using it, clients can express whether the service output is affected by some locally stored values.
- `write`(v): v is stored to a local location. With respect to the confidentiality of clients data, for example, a client can use this action to check whether their data is stored by the service.
- `recv`(ip, v): v is obtained from the network location ip (e.g., ip is a network address for a web service). Like the `read` action, this action can express the integrity of service outputs. In addition, it can specify for a composite service which component services are expected. For example, clients may specify that a trip-planning service depends on a weather forecast service in the country they will visit.
- `send`(ip, v): v is sent to the network location ip. Like `write`, this action can express the confidentiality of clients data. On the other hand, this action can check whether a composite service sends data to an expected component service. For example, clients may expect a tax agent service to send the tax report to the tax office.

4.2 Trust Policies

A trust policy is expressed as an automaton $(Q, \Sigma, q_0, F, \delta)$, where Q is a set of states, Σ a set of data processing actions as defined above, $q_0 \in Q$ the initial state, $F \subseteq Q$ a set of final states and δ a set of transition rules. A transition rule has the form $(q, a, cond, q')$, meaning that there is a transition from state q to q' when an action a happens with the condition $cond$ satisfied.

Before defining conditions, we first describe a linearity requirement to policy automata which captures that a state is required to have *at most* one subsequent state. Although this appears to be restrictive in the first instance, it does not actually restrict the expressiveness of policies. If a state needs to have multiple subsequent states, a client can write multiple policies to cover each subsequent state. This linearity property makes it easier to enforce trust policies, since we do not need to consider how to combine the verification results from different transition paths. The access control language XACML includes several operators to combine policies, which however has been shown not flexible enough to capture all possible policy combinations [16]. Our design principle is to let service clients determine whether a verified service is acceptable or not when and if there are conflicting verification results for multiple policies.

Suppose $(q, a, cond, q')$ is a rule in a policy and q'' is a preceding state of q. The condition $cond$ is logical formula built from the following basic formulas with standard boolean connectives: $v = c, v < c, v > c$ and $(q'', v') \rightarrow v$, where v is an argument of action a and c is a constant. Note that the last condition formula is not usual. It means that there is information flow from v' to v, where v' is an argument of the action in the transition starting from state q''. That is, some information about v' can be inferred from v. For example, a service does not directly send a credit card number v' to a malicious service. However, if it sends v, where $v = v' + 1$, then the confidentiality of v' is actually violated. The condition $cond$ is explained further by the policy examples below. Compared to the existing security automata [17], the automata presented here have the advantage of being able to express information flow policies.

A trust policy may be either positive or negative. A policy is positive if its last state is a final state, otherwise it is negative. A last state does not have subsequent states and is reachable from the initial state. A positive policy is used to express a liveness property, and a negative is used to express a safety property. For example, a tax report that must be sent to the tax office finally is a positive policy (liveness), while a credit card number not being sent to a malicious web service is a negative policy (safety).

The trust authority verifies services differently for the two kinds of policies. It over-approximates the service behavioral models for positive policies, while under-approximates the models for negative policies. Approximation is necessary for static verification due to the lack of actual values of program variables at the verification time [18]. If a positive policy is satisfied by a service behavioral model, then it must be satisfied by the real execution of the service. If a negative policy is not satisfied by a service behavioral model, then it must not be satisfied by the execution of the service. These properties are other advantages of the policy automata developed here to be able to express both liveness and safety properties.

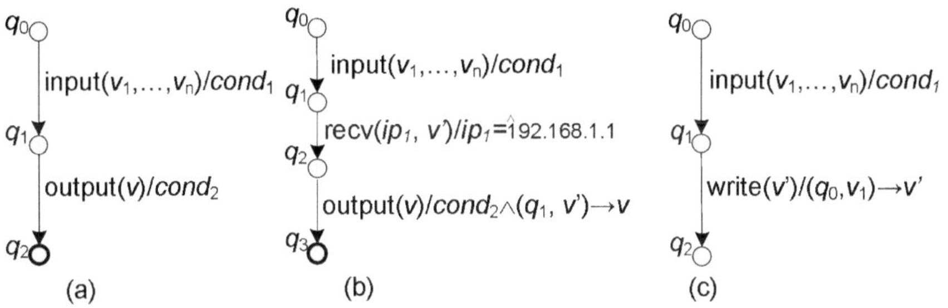

Fig. 3. Examples of Trust Policies

Figure 3 shows three examples of trust policies. The node q_0 is the initial state and the state with a bold circle (e.g., q_2 in example (a)) represents the final state. The policy (a) is positive, which expresses the precondition ($cond_1$) and postcondition ($cond_2$) found in existing semantic service modeling languages such as [19,20]. Moreover, the policy (b) shows that clients have the flexibility to refine the preconditions and postconditions requirements by specifying the output v is dependent on the information received from the location 192.168.1.1. The policy (c) is negative, which shows that any information dependent on the input v_1 cannot be stored by the service.

4.3 Enforcement of Trust Policies

Trust polices are enforced against service behavioral models. Recall that a behavioral model is a tree, and so a behavioral model is enforced by checking each path from `entry` to `exit` separately. A positive policy is satisfied if all model paths bring the policy automaton to its last state. On the contrary, a negative policy is satisfied if there is no model path to take the policy automaton to its last state. In the following, we informally describe how policies are enforced with respect to a model path.

The basic enforcement mechanism is to use the policy automaton to monitor the symbolic execution of a model path. The existing security automata [17] are used to monitor real program or system executions. That is, we bring security automata into the area of static analysis of services.

A policy automaton is enforced from its initial state and a model path is symbolically executed from its first node. The current node is checked against the current state, and then the subsequent node becomes the new current node. If the current node matches the data processing action expected by the current state and the transition condition also holds, then the policy automaton moves to the next state, which then becomes the new current state. Otherwise, the current state is not changed. At present, we define the following three matching relations between model nodes and automaton actions. The `entry` and `exit` nodes match the `input` and `output` actions, respectively; the nodes of calling Java library for reading and writing files or databases match `read` and `write` actions, respectively; the nodes of calling Java library for sending and receiving network packets match `send` and `recv` actions, respectively.

5 A Case Study

We describe a case where a behavioral model is constructed for a piece of service code and a trust policy is enforced against this model. Figure 4 shows the Java code for a

```
public class Bank{
   static public int isvalid(int cardno){
      int[] validcards = initcards();
      for(int i=0; i < validcards.length; i=i+1){
         if(cardno==validcard[i])    return 1;
      }
      return 0;
   }
   static private int[] initcards(){
      return an array of valid card numbers
   }
}
```

Fig. 4. The Bank Service

simplified bank service, which has a `isvalid` method to check the validity of card numbers. The `isvalid` method accesses all valid card numbers by using a private method `initcard`. Figure 5 shows the bytecode of the `isvalid` method compiled by a Java compiler. All instructions have been described in Section 3.1 except the instruction `iflt 6` at line 20, which transfers control to line 6 if the index for accessing the array of valid card numbers is less than the array length.

```
1:  invokes (Bank,initcards,ϵ → int[])
2:  store   1  //put validcards to variable 2
3:  iconst  0
4:  store   2  //put 0 to variable 3
5:  goto    17
6:  load    1  //get cardnum from variable 1
7:  load    1  //get validcards from variable 2
8:  load    2  //get the array index
9:  aload      //get item v at the index
10: ifne    13 //compare cardnum and v
11: iconst  1
12: return     //return 1 for cardnum = v
13: load    2  //get the array index
14: iconst  1
15: add        //increase the index by 1
16: store   2  //put the updated index back
17: load    2  //get the array index
18: load    1  //get validcards from variable 2
19: alength    //get the length of validcards
20: iflt    6  //compare index and length
21: iconst  0
22: return     //return 0 for index not less
               //than the array length
```

Fig. 5. The Bytecode of `isvalid` Method

Figure 6 is the behavioral model of the `isvalid` method. In this model example, a symbolic value is represented as a concatenation of $\sharp$ and a number (e.g., $\#1$, $\#2$). We can check that the card number is processed in the same way by the model and the bytecode. Hence, the model has the same semantics as the bytecode. In addition, the model has four branches that cover all possible execution paths of the bytecode, and hence captures all data flow within the bytecode. For example, the branch ended with exit($\sharp$12) covers the following path (represented as a sequence of instruction labels):

$$1 \cdot 2 \cdot 3 \cdot 4 \cdot 5 \cdot 17 \cdot 18 \cdot 19 \cdot 20 \cdot 6 \cdot 7 \cdot 8 \cdot 9 \cdot$$
$$10 \cdot 13 \cdot 14 \cdot 15 \cdot 16 \cdot 17 \cdot 18 \cdot 19 \cdot 20 \cdot 21 \cdot 22$$

The bytecode of `isvalid` method may lead to an infinite model due to the loop between line 6 and 20. The model here covers the execution path between line 6 and 20 only once, so it can be finite.

Suppose a client wants to use this service to check the validity of his credit card number, and allows the service to send some information about his card number for further check to a service either at location $visa\_ip$ or at location $master\_ip$. Then the client prepares two policies in Figure 7 and asks the trust authority to verify the service. The policy (a) says the information about card number cannot be sent to $master\_ip$ if such information has been sent to $visa\_ip$, while the policy (b) says the reverse case. There is no condition on the $cardno$ variable in the input action, meaning that any card number can be an input. Both policies are not violated by the service since no path in the model of Figure 6 sends the card number to other services.

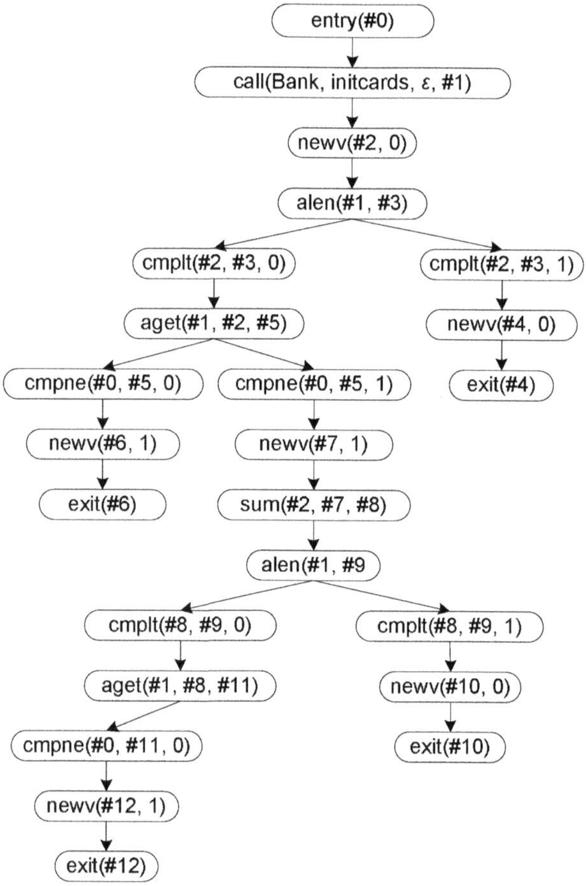

Fig. 6. The Model of `isvalid` Method

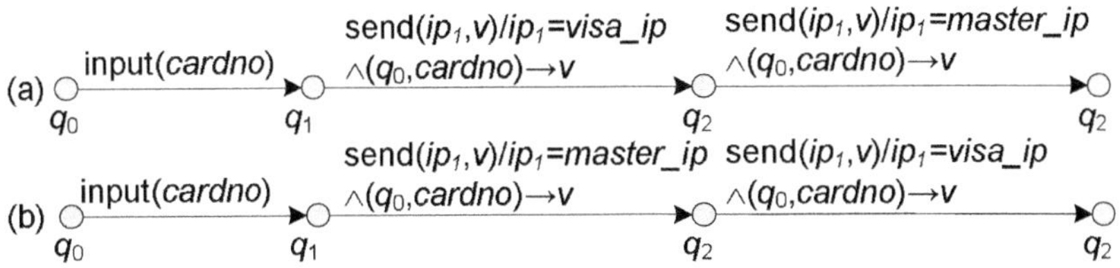

Fig. 7. Policies for Restricting Locations

6 Related Work

We have discussed some related work of semantic or property based remote attestation in trusted computing in the first section [3,4,5]. In the following, we discuss the related work for building trusted services.

The Tisa framework [21] delivers trusted services by making sure the service monitors trusted by using the TPM-based remote attestation technique [9]. A service provider may have a large number of clients at the same time, and this represents a burden for the provider to run a service monitor for all clients. Our framework does not use monitors, and hence minimizes the communication and computation overheads of Tisa. However, our framework does need the service provider to do extra work when developing services, and not just at runtime. In addition, our framework does allow a large number of trust authorities (just like a large number of service registries in SOA) to process the service certification and verification requests.

The framework in [22] allows clients to verify whether a service satisfies their privacy policies by asking providers to send a service model to clients. Thus, this framework needs an assumption that the service providers are trusted to send a right model. Our framework does not assume the trustworthiness of service providers. In addition, a service model may contain the confidential information for providers, so it is not always suitable to send the service model to clients.

The WS-Attestation architecture [23] proposes a remote attestation mechanism (resulting in a service hash being generated). Though the WS-attestation allows the binding of attestation with application contexts, it is not flexible enough for clients to check the service properties they are interested in. Our framework allows clients to define their specific trust requirements.

We have developed a similar framework [24] for delivering rigorously trusted services. In our previous framework, the service registries are also involved in the trust-establishment protocol. Hence, in order to deploy the previous framework, we have to change the existing service registries. The framework proposed in this paper does not need any change to the existing service registries, hence easier to deploy.

7 Conclusion

We have presented the framework for delivering rigorously trusted services through the use of a protocol that ties together Trust Authorities, Service Providers and Clients. This protocol aims to ensure that a provider and a client trust each others' behaviors. We believe rigorous trust will be a desirable feature for massively distributed service-oriented computing. The framework can be deployed by using the current SOA standards and protocols after introducing the new component Trust Authorities.

One limitation of our framework is that Trust Authorities verify the models of a set of collaborative services independently. In other words, they do not verify the trust policies of clients against a comprehensive model for these collaborative services. Hence, the verification result of trust authorities is only sound locally with respect to the verified service model and clients have to verify each used service separately. For example, suppose service A is composed from service B and service C, and a client does not want his sensitive data to be released to a malicious service. Then, in our current framework the client has to verify these three services one by one against his trust requirement. We will improve our framework to consider the data flows among collaborative services.

Out framework is particular useful for an organization that wants to outsource some of its services to third parties. For example, in the application of eGovernment, the governments can maintain some Trust Authorities, and when they outsource services, they ask the service providers to use the Trust Authorities to certify the outsourced services and then they can verify the services by formulating appropriate policies. In addition, they also can ask the service providers to use some well-known operating systems and service engines so as to attest the integrity of their platforms as the complement of the behavior attestation.

References

1. Resnick, P., Kuwabara, K., Zeckhauser, R., Friedman, E.: Reputation systems. ACM Commun. 43(12), 45–48 (2000)
2. Parno, B., McCune, J.M., Perrig, A.: Bootstrapping trust in commodity computers. In: Proceedings of the IEEE Symposium on Security and Privacy (May 2010)
3. Garfinkel, T., Pfaff, B., Chow, J., Rosenblum, M., Boneh, D.: Terra: a virtual machine-based platform for trusted computing. SIGOPS Oper. Syst. Rev. 37(5), 193–206 (2003)
4. Haldar, V., Chandra, D., Franz, M.: Semantic remote attestation: a virtual machine directed approach to trusted computing. In: VM 2004: Proceedings of the 3rd conference on Virtual Machine Research And Technology Symposium, p. 3. USENIX Association, Berkeley (2004)
5. Sadeghi, A.R., Stüble, C.: Property-based attestation for computing platforms: caring about properties, not mechanisms. In: NSPW 2004: Proceedings of the 2004 Workshop on New Security Paradigms, pp. 67–77. ACM, New York (2004)
6. Necula, G.C.: Proof-carrying code. In: Proceedings of the 24th ACM SIGPLAN-SIGACT Symposium on Principles of Programming Languages, pp. 106–119. ACM, New York (1997)
7. Sabelfeld, A., Myers, A.C.: Language-based information-flow security. IEEE Journal on Selected Areas in Communications 21(1), 5–19 (2003)
8. Papazoglou, M.P., Georgakopoulos, D.: Service-oriented computing: Introduction. ACM Commun. 46(10), 24–28 (2003)
9. Sailer, R., Zhang, X., Jaeger, T., van Doorn, L.: Design and implementation of a tcg-based integrity measurement architecture. In: Proceedings of the 13th conference on USENIX Security Symposium, p. 16 (2004)

10. Corbett, J., Dwyer, M., Hatcliff, J., Laubach, S., Păsăreanu, C., Robby, Z.H.: Bandera: extracting finite-state models from java source code. In: Proceedings of the 22nd International Conference on Software Engineering (2000)
11. Ball, T., Rajamani, S.K.: The SLAM project: debugging system software via static analysis. In: Proceedings of the 29th ACM Symposium on Principles of Programming Languages, pp. 1–3 (2002)
12. Wagner, D., Dean, D.: Intrusion detection via static analysis. In: IEEE Symposium on Security and Privacy (2001)
13. King, J.C.: Symbolic execution and program testing. ACM Commun. 19(7), 385–394 (1976)
14. Higuchi, T., Ohori, A.: A static type system for jvm access control. ACM Trans. Program. Lang. Syst. 29(1), 4 (2007)
15. Liu, D.: Bytecode verification for enhanced jvm access control. In: ARES 2007: Proceedings of the The Second International Conference on Availability, Reliability and Security, Washington, DC, USA, pp. 162–169. IEEE Computer Society, Los Alamitos (2007)
16. Li, N., Wang, Q., Qardaji, W., Bertino, E., Rao, P., Lobo, J., Lin, D.: Access control policy combining: theory meets practice. In: Proceedings of the 14th ACM Symposium on Access Control Models and Technologies, pp. 135–144 (2009)
17. Schneider, F.B.: Enforceable security policies. ACM Trans. Inf. Syst. Secur. 3(1), 30–50 (2000)
18. Cousot, P., Cousot, R.: Abstract interpretation: a unified lattice model for static analysis of programs by construction or approximation of fixpoints. In: POPL 1977: Proceedings of the 4th ACM SIGACT-SIGPLAN Symposium on Principles of Programming Languages, pp. 238–252 (1977)
19. W3C: OWL-S: Semantic markup for web services, `http://www.w3.org/Submission/OWL-S/`
20. W3C: Web service modeling language (WSML), `http://www.w3.org/Submission/WSML/`
21. Rajan, H., Hosamani, M.: Tisa: Towards trustworthy services in a service-oriented architecture. IEEE Transactions on Services Computing (TSC) 1(4) (2008)
22. Xu, W., Venkatakrishnan, V.N., Sekar, R., Ramakrishnan, I.V.: A framework for building privacy-conscious composite web services. In: Proceedings of the IEEE International Conference on Web Services, pp. 655–662 (2006)
23. Yoshihama, S., Ebringer, T., Nakamura, M., Munetoh, S., Maruyama, H.: Ws-attestation: Efficient and fine-grained remote attestation on web services. In: Proceedings of the IEEE International Conference on Web Services (2005)
24. Liu, D., Zic, J.: A framework for building privacy-conscious composite web services. In: Proceedings of the IEEE International Conference on Web Services (Work-in-Progress Track), pp. 648–651 (2010)

Collecting, Annotating, and Classifying Public Web Services

Mohammed AbuJarour[1], Felix Naumann[1], and Mircea Craculeac[2]

[1] Hasso-Plattner-Institut, University of Potsdam, Germany
firstname.lastname@hpi.uni-potsdam.de
[2] Neofonie, Berlin, Germany
mircea@neofonie.de

Abstract. The limitations of the traditional SOA operational model, such as the lack of rich service descriptions, weaken the role of service registries. Their removal from the model violates the basic principles of SOA, namely, *dynamic binding* and *loose coupling*. Currently, most service providers publish their Web Services on their websites instead of publishing them in service registries. This results in poor usability of these Web Services especially wrt. service discovery and service composition.

To handle this problem, we propose to increase the usability of public Web Services by collecting them automatically from the websites of their providers with the help of web crawling techniques. Additionally, the collected services are annotated with descriptions that are extracted from the crawled web pages and tags that are generated from the same web pages. These annotations are then used to derive a classification for each Web Service into different application domains. In this paper, we introduce the details of our approach and show its practical feasibility through several evaluation experiments.

Keywords: Web Service, Service Description, Tagging, Classification.

1 SOA in Theory and Practice

Due to the increasing complexity of modern software systems, distributed computing has been the typical approach in several application domains, such as banking, medicine, earth sciences, etc. Additionally, the wide and rapid spread of Internet technology has been a major driving force that led to the emergence of new software paradigms, such as the Service-oriented Architecture (SOA) [11].

The basic principles of SOA are captured in the triangular SOA operational model [17] depicted in Figure 1 (left). Three roles are identified in this model, namely, service-provider, -consumer, and -registry. Theoretically, service providers register their services into one or more service registries that play the role of service brokers. Service consumers use these registries to find services that satisfy their needs. Afterwards, a direct binding between service consumers and service providers is done to call the required service(s).

R. Meersman et al. (Eds.): OTM 2010, Part I, LNCS 6426, pp. 256–272, 2010.

The goal of this operational model is to achieve the main features of SOA, e.g., high interoperability, flexibility, scalability, fault tolerance, etc. However, to achieve such goals service consumers should have sufficient knowledge about the considered services. Much of this knowledge comes from service providers themselves in the form of service descriptions that they give during the registration of their services. Service descriptions play a key role in Service-oriented Computing (SOC). However, service descriptions are typically poor, because service providers focus on the implementation aspects of their services rather than providing rich service descriptions.

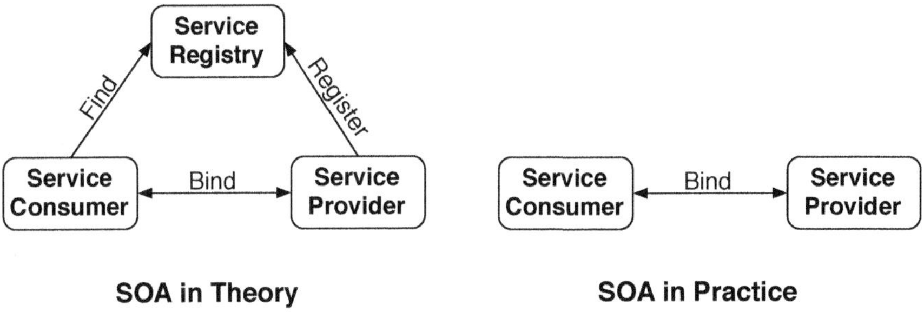

Fig. 1. SOA in theory and practice [13]

Service registries do not have control over service providers to force them to keep the descriptions about their registered Web Services up-to-date. This lack of control results in a passive and limited role of service registries. On the contrary, service providers often do keep the published information and descriptions about their offered Web Services up-to-date via their own websites.

In practice, the role of service registries is typically ignored [13] because of such limitations. For instance, 48% of a production `UDDI` registry has links that are unusable (tModels tested only); these links point to contain missing, broken or inaccurate information [4]. Removing the role of the service registry (and thus breaking the triangle) violates the basic SOA principles of *loose coupling* and *dynamic binding* (cf. Fig. 1).

A common approach used by service providers to offer public Web Services is to provide a list of services with a textual description attached to each service to explain their functionality. Moreover, several service providers offer a *try* option, where one can try their services online. Such options typically include web forms to collect input parameters from the user. Much of the information provided on such web pages is not provided in the `WSDL` description of the corresponding Web Service. We view such `HTML` pages and forms as rich sources of information and descriptions about the considered Web Services.

For instance, Amazon.com provides several public Web Services, e.g., Amazon Relational Database Service (Amazon RDS). Typically, Amazon provides a detailed description for each of their Web Services in the form of `HTML`. For example, Amazon RDS is described in detail on `https://aws.amazon.com/rds`. Much of this information, such as the fact that it is based on MySQL, is not provided in its WSDL description available at

`https://rds.amazonaws.com/doc/2010-01-01/AmazonRDSv2.wsdl`.

In our approach, we extract the information that service providers release about their offered Web Services on their websites and generate richer service descriptions from this information.

We propose an approach where service registries take the initiative to collect public Web Services from the websites of their providers through web crawling techniques, extract descriptions for these Web Services, generate tags associated with the collected Web Services from the contents provided by their service providers, and classify the collected Web Services into several application domains based on their enriched annotations. Our Web Service crawler is limited to so-called Big Web Services (SOAP-based) only. Further decision rules are required to incorporate RESTful Web Services.

In [1], we introduced a system that enables users to discover, aggregate, and consume public Web Services. However, we have observed that choosing the best services that match some users' requirements from the service catalog requires additional information to enhance the quality of the result list. This paper tackles this problem and serves as an extension to our previous work.

The main contributions of this paper are:

- Automatic collection of public Web Services over the web.
- Automatic enrichment of poor service descriptions with extracted descriptions from the HTML pages of their providers.
- Automatic generation of tags that are associated with collected Web Services.
- Supervised classification of collected Web Services.

The remainder of this paper is organized as follows: In Section 2, we give an overview of the related work. A use-case is introduced in Section 3 to highlight the targeted problems. In Section 4, we introduce our approach in detail. Section 5 shows our experiments, and a summary and future work are given in Section 6.

2 Related Work

The limitations in the traditional SOA operational model have been highlighted by several researchers in the community. In [13], the authors showed that the triangular model is not used widely in practice because of the limited role of service registries. Removing the role of the service registry (breaking the triangle) violates the basic principles of Service-oriented Computing (SOC), namely *loose coupling* and *dynamic binding*. To restore this broken triangle, the authors proposed a software engineering approach that enables dynamic binding and invocations of Web Services. Our approach tackles the limited role of service registries problem and aims at increasing the active role of service registries in SOC.

Another approach to achieve active Web Service registries was introduced in [16]. The authors use RSS feeds to announce changes in the registered services to interested service consumers. The information provided by such feeds is generated by service providers, who tend to focus on the technical part of their services rather than providing documentation or descriptions. Moreover, such a service registry cannot force service providers to notify them about any updates so that they can add RSS feeds to announce the corresponding changes.

The main reason behind the highlighted limitations of the triangular model in the aforementioned work is the lack of rich service descriptions [12]. Therefore, researchers have proposed several approaches to gather additional information about Web Services to handle the problem of poor service descriptions.

In [2], the authors use a specialized crawler to collect Web Services from multiple UDDI registries. Although the idea of using crawlers to collect Web Services is innovative, restricting it to UDDI registries does not give the maximum benefit of web crawling, as such an approach is still limited to what service providers announce during service registration.

A more advanced Web Service crawler has been introduced by the EU project Seekda (http://www.seekda.eu). In this recent project, the authors use a specialized crawler to collect public Web Services over the web, and present them in a web 2.0 environment, which allows users to annotate, tag, and use the collected Web Services. We extend this approach by annotating the collected Web Services with automatically extracted descriptions and generate tags, as we show in Section 4.2.

The automatic assignment of classes to Web Services is known as service classification. This problem is vital in SOC, because of the increasing number of Web Services. Therefore, it has been investigated by several researchers in the community. Typically, machine learning techniques are used to perform automatic service classification, where different approaches are based on argument definitions matching [6], document classification techniques [8], or semantic annotation matching [5]. In most of these approaches, the authors classify formal service descriptions, e.g., WSDL, or they assume the presence of additional information, e.g., ontology annotations. Service descriptions appear mostly in the form of comments written by service developers [15]. In general, these comments are written in English, have a low grammatical quality, punctuation is often ignored, and several spelling mistakes and snippets of abbreviated text is present. Assuming the existence of ontology annotations is not realistic [12]. In our approach, we use formal service descriptions provided by service providers, e.g., WSDL, in addition to annotations that we extract from the websites of the providers to apply a machine learning approach to classify Web Services.

3 Example: Gene Trek in Procaryote Space (GTPS)

Gene Trek in Procaryote Space (GTPS) is a service offered by the National Institute of Genetics (NIG) in Japan. The purpose of GTPS is to re-annotate the ORFs[1] among microorganisms in Genome Information Broker data by using a common protocol and diffuse the results to users as a resource for gnome-scale analysis on microbes.

The GTPS Web Service is published with several additional services on the website of the NIG under `http://xml.nig.ac.jp`. Figure 2 shows a screenshot of the web page that shows the details of the GTPS Web Service. Along with the name of the service, they provide a service description, a hyperlink to the WSDL file of this service, and a list of methods it offers. The service name is obviously provided in its WSDL file, but, the description is not. The hyperlink to the WSDL file represents a candidate place to start searching for service descriptions.

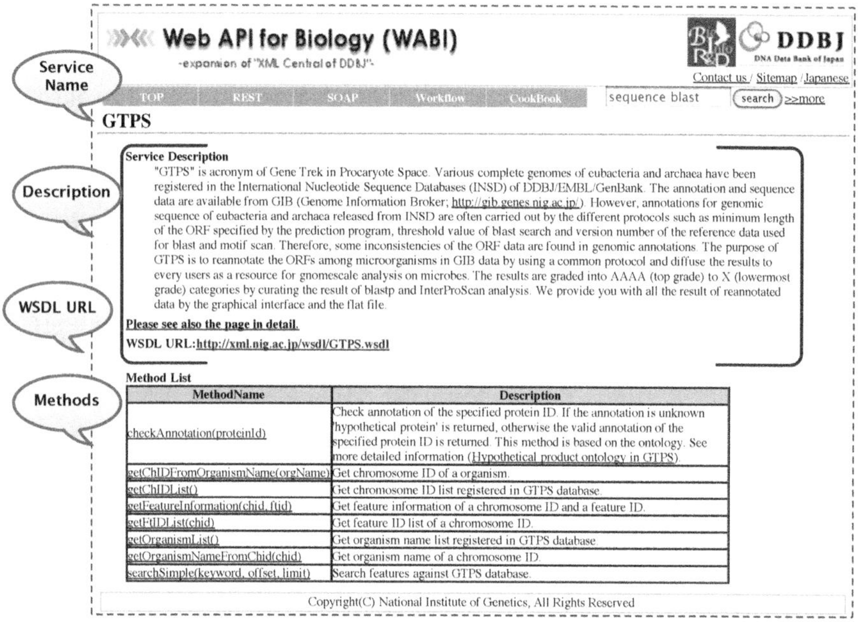

Fig. 2. The web page of the Gene Trek in Procaryote Space (GTPS) Web Service

A simplified version of the HTML source code of the same web page is shown in Figure 3. An important aspect in this code is the relationship between the element that holds the description (line 3) and the element that holds the WSDL hyperlink (line 13). These two elements usually have either the *sibling* or *parent-child* relationship. Typically, service providers describe their Web Services and then provide their links, or provide the links to their Web Services and then describe their functionalities. Other cases include more complex relationships, especially, when tables are used. In our example, the simple *sibling* relationship holds.

[1] ORF stands for Open Reading Frame, which is a DNA sequence that could potentially encode a protein.

```
<div class=message_indent>
    <div class=itemTitle>Service Description</div>
    <div class=itemContent>
     "GTPS" is acronym of Gene Trek in Procaryote Space. Various complete genomes of eubacteria and archaea have been
     registered in the International Nucleotide Sequence Databases (INSD) of DDBJ/EMBL/GenBank. The annotation and sequence
     data are available from GIB (Genome Information Broker; <a href="http://gib.genes.nig.ac.jp/">http://
     gib.genes.nig.ac.jp/</a>). However, annotations for genomic sequence of eubacteria and archaea released from INSD are
     often carried out by the different protocols such as minimum length of the ORF specified by the prediction program,
     threshold value of blast search and version number of the reference data used for blast and motif scan. Therefore, some
     inconsistencies of the ORF data are found in genomic annotations. The purpose of GTPS is to reannotate the ORFs among
     microorganisms in GIB data by using a common protocol and diffuse the results to every users as a resource for
     gnomescale analysis on microbes. The results are graded into AAAA (top grade) to X (lowermost grade) categories by
     curating the result of blastp and InterProScan analysis. We provide you with all the result of reannotated data by the
     graphical interface and the flat file.
    </div>
    <div class=itemTitle>
        <a href="http://gtps.ddbj.nig.ac.jp/" target=_blank>
           Please see also the page in detail.
        </a>
    </div>
    <div class=itemTitle>
        WSDL URL:
        <a href="http://xml.nig.ac.jp/wsdl/GTPS.wsdl">
           http://xml.nig.ac.jp/wsdl/GTPS.wsdl
        </a>
    </div>
</div>
```

Fig. 3. Part of the HTML source of the web page of the Gene Trek in Procaryote Space (GTPS) Web Service shown in Figure 2

An interesting observation is the lack of similar documentation or descriptions in the WSDL file of the GTPS Web Service.[2] This situation makes it difficult for biologists, who do not have sufficient technical background, to use such important Web Services. Moreover, discovering such a Web Service is not an easy task, unless, it is augmented with this description.

By applying our approach to this URL (`http://xml.nig.ac.jp`), we were able to find 23 Web Services, and we were able to extract the descriptions provided in the form of HTML, and generate tags that describe the extracted Web Services. The list of tags for the GTPS Web Service is `[id, chromosome, annotation, list, chid]`. Attaching these annotations to this Web Service increases its usability, because it becomes more convenient for biologists to find and use it.

4 Architecture Overview

Our proposed approach to increase the usability of public Web Services incorporates four components: a Web Service crawler, a Web Service parser, an annotation extractor, and a Web Service classifier. The architecture of our proposed approach is depicted in Figure 4.

In our approach, a service registry takes the initiative to collect public Web Services from the websites of their providers. This task is achieved using a Web Service crawler (component number 1 in Fig. 4). The main task of this crawler is to collect XML and HTML resources and store them in a special archive. The collected XML resources are then parsed and validated through a Web Service parser (component number 2) to identify valid Web Services. Valid Web Services

[2] Available at: `http://xml.nig.ac.jp/wsdl/GTPS.wsdl`

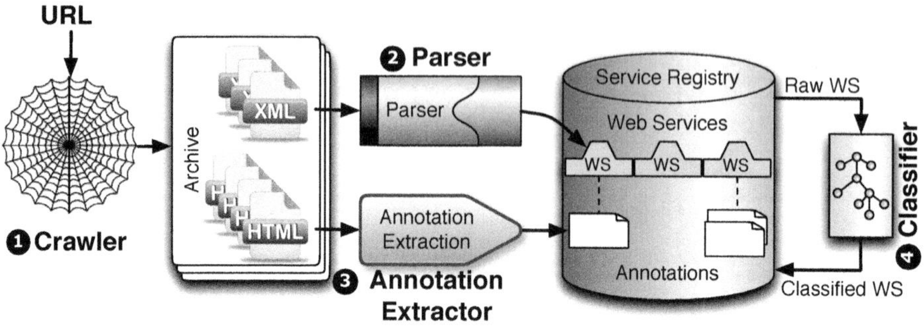

Fig. 4. An overview of the architecture of our approach

are stored in the service registry. Further details about the crawler and the parser are given in Section 4.1.

The annotation extractor (component 3 in Fig. 4) has the task of analyzing the collected `HTML` resources by the crawler to extract annotations that enrich the descriptions of the collected Web Services. The extracted annotations are stored in the service registry. Two types of annotations are generated by this component: service descriptions and tags. We give further details about this component in Section 4.2.

The annotations generated by the annotation extractor are used to classify the collected Web Services into several application domains, e.g., education, telecommunications, finance, government, etc. This task is performed by a service classifier (component number 4 in Fig. 4). Further details about this component are given in Section 4.3.

4.1 Crawling and Parsing Public Web Services

To collect public Web Services, we employ web crawling techniques to the web. We have implemented a focused crawler that targets `XML` and `HTML` resources only. `XML` files are potential candidates for Web Services descriptions, e.g., `WSDL`, whereas, `HTML` files are potential places to find further information about the collected Web Services. In this section, we consider `XML` files only. `HTML` files are considered in the following section.

The architecture of our Web Service crawler is shown in Figure 5. We use the `Heritrix` [10] crawling framework in our approach. The client on the left hand side starts the crawler by providing a seed `URI` that has to be crawled. The crawler crawls the entire domain of the given seed `URI` for `WSDL` documents. If it is able to gather `WSDL` files from that domain, then it stores the collected files into a compressed archive file, called ARC file. This ARC file is passed to the `WSDL` parser that extracts the found `WSDL` documents. Then, each of these `WSDL` documents is parsed with the WSDL4J API [9] to extract its port types, bindings, operations and descriptions if available. If the `WSDL` file is valid and no

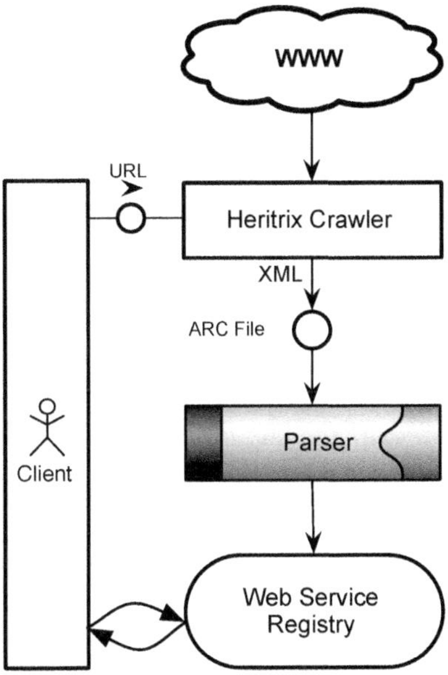

Fig. 5. The architecture of our Web Service crawler

parsing errors occurred, the file is stored in the Web Service registry that can be directly accessed by the user.

The implementation of our focused crawler incorporates a series of "DecideRules" to filter `URIs`. To determine whether a `URI` falls within the required scope, all decision rules are applied to it. Accepted `URIs` should pass all checks represented by the decision rules. The most important DecideRule that are used are:

- **PathologicalPath:** This rule is used to avoid crawler traps. It adds a constraint on how many times a path-segment pattern in the `URI` may be repeated. The `URI` is rejected if the pattern is repeated more than two times, e.g., "`www.example.com/foo/foo/foo`" is rejected.
- **MatchesRegExp:** The goal of this rule is to filter all resources that are not relevant to our crawling task. Because our goal is to identify `WSDL` files, we discard all crawled resources except `XML` and `HTML` documents. `XML` files could represent `WSDL` files and `HTML` files could contain `URIs` to `WSDL` files, in addition to descriptive text that explains the functionality of the Web Services in the linked `WSDL` files. All other document types, such as audio, video, image files, etc. are ignored by the crawler using the regular expression provided by this rule.
- **WSDLRegExp:** This second regular expression explicitly accepts all `URIs` ending with the case insensitive phrase "`wsdl`".

4.2 Annotating Web Services

In the previous section, we explained the process of collecting public Web Services over the web using a focused crawler by identifying their formal descriptions that have XML as a content type. The collected Web Services are then parsed and validated to identify valid Web Services. This step is then followed by a step to extract further information about the collected Web Services from the crawled HTML pages. In this section, we show the types of this additional information that we extract and the techniques we use to achieve this step.

Because of the lack of rich service descriptions, we propose to extract further information about public Web Services from the websites of their providers to enrich poor service descriptions. This extraction is achieved by the annotation extractor component (cf. Fig. 4). The process of annotation extraction is shown in Figure 6.

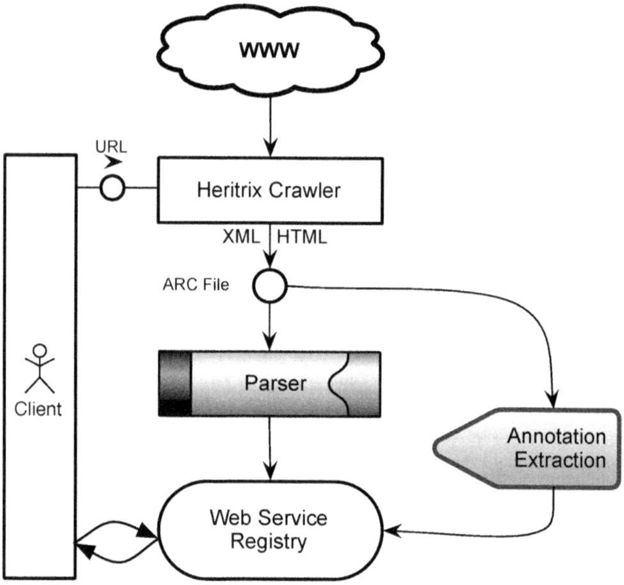

Fig. 6. The Architecture of our Web Service crawler and its annotation extractor (HTML parser)

According to our set of "DecideRules", the resulted ARC file contains URIs whose content type is either XML or HTML. We perform two iterations of parsing on this ARC file: the first iteration is done by the WSDL parser to identify WSDL URIs (cf. Sec. 4.1), and the second iteration is done by the annotation extractor to identify further information about the identified WSDL URIs.

The result of this recent step is formalized in Equation 1. Given a valid URL where some Web Services are offered, the expected outcome is a list of collected

Web Services ({ws}), extracted descriptions for each Web Service (Desc(ws)), and a list of tags associated with that Web Services (Tags(ws)).

$$ExtraWS(url) = \{\{ws, Desc(ws), Tags(ws)\}\} \qquad (1)$$

The extracted description for each of the collected Web Services, Desc(ws), is captured in Equation 2. In our approach, we use the heuristic that the place where the WSDL of a Web Service is referenced represents a good candidate place where its description can be found. Typically, service providers describe their Web Services and then provide their links, or provide the links and then describe what they do. According to our experiments, this heuristic works in more than 90% of our crawled URLs. In the remaining 10%, service providers either do not provide textual descriptions on their web pages or they use complex HTML pages, such as Amazon Web Services, where our heuristic did not find the appropriate text. Identifying the templates used in such complex HTML structures and smart extraction of such textual descriptions are part of our future work. This heuristic is also useful in the case where a web page describes more than one Web Service. Different descriptive texts can be extracted from the same web page for different Web Services. However, such Web Services are annotated with the same tags, unless, they are described in other web pages.

The content of an HTML page that references a WSDL file is parsed as a DOM tree of HTML elements. The content of an HTML element represents the concatenation of its textual content with the textual content of its sub-elements. The content of the root element represents the entire text in the HTML page. We refer to the element that contains a link to a WSDL file as (e) in Equation 2. The element that contains the description is referred to as (d). If element (d) has either the *sibling* or the *parent* relationship (R) with (e), the content of element (d) represents the extracted description of the considered Web Service (ws).

$$Desc(ws) = content(d) | R(d, e) \in \{sibling, parent\} \qquad (2)$$

Web Services can be referenced from multiple web pages. A descriptive text can be extracted from each web page. In our approach, such Web Services can have several extracted descriptive texts for each Web Service.

The remaining parts of an HTML page that references a Web Service have their impact on the generated tags for the considered Web Service. Equation 3 captures this impact. A list of tags for a Web Service contains the most frequent terms (t) in the HTML page (p) where this considered Web Service (ws) is referenced. All terms in the web page are ranked and the most frequent k terms represent its list of tags, where k is an application parameter, e.g., k=5 (cf. Sec. 5.2). Common terms are ignored through stop words removal.

$$Tags(ws) = \{t | t \in rank(content(p))\} \qquad (3)$$

However, this tag generation method can miss some important keywords. For instance, the tags of GTPS (cf. Table 2) do not include "GIB data", "microbes", "Converts", or "US" as tags. These keywords are important, but they do not appear frequently in the text. Moreover, tags give hints to service consumers about the managed Web Services because selecting proper keywords for service discovery requires domain knowledge. Such important keywords are still indexed and involved in the Web Service discovery process.

The main limitation of this approach is the use of a single source of information about Web Services, namely, the websites of their service providers. Service providers may not provide textual descriptions about their offered Web Services on their websites. In this case, our approach can only identify and collect such Web Services, but it cannot annotate or classify them. Further information about such Web Services is still required to increase their usability.

4.3 Classifying Web Services

Gathering Web Services through the crawler results in a large list of Web Services that do not have categories. This situation makes it difficult to browse through these Web Services and retrieve the relevant ones upon request. To handle this issue, we use an automatic classifier that classifies the collected Web Services into a set of predefined categories, e.g., finance, education, entertainment, etc. We have compiled this list of categories from well-known service providers and service registries on the web, such as `http://www.programmableweb.com`. A complete list of categories is shown in Section 5.3.

Machine learning techniques are used in our approach to classify Web Services, where the features used by the classifier are the `WSDL`, *description*, and *tags* of each Web Service. The name of the Web Service is not included explicitly, because it is included in the `WSDL` file. The size of some features can grow unexpectedly or cannot be predicted in advance. The `WSDL` file of a Web Service can have a few lines or thousands of lines. The generated tags are domain-specific and cannot be expected in advance. To meet this challenge, we hash the contents of each feature using the `simHash` [3] algorithm into a fixed length digest. `SimHash` produces similar hash values for similar documents. Therefore, it combines the advantages of the word-based similarity measures with the efficiency of fingerprints based on hashing.

Most similar approaches (cf. Sec. 2) use `WSDL` files to classify Web Services, but such files contain – mainly – technical descriptions. Using the extracted descriptions and tags to classify Web Services is one of the main contributions of our approach. Common terms, e.g., articles, pronouns, etc., in service descriptions and `WSDL` files are removed through stopword removal techniques before applying the `simHash` algorithm to get the digest of each feature. Additionally, the `snowball` stemmer [14] is used to capture the similarity between several derivations of the same word, e.g., walk, walk*ing*, walk*s*.

Our machine learning approach uses a supervised classifier that is trained on a set of manually classified Web Services. Then, it is tested on the newly collected unclassified Web Services to infer their classes based on the training set. The features of each Web Service (i.e., the digests of the `WSDL`, description, tags) are then used to infer classes for the unclassified Web Services from the already (manually) classified ones. The Weka [7] tool has been used to achieve this goal. Further technical specifications are given in Section 5.3.

5 Experiments and Evaluation

We have implemented a prototype that achieves the aforementioned contributions. To evaluate its feasibility, we have carried out three sets of experiments. A set of experiments to evaluate our focused crawler, another set of experiments to evaluate the extracted annotations, and a third set of experiments to evaluate the classifier. In this section, we describe these experiments, show the results, and discuss them.

5.1 Evaluating the Service Crawler

To test our Web Service crawler, we selected a number of service providers and crawled their websites using our crawler. We compare the number of collected Web Services from each service provider with the number of Web Services found by `seekda` (cf. Section 2) on the same website.

Table 1 shows a list of `URLs` of service providers (second column), the number of services found by `seekda` (third column), and the number of Web Services found using our crawler (fourth column).

Table 1. Number of collected Web Services per `URL`

ID	Service Provider URL	Seekda Result	Our Crawler
1	`webservice.genotec.ch`	8	8
2	`api.bioinfo.no`	8	9
3	`www.servicex.co.uk`	9	9
4	`xml.nig.ac.jp`	2	23
5	`www.ecocoma.com`	25	25
6	`ws.adaptivedisclosure.org`	26	26
7	`ws.serviceobjects.com`	31	31
8	`www.webservicex.net`	70	70
9	`www.strikeiron.com`	59	72
10	`splices.xignite.com`	58	190

In most cases, we are as good as `seekda` in finding published Web Services on a website. For instance, `URLs` in case 1,3,5–8. In other cases, e.g., case 2, 4, 9, 10, we managed to find more Web Services than `seekda`. One potential reason for this behavior, can be the release of new Web Services on a `URL` after `seekda` had crawled it. This situation requires incremental and iterative crawling of `URLs` to keep the list of collected Web Services up-to-date.

5.2 Evaluating the Extracted Annotations

Evaluating the extracted service descriptions is not straightforward. It requires manual checking to determine their quality. Due to space limitations, we show only the extracted service description for the example Web Service, GTPS introduced in Section 3.

> "GTPS" is acronym of Gene Trek in Procaryote Space. Various complete genomes of eubacteria and archaea have been registered in the International Nucleotide Sequence Databases (INSD) of DDBJ/EMBL/GenBank. The annotation and sequence data are available from GIB (Genome Information Broker; http://gib.genes.nig.ac.jp/). However, annotations for genomic sequence of eubacteria and archaea released from INSD are often carried out by the different protocols such as minimum length of the ORF specified by the prediction program, threshold value of blast search and version number of the reference data used for blast and motif scan. Therefore, some inconsistencies of the ORF data are found in genomic annotations. The purpose of GTPS is to reannotate the ORFs among microorganisms in GIB data by using a common protocol and diffuse the results to every users as a resource for gnomescale analysis on microbes. The results are graded into AAAA (top grade) to X (lowermost grade) categories by curating the result of blastp and InterProScan analysis. We provide you with all the result of reannotated data by the graphical interface and the flat file. Please see also the page in detail.

Fig. 7. The extracted service description for the GTPS Web Service from `http://xml.nig.ac.jp/wabi/Method?serviceName=GTPS&mode=methodList&lang=en`

Table 2. Examples of generated tags for collected Web Services

ID	Service URL	Generated Tags
1	Returns a map at a fixed scale or according to a specific scale. `http://www.servicex.co.uk/wsMapper/mapping.asmx?WSDL`	`method, scale, map, overlaid, icon`
2	Re-annotates the ORFs among microorganisms in GIB data by using a common protocol and diffuse the results to every users as a resource for gnomescale analysis on microbes. `http://xml.nig.ac.jp/wsdl/GTPS.wsdl`	`id, chromosome, annotation, list, chid`
3	Converts a chinese text from traditional to simplified characters, vice versa, unicode version to its characters version, or vice versa. `http://service.ecocoma.com/convert/chinese.asmx?WSDL`	`text, unicode, chinese, simplified, traditional`
4	Returns latitude and longitude of a given US address or vice versa. `http://ws.serviceobjects.com/gcr/GeoCoder.asmx?WSDL`	`latitude, longitude, address, estimate, location`
5	Gets domain name registration record by Host Name/Domain Name. `http://www.webservicex.net/whois.asmx?WSDL`	`whois, domain, formal, host, record`

The GTPS Web Service is intended to be used by biologists and not IT specialists. Its WSDL file gives technical details (`http://xml.nig.ac.jp/wsdl/GTPS.wsdl`), but, this description is not useful for biologists. However, the extracted semantic description – shown in Figure 7 – gives a good overview of its functionality and its inputs and outputs in a natural language that is easy to understand by biologists.

Each found Web Service is annotated with a list of tags that are generated from the content provided by its service provider. Typically, the content where a Web Service is referenced represents a potential place for generating tags for that Web Service. In our approach, we generate up to 5 tags per Web Service. Common terms, e.g., pronouns, articles, etc., are ignored using stopword removal. Table 2 shows a list of collected Web Services with a list of generated tags attached to each Web Service.

For instance, according to the description of the GTPS Web Service (cf. Section 3), the list of its extracted terms `[id, chromosome, annotation, list, chid]` looks reasonable.

5.3 Evaluating the Web Service Classifier

We use a supervised classification approach to classify newly collected Web Services. Each Web Service is assigned a class from a predefined set of classes (categories), such as finance, education, computer, entertainment, news, etc. We classified the first 200 Web Services manually, and used them as a training set to train the Weka tool to classify new unclassified Web Services. We use three

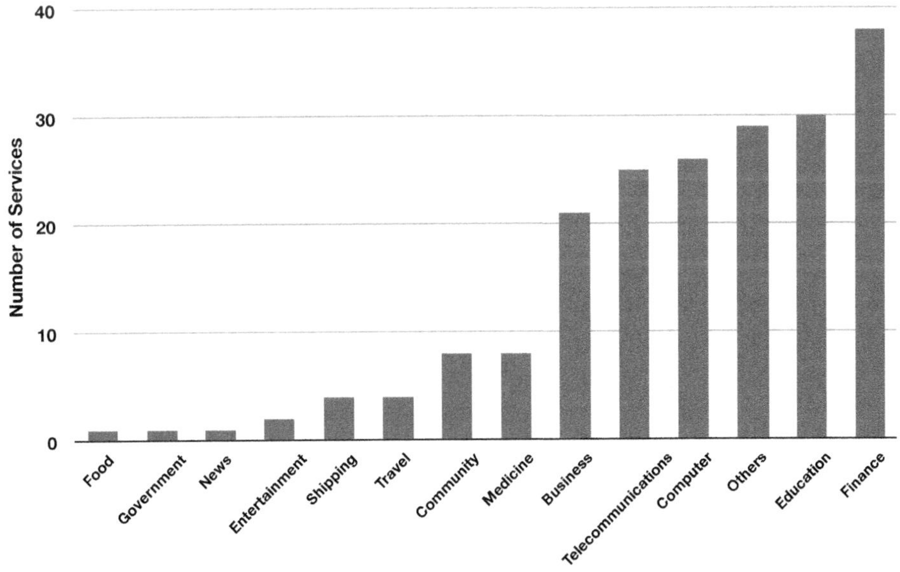

Fig. 8. The distribution of the 200 *manually* classified Web Services over 14 categories

Table 3. Examples of automatically classified Web Services

ID	Web Service	Category
1	Cocoma AOL Video Web Services. `http://service.ecocoma.com/video/aol.asmx?WSDL`	Entertainmnet
2	Gives in-depth financial and corporation information for companies `http://wsparam.strikeiron.com/GaleGroupBusinessInformation?WSDL`	Business
3	Retrieves phone number information. `http://wsparam.strikeiron.com/PhoneNumberEnhancement5?WSDL`	Telecommunication
4	Converts RSS feed into HTML `http://webservice.genotec.ch/utilities.asmx?WSDL`	Computer
5	Keyword search against over 20 life sciences databases `http://xml.nig.ac.jp/wsdl/ARSA.wsdl`	Education
6	Returns a SIC code for a company at the given address `http://ws.serviceobjects.com/sa/SICAppend.asmx?WSDL`	Finance
7	US Government Web Services and XML Data Sources `http://usgovxml.com/examples/public/armwsdls/arm.wsdl`	Government
8	Allows file upload, listing of files and file download. `http://api.bioinfo.no/wsdl/FileDepot.wsdl`	Others

features to classify Web Services, namely, the service `WDSL`, descriptions, and tags. Further details are given in Section 4.3.

Figure 8 shows the categories used to classify Web Services and the number of Web Services in each category. For instance, among the collected Web Services, there are 38 Finance, 21 Business, 1 Government Web Services, etc. This figure represents our training set.

We did several experiments with several classification algorithms, such as, Naive Bayes, Decision Table, etc. Our experiments showed that the Naive Bayes classification algorithm gives the best results in our case. Therefore, we used it to classify about 100 newly collected Web Services. The classifier distributed the 100 Web Services among 8 categories, shown in Table 3.

To show the correspondence between the classified Web Services and the automatically assigned categories, we give one example per category. Table 3 shows a list of 8 Web Services and their corresponding categories. The "Cocoma AOL Video Web Service" takes a keyword, and returns a list of AOL videos that match it. According to its `WSDL`, extracted description, and generated tags, the classifier classified it as an "Entertainment" Web Service. The classification in this case looks acceptable. However, in the case of Web Service number 8, this Web Service can be classified as "Computer" rather than "Others".

6 Summary and Future Work

The increasing number of public Web Services over the web has been reflected in limiting the usability of these Web Services. The main limitation behind the current poor usability of Web Services is the lack of rich service descriptions. Service providers tend to focus on the functionality of their services rather than providing rich service descriptions, especially, for non-technical consumers, such as biologists.

In this paper, we introduced an approach to increase the usability of the wealth of public Web Services over the web by crawling the websites of their providers to collect their offered Web Services in addition to extract further information about the collected Web Services in the form of service descriptions and tags. This extracted information is used to automatically classify these Web Services into several application domains, e.g., finance, education, entertainment, etc.

We implemented a Web Service crawler that crawls the web for public Web Services, collects, annotates, and classifies the collected services. Our focused crawler identifies `WSDL` files and `HTML` pages that reference them. These `HTML` pages are then used to enrich the collected Web Services with extracted annotations. We consider two types of annotations: service descriptions and tags. Service descriptions are information expressed in natural languages to explain their functionalities, inputs, outputs, etc. Tags are common terms that describe a Web Service. Both types are then used to classify the collected Web Services through a supervised classifier.

Our focused crawler is limited to so-called big Web Services (`SOAP`-based). Extending our approach to incorporate RESTful Web Services by adding additional specialized decision rules is part of our future work. Additionally, our plans include smart annotation extractions by identifying `HTML` templates, such as the ones used by `Amazon Web Services`.

Acknowledgment. The authors would like to thank Dustin Lange for his hints on service classification and Matthias Pohl for his implementation of `SimHash`.

References

1. AbuJarour, M., Craculeac, M., Menge, F., Vogel, T., Schwarz, J.-F.: Posr: A Comprehensive System for Aggregating and Using Web Services. In: Services, IEEE Congress on Services – I, pp. 139–146 (2009)
2. Al-Masri, E., Mahmoud, Q.H.: Investigating web services on the world wide web. In: WWW 2008: Proceeding of the 17th international conference on World Wide Web, pp. 795–804. ACM, New York (2008)

3. Charikar, M.S.: Similarity estimation techniques from rounding algorithms. In: STOC 2002: Proceedings of the thiry-fourth annual ACM Symposium on Theory of computing, pp. 380–388. ACM, New York (2002)
4. Clark, M.: UDDI weather report (2001), http://www.webservicesarchitect.com/content/articles/clark04.asp (accessed June 2010)
5. Corella, M.Á., Castells, P.: Semi-automatic semantic-based web service classification. In: Eder, J., Dustdar, S. (eds.) BPM Workshops 2006. LNCS, vol. 4103, pp. 459–470. Springer, Heidelberg (2006)
6. Duo, Z., Juan-Zi, L., Bin, X.: Web Service Annotation Using Ontology Mapping. In: SOSE 2005: Proceedings of the IEEE International Workshop, pp. 243–250. IEEE Computer Society, Washington (2005)
7. Hall, M., Frank, E., Holmes, G., Pfahringer, B., Reutemann, P., Witten, I.H.: The WEKA data mining software: an update. SIGKDD Explor. Newsl. 11(1), 10–18 (2009)
8. Heß, A., Kushmerick, N.: Learning to Attach Semantic Metadata to Web Services. In: Fensel, D., Sycara, K., Mylopoulos, J. (eds.) ISWC 2003. LNCS, vol. 2870, pp. 258–273. Springer, Heidelberg (2003)
9. IBM developerWorks: Web Services Description Language for Java Toolkit (WSDL4J), http://sourceforge.net/projects/wsdl4j
10. Internet Archive: Heritrix Web Crawler Project, http://crawler.archive.org
11. Josuttis, N.: SOA in Practice: The Art of Distributed System Design. O'Reilly Media, Inc., Sebastopol (2007)
12. Kuropka, D., Tröger, P., Staab, S., Weske, M.: Semantic Service Provisioning. Springer Publishing Company, Incorporated, Heidelberg (2008)
13. Michlmayr, A., Rosenberg, F., Platzer, C., Treiber, M., Dustdar, S.: Towards recovering the broken SOA triangle: a software engineering perspective. In: IW-SOSWE 2007: 2nd International Workshop on Service-oriented Software Engineering, pp. 22–28. ACM, New York (2007)
14. Porter, M.F.: Snowball: A language for stemming algorithms (October 2001), http://snowball.tartarus.org/texts/introduction.html (accessed June 2010)
15. Sabou, M., Wroe, C., Goble, C., Mishne, G.: Learning domain ontologies for Web service descriptions: an experiment in bioinformatics. In: WWW 2005: Proceedings of the 14th international conference on World Wide Web, pp. 190–198. ACM, New York (2005)
16. Treiber, M., Dustdar, S.: Active Web Service Registries. IEEE Internet Computing 11(5), 66–71 (2007)
17. Zhang, L.-J., Zhang, J., Cai, H.: Services Computing. Springer, Tsinghua University Press, New York, Beijing (2007)

Managing Conflict of Interest in Service Composition

Haiyang Sun, Weiliang Zhao, and Jian Yang

Department of Computing, Macquarie University,
Sydney, NSW2109, Australia
{hsun,wzhao,jian}@ics.mq.edu.au

Abstract. Web services can be composed of other services in a highly dynamic manner. The existing role based authorization approaches have not adequately taken component services into account when managing access control for composite services. In this paper, we propose a service oriented conceptual model as an extension of role based access control that can facilitate the administration and management of access for service consumers as well as component services in composite web services. Various types of conflict of interest are identified due to the complicated relationships among service consumers and component services. A set of authorization rules are developed to prevent the conflict of interest. This research is a step forward to addressing the challenge in authorization in the context of composite web services.

Keywords: Authorization, Conflict of Interest, Composite Web Services.

1 Introduction

The nature of web service creates the opportunity for building composite services by combining existing elementary or complex services (referred to as component services) [1]. Authorization of composite web services is different from traditional authorization in a close system due to the dynamic and complex relationships among service consumers and component services. Let us look at an example of Tom & Brothers which is a vehicle parts dealer that provides vehicle engines and engine accessories for both military and civil use. An *Order Service* is set up in Tom & Brothers including five operations: (1) *Order Engine*, (2) *Order Engine Accessory*, (3) *Payment*, (4) *Payment Verification* and (5) *Logistics* (See Fig. 1). Note, the *Logistics* operation is not available to the military customers since they organize parts shipment by themselves. When receiving a part order from a customer, the Tom & Brothers will order the parts from various parts suppliers. As soon as the payment has been verified, the goods will be transported to the customer. We observe that the following features exist in *Order Service* in Tom & Brothers that make authorization of composite web services complicated:

- **Complicated Authorization Constraints:** The component services of a composite web service may belong to different organizations, come from

R. Meersman et al. (Eds.): OTM 2010, Part I, LNCS 6426, pp. 273–290, 2010.

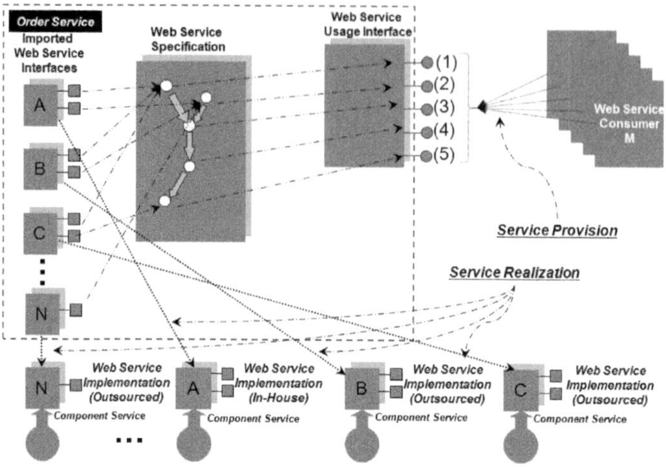

Fig. 1. *Order Service* in Tom & Brothers

different security domains, and have different security and interest requirements. The authorization constraints of a composite web service can be very complicated. For example, in Fig. 1, the operation (1)-*Order Engine* can be supported by the component web services A, B and C. Therefore before authorization is granted to a service consumer for the *Order Engine* operation, the policies of component web services A, B and C need to be checked. The complicated authorization constrains of composite services change the basic authorization question "`who can do what?`" to a more complicated one as "`who can do what under what conditions`".

– **Dynamicity of Component Services:** There may be several web services that can provide the same or similar operations. The specifications and policies of individual component services can change frequently. For example, if a component service changes its authorization policy from asking Tom & Brothers for professional engineer certificate to requiring sales representative qualification, then all the service operations in Tom & Brothers that are supported by the component service need to update their authorization policies accordingly. In Fig. 1, component services A, B, and N can support the same type of engine accessories to Tom & Brothers. If the changes occur frequently or happen in many web services, an efficient way to manage these changes is needed.
– **Conflict of Interest:** Authorization in composite services must prevent conflicts of interest among service consumers, among component services, and between consumers and component services. When there is a conflict of interest between a specific service consumer and a specific component service, the *Order Service* in Tom & Brothers should not be authorized to the service consumer when this component service is essentially needed in the composite service. For example, USA military customers may have a conflict

of interest with a component web service from a Chinese part supplier. The existing role based access control employs the mechanism of separation of duty to deal with conflict of interest for consumers, which is inadequate in dealing with the complicated situations occurred in the service setting.

In Role Based Access Control (RBAC) [2], users acquire permissions through their roles rather than that they are assigned permissions directly. This greatly reduces the administrative overhead associated with individual users and permissions. All existing role-based models in web service paradigm have not brought the administration of component services into the picture. The component services are normally remote resources or related with remote resources (the term resource will be used instead of component service later in the paper). The quantity of resources can be very large and they can be prone-to-change, which must be considered in web service authorization. In research work [8, 10, 11], roles are assigned to service consumers for service authorization. However all these researches have not put resources into the picture or they simply employ an unrealistic assumption that there is a *global* coordination on internal authorization policies of each autonomous web services to enforce the access control in service composition. Furthermore, resources in composite web services can introduce new types of conflict of interest on top of the conflict of interest between service consumers defined in the traditional RBAC approaches. The conflict of interest can occur among service consumers, among resources, and between service consumers and resources.

In this paper we propose a general approach for the authorization of composite web services as an extension of role based access control, which grants authorization to a service consumer based on the authorization constraints of the composite web services as well as those of the resources. Based on the previously proposed Service Oriented Authorization Control (SOAC) in [4], four types of conflict of interest are identified regarding to both service consumers and resources invoked in composite web services. The authorization rules are devised for these identified types of conflict of interest. Comparing with existing work, our proposed approach has the following merits:

- The characteristics and requirements for both service consumers and resources in composite web services can be explicitly captured.
- The proposed approach provides an efficient way to administrate and manage large number of service consumers and dynamic resources in relation to authorization in composite web services.
- The proposed approach has the capability to detect the conflict of interest among service consumers, among resources, and between service consumers and resources that are far more complicated than the ones identified in the existing role based authorization approaches for web services.

The rest of paper is organized as follows. Section 2 describes the conceptual model for the service oriented authorization. Section 3 identifies the various types of conflict of interest and provides the rules to prevent the conflict of interest in authorization of composite web services. Section 4 overviews some related work. Concluding remarks and discussion of future work are presented in Section 5.

2 Conceptual Model of Service Oriented Authorization Control

In this section, we describe a conceptual model, named as *Service Oriented Authorization Control (SOAC)* for managing the authorization of composite web service. SOAC is divided into two parts, *service provision* and *service realization* (See Fig. 2). We express the SOAC conceptual model by using the notation of **Entity-Relationship (E-R) Diagram**. In Fig. 2, rectangles represent elements and diamonds represent relationships.

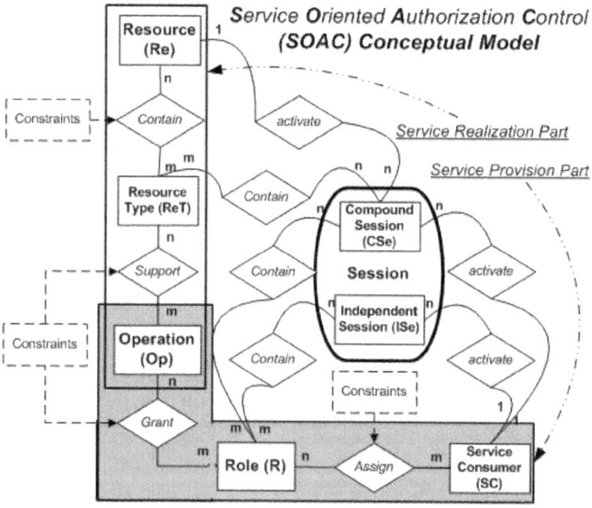

Fig. 2. Service Oriented Authorization Control (SOAC) Conceptual Model

2.1 *Service Provision* Specification

In *service provision*, a service consumer can get the authorization by fulfilling constraints of the composite service (See *Constraint* enacted between the elements of Role (**R**) and Service Consumer (**SC**) in Fig. 2). In Fig. 2, we define service consumer as the element that requires to access the composite web service's operations (**Op**). Since service consumers are prone to change and the quantity of consumers can be vary large, directly specifying the assignment of operations to individual service consumers needs tedious administration efforts. In SOAC, we follow the philosophy of RBAC to have concept role to encapsulate the service consumers that can satisfy the common authorization constraints of composite web services. A role will be assigned to a service consumer based on its characteristics (typically a credential that service consumer submits to the composite web service). Each role binds with a group of operations that can be accessed. The roles guarantee that the composite web service's operations can only be accessed by the qualified service consumers. The mapping between service consumers and roles are considered in the *service provision* part of SOAC with the following formal specification.

Definition 1. *The service provision in SOAC includes:*

- ***SC**, **R** ,and **Op** are elements representing Service Consumer, Role, and Operation.*
- **SCA** $\subseteq$ ***SC*** $\times$ ***R***, *a many-to-many relation to map service consumer to role assignment. Formally,* $\forall s^c \in SC$, $\forall r \in R$, $(s^c, r) \in SCA \Rightarrow s^c.credential = r.credential$, *where the credential that the service consumer submits is consistent with the credential that the role requires.*
- ***assigned_sc:(r:R)*** $\rightarrow 2^{SC}$, *the mapping of role r onto a set of service consumers. Formally,* $assigned\_sc(r) = \{s^c \in SC | (s^c, r) \in SCA\}$.
- **OPA** $\subseteq$***Op***$\times$***R***, *a many-to-many relation to map operation to role assignment.*
- ***assigned_op:(r:R)*** $\rightarrow 2^{Op}$, *the mapping of role r onto a set of operations. Formally,* $assigned\_op(r) = \{op \in Op \mid (op, r) \in OPA\}$.

2.2 *Service Realization* Specification

Due to the feature of **Dynamicity** of resources, it is unrealistic to specify the relationships between resources and the supported operations of composite web services individually. Resource type is defined for a set of resources by identifying their characteristics and authorization constraints (See Fig.2). The composite web service can bear multiple resource types that cover many resources. The resources can be accessed to support the operation if the operation is mapped with a resource type that covers these resources. Resources are linked with resource types with constraints. (See *Constraint* between the elements of Resource Type (**ReT**) and Resources (**Re**) in Fig. 2). The mapping between resources and resource types is the major concern in *service realization* part of SOAC. The formal specification of *service realization* is presented here.

Definition 2. *The service realization in SOAC includes:*

- ***Op**, **ReT**, and **Re** are elements representing Operation, Resource Type, and Resource.*
- **SPA** $\subseteq$ ***Op*** $\times$ ***ReT***, *a many-to-many relation to map operation to resource type.*
- ***assigned_ret:(ret:ReT)*** $\rightarrow 2^{Op}$, *the mapping of resource type ret onto a set of operations. Formally,* $assigned\_ret(ret) = \{op \in Op | (op, ret) \in SPA\}$.
- **RTA** $\subseteq$***Re***$\times$***ReT***, *a many-to-many relation to map resource to resource type. Formally,* $\forall re \in Re$, $\forall ret \in ReT$, $(re, ret) \in RTA \Rightarrow re.constraint = ret.constraint$, *where the constraint that restricts the access on the resource is consistent with the constraint that the resource type can fulfill.*

– ***assigned_re:****(ret:****ReT****)* $\rightarrow 2^{Re}$*, the mapping of resource type ret onto a set of resources. Formally, assigned_re(ret)=*$\{re \in Re | (re, ret) \in RTA\}$.

2.3 Integration of Service Provision and Service Realization

Service provision and *service realization* in SOAC must be worked together for authorization of composite web services. In Fig. 2, the mappings between the elements of Role (**R**), Operation (**Op**), and Recourse Type (**ReT**) integrate the *service provision* and *service realization.* The access to the composite web service can be assigned to a service consumer if all the constraints of the composite web service and its resources can be satisfied. In *service provision,* the service consumer is assigned a specific role for the access to the operations; while in *service realization,* the operations are mapped with resource types that cover all resources required.

In order to check conflict of interest at runtime, element **Session** is introduced at integration of *service provision* and *service realization* in SOAC (see Fig. 2). There are two types of sessions, *Independent session* (**ISe**) and *Compound session* (**CSe**). **ISe** is used to check runtime conflict of interest in *service provision*; while **CSe** is used to check runtime conflict of interest at integration of *service provision* and *service realization.* After a service consumer starts to send message to the composite web service for accessing its operations, the service consumer activates the assigned specific roles in an independent session. The resource types are involved when resources are required in composite web services. A compound session is established when the message from service consumer is transferred to resource. In this case, specific resource type is activated by the resource as well as the role is activated by the service consumer in a compound session. Note, the resource type and associated resources can not be included in the independent session, since a composite web service can not use the resource type without receiving the authorization request from the service consumer. Below is the formal definition of **Session**.

Definition 3. ***Session*** *includes two types, Independent Session (****ISe****) and Compound Session (****CSe****).*

– ***Independent Session (ISe)*** *is used by service consumer* s^c *to map the set of activated roles* $\{r_1..r_j\}$, $j \geq 1$.
– ***Compound Session (CSe)*** *is used by a pair of service consumer and resource* $< s^c, re >$ *to map a set of activated roles and resource types* $\{< r_1, ret_1 >..< r_j, ret_k >\}$, *(Note, the operations that the service consumer* s^c *requires to access are the same operations that the resource re can provide support to.) where:*
  - $r_1..r_j$, $j \geq 1$, *is a subset of roles assigned to and activated by the specific service consumer* s^c.
  - $ret_1..ret_k$, $k \geq 1$ *is a subset of resource type assigned and activated by the specific resource.*
– ***Service Consumer Independent Session:*** *SCSi:(*s^c*:****SC****)*$\rightarrow 2^{ISe}$*, the mapping of service consumer* s^c *onto a set of independent sessions ISe.*

- ***Service Consumer Compound Session:*** *$SCSc : (s^c : SC) \rightarrow 2^{CSe}$, the mapping of service consumer s^c onto a set of compound sessions CSe.*
- ***Role Independent Session: RSi:(se_i:ISe)$\rightarrow$** 2^R, the mapping of independent session se_i onto a set of roles.*
- ***Role Compound Session:*** *$RSc : (se_c : CSe) \rightarrow 2^R$, the mapping of compound session se_c onto a set of roles.*
- ***Resource Session:*** *$RES(re{:}Re) \rightarrow 2^{CSe}$, the mapping of resource re onto a set of compound session CSe.*
- ***Resource Type Session:*** *$RTS(se_c{:}CSe) \rightarrow 2^{ReT}$, the mapping of compound session se_c onto a set of resource types.*

3 Management of Conflict of Interest

Four types of **Conflicts of Interest** are identified based on SOAC. Authorization rules are defined to prevent the various types of conflict of interest at both design time and run time.

The relationships between two elements with the same type in SOAC are defined as *Exclusive* $\otimes$ or *Non-exclusive* $\ominus$. *Exclusive* relationship means that two elements of SOAC, e.g., two service consumers, two roles, or two operations, are ostracized each other; while *Non-exclusive* relationship means that two elements of SOAC are not ostracized each other. The relationship between elements with the same type in different authorizations should be the same; Otherwise, conflict of interest will occur.

3.1 Conflict of Interest between Service Consumers

In *service provision*, the relationship between two service consumers should be the same as the relationship between the assigned roles for these two consumers to prevent conflict of interest. In Fig. 3, if Op_a and Op_b are *exclusive* ($Op_a \otimes Op_b$), then the relationship between R_i and R_j that are mapped to the operations Op_a and Op_b respectively should reflect the *exclusive* relationship ($Op_a \otimes Op_b \Rightarrow R_i \otimes R_j$). The relationship between assigned roles for service consumers SC_n and SC_m must be matched with the relationship between these two consumers. If service consumers SC_n and SC_m are *non-exclusive* with each other ($SC_n \ominus SC_m$), then SC_n and SC_m can not be assigned roles R_i and R_j respectively at the same time because the roles have the *exclusive* relationship.

Two special cases are illustrated in Fig. 3, where (1) two service consumers become the same one in special case A, and (2) two operations become the same one in special case B. Moreover, the relationship between the element and itself can be *non-exclusive* or *exclusive* according to its situation.

For example, *Payment* and *Payment Verification* are *exclusive* operations that need to be mapped to different roles, and such roles are recognized as *exclusive* roles as `Payer` and `Verifier`. If a service consumer is assigned with both `Payer` and `Verifier` (Special case A in Fig.3), the conflict of interest will occur, since `Payer` and `Verifier` must have relationship-*Exclusive* for access *exclusive* operations.

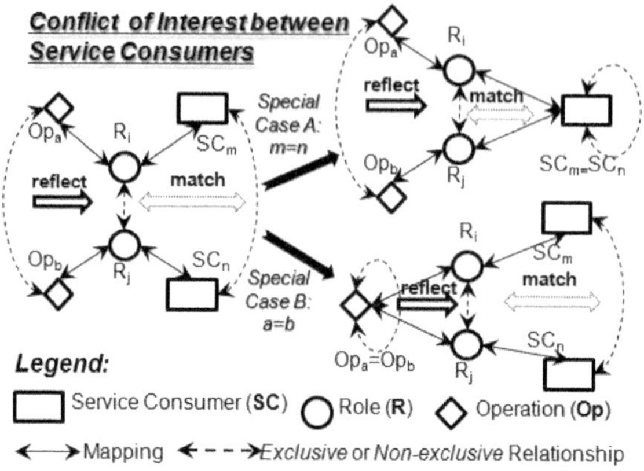

Fig. 3. Role Relationship Check (R-RC)

Let us take another example. "Double Check" policy is enforced in Tom & Brothers on operation of *Payment Verification*, i.e., two financial institutes are required to ensure the payment from purchaser. In order to avoid fraudulent payment assessment on purchase, an *exclusive* relationship between the `Initial Verifier` and `Second Verifier` must be enforced. Westpac Financial Service and St. George Financial Consultant Company are two financial institutes with *non-exclusive* relationship because they belong to the same financial group. Westpac Financial Service and St. George Financial Consultant Company can not be assigned the roles `Initial Verifier` and `Second Verifier` to do payment verification for one transaction due to their *non-exclusive* relationship.

To prevent conflict of interest among service consumers, the following authorization rule named as Static Role Relationship Check (**S-R-RC**) is specified as follows:

Authorization Rule 1. S-R-RC: *Let $\mathbb{SC}$ be a set of Service Consumers. Let $\mathbb{R}$ be a set of Roles. We say that, there is no conflict of interest between service consumers, formally $\exists r_i \in \mathbb{R}, \exists sc_m \in \mathbb{SC}, (r_i, sc_m) \in SCA$, if there exists a subset of Role $\mathbb{R}$ named as $\widetilde{R_a}$, which includes all roles that have been mapped with service consumers, and the relationships between r_i and roles in $\widetilde{R_a}$ are the same as the relationships between sc_m and service consumers that have been mapped to the roles in $\widetilde{R_a}$. Formally, $\exists \widetilde{R_a} \subseteq \mathbb{R}\text{-}\{r_i\}, \forall\, r_j \in \widetilde{R_a}, (r_j, assigned\_sc(r_j)) \in SCA$, $\forall r'_j \in \mathbb{R}\text{-}\{r_i\}\text{-}\widetilde{R_a}$, $assigned\_sc(r'_j) = \emptyset$, $\mathcal{RL}(r_i, r_j) = \mathcal{RL}(sc_m, assigned\_sc(r_j))$, where $\mathcal{RL}(element, element) = \{\otimes, \ominus\}$ reflecting the exclusive, or non-exclusive relationships between elements.*

As an alternative solution, roles can be assigned without using the above authorization rule but the conflict of authorization between consumers will be checked at run time. The mapping between service consumers and roles can be stored in the system at design time. The conflict of interest between consumers are checked when the assigned roles are activated simultaneously by a specific consumer. The authorization rule named as Dynamic Role Relationship Check (**D-R-RC**) is specified as follows:

Authorization Rule 2. D-R-RC: *Let* $\mathbb{SC}$ *be a set of Service Consumers. Let* $\mathbb{R}$ *be a set of Roles. We say that, there is no runtime conflict of interest between service consumers, formally* $\exists r_i \in \mathbb{R}, \exists sc_m \in \mathbb{SC}, (r_i, sc_m) \in SCA$, *and* $r_i \in RSi(SCSi(sc_m))$ *and/or* $r_i \in RSc(SCSc(sc_m))$, *if there exists a subset of Role* $\mathbb{R}$ *named as* $\widetilde{R_b}$, *which includes all roles that are being activated; the relationships between* r_i *and all roles in* $\widetilde{R_b}$ *are the same as the relationships between* sc_m *and service consumers that are activating these roles in* $\widetilde{R_b}$. *Formally,* $\exists \widetilde{R_b} \subseteq \mathbb{R}\text{-}\{r_i\}$, $\forall r_k \in \widetilde{R_b}$, $\exists sc_n \in \mathbb{SC}$, $r_k \in RSi(SCSi(sc_n))$ *and/or* $r_k \in RSc(SCSc(sc_n))$, $\forall r'_k \in \mathbb{R}\text{-}\widetilde{R_b}\text{-}r_i$, $\forall sc'_n \in \mathbb{SC}$, $r'_k \notin RSi(SCSi(sc'_n))$, *and* $r'_k \notin RSc(SCSc(sc'_n))$, $\mathcal{RL}(r_i, r_k) = \mathcal{RL}(sc_m, sc_n)$.

3.2 Conflict of Interest between Resources

If two resources have the relationship *Exclusive* or *Non-exclusive*, the mapped resource types for these two resources must have the same relationship as *exclusive* or *non-exclusive* to prevent conflict of interest.

In Fig.4, if Op_a and Op_b have *exclusive* relationship ($Op_a \otimes Op_b$), then the relevant resource type ReT_i and ReT_j should be *exclusive* ($Op_a \otimes Op_b \Rightarrow ReT_i \otimes RetT_j$). The relationship between the resource types mapped with resources Re_k and Re_h must be the same as the relationship between these two resources. If the resources Re_k and Re_h are *non-exclusive* with each other ($Re_k \ominus Re_h$), e.g., belonging to one company group, then Re_k and Re_h can not be mapped to resource type ReT_i and ReT_j respectively at the same time, since ReT_i and ReT_j are *exclusive*. To avoid conflict of interest, two resources with relationship $\otimes$ or $\ominus$ must be included in the associated two resource types with the same relationship $\otimes$ or $\ominus$.

Two special cases are described in Fig.4, where operations (Special Case A in Fig.4) and resources (Special Case B in Fig.4) become one operation and one resource respectively. Let us take an example as special case B in Fig. 4. For the security reason, *Order Engine* and *Order Engine Accessory* are *exclusive* operations in Tom & Brothers (particularly for military customer), where the mapped resource type, `Engine Supplier` and `Engine Accessory Supplier`, are *exclusive*. Hence, if the resource mapped to `Engine Supplier` and `Engine Accessory Supplier` are the same one, *non-exclusive* relationship exists between the resource and itself, and the resource can not be included in resource type `Engine Supplier` and `Engine Accessory Supplier` at the same time.

We devise the authorization rule named as Static Resource Type Relationship Check (**S-RT-RC**) on the mapping of resources and resource types to prevent the conflict of interest between resources. Here we formally define the authorization rule at design time as follows:

Authorization Rule 3. S-RT-RC: *Let* $\mathbb{R}e$ *be a set of Resources. Let* $\mathbb{R}e\mathbb{T}$ *be a set of Resource Types. We say that, there is no conflict of interest between*

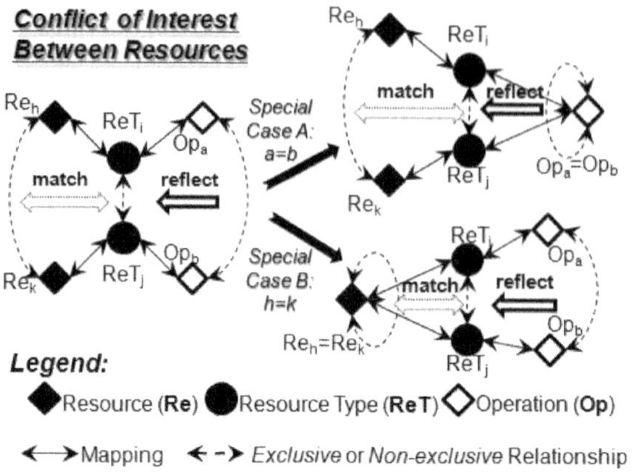

Fig. 4. Resource Type Relationship Check (RT-RC)

resources, formally $\exists ret_i \in \mathbb{R}e\mathbb{T}, \exists re_h \in \mathbb{R}e, (re_h, ret_i) \in RTA$, *if there exists a subset of* $\mathbb{R}e\mathbb{T}$ *named as* $\widetilde{ReT_a}$ *that includes all resource types that have been mapped with resources, and the relationships between* ret_i *and resource types in* $\widetilde{ReT_a}$ *are the same as the relationships between* re_h *and the resources mapped with resource types in* $\widetilde{ReT_a}$*. Formally* $\exists \widetilde{ReT_a} \subseteq \mathbb{R}e\mathbb{T}\text{-}\{ret_i\}$, $\forall\ ret_j \in \widetilde{ReT_a}$, $(ret_j,\ assigned\_re(ret_j)) \in RTA$, $\forall ret'_j \in \mathbb{R}e\mathbb{T}\text{-}\{ret_i\}\text{-}\widetilde{ReT_a}$, $assigned\_re(ret'_j) = \emptyset$, $\mathcal{RL}(ret_i, ret_j) = \mathcal{RL}(re_h, assigned\_re(ret_j))$.

Alternatively, the resource can be mapped to resource types without using the above authorization rule, but the conflict of interest between resources will be checked at run time. The mapping between resources and resource types can be stored in system at design time. The conflict of interest between resources are checked when the resource types are activated simultaneously by employing the resources to provide support to the operations. Here we formally define the Dynamic Resource Type Relationship Check (**D-RT-RC**) on preventing runtime conflict of interest between resources.

Authorization Rule 4. D-RT-RC: *Let* $\mathbb{R}e$ *be a set of Resources. Let* $\mathbb{R}e\mathbb{T}$ *be a set of Resource Types. We say that, there is no runtime conflict of interest between resources, formally* $\exists ret_i \in \mathbb{R}e\mathbb{T}, \exists re_h \in \mathbb{R}e, (re_h, ret_i) \in RTA$, *and* $ret_i \in RTS(RES(re_h))$, *if there exists a subset of* $\mathbb{R}e\mathbb{T}$ *named as* $\widetilde{ReT_b}$ *includes all resource types that are being activated; The relationships between* ret_i *and resource types in* $\widetilde{ReT_b}$ *should be the same as the relationships between* re_h *and resources that are employed to support operations by specific resource types in* $\widetilde{ReT_b}$*. Formally,* $\exists \widetilde{ReT_b} \subseteq \mathbb{R}e\mathbb{T}\text{-}\{ret_i\}$, $\forall ret_k \in \widetilde{ReT_b}$, $\exists re_l \in \mathbb{R}e$, $ret_k \in RTS(RES(re_l))$, $\forall ret'_k \in \mathbb{R}e\mathbb{T}\text{-}\widetilde{ReT_b}\text{-}\{ret_i\}$, $\forall re'_l \in \mathbb{R}e$, $ret'_k \notin RTS(RES(re'_l))$, $\mathcal{RL}(ret_i, ret_k) = \mathcal{RL}(re_h, re_l)$.

3.3 Conflict of Interest between Service Consumers and Resources

Resources and service consumers can have relationship as *exclusive* or *non-exclusive* that must be the same as the relationship of mapped roles and resource types. The relationship between a resource type and a role reflects the relationship between the operation that the role need to access and the operation that the resource type can support. The conflict of interest between service consumers and resources can occur, if the relationship between the service consumers and the resources is not the same as the relationship of mapped role and resource type.

Two special case are also presented in Fig. 5, where (1) the operation that the role need to access and the operation that the resource type can support are the same one (Special Case A in Fig. 5), and (2) the service consumer and the resource are the same web service (Special Case B in Fig. 5). In special case A at Fig. 5, the operation that the resource type ReT_j supports is what the role R_j need to access ($Op_a = Op_b$). Their relationship is *non-exclusive* ($Op_a \ominus Op_b$). If the relationship between the mapped service consumer SC_m and resource Re_k is *exclusive* ($SC_m \otimes Re_k$), e.g., the Chinese manufactory as the resource and the USA military customer as the service consumer, the mapping between the service consumer SC_m to the specific role R_j and the mapping between the resource Re_k to the specific resource type ReT_j can not be made simultaneously.

Let us take another example, in special case B at Fig. 5, a service consumer and a resource belong to one web service ($SC_m = Re_k$). Their relationship is *non-exclusive* ($SC_m \ominus Re_k$). If the operation that the web service supports as resource is *exclusive* with the operation that the web service need to access as the service consumer ($Op_a \otimes Op_b$), there is a conflict of interest between the consumer and the resource. If the web service is assigned with specific role R_i to access the operation Op_a, it can not be mapped to resource type ReT_j to support operation Op_b; vise versa.

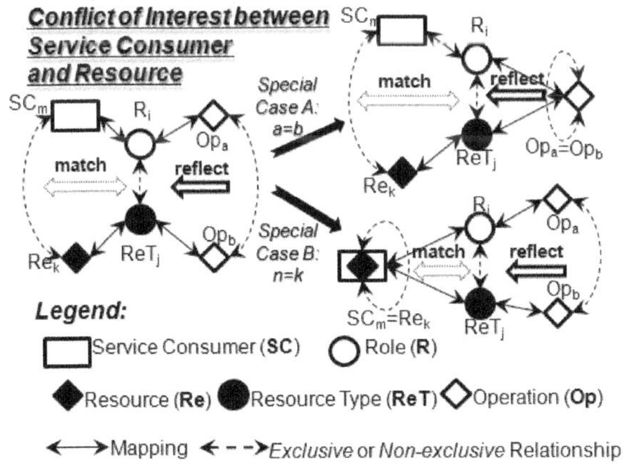

Fig. 5. Role & Resource Type Relationship Check (RRT-RC)

We define authorization rule named as Static Role & Resource Type Relationship Check (S-RRT-RC) to prevent the conflict of interest between the consumer and the resource. The formal specification is as follows:

Authorization Rule 5. S-RRT-RC: *Let $\mathbb{R}e$ be a set of Resources, and $\mathbb{SC}$ be a set of Service Consumers. Let $\mathbb{R}$ be a set of Roles, and $\mathbb{R}e\mathbb{T}$ be a set of Resource Types. We say that, there is no conflict of interest between service consumer and resource if (1) and (2) are satisfied:*

1. *service consumer sc_m and role r_i can be mapped in SCA, formally $\exists r_i \in \mathbb{R}, \exists sc_m \in \mathbb{SC}, (r_i, sc_m) \in SCA$, if there exists a set named as $\widetilde{ReT_a}$ that is a subset of Resource Types and includes all resource types that have been mapped with specific resources; The relationships between r_i and resource types in $\widetilde{ReT_a}$ should be the same as the relationships between sc_m and the resources that are mapped with the resource types in $\widetilde{ReT_a}$. Formally, $\exists \widetilde{ReT_a} \subseteq \mathbb{R}e\mathbb{T}$, $\forall\ ret_j \in \widetilde{ReT_a}$, $(ret_j,\ assigned\_re(ret_j)) \in RTA$, $\forall ret'_j \in \mathbb{R}e\mathbb{T} - \widetilde{ReT_a}$, $assigned\_re(ret'_j) = \emptyset$, $\mathcal{RL}(ret_j, r_i) = \mathcal{RL}(assigned\_re(ret_j), sc_m)$.*
2. *resource type ret_i and resource re_h can be mapped in RTA, formally $\exists ret_i \in \mathbb{R}e\mathbb{T}, \exists re_h \in \mathbb{R}e, (re_h, ret_i) \in RTA$, if there exists a set R_a as a subset of Roles that includes all roles which have been assigned to specific service consumers, and the relationships between ret_i and all roles in R_a should be the same as the relationship between re_h and service consumers that are assigned as specific roles in R_a. Formally, $\exists \widetilde{R_a} \subseteq \mathbb{R}$, $\forall\ r_j \in \widetilde{R_a}$, $(r_j,\ assigned\_sc(r_j)) \in SCA$, $\forall r'_j \in \mathbb{R} - \widetilde{R_a}$, $assigned\_sc(r'_j) = \emptyset$, $\mathcal{RL}(ret_i, r_j) = \mathcal{RL}(re_h, assigned\_sc(r_j))$.*

The mappings between roles and service consumers, and the mappings between resources and resource types can be made without using the above authorization rule. The conflict of interest between service consumers and resources will be checked at runtime. The mappings between role and service consumer, and the mapping between resource and resource type can be stored in system at design time. The conflict of interest between service consumer and resource is checked when the assigned role and resource type are activated simultaneously in the execution of the composite web service requested by the specific service consumer. The authorization rule named as Dynamic Role & Resource Type Relationship Check (D-RRT-RC) is specifies as follows:

Authorization Rule 6. D-RRT-RC *Let $\mathbb{R}e$ be a set of Resources, and $\mathbb{SC}$ be a set of Service Consumers. Let $\mathbb{R}$ be a set of Roles, and $\mathbb{R}e\mathbb{T}$ be a set of Resource Types. We say that, there is no runtime conflict of interest between service consumer and resource if (1) and (2) are satisfied:*

1. *service consumer sc_m can activate assigned role r_i, formally $\exists r_i \in \mathbb{R}, \exists sc_m \in \mathbb{SC}, (r_i, sc_m) \in SCA$, and $r_i \in RSc(SCSc(sc_m))$, if there exists a subset of Resource Types named as $\widetilde{ReT_b}$ that includes all resource types that are activated (when resources mapped to these resource types are required to provide support to operations); the relationship between r_i and all resource types*

in $\widetilde{ReT_b}$ *should be the same as the relationship between* sc_m *and resources that are activating the resource types in* $\widetilde{ReT_b}$*. Formally,* $\exists \widetilde{ReT_b} \subseteq \mathbb{ReT}$, $\forall ret_g \in \widetilde{ReT_b}$, $\exists re_h \in \mathbb{Re}$, $ret_g \in RTS(RES(re_h))$, $\forall ret'_g \in \mathbb{ReT} - \widetilde{ReT_b}$, $\forall re'_h \in \mathbb{Re}$, $ret'_g \notin RTS(RES(re'_h))$, $\mathcal{RL}(ret_g, r_i) = \mathcal{RL}(re_h, sc_m)$.

2. *resource type* ret_i *is being activated by resource* re_h*, formally* $\exists ret_i \in \mathbb{ReT}$, $\exists\, re_h \in \mathbb{Re}, (re_h, ret_i) \in RTA$*, and* $ret_i \in RTS(RES(re_h))$*, if there exists a subset of* $\mathbb{R}$ *named as* $\widetilde{R_b}$ *that includes all of roles that have been activated; The relationship between* ret_i *and roles in* $\widetilde{R_b}$ *should be the same as the relationship between* re_h *and service consumers that activate the roles in* $\widetilde{R_b}$*. Formally,* $\exists \widetilde{R_b} \subseteq \mathbb{R}$, $\forall r_g \in \widetilde{R_b}$, $\exists sc_m \in \mathbb{SC}$, $r_g \in RSc(SCSc(sc_m))$, $\forall r'_g \in \mathbb{R}$-$\widetilde{R_b}$, $\forall sc'_m \in \mathbb{SC}$, $r'_g \notin RSc(SCSc(sc'_m))$, $\mathcal{RL}(ret_i, r_g) = \mathcal{RL}(re_h, sc_m)$.

Conflict of interest between one pair of service consumer/resource and other pairs of service consumer/resource is another new type of conflict of interest which can be identified in SOAC. A service consumer and a resource is put in one pair when the service consumer request the access of the operation of a composite web service and the operation needs the support of the resource. The relationships between pairs of role/resource type reflect the relationships between operations mapped to these pairs of role/resource type. If two pairs of service consumer/resource have the relationship *Exclusive* or *Non-exclusive*, the pairs of mapped roles and resource types must have the same relationship as *Exclusive* or *Non-exclusive*

For example, in Fig. 6, if the operations are *exclusive* ($Op_a \otimes Op_b$), the relationship between the pairs of mapped roles and resource types must also be *exclusive* ($Op_a \otimes Op_b \Rightarrow (R_i, ReT_i) \otimes (R_j, ReT_j)$). Note, here the relationship between operations will be reflected by the relationship between the pairs of roles and resource types rather than considering the relationship between roles or resources types individually which are discussed in previous subsections 3.1 and 3.2. If the relationship between two pairs of service consumer and resource are *non-exclusive* ($(SC_n Re_h) \ominus (SC_m, Re_k)$), the pairs of mapped roles and resource types must also be *non-exclusive* to prevent the conflict of interest.

Two special cases are illustrated in Fig. 6, where (1) the pairs of service consumer and resource are the same one (Special case A in Fig. 6 ($SC_m = SC_n$ and $Re_h = Re_k$)), and (2) the operations in different authorizations are the same one (Special cased B in Fig. 6 ($Op_a = Op_b$)). Let us take an example in special case A. When a service consumer is mapped with the role `Military Customer` by Tom & Brothers, and the goods it orders need to be supplied by part manufactory mapped with resource type `Vehicle Engine Supplier`, it will violate the law if Tom & Brothers also use the same manufactory that is mapped with resource type `Vehicle Engine Accessory Supplier` to supply the engine accessory to the same consumer that is mapped with role `Commercial Customer`. In this case, the *exclusive* relationship between operations of *Order Engine* and *Order Engine Accessory* requires that the relationship between the pair of `Military Customer` and `Vehicle Engine Supplier` and the pair of

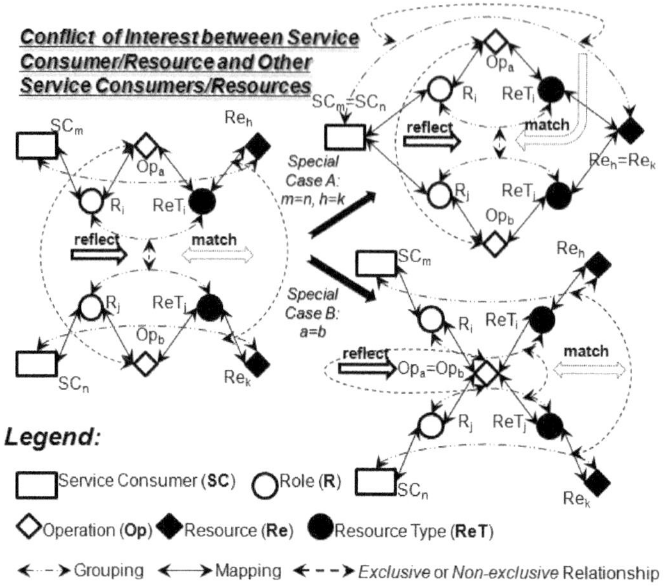

Fig. 6. Pairs of Role & Resource Type Relationship Check (PRRT-RC)

`Commercial Customer` and `Vehicle Engine Accessory Supplier` are *exclusive* also. If the two pairs of role and resource type are mapped to the same pair of service consumer and resource with a *non-exclusive* relationship, the conflict of interest occurs. This conflict of interest is identified to prevent the following two things happening at the same time. The first thing is to assemble the engine for military use with the engine accessory for civil use and the second thing is to purchase engine and engine accessory from the same part suppliers. We can observe that the service consumer can be mapped with both roles `Military Customer` and `Commercial Customer` without causing conflict of interest between customers (discussed in subsection 3.1). We can also observe that the manufactory can be mapped with both resource types `Vehicle Engine Supplier` and `Vehicle Engine Accessory Supplier` without causing conflict of interest between resources (discussed in subsection 3.2). The conflict of interest occurs when the service consumer is mapped with both roles and the resource is mapped with both resource types. In a summary, if the manufactory as `Vehicle Engine Supplier` to provide engine to a service consumer as `Military Customer`, it should not provide engine accessory to the same service consumer that is identified as `Commercial Customer`; vise versa.

We set up authorization rule named as Static Pairs of Role & Resource Type Relationship Check (S-PRRT-RC) to prevent conflict of interest between two pairs of service consumer/resource. Here we formally define the authorization rule at design time as follows:

Authorization Rule 7. S-PRRT-RC *Let* $\mathbb{R}e$ *be a set of Resources, and* $\mathbb{SC}$ *be a set of Service Consumers. Let* $\mathbb{R}$ *be a set of Roles, and* $\mathbb{R}e\mathbb{T}$ *be a set of Resource Types. We say that, there is no conflict of interest between one pair of service consumer/resource and another pair of service consumer/resource, formally* $\exists r_i \in \mathbb{R}, \exists sc_m \in \mathbb{SC}, (r_i, sc_m) \in SCA$, $\exists ret_i \in \mathbb{R}e\mathbb{T}, \exists re_h \in \mathbb{R}e$, $(re_h, ret_i) \in RTA$, $assigned\_op(r_i) \cap assigned\_ret(ret_i) \neq \emptyset$, *if there exists a set named as* $\widetilde{ReT_a}$ *that is a subset of Resource Types and includes all resource types which have been mapped with specific resources, and exists a set named as* $\widetilde{R_a}$ *that is a subset of Roles and includes all roles which have been assigned to specific service consumers; There must exist a resource type* (ret_k) *and a role* (r_k) *that map to the same operations; the relationship between* (ret_i, r_i) *and* (ret_k, r_k) *should be the same as the relationships between* (re_h, sc_m) *and pairs of resources and service consumers that are mapped to* ret_k *and* r_k *respectively. Formally,* $\exists \widetilde{ReT_a} \subseteq \mathbb{R}e\mathbb{T}$, $\forall\ ret_j \in \widetilde{ReT_a}$, $(ret_j,\ assigned\_re(ret_j)) \in RTA$, $\forall ret'_j \in \mathbb{R}e\mathbb{T} - \widetilde{ReT_a}$, $assigned\_re(ret'_j) = \emptyset$, $\exists \widetilde{R_a} \subseteq \mathbb{R}$, $\forall\ r_j \in \widetilde{R_a}$, $(r_j,\ assigned\_sc(r_j)) \in SCA$, $\forall r'_j \in \mathbb{R} - \widetilde{R_a}$, $assigned\_sc(r'_j) = \emptyset$, $\exists r_k \in \widetilde{R_a}, \exists ret_k \in \widetilde{ReT_a}$, $assigned\_op(r_k) \cap assigned\_ret(ret_k) \neq \emptyset$, $\mathcal{RL}((ret_i, r_i), (ret_k, r_k)) = \mathcal{RL}$ $((re_h, sc_m), (assigned\_re(ret_k), assigned\_sc(r_k)))$.

Without using the above authorization rule, the conflict of interest between pairs of service consumer and resource can be checked at runtime. The mapping between service consumer and role, and the mapping between resource type and resource are stored in system. The conflict of interest between pairs of service consumer/resource is checked when the associated roles and resource types are activated simultaneously. The authorization rule named as Dynamic Pairs of Role & Resource Type Relationship Check (D-PRRT-RC) is specified as follows:

Authorization Rule 8. D-PRRT-RC *Let* $\mathbb{R}e$ *be a set of Resources, and* $\mathbb{SC}$ *be a set of Service Consumers. Let* $\mathbb{R}$ *be a set of Roles, and* $\mathbb{R}e\mathbb{T}$ *be a set of Resource Types. We say that, there is no runtime conflict of interest between one pair of service consumer/resource and another pair of service consumer/resource, formally* $\exists r_i \in \mathbb{R}, \exists sc_m \in \mathbb{SC}, (r_i, sc_m) \in SCA$, $\exists ret_i \in \mathbb{R}e\mathbb{T}, \exists re_h \in \mathbb{R}e, (re_h, ret_i) \in RTA$, $assigned\_op(r_i) \cap assigned\_ret(ret_i) \neq \emptyset$, $r_i \in RSc\ (SCSc(sc_m))$, *and* $ret_i \in RTS(RES(re_h))$, *if there exists a subset of* $\mathbb{R}e\mathbb{T}$ *named as* $\widetilde{ReT_b}$ *which includes all resource types that are being activated, and there also exists a subset of* $\mathbb{R}$ *named as* $\widetilde{R_b}$ *which includes all roles that are being activated. There must exists a resource type* ret_k *belonging to* $\widetilde{ReT_b}$ *and a role* r_k *belonging to* $\widetilde{R_b}$ *that are supporting and accessing the same operations respectively; The relationship between* (ret_i, r_i) *and* (ret_k, r_k) *should be the same as the relationship between* (re_h, sc_m) *and pairs of resources and service consumers that are activating* ret_k *and* r_k *respectively. Formally* $\exists \widetilde{ReT_b} \subseteq \mathbb{R}e\mathbb{T}$, $\forall ret_x \in \widetilde{ReT_b}$, $\exists re_y \in \mathbb{R}e$, $ret_x \in RTS(RES(re_y))$, $\forall ret'_x \in \mathbb{R}e\mathbb{T} - \widetilde{ReT_b}$, $\forall re'_y \in \mathbb{R}e$, $ret'_x \notin RTS(RES(re'_y))$, $\exists \widetilde{R_b} \subseteq \mathbb{R}$, $\forall r_x \in \widetilde{R_b}$, $\exists sc_y \in \mathbb{SC}$, $r_x \in RSc(SCSc(sc_y))$, $\forall r'_x \in \widetilde{R_b}$, $\forall sc'_y \in \mathbb{SC}$, $r'_x \notin RSc(SCSc(sc'_y))$, $\exists r_k \in \widetilde{R_b}, \exists ret_k \in \widetilde{ReT_b}$, $assigned\_op(r_k) \cap assigned\_ret(ret_k)$

$\neq \emptyset$, $\exists sc_n \in \mathbb{SC}$, $r_k \in RSc(SCSc(sc_n))$, $\exists re_g \in \mathbb{R}e$, $ret_k \in RTS(RES(re_g))$, $\mathcal{RL}((ret_i, r_i), (ret_k, r_k)) = \mathcal{RL}((re_h, sc_m), (re_g, sc_n))$.

4 Related Work

Role based access control [2, 3] is a widely accepted approach to restrict system access to authorized users. In RBAC, users acquire permissions through their roles rather than they are assigned permissions directly. Traditional RBAC models deal with authorization of resources which belong to an individual organization. In web service paradigm, the component services of composite web services and their related resources normally spread over multiple organizations and are invoked in a highly dynamic manner. Traditional RBAC models can not be used directly as ready solutions for authorization of web services. There have been quite a lot of researches about authorization of web services. We will overview some representative work in the follows.

In [5, 6], the authors propose a RBAC framework to manage access control in WS-BPEL [7], named RBAC-WS-BPEL. In RBAC-WS-BPEL, authorization constrains are specified on the execution activities and roles are assigned to users for gaining permissions on execution activities. This research only focuses on the service orchestration level and it has no capability to consider characteristics of resources required by composite web services.

In [8, 9], the authors provide an enforcement and verification approach to guarantee that a service choreography can be successfully implemented between a set of web services (service consumer and the composite web service) based on their authorization constraints. This research only focuses on enforcement and verification of authorization between service consumer and composite web service. The component web services in authorization of composite web service are not taken into account.

An access control model CWS-RBAC was proposed in [10] which takes the composite service into consideration and is comparable to our proposed approach. In CWS-RBAC, a global role is assigned to service consumers to gain the permission to access the composite service and a local role mapped from global role is assigned to service consumer to access the other component services. The authors in [11] propose another concept-*Role Composition* where global role and local role are composed together. It analyzes how a local role issued by an individual component service is mapped to a global role from the composite services. In that case, if the service consumer is assigned with a global role, then it automatically bears the permissions of the bound local role on the component service. In these approaches, the "role" as a concept used by a specific service to manage the authorization is part of internal security policy within an individual web service and can not be identified by other services. For example, the composite web service can not identify which role that it can be assigned by the component web service that it needs to access. Actually, the composite web service can only perceive the permissions based on credentials, i.e, the authorization constraints (the public part of authorization policy of each web service). Hence, the mapping of the global role issued from the composite service with the local role generated in other component services is not realistic. In our proposed approach, we introduce the resource type (**ReT**) to explicitly express characteristics and requirements of resources associated with component services. **ReT** can support an efficient way for the management of dynamically involved and prone-to-change component services in composite web services. Furthermore, **ReT** provides the fundamental concept for defining the conflict of interest related with component services.

Conflict of interest is a major concern in traditional RBAC models. In order to deal with conflict of interest, static and dynamic separation of duty mechanisms are defined in RBAC standard [12, 14]. The authors in [13] have discussed the conflict of interest in the authorization of web services. However, this research deals with the authorization of web services using the same way as those authorizations in close systems. In particular, the features of composite web services have not been taken into consideration. It is lacking of existing work to identify and deal with possible types of conflict of interest among service consumers, among component services, and between service consumers and component services in composite web services.

Existing approaches about authorization of composite web services have the limitations: (1) ignoring the dynamic nature of composite web services that require resources based on-demand; (2) missing an efficient way to the administration of the resources in service-oriented authorization; (3) hard coding the roles issued from resources and composite service; and (4) lacking of authorization rules for preventing conflict of interest in composite web service authorization. This paper reports our research for the authorization of composite web services to address the above mentioned limitations of existing approaches.

5 Conclusion and Future Work

The proposed approach for authorization of composite web services can provide an efficient way to administrate and manage a large number of service consumers and dynamic component services. This research addresses the conflict of interest issue regarding to both service consumers and component services in composite web services. Four types of conflict of interest are identified. Authorization rules at both design time and run time to deal with various types of conflict of interest are provided and illustrated. In the future, we plan to investigate the possibility of employing the hierarchical structure to represent resource types and the mechanism of mapping between resource types and individual resources.

References

[1] Papazoglou, M., Georgakopoulos, D.: Service-Oriented Computing. Communications of the ACM 46(10), 25–28 (2003)

[2] Sandhu, R.S., Coyne, E., Feinstein, H., Youman, C.: Role-based Access Control Models. IEEE Computer 29(2), 38–47 (1996)

[3] Ferraiolo, D., Cugini, J., Kuhn, R.: Role Based Access Control: Features and Motivations. In: Proceedings of ACSAC (1995)

[4] Sun, H., Zhao, W., Yang, J.: SOAC: A Conceptual Model for Managing Service-Oriented Authorization. In: Proceedings of the IEEE International Conference on Service Computing, pp. 546–553 (2010)
[5] Bertino, E., Crampton, J., Paci, F.: Access Control and Authorization Constraints for WS-BPEL. In: Proceedings of the IEEE International Conference on Web Services, pp. 275–284 (2006)
[6] Paci, F., Bertino, E., Crampton, J.: An Access Control Framework for WS-BPEL. International Journal of Web Service Research 5(3), 20–43 (2008)
[7] Jordan, D., et al.: Web Services Business Process Execution Language Version 2.0 (WS-BPEL 2.0) (August. 2006), http://docs.oasis-open.org/wsbpel/2.0/
[8] Mecella, M., Ouzzani, M., Paci, F., Bertino, E.: Access Control Enforcement for Conversation-based Web Service. In: Proceedings of the International World Wide Web Conference, pp. 257–266 (2006)
[9] Paci, F., Ouzzani, M., Mecella, M.: Verification of Access Control Requirements In Web Servies Choreography. In: Proceedings of SCC, pp. 5–12 (2008)
[10] Wonohoesodo, R., Tari, Z.: A Role Based Access Control for Web Services. In: Proceedings of SCC, pp. 49–56 (2004)
[11] Fischer, J., Majumdar, R.: A Theorey of Role Composition. In: Proceedings of ICWS, pp. 49–56 (2008)
[12] Ferraiolo, D., Sandhu, R., et al.: Proposed NIST Standard for Role-Based Access Control. ACM Trans. on Information and System Security (TISSEC) 4(3), 224–274 (2001)
[13] Giblin, C., Hada, S.: Towards Separation of Duties for Services. In: The 6th Int. Workshop on SOA & Web Services Best Practices Committee, OOPSLA, Nashville, October 19 (2008)
[14] Ahn, G., Sandhu, R.: Role-Based Authorization Constraints Specification. ACM Transactions on Information and System Security (TISSEC) 3(4), 207–226 (2000)

Modelling and Automated Composition of User-Centric Services

Raman Kazhamiakin[1], Massimo Paolucci[2], Marco Pistore[1], and Heorhi Raik[1]

[1] Fondazione Bruno Kessler, via Sommarive 18, Trento TN 38050, Italy
{raman,pistore,raik}@fbk.eu
[2] DoCoMo Euro-Labs, Landsberger Strasse 312, 80687 Munich, Germany
paolucci@docomolab-euro.com

Abstract. User-centric services bring additional constraints to the problem of automated service composition. While in business-centric settings the services are orchestrated in order to accomplish a specific business task, user-centric service composition should allow the user to decide and control which tasks are executed and how. This requires the ability not only to automatically compose different, often unrelated, services on the fly, but also to generate a flexible interaction protocol that allows the user to control and coordinate composition execution. In this paper we present a novel automated composition approach that aims to support user-centric service provisioning. Specifically, we associate the service to so-called service objects and provide a declarative notation to express composition requirements in terms of the evolution of those objects. On top of these objects we also define the user control activities and constraints. Using the automated planning techniques, our approach generates a service composition that orchestrates services in a way it is requested by the user.

1 Introduction

In the past decade, the advances in technology allowed numerous service providers to introduce thousands of new electronic services as well as to create service-oriented adapters for conventional services. In these settings, the ability to efficiently integrate and compose those services in order to obtain new functionalities becomes one of the key factors for the wide adoption of the service-oriented paradigm. A variety of technologies and approaches is already available to facilitate the development of service compositions.

With the growth of the service market more and more prominent role is gained by the *user-centric services*, i.e., the services that are intended to be consumed directly by the user (e.g., personal agenda, electronic maps, on-line flight booking and check-in, restaurant finder, etc.), as opposed to business-centric (or B2B) services, which are used to provide business-to-business cooperation. Although the rapid emergence of user-centric services is the trend of the last few years, some works already distinguished them as a separate group of services [5], and some even considered their features from the service composition perspective ([6] and [9]). While from the technological viewpoint user-centric composition may rely on similar composition solutions and standards, the way such services are composed and delivered to the users should adhere to some specific yet significant requirements and constraints. In particular:

R. Meersman et al. (Eds.): OTM 2010, Part I, LNCS 6426, pp. 291–308, 2010.

- B2B service composition aims at realizing a specific business task in a structured way (e.g., by implementing a corresponding business process). In the user-centric settings the goal is to continuously support the user in performing variety of different tasks, being able to react to the changes in her plans and decisions and to propagate those changes to the composed services. This requires different ways to capture composition requirements, shifting from the definition of an ultimate composition goal to the definition of the rules and constraints on continuous service coordination.
- The execution of the business-centric composition is driven and controlled by the rationale defined by the business goal behind that composition. The execution of the composed user-centric services is driven and controlled by the user deciding which activity to execute, when it should be executed and how. The key issue here is to identify appropriate interaction means that would deliver controllability and awareness of the execution to the user in an intuitive way.
- In both cases the composition is being constructed from the service models and composition requirements defined by the designer at design time. In the user-centric settings, however, the decision of which services should be integrated and composed is left to the user, which makes the service composition a purely run-time activity. First, this makes the use of automated service composition techniques unavoidable. Second, there is a need for the appropriate modelling techniques, where the composition requirements are sufficiently abstracted from the service implementations. Third, this makes the problem of controlling the execution of the composition by the user even more complex, since the corresponding interaction protocols should be constructed and provided to the user at run-time, in a composition-specific manner.

In this paper we present a novel service composition framework which aims to address these challenges. Building upon our previous techniques for automated service composition [4], this approach provides the capabilities specifically targeting the needs of user-centric service compositions. In this framework, we propose:

- A simple yet expressive language for control flow composition requirements, being able to deal with the problems specific to user-centric service compositions just discussed. The language relies on the service model, where the essential service properties are abstracted from the low-level service implementations, thus enabling dynamic re-use of those models at run-time.
- A set of principles capturing the patterns of interaction with the user, so that he is always in control and aware of the execution of his services in an intuitive way.
- An automated support for the service composition and derivation of the corresponding user protocol, through which the user can trigger different activities, control their execution, and receive relevant information about the execution flow.

The rest of the paper is structured in the following way. In Section 2 we present out motivating example and discuss the main challenges we face. In Section 3, the general approach is outlined. Section 4 contains some background on wired planning. In Section 5, the formalization of the composition model is given. Section 6 is devoted to the implementation of the composition framework and experiments. In Section 7 we discuss related work.

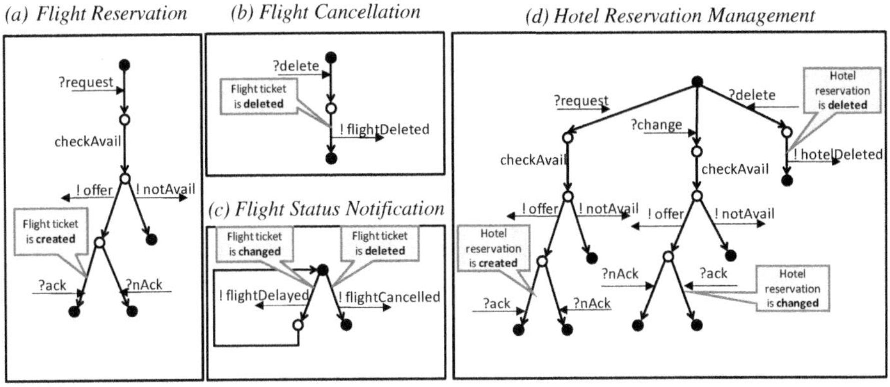

Fig. 1. Protocols of components in travel domain scenario

2 Motivating Example

For the illustration purposes, we use a case study from the travel domain, which is widely used in the literature on service composition. In this case study, the user deals with services that manage different activities over flight bookings and hotel reservations. More precisely, these services are (Fig. 1):

1. *A flight booking service (a).* Upon the user request, it sends an offer and waits for the confirmation.
2. *A flight cancellation service (b).* It simply cancels the flight upon the user request.
3. *A flight status notification service (c).* It notifies the user about flight delays and cancellations.
4. *A hotel reservation management service (d).* This is a complex service that provides means to create, modify and cancel hotel reservations.

In this scenario our goal is not simply to allow the user to book a flight and a hotel for the same trip, but to continuously coordinate their evolution when the changes are required by the user (e.g., the user wants to cancel the flight) or triggered by exogenous events (e.g., flight is delayed). Specifically, the coordination requirements may be:

- a flight ticket and hotel reservation should be booked together (i.e., transactionally).
- when the flight is delayed, the hotel reservation should be postponed, and if this is not possible, both should be cancelled.
- when the flight is cancelled, the hotel reservation should be cancelled too.

Furthermore, the composition should enable the user to control the execution. That is, the user should be able to change his objects (e.g., to cancel the flight or to modify the hotel reservation), to be aware of the changes (e.g., to receive notifications), and to make important decisions (e.g., to accept or reject proposed hotel options).

Finally, we expect that the specific service implementations (i.e., specific flight and hotel booking services) are selected dynamically, and the concrete composition is created at run-time.

The requirements posed by the presented scenario make the service composition problem much more challenging than in the similar scenarios used to evaluate existing composition approaches. In particular, the following problems should be addressed:

- *Heterogeneity of service implementations.* There may be no single service that can completely manage an entity (e.g., a flight ticket is managed by three different services, some of them may even belong to different service providers). Moreover, different provider may define the same service in different ways.
- *Continuous service coordination.* There is a need to continuously coordinate a few entities (a flight ticket and a hotel reservation) rather than simply perform a single task.
- *Re-use of composition requirements.* The complexity of control-flow requirements and dynamicity of composition instantiation raises the question of reusing them with different service implementations. In our example, once specified, composition requirements should be applicable to different implementations of flight and hotel management services.
- *Dynamicity of user protocols.* While there is clearly a need to enable the user to manipulate services and to control the composition execution, the way the user interacts with the composition, i.e., user protocol, strictly depends on the participating services and on their implementations. Such a protocol can hardly be predefined for all possible realizations.

3 Overview

In order to address the problems outlined in Section 2, we introduce a novel service modelling and composition approach. In this section we present the key elements of the approach, namely, the composition model and the composition construction process.

Composition Model. Our composition model is shown in the following figure:

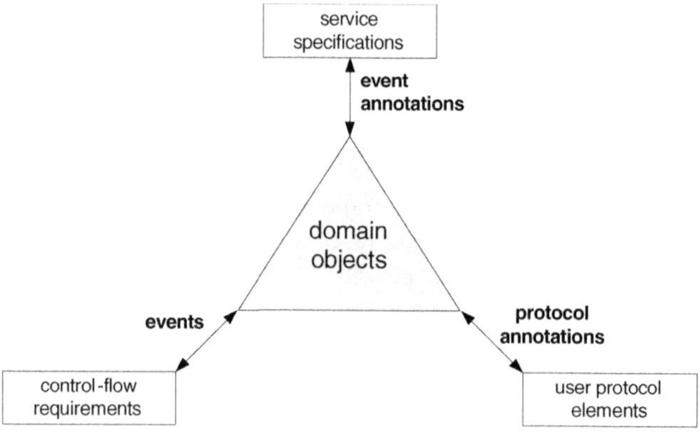

The central element of this model is the definition of *domain objects* used to represent the entities participating to the composition (e.g., a flight ticket, or a hotel reservation) and their evolution at a high level of abstraction. Details of concrete service implementations are captured in the definition of *service specifications*. These specifications are related to domain objects through event annotations that define how the execution of services makes the corresponding object evolve. The specification of the *control-flow requirements* over the service composition is given in terms of evolution of domain objects only, regardless of the specific services realizing those objects. Similarly, the *user protocol elements* capturing the requirements on the user interactions with the composition are related to the composed objects, and not to the service implementations nor to composition requirements. We remark that with this distinction we are able to address the problem of service implementation heterogeneity, re-use of composition requirements in different settings, and automatically come up with the necessary user protocol regardless of specific composition scenario and the services participating in it.

The domain objects used in our model are represented with an *object diagram*, a state diagram that defines possible object states and transitions between them (e.g., a flight ticket can be booked, then paid, then checked-in or cancelled or delayed etc.). In fact, an object diagram is the representation of an object life-cycle, where transitions correspond to the activities that can be performed over the object (e.g., flight cancellation) or external event that can happen to the object (e.g., flight delay committed by the airline).

Following the real-world phenomena, in our model we allow for stateful services with complex protocol, asynchronous and non-deterministic behavior. These services may be defined using standard notations (e.g., BPEL). To link service specifications and domain objects, we annotate some of the actions in service protocols with the events of object evolutions. As such, through domain objects our model is able to capture complex and diverse service implementations and to relate independent services managing the same entity.

The language for the specification of control-flow requirements is defined on top of object diagrams, i.e., in terms of states and events. The language aims to express various coordination goals, i.e., alignment of states of different domain objects, reaction to various events, and so on. With this language our approach supports continuous coordination requirements, enabling their reuse since the requirements are detached from service implementations.

When the composition instance and constituent services are defined, our approach automatically derives a specific user protocol for the composition. Doing this, the following requirements are considered:

- The user should have a way to manipulate the objects using available services.
- The user should be able to receive notifications about object evolution.
- During the execution, critical decisions should be delegated to the user.

Following these requirements, the corresponding protocol elements are defined in our model. Specifically, these elements are used to enable and control the activation of certain object transitions by the user, to inform the user about the changes, and to capture critical decisions and the interaction with the user on those decisions. Formal definition of the elements is given in Section 5.4.

Composition Process. The composition process consists of two major phases: design time and run time. At *design time*, IT experts model the domain objects and associate the existing services to those objects through service annotations. After that, it is possible to define groups of domain objects that are likely to be composed with each other (e.g., a flight ticket, a hotel reservation and a car rental are likely to be coordinated in the context of trip planning). For each such group of objects, a set of control-flow requirements is specified which defines how to coordinate them. In fact, these requirements define a sort of *composition template* for coordinating certain objects (e.g., the template on how to manage a trip consisting of a flight, a hotel and a car rental). Finally, the resulting specifications, namely domain objects, services, and composition templates, are stored in some service repositories. The way the repositories are defined, accessed, and managed is outside of the scope of this paper.

At *run time*, the template is instantiated with concrete objects, and services that can manage these objects are offered to the user. Once the service implementations are chosen, we use planning techniques to automatically build a composite service. Our planning-based composition tool takes as input the models of object diagrams, annotated service specifications, and control-flow requirements, we translate these models into a planning domain with planning goals over this domain. The plan obtained is intended to implement the behaviour of the composite service that meets the composition requirements specified. Finally, it is translated back to one of the standard composition languages (e.g., BPEL).

We remark that the ability to select service implementations at run time is a very important capability that we consider. The fact that implementations of the same services can be radically different (e.g., implementations of a flight booking service provided by various airlines) makes the realization of such capability far from trivial and indeed requires advanced planning techniques available at run time.

4 Background on Service Composition via Planning

In our approach to service composition we rely on the composition framework presented in [10] (planning in asynchronous domains). In that research, a planning domain is derived from service specifications, composition requirements are formalized as a planning goal, and advanced planning algorithms are applied to the planning problem to generate the composite service. The advantages of the approach are an asynchronous communication model, the ability to deal with stateful and non-deterministic services, considering preference-based (reachability) requirements on services. This is why it provides a good basis to build upon. Here we discuss the main concepts of that formal framework.

A planning domain is formally defined as a state transition system, i.e., a dynamic system that can be in one of its *states* (some of which are *initial states* and/or *accepting states*) and can evolve to new states as a result of performing some *actions*. Actions can be *input* actions, which represent the reception of messages, *output* actions, which represent messages sent to external services, and internal action τ, modelling internal computations and decisions.

Definition 1 (STS). *A state transition system is a tuple* $\langle \mathcal{S}, \mathcal{S}^0, \mathcal{I}, \mathcal{O}, \mathcal{R}, \mathcal{S}^F, \mathcal{F} \rangle$, *where:*

- $\mathcal{S}$ *is the set of states and* $\mathcal{S}^0 \subseteq \mathcal{S}$ *are the initial states;*
- $\mathcal{I}$ *and* $\mathcal{O}$ *are the input and output actions respectively;*

- $\mathcal{R} \subseteq \mathcal{S} \times Bool \times (\mathcal{I} \cup \mathcal{O} \cup \{\tau\}) \times \mathcal{S}$ *is a transition relation, where Bool represents all boolean expressions over propositions* $\mathcal{P}$*;*
- $\mathcal{S}^F \subseteq \mathcal{S}$ *is the set of accepting states;*
- $\mathcal{F} : \mathcal{S} \rightarrow 2^{\mathcal{P}}$ *is the labelling function.*

Given a labeling function the $\mathcal{F} : \mathcal{S} \rightarrow 2^{\mathcal{P}}$, we can define whether a boolean expression $b \in Bool$ over propositions in $\mathcal{P}$ holds in state $s \in \mathcal{S}$, written $s, \mathcal{F} \models b$. The definition is the classical one for validity of boolean expressions.

The transitions of STS are guarded: a transition $\langle s, b, a, s' \rangle$ is possible in the state s only if the guard expression b holds in that state, i.e., $s, \mathcal{F} \models b$. A run π of STS is a finite sequence of transitions $\pi = \langle s_0, b_0, a_0, s_1 \rangle, \ldots, \langle s_n, b_n, a_n, s_{n+1} \rangle$, with $a_i \in \mathcal{I} \cup \mathcal{O} \cup \{\tau\}$, $s_i, \mathcal{F} \models b_i$, $s_0 \in \mathcal{S}^0$, and $s_{n+1} \in \mathcal{S}^F$. The set of all runs of a STS Σ is denoted with $\Pi(\Sigma)$.

Component services can be recast as STSs, and, given a set of component services $W_1, \ldots, W_n$, the planning domain Σ is defined as a synchronous product of the all the STSs of the component services: $\Sigma = \Sigma_{W_1} \| \ldots \| \Sigma_{W_n}$. The synchronous product $\Sigma_1 \| \Sigma_2$ models the fact that the systems Σ_1 and Σ_2 evolve simultaneously on common actions and independently on actions belonging to a single system. A composed service can also be represented as a state transition system Σ_c. Its aim is to control the planning domain defined by the component services. The interactions of Σ_c and Σ are modelled by the following notion of a controlled system.

Definition 2 (Controlled System)
Let $\Sigma = \langle \mathcal{S}, \mathcal{S}^0, \mathcal{I}, \mathcal{O}, \mathcal{R}, \mathcal{S}^F, \mathcal{F} \rangle$ *and* $\Sigma_c = \langle \mathcal{S}_c, \mathcal{S}_c^0, \mathcal{I}, \mathcal{O}, \mathcal{R}_c, \mathcal{S}_c^F, \mathcal{F}_c \rangle$ *be two state transition systems. The state transition system* $\Sigma_c \triangleright \Sigma$*, describing the behaviors of system* Σ *when controlled by* Σ_c*, is defined as follows:*

$$\Sigma_c \triangleright \Sigma = \langle \mathcal{S}_c \times \mathcal{S}, \mathcal{S}_c^0 \times \mathcal{S}^0, \mathcal{I}, \mathcal{O}, \mathcal{R}_c \triangleright \mathcal{R}, \mathcal{S}_c^F \times \mathcal{S}^F, \mathcal{F}_c \cup \mathcal{F} \rangle$$

where:

$$\langle (s_c, s), (b_c \wedge b), a, (s'_c, s') \rangle \in (\mathcal{R}_c \triangleright \mathcal{R}),\ \mathit{if}$$
$$\langle s_c, b_c, a, s'_c \rangle \in \mathcal{R}_c \ \mathit{and}\ \langle s, b, a, s' \rangle \in \mathcal{R}.$$

In this setting, generating a composed service Σ_c that guarantees the satisfaction of a composition goal ρ is formalized by requiring that the controlled system $\Sigma_c \triangleright \Sigma$ satisfies the requirement ρ: $\Sigma_c \triangleright \Sigma \models \rho$. In [11] it is shown how planning for preference-ordered goals may be applied for this purpose, considering a list $\rho = (g_1, g_2, \ldots, g_n)$ of alternative requirements where each g_i is a reachability goal.

In our work, we will use this idea as a basis on top of which we will build our composition model.

5 Formal Model

In this section, we formally describe each part of our composition framework introduced in section 3. The model is an extension of the formalization presented in [4]. This extension, on the one hand, enriches the modelling capabilities of the approach and, on the other hand, allows for capturing specific properties of user-centric service composition.

5.1 Domain Objects

A domain object is intended to model some entity that we can manage using services. One service composition is likely to manage more than one domain object (in the motivating example, we manage two domain objects: a flight ticket and a hotel reservation). Every domain object is modelled with an object diagram, which is a state transition system. Transitions in an object diagram stand for activities that can be performed over the object (e.g., to book a flight ticket). To address object diagram transitions in control-flow requirements and service annotations, we label transitions with object events. Differently from [4], in this work we distinguish between two types of transitions. Transitions that are triggered by executing a certain service are called *controllable* (e.g., hotel booking) because the user can decide whether to execute them and when. These type of transitions can have more than one final state corresponding to different non-deterministic outcomes of service execution. Each non-deterministic outcome is labelled with its own event. Transitions corresponding to external notifications (e.g., flight delay notification) are called *uncontrollable* because they can happen at any time and are out of the user's control. These transitions are deterministic and have exactly one final state.

Definition 3 (Object Diagram). *An* object diagram *representing object O is a tuple $\langle L, L_0, \mathcal{E}, T\rangle$, where:*

- *L is a finite set of object configurations and $L_0 \subseteq L$ is a set of initial configurations;*
- *$\mathcal{E}$ is a set of possible events that reflect the evolution of the object;*
- *$T \subseteq L \times (\mathcal{E} \times L)^+$ is a transition relation that defines non-deterministic evolution of an object, based on events. We distinguish between controllable transitions T_c and uncontrollable transitions T_u such that $T = T_c \cup T_u$ and $T_c \cap T_u = \emptyset$.*

We remark that transition relation in domain objects allows for a few effects per transition, each leading to its own final state. Such a model takes into account that each activity over object may have a few possible non-deterministic outcomes (see the example below).

Example 1 (Flight Ticket). A possible object diagram for domain object Flight Ticket may be represented as follows:

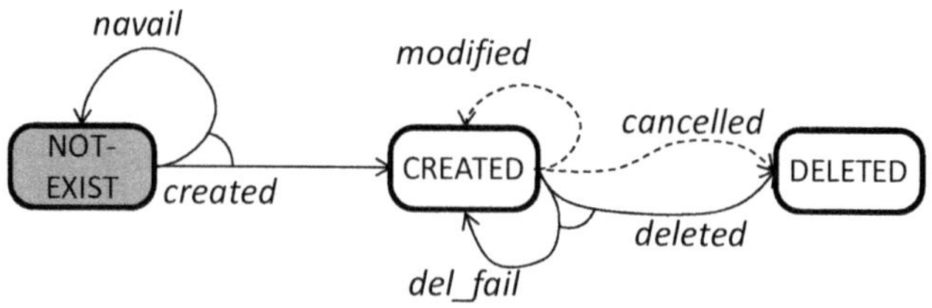

In this diagram, solid lines correspond to controllable and dashed lines to uncontrollable transitions. Non-deterministic outcomes of the same transition are marked with an arc. The diagram has three different configurations *not-exist*, *created* and *deleted*. The transition corresponding to flight booking is an example of a controllable transition with non-deterministic outcomes. The object moves to state *created* when the flight booking service is executed successfully (event "created"). At the same time, non-deterministic fail of this service is still possible (e.g., event "navail" represents non-availability of the flight with requested attributes). Formally, this transition can be represented as $T_{cr} = (\textsf{\textit{not-exist}}, \{(created, \textsf{\textit{created}}), (navail, \textsf{\textit{not-exist}})\})$. In state *created*, two uncontrollable transitions are presented: if the flight is delayed (event "modified") or cancelled (event "cancelled") by the airline. The ticket cancellation can also be performed in a controllable way using a corresponding service (events "deleted" and "del_fail").

5.2 Services

In this research, we reuse the model of annotated services presented in [4]. We deal with stateful services represented with a service protocol (e.g., a BPEL process) and a stateless interface (e.g., a WSDL specification). Every service is related to a specific domain object through special annotations (in certain sense, we use a service to produce some effect on a corresponding object). These annotations appear within the activities of the service protocol: an activity may be annotated with a set of events pertaining to the corresponding object. This implicitly defines how the execution of the service changes the object.

We use *annotated state transition system* (ASTS) as a model of service. "Annotated" means that each transition in such an STS may be labelled with object diagram events. The execution of a labelled transition propagates labelling events to the object. If, for example, a service transition is annotated with event $to^{\mathsf{e}}(l, o)$, then object o moves to configuration l when this transition takes place.

Definition 4 (Annotated State Transition System). *An annotated STS Σ is a tuple $\langle \mathcal{S}, \mathcal{S}^0, \mathcal{I}, \mathcal{O}, \mathcal{E}, \mathcal{R} \rangle$ where:*

- *$\mathcal{E}$ is the set of events;*
- *$\mathcal{R} \subseteq \mathcal{S} \times (\mathcal{I} \cup \mathcal{O} \cup \{\tau\}) \times \mathcal{E}^* \times \mathcal{S}$ is the transition relation.*

The semantics of the annotated transition is intuitively described as follows. Let object o have a set of events $\mathcal{E}$, and a service transition $(s, a, \varepsilon, s') \in \mathcal{R}$, where $s, s' \in \mathcal{S}$, $a \in (\mathcal{I} \cup \mathcal{O} \cup \{\tau\})$, and $\varepsilon \subseteq \mathcal{E}$.

The transition is considered to be *applicable* to the object o if the object is in some configuration l, and either $\varepsilon = \emptyset$, or there exists an object transition (l, ε', l'), such that $\varepsilon' \subseteq \varepsilon$. Once this transition is performed, in the first case the object will remain in the same configuration, while in the second case it will evolve to the configuration l'.

Example 2. An annotated STS of the Flight Cancellation Service (Fig. 1, b) is defined as $\Sigma = \langle \{s_0, s_1, s_2\}, s_0\}, \{delete\}, \{flightDeleted\}, \mathcal{E}, \mathcal{R} \rangle$. The output operation "flightDeleted" is annotated with the event $d^{\mathsf{e}}(f)$ (flight is "deleted"), as the service provider confirms the flight ticket cancellation. That is, $\mathcal{E} = \{d^{\mathsf{e}}(f)\}$, and $\mathcal{R} = \{(l_0, ?delete, \emptyset, l_1), (l_1, !flightDeleted, \{d^{\mathsf{e}}(f)\}, l_2)\}$.

We remark that service protocols can feature branching. For example, in the flight booking service (Fig. 1(a)) after the flight options are offered, it is possible either to accept or to reject the offer. For such protocols, more than one execution path is available. At any branching point, the decision on which branch to take is delegated to the user and is a part of the derived user protocol (for details see subsection 5.4).

5.3 Control Flow Requirements

To express control-flow requirements, we use an easy-to-specify language that is independent from service implementations and expressive enough to specify complex requirements and can take into account the user's behaviour. For those reasons, this language (i) expresses requirements on the evolution of objects, synchronizing object diagrams and defining "stable" configurations for the system of object; (ii) specifies requirements as reaction rules, which define how the composite service shall react to object events in different situations. Differently from [4], we introduce a "try-catch" construction. The intuition is to handle the situation where we want some effect to be provided, but expect that while executing services some fails may happen and these fails will require additional reaction.

Definition 5 (Composition Constraint). *A composition requirement is defined with the following generic template*

$$premise \Longrightarrow (reaction_1 \succ \ \ldots \ \succ reaction_n),$$

where $premise \equiv s^{\mathsf{s}}(o) \mid e^{\mathsf{e}}(o) \mid pr_1 \vee pr_2 \mid pr_1 \wedge pr_2$

and $reaction \equiv s^{\mathsf{s}}(o) \mid e^{\mathsf{e}}(o) \mid r_1 \vee r_2 \mid r_1 \wedge r_2 \mid \ try(r)$

$$catch(pr_1) : r_1$$

$$\ldots$$

$$catch(pr_n) : r_n$$

Here pr_1, pr_2 *and* pr_n *are premises,* r, r_1, r_2 *and* r_n *are reactions,* $s^{\mathsf{s}}(o)$ *is used to define the fact that the object o is in the configuration s, and* $e^{\mathsf{e}}(o)$ *defines that the event e of the object o has taken place,* $try(r)catch(pr_i) : r_i$ *construction means that it is necessary to do all possible to provide reaction* r*, but if, while trying to provide this reaction, situation* pr_i *(premise of the catch block) has happened,* r_i *should be provided instead.*

The left side of the constraint defines the "premise" and the right side defines a set of "reactions" that we expect from the composite service (reactions are ordered according to their priorities). More precisely, the constraint states that if the situation described in the "premise" has happened, one of the situation described in the corresponding "reactions" has to be provided with respect to given priorities. Expression $try(r)$ has to be interpreted as "do your best to provide r, bur even if you finally failed you are successfully done with $try(r)$".

Example 3. The composition requirements of the motivating example in Section 2 can be written down using our language in the following way:

1. $cr^{\mathsf{s}}(h) \vee cr^{\mathsf{s}}(f) \Longrightarrow (cr^{\mathsf{s}}(f) \wedge cr^{\mathsf{s}}(h))$

Here, the transactional creation of two objects h (hotel reservation) and f (flight ticket) is defined, i. e., mandatory bring both objects to the state "cr" (created) in case at least one of them is created. In such way we define "stable" configuration of a system of objects (both are created).

2. $mod^{\mathsf{e}}(f) \Longrightarrow try(mod^{\mathsf{e}}(h))$

$$catch(refused^{\mathsf{e}}(h) \vee mod\_navail^{\mathsf{e}}(h) :$$
$$try(del^{\mathsf{s}}(h)) \wedge try(del^{\mathsf{s}}(f))$$

   This constraint states that once the flight is delayed (event $mod^{\mathsf{e}}(f)$), the composition has to do its best to modify the hotel reservation (i. e., to trigger event $mod^{\mathsf{e}}(h)$ for the hotel reservation). If specific types of fails happen while changing the hotel reservation (non-availability $mod\_navail^{\mathsf{e}}(h)$ or the user's refusal of the new hotel offer $refused^{\mathsf{e}}(h)$) then the composition has to try to delete both objects. This is an example of requirements that specify reaction to events that the composite service has to provide.

3. $d^{\mathsf{e}}(f) \Longrightarrow (try(d^{\mathsf{e}}(h))$.

   If the flight is cancelled (event $d^{\mathsf{e}}(f)$), the composition tries to cancel the hotel reservation (event $d^{\mathsf{e}}(h)$).

The resulting composite process is supposed to continuously satisfy all the control-flow requirements specified and thus consistently manage the whole life cycle of two object.

We want to emphasize that, due to the fact that the language expresses requirements purely in terms of the evolution of objects, the requirements themselves remain independent from the implementation of services. As such, the same requirements can be used with various implementations of a conceptual service once these implementations are properly annotated with object evolution information.

5.4 User Protocol

The user protocol of the composite service should give the user enough control over the execution of component services. We distinguish three main types of user control activities that have to be reflected in the user interface and protocol of the composite service. They are:

1. **Execution activation.** Each controllable transition in an object diagram can be triggered through the execution of a particular service. We extend the user interface of the composite service with additional operations that let the user control the activation of each controllable transition (Fig. 2(a)). To activate a certain transition (i. e., to ask the composite service to execute the corresponding service), the user calls special operation $call_i$. If the composite service needs to trigger some controllable transition itself (e. g., in order to meet composition requirements) if first has to receive the user's permission for that and only then to proceed. To implement such interaction we add three more operations: ask_i, $accept_i$ and $reject_i$. First, the composite service sends ask_i and then the user replies with $accept_i$ if the permission is granted and $reject_i$ if not. We impose additional restriction which requires that the user may request the execution of a service only if the composition is not busy with any other task.

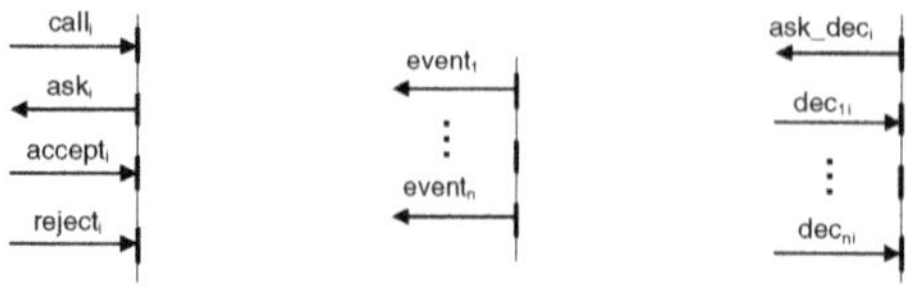

(a) *activation* (b) *reporting* (c) *decision*

Fig. 2. Interface for user control elements

2. **Event reporting.** Every event that happens to a domain object has to be reported to the user. Therefore, for each event we add operation $event_i$ to the composition interface (Fig. 2(b)). They let the user stay informed about the dynamics of the domain objects.
3. **Decision-making.** If a service protocol features branching, we allow the user to make decisions at any branching point. Particularly, for each branching point we add to the composition interface the following operations: ask_dec_i, dec_1_i, $\ldots$, dec_n_i (Fig. 2(c)). At a branching point, the composition sends ask_dec_i and then receives one of possible decisions $dec\_1_i, \ldots, dec\_n_i$.

6 Composition as Planning Problem

In order to use planning techniques for composing services, we need to replace a service composition problem with the planning one. More precisely, the formal model has to be transformed into a set of synchronized state transition systems (STS) that form a planning domain, and the composition requirements have to be rephrased in terms of the goal states of these STS's.

In this section, we define transformation rules for each part of our formal model and demonstrate how composition requirements can be expressed as planning goals. We further outline the work of the algorithm and explain how to interpret its results.

Service Transformation. To transform component services we replace a given annotated STS $\langle \mathcal{S}, \mathcal{S}^0, \mathcal{I}, \mathcal{O}, \mathcal{E}, \mathcal{R} \rangle$ with a corresponding STS $\langle \mathcal{S}, \mathcal{S}^0, \mathcal{I}, \mathcal{O}, \mathcal{R}', \mathcal{S}^F, \mathcal{F} \rangle$. In order to perform such transformation, for each transition $(s, a, \varepsilon, s') \in \mathcal{R}$ we define a corresponding transition $(s, \top, a, s') \in \mathcal{R}'$, and the states are not labeled (for each $s \in \mathcal{S}$ $\mathcal{F}(s) = \emptyset$). In order to state that each service once started has to be executed to one of its final states all the terminating and initial states of the ASTS are marked as accepting states in the STS.

Object diagrams transformation. First, we define a set of atomic propositions $\mathcal{P} \equiv \{s_j{}^{\mathsf{s}}(o_i)\}$, which specify that an object o_i is in state s_j for all objects and their states. This will allow us to capture object states in requirements. Object diagram $\langle L, L_0, \mathcal{E}, T \rangle$ in transformed into an STS $\langle \mathcal{S}, \mathcal{S}^0, \mathcal{I}, \mathcal{O}, \mathcal{R}, \mathcal{S}^F, \mathcal{F} \rangle$, where $\mathcal{S} = L$, $\mathcal{S}^0 = L_0$, every state is labelled with the corresponding proposition (i. e., $\forall s \in \mathcal{S} : \mathcal{F}(s) = \{s^{\mathsf{s}}(o)\}$), and all object configurations are accepting (i. e., $\mathcal{S}^F = \mathcal{S}$). To obtain the transition

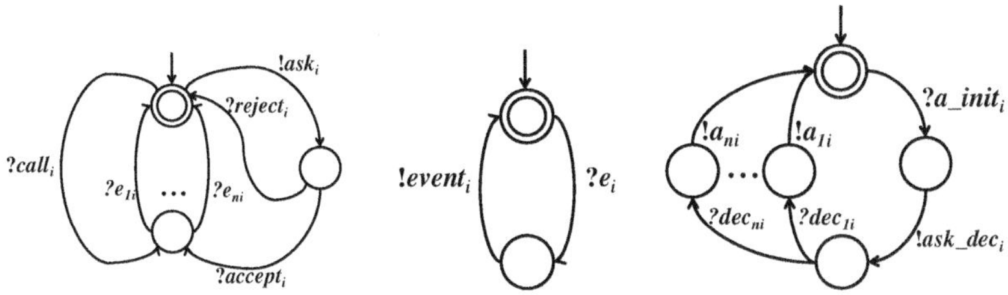

(a) Activation STS (b) Event reporting STS (c) Decision making STS

Fig. 3. STS diagrams of user control elements

relation of a new STS, for each non-deterministic transition in the object diagram $(l, c, \{(\varepsilon'_1, l'_1), \ldots, (\varepsilon'_n, l'_n)\}) \in T$ and for any transition (s, a, ε, s') of some ASTS such that $\varepsilon'_i \subseteq \varepsilon$ we define a (non-guarded) transition $(l, \top, a, l'_i) \in \mathcal{R}$.

User Protocol Transformation. For each user control element mentioned in subsection 5.4 we provide an STS implementing its semantics:

- The STS for execution activation (Fig. 3(a)) blocks a corresponding controllable transition in an object diagram (by blocking all events associated $e_{1i} \ldots e_{ni}$) until either the user sends a request ($?call_i$)) or the composite service gets user's authorization to trigger the transition ($accept_i$).
- The STS for event reporting (Fig. 3(b)) sends a report to the user ($!event_i$) every time an associated event ($?e_i$) happens to an object.
- The STS for making decisions (Fig. 3(c)) blocks service execution as soon as a branching point is reached ($?a\_init_i$). It asks the user for a decision ($!ask\_dec_i$) and when the user chooses one of the possible options ($?dec_{1i} \ldots dec_{ni}$) it unblocks a corresponding service action ($!a_{1i} \ldots !a_{ni}$).

Transformation of constraints. The composition constraints speak of both object states and occurrences of object events. For every constraint we define a corresponding STS that reflects the satisfiability of the requirement. Given a clause cl, we define a corresponding STS that contains a single output action e_{cl} representing the completion of the clause. The diagrams corresponding to different clauses and their combinations, and to the constraint diagram itself are represented in Fig. 4.

The STS for $s^{\mathsf{s}}(o)$ (Fig. 4(a)) is blocked until the object is not in the required state: the transition is guarded with the corresponding proposition. We denote the fact that object o is in state s with event e_s. The STS for $e^{\mathsf{e}}(o)$ (Fig. 4(b)) waits for any of the service actions that contain the corresponding event in its effects: for any transition (s, a, ε, s') of some ASTS such that $e^{\mathsf{e}}(o) \in \varepsilon$ a corresponding transition is defined. When it happens, a completion is reported. The STS for $cl_1 \vee cl_2$ (Fig. 4(c)) waits for any of the sub-clauses to complete, while the STS of the $cl_1 \wedge cl_2$ (Fig. 4(d)) waits for both of them to be completed.

The transformation of the $try - catch$ construction (Fig. 4(e)) includes a try-STS and one STS for each $catch$ block. For each $catch(pr_i) : r_i$ we create an STS enforcing that every failure pr_i is entailed with appropriate reaction r_i. $try(r)$ is reported to

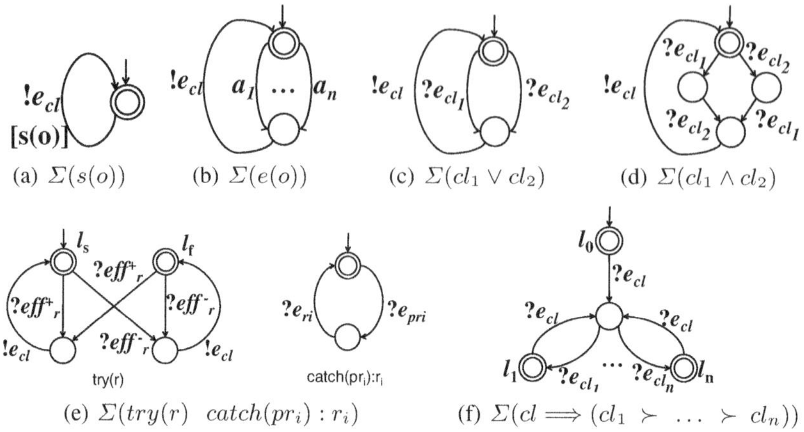

Fig. 4. STS diagrams of composition constraints

be completed when either the needed reaction r has been provided successfully (we denote this situation with event $\mathit{eff}^+(r)$) or some fail happened while trying to provide r (event $\mathit{eff}^-(r)$). Given a transition $t = (l_0, \{e_i, l_i\})$ of object o let $finals(t) = \{l_i\}$, $events(t) = \{e_i\}$, $to(t, e) = l'$ if $(e, l') \in \{e_i, l_i\}$ and $reject(t)$ corresponds to a situation when permission for triggering t is not granted (transition $reject_i$ in 3(a)), which can be considered as transition failure. Then $\mathit{eff}^+(r)$ and $\mathit{eff}^-(r)$ can be defined for different reactions as follows:

- $\mathit{eff}^+(s^{\mathsf{s}}(o)) = e_s$,
  $\mathit{eff}^-(s^{\mathsf{s}}(o)) = \{e' : (\exists t \in T, e'' \in \mathcal{E} : to(t, e'') = s) \wedge (e \in events(t))\} \bigcup \{reject(t) : t \in T_c \wedge s \in finals(t)\}$;
- $\mathit{eff}^+(e^{\mathsf{e}}(o)) = e^{\mathsf{e}}(o)$,
  $\mathit{eff}^-(e^{\mathsf{e}}(o)) = \{e' : (\exists t \in T : e \in finals(t) \wedge e' \in finals(t) \wedge e \neq e')\} \bigcup \{reject(t) : t \in T_c \wedge e \in events(t)\}$;
- $\mathit{eff}^+(cl_1 \vee cl_2) = \mathit{eff}^+(cl_1) \cup \mathit{eff}^+(cl_2)$, $\mathit{eff}^-(cl_1 \vee cl_2) = \mathit{eff}^-(cl_1) \times \mathit{eff}^-(cl_2)$;
- $\mathit{eff}^+(cl_1 \wedge cl_2) = \mathit{eff}^+(cl_1) \times \mathit{eff}^+(cl_2)$, $\mathit{eff}^-(cl_1 \wedge cl_2) = \mathit{eff}^-(cl_1) \cup \mathit{eff}^-(cl_2)$;
- $\mathit{eff}^+(try(r)) = \mathit{eff}^+(r) \cup \mathit{eff}^-(r)$, $\mathit{eff}^-(try(r)) = \emptyset$.

Intuitively, these definitions can be explained in the following way. The attempt to reach a state fails when the composition tries to trigger one of the transitions potentially leading to this state but fails. The attempt to cause some event fails when the composition tries to trigger one of the transitions potentially causing this event but fails. The attempt to provide $try(r)$ is always successful (any outcome of the attempt to trigger a transition is affordable). It is important to notice that $\mathit{eff}^-(r)$ for controllable transitions includes additional events that do not appear explicitly in an object diagram. These events correspond to the situations where the user does not authorize the composite service to execute a service (message $?reject_i$ in Fig. 3(a)). Indeed, when the system, according to requirements, is supposed to *try* to do something, but the user does not grant permission to start necessary service execution, we can conclude that the composition has actually tried to react but failed. In try-STS, state l_s is more preferable than state l_f. The corresponding goal with preferences will be:

$$\rho_t = (l_s, l_f) \tag{1}$$

The STS that represents the evolution of a composition constraint is represented in Fig. 4(f). The STS is initially in an accepting location (l_0). If the premise of the constraint takes place (e_{cl} is reported), then it moves to a non-accepting state, from which it may be satisfied by completing one of the clauses $e_{cl_1}, \ldots, e_{cl_n}$ (moving to locations $l_1, \ldots, l_n$ respectively). The corresponding goal with preferences will have the following form:

$$\rho_c = (l_0, l_1, \ldots, l_n). \tag{2}$$

That is, we require that whenever the premise take place, the composition tries to move the constraint STS to one of the accepting states, respecting the ordering of preferences.

Example 4. The constraint $d^{\mathsf{e}}(f) \implies try(d^{\mathsf{e}}(h))$ is modelled with the following STSs:

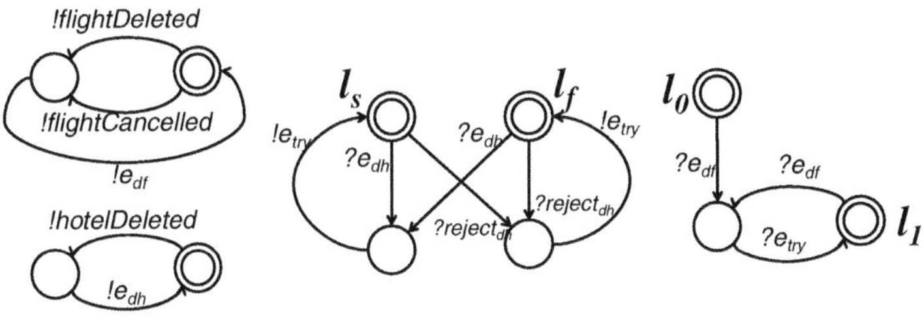

Although the hotel cancellation process is deterministic and cannot fail during the execution, negative outcome $\mathit{eff}^-(d^{\mathsf{e}}(f))$ for event $d^{\mathsf{e}}(h)$ is not empty because, as we discussed earlier, the user's refusal to grant permission to execute some service (here $reject_{dh}$) is also considered to be a failure.

6.1 Generating a Composite Service

The approach to automated service composition that we use here refers to the one presented in [10]. In particular, having a set of n services $(W_1, \ldots, W_n)$, m objects $(O_1, \ldots, O_m)$, k composition constraints $(C_1, \ldots, C_k)$ and l user control elements $(U_1, \ldots, U_l)$ we transform them into STSs using the transformation rules presented above so that we get an STS for each part of the model (respectively $\Sigma_{W_1} \ldots \Sigma_{W_n}$, $\Sigma_{O_1} \ldots \Sigma_{O_m}$, $\Sigma_{C_1} \ldots \Sigma_{C_k}$ and $\Sigma_{U_1} \ldots \Sigma_{U_l}$).

The planning domain Σ is a synchronous product of all the STSs of the component services, objects, constraints and user control elements while composition goal is constructed from the requirements defined according to the formulae (1) and (2):

$$\Sigma = \Sigma_{W_1} \| \ldots \| \Sigma_{W_n} \| \Sigma_{O_1} \| \ldots \| \Sigma_{O_m} \| \Sigma_{C_1} \| \ldots \| \Sigma_{C_k} \| \Sigma_{U_1} \| \ldots \| \Sigma_{U_l}$$

$$\rho = \bigwedge_c \rho_c \wedge \bigwedge_t \rho_t.$$

Finally, we apply the approach of [10] to domain Σ and planning goal ρ and generate a controller Σ_c, which is such that $\Sigma_c \triangleright \Sigma \models \rho$. The state transition system Σ_c is further translated into executable BPEL process, which implements a composite service required. The back translation from STS into BPEL is quite simple: input actions in Σ_c model an incoming message from a component service or from the user, while output actions in Σ_c model an outcoming message to a component service or to the user.

Correctness of the approach. The proof of the correctness of the approach consists in showing that all the executions of the composed service (controller Σ_c) satisfy the control flow requirements defined. Here we outline the key points of the proof. It is easy to see that each execution π of the composed service is also a run of the domain, i. e., if $\pi \in \Pi(\Sigma_c)$ then $\pi \in (\Sigma)$. Under the requirement that all the executions of constraint STS terminate in accepting states, we get that the executions of the domain satisfy the composition requirements. As a consequence, the following theorem holds.

Theorem 1 (Correctness of the approach). *Let:*

- $\Sigma_{W_1}, \ldots, \Sigma_{W_n}$ *be the STS encoding of component services* $W_1, \ldots W_n$,
- $\Sigma_{C_1}, \ldots, \Sigma_{C_k}$ *be the STS encoding of the constraints* $C_1, \ldots C_k$,
- $\Sigma_{O_1}, \ldots, \Sigma_{O_m}$ *be the STS encoding of the domain objects* $O_1, \ldots, O_m$, *and*
- $\Sigma_{U_1}, \ldots, \Sigma_{U_l}$ *be the STS encoding of the user control elements* $U_1, \ldots, U_l$.

Let Σ_c *be the controller for a particular composition problem*

$$\Sigma = \Sigma_{W_1} \| \ldots \| \Sigma_{W_n} \parallel \Sigma_{O_1} \| \ldots \| \Sigma_{O_m} \parallel \Sigma_{C_1} \| \ldots \| \Sigma_{C_k} \parallel \Sigma_{U_1} \| \ldots \| \Sigma_{U_l}.$$

Then the executions $\Pi(\Sigma_c)$ *satisfy the requirements* $C_1, \ldots, C_k$.

6.2 Experiments

We evaluate the potential of our approach by implementing the preliminary version of the composition framework and testing it with a reference case study. Having service specifications, object diagram descriptions, composition requirements and user control elements the composition framework generates a planning domain specification with the goals defined over this domain. After the planning algorithm is applied to the planning problem, the plan, which encodes the expected behaviour of the composite process, is translated back into BPEL.

The composed process implements the composition requirements presented. The process first waits for the request to create a flight ticket or a hotel reservation and then transactional books both items processing fails when happened. After both object are created, if the flight is delayed or cancelled, the appropriate reaction follows. The interaction with the user is embedded into the composite process. In particular, at stable point of the execution, where all the requirements are satisfied, the user is allowed to request certain operations on objects (i.e., service executions). Whenever some event happens, it is reported to the user. Finally, at branching points in service protocols, the composition asks for the user's decision and takes it into account later on.

As we shown in Fig. 1, the implementations of component services have fairly complex structure with 14 BPEL activities (such as receive, response etc.) in the most complex process. However, the composed executable process composed is much more complicated, with around 100 BPEL activities, including those providing interaction with the user. The process features very complex structure with multiple branching points and several loops. No doubt, its manual coding would take a significant amount of time.

The run of the experiment took less than 15 seconds on a Windows-machine with dual core 2 GHz CPU and 4Gb of memory. Taking into account further possible optimization, we consider these results to be very promising.

7 Related Work and Conclusions

In this paper, we have presented a novel approach to modelling and composing user-centric services. Being based on the notion of domain objects, the approach features an expressive language for control-flow requirements allowing for continuous orchestration of services using reactive rules and coordination constraints. The language is detached from service implementations and expresses the requirements in terms of domain object evolution. The approach also provides the automatic derivation of the user protocol, which enables the user to control the composition execution and to be aware of the current execution progress. While some parts of the composition model have to be specified manually, the model resolution, which is the most time and effort demanding phase of the composition process, is completely automated using planning techniques. The paper also provides some preliminary experimental results, which prove the potential of our approach.

The new model proposed in this paper is a further development of the model of [4]. Our composition engine relies on the service composition via automated planning presented in [10]. In this paper, we focused on control-flow composition requirements and did not consider data-flow composition requirements. We plan to integrate data-flow requirements as future work, exploiting the approach described in [8], which is also based on [10] and is hence compatible with our approach.

There is a wide literature on service composition. Most of the proposed approaches, however, model services as atomic entities (e.g., [1], [12] and [13]), while we consider services to be non-deterministic, stateful and asynchronous. In particular, while there are some other user-centric services composition approaches (e.g., [6], [9], [5]), they give a very different meaning to "user-centricity" than the one we used in this paper, and they address problems that are quite different from ours. The new language for control-flow requirements and the ability to derive complex user protocol also make our approach different from [10], [4], [3] and [7]. The representation of services by more abstract "object" entities is close to WS-Conversation language [2]. To some extent, our composition model is closer to the concept of mash-ups [15]. However, mash-ups are usually exploited for integration of data and of information services, and the extension to the full-fledged services considered here is not trivial. The mash-up approach described in [14] is more related to ours. There, mash-up techniques are exploited to guarantee that the coordination is maintained among the status of a set of components to be integrated, and that changes in one of the components is reflected in the others. A key difference is that in [14] the integration and coordination is done at the presentation layer (i.e., user interface), while our approach addresses the problem at the application layer. A better comparison, and possible integration, of the two approaches is part of our plan to extend out composition approach to cover the presentation layer.

Acknowledgement. The research leading to these results has received funding from the European Community Seventh Framework Programme FP7/2007-2013 under grant agreement 215483 (S-Cube).

References

1. Aggarwal, R., Verma, K., Miller, J.A., Milnor, W.: Constraint Driven Web Service Composition in METEOR-S. In: Proc. of SCC 2004, pp. 23–30 (2004)
2. Banerji, A., Bartolini, C., Beringer, D.: Web Services Conversation Language (WSCL) 1.0 (2002), `http://www.w3.org/TR/wscl10/`
3. Berardi, D., Calvanese, D., Giacomo, G.D., Mecella, M.: Composition of Services with Nondeterministic Observable Behaviour. In: Benatallah, B., Casati, F., Traverso, P. (eds.) ICSOC 2005. LNCS, vol. 3826, Springer, Heidelberg (2005)
4. Bertoli, P., Kazhamiakin, R., Paolucci, M., Pistore, M., Raik, H., Wagner, M.: Control flow requirements for automated service composition. In: ICWS, pp. 17–24 (2009)
5. Chang, M., He, J., Tsai, W., Xiao, B., Chen, Y.: Ucsoa: User-centric service-oriented architecture. In: IEEE International Conference on E-Business Engineering, pp. 248–255 (2006)
6. Corradi, A., Lodolo, E., Monti, S., Pasini, S.: A user-centric composition model for the internet of services. In: ISCC, pp. 110–117 (2008)
7. Hull, R.: Web Services Composition: A Story of Models, Automata, and Logics. In: Proc. of ICWS 2005 (2005)
8. Marconi, A., Pistore, M., Traverso, P.: Specifying Data-Flow Requirements for the Automated Composition of Web Services. In: Proc. SEFM 2006 (2006)
9. Nestler, T., Dannecker, L., Pursche, A.: User-centric composition of service front-ends at the presentation layer. In: 1st International Workshop on User-generated Services, UGS 2009 (2009)
10. Pistore, M., Traverso, P., Bertoli, P.: Automated Composition of Web Services by Planning in Asynchronous Domains. In: Proc. ICAPS 2005 (2005)
11. Shaparau, D., Pistore, M., Traverso, P.: Contingent planning with goal preferences. In: Proc. AAAI 2006 (2006)
12. Thakkar, S., Ambite, J.-L., Knoblock, C.: A data integration approach to automatically composing and optimizing web services. In: Proceedings of 2004 ICAPS Workshop on Planning and Scheduling for Web and Grid Services, Whistler, BC, Canada (2004)
13. Wu, D., Parsia, B., Sirin, E., Hendler, J., Nau, D.: Automating DAML-S Web Services Composition using SHOP2. In: Fensel, D., Sycara, K., Mylopoulos, J. (eds.) ISWC 2003. LNCS, vol. 2870, Springer, Heidelberg (2003)
14. Yu, J., Benatallah, B., Saint-Paul, R., Casati, F., Daniel, F., Matera, M.: A framework for rapid integration of presentation components. In: Proc. WWW 2007 (2007)
15. Zang, N., Rosson, M.B., Nasser, V.: Mashups: who? what? why? In: Proc. CHI 2008 (2008)

Coordinating Services for Accessing and Processing Data in Dynamic Environments

Víctor Cuevas-Vicenttín[1] Genoveva Vargas-Solar[1,2], Christine Collet[1], Noha Ibrahim[1], and Christophe Bobineau[1]

[1] Grenoble Institute of Technology, CNRS, UJF
Grenoble Informatics laboratory (LIG)
681, rue de la Passerelle, BP. 72, 38402
Saint Martin d'Hères Cedex, France
[2] French Mexican Laboratory of Informatics and Automatic Control
Exhacienda Sta. Catarina Mártir s/n 72820
San Andrés Cholula, Puebla, México
Firstname.Lastname@imag.fr

Abstract. This paper presents an approach and an associated system named HYPATIA for accessing and processing data by coordinating services in dynamic environments. A dynamic environment consists of applications, servers and devices that can be static and nomad, and that produce or consume data on demand (e.g., online applications, Web-hosted DBMS) or continuously (messaging systems, mobile services). In such an environment, data are hidden behind services that export application programming interfaces (API) through heterogeneous networks and that provide functions for retrieving and processing data. In order to have an aggregated and integrated view of the dynamic environment at every moment (e.g., accessing Google's agenda service and feeding a Twitter service for continuously locating friends as we all stroll in a city), data consumers have to execute sets of service calls, i.e., subscribe to continuous data producers, aggregate results and feed other services and then obtain results and eventually start over again. No off-the-shelf DBMS provides such service oriented querying approach including continuous, one-shot, mobile and static query evaluation.

Our work introduces the notion of hybrid query that declaratively expresses data consumers requirements and an associated query evaluator, HYPATIA, that executes data oriented query service coordinations; taking advantage of the services available in the network (data providers and devices computing capacity) and yielding the query result.

1 Introduction

This paper presents an approach and an associated system named HYPATIA for accessing and processing data by coordinating services in dynamic environments. A dynamic environment consists of applications, servers and devices that can be static and nomad, and that produce or consume data on demand (e.g., online

R. Meersman et al. (Eds.): OTM 2010, Part I, LNCS 6426, pp. 309–325, 2010.

applications, Web-hosted DBMS) or continuously (messaging systems, mobile services). In such an environment, data are hidden behind services that export application programming interfaces (API) through heterogeneous networks and that provide functions for retrieving and processing data. In this context we speak of hybrid queries, which involve on-demand and streaming data accessible through services, featuring in some cases temporal and mobile properties.

Consider the scenario depicted in Figure 1. Multiple users find themselves in an urban area carrying GPS-enabled mobile devices that periodically transmit their location. A user in this scenario may want to *Find friends which are no more than 3 km away from her/him, which are over 21 years old, and that are interested in art.*

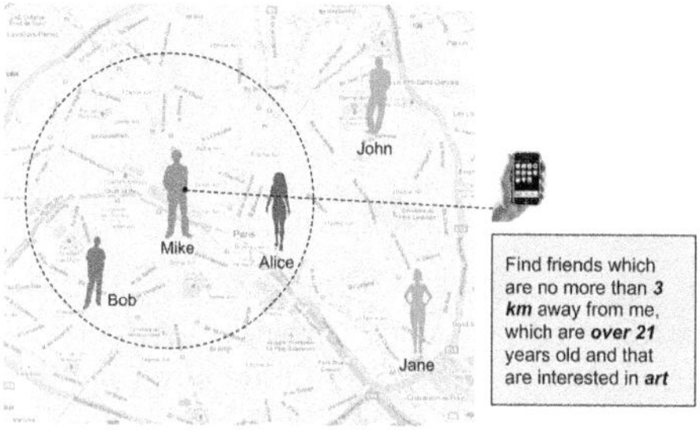

Fig. 1. Example scenario

Data are provided by services that produce data on demand or as streams according to their exported interfaces. In the example suppose the services `location`, `profile` and `interests` are available and export the following methods in their API. The service `location` is a streaming service that exports:

`subscribe()` $\rightarrow$ $\lceil$`location:`$\langle$`nickname, coor`$\rangle\rceil$

consisting of a subscription method that after invocation, will produce a stream of `location` tuples with a nickname that identifies the user and his/her coordinates[1].

The rest of the data about profiles and interests is produced by two on-demand data services, each exporting respectively the following methods:

`profile(nickname)` $\rightarrow$ `person:`$\langle$`age, gender, email`$\rangle$
`interests(nickname)` $\rightarrow$ `[s_tag:`$\langle$`tag, score`$\rangle$`]`

The first provides a single `person` tuple denoting a profile of the user, once given a request represented by his/her nickname. The second produces, given the nickname as well, a list of `s_tag` tuples, each with a tag or keyword denoting a particular interest of the user (e.g. music, sports, etc.) and a numeric score indicating the corresponding degree of interest.

[1] A stream is a continuous (and possibly infinite) sequence of tuples ordered in time.

In order to have an aggregated and integrated view of the dynamic environment at every moment (e.g., accessing Google's agenda service and feeding a Twitter service for continuously locating friends as we all stroll in a city), data consumers have to execute sets of service calls, i.e., subscribe to streaming producers, aggregate results and feed other services and then obtain results and eventually start over again.

Classical distributed query evaluation techniques alone do not suffice for such queries, as new capabilities become necessary to deal with aspects such as data stream processing, temporal and spatial data management and mobility. No off-the-shelf DBMS provides such service oriented querying approach including continuous, one-shot, mobile and static query evaluation on top of services. Our work introduces the notion of hybrid query that declaratively expresses data consumers requirements and an associated query evaluator, HYPATIA, that enacts data oriented query service coordinations; taking advantage of the services (data providers and devices computing capacity) and yielding the query result.

The remainder of the paper is organized as follows. Section 2 defines the notion of hybrid query as service coordination and its underlying data model. Section 3 details the enactment of a service coordination to evaluate a given hybrid query and the current implementation of HYPATIA which is a coordination engine specialized for query service coordinations execution. The section also presents the experimental validation that we conducted and experimental results. Section 4 discusses related work. Finally, Section 5 concludes and gives perspectives for this work.

2 Defining Hybrid Queries

A hybrid query is a query that can be mobile and continuous, and evaluated on top of on demand or streaming static or nomad data services. In our approach, in order to evaluate a hybrid query expressed in a declarative language, we transform it into an executable form which is a workflow. The workflow specifies a service coordination, which we refer to as a *query service coordination*. It implements the coordination of the necessary service calls for retrieving and processing data using services. Specifically, two types of services take part in a query service coordination: data services and computation services. Data services provide data either in a streaming or an on-demand fashion. Computation services, on the other hand, enable data processing and can be used for implementing operations like aggregation, filtering and correlation. Before explaining how a query service coordination is enacted to obtain the result of a given hybrid query, we present the underlying data model that we have adopted for hybrid queries, which applies to data and computing services. We also describe the workflow that implements the *query service coordination*.

2.1 A Data Model for Hybrid Queries

The workflow that corresponds to a query service coordination represents a program that retrieves on demand data and streams. Therefore, we need to assume an underlying pivot data model for representing the data flowing along the control flow. In our approach, data are represented using the JavaScript Object Notation with complex values complying with the JSON format, and hence can be nested or even multi-valued (e.g. a list of tuples).

In order to represent tuple streams we adopt the notion of *time-varying relation* presented in [11]. A time-varying relation is defined over a *tagged stream*, which consists of a stream of timestamped tuples with an additional sign attribute indicating whether the tuple should be added or removed from the corresponding time-varying relation.

On-demand data services provide data operations that synchronously produce data in response to an invocation. Coming back to our example, the method `profile` receives a `nickname` value of an atomic type and produces a tuple `person` with attributes `age`, `gender`, and `email`.

The result of a hybrid query is a set of tuples, each of which (along with its attributes) represents a complex value. Therefore, the result of our example query consists of a tagged stream that states which persons (represented by their respective tuples) are added or deleted from the corresponding time-varying result relation, which can then be materialized or visualized by a client application. We present next an abbreviated example of such a tuple in which the `tuplesign` attribute denotes it is a positive tuple (i.e., added to the result).

```
{"nickname":"Bob",
 "age":25,
 "gender":"M",
 "email":"bob@gmail.com",
 "timestamp":1262185366468 }
 "tuplesign":1 }
```

2.2 Query Service Coordination

As said before, a query service coordination is implemented by a workflow represented as a directed graph whose vertices and edges denote the parallel and sequential composition of activities. Each activity in turn is associated with a data or a computation service, thus specifying a service coordination. An example of a query service coordination specified as a workflow is given in Figure 2. It consists of two main branches, the one devoted to retrieving interests from the on-demand data service `interests` and the second, using the services `interests`, `time window` and, `distance` for computing the nearest neighbors and thereby locating closest friends. This is done by computing the distance of friends from the current position of the user; and filtering the profiles according to common interests and locations according to temporal constraints. The location, profile, and interests of friends are correlated in order to produce the result using a symetric-hash join algorithm[2].

[2] Note that this algorithm is implemented itself by a workflow using using computing services.

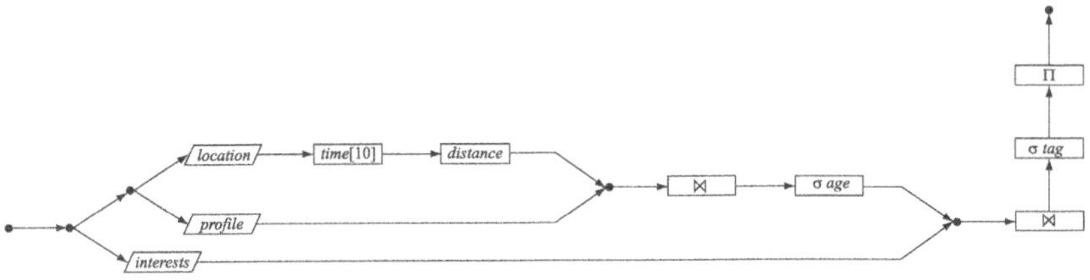

$$\pi_{p.nickname,\ age,\ gender,\ email}(\sigma_{'art'>15}(interests \bowtie_{i.nickname=p.nickname} (profile \bowtie_{p.nickname=l.nickname} \sigma_{'art' \in interests}(\mathcal{W}_{t=10}(location)))))$$

Fig. 2. Query service coordination for the query presented in Section 1

As shown in Figure 2, the query service coordination is composed of the two types of services.

- Data services appear as parallelograms at the left, they include particularly the `location`, `profile`, and `interests` data services.
- Computation services, specifically the `distance`, `correlation`, `filtering`, and `projection` services appear as rectangles and correspond to data processing operations.

The methods of a data service interface, follow a function-like pattern of the form $f : X \to y$, where f denotes the name of the operation, X a set of input parameters, and y a single output parameter.

The workflow is based on a workflow model we developed and that represents an extension of our previous work[9]. The constructs of the model and their semantics are defined using the Abstract State Machines[13] (ASM) formalism. Due to space limitations we present only a general description of it in Table 8 in the Appendix.

Data service. We define the on-demand and streaming variants of this type of service. Data is gathered from on-demand data services by invoking their methods with the appropriate parameters, producing tuples as output. This process is depicted in Figure 3 a) for the `profile` service of our example.

Streaming data services are treated in an analogous manner, except that a single invocation is performed on their `subscribe` method, after which they produce a data stream. To receive the data stream, a `gateway` service is added to the

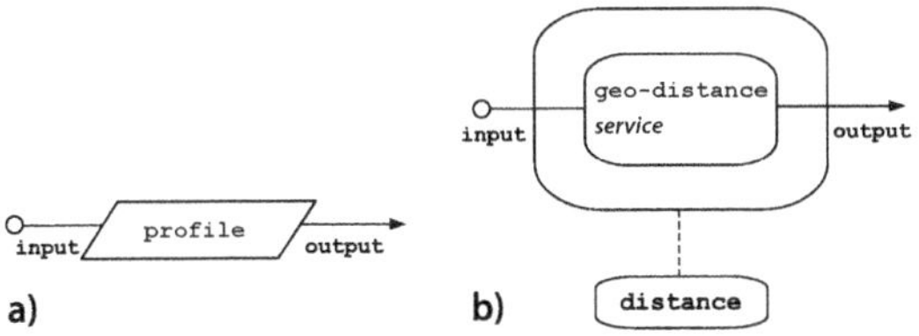

Fig. 3. a) Data service and b) Simple computation service

query service coordination, whose address is supplied during the subscription. For instance, this applies to the `location` service of the example.

Simple computation service. A computation service is considered *simple* whenever its execution is performed by a single service method invocation. Figure 3 b) illustrates such a service. The `distance` computation service relies on a `geo-distance` service, which computes the geographical distance between two points, for instance, by using Vincenty's formulae[3]. This is achieved by the invocation of its `distance` method with the appropriate parameters.

Composite computation service. A computation service is *composite* whenever its execution involves multiple method invocations, possibly also to different services. The method invocations and additional operations are organized in a (sub)workflow that specifies a service coordination that we refer to as *data processing service coordination.*

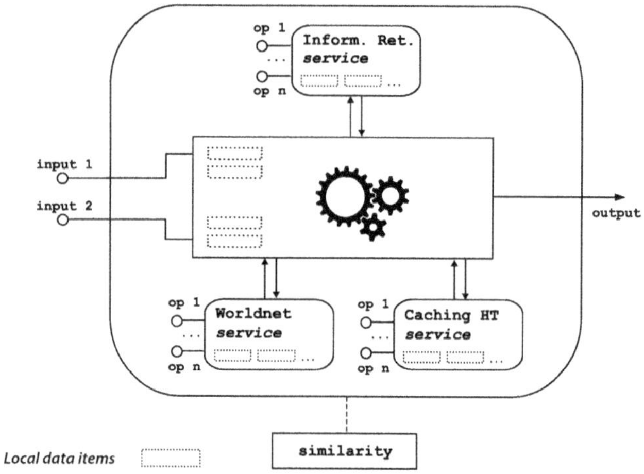

Fig. 4. Composite computation service

As an example let us consider a variant of our example query. Suppose the user issuing the query is interested not only in users within a certain geographical distance, but that also have, in general, interests similar to his or hers. The challenge is to compute similarity using available computing services. For instance, assume that we decide that three services are required to construct a `similarity` service. The service will compute the similarity between the interests of two users adopting the well-known vector cosine measure used in information retrieval. To improve accuracy, similarity will not be computed between the scored interest tags of the users as they are retrieved, but with vectors substituting each tag with its hypernym (e.g. 'fiction' for 'novels' or 'creation' for 'art'), and assigning to them the same scores as for the original tags.

[3] http://en.wikipedia.org/wiki/Vincenty%27s_formulae

Therefore, we will assume that we rely on a service called `myworldnet` offering a functionality similar to that of Worldnet for obtaining the hypernym associated with a given word. Since the invocation of this service can be expensive, we introduce the service `caching` exporting a hash table interface that will store the hypernym associated with a particular word or tag. In this manner, for a particular input tuple representing an user, we obtain a vector of hypernym-score elements relying on the service `caching` whenever possible. Then we compute the cosine between the constant vector representing interests of the user issuing the query, and the interests vector of the retrieved tuple. If the cosine is larger than a given threshold (i.e. the interests are very similar), we output the input tuple.

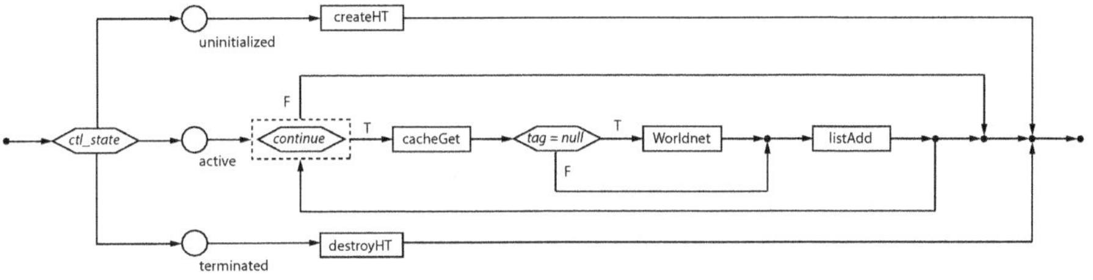

Fig. 5. User similarity composite service

Figure 4 gives an overview of the `similarity` composite computation service implementing similarity based on the aforementioned services. The application logic is specified as an ASM that can be represented as a workflow. Figure 5 presents the workflow in a simplified form, while Listing 1.1 presents a fragment of the full ASM specification of the composite computation service implementing the algorithm just described.

Listing 1.1. Fragment of the similarity service ASM

```
seq
  iterate(continue = true)
    seq
      s_tag := get(i, inTuple.interests)
      continue := s_tag != null
      hypernym := cacheHT.get(s_tag.tag)
      if(hypernym = null)
        hypernym := worldnet.hypernym(s_tag.tag)
      add(list2, create_s_tag(hypernym, s_tag.score))
      i := i + 1
    endseq
  cos := IR.cosine(list1, list2)
  if(cos > 0.6)
    output(inTuple)
endseq
```

The computation services implementing data processing in a query service coordination communicate via asynchronous *input operations* exposed by its executing environment. The production and consumption of tuples by the computation services is continuous (depending on the availability of input), yielding at the end of the processing chain specified by the workflow a data stream representing the hybrid query result.

2.3 Rationale of Query Service Coordinations

Computation services perform common tasks associated with data management (e.g. indexation or storage) or particular calculations (e.g. mathematical functions), which can be useful for processing data. They are specified as a workflow-based service coordination of basic computation services. Thereby our approach enables to take advantage of existing services for programming more complex data processing operations. By developing data processing operations by either simple or composite computation services, we can develop the core functionality required to evaluate a hybrid query. This is interesting when there is no full-fledged data management system that can fulfill changing data management requirements.

3 Enacting a Query Service Coordination

We have developed a proof of concept of our approach by implementing a service-based hybrid query processor named HYPATIA for enacting query services coordinations. Figure 6 presents its architecture. The system is implemented on the Java platform. Queries in HYPATIA are entered via a GUI and specified in a query language similar to CQL[2] and complemented with services calls, spatio-temporal and mobility aspects. Once a query is provided to the system it is parsed and then its corresponding query coordination is generated according to an algorithm that we have proposed [8]. The principle of the algorithm is to determine which simple data and computing services are implied in the

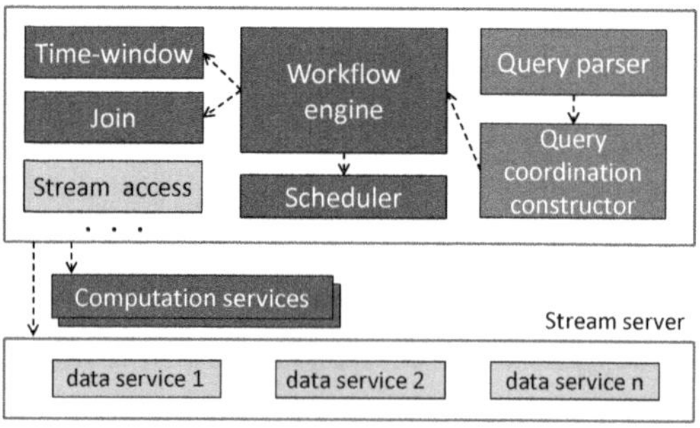

Fig. 6. Architecture of HYPATIA

coordination, determine the set of activities that define the workflow and their interdependencies in order to define the control flow. The query parser and the query service coordination constructor components perform these tasks. The parser was developed using the ANTLR[4] parser generator. The GUI also enables the user to visualize the query coordination, which is facilitated by the use of the JGraph[5] library.

The evaluation of a query is enabled by two main components that support the computation services corresponding to data processing operations. A scheduler determines which service is executed at a given time according to a predefined policy. Composite computation services communicate via asynchronous queues and are executed by a workflow engine that implements our workflow model. The workflow corresponding to the coordination of a computation service is specified in a text file using the language presented in the Appendix (whose formal foundations are based in [13]) and then interpreted by the engine, also developed with the ANTLR parser generator.

We developed a set of computation services that correspond to well known data processing operations and that are necessary for implementing hybrid query service coordinations. Table 1 below gives the operations that we implemented, with their corresponding computation services. In our experiment, these services run on a Tomcat container supported by the JAX-WS reference implementation[6].

Table 1. Data processing computation services

Operator	Description	Basic computation service
filter	filter tuples by a predicate	hash index
correlation	correlates two input sets of tuples	hash index
tuple-window	window on the n most recent tuples	queue
time-window	window on time interval t	calendar queue
duplicate-elimination	eliminate duplicates	hash table
grouping	group tuples with common attributes	hash table
correlation with caching	access data services through binding patterns (bind-join algorithm)	hash table
spatial filtering	filters tuples representing objects located in a particular region	r-tree

Table 3 in the Appendix shows the implementation of three of the data processing operators that we implemented, namely, tuple and temporal filters and a correlation based on the algorithm of the symmetric hash join. The table includes the service coordination that implements these operators and the corresponding ASM code. In the case of filters, both use a simple computation service named

[4] http://www.antlr.org/
[5] http://www.jgraph.com/
[6] https://jax-ws.dev.java.net/

queue that manages a queue of tuples and exports the methods enqueue and dequeue. The workflow includes other internal activities used for receiving the tuples and operating on them. In the particular case of the temporal window, old tuples have to be extracted from the window and the workflow includes the activities for managing expired tuples. Finally, in the case of the correlation, the coordination uses the simple service hash which is called by two activities in order to manage the right and left hand operands and then there is a third activity for performing the correlation according to the values of the common attributes of the tuples.

3.1 Validation

We implemented two test scenarios and their corresponding data services to validate our approach. The first one, mainly a demonstration scenario, is the location-based application introduced in Section 1. In order to implement the Friend Finder scenario described in the Introduction we developed a test dataset using GPS tracks obtained from everytrail.com. Concretely, we downloaded 58 tracks corresponding to travel (either by walking, cycling, or driving) within the city of Paris. We converted the data from GPX to JSON and integrated it to our test stream server to create the location service. For the profile and interests services we created a MySQL database accessible via JAX-WS Web Services running on Tomcat. The profile data is artificial and the interests were assigned and scored randomly using the most popular tags used in Flickr and Amazon.

The second scenario was developed to measure the efficiency of our current implementation in a more reliable manner; it is based on the NEXMark benchmark[7]. Our main goal was to measure the overhead of using services, so we measured the total latency (i.e. the total time required to process a tuple present in the result) for a set of six queries (see Table 2); first for our service-based system and then for an equivalent system that had at its disposal the same functionality offered by the computation services, but supported by objects inside the same Java Virtual Machine.

NEXMark proposes an auctions scenario consisting of three continuous data services, person, auction and, bid, that export the following interfaces:

$\texttt{person:}\langle \texttt{person\_id}^f, \texttt{name}^f, \texttt{phone}^f, \texttt{email}^f, \texttt{income}^f \rangle$
$\texttt{auction:}\langle \texttt{open\_auction\_id}^f, \texttt{seller\_person}^f, \texttt{category}^f, \texttt{quantity}^f \rangle$
$\texttt{bid:}\langle \texttt{person\_ref}^f, \texttt{open\_auction\_id}^f, \texttt{bid}^f \rangle$

Auctions work as follows. People can propose and bid for products. Auctions and bids are produced continuously. Table 2 shows the six queries that we evaluated in our experiment, they are stated using algebra and CQL like expressions and they are associated to the query service coordination that implements them (generated by HYPATIA). Queries Q_1 - Q_3 mainly exploit temporal filtering using window operators, filtering and correlation with and/split-join control flows. Q_4 shows a sequence of data processing activities with filtering and projection

[7] http://datalab.cs.pdx.edu/niagara/NEXMark/

Table 2. NEXMark queries

- For the last 30 persons and 30 products offered, retrieve the bids of the last 20 seconds greater than 15 euros

1)

```
SELECT bids.person_ref, bid.auction_id, bid.bid
FROM bid [RANGE 20], auction [ROW 30], person [ROW 30]
WHERE bid.auction_id = auction.auction_id AND
auction.seller_person = person.person_id
AND bid.bid > 15;
```

$\pi_{person\_ref,\ bid.auction\_id,\ bid}(\sigma_{bid>15}(\mathcal{W}_{n=30}(person) \bowtie_{person\_id=seller\_person} (\mathcal{W}_{n=30}(auction) \bowtie_{auction.auction\_id=bid.auction\_id} \mathcal{W}_{t=20}(bid))))$

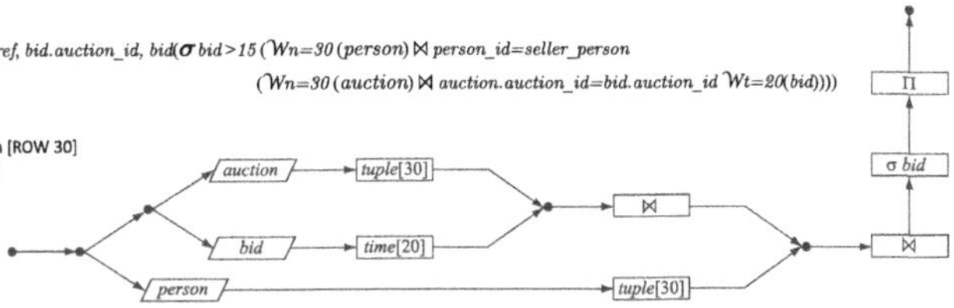

- For the persons joining and the products offered during the last minute, generate the name and email of the person along with the id of the product he/she offers

2)

```
SELECT P.name, P.email, A.auction_id
FROM auction [RANGE 60] as A, person [RANGE 60] as P
WHERE A.seller_person = P.person_id;
```

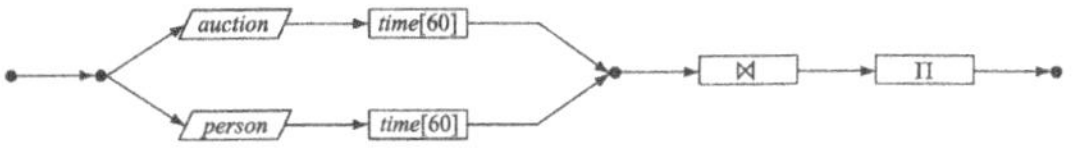

$\pi_{name,\ email,\ auction\_id}(\mathcal{W}_{t=60}(person) \bowtie_{person\_id=seller\_person} \mathcal{W}_{t=60}(auction))$

- For the last 50 products, find those whose quantity is greater than 5

3)

```
SELECT A.auction_id, A.category, A.seller_person, A.quantity
FROM auction [ROWS 50] as A
WHERE A.quantity > 5;
```

$\pi_{auction\_id,\ category,\ seller\_person,\ quantity}(\sigma_{quant>5}(\mathcal{W}_{t=60}(auction)))$

- Among the bids made in the last 5 seconds, find those whose amount is between 50 and 100 euros

4)

```
SELECT bid.person_ref, bid.auction_id, bid.bid
FROM bid [RANGE 5]
WHERE bid.bid > 50.0 and bid.bid < 100.0;
```

$\pi_{person\_ref,\ auction\_id,\ bid}(\sigma_{quant>50 \text{ and } quant<100}(\mathcal{W}_{t=5}(auction)))$

- For the last 100 persons, products and bids; give the id of the seller person, the id of the product, and the amount of the bid

5)

```
SELECT bid.person_ref, bid.open_auction_id, bid.bid
FROM bid [ROW 100], auction [ROW 100], person [ROW 100]
WHERE bid.auction_id = auction.auction_id AND
auction.seller_person = person.person_id;
```

$\pi_{person\_ref,\ bid.auction\_id,\ bid}(\mathcal{W}_{n=100}(person) \bowtie_{person\_id=seller\_person} (\mathcal{W}_{n=100}(auction) \bowtie_{bid.auction\_id=auction.auction\_id} \mathcal{W}_{n=100}(bid))$

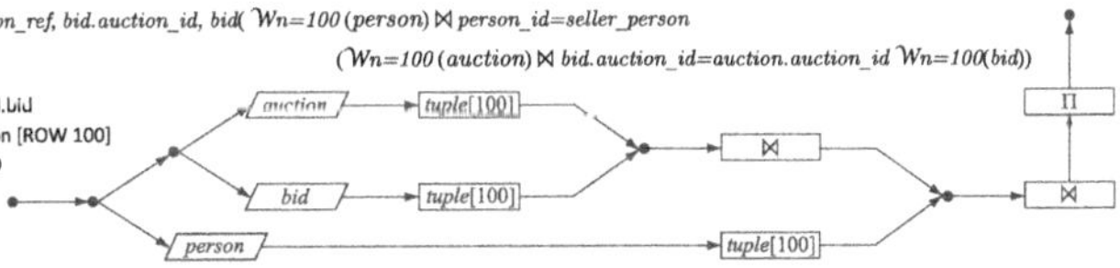

- For the last 20 persons, products and bids; give the id of the seller person, the id of the product, and the amount of the bid, whenever that amount is greater than 30

6)

```
SELECT bid.person_ref, bid.auction_id, bid.bid
FROM bid [ROW 20], auction [ROW 20], person [ROW 20]
WHERE bid.auction_id = auction.auction_id AND
auction.seller_person = person.person_id
AND bid.bid > 30;
```

$\pi_{person\_ref,\ bid.auction\_id,\ bid}(\sigma_{bid>30}(\mathcal{W}_{n=20}(person) \bowtie_{person\_id=seller\_person} (\mathcal{W}_{n=20}(auction) \bowtie_{auction.auction\_id=bid.auction\_id} \mathcal{W}_{n=20}(bid))))$

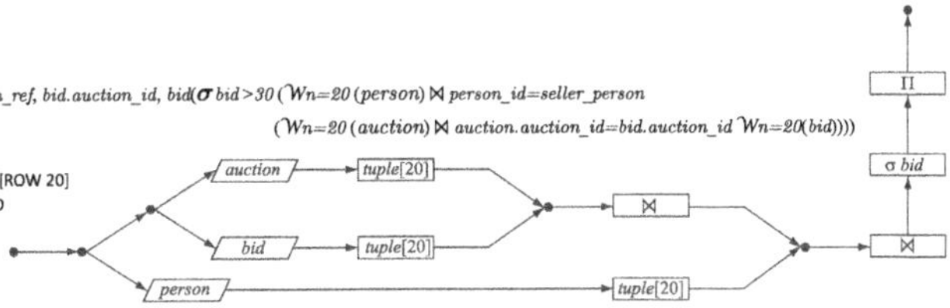

operations. Finally, Q_5 - Q_6 address several correlations organized in and/split-join control flows.

3.2 Experimental Results

For our experiments we used a local machine used in the experiment was a Dell D830 laptop with an Intel Core2 Duo (2.10 GHz) processor and equipped with 2 GB of RAM. While the remote machine was a Dell Desktop PC with a Pentium 4 (1.8 GHz) processor and 1 GB of RAM. In both cases running JSE 1.6.0_17, the local machine under Windows XP SP3 and the remote under Windows Server 2008.

As said before, to validate our approach we established a testbed of six queries based on our adaptation of the NEXMark benchmark. These queries include time and tuple based windows as well as joins. We measured tuple latency, i.e. the time elapsed from the arrival of a tuple to the instant it becomes part of the result, for three different settings. The first setting corresponds to a query processor using the same functionality of our computation services, but as plain java objects in the same virtual machine. In the second we used our computation services, which are based on the JAX-WS reference implementation, by making them run on a Tomcat container in the same machine as the query processor. For the third setting we ran the Tomcat container with the computation services on a different machine connected via intranet to the machine running the query processor.

The results are shown in Figure 7, and from them we derive two main conclusions. First, the use of services instead of shared memory resulted in about twice the latency. Second, the main overhead is due to the middleware and not to the network connection, since the results for the local Tomcat container and the remote Tomcat container are very similar. We believe that in this case the

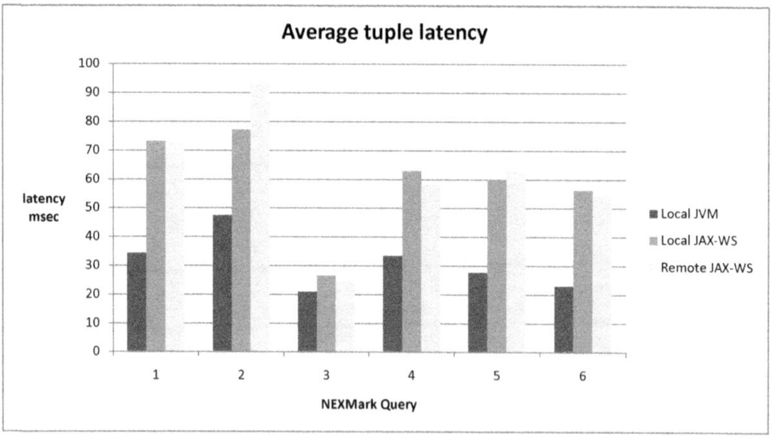

Fig. 7. Tuple latency for a services-based vs. a single Java application query processor

network costs are balanced-out by resource contingency on the query processor machine, when that machine also runs the container. We consider the overhead to be important but not invalidating for our approach, especially since in some cases we may be obligated to use services to acquire the required functionality.

From our experimental validation we learned that it is possible to implement query evaluation entirely relying on services without necessarily using a full-fledged DBMS or a DSMS. Thereby, hybrid queries that retrieve on demand data and streams are processed by the same evaluator using well adapted operators according to their characteristics given the composition approach. The approach can seem costly because of the absence of one DBMS, the use of a message based approach for implementing the workflow execution, and because there is no optimization in the current version of Hypatia. Now that we have the first implementation of our approach we can address performance issues in order to reduce cost and overhead.

4 Related Work

Our work addresses issues related to several domains. First, in relation with query processing over data services, we find similarities with heterogeneous databases and mediation systems; as well as more recently with queries over Web Services. In particular, SoCQ[12] enables to evaluate queries involving data services (including streams) in a pervasive environment. A major difference is that we adopt a service-based approach, not only to access data available as services, but to process the retrieved data in order to produce the result of the query, thus gaining in flexibility and resource sharing.

We find several projects that have followed a similar direction, but with significant differences. ObjectGlobe[6] offers the capability to share resources to evaluate queries, but limited to the granularity of operators defined as standard Java classes, which depend on a custom dynamic class loading infrastructure. OGSA-DQP[14] goes further by enabling the evaluation of relational queries using Grid services, thus achieving platform-interoperability, but still adopting a traditional architecture. Our service-based approach, on the other hand, facilitates the use of services at different granularities, via our service-coordination approach. Services of such finer granularity, particularly Amazon S3 services, are used in [5] to build the storage component of a database system. Our work differs in that we further use computation services for the evaluation of operators; while our on-demand data services abstract storage and ignore its related transactional aspects, since we focus on information access.

Our query service coordinations and their construction algorithm share some similarities with the work presented in [4]. Significant differences are that [4] considers ranking and paging data services as opposed to streams, and that they use branch-and-bound search for optimization. Currently, we are considering extending our approach with similar techniques to perform query optimization.

Hybrid queries integrate aspects found in traditional, data stream, spatio-temporal, and mobile object queries; we have incorporated many of the techniques developed for them. Data stream queries have received a lot of attention in recent years and resulted in several prototypes[1,3,7]. The queries we address follow many of their ideas, but the evaluation process in our case is service-based. In relation to spatio-temporal and mobile object queries, supported by systems such as SECONDO[10], our objective is to query provide the posiblity of querying spatio-temporal queries for retrieving data in a one-shot and in a continuous manner.

5 Conclusion and Perspectives

This paper presented a novel approach for query processing using service coordination. This technique is pertinent when queries are evaluated over data services in dynamic environments, where no full-fledged DBMS is available for their evaluation, but data processing and computation services can be used for providing the required functionality. Our work also introduced an approach that integrates continuous, stream, snapshot, and spatio-temporal queries for accessing data in ambient computing environments through the notion of hybrid query. In addition, this paper described the design and implementation o HYPATIA system for evaluating hybrid queries based on service coordination; thus demonstrating the feasibility of our approach. Our system supports the evaluation of several known types of queries.

Future work concerns two main aspects. First, we are studying the properties of consistency and completeness for hybrid queries. Since we want to verify that our service-based evaluation finds the desired results in an intrinsically dynamic environment. Second, we are working on query optimization techniques for our approach based on service coordination. Our starting point is the definition of cost models suited to ambient computing; since unlike in traditional query processing, in ambient computing environments it is difficult to obtain statistics over the data. We then plan to take into consideration the optimization techniques that have been proposed for mediation systems, as well as those available (although in lesser quantity) for data stream, spatio-temporal, and mobile object queries.

Acknowledgment

This work has been supported by the OPTIMACS ANR-08-SEGI-014 Project (optimacs.imag.fr), financed by the French National Research Agency (ANR).

References

1. Arasu, A., Babcock, B., Babu, S., Cieslewicz, J., Datar, M., Ito, K., Motwani, R., Srivastava, U., Widom, J.: Stream: The stanford data stream management system. Technical Report 2004-20, Stanford InfoLab (2004)
2. Arasu, A., Babu, S., Widom, J.: The cql continuous query language: semantic foundations and query execution. The VLDB Journal 15(2), 121–142 (2006)

3. Balakrishnan, H., Balazinska, M., Carney, D., Çetintemel, U., Cherniack, M., Convey, C., Galvez, E., Salz, J., Stonebraker, M., Tatbul, N., Tibbetts, R., Zdonik, S.: Retrospective on aurora. The VLDB Journal 13(4), 370–383 (2004)
4. Braga, D., Ceri, S., Corcoglioniti, F., Grossniklaus, M.: Panta Rhei: Flexible Execution Engine for Search Computing Queries. In: Ceri, S., Brambilla, M. (eds.) Search Computing. LNCS, vol. 5950, pp. 225–243. Springer, Heidelberg (2010)
5. Brantner, M., Florescu, D., Graf, D., Kossmann, D., Kraska, T.: Building a database on s3. In: SIGMOD 2008: Proceedings of the 2008 ACM SIGMOD international conference on Management of data, pp. 251–264. ACM, New York (2008)
6. Braumandl, R., Keidl, M., Kemper, A., Kossmann, D., Kreutz, A., Seltzsam, S., Stocker, K.: Objectglobe: Ubiquitous query processing on the internet. The VLDB Journal 10(1), 48–71 (2001)
7. Chandrasekaran, S., Cooper, O., Deshpande, A., Franklin, M.J., Hellerstein, J.M., Hong, W., Krishnamurthy, S., Madden, S.R., Reiss, F., Shah, M.A.: Telegraphcq: continuous dataflow processing. In: SIGMOD 2003: Proceedings of the 2003 ACM SIGMOD International Conference on Management of Data, pp. 668–668. ACM, New York (2003)
8. Cuevas-Vicenttín, V., Collet, C., Vargas-Solar, G., Ibrahim, N.: Hypatia: Flexible processing of hybrid queries using service coordination. Under submission for BDA 2010: 26mes journes Bases de Donnes Avances (2010)
9. Cuevas-Vicenttín, V., Vargas-Solar, G., Collet, C.: Web services orchestration in the webcontent semantic web framework. In: ENC 2008: Proceedings of the 2008 Mexican International Conference on Computer Science, Washington, DC, USA, pp. 271–282. IEEE Computer Society, Los Alamitos (2008)
10. de Almeida, V.T., Guting, R.H., Behr, T.: Querying moving objects in secondo. In: MDM 2006: Proceedings of the 7th International Conference on Mobile Data Management, Washington, DC, USA, p. 47. IEEE Computer Society, Los Alamitos (2006)
11. Ghanem, T.M., Elmagarmid, A.K., Larson, P.-Å., Aref, W.G.: Supporting views in data stream management systems. ACM Trans. Database Syst. 35(1), 1–47 (2010)
12. Gripay, Y., Laforest, F., Petit, J.-M.: A simple (yet powerful) algebra for pervasive environments. In: EDBT 2010: Proceedings of the 13th International Conference on Extending Database Technology, pp. 359–370. ACM, New York (2010)
13. Gurevich, Y.: Evolving algebras 1993: Lipari guide, pp. 9–36 (1995)
14. Lynden, S., Mukherjee, A., Hume, A.C., Fernandes, A.A.A., Paton, N.W., Sakellariou, R., Watson, P.: The design and implementation of ogsa-dqp: A service-based distributed query processor. Future Gener. Comput. Syst. 25(3), 224–236 (2009)

Appendix

Construct	Graphical representation	Notation	Description
Computation activity		data_item := new_value [1] data_item := s.op(params) [2]	activity *A* modifies a data item (1), or invokes a service operation (2)
Conditional rule	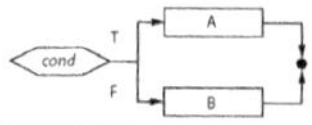	**if** (*cond*) **then** *A* else *B*	execute *A* if *cond* is satisfied, otherwise execute *B*
Parallel composition	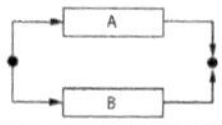	**par** *A B* **endpar**	execute *A* and *B* in parallel, changes are visible until both complete
Sequential composition		**seq** *A B* **endseq**	execute *A* followed by *B*, changes made by *A* are visible to *B*
Iteration	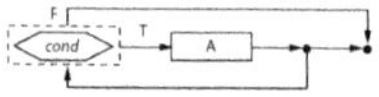	**iterate**(*cond*) *A*	execute *A* repeatedly if *cond* is satisfied, changes are visible after each iteration
Control state		**if** (*cst_item* = *val*) **then** *A*	structure activities and monitor execution via the *cst_item* control state data item

Fig. 8. Workflow constructs based on the Abstract State Machines (ASM) formalism

Table 3. Simplified specification of selected operators

Tuple-based window

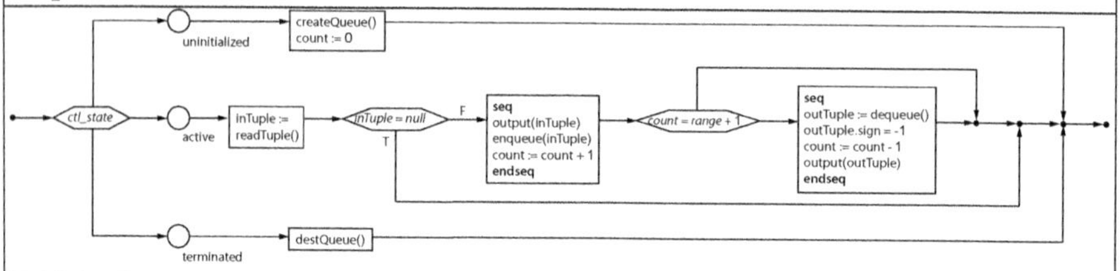


```
if( ctl_state = 'active')
  seq
     inTuple := readTuple()
     if(inTuple = null)
        skip
     else
        seq
           output(inTuple)
           q.enqueue(inTuple)
           count := count + 1
           if(count = range + 1)
              seq
                 outTuple := q.dequeue()
                 outTuple.sign = -1
                 count := count - 1
                 output(outTuple)
              endseq
        endseq
  endseq
```

Table 3. *(continued)*

Time-based window

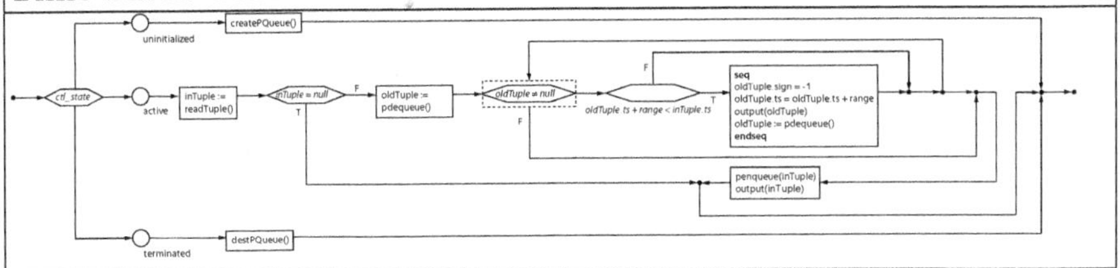


```
if( ctl_state = 'active')
  seq
     inTuple := readTuple()
     if(inTuple = null)
        skip
     else
        seq
           oldTuple := pq.dequeue()
           iterate(oldTuple != null)
              if(oldTuple.ts + range < inTuple.ts)
                 seq
                    oldTuple.sign = -1
                    oldTuple.ts = oldTuple.ts + range
                    output(oldTuple)
                    oldTuple := pq.dequeue()
                 endseq
           pq.enqueue(inTuple)
           output(inTuple)
        endseq
  endseq
```

Symmetric hash-join (abbreviated)

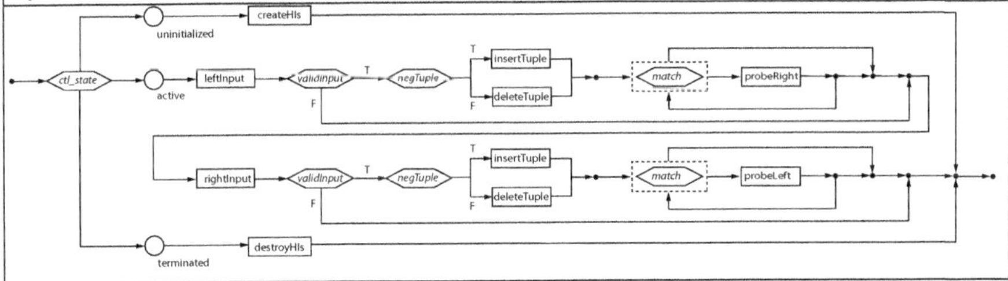


```
...
iterate(continue = true)
  seq
     tup := rhi.getData()
     outTuple := mergeTuples(inTuple, tup,
        max(inTuple.ts, t.ts), inTuple.sign)
     output(outTuple)
     continue := rhi.next()
  endseq
```

The Roles of Reliability and Reputation in Competitive Multi Agent Systems

Salvatore Garruzzo and Domenico Rosaci

DIMET, Università Mediterranea di Reggio Calabria,
Via Graziella, Località Feo di Vito,
89122 Reggio Calabria, Italy
{salvatore.garruzzo,domenico.rosaci}@unirc.it
http://www.ing.unirc.it

Abstract. In competitive multi-agent systems, the act of requesting recommendations to evaluate the reputation of an agent is a cost. On the contrary, an agent computes the reliability of another agent without paying any price. This implies the necessity for the agent to decide in which measure to use the reputation with respect to the reliability when he must select the most promising interlocutors. In the past, two main schools of thinking emerged, one assuming the necessity of always exploiting both reliability and reputation, the other declaring that the use of reputation requires, in terms of cost, more disadvantages than advantages. In this paper, we try to evaluate the role of using reputation with respect to reliability, depending on some characteristics of the involved scenario, as the size of the agent population, the percentage of unreliable agents and the percentage of agents provided with a reputation model.

Keywords: trust, reputation, competitive multi-agent systems.

1 Introduction

Over the last recent years, the introduction of trust-based approaches in multi-agent systems (MAS) has been recognized as a promising solution to improve the effectiveness of these systems [2,9,10]. It is a matter of fact that nowadays MASs are more and more exploited in several application domains to provide e-services, as e-Commerce, e-Learning and so on. In such a context, software agents are distributed in large-scale networks and interact to share resources with each other. Trust is essential in such settings to make social interactions much fruitful as possible [8]. In the context of the e-services, trust is defined as: "the quantified belief by a trustor with respect to the competence, honesty, security and dependability of a trustee within a specified context" [5]. When two agents interact with each other, one of them (the trustor) assumes the role of a service requester and the other (the trustee) acts as an e-service provider. It is important to point out that a trust relationship can involve multiple dimensions, depending on the particular perspective under which the interaction between the two agents is viewed. Some usual dimensions of trust are:

R. Meersman et al. (Eds.): OTM 2010, Part I, LNCS 6426, pp. 326–339, 2010.

- **competence:** A competent agent is capable of correctly and efficiently perform the requested tasks.
- **honesty:** A honest agent shows a truthful behaviour, and it is not fraudulent or misleading.
- **security:** A secure agent confidentially manages private data and does not allow unauthorized access to them.
- **reliability:** A reliable agent provides reliable services. In other words, reliability measures the degree of reliance that can be placed on the services provided by the agent, including the efficiency.

For each of the aspects considered above, trust augments the spectrum of interactions between two agents. Another important consideration is that the trust relationships depend on the context in which the agents interact. For instance, an e-Commerce agent might be reliable if the price of the transaction if low enough, while its reliability might significantly decrease in the case of very high price. Without loss of generality, in this paper we choose to only deal with the reliability, which is the main dimension usually considered in competitive multi-agent systems. Thus, from hereafter, we refer to trust using the term reliability.

While reliability is a subjective measure, reputation is a measure of the trust that the whole community perceives with respect to a given trustee. Reputation assumes a very important role when an agent a does not have a sufficient knowledge of another agent b. Then, a can exploit the b's reputation to decide if b is a reliable interlocutor or not.

Several reliability and reputation models have been proposed in the past for representing both reliability and reputation. However, we remark that a crucial point in the practical use of these two measures is represented by the possibility of suitably combining them to support the agent's decision.

To make this issue clear, consider an agent a that has to choose, among a set of possible interlocutors, the most suitable agents to request a service. Clearly, in order to make its choice, a has to consider the past interactions with the agents of the community, that is, its *reliability model*. However, a does not have necessarily interacted with all the agents of the community; moreover, in some cases the past interactions with an agent could be insufficient to make the trust measure credible. In such a situation, a has to also consider, besides the reliability measure, also a reputation measure, deriving by a reputation model. Finally, to operate its decision, a should combine both reliability and reputation measures, to obtain a synthetic *preference* measure, i.e., a score to assign to each candidate agents in order to choose which are the most preferable candidates for interaction. The main question is: How much the reliability should be considered with respect the reputation in determining the preference measure?

We argue that the size of agent population, as well as the capability of the agents to provide useful recommendations are two key parameters for choosing how much it is necessary to use reputation with respect to reliability. We also observe that, if we are in presence of a large agent population and there are a few of reliable agents against a lot of unreliable agents, the use of reputation becomes necessary.

1.1 Our Contribution

The main contribution of this paper is that of determining some criteria to suitably choose the weights that should be assigned to reliability and reputation.

A first difficulty to study the problem above is represented by the unsuitability, with respect to this purpose, of the existing reliability and reputation approaches. In fact, some of them provides measures of reliability and reputation, as well as a model for integrating them, but they are not designed for a competitive system and thus they do not consider the presence of reliability and reputation costs. On the other hand, the most of the existing approaches for competitive systems do not consider the necessity of integrating reliability and reputation into a unique measure. Finally, the aforementioned approaches generally do not distinguish between the reliability of an agent as service provider and the reliability of the same agent as provider of recommendations. We argue that this differentiation is crucial for a study that wants to deeply investigate the role of the reliability (that identifies with the service reliability) and that of the reputation (that strictly depends on the recommendations provided by agents).

To overcame this problem, we introduce in this paper a new reliability and reputation framework for a competitive multi-agent system, called *Reliability and Reputation Agent Framework* (RRAF). This framework allows to compute, from the viewpoint of an agent a, a measure of reliability and a measure of reputation of another agent b, where the reputation is determined by using the recommendations coming from other agents of the community, obtained paying a given price.

In this framework, reliability and reputation are integrated in an overall preference measure, and this integration is based on a parameter called β, ranging in the real interval [0,1]. In words, the value $\beta = 1$ means assigning full importance to reliability and no importance to reputation.

This framework is then used to study the role of reliability and reputation in a competitive system. More in particular, we have used the framework to test the behaviour of competitive agents in the well-known *Agent Reputation and Trust* (ART) Testbed. The RRAF agents built based to our framework have been run in different multi-agent scenarios, varying the composition of the agent population. As a result, the role of the variable β in determining the agent performances has been correlated to some crucial parameters as the size of the agent population, the percentage of the unreliable agents and the percentage of agents having a reputation model. The experimental results clarifies that the advantage of using a reputation mechanism in addition of the direct reliability is significant only for particular values of the above parameters.

The paper is organized as follows. In Section 2 we discuss some related work. In Section 3 we introduce our multi-agent scenario, while in Section 4 we describe the RRAF reliability-reputation model. In Section 5 we propose a study of the role of reputation with respect to the reliability on the ART Testbed and, finally, in Section 6 we draw our conclusions.

2 Related Work

Several reliability and reputation models have been proposed in the past [9]. All of them provide an agent a with a metric for measuring both reliability and reputation of another agent b, based on the interactions between a and b and on the recommendations that the other agents of the community generates about b.

Moreover, some different approaches have been presented in the literature dealing with the integration of reliability and reputation [3,6]. However, all these approaches leave to the user the task of setting the weights to be assigned to reliability and reputation for determining the overall preference value. Some of these approaches, as for instance that presented in [6], beside of providing measures of reliability and reputation, also introduce a model for combining them into a synthetic measure. However, these approaches do not deal with competitive systems and do not take into account the costs for computing reliability and reputation measures.

In order to provide a common platform on which different models can be compared against objective metrics the *Agent Reputation and Trust* (ART) Testbed Competition was created in 2006 [1,4]. The scenario defined for the ART platform takes place in the art appraisal domain. In such a scenario, some clients can ask the agents for appraising some paintings, and agents may ask other agents for their assessments of paintings. The assessments are based on expertise values set by the ART testbed. Each agent can have a different reliability-reputation model, for deciding which are the most suitable agents to request an opinion for appraising paintings.

Different strategies have been proposed by the participants to the ART competitions. While the most of the proposed agents exploit both reliability and reputation in their trust models, in [7] the authors propose to directly work with the reliability, without considering the reputation. Their decision is based on the consideration that there are few agents participating in a game, and therefore it is easily possible to directly evaluate all the agent population without paying the fees associated with requests of recommendation. Moreover, these authors also consider that the agent asked for the reputation of another does not have sufficient knowledge of it.

3 The Multi-agent Scenario

In our scenario, we assume the existence of some clients, that can request services to the agents of a multi-agent system. More in particular, we assume that all the services are related to the same domain $\mathcal{D}$ (e.g. e-Commerce) and each requested service falls in one of the given categories associated to that domain (e.g. the e-Commerce categories present in eBay as *Antiques*, *Art*, *Books* etc.). All the categories of $\mathcal{D}$ are contained in a pre-determined *set of categories*. We suppose that when a client needs a service falling in a given category *cat*, he sends a request to the Agent System Manager ASM of the multi-agent system, that provides to assign the request to an agent. The assignment of the client's request to an agent is performed by ASM at pre-determined temporal steps. When a new step begins, the ASM examines all the service requests performed by clients, and assigns each request to the agent considered the most suitable. The selection of the most suitable agent is performed by the ASM based on the effectiveness shown in the past by the agents in the category *cat* in which the request falls. When the assignment is realized, the client must pay to the selected agent a given price *sp* for actually obtaining the service.

In addition, during each temporal step, the agents of the community can interact each other, in order to exchange information. The interactions among agents follow this protocol:

- An agent a can decide to request the collaboration of another agent b to provide a client with a service falling in a given category *cat*. Before of requesting this collaboration, in order to understand the expertise of b in the category *cat*, the agent a can ask a third agent c for a recommendation about b. This recommendation is an evaluation of the *Quality of Service* (QoS) generally associated with the services provided by b. The agent c can accept or refuse to give the requested recommendation, and if it accepts, a must pay a given price rp to b. Moreover, a can also asks b itself for providing an auto-declaration of its expertise, paying the same price rp. The obtained recommendations can be used by a for updating its internal *reputation model* (see the next section). In words, a uses the gossips coming from the other agents to understand the reputation of b in the community. Note that the expertise declared by b about itself also contributes to form this reputation.
- If the agent a decides to obtain the collaboration of the agent b, he needs to pay a price cp to b.
- At the end of the step, the agent a receives a feedback from the system manager ASM for each service provided by a during this step. The feedback contains an evaluation of the real quality of the service, obtained by ASM directly asking the client that received the service. In addition, the feedback also informs a about the quality of the contributions provided by the agents contacted by a to realize the service. This way, a can use the feedback to update its internal *trust model* (see the next section) about the agents of the system. Moreover, the feedback can be used by a to evaluate the recommendations received about the contacted agents.

We graphically represent such a scenario in Figure 1, where the overall operation that leads to provide the client with a service is logically decomposed in 8 phases, namely: 1) the client requests a service to the ASM; 2) the ASM assigns the request to a selected agent; 3) the selected agent asks recommendations to other agents 4) who provide the recommendations; 5) the selected agent requests collaboration to other agents 6) who provide the collaboration; 7) the selected agent provide the service to the client; 8) the ASM provide a feedback to the selected agent.

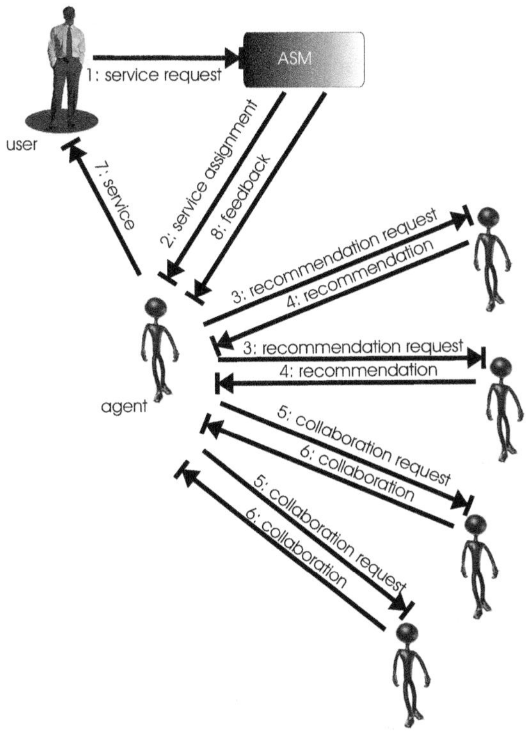

Fig. 1. The scenario in which the agents operate

4 RRAF-Model: A Representation of Trust Interactions

In this section, we introduce a framework that provides (*i*) a model to represent the scenario previously described and (*ii*) a methodology for computing the trust measures involved in this scenario. To this purpose, let A be a list containing all the agents belonging to the multi-agent systems, and let $a_i \in A$ be the i-th element of A. We associate to each agent a_i the following matrices, whose values are real numbers belonging to the interval [0,1]:

$SREL_i$: it is the *Service Reliability* matrix, where each value $SREL_i(j, cat)$ represents the *reliability* that the agent a_i assigns to the services provided by the agent a_j for the category *cat*. We remember that the reliability represents the subjective measure of the trust that an agent has in another agent. The value 0 (resp.1) means no reliability (resp. complete reliability).

REP_i: it is the *Reputation* matrix, where each value $REP_i(j, cat)$ represents the *reputation* that the agent a_i assigns to the agent a_j for the category *cat*. The reputation is a measure of trust that an agent assigns to another agent based on some recommendations coming from other agents of the community. Although the reputation is not based on a subjective evaluation of the agent, however it is not an objective measure. In fact each agent a_i computes the reputation of another agent a_j independently from how the other agents compute the reputation of a_j. Thus, it is correct to say that the value $REP_i(j, cat)$ represents how the agent a_i perceives the reputation of a_j in the community. The value 0 (resp.1) means minimum reputation (resp. maximum reputation).

$RREL_i$: it is the *Recommendation Reliability* matrix, where each $RREL_i(j, cat)$ value represents the *reliability* that the agent a_i assigns to the *recommendations* provided by the agent a_j for the category *cat*. In other words, $RREL_i(j, cat)$ is a measure of how much the agent a_i considers as reliable the suggestions coming from the agents a_j about other agents and concerning the category *cat*, i.e. it represents the reliability of the gossip coming from a_j.

$PREF_i$: it is the *Preference* matrix, where each value $PREF_i(j, cat)$ represents the overall preference that the agent a_i assigns to the agent a_j for the category *cat*, based on both the reliability and reputation perceived by a_i.

$RECC_i$: it is the *Recommendation* matrix, where each value $RECC_i(j, k, cat)$ represents the recommendation that the agent a_j provided to the agent a_i about the agent a_k for the category *cat*. Differently from the previous matrices, that have only two dimensions, $RECC_i$ is a 3-dimensions matrix.

The data structures described above are initialized by using *cold start* values, i.e. values that represents the level of trust an agent assigns to another in absence of information. A cold start value can be equal to 0, meaning a *diffident* approach, or equal to 1, meaning a *confident* approach, or equal to 0.5, meaning a *neutral* approach. Different cold start values can be used for the different matrices, since an agent can choose to use different cold start strategies for the reliability, the reputation and so one. Then, the matrices are updated at each step by the agent a_i, as follows:

- **Phase 1: Reception of the Recommendations**. The agent a_i receives, at the current step, some recommendations by the other agents, in response to previous recommendation requests. These recommendations are stored in the $RECC_i$ matrix.
- **Phase 2: Computation of SREL and RREL**: The ASM sends to a_i the feedbacks for each service s provided in the past step, where the contributions provided by other agents to a_i in realizing s are evaluated. These feedbacks are contained in a matrix $FEED_i$, where each feedback $FEED_i(s, j)$ is a real number belonging to $[0, 1]$, representing the quality of the collaboration that the agent a_j provided to the agent a_i concerning the service s. A feedback equal to 0 (resp. 1) means minimum (resp. maximum) quality of the service. Based on these feedbacks, the agent a_i updates both the matrices $SREL_i$ and $RREL_i$. More in particular, in our approach we choose to compute the current reliability shown by an agent a_j in its collaboration with a_i by averaging all the feedbacks concerning a_j. Therefore, denoting by $Services_i(j, cat)$ the set of the services of the category cat provided by a_i

with the collaboration of a_j at the previous step, the current service reliability shown by a_j, that we denote by $sr_i(j, cat)$, is computed as

$$sr_i(j, cat) = \frac{\sum_{s \in Services_i(j,cat)} FEED_i(s, j)}{|Services_i(j, cat)|} . \quad (1)$$

For each new step, this current reliability is taken into account to update the element $SREL_i$. We choose to compute this update by averaging the value of $SREL_i$ at the previous step and the current reliability computed at the new step. Formally:

$$SREL_i(j, cat) = \alpha \cdot SREL_i(j, cat) + (1 - \alpha) \cdot sr_i(j, cat) , \quad (2)$$

where α is a real value belonging to $[0, 1]$, representing the importance that a_i gives to the past evaluations of the reliability with respect to the current evaluation. In other words, α measures the importance given to the *memory* with respect to the current time. This coefficient assumes a significant importance in the design of the agent behaviour, and we will discuss in details its role in the next section.

In an analogous way, the feedbacks are used to update the recommendation reliability $RREL$. The current recommendation reliability of an agent a_j at a given step is computed by averaging all the errors made by a_j in providing a recommendation. In words, if a_j recommended to a_i the agent a_k with a recommendation $RECC_i(j, k, cat)$, and the feedback for a_k concerning a service s of the category c is $FEED_i(s, k)$, the error made by a_j by its recommendation is $|RECC_i(j, k, cat) - FEED_i(s, k)|$. By averaging all the errors concerning services of the category cat, we obtain an evaluation of the current precision of a_j with respect to the recommendations relating to a_k, that is $\left(\frac{\sum_{s \in Services_i(k,cat)} |RECC_i(j,k,cat) - FEED_i(s,k)|}{|Services_i(k,cat)|}\right)$. Finally, by averaging this precision on the set $Agents(j)$ of all the agents a_k evaluated by a_j in the previous step, we obtain the current recommendation reliability $rr_i(j, cat)$:

$$rr_i(j, cat) = \frac{\sum_{k \in Agents(j)} \left(\frac{\sum_{s \in Services_i(k,cat)} |RECC_i(j,k,cat) - FEED_i(s,k)|}{|Services_i(k,cat)|}\right)}{|Agents(j)|} . \quad (3)$$

Now, in order to update the element $RREL_i(j, cat)$, we use a weighted mean between the value of $RREL_i(j, cat)$ at the previous step and the current recommendation reliability:

$$RREL_i(j, cat) = \alpha \cdot RREL_i(j, cat) + (1 - \alpha) \cdot rr_i(j, cat) , \quad (4)$$

where α has the same meaning than for the case of the service reliability.

- **Phase 3: Computation of REP**. The recommendations contained in the matrix $RECC_i$ are used by the agent a_i to determine the reputations of the other agents of the community. In particular, a_i computes the reputation of another agent a_j as the average of all the recommendations received by the other agents of the community concerning a_j. Formally:

$$REP_i(j, cat) = \frac{\sum_{k \in A, k \neq i, k \neq j} RECC_i(k, j, cat)}{|A| - 2}, \quad (5)$$

where we denote by A the set of the agents of the community.

- **Phase 4: Computation of PREF**.The agent a_i finally computes the overall preference measure $PREF_i(j, cat)$ in the agent a_j by taking into account both the service reliability $SREL_i(j, cat)$ and the reputation $REP_i(j, cat)$. In particular, a coefficient β is used to weight the importance of the service reliability with respect to the reputation. β is a real value belonging to the interval $[0, 1]$, where $\beta = 0$ means that the agent, in order to evaluate the overall trust in another agent, does not assigns any importance to the reliability and only considers the reputation. Viceversa, if $\beta = 1$, the agent only considers the service without using the contribution of the reputation. Formally:

$$PREF_i(j, cat) = \beta \cdot SREL_i(j, cat) + (1 - \beta) \cdot REP_i(j, cat) . \quad (6)$$

At each step, the agent a_i exploits the matrix $PREF_i$ to select the most suitable candidates to request a collaboration.

5 A Study of the Role of the β Coefficient on the ART Testbed

In this section, we perform some experiments using the ART platform. On ART, each agent takes the role of an art appraiser who gives appraisals on paintings presented by its clients. In order to fulfill his appraisals, each agent can ask opinions to other agents. These agents are also in competition among them and thus, they may lie in order to fool opponents. The game is supervised by a simulator that runs in a synchronous and step by step manner, and it can be described as follows:

- The clients, simulated by the simulator, request opinions on paintings to the appraiser agents. Each painting belongs to an era. For each appraisal, an agent earns a given money amount that is stored in its bank amount BA.
- Each agent has a specific expertise level in each era, assigned by the simulator. The error made by an agent while appraising a painting depends on both this expertise and the price the appraiser decides to spend for that appraisal.
- An agent cannot appraise its paintings himself, but he has to ask other agents to obtain opinions. Each opinion has a fixed cost for the agent.
- Each agent can obtain recommendations about another agent by other players. Each recommendation has a given price. This way, the agent can build a reputation model of the other agents.
- Agents weight each received opinion in order to compute the final evaluation of the paintings.

- At the end of each step, the accuracy of agents final evaluations is compared to each other, in order to determine the client share for each agent during the next step. In other words, the most accurate agent receives more clients.
- At the end of each step, the simulator reveals the real value of each painting, thus allowing each agent to update its reliability and reputation model.
- At the end of the game, the winner of the competition is the agent having the highest bank amount BA.

The purpose of our experiments is to study how the performances of an agent changes depending on the population size N, the percentage of unreliable agents P and the percentage of agents having a reputation model R. For our experiments, we have built an agent implementing the RRAF model, and we have run some games in presence of different populations of agents. In particular, we have realized the following three experiments:

1: Relationship between the coefficient β and N. For this experiment, we have considered six different values of the agent population size, namely $N = 30$, $N = 50$, $N = 70$, $N = 100$, $N = 150$, $N = 200$. For each of these values, we have run 11 ART games, where an RRAF agent participates to each game, using a different value of β. In particular, the 11 values of β we have considered are $0.0, 0.1, 0.2, 0.3, 0.4, 0.5, 0.6, 0.7, 0.8, 0.9, 1.0$. For each game, besides the RRAF agents, we have run as competitors a population of $N-1$ Simplet agents. Simplet agent is an agent that has participated to the 2008 ART Competition, and whose software can be downloaded at the ART site [1], and that uses a reliability-reputation model. We have programmed a 50 percent of these agents with a low availability to pay for the opinions, thus generating unreliable answers to the opinion requests. This low availability is represented by the internal ART parameter $c_g = 1$. The other 50 percent

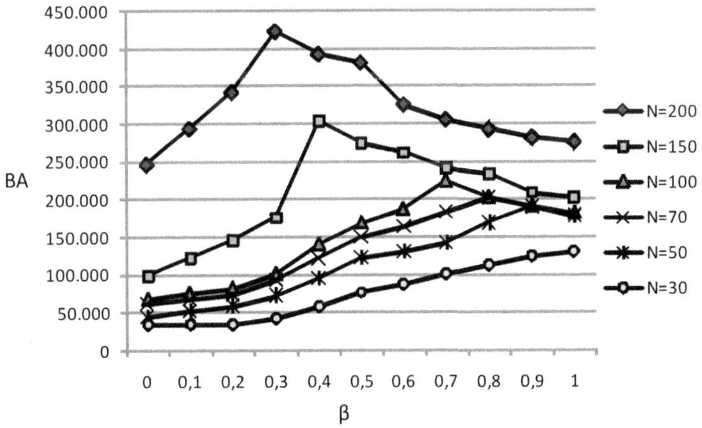

Fig. 2. Variation of the bank amount BA against the β coefficient for different sizes N of the agent population (percentage of unreliable agents P=50%, percentage of agents without reputation model R=0%)

of Simplet agent have been programmed with $c_g = 15$, that is a price for generating opinions with high reliability. This composition has been fixed for all the games, so the unique variable is the β coefficient. In Figure 2 we have reported the results of this experiment, in terms of variation of the bank amount BA of the RRAF agent against the different values of β. This variation has been represented for each population size N. We note that, if the population size is very small (e.g., $N = 30$) the maximum bank amount has been obtained using $\beta = 1$, i.e. by the agent that does not assign any importance to the reputation and only uses the reliability. On the contrary, if the population size is high (e.g. $N = 200$), the maximum bank amount has been reached using $\beta = 0.3$, that is by assigning more importance to the reputation than the reliability. Generally, the figure shows that the role of the reputation becomes more significant when the population size increases.

2: Relationship between the coefficient β and P. In this experiment, we have considered 8 different agent populations, each characterized by a different percentage P of unreliable agents. Namely, the 8 values of P we have considered are 10%, 20%, 30%, 40%, 50%, 60%, 70%, 80%. For each of these values, we have run 101 ART games, where an RRAF agent participates to each game, using a different value of β. In particular, we have considered the set of values $\{\beta_1, \beta_2, .., \beta_k\}$, where $\beta_1 = 0$, $\beta_k = 1$ and $\beta_{i+1} = \beta_i + 0.01$. For each game, besides the RRAF agents, we have run as competitors a population of 99 Simplet agents, where a percentage P of these agents generates reliable opinions, using an opinion cost $c_g = 15$, while the other agents generates unreliable opinions, using $c_g = 1$. For each population of agents, we have determined the value β_{Max}, represented the value of β that has generated the maximum bank amount for that population. In Figure 3 we have represented the variation of β_{Max} against the percentage P. We remark that,

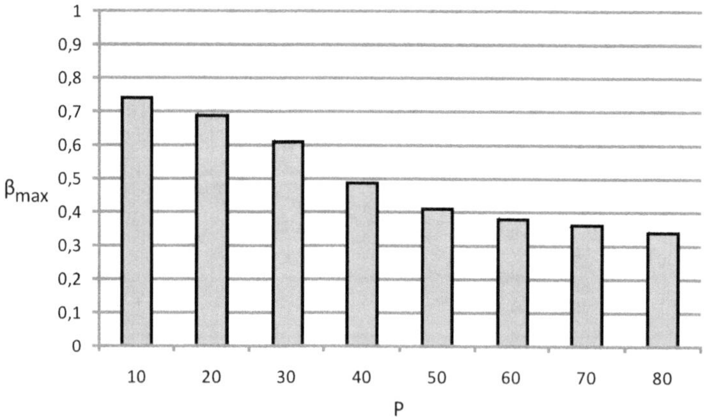

Fig. 3. Variation of the value β_{Max} against the percentage of unreliable agents, with population size $N = 150$ and percentage of agents without reputation model R=0%

in correspondence of a high value of P (e.g. $P = 80\%$), we have obtained a small value of β_{Max} (e.g. $\beta_{Max} = 0.34$), while for a small value of P (e.g. $P = 10\%$) we have obtained a high value of β_{Max} (e.g. $\beta_{Max} = 0.74$). In words, the experiment shows that the higher is the percentage of unreliable agents, the smaller will be the influence of the reputation with respect to the reliability.

3: Relationship between the coefficient β and R. In our last experiment, we have considered 8 different agent populations, each characterized by a different percentage R of agents provided with a reputation model. In particular, the 8 values of R we have considered are 0%, 10%, 20%, 30%, 40%, 50%, 60%, 70%. For each of these values, we have run 101 ART games, where an RRAF agent participates to each game, using a different value of β. In particular, as in the previous experiment, we have considered the set of values $\{\beta_1, \beta_2, .., \beta_k\}$, where $\beta_1 = 0$, $\beta_k = 1$ and $\beta_{i+1} = \beta_i + 0.01$. For each game, besides the RRAF agents, we have run as competitors a population of 99 agents, where a percentage R of these agents are Simplet agents with their reputation model, while the other agents are honest agents without reputation model. For each population of agents, we have determined the value β_{Max}, having the same meaning than in the previous experiment. Figure 4 shows the variation of β_{Max} against the percentage R. It is easy to note that, in correspondence of a high value of R (e.g. $R = 70\%$), we have obtained a high value of β_{Max} (e.g. $\beta_{Max} = 0.71$), while for a small value of R (e.g. $P = 0\%$) we have obtained a small value of β_{Max} (e.g. $\beta_{Max} = 0.41$). This experiment shows that the higher is the percentage of agents having a reputation model, the higher will be the influence of the reputation with respect to the reliability.

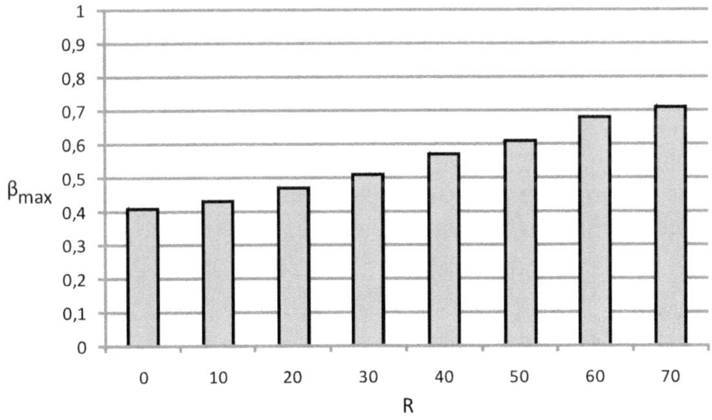

Fig. 4. Variation of the value β_{Max} against the percentage of agents having reputation model, with population size $N = 150$ and percentage of unreliable agents P=50%

6 Conclusions

The large number of trust-based approaches in competitive multi-agent systems emerged in the last recent years implies the necessity of clearly understanding what are the advantages and the limitations of using trust measures to improve the effectiveness of the systems. In particular, the two main measures considered in the past, i.e. reliability and reputation, seems to be strongly correlated to the characteristics of the agent population. However, in order to realize a sound and effective analysis, it is necessary to use a model for competitive environments that considers both the reliability of agents in providing services and in generating recommendations, as well as a mechanism to integrate both reliability and reputation for obtaining a synthetic measure to be exploited by an agent for selecting the most promising interlocutors. In this work, we propose a framework, called RRAF, that complies with the above requirements. In particular, this framework allows to built competitive agents, provided with an internal reliability-reputation model, where the importance of reliability with respect to reputation is measured by a coefficient denoted as β. We have run RRAF agents on the well-known ART testbed, in order to understand what is the correlation between the β coefficient against three main characteristics of the agent population, namely the population size, the percentage of unreliable agents and the percentage of agents provided by a reputation model. The experimental results confirm the suppositions, proposed by some authors [7], that the reputation has not a significant role if the size of the agent population is too low. However, the experiments also show that in presence of large-size agent population, the use of a reputation model can lead to an advantage of about a 40 percent with respect to the use of the only reliability. As other interesting results, our study shows that the role of the reputation becomes sufficiently significant only in presence of a sufficient percentage of unreliable agents, and only in presence of a sufficient number of agents provided with a reputation model. As for our ongoing research, we are planning to explore the dependence of β by other characteristics of the agent population, that might have, in our opinion, a significant impact as, for instance, the percentage of agents that are reliable from the viewpoint of the provided services but are unreliable as providers of recommendations. Moreover, we are thinking to exploit the knowledge of these correlations to build an agent model able to dynamically adapt its reputation model (in terms of β coefficient) to the possible variation in the time of the characteristics of the agent population.

References

1. ART-Testbed, `http://megatron.iiia.csic.es/art-testbed/`
2. Khosravifar, B., Gomrokchi, M., Bentahar, J., Thiran, P.: Maintenance-based trust for multi-agent systems. In: 8th International Conference on Autonomous Agents and Multiagent Systems, pp. 1017–1024. International Foundation for Autonomous Agents and Multiagent Systems (2009)

3. Bhuiyan, T., Xu, Y., Jøsang, A.: Integrating trust with public reputation in location-based social networks for recommendation making. In: 2008 IEEE/WIC/ACM International Conference on Web Intelligence and Intelligent Agent Technology, pp. 107–110. IEEE Press, Los Alamitos (2008)
4. Fullam, K., Klos, T., Muller, G., Sabater-Mir, J., Barber, K.S., Vercouter, L.: The agent reputation and trust (ART) testbed. In: Stølen, K., Winsborough, W.H., Martinelli, F., Massacci, F. (eds.) iTrust 2006. LNCS, vol. 3986, pp. 439–442. Springer, Heidelberg (2006)
5. Grandison, T., Sloman, M.: Trust management tools for internet applications. In: Nixon, P., Terzis, S. (eds.) iTrust 2003. LNCS, vol. 2692, pp. 91–107. Springer, Heidelberg (2003)
6. Huynh, T.D., Jennings, N.R., Shadbolt, N.R.: An integrated trust and reputation model for open multi-agent systems. Autonomous Agents and Multi-Agent Systems 13, 119–154 (2006)
7. Muoz, V., Murillo, J.: Agent uno: Winner in the 2nd spanish ART competition. Inteligencia Artificia 12, 19–27 (2008)
8. Na, S.J., Choi, K.H., Shin, D.R.: Reputation-based service discovery in multi-agents systems. In: IEEE International Workshop on Semantic Computing and Applications, pp. 126–128. IEEE Press, Los Alamitos (2008)
9. Sabater, J., Sierra, C.: Review on computational trust and reputation models. Artificial Intelligence Review 24, 33–60 (2005)
10. Sarvapali, D.H., Ramchurn, D., Jennings, N.R.: Trust in multi-agent systems. The Knowledge Engineering Review 19, 1–25 (2004)

Multilayer Superimposed Information for Collaborative Annotation in Wikis

Carlos Solís[1], José H. Canós[2], and Marcos R.S. Borges[3]

[1] Lero, The Irish Software Engineering Research Centre, University of Limerick, Limerick, Ireland
carlos.solis@lero.ie
[2] ISSI-DSIC, Universitat Politècnica de València, Camí de Vera s/n, 46022 Valencia, Spain
jhcanos@dsic.upv.es
[3] Graduate Program in Informatics, Federal University of Rio de Janeiro, 20010-974 Rio de Janeiro, Brazil
mborges@nce.ufrj.br

Abstract. Collaborative writing and editing typically use annotations to coordinate edition tasks, comment the content, add relevant references, or clarify confusing content. Despite that wikis are among the most widely used hypertext systems for performing such collaborative activities, they have little support to annotations. In this paper, we propose to use spatial hypertext layers as the solution for the management of annotations in wikis. We have extended ShyWiki, a spatial hypertext wiki environment, with Multilayer Superimposed Information features. In addition, we present the results of a study that shows the value of spatial hypertext layers for locate, organize and group annotations in interest groups under a wiki interface.

1 Introduction

Since the conception of hypertext, annotations have been used to enrich the content of hyperdocuments. Bush observed in his seminal paper [9] the importance of complementary information and pointed out that the users could insert comments to Memex trails. Later, Engelbart's NLS system [13] permitted the collaborative annotation of text. In our digital age, personal and collaborative annotations have become very popular. The former are used to assimilate contents (e.g. underlying, adding an asterisk, highlighting parts of a text, etc), whereas the latter are meant to support discussions: users form interest groups that share annotations in order to learn, think about and understand a document or group of documents.

Wiki is among the current most popular collaborative hypertext editing environments. Its simplicity and ease of use has resulted in a massive adoption as a platform for content creation and linking. The success of Wikipedia and other Wiki based systems has called the attention of the research community, whose members have developed different types of extensions of the basic Wiki

R. Meersman et al. (Eds.): OTM 2010, Part I, LNCS 6426, pp. 340–357, 2010.

implementation, (e.g. semantic wikis [23]), and have used wikis for knowledge management [30], or software engineering [2]. However, little attention has been paid to the support of annotations from readers and editors. In Wikipedia [1], annotations are inserted in the form of inline sentences, which are part of the document and may interfere the normal document reading if their number is high. To avoid this, discussion pages are used to hold user and editor comments, but such pages are in practice different entities and their content should not be considered pure annotations because they lack context (that is, they are annotations to the document, not to specific parts of it).

In this paper we face the challenge to improve wiki's collaborative annotation support. We use ShyWiki [27], a spatial hypertext wiki system that uses spatial and visual properties such as position, size, color, etc. to represent content. In ShyWiki, the elements of wiki pages are similar to sticky notes with hypermedia content; thus, annotations can be created in a simple way: a part of a wiki page may be annotated by placing a note near the text to be annotated. However, the ShyWiki system presented some usability limitations. Specifically, the risk of information overload was not controlled since both original content and annotations shared a common space, which would eventually impede the identification of each one, and difficult the access to the content when the number of annotations is high. As a solution we have enriched ShyWiki with multiple layers of information based on the concept of Superimposed Information. To evaluate the effectiveness of the solution we describe an evaluation that compares the performance of two groups of 9 subjects using the ShyWiki system. We want to examine the impact of the spatial hypertext layers in the group performance.

The paper is organized as follows: Section 2 explains the importance of collaborative annotation in wikis, and the requirements of an annotation facility. Section 3 presents the characteristics of spatial hypertext wiki (ShyWiki). Section 4 explains ShyWiki with Multilayer Superimposed Information support. Section 5 describes the user interface evaluation and its results. Section 6 describes the related work. Finally, section 7 gives the conclusions, and presents the future work.

2 Collaborative Annotation in Wikis

Collaborative annotation is part of many information management activities. For instance, in Annotative Collaboration Processes (ACPs) [29], authors and editors use annotations during the edition, review and evolution of documents to help in the coordination of the goals, tasks, resolution of conflicts, and to record comments of a group of editors. Applying ACPs in hypertext editing requires hypertext systems to meet some essential requirements: first, users must have read and write access to the content; second, users should be able to add annotations to the content; third, there should be a shared information space; and fourth, the technical access barriers to edit the content should be as low as possible, because users might not have technical knowledge about hypertext.

In the search for hypertext systems fulfilling as many of these requirements as possible, wikis appear as the best candidates. Wikis are based on the principles of ease of use, continuous improvement through incremental content creation, open structure for editing and evolution, and self organized structure according to the needs of the community [10]. Wikis are a way to provide read and write features to a hypertext, have low technical barriers, and a shared information space. However, they offer limited support to ACPs, as well as for handling annotations. In Wikipedia, for instance, the coordination to determine the path that will drive the future versions of an article is managed through a discussion page. In discussion pages, users comment and discuss the article's content including others contributions, and use it to communicate among them [16]. In other words, a discussion page is like a big annotation to another wiki page, although in practice it is a different wiki page.

Discussion pages in Wikipedia have a relevant role in the overall ACP. A study performed with Wikipedia users showed that they use discussion pages as the main way to communicate wiki article issues [8]. Additionally, there is a statistical correlation indicating that the highest quality articles in Wikipedia are the ones with more activity in their discussion pages [31].

2.1 Requirements of an Annotation Facility

Adding annotation capability to collaborative editing systems like wikis have some general requirements, which have been defined in [19]. First, the management of the annotations must be simple (lightness). Second, the superimposed information data model must be able to represent many data models (flexibility). Third, no assumptions must be made about the content being annotated. In addition, users of annotation enabled wikis should be able to:

- Add notes to a wiki page. This is the basic requirement of the system, being other requirements defined around this one.
- Add several layers of annotations to a wiki page. Since different groups of users would add information with diverse goals, such as clarify content, indicate where is additional information, coordinate tasks, etc., only one extra layer of information may become insufficient.
- View only the original information. Some users dislike reading documents that have been previously annotated by others. Annotations may interfere and distract readers [6]. The wiki has to give the choice of showing or hiding the annotations.
- View selected layers of annotations. When there are many layers, users can select those layers they want to be displayed. In this way, they can visualize just the information of their interest.
- Move annotations between layers. For example, in collaborative edition or design the relevant information in other layers (e.g. in a "draft" layer) can be incorporated to the original content.
- Organize the layers by user interest groups. In this way, a layer is presented to a user only if the layer belongs to one of the user's groups.

3 The Spatial Hypertext Wiki

Spatial hypertext [17] is a kind of hypermedia based on using visual and spatial characteristics to define relationships among hypertext elements. Users can handle and move elements in a document, or change their properties (such as color or size).In spatial hypertext, hyperlinks may become implicit because they are expressed indirectly by means of visual and spatial relationships (e.g. by positioning elements to form lists, stacks, composites and heaps [26]). Also, elements of the same type can share the visual and spatial characteristics (color, border thickness, font types, adorns, layouts, position, proximity, geometric relations, etc.). Finally, collections can be created by inserting elements into other elements.

Experience using spatial hypertext has shown that it is suitable for domains with complex structures, collaborative tasks, and where there is no difference between readers and authors [17]. We have used spatial hypertext as a solution for the requirements stated in section 2.1.

ShyWiki (Spatial Hypertext Wiki) [27,28] is a wiki which uses spatial hypertext to represent its content. ShyWiki allows its users to define visual and spatial relations among the elements of a page. A ShyWiki wiki page is a spatial hypertext document composed of notes (see Figure 1). Each note can contain elements of formatted text, images or other types of media. Properties of notes such as their colors, or positions are used for relating them.

In ShyWiki all notes include the properties: px, py, height, and background and border color. Content-Notes are notes that can display text, images, and hyperlinks. Their content is defined by means of a wiki markup language. There are two kinds of hyperlinks: external that point to web pages outside the wiki, and internal or wiki links which point to other pages in the wiki. ContentNotes can group a collection of notes, therefore they can be composite notes. ShyWiki permits the transclusion of notes, that is to say, the inclusion of notes already defined in other wiki pages by reference and without duplicating them [20]. A *TranscludedNote* is a note whose content is defined by another note.

ShyWiki provides the basic editing operations on wiki pages. Each time a wiki page is edited, a new version of the page is created. In the editing mode, a user can perform the following actions:

- Create wiki pages. When a wiki link is navigated for the first time, a new wiki page in the ShyWiki web is created. The name of the new wiki page corresponds to the link anchor text.
- Create Notes. The user can add new notes to the wiki page. The note types that can be added are ContentNote and TranscludedNotes.
- Edit Notes. The content of the notes can be changed at any time, except for transcluded notes. The content of the notes is described using the ShyWiki mark-up language.
- Move notes. Notes can be moved freely in the editing area by drag and drop actions. In this way, the user can accommodate the information at her or his convenience.

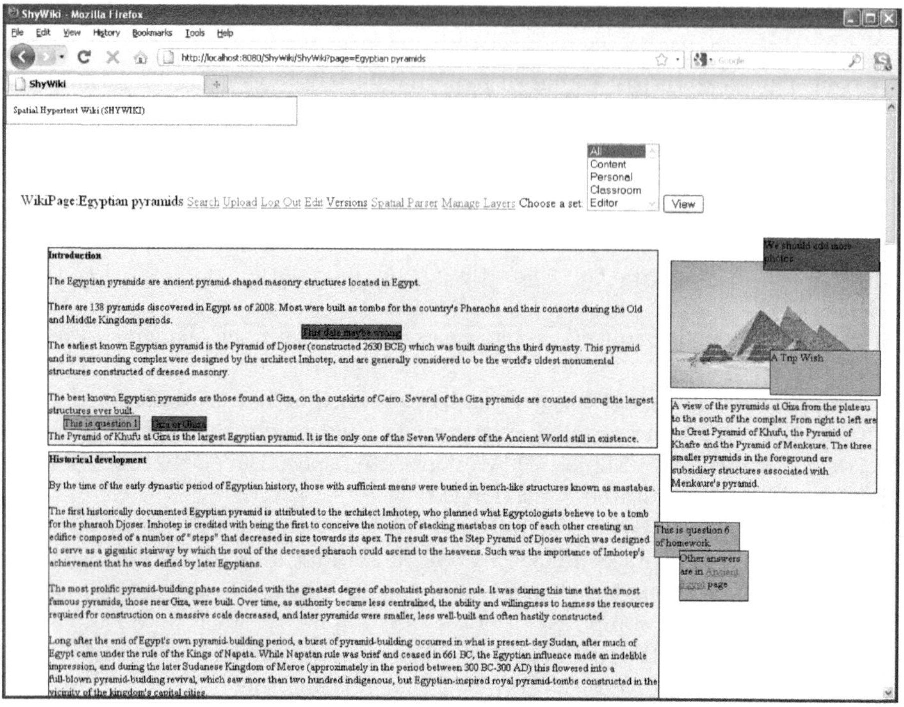

Fig. 1. A ShyWiki wiki page

- Group notes. The user can group notes to create aggregations. In this way, a note can be dragged and dropped inside another note, becoming an internal part of the latter. Once notes are grouped, a user can manipulate a set of notes as a single entity.
- Transclude notes. Users can transclude a note inside another wiki page by indicating the source document and the note identifier. The position of the transcluded note can be changed, but the remaining properties can only be modified by editing the original note.

Adding a note to ShyWiki only requires creating a note, and dragging it to a place in the wiki page; that is, the content of wiki pages is spatially organized. Notes may be placed in different regions of the page, and can be moved around. There are other two interesting features of ShyWiki: the versioning facility allows users to look at previous versions of the wiki pages, and the search facility which is used to find wiki pages and notes that contain a word or a phrase.

Despite all the above advantages, ShyWiki showed some limitations to support annotations. Using only the visual and spatial properties generates two basic problems. On the one hand, users must have a consistent and clear way to add annotations. On the other hand, it must be easy to identify which parts of a spatial hypertext document are base information, and which ones are annotations. In the case of large documents, including many annotation components, users are not able to identify which information is related to each other. In addition, the purpose of the annotations can be diverse and different users may be interested in different parts. However, a ShyWiki user cannot suppress the implicit structures that represent the annotations.

4 ShyWiki with Multilayer Superimposed Information

To make ShyWiki compliant with the requirements of section 2.1, we have extended it by incorporating multiple layers of Superimposed Information as defined in [19]. A document is a layered structure composed of an original content (called the base information) that is placed in the base of the layer stack, and the superimposed information layers, where annotations and other types of extra information can be placed. The aggregated layer is the result of adding the base layer and the superimposed information layers, and is at the top of the stack. Figure 2 shows an example of document with superimposed information. The document is the result of aggregating two superimposed information layers to a base information layer. The base information layer is composed of three notes, whereas each of the superimposed information layers has two notes that annotate the base information.

Layered documents can permit controlling which layers to include in or exclude from the aggregated layer, as well as the order they should be added. The superimposed information in each layer can be added to the base information incrementally, and the final look of the aggregated document depends on the order each superimposed information layer is added. We can observe in Figure 1 that the aggregated document would look different if the order of the superimposed information layers were different.

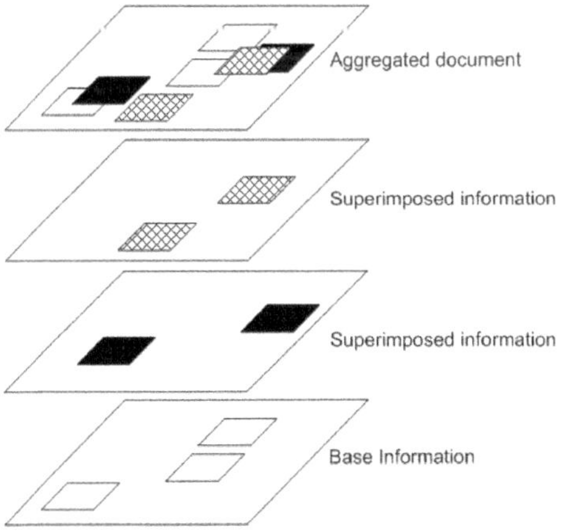

Fig. 2. Superimposed Information Spatial Hypertext Document

Using superimposed information layers adds some new possibilities for displaying the spatial hypertext content and for navigating. Each superimposed information layer is an addressable document, which makes the superimposed information accessible and searchable as other documents in a hypertext system. As a result, it is possible to define hyperlinks between layers of superimposed information in any document. In addition, the search of notes can be performed over some specific layers.

Our extension to ShyWiki considers documents as aggregations of base and superimposed information. It is possible to classify the different kinds of superimposed information notes in sets. The information in every set can be added to the base information incrementally in order to create an aggregated document. In this way, each superimposed information set is a layer of information, and spatial hypertext documents become a kind of view of three dimensional objects which are observed from the top.

4.1 ShyWiki's Superimposed Information Features

The management of the superimposed information is performed using the mechanisms that ShyWiki provides for editing wiki pages. In this way, editing superimposed information only requires knowledge of the wiki markup language.

Figure 3 shows the ShyWiki model which includes superimposed information layers. The wiki pages of ShyWiki are no longer composed by notes; rather, they are composed by objects called Information Layers, which are in turn composed by notes. As mentioned earlier, a wiki page has one base information layer, and can have many superimposed information layers.

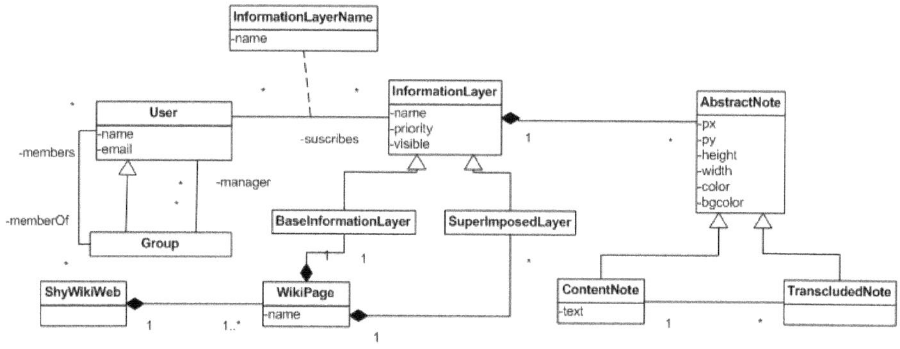

Fig. 3. ShyWiki conceptual model

Information layers are partial views of wiki pages. An information layer has a name, a description, a priority, and a visibility. The name of the layers is used to select the layers users want to display. The description of the layer is a metadata property that is used to indicate the goal of the information layer. The priority and visibility attributes are used to indicate when the superimposed information layers are displayed.

A base information layer is an information layer that is going to be complemented with superimposed information, and stores the original content of a wiki page. Every wiki page has one base information layer that is created at the page creation time. Moreover, the base information layer is always the first layer to be displayed.

A superimposed information layer is an information layer that is aggregated to a base information layer. The priority attribute permits to add the superimposed information layers in a specific order. The priority attribute is a positive integer, the highest priority is 1. If two layers of superimposed information have the same priority, it means that the order in which they are displayed is not relevant. When creating the aggregated layer, layers with lower priority value are aggregated first.

The superimposed information layers can be associated to the individuals and groups that compose the social network that builds and interacts through the wiki, and that can control the access to their annotations. Figure 3 shows also the relations among users, groups, and superimposed information layers in the ShyWiki model. A group is a specialization of a user, and represents a set of users. A layer name is associated with a set of superimposed information layers.

If a user or a group in which she or he is member is associated with a layer name, then the user is subscribed to a layer name. A user subscribes to a layer name in order to view the superimposed information layers with the same name when she or he navigates through the wiki. For example, a user subscribes to a layer name called Biology First Course, then when he or she visits any wiki page that has a superimposed information layer named Biology First Course, then it is displayed in the aggregated document.

In summary, the rule for visualizing the aggregate information layer is: A layer in a wiki page is displayed if it belongs to the user or user's group subscriptions. If a layer does not belong to any subscription, then the visibility criteria is used. The order of the visible layers is defined by their priority.

If a wiki page in ShyWiki has superimposed layers, then the wiki page allows the possibility of filtering the content by selecting the superimposed layers that the user wants to display. The operations added for visualizing superimposed information are:

- Display layers. Permits to visualize a set of superimposed information layers.
- Display base layer. Permits to visualize only the base layer.

The use of superimposed information layers has also effects in the editing mode. As users can add several superimposed layers to a wiki page, they have to indicate for each one its name and its priority. When a note is added, the user can indicate in which information layer the note must be situated; by default, a note belongs to the base information layer. A note can be moved to a different superimposed layer in the same wiki page when the properties of the note are edited. The superimposed information management operations are:

- Add layer. Adds a superimposed information layer to a wiki page.
- Remove layer. Removes a superimposed information layer including all its notes.
- Add note. Adds a note to a superimposed information layer, by default notes are added to the base level.
- Move note. Moves a note to a superimposed information layer.
- Move all. Moves all the notes in a superimposed information layer to another.

Navigation in the wiki is also affected by the superimposed information layers. The wiki markup language has been extended to allow the definition of hyperlinks pointing to a specific information layer or to a group of them. Table 1 shows the wiki mark up syntax for hyperlinks to layers.

Table 1. Wiki mark up syntax to define hyperlinks

Hyperlink to a wiki page	[[Wiki Page Name]]
Hyperlink to a layer	[[Wiki Page Name [[$LayerName_1$]]]]
Hyperlink to a layer set	[[Wiki Page Name [[$LayerName_1$]][[$LayerName_n$]]]]

ShyWiki architecture is based on Asynchronous JavaScript and XML (AJAX) services, and in the manipulation of documents content is performed using the Document Object Model interface (DOM) [27]. The superimposed information features have been implemented in the same way.

4.2 Example

Figure 1 shows a wiki page about the Egyptian pyramids. The evolution of the wiki page content is discussed in the editors layer, which includes the notes: *This date maybe wrong*, *Giza or Ghiza*, and *we should add more photos.* There is layer called *classrom* which includes the annotations created by a groups of students solving a homework. The *classroom* annotations are: *This is question 1*, *This is question 6 of homework*, and *other answers are in ancient Egypt page.* In addition, there is a layer called *personal*, which includes one annotation: *A trip wish.*

Other users cannot view the personal annotation of the student. The annotations of the *classroom* layer are shown to all the students that are subscribed to the group. The student is not subscribed to the editor's layer, then the student can see when she arrives to the page the base content and the annotations in the *personal* and *classroom* layers. The *personal* layer is only visible to one student, while the *classroom* layer is shared and build only by the classroom students. Figure 4 presents the wiki page of the pyramids after filtering all the annotations.

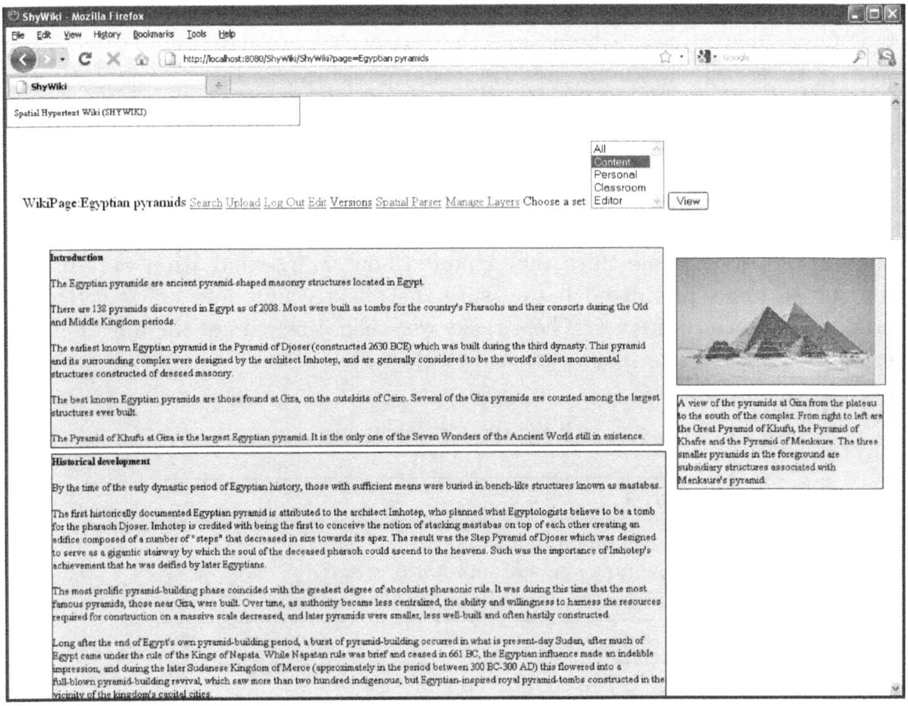

Fig. 4. A wiki page displaying the base content

5 Evaluation

For understanding if the spatial hypertext layers are found useful by users, we have performed a study that permits to compare the effectiveness and efficiency of users using annotations in a wiki with spatial layered annotations against a wiki with inline annotations.

5.1 Evaluation Design

The experiment was performed by 18 subjects (15 males and 3 females), students and staff at a large university. The subjects were split into two groups of 9 persons. One group used ShyWiki with spatial hypertext layers and annotations, and the other group used ShyWiki without spatial hypertext layers, and with inline annotations. The control group interacted with the wiki with inline annotations, and the experimental group interacted with the wiki with layered spatial annotations. The null hypothesis of the study is that the experimental group would perform better than the control group.

Both groups interacted with a wiki page which content was the same: a wiki page with three paragraphs, one image, and three sets of annotations. The annotation sets were the following: editors set that indicated the evolution direction of the content, classroom annotations that indicated interesting parts of the content for people solving a homework, and a set of personal annotations. There were 3 editors, 3 classroom and 1 personal annotations. In the wiki page with inline annotations, it was not possible to hide or filter the annotations, while in the spatial one it can be performed. The inline annotations indicated the set they belonged with a word and a colon symbol before the annotation.

In the first part, users performed three tasks: in the first task they counted the number of annotations, in the second they counted the number of sets of annotations, and in the third they counted how many annotation were in each set. These tasks permitted to measure the effectiveness and efficiency of the users using both interfaces. These tasks were the first part of the questionnaire answered by the users (shown in table 2 Part 1).

Table 2. Questionnaire

	Part 1
Q1	How many annotations are?
Q2	How many sets of annotations are?
Q3	How many annotations are in each set?
	Part 2
S4	It is useful to have annotations
S5	The annotations are intrusive
S6	The annotations are distinguishable from the content
S7	The annotations are easy to locate
S8	It would be useful to be able to hide or show the annotations
S9	It is useful to have sets of annotations
S10	It would be useful to filter the annotations by set
S11	It would be useful to subscribe to annotation sets
S12	A wiki page should show the annotations sets you are subscribed

The second part of the questionnaire contained sentences about the experience of the user interaction with the system (see table 2 Part 2). Part2 has three groups of sentences. The first groups is integrated by S4 that is about users' opinion of annotations usefulness. The second group is integrated of S5 to S8 that are question about the annotations in the interface. The third part from S9 to S12 is about the sets of annotations. These sentences were answered using a likert scale from 1 to 5 (strongly disagree, disagree, neither, agree, and strongly agree).

5.2 Results

The results analysis was performed in the following way. For comparing the effectiveness we have used Fisher's exact of a contingency table of 2x2 in order to measure the proportions of failures and success in each group. For example for Q1 the contingency table has two rows: Control(5 success, 4 failures) and Experimental(9 success, 0 failures). We used Fisher's exact test instead of Chi-square due to the small sample size. For comparing the results of the two groups for questions in part 2 and for analyzing the response times, we have used the Mann-Whitney nonparametric test or U-test. Because there is not any assumption about a normal distribution of the data. In addition, the U-test is suitable for the analysis of ordinal data such as likert questionnaires.

Table 3 presents the results of part 1 for the control and experimental group. For each question, the table presents the percentage of effectiveness users had to find right answer, and the two tailed p-value of Fisher's exact test. The times to find the answers are also show in table 3.

Table 3. Questions in part 1

	Effectiveness		Fisher	Time *secs*		U-Test
Id	Control	Experimental	exact 2 tailed	Control	Experimental	exact 2 tailed
Q1	0.55	1.00	0.082	45.74	28.80	0.063
Q2	0.44	1.00	0.029	33.63	23.97	0.063
Q3	0.44	0.88	0.131	34.38	23.84	0.297

Table 4 presents the results of the questionnaire part 2. For each question and user group, it presents the median obtained, and the two tailed p-value of the exact U-test.

Table 4. Part 2 Results - Medians

Id	Control	Experimental	U-test exact (2 tailed)
S4	4.0	4.0	0.371
S5	2.0	3.0	0.745
S6	4.0	5.0	0.190
S7	4.0	5.0	0.026
S8	4.0	4.0	0.297
S9	4.0	5.0	0.019
S10	4.0	4.0	0.699
S11	4.0	4.0	0.347
S12	4.0	5.0	0.534

5.3 Discussion

In Q1 (which is total number of annotations?), the experimental group was able to locate all the annotations in a more effective way 100% against 55% in the control group. The two tailed p-value cannot reject the hypothesis that the proportion of effectiveness are different between the control and the experimental.

However, we expected before the experiment that the experimental group performed better, then it could be possible to use a one tailed p-value, which is 0.041, which indicates that the experimental group performed better and is not independent of the interface. In the case of Q2 (How many annotation set are?), users in the experimental group were able to locate in a more effective way the sets of related annotations and the notes that belong to those sets, 100% against 44%. The p-value is 0.029, that indicates that users of the layered interface performed better. In the case of Q3(how many annotations are in each set?), the greater effectiveness in the experimental group (88% against 44%) cannot be attributed to the use of the layered interface. However, the effectiveness in Q3 for the experimental group was the double of the control one.

The times to find the answers are show in table 3, and were better for the experimental group for the three tasks. In the case of Q1 and Q3, if we interpret the result from the point of view that an improvement was expected, then a one tail p-value can be used again and it is 0.031. Therefore, the improvement in time can be attributed to the use of the layered interface. Q3 had a better time for the experimental than for the control group, however the p-value is far from 0.05.

Users of both interfaces believe that annotations are useful (S4). The control and the experimental group had a median of 4.0 (p-value 0.371). It does not matter the interface, users would like to have annotations.

In relation to the annotations in the interface, users think that inline are slightly less intrusive that spatial annotations (S5), the medians were 2.0 and 3.0 for the and experimental groups respectively (p-value 0.745). A possible, answer is that some of the spatial annotations were over the content. Although inline annotations may interrupt the lecture flow, they do not need to be removed like an annotation that is over the content. Spatial annotations were more distinguishable than inline annotations (S6), the medians were 4.0 for the control and 5.0 for the experimental group (p-value 0.190). The spatial annotations were easier to locate (S7), 4.0 was the median for the control group, and 5.0 for the experimental (p-value 0.060). Inline annotation can be located if users are reading the content, while the spatial ones can be displayed or removed by the users, and may have a special size, colour or position. It would be useful to be able to hide or show the annotations (S8), users of both interfaces had a median of 4.0 and p-value 0.297. In the case of the inline annotations it indicates that users had a requirement, while in the spatial wiki, that actually provide the feature, users found it useful. In addition, this point that users want to see the actual content with and without annotations.

The results about the sentences of sets of annotations indicate that the experimental group had a median of 5.0 for S9 (Is it useful to have sets of annotations?), while users of the control group had a median of 4.0, and the p-value was 0.019, which indicates that the feature provided in the spatial wiki influenced this answer. Users observed the annotations which were the result of the subscriptions of the wiki user used in the test. They were asked, if it is useful to have subscriptions (S10). In both interfaces they had a median of 4.0 (p-value

0.699). As a result, users believe that it is useful in any case. In addition, users think that the annotations of their subscriptions have to be shown in the wiki page (S11), the medians were 4.0 for the two groups and the p-value was 0.347. Users prefer to be aware of the annotations that are in the wiki page, instead of missing an important annotation for the tasks they are performing. As a result, questions S10 and S11 indicate that there is need of having subscriptions and show such annotations. Users of both groups found that it is useful to have sets of annotations (S12), the medians were 4.0 for the control and 5.0 for the experimental group, having a p-value of 0.534. This indicates that the control group users found useful to have the name of the set in the inline annotations, while users in the experimental group found useful to have sets that can be managed (hide/show and filter). However, for the control group this answer is not consistent with the effectiveness of answering successfully Q2.

The result give a positive feedback about the experience of the users with the layered interface. In particular the results of questions Q1 and Q2, and sentences S7 and S9 indicate an improvement in the experimental groups that can be attributed to the layered interface. In addition, the times to perform the tasks were lower in the layered interface.

6 Related Work

There are several spatial hypertext systems that provide interfaces which allow the information triage to their users. VIKI [18], is one of first spatial hypertext systems, and is focused in the emergent structure of hypertext documents. VKB [25] is a descendant of VIKI, which improved the presentation features of VIKI, and added new ones such as navigable history and global links. WARP [14] is a Web-based dynamic spatial hypertext system that is based on applets and javascript. Its most remarkable feature is an interactive user interface. None of the above mentioned systems offer facilities to manage superimposed information, nor to create it collaboratively. TinderBox [7] is a personal content assistant for visualizing, analyzing, and sharing notes, and it is a standalone application that can generate HTML documents for the Web. However, it has no wiki-like facilities to create spatial hypertext collaboratively.

Open hypermedia systems such as Microcosm [11] and Chimera [4] permit to extend documents with annotations and hyperlinks. Open hypertext could be a solution to add annotations to a wiki page. However, current open hypermedia solutions have some drawbacks. The open hypermedia data needs special servers and browsers that are not yet integrated with web servers and wikis. A group of users could share an open hypermedia solution, but they would not be able to collaborate with other wiki users world wide. Another drawback of the open hypermedia approaches, is that they need to copy the web pages in order to annotate them, that is, they are not integrated with the versioning systems provided by most wikis. As a consequence, if wiki editors are not aware of the existence of these annotations, they will not consider them when changing wiki pages.

Similar problems are present in other works focusing on the annotation of web content. Annotea [15] is an annotation framework based on RDF. Fluid documents [32] is an extension to the open hypermedia framework Arakne for defining annotations in web documents. Other systems allow personal annotation of web documents, such as Web Annotator [22], which is a web browser plug-in. These systems use specialized repositories that store the annotations and the versions of the web pages that were annotated. The version control and annotations are completely independent of the web pages annotated, so they may require additional infrastructures such as annotation servers and browsers.

Classic wikis have been used for tasks where there is a need to support collaborative writing and editing, and argumentation and design rationale management. In software engineering, for instance, they are used for capturing requirements [3,12], and for documenting software architectures designs [5,24].

7 Conclusions and Future Work

Wikis are widely used for collaborative writing and editing, and supporting annotation is a requirement of collaborative hypertext systems. However, current wikis lack features to effectively support annotation. In this paper, we have shown how to add support to annotation in wiki systems using spatial hypertext.

The characteristics of spatial hypertext make it suitable to deal with annotations in a very natural way. Essentially, the solution proposed is to use layers of spatial hypertext as elements of the wiki pages. In this way, a wiki page is composed by a set of spatial hypertext documents that are aggregated in order to build the wiki page that is displayed to the user. The use of layers permits to create different views of the information, and create hyperlinks to these views. In addition, users can subscribe to the superimposed information layers whose content is interesting for them. The original spatial hypertext wiki system has been extended to implement the solution described in the paper. Now, it provides the operations and features needed for superimposed information management, which provides support to annotation.

The study performed shows that users are willing to annotate the content, and to know the annotations that are performed by other users, in particular the ones performed by users of the same interest groups. Spatial hypertext layers help users to organize and locate the annotations in a better way than in a wiki without superimposed information support.

In the future work, the relations between layered spatial hypertext interfaces and multidimensional hypertext such as ZigZag and Xanadu [21] structures are going to be explored. Perhaps more sophisticated ways for displaying information can be provided in the spatial layers. In addition, we plan to analyze how the superimposed information layers are used, and improve the current prototype implementation.

Another future work is to support independent and parallel sub-group work. Each sub-group could work on a different layer of the shared document without reflecting on the main discussion. Meanwhile, the discussions conducted by this sub-group could be also registered and, if acceptable, even be incorporated to the main collaborative document. In addition, we plan to experiment whether layers can be used to manage an edition process as if they were based on annotation statuses or not.

Acknowledgments

The work of Carlos Solís has been funded by Science Foundation Ireland grant 03/CE2/I303_1 to LERO - the Irish Software Engineering Research Centre (http://www.lero.ie). The work of José H. Canós is partially funded by the Spanish MEC-DEEPEN project (TIN2009-08084), Junta CLM-INGENIO project (PAC08-0154-9262) and GV-grant ACOMP07/216. The work of Marcos R. S. Borges is partially supported by grants No.304252/2008-5 and 480461/2009-0 from CNPq (Brazil). The cooperation between the Brazilian and the Spanish research groups was partially sponsored by CAPES/MECD Cooperation Program, project #169/PHB2007-0064-PC.

References

1. Wikipedia, the free encyclopedia (2009), http://www.wikipedia.org
2. Aguiar, A., Dekel, U., Merson, P.: Wikis4se 2009: Wikis for software engineering. In: ICSE Companion, pp. 480–481. IEEE, Los Alamitos (2009)
3. de Almeida Ferreira, D., da Silva, A.M.R.: An enhanced wiki for requirements engineering. In: EUROMICRO Conference on Software Engineering and Advanced Applications, pp. 87–94. IEEE Computer Society, Los Alamitos (2009)
4. Anderson, K.M., Taylor, R.N., Whitehead Jr., E.J.: Chimera: hypermedia for heterogeneous software development enviroments. ACM Transactions on Information Systems 18(3), 211–245 (2000)
5. Ben-Chaim, Y., Farchi, E., Raz, O.: An effective method for keeping design artifacts up-to-date. In: WIKIS4SE 2009: ICSE Workshop on Wikis for Software Engineering, pp. 1–6 (May 2009)
6. Bernstein, M.: The bookmark and the compass: Orientation tools for hypertext users. SIG OIS Bulletin 9(4) (October 1988)
7. Bernstein, M.: Collage, composites, construction. In: HYPERTEXT 2003: Proceedings of the Fourteenth ACM Conference on Hypertext and Hypermedia, Nottingham, UK, pp. 122–123 (2003)
8. Bryant, S.L., Forte, A., Bruckman, A.: Becoming wikipedian: transformation of participation in a collaborative online encyclopedia. In: GROUP 2005: Proceedings of the 2005 International ACM SIGGROUP Conference on Supporting Group Work, pp. 1–10. ACM, New York (2005)
9. Bush, V.: As we may think. The Atlantic Monthly (July 1945)
10. Cunningham, W.: Design principles of wiki: how can so little do so much? In: WikiSym 2006: Proceedings of the 2006 international symposium on Wikis, pp. 13–14. ACM, New York (2006)
11. Davis, H.C., Hall, W., Heath, I., Hill, G.J., Wilkins, R.J.: Microcosm: An open hypermedia environment for information integration. Tech. Rep. CSTR 92-15, University of Southampton (1992), http://eprints.ecs.soton.ac.uk/713/

12. Decker, B., Ras, E., Rech, J., Jaubert, P., Rieth, M.: Wiki-based stakeholder participation in requirements engineering. IEEE Software 24(2), 28–35 (2007)
13. Engelbart, D.C.: Augmenting human intellect: A conceptual framework. Tech. rep., AFOSR-3233, Stanford Research Institute (October 1962)
14. Francisco-Revilla, L., Shipman, F.M.: Warp: a web-based dynamic spatial hypertext. In: HYPERTEXT 2004: Proceedings of the Fifteenth ACM Conference on Hypertext and hypermedia, pp. 235–236 (2004)
15. Kahan, J., Koivunen, M.R.: Annotea: an open rdf infrastructure for shared web annotations. In: WWW 2001: Proceedings of the 10th International Conference on World Wide Web, pp. 623–632. ACM, New York (2001)
16. Kittur, A., Suh, B., Pendleton, B.A., Chi, E.H.: He says, she says: conflict and coordination in wikipedia. In: CHI 2007: Proceedings of the SIGCHI conference on Human factors in computing systems, pp. 453–462. ACM, New York (2007)
17. Marshall, C.C., Shipman, F.M.: Spatial hypertext: designing for change. Communications of the ACM 38(8), 88–97 (1995)
18. Marshall, C.C., Shipman, F.M., Coombs, J.H.: Viki: spatial hypertext supporting emergent structure. In: ECHT 1994: Proceedings of the 1994 ACM European Conference on Hypermedia Technology, pp. 13–23 (1994)
19. Murthy, S., Maier, D., Delcambre, L., Bowers, S.: Putting integrated information in context: superimposing conceptual models with sparce. In: APCCM 2004: Proceedings of the first Asian-Pacific Conference on Conceptual Modelling, pp. 71–80. Australian Computer Society, Inc. (2004)
20. Nelson, T.H.: The heart of connection: hypermedia unified by transclusion. Communications of the ACM 38(8), 31–33 (1995)
21. Nelson, T.H.: A cosmology for a different computer universe: Data model, mechanisms, virtual machine and visualization infrastructure. Journal of Digital Information 5(1) (2004)
22. Reed, D., John, S.: Web annotator. In: SIGCSE 2003: Proceedings of the 34th SIGCSE Technical Symposium on Computer Science Education, pp. 386–390. ACM, New York (2003)
23. Schaffert, S., Bry, F., Baumeister, J., Kiesel, M.: Semantic wikis. IEEE Software 25(4), 8–11 (2008)
24. Shahin, M., Liang, P., Khayyambashi, M.R.: Architectural design decision: Existing models and tools. In: Joint Working IEEE/IFIP Conference on Software Architecture 2009 and European Conference on Software Architecture 2009, pp. 293–296 (2009)
25. Shipman, F.M., Hsieh, H., Maloor, P., Moore, J.M.: The visual knowledge builder: a second generation spatial hypertext. In: HYPERTEXT 2001: Proceedings of the 12th ACM Conference on Hypertext and Hypermedia, pp. 113–122. ACM, New York (2001)
26. Shipman, F.M., Marshall, C.C., Moran, T.P.: Finding and using implicit structure in human-organized spatial layouts of information. In: CHI 1995: Proceedings of the SIGCHI conference on Human factors in computing systems, pp. 346–353. ACM Press/Addison-Wesley Publishing Co. (1995)
27. Solis, C., Ali, N.: ShyWiki-a spatial hypertext wiki. In: WikiSym 2008: Proceedings of the 2008 International Symposium on Wikis, ACM, New York (2008)
28. Solis, C., Ali, N.: A spatial hypertext wiki for knowledge management. In: CTS 2010: International Symposium on Collaborative Technologies and Systems, 2010, pp. 225–234. IEEE, Los Alamitos (2010)

29. Trigg, R.H., Suchman, L.A., Halasz, F.G.: Supporting collaboration in notecards. In: CSCW 1986: Proceedings of the 1986 ACM Conference on Computer-Supported Cooperative Work, pp. 153–162. ACM, New York (1986)
30. Wagner, C., Bolloju, N.: Supporting knowledge management in organizations with conversational technologies: Discussion forums, weblogs, and wikis. Journal of Database Management 16(2), 1–8 (2005)
31. Wilkinson, D.M., Huberman, B.A.: Cooperation and quality in wikipedia. In: WikiSym 2007: Proceedings of the 2007 International Symposium on Wikis, pp. 157–164. ACM, New York (2007)
32. Zellweger, P.T., Bouvin, N.O., Jehoj, H., Mackinlay, J.D.: Fluid annotations in an open world. In: HYPERTEXT 2001: Proceedings of the 12th ACM Conference on Hypertext and Hypermedia, pp. 9–18. ACM, New York (2001)

Supporting Complex Changes in Evolving Interrelated Web Databanks

Yannis Stavrakas and George Papastefanatos

Institute for the Management of Information Systems
Athens, Greece
{yannis,gpapas}@imis.athena-innovation.gr

Abstract. In this paper we deal with problems occurring in evolving interrelated Web databanks. Examples of such databanks are networks of interlinked scientific repositories on the Web, managed independently by cooperating research groups. We argue that changes should not be treated solely as transforming operations, but rather as first class citizens retaining structural, semantic and temporal characteristics. We propose a graph model called *evo-graph* for capturing in a coherent way the inherent relationship between evolving data and changes applied on them. Evo-graph represents changes as arbitrarily complex objects, similarly to data objects. We discuss the temporal characteristics of the evo-graph, and show how the evo-graph can provide past snapshots of the data. To uniformly express temporal and provenance queries we introduce *evo-path*, a path expression language based on XPath. Evo-path takes advantage of complex changes in the evo-graph in order to answer queries that interpret and elucidate data evolution.

Keywords: Evolution of semistructured data, change-centric management.

1 Introduction

The wide availability and fast publishing of information enabled by the Web unlocked new potential as well as new problems for data management. Particularly, an emerging issue concerns collections of Web data (often scientific) that evolve independently, but remain in some ways interconnected. Those interconnections stem from the cooperative nature of the teams maintaining the collections. Consider, for example, biology research communities [2,13], that produce, consume, and archive rapidly large amounts of data. Scientific communities like that rely increasingly on the Web for collaboration, through the publication and integration of experimental and research results. Moreover, scientists in those communities would often like to review how and why the recorded data have evolved, in order to compare and re-evaluate previous and current conclusions. Such an activity may require a search that moves backwards and forwards in time, spreads across various databanks, and performs complex queries on the semantics of the changes that modified the data. In those cases, simply revising past document snapshots and differences between versions may not be enough.

R. Meersman et al. (Eds.): OTM 2010, Part I, LNCS 6426, pp. 358–375, 2010.

As a simplified example, consider two Web databanks, A and B, maintained by two biology research teams. Databank A is an authoritative source in *miRNAs*. A miRNA is a part of the DNA chain associated with the production of proteins, and is defined by a *start point* in the chain and a *length*. Under certain circumstances different miRNAs can attach themselves at different points on the DNA chain, causing important effects. Databank B contains results of experiments and performs time-consuming calculations for estimating these possible points of attachment for every miRNA. These points of attachment are called *targets*. In Fig. 2, databank A models a miRNA as an ID, a position, and a length, while databank B contains "predictions" that associate miRNA IDs with possible targets.

Databank B, like many other databanks, relies on databank A to get the most recent developments. Knowledge on miRNAs advances rapidly, and A changes often to reflect this. A miRNA in A may change name and properties, split into two distinct miRNAs, merge with another to form a new miRNA, etc. Other databanks, like B, have to check the contents of A regularly, and synchronize their contents with those of A. Research teams will probably need to repeat experiments or calculations in order to adapt to the new facts exposed in A. Such databanks form a *network of interdependent data* that evolve independently. In this network, issues of evolution and provenance are closely related; *evolution information is needed in order to be able to answer provenance queries, not only within a single databank, but across many databanks as well.* Interdependencies among databanks occur because it is common practice for scientific databanks to copy information objects from other scientific databanks.

Until now significant work has been done separately on evolution [5,8,14] and provenance [4] of XML and semistructured data. Specifically in [4] the issue of interdependent Web data has been recognized and studied. However, previous approaches do not cover all the aspects of the problem presented above, since each of them focuses on the specific questions regarding the framework it addresses. From the example above it becomes clear that in some cases evolution cannot be studied separately from provenance.

In this paper we argue that in cooperative systems where evolution and provenance issues are paramount, changes should not be treated solely as transformation operations on the data, but rather as first class citizens retaining structural, semantic, and temporal characteristics. Modeling complex changes explicitly can leverage a number of new interesting queries, and provide additional semantic information for interpreting past data. We propose a graph model called *evo-graph* for capturing in a coherent way the inherent relationship between evolving data and changes applied on them. We employ this model for representing simple as well as composite evolution operations. We discuss in detail the temporal characteristics of the evo-graph, and show how the evo-graph can provide past snapshots of the data. Finally, we introduce *evo-path*, a path expression language for evo-graph that extends XPath. Evo-path takes advantage of the complex changes in the evo-graph in order to answer queries about the provenance of data, and the interpretation of data evolution.

The structure of the paper is as follows. In section 2 we discuss related work. In section 3 we define evo-graph and give an extended example based on databanks A and B mentioned earlier. In section 4 we present the temporal properties of the evo-graph, and show how temporal snapshots can be extracted from the evo-graph. In section 5 we introduce evo-path and give example queries that take advantage of the complex changes represented in evo-graph. Finally, section 6 concludes the paper.

2 Related Work

Modeling and managing evolving Web data have recently attracted a growing interest in the database research community. We classify the various approaches as follows.

Change Detection, Versioning and XML Diffs. In one of the early approaches [5], the authors deal with the representation of changes in semistructured data, and propose DOEM, an extension of OEM capable of representing changes as annotations on nodes and edges. They propose a query language, named CHOREL, for retrieving information related to the history of nodes and edges, exploiting the change annotations. In [14] a change-centric method for managing versions in XML data is presented. The authors employ a *diff* algorithm for detecting changes between two versions of a document. Changes are represented either as edit scripts, simple deltas or completed deltas. A similar approach is introduced in [7,8], where instead of deltas calculations, a referenced-based identification of each object is used across different versions. New versions hold only the elements that are different from the previous version whereas a reference is used for pointing to the unchanged elements of past versions. In [11] the authors propose MXML, a extension of XML that uses context information to express time and models multifaceted documents. Other approaches, such as the X-Diff algorithm [19] and [6], focus mainly on the detection and less on the representation of the changes between two documents. Recently, there are works that deal with the detection of changes in semantic data, such as [16].

Temporal approaches to evolving data. An annotated bibliography on temporal and evolution aspects for Web data is presented in [12]. Most temporal approaches [1,5] enrich data elements with temporal attributes for holding valid and / or transaction time, and extend query syntax with conditions on the time validity of data [9]. In [17], a temporal model for XML is introduced, which models an XML document as a directed graph, and attaches transaction time information at the edges of the graph. The authors provide techniques for implementing the model with XML, for indexing temporal documents, and for performing temporal queries. Techniques for evaluating temporal queries on semistructured data are presented in [10,18]. In [10] the authors propose a temporal query language for adding valid time support in XQuery. In [18] the notion of a temporally grouped data model is employed for uniformly representing and querying successive versions of a document. In a more recent work [15], the authors extend this technique for publishing the history of a relational database in XML. The authors introduce the PRIMA system, where they employ a set of schema modification operators (SMOs) for representing the mappings between successive schema versions.

Archiving and Provenance in semistructured data. Work on data provenance has been mainly directed towards relational data. As far as XML and semistructured data are concerned, the archiving and management of curated databases is addressed in [3].

The authors develop an archiving technique for scientific data that uses timestamps for each version, whereas all versions are merged into one hierarchy. By identifying the semantic continuity of elements and merging them into one data structure, this approach is capable of providing meaningful change descriptions. The authors exploit the archive to answer certain temporal queries, such as retrieval of any specific version, and retrieval of the history of an element. In [4] the authors provide a technique for modeling and recording provenance information in curated databases. They consider evolution operations that span across multiple databases, such as copying and pasting data from one database to another.

Compared to the above approaches, ours has the following distinctive characteristics. First of all, we do not detect changes through *diffs*, but rather we assume that changes are introduced in our model as they occur. Changes in our approach are complex objects operating on data, and exhibit structural, semantic, and temporal properties: they can be part of other changes, correlate to each other, be transactional, long-termed or instant. These properties allows our evolution model to answer queries about "what" has evolved over time, but also to provide information about "why" and "how" data have evolved. Second of all, temporal information is assigned to the changes rather than the data, and characterizes the time that a change occurred. Based on this, the validity timespan of each version of an evolving object is determined. As a result, temporal conditions can be expressed uniformly in both data and changes. Third of all, our approach employs the same principles for modeling evolution events within a single database, as well as capturing interdependencies between disparate databases. Structuring changes into complex objects enable us to address provenance and evolution issues in a uniform manner.

3 Modeling Evolution Using Complex Changes

In this section we propose *evo-graph*, a graph model for interrelated evolving data, where changes are given equal importance as data. We present a set of basic change operations, we define evo-graph and discuss how it is constructed, and we give an example of using evo-graph in an extensive biological data scenario.

3.1 Evo-Graph: Changes as First-Class Citizens

A number of data models have been proposed in the past for semistructured data and XML [5,21]. In general, those models represent data using labeled rooted directed graphs, with values on the leaves. In this paper, we assume that Web data are represented at any given instance by a rooted acyclic graph, called from now on by the generic name *snap-graph* (see Fig. 2). A snap-graph consists of data nodes (complex and atomic), and edges connecting the nodes. In addition to the snap-graph components, we introduce the following new concepts in evo-graph (see Fig. 3):

- *Change nodes* are nodes that represent change events: basic change operations, and complex changes. Change nodes appear as triangles, to distinguish from conventional circular data nodes.
- *Change edges* connect a complex change node to the (complex or atomic) change nodes it consists of. Change edges are represented by dashed lines.

- *Evolution edges* connect each change node with two data nodes: the object version before the change and the object version after the change. Evolution edges appear as thick lines.

The evo-graph is constructed step by step, as changes occur at the current version of the snap-graph. We will use the following five *basic change operations* for the snap-graph:

- *create*: creates a new child node, and connects it with the parent node.
- *add*: adds an edge between two existing nodes, effectively adding a child node.
- *remove*: removes an edge, deleting a child.
- *update*: updates the value of an atomic node.
- *clone*: creates a deep copy B of a subtree A, and connects B under the same parent node as A.

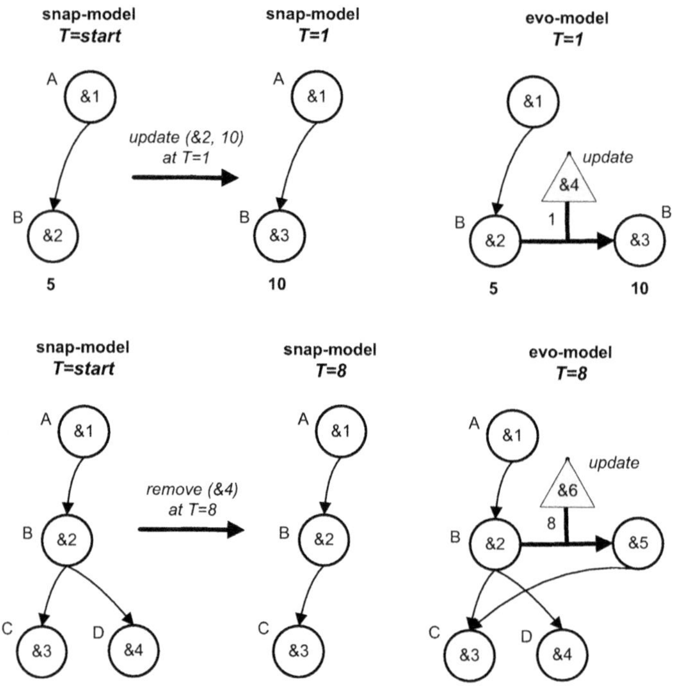

Fig. 1. Modeling of basic change operation with evo-graph

Our approach is to create a new version of an object in the evo-graph whenever a change occurs to a child of that object. Each change creates a new change node and a new evolution edge, connecting the previous version with the new version of the object. Fig. 1 shows how the basic change operations *update* and *remove* are represented in the evo-graph. Nodes contain their respective node ID, and node labels are placed next to each node. In the case of *remove*, when node &4 is removed from the children of node &2, a new version of node &2 with ID &5 is created in the evo-graph to reflect this change. As a general rule, changes that affect child nodes create new versions of the parent nodes. The same holds for *update*, since the atomic node &2 can be considered as the parent of an implied "value node".

The definition of evo-graph follows.

Evo-graph definition. The *evo-graph* is a finite directed acyclic graph $G = (V_D, V_C, E_D, E_C, E_E, r_D, r_C, f^L, f^V)$, such that:

1. *Data nodes* are divided into *complex* and *atomic*: $V_D = V_D^c \cup V_D^a$.
2. *Change nodes* are divided into *complex* and *atomic*: $V_C = V_C^c \cup V_C^a$.
3. *Data edges* depart from every complex data node, $E_D \subseteq (V_D^c \times V_D)$. Only one data edge may exist between two nodes.
4. *Changes edges* depart from every complex change node, $E_C \subseteq (V_C^c \times V_C)$, with each $v_C \in (V_C - r_C)$ having exactly one parent.
5. *Evolution edges* are directed edges that connect one change node with two data nodes: $E_E \subseteq (V_D \times V_C \times V_D)$. For every change node $v_C \in V_C$ there exists in E_E an evolution edge $e_E = (v_D, v_C, v_D')$, with $f^L(v_D) = f^L(v_D')$. The following directions are implied by e_E: $v_D \rightarrow v_D'$, $v_D \rightarrow v_C$, and $v_C \rightarrow v_D'$.
6. $r_D \in V_D$ is the *data root*, with the property that there exists a path formed by data edges and evolution edges from r_D to every other node in V_D.
7. $r_C \in V_C$ is the *change root*, with the property that there exists a path formed by change edges from r_C to every other node in V_C.
8. f^L is a function that assigns labels to nodes, such that:
   - $f^L(x) \in C$ if $x \in V_C^a$, where C is the set of names of the *basic change operations*, and
   - $f^L(x) \in L$ if $x \in V_C^c \cup V_D$, where L is the set of all other labels.
9. f^V is a function that assigns values to nodes, such that:
   - $f^V(x) \in A$ if $x \in V_D^a$, where A is the set of atomic values, and
   - $f^V(x) \in T$ if $x \in V_C^a$, where T is the set of timestamps.

The number assigned to each atomic change represents the time instance the change occurred. We assume a linear time domain and two special time instances: *start*, representing the beginning of time, and *now*, representing the current moment. The next section presents how those time instances propagate to complex changes and to the rest of the evo-graph, in order to get temporal snapshots of the data.

Intuitively, the evo-graph consists of two correlated graphs: a data graph, and a tree of changes. The data graph defines the structure of data, while the change graph defines the structure of changes on data. These two graphs interconnect by means of evolution edges, which denote the data object affected by each change. Consequently there are two roots, the data root and the change root. The change root is assumed to be always linked to an evolution edge that originates from the version *T=start* of the

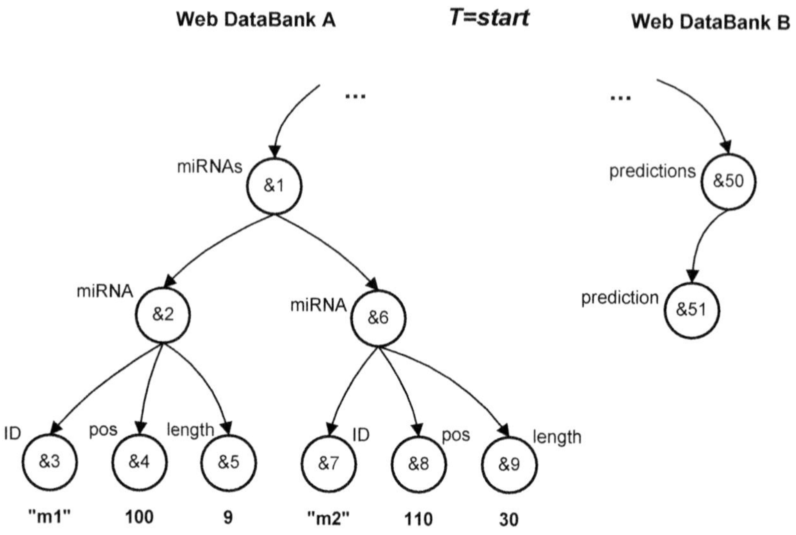

Fig. 2. State of Web databanks A and B at *T=start*

data root, and points to the version *T=now* of the data root. Moreover, there are two types of paths: the change paths that follow successive change edges, and the data paths that follow successive data and / or evolution edges.

The main objective of the evo-graph is to represent arbitrarily complex changes. The semantics of a complex change is implied by the structure of the change, as defined by the users of the databank. An atomic change can only represent one of the basic change operations, however there is no restriction on how atomic changes are combined to form complex changes. Note that, as long as the set of basic change operations is *complete* (operations can lead the snap-graph to any possible state), *the choice of basic change operations is not restricted* by the evo-graph: alternative sets of may be adopted, while the properties of evo-graph remain largely insensitive to which set is selected.

3.2 Recording Evolution and Databank Interrelations Using Complex Changes

Based on the example introduced in section 1, in this section we present a simple scenario which demonstrates how the evo-graph can be used to record dependencies and changes in two evolving interrelated Web databanks that publish bioscientific data: databank A, and databank B. Through this example we attempt to establish the importance of treating complex changes as first class citizens, since they convey indispensable semantic information for interpreting the evolution of data as well as the reasons for their current and previous states.

We assume that databank A initially contains only two miRNAs, while databank B contains a single prediction object without any data yet, as it is depicted in Fig. 2.

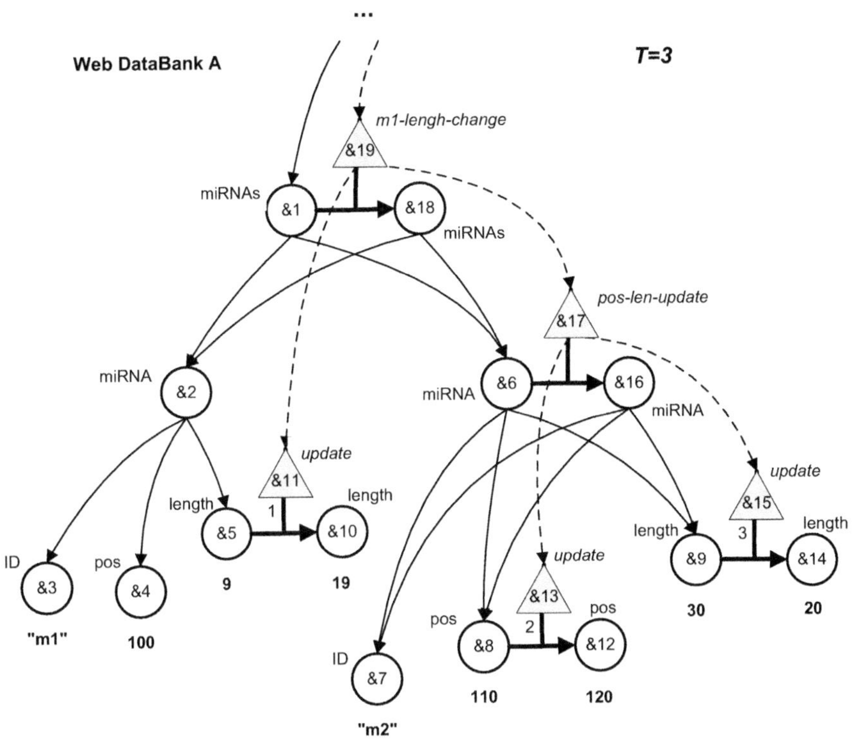

Fig. 3. Evo-graph for Web databank A at *T=3*

Fig. 3 shows the evo-graph for databank A at T=3. For simplicity, the data root and the change root are omitted. At time instance 1 (T=1) the length of the miRNA with ID "m1" is updated from 9 to 19. This basic change operation is expressed by the change node &11 that creates a new version of the length (node &10). For simplicity, the arguments of change operations are implied and do not appear on the figures. After this update, "m1" occupies the positions 100 to 119. This, however, causes a collision with miRNA "m2", which on T=1 starts at position 110. Therefore, the start position of "m2" (node &8) must be updated as a consequence of the change occurred to "m1". For the sake of the example, we assume that the end position of "m2" at the DNA chain remains fixed. Therefore, an update of the start position of "m2" must be followed by an update of its length, so that its end position remains the same. This is modeled by the complex change *pos-len-update* that appears in Fig. 3 as node &17. This complex change creates a new version of the specific miRNA, and consists of two atomic changes: an *update* of the start position of "m2" (node &13 introduces node &12), and an *update* on the length of "m2" (node &15 introduces node &14).

Change nodes &11 and &17 are further composed into the complex operation *m1-length-change*, represented by node &19. This operation is associated with node &1

and causes the creation of a new version of the *miRNAs* node (node &18). Complex change nodes can represent relationships between changes that take place in disparate places of the databank, *and would otherwise be treated as unrelated*. In this way, it is possible to *model any change operation*, like for instance, *move*, *split*, *merge*, etc.

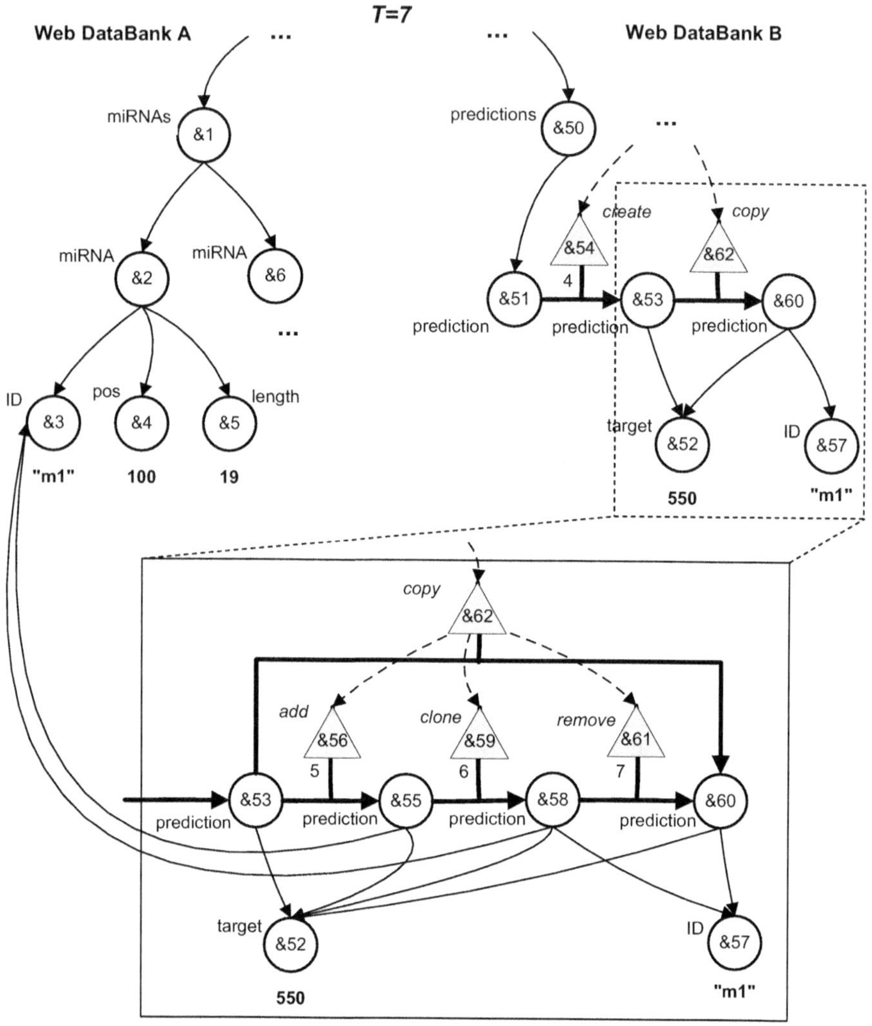

Fig. 4. Evo-graph for Web databank B at *T=7*

Fig. 4 depicts the evo-graph for databank B at T=7. Databank B decides to include miRNA "m1", and publish a prediction for its target. At T=4 a new *target* node is added under the *prediction* node in databank B. The new data node (&52) with label *target* and value 550 is created by the basic change operation *create*, which is represented by the change node &54. Instead of placing node &52 under the existing prediction node &51, a new version of the prediction node is introduced (&53).

Therefore, the change operation represented by &54 transforms the data node &51 to the data node &53 by creating the child node &52.

Now that the *target* data is inserted, the next step is to insert the ID of the miRNA associated with this target. We assume that the ID in question is copied from databank A to databank B. It is common practice to copy data among Web databanks, which leads to a number of issues related to data provenance [4]. The main objective is to *copy data from independently managed databanks, while maintaining evidence of this transaction.*

The *copy* change operation is a complex operation represented in Fig. 4 by the change node &62. The change node &62 transforms node &53 to node &60, by adding the child node &57, which is a copy of the node &3 in databank A. Due to space limitations, the *copy* operation is fully presented at the bottom of Fig. 4. It consists of three basic change operations, *add*, *clone*, and *remove*, that take place at T=5, T=6, and T=7 respectively. The basic change operation *add* connects a new version (&55) of the *prediction* node to the child node &3 of the databank A (we assume here a mechanism for referring to nodes residing at disparate sites). The basic change operation *clone* creates a (deep) copy of node &3 as node &57. Finally, the basic change operation *remove* deletes the edge from node &58 to node &3, leading to the final version of the *prediction* node (&60).

Summarizing, this example demonstrates how the evo-graph models evolution using arbitrarily complex changes, with sub-changes applied to objects that can reside far from each other in the data graph. It also shows how the same principles can be used to create and maintain links between disparate databanks, as in the case of copying and pasting information.

4 Temporal Properties of the Evo-graph

Evo-graph captures in a uniform way multiple data versions along with the evolution operations applied on each version, and represents them in a coherent graph enriched with temporal information. A key difference from existing versioning and temporal approaches on XML and semistructured data is that the time dimension is not assigned on the data elements of the graph (i.e., data nodes and edges); instead it is the change nodes that retain and propagate all temporal information on the evo-graph. A timestamp t is assigned to each atomic change node v_C^a, denoting the time on which this change occurred. Two or more change nodes may have identical timestamps as long as they correspond to changes that occurred at the same time.

In this section, we present the main mechanisms for propagating time information from the atomic change nodes towards the rest of the graph elements. Furthermore, we provide a technique for reducing the evo-graph to the snap-graph that holds under a given timestamp.

4.1 Propagation of Timespans

As already mentioned, each atomic change node in the evo-graph is assigned a timestamp denoting the time instance that the change occurred. The timestamp of a complex change is then considered to be the timestamp of its most "recent" child, and denotes the time instance the complex change is completed. Thus, timestamps propagate upwards in the change tree, imposing a partial order on changes. Notice that different change nodes with the same timestamp are allowed in our model, implying the concurrent occurrence of the respective changes. In this case, concurrent change nodes must not belong to the same direct parent, i.e., they cannot be siblings.

Change timestamps determine the *validity timespan* of data nodes and data edges. Every change affects the validity timespan of the two data nodes it is connected with (through the respective evolution edge), in the sense that the previous version of an object stops being valid the moment a new version is created. Timespans propagate to child data nodes, since a child can only exist if it has a valid parent.

In what follows we specify the process for obtaining the validity timespans for the data nodes in the evo-graph. We give two different procedures: one *top-to-bottom*, for batch processing the timespans of an evo-graph, and one *incremental*, for updating the timespans in the evo-graph after a single modification has taken place. We define timespans as unions of time intervals of the form [t1..t2) ∪ [t3..t4] ∪ ..., and we use two special values, *start* and *now*, to represent the beginning of time and the current time, respectively. Note that intervals may be open or closed on the borders, excluding or including their left / right values.

Top-to-bottom propagation. The top-to-bottom propagation goes through the entire graph and calculates all the timespans from scratch. It performs a DFS (depth first search) traversal on the graph starting from data root r_D and assuming an initial timespan `[start..now]`, and assigns a timespan to all nodes and edges. Whenever encountering a change node, the algorithm propagates the timestamp of the change node to the data nodes and edges of the graph. The steps of the algorithm are given below.

- *Step 1.* Set as the current node the data root r_D
- *Step 2.* For each outgoing data edge $e_i=(r_D,x_i) \in E_D$ set $T(e_i)=T(r_D)$, i.e. the timespan of each node is propagated to all outgoing edges.
- *Step 3.* Set $T(x_i)=\cup T(x_k,x_i)$, i.e. the timespan of a node is equal to the union of the timespans of all incoming edges, or equivalently as stated in step 2 to the union of all timespans of its parents.
- *Step 4.* If an evolution edge $e_{ev}=(x_i,c,x'_i) \in E_E$ exists, then for each outgoing evolution edge $e_{ev}=(x_i,c,x'_i) \subseteq E_E$ with timestamp t_c do steps *4a* to *4d*.
- *Step 4a.*The timespan of x_i becomes equal to $T(x_i)=T(x_i)\cap[0..t_c)$.
- *Step 4b.*The timespan of x'_i becomes equal to $T(x'_i)=T(x'_i)\cup[t_c..now]$.
- *Step 4c.* Consider x_i as root and return to step 2, i.e. propagate the new timespan of x_i towards the paths starting from this node.
- *Step 4d.* Set $x_i = x'_i$ and repeat step 4, i.e., check if an evolution edge starts from x'_i.
- *Step 5.* Else, consider x_i as root and return to step 2.

The evo-graph of Fig. 3 is shown with time annotations in Fig. 5.

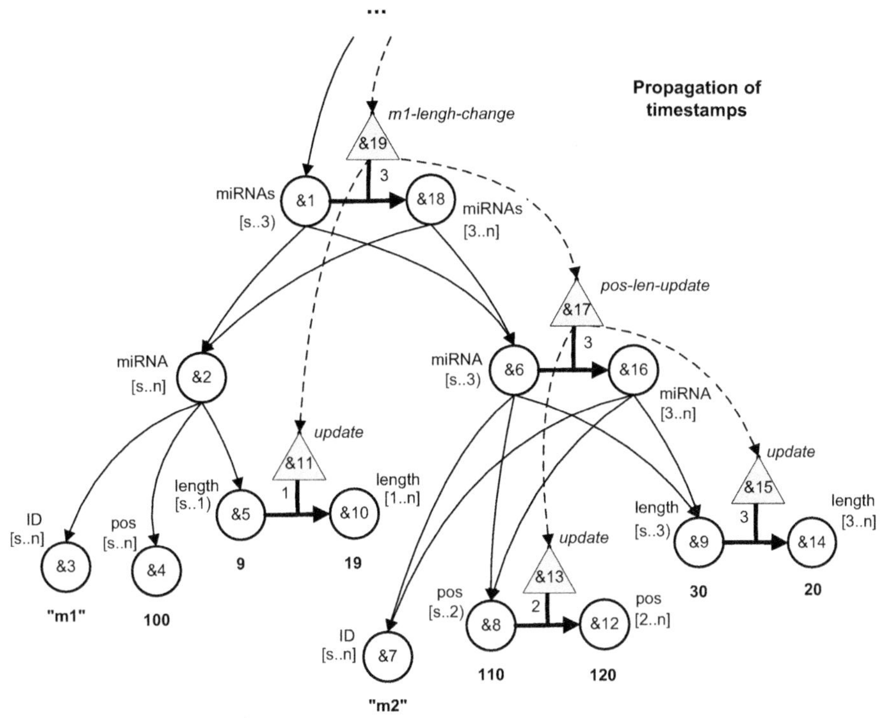

Fig. 5. Time annotated evo-graph of Fig. 3

Incremental propagation. When a new change occurs on a node of the graph, the timestamp assigned to the new change node affects only the time validity of the previous and current version of the node sustaining the change. The incremental propagation adjusts the timespans of these nodes and propagates the new timespans to their descendants only. Let us assume that an evolution change c with timestamp t_c is applied on node x_i with a timespan $T(x_i)$, creating a new evolved node x'_i and an evolution edge (x_i, c, x'_i). Then:

- The timespan of x_i becomes $T(x_i)=T(x_i)\cap[0..t_c)$. The timespan is propagated to all accessible paths, considering x_i as root and executing the top-to-bottom propagation at step 2.
- The timespan of x'_i becomes $T(x'_i)=T(x'_i)\cup[t_c..now]$. Similarly, we consider x'_i as root and propagate the timespan to all accessible paths.

The assignment of timespan to graph elements can be optimized by omitting the step 4d that propagates downwards the two subtrees, and by retaining the timespans only for the nodes involved in an evolution edge. For all other nodes, we assume that they inherit the union of the timespans of their parents.

4.2 Snapshot Reduction of the Evo-graph

The temporal information on the evo-graph allow us to perform a special operation called *snapshot reduction*, for extracting the specific version holding under a given time instance. Snapshot reduction takes as input an evo-graph plus a time instance, and produces a snap-graph consisting only of those data nodes and data edges for which their validity timespan contains the given time instance. The algorithm is presented in Table 1.

Table 1. Snapshot Reduction algorithm

```
Input: an evo-graph
    G= (V_D, V_C, E_D, E_C, E_E, r_D, r_C)
    a requested time instance t
Output:
    a snapshot graph G'=(V_D',E_D')
begin
    V_D' = r_D
    get_snapshot(G, G', t , r_D)
end

get_snapshot(G, G', t , x_0)
begin
for each edge(x_0,x_i)⊆E_D {
  if e_ev=(x_i,c,x'_i)⊆E_E exists {
    x_i=get_version(G,G',t,x_i)}
  if t⊆T(x_i){
    E_D' = E_D'∪(x_0,x_i)
      if (x_i⊄V_D'){
        V_D'=V_D'∪x_i
        get_snapshot(G, G', t , x_i)}}
}
End
```

```
get_version(G, G', t , x_i)
begin
stack s, list visited
s->put(x_i)
while(!s->empty){
  s->pop(x_i), visited->add(x_i)
  if t⊆T(x_i):
    return(x_i)
  else:
    for each (x_i,c,x'_i)⊆E_E {
      if x'_i⊄ visited:
        s->put(x'_i)}
}
end
```

The algorithm starts from the data root and calls the `get_snapshot` method, which performs a recursive DFS on the evo-graph. When a data node attached to an evolution edge is met, an inner DFS traversal (named `get_version`) is performed across the successive versions of this node for retrieving the version which is valid for the requested time instance. The algorithm connects this version with its parent, and continues the traversal downwards all paths starting from this node.

The resulting snap-graph does not contain any change nodes or evolution edges, and can be easily transformed to XML format, following a non replicated top-down traversal [17*]. The snap-graph for the time instance T=3* of the evo-graph in Fig. 5 *is shown in* Fig. 6.

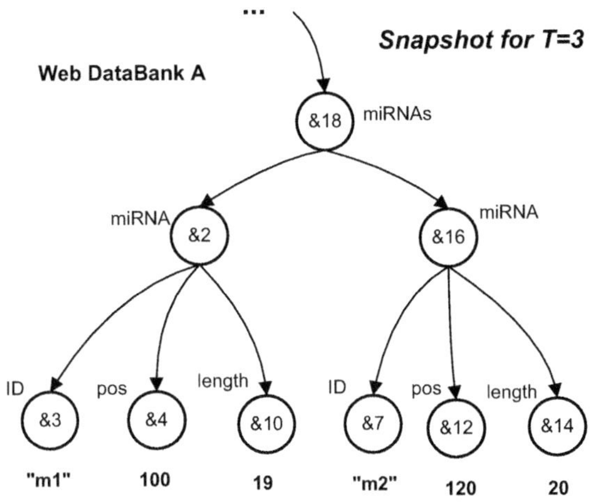

Fig. 6. Snap-graph for *T=3* of the evo-graph in Fig. 5

5 Introducing Evo-Path Expressions

XPath (XML Path Language) [20] *is a language proposed* by W3C for addressing portions of a XML document. The basic structural unit of XPath is the *XPath expression*, which may return either a node-set, a string, a Boolean, or a number. The most common kind of XPath expression, which is used in XPath to select nodes or node-sets in an XML document, is the *path expression* (or *location path expression*).

In this section we propose *evo-path* as an extension of XPath used to navigate through evo-graphs. Similarly to XPath, evo-path uses path expressions as a sequence of steps to get from one data node to another data node (or set of data nodes). In addition to XPath, evo-path uses constructs that allows the navigation through change nodes, plus predicates that express conditions on the connections between change nodes and data nodes (conditions on evolution edges).

5.1 Extending XPath for Accommodating Change Path Expressions

There are two kinds of path expressions in evo-paths: *data path expressions*, and *change path expressions*.

Data path expressions start from the data root of the evo-graph and return data nodes. Similarly to XPath they are written as a sequence of *location steps* that get from one node (the current *context node*) to another node or set of nodes. The location steps are separated by "/" characters, and have the following syntax [20]:

```
axis::node_test[pred_1][pred_2]...[pred_n]
```

Like XPath, in evo-path a predicate consists of an expression enclosed in square brackets. A predicate serves to filter a sequence, retaining some items and discarding others. Multiple predicates are allowed. For each item in the input sequence, the predicate expression is evaluated and a truth value is returned. The items for which the truth value of the predicate is true are retained, while those for which the predicate evaluates to false are discarded. Shortcuts can be applied in data path expressions just like in XPath, as shown by the following two equivalent evo-paths:

```
/child::A/descendant-or-self::node()/child::B/
                                  child::*[position()=1]
/A//B/*[1]
```

Change path expressions start from the change root of the evo-graph and return change nodes. They have the same syntax as data path expressions, but are enclosed in square brackets:

```
</location_step_1/location_step_2/…/location_step_N>
```

A *temporal predicate* is introduced in evo-path in order to express temporal conditions on the evo-graph nodes. The form of the temporal predicate is as follows:

```
[ts() operator {timespan_1, timespan_2, …, timespan_N}]
```

where `operator` is one of the `in`, `contains`, `meets`, and `equals`. The `ts()` evaluates to the timespan of the context node, which is calculated through the process described in section 4.1. The operators cover the standard operations between sets. The use of `not` is allowed in front of any of the operators.

Evolution predicates are used in evo-path to assert the existence of evolution edges connecting data and change nodes at specific points of the graph. The form of the evolution predicate is as follows:

```
[evo-filter data_path_expr | change_path_expr]
```

The `evo-filter` can be one of: `evo-before()`, `evo-after()`, and `evo-both()`. The following examples explain the use of evolution predicates in data path expressions and change path expressions.

```
</a/b [evo-both /A/B]>
/A/B [evo-after() <//update>]
```

The first example returns the change nodes `b` that are children of the change root `a`, but only if they are applied (through an evolution edge) to some data node `B`, child of the data root `A`. The second example returns the data nodes `B`, children of the data root `A`, only if they are the *result* of an *update* basic change operation. Note that in case there exists a sequence of data nodes `B` connected though consequent evolution edges, the data path expression `/A/B` will evaluate to all of these data nodes. The filters `evo-before()` and `evo-after()` retain only those data nodes that are on the correct side (left and right respectively) of the change specified by the evolution predicate. On the other hand, `evo-both()` returns *true* for the data nodes on both sides of the evolution edge.

5.2 Evo-path Example Queries

In this section we give a few examples to demonstrate the expressiveness of evo-path on a number of query categories (in italics). Moreover, we discuss the evaluation of evo-path expressions against the figures of section 3.2.

History of a data element (temporal queries). While browsing the current snapshot of the databank A (see Fig. 6*)* a bio-scientist named Brian realizes that the length of the miRNA with ID 'm2' is not what he expected, and engages in finding out what has happened and why. He starts by retrieving the previous versions of the data node &14 (see Fig. 3*):*

```
//miRNA [ID='m2'] /length [ts() not covers {now}]
```

This is a data path expression that returns the `length` data nodes of miRNA objects with `ID='m2'`. The temporal predicate `ts()` evaluates to *false* for the current version of `length` (&14) that holds under now, and *true* for every other version. The evo-path returns node &9 in Fig. 3.

Changes applied on data elements (evolution queries). Brian checks the value of node &9 and wants to learn more about the hows and whys for updating the value 30 of `length` to the current value 20. He wants to get all the complex changes that contain the relevant `update` operation (node &15), and check whether this `update` was part of a larger modification within the *miRNAs* subtree:

```
<//* [evo-both() //miRNAs//*]
     [.//update [evo-after() //length
                     [ts() covers {now}] = 20]]>
```

The first predicate of the above evo-path returns all the change nodes that are applied to a `miRNAs` data node or any of their descendants. On the next lines, the second predicate dictates that only the changes that have an `update` descendant applied on a `length` object with current value 20 can be returned. The evo-path returns nodes &19 and &17 of Fig. 3.

Relationships between change elements (causality queries). Realizing that the update of the length of 'm2' has something to do with the complex change &19 `m1-length-change`, Brian decides to check all the prior versions of the data objects affected by `m1-length-change` and its descendant changes.

```
//* [evo-before() <//m1-length-change//*>]
```

Not taking the predicate into account, the data path expression evaluates to all the data nodes in Fig. 3. *The evolution predicate evaluates to true* only for the data nodes that are connected through an evolution edge with a `m1-length-change` change node (&19) or one of its descendant change nodes (&11, &17, &13, &15). These nodes are &1, &18, &5, &10, &6, &16, &8, &12, &9, and &14. However, due to `evo-before()` in the evolution predicate, only the following nodes are returned as the result: &1, &5, &6, &8, &9. Brian links the dots and realizes that the updates on the miRNA 'm2' are a consequence of the change of the `length` of 'm1'.

Relationships between disparate data elements (provenance queries). After a while (say at *T=100*), Betty, a bio-scientist navigating databank B, comes across the prediction for the target 550 (node &52 in Fig. 4*), which seems interesting. She sees that this ta*rget is attributed to a miRNA with ID 'm1' (node &57). See looks it up on a number of sources, but she cannot find anything relevant, because 'm1' has been merged some time ago with 'm2' forming a new miRNA with ID 'm1-2' (not shown in the figures). Betty wants to follow back the trace of the node &57, and being aware of the common practice of copying data between databanks, checks whether node &57 was copied:

```
<//clone [evo-after() //prediction[ID='m1']]>
```

The evo-path above returns the change `clone` whose result was a `prediction` data node with an `ID` child node that has value 'm1'. The node returned is &59, which stands for the basic change operation `clone(&3,&57)`. The arguments of the `clone` basic change operation reveal node &3 as the origin of node &57 (we assume a mechanism for referring across databanks). Now Betty can follow the evolution of node &3 in databank A, and see it is now known under another ID.

Summarizing, the modeling of complex changes in evo-graph enables a wide range of useful queries to be expressed in a uniform way. Building a full-fledged query language based on evo-paths will allow for much more interesting queries like, for example, "retrieve the data objects that have been copied from databank A to other databanks", that would return node &57 in Fig. 4. Such queries will leverage the exploration of interdependencies between databanks, and will greatly facilitate the synchronization between their contents. This will promote the cooperation of scientific teams, since currently they devote a lot of time for manually monitoring related databanks and keeping their data updated.

6 Conclusions

In this paper we have argued that treating changes as first class citizens in data management systems enables a uniform solution to a number of evolution and provenance issues in collections of interrelated Web data. We proposed evo-graph, a graph model that represents, in addition to data, arbitrarily complex changes. We discussed the temporal characteristics of evo-graph, and showed how it can produce temporal snapshots of the data. We introduced evo-path, an extension of XPath for navigating and querying evo-graphs. Using throughout the paper a simplified biology-inspired example, we showed how evo-graph and evo-path can be used in a scenario that employs evolving scientific data. Summarizing, the paper asserts the potential of using *change objects* just like data objects in models and queries.

Future work will be directed towards: (a) building a query language around evo-path, (b) specifying a language for defining types (templates) for complex changes, (c) implementing prototype tools, and (d) experimenting and evaluating our approach in terms of modeling complexity, query language expressiveness, and efficiency.

References

1. Amagasa, T., Yoshikawa, M., Uemura, S.: A Data Model for Temporal XML Documents. In: Ibrahim, M., Küng, J., Revell, N. (eds.) DEXA 2000. LNCS, vol. 1873, p. 334. Springer, Heidelberg (2000)
2. Bairoch, A., et al.: The Universal Protein Resource (UniProt). Nucleic Acids Research 33, D154–D159 (2005) Database issue, http://www.uniprot.org/
3. Buneman, P., Khanna, S., Tajima, K., Tan, W.C.: Archiving Scientific Data. ACM Transactions on Database Systems 20, 1–39 (2004)
4. Buneman, P., Chapman, A.P., Cheney, J.: Provenance Management in Curated Databases. In: SIGMOD 2006 (2006)
5. Chawathe, S., Abiteboul, S., Widom, J.: Managing Historical Semistructured Data. Journal of Theory and Practice of Object Systems 24(4), 1–20 (1999)
6. Chawathe, S., Rajaraman, A., Garcia-Molina, H., Widom, J.: Change Detection in Hierarchically Structured Information. In: SIGMOD 1996 (1996)
7. Chien, S.-Y., Tsotras, V.J., Zaniolo, C., Zhang, D.: Storing and Querying Multiversion XML Documents using Durable Node Numbers. In: WISE 2001 (2001)
8. Chien, S.-Y., Tsotras, V.J., Zaniolo, C.: Efficient Management of Multiversion Documents by Object Referencing. In: VLDB 2001, pp. 291–300 (2001)
9. Dyreson, C.: Observing Transaction-Time Semantics with TTXPath. In: WISE 2001 (2001)
10. Gao, D., Snodgrass, R.T.: Temporal Slicing in the Evaluation of XML Queries. In: VLDB 2003 (2003)
11. Gergatsoulis, M., Stavrakas, Y.: Representing Changes in XML Documents using Dimensions. In: Bellahsène, Z., Chaudhri, A.B., Rahm, E., Rys, M., Unland, R. (eds.) XSym 2003. LNCS, vol. 2824, pp. 208–222. Springer, Heidelberg (2003)
12. Grandi, F.: Introducing an Annotated Bibliography on Temporal and Evolution Aspects in the World Wide Web. SIGMOD Record 33(2), 84–86 (2004)
13. Harris, M.A., et al.: The Gene Ontology (GO) database and informatics. Nucleic Acids Research, Database issue D258–D261 32(1) (2004), http://www.geneontology.org/
14. Marian, A., Abiteboul, S., Cobena, G., Mignet, L.: Change-Centric Management of Versions in an XML Warehouse. In: VLDB 2001 (2001)
15. Moon, H.J., Curino, C., Deutsch, A., Hou, C.Y., Zaniolo, C.: Managing and querying transaction-time databases under schema evolution. In: VLDB 2008, pp. 882–895 (2008)
16. Papavassiliou, V., Flouris, G., Fundulaki, I., Kotzinos, D., Christophides, V.: On Detecting High-Level Changes in RDF/S KBs. In: Bernstein, A., Karger, D.R., Heath, T., Feigenbaum, L., Maynard, D., Motta, E., Thirunarayan, K. (eds.) ISWC 2009. LNCS, vol. 5823, pp. 473–488. Springer, Heidelberg (2009)
17. Rizzolo, F., Vaisman, A.A.: Temporal XML: modeling, indexing, and query processing. VLDB J. 17(5), 1179–1212 (2008)
18. Wang, F., Zaniolo, C.: Temporal Queries in XML Document Archives and Web Warehouses. In: TIME 2003, pp. 47–55 (2003)
19. Wang, Y., DeWitt, D.J., Cai, J.: X-Diff: An Effective Change Detection Algorithm for XML Documents. In: ICDE 2003 (2003)
20. W3C. XML Path Language (XPath) 2.0 (January 2007), http://www.w3.org/TR/xpath20/
21. W3C. The XML data model (August 2005), http://www.w3.org/XML/Datamodel.html

Workflow ART

Ganna Monakova and Frank Leymann

University of Stuttgart, Stuttgart, Germany
lastname@iaas.uni-stuttgart.de
http://www.iaas.uni-stuttgart.de

Abstract. Business processes are obliged to follow numerous constraints, such as compliance regulations, service level agreements, security regulations, and budget constraints. To be able to understand relations between different constraint types and their impact on the business, a common constraint specification framework is required. This work presents a framework that provides visual support for analysis of the dependencies between the different constraints a business process has to adhere to by mapping logical constraints to the spatial restrictions. This enables a business process designer to gain insight into how different constraints influence the process as a whole.

Keywords: workflow modelling, workflow analysis, workflow constraints, constraint classification, workflow dimensions, workflow design.

1 Introduction

Business processes are obliged to follow numerous constraints, such as compliance regulations, service level agreements, security regulations, and budget constraints. To be able to understand the relations between different constraint types and their impact on the business, a common constraint specification framework is required. Currently there are two main approaches to constraint specification: action based and resource based. Action based approaches are used to specify the model of the business process, either imperatively using BPEL or BPMN, or declaratively using, for example, Linear Temporal Logic (LTL) to specify temporal and causal dependencies between actions executions. However, to enable execution of a specified workflow, resource based constraints have to be considered as suitable resources must be available to execute the process. Resource based constraints include restrictions on resource allocations, resource availability, and capacity. These types of constraints are particularly important for the scheduling algorithms used in production and scientific workflows, for example. Whilst both types of constraints are required for a workflow specification and execution, the relations between the two constraint types have not been analysed sufficiently.

In general constraints can be divided into two categories: constraints which directly express business semantic of a process and constraints which put restrictions on realisation of the specified semantic. An example of the first type

R. Meersman et al. (Eds.): OTM 2010, Part I, LNCS 6426, pp. 376–393, 2010.

of constraint is *Shipment can only happen after Payment*, and *Shipment must happen within 24 hours after Payment* which put dependencies on execution of activities Shipment and Payment and specifies a quality of service. An example of the second type of constraints is *Shipment company is closed on Sunday.* Consider these constraints are placed on the same workflow. As this example shows, the constraints can conflict with each other: if *Payment* finishes on Saturday evening, the *Shipment* will take more than 24 hours. This simple example demonstrates dependency of quality of service constraints with the business logic constraints and with the resource availability constraint.

Different workflow dimensions have been widely considered in literature [10,9, 5]. A workflow dimension is normally used to define a view point on a workflow model or workflow execution. However, connections between different views, and thus between different dimensions of a workflow each of which represents a different workflow aspect, are often neglected or hard to understand. The reason for this is the isolated analysis of every dimension due to the complexity of the complete workflow and lack of the appropriate visualisation tools and frameworks. As a result, analysis of dependencies between different workflow aspects becomes nearly impossible for a process designer. One of the reasons for the complexity is that constraints influencing a workflow come from the different sources. Different parties involved in the business process design have different constraints and require different views on the workflow that provides them the specification and verification of their constraints. An example of a view on a business process is from the perspective of a human involved in the process. A human has certain criteria on the task executions in a business process. For example, a human resource is only available from $8am$ until $5pm$. In addition each human resource has certain qualifications assigned to it which specify what types of activities this person can execute. A manager can also specify that none of the human resources should be assigned to more than 2 tasks at the same time. All of these constraints need to be analysed together, but still allow different parties to have different views on their respective aspects. This work introduces a workflow and constraint specification and visualisation framework that addresses these issues.

1.1 Motivating Example

The following example is used to illustrate the problem area considered by this work. A company X wants to design an incident management process. Thereby it has to take into account available resources and constraints from other departments that the process must satisfy, such as those from the Customer satisfaction department, Quality assurance department, and Financial department. The constraints are the following:

The Customer satisfaction department wants to ensure that every high priority complaint received before $12pm$ is resolved by the end of the day.

The Quality control department wants to assure that the solution is approved by a domain *Expert*. Furthermore, the approval has to be done by a different person than the person who found the solution.

The company has the following resources: *CustomerSupport*, *Developer*, and *Expert*. Each of these resources have different availability times, based on their working hours. *CustomerSupport* works from $8am$ until $5pm$ with a lunch break from $12pm$ to $1pm$. A developer works from $9am$ until $6pm$ with a break from $12pm$ until $1pm$. An expert works from $8am$ until $4pm$ without a break.

The process designer has to create a process model that satisfies all these constraints. Furthermore, every party that provides their constraints wants to have evidence that the specified constraints are satisfied. To be able to do that, it is vital to understand how the constraints relate to each other and retain an overview over the satisfied and violated constraints.

1.2 Goals and Scope

The goal of this work is to develop a modelling framework that addresses the above challenges and enables analysis of the different aspects of a workflow, as well as uncovering dependencies between them. The framework should provide a better understanding of the relations between different constraints and their impact on the workflow model. In summary, the framework should satisfy the following criteria:

1. The framework should intuitively provide views on a workflow model from the point of view of different aspects.
2. The framework should uncover dependencies between different workflow aspects to enhance understanding of the workflow model.
3. The framework should allow specification and visualisation of the constraints in a way that allows analysis of dependencies between constraints.
4. The framework should support workflow designer by prevention of constraints violation or by visualisation of violated constraints.
5. The framework should provide different views for different constraint types and different constraint owners.

This paper presents the fundamental description of the ART framework that aims to provide a complete picture of the work and its possibilities. The intention of this work is therefore to build the foundation for the detailed specification of the framework.

2 Workflow Dimensions

A specification of a single workflow task is based on three main aspects: it specifies *what* must be done, *with* what resources (including human resources) and *when* it must be done. Thereby the *when* aspect can be specified absolute or relative. An example of a workflow task is *A developer must solve the problem in time* $[t, t+3]$. Here *developer* represents a resource, *solve the problem* is the action specification and $[t, t+3]$ is the time interval for the task execution where t can be defined relatively to the time aspects of other tasks. From this specification, the following three dimensions of a workflow task can be identified:

- The *A*ction dimension represents all actions involved in a workflow. An action defines the *type* of a workflow task and specifies *what* happens if a task is executed.
- The *R*esource dimension represents all resources required for a workflow execution. In this case the human resources (known as the *who* dimension [10]) as well as the technical resources (known as the *with*-dimension [10]) are represented by the *Resource* dimension. The reason for this is that the common resource properties, such as resource availability and resource capacity, can be applied to both technical and human resources. Another reason is that both human and technical resources can be passive and active resources of a workflow task. A resource is active if it has a relation *performs* (also called activity *executor*) to the task, and passive if has a relation *usedBy* (also called task *target*) to the task. For example a patient is a *target* of the *medicate* activity, but the *executor* of the *takeDrugs* activity. Similarly, a technical resource, such as a computer, can perform a task *Compute* or can be used by a task *SwitchOff*.
- The *T*ime dimension represents the temporal aspects of a workflow. Temporal aspects include temporal dependencies between the task order execution, as well as task duration, and task deadlines.

These three dimensions constitute the basis for the *A*ction-*R*esource- *T*ime (ART) framework. A workflow task defined in the ART framework can be visualised in 3D space. This work is restricted to the tasks that use one resource and are non-interruptible, which means that each workflow task can be represented by a single cuboid as shown in Figure 1.

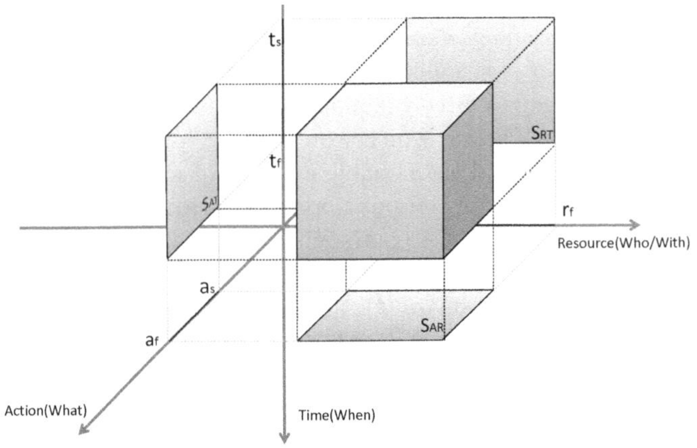

Fig. 1. A workflow task in Action, Resource and Time dimensions

Projections that a task cuboid produces on the plane defined by two dimensions yield the relationships between each: what resource is used at what time (*RT*-plane projection), what action uses which resource (*AR*-plane projection), and what action was executed at which time (AT-plane projection). The projections on the axes reflect the resource, action and time used for this task. To help better focus this work for discussion, we assume that a task is defined by exactly one action type, only uses one resource, and its execution is not interruptible. This implies that every task produces exactly one projection on every plane.

Every interval on every axis is characterised by its $start$, end and $length = end - start$ properties. To specify relations between two intervals, integer comparison operators are used. For instance, $a.end = b.start$ specifies that b follows a immediately, while $a.end < b.start$ specifies that b is placed after a on the axis.

The location of the actions, resources, and time intervals on the axes is determined by the positioning functions $p_{D_i} : D_i \rightarrow I(X_i)$ that assigns an interval on the axis X_i to every element from domain D_i. Positioning functions determine the visualisation criteria for a workflow. By changing the positioning function, the visual representation of the workflow will similarly change, enabling different views which highlight different aspects of the workflow to be viewed. For instance, the following positioning functions p_A, p_R and p_T can be chosen for the ART dimensions.

Actions can be arranged in a taxonomy $A_1, ..., A_n$ based on different criteria. A positioning function p_A based on this taxonomy should preserve subclass relations between each action, which means the following property must be satisfied: $\forall i, j \in [1, n] : SubclassOf(A_i, A_j) \rightarrow p_A(A_i) \subseteq p_A(A_j)$ Depending on the criteria used for the taxonomy, the workflow model will highlight different aspects. This also enhances constraint specification, as it allows constraints to be specified in more general classes, which are then inherited by all subclasses. For example, stating that any activity of type *CustomerInteraction* must be followed by *GetCustomerSatisfaction* can be modelled on the *CustomerInteraction* interval and applied to all intervals within this interval, and thus all subclasses of the action class *CustomerInteraction*.

Similar to the action positioning function, the resource positioning function p_R can be based on the resource taxonomy. A resource taxonomy can be built based on the resource location, which would group all resources located in one place into one class. This will then enable analysis of where tasks are performed. Another possible criterion for the positioning function is cost-based. In such a way a high-level overview of the cost spent can be given by simply analysing how many tasks are performed on the further end of the resource axis.

A Time positioning function $p_T(t) = t$ naturally reflects the time value on the T-axis. Thereby a unit on the T-axis can correspond to a second, to a day, or represent an abstract time interval. Placement of the task cuboids along the T-axes with respect to this time positioning function automatically identifies execution order of the workflow tasks[1].

A task S in the ART framework is specified by a triple (a, r, t), where a, r, and t are intervals on the corresponding axes defining the type of the action, the type of the resource, and the time interval. Note that the action and resource

[1] This work is restricted to acyclic workflows, however cycles can be represented by specifying task occurrence constraints on an abstract time interval.

type does not necessarily have to represent the bottom class of the action and resource taxonomy, which allows for a more general task definition to be used.

3 Constraints in the ART Framework

A workflow in the ART framework is specified by adding constraints to the workflow tasks execution. The constraints can refer to the execution order of the workflow tasks, to the resource allocation conditions (for example, Separation of Duty (SoD)), temporal properties of a task (deadlines), exclusive execution of the tasks (switch) and other workflow parameters. In addition, other constraints that are not directly specified in a workflow model can influence a workflow execution. An example of such a constraint is resource capacity and resource availability. For example, if a workflow specification defines a deadline for an activity A which requires two hours and must be performed by *Expert* using resources X and Y, then the capacity of the resources X and Y and the working hours of *Expert* must be considered.

In general, constraints can be classified based on the workflow aspects they restrict. Figure 2 gives an overview of the constraint types in the ART framework including some representative predicates which are discussed below. This section shows how these different constraint types are mapped to the spatial constraints and how they can be visualised and validated in the ART framework.

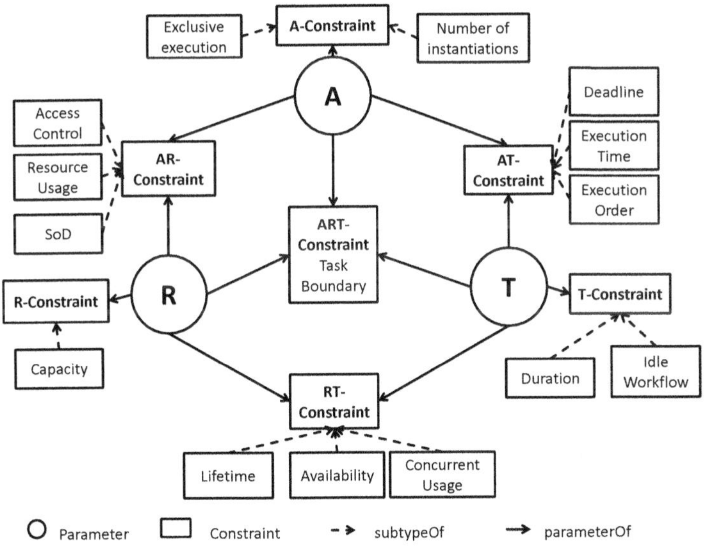

Fig. 2. Constraint Classification

3.1 Mapping of the Logical Constraints to the Spatial Restrictions

The semantic of the constraints in the ART space is given by the restriction a constraint produces on the occurrence of the tasks in the ART space. If no constraints exist, any part of the ART space can be used for the task placement. This means that theoretically any action can be executed with any resources at any time point. Constraints restrict these possibilities by defining the areas where the cuboids representing tasks can and cannot be placed, and by putting restrictions on the number of task occurrences.

To map logical constraints to the spatial restrictions we introduce the *Count* function:

$$Count : A \times R \times T \rightarrow \mathbb{N}$$

The *Count* function maps a 3D area in the ART framework to the number of the task occurrences in this area. Using this function, an area in the ART framework can be restricted with the following basic ART constraint, where $\bullet$ denotes an integer comparison operator:

$$Count(A, R, T) \bullet \mathbb{N}$$

Any of the *Count*-function parameters can encapsulate a complete dimension, in which case a constraint can be viewed as a projection of 3D space on the 2D plane. For example, the $Count(A_1, R_1, \top) \geq 1$ constraint, where $\top$ denotes the top class (in this case the complete time axis), says that a workflow projection on the *AR*-plane should produce at least one rectangle in the A_1R_1 area, see Figure 3(a). The semantic of this constraint is that in a workflow action of type A_1 has to be executed at least once with the resource R_1. On the other hand the $Count(A_1, R_1, \top) = 0$ predicate says that the action A_1 can never use the resource R_1. Similarly, the $Count(A_1, \top, T_1) \geq 1$ constraint says that action of type A_1 has to be instantiated at least once in the time interval T_1, but it does not put any restrictions on the resource usage for this action. The $Count(\top, R_1, T_1) \leq 1$ constraint means that resource R_1 can be used maximum once in time interval T_1.

Similarly, if the area defined by the triple in the *Count* function is opened in two dimensions, it counts all projections on the remaining dimension. For example $Count(A_1, \top, \top) \geq 2$ means that there must occur a task that performs action of type A_1 at least 2 times. In the ART space it means that there must be at least 2 tasks in the area defined by $(A_1, \top, \top)$, as Figure 3(b) shows.

Having the spatial constraint semantic defined, related constraints can be identified as the ones that share the restricted space: let $Region(C)$ denote the region that is restricted by constraint C, then two constraints C_1 and C_2 are related if $Region(C_1) \cap Region(C_2) \neq \emptyset$. Conflicting constraints can be identified through the conflicts of the minimal and maximum counts in the shared area. Figure 4 shows an example of conflicting constraints. Figure 4(a) shows three constraints: C_1 specifies that $Count(A_1, R_1 \cup R_2, T_1) > 0$, which means that action A_1 must be executed at least one with resource R_1 or R_2 in time interval T_1; C_2 specifies that $Count(\top, R_1, T_2) = 0$ which means that resource R_1 is not

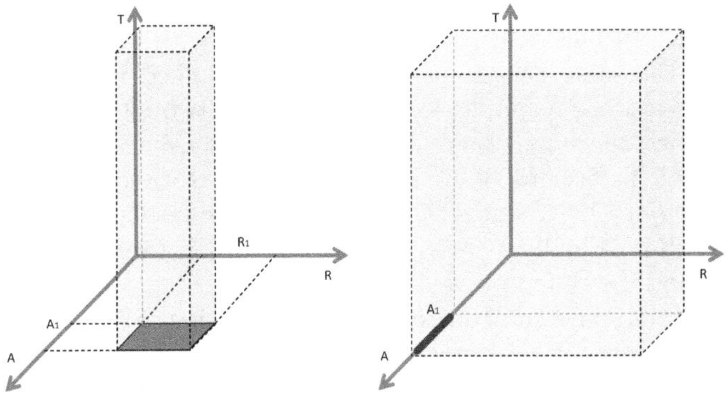

(a) 2D semantic (b) 1D semantic

Fig. 3. *Count* 3D semantic

available at time T_2; C_3 specifies that $Count(A_1, R_2, \top) = 0$, which means that resource R_2 cannot perform action A_1. Figure 4(b) shows a conflict between the constraint regions and their maximum and minimum counts: if a cuboid is placed in the region of constraint C_1 to satisfy the minimum count constraint, one of the constraints C_2 or C_3 will be violated, as $Region(C_1) \subset Region(C_2) \cup Region(C_3)$.

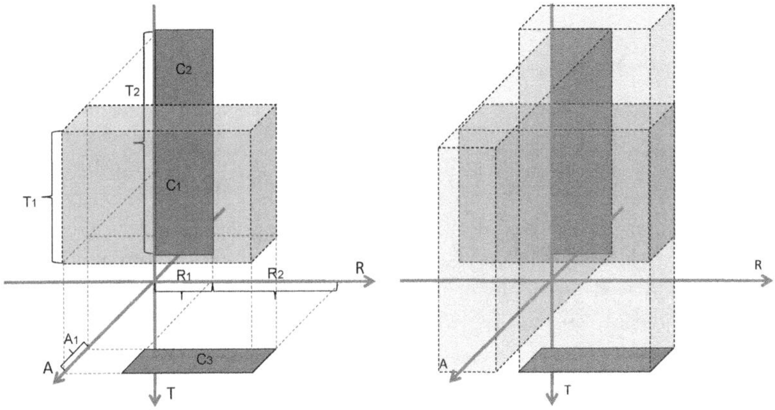

(a) (b)

Fig. 4. Conflicting constraints

Using the dimension abstraction, some constraints from Figure 2 can be defined as follows: A resource R_1 cannot be used concurrently by different tasks (Concurrent Usage): $\forall T_i \in T : Count(\top, R_1, T_i) \leq 1$. Any human resource can only execute maximal 3 tasks in parallel:$\forall T_i \in T : Count(\top, R_1, T_i) \leq 3$. Resource R_1 capacity of 10: $Count(\top, R_1, \top) \leq 10$, which says that maximum of 10 projections in the interval R_1 can exist, which implies that a maximum of 10 resources can be used. Action A_1 can only be executed by resource X:

$\forall r \in R \setminus X : Count(A_1, r) = 0$, which says that no projection can occur on the AR-plane in the A_1 lane, except in the intersection with the X resource.

In general, the same constraint types can be applied to actions, resources and time intervals. For example, exclusive usage of two intervals I_1 and I_2 can be modelled for exclusive actions as $Count(A_1 \cup A_2, \top, \top) \leq 1$, which states that only one of the actions A_1 or A_2 can be executed in a workflow. Similarly, $Count(\top, R_1 \cup R_2, \top) \leq 1$ states that only one of the resources R_1 or R_2 can be used in a workflow. Finally, $Count(\top, \top, T_1 \cup T_2) \leq 1$ states that only one task can occur during the time intervals T_1 and T_2.

Basic constraints and interval relations (see Section 2) can be combined in compound constraints using logical connectives $\wedge$, $\vee$ and $\neg$. A compound constraints combines different restrictions and can refer to different areas of the ART space. Every clause in a disjunctive normal form (DNF) form of a compound constraint represents an alternative space that the final model can satisfy. Every clause in a conjunctive normal form (CNF) form of a compound constraint represents alternative restrictions that must be considered in one ART space. An example of a compound constraint is that A_1 must be followed by A_2, which is specified as follows: $((Count(A_1, T_1, \top) > 0) \rightarrow (Count(A_2, T_2, \top) > 0)) \wedge T_2.start > T_1.end$. The CNF form of this constraint is $((Count(A_1, T_1, \top) = 0) \vee Count(A_2, T_2, \top) > 0)) \wedge T_2.start > T_1.end$, which means that a relation between two intervals must always hold and restrictions on occurrence of cuboids in two different areas are alternative.

4 Workflow Views

Sophisticated visualisation of the business process is key to understanding the business process model [13]. A good visualisation tool must enable analysis of the business process from different perspectives. The ART framework intuitively provides different perspectives depending on the aspects of interest. A 3D representation of a workflow activity visualises the dependencies between three activity dimensions. A task projection on the axis T shows the time when the task is active, the projection on the axis R shows which resources are required for this task, and the projection on the axis A contains logical actions which constitute this task. This section shows how a 3D workflow model can be analysed using different workflow views for analysis of different workflow aspects.

4.1 Workflow Projections

Figure 5 shows how projections of the 3D model on the planes can enhance the understanding of the workflow. Figure 5(a) shows an example 3D workflow while Figure 5(b) shows the projections of this workflow on the AR, AT and RT planes.

By analysing the projections of a 3D workflow model on the 2D planes, the following information can be obtained:

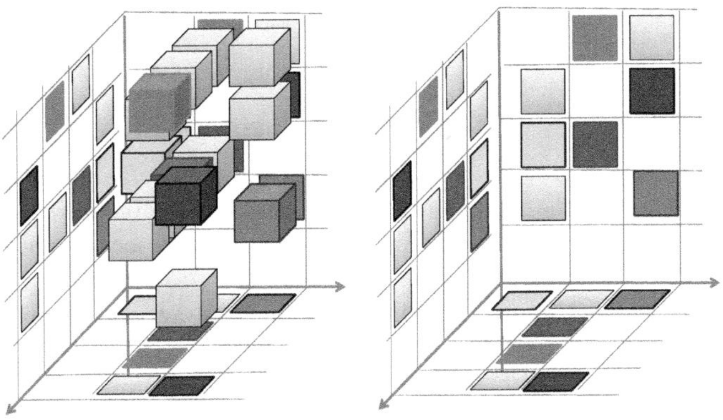

(a) 3D workflow (b) 2D projections

Fig. 5. Workflow projections

- Projection on the *AR*-plane represents all activities participating in the workflow and all resources these activities require. This gives an overview of the required capabilities needed to implement the specified workflow. An intersection in this dimension denotes that the same action type is used more than once with the same resource type.
- Projection on the *RT*-plane shows which resources are required at what time to enable execution of the specified workflow. This supports resource planning for the specified workflow. For example, if the workflow projection on the *RT*-plane produces an intersection of the activities projections, then the same resource (or resource type, depending on the resource dimension specification) will be used by more than one task at the same time. This implies that at least two resources of the resource type which contains this intersection must be available at the time specified by the intersection, otherwise a remodelling of the workflow is required.
- Projection of a 3D workflow on the *AT*-plane gives the most common view on the workflow specification. It shows the logical ordering of the task executions and their duration. An intersection in this plane denotes a parallel execution of the same functionality.

A projection of the 3D workflow model on a 2D plane abstracts the model from the third dimension. Thus, a 2D projection can be viewed as an abstract view of the complete model. Similarly, a 2D model can be further abstracted through the projection on 1D, which would give an overview of one aspect for the whole workflow, e.g. what resources are required and what actions constitute a workflow. As 2D model is an abstraction of a 3D model, 3D model is an abstraction of a 4D model. Thus, if a new dimension is added to the ART framework, there are four 3D projections that gain different views on the 4D model, depending on the selection of different aspects. Thereby the information from the abstracted dimension can be represented as task parameters or annotations.

This will not allow the same degree of dimension analysis but will give an overview of the abstracted aspects.

4.2 Workflow Cut Planes

Cut planes provide a view on the workflow from the point of view of a single resource, single activity or a single point of time. Figure 6 shows an example of a workflow cut for the resource R. Figure 6(b) shows projections of the resource specific workflows on the planes. In particular, the projection on the AR-plane shows the resource specific workflow. It shows in what actions at what time point this particular resource participates.

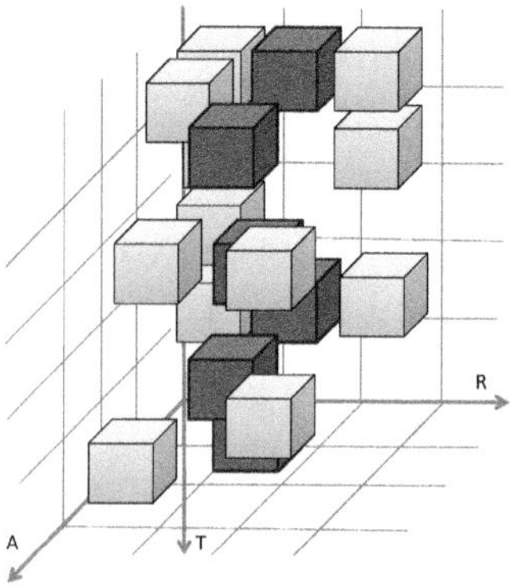

(a) 3D workflow

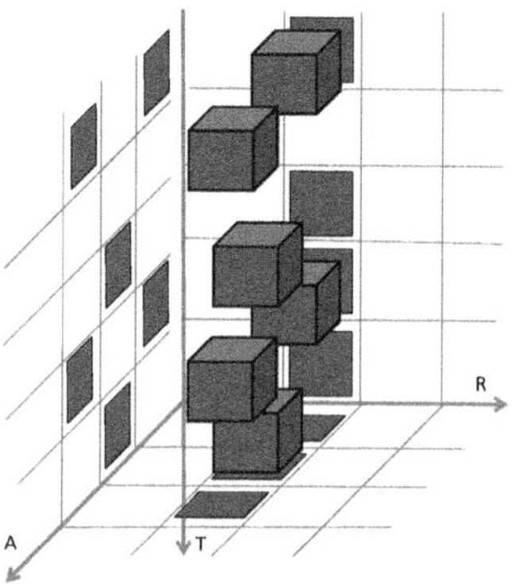

(b) Workflow cut

Fig. 6. Workflow cut planes

A resource cut plane for the resource R_1 is the plane $R = R_1$. A resource cut plane contains all activities which are executed with this specific resource. A resource cut plane can be viewed as a resource oriented workflow, which is especially interesting for the human resources. If the resource $R1$ is a human, the resource cut plane results in a personalised workflow for this human. Another interpretation for an R-cut when R_1 represents an active resource, or resource that executes the specified task, is a swim-lane. If the fixed resource is a technical component, for example a machine in a factory, the utilisation of this machine can be determined by analysing how often this machine is being idle for this workflow. Thus, it allows discovery of inefficient or unevenly distributed use of a resource. Such analysis also helps to share resources between different business process instances (in the same or different process models). Furthermore, resource specific constraints like *resource* R_1 *cannot be used by action* A_1 can be checked in this cut plane. Figure 6(b) shows an example of a resource oriented workflow obtained by cutting workflow for resource R.

A cut surface $A = A_1$ provides a view on the workflow from the point of view of a single functionality: it gives an overview when this functionality is used, who performs it and which resources are required at which point of time. Such cut surfaces can be used to check the action related properties or constraints, like *action A_1 cannot be executed more than once on the same resource*

A $T = T_1$ cut gives a snapshot of the workflow process at the specified point of time (or more general time interval) T_1. Such a cut plane can be used to check the time specific properties, like *no resources of type R can be used at time t_1*.

4.3 Other Views

As mentioned above, actions and resources are classified in a taxonomy and their placement on the axes corresponds to this taxonomy. As there are different ways to classify the actions and resources, there can be different views generated for the same workflow model. For example, one of the aspects for building a resource taxonomy can be based on the resource location, where, for example, resources located in the same city belong to the same class, which is a subclass of a class representing the resources located in the country. If the location of the resources on the R-axis corresponds to this taxonomy, then by abstracting resource level to the cities or countries, a high-level overview on the workflow distribution will be gained.

Taking the process-subprocess relation as the basis for the action taxonomy building and by mapping subprocess relation to a subclass relation between actions, the subprocesses can be naturally represented in the ART space. Thereby a cuboid that corresponds to a subprocess will be placed inside the cuboid that represents its super-process based on the action taxonomy. Note, that as the traditional subprocess specification does not consider resource dimension, the subprocess cuboids will be open on the R-axis. In addition to the traditional subprocesses that are defined through a set of actions in a specified order, the ART framework allows specification of action- , resource- and time-based subprocesses, as well as any combination of these. For example, a subprocess can be defined through a set of resources $R_1, ..., R_k$ and time interval $[t_1, t_2]$. By arranging resources $R_1, ..., R_k$ next to each other on the R-axis, the subprocess defined in such a way can be represented through a single open cuboid over the intervals containing all actions, resources $R_1, ..., R_k$ and time interval $[t_1, t_2]$. In general, any cut plane can be viewed as a subprocess of the complete workflow. Based on the cut type, such a subprocess can be based on the resource type, action type or time interval. In contrast to a traditional hierarchical decomposition of a workflow, the cross-cutting decomposition highlights different aspects of a workflow. For example, resource cut planes create a set of resource-oriented workflows that constitute the whole workflow.

Changing the size of the intervals on the action, resource and time axes changes the level of workflow abstraction. The gained workflow representation in this case consists of less cuboids, each of which is an abstraction of the smaller cuboids placed inside it. Thereby the details of the abstract cuboids, such as the ordering of the single actions as well as resources used by the actions, are omitted.

5 Motivating Example in the ART Framework

To model the example from from Section 1.1, the process designer needs action types *ReceiveComplaint*, *SolveProblem* and *ApproveSolution*. If the action types do not exist yet in the action taxonomy, then new classes representing these actions are created as sub-classes of the corresponding actions. For instance, *ReceiveComplaint* can be a sub-class of the *CustomerInteraction* action. In this case all constraints referring to the *CustomerInteraction* action would have to be applied to the *ReceiveComplaint* action as well.

ART-constraints are visualised in the 3D space, *AR*-, *RT*- and *AT*-constraints are visualised on the corresponding planes, *A*-, *R*-, and *T*-constraints are visualised on the corresponding axes (see Figure 2). Constraints produce patterns and anti-patterns on the axes and planes. A pattern is a combination of the projections a workflow has to create. An anti-pattern is a combination of the projection a workflow is not allowed to create.

The example constraints defined in Section 1.1 can be formalised as follows. *Support is qualified for acceptance of complaint, but is not qualified to find a solution* constraint is modelled as $Count(Solve, CustomerSupport, \top) = 0$. *Developer is not qualified to talk to the Customers* constraint corresponds to $Count(Accept, Developer, \top) = 0$. *Approval has to be always done by an Expert* constraint is modelled as $\forall r \in R \setminus Expert : Count(Approve, r, \top) = 0$. *Expert is qualified for solving the problems and for the solution approval* constraint is modelled as $\forall a \in A \setminus (Solve \cup Accept) : Count(a, Expert, \top) = 0$.

These constraints belong to the *AR* type of constraint, and can be modelled by restricting projections on the *AR*-plane. The formal specification of the constraints states that no projections can occur in the indicated areas. This is visualised by anti-patterns placed on the *AR*-plane as shown in Figure 7(a). The anti-pattern matches if at least one projection occurs in the red areas ($count > 0$).

Another *AR*-constraint defined in the example is the separation of duty constraint on actions *Solve* and *Accept*. This constraint can formally be described as $\forall r \in R : Count(Solve \bigcup Approve, r, \top) \leq 1$. The anti-pattern form for this constraint is $\exists r \in R : Count(Solve \bigcup Approve, r, \top) > 1$. Figure 7(b) shows the visualisation of this anti-pattern on the *AR*-plane.

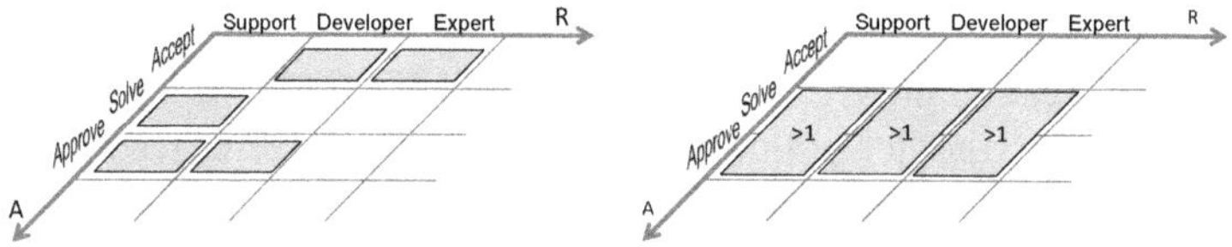

(a) Access Control (b) Separation of Duty

Fig. 7. AR-Constraints

Constraints *Solve happens after Accept*, *Approve happens after Solve*, and action durations define temporal dependencies between actions and belong to the *AT*-type of the constraints. Figure 8(a) shows how these constraints can be visualised on the *AT*-plane. The anti-pattern here is represented by red area, which means no projection is allowed to occur in this area. In this case however the anti-pattern can be changed by moving the black lines denoting the anti-pattern borderline. The black lines denote the relations between intervals, in this case defining that time interval for *Solve* is after time interval for *Accept*, and time interval for *Approve* is after *Solve*. The numbers on the virtual projections on the *AT*-plane denote the projection height and prevents the designer from moving the borderlines too far.

Availability is a property of a resource type, and specifies that the *RT*-plane can contain projections in the specified area. More important, in the time intervals where a resource type is not available, no task projections can occur, which means that no task regardless of the action type can use this resource at the specified time interval. Figure 8(b) shows resource availability constraints on the *RT*-plane. Figure 8(c) shows all the anti-patterns together.

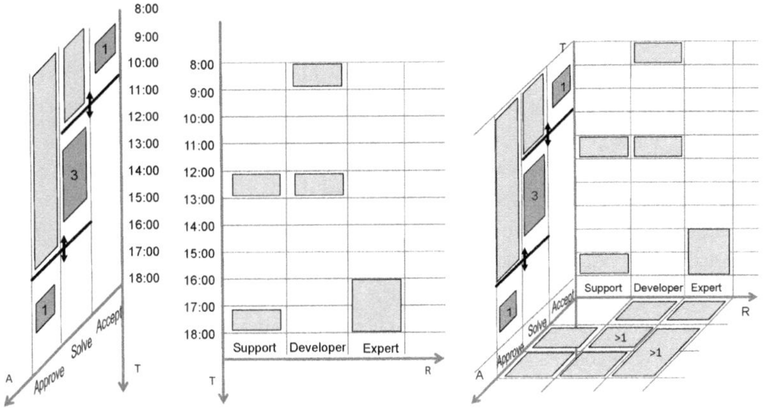

(a) AT-Constraints (b) RT-Constraints (c) Constraints merged

Fig. 8. Constraint Merge

After the anti-patterns for the workflow have been specified, the designer can place tasks in the 3D space. Every task produces 3 projections on the planes. If the projections match an anti-pattern, it is highlighted indicating that the workflow has to be changed.

The customer satisfaction constraint specifies that an important complaint has to be resolved by the end of the day if it was accepted before 12pm. Therefore the chosen planning time interval ends at 6pm, indicating the end of the day. Figure 9(a) shows an example workflow satisfying all the specified constraints, where the complaint is accepted before 9am. If a designer tries to simulate a situation in which a task performing *Accept* finishes at 12pm and tries to assign the task performing action *Solve* to the *Developer*, then the resource availability constraint for the *Expert* is violated as shown in Figure 9(b). When the designer tries to assign the *Solve* action to the *Expert*, then the separation of duty constraint is violated as shown in Figure 9(c).

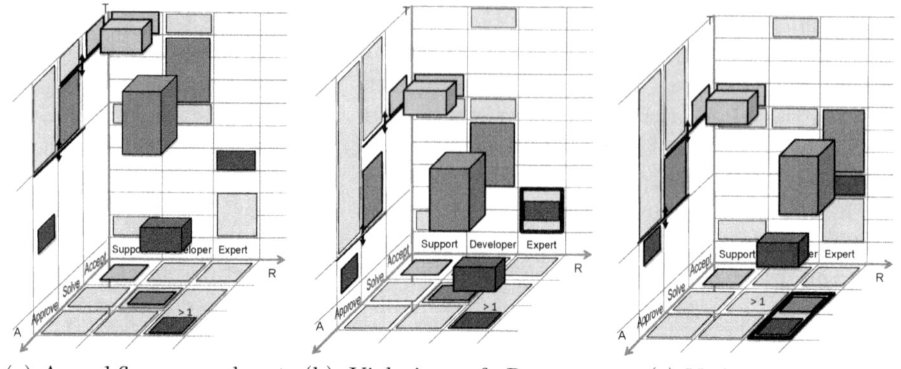

(a) A workflow example satisfying the constraints (b) Violation of Resource Availability (c) Violation of SoD

Fig. 9. Workflow examples

The given example demonstrates usage of the constraints at the design time. The framework supports workflow designer by highlighting the constraints violated, however it still requires skills from designer to be able to detect potential problems. Current work investigates how the designer can be better supported in finding a workflow model satisfying all the specified constraints.

The goal of the design time support is to ensure that the workflow model fulfils the specified constraints. However, the design time constraint enforcement is not always possible due to the dynamic changes in the environment. Similarly to the design time, the ART framework can be used at runtime for constraint monitoring. In this case, a task execution is reflected by a cuboid with the corresponding action, resource and time parameters. Thus, a cuboid at runtime does not represent an abstract specification of a task, but an instantiation of the specified task. Thereby the task instantiation cuboid should always occur inside the task specification cuboid. A violation of this rule would denote an error in the workflow engine that is responsible for the execution of workflow according to its definition. Thus, a task specification cuboid can be viewed as a constraint region that restrict occurrence of task instantiation cuboids. Runtime changes in the environment are reflected by the changes in the ART space. For instance, resource unavailability disables a piece of ART space corresponding to this resource and the time when the resource is unavailable, denoting that no task instantiation can happen in this region. Similarly, if the maximum count of a constraint region is reached, the rest of the region is disabled, which can be used for example to monitor exclusive usage of a resource. Moreover, runtime usage of the ART framework allows combining and analysing different workflow instances, which enables cross-workflow and cross-instance constraint monitoring.

6 Related Work

Related work can be divided in two main categories: business process visualisation and modelling of business processes constraints. In the business process visualisation area most of the work concentrate on visualisation of the process behaviour, while this work concentrates on visualisation of the workflow constraints in a way that allows workflow analysis with regard to different constraint types. In the area of constraint modelling and analysis, the proposed approach presented a mapping from the logical constraints to the spatial restrictions. The mapping combines logic and geometry, which allows usage of geometrical operations, such as cut and projection, for the analysis of the logical dependencies between constraints. Section 6.1 positions this work in the process visualisation area, and Section 6.2 addresses related work on constraint modelling.

6.1 Business Process Visualisation

Business Process Modelling Notation (BPMN) [14] provides a standard way for a business process to be graphically represented. Wide acceptance of BPMN (for example, by SAP NetWeaver BPM [16]) shows the importance of business process visualisation. While BPMN is widely used, the intention of the notation is to support visual exchange of knowledge between different parties, rather than to support deep analysis of the process. For example different views on the process e.g. to analyse resources and time requirements, are not provided in BPMN standard. [9] proposes a perspective oriented process modelling (POPM) approach. They define different perspectives for a modelling construct, which then enables the generation of different views on a business process. The main perspectives identified are functional, data, operational, organisational and control flow perspectives. A layered meta model of the POPM supports extensibility of the identified perspectives.

Much work exists that investigates how a better process visualisation can enhance understanding of the processes. Several use cases motivating the need for a proper business process visualisation as well as a business process graph layouting approach were introduced in [15]. In [17] the authors introduce a case study on visualisation of a business process based on a set of 3D gadgets. In [2] a Petri-net based workflow model is visualised in 3D, where the third dimension is used to represent process resources and relationships between the resources and between the resources and activities. In [4] a 2.5D representation of BPMN based process models is presented. The idea of 2.5D is the layering of the two dimensional (2D) visualization, whereby the layers are arranged in a three-dimensional space. The authors argue that such representation of a model allows them to obtain a more abstract view on business process models and eventually increases readability of the BPMN model compared to 2D. In [3] an approach for personalised visualisation of processes and process data is presented. The approach is based of the independent definition of the process symbols from the process model data. In [11] the authors investigate how usage of the icons representing the task type improves understanding of the process model. The last approach can be combined with the presented work by placing the icons representing the task type or the action a task performs on the A-axis and projecting it on one of the task cuboid faces.

6.2 Modelling and Usage of Constraints

Constraints have been widely used in the business process area for process specification, annotation, verification and validation. This work presented an approach for the constraints modelling and validation based on the geometrical shape of a business process. In [6] an extension to UML Activities notation was proposed that enables modelling both business processes and temporal constraints in the same language. The constraints can then be mapped to LTL and verified on the process model. In [8] the authors describe a Formal Contract Language (FCL) that uses deontic operators to model obligations and permissions in a contract. They use event language to represent BPMN semantic and to check if a formalisation of BPMN is compliant with the specified rules. In [18] a pattern ontology is presented which is used to specify properties on service compositions. Every pattern is translated to a corresponding state machine, which is then used to verify this property on a BPEL process. In [7] the authors first model the organisation and then specify a rule set over the concept model using an extension of LTL, which is monitored by a rule engine. In [1] temporal logic constraints are used to specify a workflow. In every step of a workflow execution a set of the reachable is computed, so that a user cannot execute an activity which does not lead to a successful process termination. In [12] the constraints are used to model the semantic of a BPEL process. This allows verification of other constraints against the set of constraints representing a BPEL process by reducing the constraint verification problem to the constraint satisfiability problem.

7 Conclusions and Outlook

The work presented a novel workflow modelling and analysis paradigm. The three main dimensions of a workflow - *A*ction, *R*esource and *T*ime - constitute the basis for the framework. By visualising a business process in the ART space, the dependencies between different aspects of the process become visible and constraints coming from different directions can be easily integrated. The logical constraints are classified and mapped to the spatial restrictions of the ART space. This combines logic and geometry and enhances understanding of the logical dependencies through the use of the geometrical operations. Thereby constraint validation is based on the geometrical properties of a business process and (anti)patterns representing the constraints.

The ongoing work extends the presented approach to the n-dimensional space, which allows representation of other workflow aspects, such as costs and location, and therefore allows n-dimensional constraint specification. Another direction compares different visualisation possibilities for different constraint types. Future work includes addition to the ART framework of the data-based decisions and process collaborations.

Acknowledgments. The work published in this article is partially funded by the MASTER project under the EU 7th Framework Programme (contract no. FP7-216917).

References

1. van der Aalst, W.M.P., Pesic, M.: Decserflow: Towards a truly declarative service flow language. In: Bravetti, M., Núñez, M., Zavattaro, G. (eds.) WS-FM 2006. LNCS, vol. 4184, pp. 1–23. Springer, Heidelberg (2006)
2. Betz, S., Eichhorn, D., Hickl, S., Klink, S., Koschmider, A., Li, Y., Oberweis, A., Trunko, R.: 3d representation of business process models. In: MobIS, pp. 73–87 (2008)
3. Bobrik, R., Bauer, T., Reichert, M.: Proviado - personalized and configurable visualizations of business processes. In: Bauknecht, K., Pröll, B., Werthner, H. (eds.) EC-Web 2006. LNCS, vol. 4082, pp. 61–71. Springer, Heidelberg (2006)
4. Effinger, P., Spielmann, J.: Lifting business process diagrams to 2.5 dimensions. Society of Photo-Optical Instrumentation Engineers Conference Series (2010)
5. Ferrari, B.: Global and north america supply chains 2007 top 10 predictions. Tech. Rep. LOOKING AHEAD MI204900, IDC (2007)
6. Förster, A., Engels, G., Schattkowsky, T., Straeten, R.V.D.: Verification of business process quality constraints based on visual process patterns. In: TASE (2007)
7. Giblin, C., Liu, A.Y., Müller, S., Pfitzmann, B., Zhou, X.: Regulations expressed as logical models (realm). In: JURIX, pp. 37–48 (2005)
8. Governatori, G., Milosevic, Z., Sadiq, S.W.: Compliance checking between business processes and business contracts. In: EDOC, pp. 221–232 (2006)
9. Jablonski, S., Götz, M.: Perspective oriented business process visualization. In: Business Process Management Workshops, pp. 144–155 (2007)
10. Leymann, F., Roller, D.: Production Workflow – Concepts and Techniques. Prentice Hall PTR, Englewood Cliffs (2000)
11. Mendling, J., Recker, J.: Towards systematic usage of labels and icons in business process models. In: 13th International Workshop on Exploring Modeling Methods for Systems Analysis and Design (2008)
12. Monakova, G.: et al.: Verifying Business Rules Using an SMT Solver for BPEL Processes. In: BPSC (2009)
13. Norton, D., Blechar, M., Jones, T.: Magic quadrant for business process analysis tools. Tech. Rep. RAS Core Research Note G00174515, Gartner (2010)
14. Object Management Group: Business process modelling notation (BPMN)
15. Rinderle, S., Bobrik, R., Reichert, M., Bauer, T.: Business process visualization - use cases, challenges, solutions. In: ICEIS, vol. (3), pp. 204–211 (2006)
16. SAP: Sap solution brief, sap netweaver business process management. Tech. rep., SAP (2009)
17. Schönhage, B., van Ballegooij, A., Eliëns, A.: 3d gadgets for business process visualization - a case study. In: Web3D, pp. 131–138 (2000)
18. Yu, J., Manh, T.P., Han, J., Jin, Y., Han, Y., Wang, J.: Pattern based property specification and verification for service composition. In: Aberer, K., Peng, Z., Rundensteiner, E.A., Zhang, Y., Li, X. (eds.) WISE 2006. LNCS, vol. 4255, pp. 156–168. Springer, Heidelberg (2006)

All links were last followed on April 19, 2010.

A Behavioral Similarity Measure between Labeled Petri Nets Based on Principal Transition Sequences
(Short Paper)

Jianmin Wang[1,2,3], Tengfei He[1,2], Lijie Wen[1,2,3], Nianhua Wu[1,2], Arthur H.M. ter Hofstede[4,5,⋆], and Jianwen Su[6]

[1] School of Software, Tsinghua University, 100084, Beijing, China
[2] Key Laboratory for Information System Security, Ministry of Education
[3] Tsinghua National Laboratory for Information Science and Technology, China
[4] Queensland University of Technology, Brisbane, Australia
[5] Eindhoven University of Technology, Eindhoven, The Netherlands
[6] University of California, Santa Barbara, CA 93106-5110, U.S.A.

Abstract. Being able to determine the degree of similarity between process models is important for management, reuse, and analysis of business process models. In this paper we propose a novel method to determine the degree of similarity between process models, which exploits their semantics. Our approach is designed for labeled Petri nets as these can be seen as a foundational theory for process modeling. As the set of traces of a labeled Petri net may be infinite, the challenge is to find a way to represent behavioral characteristics of a net in a finite manner. Therefore, the proposed similarity measure is based on the notion of so-called "principal transition sequences", which aim to provide an approximation of the essence of a process model. This paper defines a novel similarity measure, proposes a method to compute it, and demonstrates that it offers certain benefits with respect to the state-of-the-art in this field.

1 Introduction

Business process models form an essential part of many of today's enterprises. They represent valuable intellectual property and they may e.g. be used for communicating business practices (both for internal and external purposes), for business process improvement, and as a basis for workflow automation. Therefore it is not surprising that business process model collections can become quite large. Business process models are often not created from scratch, they need to comply with existing policies, and duplication of models, or parts of models, is to be avoided. Therefore being able to find similar process models effectively is useful, if not essential. The potential size of process model repositories mandates automated support for such similarity searches. The effectiveness of this support hinges on the chosen *similarity measure* for process model comparisons.

⋆ Senior Visiting Scholar of Tsinghua University.

R. Meersman et al. (Eds.): OTM 2010, Part I, LNCS 6426, pp. 394–401, 2010.

The concept of business process model similarity has attracted attention in the recent BPM literature but, more broadly, similarity measures also have applications in the area of web services (see [3]) for the purposes of matchmaking, mining and clustering in web service directories.

Recent efforts in the BPM community have tended to focus on similarity measures based on task labels or on relationships between tasks as specified in the process model (or both). This has meant that algorithms from the fields of information retrieval and graph theory could be exploited. However, such approaches may not adequately take the behavior of a process model into account, as it is pointed out in [2] that two processes may look quite similar, considering the tasks labels and the process structure, but may behave quite differently.

In this paper focus is therefore on a similarity measure that is based on the behavior of process models. In order to concretise our approach we have chosen labeled Petri nets as the process modeling formalism [1,6]. From a fundamental perspective, behavioral similarity of labeled Petri nets can be directly determined through the use of the complete set of firing sequences [5,10]. For a Petri net with loops this set may not be finite however, and an approach based on the use of all firing sequences therefore does not provide a good basis for determining behavioral similarity. Consequently, in our approach we introduce the notion of "principal transition sequence", to provide a finite approximation of the essence of the behavior of a process model. This notion is then used to define a measure for business process model similarity. Therefore the key contributions of this paper are the definition of a similarity measure based on process behavior, an approach to computing this measure, and an exploration of its significance.

The remainder of this paper is organized as follows. Section 2 introduces the notion of principal transition sequence, Section 3 presents the proposed similarity measure that is based on such sequences, and Section 4 is concerned with its evaluation. Section 5 concludes the paper and discusses some future work.

2 Principal Transition Sequences

Petri net theory has been widely accepted as a foundation for business process modeling and analysis. As to the basic notions of Petri nets, we refer the reader to [7,9].

Definition 1 (Labeled Petri Net). *A labeled Petri net is a six-tuple* $L\Sigma = (S, T, F, A, L, M_0)$*, where* (S, T, F, M_0) *is a Petri net,* A *is a finite set of action names, and* L *is a mapping from* T *to* $A \cup \{\varepsilon\}$ *(*ε *represents a transition not visible to the outside world).*

Fig. 1 gives three examples of labeled Petri nets. Having assigned names, including ε, to transitions, we can capture duplicate and hidden tasks naturally. We refer to a labeled Petri net as a Petri net when no confusion can occur.

Given a labeled Petri net, starting from its initial marking M_0 we can start to explore the state space of reachable markings. This state space is potentially infinite and then the associated reachability tree is infinite. To deal with this

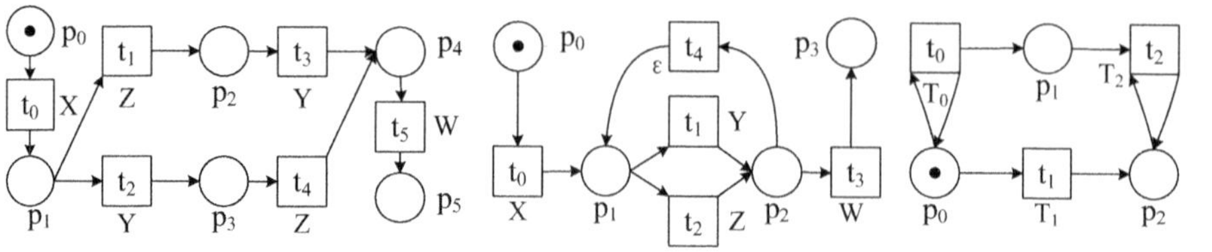

(a) $L\Sigma_1$ with duplicate labels (b) $L\Sigma_2$ with loop structure (c) $L\Sigma_3$ with unbounded places

Fig. 1. Labeled Petri nets: a) without loop b) with a loop c) with unbounded places

problem one can consider *coverability trees*. In [7] an algorithm is presented for the construction of a coverability tree and in [9] it is shown that a coverability tree is always finite.

Fig. 2 presents the corresponding coverability trees of the labeled Petri nets of Fig. 1. We denote the root node of the coverability tree as v_r. A leaf node whose marking does not have a succeeding marking is called a dead-end. A leaf node, v_o, whose marking is also the marking of an other node on the path from v_r to v_o, is called old. The node that has a marking identical to the marking of v_o and which is the closest such node to the root node v_r is called the anchor node of v_o, denoted by anchor(v_o).

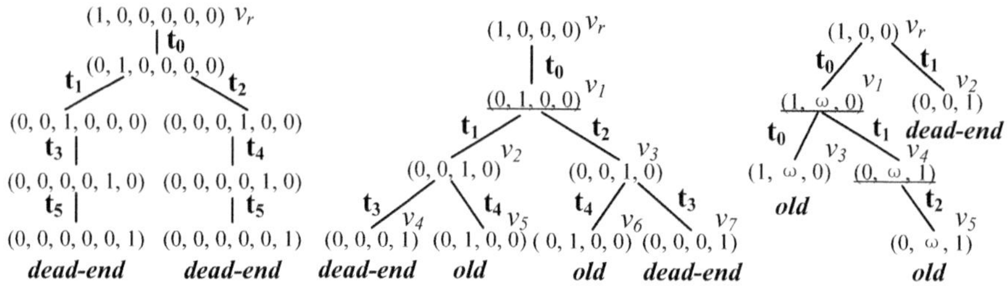

(a) (b) (c)

Fig. 2. Coverability trees of $L\Sigma_1$, $L\Sigma_2$ and $L\Sigma_3$

Based on the coverability tree of a labeled Petri net, we define its principal transition sequence by using the auxiliary function $\mathsf{ts}(v_1, v_2, CT_{L\Sigma})$ which yields the transition path from node v_1 to node v_2 in coverability tree $CT_{L\Sigma}$.

Definition 2 (Principal Transition Sequence). *Let* $L\Sigma = (S, T, F, A, L, M_0)$ *be a labeled Petri net,* $C_{L\Sigma}$ *its incidence matrix,* $CT_{L\Sigma}$ *its coverability tree with root* v_r*,* V_d *its set of dead-end nodes and* V_o *its set of old nodes. The set of principal transition sequences (PTSs) of* $L\Sigma$*,* $\mathsf{pts}(L\Sigma)$*, is the minimal set defined by:*

(1) If $v_d \in V_d$ *then* $\mathsf{ts}(v_r, v_d, CT_{L\Sigma}) \in \mathsf{pts}(L\Sigma)$*;*
(2) If $v_o \in V_o$ *then* $\mathsf{ts}(v_r, \text{anchor}(v_o), CT_{L\Sigma}) \in \mathsf{pts}(L\Sigma)$*;*
(3) If $v_o \in V_o$ *then* $\mathsf{ts}(\text{anchor}(v_o), v_o, CT_{L\Sigma}) \in \mathsf{pts}(L\Sigma)$

As the different kinds of principal transition sequences correspond to different behavior we classify them as follows. The *primary* PTSs of a Petri net $L\Sigma$, denoted as $\mathcal{P}_1(L\Sigma)$, are those PTSs that fall into category (1) or (2). These are the PTSs that correspond to nonrepeatable transition sequences. A principal transition sequence σ is an element of the set of *finitely repeatable* PTSs of $L\Sigma$, denoted as $\mathcal{P}_2(L\Sigma)$, iff it falls into category (3) and $C_{L\Sigma} \cdot X_\sigma^{\mathrm{Tr}}$ contains a negative number. Otherwise, it is an element of the set of *infinitely repeatable* PTSs, denoted as $\mathcal{P}_3(L\Sigma)$.

Now we present the algorithm for computing the various types of principal transition sequences. In this algorithm, apart from auxiliary function $\mathsf{ts}(v_1, v_2, CT_{L\Sigma})$, we also use the auxiliary predicate $\mathsf{neg}(V)$ which determines whether there are any negative values in vector V.

Algorithm 1: Generation of the various PTS sets
Input: A coverability tree $CT_{L\Sigma}$ for a labeled Petri net $L\Sigma$
In this tree V_d is the set of dead-end nodes, V_o is the set of old nodes, and v_r is the root node
Output: $\mathcal{P}_1(L\Sigma)$, $\mathcal{P}_2(L\Sigma)$, $\mathcal{P}_3(L\Sigma)$
$\mathcal{P}_1(L\Sigma) := \varnothing$; $\mathcal{P}_2(L\Sigma) := \varnothing$; $\mathcal{P}_3(L\Sigma) := \varnothing$;
for each $v_f \in V_d \cup V_o$
  begin
  if $v_f \in V_d$ **then** $\mathcal{P}_1(L\Sigma) := \mathcal{P}_1(L\Sigma) \cup \mathsf{ts}(v_r, v_f, CT_{L\Sigma})$;
  if $v_f \in V_o$ **then** $\mathcal{P}_1(L\Sigma) := \mathcal{P}_1(L\Sigma) \cup \mathsf{ts}(v_r, \mathrm{anchor}(v_f), CT_{L\Sigma})$;
  if $v_f \in V_o$ **then**
    begin
    $\sigma := \mathsf{ts}(\mathrm{anchor}(v_f), v_f, CT_{L\Sigma})$;
    if $\mathsf{neg}(C_{L\Sigma} \cdot X_\sigma^{\mathrm{Tr}})$ **then** $\mathcal{P}_2(L\Sigma) := \mathcal{P}_2(L\Sigma) \cup \sigma$
    else $\mathcal{P}_3(L\Sigma) := \mathcal{P}_3(L\Sigma) \cup \sigma$
    end
  end

3 PTS-Based Similarity

In this section a similarity measure between labeled Petri nets is defined which is based on PTSs. As the set of PTSs of a labeled Petri net provides an approximation of its behaviour, this measure takes the semantics of the nets involved into account.

Transition labels describe the intended actions of the various transitions in a labeled Petri net. For a transition t, its label is given by $L(t)$ and this notation can be naturally extended to transition sequences. Hence $L(\sigma)$ captures the trace associated with transition sequence σ. This trace can be seen as a string in the language defined by alphabet A of the net.

Definition 3 (Similarity of Two Principal Transition Sequences). *Let $L\Sigma$ and $L\Sigma'$ be labeled Petri nets and σ and σ' be transition sequences of $L\Sigma$ and $L\Sigma'$ respectively. The similarity of σ and σ', $\mathrm{Sim}(\sigma, \sigma')$, is based on their longest common subsequence given by $\mathrm{lcs}(\sigma, \sigma')$, and is defined as:*

$$\mathrm{Sim}(\sigma, \sigma') = \frac{\mathrm{length}(\mathrm{lcs}(L(\sigma), L(\sigma')))}{\max(\mathrm{length}(L(\sigma)), \mathrm{length}(L(\sigma')))}$$

Example 1. Let $\sigma = t_0 t_1 t_3$ and $\sigma' = t_0 t_1 t_4 t_2 t_3$ be transition sequences in Petri net $L\Sigma_2$. Then $L(\sigma) = XYW$, $L(\sigma') = XYZW$, and $\text{lcs}(L(\sigma), L(\sigma')) = XYW$. Therefore $\text{Sim}(\sigma, \sigma') = 0.75$.

Definition 4 (Similarity of Two Sets of Transition Sequences). *Let P and Q be sets of transition sequences, then if neither P nor Q is the empty set:*

$$\text{Sim}(P, Q) = \frac{\sum_{\sigma \in P} \max_{\sigma' \in Q} \text{Sim}(\sigma, \sigma') + \sum_{\sigma' \in Q} \max_{\sigma \in P} \text{Sim}(\sigma', \sigma)}{|P| + |Q|}$$

If either P or Q equals the empty set, but not both, then $\text{Sim}(P, Q) = 0$, *while if both P and Q are the empty set* $\text{Sim}(P, Q) = 1$.

Definition 5 (Similarity of Two Labeled Petri Nets). *The degree of similarity between labeled Petri nets $L\Sigma$ and $L\Sigma'$,* $\text{Sim}(L\Sigma, L\Sigma')$, *is defined as:*

$$\text{Sim}(L\Sigma, L\Sigma') = \sum_{i=1}^{3} \lambda_i \times \text{Sim}(\mathcal{P}_i(L\Sigma), \mathcal{P}_i(L\Sigma')), \lambda_i = \frac{|\mathcal{P}_i(L\Sigma)| + |\mathcal{P}_i(L\Sigma')|}{|\mathsf{pts}(L\Sigma)| + |\mathsf{pts}(L\Sigma')|}$$

Hence, they capture the ratios between the numbers of the various types of PTSs and the total number of PTSs.

4 Experimental Evaluation

The algorithms for the PTS-based similarity measure (abbreviated as PTS), TAR similarity measure (abbreviated as TAR) [10] and Bae's similarity measure (abbreviated as Bae) [3] were implemented in the BeehiveZ system[1], which aims to provide a general framework for process data management. The code of the algorithm for the causal footprint similarity measure (abbreviated as CFP) [4] was directly taken from the open source process mining environment ProM 5.2[2] and integrated into the BeehiveZ system.

4.1 Experiment I

In Fig. 3 six simple and interrelated models are shown. For this collection of six artificially created models, PTS (Sim) and CFP (Sim′) are computed for three different groupings. The degrees of similarity between the various pairs of process models in the three groupings are shown in Table 1.

As can be seen from Table 1 CFP considers models (a) and (c) as quite similar (more so than PTS) even though one involves a choice between Y and Z and in the other both Y and Z need to be executed. On the other hand, when for each model of this pair of models only a loop is added (which results in models (a') and (c')), the degree of similarity is reduced much more than in PTS. As

[1] http://sourceforge.net/projects/beehivez/files/
[2] www.processmining.org

the set of traces is the same for models (b) and (c) as well as for models (b') and (c') PTS rates their degree of similarity as 100%. Especially for the latter combination this constitutes a real difference with the degree of similarity as measured through CFP.

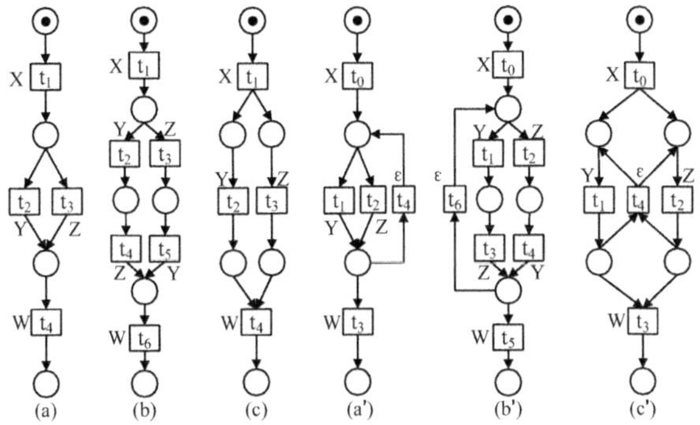

Fig. 3. Six interrelated models

Table 1. Degrees of similarity between various combinations of the six process models

	λ_1	λ_2	λ_3	$Sim(L\Sigma, L\Sigma')$	$Sim'(L\Sigma, L\Sigma')$
(a,b)	1	0	0	75%	66.74%
(a,c)	1	0	0	75%	92.85%
(b,c)	1	0	0	100%	92.85%
(a,a')	5/7	0	2/7	61.9%	67.02%
(b,b')	5/7	0	2/7	60.7%	41.70%
(c,c')	5/7	0	2/7	60.7%	85.86%
(a',b')	6/10	0	4/10	70%	62.22%
(a',c')	6/10	0	4/10	70%	72.47%
(b',c')	6/10	0	4/10	100%	72.47%

4.2 Experiment II

In this section, PTS is evaluated using 114 real-life process models from an industrial boiler manufacturer in the south-east of China. These models were created by an external consulting company using EPCs [8].

In these 114 EPCs, the total number of events is 839 and the total number of functions is 550 indicating a relatively high use of control-flow constructs. There are 23 EPCs that contain loops, 20% of the total number of models. There are 13 EPCs that contain parallel structures, where the maximum number of parallel functions is 17. The similarity between each pair of the 114 converted LPNs is computed and the results are contrasted with TAR, Bae and CFP using the following three metrics. The first metric is the average time (AvgT) it takes to compute the degree of similarity between two LPNs (only for those computations which can be done within the time limit, which for this experiment was set at 1 hour). The second metric is the percentage of pairs that satisfies the triangular inequality (TriR). A pair of LPNs x and y satisfies the triangular inequality iff for every LPN z: $\mathrm{Sim}(x, z) + \mathrm{Sim}(z, y) \geq \mathrm{Sim}(x, y)$. The third and final metric is the computability fraction (ComF), which is the percentage of LPNs for which the similarity measure could be computed (as mentioned, the limit is set at 1 hour). Note that focus is on a single LPN and whether for this LPN the preparation for the computation of the degree of similarity with other LPNs can be completed in time. The results of the comparison of the four algorithms identified earlier along these metrics can be found in Table 2.

Table 2. Results of the comparison of the four algorithms applied to 114 real-life LPNs

	PTS	CFP	Bae	TAR
AvgT (ms)	25.6	14800	4.4	0.9
TriR (%)	99.98	98.96	99.69	98.33
ComF (%)	100	96.49	100	100

4.3 More Discussion about the PTS Algorithm

To examine the worst case complexity of the PTS algorithm in an intuitive manner, we have constructed an LPN with a large parallel structure and drawn it using PIPE 2.5[3]. This LPN is shown in Figure 4.

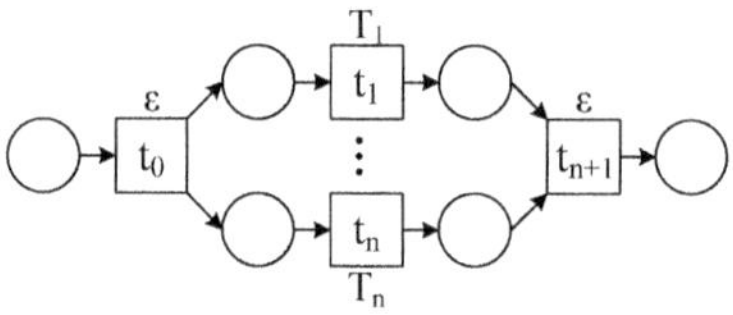

Fig. 4. A special kind of LPNs that cannot be handled easily by the PTS algorithm

The time complexity for calculating the coverability graph of an LPN such as shown in Figure 4 is $O(n!)$ according to Murata [7], while the space complexity of it is $O(2^n)$. However, as shown in Section 4.2, this limitation may not be too significant in practice as LPNs such as shown in Figure 4 with more than 15 tasks in a parallel structure may not occur that often in reality.

5 Conclusions

In this paper a new similarity measure for labeled Petri nets was proposed that takes behavioral aspects into account. The method for determining the degree of similarity between two nets circumvents the problem of having to deal with infinite trace sets or infinite reachability graphs by computing the sets of principal transition sequences. Experiments, both with artificial and real-life models, were conducted to explore characteristics of the proposed similarity measure.

[3] http://pipe2.sourceforge.net/

There are some limitations to the work presented. For example, while the proposed similarity measure takes behavioral aspects into account, the set of principal transition sequences of a net do not fully characterize its behavior. It remains an open question to what extent the resulting loss of information affects the quality of the similarity measure. If this loss is significant, refinement of the proposed similarity measure is required. In addition, the computational complexity of the proposed approach relies on the computation of coverability trees. More work is required to explore to what extent this poses limitations in practice and what can be done to manage this complexity.

Acknowledgements. This work is partially supported by the 973 Program of China (No. 2009CB320700 and No. 2007CB310802) and the 863 Program of China (No. 2008AA042301, No. 2007AA040607 and No. 2007AA040602).

References

1. van der Aalst, W.M.P.: The Application of Petri Nets to Workflow Management. Journal of Circuits, Systems, and Computers 8(1), 21–66 (1998)
2. van der Aalst, W.M.P., Alves de Medeiros, A.K., Weijters, A.J.M.M.: Process Equivalence: Comparing Two Process Models Based on Observed Behavior. In: Dustdar, S., Fiadeiro, J.L., Sheth, A.P. (eds.) BPM 2006. LNCS, vol. 4102, pp. 129–144. Springer, Heidelberg (2006)
3. Bae, J., Liu, L., Caverlee, J., Zhang, L., Bae, H.: Development of Distance Measures for Process Mining, Discovery and Integration. Int. J. Web Service Res. 4(4), 1–17 (2007)
4. Dijkman, R.M., Dumas, M., van Dongen, B.F., Käärik, R., Mendling, J.: Similarity of Business Process Models: Metrics and Evaluation. BETA Working Paper Series, WP 269, Eindhoven University of Technology, Eindhoven, The Netherlands (2009)
5. Lin, D.: An Information-Theoretic Definition of Similarity. In: Shavlik, J.W. (ed.) Proceedings of the Fifteenth Int. Conf. on Machine Learning (ICML 1998), Madison, Wisconsin, USA, July 24-27, pp. 296–304. Morgan Kaufmann, San Francisco (1998)
6. Liu, D., Wang, J., Chan, S.C.F., Sun, J., Zhang, L.: Modeling Workflow Processes with Colored Petri Nets. Computers in Industry 49(3), 267–281 (2002)
7. Murata, T.: Petri Nets: Properties, Analysis and Applications. Proceedings of the IEEE 77(4), 541–580 (1989)
8. Scheer, A.-W., Thomas, O., Adam, O.: Process Modeling Using Event-Driven Process Chains. In: Process Aware Information Systems: Bridging People and Software Through Process Technology, pp. 119–146. John Wiley & Sons, Hoboken (2005)
9. Yuan, C.: Principles of Petri Nets (Chinese version). Publishing House of Electronics Industry, Beijing (1998)
10. Zha, H., Wang, J., Wen, L., Wang, C., Sun, J.: A Workflow Net Similarity Measure based on Transition Adjacency Relations. Computers in Industry 61(5), 463–471 (2010)

Efficient and Accurate Retrieval of Business Process Models through Indexing
(Short Paper)

Tao Jin[1,2,⋆], Jianmin Wang[1,2], Nianhua Wu[2], Marcello La Rosa[3], and Arthur H.M. ter Hofstede[3,4,⋆⋆]

[1] Department of Computer Science and Technology, Tsinghua University, China
[2] School of Software, Tsinghua University, China
[3] Queensland University of Technology, Australia
[4] Eindhoven University of Technology, The Netherlands
{jint05,wnh08}@mails.thu.edu.cn, jimwang@tsinghua.edu.cn, {m.larosa,a.terhofstede}@qut.edu.au

Abstract. Recent years have seen an increased uptake of business process management technology in various industries. This has resulted in organizations trying to manage large collections of business process models. One of the challenges facing these organizations concerns the retrieval of models from large business process model repositories. As process model repositories may be large, query evaluation may be time consuming. Hence, we investigate the use of indexes to speed up this evaluation process. Experiments are conducted to demonstrate that our proposal achieves a significant reduction in query evaluation time.

Keywords: business process model, index, exact query, repository.

1 Introduction

Through the application of Business Process Management (BPM), organizations are in a position to rapidly build information systems and to evolve them due to environmental changes. Therefore, BPM has matured in recent years and has seen significant uptake in a variety of industries and also in government. This has led to the proliferation of large collections of business process models.

Managing such large business process model repositories can be challenging. For example, when new process models are to be created one may wish to leverage existing process models in order to preserve best practice or simply to reuse process fragments. Therefore, one needs to have the ability to query a business process model repository. Due to the potential size of such a repository, it is important that these queries can be executed in an efficient manner.

In this paper focus is on providing efficient support for querying business process model repositories. Given a process fragment (the model query), we are

⋆ Visit to QUT funded by China Scholarship Council.
⋆⋆ Senior Visiting Scholar of Tsinghua University.

R. Meersman et al. (Eds.): OTM 2010, Part I, LNCS 6426, pp. 402–409, 2010.

concerned with finding all process models in the repository that contain this fragment. The complexity of finding all subgraph isomorphisms is known to be NP-complete [1]. To overcome this issue, and in line with graph database techniques [1,2,3,4,5,6,7], we propose a two-stage approach that reduces the number of models needed to be checked for subgraph isomorphism. First, we filter the model repository through the use of indexes and obtain a set of candidate process models. Second, we apply an adaptation of Ullman's subgraph isomorphism check [8] to refine the set of candidate models by extracting those models containing the model query. The advantage of using indexes is that the subgraph isomorphism check is only performed on a subset of the models in the repository, which is typically much smaller than the total number of models in the repository.

In order to be able to focus on a uniform representation of business processes, we assume business processes are modeled as Petri nets or mapped from other formalisms into Petri nets. In fact, it has been shown that a wide range of business process modeling languages used in practice, e.g. BPMN, EPCs, UML Activity Diagrams and BPEL, or at least significant subsets of them, can be mapped to Petri nets (see [9] for a survey of mappings). In addition, our focus is on the control flow perspective of business process modeling.

The remainder of this paper is organized as follows. Section 2 defines the semantics of a business process model query and the notation of path-based index. Section 3 discusses the construction of indexes while Section 4 shows how these indexes can be used to query a business process model repository. Next, Section 5 analyzes the use of our approach through experiments. Section 6 discusses related work and Section 7 concludes this paper. For a more detailed treatment of our work, we refer the reader to [10].

2 Preliminaries

A query on a business process model repository is a Petri net, and the result is defined as all Petri nets in the repository that cover that query.

Definition 1 (Petri Net Cover). *Labeled Petri net $pn_1 = (P_1, T_1, F_1, L_1)$ is covered by labeled Petri net $pn_2 = (P_2, T_2, F_2, L_2)$, denoted as $pn_1 \sqsubseteq pn_2$, iff there exists a one-to-one function $h : P_1 \to P_2 \cup T_1 \to T_2 \cup F_1 \to F_2$ such that:*

1. *for all $t \in T_1$: $L_1(t) = L_2(h(t))$, i.e. function h preserves transition labels;*
2. *for all $(n_1, n_2) \in F_1$: $h(n_1, n_2) = (h(n_1), h(n_2))$, i.e. h preserves arc relations.*

Let R be a Petri net model repository and let q be a Petri net query. The result of issuing q over R is $R_q = \{r \in R \mid q \sqsubseteq r\}$. To enhance the efficiency of queries, we use indexes. These indexes are constructed from transition paths.

Definition 2 (Transition Path). *Given a labeled Petri net $pn = (P, T, F, L)$, a sequence of transitions $t_1, \ldots, t_n$ with $n \geq 1$ is a transition path iff $n = 1$ or for all $1 \leq k \leq n-1$ there is place p_k such that $p_k \in t_k \bullet \cap \bullet t_{k+1}$. For*

$n = 1$ we write the path as $\phi = L(t_1)$, and for $n > 1$ we write the path as $\phi = L(t_1) \rightarrow \ldots \rightarrow L(t_n)$. The length of this path, $\phi.length$, is n.

We use LnP_R to denote the set of all transition paths with length n, where $n \geq 1$, in all the models of a repository R. If R is clear from the context we will simply write LnP. If m is a process model, the notation LnP_m is equivalent to $LnP_{\{m\}}$. We use $LnCP_R$ to denote the set of all transition paths with lengths up to n, i.e. $LnCP_R = \bigcup_{i=1}^{n} LiP_R$.

Definition 3 (Path-based Index). *A path-based index I_R^n of length n in repository R is a set of items of the form $(\phi_i, \phi_i.list)$, where ϕ_i is a transition path of length n in a model of R and $\phi_i.list$ is the set of identifiers of all models that contain ϕ_i.*

The expression *LnP index* denotes a path-based index of length n in repository R. The expression *LnCP index* captures all path-based indexes of lengths upto n in repository R.

3 Index Construction

To enhance the efficiency of path-based indexes, we do not store the items (ϕ_i,$\phi_i.list$) directly. Instead, we use B+ trees to store items ($\phi_i.hashcode$, $\phi_i.list.pointer$) and use inverted lists to store information about ($\phi_i.list.pointer$, $\phi_i.list$), where $\phi_i.hashcode$ is the hash code of ϕ_i[1] and this code acts as a key in a B+ tree, and $\phi_i.list.pointer$ is a pointer referring to the list $\phi_i.list$. To improve I/O performance, these lists ($\phi_i.list$) are stored as slots of fixed length. When a list requires more than one slot, the first slot contains a reference to the second slot and so on. $\phi_i.list.pointer$ essentially corresponds to a reference to its first slot. It is conceivable that the application of the hash function to two different transition paths yields the same result. Hence leaf entries in these B+ trees correspond to one or more transition paths and provide a reference to a list containing all the models in which these paths occur. In our approach, the roots of B+ trees are kept in memory while the other nodes, as well as the inverted lists, are stored on disk in different files. Cache memory can be used for B+ tree nodes and inverted lists to further improve the efficiency.

As we aim to minimise retrieval time, it is beneficial to keep the depth of B+ trees minimal and to avoid hash collisions as much as possible. Therefore, transition paths of different lengths are indexed in separate B+ trees (since any process model fragment should be allowed as a query, *L1P* must be indexed).

We now present a generic algorithm for the creation of *LnP* indexes. This algorithm is described in pseudocode as Algorithm 1. Line 1 extracts all the transition paths of length n from the given model *pn*. In lines 2-6 all transition paths are processed sequentially. Line 3 computes the $\phi_i.hashcode$ of path ϕ_i. Line 4 adds the $\phi_i.hashcode$ to the B+ tree and obtains the $\phi_i.list.pointer$ to

[1] For a path of length more than one the hashcode is computed on the string "$L(t_1)->\ldots->L(t_n)$".

Algorithm 1. PathIndexConstruction

```
  input: pn: a Petri net
         n: the length of the path
1 sps ← PathExtraction(pn,n);
2 foreach path in sps do
3 |   hashcode ← DEKHash(path);
4 |   sid ← AddToBplusTree(hashcode);
5 |   AddToInvertedList(sid, pn);
6 end
```

the inverted list. Line 5 adds the identifier of model *pn* to the inverted list $\phi_i.list$ found at the address provided by $\phi_i.list.pointer$.

As shown in Algorithm 1, when a new model is added to the repository, the *LnP index* can be updated incrementally (when multiple indexes are used, all these indexes will be updated). When a model is updated, the old version is deleted and the new version is added. When models are deleted from the repository, which rarely happens in a retrieval system, we can use a list to record the identifiers of these models rather than remove them immediately from the index structure as this would not be very efficient. When the number of models recorded in this list exceeds a certain threshold, we can reconstruct the index from scratch.

4 Query Processing

Petri net query processing is divided into two stages. The first stage of query processing only acts as a filter. The first reason is that the result from the first stage may not be exact due to hash collisions where different paths may be mapped to the same list of process models. The second reason is that by focussing on transition paths context information is not taken into account, e.g. the fact that a choice may exist between two subsequent transitions in a model is lost as well as the order of such paths with respect to the query. In order to further refine the set of process models so that it corresponds to an exact result, a match operation needs to be performed in the second stage.

When multiple indexes are available during the first stage of query processing, those indexes whose lengths correspond to paths in the query can be exploited to obtain a set of candidate models. It is best to try to use an index with the largest length first for those transition paths that match the length of this index. During this process we can determine those transitions that do not occur in any path of this length. These transitions can then be used when checking another index with the next maximal length and so on.

The procedure for query processing is described in Algorithm 2. Line 1 extracts all transition paths of some length from the Petri net acting as the query. For example, if the *L1P index* is used, all paths of length one are extracted. If the *L2CP index* is used, all paths of length two are extracted, and then all paths

Algorithm 2. PetriNetQuery

```
   input  : pn: the Petri net query
   output: R: a set of Petri nets cover pn
1  sps ← PathExtraction(pn);
2  foreach path ∈ sps do
3  |  list ← PathIndexQuery(path);
4  |  add list to lists;
5  end
6  R ← Intersection(lists);
7  foreach respn ∈ R do
8  |  if CBMTest(pn, respn) fails then
9  |  |  delete respn from R;
10 |  end
11 end
12 return R;
```

of length one for those transitions that have not been used in any transition path of length two are also extracted. Lines 2-6 work as a filter and a set of candidate models is obtained, that is, the first stage of query processing. Given a path ϕ_i, Line 3 obtains a list of models $\phi_i.list$ containing this path using the index whose length equals $\phi_i.length$. In Line 6 the intersection of the resulting candidate sets is computed so as to retain only those candidate models that contain all the path queries. If some models were deleted from the repository, we would need to remove them from this intersection (this is not shown). In Lines 7-11 each candidate model is checked in order to determine whether it exactly covers the query, thus implementing the second stage of query processing. Function `CBMTest` implements the Petri net cover check according to Definition 1. It is an adaptation of Ullman's graph isomorphism algorithm [8] to Petri nets.

5 Tool Support and Evaluation

In order to validate our approach, we developed a system called BeehiveZ[2]. BeehiveZ is a java application, which makes use of the Derby RDBMS to store process models as data type CLOB. Based on the generic *LnP index*, we implemented the *L1P index* and *L2CP index*. The ProM library was used for the representation and display of Petri nets.

We conducted a number of experiments, both on a synthetic dataset and on a dataset consisting of SAP Reference Models (for this latter experiment we refer to [10]) to determine efficiency of the algorithms presented in the previous section. To this end a computer with Intel(R) Core(TM)2 Duo CPU E8400 @3.00GHz and 3GB memory was used. This computer ran Windows XP Professional SP3 and jdk6. All synthetic models were generated automatically using an algorithm

[2] BeehiveZ can be downloaded from http://sourceforge.net/projects/beehivez/

that produces a collection of Petri nets randomly. The rules used in our generator come from [11]. In the experiments on the synthetic dataset 10 models were generated to act as queries and more than 40,000 models were generated to populate the business process model repository. The number of transitions in the various models ranged from 1 to 198, the number of places from 2 to 140, the number of arcs from 2 to 765, and there were at most 242,234 differently labeled transitions out of 2,201,573 transitions in total. The 10 queries were evaluated each time after the addition of a certain number of freshly generated process models.

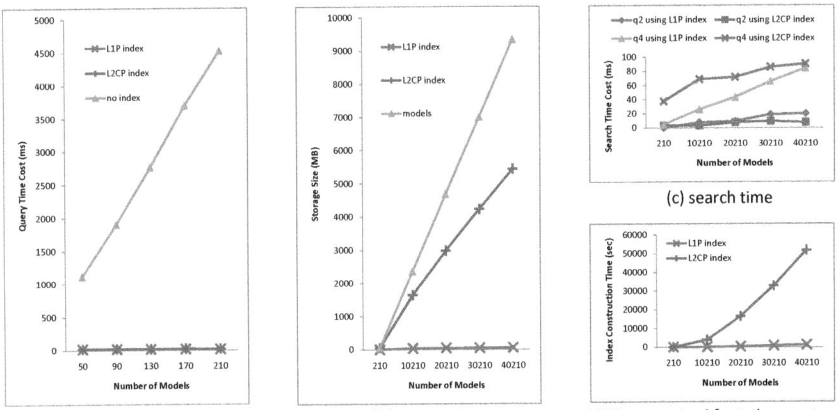

(a) query time comparison on q_2 (b) storage size (d) time required for index construction

Fig. 1. Performance of path-based indexes

As the number of candidate models is often much smaller than the size of the repository, the use of an index can save a significant amount of time, as shown in Fig. 1(a). Fig. 1(c) shows the search time for queries q_2 and q_4 using both the *L1P index* and the *L2CP index*. It can be observed that the performance of one index is not always better than the other one. Fig. 1(d) shows the time required for index construction. Here it can be observed that the *L1P index* performs better than the *L2CP index*. Whenever a new model is added to the repository, the index does not need to be reconstructed but can simply be modified. Therefore the time required for index construction is acceptable. The storage size of path-based indexes is shown in Fig. 1(b). Here too the *L1P index* performs better than the *L2CP index*. From Fig. 1, one can deduce that for the *LnCP index* if the length of paths is too large, the storage size may exceed the size required for storing the models, and the index construction would be more time consuming. This is a consequence of the fact that there are more paths in the models. Therefore the *L1P index* may be more suitable in practice.

In the above experiments, the order of B+ trees was 100, every inverted list slot contained at most 100 model identifiers, and caching for B+ trees and inverted lists was disabled. The performance of path-based indexes would be enhanced if we used cache for B+ trees and inverted lists. The size of cache for

B+ trees and inverted lists can be configured in the BeehiveZ system, and the *LRU* (Least Recently Used) algorithm is used.

6 Related Work

Our work is inspired by the *filtering and verification* approach used in graph indexing algorithms. Given a graph database and a graph query, these algorithms are used to improve the efficiency of finding all graphs in the database that contain the graph query as a subgraph, by discarding the models that do not have to be checked for subgraph isomorphism. Different graph indexing algorithms [1,2,3,4,5,6,7] use different graph features as indexes. All these approaches work on abstract graphs with one type of node, while our approach operates on Petri nets which are bipartite graphs. Additionally, in [2,3,4,6], focus is on frequent sub-structures and thus they cannot efficiently deal with queries consisting of isolated nodes or infrequent sub-structures. Hence, they are not suitable for process models, where each task may have a different label (thus reducing the frequency of common sub-structures) and queries may be made up of isolated tasks only. Moreover, extraction of sub-structures is more time-consuming and the storage space required increases. Another common drawback of these graph indexing algorithms is that the index is constructed using statistics on frequent features which are usually computed off-line, thus indexes cannot be easily updated when a new model is inserted into the graph database. Our approach on the other hand allows us to update the current indexes whenever a new model is added to the repository.

Our work has also commonalities with query languages for process models [12,13,14,15]. As opposed to our approach, all these approaches do not focus on query efficiency. For this reason, our approach is complementary to these approaches.

An indexing technique is used in [16] to search for matching process models. However, here models are represented as annotated finite state automata whereas we use generic Petri nets. Moreover, while there is support for a filtering stage, there is no refinement stage, thus reducing the accuracy of the result.

7 Conclusion and Future Work

We propose path-based indexes to speed up queries on business process model repositories in this paper. We follow a two-stage approach for query evaluation. In the first stage (filtering), we obtain an approximate result through the use of indexes. In the second stage (verification), we refine this set by using an adaptation of Ullman's subgraph isomorphism algorithm to Petri nets, in order to discard those models that do not contain the model query as a subgraph. We conducted experiments to demonstrate that the use of these indexes speeds up queries in a significant manner.

In this paper, our focus is solely on the control flow perspective of business processes. It would be interesting to enrich queries with information concerning data manipulation and resource allocation in the future.

Acknowledgments. We thank Lijie Wen for his helpful suggestions. We also thank Haiping Zha, Tengfei He and Tao Li for their contribution to the development of BeehiveZ. The work is supported by the National Basic Research Program (973 Plan) of China (No. 2009CB320700 and No. 2007CB310802), the National High-Tech Development Program (863 Plan) of China (No. 2008AA042301 and No. 2007AA040607) and CSC (China Scholarship Council).

References

1. Shasha, D., Wang, J.T.-L., Giugno, R.: Algorithmics and Applications of Tree and Graph Searching. In: PODS, pp. 39–52 (2002)
2. Yan, X., Yu, P.S., Han, J.: Graph Indexing: A Frequent Structure-based Approach. In: SIGMOD, pp. 335–346 (2004)
3. Zhang, S., Hu, M., Yang, J.: TreePi: A Novel Graph Indexing Method. In: ICDE, pp. 966–975 (2007)
4. Cheng, J., Ke, Y., Ng, W., Lu, A.: Fg-index: Towards Verification-free Query Processing on Graph Databases. In: SIGMOD, pp. 857–872 (2007)
5. Williams, D.W., Huan, J., Wang, W.: Graph Database Indexing Using Structured Graph Decomposition. In: ICDE, pp. 976–985 (2007)
6. Zhao, P., Yu, J.X., Yu, P.S.: Graph Indexing: Tree + Delta >= Graph. In: VLDB, pp. 938–949 (2007)
7. Zou, L., Chen, L., Zhang, H., Lu, Y., Lou, Q.: Summarization Graph Indexing: Beyond Frequent Structure-Based Approach. In: Haritsa, J.R., Kotagiri, R., Pudi, V. (eds.) DASFAA 2008. LNCS, vol. 4947, pp. 141–155. Springer, Heidelberg (2008)
8. Ullmann, J.R.: An Algorithm for Subgraph Isomorphism. Journal of the ACM 23(1), 31–42 (1976)
9. Lohmann, N., Verbeek, E., Dijkman, R.M.: Petri Net Transformations for Business Processes - A Survey. Transactions on Petri Nets and Other Models of Concurrency 2, 46–63 (2009)
10. Jin, T., Wang, J., Wu, N., La Rosa, M., ter Hofstede, A.H.M.: Efficient and accurate retrieval of business process models through indexing. Technical report, Tsinghua University (2010)
11. Chrzastowski-Wachtel, P., Benatallah, B., Hamadi, R., O'Dell, M., Susanto, A.: A Top-Down Petri Net-Based Approach for Dynamic Workflow Modeling. In: van der Aalst, W.M.P., ter Hofstede, A.H.M., Weske, M. (eds.) BPM 2003. LNCS, vol. 2678, pp. 336–353. Springer, Heidelberg (2003)
12. Momotko, M., Subieta, K.: Process Query Language: A Way to Make Workflow Processes More Flexible. In: Benczúr, A.A., Demetrovics, J., Gottlob, G. (eds.) ADBIS 2004. LNCS, vol. 3255, pp. 306–321. Springer, Heidelberg (2004)
13. Awad, A.: BPMN-Q: A Language to Query Business Processes. In: EMISA, pp. 115–128 (2007)
14. Di Francescomarino, C., Tonella, P.: Crosscutting Concern Documentation by Visual Query of Business Processes. In: Business Process Management Workshops, pp. 18–31 (2008)
15. Hornung, T., Koschmider, A., Oberweis, A.: A Recommender System for Business Process Models. In: Proceedings of the 17th Workshop on Information Technologies and Systems (2007)
16. Mahleko, B., Wombacher, A.: Indexing business processes based on annotated finite state automata. In: ICWS, pp. 303–311 (2006)

The Biconnected Verification of Workflow Nets

Artem Polyvyanyy, Matthias Weidlich, and Mathias Weske

Business Process Technology Group
Hasso Plattner Institute at the University of Potsdam
Prof.-Dr.-Helmert-Str. 2–3, D-14482 Potsdam, Germany
{Artem.Polyvyanyy,Matthias.Weidlich,Mathias.Weske}@hpi.uni-potsdam.de

Abstract. Formal representations of business processes are used for analysis of the process behavior. Workflow nets are a widely used formalism for describing the behavior of business processes. Structure theory of processes investigates the relation between the structure of a model and its behavior. In this paper, we propose to employ the connectivity property of workflow nets as an angle to their structural analysis. In particular, we show how soundness verification can be organized using biconnected components of a workflow net. This allows for efficient identification and localization of flaws in the behavior of workflow nets and for supporting process analysts with diagnostic information.

1 Introduction

Business process modeling is the basis for understanding, improving, and implementing working procedures in organizations. Execution semantics of common business process definition languages, such as BPEL or UML activity diagrams, are described rather informally. However, formal investigations rely on a mapping of these languages into a formalism. To this end, various mappings from process definition languages to Petri nets have been proposed, e.g., [1,2].

Workflow nets are a structural subclass of Petri nets with a dedicated source (start) place and a dedicated sink (end) place. *Soundness* is a desirable correctness property of workflow nets [3], since a sound workflow net always terminates properly and each task can contribute to the completion of a process. Consequently, a business process is considered to be correct if the corresponding workflow net is sound.

Soundness verification is a well-studied problem. Most approaches use state space analysis to solve it, so that the resulting state space explosion problem has to be faced. In this paper, we advocate to use structural analysis of workflow nets to investigate soundness, providing insight into an alternative – and in many cases, preferable – way to check soundness. In particular, we employ the biconnected decomposition of workflow nets. That is, we identify components based on cut-vertices, i.e., nodes of the net that when removed yield the net disconnected. Based thereon, we point out how the soundness verification can be organized from the derived components of a workflow net. Where applicable, we draw conclusions on soundness for the general class of workflow nets; otherwise, the results are restricted to safe nets. Besides formal results on the biconnected decomposition of

R. Meersman et al. (Eds.): OTM 2010, Part I, LNCS 6426, pp. 410–418, 2010.

workflow nets, we provide an outlook on how the triconnected decomposition of biconnected components of workflow nets might also be used to verify soundness. Despite the variety of existing soundness verification techniques, the efficiency and the structural diagnostic information for the general class of workflow nets are unique characteristics of our approach, coming at the expense of verification completeness. Withal, we see a great potential in combining our approach with existing techniques to achieve more mature process model verification.

The paper is structured as follows. The next section provides formal preliminaries for our work. In Sect. 3, we show how soundness verification can be organized following on the biconnected decomposition of workflow nets. A discussion on how this approach can be extended using triconnected decomposition techniques is presented in Sect. 4. Finally, the paper closes with a discussion of related work and conclusions.

2 Preliminaries

We use Petri nets as our formal grounding. A Petri net has a structure given by a net, a marking that represents a state of the net, and the execution semantics that describes the principles of state transitions.

Definition 1 (Petri net). A *Petri net*, or a *net*, is a tuple $N = (P, T, F)$, with P and T as finite disjoint sets of places and transitions, $P \cap T = \emptyset$, and $F \subseteq (P \times T) \cup (T \times P)$ as the flow relation.

We write $X = (P \cup T)$ for all nodes of a net. The transitive closure of F is denoted by F^+. For a node $x \in X$, $\bullet x = \{y \in X \mid (y, x) \in F\}$, $x\bullet = \{y \in X \mid (x, y) \in F\}$. A node $x \in X$ is an *input* (*output*) node of a node $y \in X$, iff $x \in \bullet y$ ($x \in y\bullet$). $in_N(x) = \{(n, x) \mid n \in \bullet x\}$ are the *incoming* flows of x and $out_N(x) = \{(x, n) \mid n \in x\bullet\}$ are the *outgoing* flows of x.

Definition 2 (Net semantics). Let $N = (P, T, F)$ be a net.

- $M : P \to \mathbb{N}_0$ is a *marking* of N, $\mathbb{M}$ denotes all markings of N. $M(p)$ returns the number of *tokens* in place p. $[p]$ denotes the marking when place p contains just one token and all other places contain no tokens.
- For any transition $t \in T$ and any marking $M \in \mathbb{M}$, t is *enabled* in M, denoted by $(N, M)[t\rangle$, iff $\forall p \in \bullet t : M(p) \geq 1$.
- Marking M' is reached from M by *firing* of t, denoted by $(N, M)[t\rangle(N, M')$, such that $M' = M - \bullet t + t\bullet$, i.e., one token is taken from each input place of t and one token is added to each output place of t.
- A *firing sequence* of length $n \in \mathbb{N}$ is a function $\sigma : \{0, \ldots, n-1\} \to T$. For $\sigma = \{(0, t_x), \ldots, (n-1, t_y)\}$, we also write $\sigma = t_0, \ldots, t_{n-1}$.
- For any two markings $M, M' \in \mathbb{M}$, M' is *reachable* from M in N, denoted by $M' \in [N, M\rangle$, iff there exists a firing sequence σ leading from M to M'.
- A *system* is a pair (N, M_0), where N is a net and M_0 its *initial marking*.

Workflow (WF-)nets form a subclass of Petri nets. WF-nets were proposed in [4] for modeling workflow definitions. A WF-net is a net with two special places: one to mark the initialization and the other to mark the completion of a workflow.

Definition 3 (WF-net, Short-circuit net, WF-system)
A Petri net $N = (P, T, F)$ is a *workflow net* (or a *WF-net*), iff N has a dedicated *source* place $i \in P$, with $\bullet i = \emptyset$, N has a dedicated *sink* place $o \in P$, with $o\bullet = \emptyset$, and the *short-ciruit* net $N' = (P, T \cup \{t^*\}, F \cup \{(o, t^*), (t^*, i)\})$, $t^* \notin T$, of N is strongly connected. A *WF-system* is a pair (N, M_i), where $M_i = [i]$.

Soundness is the basic correctness property of workow nets [3]. A sound workow net always terminates and each transition can contribute to the completion of the workflow by following certain route through the net.

Definition 4 (Liveness, Boundedness, Safeness, Soundness)
- A system (N, M_0) is *live*, iff for every reachable marking $M \in [N, M_0\rangle$ and $t \in T$, there exists a marking $M' \in [N, M\rangle$ such that $(N, M')[t\rangle$.
- A system (N, M_0) is *bounded*, iff the set $[N, M_0\rangle$ is finite.
- A system (N, M_0) is *safe*, iff $\forall\ M \in [N, M_0\rangle\ \forall\ p \in P : M(p) \leq 1$.
- A WF-system (N, M_i) with $N = (P, T, F)$ is *sound*, iff the short-circuit system (N', M_i) is live and bounded.

For the purpose of structural analysis of nets, we give the following definitions.

Definition 5 (Subnet, Path)
Let $N' = (P', T', F')$ and $N = (P, T, F)$ be two nets, and let $P' \subseteq P$, $T' \subseteq T$. N' is a *subnet* of N, denoted $N' \subseteq N$, iff $F' = F \cap ((P' \times T') \cup (T' \times P'))$. A *path* is a non-empty sequence $\langle x_1, \ldots, x_k \rangle$ of nodes, $k > 1$, denoted by $\pi(x_1, x_k)$, which satisfies $(x_1, x_2), \ldots, (x_{k-1}, x_k) \in F$. We write $x_i \in \pi$, if x_i is on the path.

The structure of a Petri net (P, T, F) is defined by the graph (X, F). Connectivity is a basic property of a graph. A graph is *connected* if every pair of distinct vertices in the graph is connected; otherwise the graph is *disconnected*. A graph is *biconnected* if there exists no vertex whose removal renders the graph disconnected. If such a vertex exists, it is called a *cutvertex*. Note that removal of a vertex implies removal of all incident edges. After removing a cutvertex from a graph, the graph gets decomposed into disconnected subgraphs (or *components*).

3 Biconnected Verification of WF-Nets

The soundness of a WF-net can be verified by checking liveness and boundedness of the corresponding short-circuit net. Short-circuit nets are connected, but not necessarily biconnected. This section explains how soundness verification of a WF-net can be broken down into checks of its biconnected components.

The classic sequential algorithm for computing biconnected components in a connected graph, proposed in [5], runs in linear time. Let (X, F) be a connected graph, then the algorithm requires time and space proportional to $max(|X|, |F|)$. Biconnected components can be arranged in a tree structure—the *tree of the biconnected components*. The tree has two types of nodes that refer either to cutvertices or to biconnected components. Edges of the tree connect cutvertices with associated biconnected components, i.e., there is an edge between a cutvertex and a biconnected component if the biconnected component contains the

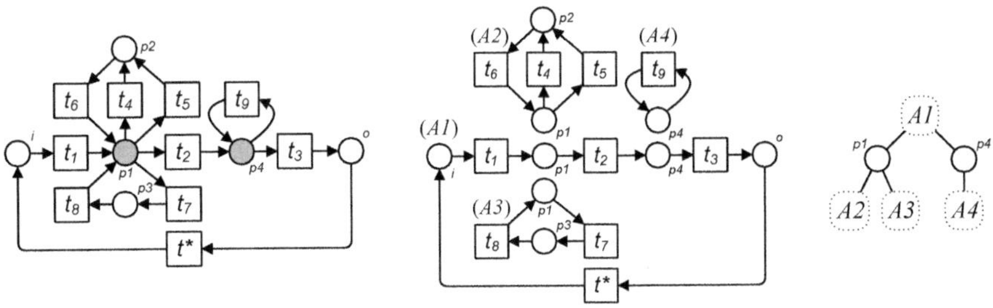

Fig. 1. (a) A short-circuit net, (b) biconnected subnets, and (c) the 2-WF-tree

cutvertex. The number of nodes in the tree is $O(|X|)$ and, hence, the space required to store the tree and all the biconnected components is $O(max(|X|, |F|))$.

A *biconnected subnet* is a biconnected component of a short-circuit net. The *tree of the biconnected subnets*, or the *2-WF-tree*, is the tree of the biconnected components of a short-circuit net.

Definition 6 (The tree of the biconnected subnets)
Let $N = (P, T, F)$ be a WF-net and let N' be its short-circuit net with the extra transition t^*. The *tree of the biconnected subnets*, or the *2-WF-tree*, of N is a tuple $\mathcal{T}_N^2 = (\mathcal{B}, \mathcal{C}, \rho, \eta, \triangle)$, where:

- $\mathcal{B}$ is a set of all biconnected subnets and $\mathcal{C}$ is a set of all cutvertices of N',
- $\rho = (P_\rho, T_\rho, F_\rho) \in \mathcal{B}$ is the root of $\mathcal{T}_N^2$, iff $t^* \in T_\rho$,
- $\eta : \mathcal{B} \to \mathcal{P}(\mathcal{B})$ assigns to biconnected subnet its child biconnected subnets,
- $\triangle \subseteq \mathcal{B} \times \mathcal{C} \times \mathcal{B}$, $(b_1, c, b_2) \in \triangle$, iff c is shared by b_1 and b_2, and $b_2 \in \eta(b_1)$.

Fig. 1 exemplifies the biconnected decomposition of a WF-net: Fig. 1(a) shows a short-circuit net. The net has two place cutvertices $p1$ and $p4$, which are highlighted with grey background. The cutvertices induce four biconnected subnets $A1$–$A4$, cf., Fig. 1(b). Finally, Fig. 1(c) organizes the subnets in the 2-WF-tree with the root node that corresponds to the biconnected subnet $A1$.

One observation is that a WF-net can be sound only if all the cutvertices of the corresponding short-circuit net are places.

Lemma 1. *Let (N, M_i), $N = (P, T, F)$, be a WF-system and N' be the short-circuit net of N. If $t \in T$ is a cutvertex of N', then (N, M_i) is not sound.*

Proof. Because t is a cutvertex of N', there exists $p' \in \bullet t$, $p' \neq i$, such that t is on every path $\pi(i, p')$. We show now by induction that t is never enabled, i.e., for every marking $M \in [N, M_i\rangle$ holds $\neg(N, M)[t\rangle$.

base: $\neg(N, M_i)[t\rangle$ as $M_i(p') = 0$, i.e., t is not enabled by the initial marking.

step: Let M' be a marking reachable from M_i by a firing sequence σ that does not contain t, i.e., t was never enabled. Let $t' \in T$ be such that $(N, M')[t'\rangle$. Assume that $t' = t$, then $M'(p') \geq 1$. If $M'(p') \geq 1$, then σ contains all the transitions of some path $\pi(i, p')$ and, hence, contains t. We have reached the contradiction and, therefore, $t' \neq t$.

As t is never enabled, (N', M_i) is not live. Thus, (N, M_i) is not sound. □

A transition cutvertex hints at unsoundness of the net and, therefore, constitutes valuable diagnostic information. In case all cutvertices of a short-circuit net are places, verification procedure should proceed. We show how the verification procedure can be broken down into checks of biconnected subnets of the short-circuit net. First, we explain how to derive WF-nets from biconnected subnets.

Definition 7 (Biconnected sub-WF-net). Let $N = (P, T, F)$ be a WF-net, $\mathcal{T}_N^2 = (\mathcal{B}, \mathcal{C}, \rho, \eta, \Delta)$ its 2-WF-tree, and $b = (P_b, T_b, F_b) \in \mathcal{B}$. A *biconnected sub-WF-net* of N, denoted $b^\star$, $b^\star = (P_{b^\star}, T_{b^\star}, F_{b^\star})$, is obtained from b as follows:
- ◦ If $b = \rho$, then $P_{b^\star} = P_b$, $T_{b^\star} = T_b \cap T$, and $F_{b^\star} = F_b \cap F$.
- ◦ If $b \neq \rho$ and $a \in \mathcal{B}$, $c \in \mathcal{C}$ are such that there exists $(a, c, b) \in \Delta$, then $P_{b^\star} = (P_b \setminus \{c\}) \cup \{i, o\}$, $T_{b^\star} = T_b$, and $F_{b^\star} = \{(x_1, x_2) \in F_b \mid x_1 \neq c \wedge x_2 \neq c\} \cup \{(i, x) \in \{i\} \times T_b \mid (c, x) \in F_b\} \cup \{(x, o) \in T_b \times \{o\} \mid (x, c) \in F_b\}$.

A WF-net that corresponds to a subtree of b, denoted b^Δ, is obtained by merging sub-WF-net $b^\star$ and all subnets that are descendants of b at shared cutvertices. Biconnected sub-WF-nets are also referred to as biconnected WF-nets.

Fig. 2 presents sub-WF-nets of the short-circuit net provided in Fig. 1(a). The sub-WF-nets correspond to the biconnected subnets in Fig. 1(b). Sub-WF-net $A1$ is obtained from the corresponding biconnected subnet by ignoring transition t^* and adjacent flow relations. In the case when a biconnected subnet is not the root of the 2-WF-tree, cf., Fig. 1(c), the corresponding sub-WF-net is obtained as follows: The cutvertex that corresponds to the parent node in the 2-WF-tree is removed from the subnet and two fresh places are added, a source place i and a sink place o. The flow relations of the cutvertex are rerouted to originate from i or to terminate at o, respectively.

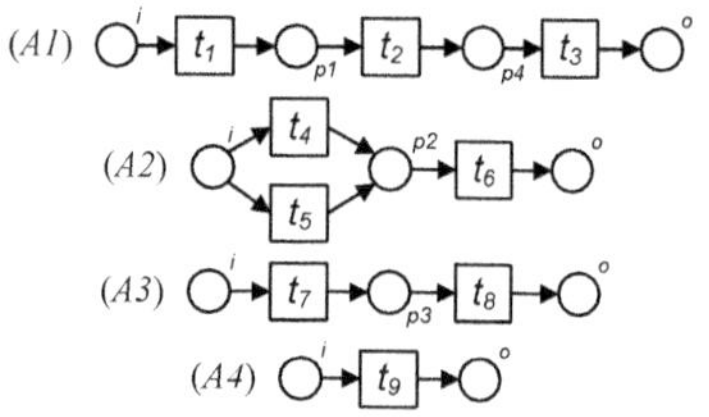

Fig. 2. Biconnected sub-WF-nets

Construction of a WF-net that corresponds to a subtree in the 2-WF-tree is supported by two types of transformations, viz., refinements, of nets.

Definition 8 (Self-loop place refinement, Transition refinement)
- ◦ Let $N_1 = (P_1, T_1, F_1)$ be a net, $p \in P_1$ a place. A *self-loop place refinement* of p yields a net $N_2 = (P_1, T_1 \cup \{t_p\}, F_1 \cup \{(p, t_p), (t_p, p)\})$, denoted $N_1[p]$.
- ◦ Let $N_1 = (P_1, T_1, F_1)$ be a net, $N_2 = (P_2, T_2, F_2)$ a WF-net with source i and sink o, $T_1 \cap T_2 = \emptyset$, $P_1 \cap P_2 = \emptyset$, and $t \in T_1$. A *transition refinement* of t by N_2 yields a net $N_3 = (P_3, T_3, F_3)$, denoted $N_1[t/N_2]$, such that:
  - – $P_3 = P_1 \cup (P_2 \setminus \{i, o\})$, $T_3 = (T_1 \setminus \{t\}) \cup T_2$, and
  - – $F_3 = \{(x_1, x_2) \in F_1 | x_1 \neq t \wedge x_2 \neq t\} \cup \{(x_1, x_2) \in F_2 | \{x_1, x_2\} \cap \{i, o\}\}$
    $\cup \{(x_1, x_2) \in P_1 \times T_2 \mid (x_1, t) \in F_1 \wedge (i, x_2) \in F_2\}$
    $\cup \{(x_1, x_2) \in T_2 \times P_1 \mid (t, x_2) \in F_1 \wedge (x_1, o) \in F_2\}$.

A self-loop place refinement preserves liveness and safeness, cf., [6]. The concept of transition refinement is borrowed from [7,8]. Fig. 3(a) shows the self-loop refinement of place p_1 in the WF-net $A1$ from Fig. 2, whereas Fig. 3(b) depicts the transition t_{p_1} refinement in the WF-net from Fig. 3(a) by WF-net $A2$.

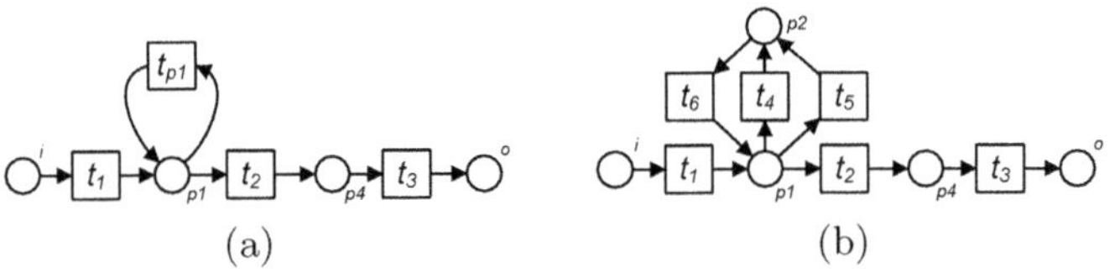

Fig. 3. (a) A self-loop place refinement, and (b) a transition refinement

By using biconnected sub-WF-nets of a WF-net and the net transformations from Definition 8 it is possible to organize soundness verification of the WF-net. In the class of safe systems, the soundness of a system is closely related to the soundness of its biconnected sub-WF-nets.

Theorem 1. *Each biconnected sub-WF-net of a WF-net is safe and sound, iff the WF-net is safe and sound.*

Proof. Let N be a WF-net and let $\mathcal{T}_N^2 = (\mathcal{B}, \mathcal{C}, \rho, \eta, \triangle)$ be the 2-WF-tree of N.
($\Rightarrow$) By structural induction on the tree of the biconnected subnets.

base: If $\mathcal{T}_N^2$ contains only one biconnected subnet, i.e., $|\mathcal{B}| = 1$, then N is a biconnected WF-net. Obviously, the claim holds.

step: Let $b \in \mathcal{B}$ be a biconnected subnet. Suppose that the claim holds for all $a^\triangle$ such that $a \in \eta(b)$. We show by induction that the claim is also true for $b^\triangle$.
$b^\star$ is a biconnected sub-WF-net of N and, hence, is safe and sound. Let $a \in \eta(b)$ and $c \in \mathcal{C}$ be such that $(b, c, a) \in \triangle$. A WF-net $b' = b^\star[c]$ with a self-loop transition t_c is safe and sound. A WF-net $b'[t_c/a^\triangle]$ is safe and sound, cf., statement 4 of Theorem 3 in [8]. Therefore, after refining $b^\star$ with all the biconnected WF-nets that correspond to subnets from $\eta(b)$ one obtains a safe and sound WF-net that is equal to $b^\triangle$.

As $\rho^\triangle$ is equal to N, the claim holds.
($\Leftarrow$) The claim trivially holds by following ($\Rightarrow$) in the reverse direction. □

Therefore, it suffices to show that at least one biconnected sub-WF-net is not safe and sound in order to conclude that the WF-net is not safe and sound. This biconnected sub-WF-net causes unsoundness and constitutes valuable diagnostic information. Finally, because biconnected sub-WF-nets can be computed in time linear to the size of a net, the biconnected decomposition step does not add to the overall complexity of soundness verification.

4 Towards Triconnected Verification of WF-Nets

This section sketches the connectivity-based soundness verification of biconnected WF-nets. Biconnected WF-nets contain no cutvertices; they can, however, contain pairs of vertices that when removed yield the *triconnected* subnets. The sequential algorithm for computing triconnected components in a biconnected graph runs in linear time, cf., [9]. In [10], the authors discuss implementation aspects of the algorithm. Let (X, F) be a biconnected graph, then the algorithm requires time and space proportional to $max(|X|, |F|)$.

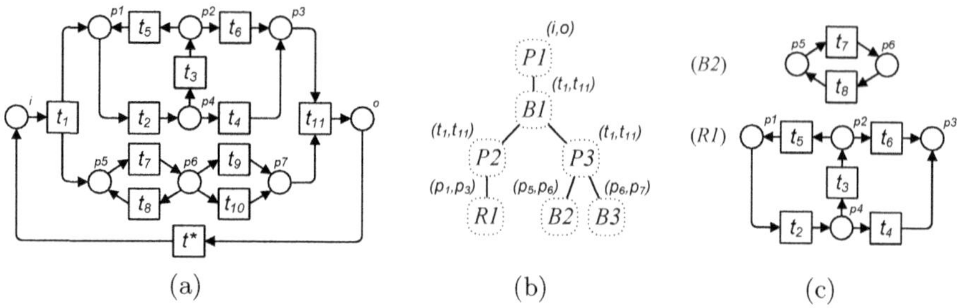

Fig. 4. (a) A short-circuit net, (b) the 3-WF-tree, and (c) triconnected subnets

The triconnected decomposition of WF-nets is illustrated in Fig. 4. Fig. 4(a) shows a WF-net that is biconnected, but not triconnected. That is, it contains several triconnected subnets. For instance, the subnet between places $p1$ and $p3$ is such triconnected subnet, as the removal of both nodes yields the graph disconnected. According to [11], there are four structural classes of triconnected components and, therefore, of triconnected subnets. A subnet is *trivial* if its a flow; a *polygon* if it decomposes into a sequence of subnets where the exit of a subnet is the entry of the next subnet in the sequence; a *bond* if it decomposes into a set of subnets that share boundary nodes; or a *rigid* otherwise. These subnets form a hierarchy that yields the tree of triconnected subnets, similar to the tree of biconnected subnets introduced above. Fig. 4(b) shows this tree for the example net in Fig. 4(a), while Fig. 4(c) also depicts two exemplary triconnected subnets. Note that names of subnets hint at their structural class.

The subnets derived by triconnected decomposition of a WF-net may be leveraged for soundness verification. While a detailed investigation of these nets is beyond the scope of this paper, initial results have been presented already for free-choice nets in [12]. There it was shown that for this class of nets soundness imposes certain requirements on the boundary nodes of triconnected components. For instance, all bond components of a free-choice sound WF-net are either place-bordered or transition-bordered. Moreover, heuristics for soundness verification based on triconnected components have also been proposed in [13].

5 Related Work and Conclusion

In this paper, we have investigated the relation between the connectivity property of a WF-net and its behavioral correctness. We organized soundness verification based on the biconnected decomposition of a WF-net and discussed the potential for leveraging its triconnected decomposition.

Our approach relates to other work on the verification of process models. Verification of workflow graphs might be organized based on fragments that have a single-entry edge and a single-exit edge [14]. Albeit related, this work leverages edge-connectivity, whereas our work uses node-connectivity. Soundness checking based on heuristics and state space exploration for a triconnected decomposition of a (free-choice) process graph has been proposed in [13]. Our technique complements this approach and might be integrated to achieve more mature soundness verification. Verification of Petri nets can be based on structural reductions. Besides the rules by Murata [6], Berthelot proposed a set of rules that reduce live and bounded marked graphs to a single transition [15], while there is a complete kit of rules for free-choice Petri nets [16]. All these rules are incomplete when applied to nets of arbitrary structure.

Despite the large body of related work on the formal verification of process models, we are not aware of any work that employs the connectivity property as an angle to their structural analysis. The biconnected decomposition allows for a *divide and conquer* strategy as suggested by the principles of connectivity-based decomposition outlined in [17]. In future work, we aim at extending our approach towards a holistic verification framework that allows for verification of ordinary Petri nets using step-wise connectivity-based decomposition.

References

1. Lohmann, N.: A feature-complete Petri net semantics for WS-BPEL 2.0. In: Dumas, M., Heckel, R. (eds.) WS-FM 2007. LNCS, vol. 4937, pp. 77–91. Springer, Heidelberg (2008)
2. Eshuis, R., Wieringa, R.: Tool support for verifying UML activity diagrams. IEEE Trans. Software Eng. 30(7), 437–447 (2004)
3. Aalst, W.: Verification of workflow nets. In: Azéma, P., Balbo, G. (eds.) ICATPN 1997. LNCS, vol. 1248, pp. 407–426. Springer, Heidelberg (1997)
4. Aalst, W.: The application of Petri nets to workflow management. Journal of Circuits, Systems, and Computers 8(1), 21–66 (1998)
5. Hopcroft, J., Tarjan, R.: Algorithm 447: efficient algorithms for graph manipulation. ACM Commun. 16(6), 372–378 (1973)
6. Murata, T.: Petri nets: Properties, analysis and applications. Proceedings of the IEEE 77(4), 541–580 (1989)
7. Valette, R.: Analysis of petri nets by stepwise refinements. J. Comput. Syst. Sci. 18(1), 35–46 (1979)
8. Aalst, W.: Workflow verification: Finding control-flow errors using petri-net-based techniques. In: van der Aalst, W.M.P., Desel, J., Oberweis, A. (eds.) BPM 2000. LNCS, vol. 1806, pp. 161–183. Springer, Heidelberg (2000)
9. Hopcroft, J., Tarjan, R.: Dividing a graph into triconnected components. SIAM Journal on Computing 2(3), 135–158 (1973)
10. Gutwenger, C., Mutzel, P.: A linear time implementation of SPQR-trees. In: Marks, J. (ed.) GD 2000. LNCS, vol. 1984, pp. 77–90. Springer, Heidelberg (2001)
11. Polyvyanyy, A., Vanhatalo, J., Voelzer, H.: Simplified computation and generalization of the refined process structure tree. In: WS-FM, Hoboken, NJ, US, (to appear, September 2010)
12. Weidlich, M., Polyvyanyy, A., Mendling, J., Weske, M.: Efficient computation of causal behavioural profiles using structural decomposition. In: Lilius, J., Penczek, W. (eds.) Applications and Theory of Petri Nets. LNCS, vol. 6128, pp. 63–83. Springer, Heidelberg (2010)
13. Fahland, D., Favre, C., Jobstmann, B., Koehler, J., Lohmann, N., Völzer, H., Wolf, K.: Instantaneous soundness checking of industrial business process models. In: Dayal, U., Eder, J., Koehler, J., Reijers, H.A. (eds.) BPM 2009. LNCS, vol. 5701, pp. 278–293. Springer, Heidelberg (2009)

14. Vanhatalo, J., Völzer, H., Leymann, F.: Faster and more focused control-flow analysis for business process models through SESE decomposition. In: Krämer, B.J., Lin, K.-J., Narasimhan, P. (eds.) ICSOC 2007. LNCS, vol. 4749, pp. 43–55. Springer, Heidelberg (2007)
15. Berthelot, G.: Transformations and decompositions of nets. In: Brauer, W., Reisig, W., Rozenberg, G. (eds.) APN 1986. LNCS, vol. 254, pp. 359–376. Springer, Heidelberg (1987)
16. Desel, J., Esparza, J.: Free Choice Petri Nets. Cambridge University Press, Cambridge (1995)
17. Polyvyanyy, A.: Structural abstraction of process specifications. In: ZEUS (2010)

Business Process Scheduling with Resource Availability Constraints

Jiajie Xu[1], Chengfei Liu[1], Xiaohui Zhao[2], and Sira Yongchareon[1]

[1] Faculty of Information and Communication Technologies
Swinburne University of Technology, Australia
{jxu,cliu,syongchareon}@groupwise.swin.edu.au
[2] Department of Industrial Engineering and Innovation Sciences
Eindhoven University of Technology, The Netherlands
x.zhao@tue.nl

Abstract. Resources tend to follow certain availability patterns, due to the maintenance cycles, work shifts, etc. Such availability patterns heavily influence the efficiency and effectiveness of enterprise process scheduling. Most existing process scheduling and resource management approaches focus on process structure and resource utilisation, yet neglect the resource availability constraints. In this paper, we investigate how to plan the business process instances scheduling in accordance with resource availability patterns, so that enterprise resources can be rationally and sufficiently used. Three planning strategies are proposed to maximise the process instance throughput using different criteria.

1 Introduction

Resource planning is a classical issue for enterprise operation management, whilst the global financial crisis further urges enterprises to seek optimal resource utilisation for cost effectiveness. Planning resources for a large number of process instances before execution guarantees the business requirements to be satisfied and benefits enterprises for intelligent marketing-decision support, and such planning for enterprise operations is always subject to resource capacity and availability [3, 5]. However, most existing works [1, 3, 5, 6] focus on handling this problem at the run time. This paper incorporates the resource availability constraints and process structures into build time process scheduling, and devises a comprehensive framework for maximising process instance throughput with a set of strategies.

Apart from the deadline constraint in classical resource management for business processes, high process instance concurrency is highly sought after in most application scenarios. This is because that the concurrently running instances lead to high instance throughput and efficient resource utilisation for resource management and process scheduling. However, it is not realistic to increase the process instance concurrency by pushing all resources together to serve instances, because resources themselves are only available in certain time periods in practice, e.g., a worker is not supposed to work after hours. Thus, the process scheduling should take into account

R. Meersman et al. (Eds.): OTM 2010, Part I, LNCS 6426, pp. 419–427, 2010.

the resource availability, resource capability, process task dependency, instance deadline, as well as the inter-influence among these factors.

As a classical enterprise management topic, process scheduling has attracted a lot of research efforts. Some algorithms in this area using different heuristics (such as GA, SA, etc.) are compared in work [12]. However, most of these approaches assume that the availability information of resources can only be known at run time. In our previous work [4], we assume that the availability of resources can be tailored to tasks. To the best of our knowledge, so far no work has addressed the influence of resource availability on scheduling large scale of process instances at the build time, which is an important issue. To tackle this problem and further improve the process scheduling performance, in this paper we propose a comprehensive scheduling framework in this paper to deal with the scheduling of heterogeneous process instances under resource availability constraints at build time, so as to maximise the number of instances to be successfully scheduled in different criteria.

The rest of this paper is organised as follows: Section 2 introduces a model including the key notions for process instance scheduling, and formally defines the problem we intend to address. Three strategies for process scheduling are proposed in Section 3. Section 4 reviews the related work and discusses the advantages of our approach. Lastly, concluding remarks and future works are given in Section 5.

2 Model and Problem Definition

In this section, we first present a model comprising resources, tasks, process instances and resource allocation. Based on the definitions, the problem we intend to investigate in this paper is formally defined.

Definition 1. (Resource) Resource is used to perform tasks in business processes. A resource satisfies time availability constraints defined by a sequence of available time periods.

Definition 2. (Task) A task in a business process can be executed by a set of capable resources. For each resource capable of executing a task, the time required for executing this task may be different.

Definition 3. (Resource Slot) Resource slot measures a time duration (within the available time periods) of a particular resource. The resource of this slot may be *available* for use in a time duration (e.g., from start time *st* to end time *et*), or has been *assigned* to perform a task for a business process.

Definition 4. (Process Instance) A business process instance *ins* has a task set T and an edge set E, which defines the dependency between tasks. An edge $e(t_i, t_j) \in E$ indicates that t_j can only start after t_i finishes. The instance *ins* is required to be executed within a range $[D_s(ins), D_f(ins)]$, where $D_s(ins)$ stands for the earliest start time and $D_f(ins)$ the latest finishing time (deadline).

Definition 5. (Allocation) Allocation is the resource assignment to a task t of a process instance *ins*. An allocation <*ins*, *t*, *r*, *st*, *et*> indicates that an available slot *slt* of resource r is able to be allocated for executing task t of *ins* from time *st* to *et*. Such allocation may result in adjustment on those slots of r before or after *slt*.

Problem Statement
Given a set of resources *R*, and a number of instances *I*, the problem is to find a scheduling scheme *S* (which consists of a set of allocations) to schedule instances in *I* using resources in *R* such that maximal number of instances can be scheduled. During scheduling process, four constraints must be satisfied: **(C1)** Time constraint of instance - each instance *ins* must be executed between a required duration within the time range $[D_s(ins), D_f(ins)]$; **(C2)** Availability constraint of resource – each schedule from a task *t* to resource *r* must be in such a time duration that *r* is available; **(C3)** Process structural constraints – if there is an edge from task t_1 to task t_2 in the business process, then t_2 cannot start until t_1 finishes; **(C4)** Conflict free – at one time, one resource can only be used for executing one task.

3 Scheduling Strategies

Finding the optimal solution to the above defined problem is computationally hard. As such, near optimal strategies based on reasonable heuristic rules are sought after. To reduce the calculation for each allocation of a resource to a task, we first apply a so-called optimistic pre-allocation scheme to all instances by only satisfying constraints C1, C2 and C3 while ignoring constraint C4 between different instances (C4 on the single instance level is satisfied) at the beginning. For each allocation of the optimistic scheme, the most efficient resource is used. This pre-allocation sets a basis for the following process scheduling because after the pre-allocation, the time gap denoted as $g(ins)$ for each instance *ins* can be easily calculated as the difference between $D_f(ins)$ (the deadline of *ins*) and the finishing time of *ins* in the optimistic allocation. It is obvious that if $g(ins)$ is negative, then *ins* cannot be scheduled because the most efficient resources are used. We also know that this initial time gap is obtained by allowing conflict resource allocation. The scheduling process then is to re-allocate tasks such that constraint C4 can also be satisfied.

The time gap is an important indicator for the priority of instance allocation. An instance with smaller time gap is considered to be more "dangerous". Our first scheduling strategy is based on the rule to iteratively save the most "dangerous" instance *ins* which owns the minimum value in $g(ins)$. This strategy operates in a depth first manner and falls into the category of greedy algorithm as only local optimisation is applied to one instance (i.e., the most dangerous one) at a time. Sometimes, this strategy is practical because it guarantees that an instance is scheduled once it is processed. However, allowing one instance to go through may be at the cost of sacrificing other instances.

Given the limitation of the first strategy which is local optimisation based, we propose some holistic strategies that are global optimisation in nature. A holistic approach operates more or less in breadth first manner. Instead of scheduling one instance at a time, it allocates resource to a task of an instance at a time based on a particular rule. So this approach allows balanced scheduling and thus gives chances to all instances. It focuses more on dependencies among instances. Compared with the greedy strategy, instances scheduled in this approach tend to success or fail together. In most cases, the balanced scheduling approach enables more instances to be schedulable. However when resource is extremely limited, a holistic approach may cause more instances non-schedulable compared with the greedy strategy. In the holistic approach, we would like to allocate resource to the current task of an instance at a time. As to which instance to select, we design two strategies. The first strategy is to select the instance based on several heuristic rules about that instance, including whether it owns the minimum time gap. We call the current task in such an instance the most urgent task. This strategy is different from the greedy strategy because after the allocation, the time gap for other instances will be adjusted to use the remaining available resources in an optimistic way, and the instance with minimum time gap may be changed to another instance after the adjustment. However, it does bear similarity with the greedy strategy so we call it a dynamic local optimization strategy. The second strategy is dynamic global optimization. The holistic rules designed for this strategy are based on the penalty calculated from all instances, including the summation of the gap increases of all instances. This strategy chooses the instance with the minimum penalty to schedule.

Table 1. Scheduling strategies

Strategy	Priority
DM – Depth first/Min gap	Most dangerous instance (instance with the minimum time gap)
BL – Breadth first/dynamic Local optimisation	Most urgent task (mainly determined by the task in the most dangerous instance)
BG – Breadth first/dynamic Global optimisation	Least penalised task (the allocation of the task that results in the minimum time gap increases of all instances and other factors)

Table 1 summarises the three strategies introduced. The details of these strategies will be introduced in 3.1, 3.2, and 3.3, respectively. Also, a discussion about the comparison among three proposed strategies will be conducted in 3.4.

3.1 DM Scheduling Strategy - Depth First/Min Gap

This strategy is based on a greedy algorithm for process scheduling. Resource allocation is applied for the most dangerous instance one by one. The allocating sequence is in descending order of instance time gap. Given a set of instances, the instance *ins* with the minimal time gap has the least room to delay. If the resources are allocated to other instances first, this instance is most likely affected, i.e., re-allocation even using the remaining best available resources may cause it to exceed its deadline ($D_f(ins)$). Therefore the capable resources, we set the highest priority to this instance for occupying most efficient ones. The algorithm proceeds as follows. We first pre-allocate all instances in optimistic way such that each instance has a time gap initially. Then we select the instance with minimum time gap and keep the optimistic allocations for the instance. Once an instance is scheduled, due to the allocated resources to the instance, we have to adjust those affected allocations of other instances by using the remaining resources. After that, we continue to select the instance with minimum time gap among the un-scheduled instances. The selection and scheduling of the instance with the minimum time gap and allocation adjustment are repeated until none of the remaining instances are schedulable. The algorithm is conducted as the following steps.

1. Initial optimistic allocation. Firstly, we pre-allocate all instances and calculate their time gap to deadline before allocation, without considering the resource conflict (constraint C3). It provides the best scenarios for all the instances. Given instance set *I* and resource set *R*, we first find the current task *t* (or the task to be scheduled next) of *ins*, and then calculate the minimal end time of *t* with available resources by function. If the end time of *t* exceeds deadline, this instance is dropped out as it is definitely non-schedulable. Otherwise, *t* is allocated with the most efficient resource. This pre-allocation procedure continues until all instances have been processed.

2. Resource allocation. Based on the time gap of un-scheduled instances, resource allocation becomes easy. Basically, we use the criterion of time gap to deadline to evaluate the priority of instances. The less the time gap between the finishing time to deadline, the more dangerous this instance is and hence more priority for allocation. After the most dangerous instance i_s is selected, resource allocation is made on it. When an instance is successfully scheduled, it is removed from the scheduling list.

3. Optimistic allocation adjustment. After resource allocation of instance *ins*, the optimistic allocation of other instances must be adjusted due to the resource availability change. We only need to adjust the optimal allocations of some instances, which use any resource slot occupied by the instance *ins*. The adjustment is made by selecting the most efficient slot from the remaining available resources. For each remaining instance *ins'*, the task set *T* conflicting with previous allocation is generated for possible re-allocation. For each task *t* in *T*, the new finishing time of optimistic allocation is re-calculated. If the updated finishing time is within the deadline, optimistic allocation is re-applied for *t* of *ins'*. Otherwise, this instance is dropped out. Resource allocation and optimistic allocation adjustment are repeated until all instances are processed, i.e., either scheduled or dropped out.

Above three steps continue until no remaining instance is schedulable. Success rate is finally returned together with the process schedules.

3.2 BL Scheduling Strategy - Breadth First / Dynamic Local Optimisation

The BL strategy attempts to plan resources for instances in a holistic way yet using dynamic local optimisation. We know that the DM strategy allocates resources to one instance at a time. The BL strategy is different in that resource allocation is made to one task of one instance at a time. In this way, it balances all instances by giving them the same chance for occupying resources. Among those current tasks competing for a resource, allocation will be made to schedule the most urgent task, and task urgency is evaluated by certain criteria on the instance this task belongs to. Specifically, in each round we select a next available resource slot for allocation, and this resource is supposed to be used for the most urgent task according to a set of heuristics for local optimisation. Initially, the result of pre-allocation is used as input for BL strategy. Then instance scheduling is conducted in an iterative approach using the following three steps until no remaining instance is schedulable.

1. Selecting resource and generating candidate task set. First we select a resource slot. We choose the resource slot *slt* that is the one first in use among all available resource slots. This optimistically allocated resource slot may be conflicting with more than one current task of different instances. Obviously only one of them can be allocated with the slot (i.e., satisfying constraint C3 for conflict free allocation). In this step, we first find the conflicting task set on this resource slot. Assume task t is the earliest one using *slt*, the time period *tp* of the allocation on t is derived. The conflicting task set T includes all un-scheduled tasks using resource slot *slt* during a period overlapping with *tp*. Afterwards, we select the most urgent task from T based on a set of heuristics.

2. Resource allocation. Given resource slot *slt* and conflicting task set T from 3.3.1, this step is to choose the most urgent task. In the BL strategy, the urgency of a task is determined by a set of heuristic rules about the instance containing the task.

> ***Rule 1.*** The priority of a task t for allocation is influenced by the time gap of the instance it belongs to. The smaller value of time gap, the higher priority of t for allocation as the instance is more likely to exceed the deadline otherwise.
>
> ***Rule 2.*** The number of alternative resource slots to resource slot *slt* influences the priority of a task t. If t has many alternative resource slots (capable resources to which t can be re-allocated), t has abundant allocation choices hence may not have the priority of to be allocated using the slot *slt*.
>
> ***Rule 3.*** If a task t is not allocated and there is no alternative resource slot for t, time gap of the instance *ins* that t belongs to may reduce from $g(ins)$ to $g(ins)'$. An instance with a higher ratio = $g(ins)' / g(ins)$ is more likely to exceed deadline, hence has more priority to be scheduled immediately.

For each task t of instance *ins* in conflicting task set T, we generate the alternative resource set S_a according to Rule 2. Based on the heuristic rules, the priority of each task for requesting this resource is calculated by function $u(t)$. Assume $x = 1 + | S_a |$ and $r = g(ins)' / g(ins)$ for task t, the urgency of this task of being selected is computed as *formula 1*:

$$u(t) = r \Big/ g(ins) \times \sqrt{x} \qquad (g(ins) \neq 0) \tag{1}$$

In formula 1, the urgency of task t is in reverse proportion to $g(ins)$, because resources tend to save tasks in dangerous instances according to Rule 1. Urgency is also in reverse proportion to $\sqrt{x}$, because the task with more alternative resources can be more likely scheduled by other resources without affecting optimistic allocation (Rule 2). To reduce the effect of x, square root of x is used. In contrast, the urgency of task is in proportion to the ratio r. If a missed allocation of a task to this resource will cause a dramatic decrease of the time gap from $g(ins)$ to $g(ins)'$, this task has a high value of r and is more urgent to be allocated at this time (Rule 3). Among task set T we select and schedule the task t_s with maximum value of $u(t_s)$.

3. Allocation adjustment. After resource allocation in the previous step, the allocations of some instances may be affected and required to change accordingly. Similar to the DM strategy, affected allocations are adjusted. But if an instance becomes unschedulable with remaining resources, its occupied resources are released. After optimistic pre-allocation, steps from 3.2.1 to 3.2.3 are repeated until no remaining instance is schedulable. Lastly, we try to re-schedule the allocated tasks to save the other instances. Finally, the process scheduling result is returned.

3.3 BG Scheduling Strategy - Breadth First / Dynamic Global Optimisation

The BG strategy uses a different optimisation criterion for holistic process scheduling compared with the BL strategy. Process scheduling is also carried out for one task of one instance in each round, and the instances are scheduled in a balanced way. However, this strategy targets a global optimisation for every allocation. Resources are used to schedule the task with minimal penalty based on all instances rather than a single instance. We propose three heuristic rules, and based on these rules the penalty of each task for allocation can be calculated by a formula. In comparison, this strategy considers more impact among different instances than the previous two strategies. Given a resource slot *slt* and a conflicting task set *T* on *slt*, task priority is determined by the following rules:

Rule 1. When *slt* is allocated to $t \in T$ of an instance, the total time gap increase of all instances influences the task penalty. The more the total time gap increases, the more penalty it will get and hence the less priority this task will be scheduled from the overall perspective.

Rule 2. The task gets lower penalty if it belongs to an instance with less number of un-scheduled tasks. If the instance of a task has fewer un-scheduled tasks, the task has more priority to be scheduled because we are more likely to guarantee that the instance can be finished.

Rule 3. The task gets higher penalty if it results in more instances become un-schedulable. Each allocation is aimed to cause the least number of instances becoming un-schedulable.

Based on the result of pre-allocation, we select the next available resource slot that is first used (minimal start time) in all un-allocated instances, and then generate the task candidate set of the resource slot. The penalty of task candidates are evaluated according to the heuristic rules proposed above, and the resource slot is allocated to the task with minimal penalty from the global view. Given a task *t* of instance *ins*, the penalty *p*(*t*) for scheduling this task using resource slot *slt* is calculated as:

$$p(t) = (1 - \frac{1}{2x}) \cdot y^2 \cdot \left(\sum_{i \in I} (g(i)' - g(i)) \right) \tag{2}$$

where x is the number of remaining tasks of *ins* including *t*, y is the number of un-schedulable instance resulted from the allocation of *t*, and $\sum_{i \in I} (g(i)' - g(i))$ is the total time gap increase. The penalty has direct relationship with the total time gap increase of all instances (Rule 1). Also, the penalty is in proportion to x because when an instance is about to finish, we tend to finish it (Rule 2). However, Rule 2 is less dominant so we design $(1 - 1/2x)$ as the coefficient in range [0.5, 1) to restrict its effect. In addition, task penalty is also in proportion to y because the allocation should avoid affecting other instances (Rule 3). We emphasise its effect with y^2. In each round, the task t_s with minimal penalty is selected, and resource slot *slt* is allocated to schedule this task for global optimisation. Optimistic allocations are updated after task scheduling. Similar to the BL strategy, these three steps continue until no remaining instance is schedulable.

3.4 Discussion

A preliminary experiment is implemented to evaluate the performance of the above three strategies. Experimental results will not be introduced in this paper because of the limitation of space. Through the experiment, we observe that the BG strategy has higher success rate when resource is sufficient and performs worse when resource becomes tighter. This coincides with our early analysis that instances scheduled in this strategy tend to success or fail together. When resources are insufficient, the DM strategy becomes a practical scheduling strategy. This also coincides with our analysis due to the nature of the depth first scheduling. Compared with BG and DM, the BL strategy adopts the method in between and it performs best when the resource sufficiency is in middle of BG (sufficient mode) and DM strategy (skewed mode).

4 Related Work

Workflow scheduling is to investigate resource management while considering the complex task dependencies of workflows. Related work in this area can be classified into two categories. The first category is to allocate suitable resources for workflow instances at run time. In [11], Yu and Buyya developed a genetic approach to solve the deadline constrained scheduling problem. The fitness function combines time fitness and cost fitness. Based on the fitness value, their algorithm searches for a solution which has minimal execution cost with the deadline by two types of mutation operations: the swapping mutation and replacing mutation. YarKhan and Dongarra [10] proposed a solution using simulated annealing to select a suitable size of a set of resources for scheduling ScaLAPACK application in Gird environment. Work [6] presented architecture of workflow scheduling under the resource constraints. In work [7], a novel framework of resource patterns for workflow resource management is proposed by Senkul and Toroslu. In contrast, the second category is to plan resources for the workflow instances at the build time. In this category, more instance dependency information is assumed to be available and therefore can be explored for resource planning at build time. In work [9], two strategies are proposed to plan resources for a massive number of process instances before execution, in order to meet the deadline and minimise total cost. Also, resource planning for service oriented workflows is investigated in [2]. It firstly introduces both the required architecture for resource planning and workload prediction, and then presents the optimization approaches and heuristics for solving the resource planning with low computational overhead. Work [8] incorporates process structural improvement into resource allocation to optimize the process execution in meeting certain requirements.

As far as we know, none of them considers the time availability patterns of resources, which is a crucial issue for rational use of resource in practice. Compared with these works, this paper focuses on the scheduling of process instances with resource availability constraints before execution. In particular, our approach considers the resource work shift constraints and supports both homogeneous and heterogeneous structured process instances.

5 Conclusion

In this paper, we tackled the problem of business process instance scheduling satisfying certain availability constraints. We investigated how to allocate resources for process instances before execution such that the success rate of scheduling is maximised. As the problem is computationally hard, we explored a set of heuristic rules and proposed one greedy algorithm and two holistic algorithms.

Acknowledgement. The research work reported in this paper is supported by Australian Research Council under Linkage Grant LP0990393.

References

1. Avanes, A., Freytag, J.C.: Adaptive workflow scheduling under resource allocation constraints and network dynamics. Proceedings of VLDB 1(2), 1631–1637 (2008)
2. Eckert, J., Ertogrul, D., Miede, A., Repp, N.: Ralf Steinmetz: Resource Planning Heuristics for Service-Oriented Workflows. In: Web Intelligence, pp. 591–597 (2008)
3. Iosup, A., Jan, M., Sonmez, O., Epema, D.H.J.: On the dynamic resource availability in grids. In: Proceedings of GRID, pp. 26–33 (2007)
4. Jensen, M.T.: Generating robust and flexible job shop schedules using genetic algorithms. IEEE Trans. Evolutionary Computation 7(3), 275–288 (2003)
5. Rood, B., Lewis, M.J.: Scheduling on the Grid via multi-state resource availability prediction. In: Proceedings of GRID, pp. 126–135 (2008)
6. Russell, N., van der Aalst, W.M.P., ter Hofstede, A.H.M.: Workflow Resource Patterns: Identification, Representation and Tool Support. In: Pastor, Ó., Falcão e Cunha, J. (eds.) CAiSE 2005. LNCS, vol. 3520, pp. 216–232. Springer, Heidelberg (2005)
7. Senkul, P., Toroslu, I.K.: An architecture for workflow scheduling under resource allocation constraints. Inf. Syst. 30(5), 399–422 (2005)
8. Xu, J., Liu, C., Zhao, X.: Resource Allocation vs. Business Process Improvement: How They Impact on Each Other. In: Dumas, M., Reichert, M., Shan, M.-C. (eds.) BPM 2008. LNCS, vol. 5240, pp. 228–243. Springer, Heidelberg (2008)
9. Xu, J., Liu, C., Zhao, X.: Resource planning for massive number of process instances. In: Proceedings of CoopIS, pp. 219–236 (2009)
10. YarKhan, A., Dongarra, J.J.: Experiments with scheduling using simulated annealing in Grid Environment. In: Proceedings of GRID, pp. 232–242 (2002)
11. Yu, J., Buyya, R.: Scheduling scientific workflow applications with deadline and budget constraints using genetic algorithms. Scientific Programming 14, 217–230 (2006)
12. Yu, J., Buyya, R.: A taxonomy of workflow management systems for grid computing. J. Grid Comput. 3(3-4), 171–200 (2005)

Achieving Recovery in Service Composition with Assurance Points and Integration Rules
(Short Paper)

Susan D. Urban, Le Gao, Rajiv Shrestha, and Andrew Courter

Texas Tech University, Department of Computer Science
Lubbock, TX 79409
Tel.: +1-806-742-2484
{susan.urban,le.gao,rajiv.shrestha,s.courter}@ttu.edu

Abstract. This paper defines the concept of Assurance Points (APs) together with the use of integration rules to provide a flexible way of checking constraints and responding to execution errors in service composition. An AP is a combined logical and physical checkpoint, providing an execution milestone that stores critical data and interacts with integration rules to alter program flow and to invoke different forms of recovery depending on the execution status. During normal execution, APs invoke rules that check pre-conditions, post-conditions, and other application rules. When execution errors occur, APs are also used as rollback points. Integration rules can invoke backward recovery to specific APs using compensation as well as forward recovery through rechecking of preconditions before retry attempts or through execution of contingencies and alternative execution paths. APs together with integration rules provide an increased level of consistency checking as well as backward and forward recovery actions.

Keywords: service composition; data consistency, recovery, compensation, contingency, retry, checkpoints.

1 Introduction

Web Services and service-oriented computing are becoming widely used for business-to-business integration. Prevalent techniques [7, 19, 24] have been widely adopted for process modeling, with execution engines based on standards such as the Business Process Execution Language (BPEL) [10] providing a framework for execution of processes composed of services. Service composition for business integration, however, creates challenges for traditional process modeling techniques.

In a service execution environment, a process must be flexible enough to respond to errors, exceptions, and interruptions. Backward and forward recovery mechanisms [13] can be used to respond to such events. For example, compensation is a backward recovery mechanism that performs a logical undo operation. Contingency is a forward recovery mechanism that provides an alternative execution path to keep a process running. Nevertheless, most service composition techniques do not provide flexibility with

R. Meersman et al. (Eds.): OTM 2010, Part I, LNCS 6426, pp. 428–437, 2010.

respect to the combined use of compensation and contingency. Service composition models need to be enhanced with features that allow processes to assess their execution status to support more dynamic ways of responding to failures, while at the same time validating correctness conditions for process execution.

This paper presents our investigation of *Assurance Points* (APs) and *integration rules* to provide a more flexible way of checking constraints and responding to execution failures. An AP is a combined logical and physical checkpoint. As a physical checkpoint, an AP provides a way to store data at critical points in the execution of a process. Unlike past work with checkpointing [6, 15], our work focuses on the use of APs for user-defined consistency checking and rollback points that can be used to maximize forward recovery options when failures occur. In particular, an AP provides an execution milestone that interacts with integration rules. The data stored at an AP is passed as parameters to integration rules that are used to check pre-conditions, post-conditions, and other application conditions. Failure of a pre or post-condition or the failure of a service execution can invoke several different forms of recovery, including backward recovery of the entire process, retry attempts, or execution of contingent procedures. The unique aspect of APs is that they provide intermediate rollback points when failures occur that allow a process to be compensated to a specific AP for the purpose of rechecking pre-conditions before retry attempts or the execution of contingent procedures.

In this paper, we describe the interaction among APs, integration rules, and the different forms of recovery actions as defined in [20], illustrating the functionality of these concepts using an online shopping scenario. We then provide a comparison of our approach to the fault handling and recovery procedures in BPEL [11]. The primary contribution of our work is found in the explicit support provided for user-defined constraints, with rule-driven recovery actions for compensation, retry, and contingency procedures that support flexibility with respect to the combined use of backward and forward recovery options.

2 Related Work

From a historical point of view, our work is founded on past work with Advanced Transaction Models (ATMs). ATMs provide better support for Long Running Transactions (LRTs) that need relaxed atomicity and isolation properties [4]. In the work of [8], sagas were defined as a mechanism to structure long running processes, with each sub-transaction having a compensating procedure to reverse the affects of the saga when it fails. Other advanced transaction models have also made use of compensation for hierarchically structured transactions [18].

More recently, events and rules have been used to dynamically specify control flow and data flow in a process by using Event Condition Action (ECA) rules [17]. ECA rules have also been successfully implemented for exception handling in work such as [2, 14]. The work in [14] uses ECA rules to generate reliable and fault-tolerant BPEL processes to overcome the limited fault handling capability of BPEL. Our work with assurance points also supports the use of rules that separate fault handling from normal business logic. Combined with assurance points, integration rules are used to integrate user-defined consistency constraints with the recovery process.

Several efforts have been made to enhance the BPEL fault and exception handling capabilities. BPEL4Job [21] addresses fault-handling design for job flow management with the ability to migrate flow instances. The work in [16] proposes mechanisms like external variable setting, future alternative behavior, rollback and conditional re-execution of the Flow, timeout, and redo mechanisms for enabling recovery actions using BPEL. The Dynamo [1] framework for the dynamic monitoring of WS-BPEL processes weaves rules such as pre/post conditions and invariants into the BPEL process. Most of these projects do not fully integrate constraint checking with a variety of recovery actions as in our work to support more dynamic and flexible ways of reacting to failures. Our research demonstrates the viability of variegated recovery approaches within a BPEL-like execution environment.

In checkpointing systems, consistent execution states are saved during the process flow. During failures and exceptions, the activity can be rolled back to the closest consistent checkpoint to move the execution to an alternative platform [6, 15]. The AP concept presented in this paper also stores critical execution data, but uses the data as parameters to rules that perform constraint checking and invoke different types of recovery actions.

The work in [3] illustrates the application of aspect-oriented software development concepts to workflow languages to provide flexible and adaptable workflows. AO4BPEL [4] is an aspect-oriented extension to BPEL that uses AspectJ to provide control flow adaptations [12]. Assurance Points are similar to aspect-oriented programming but are more fully integrated into the process execution engine for support of recovery actions.

3 Service Composition and Recovery with Assurance Points

This section summarizes the service composition and recovery model from [25]. We then define and illustrate the use of assurance points and integration rules in the context of this model.

3.1 Overview of the Model

In [25], a process is defined as a top-level execution entity that is composed of other execution entities. A process is denoted as p_i, where p represents a process and the subscript i represents a unique identifier of the process. An operation represents a service invocation, denoted as $op_{i,j}$, such that op is an operation, i identifies the enclosing process p_i, and j represents the unique identifier of the operation within p_i. Compensation ($cop_{i,j}$) is an operation intended for backward recovery, while contingency ($top_{i,j}$) is an operation used for forward recovery.

Atomic groups and composite groups are logical execution units that enable the specification of processes with complex control structure, facilitating service execution failure recovery by adding scopes within the context of a process execution. An atomic group (denoted $ag_{i,j}$) contains an operation, an optional compensation, and an optional contingency. A composite group (denoted $cg_{i,k}$) may contain multiple atomic groups, and/or multiple composite groups that execute sequentially or in parallel. A composite group can have its own compensation and contingency as optional elements. Contingency is always tried first upon the failure of an atomic or composite group. Compensation, on the other had, is a recovery activity that is only applied as a way to reverse the effects of completed atomic and composite groups.

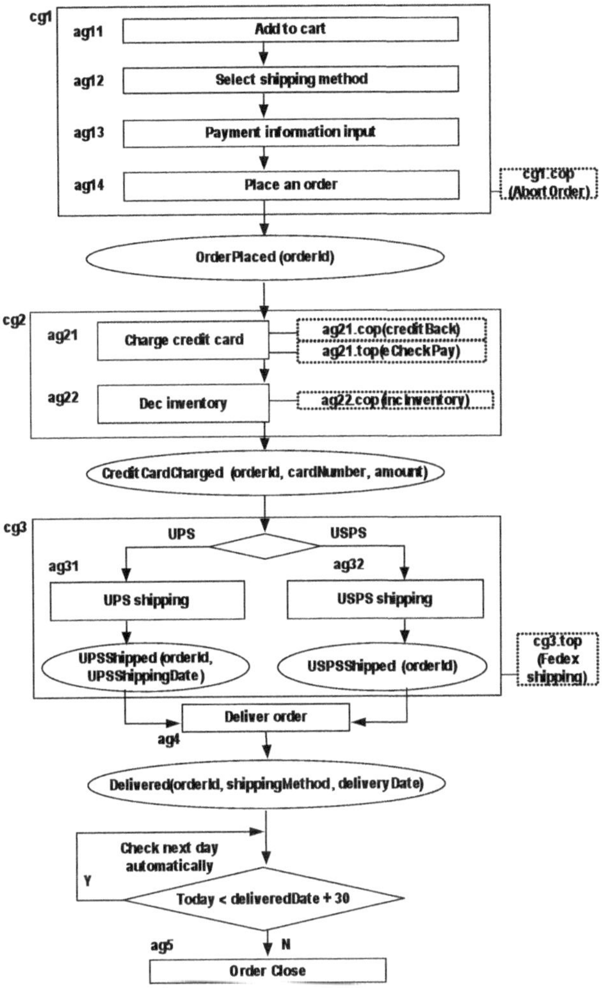

Fig. 1. Online Shopping Process with APs

Figure 1 shows an online shopping process that is used as an example in the remainder of the paper. The process is composed of three composite groups (cg_1, cg_2 and cg_3). The group cg_1 contains four atomic groups and a compensating procedure (cg1.cop) that is attached to the entire group, which is known as shallow compensation. Shallow compensation involves the execution of a compensating procedure that will reverse the effects of the entire composite group. In comparison, cg_2 is composed of two atomic groups, where each atomic group has its own compensating procedure (ag_{21}.cop and ag_{22}.cop), which is known as deep compensation. Deep compensation involves the execution of compensating procedures for each group within a composite group. In addition, the atomic group ag_{21} also has a contingent procedure (ag_{21}.top) that will be executed if ag_{21} fails. The composite group cg_3 also has a contingent procedure (cg_3.top). The reader should refer to [25] for a more formal presentation of the recovery semantics for shallow compensation, deep compensation, and contingency in the context of the service composition model.

3.2 Assurance Point and Rule Extensions

Our work has extended the model described in the previous section with the concept of assurance points, which are depicted in Figure 1 as ovals. An AP is a process execution correctness guard as well as a potential rollback point during the recovery process. Given that concurrent processes do not execute as traditional transactions in a service-oriented environment, inserting APs at critical points in a process is important for checking consistency constraints and potentially reducing the risk of failure or inconsistent data. An AP also serves as a milestone for backward and forward recovery activities. When failures occur, APs can be used as rollback points for backward recovery, rechecking pre-conditions relevant to forward recovery. In the current version of our work, we assume that APs are placed at points in a process where they are only executed once, and not embedded in iterative control structures.

An AP is defined as: AP = <apId, apParameters*, IR_{pre}?, IR_{post}?, IR_{cond}*>, where apID is the unique identifier of the AP, apParameters is a list of critical data items to be stored as part of the AP, IR_{pre} is an integration rule defining a pre-condition, IR_{post} is an integration rule defining a post-condition, and IR_{cond} is an integration rule defining additional application rules. In the above notation, * indicates 0 or more occurrences, while ? indicates zero or one optional occurrences.

IR_{pre}, IR_{post}, and IR_{cond} are expressed as Event-Condition-Action (ECA) rules based on the use of integration rules to interconnect software components [9, 22]. An IR is triggered by a process reaching an AP during execution, where an AP serves as the event of an integration rule. Upon reaching an AP, the condition of an IR is evaluated.

The action specification is executed if the rule condition evaluates to true. For IR_{pre} and IR_{post}, a constraint C is always expressed in a negative form (not(C)). An action (action 1) is invoked if the pre or post condition is not true, invoking a recovery action or an alternative execution path. If the specified action is a retry activity, then there is a possibility for the process to execute through the same pre or post condition a second time. As a result, integration rules support the capability of specifying a second action (action 2).

In its most basic form, a recovery action simply invokes an alternative process. Recovery actions can also be one of the following actions:

- **APRollback:** APRollback is used when the entire process needs to compensate its way back to the start of the process according to the semantics of the service compensation model.
- **APRetry:** APRetry is used when the running process needs to be backward recovered using compensation to a specific AP. By default, the backward recovery process will go to the first AP reached as part of the shallow or deep compensation process within the same scope. The pre-condition defined in the AP is re-checked. If the pre-condition is satisfied, the process execution is resumed from that AP by re-trying the recovered operations. Otherwise, the action of the pre-condition rule

is executed. The APRetry command can optionally specify a parameter indicating the AP that is the target of the backward recovery process.

- **APCascadedContingency (APCC):** APCC is a backward recovery process that searches backwards through the hierarchical nesting of composite groups to find a possible contingent procedure for a failed composite group. During the APCC backward recovery process, when an AP is found before a composite group, the pre-condition defined in the AP will be re-checked before invoking any contingent procedures for forward recovery. APC is specifically used as a means of forward recovery from nested composite groups.

The most basic use of an AP together with integration rules is shown in Figure 2, which shows a process with three composite groups and an AP between each composite group. The shaded box shows the functionality of an AP using AP2 as an example. Each AP serves as a checkpoint facility, storing execution status data in a checkpoint database (AP data in Figure 2). When the execution reaches AP2, IRs associated with the AP are invoked. The condition of an IR_{post} is evaluated first to validate the execution of cg_2. If the post-condition is violated, the action invoked can be one of the pre-defined recovery actions as described above. If the post-condition is not violated, then an IR_{pre} rule is evaluated to check the pre-condition for the next service execution. If the pre-condition is violated, one of the pre-defined recovery actions will be invoked. If the pre-condition is satisfied, the AP will check for any additional, conditional rules (IR_{cond}) that may have been expressed. IR_{cond} rules do not affect the normal flow of execution but provide a way to invoke additional parallel activity based on application requirements. Note that the expression of a pre-condition, post-condition or any additional condition is optional.

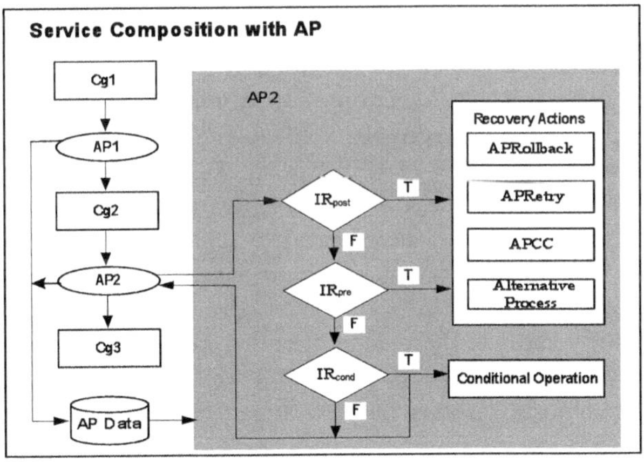

Fig. 2. Basic Use of AP and Integration Rules

3.3 Case Study: Assurance Points and Rules

This section provides an example of assurance points, integration rules, and conditional rules using the online shopping application in Figure 1. APs are shown as ovals between composite and/or atomic groups, where each AP has a name and a list of parameters that are stored at the AP.

Table 1 shows rules associated with the APs in Figure 1. The orderPlaced AP follows the execution of cg_1, which is a composite process that supports adding items to a cart, selecting a shipping method, entering payment information, and submitting an order. The orderPlaced AP marks the transition from placing the order to actually processing the order. The AP has a pre-condition called the QuantityChecked1 rule that serves as verification that the store has enough goods in stock to proceed with the order. The condition validates the status of the inventory and, if the availability has changed since the customer began adding items to the cart, the rule invokes the backOrderPurchase process. In this case, the rule does not invoke one of the predefined recovery actions but, instead, invokes an alternate execution path.

If the process passes the pre-condition verification, the process then executes cg_2, which charges the customer's credit card and decrements the inventory. The composite group is followed by the CreditCardCharged AP, which has a post-condition that further guarantees the in-stock quantity is greater than zero after the inventory has been decremented. If the post-condition is violated, the APRetry action is invoked. APRetry will perform a logical rollback of cg_2 by performing deep compensation (i.e., executing ag_{22}.cop followed by ag_{21}.cop). According to the retry semantics, when the process reverses itself to the orderPlaced AP, the pre-condition of the orderPlaced AP will be rechecked. The retry of cg_2 will only be allowed if the pre-condition is satisfied. Otherwise, the backOrderPurchase process will be invoked. In the case where the precondition of the orderPlaced AP is satisfied, the cg_2 process will be re-executed. If the post-condition of the orderPlaced AP fails a second time, the entire process will go through a rollback process by performing deep compensation on cg_2 and shallow compensation on cg_1. Note that in Table 1, the CreditCardCharged AP also has a conditional rule that sends a message notification for large charges.

The APCC recovery action can be specified as a rule action, but it is also the default action to take when the execution of an atomic group and the contingency of an atomic group fails. As an example, suppose the process is executing inside cg_3 and fails during the execution of UPSshipping. Since there is no contingency attached to UPSshipping, the process will enter APCC mode, which attempts to reverse the process to the beginning of the most enclosing composite group, which in this case is cg_3. The APCC recovery process will then execute the contingency of the composite group (cg_3.top). The APCC recovery process will alway check for an AP with a precondition and test the precondition before executing a contingent procedure. The APCC recovery process provides a well-defined procedure for backing out of nested composite groups and checking for contingent, forward recovery procedures.

Since no pre or post condition is specified for the Delivered AP, only the conditional rule shippingRefund is evaluated. Assume the delivery method was overnight through UPS with an extra shipping fee. If UPS has delivered the item on time, then the Delivered AP is complete and execution continues. Otherwise, refundUPSShipping-Charge is invoked to refund the extra fee while the main process execution continues.

Table 1. AP Rules in the Online Shopping Process

Integration Rule	Conditional Rule
create rule QuantityCheck1::pre **event:** ***OrderPlaced*** (orderId) **condition:** exists(select L.itemId from Inventory I, LineItem L where L.orderId=orderId and L.itemId=I.itemId and L.quantity>I.quantity) **action:** backOrderPurchase(orderId)	**create rule** Notice::cond **event:** ***CreditCardCharged*** (orderId, cardNumber , amount) **condition:** amount > $1000 **action:** highExpenseNotice(cardNumber)
create rule QuantityCheck2::post **event:** ***CreditCardCharged*** (orderId, cardNumber, amount) **condition:** exists(select L.itemId from Inventory I, LineItem L where L.orderId=orderId and L.itemId=I.itemId and I.quantity<0) **action1**: APRetry **action2:** APRollback	**create rule** ShippingRefund::cond **event**: ***Delivered*** (orderId, shippingMethod, deliveryDate) **condition:** shippingMethod = UPS && deliveryDate != UP-SShipped.UPSShippingDate+1 **action:** refundUPSShippingCharge(orderId)

4 Comparison to Recovery in BPEL

We have developed a prototype implementation of the AP concept and also conducted a comparison of our work with BPEL. The work in [11] highlights the two main problems with the BPEL fault and compensation mechanism: 1) compensation order can violate control link dependencies if control links cross the scope boundaries, and 2) high complexity of default compensation order due to default handler behavior. Unlike BPEL, the order of the AP compensation approach is clear since APs support a hierarchical process structure and do not support control links between non-peer scopes, making the semantics of compensation in the AP approach unambiguous.

In general, the notion of compensation should also be capable of handling constraint violations [5]. Since BPEL's compensation handling mechanism through the <compensate> activity can only be called inside a fault handler, this limits the ability to call compensation outside a fault handling. In the case of the AP model, compensation can be invoked during normal execution (no error has yet occurred) when integration rules are not satisfied. This allows a flexible way to recover the process through compensation in response to constraint violations.

BPEL does not explicitly support a contingency feature other than fault, exception, and termination handlers. The designer is responsible for complex fault handling logic, which, as pointed out in [5, 11] has the potential to increase complexity and create unexpected errors. The AP model provides explicit contingency activities so that forward recovery is possible.

5 Conclusions and Future Directions

This research has defined the use of assurance points, integration rules, and recovery actions to 1) provide a way of expressing user-defined constraints for process execution and 2) provide greater flexibility for use of forward and backward recovery options when constraints are not satisfied or execution fails. Assurance points enhance traditional work with checkpointing, providing logical points for backward recovery with semantics that increase the potential for forward recovery by rechecking preconditions, retrying services, and looking for contingencies. Planning for failure and recovery should be an important part of every process specification.

There are several directions for future work. We are currently extending the recovery algorithms to support parallel execution as in the flow activity of BPEL. Another direction involves formalization of the assurance point concept using Petri-nets and model-checking. Methodological issues for the specification of APs, integration rules, and recovery procedures will also be addressed, together with refinement of recovery actions for concurrent and iterative activity. We are also investigating the integration of assurance points with our work on decentralized data dependency analysis [23] in Process Execution Agents (PEXAs), where PEXAs communicate about data dependencies so that when one process fails and recovers, other data dependent processes can be notified of potential data inconsistencies. The AP concept can be used to enhance decentralized PEXAs with greater flexibility for process recovery options.

Acknowledgments. This research has been supported by NSF Grant CCF-0820152. Opinions, findings, conclusions or recommendations expressed in this paper are those of the author(s) and do not necessarily reflect the views of NSF.

References

1. Baresi, L., Guinea, S., Pasquale, L.: Self-Healing BPEL Processes with Dynamo and the JBoss Rule Engine. In: ACM Int. Workshop on Eng. of Software Services for Pervasive Environments, pp. 11–20. ACM, New York (2007)
2. Brambilla, M., Ceri, S., Comai, S., Tziviskou, C.: Exception Handling in Workflow-Driven Web Applications. In: Proc. of the14th Int. Conf. on World Wide Web, pp. 170–179. ACM, New York (2005)
3. Charfi, A., Mezini, M.: Aspect-Oriented Workflow Languages. In: Meersman, R., Tari, Z. (eds.) OTM 2006. LNCS, vol. 4275, pp. 183–200. Springer, Heidelberg (2006)
4. Cichocki, A.: Workflow and Process Automation: Concepts and Technology. Kluwer Academic Pub., Dordrecht (1998)
5. Coleman, J.: Examining BPEL's Compensation Construct. In: Workshop on Rigorous Eng. of Fault-Tolerant Systems (2005)
6. Dialani, V., Miles, S., Moreau, L., De Roure, D., Luck, M.: Towards a CSCW Framework for Scientific Cooperation in Europe. LNCS, pp. 889–898. Springer, Heidelberg (1995)
7. Engels, G., Förster, A., Heckel, R., Thöne, S.: Process Modeling using UML. In: Process-Aware Information Systems: Bridging People and Software through Process Technology, pp. 85–117. Wiley, Hoboken (2005)
8. Garcia-Molina, H., Salem, K.: Sagas. Morgan Kaufmann Publishers Inc., San Francisco (1994)

9. Jin, Y.: An Architecture and Execution Environment for Component Integration Rules. Ph.D. Diss., Arizona State University (2004)
10. Jordan, D., Evdemon, J., Alves, A., Arkin, A., Askary, S., Barreto, C., Bloch, B., Curbera, F., Ford, M., Goland, Y.: Web Services Business Process Execution Language Version 2.0. OASIS Standard 11 (2007)
11. Khalaf, R., Roller, D., Leymann, F.: Revisiting the Behavior of Fault and Compensation Handlers in WS-BPEL. In: Meersman, R., Dillon, T., Herrero, P. (eds.) OTM 2009. LNCS, vol. 5870, pp. 286–303. Springer, Heidelberg (2009)
12. Kiczales, G., Hilsdale, E., Hugunin, J., Kersten, M., Palm, J., Griswold, W.G.: An Overview of AspectJ. In: Knudsen, J.L. (ed.) ECOOP 2001. LNCS, vol. 2072, pp. 327–353. Springer, Heidelberg (2001)
13. Lee, P.A., Anderson, T., Laprie, J.C., Avizienis, A., Kopetz, H.: Fault Tolerance: Principles and Practice. Springer, New York (1990)
14. Liu, A., Li, Q., Huang, L., Xiao, M.: A Declarative Approach to Enhancing the Reliability of BPEL Processes. In: Proc. of the Int. Conf. on Web Services, pp. 272–279 (2007)
15. Luo, Z.W.: Checkpointing for Workflow Recovery. In: Proc. of the 38th Annual Southeast Regional Conf., pp. 79–80. ACM, New York (2000)
16. Modafferi, S., Conforti, E.: Methods for Enabling Recovery Actions in WS-BPEL. In: Meersman, R., Tari, Z. (eds.) OTM 2006. LNCS, vol. 4275, p. 219. Springer, Heidelberg (2006)
17. Paton, N.W., Díaz, O.: Active Database Systems. ACM Computing Surveys 31 (1999)
18. Rolf, A., Klas, W., Veijalainen, J.: Transaction Management Support for Cooperative Applications. Kluwer Academic Pub., Dordrecht (1997)
19. Scheer, A.W., Thomas, O., Adam, O.: Process Modeling Using Event-driven Process Chains. In: Process-aware Information Systems: Bridging People and Software through Process Technology, pp. 119–145. Wiley, New Jersey (2005)
20. Shrestha, R.: Using Assurance Points, Events, and Rules for Recovery in Service Composition. M.S. Thesis, Texas Tech University (2010)
21. Tan, W., Fong, L., Bobroff, N.: Bpel4job: A Fault-Handling Design for Job Flow Management. In: Krämer, B.J., Lin, K.-J., Narasimhan, P. (eds.) ICSOC 2007. LNCS, vol. 4749, p. 27. Springer, Heidelberg (2007)
22. Urban, S.D., Dietrich, S.W., Na, Y., Jin, Y., Sundermier, A., Saxena, A.: The IRules Project: Using Active Rules for the Integration of Distributed Software Components. In: Proc. of the 9th IFIP Working Conf. on Database Semantics: Semantic Issues in E-Commerce Systems, pp. 265–286 (2001)
23. Urban, S.D., Liu, Z.A., Gao, L.: Decentralized Data Dependency Analysis for Concurrent Process Execution. In: Proc. of the 13th Enterprise Dist. Object Computing Conf. Workshops (Edocw 2009), pp. 74–83 (2009)
24. White, S.A.: Business Process Modeling Notation, BPMN (2004), `http://www.bpmi.org/bpmi-downloads/BPMN-V1.0.pdf`
25. Xiao, Y., Urban, S.D.: The DeltaGrid Service Composition and Recovery Model. Int. Journal of Web Services Research (2009)

Business Protocol Adaptation for Flexible Chain Management

Ricardo Seguel, Rik Eshuis, and Paul Grefen

Information Systems Group, School of Industrial Engineering,
Eindhoven University of Technology, The Netherlands
{r.e.seguel,h.eshuis,p.w.p.j.grefen}@tue.nl

Abstract. Nowadays, organizations collaborate in business chains using dynamic service outsourcing to deliver complex products and services. To enable the flexible formation of business chains, organizations need to ensure that their business protocols are compatible. If the business protocols are incompatible, then the organizations cannot form a business chain. Protocol adaptors can resolve incompatibilities between business protocols during chain formation. By using the customer order decoupling point, we identify three different business chain structures. For each chain structure, we identify how adaptation can be used to support flexible chain formation.

Keywords: Business Chains, Dynamic Service Outsourcing, Interacting Services, Protocol Adaptor, Service Adaptation.

1 Introduction

In competitive markets, the production of complex products and services involves a number of autonomous organizations [7] that collaborate in business chains. Different business chain structures or types of business chains can be identified by using the customer order decoupling point (CODP) [8], which indicates how deeply the customer order penetrates into a business chain. Locating the CODP at the different organizations in Figure 1 results in three different chain structures. In a demand chain, all organizations produce to order since the CODP is at the last provider in the chain (order-driven). In a supply chain, all organizations produce to stock since the CODP is at the first provider in the chain (forecast-driven). In a hybrid demand/supply chain, the CODP divides the chain in two: downstream, organizations produce to order and upstream, organizations produce to stock. For example, in Figure 1 the CODP at the service provider indicates that the service consumer and provider operate in demand chain mode while the provider and the 2nd-tier providers operate in supply chain mode. Note that the hybrid supply/demand chain case cannot exist by definition of the CODP. We describe the formation of business chains later in Section 3.

Due to the shorter life-cycles and increasing complexity of products and services, the autonomous organizations in a business chain set up their collaboration in a just-in-time fashion, using dynamic service outsourcing. In dynamic service

R. Meersman et al. (Eds.): OTM 2010, Part I, LNCS 6426, pp. 438–445, 2010.

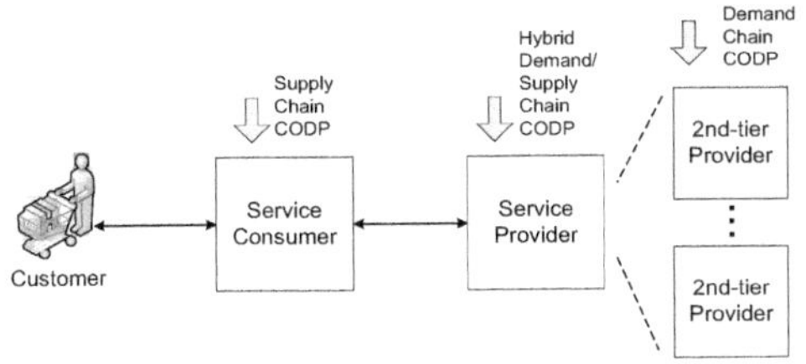

Fig. 1. Business Chain Management Cases

outsourcing, an organization outsources a part of its business process, for instance order fulfillment, to a partner that is selected at the last possible moment from the marketplace [6]. Note that dynamic service outsourcing can be used both downstream and upstream the CODP. Once the organizations have established a B2B relation using dynamic service outsourcing, they can collaborate by invoking functionalities from each other according to their business protocols in their public process view [2,4]. Each public process view abstracts an underlying private business processes that is executed by the organization. In a business chain, the 2nd-tier providers do not observe the business protocols shared by the service consumer and the service (1st-tier) provider in their public process views, and vice versa.

In current dynamic service outsourcing approaches [7], the tacit assumption is made that interacting protocols are compatible: each sent message being received and processed by the other party, and thus no deadlocks occur. However, this assumption is not very realistic since in practice each organization has its own protocol that specifies its own way of working. Two collaborating organizations may easily have incompatible protocols. Moreover, the underlying business processes can be implemented by legacy information systems that cannot be modified easily in case of incompatibilities. Therefore, organizations need to ensure that their business protocols are compatible to enable the flexible formation of business chains.

The goal of this paper is to identify how protocol adaptation can be used to support flexible chain formation, resolving protocol incompatibilities between partner organizations. A protocol adaptor ensures that the interaction between two protocols proceeds properly by intercepting and reordering messages such that they are delivered to the receiving side in the order that this side expects [11]. For each business chain structure, we describe how protocol adaptors can be used to resolve (if possible) incompatibilities between interacting services during chain formation.

There is a large body of work on protocol adaptation [1,9,10,11,12]. However, none of these works discuss how adaptation can be used to improve the formation of supply and demand chains, which is the topic of this paper. Note that any of these existing protocol adaptation approaches can be used to realize the actual adaptation between incompatible protocols. Thus, our work complements the existing work by showing how it can be applied to enable the flexible formation of business chains. In this paper, we focus on adaptation of behavioral mismatches rather than interface mismatches. An interface mismatch is due to differences in the formats and specifications of messages exchanged. Such a mismatch can be resolved using schema mapping and transformation tools [10,12]. We will extend our approach adding interface adaptation in future work.

The remainder of this paper is organized as follows. Section 2 illustrates a motivating example. Section 3 explains the business chain structures. Section 4 describes the three flexible chain formation cases. Section 5 presents the conclusions and future work.

2 Motivating Example

We introduce our running example to explain and illustrate our approach. In Figure 2, we illustrate a dynamic service outsourcing scenario in which a hybrid demand/supply chain structure cannot be configured since the interacting services have incompatible business protocols.

In this complex scenario, the company W outsources a fulfillment service to the company X collaborating in demand chain mode, and the company X outsources a delivery service to the company Y collaborating in supply chain mode. Each interacting service composes three services describing the business protocols in which they are invoked at the public process view. Note that the arrows between the interacting services indicate send (source) and receive (target) actions. Moreover, the private process view of a fulfillment service X is not known

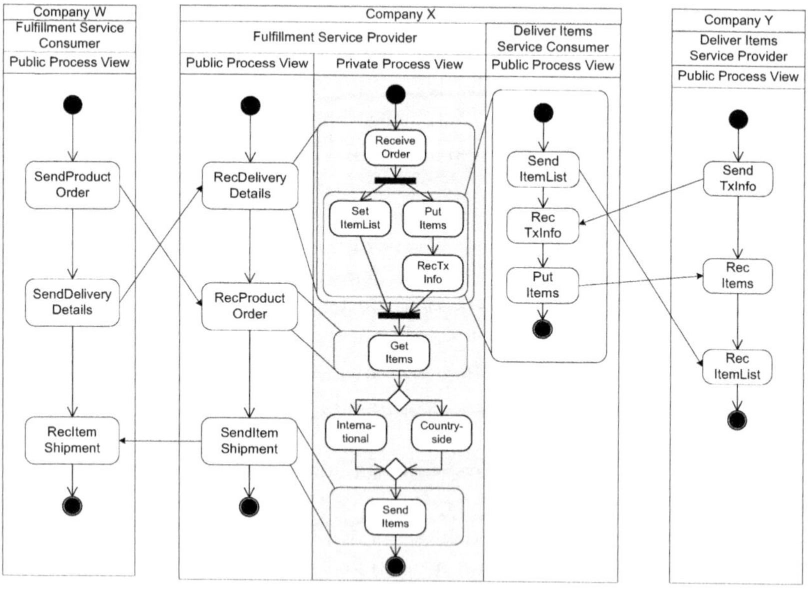

Fig. 2. Hybrid Demand/Supply Chain Formation with Mismatches between the Business Protocols

by the other parties and vice versa. To enable the configuration of the hybrid demand/supply chain, companies W, X and Y have to ensure that their business protocols are compatible. For that, they have to construct a protocol adaptor to resolve mismatches. However, the responsibility of constructing an adaptor is determined according to each business chain structure.

3 Business Chain Management

Dynamic service outsourcing enables the formation of a business chain between autonomous organizations collaborating in specific markets; for example, in financial, insurance and logistics markets [7]. The business chain is formed dynamically by the (automatic) integration of business protocols of the collaborating organizations. This way, there are three chain management cases for collaborating organizations using dynamic service outsourcing:

1. In a *demand chain formation* case, the service consumer defines the business protocol according to its customer business requirements. The CODP is defined at the latest provider in the chain. For example, in Figure 1 the decoupling point is at the 2nd-tier provider. To configure the demand chain, the service consumer searches the service provider in the marketplace to outsource its non-core protocol part. The service provider offers a business protocol in conformance with the consumer business protocol. Then, the provider outsources either part of or its complete process to 2nd-tier providers found in the marketplaces. The service provider is the orchestrator that composes interacting services of 2nd-tier providers to offer a business protocol that meets the consumer business protocol.
2. In a *supply chain formation* case, the service provider defines the business protocol to offer a standard service to many service consumers; for instance, in conformance with reference models like SCOR [3] or eTOM [5]. The CODP is defined close to the customer; for example, in Figure 1 the decoupling point is at the service consumer. The service provider acts as orchestrator, it searches 2nd-tier providers in the marketplace to outsource either part of or its complete process to meet the standard service. Then, the service consumer defines its business protocol according to the standard service provider, found in the marketplace.
3. In a *hybrid demand/supply chain formation* case, the chain between the service consumer and the service provider operates in demand mode (produce to order) while the chain between the service provider and the 2nd-tier providers operates in supply mode (produce to stock). This way, the CODP is defined at the service provider; see Figure 1. The service consumer sets its business protocol to meet its customer business requirements. Then, it finds the service provider in the marketplace that defines a business protocol according to the customer demands. On the other hand, the service provider sets its business protocol according to the standard services offered by the 2nd-tier providers.

In dynamic service outsourcing, some partner business protocols cannot be selected from the marketplace during business chain formation since they are incompatible. Note that resolving mismatches using human intervention will depend of the time constraints of the business transaction. Therefore, in just-in-time service collaborations an efficient and automated adaptation method has to be introduced for the business chain formation. In [11] we describe the existing work on adaptation.

4 Flexible Business Chain Management

We describe the flexible chain formation cases using protocol adaptation in dynamic service outsourcing. Next, we explain a flexible chain configuration case using our running example.

4.1 Flexible Business Chain Formation Cases

The mismatches found during the business chain formation can be resolved by constructing a protocol adaptor between the interacting services. This way, the partners that are discarded for incompatible business protocols can build an adaptor to be protocol compatible. Then, the searching space for potential partners in the marketplace grows, and thus there are more partners for selection that meet both protocol compatibility and other matching specific characteristics.

We show in Figure 3 a business chain (similar to Figure 1) to illustrate the adaptation cases between the interacting services. The letters outside the services in Figure 3 represent the place where the protocol adaptor is constructed. For example, the symbol ⓐ represents that the service consumer builds a protocol adaptor to resolve mismatches with the service provider. We have identified the following adaptation cases to define the adaptation responsibility of a partner that participates in the flexible business chain formation:

1. In a *flexible demand chain formation* scenario, the service consumer defines its business protocol according to the customer business requirements. Then, the service consumer searches a service provider in the marketplace according to the customer requirements and its business protocol. If the provider business protocol offered in the marketplace is incompatible, then the provider has to construct a protocol adaptor to resolve the mismatches with the service consumer for later selection; see ⓑ in Figure 3. This way, the service

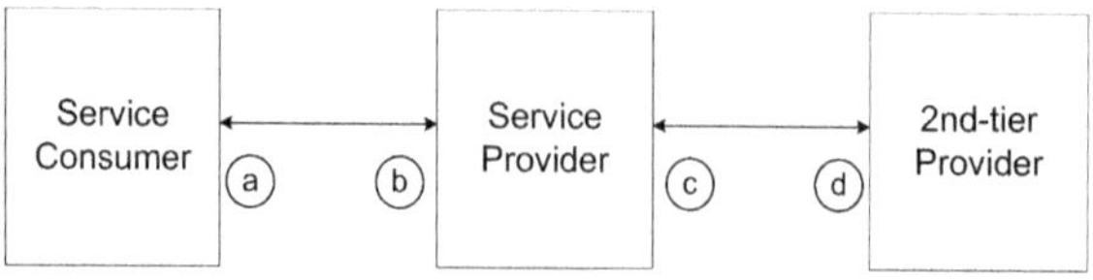

Fig. 3. Business Chain to Identify Adaptation Cases

Table 1. Flexible Business Chain Formation Cases

Cases	Consumer		Provider				2nd-tier Provider	
	BP to Provider	Adaptor ⓐ	Adaptor ⓑ	BP to Consumer	BP to 2nd-tier Provider	Adaptor ⓒ	Adaptor ⓓ	BP to Provider
Demand chain	Defined		✓	Incompatible	Defined		✓	Incompatible
Supply chain	Incompatible	✓		Defined	Incompatible	✓		Defined
Hybrid chain	Defined		✓	Incompatible	Incompatible	✓		Defined

consumer has more potential partners for selection based on both protocol compatibility and other matching characteristics. Since the CODP is moved to the last provider in the demand chain, the responsibility of constructing an adaptor is always of the provider. Thus, the 2nd-tier provider is responsible of building an adaptor to be compatible with the (1st-tier) service provider; see ⓓ in Figure 3.

2. In a *flexible supply chain formation* scenario, the service provider sets its business protocol in conformance with market standards. The service consumer searches the standard service provider in the marketplace to define its business protocol. If the consumer business protocol is incompatible with the standard business protocol, then the consumer has to build a protocol adaptor to resolve mismatches with the service provider; see ⓐ in Figure 3. Thus, the consumer can find more potential standard providers based on both protocol compatibility and other matching characteristics. In the supply chain, the CODP is moved to the service consumer, and thus the responsibility of building an adaptor is always of the service consumer. Therefore, the service provider is responsible of building the adaptor to resolve mismatches with the 2nd-tier provider; see ⓒ in Figure 3.
3. In a *flexible hybrid demand/supply chain formation* scenario, the service consumer and service provider form a demand chain while the service (1st-tier) provider and the 2nd-tier provider form a supply chain. Then, the CODP is at the service provider. This way, the responsibility of building an adaptor is always of the service (1st-tier) provider: it has to build an adaptor to resolve mismatches with the service consumer; see ⓑ in Figure 3. On the other hand, it has to build an adaptor to resolve mismatches with the 2nd-tier provider; see ⓒ Figure 3.

We summarize the three adaptation cases in Table 1, using the business chain depicted in Figure 3. The rows correspond to the demand, supply and hybrid demand/supply chain formation cases. The columns correspond to the interacting services in the business chain. The sub-columns BP to Provider, BP to Consumer and BP to 2nd-tier Provider represent the business protocol shared by the services at the public view, and thus they can be either defined by the service (Defined) or incompatible with the partner (Incompatible). The sub-columns Adaptor ⓐ–ⓓ represent the place where the adaptor is constructed and it is indicated with a check mark (✓). The adaptation cases illustrated in Table 1 are very relevant to easily identify the responsibility of building a protocol adaptor during the configuration of a business chain at design-time. This way, it enables

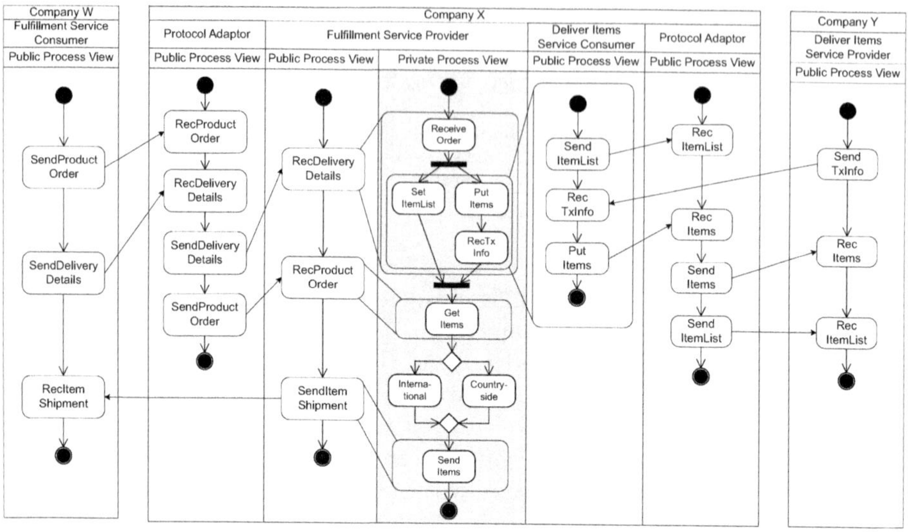

Fig. 4. Adaptation Case for Flexible Hybrid Demand/Supply Chain Formation

the proper deployment of the business protocols and the adaptor to preserve the dynamism of the business chain at run-time.

4.2 An Example of Flexible Business Chain Formation

To describe the flexible formation of a business chain, we explain the hybrid demand/supply chain case since it includes the other two business chain cases. We use our running example shown in Figure 2 to illustrate the solution in Figure 4. Companies W and X operate in demand chain mode. Then, the company X constructs a protocol adaptor to resolve the mismatches with the company W, using one of the adaptation methods presented in [1, 9, 10, 11, 12]. In this example we use the method presented in [11]. The company X constructs the protocol adaptor at the public process view and it deploys the adaptor in front of its business protocol. Then, the company X offers the protocol adaptor and its business protocol in the marketplace. Note that the communication of messages is shown in the figure by the arrows crossing the organization borders, indicating send (source) and receive (target) actions. On the other hand, in Figure 4 the company X outsources the delivery of items (Deliver Items service) to the company Y. Since companies X and Y operate in supply chain mode, the company X builds a protocol adaptor.

Note that the interacting services in the business chain use fine-grained process synchronization to control and monitor the execution of the business protocols, which is independent of the synchronous/asynchronous communication that they use. For instance, in Figure 4, the interacting services are using asynchronous communication while they execute the business protocols.

5 Conclusions and Future Work

We have presented three different cases for the flexible formation of business chain structures, considering protocol adaptation as a key enabler. Any existing protocol adaptation approach can be used to realize the actual adaptation. The presented approach enables the flexible formation of business chains between organizations that collaborate in a just-in-time fashion to meet a solution objective. The flexible formation of business chains is very important for organizations in competitive markets where the complexity of products and services increases while the life-cycles are shortened.

There are several directions for future work. We plan to extend our approach adding interface adaptation. We are currently extending our approach to define a software architecture in which the presented three cases can be described. Although this paper is focused on flexible formation of business chains, we will extend our approach to deal with adaptation of running business chains that deadlock due to the propagation of changes on the partner business protocols.

References

1. Brogi, A., Popescu, R.: Automated generation of BPEL adapters. In: Dan, A., Lamersdorf, W. (eds.) ICSOC 2006. LNCS, vol. 4294, pp. 27–39. Springer, Heidelberg (2006)
2. Chiu, D., Cheung, S., Till, S., Karlapalem, K., Li, Q., Kafeza, E.: Workflow view driven cross-organizational interoperability in a web service environment. Information Technology and Management 5(3-4), 221–250 (2004)
3. Supply Chain Council. SCOR: Supply-Chain Operations Reference model; version 9.0 (2008), `http://www.supply-chain.org`
4. Eshuis, R., Grefen, P.: Constructing customized process views. Data and Knowledge Engineering 64(2), 419–438 (2008)
5. TM Forum. eTOM: enhanced Telecom Operations Map; release 8.0 (2008), `http://www.tmforum.org/`
6. Grefen, P.: Mastering E-Business. Routledge, New York (2010)
7. Grefen, P., Eshuis, R., Mehandjiev, N., Kouvas, G., Weichhart, G.: Internet-based support for process-oriented instant virtual enterprises. IEEE Internet Computing 13(6), 65–73 (2009)
8. Gunasekaran, A., Ngai, E.W.T.: Build-to-order supply chain management: a literature review and framework for development. Journal of Operations Management 23(5), 423–451 (2005)
9. Mateescu, R., Poizat, P., Salaün, G.: Adaptation of service protocols using process algebra and on-the-fly reduction techniques. In: Bouguettaya, A., Krueger, I., Margaria, T. (eds.) ICSOC 2008. LNCS, vol. 5364, pp. 84–99. Springer, Heidelberg (2008)
10. Motahari Nezhad, H.R., Xu, G.Y., Benatallah, B.: Protocol-aware matching of web service interfaces for adapter development. In: Proc. WWW 2010, pp. 731–740. ACM, New York (2010)
11. Seguel, R., Eshuis, R., Grefen, P.: Minimal protocol adaptors for loosely coupled services. In: Proc. ICWS 2010, pp. 417–424. IEEE, Los Alamitos (2010)
12. Shan, Z., Kumar, A., Grefen, P.: Towards integrated service adaptation - a new approach combining message and control flow adaptation. In: Proc. ICWS 2010, pp. 385–392. IEEE, Los Alamitos (2010)

Business Process Monitoring with BPath*
(Short Paper)

Samir Sebahi and Mohand-Said Hacid

Université de Lyon
Université Claude Bernard Lyon 1
LIRIS, CNRS, UMR5205, France
{samir.sebahi,mohand-said.hacid}@liris.cnrs.fr

Abstract. Enterprise information systems allow more automation of tasks and complex interconnections, particularly with the emergence of new paradigms like Service Oriented Architecture (SOA). These new environments make checking correctness of systems at design-time as well as at run-time particularly challenging. In this paper, we propose a new monitoring framework that makes use of business protocols as a simple abstraction of business processes. We provide a monitoring language called BPath, which is an XPath-based language for both expressing and checking temporal and hybrid logical properties at run-time, making the execution of a business process visible by expressing and evaluating statistical queries over execution traces.

Keywords: Service based systems, hybrid logic, XPath, monitoring, business process, business protocol.

1 Introduction

The advent of web services and Service Oriented Architecture (SOA) has made a considerable progress in the way applications are developed and used, leading to the opening of new borders for information systems, with more automation of tasks and complex and multiple interconnection scenarios between applications within the same system and across different systems. In this context, the task of checking correctness of a system at design-time as well as at run-time becomes particularly challenging.

In this paper we present a new monitoring framework based on messages abstraction. This abstraction is called business protocol [1]. We provide an extension of XPath [2] to accommodate verification issues. The resulting language (called BPath) is also a query language that can be used to track and make visibility on business process execution.

In order to give an intuitive idea about our monitoring approach, let us consider the following scenario, inspired from [6], of an online Car Rental System (CRS) shown Fig. 1(a) and Fig. 1(b). CRS offers a car location service: whenever a rent car request is received (*RentCar*), the availability of the requested car will be checked

* This work is a part of the research project "COMPAS: Compliance-driven Models, Languages and Architectures for Services", which is funded by the European commission, funding reference FP7-215175.

R. Meersman et al. (Eds.): OTM 2010, Part I, LNCS 6426, pp. 446–453, 2010.

(*checkCarAavailability*). If it is not available, then a list of cars will be sent to the client, otherwise, the requested car is reserved, and a confirmation message is sent to the client. Then, the client will send her/his bank information (*BankInfo*), which will be validated (*CheckBankInfo*), before sending the keys. After returning the keys, the client receives a payment confirmation. But in case the bank information is not valid, *BankInfo rejected* message will be sent to the client and the process instance is completed. The black box in the diagram refers to activities which make reference to internal modules in the business process. The first one is a sensor module which checks the availability of a given car in the parking, and the second is a bank module which offers the ability to check bank information.

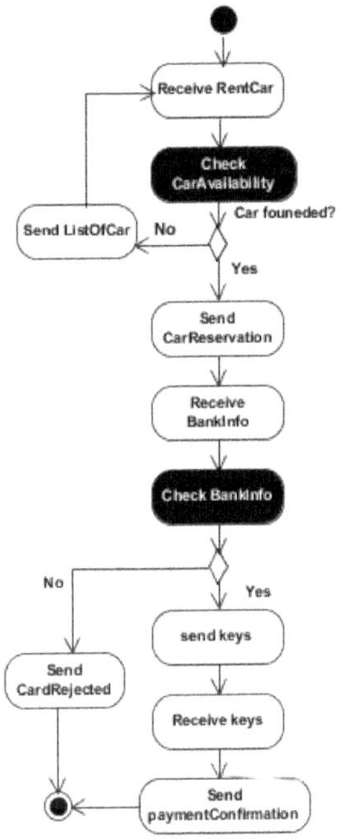

(**a**) Business process

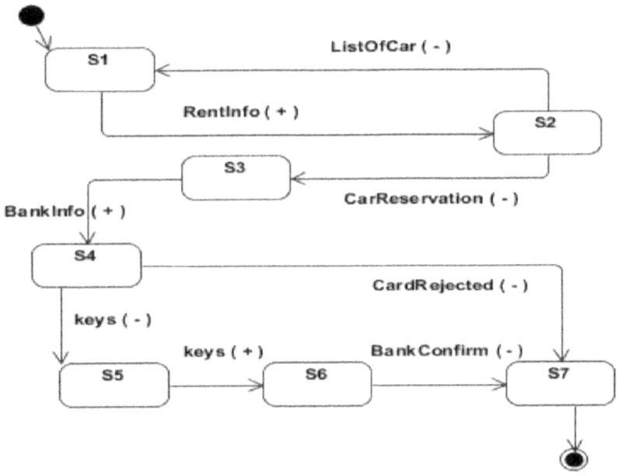

(**b**) Business protocol

Fig. 1. Car Rental System

The paper is organized as follows: Section 2 describes architectural and design principles of our approach for monitoring. In section 3 we present our monitoring language, and then we show its application to monitoring in Section 4. In section 5, we present some related works, and we conclude in section 6 by summarizing our work and anticipating on necessary extensions.

2 The Overall Architecture

Fig. 2 depicts the main components of the monitoring framework. First, a BPEL business process specification (Fig. 1(a)) is transformed into a business protocol shown in

Fig. 1(b). Then, monitoring properties and queries are formulated using BPath monitoring language over the business protocol. At run-time, all incoming or outgoing messages will be captured by the business protocol monitor component before reaching their original destination. The process engine as well as the monitoring framework will publish respectively the execution and monitoring events, which will be stored in the execution log. The execution log is of two types: states log, generated by the business protocol monitor, and events log generated by the process engine.

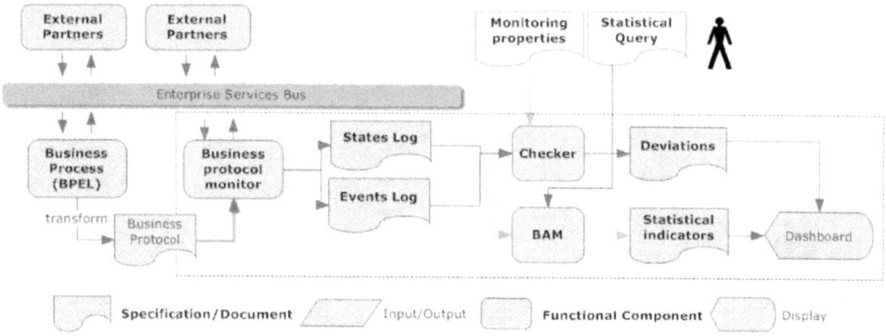

Fig. 2. Monitoring framework

On the basis of these generated execution logs, a checker component will check the correctness of the current execution and a Business Activity Monitor (BAM) component will evaluate the specified statistical query to return statistical indicators on the execution of the process, and then both of these monitoring results will be published on a dashboard component.

3 Monitoring Language

BPath is built on top of XPath, and evaluated over a special tree of nodes (each node has only one child node, and no sibling nodes) forming a linear structure. BPath accommodates the notion of static and dynamic attributes and allows variable assignment inside path expressions. BPath offers a mean to express properties in first order hybrid logic.

First order Hybrid logic [3] is an extension of first-order modal logic in which it is possible to name states and to assert that a formula is true at a named state. It may contain: nominals, satisfaction operators, and the $\downarrow$-binder. A Nominal is a propositional symbol, which is true at exactly one possible state. A State variable is a variable that makes reference to a state. A satisfaction operator $@s$ where s is a nominal or a state variable gives access to the state named or referenced by s. A formula of the form $@_s\varphi$ asserts that φ is true at the state named or referenced by s. Finally, a formula of the form $\downarrow s.\varphi$ binds all occurrences of the state variable s in φ to the current state of evaluation.

A BPath formula is built according to the following abstract syntax:

$\varphi ::= T \mid T = T \mid P(T, \ldots, T) \mid not\ \varphi \mid \varphi\ and\ \varphi \mid \varphi\ or\ \varphi \mid (\varphi) \mid @_s\varphi \mid \downarrow s,\varphi \mid \downarrow_\pi s,\varphi$
$\mid \downarrow_T x,\varphi \mid \exists x\ \varphi \mid \forall x\ \varphi \mid X\ \varphi \mid F\ \varphi \mid G\ \varphi \mid \varphi\ U\ \psi$
$T ::= \pi \mid x \mid c \mid \pi/@q \mid \$s \mid \$s/@q$
$\pi ::= Axis::N \mid (\pi) \mid \pi[\varphi] \mid \pi/\pi \mid$
$N ::= n \mid *$
Axis ::= child | *descendant* | *self* | *descendant-or-self*| *parent* | *ancestor*| *ancestor-or-self*

Where: $x \in$FVAR (a set of first-order variables), $n \in$LAB (a set of first-order constants). We define a function *lablel*: W→LAB, such that for each element of *W* associates an element of LAB. $s \in$ SVAR (a set of state variables). $q \in$ATTS (a set of unary function symbols, called static attributes) $\cup$ ATTD (a set of unary function symbols, called dynamic attributes) $\cup$ FUN (a set of one or more arity functions). To simplify some expressions, we consider that "π/*child::N*" can be written as "π/N", that "*self::*/@q*" can be simply written as "*@q*", and that "not (φ) ∨ α" can be abbreviated as "φ→ α".

X, F, G, and U are linear temporal logic operators. Temporal logic is a special type of modal logic: it provides a formal system for qualitatively describing and reasoning about how the truth values of assertions change over time [4]. These operators have the following meaning: X(φ): φ should be true on the next state, F(φ): mean that φ should be true at least once in the future, G(φ): φ should be true every time in the future, φ U ψ: φ has to be true at least until ψ, which is true now or in the future.

4 Application Scenario

In this section, we will show, through a concrete execution scenario, how BPath can be used to monitor business process execution. Let us assume that the car rental system manages three cars (RedCar, GreenCar, BlueCar), and receives requests from three clients (John, Mark and Bob), that we consider as web services interacting with the CRS business process: First, John sends a request for red car, but his credit card will be rejected, but he tries again and gets the car. Mark requests a green car, gets a reservation and keys, and then receives a payment confirmation after returning the keys. Bob requests the same car as Mark and obtains a reservation.

At run time, different instances of the CRS business process will execute simultaneously, and generate different kinds of events, including messages exchanged between different instances of the process and external partners. These events will be captured and stored by the events log component.

Definition 1. An events log is a collection of entries *el = (name, (key=value), (key=value)...., InsId, T),* where: *name* is the name of the event, *(key=value)* ...are list of items and their values contained within the event, *InsId* is an Instance identifier of the process instance concerned with the event, *and T* is a timestamp recording the time the event occurred.

Listing 1 shows an example of an event log from the supposed execution scenario of the CRS business process:

L1 : RentInfo: ClientInfo=John, CarInfo=RedCar, InstId=1, T=1

L2: CarReservation: carReserved=yes, InstId=1, T=3

L3: CardRejected: cardInfo=798799979879, InstId=1, T=5

L4: RentInfo: ClientInfo=Mark, CarInfo=GreenCar, InstId=2, T=8

L5: CarReservation: carReserved=yes, InstId=2, T=10

L6: BankInfo: cardInfo=798799979879, InstId=2, T=12

L7 : RentInfo: ClientInfo=John, CarInfo=BlueCar, InstId=3, T=15

L8: CarReservation: carReserved=yes, InstId=3, T=17

L9: Keys: keysOut=KY123, InstId=2, T=19

L10: RentInfo: ClientInfo=Bob, CarInfo= GreenCar, InstId=4, T=22

L11: CarReservation: carReserved=yes, InstId=4, T=24

L12: Keys: keysIn=KY123, InstId=2, InstId=2, T=26

L13: BankConfirm: payeConfirmed =yes, BankTransation=Trans0001, InstId=2, T=28

Listing 1. Events log

Additionally, the business protocol will generate events related to a transition from a state to another state, when a message is received or sent to or by an instance of the process. These events are stored in a states log.

Definition 2. A state log (SL) is an XML tree of nodes (states-nodes): w_1, w_2, w_3...where w_2 is the unique child node of w_1, w_3 the unique child node of w_2, etc. Each state-node has a name $s_j \in LAB$ such that $s_j = label(w_i)$,. and two attributes, *InsId (instance identifier)*$\in$*ATTS,* and *T (timestamp)*$\in$ *ATTS*. Listing 2 shows the states log generated from the supposed execution scenario of the CRS business process.

A BPath expression will be evaluated over the state log. But as we can see, states log do not contain a lot of information about the execution, because the real execution events are stored in the events log. Execution information can be retrieved and linked to a state-node through dynamic attributes. In BPath, the value of a dynamic attribute at state-node w is defined by a function θ (q, w), which extracts the last value of q from the events log, before that state node w occurs. For instance, the following BPath expressions, when evaluated at $T>4$, will return:

S1/S2/@ClientInfo = { John }, S1/S2/S3/@ClientInfo = {john}, and S1/S2/S3/@ carReserved = {yes}.

```
<S1 InstId="1" T="0">
 <S2 InstId="1" T="2">
  <S3 InstId="1" T="4">
   <S4 InstId="1" T="6">
    <S1 InstId="2" T="7">
     <S2 InstId="2" T="9">
      <S3 InstId="2" T="11">
       <S4 InstId="2" T="13">
        <S1 InstId="3" T="14">
         <S2 InstId="3" T="16">
          <S3 InstId="3" T="18">
           <S5 InstId="2" T="20">
            <S1 InstId="4" T="21">
             <S2 InstId="4" T="23">
              <S3 InstId="4" T="25">
               <S6 InstId="2" T="27">
                <S7 InstId="2" T="29"/>
               </S6>
              </S3>
     {...}
</S1>
```

Listing 2. States log

To show how the monitoring framework is able to monitor different kinds of properties and queries, we propose to consider the following list which should be continuously evaluated at run-time:

P1 (Not rejected customer): check that in case where credit card of a client is rejected, the client should wait one hour to be able to get a car reservation. We formulate this property in BPath as follows:

$$\mathbf{G}(\mathit{self::S7}[\downarrow S7,\ @\mathit{CardRejected} \rightarrow \mathit{not}(\ \mathbf{F}(\mathit{self::S3}[@\mathit{CleientInfo}=\$S7/@\mathit{ClientInfo}\ \mathit{and}\ \ (@T-\$S7/@T)<60\ ]))]) \tag{1}$$

In this property, we check that every time in the future where credit card of a client is rejected (can be checked at state S7), the concerned client should not get a car reservation (can be checked at the state S3 following S7), knowing that the elapsed time (between S3 and S7) is less than an hour.

P2 (Sensor coherence): A client should not get a car reservation when the keys are taken by another client. This property can be expressed using BPath as follows:

$$\mathbf{G}(\mathit{self::S5}[\downarrow S5,\ \mathbf{F}(\mathit{self::S3}\ [\downarrow S3,\ @\mathit{CarInfo}=\$S5/@\mathit{CarInfo}\ ]) \rightarrow \$S5[\mathbf{F}(\mathit{slef::S7}[@\mathit{CarInfo}=\$S5/@\mathit{CarInfo}\ \mathit{and}\ @T<\$S3/@T])])) \tag{2}$$

In this property we express that whenever keys of a car is sent (at state S5), every time in the future where a reservation for the same car is requested (at state S3), it should be the case that the keys of this car were returned before (if there exists a state S7 after S5 but before S3, where the keys of the car are returned)

As we can see from the previous execution log, the properties (P1, P2) are violated respectively at:

1. L8 (see events log): when John obtains a car reservation, knowing that his credit card was rejected since less than one hour (see L3).
2. At line L11: the green car was reserved for Bob (at L11), but this car is still assigned to Mark (L9), and the keys of the car are returned by Mark only after (L11), exactly at (L12).

BPath is also a query language that can be used to return statistical indicators on the execution of a business process:

Q1 (Average time car reservation): calculating average time to make a car reservation.

$$\textbf{Sum}(\textit{descendant-or-self::S1}[\downarrow S1,\ \textit{descendant::S3}[\downarrow S3,\ (@InstId=\$S1/@InstId)\ ]\ ]/@(\$S3/@T\text{-}@T)\ )\ \textit{div count}(\textit{descendant::S3}). \tag{3}$$

In this query we start by calculating the sum for all process instances of the time to reach the state S3 (the reservation state) from the state S1 (the start state), then dividing the obtained sum on the number of reservations. We use two functions (sum and count) to respectively calculate the sum and the number of elements of a sequence.

Q2 (Rejected bank info): to count the number of rejected credit cards we write in BPath:

$$\textbf{Count}\ (\textit{descendant-or-self::S7}[@CardRejected]) \tag{4}$$

5 Related Work

Recently, a few approaches were designed to deal with the problem of monitoring business processes. Some of them are directly related to our work. [5] Proposes a language (WSCoL) for specifying constraints on execution by defining a set of monitoring rules, for both functional and non-functional constraints like with BPath. In [6], monitoring properties are specified using event calculus language, and checked in post-mortem way against the stated behaviors and the recorded behavior in execution log at runtime, making the monitoring framework non intrusive regarding the execution of the business process, which is also the same case in our monitoring framework. Like BPath, [7, 8] propose monitoring languages that are built on top of XPath. [7] Proposes an approach to the monitoring of business processes specified in BPEL. A visual language, called Business Process Query Language (BPQL), with query capabilities, over BPEL processes, was introduced. XQuery expressions are generated, in the same way that graphical notations help BPEL designers generate specification code, using dedicated icons for each activity. [8] Proposes an approach for monitoring web service choreography by means of the XQuery engine. Linear temporal logic properties are translated into an equivalent XQuery expression, and then evaluated over XML message traces representing the choreography. Our monitoring framework is distinguished by using a simple messages based abstraction, and an expressive hybrid logic based language.

6 Conclusion and Future Work

In this work, we provided a preliminary framework for business process monitoring. First, we have presented BPath, the underlying monitoring language. Then, through a case study, we have shown how the monitoring framework can be used to monitor a business process. To summarize, we have developed a monitoring framework that mainly displays the following features:

- The use of simple messages as an abstraction mechanism;
- A single expressive language for expressing both monitoring properties and queries. However, BPath is familiar to those who already use XPath.
- Monitoring properties and queries can be dynamically specified during the execution of the process,
- Non-intrusive monitoring framework, because it is executed in completely separated way from the business process.

Our future work will be devoted to the design of methods to analyze and explain the reason of the deviations when they occur, and move towards resolving them as soon as they occur.

References

1. Benatallah, B., Casati, F., Toumani, F.: Analysis and Management of Web Service Protocols. In: Atzeni, P., Chu, W., Lu, H., Zhou, S., Ling, T.-W. (eds.) ER 2004. LNCS, vol. 3288, pp. 524–541. Springer, Heidelberg (2004)
2. Clark, J., DeRose, S.: XML path language (XPath) version 1.0, W3C recommendation (1999), `http://www.w3.org/TR/xpath`
3. Blackburn, P., Marx, M.: Tableaux for Quantified Hybrid Logic. In: Egly, U., Fermüller, C. (eds.) TABLEAUX 2002. LNCS (LNAI), vol. 2381, pp. 259–286. Springer, Heidelberg (2002)
4. Emerson, E.A.: Temporal and modal logic. Handbook of theoretical computer science: formal models and semantics, vol. B, pp. 995–1072. MIT Press, Cambridge (1990)
5. Baresi, L., Guinea, S.: Towards Dynamic Monitoring of WS-BPEL Processes. In: Benatallah, B., Casati, F., Traverso, P. (eds.) ICSOC 2005. LNCS, vol. 3826, pp. 269–282. Springer, Heidelberg (2005)
6. Mahbub, K., Spanoudakis, G.: A framework for requirents monitoring of service based systems. In: Proceedings of the 2nd International Conference on Service Oriented Computing, pp. 84–93. ACM, New York (2004)
7. Beeri, C., Eyal, A.: Monitoring business processes with queries. In: The Proceedings of the 33rd International Conference on Very Large Data Bases VLDB 2007, pp. 603–614 (2007)
8. Hallé, S., Villemaire, R.: XML Methods for Validation of Temporal Properties on Message Traces with Data. In: Meersman, R., Tari, Z. (eds.) OTM 2008. LNCS, vol. 5332, pp. 337–353. Springer, Heidelberg (2008)

CoMaP: A Cooperative Overlay-Based Mashup Platform

Osama Al-Haj Hassan, Lakshmish Ramaswamy, and John A. Miller

Computer Science Department, University of Georgia,
Athens, GA 30602, USA
{hasan,laks,jam}@cs.uga.edu

Abstract. Recently, mashups have emerged as an important class of Web 2.0 collaborative applications. Mashups can be conceived as personalized Web services which aggregate and manipulate data from multiple, geographically-distributed Web sources. Mashups, while enhancing personalization, bring up new scalability and performance challenges. The fact that most existing mashup platforms are centralized further exacerbates the scalability challenges. Towards addressing these challenges, in this paper, we present the design, implementation, and evaluation of *CoMaP* – a cooperative information system for mashup execution. The design of *CoMaP* is characterized by a scalable architecture with multiple cooperative nodes distributed across the Internet and possibly multiple controllers which plan and coordinate mashup execution. In our architecture, an individual mashup can be executed at several collaborative nodes with each node executing part of the mashup. *CoMaP* includes a unique mashup deployment scheme that decides which nodes would be involved in executing an individual mashup and what operators they would host. Also, *CoMaP* continuously adapts to overlay dynamics and to user actions such as creation of new mashups or deletion of existing ones. Furthermore, *CoMaP* possesses failure resiliency feature which is necessary for cooperative information systems. Our experimental study indicates that the proposed techniques yield improved system performance.

Keywords: cooperative information systems, Web 2.0, mashup, collaboration.

1 Introduction

Web 2.0 continues to evolve and grow at a tremendous pace. Web 2.0 applications are characterized by high degrees of personalization and social interaction, and they enable seamless information sharing and collaboration among end-users [15]. Mashups are one such class of popular Web 2.0 applications. Mashups can be conceptualized as personalized Web services that are created by end-users. Functionally, they fetch data from one or more Web sources, which would then be aggregated, manipulated and filtered as per user specifications, and the final results would be dispatched to the end-users. Yahoo pipes [17] and Intel

R. Meersman et al. (Eds.): OTM 2010, Part I, LNCS 6426, pp. 454–471, 2010.

MashMaker [8] are among the popular mashup platforms. Mashup platforms are also considered a type of collaborative information systems that enable collaboration and sharing of data among end-users by allowing them to browse each other mashups and use them to build their own customized ones.

Mashups, while enabling high-degree of personalization, flexibility, and collaboration are also faced with unique scalability and performance limitations. First, unlike traditional Web services, mashups are designed by end-users. This implies that number of mashups hosted by a mashup platform is orders of magnitude higher than number of Web services hosted by a Web service portal. Second, mashups rely upon data from many different sources distributed across the Internet. These data sources vary widely in terms of their data characteristics, and reliability. Third, since mashups are developed by non-tech-savvy end-users, they may not be optimized from efficiency stand-point. These limitations are exacerbated by the fact that most existing mashup platforms are centralized.

This paper explores distribution as a mechanism to achieve scalability and performance of mashups. We present a dynamic cooperative mashup execution framework called *CoMaP*. *CoMaP* is based upon an overlay of nodes that collaborate to execute mashup process (either partial or complete). The collaboration between nodes is facilitated by a controller which also plans the execution of individual mashups. In designing *CoMaP*, we make three novel contributions.

- First, we present an efficient cooperative mashup architecture in which multiple nodes cooperate to execute mashups. Our architecture is distributed and mashup operators are spread across several nodes. The collaboration between mashup execution nodes is facilitated by a controller which also plans the execution of individual mashups.
- Second, we introduce a dynamic mashup distribution technique that is sensitive to the locations of the various data sources of an individual mashup as well as the destinations of its results. Our technique progressively optimizes the network load in the overlay and the latency of mashup execution.
- Third, we handle failure resiliency issues in our architecture through replicating nodes and replicating parts of mashup workflows.

We evaluate the design of *CoMaP* through series of experiments that show the effectiveness of our architecture and distribution technique.

2 Motivation and Challenges

In this section, we introduce background about mashups and current functionality of existing mashup platforms. In addition, we discuss motivations that led us to introducing *CoMaP* and challenges that we need to handle in our architecture.

Mashups are popular because of their personalization property that enables each end-user to design his own mashups based on his own needs as opposed to a Web service which is dedicated to a group of end-users. The operators involved in mashups can be operators for fetching data from data sources distributed across the Web. They can also be data processing operators such as filter operators.

Notice that each mashup operator Op_z might have multiple parents and multiple children where children operators are the source of input to Op_z and parent operators are the sinks of output of Op_z.

In addition to Yahoo pipes [17], other mashup platforms exist in literature such as MARIO [11], DAMIA [7], Marmite [16], and MashMaker [8]. These platforms work in several ways such as providing a cloud of tags from which end-users build their mashups, or allowing end-users to work on data sources using a visual interface. To the best of our knowledge, these platforms are based on a centralized server through which end-users create and execute mashups.

Since each end-user has the privilege of designing his own mashups, mashup platforms typically host large numbers of mashups and experience high mashup request rates. Because of that, a centralized mashup platform faces an increasing pressure and might not be able to keep up with increasing amount of end-users requests which raises a scalability problem. Also, a centralized mashup platform does not consider the geographical location of end-users and data sources; this implies that some end-users might observe high delays. In addition, having a centralized mashup platform implies that the centralized server is a single point of failure. The previous three points motivates the need for a distributed mashup platform where mashup execution takes part on several cooperative nodes.

2.1 Challenges

Distributing mashup execution requires the collaboration of distributed nodes in an overlay that faces network dynamics; therefore, we need to handle several challenges in distributing mashup execution.

Since we are designing a distributed system, what type of cooperation is needed between network nodes? This is important to guarantee a complete and correct mashup execution. Also, should a mashup be executed on one node or multiple nodes? Executing a mashup on multiple nodes forms a way of parallel execution. Further, what are the parameters based on which a node is selected to execute the whole mashup or part of it? Parameters such as communication links delay, bandwidth and nodes loading, should be considered.

The next challenges are related to handling dynamics of the system; what happens in the case of changing network parameters? For example, communication links delay and bandwidth between nodes is changing due to factors such as congestion. Also, node loading is changing as nodes get more mashups to execute. Therefore, a mashup that is being executed on some nodes might have to be reassigned to different nodes to adapt to changing network parameters. Also, what if more than one end-user share the same mashup or part of it? A mashup execution plan is initially designed based on a number of end-users requesting it. When more end-users request the same mashup, the mashup execution plan might change based on the geographical location of the new end-users. Further, what happens if network nodes fail? Certain recovery method should be applied to make sure system functionality is not affected?

Towards addressing the previous challenges, we proceed by introducing our distributed mashup platform *CoMaP*.

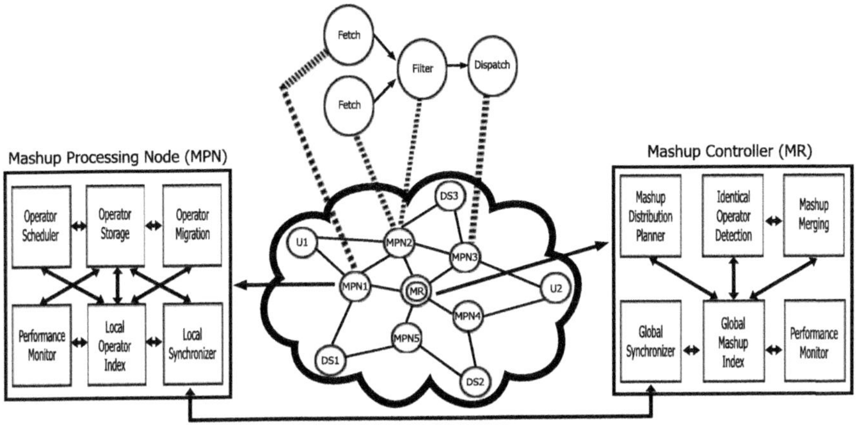

Fig. 1. CoMaP Architecture

3 CoMaP Architecture

Figure 1 illustrates *CoMaP*'s high-level design architecture. *CoMaP* is based upon an overlay of mashup processing nodes MPNs, we refer to this set of nodes as $MPNSet = \{MPN_1, MPN_2, \ldots, MPN_L\}$. These nodes are distributed across the Internet, and they collaborate to execute mashup workflows. A mashup controller MR plans the execution of each mashup. It also coordinates the activities of various processing nodes involved in the execution of a mashup. A set of end-users $USet = \{U_1, U_2, \ldots, U_N\}$ interact with *CoMaP*. Each of those end-users can design and submit his own mashups to MR using a mashup designer. Note that each MPN and end-user in *CoMaP* can tell what its coordinates are by probing a set of nodes geographically distributed over the Web (Landmarks). Landmarks [9] cooperate among each other to deliver coordinates for the node that probed them. We refer to the set of mashups that MR receives as $MpSet = \{Mp_1, Mp_2, \ldots, Mp_M\}$. Operators that form those mashups are referred to as $OpSet = \{Op_1, Op_2, \ldots, Op_Z\}$. The previous entities are connected with a set of communication links where each communication link $LNK_{e,f}$ connects node e with node f. Each communication link $LNK_{e,f}$ has a delay $DeLNK_{e,f}$ and a bandwidth $BndLNK_{e,f}$.

Each MPN is responsible for executing a set of workflows as determined by MR. An individual workflow might correspond to an entire mashup or part of it. A mashup workflow is essentially a tree of operators. When executing a workflow, one MPN may fetch data from external sources or it may receive partially processed data from other processing nodes which would have executed earlier parts of the mashup. The results are dispatched either to the end-user (if no further processing is needed for the mashup) or to another MPN (if mashup execution is not yet complete). Executing a mashup on several nodes yields better efficiency and scalability. For example, if a mashup consists of two

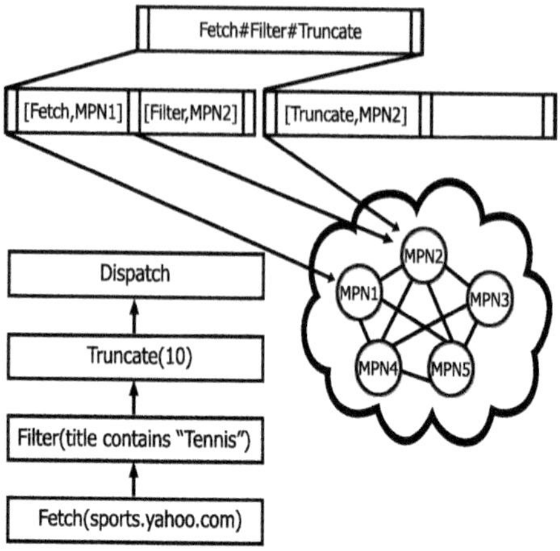

Fig. 2. A mashup stored in B+ tree which points to *MPN*s where operators are deployed

fetch operators that fetch data from two different data sources, then assigning each operator to a different node facilitates parallel execution.

As indicated in Figure 1, each *MPN* comprises of several components. Mashup workflows assigned to the processing node are stored in the operator storage, and are indexed by the operator index. The local scheduler makes the workflow scheduling decisions. The performance of each processing node is locally monitored, summary of which is communicated to the global performance monitor (located at *MR*) periodically.

End-users interact with the system through *MR* which they get to know upon joining the system. The set of interactions include creation and deployment of new mashups and deletion of existing ones. When an end-user sends a new mashup to *MR* to be executed, *MR* first checks whether the newly created mashup shares operator sequences with existing mashups. If so, *MR* modifies the mashup to utilize the results from the existing operator sequences so that duplicate computations are avoided. The global mashup index aids the detection of shared mashup operators. This index is similar to the index that we introduced in *AMMORE* [2] except that the index introduced in *AMMORE* is based on a centralized architecture. Therefore, the global index used by each *MR* is extended from *AMMORE* index so that it contains information about where each operator is deployed in the network. Figure 2 shows an example of the global operator index.

Once *MR* is done with shared operators detection, it uses its mashup distribution planner to decide where (on which execution nodes) an incoming mashup would be executed, and if multiple nodes are involved in executing a mashup what part each would execute. The mashup distribution planning considers several factors including the mashup structure, the locations of the data sources and end-users, and the current performance of the overlay. The global performance

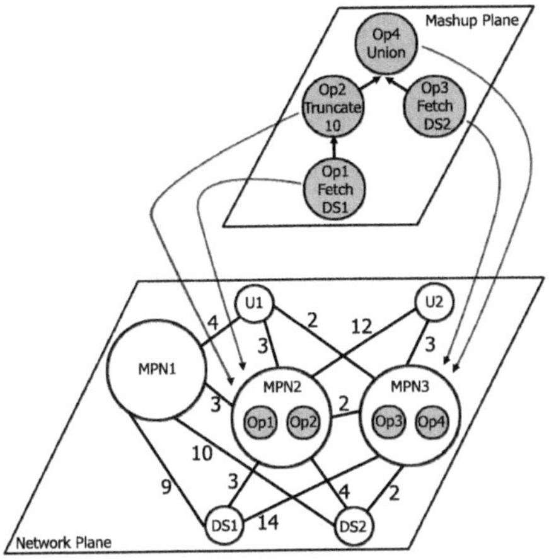

Fig. 3. The operator placement problem in CoMap

monitor at MR interacts with the local performance monitors at individual MPNs, and it maintains a global snapshot of the overlay performance. The global synchronizers coordinate the activities of the MPNs involved in executing a mashup. Figure 3 illustrates a mashup being executed on two MPNs.

Next, we explain our technique for distributing mashup execution and how it can adapt to network changes.

4 Planning Distributed Mashup Execution

This section formally describes the distributed mashup execution problem. After that, we explain how to plan the deployment of mashup operators in the overlay network and how they are executed in a distributed fashion.

4.1 Problem Statement

Figure 3 demonstrates the operator placement problem. We have a plane of mashups and a plane of network nodes, data sources, and end-users. System cost differs based on where operators are placed in the overlay network. Therefore, our goal is to place each operator in a node in the network such that system cost is minimum. Towards solving this problem, we model the distributed mashup execution problem as an optimization problem. In *CoMaP*, we consider delay, bandwidth, and nodes load as metrics for computing the cost of executing operators in different places in the overlay network.

When a certain operator is executed on a given node, the cost of that execution is partitioned into computation cost and communication cost. Computation cost results from processing time of executing the operator on the node and communication time results from transmitting operators execution output to the next set of nodes that host the operators coming next in the mashup workflow. Suppose we have an operator Op_z that belongs to mashup Mp_i, created by end-user U_j, and hosted by MPN_k. The input of this operator is coming from the operators which are executed before Op_z, we refer to this set of operators as $PrvOpSet$ and we refer to some operator in this set as Op_q. We refer to the output size of Op_q as OS_q. The computation cost of Op_z deployed on MPN_k can be formulated as the summation of the size of the output data of each operator in $PrvOpSet$ in kilobytes divided by time needed by MPN_k to process each kilobyte of the data PT_k. Thus, $CompTime_{z,k} = \sum_{q=1}^{Q} \frac{OS_q}{PT_k}$.

Once Op_z operator finishes execution, it needs to send its output to the MPNs that host the next set of operators that are expecting input from Op_z. We refer to this set of MPNs as $NxtMPNSet$ and we refer to some MPN in this set as MPN_r. Communication time resulted by operator Op_z deployed on MPN_k can be formulated as the size of operator Op_z output in kilobytes OS_z divided by outgoing communication link bandwidth $BndLNK_{k,r}$ between MPN_k and each MPN_r in $NxtMPNSet$, the result is added to outgoing link's communication delay per unit of data $DeLNK_{k,r}$ between MPN_k and each MPN_r. Therefore, $CommTime_{z,k} = \sum_{r=1}^{R} (\frac{OS_z}{BandLNK_{k,r}} + DeLNK_{k,r})$.

As a result, cost of execution of operator is the combination of computation and communication costs. Notice, that operators are executed multiple times according to their request rate, so, the total cost for an operator has to be multiplied with the operator's request rate RT_z. Therefore, cost of executing operator Op_z on MPN_k becomes $C_{z,k} = RT_z \times ((\sum_{q=1}^{Q} \frac{OS_q}{PT_k}) + \sum_{r=1}^{R} (\frac{OS_z}{BandLNK_{k,r}} + DeLNK_{k,r}))$.

System cost results from the combination of delay resulting from 1) End-users $USet$ submitting their mashups to Mashup Controller MR 2) MR performing operators merging on requested mashups 3) MR assigning mashup operators to $MPNSet$ 4) Executing mashup operators $OpSet$ on $MPNSet$. Cost in 4 can be optimized, therefore, our target in this optimization problem is to place operators $OpSet$ on $MPNSet$ such that total cost of executing operators is minimum. Let $Alloc_{z,k}$ be a {0,1} variable denoting that operator Op_z is deployed on MPN_k ($Alloc_{z,k} = 1$), otherwise, $Alloc_{z,k} = 0$. Therefore, the optimization problem is to assign values to each $Alloc_{z,k}$ variable such that $\sum_{z=1}^{Z} \sum_{k=1}^{L} Alloc_{z,k} \times C_{z,k}$ is minimized while ensuring that the following constraints are not violated: 1) For an operator Op_z, $\sum_{k=1}^{L} Alloc_{z,k} = 1$, this indicates that Op_z is deployed only on one MPN; 2) $LD_k <= LdLimit_k$ which indicates that the load of MPN_k should not exceed its maximum allowed load.

A few naive approaches can be used to deploy mashup operators in overlay network, the first one is '*Random*' deployment where mashup operators are distributed randomly on MPNs. Another approach is '*Destination*' deployment where mashup operators are deployed on MPNs that are closest to the end-user who requested the mashup. The opposite approach is '*Source*' deployment where mashup operators are deployed on MPNs that are closest to data sources that contribute to these operators. One more approach is the '*Optimal*' deployment in which an exhaustive search is performed to deploy operators on MPNs that

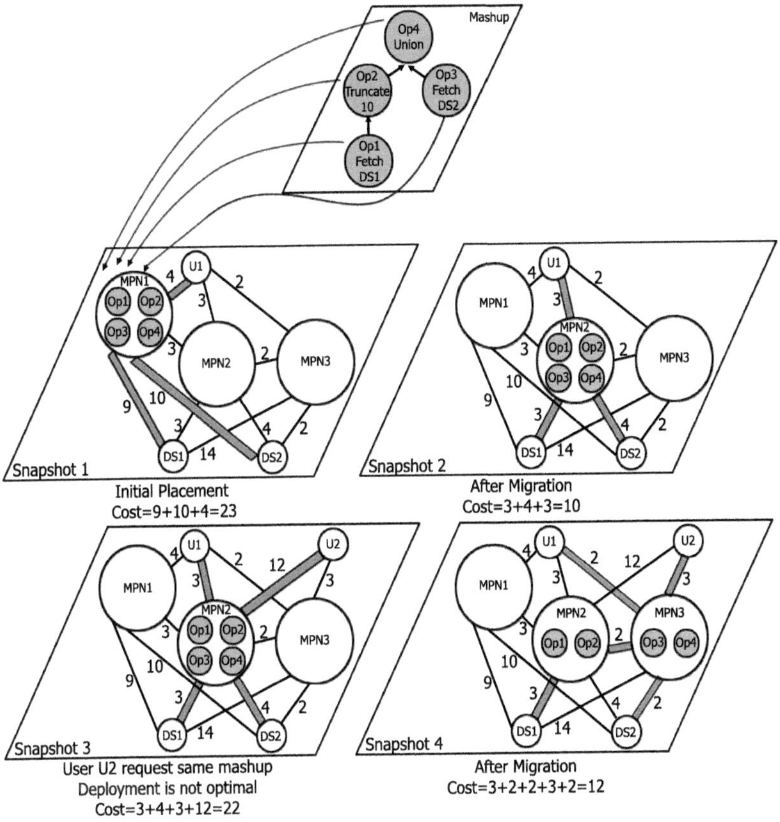

Fig. 4. A scenario of CoMaP operator placement

yield the minimum cost. The '*Optimal*' approach is expected to produce the best result but its running time is exponential due to its exhaustive search nature.

4.2 Our Scheme – DIMA

This subsection describes our approach for deploying mashup operators. Our approach is a two-stage optimization process where initial operator deployment is performed in the first stage and a migration process takes place in the second stage. We introduce a running example represented in Figure 4 throughout our discussion. In this example, a mashup consisting of four operators is to be deployed on MPNs. The mashup first uses a fetch operator (Op_1) to pull data from data source DS_1, then it uses Op_2 to truncate 10 items from the result of fetching data. Second, the mashup uses a fetch operator (Op_3) to fetch data from data source DS_2. Finally, the results of Op_2 and Op_3 are combined using a union operator (Op_4), and the final result is dispatched to end-user (U_1). Figure 4 consists of 4 parts representing in-order snapshots of the system. Link delays on the figure represent the final delay (in seconds) resulting from taking propagation delay, bandwidth, and data source sizes into consideration. For the sake of clarity in this figure, we assume all MPNs have the same processing power. One thing to mention is that geographical location of a node is reflected by its location in the layout. For example, by looking at part 1 of the figure, we can see that MPN_1 is closer to U_1 than MPN_2. Communication links that contribute to system cost are shaded in grey.

Stage1: Initial Deployment. Mashup Controller MR has information about all MPNs in the system, including load of MPNs and their coordinates in the network distance graph. Such information is transferred to MR by MPNs upon joining the network. The load information for MPNs is then updated as MR deploys mashup operators on MPNs. Once an end-user sends his mashup to MR, the coordinates for the end-user machine is also sent to MR.

In this stage, when the mashup arrives to MR, MR uses end-user coordinates and MPNs coordinates to compute Euclidian distance between each pair of end-user and MPN. This distance is then used to estimate delay of sending data from MPN to end-user. Each operator is then initially deployed on the MPN that has the minimum delay from the end-user. In our running example, part 1 of Figure 4 shows the initial deployment stage for the four operators. Notice that delay in this stage is only computed based on coordinates (Euclidean distance). Here, since MPN_1 is geographically closer to U_1 than MPN_2 and MPN_3, all operators are initially deployed on MPN_1.

This initial operator deployment may not always be optimal for the following reasons. First, this stage depends on Euclidian distances to estimate delays which is not accurate as relying on current network conditions. In part 1 of our running example, actual link delays do not comply with geographical location of nodes. This can happen because some nodes reside on fast links, others might reside on slower links. It can also happen because of congested links. Second, operator deployment in this stage is based on distances from end-users, if distances from end-users and data sources are taken into consideration; better deployment decisions might be achieved. In part 1 of our running example, delays between MPN_1 and data sources DS_1 and DS_2 are not considered. However, distances from data sources are unknown at this stage because the coordinates of data sources are not known. The number of data sources on the Web is huge, this is why the system cannot store and maintain coordinates of that large number of data sources. Third, as we will explain in the next subsection, mashup operator deployment becomes sub-optimal when more end-users share mashups.

Once the initial placement of each operator is decided, the entry for that operator in the global mashup index is updated with the new deployment information that specifies at which MPN the operator is deployed. Although this initial step may not lead to optimal deployment decision, it is a good initial step. Next, the optimization process seeks to improve deployment by going through a migration process.

Stage2: Operator Migration. To minimize system cost, operators should migrate from the MPN on which they are deployed to a new MPN that leads to a better deployment decision. This migration process has to be fully distributed to preserve the scalability feature of *CoMaP*.

Each MPN has to decide if migrating operators to one of its neighbors decreases the total system cost; the total system cost is not available for MPN nodes due to the distributed nature of *CoMaP*. Basically, the total system cost is the summation of operators execution costs all over the network. So, if each MPN minimizes operator execution cost within its neighborhood, that will eventually decrease the total system cost.

To compute the amount of cost change resulting from migrating operators from MPN_i to MPN_j, first, we introduce the cost of a migration *state*. Each migration step has two states; $CurrentSate$ and $NewState$ where the $CurrentState$ represents hosting operators on MPN_i (Before migration) and the $NewState$ represents hosting operators on MPN_i in addition to hosting migrated operators on MPN_j (After migration). Therefore, we have two costs; $CurrentStateCost$ and $NewStateCost$ where the cost of each state includes the cost of hosting operators in that state; such that the cost of hosting an operator on some MPN is given as follows; 1) the cost of sending input to MPN by the nodes that host the children of this operator. 2) The cost of processing the input on MPN. 3) The cost of sending output by MPN to nodes that host parents of this operator. 4) The cost of communication between MPN and the end-users sharing the operator which is evaluated by pinging end-users machines. When MPN_i is considering migrating operators to MPN_j, it computes $NetB = CurrentStateCost - NewStateCost$ and it also considers all direct neighbors MPN_j (number of hops=1). After that, operators migrate to the neighbor with maximum positive $NetB$ value. A positive $NetB$ value indicates that this migration step leads to minimization of system cost.

Now, we demonstrate this stage in part 2 of our running example, MPN_1 is considering migrating all 4 operators to MPN_2. In this case, MPN_1 uses ping pong messages to estimate cost of fetching data from DS_1 and DS_2. Then, it uses ping pong messages to estimate cost of sending the result to U_1. Accordingly, $CurrentStateCost = 23$. Now, MPN_1 asks its neighbor MPN_2 about the cost of hosting the 4 operators on it. Here, MPN_2 uses ping pong messages to estimate the cost of fetching data from DS_1 and DS_2 plus the cost of sending result to U_1; then MPN_2 sends the result back to MPN_1. Based on MPN_2 feedback, MPN_1 finds out that $NewStateCost = 10$. After that, MPN_1 calculates the net benefit ($NetB = 13$) and decides to migrate all 4 operators to MPN_2.

Notice that if no such **direct** neighbor with $NetB > 0$ is found, MPN_i widens its search process by looking at indirect neighbors where the number of hops = 2. This increase in the tested neighborhood helps '$DIMA$' scheme to avoid local optima. At the same time, the maximum number of hops we use for the local search process is 3, it is kept low so that *CoMaP* efficiency is not degraded. Also, this parameter can be set by the system administrator.

Part 3 of our running example considers the case when a new user U_2 requests the same mashup which U_1 initially requested. Because U_1 and U_2 share mashups, the previous operators deployment which is based on U_1 requesting the mashup is not optimal any more. This happens because communication between MPN_2 and U_2 results in high delay. Therefore, migration is needed again. In this example, MPN_2 is considering migrating Op_3 and Op_4 to MPN_3 as a target neighbor. MPN_2 repeats the same migration steps which results in $NewStateCost = 12$, $CurrentStateCost = 22$, and $NetB = 10$. As a result, MPN_2 decides that Op_3 and Op_4 should migrate to MPN_3 which is reflected in part 4 of Figure 4.

When an operator migrates from MPN_i to MPN_j, MPN_i informs the MPNs on which children and parent operators are deployed with such a change. In addition, MPN_i informs the mashup controller about the new change. The mashup controller in turn updates its mashup index with the new deployment decisions. Therefore, when new requests for mashups arrive to the mashup controller, the controller is able to consult the up to date mashup index to find out to which MPNs the mashup execution should be directed.

The migration process is performed periodically to ensure that *CoMaP* adapts to newly requested mashups and to changes in the number of end-users sharing operators. Moreover, the migration process needs to be executed periodically to adapt to changes in network links delay and bandwidth. Note that communication costs between MPNs is calculated such that delay and bandwidth values are the actual values of the links in the overlay network.

Notice that the cost of probing nodes done in the migration process is considered tolerable for the system because probing only occurs periodically when the migration process is performed. In addition, the migration process happens within each MPN locality which means that the migration process is performed smoothly without the system functionality being affected.

In the next section, we discuss failure resiliency which is an important quality for cooperative distributed information systems.

5 Failure Resiliency

The sources of failure in *CoMaP* could come from 1) Failure of Mashup Controller (MR) or 2) Failure of Mashup Processing Nodes (MPNs). Failure of a mashup controller is handled by replicating it which helps to avoid a single point of failure in the system. Among those controllers, one of them is the main controller and the other replicas are secondary controllers. All mashup controllers are identical to one another in terms of system information they posses and each one of them plays the same role in terms of receiving and handling end-user requests. However, the main controller plays slightly different role than secondary controllers in failure resiliency process. All mashup controllers are chosen to be distributed geographically in the network such that each controller serves the end-users closer to it.

To guarantee correct functionality of *CoMaP*, certain interaction between controllers is needed. For example, detecting shared operators requires that each controller knows about all operators in all mashups sent by end-users. Therefore, when one controller receives a mashup from an end-user, it directly sends the mashup information to all other controllers. This way, detecting shared operators becomes identical in all controller nodes. However, when a mashup is sent to a controller, that controller is the only one responsible of directing the execution of that mashup.

Another type of communication is needed between controllers in the case of controller failure. Basically, each controller has one identical list of nodes which specifies three pieces of information. First, who is currently the main controller? Second, what is the current set of secondary controllers? Third, what is the set of candidate nodes that can be replacements of secondary controllers? The main controller exchange heart beat messages with secondary controllers to ensure they are still alive. If the main controller did not receive a reply from one of the secondary controllers, it assumes it failed and responds by performing the following operations. First, it uses the candidate set to assign a new secondary controller. Second, its current state is duplicated on to the new secondary controller so that it can start operating. Third, it notifies all other secondary controllers about the failure of the old controller and the existence of the new replacement.

Failure of the main controller is handled as follows, in case secondary controllers do not receive heart beat messages from the main controller, they assume it failed. Here, the current set of secondary controllers is used to recover from such a failure. Basically, what happens is that the current set of secondary controllers is ordered such that the first controller in the list has the responsibility of replacing the main controller when it fails. In this case, the previously mentioned secondary controller (new main controller) performs the following operations. First, it eliminates itself from the current secondary controllers list. Second, it propagates the change in this list to all other controllers. Third, it announces itself as the new main controller to all other secondary controllers. The introduction of coordinator replicas only causes one change on '$DIMA$' operator deployment scheme. When an operator migrates from MPN_i to another MPN, MPN_i contacts the coordinator in its area to inform it about operator migration. That coordinator in turn distributes the information to all other coordinators.

So far, we discussed failure within controllers, now, we discuss failure of Mashup Processing Nodes (MPNs). MPNs exchange heart beat messages with direct neighbors, if one MPN did not receive a reply from one of the neighbors, it assumes failure of that neighbor and reports the failure to the controller in its area. Once the controller receives the failure notification, it reallocates the operators which used to be hosted by the failed MPN to a new MPN. This new allocation is propagated to the main controller and all secondary controllers.

Moreover, if failure occurred to one of the mashup processing nodes (MPNs), then the effect of this failure is alleviated by replicating operators. If one MPN hosting an operator fails, then the operator can still be accessed through its replica. Since a huge number of operators exist in *CoMaP*, we cannot replicate each one of them. So, we select a percentage of the most overloaded MPNs in the system and we replicate their operators. This percentage is selected by the system administrator based on observed system performance. When one MPN replicates an operator to another MPN, it also informs the controller in its area of the replication process, and that controller propagates this change to all other controllers.

6 Experimental Evaluation

We use simulation to perform our experiments. The goal of experiments is to evaluate '$DIMA$' approach by showing its effect on *CoMaP* performance. Also, we discuss the effect of applying failure resiliency on our system.

6.1 Experimental Setup

CoMaP environment simulates several operators which is similar to yahoo pipes, these operators are Fetch, Filter, Sort, Union, Truncate, Tail, Sub-Element, Reverse, Unique, and Count. Our system consists of 4 mashup controllers, 100 data sources, 100 end-users, and a number of MPNs varying from 1000 to 4000. The total number of mashups requested by end-users varies from 1000 to 10000 where mashups request rate varies from 5 to 65 requests per unit time. The data sources are extracted from syndic8 [3] which is a repository for RSS and Atom feeds, the popularity distribution of data sources is also extracted from syndic8 where the number of subscriptions for a data source reflects its popularity. The number of operators per mashup varies from 10 to 40 where two of these operators are fetch operators and their data sources are selected based on data sources popularity, the rest of operators are selected randomly. Data source sizes vary from 1000 KB to 10000 KB. Our overlay topology is the Internet topology in 2008 measured by DIMES [13]. The number of nodes we use from this topology varies from 1204 to 4204.

6.2 System Evaluation

System cost in *CoMaP* is measured based on two factors, first, the average delay per mashup resulting from deploying and executing mashups operators, second, the average network usage per mashup which is defined as the average number of bytes transferred within the network caused by executing mashups. The '$DIMA$' approach is compared to '*Random*', '*Source*', '*Destination*', and '*Optimal*' approaches. In all experiments we vary one parameter and keep the others constant. Unless mentioned, the constant values for number of mashups, number of operators, mashup request rate, data source size, and number of MPNs are 1000 mashup, 10 operators per mashup, 25 requests per unit time, 1000 KB, and 2000 MPNs, respectively.

In the first experiment we vary number of operators in *CoMaP* from 10 to 40 and we measure delay and network usage for the different schemes; Figures 5 and 6 show that '*Random*' scheme leads to high delays and high network usage

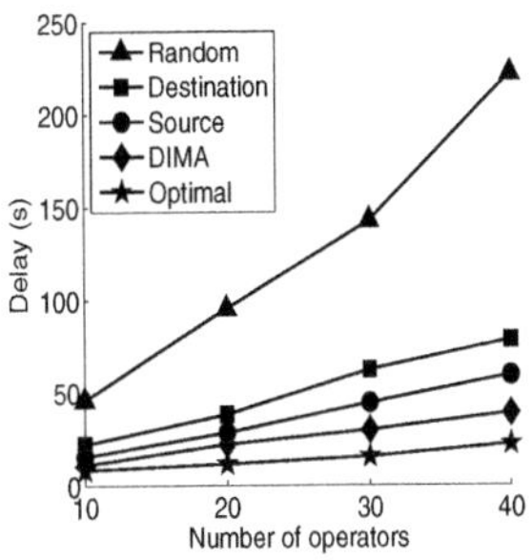

Fig. 5. Average delay per mashup when number of operators varies

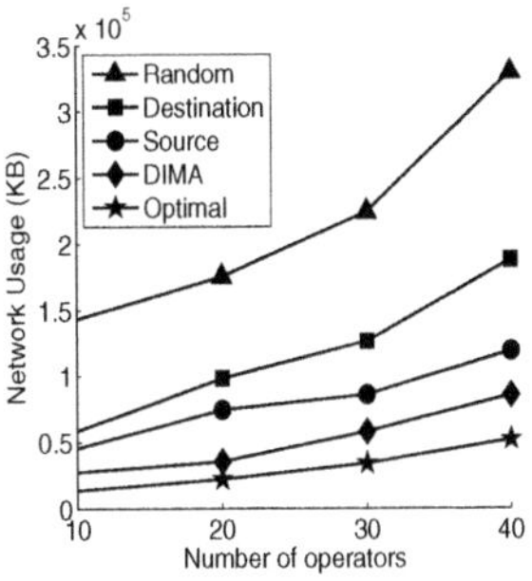

Fig. 6. Average network usage per mashup when number of operators varies

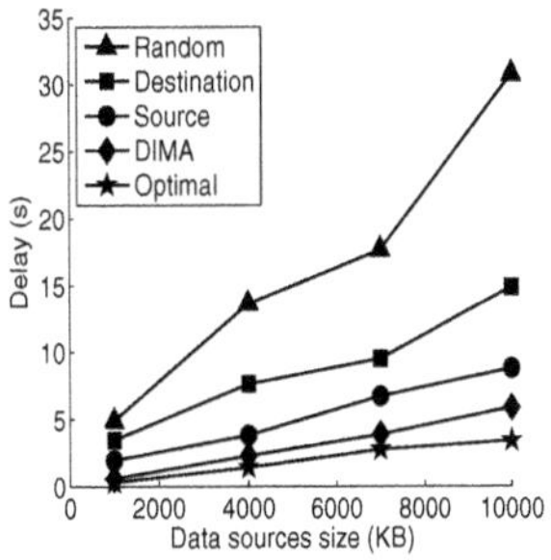

Fig. 7. Average delay per mashup when data source size varies

and it is the worst among all schemes because it does not follow any kind of heuristics to deploy operators. The '*Source*' and '*Destination*' schemes lead to lower delay and network usage than the '*Random*' deployment. The results of the '*Source*' and '*Destination*' schemes might vary depending on how many end-users share operators. The '*Optimal*' scheme generates the lowest delay and network usage which is expected because of the exhaustive search performed by this scheme. This scheme is not practical because it requires long exhaustive search. '*DIMA*' approach beats '*Random*', '*Source*', and '*Destination*' approaches in terms of delay and network usage. This better performance is the result of a more dynamic two-stage optimization scheme that depends on distances from data sources and end-users at the same time, and it depends on operator migration which keeps *CoMaP* adapting to changes in network links delay and bandwidth and to changes in number of end-users sharing operators. Notice that '*DIMA*' performance is also close to the '*Optimal*' approach which proves its effectiveness. Figures 5 and 6 also show that the gap between each scheme and the '*Optimal*' scheme widens as more operators are used in mashups, this occurs because as more operators are used, more delay results normally from executing those operators. This delay is minimum in '*DIMA*'; because it uses migration to find better deployment options while migration is not used by the other schemes causing their delay of executing operators to increase rapidly.

We performed another experiment where sizes of data sources varies from 1000 KB to 10000 KB, as figures 7 and 8 show, the system cost increases for all schemes as data source sizes increase, this is due to increasing computation and communication costs resulted from increasing volume of data. In the next experiment, we vary number of *MPN*s in the network from 1000 to 4000 and measure delay and network usage. The results are plotted in Figures 9 and 10. The important point to take from these two figures is that the gap between '*DIMA*' scheme and '*Optimal*' scheme increases because as more *MPN*s are used, the search space size increases which adds more challenge for the '*DIMA*' scheme to find close to optimal deployment decisions.

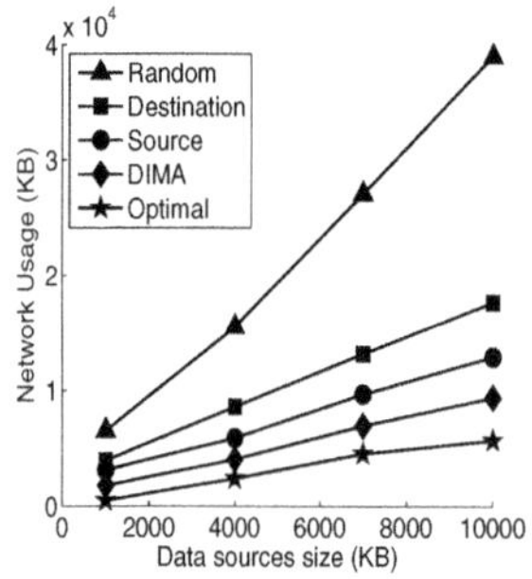

Fig. 8. Average network usage per mashup when data source size varies

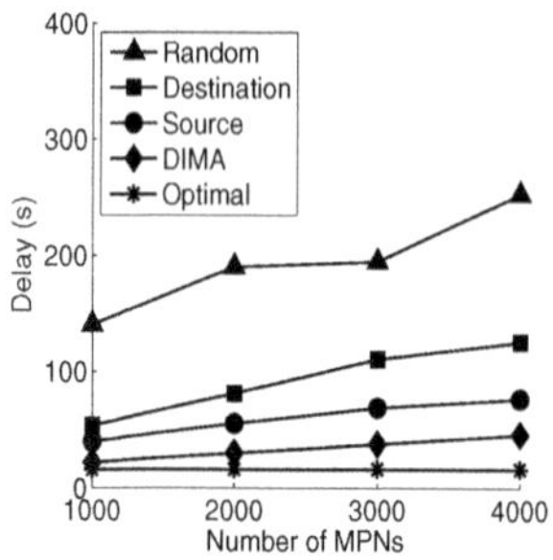

Fig. 9. Average delay per mashup when number of MPNs varies

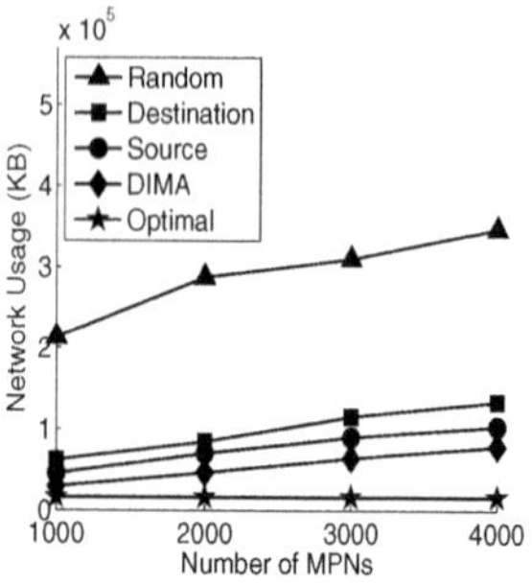

Fig. 10. Average network usage per mashup when number of MPNs varies

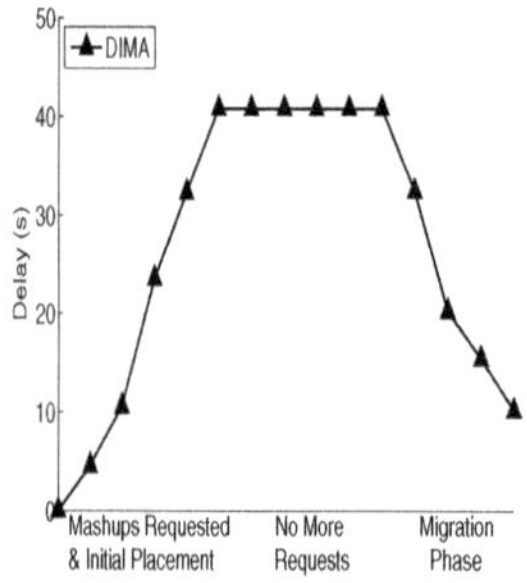

Fig. 11. Average delay per mashup in different execution periods

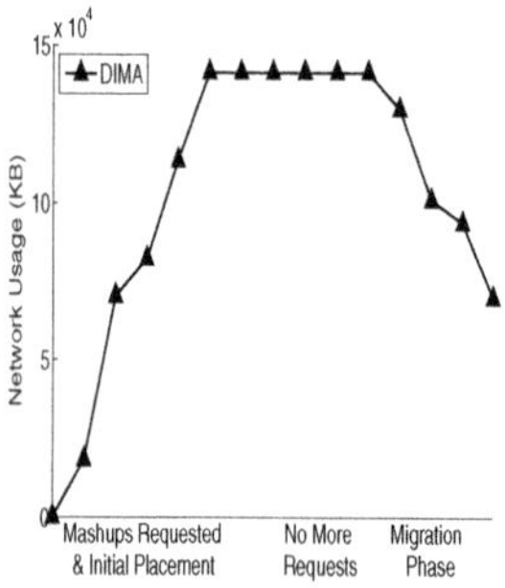

Fig. 12. Average network usage per mashup in different execution periods

We conducted an experiment to evaluate the effect of migration on system cost where we measure delay and network usage in three different periods of system execution. In the first period, mashups are requested, '$DIMA$' initial operator placement is executed (stage 1), and mashups are executed. The second period continues mashup execution without further requested mashups. The third period is when '$DIMA$' migration process (stage 2) starts and no further mashups are requested. As captured in Figures 11 and 12, delay and network usage increase when more mashups are requested in the first period, the system then stabilizes on the highest costs in the second period when no more mashups are requested, then delay and network usage drop significantly when the migration process starts. This cycle continues through the life time of *CoMaP*.

In the next experiment, we study the effect of enforcing failure resiliency in *CoMaP*. Here, the number of mashups is fixed at 10,000, replication percentage is fixed at 25 percent of the most overloaded MPNs. Figure 13 shows the average delay per mashup resulting from executing mashups in '$DIMA$' approach in two cases, the first uses failure resiliency and the second does not use it. In the later case, the delay is constant because no failures are assumed in the system. In the former case, MPNs failure is simulated in the system based on

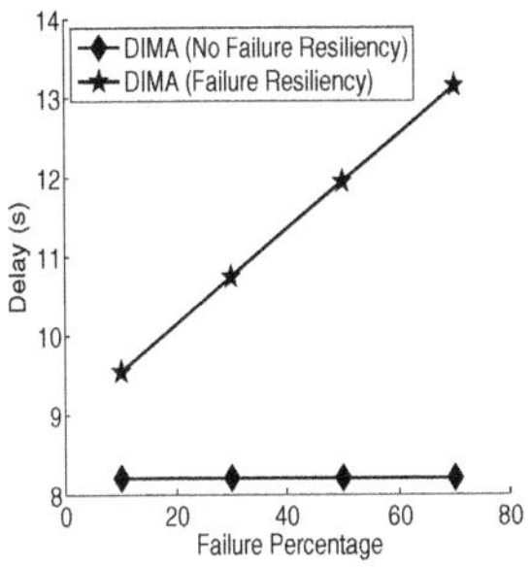

Fig. 13. Average delay per mashup in DIMA in the presence and absence of failure resiliency

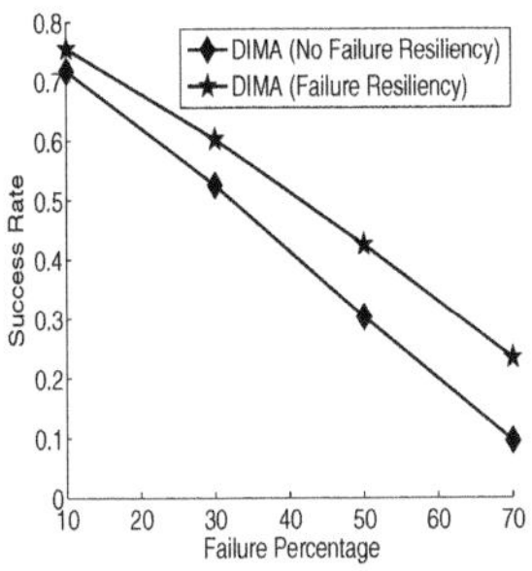

Fig. 14. Success rate of executing mashups in DIMA in the presence and absence of failure resiliency

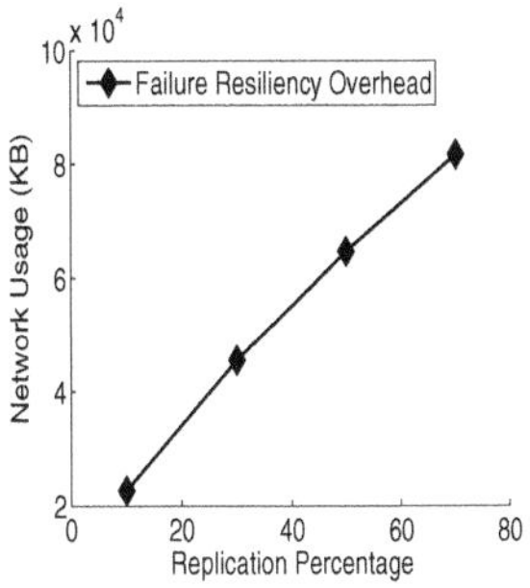

Fig. 15. Total overhead of applying failure resiliency when replication percentage is variable

a variable failure probability (10 percent - 70 percent) and only one mashup controller fails. We notice that applying failure resiliency increases delay. This can be explained in three points. First, end-users normally send their mashups to the mashup controller closer to them, now, when that mashup controller fails, end-users would have to send their mashups to a different farther away controller. Second, since operators are replicated on different MPNs, mashup execution might not go through the MPN that yields less delay; this happens because mashup execution is sometimes directed to different MPNs because the MPNs that yield minimum delay failed. Third, when failure probability increases, more MPNs that yield minimum delay fail which forces communication to be directed to other MPNs which do not lead to minimum delay.

In the next experiment, we measure the success rate of executing mashups by using the same parameters as the previous experiment except that failure is assumed in both cases of existence and absence of failure resiliency. Figure 14 shows that success rate decreases as failure probability increases and that is a direct effect of increasing nodes failures. The same figure shows that using failure resiliency results in higher success rate than the case where failure resiliency is absent; this is because operators are replicated which increases their availability.

In the last experiment, we show the overhead of failure resiliency. In Figure 15, failure probability is set to 20 percent, one mashup controller fails, number of mashups is set to $1,000$. The replication percentage varies between 10 percent and 70 percent which reflects the percentage of nodes their operators gets replicated. The figure shows the total overhead needed to maintain state of the system when applying failure resiliency. The overhead is measured in terms of network usage in kilobytes resulting from exchanged messages due to failure resiliency and replications. The state of the system includes keeping mashups information on mashup controllers identical. It also includes the cost of communication between controllers in case one of them fails. It also includes the communication between MPNs and controllers in case of replicating operators and failed MPNs. We notice that the overhead increases as replication percentage increases, this happens because more operators are replicated and therefore more communication occurs between MPNs and controllers. The system faces this kind of overhead only when the system is initialized with replicas, during a failure, and when replicating operators. Other than these times, the system does not deal with this overhead.

The previous set of experiments show the effectiveness of the '$DIMA$' scheme in reaching operator deployment decisions leading to low network delay and usage. Despite of the overhead of applying failure resiliency in *CoMaP*, using it decreases the failure probability of *CoMaP* by avoiding single point of failures.

7 Related Work

Since the advent of Web 2.0, several mashup platforms have been proposed in the literature [14] [16] [6] [7] [11]. Karma [14] offers a build by example approach for end-users. Marmite [16] works at the user end as a Firefox plug-in. MashMaker [6] is a tool for building mashups from widgets, it also enables end-users to share mashup widgets. DAMIA [7] is a data integration service dedicated for enterprise domain and situational applications. MARIO [11] is a mashup platform in which a planning algorithm for mashup execution is proposed where mashups are created using tags. None of the previous mashup platforms is distributed which limits their scalability.

Several platforms for distributed component execution have been investigated in literature [10] [1] [4] [5] [12]. A platform for distributed stream processing is proposed in [10]. Each stream is processed in several broker nodes in an overlay network; authors propose a scheme for placing stream processing operators. The cost metric we propose in *CoMaP* is more comprehensive than the metric they use. Also, authors do not consider failure issues while we do target this issue. Another operator deployment environment is proposed in [1] where deployment is based on Distributed Hash Tables (DHT) routing. However, as explained in [10], using DHT for selecting nodes where operators are deployed can lead to poor node selections. Borealis [4] is a distributed stream processing system, where operator deployment in their system does not consider network overlay changes such as changes in links delay and bandwidth. Medusa [5] is another distributed stream processing environment that deploys operators in a way to achieve load balancing. Analysis for node placement in overlay networks is investigated in [12]. However, they focus on placing machines on network infrastructure, while *CoMaP* focuses on mashup operator placement in overlay networks.

8 Conclusion

As one of the collaborative Web 2.0 applications, mashups are faced with a number of scalability and performance limitations. In this paper, we presented *CoMaP* – a dynamic cooperative overlay-based mashup platform. *CoMaP* incorporates several novel features. First, we presented a scalable and efficient architecture for *CoMaP* comprising of a multitude of cooperative mashup processing nodes and a set of mashup controllers. Second, we introduced a dynamic mashup distribution technique that is sensitive to the relative locations of the sources and the destinations of a mashup, and optimizes data flow within the overlay. Third, we described how we enforce failure resiliency feature in our system. Load balancing is an important feature to be applied in our system as a future work. Our experimental study demonstrated that *CoMaP* yields improved system performance and scalability.

References

1. Ahmad, Y., Cetintemel, U., Jannotti, J., Zgolinski, A., Zdonik, S.: Network awareness in internet-scale stream processing. IEEE Data Eng. Bulletin 28(1), 63–69 (2005)
2. Al-Haj Hassan, O., Ramaswamy, L., Miller, J.A.: Enhancing scalability and performance of mashups through merging and operator reordering. In: ICWS (to appear, 2010)
3. Barr, J., Kearney, B.: Syndic8 feeds repository (2001), `http://www.syndic8.com`
4. Centintemel, U., Cherniack, M., Hwang, J.H., Lindner, W., Maskey, A.S., Rasin, A., Ryvkina, E., Tatbul, N., Xing, Y., Zdonik, S.: The design of the borealis stream processing engine. In: CIDR (2005)
5. Cherniack, M., Balakrishnan, H., Balazinska, M., Carney, D., Cetintemel, U., Xing, Y., Zdonik, S.: Scalable distributed stream processing. In: CIDR (2003)
6. Ennals, R.J., Garofalakis, M.N.: Mashmaker: mashups for the masses. In: ACM SIGMOD, pp. 1116–1118 (2007)
7. IBM Corp.: Damia (2007), `http://services.alphaworks.ibm.com/damia/`
8. Intel Corp.: Mash maker (2007), `http://mashmaker.intel.com/web/`
9. Ng, E.T.S., Zhang, H.: A network positioning system for the internet. In: USENIX Annual Technical Conference (2004)
10. Pietzuch, P., Ledlie, J., Shneidman, J., Roussopoulos, M., Welsh, M., Seltzer, M.: Network-aware operator placement for stream-processing systems. In: ICDE (2006)
11. Riabov, A., Bouillet, E., Feblowitz, M., Liu, Z., Ranganathan, A.: Wishful search: interactive composition of data mashups. In: WWW, pp. 775–784 (2008)
12. Roy, S., Pucha, H., Zhang, Z., Hu, Y.C., Qiu, L.: Overlay node placement: Analysis, algorithms and impact on applications. In: ICDCS, pp. 53–53 (2007)
13. Shavitt, Y., Shir, E.: Dimes: let the internet measures itself. ACM SIGCOMM 35(5), 71–74 (2005)
14. Tuchinda, R., Szekely, P., Knoblock, C.: Building mashups by example. In: International Conference on Intelligent User Interfaces, pp. 139–148 (2008)
15. Wikipedia: Web 2.0 (2007), `http://en.wikipedia.org/wiki/Web_2.0`
16. Wong, J., Hong, J.: Making mashups with marmite: towards end-user programming for the web. In: CHI, pp. 1435–1444 (2007)
17. Yahoo Inc.: Yahoo pipes (2007), `http://pipes.yahoo.com/`

Composing Near-Optimal Expert Teams: A Trade-Off between Skills and Connectivity

Christoph Dorn and Schahram Dustdar

Distributed Systems Group, Vienna University of Technology, 1040 Vienna, Austria
lastname@infosys.tuwien.ac.at
http://www.infosys.tuwien.ac.at/staff

Abstract. Rapidly changing business requirements necessitate the ad-hoc composition of expert teams to handle complex business cases. Expert-centric properties such as skills, however, are insufficient to assemble an effective team. The given interaction structure determines to a large degree how well the experts can be expected to collaborate. This paper addresses the team composition problem which consists of expert interaction network extraction, skill profile creation, and ultimately team formation. We provide a heuristic for finding near-optimal teams that yield the best trade-off between skill coverage and team connectivity. Finally, we apply a real-world data set to demonstrate the applicability and benefits of our approach.

Keywords: social network, team formation, simulated annealing, skill connectivity tradeoff.

1 Introduction

Over the past years we have observed a trend towards online knowledge creation and sharing (e.g., Slashdot[1], Yahoo! Answers[2]). People increasingly apply their expertise online to answer other users' questions or provide additional information on topics under discussion. Rapidly changing business requirements keep individual companies from employing a large set of experts that continuously cover the required skill set. Exploration of online communities allows dynamic access to the top experts of the desired expertise.

Previous work focused on identifying the most important experts in an online community (e.g., [21]). Complex business cases, however, require the complementary expertise of multiple experts that need to collaborate closely. A team of top experts will be most effective if they have interacted before and thus exhibit confidence in each other's expertise. The problem is finding the best trade-off between maximum skill coverage and maximum interaction connectivity. Finding an optimal team configuration is non-trivial as the search space grows exponentially with the number of required skills and available experts.

[1] http://slashdot.org/

[2] http://answers.yahoo.com/

R. Meersman et al. (Eds.): OTM 2010, Part I, LNCS 6426, pp. 472–489, 2010.

In this paper we present a mechanism for extracting an expert network and corresponding expert skill profiles from online discussion threads. Our novel trade-off model allows fine-grained preference configuration of team connectivity over maximum skill coverage. We provide a heuristic to extract the optimum team composition from an expert network for a given trade-off configuration. As the skill data originates from discussion sites, we envision the resulting team compositions to collaborate well over the internet rather than work face to face.

Section 2 compares our work to previous research efforts. Section 3 outlines our approach in more detail based on a motivating example. Subsequently, Section 4 describes the mechanism for extracting an expert network and corresponding skill profiles from discussion threads. Section 5 provides the formal definition of the team formation problem. Section 6 demonstrates the adaptation of Simulated Annealing to our problem. The evaluation in Section 7 applies a real-world data set to demonstrate the effectiveness and efficiency of our approach. The paper concludes with an outlook on future work.

2 Related Work

Team formation is an intensely studied problem in the operation research domain. Most approaches model the problem as finding the best match of experts to required skills taking into account multiple dimensions from technical skills, cognitive properties, and personal motivation [4,11,23]. Such research focuses only on properties of individual experts that are independent of the resulting team configuration.

Recent efforts introduce social network information to enhance the skill profile of individual members. Hyeongon et al. [23] measure the *familiarity* between experts to derive a person's *know-who*. Cheatham and Cleereman [8] apply social network analysis to detect common interests and collaborations. The extracted information, however, is applied independently from the overall team structure. These mechanisms present opportunities for refinement of the skill modeling and configuration aspects of our approach but remain otherwise complementary.

To the best of our knowledge, Theodoros et al. [16] discuss the only team formation approach that specifically focuses on the expert network for determining the most suitable team. Our approach differs in two significant aspects. First, we model a trade-off between skill coverage and team connectivity whereas [16] treats every expert above a certain skill threshold as equally suitable and ignores every expert below that threshold. Second, our algorithm aims for a fully connected team graph (i.e., relations between every pair of experts). Theodoros et al. optimize the team connectivity based on a minimum spanning tree (MST). We argue that it is more important to focus on having most members well connected (i.e. everybody trusts (almost) everybody else) within the team than focusing only on the strongest ties within the team.

Analysis of various network topologies [12] has demonstrated the impact of the network structure on efficient team formation. General research on the formation of groups in large scale social networks [2] helps to understand the involved dynamic aspects but does not provide the algorithms for identifying optimal team configurations. Investigations into the structure of various real-world networks provides vital understanding of the underlying network characteristics relevant to the team formation problem [18,9]. Papers on existing online expert communities such as Slashdot [13] and Yahoo! answers [1] yield specific knowledge about the social network structure and expertise distribution that need to be supported by a team formation mechanism. Complementary approaches regarding extraction of expert networks and their skill profile include mining of email data sets [5] or open source software repositories [6].

Related research efforts based on non-functional aspects (i.e., non-skill related aspects) can also be found in the domain of service composition [10]. Here, services with the required capabilities need to be combined to provide a desirable, overall functionality. Composition (i.e., formation) is driven by the client's preferences [24], environment context [19,17], or service context (i.e., current expert context) [3]. We can take inspiration from such research to refine the properties and requirements of teams to include context such as expert availability or location. Nonetheless, the network structure remains equally unexplored in service composition.

In contrast, the network structure has gained significant impact for determining the most important network element. A prominent example of a graph-based global importance metric is Google's page rank [7]. An extended version [14] yields total ranks by aggregating search-topic-specific ranks. Inspired by the page rank algorithm, Schall [20] applies interaction intensities and skills to rank humans in mixed service-oriented environments. These algorithms provide additional means to determine person-centric metrics but do not address the team formation problem.

3 Approach

Expert team composition consists of three phases. First, we extract experts from discussion threads and form a social network (Fig. 1 Step 1). Basically, each reply to a posting results in an edge between the author of the original posting and the reply's author.

Next, we derive expert skill profiles from titles and tags of discussion threads (Fig. 1 Step 2). Each word represents a particular skill. Identification of meaningful words from tags and titles is considered outside the scope of this work as ultimately it is up to the user which skills (i.e., words) he/she defines as required to be provided by the team of experts. The number of postings in a thread associated with a particular skill determines the expert's skill level.

Finally, we solve the team formation subproblem applying a heuristic that searches the generated social network for the optimum team (Fig. 1 Step 3). The optimum team configuration depends on the trade-off between skill coverage and expert connectivity. We can recommend the top expert for each skill or accept less qualified team members which, however, yield a more tightly connected interaction network. The motivating example in the following subsection outlines these steps in more detail.

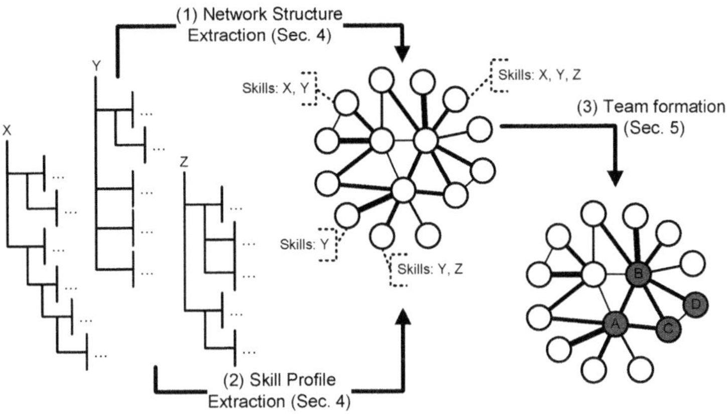

Fig. 1. Extracting network structure (1) and skill profile (2) from discussion threads for expert team formation (3)

Motivating Example. We observe the postings of five experts (Alice, Bob, Carol, Dave, and Eve) across three posting threads on mobile computing (*Mobile*), web technologies (*Web*), and streaming mechanisms (*Streaming*). Fig. 2 (left) provides the posting structure of these three discussions, displaying only the author of a posting. The corresponding interaction structure is outlined in Fig. 2 (right). In the discussion on mobile technologies Alice replied to a posting by Bob. Therefore, we create an edge between these to experts. Carol also participated in the discussion but did not respond directly to any of the observed experts. Consequently we raise only her expertise level without creating any edges. The same holds true for Alice's second posting. Eventually we derive following top experts for the three skills *Mobile*, *Web*, and *Streaming*: Alice is the top expert for *Mobile* with two postings, Eve yields best expertise for *Web* with three postings, and Bob and Carol share the most postings for *Streaming*.

We select Alice, Carol, and Eve to obtain one potential best qualified team. They have, however, never directly interacted and thus share no common edge in the network. An immediate improvement results from exchanging Carol for Bob

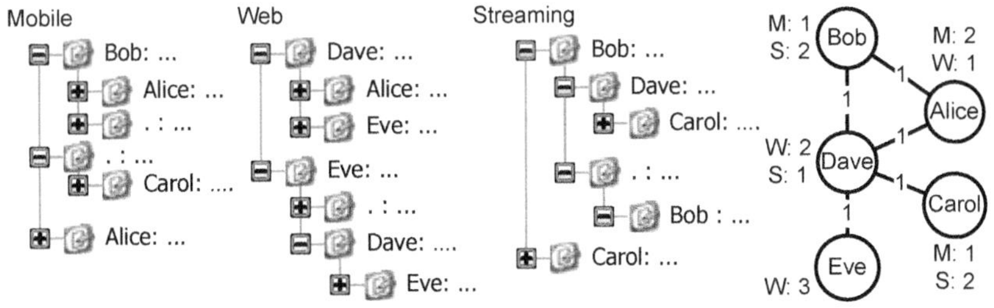

Fig. 2. Example transformation of discussion threads to interaction network and skills. (Edge labels equal interaction count; M/W/S: *Mobile*, *Web*, and *Streaming* skills).

who is connected to Alice and yields the same expertise level as Carol. Ultimately, a sensible trade-off consists of introducing Dave to the team for providing the *Web* skill although he is not the most qualified expert. This trade-off, however, produces an even better connected team where everyone knows everyone else. In this paper, we will also consider edge weights to derive tighter connected teams. We ignore them here, as the edge weights are all equal in this example.

4 Network and Skill Extraction

A posting thread is mapped to a tree graph $\mathcal{F}(\mathcal{P},\mathcal{R})$ with postings $p \in \mathcal{P}$ linked by directed, weighted edges $r \in \mathcal{R}$. Any edge r_i points from a reply to its parent posting and initially yields weight $w(r_i) = 1$.

The expert social network is modeled as an undirected graph $\mathcal{SN}(\mathcal{V},\mathcal{E})$. The nodes are experts $v \in \mathcal{V}$, the weighted edges $e \in \mathcal{E}$ link two experts if at least one of them has once posted a reply to the other. Applying undirected edges is more appropriate than directed edges as without in-depth semantic analysis we cannot distinguish between an expert correcting a novice, or a novice requesting clarification from an expert. We, therefore, interpret each link as an interaction. The edge weight $w(e)$ derives from the amount of replies between two experts.

Each expert exhibits a skill profile $\mathcal{SP}$ comprising of multiple skills s. During thread transformation, we first extract the topics from the thread and interpret them as skills[3]. We then count for each expert active in the underlying thread the number of postings and increase his/her skill counter $k_i(s)$ correspondingly. Each posting increases the skill counter by 1 as this is the simplest assumption when the content of the posting remains unknown. Some online discussion sites apply a moderation scheme that allows moderators and/or other users to evaluate the quality of individual postings (e.g., `http://slashdot.org`). Filtering out of low quality posts can then be applied to better represent a user's expertise and deter non-experts to boost their expert-level through flooding a forum with irrelevant posts. Scores provide a refined expertise structure, however our general approach works on any discussion tree.

The absolute skill values are only an intermediary metric, as we need to be able to compare multiple skills. To this end, we measure for each expert and each skill the expertise level $q_i(s)$ in the interval $[0; 1]$. A linear transformation maps the absolute skill counter to the relative expertise level: $q_i(s) = k_i(s)/max(k(s))$ such that the expert with most postings of a given skill s yields expertise $q(s) = 1$. The overall aggregation of skills from every expert determines the network's skill portfolio $\mathcal{S}_{\mathcal{SN}}$. Note that the transformation from thread structure to interaction network doesn't necessarily create a new social network but rather updates the edges between experts as well as skills of experts in an already existing network. Transformation of the posting structure to social network links is, however, not immediately applicable on raw threads in the presence of anonymous postings.

[3] Consideration of synonyms and/or additional skill reasoning based on knowledge models is outside the scope of this paper.

Thread Reduction. Most discussion sites allow anonymous postings. The challenge is to remove those postings without jeopardizing the transformation of remaining postings to the interaction network. There are two ways to deal with such postings. On the one hand, we can ignore them and rely solely on direct replies between known experts. When the number of anonymous postings is high, however, this will reduce the likelihood of having a sensible set of interactions. On the other hand, we can simply bridge the anonymous postings, thereby risking to introduce interactions between experts that do not reflect reality. Take the initial thread in Figure 3 (left part) as an example. In the first case, we would merely derive a link between Eve and Dave. The second case would yield an overrated link between Eve and Dave (4 replies) and also an overly strong link between Dave and Alice (1 reply).

Fig. 3. Reduction of posting threads and transformation to interaction network

Algorithm 1. Thread Reduction Algorithm $\mathcal{TRA}(\mathcal{F}(\mathcal{P}, \mathcal{R}))$.

for $Posting\ m \in \mathcal{P}$ **do**
  if $isAnonymousCreator(m)$ **then**
    $Posting\ parent \leftarrow getSuccessor(\mathcal{F}, m)$
    $ReplyEdge\ mp \leftarrow getEdge(\mathcal{T}, m, parent)$
    /* Remove the edge from the anonymous posting to its parents */
    $removeEdge(\mathcal{F}, mp)$
    for $Posting\ child \in getPredecessors(\mathcal{F}, m)$ **do**
      /* For each reply */
      $ReplyEdge\ cm \leftarrow getEdge(\mathcal{F}, child, m)$
      /* Remove the edge from the reply to the posting */
      $removeEdge(\mathcal{F}, cm)$
      /* Add a new reply edge bridging the anonymous posting */
      $ReplyEdge\ cp \leftarrow createEdge(\mathcal{F}, child, parent)$
      /* Reduce the edge weight */
      $setEdgeWeight(cp, getWeight(mp) * getWeight(cm) * 0.5)$
    end for
  end if
end for

Our thread reduction algorithm (Alg. 1) mitigates both disadvantages by combining link bridging with link dampening. The link strength between a posting and a reply is halved for each intermediary anonymous posting, thereby rapidly decreasing with distance. Figure 3 (middle part) displays the reduced thread and the link strength of each reply towards its parent. Ultimately, all non-anonymous users from a discussion tree become part of the social network. When extracting an optimal team, however, filtering out experts below a minimum level of expertise improves processing speed.

5 Formalizing the Team Formation Problem

The team formation problem defines a set of required skills $\mathcal{S}_\mathcal{R} \subseteq \mathcal{S}_{\mathcal{SN}}$. The importance of each contained skill $s \in \mathcal{S}_\mathcal{R}$ is given by weight $w(s)$ in the interval $]0;1]$ with $\sum_i w_i(s) = 1$. The goal is finding the set of experts $\mathcal{T} \subseteq \mathcal{V}$ that exhibits a good-enough match of the required skill while providing a sufficient degree of connectivity within the team. Here the exact meaning of the terms *good-enough* and *sufficient* are subject to the trade-off between *skill coverage* and *team distance.*

Skill coverage measures how well the set of experts match the required set of skills $\mathcal{S}_\mathcal{R}$. For each skill s, the best match is the team member with the highest corresponding expertise level $q(s)$. A single expert potentially yields the highest expertise level for multiple skills. Subsequently, the team's overall skill fulfillment $\mathcal{C}_\mathcal{T}$ is defined as:

$$\mathcal{C}_\mathcal{T} = \sum_i max(q_j(s_i)) * w(s_i) \qquad where\ v_j \in \mathcal{T} \qquad \forall s_i \in \mathcal{S}_\mathcal{R} \tag{1}$$

The team with maximum achievable coverage is denoted as $Top(\mathcal{S}_\mathcal{R})$ and yields for every required skill an expert with maximum expertise level $q(s) = 1$. The top team, however, is not the best choice when its members have little interacted before. The team distance $\mathcal{D}_\mathcal{T}$ quantifies the amount and strength of inter-team links compared to the maximum possible connectivity:

$$\mathcal{D}_\mathcal{T} = \sum_{\mathcal{E}_\mathcal{T}} \frac{1}{w(e_{ij})} + (\frac{|\mathcal{T}| * (|\mathcal{T}| - 1)}{2} - |\mathcal{E}_\mathcal{T}|) * \beta * max(\frac{1}{w(e)}) \qquad \forall i,j \in \mathcal{T} \tag{2}$$

where $|\mathcal{E}_\mathcal{T}|$ is the number of intra-team edges whereas $max(\frac{1}{w(e)})$ determines the weight of the weakest link in the overall social network. As we aim to minimize $\mathcal{D}_\mathcal{T}$, we sum across all inverted edge weights and add a penalty for every non-existent edge. The penalty parameter β determines the impact of such a non-existing edge. For $\beta = 1$ a missing edge between two experts receives the minimum interaction weight, thus switching to a configuration with an additional edge has almost no impact on distance. As $\beta \to \infty$ the existing edge weights loose their significance and teams exhibiting a fully connected graph will yield the lowest distance. A sensible value derived from our experiments is $\beta = 4$ which we will use throughout this paper.

The overall team quality $\mathcal{Q}_{\mathcal{T}}$ is ultimately obtained though aggregating skill coverage $\mathcal{C}_{\mathcal{T}}$ and team distance $\mathcal{D}_{\mathcal{T}}$. We introduce the trade-off parameter α that configures acceptable combinations of coverage and distance:

$$\mathcal{Q}_{\mathcal{T}} = \alpha * \mathcal{C}_{\mathcal{T}} + (1 - \alpha) * (1 - \frac{\mathcal{D}_{\mathcal{T}}}{\mathcal{D}_{MAX}}) \qquad \alpha = [0; 1] \tag{3}$$

where $\mathcal{D}_{MAX}$ is the maximum distance for a team of $|\mathcal{S}_{\mathcal{R}}|$ experts what yield no direct inter-team edges ($|\mathcal{E}_{\mathcal{T}}| = 0$). The top team $Top(\mathcal{S}_{\mathcal{R}})$ will yield the highest quality when α approaches 1, whereas the best connected team will provide the best quality for $\alpha \to 0$. We can guarantee a minimum skill coverage level if we include only experts that exhibit a given expertise threshold.

For the example team formation problem in Figure 2, we derive following quality measurements for the three considered teams when applying $\alpha = 0.5$. A team comprising Alice, Carol, and Eve will yield quality $\mathcal{Q}_{ACE} = 0.5$ with $\mathcal{C}_{ACE} = 1$ and $\mathcal{D}_{ACE} = 12$. The team consisting of Alice, Bob, and Eve achieves better distance, and thus also better quality: $\mathcal{Q}_{ABE} = 0.625$, with $\mathcal{C}_{ABE} = 1$ and $\mathcal{D}_{ABE} = 9$. Finally, the combination of Alice, Bob, and Dave provides the best quality (for the given trade-off parameter): $\mathcal{Q}_{ABD} = 0.82$, with $\mathcal{C}_{ABD} = 0.\dot{8}$ and $\mathcal{D}_{ABD} = 3$. In all three cases, $\mathcal{D}_{MAX} = 12$ as $3\ edges * (\beta = 4) * (max(1/w(e)) = 1) \to 12$.

6 Team Formation Heuristic

In the search of a better trade-off between skill coverage and team distance, we need to test various expert combinations. Investigations of the rich-club phenomenon in scientific collaboration networks (e.g., [9]) have shown that a sufficiently well connected team is unlikely to be amongst the very top ranked experts. A network exhibiting rich-club properties has the best-connected nodes form tightly connected communities. In the case of expert networks — such as scientific author networks — such tight collaborative groups exist only within particular research domains but not beyond. Consequently, we need to include also experts below the top 10 in our search for acceptable team configurations when skills are increasingly different (e.g., when skills belong to distinct domains).

Brute-force testing of every possible combination, however, quickly becomes unfeasible. Testing the top m experts for $\mathcal{S}_{\mathcal{R}}$ skills has $\mathcal{O}(m^{\mathcal{S}_{\mathcal{R}}})$ computational complexity (i.e., already for 10 experts and 10 skills, we would need to analyze 10 billion combinations). Our goal is to find a better connected team than the aggregation of the top experts for each skill but not necessarily the best possible solution. Simulated Annealing [15] is a suitable optimization heuristic for this problem.

6.1 Simulated Annealing

Simulated Annealing (SA) is a heuristic for approximating a global optimum in complex mathematical problems. It is well suited for problems with discrete search space such as the order of cities in the traveling sales man problem. We briefly outline the generic heuristic aspect and discuss the problem specific parts in the subsequent subsections in more detail. Simulated annealing is an iterative process building on following basic components:

Candidate Solution contains the current best problem solution which is gradually improved. In the team formation problem, the current solution $\mathcal{T}$ assigns one expert to each skill, potentially having one expert covering multiple skills.

Solution Energy Function measures the quality of a given solution. SA aims to find a solution with the lowest possible energy. The current quality function $\mathcal{Q}_{\mathcal{T}}$ returns higher values for better team configurations. We provide the restructured equation in the following subsection to derive a suitable energy function.

Neighborhood Function provides a new candidate solution based on the current solution. A good neighborhood function traverses the search space quickly, but produces new solutions that yield similar energy level to the preceding solution. The neighborhood function takes a team configuration and replaces the expert of a random skill.

Transition Function decides whether to accept a new solution or to stick with the current one. Simulated Annealing also accepts team configurations that yield worse quality than the current one to avoid local optima.

Cooling function gradually reduces the temperature. Large solution changes are less likely for lower temperatures. As the temperature falls, worse solutions are less likely to be accepted.

We briefly outline the iterative process in Algorithm 2 as provided in the JUNG 1.7.6 framework[4]. We omit some configuration parameters for sake of clarity. Transition function and Cooling function are problem independent, thus introduced here. We discuss neighborhood function and energy function in the subsequent subsections. For now, we treat these as blackboxes.

Simulated annealing takes an initial solution (i.e., the top expert for every skill) and derives the corresponding energy. Simulated Annealing continues to evaluated similar solutions as long as the temperature has not reached zero and there are more available iterations. A new solution is always accepted when it yields lower energy (Alg. 2 line 12). Worse solutions are accepted with probability p_{SA} defined as:

$$p_{SA} = e^{-\frac{\delta_{energy}}{temp}} \tag{4}$$

where δ_{energy} is the energy difference between the current and new solution, *temp* is the current annealing temperature, and e is Euler's number. A transition to a solution with higher energy is possible as long as the temperature remains high, or the energy difference is very small.

The freezing process depends on the cooling rate and current iteration state. As long as the number of successful transitions is high (i.e., *success* close to *tries*)

[4] `http://jung.sourceforge.net/`

the system remains in a search space region that still provides many solutions with lower energy. The function for the temperature in the next iteration is defined as:

$$temp_n = r_{cooling}^{(limit_{accept} - \frac{success}{tries})*tries} * temp \qquad (5)$$

where $tries$, $r_{cooling}$, and $limit_{accept}$ are configuration parameters. For our experiments, we apply $tries = 100$, $r_{cooling} = 0.99$, and $limit_{accept} = 0.97$

Algorithm 2. Simulated Annealing Algorithm $\mathcal{SA}(maxIt, startTemp)$.

```
T ← calcNewSolution(startTemp)
nrg ← calcEnergy(T)
temp ← startTemp
iteration ← 0
while temp > 0 ∪ iteration < maxIt do
    success ← 0
    for tries do
        /* Neighborhood function provides a new solution. */
        newSolution ← calcNewSolution(T, temp)
        nrg_new ← calcEnergy(newSolution)
        δ_energy ← nrg − nrg_new
        if doTransition(δ_energy, newSolution, temp) then
            T ← newSolution
            nrg ← nrg_new
            success + +
        end if
    end for
    temp ← calcTemperature(temp, success)
    iteration + +
end while
return T
```

6.2 Simulated Annealing Energy Function

The energy function provides the tradeoff between skill coverage $\mathcal{C}_\mathcal{T}$ and team distance $\mathcal{D}_\mathcal{T}$. A solution consists of an expert for each skill. We cannot directly reuse the overall team quality function $\mathcal{Q}_\mathcal{T}$ as SA requires an energy function that decreases with raising solution quality. The initial solution consists of the top expert for each required skill in $\mathcal{S}_\mathcal{R}$. This composition provides an upper boundary to the possible skill coverage. Any better solution must exhibit lower energy by reducing the distance $\mathcal{D}_\mathcal{T}$. Expert compositions that additionally come with lower coverage need to yield proportionally even lower distance. The proportion is determined by the tradeoff factor α. The initial solution has energy $=$ 1. Any solution that reduces coverage and distance to similar extent yields also energy $= 1$. Ultimately, the energy function for a solution $\mathcal{T}$ is defined as:

$$nrg_\mathcal{T} = \frac{1 - (\alpha * \mathcal{C}_\mathcal{T} + (1-\alpha) * (1 - \mathcal{D}'_\mathcal{T} * \mathcal{D}_{top}^{-1}))}{1-\alpha} \qquad (6)$$

where $\mathcal{D}'_T$ is the normalized distance $\mathcal{D}_T/\mathcal{D}_{MAX}$ and $\mathcal{D}_{top}$ is the normalized distance of the initial solution. As no solution can yield higher coverage than the top experts, any solution with higher distance than $\mathcal{D}_{top}$ will yield an energy value greater than 1 and thus can safely be ignored. Dividing the aggregation of skill coverage and distance by $1 - \alpha$ ensures that regardless of α the initial solution and any proportional tradeoff will always yield $nrg = 1$.

6.3 Simulated Annealing Neighborhood Function

The neighborhood function generates a new solution given a current solution. The function needs to be able to (a) traverse the search space in short time and (b) find neighboring configuration with similar energy. The first requirement guarantees that the simulated annealing algorithms is able to reach all states in a timely manner, thus potentially identifying the optimum solution. The second requirement ensures the algorithm's convergence. A random solution is more likely to be worse (rather than better) than the current solution. Jumping between high energy states maintains a high temperature level, thereby keeping the system from cooling down and finding the desired areas of low energy.

Our neighborhood function addresses both concerns. We randomly select a required skill s and exchange the current expert v_{old} with another expert v_{new} with probability p_{nh}. The neighborhood probability p_{nh} depends on the interaction proximity and threshold parameter s_{nh}

$$s_{nh} = \frac{temp}{maxTemp} * (prox_{max} - prox_{min}) + prox_{min} \tag{7}$$

$$p_{nh}(e_{new}) = \begin{cases} \frac{1}{m-1} & if\ prox(v_{old}, v_{new}) \geq s_{nh} \\ \frac{\psi}{m-1} & otherwise \qquad with\ \psi = \frac{prox(v_{new}, v_{old}) - prox_{min}}{s_{nh} - prox_{min}} \end{cases} \tag{8}$$

where m is the number of candidate experts. The proximity $prox(v_{old}, v_{new})$ between two experts is defined by the shortest hop path (SHP) with maximum edge weights. We sum across all traversed edges and take the hop count into account to penalize for the number of intermediary experts. The stronger two experts are connected, the higher their proximity.

$$prox(v_i, v_j) = \frac{\sum_k w(e)}{k * (k-1) + 1} \qquad \forall w(e) \in max[SHP(v_i, v_j)] \tag{9}$$

For the expert selection probability p_{nh} we define $prox_{max} = max[prox(v_{old}, v_i)]$ and analog $prox_{min} = min[prox(v_{old}, v_i)]$ where v_i is any expert that provides a minimum expertise level of the selected skill ($q(s) > 0$). This prevents the selection of experts that are in close proximity but who do not provide the required skill. When the expected workload requires a minimum number of members t_{min}, we simply remove members of the current solution from the candidate set. We first remove the worst ranked existing expert until no expert from the candidate set (if selected) would violate the size constraint.

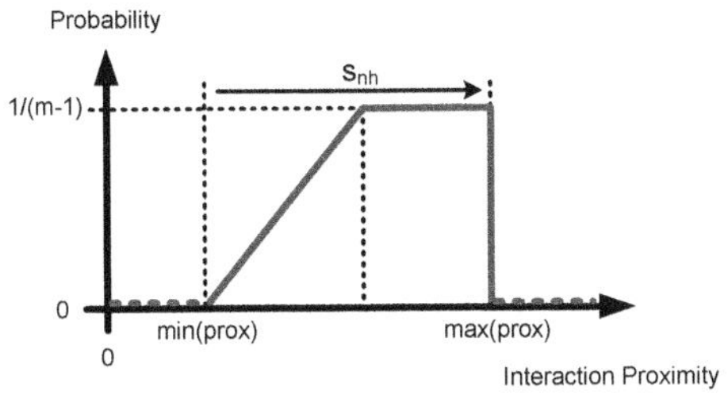

Fig. 4. Probability function for selecting a particular expert based on annealing temperature and interaction proximity

The neighborhood probability function ensures that experts that are in proximity of the current solution are more likely to be selected, than experts further away. Besides interaction proximity, also the current temperature affects this probability. In the beginning, when temperature is still high, proximity has little effect and every expert is equally like being selected. Later in the process, the probability of selecting a particular expert decreases linearly with distance. As shown in Figure 4, s_{nh} moves from $prox_{min}$ to $prox_{max}$ as the temperature falls towards zero. Note that the neighborhood probability function p_{nh} is not a classical probability density function as the sum of probabilities for all observed experts does not add up to 1.

This neighborhood function enables to quickly traverse the complete search space at the beginning. Later, we still can reach every solution, but require more steps to do so. We assume two experts in proximity to yield similar links to common neighbors. Thus, as we increasingly select new experts that are close to their replaced predecessor, the total connectivity will improve on average more than selecting random experts. Subsequently, two candidate solutions will yield similar energy values. This avoids fruitless testing of solutions with high energy.

7 Evaluation

We evaluate our team formation mechanism with a real world data set extracted from Slashdot. We provide a brief introduction to the data set. The experiments consist of 8 sets of 5 skill configurations for a total of 45 different skill configurations. We present one example for in-depth discussion of the effect and successful results of our approach.

Experiment Setup. Slashdot is a well understood and rich data set [13] describing a large user community. Users submit information technology related news items which the editors decide to publish or not. News fall into multiple categories (i.e., subdomains) such as *linux*, *apple*, or *games*. A published piece of news becomes a *story* which all users—anonymous or logged-in—can comment on. These comments create a posting hierarchy. Slashdot exhibits the characteristics of a large-scale expert network. Some users remain consistently active throughout all subdomains. Other users join in an ad-hoc manner, participate for a limited period, and then vanish again. Users are interested in providing their knowledge to improve the quality and information content of a story. They rarely engaging in long running personal communication threads with other users [13,22].

The subdomain names are directly mapped to skills. Each story maps to the skill represented by its parent subdomain. The slashdot moderation system also enables classification of postings according to *Insightful*, *Interesting*, *Informative*, *Funny*, etc. content which we combine with subdomains to generate more fine-grained skills. We group the experiment set in two rough categories: (i) cross-subdomain teams and (ii) mixed inter-intra subdomain teams.

The first three experiment sets ($Ex_1 \rightarrow Ex_3$) yield 6, 7, and 8 skills, respectively, out of 10 available subdomains. When ever a user posts in a story within a subdomain, his/her corresponding skill is raised by 1. The first skill set $\mathcal{S}_{SUB}$ contains $S1 = apple$, $S2 = ask$, $S3 = entertainment$, $S4 = mobile$, $S5 = linux$, $S6 = developers$, $S7 = games$, $S8 = news$, $S9 = slashdot$, and $S10 = it$. The remaining 5 experiment sets introduce skills combined from predicates and subdomains; thus only postings with predicates are considered. When a user's posting within subdomain X receives a predicate Y, then the user's skill XY is increased (e.g., an *Interesting* posting within subdomain *linux* increases skill *linuxInteresting*. The experiment sets ($Ex_4 \rightarrow Ex_8$) are derived from 2x4, 6x2, 4x3, 3x4, and 4x4 subdomain-predicate combinations. The second skill set is the combination of $\mathcal{S}_{SUB}$ and $\mathcal{S}_{PRED} = \{P1 = Informative,\ P2 = Interesting,\ P3 = Funny,\ P4 = Insightful\ \} \rightarrow \{S1P1,\ \ldots,\ S10P4\}$ for a total of 40 skills.

All experiment rounds applied $\alpha = 0.5$ and experts had to yield $q(s) \geq 0.5$ to be considered for a particular skill s. Experts that did not provide a single required skills were temporarily removed from the social network to improve processing speed. Each skill was considered of equal importance, thus the skill weights $w(s)$ were uniformly set to $1/|S_R|$.

Experiment Results. We analyze experiment set Ex_1 configuration 4 in more detail. The required eight skills are $S_R = \{S1, S2, S3, S4, S7, S8, S9, S10\}$. Figure 5 visualizes the interaction structure of the initial and the optimal team. The initial team of top experts are $T_{top} = \{V5, V6, V7, V8, V9, V10\}$. The optimal team $T_{opt} = \{V1, V2, V3, V4, V7, V10\}$ keeps $V7$ and $V10$ from the initial team but introduces four new experts[5]. Note that expert $V7$ and $V10$ provide two skills each (see also Table 1). The optimal team improves the distance by 90% (from $D_{TOP} = 0.40$ down to $D'_T = 0.04$) while reducing the skill coverage to $C_T = 0.67 (\equiv 33\%)$. The optimal team graph is fully connected, and in addition, also exhibits stronger links between members than the initial team.

[5] These 10 experts make up T_{top} and T_{opt}. The corresponding slashdot IDs are: $V1$:622222, $V2$:987471, $V3$:595695, $V4$:71849, $V5$:25149, $V6$:912633, $V7$:957197, $V8$:18001, $V9$:727027, and $V10$:835522. In total, 49 experts qualified as team member candidate (at least one $q(s) > 0.5$) embedded in a social network of 17765 experts.

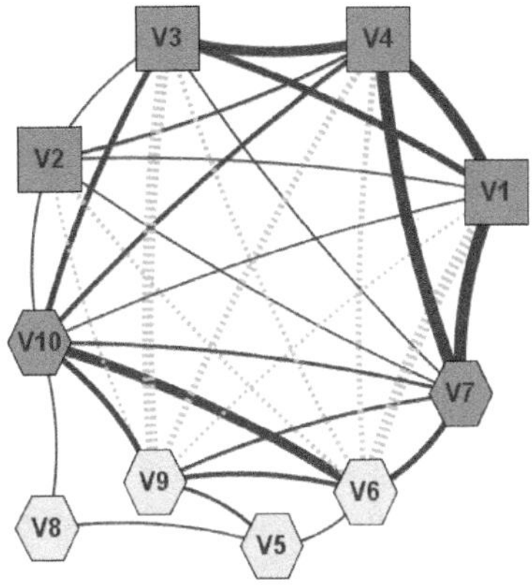

Fig. 5. Optimal expert team (green squares) and initial expert team (yellow hexagons) for experiment set Ex_1 skill configuration 4. Line thickness represents interaction distance; with solid intra-team links and dashed inter-team links. (Colors online).

Table 1. Expert skills for initial T_{TOP} and optimal team T_{OPT} for Ex_1 configuration 4. Rank $r(s)$ and utility $q(s)$ of each expert for the provided skill are in brackets. All experts in T_{TOP} yield rank $r = 1$ and utility $q(.) = 1$.

Skill	T_{top}	T_{opt}	$r(s)$	$q(s)$
$S1$	$V8$	$V1$	5	0.594
$S2$	$V7$	$V7$	1	1.0
$S3$	$V6$	$V10$	12	0.535
$S4$	$V5$	$V10$	6	0.515
$S7$	$V9$	$V2$	4	0.524
$S8$	$V7$	$V7$	1	1.0
$S9$	$V10$	$V3$	5	0.577
$S10$	$V7$	$V4$	7	0.648

We have printed the energy of the initial, optimal, and next top-30 solutions in Figure 6. The best and second best solution yield almost identical energy and are also distance and skill fulfillment wise rather similar. The team configuration, however, differs by one dropped, and two additional members. Most top-30 solutions for this skill configuration remain around $nrg_T = 0.83$. Within those solutions a broad spectrum of teams exist that cover the range from low distance/low skill coverage to high distance/high skill coverage. We can then apply a-posteriori preferences towards higher skilled or lower skilled expert compositions from such a set of equally qualified teams. Our algorithm found in total more than 100 team configurations which yield a better trade-off than the initial team T_{top}.

The results of configurations $Ex_1 \rightarrow Ex_3$ reveal that the team formation heuristic finds significantly better solutions for all of the observed skill combinations. The normalized team distance D'_T of the optimal solutions (Figure 7 blue squares) amounts to 0.004 up to 0.17 of the initial distance while skill fulfillment remains comparatively high between 0.67 and 0.93. For each required skill configuration, our approach found more than 100 solution that all provide a better tradeoff than the initial team configuration T_{top}. When we compare the absolute distance values (D_T) in Figure 8, we note that the initial distance does not affect the heuristic's ability to find significantly well connected teams.

In experiment sets $Ex_4 \rightarrow Ex_8$, we tested for the effect of correlated skills (i.e., predicates within the same subdomain) and larger skill sets. The heuristic still determines better solutions (except for configuration 5 in set 8 having 16 skills) but does not achieve as high quality tradeoffs as in $Ex_1 \rightarrow Ex_3$ (compare the red

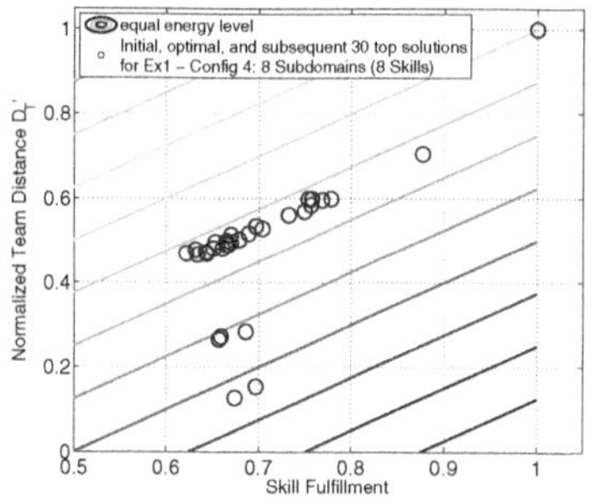

Fig. 6. Initial (top right), optimal (bottom left), and top 30 solutions (normalized values) for Ex_1 configuration 4

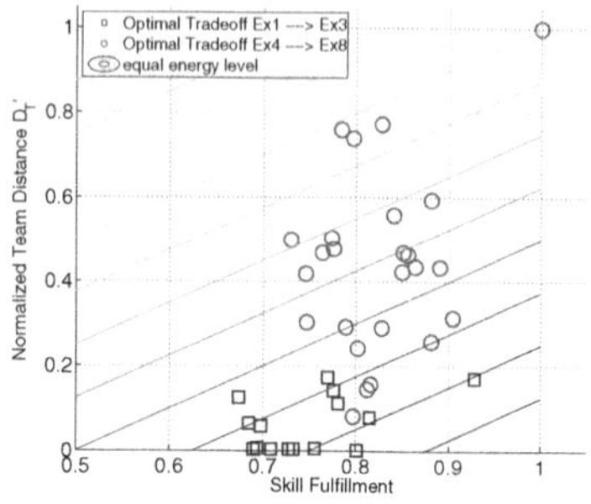

Fig. 7. Normalized optimal solutions for $Ex_1 \rightarrow Ex_3$ (squares) and $Ex_4 \rightarrow Ex_8$ (circles). (All initial solutions reside at [1, 1].

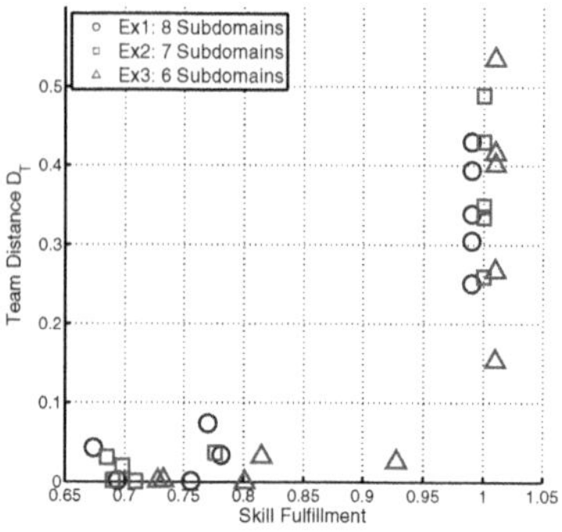

Fig. 8. Initial and optimal solutions for the 15 skill configurations in $Ex_1 \rightarrow Ex_3$. Initial solutions are slightly shifted (+/-0.01) for sake of clarity.

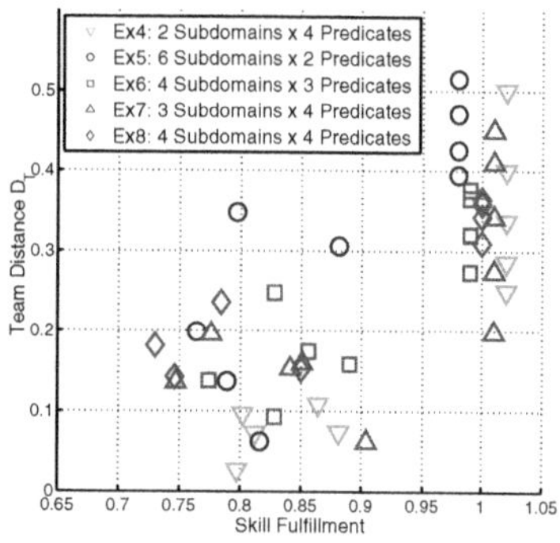

Fig. 9. Initial and optimal solutions for the 25 skill configurations in $Ex_4 \rightarrow Ex_8$. Initial solutions are slightly shifted (+/-0.02) for sake of clarity.

circles to the blue squares in Figure 7). Increasing the skill set results in larger teams which are unlikely to exhibit similar dense connectivity as smaller groups. Larger skill sets come also with lower alternative trade-off solutions. For the $Ex_4 \rightarrow Ex_8$, there exist on average 84.2, 76.4, 48.6, 49.6, and 17.2 alternatives, respectively. The effect of similar skills becomes apparent in Ex_8 which contains all four predicates from 2 subdomains (ocher, upside down triangles in Figure 9). Although team distance is significantly lower, the improvement remains en par with the worst improvements in experiment 1. The average distance of set Ex_8 $\overline{D'_{EX8}} = 0.23$ remains significantly above the distance of set Ex_1 $\overline{D'_{EX1}} = 0.08$ (having also 8 skills).

Evaluation Summary. Our team composition algorithm provides excellent results across all experiment sets. Figure 10 compares the average and standard deviation of energy, distance, and coverage for all eight experiment sets. Our approach yields for all set consistently high skill coverage (~ 0.8). The overall energy is, hence, mostly determined by team distance. Increasing skills and skill similarity limit the achievable distance reduction. We are able to detect significantly better connected teams for configurations of up to 12 skills, and still some improvement for up to 16 skills. Teams without explicit management structure, however, rarely exceed 10 to 12 members. We therefore did not test any configurations larger than 16 skills.

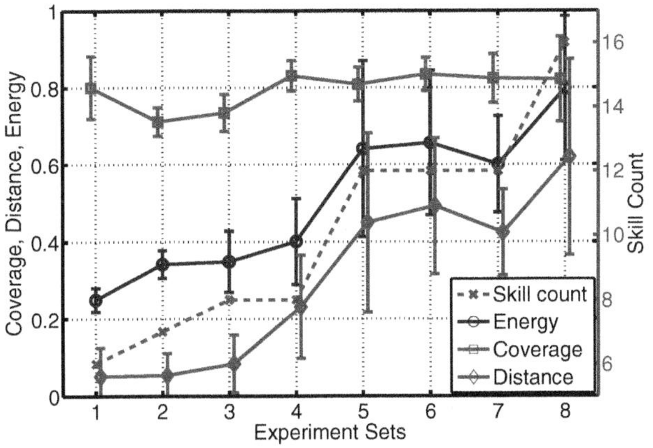

Fig. 10. Average and standard deviation of energy, distance, and coverage for all experiment sets (full lines). The respective skill count for each experiment set is given by the dashed, green line. (Colors online)

8 Conclusion

Online communities provide both the raw data for deriving expert skill profiles and their interaction structure. Considering only independent expert properties is insufficient for finding the best suited team. Optimal team composition requires a trade-off between skill coverage and expert connectivity. We have demonstrated the benefit of our heuristic for finding well connected experts that simultaneously yield high expertise level in a social network. In the future, we will investigate mechanisms to support skill dependencies (i.e., respective experts connected tighter). This allows for finding optimally structured teams without having to focus on neither fully connected graphs nor minimum-spanning tree graphs. Such skill dependencies also provide the basis for composing optimally structured teams beyond 12 members in combination with management skills. At the same time, we plan to evaluate our algorithm with other online communities that exhibit a larger overall skill set. A qualitative comparison to other team formation algorithms is also an open topic.

Acknowledgment. The authors would like to thank Daniel Schall and Florian Skopik for providing the slashdot data set. This work has been partially supported by the EU STREP project Commius (FP7-213876).

References

1. Adamic, L.A., Zhang, J., Bakshy, E., Ackerman, M.S.: Knowledge sharing and yahoo answers: everyone knows something. In: WWW 2008: Proceeding of the 17th Int. Conference on World Wide Web, pp. 665–674. ACM, New York (2008)
2. Backstrom, L., Huttenlocher, D., Kleinberg, J., Lan, X.: Group formation in large social networks: membership, growth, and evolution. In: KDD 2006: Proceedings of the 12th ACM SIGKDD International Conference on Knowledge Discovery and Data Mining, pp. 44–54. ACM, New York (2006)
3. Baresi, L., Bianchini, D., Antonellis, V.D., Fugini, M.G., Pernici, B., Plebani, P.: Context-aware composition of e-services. In: Benatallah, B., Shan, M.-C. (eds.) TES 2003. LNCS, vol. 2819, pp. 28–41. Springer, Heidelberg (2003)
4. Baykasoglu, A., Dereli, T., Das, S.: Project team selection using fuzzy optimization approach. Cybern. Syst. 38(2), 155–185 (2007)
5. Bird, C., Gourley, A., Devanbu, P., Gertz, M., Swaminathan, A.: Mining email social networks. In: MSR 2006: Proceedings of the 2006 Int. Workshop on Mining Software Repositories, pp. 137–143. ACM Press, New York (2006)
6. Bird, C., Pattison, D., D'Souza, R., Filkov, V., Devanbu, P.: Latent social structure in open source projects. In: SIGSOFT 2008/FSE-16: Proceedings of the 16th ACM SIGSOFT International Symposium on Foundations of software engineering, pp. 24–35. ACM, New York (2008)
7. Brin, S., Page, L.: The anatomy of a large-scale hypertextual web search engine. Computer Networks and ISDN Systems 30(1-7), 107–117 (1998); Proceedings of the Seventh International World Wide Web Conference
8. Cheatham, M., Cleereman, K.: Application of social network analysis to collaborative team formation. In: CTS 2006: Proceedings of the International Symposium on Collaborative Technologies and Systems, pp. 306–311. IEEE Computer Society, Washington (2006)
9. Colizza, V., Flammini, A., Serrano, M.A., Vespignani, A.: Detecting rich-club ordering in complex networks. Nature Physics 2, 110–115 (2006)
10. Dustdar, S., Schreiner, W.: A survey on web services composition. Int. J. Web Grid Serv. 1(1), 1–30 (2005)
11. Fitzpatrick, E.L., Askin, R.G.: Forming effective worker teams with multi-functional skill requirements. Comput. Ind. Eng. 48(3), 593–608 (2005)
12. Gaston, M.E., Simmons, J.: desJardins, M.: Adapting network structure for efficient team formation. In: AAMAS 2004 Workshop on Learning and Evolution in Agent Based Systems (July 2004)
13. Gómez, V., Kaltenbrunner, A., López, V.: Statistical analysis of the social network and discussion threads in slashdot. In: WWW 2008: Proceedings of the 17th Int. Conference on World Wide Web, pp. 645–654. ACM, New York (2008)
14. Haveliwala, T.: Topic-sensitive pagerank: a context-sensitive ranking algorithm for web search. IEEE Transactions on Knowledge and Data Engineering 15(4), 784–796 (2003)
15. Kirkpatrick, S., Gelatt, C.D., Vecchi, M.P.: Optimization by simulated annealing. Science 220(4598), 671–680 (1983)
16. Lappas, T., Liu, K., Terzi, E.: Finding a team of experts in social networks. In: KDD 2009: Proceedings of the 15th ACM SIGKDD Int. Conference on Knowledge Discovery and Data Mining, pp. 467–476. ACM, New York (2009)
17. Maamar, Z., Benslimane, D., Thiran, P., Ghedira, C., Dustdar, S., Sattanathan, S.: Towards a context-based multi-type policy approach for web services composition. Data Knowl. Eng. 62(2), 327–351 (2007)

18. McAuley, J.J., da Fontoura Costa, L., Caetano, T.S.: Rich-club phenomenon across complex network hierarchies. Applied Physics Letters 91(8), 084103 (2007)
19. Quitadamo, R., Zambonelli, F., Cabri, G.: The service ecosystem: Dynamic self-aggregation of pervasive communication services. In: First International Workshop on Software Engineering for Pervasive Computing Applications, Systems, and Environments, SEPCASE 2007, pp. 1–10 (May 2007)
20. Schall, D.: Human Interactions in Mixed Systems - Architecture, Protocols, and Algorithms. PhD Thesis, Vienna University of Technology, Karlsplatz 13, 1040 Vienna, Austria (2009)
21. Skopik, F., Schall, D., Dustdar, S.: Modeling and mining of dynamic trust in complex service-oriented systems. Information Systems Journal 35(7), 735–757 (2010)
22. Skopik, F., Truong, H.L., Dustdar, S.: Trust and reputation mining in professional virtual communities. In: Gaedke, M., Grossniklaus, M., Díaz, O. (eds.) ICWE 2009. LNCS, vol. 5648, pp. 76–90. Springer, Heidelberg (2009)
23. Wi, H., Oh, S., Mun, J., Jung, M.: A team formation model based on knowledge and collaboration. Expert Syst. Appl. 36(5), 9121–9134 (2009)
24. Yang, Y., Mahon, F., Williams, M.H., Pfeifer, T.: Context-aware dynamic personalised service re-composition in a pervasive service environment. In: Ma, J., Jin, H., Yang, L.T., Tsai, J.J.-P. (eds.) UIC 2006. LNCS, vol. 4159, pp. 724–735. Springer, Heidelberg (2006)

Complementarity in Competence Management: Framework and Implementation

Nacer Boudjlida and Dong Cheng

Nancy University, UHP Nancy 1, LORIA, UMR 7503, France
Nacer.Boudjlida@loria.fr, Dong.Cheng@loria.fr

Abstract. Retrieving and composing individuals' capabilities are the matter of several research fields, like competence-based management, human resources management, enterprise knowledge management systems, knowledge representation systems, etc. This work focuses on capability representation, discovery and composition in heterogeneous, and possibly distributed, knowledge representation environments. We define a capability representation language in Description Logics, and we propose approaches and algorithms for capability management and discovery. In addition, we outline how our proposals are implemented in a mediator-based prototype system.

Keywords: Capability discovery, Heterogeneous, Composite Answer, Description Logics, Mediation, Mediator Federation.

1 Introduction

The driving motivation of this work is to provide a contribution to the satisfaction of the need for retrieving individuals (we will also call entities) who may carry out actions, as well as the need for retrieving individuals who, when putting their competences together, may carry out actions.

Representation, location and composition of individuals' skills and competences are parts of the theory of competence-based strategic management, which is established as a theory since the early 1990's [26]. Along this view, [4] identifies four processes as components of a competence management system: competence identification, competence assessment, competence acquisition, competence usage. The process of *competence identification* aims at representing competencies in a formal format which can be read in the processes of competence assessment and competence usage. The process of *competence assessment* fixes the relationship between individuals and some required competencies, while *competence usage* concerns individuals whose competencies meet the given requirements.

A similar way, in the frame of enterprise knowledge management, [22] identifies various facets of enterprise knowledge (figure 1). Enterprise knowledge (*explicit knowledge*) as well as enterprise Know-How (*tacit knowledge*) are essential for the decision processes and for the execution of the main processes which constitute the activity of an enterprise. Therefore, they need to be identified, located,

R. Meersman et al. (Eds.): OTM 2010, Part I, LNCS 6426, pp. 490–506, 2010.

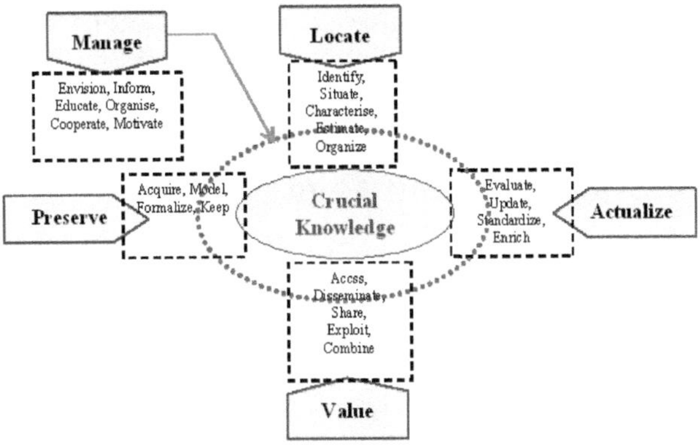

Fig. 1. Entreprise Knowledge [22]

characterized, organized into maps [25], evaluated and organized into hierarchies in order to serve for the enterprise purposes.

In *computer science*, capabilities may be provided by some intelligent agents in the domain of Artificial Intelligence (AI), and these capabilities are essentially the actions an agent can perform solely or cooperatively [27,12].

On the other hand, the (dynamic) *discovery* of the capabilities (or the services) an "entity" offers has different application domains. Component-based programming, electronic business (*e-business*) and even enterprise knowledge management [22,25] are among the application domains in which there is a need for the discovery of services or capabilities an "entity" offers. For these purposes, the only syntactic description of an entity's capability (like the *signature* of a software component or a Web service) is not satisfactory when using that description for answering a request: an additional semantic description is required [6]. Moreover, the elicitation of possible relationships among the services may contribute to find out "the best" service or the "best complementary" services that satisfy a request.

For instance, in *e-business*, considered as a possible application domain of this work, this notion of complementarity (similar to the notion of *pooling of individual skills* in [26]) can be applied when attempting to constitute business alliances or when looking for business partners.

In this work, we propose a formal foundation and a pragmatic solution to implement a competence management system fitted with facilities to describe, organize and discover competencies, as well as facilities to discover complementary competencies.

The presentation is structured as follows. In section 2, we expose some general situations of *capability discovery* and *management*, together with the architecture of the target system, viewed as an heterogeneous and distributed knowledge management system. Section 3 briefly introduces a capability representation language which is founded on description logics (DLs) [2]. Section 4 shows how methods and algorithms are used for capability management and retrieval.

Section 5 briefly introduces the architecture of the prototype we implemented in order to validate our proposals. Concluding remarks and further research directions are in section 6.

2 Problem Statement and Contributions

The ultimate goal is to study and to implement an interoperable query service between heterogeneous knowledge management systems. The ideal of this work is to use "capability requirements" as queries in heterogeneous knowledge management environments.

From a system architecture point of view, the target system is a trader (also called mediator) based architecture [28,8] very similar to the notion of *discovery agency* in Web services architectures[1] [1]. In this architecture, an "entity", called *exporter*, publishes its capabilities at one or several mediator sites (see figure 2). Entities, called *importers*, send requests to the mediator asking for exporters fitted with a given set of capabilities. The *capability discovery* process tries to retrieve which kinds of entities own the requested capabilities, and who these entities are. The *query evaluation* process will then act on a repository that is expressed in a given Knowledge Representation (KR) language. In addition, many repositories may be available and they are possibly distributed or heterogeneous. Therefore, one requires to deal with distributed and heterogeneous knowledge management. From our concern, we approached this situation thanks to the design and the partial implementation of a federation of capability management systems which is described in section 5.

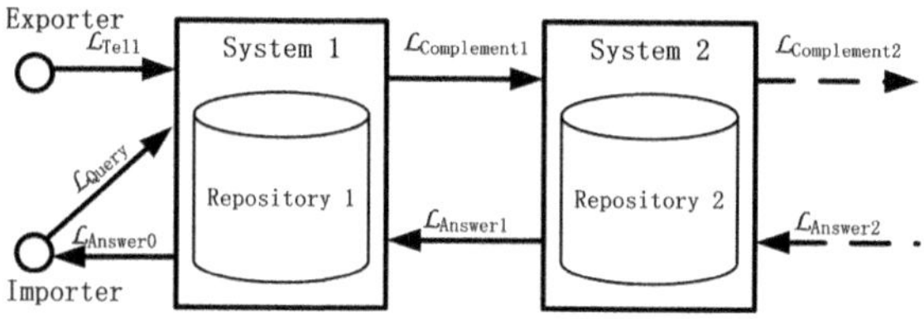

Fig. 2. The Mediator-based Architecture

More precisely, among central objectives and original contributions of our work, we propose:

1. a formal framework for describing and organizing capabilities: we emphasize the need for an appropriate formal and sound basis for the representation and the organization of the capabilities we intend to describe and to manage. From our concern, we opted for the description logic family of languages [2] as a KR language[2].

[1] http://www.w3.org/2002/ws/

[2] A complementary work is running using Conceptual Graphs [16].

2. a single concept (the *complement concept* [23]) and associated mechanisms that enable:
   (a) comparing *intentionally* defined entities (i.e. entities described by a set of capabilities),
   (b) identifying capability gaps between given intentionally defined entities,
   (c) identifying *actual* entities that are candidates for filling-up the identified gaps,
   (d) constraining the set of candidates that contribute to the fulfillment of identified gaps.

These contributions are validated thanks to a mediation architecture we have designed and (partly) implemented as a proof of concepts for capability management applications.

The fundamental concept which underlies this work is the *complement concept* which intuitively means *"what piece of knowledge is missing to an entity A to be an entity B"*. This concept is very central in this work since it provides the accurate basis, at the same time, for *(a)* comparing intentionally defined entities, *(b)* identifying the possible gaps, *(c)* full filling these gaps. The algorithm we developed and that is detailed in section 4 covers all these situations.

In this conceptual model of mediator-based architecture, we also introduced the capability discovery problem, where the results of the *capability discovery* process may be described by a composition of partial answers [10], which consists of two parts: $\mathcal{L}_{Satisfaction}(Q)$ and $\mathcal{L}_{Complement}(Q)$.

$\mathcal{L}_{Satisfaction}$ and $\mathcal{L}_{Complement}$ are sublanguages of $\mathcal{L}_{Answer}$. $\mathcal{L}_{Satisfaction}(Q)$ describes a satisfaction, that is, a single entity or a set of entities satisfying a query Q. If Q is fully satisfied, its complement (denoted as $\mathcal{L}_{Complement}(Q)$) is empty. In the contrary, the system will try to determine a complement for this answer. Intuitively, this complement designates "the missing part" in an entity in order for that entity to satisfy the query: the complement, when it exists, is a single capability description or a conjunction of capability descriptions.

Before presenting the *capability discovery* process and the *composite answer* notion, we briefly introduce the capability representation language we have used.

3 Representing Capabilities as Roles in DL

In this work, we rely on the Description Logic family of languages (DL) [2], that are intensively developed and studied in the field of Knowledge Representation. So it is not surprising that they are particularly adapted for representing the semantics of real world situations, including data semantics [5,3,11].

In DL, *concepts* model classes of individuals (sets of individuals) and they correspond to generic entities in an application domain. An *individual* is an instance of a concept. *Roles* model binary relationships among the individual classes. A concept is specified thanks to a structured description that is built giving *constructors* that introduce the roles associated with the concept and possible restrictions associated with some roles. Usually, the restrictions constrain the range of the binary relationship that is defined by a role and the role's cardinal fixes the minimum and the maximum numbers of elementary values of the role. As for classical logic, a formal semantics may be associated with the defined concepts and roles. Indeed, using an interpretation domain, one can then define the notions of concept and role interpretations as well as the notions of concept satisfiability, equivalence and incompatibility (see [2,13] for further details).

$\mathcal{ALN}_{r+}$ is the DL-based language we propose for the formal representation of capabilities. Before starting with the definition of $\mathcal{ALN}_{r+}$ (an initial version of this capability representation language has been proposed in 2006 [14]), let us introduce some notations. The letters A, B are often used for *primitive concepts*, and C, D for *non primitive concept* descriptions (a *non primitive concept* is defined thanks to a formula that may encompass *primitive concepts* as well as *non primitive* ones). A similar way, considering *roles*, the letters r, s will often be used for *primitive roles*, the letters R, S for non primitive role descriptions, and finally, the letters f, g denote role functional restrictions. Non negative integers (in numbered restrictions) are often denoted by n, m, and individuals are denoted a, b, c, d.

Thanks to these notations, *concept* descriptions and capability descriptions are formed according to the syntactic rules depicted in figure 3. The higher part of the figure contains a list of syntactic rules for $\mathcal{ALN}_{r+}$-*concept* description, and the lower part is the list of syntactic rules for $\mathcal{ALN}_{r+}$-role description.

Name	Abstract syntax	Concrete syntax
primitive concept	$C, D \rightarrow A \mid$	`A`
universal concept[3]	$\top \mid$	`TOP`
bottom concept	$\bot \mid$	`BOTTOM`
primitive negation	$\neg A \mid$	`(not A)`
at-least restriction	$(\geq n\ r) \mid$	`(atleast n r)`
at-most restriction	$(\leq n\ r) \mid$	`(atmost n r)`
concept conjunction	$C \sqcap D \mid$	`(and C D)`
value restriction on roles	$\forall R.C$	`(all R C)`
role name	$R, S \rightarrow r \mid$	`r`
universal role	$\top_{role} \mid$	`TOProle`
bottom role	$\bot_{role} \mid$	`BOTTOMrole`
role disjunction	$R \cup S \mid$	`(or R S)`
symmetric closure	$R^- \mid$	(R^-)
transitive closure	$R^+ \mid$	(R^+)
reflexive-transitive closure	$R^* \mid$	(R^*)
role functional restriction	RfS	(RfS)

Fig. 3. Syntax of $\mathcal{ALN}_{r+}$

The *and* constructor enables defining *concepts* as a conjunction of *concepts*: these *concepts* are the immediate ascendants of the defined one. The *all* constructor constrains a role's range and the *at-least* and *at-most* constructors enable specifying the role's cardinality. Finally, the *not* constructor only applies to primitive concept.

In this work, we consider a *capability* description concept as a role description under the form $\forall R.\top$. Intuitively, this description means *"anything fitted with a capability R"* and it acts as a query addressed to existing capability repositories.

Now, let us consider the extension $\mathcal{ALN}_{r+}$: the part of $\mathcal{ALN}_{r+}$-*concept* description (the lower part in figure 3) is exactly as the $\mathcal{ALN}$-*concept* description syntax (some extensions to $\mathcal{ALN}$-role descriptions have already been mentioned and proved in [2], like $\mathcal{ALN}^*$ which extends $\mathcal{ALN}$ by the role constructors). For example, the $\mathcal{ALN}_{r+}$-*concept* description $\texttt{Flight} \doteq \forall\ \texttt{has-flight}^*.\texttt{AirPort}$ intuitively describes all air travels that include Non-stop flights and transfers. In particular, $\texttt{has-flight}^*$ has to be interpreted as the reflexive-transitive closure of the role `has-flight`, thus representing the role "transfers".

In addition, we suppose that f is a limited predicate logic form in $\mathcal{ALN}_{r+}$, which describes the relationship between two *roles* and four related *concepts*, as sketched in figure 4. Indeed, the figure 4 draws a general model of the functional restriction of roles. The role functional restriction model can be used in many relationships between roles. Hence, this formal f is an open model for the relation between descriptions of roles. Many formal relationship descriptions could be accepted by this model, such as composition, equivalence and subsumption which are then usable in the capability discovery process. As an example, the following role functional restriction f defines the role composition relationship: $RfS,\ where\ f = \{(a,c) \in \Delta^{\mathcal{I}} \times \Delta^{\mathcal{I}} \mid \exists b\ \forall R\ \forall S.(a,b) \in R^{\mathcal{I}} \wedge (b,c) \in S^{\mathcal{I}}\}$ Thanks to the composition description, we can represent the relationship between two capability descriptions: for instance, `has-train` and `has-flight`, that intuitively describes the fact that "trains can transfer to flights".

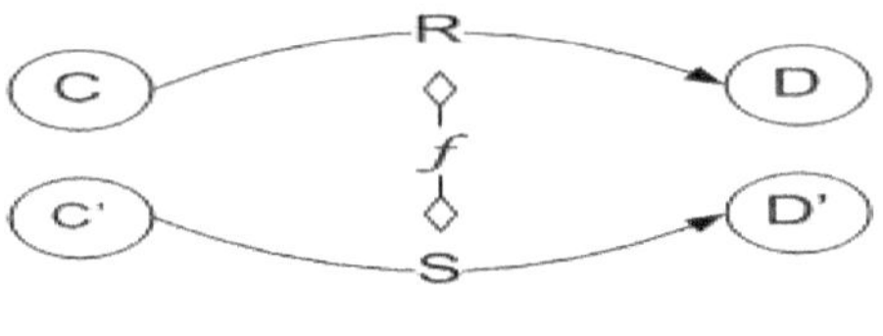

Fig. 4. A Model of Functional Restriction of Roles

$\mathcal{ALN}_{r+}$ offers basic concept description syntax and it increases role restrictions since it enables formulating *relationships between relationships* (remember that roles are relationships between concepts). These description structures will be applied to the capability discovery process in the next section.

4 Capability Management and Discovery

Capability management and discovery are two main processes that are considered in this work. They are implemented thanks to basic inference mechanisms and algorithms. These processes are detailed in this section. They are based on what is available in DL: concepts classification and the subsumption relationship.

Indeed, we use a *classification* method to organize and maintain terminologies into two hierarchies: a *concept hierarchy* and a *role hierarchy*. The classification process aims at determining the position of a new *concept* in a given hierarchy. In the capability discovery process, the classification method also determines the satisfactions description, considering the query as a *concept/role* description Q. The result of the query Q, when it exists, is the set of instances of the *concepts/roles* that are subsumed by Q or that are equivalent to Q.

For clarity purposes, we define very briefly the subsumption relationship and the classification process.

4.1 Subsumption and Classification

Subsumption is the fundamental relationship that may hold among described concepts. Intuitively, a concept C (PERSON, for example) *subsumes* a concept D (WOMAN, for example) if the set of individuals represented by C contains the set of individuals represented by D. More formally, C subsumes D (or D is subsumed by C and it is denoted as $D \sqsubseteq C$) if and only if $D^I \subseteq C^I$ for every possible interpretation I. C is called the *subsuming* concept and D the *subsumed* one.

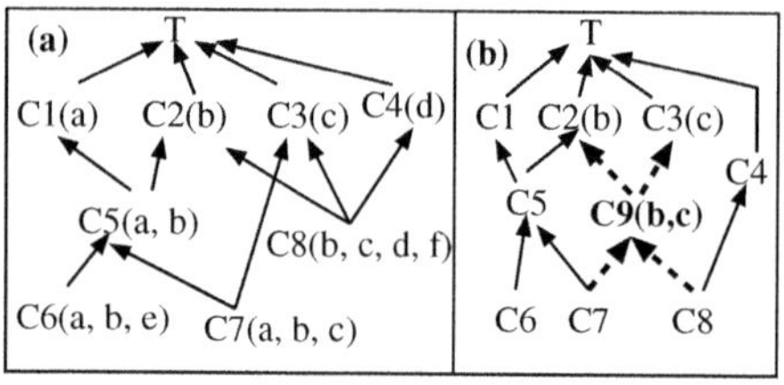

Fig. 5. (a) A hierarchy H of concepts; (b) H after inserting concept C9

The subsumption relationship defines a hierarchical structure among a set of concepts and it may graphically be represented as an acyclic oriented graph rooted at $\top$ (see the left hand-side of figure 5). In the graph, the nodes are concepts and the edges are instances of the relationship. The classification process operates on that hierarchy of concepts. The least subsumer concept (LSCs) and the most specific concepts(MSCs) are the foundations of the classification process which is decomposed into 3 steps:

1. Retrieve the most specific concepts of X (denoted $MSCs(X)$);
2. Retrieve the least subsumers concepts of X (denoted $LSCs(X)$);

3. (possibly) Remove the direct links between MSCs and LSCs of X, and then update the links between X and its MSCs and LSCs (The right hand-side of figure 5 illustrates the process as applied to the concept $C_9(b, c)$).

In a query/answer process, if the query is described as a concept description X, the MSCs(X) will be the "best satisfaction" for the query.

However, if MSC(X) only includes the $\perp$ concept, LSCs(X) will be the possible satisfactions. Therefore, MSCs and LSCs are useful concepts for the coverage of the objectives we mentioned in section 2.

A similar way, in this work, we extend the classification method to the role hierarchy which is based on a similar couple of concepts: least subsumers roles (LSRs) and most specific roles (MSRs). The subsumption relationship testing is the foundation for calculating the two couples of concepts: MSCs and LSCs, MSRs and LSRs; this is performed thanks to a subsumption testing algorithm which has, as an important additional duty, to determine the complement concept.

4.2 Complement Concept

Given two concept descriptions, a subsumption testing algorithm checks whether one description can be "embedded into the other". We apply a Normalize-Compare algorithm (NC algorithm) for testing the subsumption relationships. The NC algorithm is a structural subsumption algorithm. Indeed, the algorithm compares the syntactic structures of the concept descriptions. Despite the fact that the structural subsumption algorithm cannot handle well the negation and the disjunctive syntactic structures, it reveals convenient for the calculation of the *complement* concept.

The NC algorithm proceeds in two phases: normalization and comparison. First, the concept descriptions to be tested for subsumption are normalized, and then the syntactic structures of the normal forms are compared. These phases are successively discussed hereafter.

For short (see details in [15]), the normalization process[4] reduces the "before normalization" class diagram in figure 6 into the "after normalization" class diagram in figure 7. We syntactically denote $\mathcal{ALN}_{r+}$ normal forms as simplified conjunctive forms. For example, C and D are denoted as C = (and $C_1, \ldots, C_n$) (or alternatively as $C_1 \sqcap \cdots \sqcap C_n$) and D = (and $D_1, \ldots, D_m$), where C_i or D_j are atomic concepts, present in the *capability* descriptions.

Under these forms, two *concepts* can be easily compared to check whether the subsumption relationship holds between them or not: giving C = (and $C_1, \ldots, C_n$) and D = (and $D_1, \ldots, D_m$), the test "does the concept A subsume the concept B?" returns "true", if and only if $\forall C_i$ (i $\in$ 1, …, n) $\exists$ D_j (j $\in$ 1, …, m) such that $D_j \sqsubseteq C_i$ and where $\sqsubseteq$ denotes the subsumption relationship.

When applied for capability retrieval, a concept description C represents the requirement in a query Q as $C_1 \sqcap \cdots \sqcap C_n$, i.e. C represents the required

[4] Roughly speaking, the normalization process resembles a macro substitution one: non primitive concepts are recursively replaced by their definition.

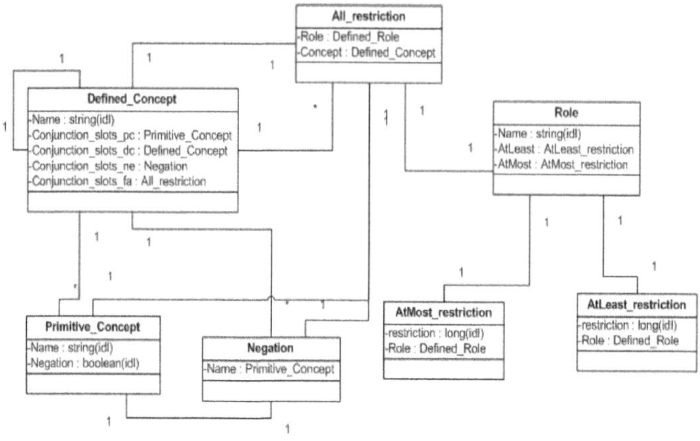

Fig. 6. Description Form in $\mathcal{ALN}_{r+}$, before Normalization

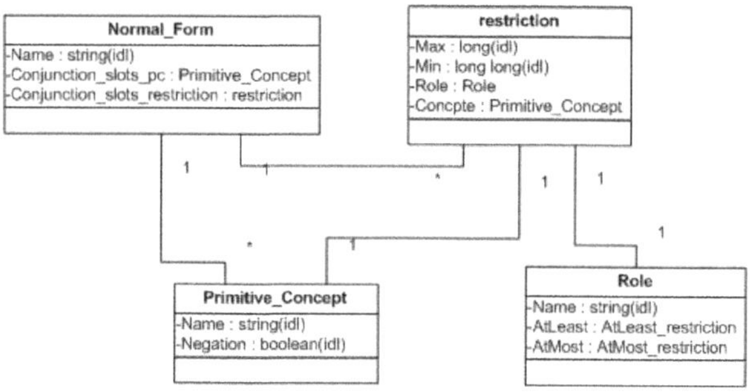

Fig. 7. Description Form in $\mathcal{ALN}_{r+}$, after Normalization

capabilities. Then, the possible answers to Q is a concept description D, which is also under the conjunctive form $D_1 \sqcap \cdots \sqcap D_n$. The conjunctive normal forms are then used to determine the *satisfaction* part and the *complement* part for a given query. Figure 8 sketches the determination of the *complement* between two concept descriptions. In that figure, the subsumption relationship holds between $C_1, \ldots, C_k$ and $D_1, \ldots, D_k$ (i.e. according to the notation we are using: $\mathcal{L}_{Satisfaction}(Q) = D_1 \sqcap \cdots \sqcap D_k$). On the other hand, the remaining concepts $C_{k+1}, \ldots, C_n$ are not satisfied and they will therefore describe the complement to be determined: $\mathcal{L}_{Complement}(Q) = C_{k+1} \sqcap \cdots \sqcap C_n$.

As an example, consider the concept CITY-AIRPORT which characterizes cities that offer air transportation facilities and the concept PORT-AIR that characterizes cities fitted with air and sea transportations facilities. The normal forms of these concepts are given below.

$$
\begin{array}{lll}
C: \texttt{PORT-AIR}= & (\sqcap\ \texttt{CITY} & (C_1) \\
 & ((\geq\ \infty\ 1\ \texttt{has-flight}^{-}).\texttt{CITY}) & (C_2) \\
 & ((\geq\ \infty\ 1\ \texttt{has-ferry}).\texttt{CITY})) & (C_3)
\end{array}
$$

$$
\begin{array}{lll}
D: \texttt{CITY-AIRPORT}= & (\sqcap\ \texttt{CITY} & (D_1) \\
 & ((\geq\ \infty\ 1\ \texttt{has-flight}^{-}).\texttt{CITY})) & (D_2)
\end{array}
$$

Assume that PORT-AIR is the query (denoted as C) and CITY-AIRPORT, denoted as D is a concept in the knowledge base. In these descriptions, $D_1 \sqcap D_2$ is a partial satisfaction of the query C), and C_3 is the complement to be satisfied.

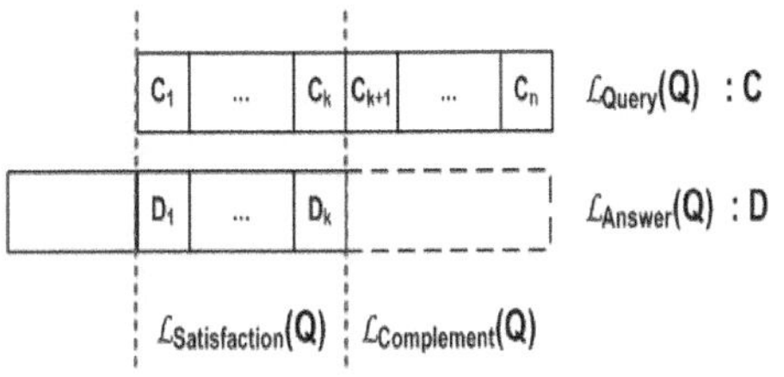

Fig. 8. Determination of a Composite Answer

In addition, we already mentioned that multiple satisfactions may exist and that they have to be composed to satisfy the requirement of a query. In order to calculate the satisfaction and the complement parts, beside the classification algorithm, we introduce an array of Boolean (called Satisfaction Table further, and ST for short). The Boolean array records the results of the evaluation of the subsumption relationship (see table 1). In that table, $C_1, C_2, C_3, \ldots, C_n$ denote the query concept under its normal form and $D_1, D_2, D_3, \ldots, D_m$ denotes *concepts* under a normal form too, i.e. every D_j has to be viewed as $(and\, D_j^1, D_j^2, \ldots, D_j^{nj})$. Therefore, $ST[D_j, C_i] = true \leftrightarrow\ D_j^i \sqsubseteq C_i$ (more details are given in [15]).

That means that the *complement* is given by the conjunction of all the *atomic concepts* for which the corresponding values in the satisfaction table are "false".

Table 1. Three observed values and the satisfaction table

	C_1	C_2	...	C_n
D_1	False	False	...	True
D_2	False	True	...	True
...	...	...	...	...
D_m	False	False	...	False
ORoD	False	True	...	True

ORoS	ANDoS
True	False

Afterward, in order to attempt to actually satisfy the identified complement, we introduce three observed values, in addition to the satisfaction table: ORoD, ORoS, and ANDoS.

- $ORoD[1..n]$ is defined as $ORoD[i] = \bigvee_{j=1}^{m} ST[D_j^i, C_i], \forall i \in [1..n]$, i.e. $ORoD[i]$ is the disjunction of the boolean values in $ST[*, i]$ and when it evaluates to true it means that the concept C_i in the query C is satisfied by at least one concept among the concepts $D_k^i, k \in [1..m]$.
- If the conjunction $ANDoS$ of the values of $ORoD$, defined as $ANDoS = \bigwedge_{i=1}^{n} ORoD[i]$, is true, then that means that all the C_is are satisfied, and therefore the query is fully satisfied too.
- Finally, when $ANDoS$ is false, the logical disjunction of the values of $ORoD$, noted $ORoS$ and defined as $ORoS = \bigvee_{i=1}^{n} ORoD[i]$, enables to determine a possible partial satisfaction. Indeed, if $ORoS = True$, that means that there exists some C_k that are satisfied, i.e. a partial answer is found for the query. But, if both $ORoS$ and $ANDoS$ are false then no atomic concept description D_j^k $(j \in 1..m)$ satisfies any C_i, i.e. even a partial answer to the query cannot be found.

Thanks to the analysis of the results of the classification (which identifies the *Least Common Subsumer (LCS)* and the *Most Specific Concept (MSC)*) and thanks to the results of the Normalize-and-Compare algorithm, which delivers the ORoS and ANDoS values, the cases for a composite answer are covered. These cases intuitively mean:

1. *Exact satisfaction*: There exist individuals who are fitted with the only requested capabilities;
2. *Wider Satisfaction*: There exist individuals who are fitted with more than the requested capabilities;
3. *Complementary Satisfaction*: No individual possesses the requested capabilities, but there exist individuals whose union of capabilities meets the requested ones
4. *Partial Satisfaction*: There exist individuals who are fitted with part of the requested capabilities
5. *Failure*: No individual is fitted with any of the requested capabilities

Table 2 summarizes the above discussion. In this table, X and Y are two concept descriptions, $\top$ is the TOP concept and $\bot$ is the BOTTOM concept.

Table 2. Analysis of the Satisfaction Cases

Case	LCS(Q)	MSC(Q)	ORoS	ANDoS
1: Exact Satisfaction	X	Y	True	True
2: Wider Satisfaction	X	$\bot$	True	True
3: Complementary Satisfaction	$\top$	$\bot$	True	True
4: Partial Satisfaction	$\top$	$\bot$	True	False
5: Failure	$\top$	$\bot$	False	False

In addition, the content of the table can be expressed a more formal way as follows:

1. *Exact satisfaction*: $Y \sqsubseteq Q \sqsubseteq X$ iff $(LCS(Q) = X) \wedge (MSC(Q) = Y) \wedge (ORoS = True) \wedge (ANDoS = True)$;
2. *Wider Satisfaction*: $Q \sqsubseteq X$ iff $(LCS(Q) = X) \wedge (MSC(Q) = \bot) \wedge (ORoS = True) \wedge (ANDoS = True)$;
3. *Complementary Satisfaction*: $\exists X_1, \ldots, \exists X_n, Q \sqsubseteq \bigcup_{i=1}^{n} X_i$ iff $(LCS(Q) = \top) \wedge (MSC(Q) = \bot) \wedge (ORoS = True) \wedge (ANDoS = True)$;
4. *Partial Satisfaction*: $\exists X_1, \ldots, \exists X_n, \bigcup_{i=1}^{n} X_i \sqsubset Q \wedge \neg(\exists Y_1, \ldots, \exists Y_m, Q \sqsubseteq \bigcup_{j=1}^{m} Y_j)$ iff $(LCS(Q) = \top) \wedge (MSC(Q) = \bot) \wedge (ORoS = True) \wedge (ANDoS = False)$;
5. *Failure*: $\forall X \in \mathcal{T}, X \cap Q = \emptyset$ iff $(LCS(Q) = \top) \wedge (MSC(Q) = \bot) \wedge (ORoS = False) \wedge (ANDoS = False)$.

The three observed values are used to determine the variety of situations in the capability discovery. When the query is not fully satisfied giving a mediator's capability description repository, the complement concept (i.e. the conjunction of all the *atomic concepts* for which the corresponding values in the satisfaction table are "false") may be sent to an other mediator which in turns performs the same process, considering the description of the identified complement as a query. Furthermore, the cooperating mediators may be homogeneous (i.e. they use the same capability representation language) as well as heterogeneous (i.e. they use different capability representation languages). In the later case, mappings between terms and concepts are required. This is sketched in the next section (see also section 5 for some words about the actual implementation of these features).

4.3 Heterogeneous Capability Discovery

The capability discovery is serial steps in a heterogeneous repository environment, which includes the classification, the NC algorithm, the satisfaction table and the complement determination, as explained in the previous sections. We focus hereafter on heterogeneous KR languages problems.

The structure of atomic concepts are one by one satisfied in the satisfaction table in the previous section. The unsatisfied structures in the *complement* may be satisfied by other systems.

The atomic concept structure ($\forall R.A$) is written using three symbols: universal quantification $\forall$, *Role* identity R, and *Concept* identity A, that means that all assertions of an entity A own the capability R. If the atomic concept structure represents a query $\mathcal{L}_{Query}(Q) = \forall R.A$, it means that we are looking for an entity A which owns the capability R, where A is the identity of one entity and the capability R is the one which is looked for. Therefore, the concept description is translated into a *universal concept*, like the *top concept* $\top$ in DLs, and the *"thing"* concept in Frame-Logic [19] (F-Logic) and Conceptual Graphs [18] (CGs). In addition, in order to deal with multiple KR languages, the vocabulary of R

must be translated between the heterogeneous systems. In this frame, the *lexical translation* of the terms used in R is independent of the *syntax translation.*

Considering lexical translation, term mapping may be facilitated by the use of a common ontology. The most basic method simply computes the "distance" between two concepts in the common ontology. The vocabularies in the *capability description* may be included in the common ontology, or serve to determine similar terms in a local repository. The similarity determination, not central in our work, is implemented thanks to hierarchical dictionaries, like WordNet [21]. However, classically, we need to tackle situations where exact mappings between terms do not exist. We dealt with such situations thanks to similarity distance measurement among terms.

From the syntactic point of view, we have to consider syntactic mappings between the considered KR languages. For example, a query of role R can be easily expressed in the three KR languages we considered:

$$\begin{aligned} \mathcal{Q}_{DL} &\doteq \forall R.X; \\ \mathcal{Q}_{F-Logic} &\doteq \text{FORALL } X \leftarrow R(X); \\ \mathcal{Q}_{CGs} &\doteq [\text{Object:*}X]\ [\text{Object:}Y]\ (R\ ?X\ ?Y); \end{aligned}$$

Therefore, the query is processed alike the initial one. The cooperating mediator returns a positive or a negative answer (as a boolean value), that means that the *capability* is satisfied or not, then the result can be processed in the satisfaction table as a satisfaction candidate in DLs.

5 Complementary Capabilities and Implementation

In this work, we approached the *capability discovery* at four levels:

1. Firstly, the query may be fully satisfied by individuals that are identified in a single repository. The classification method locates the satisfaction in the knowledge hierarchy of the repository. This level is called *local full satisfaction.*
2. Otherwise, the query is satisfied by a "group" of individuals in a single repository. This level focuses on the capabilities matching calculation and composite answer calculation. We call this level *local composite satisfaction.*
3. The query and the repository are in the same KR language and the repository is distributed in several independent servers. To handle this situation, we use the calculus that are used for the *local composite satisfaction.* Therefore, this situation focuses on the solution of distributed calculation problem. We call this level the *homogeneous distributed satisfaction.*
4. The final level is called *heterogeneous satisfaction.* The query and the repositories are in different KR languages, and the repository may be distributed. This situation focuses on the problem of communication and interoperation between different KR languages.

We implemented a mediator federation prototype system (figure 9) to validate our proposals. The prototype consists of two parts: *(i)* the capability application

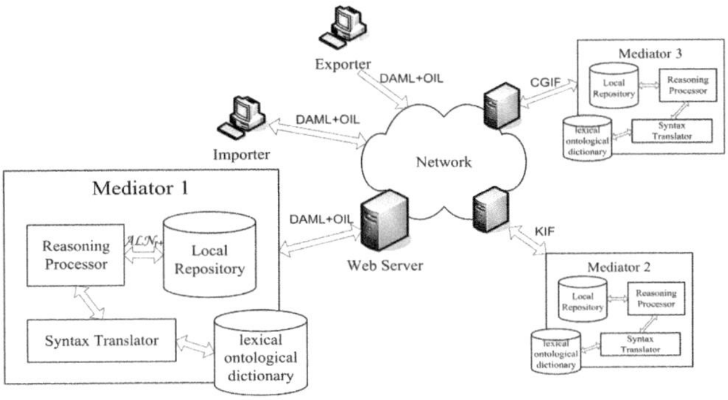

Fig. 9. The Mediators Federation

approaches in $\mathcal{ALN}_{r+}$ Knowledge Base, and *(ii)* the mediator server composition in heterogeneous environments. In the first part, all the facilities, which were mentioned in the previous section and that are required by a capability management system, has been developed in *Java*. These include:

- a service for testing the subsumption relationship,
- a service for the determination of the *complement* and the *satisfaction* concepts,
- and a service for the calculation of the *composite answers*, when required.

In the second part, we experimented composite heterogeneous mediation services in an environment as drawn in figure 9. The three federated mediators show a heterogeneous and distributed environment where:

- Mediator 1 supports the increased DLs language $\mathcal{ALN}_{r+}$, which loads all the programs of capability application in the first part;
- Mediator 2 supports F-Logic, and its communication language format is KIF [17];
- Mediator 3 supports Conceptual Graphs (CGs), and its communication language is CGIF [20].

The federated mediator architecture conforms to the Service Oriented Architecture (SOA) [1], and it is implemented using Web Services techniques. The prototype is written in Java (Sun Microsystem's JDK1.2 and Java Web Services Developer Pack 1.6). It has been tested under various operating systems like Miscrosoft Windows (95, 98, Me, XP, 2000, 2003) et Linux (Red Hat 7.X et Mandrake 8.x). Considering the Peer-to-Peer (P2P) systems characteristics the prototype have the following ones:

1. *Considering autonomy*: autonomy is reached thanks to the fact that every mediator offers services to its clients (exporters and importers) to publish their capabilities and to search for capabilities, respectively.

2. *Considering dynamicity*: in its current state, the prototype relies on an OWL-S document for the management of the federation. Clearly, this solution is not adequate for real-life applications. UDDI [24] enables describing how entities publish their services and discover each other. It also enables defining how services or software applications can interact over Internet. This principle may be used in the federated architecture for implementing the management and the dynamic discovery of the mediators and their services. This obviously needs additional mechanisms to be available, like mechanisms that enable a mediator to join or to leave (temporarily or definitely) a federation. However, this feature has not been considered in this work since it is not central for us.
3. *Considering decentralization*: the architecture is *par essence* decentralized since a mediator may address a query to any other one in the federation.
4. *Considering cooperation*: it is also a characteristic of the prototype since, when a local mediator fails in satisfying a query, it may cooperate with some other mediators in order to compute a composite answer to the query.

On an other hand, with regard to mediator's characteristics, like *context management* and *query propagation*:

1. the current prototype does not offer sophisticated mechanisms for *context management*. It implements simple strategies for the computation of composite answers (like find the *the first fit* or limit to *at most* x components in the answer for a query). Further investigations and developments are required to fully support the variety of the required strategies.
2. based on this simple context management, *query propagation* is done according to a *proximity criteria* (as opposed to a *semantic criteria*): queries are forwarded to nearest mediator as an OWL-S document.

6 Concluding Remarks and Further Work

In this work, we consider that two main results have been achieved: firstly defining a *capability* description language $\mathcal{ALN}_{r+}$ to support capability management and inference services; secondly designing a mediation federation system in order to implement the composite answer approach for capability discovery in heterogeneous knowledge representation environments.

$\mathcal{ALN}_{r+}$ inherits and extends the knowledge representation theory and technology of Description Logic. We implemented inference services which may be used for capability management and capability discovery. We also introduced an open model of restriction f to describe the relationships between *roles*. Nevertheless, more complex relationships between the relationships of capabilities may exist, and *modal logic* and/or *second-order logic* theories may be used in the description and in the inference on the relationships between the relationships among capabilities. Further, the implemented services are easily extendible to handle constraints on the types of the expected answers to a query, like constraining the number of fragments that constitute a composite answer. This type of extension may serve, for example, to find out *at most n/at least m* individuals who have complementary capabilities. In addition, the availability of a kind of *"common and shared understanding"* will very probably ease the interoperability of the mediators within a federation: this is one of our running investigation [7].

From an implementation point of view, the whole mediator federation prototype is under a hybrid system architecture, where an importer, an exporter and a mediator server compose a typical SOA system. But the mediators' federation is a pure P2P architecture whose characteristics are more deeply discussed in [9]. This prototype depends on a manual OWL-S document to manage the whole mediator federation inter-actions: that cannot work in a "'real-life"' applications. Therefore, dynamic federation management, context management and semantic criteria for query propagation and how they interact need further investigations and developments.

References

1. Alonso, G., Casati, F.: Web services and service-oriented architectures. In: ICDE, p. 1147. IEEE Computer Society, Los Alamitos (2005)
2. Baader, F., Calvanese, D., McGuinness, D.L., Nardi, D., Patel-Schneider, P.F. (eds.): The Description Logic Handbook: Theory, Implementation, and Applications. Cambridge University Press, Cambridge (2003)
3. Beeri, C., Levy, A., Rousset, M.C.: Rewriting Queries Using Views in Description Logics. In: ACM Symposium on Principles Of Database Systems, pp. 99–108. Tucson, Arizona (1997)
4. Berio, G., Harzallah, M.: Knowledge management for competence management. Journal of Universal Knowledge Management 0(1), 21–28 (2005)
5. Borgida, A.: Description Logics in Data Management. IEEE Transactions on Knowledge and Data Engineering 7(5), 671–682 (1995)
6. Borgida, A., Devanhu, P.: Adding more "DL" to IDL: Towards more Knowledgeable Component Interoperability. In: 21rst International Conference on Software Engineering, ICSE 1999, pp. 378–387. ACM Press, Los Angeles (May 1999)
7. Bouchaib, F., Boudjlida, N., Talantikite, H.N.: A generic model of knowledge and competence of domains. In: Abdelwahed, E.H., Mountassir, H. (eds.) Proceedings of the 3rd International Conference on Web and Information Technologies, ICWIT 2010, Marrakech, Morocco, pp. 209–220 (June 2010)
8. Boudjlida, N.: A Mediator-Based Architecture for Capability Management. In: Hamza, M. (ed.) Proceedings of the 6th International Conference on Software Engineering and Applications, SEA 2002, pp. 45–50. MIT, Cambridge (November 2002)
9. Boudjlida, N., Cheng, D.: Gestion distribuée de compétences et de leurs complémentarité. In: Obaid, A. (ed.)Proc. 9ème Conférence Internationale sur les NOuvelles TEchnologies de la REpartition, NOTERE 2009, Montréal, Canada, pp. 64–75 (June-July 2009) ISBN 978-2-9809407-1-2
10. Boudjlida, N., Dong, C.: Federated Mediators for Query Composite-Answers. In: Enterprise Informations Systems, vol. VI, pp. 31–38. Kluwer Academics Publishers, Dordrecht (2006) ISBN10 1-4020-3674-4
11. Calvanese, D., de Giacomo, D., Lenzerini, M., Nardi, D., Rosati, R.: Information Integration: Conceptual Modeling and Reasoning Support. In: 6th International Conference on Cooperative Information Systems, CoopIS 1998, pp. 280–291 (1998)

12. Dennis, J., Horn, E.V.: Programming semantics for multiprogrammed computations. Communications of the Association of Computing Machinery, 143–155 (March 1966)
13. DL-org: Description logics (2007), http://dl.kr.org/
14. Dong, C.: Capability representation on increased $\mathcal{ALN}$. In: Doctoral Symposium of Interoperability for Enterprise Software and Applications Conference, Bordeaux, France (March 2006)
15. Dong, C.: Capability Management and Discovery in Heterogeneous Environments. Ph.D. thesis, Nancy University, UHP Nancy 1, LORIA (F) (November 2008)
16. Gasmi, B., Boudjlida, N., Talantikite, H.N.: Conceptual graphs for competence management. In: Ghenima, M., Smaili, K., Sidhom, S. (eds.) Proceedings of the 3rd International Conference on Information Systems and Business Intelligence, SIIE 2010, pp. 505–514. IHE Editions, Sousse (February 2010)
17. Genesereth, M.R.: Knowledge Interchange Format (1998)
18. ISO: Standard for conceptual graphs (2003), http://www.jfsowa.com/cg/
19. Kifer, M., Lausen, G., Wu, J.: Logical foundations of object-oriented and frame-based languages. Journal of the Association for Computing Machinery 42, 741–843 (1995), citeseer.ist.psu.edu/kifer90logical.html
20. Martin, P.: Knowledge representation in CGLF, CGIF, KIF, frame-CG and formalized-english. In: Priss, U., Corbett, D.R., Angelova, G. (eds.) ICCS 2002. LNCS (LNAI), vol. 2393, pp. 77–91. Springer, Heidelberg (2002), http://link.springer.de/link/service/series/0558/bibs/2393/23930077.htm
21. Miller, G.A., et al.: Wordnet 2.0 (2003), http://www.cogsci.princeton.edu/~wn/
22. Nonaka, I., Takeuchi, H.: The Knowledge - Creating Company: How Japanese Companies Create the Dynamics of Innovation. Oxford University Press, Oxford (1995), http://www.loc.gov/catdir/enhancements/fy0604/94040408-d.html
23. Schmidt-Schauss, M., Smolka, G.: Attribute Concepts Description with Complements. Artificial Intelligence Journal 48(1), 1–26 (1991)
24. UDDI.org: Uddi: Universal description, discovery and integration. Technical White Paper (September 2003), http://uddi.org
25. Velardi, P., Cucchiarelli, A., Petit, M.: Supporting scientific collaboration in a network of excellence through a semantically indexed knowledge map. In: Doumeingts, G., Muller, J., G.M., Vallespir, B. (eds.) Proceedings of the 2nd International Conference On Interoperability for Entreprise Software and Applications, I-ESA 2006, pp. 231–241. Springer, Bordeaux (March 2006)
26. Vernhout, A.: Management challenges in the competence-based organization. Competence-Based Management Website (2007)
27. Wickler, G.J.: Using Expressive and Flexible Action Representation to Reason about Capabilities for Intelligent Agent Cooperation. Ph.D. thesis, University of Edinburgh (1999)
28. Wiederhold, G.: Mediators in the architecture of future information systems. IEEE Computer 25(3), 38–49 (1992)

Scalable XML Collaborative Editing with Undo
(Short Paper)

Stéphane Martin[1], Pascal Urso[2], and Stéphane Weiss[2]

[1] Laboratoire d'Informatique Fondamentale
39 rue F. Jolio-Curie,
13013 Marseille, France
stephane.martin@lif.univ-mrs.fr
[2] Université de Lorraine
LORIA, Campus Scientifique,
54506 Vandoeuvre-lès-Nancy, France
{pascal.urso,stephane.weiss}@loria.fr

Abstract. Commutative Replicated Data-Type (CRDT) is a new class of algorithms that ensures scalable consistency of replicated data. It has been successfully applied to collaborative editing of texts without complex concurrency control.

In this paper, we present a CRDT to edit XML data. Compared to existing approaches for XML collaborative editing, our approach is more scalable and handles all the XML editing aspects : elements, contents, attributes and undo. Indeed, undo is recognized as an important feature for collaborative editing that allows to overcome system complexity through error recovery or collaborative conflict resolution.

Keywords: XML, Collaborative Editing, P2P, Group Undo, Scalability, Optimistic Replication, CRDT.

1 Introduction

In large-scale infrastructures such as clouds or peer-to-peer networks, data are replicated to ensure availability, efficiency and fault-tolerance. Since data are the heart of the information systems, the consistency of the replicas is a key issue. Mechanisms to ensure strong consistency levels – such as linear or atomic – do not scale, thus modern large-scale infrastructures now rely on eventual consistency.

Commutative Replicated Data Types [12,16] (CRDT) is a promising new class of algorithms used to build operation-based optimistic replication [14] mechanisms. It ensures eventual consistency of replicated data without complex concurrency control. It has been successfully applied to scalable collaborative editing of textual document but not yet on semi-structured data types. EXtensible Markup Language (XML) is used in a wide range of information systems from semi-structured data storing to query. Moreover, XML is the standard format for exchanging data, allowing interoperability and openness.

Collaborative editing (CE) provides several advantages such as obtaining different viewpoints, reducing task completion time, and obtaining a more accurate final result.

R. Meersman et al. (Eds.): OTM 2010, Part I, LNCS 6426, pp. 507–514, 2010.

Nowadays, collaborative editing becomes massive and part of our every day life. The online encyclopedia Wikipedia users have produced 15 millions of articles in a few years.

Undo has been recognized as an important feature of single and collaborative editors [2,3]. The undo feature provides a powerful way to recover from errors and vandalism acts or to manage edit conflicts. So, it helps the user to face the complexity of the system. However, designing an undo feature is a non-trivial task. First, in collaborative editing, this feature must allow to undo any operation – and not only the last one – from any user. This is called global selective undo (or anyundo). Second, this undo must be correct from the user's point of view. The system must return in a state such as the undone operation has never been performed.

We propose to design an XML CRDT for collaborative editing. This CRDT handles both aspects of XML trees : elements' children and attributes. The order in the list of the elements' children are treated as in linear structure CRDT. Elements' attributes are treated using a last-writer-wins rule. Our undo is obtained by keeping the previous value given to attributes and operations applied on elements, and then counting concurrent undo and redo operations. A garbage collection mechanism is presented to garbage old operations.

2 State of the Art

The Operational Transformation (OT) [13] approach is an operation-based replication mechanism. OT relies on a generic integration algorithm and a set of transformation functions specific to the type of replicated data. Some integration mechanism use states vectors – or context vectors [15] in the presence of undo – to detect concurrency between operations; such mechanisms are not adapted to large-scale infrastructures. Ignat et al. [4] propose to couples an integration mechanism that uses anti-entropy, with some specific transformation functions [11] to obtain P2P XML collaboration. However, this proposition replaces deleted elements by tombstones in the edited document to ensure consistency, making the document eventually growing without limits and proposes no undo.

Martin et al. [9] proposes an XML-tree reconciliation mechanism very similar to a CRDT since concurrent operations commute without transformation. However, this approach does not treat XML element's attributes, which require a specific treatment, since they are unique and unordered. Furthermore, it uses state vector that limits its scalability and proposes no undo feature.

In the field of Data Management, some works give attention to XML replication. Some of them [6,1] suppose the existence of some protocol to ensure consistency of replicated content without defining it. Finally, [8] proposes a merging algorithm for concurrent modifications that can only be used in a centralized context.

3 XML CRDT without Undo

In a collaborative editor, to ensure scalability and high-responsiveness of local modifications, data must be replicated. This replication is optimistic since local modifications are immediately executed. The replicas are allowed to diverge in the short time, but the system must ensure eventual consistency. When the system is idle (i.e., all modifications are delivered), the replicas must have the same content.

A Commutative Replicated Data Type(CRDT) [12] is a data type where all concurrent operations commute. In other words, whatever the delivery order of operations, the resulting document is identical. As a result, a CRDT ensure eventual consistency as proven in [12].

Thus, we see an XML collaborative editor as a set of network nodes that host a set of replicas (up to one per node) of the shared XML document. Local modifications are immediately executed and disseminated to all other replicas. We assume that every replica will eventually receive every modification.

We consider an XML tree as an *edge e* with three elements : $e.identifier$ the unique identifier of the edge (a timestamp), $e.children$ the children of the edge (a set of edge), and $e.attributes$ the attributes of the edge (a map string to value). The key of the map are the attribute's name (a string), and a value av has two elements, $av.value$: the current value of the attribute (a string), $av.timestamp$: the current timestamp of the attribute. The basic operations that affect an XML tree are :

- $Add(id_p, id)$: Adds a edge with identifier id under the edge id_p. This edge is empty, it has no tag-name, child or attribute.
- $Del(id)$: Deletes the edge identified by id.
- $SetAttr(id, attr, val, ts)$: Sets the value val with the timestamp ts to the attribute $attr$ of the edge identified by id. The deletion of an attribute is done by setting is value to nil.

To allow *Add* and *Del* operations to commute, we use a unique timestamp identifier. Timestamp identifiers can be defined as follows: each replica is identified by a unique identifier s and each operation generated by this site is identified by a clock h_s (logical clock or wall clock). An identifier id is a pair $(h_s : s)$. For instance $(3 : 2)$ identifies the operation 3 of the site number 2. The set of the identifiers is denoted by ID. Thus, two edges added concurrently at the same place in the tree have different identifiers.

To allow *SetAttr* operations to commute, we use a classical last-writer-wins technique. We associate to each attribute a timestamp ts. A remote $SetAttr$ is applied if and only if its timestamp is higher than the timestamp associated to the attribute. Timestamps are totally ordered. Let $ts_1 = (h_1 : s_1)$ and $ts_2 = (h_2 : s_2)$, we have $ts_1 > ts_2$ if and only if $h_1 > h_2$, or $h_1 = h_2$ and $s_1 > s_2$. Clocks are loosely synchronized, i.e., when a replica receives an operation with a timestamp $(h_2 : s_2)$, it sets its own clock h_1 to $max(h_1, h_2)$.

Special attributes. The special attributes $@tag$ and $@position$ contain the tag-name and the position of an edge and cannot be nil. The position allows to order the children of a node. This position is not a basic number. Indeed, to ensure that the order among edges is the same on all replicas, this position must be *unique, totally ordered and dense*. Positions are dense if a replica can always generate a position between two arbitrary positions. This position can be a priority string concatenated with an identifier [9], a sequence of integers [16], or a bitstring concatenated with an identifier [12] all with a lexicographic ordering. Finally, to model the textual edges we use another special attribute *@text*. If this attribute has a value v, whatever the value of other attributes, the edge is considered as a textual edge with content v.

Algorithms. The function deliver(op,t) applies an operation op on an XML tree t. The function find(t, id) returns the edge identified by id. The function findFather(t, id) returns the father of the edge identified by id.

```
deliver (Add(id_p, id), t) :
  edge p = find(id_p, t), e = new edge(id);
  if p ≠ nil then p.children = p.children ∪ {e};
end
deliver (Del(id), t) :
  edge p = findFather(id, t), e = find(id, p);
  if p ≠ nil then p.children = p.children \ {e};
end
deliver (SetAttr(id, attr, val, ts), t) :
  edge e = find(id, t);
  if e ≠ nil and (e.attributes[attr] = nil or e.attributes[attr].timestamp < ts) then
      e.attributes[attr].value = val;
      e.attributes[attr].timestamp = ts;
  endif
end
```

4 XML CRDT with Undo

Obtaining a correct undo from the user's point of view is a non-trivial task. Let's have the following scenario 1. a user adds an element, 2. a user deletes this element, 3. the add is undone, 4. the delete is undone concurrently by 2 different users. At the end, since both operations add and delete are undone, the node must be invisible. And this must be true on every replica and whatever the delivery order of operations. For instance, using *Del* to undo *Add* leads to different results according to the reception order of the operations. The element is visible if an un-delete is received in last or not if it is a un-add. Such a behavior violates eventual consistency.

To obtain a satisfying undo, we keep the information about every operations applied to each edge. Then we count the *effect counter* of an operation : one minus the number of undo plus the number of redo. If this effect counter is greater than 0, the operation has an effect. An element is visible if the add has an effect counter greater than 0, and no delete with an effect counter greater than 0. The value of an attribute is determined by the more recent value with an effect counter greater than 0. Thus, we need to keep into the map of attributes, the list of values – including nil values – associated to an effect counter. The list is ordered by the decreasing timestamp.

With undo, an edge attribute $e.attributes[attr]$ becomes an ordered list of *value v*, each value containing 3 elements : $v.value$ a value of the attribute (a string), $v.timestamp$ the timestamp associated to this value, and $v.effect$ the effect counter of this value (a integer). *The list is ordered by the timestamp.* The function add(l,v) adds a value v in the list l at its place according to $v.timestamp$. The function get(l,ts) returns the value associated to ts in the list l. The special $@add$ attribute has only one value associated to the timestamp equal to the edge identifier. The special $@del$ attribute stores the list of timestamp of delete operations applied to the edge.

```
deliver (Add(id_p, id), t) :
  edge p = find(t, id_p), e = new edge(id);
  p.children = p.children ∪ {e}
  add(e.attributes[@add], new value (nil, id, 1));
end
deliver (Del(id, ts), t) :
  edge e = find (t, id);
  add(e.attributes[@del], new value (nil, ts, 1));
end
deliver (SetAttr(id, attr, val, ts), t) :
  edge e = find (t, id);
  add(e.attributes[attr], new value (val, ts, 1));
end
```

Undo of an operation is simply achieved by decrementing the corresponding effect counter. When a *Redo* is delivered, the increment function is called with a delta of $+1$.

```
deliver (Undo(Add(id_p, id)), t) :
  increment(t, id, @add, id, -1);
end
deliver (Undo(Del(id, ts)), t) :
  increment(t, id, @del, ts, -1);
end
deliver (Undo(SetAttr(id, attr, val, ts)), t) :
  increment(t, id, attr, ts, -1);
end
function increment(t, id, attr, ts, delta)
  edge e = find(t, id);
  value v = get(e.attributes[attr], ts);
  v. effect  += delta;
end
```

Example. Figure 1 presents the application of our functions on the introducing example. On every replica, the add and del operations have an effect counter lesser or equal to 0. Thus none of these operations have an effect on the XML tree and the edge is invisible.

Model to XML. As the model described above includes tombstones and operations information, it cannot be used directly by applications. Indeed, applications must not see a tombstones and only one value for each attribute. A node is visible if the effect

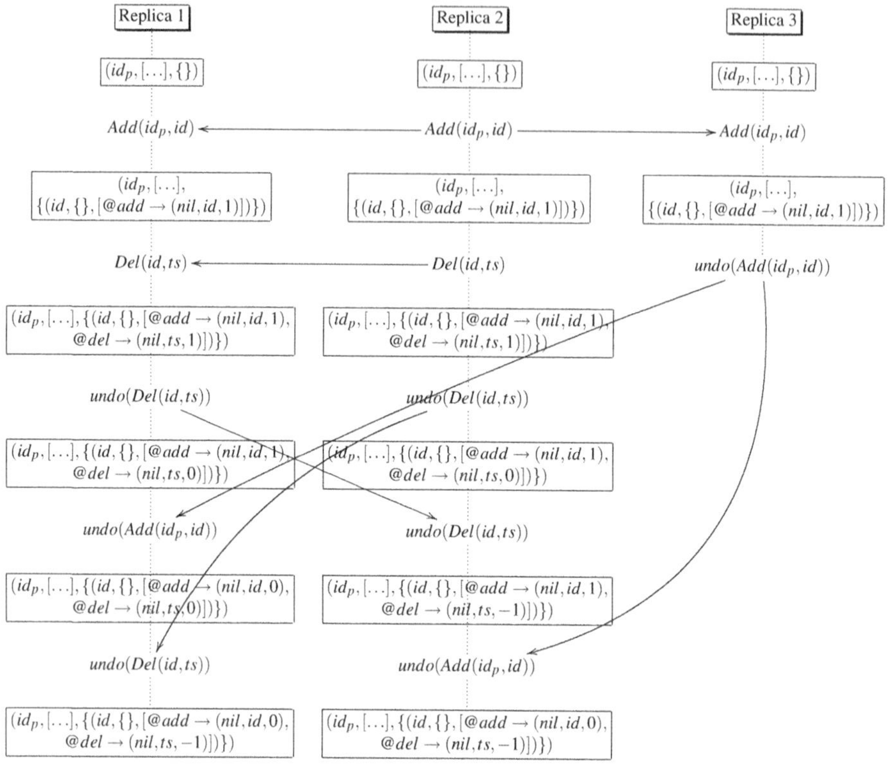

Fig. 1. Concurrent undos with effect counters

counter of the attribute $@add$ is at least one, and if all values of the attribute $@del$ have an effect counter of at most 0. If the edge is a text, i.e., the attribute $@text$ has a value, we write this value in the XML Document. If the edge is visible and is not a text, we write the tag and the attributes corresponding to that edge. Therefore, we need to compute the current value of the attributes which is the newest non-undone value of a value list. Finally, the rendering function calls itself to treat the children of the edge.

Correctness. To ensure that our data type is a CRDT and thus that eventual consistency is ensured, we must prove all our operations commutes. For a complete proof, please see [10]. The only requirement to ensure consistency of the XML CRDT without undo is to receive delete operation after insert of a node. With undo, this constraint is not required to ensure consistency since a delete can be received before an insert. The delete produces directly a tombstone.

5 Garbage Collecting

Concerning the scalability in term of operations number, the XML CRDT without undo requires tombstones for attributes as the Thomas Write Rule defined in the RFC 677 [5].

The XML CRDT with undo requires to keep an information about every operation applied to the XML document. This is not surprising since any undo system must keep a trace of an operation that can be undone, either in the document model or in a history log.

However, a garbage collecting mechanism can be designed. Such a garbage collection is similar to the one already present in the RFC 667 [5]. Each replica i maintains a vector v_i of the last clock timestamp received by all other replicas (including its own clock). From this vector the replica computes m_i the minimum of these clocks. This minimum is sent regularly to the other replicas. It can be piggybacked to operation's messages or sent regularly in a specific message. From the minimum received (including its own), each replica maintains another vector V_i. The minimum of V_i is M_i. The point is that, if communication is FIFO, a replica knows that every replica has received all potential messages with a timestamp less or equal to M_i. Thus any tombstone with a timestamp less or equal to M_i can be safely removed. This mechanism can be directly used in the XML CRDT without undo to remove old deleted attributes.

In the XML CRDT with undo, we only authorize to produce an undo of an operation whose timestamp is greater than m_i. Thus operations with a timestamp lesser than M_i will never see their effect modified. So, elements such as follows can be safely and definitively purged :

- attribute value v with $v.timestamp < M_i$ and $v.effect \leq 0$
- attribute value v with $v.timestamp < M_i$ and there exists v' with $v.timestamp < v'.timestamp < M_i$ and $v'.effect > 0$
- attribute with no value or with every value v such that $v.timestamp < M_i$ and ($v.effect \leq 0$ or $v.value = nil$)
- edge with any delete value d with $d.timestamp < M_i$ and $d.effect > 0$ or with the add value a with $a.timestamp < M_i$ and $a.effect \leq 0$.

Thus, the time and space complexity of the approach is greatly reduced to be proportional to the size of the view. Moreover, differently to the RFC 677, replicas send $m_i - k$ with k a global constant instead of m_i. Thus, even if the replicas are tightly synchronized – having m_i very close to their own clock –, the replicas can always undo the last operations. Also, the garbage collecting mechanism that can be adapted to the other tombstone-based approach is much less scalable since based on a consensus-like method [7].

6 Conclusion

We have presented a commutative replicated data type that supports XML collaborative editing, including a global selective undo mechanism. Our commutative replicated data type is designed to scale since the replicas number never impacts the execution complexity. Obviously, the undo mechanism requires to keep information about the operations we allow to undo. We presented a garbage collection mechanism that allows to purge the old operations information.

We still have much work to achieve on this topic. Firstly, we need to make experiments to establish the actual scalability and efficiency of the approach in presence of huge data. Secondly, we plan to study replication of XML data typed with DTD or XSD. This is a difficult task, never achieved in a scalable way.

References

1. Abiteboul, S., Bonifati, A., Cobéna, G., Manolescu, I., Milo, T.: Dynamic xml documents with distribution and replication. In: SIGMOD 2003: Proceedings of the 2003 ACM SIGMOD International Conference on Management of Data, pp. 527–538. ACM, New York (2003)
2. Abowd, G.D., Dix, A.J.: Giving undo attention. Interacting with Computers 4(3), 317–342 (1992)
3. Choudhary, R., Dewan, P.: A general multi-user undo/redo model. In: ECSCW 1995: Proceedings of the Fourth Conference on European Conference on Computer-Supported Cooperative Work, Norwell, MA, USA, pp. 231–246. Kluwer Academic Publishers, Dordrecht (1995)
4. Ignat, C.-L., Oster, G.: Peer-to-peer collaboration over xml documents. In: Luo, Y. (ed.) CDVE 2008. LNCS, vol. 5220, pp. 66–73. Springer, Heidelberg (2008)
5. Johnson, P.R., Thomas, R.H.: RFC 677: Maintenance of duplicate databases (January 1975), `http://www.ietf.org/rfc/rfc677.txt` (September 2005)
6. Koloniari, G., Pitoura, E.: Peer-to-peer management of xml data: issues and research challenges. SIGMOD Rec. 34(2), 6–17 (2005)
7. Letia, M., Preguiça, N., Shapiro, M.: CRDTs: Consistency without concurrency control. In: SOSP W. on Large Scale Distributed Systems and Middleware (LADIS), Big Sky, MT, USA, pp. 29–34, SIGOPS, ACM (October 2009)
8. Lindholm, T.: Xml three-way merge as a reconciliation engine for mobile data. In: MobiDe 2003: Proceedings of the 3rd ACM international Workshop on Data Engineering for Wireless and Mobile Access, pp. 93–97. ACM, New York (2003)
9. Martin, S., Lugiez, D.: Collaborative peer to peer edition: Avoiding conflicts is better than solving conflicts. In: Weghorn, H., Isaías, P.T. (eds.) IADIS AC (2), pp. 124–128. IADIS Press (2009)
10. Martin, S., Urso, P., Weiss, S.: Scalable XML Collaborative Editing with Undo. Research Report RR-7362, INRIA (August 2010)
11. Oster, G., Urso, P., Molli, P., Imine, A.: Tombstone transformation functions for ensuring consistency in collaborative editing systems. In: The Second International Conference on Collaborative Computing: Networking, Applications and Worksharing (CollaborateCom 2006), Atlanta, Georgia, USA, November 2006, IEEE Press, Los Alamitos (2006)
12. Preguiça, N.M., Marquès, J.M., Shapiro, M., Letia, M.: A commutative replicated data type for cooperative editing. In: ICDCS, pp. 395–403. IEEE Computer Society, Los Alamitos (2009)
13. Ressel, M., Nitsche-Ruhland, D., Gunzenhäuser, R.: An integrating, transformation-oriented approach to concurrency control and undo in group editors. In: CSCW, pp. 288–297 (1996)
14. Saito, Y., Shapiro, M.: Optimistic replication. ACM Computing Surveys 37(1), 42–81 (2005)
15. Sun, D., Sun, C.: Operation Context and Context-based Operational Transformation. In: Proceedings of the ACM Conference on Computer-Supported Cooperative Work - CSCW 2006, Banff, Alberta, Canada, November 2006, pp. 279–288. ACM Press, New York (2006)
16. Weiss, S., Urso, P., Molli, P.: Logoot-Undo: Distributed Collaborative Editing System on P2P Networks. IEEE Trans. Parallel Distrib. Syst. 21(8), 1162–1174 (2010)

A Cooperative Approach to View Selection and Placement in P2P Systems
(Short Paper)

Zohra Bellahsene, Michelle Cart, and Nour Kadi

LIRMM - Université Montpellier 2
161 rue Ada 34095 Montpellier cedex 5, France
firstname.name@lirmm.fr

Abstract. P2P systems are becoming increasingly popular as they enable users to exchange digital information by participating in complex networks. However, limited work has been done on employing materialized views in P2P data warehousing systems. We argue that this technique can be applied in P2P data sharing for (i) saving work for frequently asked queries and (ii) increasing availability in cases of failures. In this paper, we present an approach for dynamically selecting an effective set of views to be materialized and place them in key points in the P2P system so as to achieve the best combination of good query performance and low view maintenance cost, given a limited amount of storage space at each peer. Moreover, as the system is dynamic, our approach continuously monitors the incoming query and adjusts the system configuration by removing materialized views in order to replace the less beneficial views with more beneficial ones.

1 Introduction

In data warehousing and cloud computing systems, the presence of appropriate materialized views can significantly improve query performance. The goal of view selection process is to find a set of views that minimizes the expected cost of evaluating the queries of the workload. Traditionally, view selection has been carried out statically. With static view selection, a system administrator decides what kinds of queries might be carried out in the system. Most of the proposed approaches are based on query workload and choose accordingly the set of views to materialize. Obviously, static selection of views has several weaknesses: (i) the query workload is often not predictable; (ii) even if the workload can be predicted, the workload is likely to change, and the workload might change so quickly that the system administrator cannot adjust the view selection quickly enough. Therefore, dynamic view selection approaches have been developed [6,7].

The view materialization issue in P2P setting can be seen as two sub-problems. First, the view selection problem is to choose an appropriate set of views to be materialized that can improve the performance of the system. Second, the data placement problem is to decide where these views should be placed on the peers so that the whole query workload can be executed in the fastest possible way. The specific contributions of our work are as follows.

R. Meersman et al. (Eds.): OTM 2010, Part I, LNCS 6426, pp. 515–522, 2010.

- A cost model for selecting the candidate views taking into account query processing cost, view maintenance cost and network transfer cost, all at once.
- A view method deciding which candidate views to materialise. In addition, it provides a strategy to replace materialized views by more beneficial ones in the case of reaching the storage limit in a peer.
- Two policies for the data placement problem; each one provides a degree of cooperation between the peers in a cluster: (i) Isolated Policy: places the views closest to where they are more frequently accessed (ii) Voluntary Policy: approximates an ideal policy by trying to make the loss of replacing the already materialized views minimal.

The rest of the paper is organized as follows. In Section 2 presents the problem of view selection problem in P2P context and a framework for representing the view queries in order to detect common sub-expressions. Section 3 contains the cost model used in our approach. Then, the strategy for selecting the views to be materialized is described in Section 4. In Section 5, two data placement policies are proposed. An overview of related work is presented in Section 6. Finally, Section 7 contains the conclusion and future work.

2 View Selection Problem in P2P Systems

A view is a derived relation defined by a query in terms of source relations and/or other views. It is said to be materialized when its extent is computed and persistently stored (otherwise, it is said to be virtual). We consider Selection-Projection-Join (SPJ) views that may involve aggregation and a group by clause as well. The general problem of view selection is to select a set of views to be materialized that optimizes both the view maintenance [8] and query processing time given some constraints like storage space. To find the optimal solution satisfying all constraints is a NP-complete problem, therefore it is necessary to develop heuristics.

In P2P systems, the problem can be formulated as follows. Assume a model containing N peer nodes, in which each node n_j has associated storage B_j and query workload $Q = \{Q_{j1}, Q_{j2}, \ldots, Q_{jk}\}$, that changes over time, where each query Q_{ji} has an associated non-negative weight f_{ji} which describes the frequency of Q_{ji}. Every pair of nodes ns and nt is connected by an edge with a cost $Ct(ns, nt)$ per unit of data transferred. The issue is to dynamically materialize a set of views $M = \{V_1, V_2, \ldots, V_m\}$ and place each of them at a proper node in order to provide high query performance time and low view maintenance cost of the entire system taking into account the space constraint and the cost transfer between the peers.

We will use the Multi View Materialization Graph (MVMG) framework as in our previous work [1] for representing views to be materialized in order to exhibit common sub-expressions between different queries. The MVMG, which is similar to the AND-OR DAG representation of queries in multi query optimization, is a bipartite Directed Acyclic Graph (DAG) composed of two types of nodes: AND nodes and OR nodes (i.e., operation and view nodes respectively). In fact, the MVMG represents AND-OR DAGs of several queries in a single DAG. In this work, the MVMG is built incrementally because the view selection method is applied as a query arrives. We borrow the rule provided in [9] for identifying common sub-expressions. For example, equivalent nodes, obtained after applying join associativity property, are replaced by a single equivalence node. In addition, we consider metadata like frequency at each node of the graph.

We assume that the data warehouse is organized along with XPeer architecture [2]. The nodes are grouped into clusters; at each cluster there is a super-peer, called cluster-peer, which has extra capabilities and duties in the network. It is in charge to take the decision for materializing the appropriate set of views, which will increase the performance of the peers within this cluster. Each cluster-peer acts as a centralized server to a subset of nodes in the cluster representing clients. It can be considered as a reference for its clients as it keeps a full repository about all the materialized views at each peer in the cluster and it is the responsible for the configuration, and administration of the materialized views in its clients. Our approach consists in continuously monitoring the incoming queries at any peer of the cluster and adjusting the system configuration in order to maximize query performance at the peers of the cluster. Our method proceeds in three steps, as follows:

- Select candidate views for materialization.
- Decide which views to materialize or dematerialize.
- Place the materialized views on the appropriate peers.

3 Cost Analysis of View Selection Strategy

As mentioned earlier, a MVMG is used for modeling the workload of the entire cluster. We present the following definition for the MVMG at the cluster c.

- For any leaf node r which represents a base relation, $f_u(r)$ denotes the update frequency of r.
- For any root node q which represents a global query, $f_{p_i}(q)$ denotes the query access frequency of the query q at the peer p_i which belongs to cluster c.

The frequency of a query q, $f(q)$, at all peers within the cluster is computed as follows:

$$f(q) = \sum_{p_i \in cp} f_{p_i}(q)$$

where cp is the set of all peers in cluster c.

3.1 Cost Model

For every vertex v in the MVMG

- $C_m(v)$ denotes the view maintenance cost of v based on changes to the base relation r if v is materialized. Here, we consider the incremental maintenance, so $C_m(v)$ represents the cost of computing the differential from the data origin plus the cost of transferring it to the specified cluster.
- $C_e(v)$ denotes the cost of computing v in its data origin. It is the average cost processing time.
- $C_n(p_i \rightarrow p_j)$ denotes the network transfer cost. It is the cost per unit of data transferred for the edge between two peers p_i, p_j.

- $C_t(v, p_i \rightarrow sp)$ denotes the total cost to get v from its data origin p_i to the cluster-peer sp. It includes the processing and transfer costs. Finally, we have:

$$C_t(v, p_i \rightarrow sp) = C_e(v) + C_n(p_i \rightarrow sp) * size(v)$$

where $size(v)$ denotes estimated size of materialized view v.

3.2 Criteria of Selection

The cluster-peer assigns a value, called *goodness(v)* for each view v in MVMG. This goodness represents the cost for materializing the view at the cluster. Obviously, if the view is expensive to compute or is frequently used then it is more beneficial to keep it locally. On the other hand, if the view is frequently updated then materializing this view becomes less attractive especially if the maintenance cost is relatively high. Let $CS(v)$ be the saving if view v is materialized and let $CM(v)$ be the view maintenance cost according to the update frequency.

- $CS(v) = \sum_{q \in Q_v} f(q) * C_t(v, p_i \rightarrow sp)$
- $CM(v) = \sum_{r \in Iv} f_u(r) * C_m(v)$
  where Q_v denotes the set of queries that use view v and I_v denotes the base relation instances, which are used to produce v.

Then, the following formula calculates the goodness of view v:

$$goodness(v) = CS(v) - CM(v)$$

4 View Selection Strategy

Pre-Selection. A first phase of selection on views is performed to eliminate the views that provide no benefit. A view is considered as beneficial if and only if its materialization reduces significantly the query processing cost without increasing significantly the view maintenance cost. The first step of our approach pre-selects a set of views called candidate views V_C from the set of views from the view query. These views should be the most beneficial views for the peers of the specified cluster and are computed by the following formulae:

$$goodness(V_C) = \sum_{v \in V_C} goodness(v, V_C) \text{ be maximal} \qquad (1)$$

$$\mid V_C \mid \text{ be minimal}$$

Final Selection. As mentioned earlier, the candidate views returned from the first phase are promising for materialization, but they will not be materialized by default because we have given a limited amount of storage space. Therefore, any candidate view will be materialized if it is beneficial enough to the peers of the cluster. Now, suppose that the candidate v will be materialized in the peer p_j. If p_j has enough space to store v_i, then it will be materialized at p_j immediately. However, if the storage limit at p_j is reached, then v_i will be materialized only if it proofs to be more beneficial than those which are already materialized. In this case, the views with less benefit should be removed to free the necessary space for materializing the new candidate. Otherwise, the candidate view will be ignored.

The final decision to materialize view v is based on the notion of benefit.

$$Benefit(v) = goodness(v) - goodness(V^-)$$

where V^- is the set of already materialized views to be removed in order to free the necessary storage space.

The replacement strategy will be applied at any peer to calculate the benefit of the candidate v_{new} over the views that are already materialized at that peer. At the first, it will select all materialized views at certain peer with lower goodness value than v_{new}, and adds these views to the set of candidate (for removal) views V_c^-. Finding the set of views to be removed is formed by solving an instance of the KNAPSACK problem. Given the set of objects in V_c^-, the size of the storage space s_{max}, knapsack will find the views with highest goodness to remain materialized. The rest of views V^- will be removed from peer p in order to free enough space to materialize v_{new} according to the following formulas:

$$size(V^-) + freespace > size(v_{new})$$

$$goodness(V^-) < goodness(v_{new})$$

5 View Placement Policy

In this section, we present two policies for where to materialize each candidate view; each policy defines a degree of cooperation between the cluster peers. However, both have the same goal, which is getting better performance with lower traffic between the cluster peers.

5.1 Isolated Policy

The principle of the Isolated Policy is that the cluster-peer tries to solve the problem of each peer in the cluster separately without using the capabilities of the other peers within the cluster. In the case where there is not enough space in this peer, it will not use the free resources on the other peers but instead the replacement policy will be used to free enough space in that peer in order to store the new candidate view if it is more beneficial. For each candidate view, the cluster-peer will find the peer that uses this view more frequently. The candidate view will be materialized at that peer if it has enough space. However, if this peer reaches the storage limit, then the candidate view will be materialized only if it is more beneficial than the already materialized views in that peer. The Isolated Policy strategy is divided into two phases:

Phase 1: While there is enough storage space at a peer, the candidate views will be materialized.

Phase 2: If the storage limit in is reached, a candidate view will be materialized only if its benefit is positive. In this case, the views in V^- will be removed to free enough space to store v_{new}.

5.2 Voluntary Policy

In contrast to Isolated Policy, Voluntary Policy attempts to exploit under-utilized resources (e.g., storage space) that may exist in some neighbor peers and at the same time avoid wasting any view that has been materialized. Assume that we want to materialize the candidate v_{new}. The cluster-peer will find the peer that has the maximum frequency in using v_{new} and at the same time has enough space to materialize it. However, in the case where all the peers in the cluster reach the storage limit, then the cluster-peer will select the peer that provides the highest benefit with the lowest transfer cost for materializing v_{new}.

The strategy of Voluntary Policy is divided into two phases:

Phase 1: Try to store the new candidate v_{new} without loosing any already materialized view by finding the peers at the cluster that have enough free space to store v_{new} then select the one that has the highest frequency in using v_{new}.

Phase 2: In the case where not enough space is found at any peer in the cluster, therefore it is necessary to remove some already materialized views. In order to reduce the loss of removing already materialized views in the cluster, the set of views to be removed which are the least beneficial views to all the peers in the cluster, should be computed. For that, the cluster-peer chooses the peer associated with the maximum value of $BenPeer$. If this value is positive then the candidate v_{new} will be stored in that peer after removing the less beneficial view V^- specified by the replacement strategy. The criteria for selecting the peer is based on the value of the following expression:

$$BenPeer_{p_i} = \frac{b_i}{C_n(sp \rightarrow p_j)}$$

The first term of this formula b_i represents the benefit of materializing the candidate view v_{new} versus the loss of removing the already materialized views at the peer p_i. The second term $C_n(sp \rightarrow p_j)$ represents the cost of transferring v_{new} from the cluster-peer to p_i.

6 Related Work

6.1 Dynamic View Selection in Data Warehousing

DynaMat [7] is a system aimed to unify the view selection and the view maintenance problems. The principle of this system is monitoring constantly the incoming queries and materializing their query results given the space constraint. During the update only the most beneficial subset of materialized views is refreshed within a given maintenance window. However, Dynamat approach does not use any framework to detect common views between queries for reuse purpose.

The dynamic data warehouse design is modeled as search space problem in [11]. Rules for pruning the search space are proposed. The first rule relies on favoring the query rewriting that uses views already materialized. The second one modifies the previous rule to favor common sub-expression. However, the proposed view selection algorithm is still in exponential time. Besides, neither implementation nor evaluation of the method have been performed.

Another dynamic approach presented in [10] provides a solution for materializing the indexes which can be seen as a special case of the materialized views. The authors introduce a novel self-tuning framework that continuously monitors the incoming queries and adjusts the system configuration in order to maximize query performance. This approach doesn't react to temporary variations of the query distribution but focus on real changes of the workload. Comparing with our design, we have achieved this feature simply by taking into account the frequency of the view to compute its goodness when taking the decision of materializing it.

6.2 Caching in Distributed Database Systems

An approach, called cache investment is proposed in [5] for integrating query optimization and data placement that looks beyond the performance of a single query. The goal of this study is to place copies of data closest to where they will most likely be accessed. The authors demonstrate that there is circular dependency between caching and query plan optimization which has significant performance implications for advanced distributed database systems. The main difference is that in our approach it is not necessary to materialize the view in the same site where the query has been posed, because we take into account the cooperation between the sites to avoid wasting already materialized as much as possible. However, this point is ignored in this paper [5] as they assume the client-server architecture without any cooperation between the clients in order to invest their cache together.

6.3 Caching and Data Placement in P2P Context

The caching system presented in [4] addresses the problem of PeerOLAP architecture where a large number of peers access sporadically a number of separate data warehouses for posing On-Line Analytical Processing queries. When any query arrives at a peer p, first it is decomposed into chunks. Then, peer p tries to find some chunks locally and will broadcast a demand of the missing chunks to its neighbors. We can see from this scenario that a lot of messages would pass through the network in order to find the answer of a query. In our design we avoid this problem by using the materialized information stored as an entire view and employing the cluster-peer at each cluster which keeps a repository of the entire materialized view at the peers of the cluster.

In Piazza [3], each peer can have any of the following four roles: data origin which provides the original content, storage provider which stores materialized views, query evaluator which uses its CPU resources to evaluate a query and query initiator which poses new queries to the system. Piazza deals primarily with the data placement problem which is to distribute data and work so the full query workload is answered with lowest cost under the existing resource and bandwidth constraints. In Piazza, the data placement problem is solved by separating logically the system into smaller spheres of cooperation and advertising the set of materialized views to all the nodes of a sphere. All peer nodes that belong to the same spheres pool their resources and make cooperative decisions. In our design we avoid this advertisement by employing the cluster-peer at the cluster "sphere" so each peer has to send its catalogue only to its cluster-peer.

7 Conclusion and Future Work

In this paper, we propose a method, which decides dynamically for a given query which views, called candidates, are worthwhile to be materialized taking into account query processing cost, maintenance cost and network transfer cost. We solved the data placement problem by designing two policies: the Isolated and Voluntary policies. Each policy provides a dynamic approach for placing each candidate view. The Isolated policy was motivated by replacement policies for storage management at a peer that records the highest frequency usage of a candidate view. The Voluntary policy was designed to approximate an ideal policy by trying to make the loss of replacing the already materialized views to be minimal. This policy applies the replacement policy for all the peers within a cluster then chooses to materialize the candidate views at the peer that provides the highest benefit.

References

1. Baril, X., Bellahsene, Z.: Selection of materialized views: a cost-based approach. In: Eder, J., Missikoff, M. (eds.) CAiSE 2003. LNCS, vol. 2681. Springer, Heidelberg (2003)
2. Bellahsene, Z., Roantree, M.: Querying distributed data in a super-peer based architecture. In: Galindo, F., Takizawa, M., Traunmüller, R. (eds.) DEXA 2004. LNCS, vol. 3180, pp. 296–305. Springer, Heidelberg (2004)
3. Gribble, S., Halevy, A., Ives, Z., Rodrig, M., Suciu, D.: What Can Databases do for Peer-to-Peer. In: WebDB Workshop on Databases and the Web (June 2001)
4. Kalnis, P., Ng, W.S., Ooi, B.C., Papadias, D., Tan, K.: An Adaptive Peer-to-Peer Network for Distributed Caching of OLAP Results. In: Proceeding of the International Conference on Management of Data, SIGMOD, Madison, WI, pp. 25–36 (2002)
5. Kossmann, D.: The State of the art in distributed query processingt. Journal of ACM Computing Surveys 32(4), 422–469 (2000)
6. Kotidis, Y., Roussopoulos, N.: DynaMat: A Dynamic View Management System for Data Warehouses. In: Proceeding of the International Conference on Management of Data, SIGMOD, Philadelphia, USA (1999)
7. Kotidis, Y., Roussopoulos, N.: A case for dynamic view management. Journal of ACM Trans. Database Syst 26(4), 388–423 (2001)
8. Roussopoulos, N.: Materialized Views and Data Warehouses. ACM SIGMOD Record 27(1) (March 1998)
9. Roy, P., Seshadri, S., Sudarshan, S., Siddhesh, B.: Efficient and Extensible Algorithms for Multiquery Optimization. In: Proceeding of the International Conference on Management of Data, SIGMOD, San Diego, USA (2000)
10. Schnaitter, K., Abiteboul, S., Milo, T., Polyzotis, N.: Colt -continuous online database tuning. In: Proceeding of the International Conference on Management of Data, SIGMOD (2006)
11. Theodoratos, D., Sellis, T.: Incremental Design. Journal of Intelligent Information Systems 15, 7–27 (2000)

Satisfaction and Coherence of Deadline Constraints in Inter-Organizational Workflows

Mouna Makni[1,2], Samir Tata[1], Moez Yeddes[3], and Nejib Ben Hadj-Alouane[2]

[1] Institut TELECOM, TELECOM SudParis, UMR CNRS Samovar, France
{Mouna.Makni,Samir.Tata}@it-sudparis.eu
[2] National Engineering School of Tunis, OASIS Laboratory, Tunisia
nejib_bha@yahoo.com
[3] National School of Computer Sciences, CRISTAL Laboratory, Tunisia
yeddes@yahoo.fr

Abstract. The integration of time constraints in Inter-Organizational Workflows (IOWs) is an important issue in the workflow research field. Since each partner exposes a limited version of his business process, some information is kept hidden and not visible to all partners. The inter-enterprise business process, however, is obtained by joining all activities and control flows that have relevant roles within the context of the global operation. It should be noted that this composition process does not intrinsically guarantee the satisfaction of any critical deadline constraints that may be imposed by the partners. Obviously, expressing and satisfying time deadlines is important for modern business processes that need to be optimized for efficiency and extreme competitiveness. In this paper, we propose a temporal extension to CoopFlow, an existing approach for designing and modeling IOW, based on Time Petri Net models. A method for expressing and publishing sensible time deadlines, by the partners, is given. We also give a systematic method assuring the verification and the consistency of the published time constraints within the context of the global business process, while maintaining the core advantage of CoopFlow, that each partner can keep the critical part of his business process private.

Keywords: Inter-Organizational, Workflows, Time modeling, Deadline constraints, Time Petri Net.

1 Introduction

The design of complex inter-enterprise business processes plays a significant role in facing ever increasing industrial competition and pressures. In this new modern environment, it is important for business partners to rapidly join forces in order to create new and valuable expertise with cheaper costs and within restrictive deadlines. A short-term cooperation within virtual enterprises allows dynamic interconnection of a set of partners with complementary skills according to their needs. A virtual environment, within which companies can effectively engage each other, must fulfill some requirements. In fact, the basic supposition of a proper virtual environment is that the description of the business processes of the partners are well advertised and readily available in a common registry. A challenging issue is the preservation of industrial privacy [1,2],

R. Meersman et al. (Eds.): OTM 2010, Part I, LNCS 6426, pp. 523–539, 2010.

especially within the context of occasional collaborations, where there are serious consequences for companies fully exposing their business knowledge. Thus, abstraction is a first step used prior to advertising, and consists of eliminating details that are not absolutely necessary for cooperation needs. The next step is matching [15], which consists of identifying and selecting the appropriate partners able to provide the required services.

Within the above context, the CoopFlow approach is designed to support short-term ascending workflow cooperation within virtual enterprises, using the publish/subscribe paradigm. We have already presented the basic ideas of the CoopFlow approach and compared it with existing approaches for workflow cooperation [15]. So far, in CoopFlow, the focus has been on the structural conformance of the processes of the partners; i.e. the partners which execute complementary tasks can properly interconnect within an Inter-Organizational Workflow (IOW) structure. In this paper, we undertake the new important concern of ensuring that the timing constraints and/or expectations of the involved partners are also compatible. With regards to functional requirements, it should be noted that workflow behaviors are typically closely tied to the timing requirements. Therefore, enterprises, which are looking for cost reductions, should strive to include timing requirements early on, as part of their workflow matching process. Our purpose is to provide a time-oriented inter-organizational workflow modeling and management framework, within the context of CoopFlow. Such a framework will enable enterprises to specify temporal constraints and detect, early on, temporal contradictions that may constitute obstacles towards their cooperation, while maintaining the main advantage, that each partner can keep the critical aspects of its business process private.

Within CoopFlow, workflows are modeled using Petri Nets; we propose an extension based on Time Petri Net models and tools, for modeling temporal constraints and computing responses times. Given an abstracted version of its business process, a company should add temporal expectations for actions that will be performed by external parties, i.e., time durations after which supplied services cannot be performed anymore. On the other side, potential partners will be able to capture temporal requirements as well as business behaviors from the common registry, in order to execute, locally, temporal reasoning and verification. The running example given in this article details our approach for a deadline constraint calculation and verification in the case of a request-response pair of transitions. **Results of our work guarantee that verifying the satisfaction of the relevant deadlines, locally by each partner, leads to the temporal conformance of all deadlines within the global IOW.** This paper does not discuss all the aspects that are relevant to identifying whether two workflows can cooperate without violating timing constraints. For example, we do not deal with all possible interaction patterns between two or more candidates and we do not consider realistic timing aspect such as stochastic and probabilistic aspects.

This paper is organized as follows. Section 2 presents the necessary background from Petri Nets, Time Petri Nets and CoopFlow that is needed to understand our work. Section 3 presents the basic concepts for workflow modeling within the context of our timed extension to CoopFlow. Section 4 details our approach, based on a class of Time Petri Nets, for computing, modeling and advertising timing constraints. Section 5 presents a method relying on local partner verification, while guaranteeing the satisfaction of all the timing constraints (deadlines) within the global IOW. Section 6 concludes this paper and presents the future work.

2 Background and Preliminaries

CoopFlow uses the Petri Net formalism in order to provide powerful workflow analysis and validation techniques. In the present work, we focus on a class of Petri Nets (PNs), which we call acyclic Petri Nets (APNs), for workflow modeling. In order to incorporate timing behaviors and constraints within CoopFlow, we adopt Time Petri Nets (TPNs) which is an important time extension to PNs proposed by Merlin [13]. Temporal information, in TPNs, is defined by an interval associated with each transition, referring to its firing time limits. In this section we first recall the definition and the basic notions of Petri Nets and Time Petri Nets that are useful for our work.

2.1 Preliminaries from Petri Nets and Time Petri Nets

In this subsection, we recall relevant basic notions from Petri Nets and Time Petri Nets. We also define acyclic PNs, a sub-class of Petri Nets, which we rely on to develop our results. A Petri Net is formally defined as follows.

Definition 1 (Petri Nets). *Let P and T be disjoint sets of places and transitions, respectively; the elements of $P \bigcup T$ are called nodes. A Petri Net is a tuple $\langle P, T, Pre, Post\rangle$ with the backward and forward incidence matrices, Pre and Post, defined as Pre (respectively Post) : $P \times T \rightarrow \mathbb{N}$. We denote by $Pre(a)$ (respectively $Post(a)$) the column vector indexed by a of the matrix Pre (respectively Post).*

The preset of a place p (respectively a transition a) is defined as ${}^\bullet p = \{a \in T \text{ s.t. } Post(p,a) > 0\}$ (respectively ${}^\bullet a = \{p \in P \text{ s.t. } Pre(p,a) > 0\}$, and the postset is given as $p^\bullet = \{a \in T \text{ s.t. } Pre(p,a) > 0\}$ (respectively $a^\bullet = \{p \in P \text{ s.t. } Post(p,a) > 0\}$).

In the following, we first define the marking and the transition enabling mechanisms according to the Petri Net theory. Then we present the Petri Net language definition.

Definition 2 (Petri Net marking). *A marking of a PN is a mapping $P \rightarrow \mathbb{N}$. We call $\langle PN, M_0\rangle$ a system with initial marking M_0 for a PN. A marking M enables the transition a, which is denoted $M \xrightarrow{a}$, if $M(p) \geq Pre(p,a) \forall_{p \in {}^\bullet a}$. In this case the transition can occur, leading to the new marking M' that is given by $M' = M - Pre(a) + Post(a)$. We denote this occurrence by $M \xrightarrow{a} M'$. If there exists a chain $M_0 \xrightarrow{a_1} M_1 \xrightarrow{a_2} M_2 \xrightarrow{a_3} \ldots \xrightarrow{a_n} M_n$, denoted by $M_0 \xrightarrow{\omega} M_n$, the sequence $\omega = a_1 \ldots a_n$ is also called a computation. The marking M_0 enables the computation ω (denoted $M_0 \xrightarrow{\omega}$).*

Definition 3 (Petri Net language). *We denote by T^* the set of finite sequences of T, the set of transitions of PN. The language of the marking Peti Net $\langle PN, M_0\rangle$ is the set $L(\langle PN, M_0\rangle) = \{\omega \in T^* \mid M_0 \xrightarrow{\omega}\}$.*

In the following, we define a sub-class of Petri Nets without loops or cycles, which we call acyclic Petri Nets (APNs).

Definition 4 (Acyclic PN). *An APN is a PN* $= \langle P,T,Pre,Post\rangle$*, such that for any given computation of the language* $\omega = a_1a_2...a_n$*, it generates, using any possible initial marking, each activity or transition* $a_i \in T\ \forall_{1<i<n}$ *can appear at most once in* ω*.*
From a structural perspective, it is easiest to see an APN as a graph with a particular ordering such that a place (respectively a transition) can only be connected to transitions (respectively places) that follow it (or are placed after it).

We define Time Petri Nets as follows [14,13].

Definition 5 (Time Petri Net). *A TPN is a tuple* $\langle P,T,Pre,Post,M_0,S\rangle$ *where:*

- $\langle\langle P,T,Pre,Post\rangle,M_0\rangle$ *is a Petri Net with initial marking* M_0*;*
- $S : T \rightarrow \mathbb{Q}^+ \times (\mathbb{Q}^+ \cup \infty)$ *is a static time interval to transition mapping.*

A Time Petri Net model associates with each transition $a \in T$ *a static time interval* $S(a) = [tmin(a), tmax(a)]$*. Assuming that* τ *is the latest time instant when the transition* a *becomes enabled (i.e.,* $M > Pre(a)$*), then* $[\tau + tmin(a), \tau + tmax(a)]$ *is the time range for firing the transition* a*, on the exception that* a *is disabled by firing another conflicting transition at a prior time. We call* $tmin(a)$ *and* $tmax(a)$*, respectively, the earliest* (EFT) *and latest* (LFT) *possible firing times. A clock is associated to each validated transition to keep track of the elapsed time until its firing date. The transition* a *remains enabled at least* $tmin(a)$ *time units, and at most* $tmax(a)$ *time units before its firing. Firing a transition is instantaneous and modifies the marking in a regular PN.*

The corresponding semantic of a Time Petri Net is defined as follows.

Definition 6 (Semantics of a TPN). *The behavior of a TPN can be defined by a timed language of the possible firing sequences of pairs,* (a,τ)*, where* a *is a transition of the TPN and* $\tau \in \mathbb{Q}^+$*. Then, a sequence of transitions* $\omega = (a_1,\tau_1)(a_2,\tau_2)...(a_n,\tau_n)$ *indicates that each* a_i *in this sequence is fired at absolute time* τ_i*, with* $\tau_1 < \tau_2 < ... < \tau_n$*. A marking* M *is reachable in a TPN iff there is a timed firing sequence* ω*, leading from the initial marking* M_0 *to* M*; we denote this by* $M_0 \xrightarrow{\omega} M$*. The untimed sequence derived from the timed* $\omega = (a_1,\tau_1)(a_2,\tau_2)...(a_n,\tau_n)$ *is* $untimed(\omega) = a_1a_2...a_n$*.*

In the following, we give an overview of the basic workflow modeling concepts enabling a timed extension to the CoopFlow approach.

2.2 CoopFlow Basic Modeling Concepts

In this subsection we present basic workflow modeling concepts from CoopFlow and introduce our new temporal information modeling technique. In this work, we focus on a sub-class of well-structured workflow nets (WF-Nets) that are also acyclic. Temporal behavior is added in accordance to the Time Petri Net (TPN) formalism. To introduce the well-structured WF-Nets defined in [17], we start by recalling some definitions.

Definition 7 (Wf-Nets). *A Petri Net* $PN = \langle P,T,Pre,Post\rangle$ *is said to be a Wf-Net if:*

- *there is one source place* $p_i \in P$ *s.t.* $^\bullet p_i = \emptyset$ *and one sink place* $p_o \in P$ *s.t.* $p_o{}^\bullet = \emptyset$*;*
- *every node* $x \in P \bigcup T$ *is on a path from* p_i *to* p_o*.*

From a behavioral perspective, a WF-Net is associated with an initial marking, such that, only the source place is marked with a single token.

Definition 8 (Path, elementary, alphabet). *Let PN be a Petri net. A path C from a node n_1 to a node n_k is a sequence $\langle n_1, n_2, ..., n_k \rangle$ such that $\langle n_i, n_{i+1} \rangle \in Pre$ $\forall_{1 \leq i \leq k-1}$. $\alpha(C) = \{n_1, n_2, ..., n_k\}$ is the alphabet of C. C is elementary iff for any two nodes n_i and n_j on C, $i \neq j \Rightarrow n_i \neq n_j$.*

Definition 9 (Well-structured Workflow). *A WF-net PN is well-structured iff PN satisfies the following property: for any pair of nodes x and y such that one of the nodes is a place and the other a transition and for any pair of elementary paths C_1 and C_2 leading from x to y, $\alpha(C_1) \bigcap \alpha(C_2) = \{x, y\} \Rightarrow C_1 = C_2$.*

Informally, a well-structured workflow can be composed inductively based on four workflow patterns: sequences, alternative structure (Or join/split), parallel structure (And join/split) and structured loop [17].

Assumption 1. *In our work, we exclude cycles and repetition mechanisms. Hence, we focus only on a sub-class of well-structured WF-Nets that can be captured by acyclic PNs as defined below.*

In the timed extension of CoopFlow, we assume that each partner holds locally two versions of his business process, giving both structural and temporal information. Each workflow is also composed of two types of transitions, defined as follows.

Definition 10 (Private Workflow PWF and Private Temporal Workflow PTWF). *Each partner holds locally a business process called Private Workflow (PWF), which is a well-structured Wf-Net captured by an $APN = \langle P, T, Pre, Post \rangle$, and associated to an initial marking M_0, such that only the source node contains a single token. The temporal behavior is added by a mapping function giving firing time limits for each transition $a \in T$. Thus, the corresponding Private Temporal Workflow (PTWF) is defined by the $TPN = \langle P, T, Pre, Post, M_0, S \rangle$, s.t., S is the added set of timing intervals.*

Definition 11 (Cooperative vs local activities). *Consider a PTWF captured by an $APN = \langle P, T, Pre, Post \rangle$. We distinguish two types of transitions from T: cooperative transitions that interact with others in the global IOW, denoted Coop, and local transitions that perform local actions, denoted Loc. We assume that $Coop \bigcup Loc = T$ and $Coop \bigcap Loc = \phi$.*

Each cooperative transition a is represented by a tuple $a =< name, type, dataflow >$, s.t.,

- *a.name is the name attribute of a;*
- *a.type, is a Boolean variable that specifies whether a is supposed to receive a dataflow ($type = true$) or to send a dataflow ($type = false$);*
- *a.dataflow, represents the description of business semantics of a, according to a semantic model.*

An inter-organizational workflow can be considered as the collaboration of several workflows. In order to set up a cooperation while preserving privacy, workflows have to be abstracted, i.e, local activities have to be hidden. The abstraction process, defined in CoopFlow [11,4], produces a reduced version of the PWF, denoted Abstracted workflow (AF), which will be advertised into a registry to be found and interconnected to partners.

Example. Consider *Partner*1 and *Partner*2, two candidates for a cooperation, whose PTWF are illustrated respectively in figure 1(a) and 1(b). The filled transitions represent cooperative transitions, while the others are local activities which are hidden following the abstraction process. The corresponding abstracted workflows AF_1 and AF_2, are illustrated respectively in 2(a) and 2(b) and do not contain any temporal information.

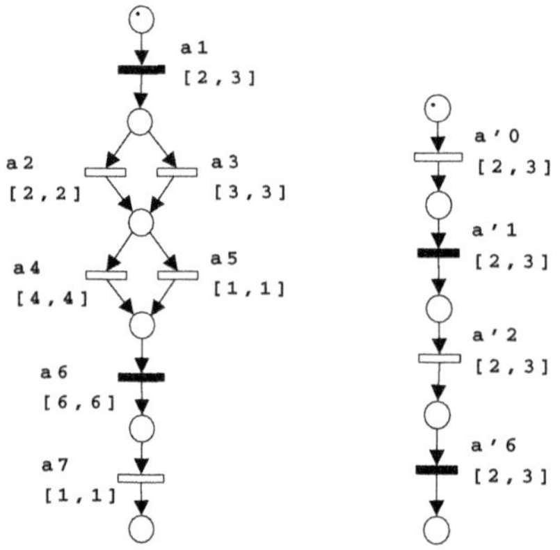

(a) $(PTWF_1)$ (b) $(PTWF_2)$

Fig. 1. The PTWF of *Partner*1 and *Partner*2

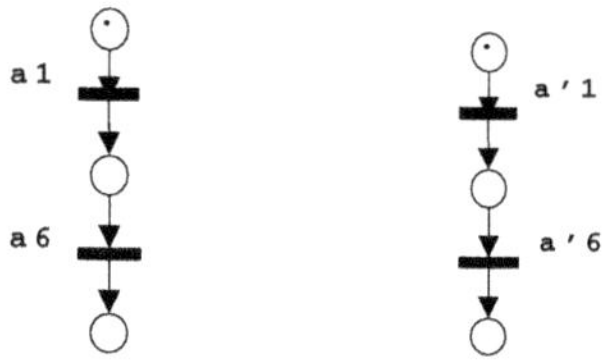

(a) (AF_1) (b) (AF_2)

Fig. 2. The *AF* of *Partner*1 and *Partner*2

The selection criteria making a choice of an effective partner is based on the observable behavior, i.e., behavior on the cooperative activities. Two cooperative transitions are considered equivalent according to their business semantics, denoted by $\sim$, if they are described using references to equivalent concepts in a semantic model [15]. In the example above, AF_1 and AF_2 are validated to be coherent following the matching process, i.e. $a_1 \backsim a'1$ and $a_6 \sim a'_6$.

The previous work concentrates on the structural conformance validation and does not guarantee the satisfaction of any temporal requirements that may be imposed by the partners. In the next section, we state this problem on the running example and present our temporal information modeling technique.

3 Deadline Constraints Modeling and Advertisement

With regards to the urgency of some critical cooperative activities, we suggest that partners specify pre-computed deadlines for their critical supplied tasks, i.e. the maximum runtime delay to monitor urgent tasks. These deadline constraints should be advertised to the potential candidates as well as the business behavior.

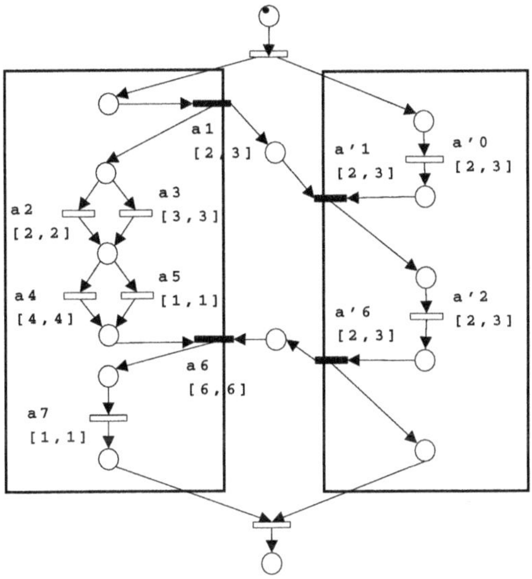

Fig. 3. The IOW resulted by *Partner*1 and *Partner*2 cooperation

Example. Figure 3 illustrates the global IOW defined following the successful matching process between *Partner*1 and *Partner*2. Even if the matching procedure validates the structural conformance of the partners, we expect that some global properties are not satisfied in the IOW. For instance deadlines constraints can be violated if all participating enterprises do not respect their allowed temporal bounds for delivering the invoked services. Consider a situation in which *Partner*1 specifies that the required service delivery (i.e. transition a_6 firing) should not exceed a specified time since the order is sent (i.e. transition a_1 firing). Abstracted workflows do not contain enough information to ensure that timing constraints of the involved partners are also compatible.

Our approach consists of adding to the abstracted representation temporal constraints between critical transitions. In this article, we focus on calculating and verifying a deadline constraint for a pair of request-response transitions which will interact with others in the global IOW in order to externalize a specified service. This is specified by the following assumption.

Assumption 2. *Let* $PTWF = \langle P,T,Pre,Post,M_0,S\rangle$ *a temporal private workflow, and the corresponding PWF is a well-structured Wf-Net that can be captured by an acyclic PN. A deadline constraint can be added between two cooperative activities* $a_i \in T$ *and* $a_j \in T$ *iff:*

- a_i *simulates a request event and* a_j *a response event, which will interact with the same partner in the global IOW, i.e.* $a_i.type = false$ *and* $a_j.type = true$*;*
- a_i *and* a_j *are two successive cooperative activities, i.e.* $\forall \omega \in L(TPWF)$*, if* $a_i, a_j \in \omega$ *then* $untimed(\omega) = \omega_i a_i \omega_l a_j \omega_j$*, s.t.,* ω_l *is a sequence formed only by local activities.*

Our idea is based on the propagation of local time constraints to the shared view, which enables partners to capture timing requirements and to check their consistency locally, and thus the temporal conformance can be achieved while preserving the partner's privacy. In the following, we present the proposed methods for calculating, modeling and advertising the deadlines constraints.

The first step consists of specifying a deadline constraint to limit, for an potential candidate, the elapsed time from the instant a service request is sent (modeled by firing transition a_i) and its delivery (modeled by transition a_j firing). In order to achieve this goal, we begin by giving a method for determining maximal execution times between the occurrence of the two critical cooperative activities a_i and a_j, denoted $Max(a_i,a_j)$. Consider the two marking states M_i and M_j, such that M_i is reached after the firing of the cooperative transition a_i (at absolute time τ_i) and M_j is reached after the firing of the cooperative transition a_j (at absolute time τ_j).

We assume that, in M_i, $\forall_{p_k \in a_i\bullet}$, $M(p_k) = 1$, and, in M_j, $\forall_{p_k \in a_j\bullet}$, $M(p_k) = 1$. The following proposition characterizes the maximum execution time between the considered cooperative transitions.

Proposition 1 (Maximum execution time). *The Maximum execution time incurred along the possible paths joining marking* M_i *and* M_j*, denoted* $Max(a_i,a_j)$*, is computed by maximizing the total* LFT *(see Definition 5) incurred along every path over all possible trajectories, such that* $\tau_j - \tau_i \leq Max(a_i,a_j)$.

Let $L_{a_i a_j} = \{w \ s.t. \ w = (a_{i+1},\tau_{i+1})(a_{i+2},\tau_{i+2})...(a_{j-1},\tau_{j-1})(a_j,\tau_j)\}$ be the set of all possible timed firing sequences that takes the workflow from M_i to M_j i.e. the set of possible runs from a_i firing time τ_i to a_j firing time τ_j. $Max(a_i,a_j)$ is determined by maximizing $Tmax(w) \ \forall_{w \in L_{a_i a_j}}$ defined as

$Tmax(w) = \sum_{k=i+1}^{j} tmax(a_k) \ \forall_{w \in L_{a_i a_j}}$ (since we consider the workflow after firing the transition a_i, we do not consider $(tmax(a_i))$.

Proof. This property is obvious from the structure of the PNs considered. As we have limited the subset of well-structured WF-Nets to acyclic PNs, we can enumerate all the possible paths joining the considered marking M_i and M_j, that should not contain any cycle. Consider the system from a_i firing instant, i.e. from τ_i absolute time. Consider two transitions a_k and a_{k+1} successively fired in the timed sequence ω. Since a_{k+1} is validated by the occurrence of transition a_k, we have the following inequalities system. $\tau_{k+1} \leq \tau_k + tmax(a_{k+1})\ \forall_{i \leq k \leq j-1}$

Then $\tau_j - \tau_i$ is characterized as follows $\forall_{\omega \in L_{a_i a_j}}, \tau_j - \tau_i \leq \sum_{k=i+1}^{j} tmax(a_k)$. This is also defined by $\forall_{\omega \in L_{a_i a_j}}, \tau_j - \tau_i \leq Tmax(\omega)$.

As $Max(a_i, a_j)$ maximizes $Tmax(\omega)\ \forall_{\omega \in L_{a_i a_j}}$, we affirm that $\tau_j - \tau_i \leq Max(a_i, a_j)$.

Now, we can specify a deadline parameter, denoted $D_{a_i a_j}$, which constrains the allowed time distance between the occurrence of a_i and a_j and should be greater than the maximum execution time between a_i and a_j, denoted $Max(a_i, a_j)$. Let C_{Coop} be a constant specified by the PWF workflow designer to give the potential partner extended time to deliver the required service, then $D_{a_i a_j} = Max(a_i, a_j) + C_{Coop}$.

Example (Deadline constraint specification for Partner1). Assuming that *Partner*1 (see figure 1(a)) is searching for a cooperation candidate. Cooperative activities are $a1$ and $a6$. *Partner*1 aims at specifying a deadline constraint for these activities. Let's calculate $Max(a1, a6)$.

$L_{a_1 a_6} = \{(a_2, \tau_2)(a_4, \tau_4)(a_6, \tau_6), (a_2, \tau_2)(a_5, \tau_5)(a_6, \tau_6), (a_3, \tau_3)(a_4, \tau_4)(a_6, \tau_6),$
$(a_3, \tau_3)(a_5, \tau_5)(a_6, \tau_6)\}$
$untimed(L_{a_1 a_6}) = \{a_2 a_4 a_6, a_2 a_5 a_6, a_3 a_4 a_6, a_3 a_5 a_6\}$
$tmax(a_2 a_4 a_6) = 2 + 4 + 6 = 12$
$tmax(a_2 a_5 a_6) = 2 + 1 + 6 = 9$
$tmax(a_3 a_4 a_6) = 3 + 4 + 6 = 13$
$tmax(a_3 a_5 a_6) = 3 + 1 + 6 = 10$
$\Rightarrow Max(a_2, a_6) = 13$
The deadline constraint is specified as follows $D_{a_1 a_6} = Max(a_1, a_6) + C_{Coop} = 13 + 7$

To advertise a pre-defined deadline constraint $D_{a_i a_j}$, a partner would have to translate such an informal requirement into the temporal model. The deadline constraint, which describes the allowed execution time between two cooperative activities, is modeled by a non-intrusive observer [16,9] and transforms the problem into a reachability analysis of a specific state *Error*. As shown in figure 4, the interval associated with the added transition *Deadline* is $[D_{a_i a_j}, D_{a_i a_j}]$. When transition *Deadline* is validated (by the existence of a token in the place *Obs*), the associated clock is enabled. The token will be used either by firing transition a_j if the constraint is satisfied or transition *Deadline* if the given time limit is reached. Checking the maximum duration becomes an analysis of the reachability of place *Error*, which is marked if the execution time is longer than the specified duration [12].

Following the constraint specification, a partner have to validate it locally, in order to ensure that all possible sequences between the critical transitions a_i and a_j do not exceed the pre-computed deadline.

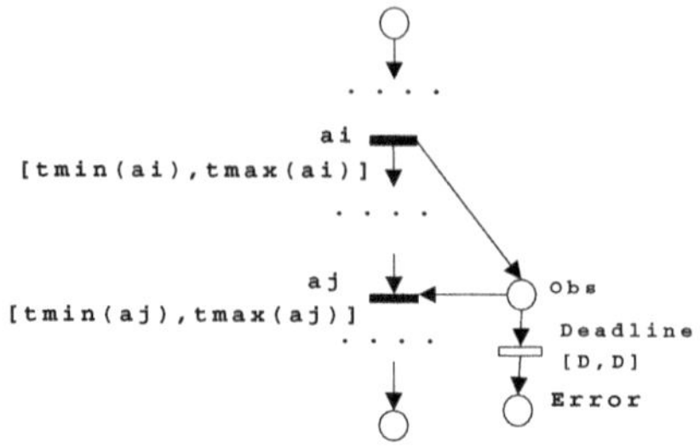

Fig. 4. The pre-defined constraint modeled by an observer

Definition 12 (Observer local validation $PTWF \mid O$**).** *In order to validate locally a specified constraint* $D_{a_i a_j}$ *within the corresponding* $PTWF = \langle P, T, Pre, Post, M_0, S \rangle$*, an observer O is added [12].*

The resulting workflow denoted $PTWF \mid O = \langle P', T', Pre', Post', M_0, S' \rangle$ *is defined as follows:*

- $P' = P \bigcup \{Obs, Error\}$ *where Obs is the place simulating the counting place of the observer and Error is the place marked if the constraint* $D_{a_i a_j}$ *is non respected;*
- $T' = T \bigcup \{Deadline\}$ *where Deadline is the transition which occurs if the transition is non respected;*
- $\begin{cases} Pre'(p,a) = Pre(p,a) & if\ (p,a) \in P \times T \\ Pre'(Obs, a_j) = 1 \\ Pre'(Obs, Deadline) = 1 \end{cases}$
- $\begin{cases} Post'(p,a) = Pre(p,a) & if\ (p,a) \in P \times T \\ Post'(Obs, a_i) = 1 \\ Post'(Error, Deadline) = 1 \end{cases}$
- $\begin{cases} S'(a) = S(a) & \forall a \in T \\ S'(Deadline) = [D_{a_i a_j}, D_{a_i a_j}] \end{cases}$

Lemma. *Let* $D_{a_i a_j}$ *be a deadline constraint calculated by a partner and modeled using an observer O, then* $L(PTWF \mid O) = L(PTWF)$*.*

Proof. This property follows directly from $D_{a_i a_j}$ computation in Proposition 1 and Definition 12. Because *Deadline* is the only added transition in $PTWF \mid O$, proving that $L(PTWF \mid O) = L(PTWF)$ is equivalent to prove that *Deadline* is a dead transition. Transition *Deadline* is validated by a_i firing which produces a token in place *Obs*. The token is used either by firing *Deadline* or the conflicting transition a_j. By definition, the bound on transition *Deadline* is greater than the maximum execution time of all transitions between the two corresponding cooperative activities i.e. $D_{a_i a_j} \geq Max(a_i, a_j)$. Since the conflicting transition a_j always occurs before *Deadline*, *Deadline* becomes a dead transition.

*Example (Deadline local validation for Partner*1*).* $D_{a_1 a_6}$ calculation above guarantees that the place *Error* is never reachable in the corresponding $PTWF \mid O$, illustrated in figure 5.

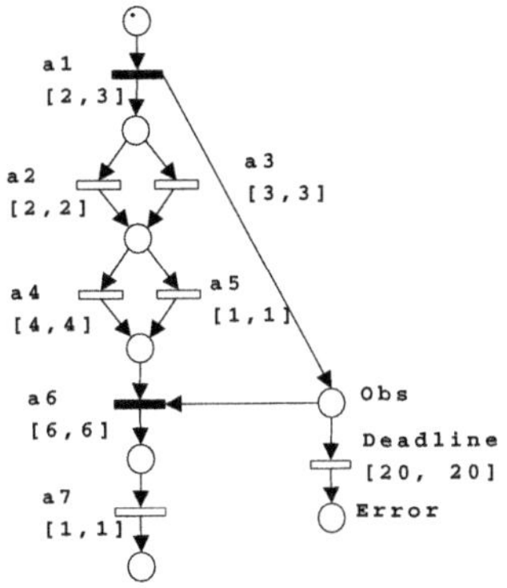

Fig. 5. The connected workflow $PTWF \mid O$ of $Partner1$

After generating the public workflow (AF) following the abstraction procedure, adding the calculated deadline constraint generates the corresponding temporal abstracted workflow, denoted (TAF). In order to advertise deadline constraints, observer can be added to the Temporal Abstracted Workflow (TAF) as follows.

Definition 13 (Deadline constraint advertisement $TAF \mid O$**)**
Let $PTWF = \langle P,T,Pre,Post,M_0,S\rangle$ *and* $AF = \langle P_a,T_a,Pre_a,Post_a\rangle$ *be the temporal private workflow and the corresponding abstracted version generated. Consider a pre-computed deadline constraint* $D_{a_ia_j}$ *between a pair of request-response transitions* a_i *and* a_j *specified and modeled by an observer O. The public temporal workflow with the added constraint* $TAF \mid O = \langle P_t,T_t,Pre_t,Post_t,M_0,S_t\rangle$ *is defined as follows:*

- $P_t = P_a \bigcup \{Obs, Error\}$;
- $T_t = T_a \bigcup \{Deadline\}$;
- $\begin{cases} Pre_t(p,a) = Pre_a(p,a) \quad if(p,a) \in P_a \times T_a \\ Pre_t(Obs,a_j) = 1 \\ Pre_t(Obs,Deadline) = 1 \end{cases}$
- $\begin{cases} Post_t(p,a) = Pre_a(p,a) \quad if(p,a) \in P_a \times T_a \\ Post_t(Obs,a_i) = 1 \\ Post_t(Error,Deadline) = 1 \end{cases}$
- $\begin{cases} S_t(a) = S(a) \forall a \in T_a \\ S_t(Deadline) = [D_{a_ia_j}, D_{a_ia_j}] \end{cases}$

Example (Deadline constraint advertisement for $Partner1$*).* As illustrated in figure 6(b), the advertised $TAF \mid O$ for $Partner1$ contains enough information to validate business conformance as well as temporal behavior suitability: it is generated by adding to the abstracted workflow AF, illustrated in figure 6(a), firing limits for visible transitions, and also by composing it with the added observer O. We note that the constrained transitions are always successive in $TAF \mid O$ (as assumed in Assumption 2).

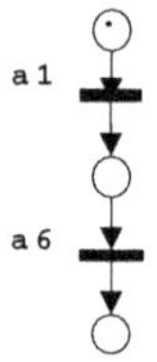

(a) $(AF1)$

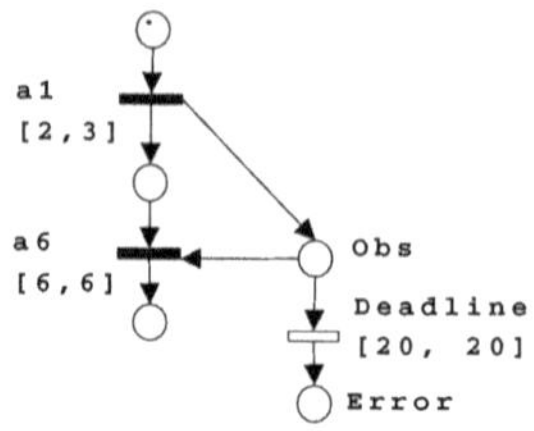

(b) $(TAF1 \mid O)$

Fig. 6. The advertisement of deadline constraint specified by *Partner*1

4 Deadline Constraints Conformance

Advertised workflows, within the temporal CoopFlow extension, contain enough information to ensure the structural and temporal suitability of the potential partners. If the business behavior complementarity is validated by the algorithms defined in CoopFlow [3], a further analysis is executed to validate whether temporal behavior of the involved is also coherent i.e. will published deadlines be respected in the global IOW? In order to give a systematic method for assuring the satisfaction and consistency of all the published time constraints, we start by formally define an interconnection of two temporal workflows.

Definition 14 (Workflow Temporal interconnection $PTWF_1 \parallel PTWF_2$**)**
Let $PTWF_1 = \langle P_1, T_1, Pre_1, Post_1, M_{01}, S_1 \rangle$ *and* $PTWF_2 = \langle P_2, T_2, Pre_2, Post_2, M_{02}, S_2 \rangle$ *be two TPN modeling temporal workflows for two cooperation candidates. Let* $Coop_1$ *(respectively* $Coop_2$*) be the cooperative transitions of* $PTWF_1$ *(respectively* $PTWF_2$*), and* i_1 *(respectively* i_2*) and* o_1 *(respectively* o_2*) be the source and sink places of* $PTWF_1$ *(respectively* $PTWF_2$*). Then the interconnection of* $PTWF_1$ *and* $PTWF_2$ *leads to the Petri net* $PTWF_1 \parallel PTWF_2 = \langle P, T, Pre, Post, M_0, S \rangle$ *defined as follows:*

- $P = P_1 \bigcup P_2 \bigcup B \bigcup \{i, o\}$, *where* B *is a set of buffer places such that:* $\exists (a_i, a_j) \in Coop_1, (a'_i, a'_j) \in Coop_2$ *and* $a_i \sim a'_i, a_j \sim a'_j$ *(simulating a request/response exchange between* $PTWF_1$ *and* $PTWF_2$*) iff* $b_{a_i,a'_i} \in B$ *and* $b_{a_j,a'_j} \in B$*;*
- $T = T_1 \bigcup T_2 \bigcup \{in, out\}$
- $\forall p \in P \setminus \{i, o\} \setminus B, \forall a \in T \setminus \{in, out\}$

$$Pre(p,a) = \begin{cases} Pre_1(p,a) & if (p,a) \in P_1 \times T_1 \\ Pre_2(p,a) & if (p,a) \in P_2 \times T_2 \end{cases}$$

$$Post(p,a) = \begin{cases} Post_1(p,a) & if (p,a) \in P_1 \times T_1 \\ Post_2(p,a) & if (p,a) \in P_2 \times T_2 \end{cases}$$

  - $\forall b_{a_i,a'_i} \in B, Pre(b, a_k) = a_k.type$ *and* $Post(a_k, b) = a_k.type \forall_{k=i,i'}$;
  - $Pre(i, in) = 1, Post(out, o) = 1, Post(in, i_k) = 1$ *and* $Pre(o_k, out) = 1 \forall_{k=i,i'}$.
- M_0 *is defined such that* $M(i) = 1$*;*
- $$\begin{cases} S(a) = S_1(a) & if a \in T_1 \\ S(a) = S_2(a) & if a \in T_2 \\ S(in) = [0,0] \\ S(out) = [0,0] \end{cases}$$

Our contribution consists of guaranteeing that a local temporal reasoning and verification method leads to the satisfaction of deadline constraints in the global IOW. This is important because the core advantage of CoopFlow, which is privacy preservation, should be maintained, even if some temporal information and processes are added. Consider $PTWF_1$ a temporal private workflow of *Partner*1 and $TAF_1 \mid O$ its abstracted temporal workflow advertised with a deadline constraint modeled by an observer O. Let *Partner*2 (associated with $PTWF_2$) be an potential collaboration candidate, which satisfies structural cooperation candidates properties. In the following, we define how a partner (in this case *Partner*2) execute local verification, before presenting our proposition.

Definition 15 (Deadline local verification process). *The deadline local verification process executed by Partner2 is defined by the state reachability analysis of place Error in the interconnected workflow* $PTWF_2 \mid\mid TAF_1 \mid O$*. This composition is defined as two temporal workflow interconnection in Definition 14.*

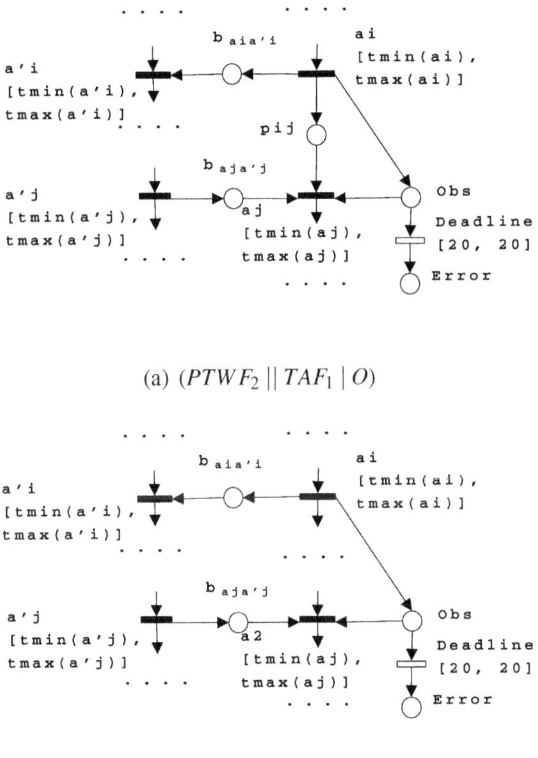

(a) $(PTWF_2 \mid\mid TAF_1 \mid O)$

(b) $(PTWF_2 \mid\mid PTWF_1 \mid O)$

Fig. 7. The reachability analysis of place *Error*

Theorem. *If the deadline local verification process executed by Partner2 is validated, then the deadline constraint conformance is respected in the resulting interconnected workflow. i.e. if the place Error is not reachable in the interconnected workflow* $PTWF_2 \parallel TAF_1 \mid O$ *then it is not reachable in* $PTWF_2 \parallel PTWF_1 \mid O$*. This guarantee that Deadline transition is a dead transition in the two interconnected processes.*

Proof. Figure 7 illustrates the observer added in both $PTWF_2 \parallel TAF_1 \mid O$ and $PTWF_2 \parallel PTWF_1 \mid O$, following Definitions 12 and 13. As assumed in Assumption 2, cooperative transitions a_i and a_j are successive, i.e., interconnected by a place in TAF and a set of local transitions in $PTWF_1$.

- First we suppose that the state reachability analysis of the interconnected workflow $PTWF_2 \parallel TAF_1 \mid O$ can not lead to the place $Error$ marking i.e. $\forall_{\omega \in L(PTWF_2 \parallel TAF_1 \mid O)}$, $Deadline \notin \alpha(untimed(\omega))$. Let's concentrate in the possible firing sequences between a_i and a_j. As specified in Definitions 14 and 15, in $PTWF_2 \parallel TAF_1 \mid O$, ${}^\bullet a_j = \{Obs, p_{ij}\} \bigcup b_{a_j, a'_j}$. Obs is marked after a_i firing, and will be used for firing transition $Deadline$ after $D_{a_i a_j}$ time units, unless it is disabled by the conflicting transition a_j. Since the supposition is that $Error$ is never reachable in $PTWF_2 \parallel TAF_1 \mid O$, then $Max(a_i, a_j) < D_{a_i a_j}$.

  Following Definition 11, $Untimed(L_{a_i a_j}) = \{a_j, a'_i w a_j \ s.t. w \in L_{a'_i a'_j}$ in$PTWF_2\} \Rightarrow tmax(a_j) < D_{a_i a_j}$ and $tmax(a'_i w' a_j) < D_{a_i a_j} \forall_{w' \in L_{a'_i a'_j}}$ in $PTWF_2$.
- Now let's prove that following the previous supposition, $\forall \omega \in L(PTWF_2 \parallel PTWF_1 \mid O)$, $Deadline \notin \alpha(\omega)$. Following Definition 11, $Untimed(L_{a_i a_j}) = \{w_1 s.t. w_1 \in L_{a_i a_j}$ in $PTWF_1, a'_i w' a_j \ s.t. w' \in L_{a'_i a'_j}$ in $PTWF_2\}$. Proving that $Error$ is not reachable means that $Max(a_i, a_j) < D_{a_i a_j}$.

  $Tmax(w_1) < D_{a_i a_j} \forall_{w_1 \in L_{a_i a_j}}$ in $PTWF_1$ is guaranteed by Definition 11. Because the pre-computed constraint have to be validated before publishing, $Deadline$ can not be fired for all timed sequences between a_i and a_j in $PTWF_1$.

  $Tmax(a'_i w' a_j) < D \forall_{w' \in L_{a'_i a'_j}}$ in $PTWF_2\}$ is guaranteed by the supposition.

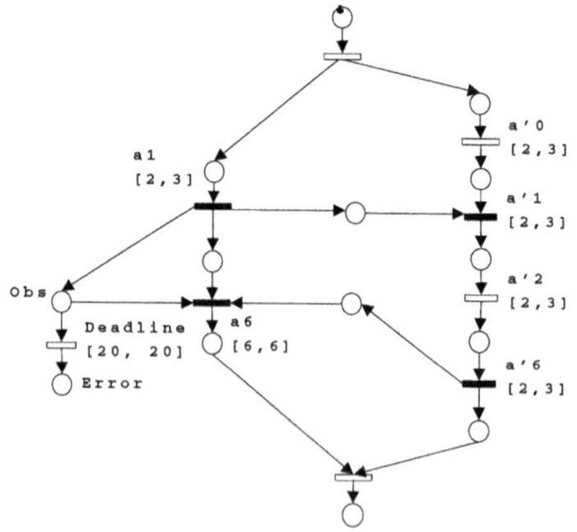

Fig. 8. The interconnected workflow ($PTWF_2 \parallel TAF_1 \mid O$)

Finally, we can assure that *Error* place is never reachable in the resulting interconnected workflows.

Example (Temporal local conformance validation by Partner2). As illustrated in figure 8, *Partner*2 assure that place *Error* is not reachable in $PTWF_2 \mid\mid TAF_1 \mid O$. This guarantee that, if the deadline constraint is respected locally, it will be the same in the global IOW, shown in figure 9.

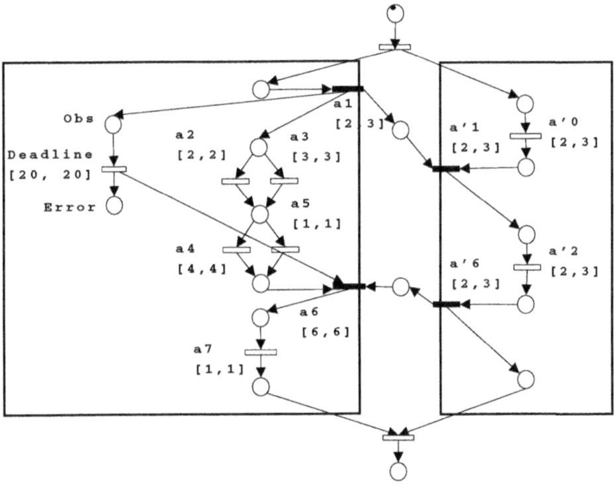

Fig. 9. The interconnected $(PTWF_2 \mid\mid PTWF_1 \mid O)$ workflow

5 Related Works

Time management in workflow-based processes has been studied among several aspects: activities duration control, scheduling and prioritization, resources management, etc.

The first important issue to deal with is time modeling, which includes specification of temporal information as well as timing constraints. In [6] and [7], a timed workflow graph extends initial workflow graphs by adding some temporal constraints to each activity. The proposed technique consists of searching for an execution plan which does not violate any time constraints. The result is a timed activity graph that includes deadline ranges for each activity. The assumption made is that activities have fixed duration and each workflow has an assigned deadline to respect. Temporal modeling have also been studied in web service compositions research field. In [5], the authors used timed automata formalism to describe the temporal information. The system temporal expectations are expressed using goal-oriented engineering and the testing of time goal requirements is done using model checking techniques. In [10], authors propose an extension of timed automata formalism to specify global timing aspects of web service compositions, called Web Service Timed State Transition Systems (WSTTS). Complex timed requirements can be specified modeling time intervals between events, time bounds or combinations of them.

In our approach, we choose one of the temporal extension of the Petri Net theory, priory used in the Coopflow approach, to integrate timing information. Time Petri Nets associate a time interval to each activity to express time range for its firing since its validation. Because transitions duration are not fixed, the execution time of an activity can depend on the cost related. In fact, when a partner imposes a given deadline, this can have implications on the possible deadlines that can be demanded by the other partners. Therefore, we advocate that deadlines and activities duration should be negotiated. Another important feature of our work is the validation of specified deadlines in the inter-organizational processes with the respect of partners' privacy. Some related works discussed the proposed approaches in situations like inter-organizational workflows or web service composition [10,1,8]. Our approach is different because deadlines can be specified to each activity and should be tested and negotiated without exposing the partners private processes.

6 Conclusions

This paper addresses the problem of incorporating and verifying deadlines constraints conformance in the context of Inter-Organizational Workflows, without exposing the private processes of the partners. Even if the business behavior complementarity of the involved parties is validated, missing deadlines while delivering the required services may lead to a global failure execution. Based on the existing CoopFlow approach and using Time Petri Net theory, we proposed a method for modeling and advertising temporal requirements for cooperative activities on the abstracted version of business behavior. State reachability analysis is used for checking temporal correctness of the resulting workflow. The main contribution of this paper is that the verification process can be executed while maintaining the core advantage of CoopFlow, i.e. that each partner can keep the critical parts of its business process private. In fact, we proved that a deadline local verification process executed by a partner can lead to a deadline conformance in the resulting interconnected workflow. We made the assumption that this technique is restricted to WF-Nets that do not contains any cycles, and we detailed an example of a deadline specification in the case of a request-request cooperation between two candidates. A further work will concentrate on generalizing this technique to other cooperation patterns (not only sender and receiver transitions), to multiple partners and even more than one deadline constraint. Our ultimate purpose is to set up an algorithm that describes how deadlines must be calculated and how the corresponding observers will be added. The resulting timed-oriented framework enables the checking for satisfaction of local time constraints within the global business process by preserving the autonomy and privacy of the internal partner processes.

References

1. Amirreza, T.N., Eder, J.: Temporal consistency of view based interorganizational workflows. In: 2nd International United Information Systems Conference, Klagenfurt, Austria, pp. 96–107 (2008)
2. Chebbi, I., Dustdar, S., Tata, S.: The view-based approach to dynamic inter-organizational workflow cooperation. Data Knowl. Eng. 56(2), 139–173 (2006)

3. Chebbi, I., Tata, S.: Coopflow: A framework for inter-organizational workflow cooperation. In: Meersman, R., Tari, Z. (eds.) OTM 2005. LNCS, vol. 3760, pp. 112–129. Springer, Heidelberg (2005)
4. Chebbi, I., Tata, S.: Workflow abstraction for privacy preservation. In: Web Information Systems Engineering Workshops, Nancy, France, pp. 166–177 (2007)
5. Diaz, G., Navarro, E., Cambronero, M.-E., Valero, V., Cuartero, F.: Testing time goal-driven requirements with model checking techniques. In: ECBS 2007: Proceedings of the 14th Annual IEEE International Conference and Workshops on the Engineering of Computer-Based Systems, Washington, DC, USA, pp. 503–514 (2007)
6. Ede, J., Gruber, W., Panagos, E.: Temporal modeling of workflows with conditional execution paths. In: Ibrahim, M., Küng, J., Revell, N. (eds.) DEXA 2000. LNCS, vol. 1873, pp. 243–253. Springer, Heidelberg (2000)
7. Eder, J., Panagos, E.: Managing time in workflow systems. In: Fischer, L. (ed.) Workflow Handbook 2001, pp. 109–132. Future Strategies Inc. (2000)
8. Eder, J., Tahamtan, A.: Temporal conformance of federated choreographies. In: Bhowmick, S.S., Küng, J., Wagner, R. (eds.) DEXA 2008. LNCS, vol. 5181, pp. 668–675. Springer, Heidelberg (2008)
9. Godary, K.: Lpt: Little parametric tool, outil pour la validation d'une borne temprelle paramétrée. In: Sixième Conférence Internationale Francophone d'Automatique, CIFA 2008 (2008)
10. Kazhamiakin, R., Pandya, P., Pistore, M.: Representation, verification, and computation of timed properties in web. In: Proceedings of the IEEE International Conference on Web Services, Washington, DC, USA, pp. 497–504 (2006)
11. Klai, K., Tata, S., Desel, J.: Symbolic abstraction and deadlock-freeness verification of inter-enterprise processes. In: Dayal, U., Eder, J., Koehler, J., Reijers, H.A. (eds.) Business Process Management. LNCS, vol. 5701, pp. 294–309. Springer, Heidelberg (2009)
12. Makni, M., Alouane, N.B.H., Yeddes, M., Tata, S.: Modeling time constraints in inter-organizational workflows. In: International Conference on Enterprise Information Systems, Madeira, Portugal (2010)
13. Merlin, P.M.: A study of the Recoverability of Computing Systems. Technical report ♯58 (phd thesis), Computer Science Department, University of California at Irvine (1974)
14. Pezze, M., Young, M.: Time petri: A primer introduction. In: Tutorial Presented at the Multi-Workshop on Formal Methods in Performance Evaluation and Applications, Zaragoza, Spain, pp. 41–46 (1999)
15. Tata, S., Klai, K., M'Bareck, N.O.A.: Coopflow: A bottom-up approach to workflow cooperation for short-term virtual enterprises. IEEE T. Services Computing 1(4), 214–228 (2008)
16. Toussaint, J., Simonot-Lion, F., Thomesse, J.-P.: Time constraints verification methods based on time petri nets. In: Proceedings of the 6th IEEE Workshop on Future Trends of Distributed Computing Systems, Washington, DC, USA, p. 262 (1997)
17. van der Aalst, W.M.P.: The application of petri nets to workflow management. Journal of Circuits, Systems, and Computers 8(1), 21–66 (1998)

An Ontological Approach for Semantic Annotation of Supply Chain Process Models

Xiaodong Wang[2], Nan Li[2], Hongming Cai[1], and Boyi Xu[3]

[1] School of Software, Shanghai JiaoTong University, Shanghai, China
[2] BIT Institute,University of Mannheim, Mannheim, Germany
[3] Antai College of Economic&Management, Shanghai JiaoTong University, Shanghai, China
{wangxd.sjtu,nanjingshandong}@googlemail.com,
{hmcai,byxu}@sjtu.edu.cn

Abstract. A Supply Chain Process involves various departments and organizations. However, terminology for supply chain process models doesn't have formalized representations. Moreover, formal definitions of dynamic semantic of process models are commonly absent. Such problems discourage the integration of various process models from different partners. Thereafter, technologies of semantic annotation for business process models are developed to solve these problems. In this paper an ontological approach is proposed to annotate supply chain process models with semantic meanings. The ontology for supply chain process model, so-called scorBPMN ontology, is introduced for such semantic annotation, which specifies semantics of supply chain process models at both meta-model level and mode level. Then the similarity-based matching functionality is developed to link process model elements with concepts in the ontology. The proposed approach presents an ontological description of semantics of supply chain processes and similarity-based annotation of process models, so that various supply chain process models can be standardized and explained with unified semantic annotations, which is the basis for process integration, implementation and analysis.

Keywords: Supply Chain Process, Semantic annotation, scorBPMN ontology.

1 Introduction

Supply Chain Process is a special business process which interrelates production, logistics and information. Different from other business processes, supply chain processes usually span departments and organizations. They are generally operated by different independent firms in order to produce and deliver a range of specified goods and services. A multitude of modeling languages for the representation of processes have been developed since the first large data processing applications [1]. Examples are Petri net, OMG's Business Process Modeling Notation (BPMN) [2], the Event-driven Process Chain (EPC) or the UML activity diagram. However, current methods

R. Meersman et al. (Eds.): OTM 2010, Part I, LNCS 6426, pp. 540–554, 2010.

of process modeling lack adequate specification of terminology used in supply chain process models, which leads to inconsistency and conflicts during the interconnecting of various process models into a complete supply chain process. Another problem is that current process modeling languages are semi-formal. An essential part of the semantic of a process model is thus always bound to the natural language, which, with its ambiguities, allows much room for interpretation [3]. Clearly defined semantics for each model element are however necessary, if process models from various modelers are combined, searched and translated or if it is planned that the semantics in the models should be automatically validated and used for the configuration of an information system [4].

SBPM (Semantic Business Process Management) [5] is introduced to solve the above problems. A key aspect of SBPM is the semantic annotation of process models. Using linkage of the elements of a process model with concepts from an ontology, semantic annotation of process models provides a basis for sharing concepts and knowledge about process, reusing process fragments, integrating of processes from various partners and automatically developing IT implementation of process models. For a process model, there are two dimensions that need to be considered: the semantics of the meta-model elements when different representations are used and the terms that describe the model elements. Therefore, an ontological foundation is necessary: i.e. the semantics of each element in a business process model must be defined in a "machine-understandable" fashion to support the whole business process management lifecycle [6].

Within this context, an ontological approach for semantic annotating of supply chain process models is proposed in this paper. In this approach, sBPMN ontology of the SUPER (Semantics Utilised for Process Management within and between Enterprises) [7] project is employed to describe semantics of the process meta-model. The sBPMN serves as a format for representing BPMN process models and featuring basic concepts and attributes for standard BPMN elements. This Supply Chain Operation Reference Model (SCOR-Model) [8] is a reference model for designing and implementation of supply chain. As a de fact standard for supply chain, SCOR-Model provides standard terminology and representations of supply chain processes. Based on SCOR-Model, a SCOR-ontology is developed to specify constructs and terminology in supply chain processes and it serves as the domain ontology in our approach. Through combining BPMN ontology with SCOR ontology, an ontology for supply chain process models, so-called scorBPMN ontology, could be derived, which specifies the semantics in supply chain processes.

To link process elements with concepts in above defined ontologies, a method which is based on ontological similarities is proposed. These similarities comprise syntactic, linguistic and structural similarity of ontology concepts. Finally a prototype tools is developed to illustrate the semantic annotating process models with supply chain process ontologies.

The proposed approach enables a formal and semantic representation for supply chain process models. Via similarities-based annotation of process models, formal description for semantic in supply chain process models can be achieved. Hereby process models from various partners can be smoothly integrated. Such semantic annotations can also facilitate process mining, reusing of process fragments and model-driven IT implementation of process models.

2 Related Work

The idea of utilizing ontology in the area of business process management is not new. For example, Wand and Weber have used ontologies to describe and evaluate certain aspects of modeling language [9].

The core related work can be found at the intersection of business process management and semantic web, which is currently promoted in the project SUPER. In the SUPER project a general ontology for business process model BPMO (Business Process Modeling Ontology) [10] is proposed, which is a general ontology which describes meta-data of process models. The related BPMO modeling environment provides basic functionality in order to enrich existing process models with semantic annotations. In contrast, the approach introduced in this paper is closely related to the sBPMN ontology and SCOR ontology. It offers a flexible and fine-granular semantic annotation of supply chain process models that are described in BPMN. The detailed introduction about sBPMN ontology can be found in [11].

There are also related works that focus on the semantic annotation of models in another certain language. For example, an approach to semantic annotation for Petri nets is proposed in [12]. In [13], a semantic extension of EPC with formal ontology is developed, in which semantics of the individual element in process models can be specified. In [14], a General Process Ontology (GPO) is proposed and the related semantic annotation framework is discussed.

Semantic annotation of business process models requires the engagement of domain ontologies which describe data objects and their states. Domain ontologies provide the normalized terminologies which specify the related information used in process models. In [15], approaches which combine domain ontologies with process meta-models ontologies to semantically annotate process models are introduced. In [16], the possibility to apply SCOR-Model for providing normalized terms in the IT implementation of supply chain process models is discussed. Extended from these works, the ontological description of SCOR-Model is introduced in our approach as domain ontology for semantically annotating of supply chain process models.

3 Main Idea

As mentioned above, the semantics of individual process model elements will be specified using concepts from formal ontologies. Hereby a combined process modeling ontology, so-called scorBPMN ontology, is firstly generated, which is derived from basic BPMN ontology and SCOR ontology. Thereafter a method to match process model elements with ontology concepts is developed. Figure 1 illustrates this approach:

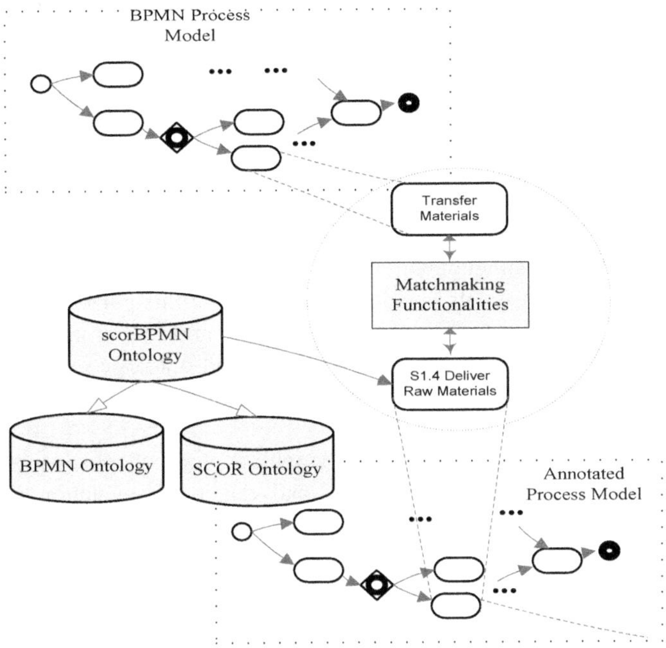

Fig. 1. The approach to semantically annotate supply chain process models

There are different levels that can be annotated with semantic information in a process model. The first level is meta-model level annotation, in which the constructs defined by meta-model can be annotated with concepts of ontology. For model-level annotation domain ontologies are utilized to specify the semantics of information in a certain context. To simplify the illustration of the approach, the supply chain process models in our works are supposed to be represented in BPMN, which is also widely accepted as modeling language for supply chain process modeling. If necessary, the process models in other modeling languages can be transformed into process models in BPMN. There are also articles for this purpose. For example, Hoyer introduced a direct transformation from process models in EPC to process models in BPMN [17]. Hereby the meta-model of a supply chain process model can be specified with BPMN ontology. The BPMN ontology used in this paper is extended from sBPMN ontology [11]. It formalizes the representation of BPMN process models and defines constructs of a process model. These process constructs include process actions, control nodes, etc. Moreover, such ontological definitions of process meta-model are not only machine-readable, but also machine-understandable, which means that they are in a form that allows computer to infer and reason new facts using an underlying ontology. For example, computer can deduce execution orders of process actions according to the dependency among them.

The semantic of information in the context of supply chain will be specified with the ontology of SCOR reference model, which provides not only the standardized terms of supply chain process models but also the related definitions of non-functionalities, such as performance metrics, inputs and outputs, pre-conditions and post-effects of process elements.

Derived from BPMN ontology and SCOR ontology, scorBPMN ontology provides ontological concepts for semantic annotation of supply chain process models. Therefore an integrated ontology for annotation is provided. The model elements need to be linked to instances in scorBPMN ontology, not to be linked to BPMN ontology and SCOR ontology simultaneously. The annotation of process models in meta-model level and model level can be achieved with an affirmatory ontology. After defining the necessary ontology, an automatic matching of process model element with ontology concepts is required for the annotation. To achieve this purpose, the similarities between them are measured. These similarities are composed of syntactic, linguistic and structural similarities between model element and ontology instance. Hence the individual process model element could be linked to ontology instance with highest similarities.

The approach will be illustrated with a graphical prototypical software tool. With this tool, similarity measuring is executed and candidate annotation will be listed during user's annotation for supply chain process model elements. Annotated process model will be outputted into OWL-DL (Web Ontology Language) [18] files.

4 Utilized Ontologies

Terms and description used in business processes may differ from one company to another. By formal descriptions in a shared ontology, all business partners would have a common understanding of term's domain. An ontology is defined through the domain's concepts and properties, both arranged in a subsumption hierarchy, instances of specific concepts, properties and axioms to infer new knowledge from already existing one [19].

Different ontologies are required for the annotation in various levels. In this paper the annotation of process meta-model will be realized with BPMN ontology, which describes basic constructs and their relationships in process models. Considering the context of supply chain, the ontology of SCOR reference model, so-called SCOR ontology formalizes the terms used in supply chain process models. The ontology concepts should be unified and consistent in order to realize annotation, hence scorBPMN ontology is derived from these two ontologies and combines the concepts in them.

4.1 BPMN Ontology

As a graphical process modeling language, BPMN receives increasing attention in modeling supply chain processes. Nevertheless, BPMN is still a graph-oriented language and lacks formal definition. The meaning of a BPD (Business Process Diagram) in BPMN could not be directly understood by a computer so that automatic execution and analysis of business process model are still challenging work. Abramowicz proposed an ontology description, so-called sBPMN, for meta-model of

BPMN process models [11]. In this section, the sBPMN is introduced for the ontological description of BPMN process model. To deduce a unified ontology for the semantic annotation of supply chain process models, a formalized description for concepts in sBPMN ontology is also proposed.

The core element of the sBPMN ontology is a BPD presenting the process model. According to the BPMN specification the four basic categories of elements in processes are Flow Objects, Connecting Objects, Swimlanes and Artifacts. Details about sBPMN ontology can be found in [11] and [20].

Nevertheless, the BPMN ontology offers only meta-model level semantic information and it needs to integrate domain ontology for the annotation of process model. For the purpose of generating certain ontology for supply chain process model, the formalized description of concepts is given as follows:

A BPMN process model could be defined with a tuple $P = (F, C, S, A)$ in which:

$F = (A_C, E, T, G)$ represents the flow object, including the activity A_C, events E, event trigger T, and gateway G.

Activity A_C denotes the kind of work which must be done in process, and it could be represented as the tuple $A_C = (T_S, P_S)$ in which T_S represents Task in process model. A task is an atomic unit of work and cannot be broken into further detail level. P_S represents sub-process in process model.

E represents the event, which denotes something that happens in process. It can be also represented as the tuple $E = (E_S, E_I, E_E)$ where E_S represents start event; E_I represents intermediate event; E_E represents end event.

T represents triggers of events. A trigger could be message, time or exception.

G represents gateway in BPD. It determines forking and merging of paths that depend on the conditions. Gateway G could also be represented as the tuple $G = (G_{EX}, G_{IX}, G_{CP}, G_{PL})$. G_{EX} represents the exclusive gateway, G_{IX} represents the inclusive gateway, G_{CP} represents the complex gateway, G_{PL} represents the parallel gateway.

$C = (C_S, C_M, C_A)$ represents the control flow relation (the connecting object in sBPMN) that means $C = F \times F$, where C_S represents sequence flow; C_M represents message flow; C_A represents association among flow objects.

$S = (S_P, S_L)$ represents the swim lane in BPD. Swim lane is a visual mechanism of organizing and categorizing activities. In the tuple $S = (S_P, S_L)$ S_P represents pool in BPD and S_L represents lane in BPD.

$A = (A_N, D_O, G_R)$ represents artifacts in BPD, in which: A_N represents the annotation in BPD; D_O represents data object in BPD; G_R represents group in BPD.

4.2 SCOR Ontology

As a result of effort for standardization of supply chain process, SCOR model is a reference model designed for the effective communication among supply chain partners. It incorporates elements like standard descriptions of processes, standard metrics and best-in-class practices [21]. SCOR model forms a conceptual frame, which provides a standardized terminology and processes enabling a general description of supply chains. However, unlike optimizing models, no mathematical formal description of a supply chain and no optimal or heuristic methods for solving a problem are given in SCOR [22], which incurs ambiguity in the process modeling and IT implementation. Hereby it is necessary to extract general concepts of supply chain from SCOR model so that a unified vocabulary for the representation of supply chain process can be built. For this purpose the formalized description of concepts in SCOR model is proposed and based on it the ontology of SCOR model is established.

A SCOR process model can be specified as the tuple: $SCOR\_P = (P^{SC}, C^{SC}, H^{SC}, M^{SC}, B^{SC})$ where

$P^{SC} = (N^{SC}, ID^{SC}, CA^{SC}, HR^{SC}, I^{SC}, O^{SC}, PF^{SC}, PP^{SC}, PM^{SC}, PB^{SC})$ represents in SCOR defined process elements, which can constitute a complete supply chain process. In detail, a process element consists of the following attributes:

N^{SC} is the name of a process element

ID^{SC} is the ID of a process element

CA^{SC} is the category of a process element

HR^{SC} is the hierarchical level related to a process element. SCOR model merely specifies three layers of hierarchy. Supply chain designers need to develop deep levels of process models till they could be implemented.

I^{SC} represents the inputs set that can be accepted by a process element.

O^{SC} represents the outputs set that a process element possibly generates.

PF^{SC} represents the previous process elements that can be executed before a process element.

PP^{SC} represents the post process elements that can be executed after a process element.

PM^{SC} represent the performance metrics which are linked to a process element.

PB^{SC} represents the best practices of a process element, it is normally depicted with textural description.

In SCOR model five categories C^{SC} are defined for process element: plan, supply, make, deliver and return. H^{SC} defines the hierarchy structure of supply chain processes. A higher level process element can be decomposed into a process chain that is comprised of series of process elements in lower-level.

M^{SC} represents performance metrics in SCOR model. The SCOR model contains more than 150 key indicators that measure the performance of supply chain operations. Similar with the process elements, SCOR metrics are organized in a hierarchical structure. The metrics are used in conjunction with performance attributes of process elements. For example, delivery performance is calculated with the ratio of punctual products delivery. Performance metrics M^{SC} have composite structures and can be also represented as the tuple: $M^{SC} = (NM^{SC}, MID^{SC}, ComME^{SC}, Aggre^{SC})$ where NM^{SC} is the name of the metric; MID^{SC} is the metric identifier; $ComME^{SC}$ represents the components of the metric; $Aggre^{SC}$ represents the aggregating relationship among the metric and its components.

B^{SC} represents the best practices. Over 430 executable practices derived from the experience of SCC (Supply Chain Council) members are available in the specification of SCOR model.

In this section, the above concepts of SCOR model and their relationships will be described with SCOR ontology. Figure 2 shows briefly the concepts of SCOR ontology.

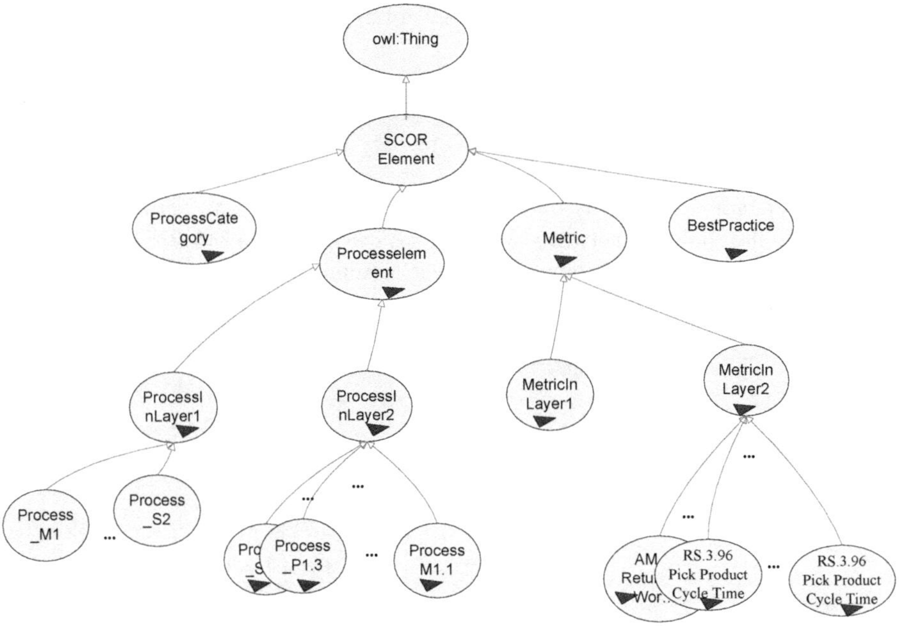

Fig. 2. The core concepts in SCOR ontology

In SCOR ontology the class *SCORElement* directly inherits from the root concept "owl:Thing". The class *ProcessElement* is defined as a general concept for process element. Its subclasses are also specified to describe process element in different level. The concrete process element definitions of SCOR model will also be depicted as OWL classes, which can be decomposed into sub-process of different supply chain partners. Similarly performance metric is described as classes, concrete performance metrics are described as instances. The linkages among metric, attributes and process elements are defined as properties of corresponding classes. The data type and value range of inputs, outputs and metric are specified with axiom in ontology. Figure 2 gives only a brief overview of SCOR ontology, the eclipse with solid triangle means the concepts has more descendants. The properties and relationships of concepts are hidden in Figure 2.

4.3 The scorBPMN Ontology

To semantically annotate supply chain process model, a set of ontology concepts are required. In this section the scorBPMN ontology is derived from BPMN ontology and SCOR ontology for this purpose.

In scorBPMN ontology, the concept *SCProcessElement* is created to integrate the concept *activity* in BPMN ontology and the concept *ProcessElement* in SCOR ontology. It means that it is a subclass of these two classes and can be treated as an activity in BPMN and in the mean time it can have all properties of the process element in

SCOR ontology. Consequently the instances of *SCProcessElement* depict the supply chain process element.

The concept *SCMetric* represents the performance metrics in SCOR model. While the performance metric is always related to process element, the *SCMetric* is derived from the concept *annotation* in BPMN ontology and the concept *Metric* in SCOR ontology.

The *association* in BPMN ontology between *annotation* and *activity* can be extended to the linkage between *SCProcessElement* and *SCMetric.* The concept *DataObject* in BPMN ontology is extended to represent the inputs and outputs of *SCProcessElement.* Correspondingly the axiom about data type and value range in SCOR ontology will be extended in scorBPMN ontology.

Figure 3 shows the core concepts in scorBPMN ontology.

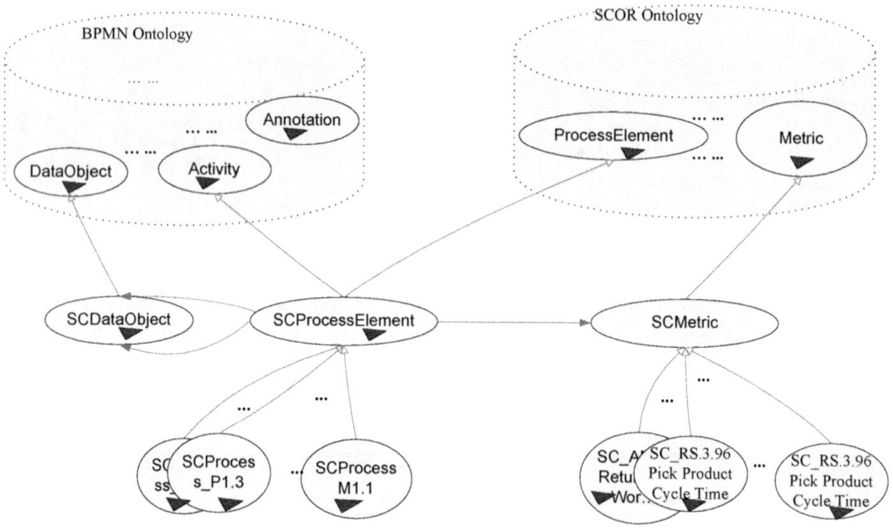

Fig. 3. The core concepts in scorBPMN ontology

5 Semantic Annotation of Process Models

In this section the semantic annotation of supply chain process models is explained. Generally, semantic annotation is mostly proposed in literature to annotate documents and web pages. In this paper, semantic annotation of a supply chain process model can be referred to the linking of process model elements with supply chain ontology concepts so that process models from various sources can obtain a standardized explanation. This linking is achieved through utilizing of scorBPMN ontology and a similarity-based matching. The steps of annotating a process model are described in Fig. 4:

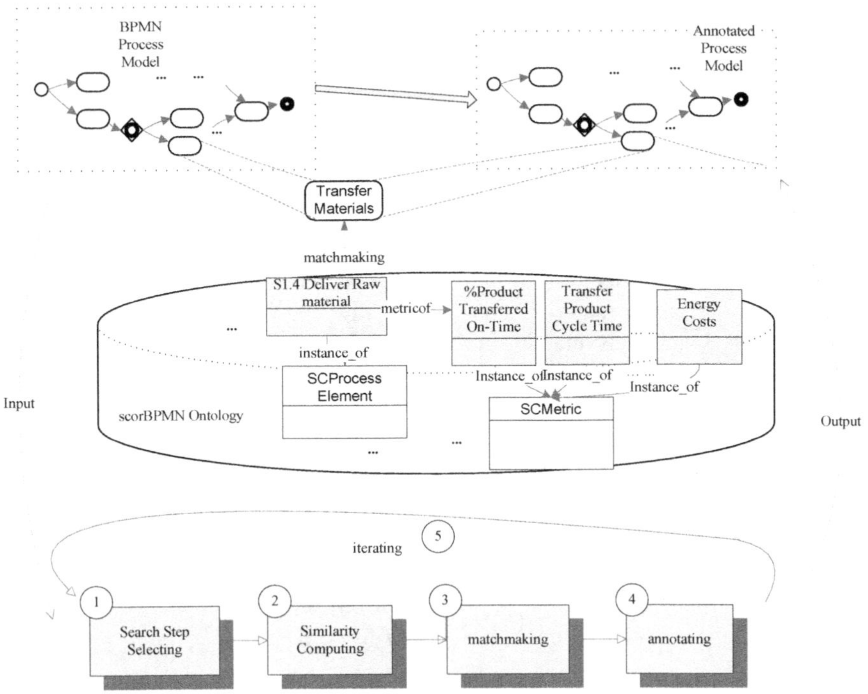

Fig. 4. The steps of annotating

Input: The input of annotating is the process models in BPMN.

Element selecting: The next step is to decide which concept in ontology can be matched with element in process model. For a process model element, the concept in ontology which has the same class will be selected to compare the similarities with itself.

Similarity computing: To select exact instance of ontology to annotate process model element, the similarities between them will be computed. The definition of similarity between them will be given in the following section.

Match making: After computing of similarities, matching will be executed. Simply speaking, for a process model element, the instance in scorBPMN ontology with highest similarity with it will be chosen to annotate it.

Iterating: The annotating of an element could affect the value of similarities of its neighboring elements. So these steps of annotating should be iterated.

5.1 Similarity Computing

In order to build linkage between process model elements and ontology instances, a solution to compare similarities between them is introduced in this section. This computation of similarities is based on string-match and comprises three aspects: syntactic similarity, linguist similarity and structural similarity.

Maedche and Staab propose a syntactic similarity measuring method which is based on the edit distance between two strings [23]. The names of process elements and the names of ontology instances are compared with this syntactic similarity. The syntactic similarity of process model element name *e* and the instance name *o* is defined as follows:

$$sim_{syn} = \frac{\min(|e|,|o|) - ed\ (e,o)}{min(|e|,|o|)} \tag{1}$$

In this definition $min(|e|, |o|)$ represents the minimal length of two strings; $ed\ (e, o)$ is the Levenshtein-edit distance of two strings [24]. For example the minimal length of two strings "Transfer material" and "deliver raw material" is 17, the Levenshtein-edit distance is 8, and the syntactic similarity is 0.529.

To solve the problems of synonym and homonym of words, the linguist similarity is introduced in the matching. The linguist similarity between names of process elements and instance is measured on the base of synonym relationships of WordNet [25]. Let the function $ç(o)$ retrieve all terms in the synonym relationship in WordNet for the phrasing of a given ontological concept instance o, the function $S = ç(o) \cap ç(e)$ denote the intersect of synonym terms of the ontology instance name o and the process model element *e* . Then the function

$$f\ (S) = \begin{cases} 1\ iff\ \ S \neq \emptyset \\ 0\ iff\ S\ = \emptyset \end{cases} \tag{2}$$

Let $max(|ç(o)|, |ç(e)|)$ denote the maximum of the cardinalities of two sets $ç(o)$ and $ç(e)$, then the linguistic similarity sim_{lin} between ontology instance o and process element *e* is defined as:

$$sim_{lin} = \frac{f(S)}{max(|ç(o)|,|ç(e)|)} \tag{3}$$

With measuring of syntactic and linguist similarities, the structural similarity can be deduced. The structural similarity is based on the features of the ontology concept and the process model element. The features of a concept mean that the set of its attributes and its neighbors. For a *SCProcessElement*, its features include inputs and outputs sets, previous process elements and post process elements, related performance metric. Hence the structural similarity sim_{strc} can be defined as:

$$sim_{strc} = \frac{\sum_{i=1}^{n} w_i^p\, sim_i(p_i^o, p_i^e)}{\sum_{i=1}^{n} w_i^p} \tag{4}$$

$sim_i(p_i^o, p_i^e)$ denotes the similarity between features and $sim_i(p_i^o, p_i^e) = sim_{syn}(p_i^o, p_i^e) + sim_{lin}(p_i^o, p_i^e)$. w_i^p denotes the corresponding weight of similarity. Currently they are simply evaluated with 1.

Finally the combined similarity is defined as following:

$$sim_{com} = \frac{w_{syn} sim_{syn}(o,e) + w_{lin} sim_{lin}(o,e) + w_{strc} sim_{strc}(o,e)}{w_{syn} + w_{lin} + w_{strc}} \tag{5}$$

w_{syn} is the weight of syntactic similarity, w_{lin} is the weight of linguist similarity and w_{strc} is the weight of structural similarity. Table 1 shows results of measuring similarities between several ontology instances and process model elements:

Table 1. Results of measuring similarities between several ontology instances and process model elements

Process model Element	Ontology instance	Syntactic similarity	Linguistic similarity	Structural similarity	Combined similarity
Deliver raw material	Transfer material	0.529	0.625	0.836	0.663
Check availability	Check inventory	0.30	0.0721	0.654	0.342
Deliver Product & Invoice	Ship Invoice	0.412	0. 787	0.425	0.541
Send confirmation	Send verification	0.8125	0.875	1.0	0.896

5.2 A Cast Study

To explain how our approach works, we give a simplified manufacturing process to illustrate the modeling of process and the generation of corresponding service description. The manufacturer receives customer order from end-customer, checks product availability, and then organizes production. To complete production, the manufacturer requires supplier for raw materials. The supplier checks inventory and then transfers raw materials to the manufacturer. After receiving raw materials, the manufacturer completes production and sends product to deliver, the deliver transfers product and invoice to customer. Figure 5 illustrates the process model with semantic annotation.

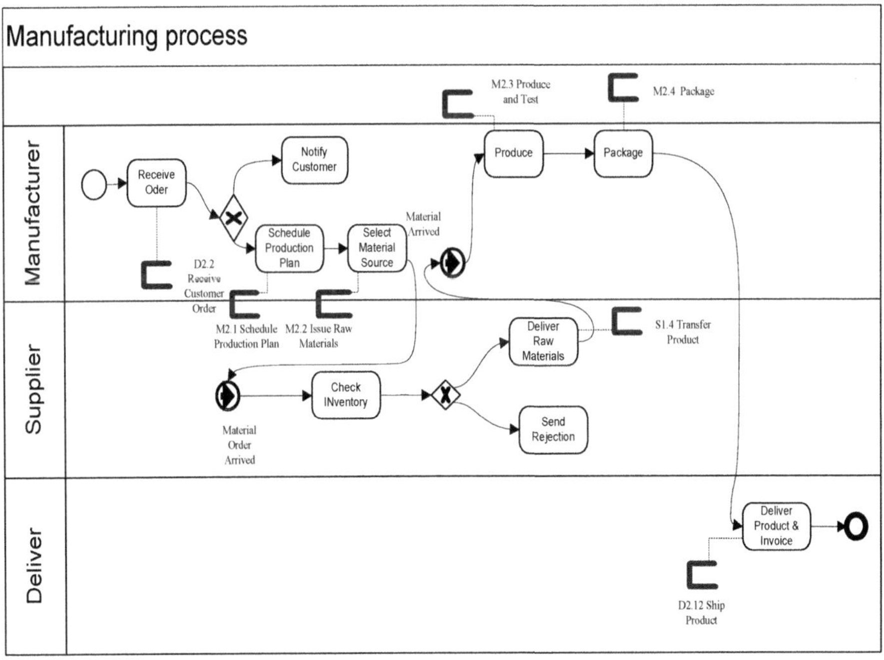

Fig. 5. An annotated manufacture process model

In this example, the supply chain process is comprised of the fragments that come from different partners: customer, manufacturer, material supplier and deliverer. Even for the same process elements of these fragments the partners might have different denotations, for example, the process element "Produce" of the manufacturer could accept the outputs of process element "deliver raw materials" which is executed by material supplier, but the material supplier might name the same process element as "Transfer Product". Such different vocabulary problems could hinder interconnecting various process fragments into a complete supply chain process. Similarly, the problems come up during the IT implementation of the process model. Through semantic annotation of the process model, such semantic ambiguity could be eliminated so that the interconnectivity of process model fragments could be achieved. The introduction of SCOR reference model, which is a de facto standard for supply chain, ensures the standardization of terms that are used in process model. Furthermore, this semantic annotation provides a basis for process searching and mining, which facilitates reusing of process models and IT implementations.

6 A Prototype Software Tool

To illustrate our, a prototype tool, so-called "scorSan (Supply Chain Process Annotating)", is developed. Figure 6 shows the framework of this prototype tool.

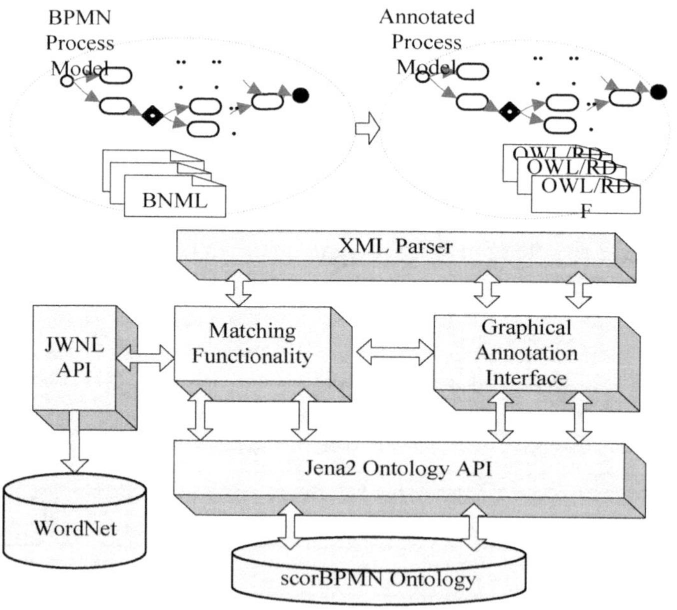

Fig. 6. The framework of the prototype tool

For the manipulation of the defined ontologies, Jena2 Ontology API is utilized, which is an open-source semantic web programmers' toolkits [27]. It is implemented in Java and offers a simple abstraction of the RDF graph as its central internal interface. WordNet is employed to exploit linguistic features of ontology, to access WordNet. JWNL API is used, which is a toolkit implemented in Java [28]. The matching functionality measures the similarities of process models elements with ontology concepts and matches them. However, this matching method could not be always succeeded and needs users' participation. Thereby a graphical interface is developed to help users to select appropriate annotation from a proposed list.

7 Conclusion

In this paper a new approach to annotate supply chain process models is proposed. This approach integrates ontological description of process models and standardized terminology of supply chains. Based on this approach, the formal semantic description of supply chain process models could be derived so that interconnectivity of process models could be achieved. Furthermore, the formal and semantic annotation improves the reusability of process models and facilitates the IT implementation.

Acknowledgement

This paper is supported by the National High Technology Research and Development Program of China ("863" Program) under No.2008AA04Z126, the National Natural Science Foundation of China under Grant No.60603080 and No.70871078.

References

1. Dumas, M., van der Aalst, W.M.P., ter Hofstede, A.H.M.: Process-aware Information Systems: Bridging People and Software through Process Technology. Wiley, Hoboken (2005)
2. Object Management Group (ed.): Business Process Modeling Notation Specification: Final Adopted Specification dtc/ 06-02-01. Object Management Group, Needham (2006)
3. Thomas, O., Fellmann, M.: Semantic EPC: Enhancing Process Modeling Using Ontology Languages. In: Proceedings of the Workshop on Semantic Business Process and Product Lifecycle Management (SBPM 2007), Innsbruck, Austria (2007)
4. Thomas, O.: Joint Reference Modeling: Collaboration Support through Version Management. In: Sprague, R.H. (ed.) Proceedings of the 40th Annual Hawaii International Conference on System Science, Big Island, Hawaii, January 3-6 (2007)
5. Hepp, M., Leymann, F., Dominique, J., Wahler, A., Fensel, D.: Semantic Business Process Management: A Vision towards Using Semantic Web Services for Business Process Management. In: Proceedings of ICEBE, pp. 535–540 (2005)
6. Lautenbacher, F., Bauer, B., Seitz, C.: Semantic Business Process Modeling – Benefits and Capability. In: AAAI 2008 Stanford Spring Symposium – AI Meets Business Rules and Process Management (AIBR), Stanford University, California, USA, March 26-28 (2008)
7. Integrated Project SUPER (Semantics Utilised for Process Management within and between Enterprises), `http://www.ip-super.org`
8. Supply Chain Council: SCOR 9.0, `https://www.supply-chain.org/resources/9.0`
9. Wand, Y., Web, R.: Research Commentary: Information Systems and Conceptual Modeling – A Research Agenda. Information System Research 13(4), 363–376 (2002)

10. Dimitrov, M., Simov, A., Stein, S., Konstantinov, M.: A BPMO Based Semantic Business Process Modeling Enviroment. In: Proceedings of the Workshop on Semantic Business Process and Product Life Management, Innsbruck, Austria (June 2007)
11. Abramowicz, W., Filpowska, A., Kaczmarek, M., Kaczmarek, T.: Semantically Enhanced Business Process Modelling Notation. In: Hepp, M., Hinkemann, K., Karagiannis, D., Klein, R., Stojanovic, N. (eds.) Proceedings of the Workshop on Semantic Business Process and Product Lifecycle Management (SBPM 2007), Innsbruck, Austria, June 7 (2007)
12. Brockmans, S., Ehrig, M., Koschmider, A., Oberweis, A., Studer, R.: Semantic Alignment of Business Processes. In: Manolopoulos, Y., Filipe, J., Constantopoulos, P., Cordeiro, J. (eds.) Proceedings of the 8th International Conference on Enterprise Information Systems (ICEIS 2006), pp. 191–196. INSTICC Press, Paphos (2006)
13. Thomas, O., Fellmann, M.: Semantic EPC: Enhancing Process Modeling Using Ontology Languages. In: Proceedings of the Workshop on Semantic Business Process and Product Lifecycle Management (SBPM 2007), 4th European Semantic Web Conference (ESWC 2007), Innsbruck, Austria, June 7 (2007)
14. Lin, Y., Strasnkas, D., Hakkarainen, S., Krogstie, S., Slvberg, A.: Semantic Annotation Framework to Manage Semantic Heterogeneity of Process Models. In: Dubois, E., Pohl, K. (eds.) CAiSE 2006. LNCS, vol. 4001, pp. 433–466. Springer, Heidelberg (2006)
15. Born, M., Dörr, F., Weber, I.: User-friendly Semantic Annotation in Business Process Modeling. In: Benatallah, B., Casati, F., Georgakopoulos, D., Bartolini, C., Sadiq, W., Godart, C. (eds.) WISE 2007. LNCS, vol. 4831, pp. 260–271. Springer, Heidelberg (2007)
16. Wang, X., Cai, H., Xu, B.: An Extended Petri-Net Based Approach for Supply Chain Process Modeling and Web Service Transformation. In: Proceedings of International Conference on Engineering Management and Service Sciences (EMS) 2009, pp. 1–5 (2009)
17. Hoyer, V., Bucherer, E., Schnabel, F.: Collaborative e-Business Process Modeling: Transforming Private EPC to Public BPMN Process Models. In: Proceedings of Business Process Management Workshops, pp. 185–196 (2008)
18. Dean, M., Schreiber, G.: Web Ontology Language (OWL) Reference Version 1.0. Technical Report, World Wide Web Consortium (W3C) (2003)
19. Staab, S., Studer, R.: Handbooks on Information System. Springer, Heidelberg (2004)
20. SUPER specification: sBPMN and sEPC to BPMO Translation, http://www.ip-super.org/res/Deliverables/M24/D4.5.pdf
21. Rabe, M., Jaekel, F., Weinaug, H.: Reference Models for Supply Chain Design and Configuration. In: Proceedings of the 2006 Winter Simulation Conference, pp. 1143–1150 (2006)
22. Meyer, H., Rohde, J., Stadtler, H., Seitz, C.: Supply Chain Analysis. In: Supply Chain Management and Advanced Planning, pp. 29–56
23. Maedche, A., Staab, S.: Measuring Similarity between Ontologies. In: Gómez-Pérez, A., Benjamins, V.R. (eds.) EKAW 2002. LNCS (LNAI), vol. 2473, pp. 251–263. Springer, Heidelberg (2002)
24. Levensthtein, I.: Binary Code Capable of Correcting Deletions, Insertions and Reversals. Cybernetics and Control Theory 10 (8), 707–710
25. W3C: RDF/OWL Representation of WordNet, W3C Working Draft (June 2006), http://www.w3.org/TR/wordnet-rdf/
26. Ehrig, M., Koschmider, A., Oberweis, A.: Measuring Similarity between Semantic Business Process Models. In: Proceedings of the 4th Asia-Pacific Conference on Conceptual Modeling, Australia (2007)
27. Wikinson, K., Sayers, C., Kuno, H.A., Reynodes, D.: Efficient RDF storage and retrieval in Jena2. In: Proceedings of 1s International Workshop on Semantic Web and Databases, pp. 131–150 (2003)
28. Didion, J.: JWNL 1.3 (2003), http://www.codezoo.com/pub/component/196?category=5

Defining Process Performance Indicators: An Ontological Approach*

Adela del-Río-Ortega, Manuel Resinas, and Antonio Ruiz-Cortés

Universidad de Sevilla, Spain

Abstract. It is increasingly important to evaluate the performance of business processes. A key instrument to carry out this evaluation is by means of Process Performance Indicators (PPIs) as suggested in many methodologies and frameworks like, for instance, COBIT, ITIL or EFQM. As a consequence, it is convenient to integrate the management of PPIs into the whole business process lifecycle from its design to its evaluation. In this paper, we focus on the definition of PPIs as a necessary step to achieve that integration. Unfortunately, current proposals are not able to specify several usual types of PPIs, specially those related to data, and are not well designed to enable the automated analysis of PPIs at design-time. In this paper, we present an ontology for the definition of process performance indicators that overcomes this issue, explicitly defines the relationships between the indicators and the elements defined in a business process modelled in BPMN, and enables the analysis of PPIs at design-time. Furthermore, this ontology has been validated by means of several real-world scenarios.

1 Introduction

An important aspect in the business process lifecycle is the evaluation of business processes performance, since it helps organisations to define and measure progress towards their goals. Performance requirements on business processes can be specified by means of Process Performance Indicators (PPIs) with target values that must be reached in a certain period. A PPI is a measure that reflects the critical success factors of a business process defined within an organisation, in which its target value reflects the objectives pursued by the organisation with that business process. Note that we use PPI as a kind of Key Performance Indicator (KPI) that focuses exclusively on the indicators defined on the business processes. Nowadays, many methodologies and frameworks like, for instance, COBIT, ITIL or the EFQM excellence model, confirm this importance by including the definition of these PPIs within their recommendations as a means to evaluate the performance of the existing business processes.

In order to make this evaluation of business processes easier, it is convenient to integrate the management of PPIs into the whole business process lifecycle [1,2]

* This work has been partially supported by the European Commission (FEDER), Spanish Government under the CICYT project SETI (TIN2009-07366); and project P07-TIC-2533 funded by the Andalusian local Government.

R. Meersman et al. (Eds.): OTM 2010, Part I, LNCS 6426, pp. 555–572, 2010.

as follows: in the design and analysis phase, PPIs should be modelled together with the business process. Furthermore, this model of PPIs should also enable their analysis by detecting the dependencies amongst them at design time and also using them as part of the business process analysis, for instance in business process simulation techniques. During the configuration phase, the instrumentation of the processes that are necessary to take the measures must be defined. During the business process enactment, when valuable execution data is gathered, the PPIs' values have to be calculated and the monitoring of these PPIs should be carried out. For instance, this can be done based on execution logs that store information about the process such as the start or end of activities. Finally, during the evaluation phase, where the monitoring information obtained in the previous phase will help to identify correlations and predict future behaviour.

An appropriate definition of PPIs is key to enable the automated support of the aforementioned PPIs lifecycle. Unfortunately, in practice, such definition is done in an informal and ad-hoc way, since there not exists any standard model to define such PPIs over business processes (defined for example in BPMN [3]). Furthermore, although there are several research proposals to define PPIs, none of them are well-suited because they cannot express commonly used PPIs or they are not ready to enable a design-time analysis of PPIs or they do not define explicitly their relationship with the business process and, hence, make it difficult their use together with business process analysis techniques (*cf.* Section 6 for more details).

To overcome this issue, we present an ontology to define PPIs whose main benefits can be summarised as follows:

1. The relation between PPIs and the business process is explicitly established. This enables the use of PPIs together with other business process analysis techniques and helps in the instrumentation of the information systems that is necessary to obtain measures automatically.
2. It supports the definition of a wide variety of PPIs, including those associated with data objects. It also supports the definition of an expressive analysis period of a PPI. In fact, our ontology supports the definition of PPIs that, as far as we know, cannot be expressed in any other similar proposal (*cf.* Section 6).
3. Dependencies between `ProcessMeasures` and `InstanceMeasures` can be automatically obtained from the ontology, which enables the analysis of PPIs at design time. Furthermore, since the ontology has been defined in OWL DL, automated reasoners can be used to make queries about the PPI model such as *how many PPIs are defined on the same* ***`MeasureDefinition`****?* or *how many PPIs are defined on a* ***`TimeMeasure`****?*.

Furthermore, we have validated the suitability of the ontology for the definition of real PPIs by using several real scenarios in different environments (the Information Technology Department of the Andalusian Health Service and the Justice and Public Administration Department of the Andalusian Local Government), in order to prove the applicability of our solution to actual scenarios.

The remainder of this paper is organised as follows. In Section 2 we present two case studies. Then in Section 3 we propose an ontology for the definition of PPIs. The ontology will be used in Section 4 to express the PPIs defined for the two case studies and to explain the way our ontology is applied to that definition. Section 5 details how dependencies between measure definitions can be inferred from the ontology. In Section 6 we present related work. Finally, Section 7 draws the conclusions from our work, summarizes the paper and outlines our future work.

2 Case Studies

In this section we introduce two real scenarios from different environments. Their processes were modelled by process modellers from each organisation using diverse languages (BPMN and flow diagrams) and the way PPIs were described by their process analysts was also different, even when it was always in a natural language (These activities were conducted before the definition of our ontology). We have unified them by modelling both scenarios in BPMN and presenting their corresponding PPIs in several tables. We intend to show the applicability of our approach to real cases from completely different organisations. Because of space constraint, in this paper we just include one process for each case study. However, more processes from these scenarios can be found at `http://www.isa.us.es/ppiontology/`.

2.1 Process of the Request For Change Management

First, we present an excerpt of a real scenario that takes place in the context of the Information Technology Department of the Andalusian Health Service. We focus on the business process of managing Request for Changes in the existing Information Systems. This process was modelled by the quality office of this department, but due to space and in order to make it easier to understand, we have simplified the real process obtaining the diagram depicted in Figure 1.

The process starts when the requester submits a Request For Change (RFC). Then, the planning and quality manager must identify the priority and analyse

Table 1. PPIs defined for the RFC management process

Description	Periodicity	id
(RFCs cancelled-registry error/RFCs registered)	annual	PPI1
Average time of committee decision	monthly and annual	PPI2
(corrective RFCs/approved RFCs)	monthly and annual	PPI3
(perfective and adaptive RFC/approved RFCs)	monthly and annual	PPI4
Average time of the "analyse RFC" activity	annual	PPI5
Number of RFCs with the state "in analysis"	monthly	PPI6
Number of RFCs per type of change	annual	PPI7
Number of RFCs per project	annual	PPI8
Number of RFCs per application	annual	PPI9
Average lifetime of a RFC	annual	PPI10

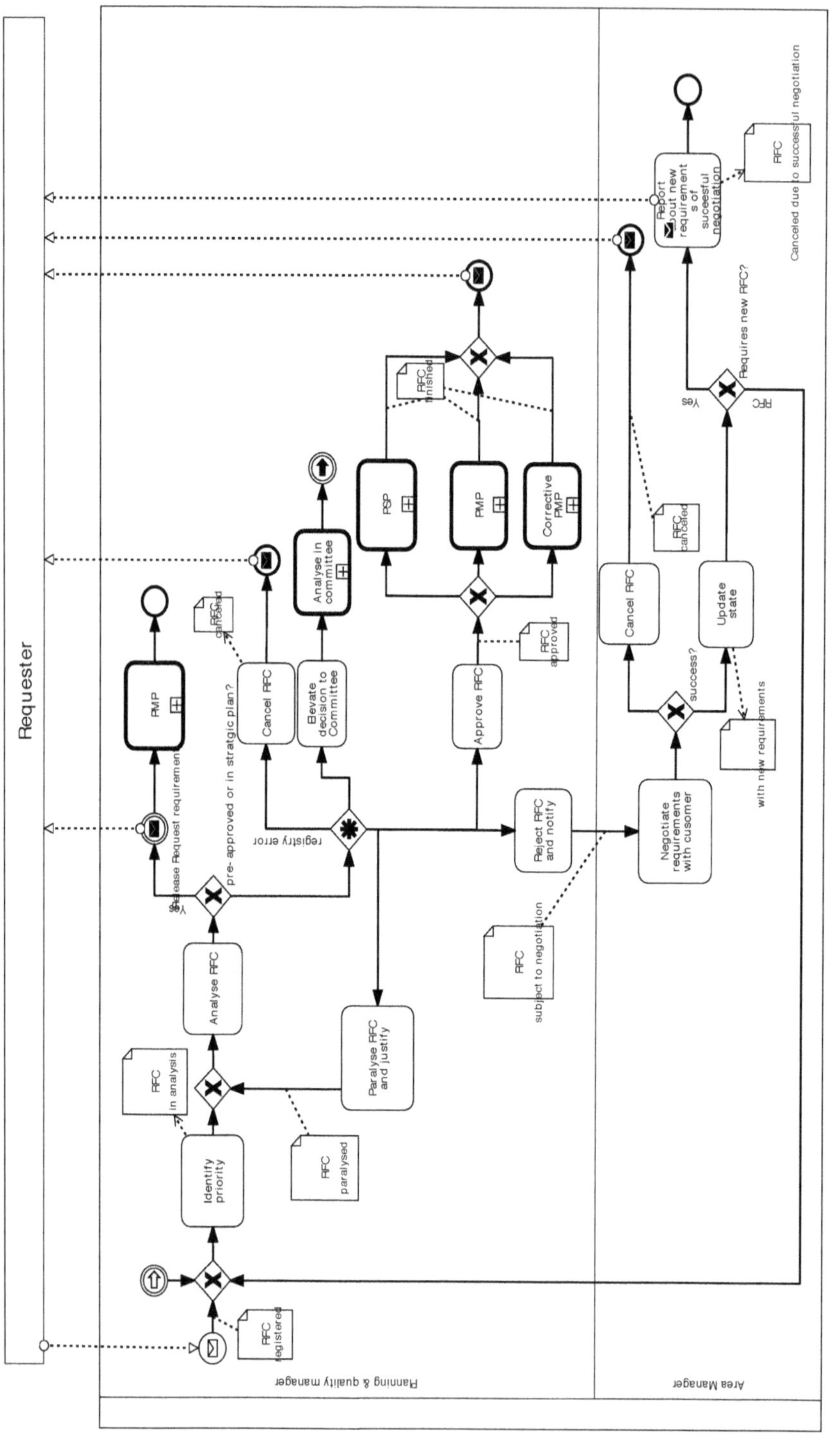

Fig. 1. Process of the request for change management

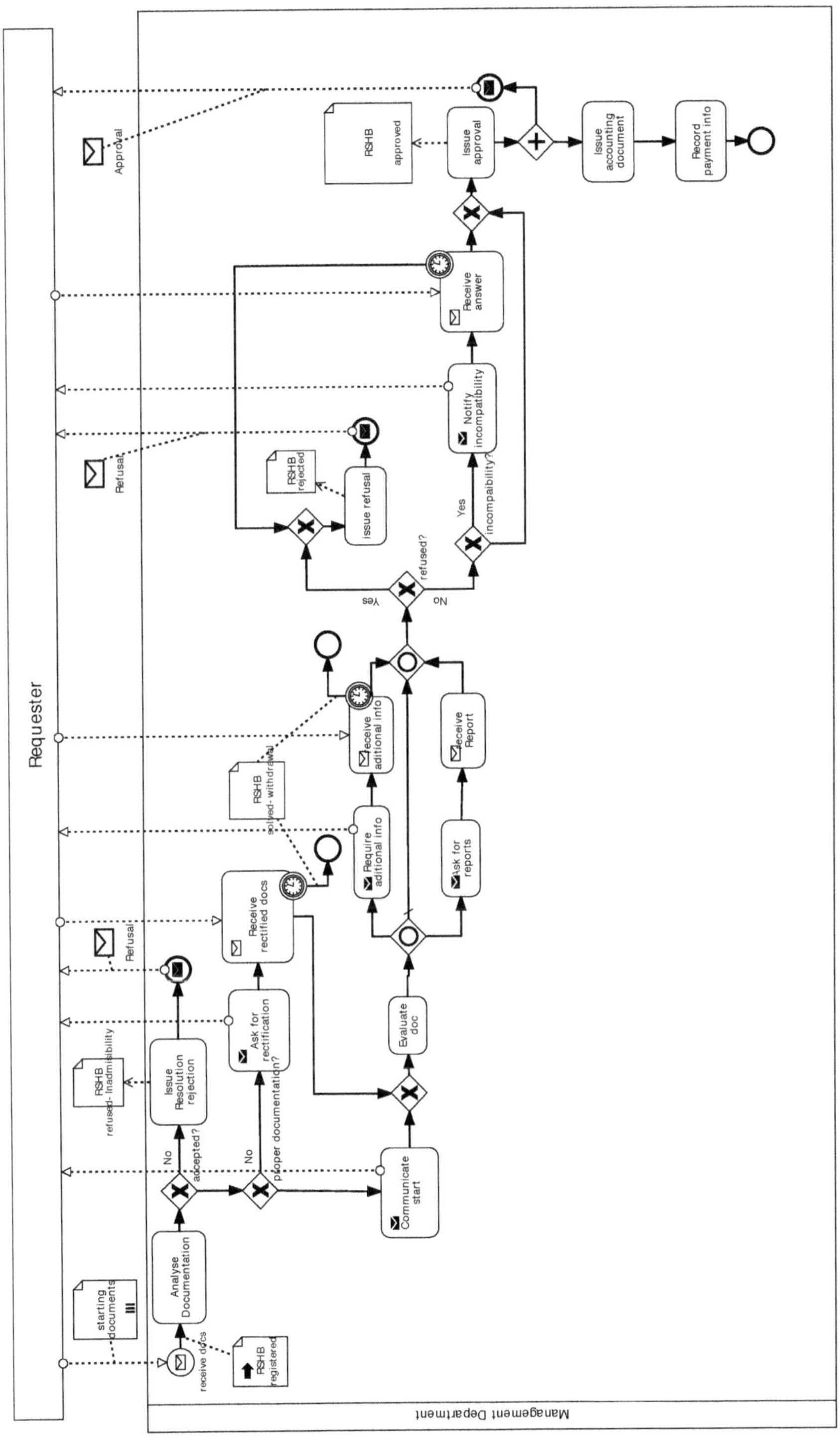

Fig. 2. Process of the social and health benefits management

the request in order to make a decision. If the RFC was in the strategic plan or pre-approved, the requester will be asked to submit a release request and the process will continue through the global Project Management Process (PMP). Otherwise, according to several factors like the availability of resources, the requirements requested, and others, the RFC will be either approved, cancelled, raised to a committee for them to make the decision, paralysed or sent to the area manager in order for her to negotiate new requirements.

In addition, throughout the process, the RFC document can pass through several states: *registered*, *in analysis*, *paralysed*, *cancelled*, *approved*, *subject to negotiation*, *with new requirements* and *cancelled due to successful negotiation.*

After modelling the process, this department also defined a set of indicators associated with it, but they did it in a spreadsheet in a natural language. Table 1 lists the PPIs they defined for the Request For Change management process.

2.2 Process of the Social and Health Benefits Management

The second case study takes place in the context of the Consejería de Justicia y Administración Pública(Andalusian Local Government). It is the business process associated with the management of social and health benefits (Figure 2).

This process starts when the requester sends the required documentation. After that, the management department analyses the documentation and decides whether to deny, ask for rectifying the documentation or evaluate the request. Sometimes further information or reports are required. Finally, the decision of rejection or approval will be sent and the payment information will be recorded. The set of PPIs defined by the process analysts of the aforementioned organisation for this process are detailed in Table 2.

Table 2. PPIs defined for the RSHB management process

Description	Periodicity	Id
Number of requests submitted	monthly and annual	PPI11
Combined budgets of requests granted	monthly and annual	PPI12
(Requests approved/requets submitted) $\times$ 100	monthly and annual	PPI13
(Requests rejected/requests submitted) $\times$ 100	monthly and annual	PPI14
(Requests rejected$_{\text{inadmissibility}}$/requests submitted) $\times$ 100	monthly and annual	PPI15
(Requests rejected$_{\text{withdrawal}}$/requests submitted) $\times$ 100	monthly and annual	PPI16
$(resolutiondate - registrationdate)/requestsregistered$	annual	PPI17
$((resolutiondate - registrationdate) - dayswithrequestsparalised)/requestsregistered$	annual	PPI18

3 PPI Ontology

In the following, we present the ontology we have defined to specify PPIs[1]. We decided to use OWL DL [4] due to the high expressivity it offers and also because

[1] The OWL file can be downloaded from `http://www.isa.us.es/ppiontology/`

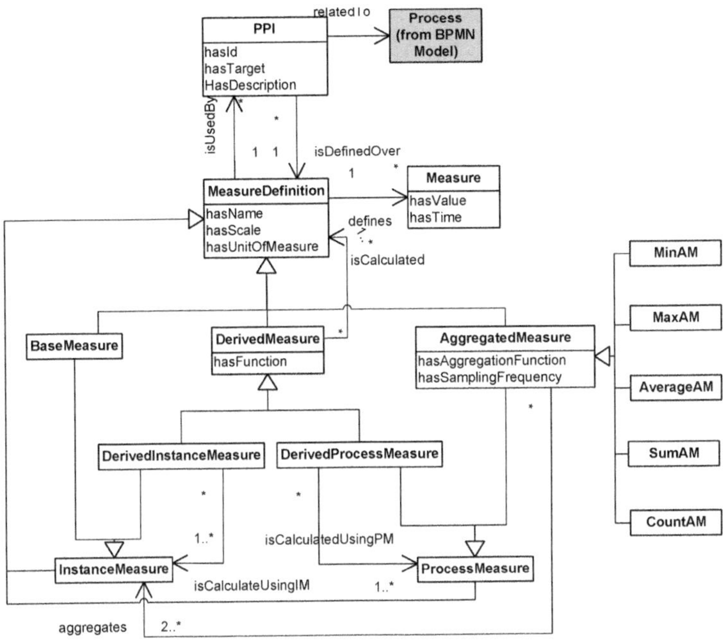

Fig. 3. PPI Ontology (overview)

there exist reasoners that allow to infer knowledge and make queries. Figure 3 depicts the high level view of our ontology. The ontology is represented using UML as proposed in [5]. Those elements depicted in a grey color do not belong to our ontology but they are concepts borrowed from BPMN.

A PPI is referred to by means of a `hasID`, described through its `hasDescription` and has a `hasTarget` restriction, which is the objective to achieve. PPIs are related to a process, and are defined by a `MeasureDefinition`. In order to define a measure, we need to specify its `hasName`, `hasScale` (set of values with defined properties, e.g. natural, integer, float, map) and, in some cases, `hasUnitOfMeasure`. `MeasureDefinitions` are used to define measures, which take values (`hasValue`) in different time instants (`hasTime`).

When formulating measures for PPIs, we can identify two classifications attending to different criteria:

- Attending to whether we consider one single process instance or we calculate the value using a set of instances by aggregating them (`aggregates`), we can distinguish between `InstanceMeasures` and `ProcessMeasures`. For instance, in our case study, an `InstanceMeasure` could be "the duration of the activity *analyse RFC*" for a given process instance, and a `ProcessMeasure` "the average duration of that activity in the last month". Usually, most PPIs will be defined using `ProcessMeasures`.

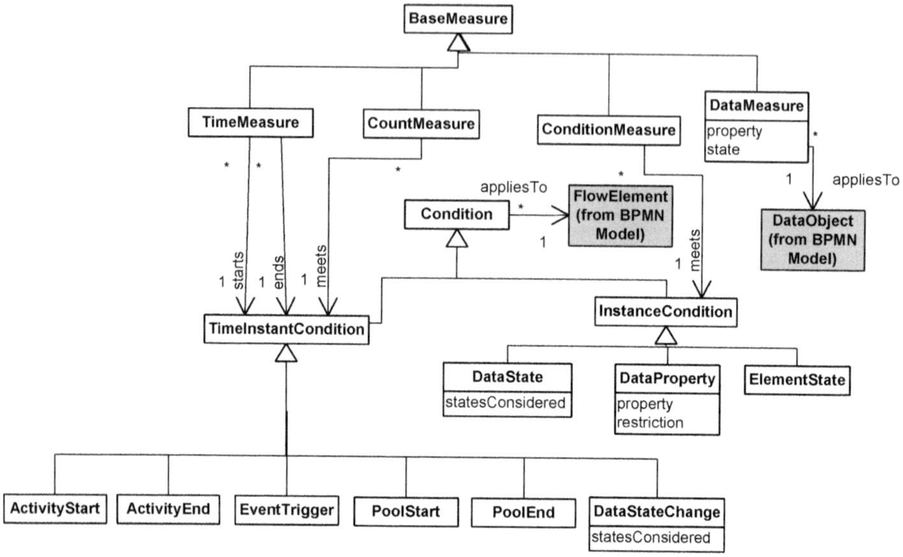

Fig. 4. PPI Ontology (`BaseMeasure` classification)

– Attending to which is the way to get the value of the measure, there are `BaseMeasures`, `AggregatedMeasures` and `DerivedMeasures`. In the following subsections we detail all of them.

3.1 BaseMeasures

In this case, the value of the measure is obtained by executing certain measurement method over a single process instance, i.e. it is an `InstanceMeasure` that is not calculated using any other measure. Depending on what needs to be measured, a different measurement method will be applied. As shown in Figure 4, we can measure time (`TimeMeasure`), the number of times that something happens (`CountMeasure`), or whether certain property of a data (`DataMeasure`), or a concrete condition (`ConditionMeasure`) is fulfilled.

TimeMeasure : In this case, the duration between two `TimeInstantConditions` (`start` and `end`) will be measured. These `TimeInstantConditions` can be associated with the start or the end of an activity or a process contained in a pool, with the trigger of an event, or with the change of the state of a data. An example of this kind of measure would be "the duration of the activity *analyse RFC*", and the start and end conditions would match the beginning and the end of this activity.

CountMeasure : It counts the number of times a `TimeInstantCondition` is met, i.e. the number of times an activity or a pool starts or ends, an event is triggered or a DataObject passes through certain states. For instance, "The number of times a RFC is analysed in an instance" is an example of this measure, and it would be measured by counting the number of times condition `activityEnd` for the activity *analyse RFC* is met. Note that it can be greater than 1 for an instance since there may be loops in the process.

`ConditionMeasure` : We can also check if certain `InstanceConditions` are being or have been met. These `ConditionMeasures` always take a boolean value for each instance. For instance, it could be useful to know whether data instances are or have finished in a given `DataState` or a set of them (e.g. "RFCs in state *paralysed*"). Or even we can check if some of the properties of a dataObject (`DataProperty`) meet a particular restriction, e.g. data with priority = "high". The last possibility we consider for `ConditionMeasures` is the `ElementState`, in which whether a `FlowElement` is currently in execution or not is checked, i.e. if it contains or not an execution token while taking the measure.

`DataMeasure` : It measures certain properties contained in the `DataObjects` themselves, e.g. number of information systems that a RFC affect to.

Note that all these `BaseMeasures` are defined (`appliesTo`) over a concrete `FlowElement` (or two in the case of `TimeMeasures`) of the associated BPMN diagram. Depending on the kind of `Condition`, this element will be an activity, a pool, an event, a data object, etc. We do not depict all these correspondences in our figure for the sake of simplicity and readability.

3.2 AggregatedMeasures

In this type of `MeasureDefinition`, the value of the measure is calculated by applying a certain `aggregationFunction` on a set of measures (belonging to different instances) to obtain one single value. Depending on whether the `aggregationFunction` applied is minimum, maximum, average, sum or count (number of "trues" for the boolean values), these measures can be `MinAM`, `MaxAM`, `AvgAM`, `SumAM` or `CountAM` respectively. An example of `AggregatedMeasure` would be "the number of RFC rejected in the last year", that would be calculated through the aggregation function SUM (it would be a `SumAM`). However, there are three issues to be considered regarding which are the process instances whose measure will be used to calculate the `AggregatedMeasure`. First, a sampling frequency can be defined, so that we do not need to measure every instance, but one out of X, being X the sampling frequency. This makes sense in environments where taking a measure is hard or costly (e.g. when the measure can not be obtained automatically). Second, when aggregating measures, it may be useful to group them by certain condition (`InstanceCondition`), for instance, "the number of RFCs per project". In such a case, the number of RFCs would be added (`SumAM`) and then they would be grouped (`isGroupedBy`) by the `DataProperty` project. The result would be a map, with a value per each project. Third, usually an `AggregatedMeasure` defines a temporal range to consider when measuring. This temporal range is defined by means of an `analysisPeriod` (depicted in

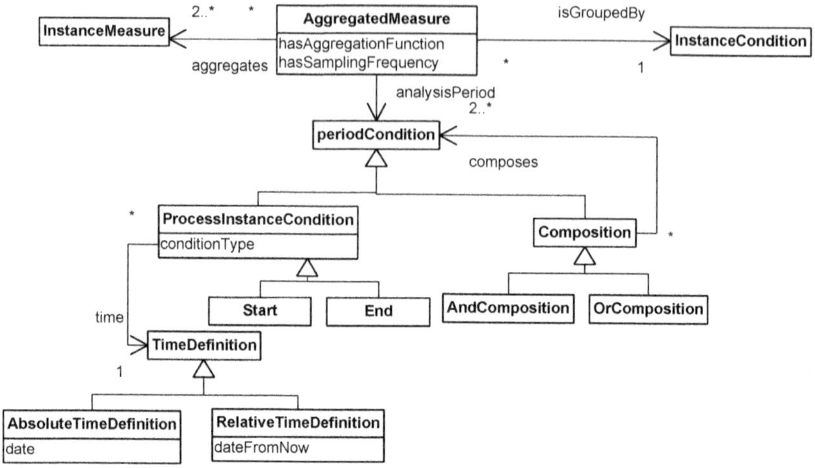

Fig. 5. PPI Ontology (Analysis period definition)

Figure 5) and must be understood as a temporal condition that must hold every process instance for its measures to be included in the aggregation.

The condition (`ProcessInstanceCondition`), which can be of different types (`conditionType`: $>$, $\geq$, $<$ and $\leq$), is defined between the start/end of process instances and the moments in time (`TimeDefinition`), usually two, that define the period(s) in which to take the measures. Moreover, these conditions can be composed by means of an AND and/or an OR operator when necessary. For instance, it could be interesting to measure the number of RFCs rejected during the last holidays' periods, both Christmas and summer. Thus, only the measures whose process instances finished between 18-12-2009 and 4-1-2010, or between 1-8-2009 and 31-8-2009 would be considered.

3.3 DerivedMeasures

Their value is calculated by performing a mathematical function to combine two or more `MeasureDefinitions`. Depending on whether the measures combined are instance or process measures, the result will be a `DerivedInstanceMeasure` or a `DerivedProcessMeasure` respectively. Examples for both cases are respectively "the percentage of time spent in the activity *analyse RFC* with respect to the duration of the whole process", and "percentage of rejected RFCs with respect to all the registered RFCs".

4 Validating Our Ontology

To validate the suitability of the ontology for the definition of real PPIs, we translate textual descriptions of indicators defined by process analysts from several real scenarios to their equivalent representation using the PPI ontology

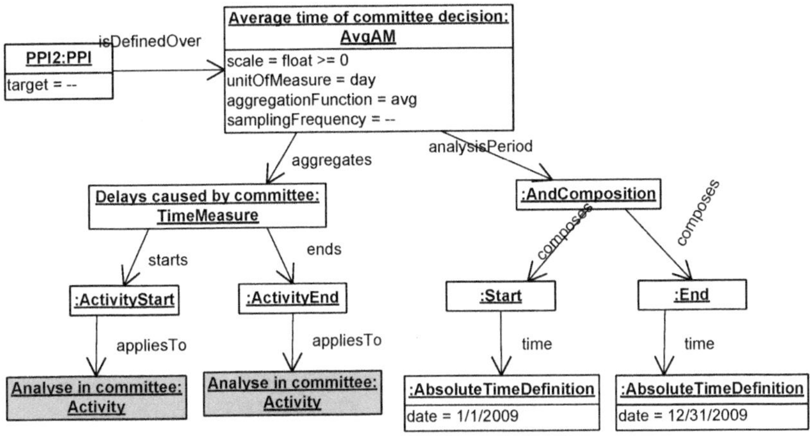

Fig. 6. Definition of the PPI2 "Delays caused by the committee"

presented in Section 3. However, due to space constraints, we only include in the paper the definition of some of the PPIs from our two case studies (the ones we considered more representative). The definition of the remaining PPIs of the processes included in this paper together with PPIs from other processes are available at `http://www.isa.us.es/ppiontology/`.

4.1 Process of the Request for Change Management

In Section 2 we introduced a real scenario in the context of the Information Technology Department of the Andalusian Health Service whose PPIs were listed in Table 1. With our ontology, we can directly express all of those PPIs.

PPI2 (Figure 6). We omit the description in the PPI box for space reasons. This PPI2 is defined over an aggregated measure that calculates the average of a time base measure. This time measure represent the duration of the activity *analyse in committee.*

PPI8 (Figure 7). It is defined over an aggregated measure that counts all the RFCs registered, grouping them by the project they belong to. The result of this PPI will be a map, with one value per project.

4.2 Process of the Social and Health Benefits Management

Anew, we proceed as we did with the previous scenario, now refereing to the process associated with the management of social and health benefits. We transform the textual descriptions of indicators contained in Table 2 to our ontology. We choose again two indicators for doing so.

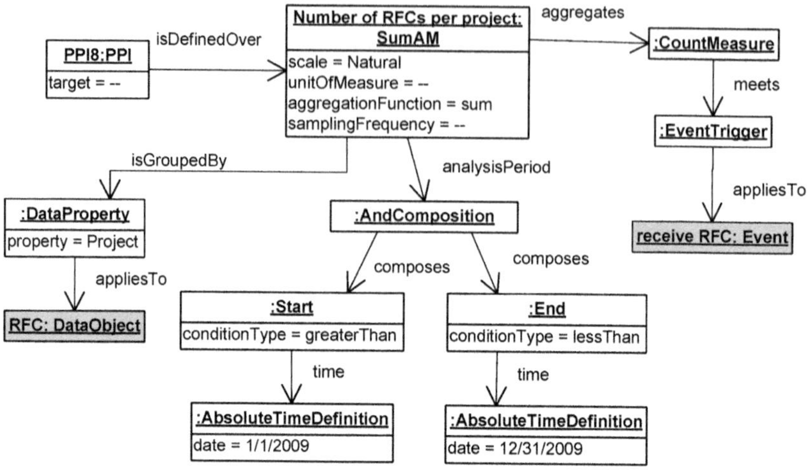

Fig. 7. Definition of the PPI8 "Number of RFCs per project"

PPI12 (Figure 8). This PPI is defined over an aggregated measure that sums the budget of each RSHB (Request of Social or Health Benefit) approved during last year (instances started on or after the first of January and ended before or on the 31st of December).

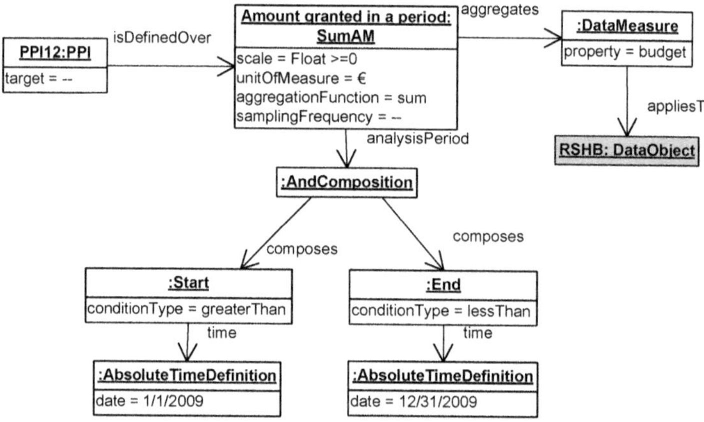

Fig. 8. Definition of the PPI12 "Amount granted in a period"

PPI13 (Figure 9). It is defined over the derived process measure *percentage of requests approved*, that is calculated using two aggregated measures, according to the defined function. The first one sums the number of requests approved last year by counting the number of times the activity *Issue approval* finished in that period. The second one sums the number of requests registered last year by

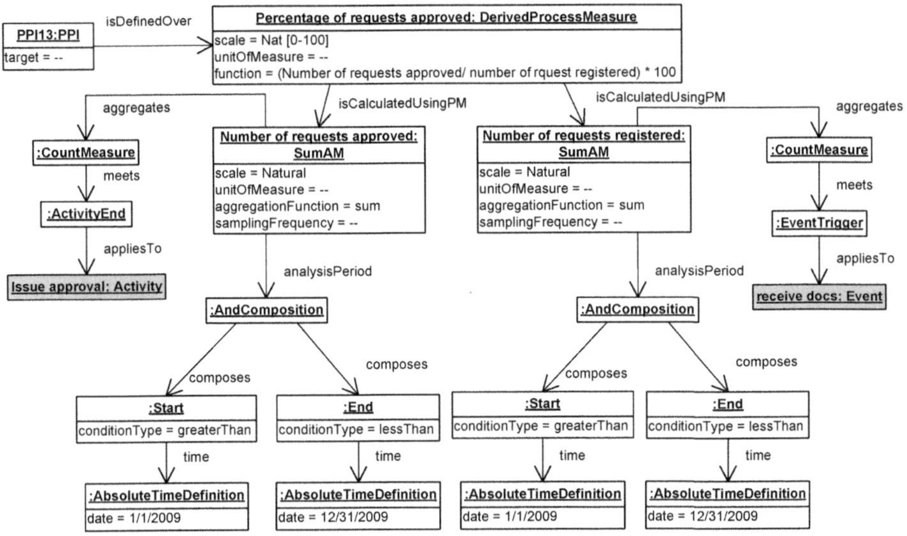

Fig. 9. Definition of the PPI13 "Percentage of requests approved"

counting the number of times the event *receive doc* is triggered. The definition of the analysis period is the same for both of them and coincides with the one of the previous PPI.

5 Modelling Dependencies on the PPI Ontology

The PPI ontology defines two types of relationships between `MeasureDefinitions`: `aggregates` and `isCalculated`. The former means that the measures defined by the `MeasureDefinition` are calculated as an aggregation of the same type of measures (i.e., defined by the same `MeasureDefinition`) from different process instances. The latter means that the measures are calculated as a mathematical function of either several different process measures, or several different measures from the same process instance. This last property can be further refined into two subproperties: `isCalculatedPositively` and `isCalculatedNegatively`, depending on whether the changes in one measure affect the other measure either in the same direction (positive) or the opposite direction (negative). For instance, if $PercentRequestsApproved = \frac{RequestsApproved}{RequestRegistered} \times 100$, then:

$$isCalculatedPositively(PercentRequestsApproved, RequestsApproved)$$
$$isCalculatedNegatively(PercentRequestsApproved, RequestRegistered)$$

These relationships define a dependency between `MeasureDefinitions` in the sense that changes in the measures defined by one `MeasureDefinition` have an influence on the measures defined by the other `MeasureDefinition`. Therefore, two new properties can be added to the ontology, namely: `dependsOn` and its inverse property, `isDepended`. Furthermore, each of these two relationships can be refined again into other two different relationships in the same way as `isCalculated`, i.e., depending on whether the changes in one measure affect the other measure either in the same direction (`dependsDirectlyOn`) or the opposite direction (`dependsInverselyOn`).

Therefore, if a `MeasureDefinition` $m1$ aggregates a `MeasureDefinition` $m2$, then $m1$ depends directly on $m2$. Similarly, if a `MeasureDefinition` $m1$ is calculated on another `MeasureDefinition` $m2$, then $m1$ depends either directly or inversely on $m2$ depending on whether $m1$ is calculated positively or negatively from $m2$ respectively. These statements can be expressed as inference rules in the ontology as follows[2]:

$$\begin{aligned} directlyAggregates(?x, ?y) &\longrightarrow dependsDirectlyOn(?x, ?y) \\ isCalculatedPositively(?x, ?y) &\longrightarrow dependsDirectlyOn(?x, ?y) \\ isCalculatedNegatively(?x, ?y) &\longrightarrow dependsInverselyOn(?x, ?y) \end{aligned}$$

Furthermore, other inference rules can be defined to propagate the dependencies throughout all `MeasureDefinitions`. These rules infer the dependencies between two `MeasureDefinitions` (x and z) by means of the dependencies they have with another `MeasureDefinition` y as follows:

$$\begin{aligned} & isCalculatedNegatively(?x, ?y), \\ & \quad dependsInverselyOn(?y, ?z) \longrightarrow dependsDirectlyOn(?x, ?z) \\ & isCalculatedNegatively(?x, ?y), \\ & \quad dependsDirectlyOn(?y, ?z) \longrightarrow dependsInverselyOn(?x, ?z) \\ & isCalculatedPositively(?x, ?y), \\ & \quad dependsDirectlyOn(?y, ?z) \longrightarrow dependsDirectlyOn(?x, ?z) \\ & isCalculatedPositively(?x, ?y), \\ & \quad dependsInverselyOn(?y, ?z) \longrightarrow dependsInverselyOn(?x, ?z) \end{aligned}$$

Since most modern OWL-DL reasoners allow the use of SWRL rules together with the ontology as a means to extend the expressiveness of OWL DL, the rules defined above can be used to infer all of the dependencies amongst MeasureDefinitions and, then, all these inferred knowledge can be used to answer queries regarding the PPIs defined in one organisation. For instance, we may identify potentially conflicting PPIs if they are defined over two `MeasureDefinitions` $m1$ and $m2$ and there is a third `MeasureDefinition` $m3$ such as $m1$ depends directly on $m3$ and $m2$ depends inversely on $m3$ or *vice versa*.

[2] Rules are expressed using a syntax close to the Semantic Web Rules Language (SWRL).

Table 3. Comparison of the analysed approaches and our proposal

Proposal	**(1)**	**(2)**	**(3)**	**(4)**	**(5)**	**(6)**
Pedrinaci et al. [6]	N/A	✓	✗	✓	~	~
Popova et al. [10]	✓	✓	N/A	✗	✓	✗
Mayerl et al. [12]	~	✗	✗	✓	~	✗
Castellanos et al. [13]	~	✗	N/A	~	✗	✗
Momm et al. [14]	✓	✗	✗	✗	✗	✗
Wetzstein et al. [15]	✓	✗	✗	✗	~	✗
Our Proposal	✓	✓	✓	✓	✓	✓

(1) Explicit relation with the business process (4) Derived measures
(2) Definition of analysis period (5) Analysis of PPIs (Design-time)
(3) Data measures (6) Queries about PPIs

6 Related Work

There already exists a number of proposals that use ontologies in business process management [6], ranging from ontologies supporting the definition of organisational structures [7], business processes [8] or even business goals to ontologies for capturing execution logs and supporting business process analysis [9]. There are also some other ontologies dedicated to define measures in different areas, like [11] for software measurement or the one introduced by Pedrinaci et al. [6], which describes a Semantic Business Process Monitoring Tool called SENTINEL, and, therefore, it is closer to our proposal. This tool can support automated reasoning, though the authors point out that one aspect to be improved is the analysis engines in order to support deviations. In this paper, they also present a metric ontology to allow the definition and computation of metrics, which take into account many of the aspects we do and it is based on the concept of population filter, which is somehow similar to our "analysis period" but not only limited to time. However, it is not clear how PPIs can be analysed and queried based on this concept nor it is clear whether it allows an explicit relation between PPIs and the elements of a business process. Furthermore, they deal with runtime analysis, but not design-time.

Outside the semantic web-based approach, there are also several approaches to evaluate the performance of business processes defined in the literature and, in some cases, implemented in products.

Popova et al. [10] present a framework for modeling performance indicators within a general organisation modeling framework. They define indicators by assigning values to a set of attributes, but they do not point out the way these indicators are calculated. They do it, instead, in [18], where they present formal techniques for analysis of executions of organizational scenarios. They also define, in this work, relations between PPIs and the processes, and relationships between PPIs (causality, correlation and aggregation), introduced briefly in [10] and explained in detail in [18]. According to the definition of the analysis period, they define temporal properties over PPIs (called PI expressions) in [19]. They do not consider derived measures nor queries in their works.

In [12] Mayerl et al. discuss how to derive metric dependency definitions from functional dependencies by applying dependency patterns. However, they do not delve into the definition of measures, they only set the semantics of some elements to consider when defining measures.

Castellanos et al.'s approach [13] is implemented in the IBOM platform, that allows, among other things, to define business measures and perform intelligent analysis on them to understand causes of undesired values and predict future values. The user can define business measures (through a GUI) to measure characteristics of process instances, processes, resources or of the overall business operations. Specifically, they characterize metrics through four attributes: name (unique), target entity (objet to be measured), data type (numeric, boolean, taxonomy or SLA) and desirable metric values. For the computation logic definition, templates are used. These templates map data and metadata about process executions into numeric and boolean measures. This approach is not focused on business processes but on the whole organisation. Anyway, during the definition of metrics, as far as we can deduce from the paper, they do not take into account some aspects we do, as the analysis period, the unit of measure, the dimension to be measured. It is not possible to know which is the set of measures than can be defined with this approach.

In [14], Momm et al. present a metamodel for the specification of the PPI monitoring, an extension of the BPMN metamodel for modeling the required instrumentation for the monitoring, and an outline of methodology for an automated generation of this instrumentation. However, the metamodel for the specification of performance indicators does not consider those related to data or events (PPI6, PPI12 and PPI16 from our examples can not be defined according to this metamodel). Moreover, it lacks some properties when defining PPIs like the analysis period or the function to calculate derived measures.

Another work which is close to ours is the one presented by Wetzstein et al. in [15]. This paper introduces a framework for BAM as part of the semantic business process management. The authors describe a KPI ontology using WSML to specify KPIs over semantic business processes. However, our ontology improves this one, since they do not take into account indicators related to data (they can not define PPI6).

To sum up all this information and establish an explicit comparison between the approaches analysed above and our proposal, we present Table 3. We highlight those benefits we assigned to our ontology in Section 1: relation between PPIs and BPs (feature 1), definition of a wide variety of PPIs (feature 2, 3 and 4), and analysis and queries on PPIs (features 5 and 6). We use the following notation: A ✓ sign means that the proposal successfully addresses the issue; a $\sim$ sign indicates that it addresses it partially; a ✗ sign indicates that it does not contemplate the issue; and N/A means the information is not available.

7 Conclusions and Future Work

In this paper, we argue the importance of integrating the management of PPIs into the whole business process lifecycle. Specifically, in the design and analysis phase, PPIs must be modelled together with the business process. This model should enable (at design-time) an automated or semi-automated analysis to, for instance, detect the dependencies and potential conflicts amongst them or to use them together with other business process analysis techniques such as simulation techniques. As a consequence the mechanism used to define PPIs must be expressive enough to allow the definition of a wide range of PPIs; it must establish explicitly the relation between PPIs and the business process, and it must enable the analysis of PPIs at design-time.

To this end, we present an ontology to describe these indicators (allowing the definition of such a variety of PPIs). We also identify how they depend on the performed activities and other business objects by establishing these relationships between PPIs and business processes explicitly. Finally the definition of PPIs using OWL-DL enables their analysis at design-time in a way that is amenable to automated reasoning, as outlined in Section 5. Furthermore, we have validated the ontology against several real-world case-studies to check its expressiveness.

Our future work focuses on increasing the number of types of PPIs that can be defined using the ontology and improving the automated analysis capabilities. Regarding the former, we want to extend our ontology to allow the specification of complex conditions, for instance, *number of RFCs approved after being previously rejected*. In the last case, complex queries on BPMN such as those defined in BPMN-Q [16] could be used as a type of `Condition`. Regarding the latter, we plan to extend the automated detection of dependencies between measure definitions to detect dependencies amongst different base measures. Furthermore, we are developing a graphical notation in order to depict these ontological concepts of PPIs over business processes and we are also integrating this notation into the web-based editor ORYX [17] as a result of a collaboration stay with the BPT group at the HPI Potsdam.

Acknowledgments

We would like to thank to the Quality Office of the Information Technology Department of the Andalusian Health Service for kindly providing us their internal business process models and its PPIs. We also would like to thank F. Casati, J. Fabra, J. M. García, C. Pedrinaci, F. Ruiz, A. Sharpanskykh and M. Weske for their helpful comments in earlier versions of this paper.

References

1. Weske, M.: Business Process Management: Concepts, Languages, Architectures. Springer, Heidelberg (2007)
2. del Río-Ortega, A., Resinas, M., Ruiz-Cortés, A.: Towards modelling and tracing key performance indicators in business processes. In: II Taller sobre Procesos de Negocio e Ingeniería de Servicios, PNIS 2009 (2009)
3. OMG: Business process modeling notation (BPMN) v2.0 (2009)

4. W3C OWL Working Group: Owl 2 web ontology language (2009)
5. Brockmans, S., Volz, R., Eberhart, A., Löffler, P.: Visual modeling of OWL DL ontologies using UML. In: McIlraith, S.A., Plexousakis, D., van Harmelen, F. (eds.) ISWC 2004. LNCS, vol. 3298, pp. 198–213. Springer, Heidelberg (2004)
6. Pedrinaci, C., Lambert, D., Wetzstein, B., van Lessen, T., Cekov, L., Dimitrov, M.: Sentinel: a semantic business process monitoring tool. In: OBI, p. 1 (2008)
7. Abramowicz, W., Filipowska, A., Kaczmarek, M., Pedrinaci, C., Starzecka, M.A.W.: Organization structure description for the needs of semantic business process management. In: 3rd international Workshop on Semantic Business Process Management colocated with 5th European Semantic Web Conference (2008)
8. Abramowicz, W., Filipowska, A., Kaczmarek, M., Kaczmarek, T.: Semantically enhanced business process modelling notation. In: Proceedings of SBPM 2007 Semantic Process and Product Lifecycle Management in conjunction with the 3rd European Semantic Web Conference, ESWC 2007 (2007)
9. Pedrinaci, C., Domingue, J., Alves de Medeiros, A.K.: A core ontology for business process analysis. In: Bechhofer, S., Hauswirth, M., Hoffmann, J., Koubarakis, M. (eds.) ESWC 2008. LNCS, vol. 5021, pp. 49–64. Springer, Heidelberg (2008)
10. Popova, V., Sharpanskykh, A.: Modeling organizational performance indicators. In: Information Systems (2009)
11. Garcia, F., Bertoa, M.F., Calero, C., Vallecillo, A., Ruiz, F., Piattini, M., Genero, M.: Towards a consistent terminology for software measurement. Information & Software Technology (48), 631–644 (2006)
12. Mayerl, C., Hüner, K., Gaspar, J.U., Momm, C., Abeck, S.: Definition of metric dependencies for monitoring the impact of quality of services on quality of processes. In: Second IEEE/IFIP International Workshop on Business-driven IT Management (Munich), pp. 1–10 (2007)
13. Castellanos, M., Casati, F., Shan, M.C., Dayal, U.: ibom: a platform for intelligent business operation management. In: Proceedings of 21st International Conference on Data Engineering, pp. 1084–1095. Hewlett-Packard Laboratories (2005)
14. Momm, C., Malec, R., Abeck, S.: Towards a model-driven development of monitored processes. Wirtschaftsinformatik (2), 319–336 (2007)
15. Wetzstein, B., Ma, Z., Leymann, F.: Towards Measuring Key Performance Indicators of Semantic Business Processes. In: 11th International Conference on Business Information Systems (BIS 2008) & Innsbruck, Austria, pp. 227–238 (2008)
16. Awad, A., Decker, G., Weske, M.: Efficient compliance checking using bpmn-q and temporal logic. In: Dumas, M., Reichert, M., Shan, M.-C. (eds.) BPM 2008. LNCS, vol. 5240, pp. 326–341. Springer, Heidelberg (2008)
17. Decker, G., Overdick, H., Weske, M.: Oryx - An Open Modeling Platform for the BPM Community. In: Dumas, M., Reichert, M., Shan, M.-C. (eds.) BPM 2008. LNCS, vol. 5240, pp. 382–385. Springer, Heidelberg (2008)
18. Popova, V., Sharpanskykh, A.: Formal analysis of executions of organizational scenarios based on process-oriented specifications. In: Applied Intelligence (2009)
19. Popova, V., Sharpanskykh, A.: Formal Goal-based Modeling of Organizationss. In: MSVVEIS, pp. 19–28 (2008)

Peer Rewiring in Semantic Overlay Networks under Churn
(Short Paper)

Paraskevi Raftopoulou[1,2] and Euripides G.M. Petrakis[2]

[1] University of Peloponnese (UOP), Tripoli, 22100, Greece
[2] Technical University of Crete (TUC), Chania, 73100, Greece
praftop@uop.gr, petrakis@intelligence.tuc.gr

Abstract. Semantic overlay networks have been proposed as a way to organise peer-to-peer networks; peers that are semantically, thematically or socially similar are discovered and logically organised into groups. Efficient content retrieval is then performed by routing the query towards peer groups based on their likelihood to match the query. In this paper, we study the behaviour of semantic overlay networks that support full-fledged information retrieval in the presence of peer churn. We adopt a model for peer churn, and study the effect of network dynamics on peer organisation and retrieval performance. The overlay network is evaluated on a realistic peer-to-peer environment using real-world data and queries, and taking into account the dynamics of user-driven peer participation. Using this evaluation, we draw conclusions on the performance of the system in terms of clustering efficiency, communication load and retrieval accuracy in such a realistic setting.

1 Introduction

The main idea behind peer-to-peer (P2P) is that instead of relying on central components, functionality is provided through decentralised overlay architectures, where peers typically connect to a small set of other peers. Specifically in Semantic Overlay Networks (SONs), peers that are semantically, thematically or socially similar are *organised* into groups. Queries are then selectively forwarded to those groups that have the potential to provide content matching the queries. SONs, while being highly flexible, improve query performance and guarantee high degree of peer autonomy [5]. Unlike what their name imply, SONs do not necessarily use semantics in the traditional sense (e.g., ontologies), however this is the term first proposed in the literature [3].

SONs technology has proven useful not only for information sharing in distributed environments, but also as a natural distributed alternative to Web 2.0 application domains, such as decentralised social networking in the spirit of Flickr or del.icio.us. Contrary to structured overlays that focus on providing accurate location mechanisms (e.g., [20]), SONs are better suited for loose P2P architectures, which assume neither a specific network structure nor total control

R. Meersman et al. (Eds.): OTM 2010, Part I, LNCS 6426, pp. 573–581, 2010.

over the location of the data. Additionally, SONs offer better support of semantics due to their ability to provide mechanisms for approximate, range, or text queries, and emphasise peer autonomy. Naturally, the one technique does not exclude the other, since semantic overlays can appear over structured overlays in an attempt to combine their good properties [4].

The management of large volumes of data in P2P networks has generated additional interest in methods supporting information retrieval (IR) (e.g., [6,2]). Most of these research proposals, while exploiting certain architectural [6] or modelling [2] aspects of peer organisation, assume for their experimental evaluation an ideal scenario where peers never leave or join the network. However, studies of P2P content-sharing systems have concluded that peers are typically dynamic (e.g., [21]). A peer joins the network when a user starts the application. While being connected, the peer can contribute resources to the network and search for resources provided by other peers. The peer leaves the system when the user exits the application. Stutzbach and Rejaie [21] define such a join-participate-leave cycle as a *session*. The independent arrival and departure of peers creates the collective effect called *churn*. These user-driven dynamics of peer participation is a critical issue, since churn affects the overlay structure [22], the resiliency of the overlay [8,25], the selection of key design parameters [9], and the content availability which in turn, affects retrieval effectiveness.

To the best of our knowledge, the work presented in this paper is the first to address the issues involved in the design and the evaluation of the SONs when introducing peer churn. We adopt a model for peer churn proposed by Yao et al. [25], and study the effect of network dynamics on peer organisation and retrieval performance. The overlay network is evaluated on a realistic P2P environment using real-world data and queries. Based on the results of this evaluation, we draw conclusions on the performance of the system in terms of clustering efficiency, communication load and retrieval accuracy.

The remainder of the paper is organised as follows. SON-like structures supporting IR functionality are reviewed in Section 2. Section 3 presents the model used to describe peer churn, while Section 4 presents a SON architecture and the related rewiring protocol. Finally, the experimental evaluation of the dynamic network is presented in Section 5.

2 Related Work and Background

Initial IR approaches implementing SON-like structures and supporting content search in a distributed collection of peers include the work of Li et al. [10], where semantic small world (SSW) is proposed. SSW aims to construct a self-organising network based on the semantics of data objects stored locally to peers. Along the same lines, Schmitz [18] assumes that peers share concepts from a common ontology and proposes strategies for organising peers into communities with similar concepts. i*Cluster* [15] extends these protocols by allowing peers with multiple and dynamic interests to form clusters.

Loser et al. [12] introduce the concept of semantic overlay clusters for super-peer networks. This work aims at clustering peers that store complex heterogeneous schemes by using a super-peer architecture. Along the same lines, Lu et al. [13] propose a two-tier architecture. In this architecture, a peer provides content-based information about neighbouring peers and determines how to route queries in the network. In [6], Klampanos et al. propose an architecture for IR-based clustering of peers. In this architecture, a representative peer (hub) maintains information about all other hubs and is responsible for query routing.

The notion of peer clustering based on similar interests rather than similar documents is introduced by Sripanidkulchai et al. [19]. According to this work, peers are organised on the top of the existing Gnutella network to improve retrieval performance. Emphasising on small world networks, Voulgaris et al. [23] propose an epidemic protocol that implicitly clusters peers with similar content. In [11], Loser et al. propose a three-layer organisation of peers (based both on peer content and usefulness estimators) and suggest combining information from all layers for routing queries.

Aberer at al. [1] introduce a decentralised process that, relying on pair-wise local interactions, incrementally develops global agreement and obtains semantic interoperability among data sources. Koloniari et al. [7] model peer clustering as a game, where peers try to maximise the recall for their local query workload by joining the appropriate clusters.

Most of the above presented research proposals, while exploiting certain architectural or modelling aspects of peer organisation, assume for their experimental evaluation an ideal scenario where peers never leave or join the network. In this paper, we address the issues involved in the design and the evaluation of the SONs when introducing the dynamics of user-driven peer participation.

3 Churn Model

Building upon previous work [25,8,21], we present a model of user behaviour characterising peer arrivals and departures in a P2P system. The model takes into account heterogeneous browsing habits, formalises recurring user participation in P2P systems and explains the relationship between the various lifetime distributions observable in P2P networks.

Churn Model. We consider a P2P network with N peers. Each peer p_i is either *alive* (i.e., present in the system) at a specific moment or *dead* (i.e., logged-off). This behaviour is modelled by a renewal process $\{Z_i(t)\}$ for each peer p_i, $0 \leq i \leq N$, as in [25]. This process is 1 if p_i is alive at time t, and 0 otherwise. The following assumptions are made:

1. To capture the independent nature of peers, we assume that peers behave independently of each other and processes $\{Z_i(t)\}$ and $\{Z_j(t)\}$, for any $i \neq j$, are independent. This means that peers do not synchronise their arrivals or departures and generally exhibit uncorrelated lifetime characteristics.
2. Although the model is generic enough to allow dependencies between cycle lengths, without loss of generality we treat all on-line processes (or lifetime) and off-time processes as independent and use identical distributed sets of variables. Thus, for each process $\{Z_i(t)\}$ its on-line durations $\{L_{i,t}\}$

are described by some distribution $F_i(x)$ and its off-line durations $\{D_{i,t}\}$ are described by another distribution $G_i(x)$. By this, for each peer its on-line and off-line durations are independent.

Lifetime Distribution. The on-line distribution commonly considered in the literature [25,8] is the heavy-tail distribution. The same consideration holds for the off-line distribution. To allow for arbitrarily small lifetimes, a Pareto distribution [25] is used to represent the on-line durations $F(x) = 1 - (x/x_m)^{-k}$, $x_m > 0$, $k > 1$, where x stands for the on-line durations. Off-line durations are respectively represented by an alike Pareto distribution $G(x)$. Each Pareto distribution is parameterised by the quantities x_m and k, which stand for the *scale* and the *shape* of the distribution respectively. The scale parameter sets the position of the left edge of the probability density function. The shape parameter determines the skewness of the distribution.

Peer Availability. The *availability* a_i of peer p_i is the probability that p_i is in the system at a random moment. Intuitively, we expect this probability to represent the lifetime of a peer over the entire lifetime of the system. Yao et al. [25] define the average on-line duration (or lifetime) of a peer p_i as $l_i = E[L_i]$ and its average off-line duration as $d_i = E[D_i]$. The availability a_i of peer p_i is then calculated, in the spirit of [17], as $a_i = \lim_{t \to \infty} P(Z_i(t) = 1) = \frac{l_i}{l_i + d_i}$.

According to this model, the only parameters that control a peer's availability are the on-line l_i and the off-line d_i durations. Notice that these parameters are *independent* and *unique* for each peer. Parameters l_i and d_i are drawn independently from two Pareto distributions. Once pair (l_i, d_i) is generated for each peer p_i, it remains constant for the entire evolution of the system.

4 A Semantic Overlay Network

The present work uses i*Cluster* P2P network [15], which extends the idea of peer organisation in small-world networks by allowing peers to have multiple and dynamic interests. i*Cluster* peers are responsible for serving both users searching for and users contributing information to the network. Each i*Cluster* peer is characterised by its information content (i.e., its document collection), which may be either automatically (by text analysis) or manually (e.g., tags or index terms) assigned to each document. To identify its *interests*, a peer categorises its documents by using an external reference system (i.e., an ontology as in [18] or a taxonomy such as the ACM categorisation system) or by clustering. Thereupon, a peer may be assigned *more than one* interests. Interests are created and deleted dynamically to reflect the documents a peer contributes to the network.

Each peer maintains (for each interest) a *routing index* (RI) holding information for short- and long-range links to other peers. Short-range links connect peers inside a SON (i.e., peers with similar interest), while long-range links are used to interconnect SONs. Entries in the routing index contain the IP addresses of the peers the links point to and the corresponding interests of these peers.

The basic protocols that determine the way peers join the overlay network, connect to and disconnect from the network, and the way queries are processed are thoroughly presented in [16]. Below, we present the protocol that specifies the way peers dynamically self-organise into SONs.

Rewiring Protocol. Peer organisation proceeds by establishing new connections to similar peers and by discarding old ones. Each peer p_i periodically (e.g., when joining the network or when its interests have changed) initiates a rewiring procedure (independently for each interest) by computing the intra-cluster (or *neighborhood*) similarity $NS_i = \frac{1}{s} \cdot \sum_{\forall p_j \in RI_i} sim(I_i, I_j)$, where s is the number of short-range links of p_i according to interest I_i, p_j is a peer contained in RI_i that is on-line, I_j is the interest of p_j, and $sim()$ can be any appropriate similarity function (e.g., the cosine similarity between the term vector representations). The neighborhood similarity NS_i is used here as a measure of *cluster cohesion*, indicating whether peers with similar interests are gathered together.

If NS_i is greater than a threshold θ, then p_i does not need to take any further action, since it considers that it is surrounded by peers with similar interests. Otherwise, p_i issues a $\textsc{FindPeers}(ip(p_i), I_i, L, \tau_R)$ message, where L is a list and τ_R is the time-to-live (TTL) of the message. List L is initially empty and will be used to store tuples of the form $\langle ip(p_j), I_j \rangle$, containing the IP address and interest of peers discovered while the message traverses the network. System parameters θ and τ_R need to be known upon bootstrapping.

A peer p_j receiving the FindPeers() message appends its IP address $ip(p_j)$ and its interest I_j (or the interest most similar to I_i if p_j has multiple interests) to L, reduces τ_R by one, and forwards the message to m random neighbouring peers ($m \leq s$). This message forwarding technique is referred to in the literature as *random walk* (RW) [18,16]. When $\tau_R = 0$, the FindPeers() message is sent back to the message initiator p_i. When the message initiator p_i receives the FindPeers() message back, it uses the information in L to update its routing index RI_i by replacing old short-range links with new links to peers with more similar interests. For the update of the long-range links, peer p_i uses a random walk in the network [16].

5 Evaluation

In this section, we evaluate the effect of peer churn on SONs, using the i*Cluster* rewiring protocol and a realistic dynamic setting. Typically, in the evaluation of P2P IR systems performance is measured in terms of *network traffic* (i.e., the number of rewiring/search messages sent over the network) and retrieval effectiveness (i.e., *recall*). In our setting precision is always 100% since only relevant documents are retrieved. Peer clustering is measured by *clustering efficiency* $\bar{\kappa}$ [14], which gives information about the underlying network structure.

5.1 Experimental Testbed

Dataset. The dataset, also used in the evaluation of [24,16], contains over 556,000 web documents from the TREC-6 collection belonging in 100 categories.

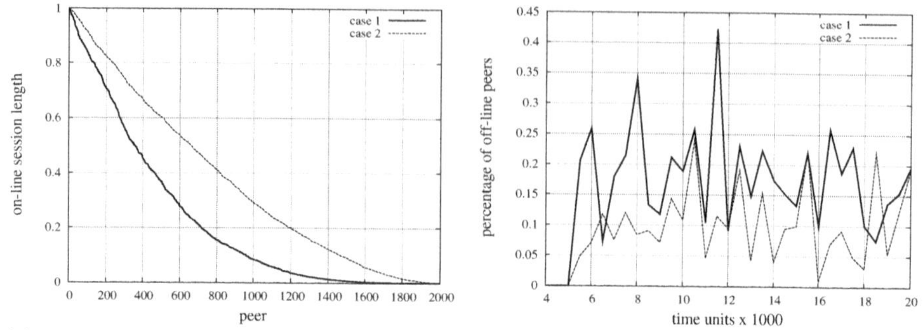

(a) Distributions of on-line session lengths (b) Off-line peers over time

Fig. 1. Lifetime distributions

The queries employed in the evaluation of the corpus are strong representatives of document categories (i.e., the topics of the categories).

Setup. We consider 2000 loosely-connected peers, each of which contributes documents in the network from a single category. At the bootstrapping phase, peers join the network and are connected as described in [16]. We experimented with different values of the parameters. We consider that a given parameter value is better than another if it results in better clustering and retrieval for less communication load. These results are out of the scope of this paper and the interested user may refer to [16]. The simulator used to evaluate the rewiring protocol was implemented in C/C++ and all experiments were run on a Linux machine. Our results were averaged over 25 runs (5 random initial network topologies and 5 runs for each topology). Query processing is carried out as described in [16].

Lifetime Distributions. We experimented with different lifetime distributions. Figure 1(a) illustrates two different on-line session length distributions. By definition, the more skewed the distribution is, the smaller the lifetimes of the most peers are. The first case in Figure 1(a) corresponds to a difficult scenario compared to the second case, since peers are on-line for shorter time periods and leave the network more often. Figure 1(b) presents the percentage of off-line peers as a function of time. In the first scenario the percentage of the peers that are logged-off reaches up to 42% ($t = 11.5K$), while in the second scenario the percentage of the logged-off peers every moment is kept under 25%.

5.2 Experimental Evaluation

Rewiring Effectiveness. Figure 2(a) presents clustering efficiency as a measure of network organisation over time. The plots presented in the figure correspond to the two dynamic scenarios discussed in the previous section. A static network (with peers always connected to the network) is used as the baseline for our evaluation. Initially ($t \leq 4K$), the clustering efficiency is very low indicating that peers are still randomly connected. We observe that during the initial convergence period ($t \leq 5K$) peers self-organise into clusters improving the clustering

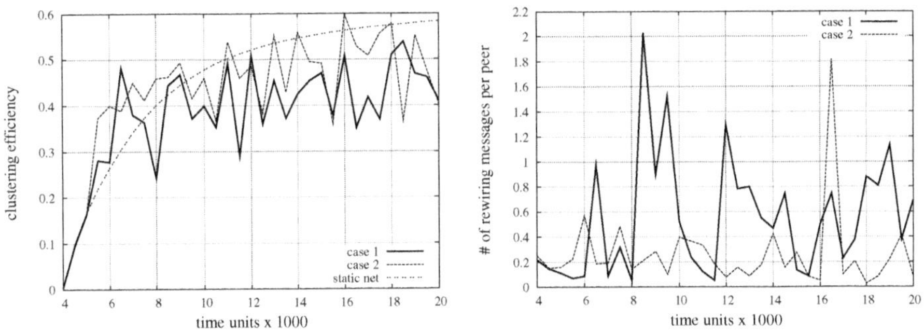

(a) Clustering efficiency (b) Rewiring messages

Fig. 2. Rewiring effectiveness over time

efficiency. In the case of the static network, rewiring finally converges towards a stable network organisation and a constant value of clustering efficiency. In the case of the dynamic network, peers arbitrarily leave and join the system and by this, links pointing to off-line peers as well as newly-connected peers emerge. As a result, peer connections continuously change and peers try (by rewiring) to recover network organisation, a situation continuously repeated.

As shown in Figure 2(a), the rewiring protocol manages to organise the network and clustering efficiency is eventually kept high compared to the unorganised network. Naturally, the network loses its clustering cohesion at moments of high churn, e.g. in the first case when $t = 8K$ and 35% of the peers are off-line, but the network manages to quickly recover in all cases. We are thus, driven to the conclusion that SONs are resilient to churn; the rewiring protocol manages to quickly reorganise the network and keep the values of clustering efficiency high. Notice, by collating Figures 2(a) and 1(b), that clustering efficiency is narrowly related to the percentage of peers that are off-line; when the percentage of off-line peers increases clustering efficiency decreases, and vice versa.

In terms of rewiring messages, peer churn imposes a continuous need for peer organisation, which in turn leads to message traffic. Figure 2(b) presents the number of rewiring messages over time. As churn increases, more peers need to rewire their links and more messages traverse the network: in the first scenario rewiring messages are on average 3 times more than the second, less dynamic, one. Compared to a static network, the rewiring procedure in a dynamic setting needs on average 2 times more and on the worst case 7 times more messages to keep the SON organised.

Retrieval Effectiveness. Figure 3(a) presents the performance of retrievals under churn as a function of time. We observe that recall attains high values throughout the entire evolution of the system. In particular, during the initial convergence period ($t \leq 5K$), the peers self-organise into clusters and the retrieval performance is almost doubled compared to the initial unorganised network. After this point, peers continuously leave and re-join the network. The arbitrarily connected peers naturally cause troubles to the retrieval performance

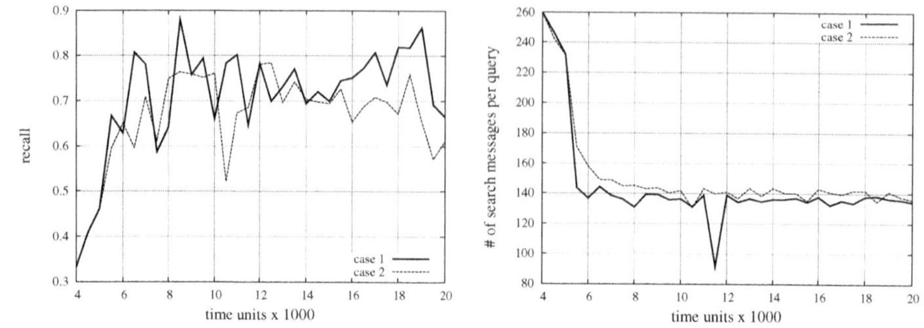

(a) Retrieval efficiency

(b) Search messages

Fig. 3. Retrieval effectiveness over time

of the network. However, Figure 3(a) shows that recall is always kept high (in the the worst case of the second scenario ($t = 10.5K$) recall is 55% better compared to the recall on an unorganised network).

Figure 3(b) shows the number of messages per query over time for the two different scenarios. When the network is not organised ($t = 4K$), a high number of search messages is needed to retrieve the available data relevant to a query. However, this message overhead is decreased (more than 85%) as peers continuously get organised into clusters with similar interests. Notice though, that the number of search messages is kept low throughout the evolution of the system, regardless the continuous changes in the network structure. This happens because the number of search messages is related to the number of neighbouring peers, that under a dynamic scenario is interpreted to the number of *available* neighbouring peers. In cases of high churn, a noticeable number of peers have gone off-line, the network size has been reduced and the overlay has lost its structure. The rewiring mechanism reinstates the network organisation, but the number of search messages is kept low since the neighborhoods are sparsely populated (notice that the lowest number of messages is achieved in the first scenario at $t = 11.5K$, when the percentage of off-line peers is the higher achieved).

References

1. Aberer, K., Cudre-Mauroux, P., Hauswirth, M.: The Chatty Web: Emergent Semanics Through Gossiping. In: WWW 2003 (2003)
2. Backes, M., Hamerlik, M., Linari, A., Maffei, M., Tryfonopoulos, C., Weikum, G.: Anonymous and Censorship-resistant Content-sharing in Unstructured Overlays. In: PODC 2008 (2008)
3. Crespo, A., Garcia-Molina, H.: Routing Indices for P2P Systems. In: ICDCS 2002 (2002)
4. Doulkeridis, C., Vlachou, A., Norvag, K., Vazirgiannis, M.: Handbook of Peer-to-Peer Networking. Springer, Heidelberg (2010)
5. Garcia-Molina, H., Yang, B.: Efficient Search in P2P Networks. In: ICDCS 2002 (2002)

6. Klampanos, I., Jose, J.: An Architecture for Information Retrieval over Semi-Collaborating Peer-to-Peer Networks. In: ACM SAC 2004 (2004)
7. Koloniari, G., Pitoura, E.: Recall-based Cluster Reformulation by Selfish Peers. In: NetDB 2008 (2008)
8. Leonard, D., Yao, Z., Rai, V., Loguinov, D.: On Lifetime-Based Node Failure and Stohastic Resilience of Decentralised Peer-to-Peer Networks. IEEE/ACM Transactions on Networking 15(3) (2007)
9. Li, J., Stribling, J., Kaashoek, F., Morris, R., Gil, T.: A Performance vs. Cost Framework for Evaluating DHT Design Tradeoffs under Churn. In: INFOCOM 2005 (2005)
10. Li, M., Lee, W.-C., Sivasubramaniam, A.: Semantic Small World: An Overlay Network for Peer-to-Peer Search. In: ICNP 2004 (2004)
11. Loser, A., Tempich, C.: On Ranking Peers in Semantic Overlay Networks. In: Althoff, K.-D., Dengel, A.R., Bergmann, R., Nick, M., Roth-Berghofer, T.R. (eds.) WM 2005. LNCS (LNAI), vol. 3782, Springer, Heidelberg (2005)
12. Loser, A., Wolpers, M., Siberski, W., Nejdl, W.: Semantic Overlay Clusters within Super-Peer Networks. In: DBISP2P 2003 (2003)
13. Lu, J., Callan, J.: Content-based Retrieval in Hybrid Peer-to-peer Networks. In: CIKM 2003 (2003)
14. Raftopoulou, P., Petrakis, E.: A Measure for Cluster Cohesion in Semantic Overlay Networks. In: LSDS-IR 2008 (2008)
15. Raftopoulou, P., Petrakis, E.G.M.: iCluster: a Self-Organising Overlay Network for P2P Information Retrieval. In: Macdonald, C., Ounis, I., Plachouras, V., Ruthven, I., White, R.W. (eds.) ECIR 2008. LNCS, vol. 4956, Springer, Heidelberg (2008)
16. Raftopoulou, P., Petrakis, E.G.M., Tryfonopoulos, C.: Rewiring Strategies for Semantic Overlay Networks. Distributed and Parallel DataBases 2–3(26) (2009)
17. Saroiu, S., Gummadi, K.P., Gribble, S.D.: A Measurement Study of Peer-to-Peer File Sharing Systems. In: MMCN 2002 (2002)
18. Schmitz, C.: Self-Organization of a Small World by Topic. In: P2PKM 2004 (2004)
19. Sripanidkulchai, K., Maggs, B., Zhang, H.: Efficient Content Location using Interest-Based Locality in Peer-to-Peer Systems. In: INFOCOM 2003 (2003)
20. Stoica, I., Morris, R., Liben-Nowell, D., Karger, D.R., Frans Kaashoek, M., Dabek, F., Balakrishnan, H.: Chord: A Scalable Peer-to-Peer Lookup Protocol for Internet Applications. IEEE/ACM Transactions on Networking 11(1) (2003)
21. Stutzbach, D., Rejaie, R.: Understanding Churn in Peer-to-Peer Networks. In: INFOCOM 2006 (2006)
22. Stutzbach, D., Rejaie, R., Sen, S.: Characterizing Unstructured Overlay Topologies in Modern P2P File-Sharing Systems. In: IMC 2005 (2005)
23. Voulgaris, S., van Steen, M., Iwanicki, K.: Proactive Gossip-based Management of Semantic Overlay Networks. Concurrency and Computation: Practice and Experience 19(17) (2007)
24. Xu, J., Croft, W.B.: Cluster-Based Language Models for Distributed Retrieval. In: ACM SIGIR 1999 (1999)
25. Yao, Z., Leonard, D., Wang, X., Loguinov, D.: Modeling Heterogeneous User Churn and Local Resilience of Unstructured P2P Networks. In: ICNP 2006 (2006)

IS'10 - PC Co-chairs Message

On behalf of the Program Committee of the OTM IS 2010 5th International Symposium on Information Security, it is our great pleasure to welcome the participants to the OTM IS 2010, held in conjunction with OnTheMove Federated Conferences OTM 2010, during October 25-26, 2010, in Crete, Greece.

In recent years, there have been very significant changes to the threat landscape brought about by the de-perimiterisation of the enterprise and the advent of cloud computing and widespread virtualisation, social networks, smartphones, NFC and RFID. The objective of the OTM IS 2010 Symposium is to promote information security related research and development activities and to encourage communication between researchers and engineers throughout the world in areas which contribute to improving our response to new and old threats.

In response to the Call for Papers, a total of 12 submissions were received, from which 7 were carefully selected for presentation. Each paper was peer reviewed by at least three members of the Program Committee.

The OTM IS 2010 Symposium program covers a variety of research topics, which are of current interest, such as authentication, access control and privacy in distributed environments. We hope you will find the program stimulating and a source of inspiration for your future research.

We would like to express our gratitude to all authors who submitted valuable papers to the OTM IS 2010 Symposium, including those whose submissions were not selected for publication, as well as to the members of the Program Committee and the additional reviewers for their constructive and insightful comments. Without their support the symposium program would not have been possible. We are grateful to the OTM General Chairs Prof. R. Meersman, Prof. T. Dillon, and Prof. Pilar Herrero, as well as to the OTM organizing and logistics team for their continuous and valuable support in all aspects of the organization of this symposium.

We hope that you enjoy the Proceedings of the OTM IS 2010 5th International Symposium on Information Security, prepared by Springer LNCS, and find it a useful source of ideas, results and recent research findings.

August 2010

Giles Hogben
Stefanos Gritzalis
IS'10

R. Meersman et al. (Eds.): OTM 2010, Part I, LNCS 6426, p. 582, 2010.

Mutual Preimage Authentication for Fast Handover in Enterprise Networks

Andreas Noack[1,2] and Mark Borrmann[2]

[1] Horst Görtz Institute for IT-Security
[2] Ruhr University Bochum

Abstract. Wireless enterprise networks with a central authentication server are very common in companies due to their simple serviceability. Roaming between wireless cells of these enterprise networks usually results in connection interrupts because of long authentication times, which are very negative for near realtime communication like VoIP calls. Fast handover in enterprise networks demands therefore a fast authentication and key exchange protocol.

We propose an extensible authentication protocol (EAP) for this purpose that is explicitely optimized to reduce authentication times, while still providing a high security level. The "Mutual Preimage Authentication" (MPA) protocol offers a secure authentication of both sides and a secure key agreement with only two cryptographic messages and symmetric cryptography. Even more, the MPA protocol provides non-repudiation for the authentication process.

Our contribution includes a formal security proof under an enhanced Canetti-Krawczyk (eCK) based security model and a practical performance analysis on the basis of a proof-of-concept implementation [4], where we demonstrate the efficiency of our protocol in comparison with common efficient EAP protocols.

Keywords: Wireless networks, Enterprise, RADIUS, Extensible Authentication Protocol, Roaming, Handover.

1 Introduction

Wireless networks play meanwhile an important role for IT infrastructures in companies and in the home environment. This is because expensive infrastructures with copper or fibre optic cables can be reduced and because there is a mobility option for wireless devices (e.g. PDAs, notebooks, smartphones, etc.) that allows a free movement of the users. An important attempt towards the propagation of the wireless technology was that security weaknesses from the first generation wireless LANs (e.g. [9][21][20][1]) can be handled with the IEEE 802.11i [10] standard for wireless security today.

The IEEE 802.11i standard provides two operation modes to establish a secure wireless infrastructure: *personal* and *enterprise* mode.

The personal mode is normally used in the small office and home office (SoHo) environment, using a common pre-shared key (PSK) to provide authentication

R. Meersman et al. (Eds.): OTM 2010, Part I, LNCS 6426, pp. 583–599, 2010.

and confidentiality. This pre-shared key must be manually configured in all mobile devices and access points. In contrast, enterprise networks use a central authentication server (e.g. RADIUS [18] or Diameter [6]) to authenticate the associated wireless clients via IEEE 802.1X [7]. Companies usually go for the enterprise mode because of the central administration ability, the possibility of linking the wireless accounts to existing authentication databases and last but not least for a higher security.

In this paper, we focus on mobile clients in the enterprise setting. These are mobile users who use small wireless devices for audio/video telephony, multimedia applications or remote control purposes. IP phones on the university campus or business premises, or video streaming to a smartphone user while being on the way, are practical examples. An important business use case (e.g. in the mining industry) is furthermore the remote controlling and monitoring of mobile machinery.

Roaming between two access points means in the most cases delay or packet loss due to long authentication times. This can be very annoying in a realtime communication or can even interrupt the connection under certain conditions. In case of remote control, delay and packet loss due to handover can easily lead to dangerous incidents. Thus the delay and packet loss rate must be minimized for these scenarios.

We demand a secure authentication solution for the enterprise setting that is optimized for fast handover to deal with (near) realtime communication in a proper way. A smaller execution time, than current widespread solutions are providing, is necessary.

1.1 Our Contribution

We present an efficient Extensible Authentication Protocol (EAP) for the use with a RADIUS or Diameter authentication server. Our EAP protocol is called Mutual Preimage Authentication (MPA) due to its use of cryptographic hash-functions for the authentication of both sides. With an improved hash chain technique, we achieve a secure key agreement and mutual authentication with only two cryptographic protocol messages that just use symmetric cryptography. Even more, the protocol provides non-repudiation for the authentication process, which is in contrast not given by trivial (two message) key derivation techniques (e.g. key derivation based on a a shared secret and exchanged random nonce). Note additionally that a secure authentication and key exchange is not possible with only two messages using conventional symmetric methods. The provided security level is underlined by a formal security proof in section 4.

Additionally we contribute an implementation of EAP-MPA within the Host AP project [14] that consists of an access point part with integrated RADIUS authentication server (*hostapd*) and a supplicant part (*wpa_supplicant*). We evaluate the runtime performance of EAP-MPA and several widespread EAP protocols (EAP-TLS, EAP-TTLS, EAP-PSK) in a practical test and provide a performance comparison in section 5 of our work.

Roaming or authentication time optimized EAP protocols are quite rare in practice. EAP-PSK is (as far as we measured) the fastest protocols that is supported by common RADIUS servers (protocol details in [15]). Cordasco et al. propose EAP-TLS-KS [8], a EAP-TLS variant that is optimized for fast roaming. While they achieve a slight improvement in the authentication time in comparison with EAP-TLS, they demand a modification of the EAP protocol messages at the authenticator which makes the protocol incompatible with the EAP standard. As we consider a scenario with standard components, we left this protocol out.

2 Protocol Overview

The mutual preimage authentication protocol (MPA) consists of two phases: A main phase (phase 1) that is optimized for fast handover and an initialization phase (phase 0) that is called once before the first run of the main phase.

Fig. 1. EAP-MPA - Main phase (1)

In the main phase (Figure 1), both participants are mutually and non-repudiatively authenticated by sending a preimage that is verified with a cryptographic hash function on the other side. Together with each preimage, an encrypted image for the next authentication process is transmitted. Obviously the protocol must prevent this image from being replaced or modified, since a successful attack would break the mutual authentication property. The authentication concept is similar to a hash chain authentication, whereby in this case the hash chains have a length of one and are overlapping. With this authentication concept, we are able to do mutual authentication and key agreement at the same time with only two protocol messages.

The protocol works as follows: Before the protocol starts, both participants know the values EK_A, EK_B (encryption keys), $AUTH_{A/B}$ (Hash value from $NXTPROOF_{B/A}$ of the other party) and $PROOF_{A/B}$ (own $NXTPROOF_{A/B}$ value) from the previous session. The server B chooses $NXTPROOF_B$ randomly and encrypts the hash value of it (NXT_B), the $NXTPROOF_B$ value from the previous session, the ID from A and an integrity protection value IP_B. The client A can decrypt the message and check if $PROOF_B$ is the preimage of NXT_B from the previous session. In this way, the current session is non-repudiatively combined with the previous session. Furthermore, the client A receives the $AUTH_B = NXT_B$ value for the authentication of server B in the next session in a confidential and integrity protected way. When all tests are successful (integrity protection and matching preimage), client A encrypts a message for server B, that is assembled in the same way as the message from server B. After reception of the encrypted message, server B decrypts and applies the same tests on the message that client A has done with the first message.

Before being able to authenticate with the normal protocol phase, an initialization phase – phase 0 – must be completed to establish the necessary images

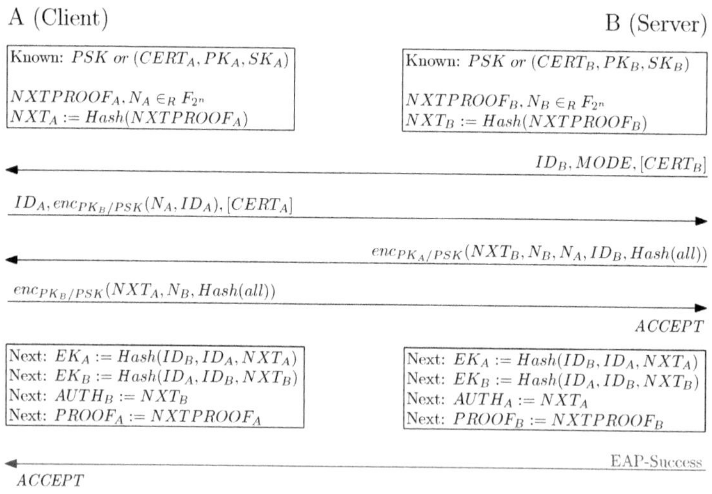

Fig. 2. EAP-MPA - Initialization phase (0)

on both sites (Figure 2). Phase 0 must provide a high security level, since the validity of the authentication in the main phase depends on a successful phase 0 authentication. Therefore the initialization phase is able to use a certificate based authentication, which actually leads to a longer handover time. However, phase 0 is only called once before a (theoretically unlimited) series of MPA main phases.

For usability reasons, we optionally provide a pre-shared key (PSK) and a hybrid authentication in the initialization phase. The pre-shared key mode is used for scenarios, where no public key infrastructure can be deployed; both sides are mutually authenticated with the PSK. In the hybrid mode, only the server is authenticated with a certificate, the user with a pre-shared key. This is similar to e.g. EAP-TTLS/CHAP, which is oftenly used in this way, because the operator does not need to issue certificates for all clients (which means lower management costs).

The first message originates from the server B and contains the chosen encryption mode (symmetric/asymmetric/hybrid), its ID and optionally the certificate of server B. Client A chooses a random nonce N_A and encrypts it together with the own ID for server B, a certificate is attached optionally. After decryption, server B chooses a random nonce N_B and a random value $NXTPROOF_B$. Then server B encrypts a message for client A that contains the hash value NXT_B from $NXTPROOF_B$, the nonce N_B, the client nonce N_A, its ID_B and an integrity protecting hash value $Hash(all)$ about all communicated messages up to this point (including the data in message 3). Client A decrypts, verifies and assembles the last cryptographic protocol message. The hash value NXT_A from the randomly chosen value $NXTPROOF_A$, the server nonce N_B and an integrity protecting hash value $Hash(all)$ about all communicated messages up to this point (including the data in message 4) are encrypted for server B. After the successful verification at server B, the EAP-Success message is sent.

3 Security Model

3.1 Protocol Participants and Keys

We have two protocol participants in our extensible authentication protocol EAP-MPA: *Client* 'C' (Supplicant) and *Authentication Server* 'S'. In a practical scenario there is another party, the *Authenticator* (Access point). But since this party just forwards the data between both other parties, it does not play a role for the protocol design nor for the security proof.

On the *Client* and the *Authentication Server* we need several preliminary values depending on which protocol phase is used. The main protocol needs a set of established values on both sides: EK_A, EK_B, $AUTH_{A/B}$ and $PROOF_{A/B}$, whereby the initialization phase (phase 0) is able to agree these values on behalf of either a pre shared key PSK (i.e. password) or a public key pair $\{PK_{A/B}, SK_{A/B}\}$ with a certificate $CERT_{A/B}$.

3.2 Instances and Protocol Sessions

The number of clients $\mathcal{C}$ may be very high and it is even likely that there are different authentication servers $\mathcal{S}$ in use. We therefore assume that it is possible that the same clients $\mathcal{C}$ *or* authentication servers $\mathcal{S}$ are participants in parallel protocol sessions. We want to extend this by saying that it is possible that there are different protocol sessions with exactly the same $\mathcal{C}$ *and* $\mathcal{S}$. The number of parallel protocol sessions is denoted by q.

We claim that there is an unlimited number of instances of $\mathcal{C}$ and $\mathcal{S}$, whereby denoting an instance as $\mathcal{X}_s$ with $\mathcal{X} \in \{\mathcal{C}, \mathcal{S}\}$ and $s \in \boldsymbol{N}$. Instances, also called oracles, have access to the longterm key of their capital, whereby they agree on different session keys in the protocol run.

In the main phase of our protocol, two instances $\mathcal{C}$ and $\mathcal{S}$ are called partnered when they have the same session id $SID := ID_A, ID_B, EK_A, EK_B$ whereby $ID_?$ are the identifiers of the participants and $EK_?$ the agreed encryption keys (session keys). To call two instances $\mathcal{C}$ and $\mathcal{S}$ partnered in the initialization phase (phase 0), they need to have the same session ID which is defined as follows: $SID := ID_A, ID_B, N_A, N_B$ whereby $N_?$ are randomly chosen nonces. Both definitions for SID are based on the idea of matching conversations that was described by Bellare and Rogaway [2].

An instance of $\mathcal{C}$, $\mathcal{S}$ in a protocol session calls ACCEPT or ABORT upon the decision if the protocol execution was successful in respect to the protocol aims.

3.3 Adversarial Model

The adversary $\mathcal{A}$ is modelled as a probabilistic polynomial time (PPT) machine and has full control over the communication and protocol invocations. $\mathcal{A}$ is allowed to do the following queries:

- **Invoke($\mathcal{X}$, m).** Upon this query, a new instance $\mathcal{X}_s$ of $\mathcal{X} \in \{\mathcal{C}, \mathcal{S}\}$ is created. Message m is sent to the new instance, whereby the answer is directed to the adversary $\mathcal{A}$.
- **Send($\mathcal{X}_s$, m).** This query sends a message m to $\mathcal{X}_s$. When $\mathcal{X}_s$ has completed processing m, the response is sent back to $\mathcal{A}$. With the help of this query, $\mathcal{A}$'s control over the communication channel is modeled, since $\mathcal{A}$ is able to stay passive by honestly forwarding each message or to become active by modifying m or even injecting a new message.
- **Corrupt($\mathcal{X}$).** As response to this query, $\mathcal{A}$ gets the longterm key of $\mathcal{X}$. That is PSK or $SK_{A/B}$ dependent on the used authentication mode of the initialization phase (phase 0). There are no longterm keys used in the main phase of the protocol. When $\mathcal{X}$ becomes corrupted, all instances $\mathcal{X}_s$ of $\mathcal{X}$ become corrupted too.
- **SessionKeyReveal($\mathcal{X}_s$).** If $\mathcal{X}_s$ has already accepted, the adversary $\mathcal{A}$ gets the session key as response to this query. The session key between $\mathcal{C}$ and $\mathcal{S}$ is EK_A and EK_B.
- **Test($\mathcal{X}_s$).** The adversary may query **TestKey()** to an accepted instance of a session. The instance $\mathcal{X}_s$ chooses a random bit b and answers with a random value on $b = 0$ and with the session key $\{EK_A, EK_B\}$ on $b = 1$.

3.4 Building Blocks

In this section, we list the cryptographic primitives that are used by both phases of our EAP protocol: the initialization and main phase.

- A *cryptographic hash function* that provides preimage, second preimage and collision resistance [17]. Hash: $\{0,1\}^* \rightarrow \{0,1\}^l$. By $\text{Succ}_{\text{hash}}^{\text{preimage}}(l)$ we denote the success probability for a PPT adversary to find a preimage for a given output $\in \{0,1\}^l$ of the hash function. $\text{Succ}_{\text{hash}}^{\text{2nd preimage}}(l)$ denotes the success probability for a PPT adversary to find a second preimage $m_2 \in \{0,1\}^*$ for a given preimage-hash pair $\langle m_1, \text{hash}(m_1)\rangle \in \langle\{0,1\}^*, \{0,1\}^l\rangle$ with $\text{hash}(m_1) = \text{hash}(m_2)$. $\text{Succ}_{\text{hash}}^{\text{collision}}(l)$ denotes the success probability for a PPT adversary to find a collision $m_1, m_2 \in \{0,1\}^*$ with $m_1 \neq m_2$ and $\text{Hash}(m_1)$=$\text{Hash}(m_2)$. Using hash functions for message authentication is discussed in [13].
- A *pseudo random function* PRF: $\{0,1\}^l \times \{0,1\}^* \rightarrow \{0,1\}^*$ for key derivation. We denote the maximum advantage over all PPT adversaries (running within time l) in distinguishing the outputs of PRF from the outputs of a random oracle better than Pr=$\frac{1}{2}$ by $\text{Adv}_{\text{hash}}^{\text{prf}}(l)$.
- An *asymmetric encryption scheme* that suffices the indistinguishability property under adaptive chosen ciphertext attacks (IND-CCA2) [5]. We denote the advantage that an adversary is able to decrypt at least one bit without knowing the used secret key as $\text{Adv}_{\text{asym. cipher}}^{\text{ind-cca2}}(l)$.
- A *symmetric encryption scheme with integrity protection* that suffices the indistinguishability property under adaptive chosen ciphertext attacks (IND-CCA2) [5]. We denote the advantage that an adversary is able to decrypt at least one bit without knowing the used key as $\text{Adv}_{\text{sym. cipher}}^{\text{ind-cca2}}(l)$. Furthermore, the symmetric encryption scheme satisfies weak unforgeability against chosen message attacks. The adversary's success probability to encrypt without the right key and gaining a valid ciphertext is $\text{Succ}_{\text{ENC}}^{\text{wuf-cma}}(l)$.

3.5 Correctness

The authentication and key establishment protocol EAP-MPA is correct, if definition 1 holds. Note that this correctness definition describes the correctness of both protocol phases: initialization and main phase.

Definition 1 (Correctness). *In the presence of a passive adversary, the protocol phases are correct, if* $\mathcal{C}$ *and* $\mathcal{S}$ *have accepted and*

- EK_A *and* EK_B *are identical on both sides*
- $AUTH_{A/B}$ *and* $PROOF_{A/B}$ *correspond to each other*

Actually the correctness of the main phase can also be proven by the occurence of the same K_{AB} on both sides, but since K_{AB} is derived from $EK_{A/B}$, $AUTH_{A/B}$ and $PROOF_{A/B}$ the given definition states the correctness implicitly.

3.6 Security Goals

Now we state the security goals that have to be achieved between an instance $\mathcal{C}_i$ of the supplicant/client ($\mathcal{C}$) and an instance $\mathcal{S}_j$ of the authentication server ($\mathcal{S}$). These are Mutual Authentication and Authenticated Key Exchange for both phases of the EAP-MPA protocol, the initialization phase 0 and the main phase.

Definition 2 (Mutual Authentication between $\mathcal{C}$ and $\mathcal{S}$). *In both phases of a correct EAP-MPA protocol run π, $Game_{\Pi}^{MA}$ decribes the interaction between the honest parties $\mathcal{C}$ and $\mathcal{S}$ with a PPT adversary $\mathcal{A}$ that is capable of asking all queries defined in section 3.3. $\mathcal{A}$ violates the Mutual Authentication property if at least one of the following events occurs:*

1. *An uncorrupted instance $\mathcal{C}_i$ of $\mathcal{C}$ accepts the protocol run with a corrupted partnered instance of $\mathcal{S}$.*
2. *An uncorrupted instance $\mathcal{S}_j$ of $\mathcal{S}$ accepts the protocol run with a corrupted partnered instance of $\mathcal{C}$.*
3. *After both uncorrupted partnered instances $\mathcal{C}_i$ and $\mathcal{S}_j$ have accepted, they share a different session key (EK_A, EK_B) or have non corresponding authentication credentials ($AUTH_{A/B}$, $PROOF_{A/B}$).*

Definition 3 (Authenticated Key Exchange between $\mathcal{C}$ and $\mathcal{S}$). *Given a uniformly chosen bit b, a PPT adversary $\mathcal{A}$ interacts with a correct protocol Π, whereby it is not allowed for $\mathcal{A}$ to query **SessionKeyReveal()** to an accepted instance or to corrupt an instance. $Game_{\Pi}^{AKE}(\mathcal{A}, l)$ is defined as the following interaction for both protocol phases:*

1. *$\mathcal{A}$ interacts with instances $\mathcal{C}_i$, $\mathcal{S}_j$ without using the **SessionKeyReveal()** and **Corrupt()** query*
2. *$\mathcal{A}$ asks a **Test()** query to an instance $\mathcal{C}_i$ or $\mathcal{S}_j$ and gets, dependent on b, a random value chosen from $\{0,1\}^l$ (if $b = 0$) or $\{EK_A, EK_B\}$ (if $b = 1$)*
3. *After further interaction, $\mathcal{A}$ terminates and outputs a bit b'*

$\mathcal{A}$ wins $\text{Game}_{\Pi}^{\text{AKE}}(\mathcal{A}, 1)$ if $b' = b$. The maximum probability of the adversarial advantage over the random guess of b, over all adversaries (running in time l) is

$$\text{Adv}_{\Pi}^{\text{AKE}}(\mathcal{A}, l) = \max_{\mathcal{A}} |2\Pr[\text{Game}_{\Pi}^{\text{AKE}}(\mathcal{A}, l) = b] - 1|.$$

4 Security Proof

In this section we state the security of the proposed EAP-MPA protocol whereby the security analysis is based on the sequences of games technique by Shoup [19], using an improved eCK security model derived from LaMacchia et al. [12] and Huang et al. [11]. We denote the security proof for the main mode and for the most secure mode of the initialization phase, the asymmetric mode. Proofs for the symmetric and hybrid mode are left out due to similarity to the proof of the asymmetric mode.

4.1 Initialization Phase (Asymmetric)

The initialization phase of EAP-MPA in the asymmetric mode uses public key encryption for the mutual authentication. That means, that all encryptions within the protocol are public key encryptions with the public key of the intended receiving party.

Theorem 1 (Mutual authentication between $\mathcal{C}$ and $\mathcal{S}$). With a second preimage resistant cryptographic hash function, an ind-cca2 secure Asymmetric encryption scheme, the protocol Π of EAP-MPA provides mutual authentication in the sense of definition 2 and

$$\mathrm{Succ}^{\mathrm{MA}}_{\mathrm{Phase\ 0\ /\ asym.}}(l) \leq \frac{4q^2}{2^l} + 4 \cdot \mathrm{Adv}^{\mathrm{ind\text{-}cca2}}_{\mathrm{asym.\ cipher}}(l).$$

The event that an adversary $\mathcal{A}$ breaks the mutual authentication between $\mathcal{C}$ and $\mathcal{S}$ is denoted by Win_i^{MA}.

Game G_0. [*Real protocol*] The real $\mathrm{Game}^{\mathrm{MA}}_{\mathrm{Phase\ 0\ /\ sym.}}(l)$ played between a PPT adversary $\mathcal{A}$ and a simulator Δ. Δ simulates all protocol queries from $\mathcal{C}$ and $\mathcal{S}$ according to the protocol specification.

Game G_1. [*Collisions for nonces N_A, N_B*] The simulation aborts, when the same random nonces N_A or N_B are chosen by the simulator Δ in different protocol sessions.

$$|Pr[\mathrm{Win}_1^{\mathrm{MA}}] - Pr[\mathrm{Win}_0^{\mathrm{MA}}]| \leq \frac{2q^2}{2^l}$$

Due to the collision avoidance for N_A and N_B, we exclude the possibility to replay the messages 3 and 4.

Game G_2. [*Collisions for NXT_A, NXT_B*] The simulation aborts, when the same values NXT_A or NXT_B are chosen by the simulator Δ in different protocol sessions.

$$|Pr[\mathrm{Win}_2^{\mathrm{MA}}] - Pr[\mathrm{Win}_1^{\mathrm{MA}}]| \leq \frac{2q^2}{2^l}$$

This game implies that there are no collisions between $NXTPROOF_A$ and $NXTPROOF_B$ as well, because if NXT_A or NXT_B collide, their preimages will also collide. By excluding collisions for $NXT_{A/B}$ we make sure that the adversary does not accidently know the preimages $NXTPROOF_{A/B}$ before they are used by the honest parties.

Game G_3. [*Information gain from encryptions*] In this game, the simulator Δ exchanges the encryption of N_A and N_B in message 2 and 3 with randomly chosen values.

$$|Pr[\mathrm{Win}_3^{\mathrm{MA}}] - Pr[\mathrm{Win}_2^{\mathrm{MA}}]| \leq 4 \cdot \mathrm{Adv}^{\mathrm{ind\text{-}cca2}}_{\mathrm{asym.\ cipher}}(l)$$

With this game, we exclude the possibility for the adversary $\mathcal{A}$ to send own $NXT_{A/B}$ values in the 3rd and 4th protocol message. This is because the messages 3 and 4 additionally include random nonces that are each chosen in the previous message. If the adversary $\mathcal{A}$ wants to forge message 3 or 4 with a higher probability than $\frac{1}{2^l}$, he needs to become aware of the according nonce. Therefore the security of this point is the amount of information gain, the adversary $\mathcal{A}$ is able to get from the symmetric encryptions of the previous (2nd or 3rd) and the current (3rd or 4th, can be interrupted) message.

Since we are using asymmetric encryption with the public key of the partnered instance in this mode of the initialization phase, a game protecting from blind manipulation of the ciphertext does not make sense. But in the asymmetric mode, we have to additionally take care of the Unknown Key Share (UKS) attack [3]. There are two possibilities: Pretend another identity towards the client $\mathcal{C}$ or the authentication server $\mathcal{S}$.
Pretending a wrong client identity ID_C (in message 2) towards the authentication server $\mathcal{S}$ is not possible, because the message (which also includes a challenge nonce N_A) is encrypted with the public key of $\mathcal{S}$. Pretending a wrong server identity ID_D towards the client is not possible due to the inclusion of the server ID_B in message 3. If the adversary $\mathcal{A}$ would exchange message 3, the client would not be able to complete the protocol with the authentication server, because nonce N_B would not match. Therefore the EAP-MPA protocol is resistant against the Unknown Key Share attack.

Finally, the mutual authentication property cannot be broken by event 3 from definition 2, because the identities cannot be spoofed (UKS is not possible) and the $NXT_{A/B}$ values cannot be forged due to game G_3. G_1 and G_2 exclude the possibility for an accidental matching of the random parameters. The success probability of an adversary $\mathcal{A}$ to break the mutual authentication property of EAP-MPA (initialization phase, *asymmetric* mode) is therefore

$$Pr[\mathrm{Win}_3^{\mathrm{MA}}] = 0.$$

Combining the previous equations, we conclude this proof.

Theorem 2 (Authenticated Key Exchange between $\mathcal{C}$ and $\mathcal{S}$). With a second preimage resistant cryptographic hash function, an ind-cca2 secure asymmetric encryption scheme, the protocol Π of EAP-MPA provides authenticated key exchange in the sense of definition 3 and

$$\mathrm{Succ}^{\mathrm{AKE}}_{\mathrm{Phase\ 0\ /\ asym.}}(l) \leq \frac{4q^2}{2^l} + 4 \cdot \mathrm{Adv}^{\text{ind-cca2}}_{\text{asym. cipher}}(l) + 2 \cdot \mathrm{Adv}^{\mathrm{prf}}_{\mathrm{hash}}(l).$$

The event that an adversary $\mathcal{A}$ breaks the mutual authentication between $\mathcal{M}$ and $\mathcal{H}$ is denoted by Win_i^{AKE}.

Game G_0. [*Real protocol*] The real $\mathrm{Game}^{\mathrm{AKE}}_{\mathrm{Phase\ 0\ /\ asym.}}(l)$ played between a PPT adversary $\mathcal{A}$ and a simulator Δ. Δ simulates all protocol queries from $\mathcal{C}$ and $\mathcal{S}$ according to the protocol specification.

Game G_1, G_2 and G_3 are equal to the according games in the proof of theorem 1.

Game G_4. [*Pseudo-randomness from* EK_A, EK_B] The simulator Δ chooses the values EK_A and EK_B at random instead of computing them with a pseudo-random function. For consistency, the simulator Δ chooses the same random values on both sides.

$$|Pr[\text{Win}_4^{\text{AKE}}] - Pr[\text{Win}_3^{\text{AKE}}]| \leq 2 \cdot \text{Adv}_{\text{hash}}^{\text{prf}}(l)$$

This game excludes that an adversary $\mathcal{A}$ has a better win probability than $\frac{1}{2^l}$ to compute the keys EK_A and EK_B. Since the adversary $\mathcal{A}$ has the knowledge of a part of the input vector for the pseudo-random function (namely $ID_{A/B}$, $IP_{A/B}$ computable), the difference between the games G_3 and G_4 is the pseudo-randomness property (with partly known input vectors) of the used prf function.

The adversary $\mathcal{A}$ will call **Test**($\mathcal{X}_S$) and gets in dependency of the chosen b: $\{EK_A, EK_B\}$ or random value as response. Since there are no collisions for $N_{A/B}$, $NXT_{A/B}$ (due to Game G_1 and G_2), there is no possibility to successfully change the values NXT_A and NXT_B (due to Game G_3) and the exchanged keys EK_A and EK_B are fully random, the success probability of the adversary $\mathcal{A}$ to choose b' with $b = b'$ is $\frac{1}{2}$. The success probability to win the game is therefore

$$Pr[\text{Win}_3^{\text{AKE}}] = 0.$$

Combining the previous equations, we conclude this proof.

4.2 Main Phase

Now we are considering the security of the main phase of EAP-MPA. Therefore we use one theorem for mutual authentication and one theorem for authenticated key exchange.

Theorem 3 (Mutual authentication between $\mathcal{C}$ and $\mathcal{S}$). With a second preimage resistant cryptographic hash function, an ind-cca2 secure symmetric encryption scheme, the protocol Π of EAP-MPA provides mutual authentication in the sense of definition 2 and

$$\text{Succ}_{\text{Phase 1}}^{\text{MA}}(l) \leq 2 \cdot \left(\frac{2q^2}{2^l} + \text{Adv}_{\text{sym. cipher}}^{\text{ind-cca2}}(l) \cdot \left(1 + \text{Succ}_{\text{hash}}^{\text{2nd preimage}}(l)\right)\right)$$

The event that an adversary $\mathcal{A}$ breaks the mutual authentication between $\mathcal{C}$ and $\mathcal{S}$ is denoted by Win_i^{MA}.

Game G_0. [*Real protocol*] The real $\text{Game}_{\text{Phase 0 / sym.}}^{\text{MA}}(l)$ played between a PPT adversary $\mathcal{A}$ and a simulator Δ. Δ simulates all protocol queries from $\mathcal{C}$ and $\mathcal{S}$ according to the protocol specification.

Game G_1. *[Collisions for NXT, $PROOF$]* The simulation aborts, when the same values NXT_A, NXT_B, $PROOF_A$ or $PROOF_B$ are chosen by the simulator Δ in different protocol sessions.

$$|Pr[\text{Win}_1^{\text{MA}}] - Pr[\text{Win}_0^{\text{MA}}]| \leq \frac{4q^2}{2^l}$$

This game excludes an accidental collision of the confidential parameters $NXT_{A/B}$ and $PROOF_{A/B}$ that would enable the adversary $\mathcal{A}$ to impersonate one or more parties.

Game G_2. *[Creating valid IP values]* The simulator Δ stops, if there is a valid integrity protection (IP) value that was not previously computed by one of the honest parties.

$$|Pr[\text{Win}_2^{\text{MA}}] - Pr[\text{Win}_1^{\text{MA}}]| \leq 2 \cdot \text{Adv}_{\text{sym. cipher}}^{\text{ind-cca2}}(l) \cdot \left(1 + \text{Succ}_{\text{hash}}^{\text{2nd preimage}}(l)\right)$$

To forge an IP value, the adversary has to collect all input data that enter the "hash"-function. These are $NXT_{B/A}$, $PROOF_{B/A}$ and $ID_{A/B}$, whereby the ID is known. The first possibility is to gain all these information from the ciphertext ($\text{Adv}_{\text{sym. cipher}}^{\text{ind-cca2}}(l)$). There is a second possibility to become aware of the $PROOF_{B/A}$ value: Decrypt the previous ciphertext *and* find a second preimage $PROOF_{B/A}$ for the previous $NXT_{B/A}$ value (current $NXT_{B/A}$ would still be missing).

However, the re-encryption of the computed IP value is not considered and for the second possibility there would be still a $NXT_{B/A}$ value missing, so the computed probability to differentiate the games is clearly an upper border.

Since the adversary $\mathcal{A}$ is not able to successfully manipulate the data (protected by IP) due to Game G_2 and there are no accidental collisions due to Game G_1, we conclude that the overall success probability for the adversary $\mathcal{A}$ to break the mutual authentication property is

$$Pr[\text{Win}_2^{\text{MA}}] = 0$$

Combining the previous equations, we conclude this proof.

Theorem 4 (Authenticated Key Exchange between $\mathcal{C}$ and $\mathcal{S}$) With a second preimage resistant cryptographic hash function, an ind-cca2 secure symmetric encryption scheme, the protocol Π of EAP-MPA provides authenticated key exchange in the sense of definition 3 and

$$\text{Succ}_{\text{Phase 1}}^{\text{AKE}}(l) \leq 2 \cdot \left(\frac{2q^2}{2^l} + \text{Adv}_{\text{sym. cipher}}^{\text{ind-cca2}}(l) \cdot \left(1 + \text{Succ}_{\text{hash}}^{\text{2nd preimage}}(l)\right) + \text{Adv}_{\text{hash}}^{\text{prf}}(l)\right).$$

The event that an adversary $\mathcal{A}$ breaks the authenticated key exchange property between $\mathcal{C}$ and $\mathcal{S}$ is denoted by Win_i^{AKE}.

Game G_0. [*Real protocol*] The real $\text{Game}^{\text{MA}}_{\text{Phase 0 / sym.}}(l)$ played between a PPT adversary $\mathcal{A}$ and a simulator Δ. Δ simulates all protocol queries from $\mathcal{C}$ and $\mathcal{S}$ according to the protocol specification.

Game G_1 and G_2 are equal to the according games in the proof of theorem 3.

Game G_3. [*Pseudo-randomness from* EK_A, EK_B] The simulator Δ chooses the values EK_A and EK_B at random instead of computing them with a pseudo-random function. For consistency, the simulator Δ chooses the same random values on both sides.

$$|Pr[\text{Win}_3^{\text{AKE}}] - Pr[\text{Win}_2^{\text{AKE}}]| \leq 2 \cdot \text{Adv}_{\text{hash}}^{\text{prf}}(l)$$

This game excludes that an adversary $\mathcal{A}$ has a better win probability than $\frac{1}{2^l}$ to compute the keys EK_A and EK_B. Since the adversary $\mathcal{A}$ has the knowledge of a part of the input vector for the pseudo-random function (namely $ID_{A/B}$, $IP_{A/B}$ computable), the difference between the games G_2 and G_3 is the pseudo-randomness property (with partly known input vectors) of the used prf function.

The adversary $\mathcal{A}$ will call **Test**($\mathcal{X}_S$) and gets in dependency of the chosen b: $\{EK_A, EK_B\}$ or random value as response. Since there are no collisions for $N_{A/B}$, $NXT_{A/B}$ (due to Game G_1), there is no possibility to successfully change the values NXT_A and NXT_B (due to Game G_2) and the exchanged keys EK_A and EK_B are fully random, the success probability of the adversary $\mathcal{A}$ to choose b' with $b = b'$ is $\frac{1}{2}$. The success probability to win the game is therefore

$$Pr[\text{Win}_3^{\text{AKE}}] = 0$$

Combining the previous equations, we conclude this proof.

5 Performance Analysis

This chapter deals with a performance analysis of EAP-MPA and the comparison with three common EAP protocols.

5.1 EAP Protocols

EAP-TLS is one of the most secure EAP protocols, due to its use of client and server certificates for authentication. Furthermore EAP-TLS is very common, since supported by a big number of implementations.

EAP-TTLS authenticates the server with a certificate while allowing the client to use an inner authentication method that can be based on simpler or even faster techniques. We have chosen CHAP as an inner authentication method since it uses only two small sized messages. Together with EAP-PEAP (which is a little bit slower due to more overhead), EAP-TTLS is one of the most used EAP protocols because it provides client authentication without a PKI and it is integrated in the Microsoft and Cisco implementations. Both, EAP-TLS and EAP-TTLS, support fast reconnection which leads to much smaller authentication times.

EAP-PSK is designed to be very efficient because the authentication just relies on symmetric cryptography (pre shared key) while using only four messages. EAP-PSK is not very widespread but therefore a candidate for the fastest EAP protocol supported by wireless scenarios.

5.2 Performance Results

The performance analysis is based on the access point software *hostapd* (version 0.6.9, [14]) und the client supplicant software *wpa_supplicant* (version 0.6.9) under Linux. Since *hostapd* did not support fast reconnection, a freeRADIUS [16] authentication server was additionally used on the access point device. All tests have been repeated 20 times, where we have noticed a small standard variance confirming their practicability [4].

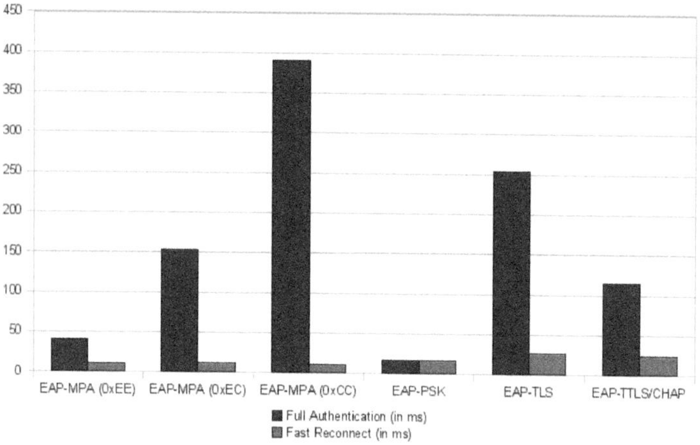

Fig. 3. Performance comparison of all protocol phases

Figure 3 shows the time in *ms* that is consumed by EAP-MPA with different modes (symmetric [0xEE], hybrid[0xEC], asymmetric [0xCC]) and the time used by the EAP protocols EAP-PSK, EAP-TLS and EAP-TTLS/CHAP. The left bars of each protocol (blue) represent the time of the first authentication, whereby this means for EAP-MPA the execution of the initialization *and* the main phase (both). Additionally there is another issue with the EAP-MPA implementation: Since there is no out-of-the-box fragmentation for large packets in hostapd, we deploy a quite inefficient fragmentation mechanism to allow the transmission of certificates. An improvement of this mechanism will probably create faster results than the corresponding EAP protocol (EAP-MPA[0xCC] vs. EAP-TLS and EAP-MPA[0xEC] vs. EAP-TTLS/CHAP). EAP-PSK, EAP-TLS and EAP-TTLS are used in the normal mode (not fast reconnect).

The right bars of each protocol block (orange) show the performance of the main phases of EAP-MPA, EAP-PSK and the fast reconnect phases of EAP-TLS and EAP-TTLS. As you can see, EAP-MPA provides the fastest results of

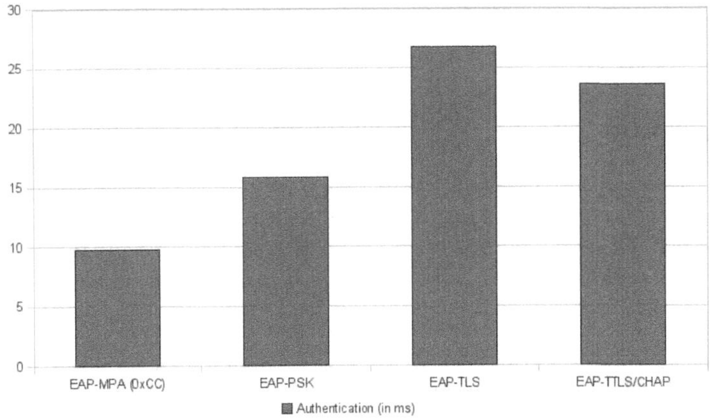

Fig. 4. Performance comparison of the "fast" protocol phases

all protocols when running in the main phase. Figure 4 underlines EAP-MPAs advantage by only comparing the fast protocol phases of the examined EAP protocols. Note that the main phase of EAP-MPA is always the same for the different operation modes.

Finally we have realized an EAP protocol that is twice as fast as EAP-TLS in fast reconnect mode and a third faster than EAP-PSK – which is one of the most efficient EAP protocols to date.

6 Conclusion

In this paper, we have introduced a new EAP protocol that is optimized for fast handover scenarios - the mutual preimage authentication protocol: EAP-MPA. The protocol consists of two phases, a high secure initialization phase that is executed only once and a fast main phase that is designed for fast execution.

We have defined a security model that is based on the enhanced Canetti-Krawczyk (eCK) model and have presented security proofs for both protocol phases and each operation mode. Therefore the security of our proposed protocol is proven formally under a strong attacker model.

Lastly we concluded our work with a practical performance analysis that compares our proof of concept implementation with several common EAP protocols regarding their authentication time. EAP-MPA (main phase) is with an authentication time of only 10ms the fastest protocol among the common EAP protocols and can therefore be recommended for fast roaming scenarios.

Future work is to provide a well tested and performance optimized EAP-MPA implementation for several operating systems. Furthermore, to enhance the wireless roaming performance, the underlying wireless network stacks must be prepared for fast roaming scenarios, i.e. implementation of smart access point selection mechanisms (best link) and optimizing network stack related timeouts.

References

1. Beck, M., Tews, E.: Practical attacks against wep and wpa. Cryptology ePrint Archive, Report 2008/472 (2008), `http://eprint.iacr.org/`
2. Bellare, M., Rogaway, P.: Entity authentication and key distribution. In: Stinson, D.R. (ed.) CRYPTO 1993. LNCS, vol. 773, pp. 232–249. Springer, Heidelberg (1994)
3. Blake-Wilson, S., Menezes, A.: Unknown key-share attacks on the station-to-station (STS) protocol. In: Lecture Notes in Computer Science, pp. 154–170 (1999)
4. Borrmann, M.: Implementierung eines effizienten eap-protokolls. Diplomathesis, Ruhr-University Bochum (2009)
5. Rackoff, C., Simon, D.R.: Non-interactive zero-knowledge proof of knowledge and chosen ciphertext attack. In: Feigenbaum, J. (ed.) CRYPTO 1991. LNCS, vol. 576, pp. 433–444. Springer, Heidelberg (1992)
6. Calhoun, P., Loughney, J., Guttman, E., Zorn, G., Arkko, J.: Diameter base protocol. RFC3588, Network Working Group (2003)
7. LAN/MAN Standards Committee. Ieee standard for local and metropolitan area networks – port-based network access control. IEEE 802.1X, IEEE Computer Society (2004)
8. Cordasco, J., Meyer, U., Wetzel, S.: Implementation and performance evaluation of eap-tls-ks. In: Securecomm and Workshops, pp. 1–12 (2006)
9. Fluhrer, S.R., Mantin, I., Shamir, A.: Weaknesses in the key scheduling algorithm of rc4. In: Vaudenay, S., Youssef, A.M. (eds.) SAC 2001. LNCS, vol. 2259, pp. 1–24. Springer, Heidelberg (2001)
10. IEEE 802.11 Working Group. Ieee standard for information technology – part 11: Wireless lan medium access control (mac) and physical layer (phy) specifications/amendment 6: Medium access control (mac) security enhancements. IEEE 802.11i, IEEE Computer Society (2007)
11. Huang, H., Cao, Z.: Authenticated key exchange protocols with enhanced freshness properties. Cryptology ePrint Archive, Report 2009/505 (2009), `http://eprint.iacr.org/`
12. LaMacchia, B., Lauter, K., Mityagin, A.: Stronger security of authenticated key exchange. Cryptology ePrint Archive, Report 2006/073 (2006), `http://eprint.iacr.org/`
13. Bellare, M., Canetti, R., Krawczyk, H.: Keying hash functions for message authentication. In: Koblitz, N. (ed.) CRYPTO 1996. LNCS, vol. 1109, pp. 1–15. Springer, Heidelberg (1996)
14. Malinen, J.: Host ap project (hostapd/wpa_supplicant). Website (2009), `http://hostap.epitest.fi/`
15. Noack, A.: Sicherheitsanalyse von eap-protokollen. Masterthesis, Ruhr-University Bochum (2007)
16. Opensource. Freeradius project (2009), `http://freeradius.org/`
17. Rogaway, P., Shrimpton, T.: Cryptographic hash-function basics: Definitions, implications, and separations for preimage resistance, second-preimage resistance, and collision resistance. In: Roy, B., Meier, W. (eds.) FSE 2004. LNCS, vol. 3017, pp. 371–388. Springer, Heidelberg (2004)

18. Rigney, C., Willens, S., Rubens, A., Simpson, W.: Remote authentication dial in user service (radius). RFC2865, Network Working Group (2000)
19. Shoup, V.: Sequences of games: a tool for taming complexity in security proofs. Cryptology ePrint Archive, Report 2004/332 (2004), http://eprint.iacr.org/
20. Tews, E.: Attacks on the wep protocol. Cryptology ePrint Archive, Report 2007/471 (2007), http://eprint.iacr.org/
21. Tews, E., Weinmann, R.-P., Pyshkin, A.: Breaking 104 bit wep in less than 60 seconds. Cryptology ePrint Archive, Report 2007/120 (2007), http://eprint.iacr.org/

Supporting Role Based Provisioning with Rules Using OWL and F-Logic

Patrick Rempel[1], Basel Katt[2], and Ruth Breu[2]

[1] Oxford Computer Group Germany, Munich, Germany
patrick.rempel@oxfordcomputergroup.com
[2] University of Innsbruck, Innsbruck, Austria
{basel.katt,ruth.breu}@uibk.ac.at

Abstract. The rule-based RBAC (RB-RBAC) model has been proposed to dynamically assign users to roles based on a set of rules. We identify two problems of this model: simplified rule language with limited expressiveness and the lack of rule reasoning capabilities. In this paper we propose an expressive and extensible provisioning framework that overcomes these drawbacks. Our framework supports complex user-role assignment rules and provides rule reasoning capabilities using OWL DL and F-Logic. Furthermore, we show how our approach supports (i) weak and strong negation to enhance expressiveness and strictness, (ii) defining static SoD constraints, and (iii) detecting conflicts. Finally, the paper describes a mechanism to deduce well-formed SPML requests from rules to provision policy systems with entitlements.

1 Introduction

In the area of access control, provisioning is the continuous process of preparing target systems with entitlements. Typically, this continuous process is driven by rules that specify what entitlements are supposed to be applied to what target system. The target system typically implements access policy mechanisms such as RBAC, MAC, or DAC to enforce the provisioned entitlements within their system domain.

Besides, provisioning is an integral component of managing the life cycle of digital identities [32]. Digital identities are electronic information associated with an individual that are used by systems to authenticate and authorize users to services protected by access control policies. By now, a vast number of software vendors have introduced so known identity management solutions in order to technically support and automate the life cycle of digital identities.

Furthermore, the OASIS provisioning services technical committee defines the XML-based language SPML [25] for exchanging user, resource, and service provisioning information. SPML specifies an abstract provisioning domain model containing requesting authorities, provisioning service provider, provisioning service target, and provisioning service object. According to SPML communication protocol, domain model entities are enabled to interact via well-formed SPML requests and responds. Though SPML defines a generic provisioning framework,

R. Meersman et al. (Eds.): OTM 2010, Part I, LNCS 6426, pp. 600–618, 2010.

the most important challenge is providing proper provisioning requests in due considerations of organizational security policies.

As a common approach, several provisioning frameworks introduce RBAC as an integral part to their platform in order to abstract user-role and role-permission assignments to a meta-level. The abstraction can be used to establish user-role and role-permission assignments on a meta-level. Provisioning systems can then automatically provision the assignments to multiple targets and save administrative effort.

Though the application of RBAC at a meta-level often comes with the risk of tremendous role explosions. When defining roles at a meta-level, often numerous exceptions must be implemented in the role model to satisfy all general and target system specific requirements. As a result, the blown role model again requires expensive administrative effort to maintain assignments of many marginally varying roles, which depresses the advantages of RBAC considerably. Especially large scale provisioning systems that serve multiple provisioning targets may suffer from the exploding amount of roles and its complexity.

The risk of role explosion in RBAC and increasing administrative effort has already been identified and discussed by Al-Kathani et al. [2]. They propose a language to assert attribute expressions on users in RBAC. With the proposed language, rules can be formulated to define dynamic sets of users depending on their attributes. The dynamic sets of users are automatically assigned to roles with further rules to decrease the administrative effort to manually establish user-role assignments. Initially the approach requires involving domain experts to setup a proper rule set. Aiming the required expert involvement to setup rules, Ni et al. [24] have recently proposed a supervised learning-based approach to automatically discover assignment rules. Domain experts are required defining meaningful sample assignments that are used as a training set.

The proposed approaches can be used to establish automated user-role assignments either by explicitly defining rules or by learning from examples. However, complex assignment rules cannot be expressed adequately, and thus the potential of assignment rules to save administrative effort in RBAC is not yet exhausted. Existing approaches did not consider RB-RBAC as provisioning meta-model and thus did not investigate algorithms to translate inferred meta-model facts into concrete provisioning operation.

Contributions: In this paper, we develop an expressive and extensible provisioning framework that supports complex user-role assignment rules and infers valid provisioning operations. Our contributions can be summarized as follows:

- We extend RBAC model to properly serve our framework as meta-model for role based provisioning.
- The meta-model of the extended RBAC is formalized as ontology using the Web Ontology Language (OWL).
- We propose a complex provisioning rule definition and reasoning mechanism with hybrid usage of OWL and F-Logic by adapting ideas from RB-RBAC.

– We describe a mechanism to translate provisioning facts, inferred from the provisioning meta-model through provisioning rules, into concrete SPML provisioning operations. Thereby we demonstrate the applicability of our proposed rule reasoning framework as role-based provisioning system supporting SPML.

The paper is organized as follows. First, we extend in section 2 the RBAC model for the usage as provisioning meta-model and formalize the model extension as ontology. In section 3 we demonstrate how complex assignment rules can be formulated within our role reasoning framework by combining OWL with logic programming. We also validate the application of rules to support RBAC features as role inheritance and separation of duty (SoD). Finally, in section 4 we show how assignment facts, inferred from our logical knowledge base, can be automatically translated into well-formed SPML requests to properly provision target systems with entitlements. Related work is discussed in section 5, and we conclude the paper in section 6.

2 RBAC Ontology and Extensions

2.1 Ontologies

Ontologies are suitable methods to describe and formalize concepts, relationships, and other distinctions of a domain. The Web Ontology Language (OWL) is a W3C standard for a family of knowledge representation languages for authoring ontologies. Its underpinning semantic is based on Description Logics (DL). Due to its prevalence and wide acceptance, OWL is supported by many software projects and vendors. The modeling, serializing, and reasoning of ontologies can be automated or at least supported by tools. DL characterizes domain concepts (classes, properties) and formalizes its terminology. Additionally, further restrictions and specifications can be expressed by DL. Another characteristic of DL is the emphasis on reasoning to infer implicitly represented knowledge from the explicitly described knowledge base.

2.2 Motivating Scenario

In order to show the feasibility of our framework and motivate the extensions of RBAC we introduce a motivating scenario in the financial domain. A fictional company is structured in cost centers to support financial planning, budgeting, and controlling. For every cost center, an annual budget and at least two responsible have to be defined. Furthermore company employees belong to at least one cost center. Costs caused by any employee are apportioned to the cost center the employee belongs to. Every cost allocation to a cost center has to be approved by at least one responsible of the involved cost center. In turn, the cost center responsible requires the "cost allocation approver" role to conduct the cost allocation approval. Cost center responsible may delegate their cost center responsibilities to other persons. To prevent cost centers from developing deficit balances, the following policies have been defined by the chief financial officer:

1. The total of all allocated costs per cost center must not exceed 110% of the assigned cost center budget.
2. The following cost allocation approver (CAA) roles are available. (*i*) **CAA Restricted**: $ApprovedCosts \leq$ €10.000 (*ii*) **CAA Medium**: €10.000 $<$ $ApprovedCosts \leq$ €100.000, and (*iii*) **CAA Unrestricted**: $ApprovedCosts >$ €100.000.
3. The most appropriate CAA roles must be granted to or revoked from the cost center responsible according to the cost center's available budget. Rules #1 and #2 must not be violated.

It is obvious that the rules, specified above, cannot be expressed with RB-RBAC since it does not provide any capabilities to specify cardinalities ("cost center must have at least two responsibles"), aggregations ("all allocated costs of a cost center"), and arithmetic expressions ("allocated costs per cost center must not exceed 110% of the cost center budget"). The attribute expressions in RB-RBAC always refer to attribute values of a single class. Attributes of related classes ("budget of the cost center a person belongs to") cannot be used in RB-RBAC attribute expressions. Due to the limitations above, RB-RBAC does not provide capabilities to formulate complex rules as required in the scenario. Therefore we propose a framework that can deal with RBAC model as well as model extensions, and provides capabilities to express complex assignment rules.

2.3 RBAC Extension

The motivating scenario illustrates the necessity to extend the RBAC model with additional classes to make it usable as provisioning framework meta-model. Typically, enterprise security policies are defined with the help of enterprise entities, such as department, location, cost center or the like (context) with the objective to put restrictions on the activities of humans (person) within the enterprise domain to comply with any legal obligation, as well as to protect it from frauds. Thereby it is the obligation of a provisioning system to translate meta-level rules into concrete entitlements of user accounts, used by humans at the application level (target).

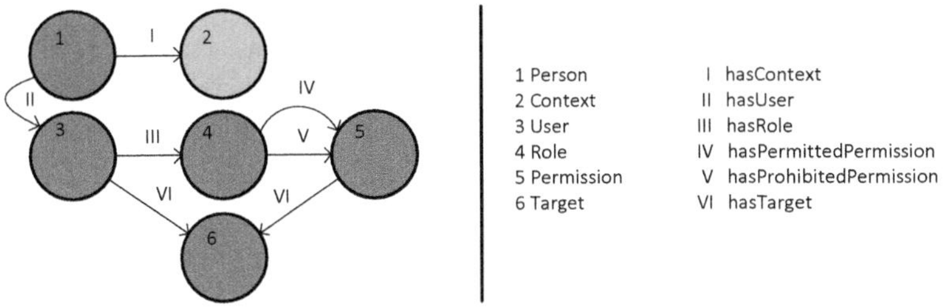

Fig. 1. Ontology of RBAC and Extensions

Therefore we propose in our provisioning framework to extend the RBAC model with three classes, namely, *target*, *person* and *context* classes. The following ontology concepts define the formal specification of all elements of RBAC model and its extensions (cf. Figure 1). Based on this formalization, we propose a rule definition scheme, where reasoners can be used to entail entitlement provisioning information.

Target. The target class represents things that serve as provisioning destination or endpoint (system, application, service etc.).

User. This class represents subjects that perform operations on a target. Each user class has exactly one target (*hasTarget*).

Permission. The permission class represents authorizations to perform security related operations on a target. Just as user classes, each permission class has exactly one provisioning target (*hasTarget*).

Role. A role class represents things that serve as roles of users. A role has one to many permissions, which must be an instance of the class permission. Since roles can explicitly permit or prohibit permissions, the class role has two distinct properties: (*i*) *hasPermittedPermission*, and (*ii*) *hasProhibitedPermission*. Role hierarchies can be represented with the property *hasSubRoles*.

Person. The person class represents a human being and its characteristics in the provisioning framework meta-model. Thereby a person can belong to one or to many contexts (*hasContext*). Due to this relation, abstract enterprise policies can be formulated at a meta-level. Apart from that a person can possess single or multiple user accounts that belong to a concrete target. That means a person utilizes users to perform security related operations on a target. Due to the person-user relation, abstract enterprise policies formulated at meta-level with context entities, can adequately be mapped to concrete target. This enables the provisioning framework to provision any target with user accounts and entitlements that comply with meta-level security policies.

Context. The context class represents entities within a domain containing information that are essential to formulate policy rules but cannot be stored as attributes of existing entities due to its complexity. Contexts are typically related to person or role and represent a certain aspect (e.g. environment, such as time or location) of the related object. Contexts can form hierarchies with OWL class inheritance. Additional domain specific properties can be added accordingly. In this section we focus on the essential properties for rule driven role based provisioning.

3 Role Based Provisioning Rule Framework

We use the formally described RBAC ontology as a starting point for the provisioning rule expression framework. The proposed framework is supposed to provide all

RB-RBAC rules expression capabilities [2]. Additionally, it provides capabilities to explicitly specify class relation *quantifiers and cardinalities*, define *aggregations* on value lists, and determine *arithmetic* expressions as part of the rule condition. It is essential that the framework supports rule expressions that can be applied to our RBAC meta-model. Because of that, the framework permits to define attribute expressions on any meta-model class and to form rules by logically combining these expressions. Thus the framework overcomes the limitation of RB-RBAC that only attribute expressions on a single class user is allowed.

Therefore we propose a provisioning framework (cf. Figure 2) that uses an extended RBAC model as meta-model. We choose RBAC instead of attribute based access control (ABAC) as meta model to utilize RBAC features such as role hierarchies or SoD constraints within our framework. The provisioning framework adapts ideas from RB-RBAC to formulate provisioning rules but extend these ideas by introducing a rich rule reasoning component. The provisioning framework consists of the following parts:

1. The OWL part. It allows to model and store (Protégé) the extended RBAC ontology (cf. Section 3.1) as well as to reason (cf. Section 3.2) on the ontology with OWL reasoner (Pellet).
2. The F-Logic part. The logical programming environment FLORA-2 provides an F-Logic inference engine (cf. Section 3.4) and adds further rule reasoning capabilities (cf. Section 3.5 and 3.6) to the framework that can not be achieved with OWL reasoner only.
3. The controller part. *Provisioning Rule Controller* (cf. Section 3.3) supervises the overall reasoning process, initiates the required knowledge representation translation and infers SPML provisioning operations from the meta-model (cf. Section 4).

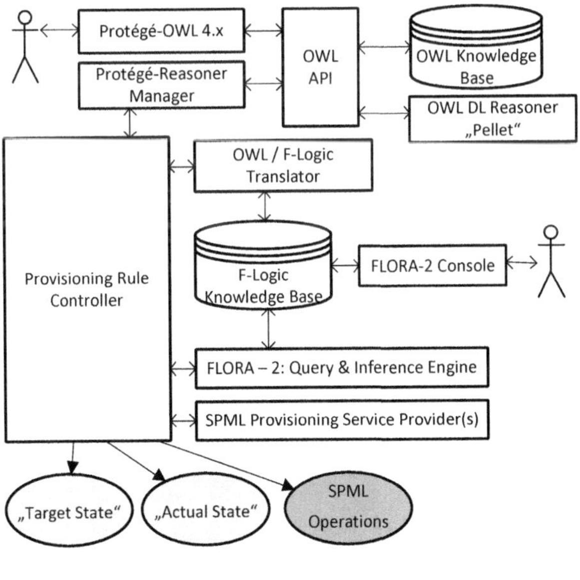

Fig. 2. Role Based Provisioning Rule Framework Architecture

3.1 OWL DL

The existing base ontology can be extended for any scenario specific purpose in a natural way with OWL DL axioms. Hierarchical relations can be defined with OWL class inheritance. Class relations can be specified with reference properties. OWL DL further enables asserting constraints on classes by specifying domains, ranges, quantifiers and cardinalities. These restrictions can be defined for any ontology class and be combined with logical operations. This means that OWL DL expressions are not limited to a single class, but can also be applied to our RBAC meta-model. The following conditions from the motivating scenario can be expressed straight forward in OWL DL, shown in Table 1:

CI *(A cost center is a context, a person can belong to.)*: This can be specified by defining cost center class as a subclass of context. The person to cost center reference does not need to be specified explicitly due to the class inheritance.

CII *(A cost center may have costs assigned.)*: OWL DL allows to further describe named ontology classes using property restrictions. We define a new property hasCosts and use the universal quantifier restriction with the filler "datatype: decimal". The restriction states that if such a relation exists, it must be with a value of the type decimal.

CIII *(A cost center must have a budget.)*: We define another property hasBudget and use again the universal restriction with the filler "datatype: decimal". We further use an existential restriction to state that every cost center must have a hasBudget property. That means all individuals without a hasBudget property or with a hasBudget property that does not satisfy the universal restriction cannot be a cost center.

CIV *(A cost center must have more than one responsible. Only a person is a valid cost center responsible.)*: We define a property hasResponsible with the filler person and the intersection of a universal and an existential restriction along the property. We also define a cardinality restriction to ensure more than one responsible is defined for each cost center. The usage of cardinality restrictions requires that the OWL reasoner supports Unique Name Assumption (UNA) to be reliable.

CV + CVI *(A cost center responsible can delegate his responsibility to another person who becomes a cost center responsible too.)*: First we define a new

Table 1. DL Axioms

#	**DL Axiom**
CI	$CostCenter \sqsubseteq Context$
CII	$CostCenter \sqsubseteq \forall hasCosts.xsd : decimal$
CIII	$CostCenter \sqsubseteq \forall hasBudget.xsd : decimal \sqcap \exists hasBudget.xsd : decimal$
CIV	$CostCenter \sqsubseteq \forall hasResponsible.Person$ $\sqcap \exists hasResponsible.Person \sqcap \geq 2\ hasResponsible$
CV	$hasDelegate+ \sqsubseteq hasDelegate$
CVI	$CostCenterResponsible \sqsubseteq \forall hasDelegate.Person \sqcap Person$ $\sqcap (\exists isResponsible.CostCenter \sqcup \exists isDelegate.CostCenterResponsible)$

subclass of person *cost center responsible*. We define an isResponsible property (inverse to hasResponsible), a hasDelegate property and the inverse property isDelegate with the filler Person to allow delegations. HasDelegate is transitive to support multi-level delegations. Thus, a cost center responsible must either have an isResponsible or isDelegate property. Therefore we define the union of an existential restriction of isResponsible and isDelegate as another cost center responsible constraint.

Figure 3 visualizes the cost center related ontology extension using crop circle visualization [27].

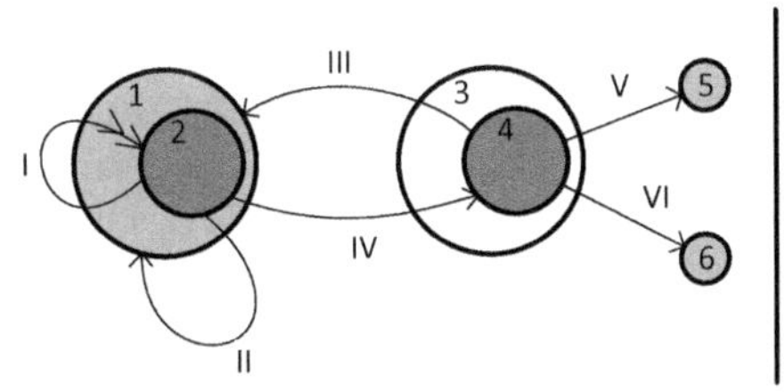

Fig. 3. Ontology Extension: Cost Center

3.2 OWL DL Reasoning

An important feature of ontologies that are described in OWL DL is that they can be computed by a reasoner. One of the key services, provided by OWL DL reasoners, is syntax and consistency checking. The OWL semantics and abstract syntax [28] formally defines ontology consistency. The OWL Web Ontology Test Cases W3C Recommendation [8] specifies the OWL conformance criteria for syntax and consistency checkers as well as consistency test cases. Based on ontology class definitions, the reasoner can validate whether or not it is possible for a class to have any instance. Classes that cannot have any instances are unsatisfiable. If a reasoner identifies unsatisfiable classes, the reasoner marks them as inconsistent. Another key feature of OWL reasoners is subsumption testing. The conditions of classes are evaluated to determine if a subclass-superclass relationship exists between classes. Thereby a complete class hierarchy, consisting of explicit and entailed subclass relations, can be computed. We use the OWL DL reasoner Pellet [26] in our framework. As a result of the reasoning process, an inferred knowledge base is constructed.

3.3 Provisioning Rule Controller

In order to further process the OWL DL reasoner output, we introduce the intermediate framework component provisioning rule controller. The purpose of the controller is to supervise the overall entailment process. As soon as changes happen to the knowledge base, the controller initiates a new reasoning iteration. To support other reasoners in future extensions, the controller utilizes the reasoner manager of the Protégé-OWL [29] inference package. The reasoner manages communication with the reasoner plug-in and provides several methods to obtain inferred information about ontology classes and individuals. The controller then initiates the translation of the inferred information into an F-Logic ontology representation, which will be discussed in the next section. The OWL to F-Logic translation is required before the second reasoning part (cf. Section 3.5) can be initiated.

3.4 F-Logic

While OWL DL has it strengths in defining ontology concepts, instances and the taxonomy of classes, especially in conjunction with OWL DL reasoners, it does not provide a sufficient support for computed properties. Especially the support of computed properties is required to express rule based user-role, role-permission, and user-permission assignments. We also require computed properties, based on logical and arithmetic expressions to adequately express assignment rules. E.g. the calculated cost center property hasCostLimit (110% of the cost center budget) must be calculated: $hasCostLimit = (budget * 110)/100$. Another important aspect of many rule languages is the capability to express aggregations (e.g. min, max, count, sum) for sets of instances and set-valued properties.

Another drawback of OWL is the way it evaluates negations. The OWL semantic, and thus OWL reasoners as well, adopts the logical model of an open world assumption to evaluate negations [19]: a statement is false if and only if it can be proved to be true that the statement contradicts other information from the ontology. This assumption accepts that the knowledge base of the ontology is incomplete. So OWL DL only enables specifying weak negations. When dealing with access control policy rules, in which permissions can be explicitly prohibited, the application of weak negation leads to an unsafe policy system (cf. Section 3.6).

In order to address OWL DL inherent limitations, different approaches try to combine or extend ontologies with rules. Several systems define a language consisting of RDF as core part and an extension to define rules, such as Jena [1], TRIPPLE [31], and N3Logic [6]. Another approach to combine rules and ontologies is Description Logic Programs (DLP), proposed in [16]. DLPs define an intersection of description logic and declarative logic program (Horn clauses). That means, DLPs allow combining rules whenever description logic axioms correspond with Horn rules. The intersection also means that description logic mapping constructors, such as disjunction, universal restriction, existential restriction, negation, and cardinality restriction, can only be used limitedly. However, disjunction, implication, and conjunction in the head (or body) of a horn rule cannot be supported by DLPs. This is because the corresponding Horn representation cannot be handled within a def-Horn framework.

Another approach of adding rules to OWL is the proposition of SWRL [18], which adds a new kind of axiom (Horn clause rules) to OWL DL. Therefore the OWL syntax and semantic is extended to include Horn clause rules [17]. Due to the usage of Horn clauses, the limitations, already discussed for DLP, also pertain for SWRL.

Due to the limited expressiveness of rules in combined approaches we use a hybrid approach within our framework. In a first step we use an existing ontology reasoner to check consistency and entail class hierarchies. In a second step we use an existing rule reasoner to support computed properties based on arithmetic expressions and aggregations as well as negation as failure, which is related to closed world assumption. Two important aspects must be covered by the rule reasoner: The reasoner (i) must provide a logical foundation which supports the required rules expressiveness and (ii) must support the object-oriented concepts of semantic web ontologies in order to allow an automated knowledge transfer between the two reasoners. We choose F-Logic [22] which extend the paradigm of logical programming and deductive database with the concepts of objects, classes, and types. Our provisioning framework avails the open-source system Flora-2 [33], which is a complete programming environment that integrates F-Logic with other formalisms such as HiLog and Transaction Logic.

The following conditions from our motivating scenario cannot be expressed with OWL DL but can be expressed through F-Logic rules, shown in Table 2:

CI *(A cost center has a calculated property which contains the total of all allocated costs.)*: The calculated property can be expressed with an object molecule as a rule head. Since allocated cost is single valued, the property can be defined as a scalar method. The object that owns the calculated property and the calculated value are defined as variables in the rule head. The rule body specifies the formation rules of the variables. An is-a assertion of the form O:C defines the class binding of the object variable. The aggregation method *sum* calculates the total of the set-valued property *hasCosts*. This property is already defined through OWL DL.

CII *(A cost center has a calculated property which specifies the limit of all allocated costs. The total of all allocated costs per cost center must not exceed 110% of the assigned budget.)*: The cost limit property can be expressed similarly, albeit we use an arithmetic expression to calculate it.

CIII *(A person has a calculated property which contains all explicit (direct delegation) and implicit (transitive delegation) delegates.)*: This can again be defined as calculated property. Thereby the transitive delegation can be resolved with a recursive rule expression.

Table 2. F-Logic Rule Expressions

#	F-Logic Syntax
CI	$?X[hasTotalAllocatedCosts \rightarrow ?Y] \longleftarrow$ $?X : CostCenter \wedge ?Y = sum\{?Z \mid ?X[hasCosts \rightarrow ?Z]\}.$
CII	$?X[hasCostLimit \rightarrow ?Y] \longleftarrow$ $?X : CostCenter \wedge ?X[hasBudget \rightarrow ?Z] \wedge ?Y\ is\ ?Z * 110/100.$
CIII	$?X[hasDelegateAll \rightarrow ?Y] \longleftarrow$ $?X : Person \wedge ?Y : Person \wedge ?X[hasDelegate \rightarrow ?Z]$ $\wedge\ (?Y = ?Z \vee ?Z[hasDelegateAll \rightarrow ?Y]).$
CIV	$?X[hasResponsibleAll \rightarrow ?Y] \longleftarrow$ $?X : CostCenter \wedge ?Y : Person$ $\wedge\ (\ ?X[hasResponsible \rightarrow ?Y]$ $\vee\ (\ ?X[hasResponsible \rightarrow ?Z] \wedge ?Z[hasDelegateAll \rightarrow ?Y])\ ).$

CIV *(A cost center has a calculated property which contains all responsible.)*: Possible members are directly assigned responsible, direct delegates, and transitive delegates. This can be expressed through a calculated property that unifies the set of directly assigned responsible (OWL property) and the set of all delegates of the responsible.

3.5 F-Logic Reasoning

Due to its object-oriented concepts and frame based syntax, F-Logic can also be used as ontology language. While OWL classes are modeled as unary predicates and properties as binary predicates, F-Logic classes and properties are modeled as terms. That means the typical ontology components such as class taxonomy, concept definition, and instance definition can be modeled in OWL and F-Logic. In our provisioning framework we combine both approaches to leverage the reasoning and expressiveness advantages of both. In order to use both reasoning approaches within our multi-step reasoning process, the knowledge base facts must be translated between OWL and F-Logic [11]. Since we only transfer entailed knowledge base facts the set of translation rules shown in Table 3 is sufficient for the needs of our framework.

Table 3. DL / F-Logic Translation

	OWL Syntax	**F-Logic Syntax**
class hierarchies	$C \sqsubseteq D$	C::D
concept definitions	$C \sqsubseteq \forall P.D$	C[P $\star \Rightarrow$ D]
instances	$I \in C$	$I : C$

3.6 RBAC Policies

One key purpose of the framework is to provide appropriate methods to establish rule based user-role and permission-role assignments. The established assignments can then be propagated to provisioning targets. While users, roles, and permissions are modeled as OWL classes, assignments are modeled as calculated properties on each class. The user-role assignment is modeled as hasRole property on the user class. The following F-Logic rules dynamically establish user-role assignments from our motivating scenario. Role-permission assignments can be defined accordingly.

Assignment rule definition for users with hasRole = "CAA RESTRICTED":

$$?X[hasRole \rightarrow CAA\_RESTRICTED] \longleftarrow$$
$$?X : User \wedge ?ZZ[hasUser \rightarrow ?X] \wedge ?Y : CostCenter[hasResponsible \rightarrow ?ZZ]$$
$$\wedge\ ?XX = sum\{?Z|?Y[hasCosts \rightarrow ?Z]\} \wedge ?Y : CostCenter[hasBudget \rightarrow ?YY]$$
$$\wedge\ ?XXX\ is\ ?YY * 110/100 - ?XX \wedge ?XXX < 10000$$

Assignment rule definition for users with hasRole = "CAA MEDIUM":

$$?X[hasRole \rightarrow CAA\_MEDIUM] \longleftarrow$$
$$?X : User \wedge ?ZZ[hasUser \rightarrow ?X] \wedge ?Y : CostCenter[hasResponsible \rightarrow ?ZZ]$$
$$\wedge\ ?XX = sum\{?Z|?Y[hasCosts \rightarrow ?Z]\} \wedge ?Y : CostCenter[hasBudget \rightarrow ?YY]$$
$$\wedge\ ?XXX\ is\ ?YY * 110/100 - ?XX \wedge ?XXX \geq 10000 \wedge ?XXX < 100000$$

Assignment rule definition for users with hasRole = "CAA UNRESTRICTED":

$$?X[hasRole \rightarrow CAA\_UNRESTRICTED] \longleftarrow$$
$$?X : User \wedge ?ZZ[hasUser \rightarrow ?X] \wedge ?Y : CostCenter[hasResponsible \rightarrow ?ZZ]$$
$$\wedge\ ?XX = sum\{?Z|?Y[hasCosts \rightarrow ?Z]\} \wedge ?Y : CostCenter[hasBudget \rightarrow ?YY]$$
$$\wedge\ ?XXX\ is\ ?YY * 110/100 - ?XX \wedge ?XXX \geq 100000$$

Hierarchies. We model role hierarchies as hasSubRoles relation property on the role class. Each role dominates its sub-roles transitively, which means that the role is senior to its transitive sub-roles. Due to the fact that senior roles acquire the permissions of their juniors, role-permissions assignments are the union of rule based role-permission assignments (calculated role property has-permissions) and inherited assignments due to the following permission inheritance rules:

Assignment rule that calculates all transitive sub-roles of a role:

$$?X[hasSubRolesAll \rightarrow ?Y] \longleftarrow$$
$$?X : Role \wedge ?Y : Role \wedge ?X[hasSubRole \rightarrow ?Z]$$
$$\wedge\ (?Y = ?Z \vee ?Z[hasSubRoleAll \rightarrow ?Y])$$

Assignment rule that calculates all permissions of a role, either due to direct assignment or role inheritance:

$$?X[hasPermissionAll \rightarrow ?Y] \longleftarrow$$
$$?X : Role \wedge ?Y : Permission$$
$$\wedge\ ?X[hasSubRolesAll \rightarrow ?Z] \wedge ?Z[hasPermission \rightarrow ?Y]$$

User memberships of roles are calculated inversely because junior roles acquire the user membership of their seniors.

Negation. Due to the existence of two distinct logical reasoners in the provisioning framework, the different reasoner semantics on how implicit knowledge is evaluated must be considered carefully. The OWL reasoner uses Open World Assumption (OWA). It only interprets information false or "negative" if the information explicitly contradicts other axioms (weak negation). Under OWA it is accepted that the knowledge base is incomplete. By contrast, the F-Logic reasoner uses Closed World Assumption (CWA) [30]. It interprets information as false or "negative" if the information is not explicitly stated in the knowledge base (strong negation), which is also known as negation-as-failure [9]. Under CWA the knowledge base is considered complete and the CWA reasoner may conclude false negatives because of missing information in the knowledge base. The uncontrolled usage of weak negation, especially in the context of security related policies and provisioning rules, is regarded unsafe. Therefore we propose to classify all predicates in the rule base either as *weak* or *strong*. The framework controls that weak predicates are evaluated under OWA and strong predicates under CWA.

Separation of Duty. The RBAC model provides separation of duty (SoD) to enforce conflict of interest policies [12]. It distinguishes static and dynamic SoD constraints. While static SoD places constraints on the assignment of users to roles, dynamic SoD places constraints on roles that can be activated within a user's session. Since the proposed framework is supposed to entail and provision user-role and role-permission assignments, only static SoD can be applied within the RBAC meta-model. Static SoD is defined as the tuple (R, n), where: R is a set of roles, n is the maximum number of roles from the set which may be assigned to a single user. In order to model static SoD in the provisioning RBAC meta-model, we introduce the new class SoD constraint to the ontology. This class consists of a set-valued property hasRoles, containing the set of constrained roles, and a single value integer property hasMaximum, defining the maximum number of roles. In addition we define calculated property hasTransgressingUser, which contains the set of users that acquires more than the maximum allowed roles.

Since we distinguish between person and user within our RBAC meta-model, it is important that we also consider conflict of interest policy for persons. By design a person can have one to many users. Due to that, a person might acquire more than the maximum allowed roles of a SoD constraint through different users without producing a SoD conflict. Therefore we add the property hasScope and the calculated property hasTransgressingPerson to the class SoD-Constraint. The scope can be used to specify whether SoD has to be applied locally (user) or globally (person). If the scope is set to global, the set of all roles acquired by a person through users is considered for calculating the users and person which are in conflict with the SoD policy. Otherwise only the set of roles acquired by a user is considered. The set of persons and users with a SoD conflict are computed by the calculated backlink property hasSoDConflict (Figure 4).

Dynamic SoD policies could be defined in the RBAC meta-model but cannot be used to deduce any SoD conflicts. It has to be applied by the target systems directly since user sessions and role activations are typically out of context of a provisioning framework.

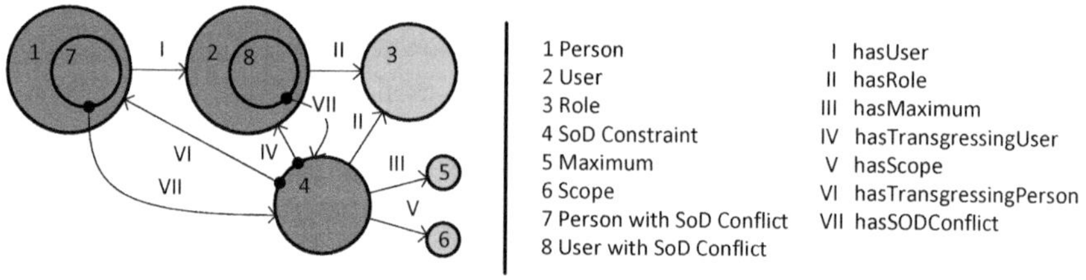

Fig. 4. Ontology Extension: Separation of Duty

4 Provisioning

Two general aspects have to be considered for role based provisioning. In the previous section we discussed the rule based reasoning part of our proposed framework to infer user-role and role-permission assignments facts from the RBAC meta-model. The set of inferred assignment facts comprise the overall target state of all RBAC policies for all provisioning targets. In this section we discuss the process of provisioning the overall target state of policies to the targets. We assume in our framework that all provisioning targets either implement SPML [25] or a dedicated provider makes the target available for SPML provisioning actions. According to the SPML domain model, our framework has the role of the Requesting Authority (RA) that issues well-formed SPML requests to a Provisioning Service Provider (PSP). SPML defines the Provisioning Service Target (PST) as an endpoint that the PSP makes available for provisioning actions. The PSP manages the PST objects in compliance with the provisioning requests. That means, our framework establishes trust relationship(s) to one or many PSP and initiates adequate requests in order to provision the inferred overall target state to all PST.

4.1 Target State

The SPML domain model defines that one PST is provisioned by exactly one PSP, but a PSP can provision multiple PST. We define in our RBAC metamodel the class target and the constraint that every user and permission must be linked with a target. Due to that the framework can determine which inferred assignment fact has to be provisioned to which PST and thereby it can determine which PSP must be contacted with well-formed SPML requests. For that reason the framework's provisioning rule controller provides the capability to query inferred assignment facts from the knowledge base and to translate them into well-formed SPML requests. Each PST has a schema that defines the structure of Provisioning Service Objects (PSO), which represents a data entity and its properties on a PST. A well-formed SPML provisioning request consists of an operation (add, modify, delete, suspend, resume) and operation parameters. Operation parameters may be serialized PSO, distinct PSO identifier, distinct PST identifier, and execution mode (synchronous/asynchronous). Therefore the provisioning rule controller must translate an assignment fact into a PSO that correspond to the PST schema. Additionally an appropriate operation type has to be deduced. While inferred facts can directly be translated to PSO by object schema translation, the appropriate operation type also depends on the existence and actual state of the PSO in the PST (refer to 4.2). SPML has another exception which is important for PSO translation: references properties that can be used to refer from one PSO to another PSO are not part of the PSO schema. Instead, an SPML reference capability defines which PSO type supports references to which other PSO type. Thus the provisioning rule controller translates reference properties into SPML reference capability data and all other properties to PSO data.

4.2 Actual State

Though the overall target state of all RBAC policies can be inferred from the provisioning framework's knowledge base, the provisioning controller also requires information on the actual state of RBAC policies, present in each PST, to deduce appropriate SPML operations. By definition the provisioning framework has information about all potentially provisioned PSP and PST. SPML defines generic methods that enable the PSR to determine the actual state of each PST. The *lookup* operation can be used to obtain serialized PSO as well as the PSO related reference capability data. The *search* operation supports the ability to retrieve all or a subset of the PSO in a PST. PSO subsets are defined by XPath expressions. For actual state reasoning we must also consider the corresponding PSP resource consumption. If the provisioning framework would search for all PSO with every actual state reasoning iteration, the requested PSP would exhaust available resources soon. Thus the *update* operation should be used to retrieve only PSO that have been created, changed, or deleted since the last actual state reasoning iteration. That means, the result of an update query represents the delta between previous and current actual state. By cumulating the deltas, the actual state can be computed without unnecessarily exhausting PSP resources.

4.3 Provisioning Operations

Contrary to PSO data and reference capability data, SPML provisioning operations depend on the inferred target state and the detected actual state of PSO. Table 4 summarizes all relevant PSO actual state/target state constellations and their corresponding SPML operations at glance. According to that mapping table the provisioning controller is able to infer well-formed SPML requests from the actual state and target state to provision entitlements correctly.

Table 4. Provisioning Operations

Actual State	**Target State**	**Operation**
PSO identifier	-	Delete
-	PSO identifier	Add
PSO identifier with data'	PSO identifier with data"	Modify
PSO identifier with reference capability data'	PSO identifier with reference capability data"	Modify
Enabled PSO	Disabled PSO	Suspend
Disabled PSO	Enabled PSO	Resume

5 Related Work

The closest to our work is the RB-RBAC model proposed by Al-Kahtani et al. [2], in which the authors proposed to automatically assign users to roles. With these rules, attribute expressions on users can be formulated to define conditions and constraints on using roles. RB-RBAC also allows to induce role hierarchies by introducing role dominance relations [3] and negative authorization [4].

The rule based provisioning approach in [21] distinguishes dynamic (provisioning with RB-RBAC) and static (RBAC administration) user-role assignments to combine advantages of roles and rules. Yu et al. [34] proposed a DL based approach to represent and reason on RB-RBAC, while similar approaches used DL to reason on RBAC via DL reasoners RACER [35] or Pellet [10] in order to verify policy correctness, capture constraints, and make access control decisions. Giunchiglia et al. [14] proposed a relation model (RelBAC) to represent access control rules and used DL as well in [15] to formalize and reason on policy rules.

Bertino et.al. [7] proposed a logical formalism for reasoning about access control models. The proposed logical language is composed of C-Datalog programs. ROWLBAC [13] defines an OWL ontology to represent RBAC and attribute based access control policies. The authors proposed the use of OWL axioms (*citizen* disjoint *resident* role) to specify SoD constraints.

The major advantage of our work against the mentioned approaches is twofold. (i) *Expressivness*: we propose a framework that provides expressive rule definition capabilities, namely, arithmetic terms, aggregations, strong negations, attribute quantifiers, attribute cardinalities, and combined attribute expressions on multiple classes but still leverages the well studied advantages of DL reasoning. (ii) *Strong negation*: all OWL/DL based approaches are based on the concept of open world assumption with weak negation. Due to that, SoD constraints containing negations ("a role that permits study must not be combined with a role that does not prohibit work") can be formulated in OWL, but can only be enforced by OWL reasoners if all roles explicitly store the information that they do or do not prohibit work. Therefore we propose to additionally use logic programs with strong negations to strictly enforce SoD. Nejdl et al. [23] formalized credential ontologies and constraints with F-Logic to specify access control policies under closed world assumption but did not consider DL. Though the pure F-Logic approach is sufficient to model ontologies in general (as discussed in [5]) and access control policies with constraints and strong negation in particular, our hybrid DL/F-Logic approach allows to represent existential information of a class without specifying any concrete instance. In pure F-Logic only an approximation can be expressed with Skolem functions.

To the best of our knowledge, no work has been done on combining OWL DL with F-Logic in the area of access control policy modeling to address shortcomings of existing approaches that focus on DL or F-Logic only. An inference engine that uses F-Logic to reason with OWL ontologies is F-OWL [36]. It researches how OWL can support multi-agent systems. Another approach combines OWL with F-Logic rules for semantic web application nodes [20]. These studies do not evaluate applicability of combined OWL and F-Logic for access control policies.

A supervised learning-based approach [24] has been recently proposed to automatically discover pseudo-rules by classifying sample assignments. Though the learning-based approach probably does not need as much expert involvement, it requires a set of sound sample assignments to be created by domain experts. Furthermore, existing sample assignments do not necessarily represent IT-security policies correctly.

6 Conclusions and Future Work

In this paper, we introduce a framework to model complex rules to dynamically establish user-role and role-permission assignments in RBAC. To overcome the drawbacks of existing rule based approaches, we propose a composition approach based on OWL ontologies, OWL DL axioms, and F-Logic expressions that provide appropriate expressiveness and flexibility.

As a foundation we define an RBAC ontology and illustrate the extensibility and the concrete necessity of domain (provisioning framework) specific extensions through a motivating example. For this purpose we extend the ontology with concepts such as *person, context, and target.* The ontology serves as RBAC meta-model that can be used to specify rules (user-role assignments), which are processed by reasoning and provisioning components.

Ontology classes, individuals, and properties are specified precisely with OWL DL axioms that assert cardinally and quantifier constraints over them. We leverage existing reasoning tools to validate model consistency and to infer class hierarchy.

To enhance the framework's rule expression and reasoning capabilities we propose to use OWL and F-Logic reasoners in a hybrid manner. While certain rules are expressed with OWL DL axioms, such as cardinally and quantifier constraints, more complex rules are defined with F-Logic due to its expressive power. However this requires that inferred OWL ontology facts must be translated into F-Logic syntax for further processing. Applying complex F-Logic assignment rules to the RBAC ontology enables to define (i) calculated properties on n-ary class relations, (ii) arithmetic expressions, (iii) aggregations, and (iv) logical expressions.

Finally we describe a method to translate assignment information, deduced from the ontology and rules, into corresponding SPML operations to provision policy systems with entitlements.

A prototypical implementation and empirical study is underway, surveying multiple OWL and F-Logic reasoners within the provisioning framework concerning performance and suitability. Additionally the hybrid reasoning approach leverages a heterogeneous group of rule definition languages. Thus we plan to investigate how the heterogeneous languages can be unified with existing rules interchange standards.

References

1. Jena - a semantic web framework for java. Internet, `http://jena.sourceforge.net`
2. Al-Kahtani, M., Sandhu, R.: A model for attribute-based user-role assignment. In: Proc. 18th ACSAC (2002)
3. Al-Kahtani, M.A., Sandhu, R.: Induced role hierarchies with attribute-based rbac. In: Proc. 8th SACMAT (2003)
4. Al-Kahtani, M.A., Sandhu, R.S.: Rule-based rbac with negative authorization, pp. 405–415. IEEE Computer Society, Los Alamitos (2004)
5. Angele, J., Kifer, M., Lausen, G.: Ontologies in F-logic. In: Handbook on Ontologies, pp. 45–70 (2009)
6. Berners-Lee, T., Connolly, D., Kagal, L., Scharf, Y., Hendler, J.A.: N3Logic: A logical framework for the World Wide Web. TPLP 8, 249–269 (2008)
7. Bertino, E., Catania, B., Ferrari, E., Perlasca, P.: A logical framework for reasoning about access control models. In: Proc. of SACMAT 2001, pp. 41–52. ACM, New York (2001)

8. Carroll, J.J., Roo, J.: OWL Web Ontology Language Test Cases. W3C recommendation W3C (2004), http://www.w3.org/tr/owl-test
9. Clark, K.L.: Negation as failure. In: Logic and Data Bases (1978)
10. Cruz, I.F., Gjomemo, R., Lin, B., Orsini, M.: A constraint and attribute based security framework for dynamic role assignment in collaborative environments. In: Proc. of the 4th CollaborateCom 2008 (2008)
11. de Bruijn, J., Heymans, S.: On the Relationship between Description Logic-based and F-Logic-based Ontologies, vol. 82. IOS Press, Amsterdam (2008)
12. Ferraiolo, D.F., Sandhu, R., Gavrila, S., Kuhn, D.R., Chandramouli, R.: Proposed nist standard for role-based access control. ACM TISSEC 4(3), 224–274 (2001)
13. Finin, T., Joshi, A., Kagal, L., Niu, J., Sandhu, R., Winsborough, W., Thuraisingham, B.: ROWLBAC: representing role based access control in OWL. In: Proc. of the 13th ACM SACMAT (2008)
14. Giunchiglia, F., Zhang, R., Crispo, B.: Relbac: Relation based access control. In: 4th Int. Conf. on SKG 2008, pp. 3–11 (2008)
15. Giunchiglia, F., Crispo, B., Zhang, R.: Design and run time reasoning with relbac. Technical report, DISI (2008)
16. Grosof, B.N., Horrocks, I., Volz, R., Decker, S.: Description logic programs: combining logic programs with description logic. In: Proc. of the 12th international conference on WWW (2003)
17. Horrocks, I., Patel-Schneider, P.F.: A proposal for an owl rules language. In: Proc. of the 13th Int. WWW (2004)
18. Horrocks, I., Patel-Schneider, P.F., Boley, H., Tabet, S., Grosof, B., Dean, M.: SWRL: A Semantic Web Rule Language Combining OWL and RuleML. W3C Member Submission W3C (2004), http://www.w3.org/Submission/SWRL/
19. Horrocks, I., Patel-Schneider, P.F., van Harmelen, F.: From SHIQ and RDF to OWL: the making of a Web Ontology Language. J. Web Sem. 1(1), 7–26 (2003)
20. Kattenstroth, H., May, W., Schenk, F.: Combining OWL with F-Logic Rules and Defaults. In: Proc. of 2nd Int. WS on ALPSWS (2007)
21. Kern, A., Walhorn, C.: Rule support for rolebased access control. In: Proceedings of the tenth ACM symposium on Access control models and technologies (2005)
22. Kifer, M., Lausen, G., Wu, J.: Logical foundations of object-oriented and frame-based languages. J. ACM 42, 741–843 (1995)
23. Nejdl, W., Olmedilla, D., Winslett, M., Zhang, C.C.: Ontology-based policy specification and management. In: Gómez-Pérez, A., Euzenat, J. (eds.) ESWC 2005. LNCS, vol. 3532, pp. 290–302. Springer, Heidelberg (2005)
24. Ni, Q., Lobo, J., Calo, S., Rohtangi, P., Bertino, E.: Automating Role-based Provisioning by Learning from Examples. In: Proc. of the 14th SACMAT (2009)
25. OASIS. Oasis service provisioning markup language (spml) v. 2 (2006), http://www.oasis-open.org/committees/tc_home.php?wg_abbrev=provision
26. Parsia, B., Sirin, E.: Pellet: An OWL DL Reasoner. In: McIlraith, S.A., Plexousakis, D., van Harmelen, F. (eds.) ISWC 2004. LNCS, vol. 3298. Springer, Heidelberg (2004)
27. Parsia, B., Wang, T., Golbeck, J.: Visualizing web ontologies with cropcircles. In: Gil, Y., Motta, E., Benjamins, V.R., Musen, M.A. (eds.) ISWC 2005. LNCS, vol. 3729. Springer, Heidelberg (2005)
28. Patel-Schneider, P.F., Hayes, P., Horrocks, I.: OWL Web Ontology Language Semantics and Abstract Syntax. W3C (2004), http://www.w3.org/tr/owl-semantics
29. Protégé, http://protegewiki.stanford.edu
30. Shepherdson, J.C.: Negation as failure: a comparison of clark's completed data base and reiter's closed world assumption. J. Log. Program. 1(1), 51–79 (1984)

31. Sintek, M., Decker, S.: Triple - a query, inference, and transformation language for the semantic web. In: Horrocks, I., Hendler, J. (eds.) ISWC 2002. LNCS, vol. 2342, p. 364. Springer, Heidelberg (2002)
32. Windley, P.J.: Digital Identity. O'Reilly, Sebastopol (2005)
33. Yang, G., Kifer, M., Zhao, C.: FLORA-2: A Rule-Based Knowledge Representation and Inference Infrastructure for the Semantic Web. In: Meersman, R., Tari, Z., Schmidt, D.C. (eds.) CoopIS 2003, DOA 2003, and ODBASE 2003. LNCS, vol. 2888, Springer, Heidelberg (2003)
34. Yu, H., Xie, Q., Che, H.: Description Logic Based Conflict Detection Methods for RB-RBAC Model. IJCSNS 6(1A), 120 (2006)
35. Zhao, C., Heilili, N., Liu, S., Lin, Z.: Representation and reasoning on rbac: A description logic approach. In: Van Hung, D., Wirsing, M. (eds.) ICTAC 2005. LNCS, vol. 3722, pp. 381–393. Springer, Heidelberg (2005)
36. Zou, Y., Finin, T.W., Chen, H.: F-OWL: an Inference Engine for the Semantic Web. In: Hinchey, M.G., Rash, J.L., Truszkowski, W.F., Rouff, C.A. (eds.) FAABS 2004. LNCS (LNAI), vol. 3228, pp. 238–248. Springer, Heidelberg (2004)

Using Real Option Thinking to Improve Decision Making in Security Investment

Virginia N.L. Franqueira[1,*], Siv Hilde Houmb[2], and Maya Daneva[1]

[1] University of Twente
Enschede, The Netherlands
{franqueirav,m.daneva}@ewi.utwente.nl
[2] SecureNOK Ltd.
Sandnes, Norway
sivhoumb@securenok.com

Abstract. Making well-founded security investment decisions is hard: several alternatives may need to be considered, the alternatives' space is often diffuse, and many decision parameters that are traded-off are uncertain or incomplete. We cope with these challenges by proposing a method that supports decision makers in the process of making well-founded and balanced security investment decisions. The method has two fundamental ingredients, staging and learning, that fit into a continuous decision cycle. The method takes advantage of Real Options thinking, not only to select a decision option, but also to compound it with other options in following decision iterations, after reflection on the decision alternatives previously implemented. Additionally, our method is supported by the SecInvest tool for trade-off analysis that considers decision parameters, including cost, risks, context (such as time-to-market and B2B trust), and expected benefits when evaluating the various decision alternatives. The output of the tool, a fitness score for each decision alternative, allows to compare the evaluations of the decision makers involved as well as to include learning and consequent adjustments of decision parameters. We demonstrate the method using a three decision alternatives example.

Keywords: Security Decision Support, Security Economics, Extended Enterprise, Bayesian Belief Network (BBN), Real Option Analysis, Outsourcing.

1 Introduction

The financial crises has brought with it an even tighter budget frame and an increased need to do well-founded and balanced investments decisions. However, this is an especially difficult task for security investments because security is not easy to understand and risks often refer to future and potential events, which may or may not happen, and for which little empirical historical data is available. Risk levels can in these cases be estimated as "guesstimates" only and are at

* Supported by the research program Sentinels, http://www.sentinels.nl

R. Meersman et al. (Eds.): OTM 2010, Part I, LNCS 6426, pp. 619–638, 2010.

best uncertain. Nevertheless, it is still widely accepted for preventive security strategies to rely on expert judgments. This is often suboptimal because experts may be more or less uncertain about the information they provide and several experts may judge the same event using different formats and based on various reference guidelines, which makes it difficult and error-prone to aggregate the opinions provided. As a result, risks events may be wrongly prioritized.

What is usually considered the solution to enhance security spending decisions is to improve on the risk estimation and prioritization processes and methods used. Although this does add value, the problem still persists because risk is only one of the dimensions to be considered in the trade-offs of security decision making. In this paper, we suggest an alternative approach, i.e. a method for tackling security investment decisions using a stage-wise investment process, achieved by Real Options thinking. The idea is to select a decision option, and compound other options on a next decision iteration. Our approach calls for a closer monitoring of an implemented decision, for example in terms of actual risks, to feed the learning process explicit in Real Options. The method is supported by a security trade-off tool implemented as a Bayesian Belief Network (BBN) topology, called SecInvest, that lets decision makers evaluate alternative investments and identify the best fitted. As we will see in the paper, this is challenging but rewarding, and ensures a tighter control and management of security investments.

The paper is structured as follows. Section 2 describes the context of this research: we present (i) the challenges of Security Investment and why they exist, (ii) the state of art in practice of decision making in Information Security, and (iii) how Real Options thinking applies to Information Security. In Section 3, we propose our method for Security Investment decision making, that builds on Real Options thinking, and the supporting tool, SecInvest. Sections 4 and 5 illustrate our method with an example. We conclude and propose follow-up work in Section 6.

2 Context

2.1 Challenges in Security Investment and Why They Exist

Making wise (meaning profitable) security decisions on how to balance security spending and make effective use of the security budget is hard. Many risk assessment approaches (e.g., CORAS [7] and ISO27005:2008[25]) aiming at supporting such a decision process are insufficient in that they focus exclusively on security and does not account for the financial aspects of security. Furthermore, it is not enough to make a number of single wise security investment decisions if these together do not represent a good overall security strategy. A holistic perspective on security is desirable, which requires to examine the dependencies between the various controls employed in the organization, across systems and across decisions. This is hard even for small organizations and small systems. In large organizations this is close to impossible, as there is unevenly distributed information (more information on some aspects and less than enough on others) and often no single person or manageable group of persons has an adequate overview of all systems and their cross-cutting dependencies over security controls. Recently, the holistic view on security investment has been recognized as critical and the research field of Enterprise Risk Management has emerged. However, this field is wide and highly immature in its current state. Moreover, we have yet to accept and address the biases involved in using experts to guide investments for security because objective assessment is crucial. If not possible at all, experts should rather be busy modeling uncertainties, e.g., with the Bayesian or subjectivistic interpretation of probability, as it happens when assessing safety of systems today. The uncertainties involved in security decisions are due to many reasons:

- There is scarce empirical data to support security decisions. It is rare for decision makers to build on earlier experience and investment data can rarely be used across systems, and across organizations. Systems are too different and not all details regarding decisions are made public, which impedes real comparisons.
- Estimating the effect of security controls employed in systems and user environments is challenging, as we refer to the future potential of a control in preventing against identified, but also unknown, security threats.
- Systems and/or procedures may change and users may neglect their responsibilities when using the control, giving rise to vulnerabilities. Hence, the space of vulnerabilities is very broad.
- Estimating the cost of security controls is difficult, as cost should include operational and maintenance parameters, i.e. cost related to all phases of the controls lifecycle (starting with the decision made and ending with phasing out or replacing the controls).

2.2 State of the Art in Practice in Information Security Decision Making

We surveyed existing literature ([11,8,18] and more) on the investment and budgeting decision processes that are currently prevailing in large and midsize businesses with respect to information security. The sources agree that security funding should be managed from an economic perspective (e.g., [14,19]). That is, a firm should invest resources into security controls up to the point at which the last dollar of information security investment yields a dollar of savings [18]. Our survey of literature revealed a variety of economic approaches (e.g. the Return on Investment for Security (ROSI), the Net Present Value (NPV), and the Annualized Loss Expectancy models, the Security Attribute Evaluation (SEAM) and the Cost Effectiveness Analysis methods) (see [10,12] for a survey of these models/methods). Each approach uses a specific form of a cost-benefit analysis. In practice, however, it is rarely achievable to set up a budget decision making process that rests solely on results of these rational economic models due to the fact that both the cost and benefit components often are too difficult to estimate, as indicated in Section 2.1. To keep cost-benefit analysis practical, companies take modified approaches to planned security funding which fall into three categories: expert judgments, algorithmic estimation, and estimation by analogy. The first category relies on the consolidated experts experiences complemented with benchmarking data from public repositories (e.g., NIST[1]). The second category relies on the application of mathematical formulas (mainly from the field of financial accounting) to quantify either the cost or the benefit component of the cost-benefit relationship. For example, Fidelity uses a cyber threat matrix that positions in a four-quadrant grid the probability of a compromise versus its business impact [14]. However, most organizations have no valid data collected for this purpose. The third category, estimation by analogy, suggests periodic reevaluation of threat levels, then, adjustment of the security budget of the previous year to derive the next year's one.

A few authors (e.g., [3,19,11]) have investigated the use of these approaches. What they indicate to work well was to first use the NPV or the ROSI model, and, then, to complement it with an analysis of (i) the dynamic impact of security risk, (ii) the flexibility inherent in most strategic information security investment decisions, and (iii) the dependencies and sequencing constraints typically associated with the implementation of security strategies. The current three categories of budget estimation models in our review do not properly account for these three aspects of the decision making processes. The inadequate decision making support of these methods is due to their built-in assumption that the future business development follows a fixed path [2]. Security decision makers who rely on these methods inevitably fall into the trap of underestimating the potential value of their security investments and, as a result, do not invest enough in uncertain but highly promising opportunities. Drawing on these results, it seems timely and appropriate to consider incorporating options thinking into the decision processes for security spendings. The next section summarizes the real options concept and explains why we think it fits the needs of today's security decision makers.

2.3 Real Option Thinking in a Security Investment Context

The Real Option Analysis (ROA) [2] was first known as a decision support technique in the area of capital investments. The concept of *real* means adapting mathematical models used to evaluate financial options to more-tangible investments. Since 1999, this concept has found its way into the area of appraising IT investments (e.g., [19,6,5]). Li and Su [27] use ROA for the analysis of security investment alternatives (as we do) but they take a profit-maximizing approach for decision making, while we take a trade-off approach that considers non-profit factors, such as risk and context, as well.

The core of the ROA for IT assets consists of: (i) the identification and assessment of optional project components, and (ii) the selection and application of a mathematical model for valuing financial options that serve to quantify the current value of choosing these components for inclusion at a later time. This is similar

[1] National Institute of Standards and Technology (`www.nist.gov`).

to that of ROSI and other models (as discussed above) but, as we will see in the following, enables a structured manner for reasoning under uncertainty, enables the decision maker to defer the decision until more information is made available, and to plan and set-up multiple decision outcomes which can be executed at a later time; i.e., ROA is tailored for reasoning over uncertain factors.

Optional components are project parts that can either be pushed ahead or pulled out at a later point in time when new information becomes available to the decision makers. The option, therefore, is the right but not the obligation to spend a budget or put resources on a project. Real-options thinking seems suitable for information security strategists because of the fields high stakes and tremendous uncertainty. We think it is worthwhile exploring the use of the ROA concept as a vehicle for security decision making because:

1. Unlike traditional techniques, it comprehends uncertainty and it responds to the dynamics inherent in today's business that drives security requirements.
2. It provides interested stakeholders of security projects in the context of a spectrum of possibilities rather than in the context of a single or three (the best, likely or worst case) discrete set-ups, and it facilitates fine-tuning of operational tactics as organizational circumstances unfold over time.
3. It allows managers to make decisions while keeping in mind the trends in their business sector.
4. It allows event-driven incremental expenditures while focusing on organizations critical assets essential to accomplish its mission.
5. It states that not all information assets are of equal value.
6. It allows stakeholders to rationally decide what level they are willing to assume with respect to the assets.

When discussing the *options* in this paper, we do not take the perspective of applying a new class of mathematical models. Instead, we look at it as a way of re-framing the discussion about security investment decisions in terms of options. Clearly, the first step in re-orienting our way of thinking about security controls is to identify the options that exist in security decisions. Only then it will be possible for practitioners to incorporate options thinking into their decision making processes. Drawing on our literature review, we identify that real options can take a number of forms (Table 1).

Each of these options in Table 1 owes its value to the flexibility it gives the organization. Flexibility adds value in two ways. First, management can defer a security investment: because of the time value of money, managers are better off paying the investment cost later rather than sooner. Second, the value of the security investment can change before the option expires. If the value goes up, decision makers are better off. If the value goes down, they are no worse off because they do not have to invest in the project. In real life, these options do not exist in isolation. More often than not, options of different types co-exist and might build upon each other to produce a combined desired effect for a company in the long run. Therefore, there is both learning and staging ingredients implicit in ROA thinking. An option in a package of options is called in literature *a*

Table 1. Description of options applied to information security-related investments

Option	Description
Postpone	Decide to not make an investment decision now, maybe because the level of uncertainties is too high, leaving it to a next cycle of investment decisions.
Abandon	Decide to back-track from a previous investment decision; usually compound with another investment option such as switch or insource.
Scope up	Decide to expand the level of investments on a previously selected investment alternative.
Scope down	Decide to contract the level of investments on a previously selected investment alternative.
Outsource	Decide to transfer an activity or business process currently performed in-house to another organization.
Insource	Decide to transfer back a previously outsourced activity or business process.
Switch	Decide to change a previously committed investment decision; e.g., change of outsourcing provider.

compound option [16][2]. It means an option on an option: the completion of one stage gives the option to start the next stage. This also means that the exercise payoff of a compound option involves the value of another option. For example, if the last selected security investment option was *outsource*; in the next cycle of decisions, the decision could be the compound option *abandon+switch* or *abandon+insource*. Note that *outsource+abandon* is also a compound option, since they make sense to happen one after the other. In the next section, we propose a method that applies ROA thinking to the process of decision making of information security investments.

3 Method for Security Investment Decision Making

The objective of our method (illustrated in Fig. 1) is twofold: to help decision makers to (i) reason about multiple alternatives that are only partly comparable and (ii) deal with uncertainties and incomplete information. To achieve this objective our method deploys the staging and learning ingredients present in ROA thinking.

The method is composed of six steps; however, we make note that there is no predefined starting point, and the numbers of the steps are used as reference purposes only and not for prescribing order. This means one can start at any step depending on the information available. Below we explain the steps briefly and indicate how we execute them in our example.

Step 1 concerns the identification of options that could be used to spend a given security budget. The output is a set of one or more possible options. This step will be the starting point of the example we present in the next section. Step 2 is a decision point where one option is selected, if there are choices. In

[2] We indicate that options A and B are compound as $A + B$.

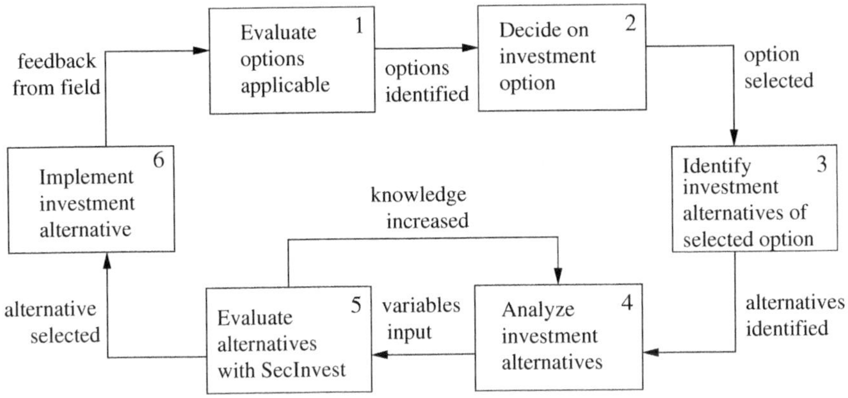

Fig. 1. Method for investment decision making

our example, we start with option **outsource** selected. Step 3 identifies investment alternatives that apply to the selected option. In our example, we identify three outsourcing alternatives. In Step 4, each stakeholder involved in the decision making process analyzes the alternatives (with the information available) in terms of four dimensions: risk, cost, context and expected benefits, and these analyses feed Step 5. The SecInvest tool (described in Section 3.1) supports the evaluation of each alternative by aggregating decision makers' analyses and produces a quantitative output that has to be interpreted. Note that this output provides insights on the alternatives, hence, there is a learning cycle comprehending of Steps 4 and 5 that incrementally increases the understanding of the investment alternatives. The result of this learning process is the decision point where one investment alternative is selected, and then implemented (Step 6).

The implemented investment alternative is to be monitored to feed information into the next cycle of investment decisions, starting from Step 1 where investment options are identified. Below, we describe the tool that supports Steps 4 and 5.

3.1 Tool Support for the Method

SecInvest is a security investment prototype tool that supports Steps 4 and 5 of our method by emulating the presence of a security expert. It takes decision makers through the evaluation of investment alternatives in a step-by-step manner, without requiring the decision maker to be an expert. SecInvest does this with the help of a number of knowledge and experience repositories, both company confidential and publicly available. The public repositories are made up of information from sources like open vulnerability websites and risk analysis report providers (e.g., NIST[3] and ENISA[4]) They also incorporate vendor-specific exploit and vulnerability information. To capture regional aspects like country-specific threat situations which may affect the investment initiative,

[3] National Institute of Standards and Technology (`www.nist.gov`).

[4] European Network and Information Security Agency (`www.enisa.europa.eu`).

SecInvest includes an additional regional risk repository. Note that in most cases very little cost details are available in public repositories, including those concerning national security. The company confidential repositories, on the other hand, are specific for an organization and will most probably include cost details, budget, and trade-off priorities, in addition to experience data.

SecInvest uses a trust-based information aggregation technique [23] to combine the disparate information and help select and link information of relevance for a particular investment decision. The tool also takes into account whether the decision maker is risk-averse, risk-taking or in-between, and lets the decision maker actively take part in the investment alternative evaluation process, as demonstrated in Section 5.

3.2 Decision Engine of SecInvest

Fig. 2 provides a schematic view of the four categories of variables involved in evaluating security investments alternatives based on fitness score: (a) Cost variables, (b) Risk variables, (c) Context variables, and (d) Benefit variables. In addition, there are priority variables which in SecInvest are modeled as a utility function across the other variable sets. The cost category includes the variables: (a1) Monetary cost, (a2) Billing model, and (a3) Cost coverage. In SecInvest these three variables are defined in terms of a qualitative relational scale and all are ranked internally and in respect to the other cost variables using conditional probability expressions. The same applies to the risk variables: (b1) New risks, (b2) Compliance, and (b3) Liability; the Context variables: (c1) Time-to-market (hereafter called TTM), (c2) B2B trust (hereafter called Trust), (c3) Cultural issues; and the Benefit variables: (d1) Cost savings, and (d2) Control retained. The risk and context variables are used to compare alternatives from a security perspective, while the cost and benefit variables hold the financial and business constraints.

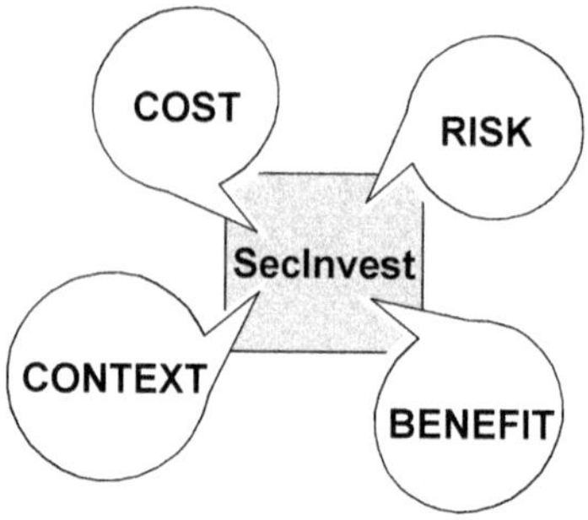

Fig. 2. Information categories involved in the decision engine

The SecInvest decision engine is implemented as a Bayesian Belief Network (BBN) topology [26], as shown in Fig. 3. BBN is a powerful tool for reasoning under uncertainty and have shown effective for both assessing the safety [20,28] and the security [22] of systems. A BBN is a directed acyclic graph (DAG) together with an associated set of probability tables, where the probability tables specify the relations between the various input variables in terms of conditional probability expressions. The DAG consists of nodes representing the variables involved, and arcs representing the dependencies between these variables. Nodes are defined as stochastic or decision variables, and multiple variables may be

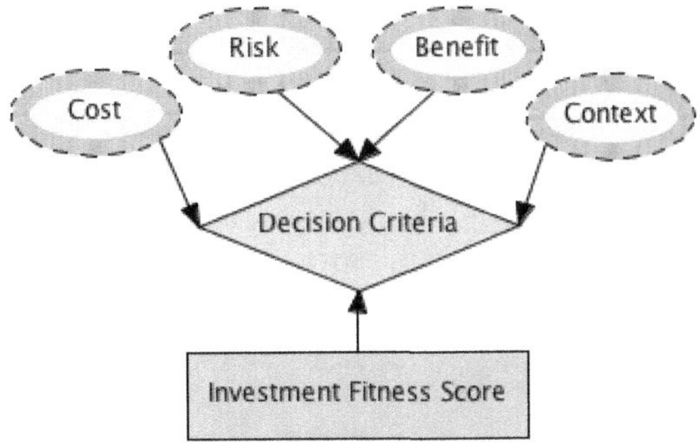

Fig. 3. BBN topology of SecInvest decision engine

used to determine the state of a node. Each state of a node is specified using probability density functions that express the confidence in the various outcomes of the set of variables connected to a node. The state depends conditionally on the status of the parent nodes of the incoming arcs.

There are three types of nodes in a DAG: (1) target nodes, (2) intermediate nodes, and (3) observable nodes. Target nodes are those that the network wants to assess. In Fig. 3, this node is *Investment Fitness Score*. The directed arcs between the nodes denote the causal relationship between the underlying variables. Evidence is entered at the observable nodes and propagated through the network using these causal relationships. The propagation algorithm is based on the underlying computational model of BBN. SecInvest is implemented using the BBN tool $HUGIN^{TM}$ [24], which includes the following additional semantics: stochastic variables are modeled as ovals, decision variables as rectangles, and the associated utility functions supporting the decision variables as diamonds (see Fig. 3). Note that each stippled oval represents a node with an associated subnet, which may be composed of any number of observable and intermediate nodes, as shown in Fig. 4.

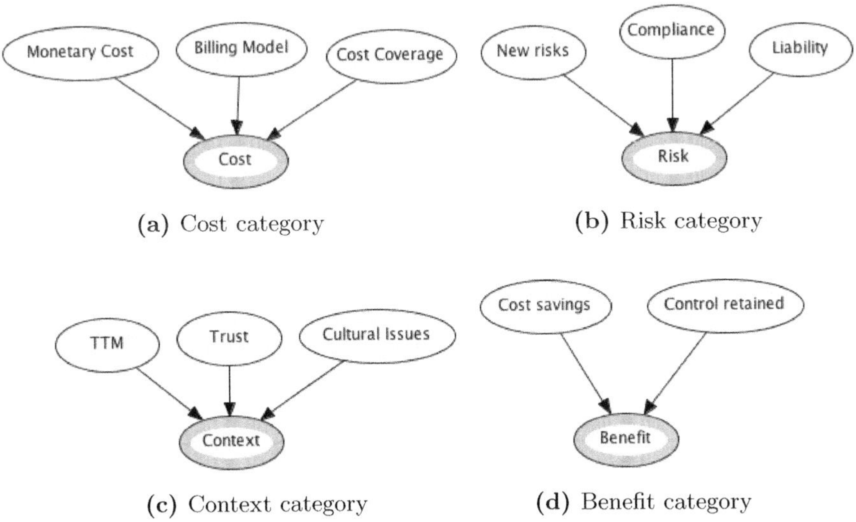

Fig. 4. SecInvest subnets

The variable *New Risks* in the Risk category subnet (Fig. 4b) could itself have an associated subnet related to the issues discussed in Section 5.2. For example, *New Risks* could be derived from: Loss of Governance, Lock-in, Isolation Failure, Data Protection, Insecure/Incomplete Data Deletion, Malicious Insider, Poor Quality of Services, Lack of Clear Policies. However, because of space limitation, we intentionally decided not to consider *New Risks* as a subnet. The same is the case for most variables (observable nodes) in Fig. 4. For more information about SecInvest, see Houmb [22] which describes its predecessor, i.e., the AORDD framework and security solution trade-off analysis.

4 Example: Retailer-Manufacturer B2B Relationship

We demonstrate our method using a typical retailer-manufacturer context, shown in Fig. 5, which illustrates the collaborative business process carried out between the retailer and the manufacturer, and the applications supporting it.

The starting point in this process is a Purchase Order (PO). Retailer employees can place PO in two ways: they either use the manufacturer sales portal or they use the manufacturer call center and have a sales desk employee place and manage their orders. The EDI-based documents, such as a PO, are usually transmitted via AS2 (Applicability Statement 2). AS2 is a standard which defines secure transmission over HTTP, used to send and receive EDI files over the Internet. The PO transmitted by the retailer or the sales desk employee is thus

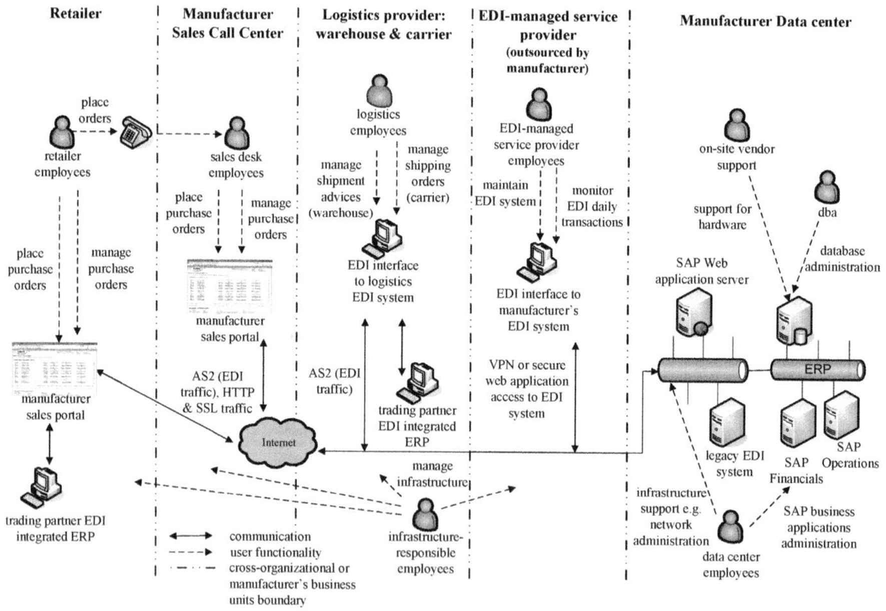

Fig. 5. Application architecture diagram of a typical retailer-manufacturer relationship

sent via AS2 connection to the EDI system located on the manufacturer data center. The EDI system basically processes the EDI files, that has to be integrated with the manufacturer ERP (Enterprise Resource Planning) infrastructure. In this example, we assume that the manufacturer has a SAP ERP[5]. The integration between EDI system and SAP ERP requires an interface based on SAP IDoc (Intermediate Document) technology; via this IDocs interface documents are transferred from EDI to ERP and vice-versa. Once the PO is approved, several exchanges of EDI-based files occur between the ERP infrastructure of the retailer, warehouse/carrier and the manufacturer. For example, employees from the logistics partner, i.e. the warehouse and carrier employees, will have an EDI interface to access their EDI system (logistics EDI system) used to manage shipping advices and shipping orders, respectively. The activities triggered at each step of the whole process are performed by different business applications part of the manufacturer ERP infrastructure. For example, the invoice triggers the update of accounts receivable on the manufacturer side. This step involves SAP Financials to issue the invoice and send the EDI-based invoice automatically to the retailer, and to update the receivable accounts.

The manufacturer's legacy EDI system (located on its data center) is managed remotely by a service provider (as in Fig. 5). Therefore, their employees basically perform tasks related to: (i) maintenance of the EDI system and (ii) monitoring of EDI daily transactions. EDI maintenance involves tasks related to disaster recovery such as archive of EDI data and backup of EDI software; while EDI daily monitoring involves tracking EDI error messages and repair or resume transmission [4]. The manufacturer's ERP, including the database, the sales portal and web server, as well as the IT infrastructure, are all assumed to be hosted and managed, in this example, by the manufacturer employees with on-site service providers support such as of hardware vendors.

5 Applying the Proposed Method to the Example

5.1 Identification of Investment Alternatives of the Selected Option

Our example in Section 4 assumes that (i) the manufacturer B2B call center and the sales portal were hosted in-house and managed by its employees, and (ii) decision makers are faced with the evaluation of investment alternatives involving the outsourcing of some of these tasks. However, different tasks can be outsourced, and each alternative to outsource brings different benefits, costs and risks. Therefore, we apply our method (see Section 3) from Step 1 assuming **outsource** as the only investment option under consideration. Thus, in Step 2, the *outsource* option is selected and we proceed with Step 3, where outsourcing investment alternatives are identified. These are the following:

- **Alternative A1: outsource the B2B portal to an e-commerce provider** A1 represents the outsourcing of the web application (i.e., the sales portal as a managed service) used either directly by the retailers or by the sales

[5] www.sap.com/solutions/business-suite/erp

agents of the B2B call center, this is indicated as the *manufacturer sales portal* on Fig. 5. This means that, while the manufacturer B2B call center will remain in-house, the manufacturer organization will contract an e-commerce provider that typically:

- develops and manages the portal application, being responsible for system updates and version upgrades, backup, application security;
- hosts and manages the infrastructure where the application runs, being responsible for hardware, software, and the supporting network;
- manages and monitors the functionalities of the portal, being responsible for purchase order and fraud management, and transactions monitoring.

In this case, we consider that the e-commerce provider will host the portal on a private infrastructure, i.e., an infrastructure that is specific to the manufacturer. Therefore, the web server will contain only the manufacturer portal that will be isolated on a private network, separate from other clients.

– **Alternative A2: outsource the sales portal to a sales cloud provider**
Similarly to alternative A1, in this case the B2B call center also remains in-house, and the manufacturer sales portal is outsourced. However, this software-as-a-service alternative relies on the economic model of cloud computing that has the following main characteristics [15]: (i) *pay-as-you-go* billing that allows cloud customers to pay according to level of usage, (ii) shared infrastructure (hardware, database, etc) and single application software (i.e. same portal with standard customizations) that potentially has a positive impact on costs for cloud consumers, (iii) on-demand, elastic, allocation of resources that allows cloud consumers to scale up or down quickly, and (iv) almost instantaneous deployment.

– **Alternative A3: outsource the B2B call center to a business process outsourcing (BPO) provider**
This case represents a step further, since it considers the outsourcing of the B2B call center as a whole, as opposed to the outsourcing of the sales portal used by the call center as in A1 and A2. This means that the call center will operate completely on the premises of the BPO provider, using its own workforce, human resources practices, and infrastructure. It does not mean, however, that the call center provider will also provide and manage the manufacturer sales portal; we assume that the portal remains in the hands of the manufacturer (otherwise the analysis of alternatives A1 or A2 would also apply in this alternative).

5.2 Analysis of Investment Alternatives

Below we first analyze the investment alternatives A1-A3 in terms of the categories risk, context and benefit, using information from public repositories. We summarize this analysis in Table 2, in terms of the variables associated with each category in Fig. 2. We use this analysis in Section 5.3 to evaluate the alternatives with the support of the SecInvest tool.

Risk Category. A general truth about risks in outsourcing that apply to all investment alternatives we consider (A1-A3) is that the responsibility of some risks is transferable to the outsource provider. However, we have to learn that "Ultimately, you can outsource responsibility but you can't outsource accountability" [15].

We analyze alternative A2, and use this analysis to comparatively analyze alternative A1 along the way. For the analysis of risks introduced by alternative A2, we take as reference results from the risk assessment performed by ENISA on Cloud Computing [15]. The main risks identified are:

- **Loss of Governance:** The cloud consumer delegates to the cloud provider control over a number of issues that affect security; Service Level Agreements (SLAs) and often used standard contracts do not provide the necessary level of liability to cover all these issues, e.g., in terms of confidentiality of sensitive data that is not measurable by quality of service (QoS) indicators. This risk is present both in A1 and A2.
- **Lock-in:** A lack of standards/regulations to guarantee interoperability and portability of data, applications and services, may render the swap of cloud providers expensive and the insourcing of previously outsourced tasks difficult. This risk is present in both A1 and A2.
- **Isolation Failure:** Virtualization that allows resource sharing is a relatively new technology. Therefore, the number of attacks reported so far is still small, and they involve high complexity. However, this may be due to the novelty of the technology and does not eliminate the risk. This risk applies to A2 but not to A1.
- **Data Protection:** Auditing standards, e.g. SAS 70 (Type 2) [1], may be used by cloud providers to show to cloud consumers that certain security controls have passed external auditors' tests over a period of time. Yet, this does not necessarily provide evidences of lawful handling of data, especially when multiple transfers of data across country borders occur. This risk is present in both A1 and A2.
- **Insecure or Incomplete Data Deletion:** "In the case of multiple tenancies and the reuse of hardware resources, this represents a higher risk to the customer than with dedicated hardware" [15]. This risk applies to A2, and on a lower scale to A1 because resources are not shared.
- **Malicious Insider:** In an outsourcing context in general, but also in a cloud computing setting, we observe a class of people that has authorized access, to a certain extent, to assets that belong to the cloud consumer, such as data it owns and thus is accountable for. However, these individuals do not fall under the legal control of the cloud consumer, therefore, although they are insiders from the perspective of the cloud producer, they are external insiders [17] from the perspective of the cloud consumer. This risk is also present in both A1 and A2.
- **Compliance Risks:** Compliance to laws and regulations is only achieved through evidences; this may become an issue when the cloud provider neither provides the necessary evidences nor allows the cloud consumer to perform auditing to generate them. It may also happen that certain compliances

cannot be achieved in a cloud computing setting. This risk applies to A2 and, on a lower scale, to A1 because B2B contracts and SLAs are customizable in non-cloud outsourcing.

For the analysis of risks introduced by alternative A3, we take as reference the Global Call Centre Report [21] that compares in-house and subcontracted call centers. A good portion of risks in outsourced call centers is related to the workforce, since "People is what matters in a call center", according to [9]. Independent on the geographic location of the call center, this report shows that:

- Job quality in outsourced call centers is poorer than at in-house call centers.
- Low quality jobs directly impact the rate of turnover; therefore, outsourced call centers have higher rate of turnover.
- In terms of human resource practices, outsourced call centers (i) have the incentive to employ more part-time temporary staff than in-house call centers; (ii) invest typically 50% less in training new employees; (iii) pay on average 12% less to their employees, probably because "Subcontractors typically have lower union coverage, lower complexity, and hire employees with lower skills and formal education" [21].

The differences uncovered by the report indicate that, although outsourced call centers may provide more flexibility to accommodate peaks of demand (e.g., during Christmas season) with part-time temporary staff, they also tend to provide a poorer quality of services.

Context Category. The alternative that provides a shorter time-to-market is alternative A2 because it does not involve development or customization phase, such as with A1, and transition phase, such as with A3.

Another important dimension in the context category is the trustworthiness on the outsourcing provider. For example, one alternative may be favored as it involves a provider that is already known by the contracting organization or that has a good reputation in the market.

Cultural issues may also represent an important aspect in the context category, and alternative A3 might be especially affected by such issues. For example, the difficulty in understanding a call center agent, as well as the difficulty in understanding the calling client [13] may both be sources of dissatisfaction, that directly affect quality of services; therefore, it should be explicitly evaluated when considering security investment alternatives.

Benefit Category. Each stakeholder's perceived benefits reflect his role in the organization he represents. Even with quantifiable variables (e.g., benefits in terms of money savings), benefits remain subjective and stakeholders evaluate them differently.

5.3 Evaluation of Investment Alternatives with SecInvest

In this section, we complement the public repositories, that we have already used to analyze alternatives A1-A3, with company-specific confidential information

Table 2. Summary analysis of investment alternatives

	Variable	**A1**	**A2**	**A3**
COST	Monetary cost	only known after providers make their offers; before that this depends on stakeholders' perceptions		
COST	Billing model	monthly fixed, established by negotiable contracts	pay-as-you-go based on usage, often established by standard contracts	monthly fixed, established by negotiable contracts
COST	Cost coverage	custom B2B portal and its usage	standard B2B portal and its usage	B2B call center operations, excluded B2B portal
RISK	New risks	loss of governance, lock-in, data protection, insecure or incomplete data deletion (lower scale than in A2), malicious insider	loss of governance, lock-in, isolation failure, data protection, insecure or incomplete data deletion, malicious insider	mainly quality of services risks, lack of clear policies
RISK	Compliance	issues related to the generation of necessary evidences to show compliance; especial requirements might be negotiable resulting in specific clauses in the contract that minimize this risk	issues related to the generation of necessary evidences to show compliance; especial requirements difficult to be negotiated	encrypted contact recording may satisfy data retention requirements; practices such as comprehensive background checks in hiring process, restricted access to Internet, prohibited mobile phones in working place, etc may provide needed evidences to assure compliance
RISK	Liability	customized contracts may provide higher level of liability; nevertheless SLAs provide quality of services guarantees but not security assurance	SLAs and standard contracts provide low level of liability related to some security issues e.g. in terms of confidentiality	full-time contact recording and clear contract clauses can help in respect to liability in disputes
CONTEXT	TTM	development or customization of the portal phase may be involved	quick deployment of portal	migration period where call center employees are trained
CONTEXT	Trust	requires search on the company confidential repositories for experience data		
CONTEXT	Cultural issues	not an especial issue	not an especial issue	may cause communication problems with offshore outsource providers
BENEFIT	Cost savings	cost savings expected when compared to in-house	payment based on usage and shared infrastructure provide the perspective of high cost savings (higher than A1)	perspective of cost savings compared to keeping activities in-house
BENEFIT	Control retained	possibility to demand periodic monitoring reports, nevertheless A1 represents a loss of control compared to in-house option but compared to alternative A2 it provides more control	lower level of control retained compared to A2	control retained comes mainly in form of measurable quality of service attributes such as average call response time and statistics on level of satisfaction perceived by customers

(that is neither publicly available nor disclosed to company partners, therefore is stored in company confidential repositories). This is used to contextualize the publicly available information. For example, a company may store experiences on various outsourcing providers in their confidential repositories.

We assume that two stakeholders are asked to evaluate the alternatives A1-A3, as summarized in Table 2: (1) the Chief Information Security Officer (CISO), responsible for all aspects of security, (2) the Chief Finance Officer (CFO), responsible for managing financial risks and perform financial planning. Furthermore, we assume that the CISO is very conscious of security risks and, therefore, deems risks more important than costs. In contrast, the CFO deems costs more important than risks. Below we demonstrate how to balance these prioritizes by using SecInvest. For each investment alternative, SecInvest computes the target node *Investment Fitness Score* (see Fig. 3) using the subnets shown in Fig. 4, and produces a fitness score based on the evaluation of each stakeholder.

Table 3. Summary of investments evaluation by the CISO stakeholder

Variable	A1	A2	A3
Monetary cost	medium	low	medium
Billing model	fixed	variable	fixed
Cost coverage	medium	low	medium
New risks	medium	high	medium
Compliance	medium	high	medium
Liability	medium	low	medium
TTM	low	low	medium
Trust	high	medium	low
Cultural issues	none	none	none
Cost savings	low	medium	low
Control retained	medium	low	low

Stakeholder 1 (CISO) evaluation. The perceived evaluation of alternatives A1-A3 from the perspective of the CISO is presented in Table 3 and serves as input data into SecInvest. The CISO has evaluated the risk level to be relatively high for all alternatives. Fig. 6 shows the resulting fitness score for alternative A2, considering the CISO input ($Fitness\_score(A2) = 0.33$). The results of the information propagation for alternatives A1 and A3 are 0.63 and 0.67, respectively ($Fitness\_score(A1) = 0.63$; $Fitness\_score(A3) = 0.67$). These fitness scores vary depending on the stakeholder-specific priorities among variables. This means that depending on the priorities, the BBN network will behave differently. Note that the CISO put focus on New Risks, Compliance, Liability, TTM and Trust.

Stakeholder 2 (CFO) evaluation. As indicated earlier, the CFO is a risk-taker and therefore his priorities give precedence to Monetary Cost, Cost Coverage, Compliance, Liability, and Cost Savings. Table 4 shows the CFO's evaluation for the three alternatives. The priorities of the CFO result in the following fitness scores:

$Fitness\_score(A1) = 0.68$;
$Fitness\_score(A2) = 0.25$;
$Fitness\_score(A3) = 0.26$.

Table 4. Summary of investments evaluation by the CFO stakeholder

Variable	A1	A2	A3
Monetary cost	low	low	low
Billing model	fixed	variable	fixed
Cost coverage	medium	medium	medium
New risks	low	low	low
Compliance	medium	high	medium
Liability	medium	low	medium
TTM	medium	low	medium
Trust	medium	medium	low
Cultural issues	none	none	none
Cost savings	high	medium	medium
Control retained	medium	low	low

Note that in Tables 3 and 4 the variable *Cultural Issues* has "none"-value assigned for all three alternatives (A1-A3). This means that the variable has not been considered by any of the stakeholders. It does not mean, however, that there are no cultural issues; such issues are especially important when offshore outsourcing providers are involved. Nevertheless, evaluating cultural issues may be easier when lessons learnt can be taken into account, i.e., in a later decision iteration.

Balancing Stakeholder Priorities. When all stakeholders have provided their inputs, the results needs to be aggregated. This is a game-like trade-off analysis. In the example, we have two competing stakeholders' priorities. Despite their differences, both stakeholders agree that A1 is the better alternative. The alternative the stakeholders cannot agree upon is A3, for which the resulting fitness scores for the CISO and the CFO are very different. The CFO is by no means in favor of A3, while for the CISO both A1 and A3 are possible investment candidates. What we now need to do is to re-confirm the information provided and the priorities assigned to the variables for both stakeholders, inform them about the result and arrange for a meeting for discussion. If time and resources do allow for such a meeting, SecInvest will advice the decision maker (e.g., the executive who ultimately makes the decision on security strategy) about the result and leave it up to the decision maker to either accept A1, as an agreed upon best investment alternative, or to take further actions.

6 Summary and Future Work

This paper sought to contribute to the research and practice in decision making for security investments. We motivated the use of staging and learning options in a multi-stakeholder decision making cycle that accommodates a variety of uncertainties faced by today's network organizations. We propose a method, supported by a tool, that leverage public and company-specific repositories to help stakeholders evaluate the fitness score of each option they deem a candidate for inclusion in their corporate security strategy. Unlike other approaches, our approach is designed for stakeholders to keep a holistic perspective on security and clearly see how each option (1) builds upon previously realized options and

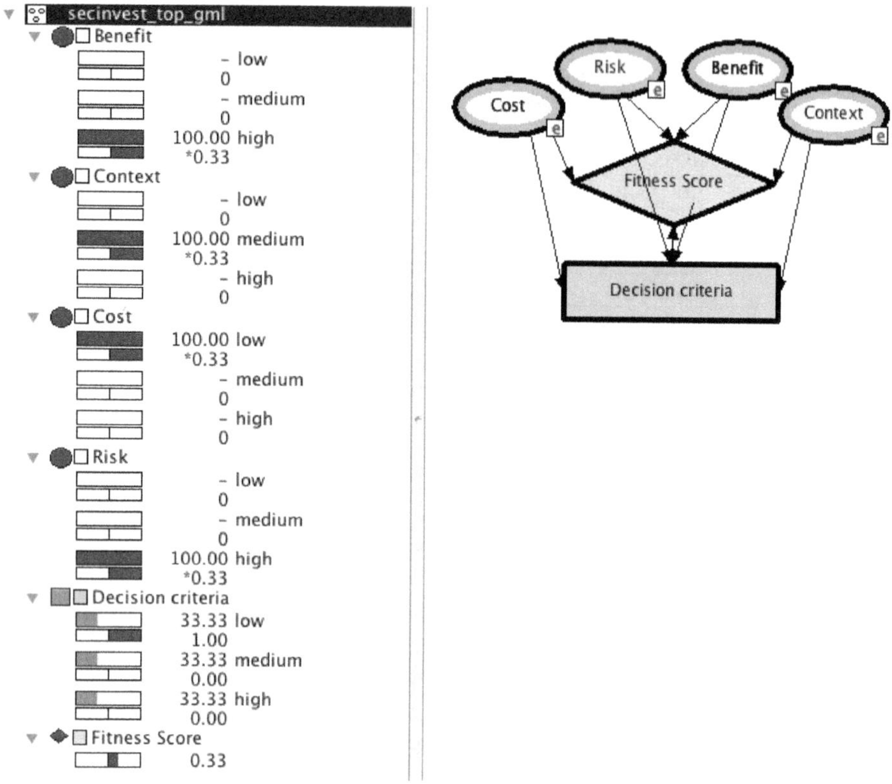

Fig. 6. Fitness score for A2, as per the CISO evaluation

(2) helps the realization of future options. This helps decision makers spot sub-optimal decision paths early in the security-strategy-planing process.

While we think that our approach is promising, we acknowledge that we need more case study research before making it available for managers and executives to use. We plan case studies in three organizations in Norway and the Netherlands to investigate the applicability of the method based on a variety of problem contexts. Such case studies also aim to apply the method to security decisions at different levels. While the example discussed in this paper relates to security investments at a strategic level, the proposed method fits equally to more tactical and technical investment decisions. A typical case could be to consider alternative technologies of Intrusion Detection Systems, e.g., signature and anomaly-based detection. This would involve the same information categories (Fig. 2) with different variables, therefore, requiring an update on SecInvest subnets (Fig. 4).

References

1. AICPA: SAS No. 70, Service Organizations (2000), http://www.aicpa.org/download/members/div/auditstd/AU-00324.PDF
2. Amram, M., Kulatilaka, N.: Real Options: Managing Strategic Investment in an Uncertain World. Harvard Business School Press, Cambridge (1999)
3. Anderson, R.: Why Information Security is Hard - An Economic Perspective. In: ACSAC 2001: Proc. 17th Annual Computer Security Applications Conference, pp. 358–365. IEEE Press, Los Alamitos (December 2001)
4. AS2 Processing for EDI, http://www.dcs-is-edi.com/AS2.html (last visited on March 2010)
5. Benaroch, M., Kauffman, R.J.: A Case for Using Real Options Pricing Analysis to Evaluate Information Technology Project Investment. Information Systems Research 10(1), 70–86 (1999)
6. Berthold, S., Bhme, R.: Valuating Privacy with Option Pricing Theory. In: Economics of Information Security and Privacy, pp. 187–209. Springer, Heidelberg (2010)
7. den Braber, F., Hogganvik, I., Lund, M.S., Stølen, K., Vraalsen, F.: Model-based security analysis in seven steps - a guided tour to the CORAS method. BT Technology Journal 25(1), 101–117 (2007)
8. Brown, W., Nasuti, F.: Sarbanes-Oxley and Enterprise Security: IT Governance and What It Takes to Get the Job Done. Information Systems Security 14(5), 15–28 (2005)
9. Interview with Carol Borghesi, MD, BT Retail Customer Contact Center. Global Services Media (December 2005), http://www.globalservicesmedia.com/BPO/Customer-Care/Interview-with-Carol-Borghesi-MD-BT-Retail-Customer-Contact-Center/23/9/0/general200705211 (last visited May 2010)
10. Butler, S.A.: Security attribute evaluation method: a cost-benefit approach. In: ICSE 2002: Proc. of the 24rd International Conference on Software Engineering, pp. 232–240. ACM Press, New York (2002)
11. Cavusoglu, H., Cavusoglu, H., Raghunathan, S.: Economics of IT Security Management: Four Improvements to Current Security Practices. Communications of the Association for Information Systems 14, 65–75 (2004)
12. Daneva, M.: Applying Real Options Thinking to Information Security in Networked Organizations. Tech. Rep. TR-CTIT-06-11, Centre for Telematics and Information Technology, University of Twente, Enschede (August 2006)
13. Dawson, K., Weston, R.: Call Centre Hang-ups. Global Services Media (December 2005), http://www.globalservicesmedia.com/BPO/Customer-Care/Call-Center-Hang-ups/23/9/0/general20070521987 (last visited May 2010)
14. Dynes, S., Eric, H.B., Johnson, M.E.: Information Security in the Extended Enterprise: Some Initial Results From a Field Study of an Industrial Firm. In: Proc. of Int. Workshop on the Economics of Information Security (2005)
15. Cloud Computing Risk Assessment. ENISA: European Network and Information Security Agency (November 2009)
16. Erdogmus, H.: Valuation of Learning Options in Software Development under Private and Market Risk. The Engineering Economist 47(3), 308–353 (2002)

17. Franqueira, V.N.L., van Cleeff, A., van Eck, P.A.T., Wieringa, R.J.: External Insider Threat: a Real Security Challenge in Enterprise Value Webs. In: Proc. of the Fifth Int. Conf. on Availability, Reliability and Security (ARES 2010), pp. 446–453. IEEE Computer Society Press, Los Alamitos (February 2010)
18. Gordon, L.A., Loeb, M.P.: Budgeting Process for Information Security Expenditures. Communications of the ACM 49(1), 121–125 (2006)
19. Gordon, L.A., Loeb, M.P., Lucyshyn, W.: Information Security Expenditures and Real Options: A Wait-and-See Approach. Computer Security Journal 19(2), 1–7 (2003)
20. Gran, B.A.: The use of Bayesian Belief Networks for combining disparate sources of information in the safety assessment of software based systems. Ph.D. thesis, Norwegian University of Sciences and Technology, Norway (2002)
21. Holman, D., Batt, R., Holtgrewe, U.: The Global Call Centre Report: International Perspectives on Management and Employment (2007)
22. Houmb, S.H.: Decision Support for Choice of Security Solution: The Aspect-Oriented Risk Driven Development (AORDD) Framework. Ph.D. thesis, Norwegian University of Science and Technology, Trondheim (November 2007)
23. Houmb, S.H., Chakraborty, S., Ray, I., Ray, I.: Using Trust-Based Information Aggregation for Predicting Security Level of Systems. In: To appear in Proc. of the 24th Annual IFIP WG 11.3 Working Conf. on Data and Applications Security and Privacy XXIV. pp. 241–256. Springer, Heidelberg (June 2010)
24. HUGIN: tool made by Hugin Expert AS (2009), `http://www.hugin.com/` (last visited on June 2010)
25. ISO/IEC-27005: Information technology. Security techniques. Information security risk management (2008)
26. Jensen, F.V.: Introduction to Bayesian Networks. Springer, New York (1996)
27. Li, J., Su, X.: Making Cost Effective Security Decision with Real Option Thinking. In: ICSEA 2007: Proc. 2nd Int. Conf. on Software Engineering Advances, pp. 14–22. IEEE Press, Los Alamitos (2007)
28. Safety and Risk Evaluation using Bayesian Nets. ESPIRIT Framework IV nr. 22187 (1999), `http://www.hugin.dk/serene/` (last visited on June 2010)

Context Sensitive Privacy Management in a Distributed Environment

Grzegorz Gołaszewski and Janusz Górski

Gdańsk University of Technology, ul. Narutowicza 11/12
80-233 Gdańsk, Poland
{grzo,jango}@eti.pg.gda.pl

Abstract. The paper presents a mechanism for privacy management developed for a distributed environment with the assumption that the nodes are subjected to severe resource constraints (processing power, memory). The basic idea is that the private data are filtered out in accordance with users' privacy policies before they become visible to other users. The decisions are highly localized which reduces the load related to privacy management on the computing nodes. The mechanism is hidden in middleware (the platform) and is transparent to the applications running on the nodes. The paper describes the problem and its solution in abstract terms and then presents the technical system which has been developed to demonstrate the proposed solution.

Keywords: privacy management, context dependence, distributed systems, mobile systems, embedded systems, Angel.

1 Introduction

Privacy protection is presently one of the major concerns related to applications of modern information technologies. Wireless, mobile and embedded applications pose multiple new threats related to privacy, including new types of data which become widely available (e.g. location), potential for automatic gathering of data without user's consent (e.g. by means of various types of sensors) and automatic linking of these data with users' identities (by means of RFIDs, mobile phones, smartcards and other personally carried tokens). One of the problems related to such dynamic and distributed environments is that privacy is highly context dependent meaning that the same data item can be subjected to different privacy requirements (from the data owner's viewpoint) depending on the context within which the data is potentially disclosed.

This paper addresses the problem of context dependence of privacy requirements with respect to environments where users have access to mobile and stationary terminals which can display their private data. The terminals are cooperating with gateways by calling services through which private data can 'leak' to terminals. The gateways are under control of (possibly multiple) users and run applications serving the specific application objectives (for instance, health monitoring, lifestyle support, home automation etc.). The gateways gather data sensed by wireless sensors, including body parameters, environmental parameters etc. and process them according to the needs.

R. Meersman et al. (Eds.): OTM 2010, Part I, LNCS 6426, pp. 639–655, 2010.

In such an environment, the problem we are dealing with in this paper is that data displayed on a terminal may undergo different privacy restrictions depending on the context of the terminal owner is currently in (basically, the contexts differentiate between different groups of subjects being able to see the data displayed on the terminal). These restrictions have their roots in the privacy policies of data owners.

In the paper we assume that such privacy policies are known. In the presented application of the method we provide an explicit mechanism by which the data owners can define their privacy policies. However, the presented mechanism would work also in the situation where the policies are acquired in a more indirect way.

The mechanism we present has two distinguishing features. Firstly, it controls interfaces through which the applications running on the gateways and the terminals cooperate. And it builds into each interface a sort of 'valve' which control leaking of the private data depending on the current context. Secondly, it is localized in the architecture of the deployed software in a way which keeps most of the software 'unconscious' of the presence of the mechanism (making it transparent to the running applications).

The paper is structured as follows. Section 2 introduces the problem, the related assumptions and constraints. Section 3 describes our solution to the problem and section 4 gives details on how this solution was demonstrated within the context of the Angel[1] project. In section 5 we compare our work with the work of others. Section 6 concludes the work.

2 Problem Statement

2.1 The Problem

Private data belong to its *owner. Privacy* is understood as the right of the data owner to decide about disclosure, storage and processing of his/her private data. This right may be implemented in different ways: by providing the data owner with means to indicate potential receivers of the data, to accept the purpose of data collection before the data being actually stored/processed and to designate the situations in which the data can be disclosed etc. For instance, Tom may implement his privacy right by deciding that his location should be confidential except that it may be disclosed to an ambulance service in case of medical emergency.

We assume that different situations for which the owner sets restrictions on his/her private data disclosure can be enumerated and we call them *contexts*. The context a given person is actually in is called her/his *current context*. In the above example, Tom defines restrictions related to his private data with respect to the context "medical emergency". Other contexts are possible for Tom, like "at home", "jogging", "having guests" etc. Tom decides that for these contexts his location remains confidential.

We assume that each data owner defines his/her *privacy policy*. For each possible current context, the policy specifies the receivers authorized to obtain the owner's

---

[1] 6th FR STREP *Advanced Networked embedded platform as a Gateway to Enhance quality of Life* (ANGEL), Contract number IST-033506.

private data. For instance, the privacy policy of Tom includes the requirement: *Tom's location can be disclosed to* ***ambulance service*** *in the* ***medical emergency*** *context.*

We assume the following model of the system:

- the system includes multiple *gateways*,
- each gateway is controlled by one or more system *users,*
- each gateway hosts a number of *applications*,
- a distinguished application called *platform* is permanently deployed on each gateway,
- applications can disclose data to data *receivers* through *interfaces*,
- data receivers are applications or *user terminals,*
- system behaviour is modelled as a sequence of system *states,*
- for each interface, the potential scope of data disclosed by the interface at a given state to different receivers can be determined statically (i.e. is known before the system starts).

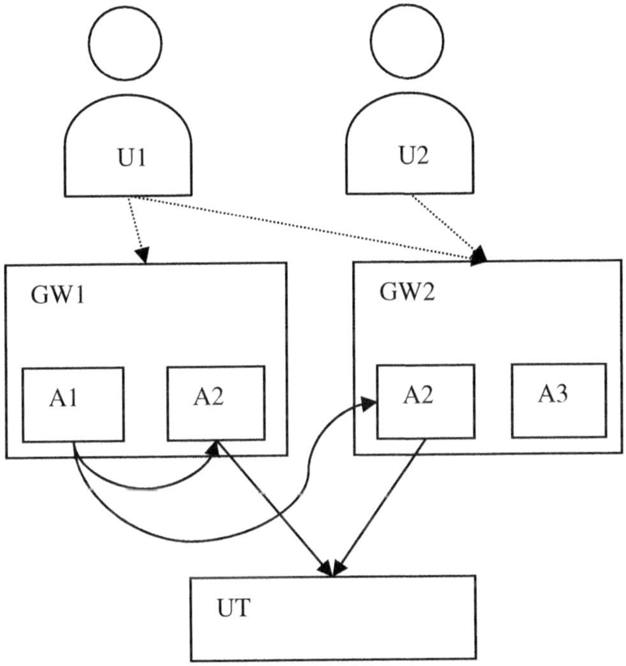

Fig. 1. An example of the system

In Fig. 1 an example system is presented. It consists of two gateways (GW1, GW2), three applications (A1, A2, A3) and a user terminal (UT). A1 and A2 are deployed on GW1 and A2 and A3 on GW2. GW1 is controlled by one user U1 and GW2 is controlled by two users, U1 and U2, which is represented by dotted arrows. Potential data flows are represented by solid arrows. These arrows originate in interfaces of the corresponding applications.

The problem statement is as follows.

> *To ensure that for each system state, data disclosure on system interfaces observes the restrictions imposed by the privacy policies of the data owners.*

Let us imagine that Tom is using a system which integrates mobile devices, including Tom's PDA (equipped with GPS) and the mobile terminal in an ambulance. In an emergency situation, Tom's PDA connects to the ambulance to call for help. In such context, the problem is how to enforce Tom's privacy policy, and make sure that Tom's location will remain confidential in all other situations except his health emergency.

2.2 Assumptions and Constraints

Before we present our solution to the above problem, we introduce several additional assumptions which constraint the problem solution space.

- For each data owner, the corresponding privacy policy distinguishes different private *data types*.
- For each interface, the scope of private data possibly released through the interface is determined at system configuration time. At run time the interface either releases all data or nothing (i.e. partial disclosure is impossible).
- For each gateway, the applications deployed on the gateway may attempt to disclose (through corresponding interfaces) only the private data of the users of the gateway.
- For each system state, the current context of each user can be determined.
- For each user, the contexts are mutually exclusive (i.e. at any time, the user is in exactly one current context); however, for different users, their current contexts can differ.
- Platform does not disclose private data. It is used for system management purposes and provides support for other applications.

In addition, we impose the following constraints on the solution sought for the problem:

- the privacy policies are defined referring to contexts and data receivers (i.e. the system structure remains transparent at this abstraction level),
- the effort required from application developers to implement the privacy policies should be minimized.

3 The Solution

3.1 General Idea

To control the users' private data disclosure we propose a mechanism that 'filters out' (depending on the current context) the data being displayed through system interfaces in accordance with the user's privacy policy requirements. This filtering process follows the changes in current contexts of the users and guarantees that the private data is not disclosed if so required by the user's privacy policy.

This filtering is effected on each interface through which private data are delivered to data receivers. The data filtering decisions are controlled by the *canAccess* (partial) function which has the following signature:

$$canAccess: O \times R \times C \times I \nrightarrow Boolean\ , \tag{1}$$

where O denotes a set of data owners, R represents a set of data receivers, C is a set of contexts and I is a set of interfaces. The function returns a Boolean value which indicates whether a given interface i can disclose data of the owner o to the receiver r in the current context c. In other words, *canAccess* decides about 'opening' or 'closing' a given interface in a specific context and for specified owner and receiver.

The function *canAccess* is derived from the privacy policies specified by the users. At system runtime, the function is continuously evaluated to adjust private data filtering to the changing contexts of the users.

To provide for efficiency of evaluation of *canAccess* values, several more specific data structures and algorithms have been proposed.

3.2 Privacy Policies

We assume that the privacy policy of a system user is represented by a *privacy matrix.* The matrix specifies the private data types to be visible to different receiver categories in different contexts. This specification is given by each data owner by setting corresponding controls in the *privacy matrix* ('√' means 'disclose' and '–' means 'do not disclose'). An example privacy matrix is shown in Table 1.

Table 1. Privacy matrix

	ReceiverCategory1		ReceiverCategory2		ReceiverCategory3	
Context1	*DataType1*	√	*DataType1*	√	*DataType2*	√
	DataType2	-	*DataType3*	-	*DataType4*	√
	DataType3	√	*DataType4*	-		
Context2	*DataType1*	-	*DataType1*	√	*DataType2*	-
	DataType2	√	*DataType3*	√	*DataType4*	√
	DataType3	-	*DataType4*	-		

Table 1 shows a privacy matrix as it is seen by a single user. Initially, the matrix includes one *default* context which is the current context of the user. Additional contexts can be added/removed by the user (the contexts are enumerated in the first column of the table). For each context, the relevant receiver categories and private data types are given. The user can declare her/his privacy policy by setting corresponding controls in the table.

In the example presented in Table 1, the user decided that while being in *Context1*, data types *DataType1*and *DataType3* are to be disclosed to *ReceiverCategory1* whereas access to *DataType2* is to be prohibited. In the same context, the data visible to *ReceiverCategory2* is just *DataType1*.

For instance, if *DataType4* = *Health information*, *ReceiverCategory2* = *Friends* and *ReceiverCategory3* = *Family*, the choices represented in Table 1 mean that Tom does not want his friends to know his health details whereas he accepts that family members can have full access to this information.

More formally, we can represent the privacy policies as a function *PrivPol* with the following signature:

$$PrivPol\colon O \rightarrow \mathbb{P}\,(C \times RC \times DT \times Boolean)\,, \tag{2}$$

where *RC* is the set of possible receiver categories and *DT* is the set of possible private data types.

The mapping of private data receivers to receiver categories is specified (by the private data owner) by means of the auxiliary *mapping* function.

$$mapping\colon O \twoheadrightarrow RC \times R\,. \tag{3}$$

Note that if a gateway *g* is controlled by users *u1* and *u2* (e.g. a gateway collecting and displaying the house environment parameters where *u1* and *u2 are inhabitants of the house*), a possibility of privacy policy conflict arises. Consider a situation where *dt* is a private data type of both, *u1* and *u2,* and the users specify in their privacy policies conflicting requirements related to releasing *dt* through interfaces of *g,* respectively for context *c1* (for *u1)* and *c2* (for *u2*). Then, if in a given state the current context for *u1* is *c1* and for *u2* is *c2*, we have conflicting requirements for interfaces of *g*.

In general, such conflict can be resolved by one of the strategies listed below:

- release *dt* if both, *u1* and *u2,* allow for this in their privacy policies (seeking for consensus),
- release *dt* if either *u1* or *u2* allow for this in their privacy policies (in case of more users, this can be generalized as a threshold based decision),
- let the data receiver to specify the intended owner of *dt* and then decide in accordance with the owner's policy (conflict elimination).

The third strategy eliminates the conflict by narrowing the scope – relating the decision about releasing *dt* to just one owner (either *u1* or *u2*). In such case, if *u1* says 'disclose *dt*' and *u2* says 'do not disclose *dt*', the request 'give me *dt* of *u1*' issued to an interface of *g* will return a data of type *dt* whereas the request 'give me *dt* of *u2*' will return an empty value.

In the mechanism described below we are following this conflict elimination strategy. Nevertheless, implementation of other strategies is also possible.

3.3 System Configuration

We assume that the following information related to system configuration is available.

For each application deployed in the system, a list of its interfaces and for each interface the list of *private data types* exposed by the interface are determined at system configuration time. And for each interface, the list of all possible *receiver categories* is given.

The above information is represented by the *appInfo* function, which for each application specifies a set of triples, where each triple include: an interface exposed by the application, private data types exposed by the interface, and receiver categories envisioned as data consumers for the interface:

$$appInfo\colon A \rightarrow \mathbb{P}\,(I \times \mathbb{P}\,DT \times \mathbb{P}\,RC)\,. \tag{4}$$

In addition, it is assumed that the following information is maintained at system runtime:

- identification of gateway users:

$$own\colon Gw \leftrightarrow O\,, \tag{5}$$

  where *Gw* is a set of all gateways,
- identification of the applications deployed on each gateway:

$$conf\colon Gw \leftrightarrow A\,, \tag{6}$$

  where *A* is the set of all applications deployed in the system.

Note that the above information can be used to automatically calculate the privacy matrix of each user in the form shown in Table 1. Initially, the user defined entries of the matrix are set to "do not disclose" default value.

3.4 Making Privacy Related Decisions

The privacy related decisions are made by continuously evaluating the value of the *canAccess* function in order to decide about private data release through system interfaces. The function is evaluated from the information submitted and maintained in the system (described in sections 3.2 and 3.3).

First, an auxiliary *canAccess'* function is calculated from *PrivPol*, *appInfo* and *conf* functions. It has the following signature:

$$canAccess'\colon O \times RC \times C \times I \nrightarrow Boolean\,. \tag{7}$$

Values of *canAccess'* are generated following the folowing rule: in a given context, an interface can disclose data to a given receiver category only if the receiver category has the permission (given in the privacy policies of the data owner) to obtain, in this context, all data types potentially disclosed by this interface.

For example, assume that Tom is doing physical exercises (the current context of Tom). Assume also that the treadmill he uses acts as a gateway under his control and exposes interface *i* used for exercise monitoring. The treadmill publishes data such as speed, distance, but also pulse and heart rate. Therefore the data published by *i* belong to both *Exercise information* and *Health information* data types. Then, if Tom wants his coach to gain access to his *Exercise information*, he has to give him/her access to his *Health information* as well. To enable Tom to separate the *Exercise information* and *Health information* data these data types should be released through separate interfaces. In present implementation of the privacy management mechanism such decision is to be made at application development time.

In case a user redefines his/her privacy policy or the system configuration changes, *canAccess'* function has to be recalculated.

From *canAccess'* and *mapping* functions we calculate values of *canAccess* following the principle that a receiver *r* can obtain data from an interface *i* if *r* belongs to at least one receiver category *rc* authorized by the data owner *o* to see his/her private data through this interface.

Following the example of Tom's exercise monitoring, let us assume that Tom uses a treadmill which exposes his *Exercise information* through interface *i*. In his privacy policy Tom lets the receiver category *Coach* to view this data. At the same time Tom denies seeing this data by the category *Friends*. In such situation Helen, a friend of Tom, would receive empty response if she tries to call the interface *i* from her user terminal. However, John, a friend of Tom and simultaneously his trainer would receive Tom's exercise data. Also Tim, who belongs to the coaching team, will have access to this data, even if he is not a friend of Tom.

3.5 The Platform

To release applications from managing privacy and to localize privacy-related decisions we use the concept of the *platform*. Platform is an application that is permanently deployed on each gateway and is charged (among others) with making privacy related decisions. The process goes as follows.

When an application receives a request to release private data through its interface, it forwards this request to the platform with the following descriptor:

<data receiver ID, called interface ID, data owner ID>.

For instance, *<John, i, Tom>* means that *John* requested from *i* data belonging to *Tom*. The platform uses the received descriptor along with information on the current context of *Tom* to evaluate *canAccess* function and responds with a Boolean decision on if to serve the request or to ignore it.

For efficiency reasons, *canAcess* can be pre-calculated and its relevant part can be stored on each gateway together with the current context information for the gateway user. In case this information changes (e.g. privacy policy change, system configuration change etc.) the new values are re-distributed to the gateways. Note that it is sufficient to restrict to the current contexts of the users controlling given gateway and maintain only this part of *canAccess* which relates to the privacy policies of these users.

The result of the above solution is that the privacy management is almost transparent to applications. The only localities where privacy management needs care are application interfaces where a simple coding protocol is to be followed: call the platform before releasing data through the interface (asking for a permission).

4 Proof of Concept

The mechanism described above was developed within the context of Angel project. The project objective was to develop and to demonstrate the wireless sensor network

(WSN) based platform integrating WSN enabling technologies (in particular Zigbee [1]) and Internet technologies for health and lifestyle supporting applications.

4.1 Privacy Requirements

In Angel the privacy protection requirements were derived following a three step process:

1. analysis of the relevant source documents like Directive 95/46/EC [2], Directive 2002/58/EC [3], OECD Privacy Guidelines [4], HIPPA Privacy Rule [5] etc. to derive *generic privacy requirements*,
2. mapping the generic requirements on the Angel application scenarios to derive *system level privacy requirements*,
3. mapping the system level privacy requirements on the Angel platform to derive the *platform level privacy requirements*. These mappings were maintained to provide for traceability of privacy requirements.

An example platform level privacy requirements are as follows: PR1: platform should enable identification of patient's health information, PR2: platform should allow for private data purge, PR3: platform should ensure confidentiality of privacy-related data over all communication routes, PR4: platform should ensure integrity of privacy-related data over all communication routes.

4.2 The System

The concept of *Angel system* has been defined comprising of three main logical components: *smart node*, *Angel gateway* and *Angel service terminal.*

Smart node is a small device with limited computational power, wireless networking capability and low energy consumption. Smart nodes are used for collecting data in two kinds of networks: Body Sensor Network (BSN) and Home Area Network (HAN). BSN comprises of wearable sensor nodes (like heart-rate sensors or pedometers), while HAN integrates nodes measuring habitat parameters, e.g. light intensity, temperature, humidity etc. In both cases, the nodes communicate gathered data via WSN protocol to an Angel gateway.

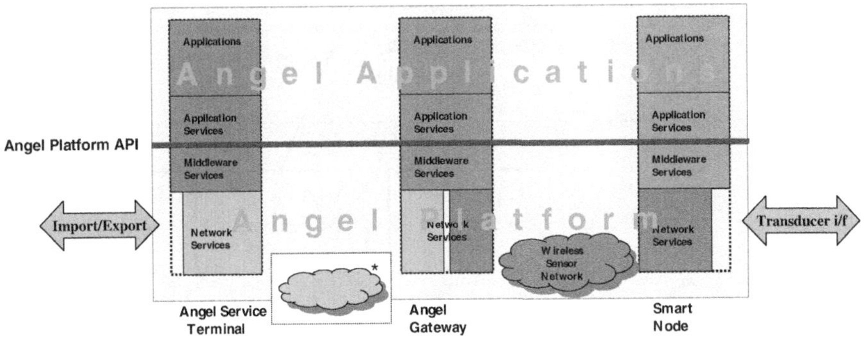

Fig. 2. The Angel Reference Architecture [6]

Gateway is a device with more computational power, equipped with both, WSN interface and IP interface. The data is collected on the gateway by dedicated applications. To disclose the gathered data, Angel applications use Web Services.

Data is disclosed to Angel service terminals, which are (logical) devices capable of receiving data from the gateways and provide related services. As system components are logical, it may happen that a terminal and a gateway reside on the same physical device (e.g. PDA) although it is not necessary. For instance, an IP television set-top box equipped with a WSN interface simultaneously hosts a gateway and a user terminal. In such case the set-top box is capable of collecting data and forwarding it to other Angel service terminals through Internet, as well as displaying the collected data on the TV-set connected to it.

All Angel enabled devices host a software layer providing common services for Angel applications (the middleware). Angel reference architecture is shown in Fig. 2 [6].

4.3 Privacy Subsystem Architecture

Our proof-of-concept implementation of the privacy management mechanism is shown in Fig. 3.

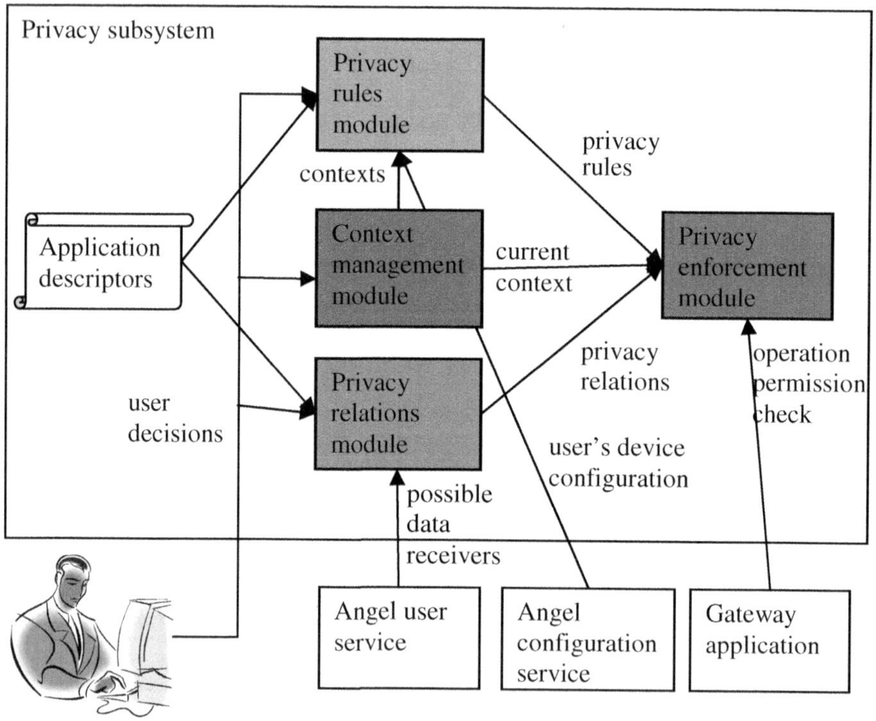

Fig. 3. Angel privacy subsystem logical architecture

Privacy rules module is responsible for constructing a privacy matrix, allowing user manipulation of the matrix, determining privacy rules (*canAccess'* function (7)) and distributing them to gateways.

Context management module is responsible for managing user contexts. This includes managing current context change (in the present implementation the context switching was left to the users; nevertheless it can be delegated to an automatic context detecting mechanism).

Privacy relations module manages receiver categories and their relation to individual Angel users.

The above three modules feed their output to *Privacy enforcement* module, which is responsible for enforcing privacy policies.

Note, that although the security subsystem is not depicted in Fig. 3, the privacy subsystem relies on it in several aspects: users and data receiver authentication, secure communication, and so on. However, these aspects are not discussed here, as they are outside the scope of this paper.

4.4 Privacy Related Information

To perform their tasks, the privacy subsystem modules need to be fed with proper information. Data carrying this information is received from other Angel subsystems, from users' input or from system configuration files.

The *appInfo* function (4) is provided in the form of *application descriptors*. An application descriptor is an XML file describing privacy properties of a single Angel application. A sample application descriptor is presented below (in this implementation of an application descriptor, interfaces are called 'methods').

```
<?xml version="1.0" encoding="utf-8" ?>

<gw-application id="101" name="DemoGWApp"
version="1.0">
     <description>Application for testing
purposes</description>

        <published-methods
           <method name="getUserInformation1">
                <data-categories><data-category>User
Information 1</data-category></data-categories>
                <receiver-purpose-groups>
                     <receiver-purpose-group>
                          <receiver-role>User
Information 1 Role</receiver-role>
                          <processing-purpose>User
Information 1 Purpose 1</processing-purpose>
                     </receiver-purpose-group>
                <receiver-purpose-group>
           </method>
...
```

Fig. 4. Example application descriptor

System configuration information (*own* (5) and *conf* (6) functions) is provided by other Angel subsystem: *Angel configuration service*.

Angel user service provides a list of all receivers registered in Angel. The information is provided to *Privacy relations module* to enable mapping of receivers to receiver categories.

4.5 Privacy Subsystem Deployment

Privacy rules and *Privacy relations* modules are deployed on a distinguished Angel service terminal called Service Centre (SC). User interface to these modules is provided by a web portal, as shown on Fig. 5.

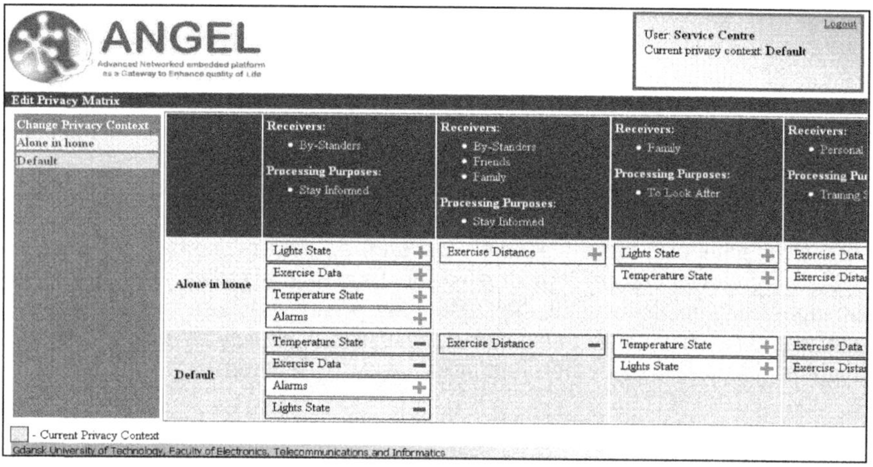

Fig. 5. Privacy management interface (privacy matrix)

Context management module is deployed on both, SC and Angel gateways. On SC it is integrated with *Privacy rules* module. On gateways it is integrated into middleware library and a dedicated Angel application (deployed on each gateway) has been created to provide its user interface. On gateways, however, the *Context management* module does not provide for defining new contexts – only switching of the current context is supported. Current context switching is broadcasted to all gateways owned by a given user from SC. In case the switch was originated on a gateway, the change is first communicated to the SC and then propagated to other relevant gateways.

Privacy enforcement module is deployed on gateways as a part of the Angel platform. It performs two main tasks:

- collects privacy configuration data,
- provides Angel applications with privacy decisions.

Privacy configuration data is distributed to gateways from SC (*canAccess'* (7) by *Privacy rules* module and *mapping* (3) by *Privacy relations* module) either on demand or when the data changes.

Provision of privacy decisions is done through a set of library functions:

- *isLocalAllowed* – a method called by a gateway application before serving any request (received through a Web Services call). It checks whether serving the indicated request is allowed from the privacy viewpoint.
- *isRemoteAllowed* – a method called before a gateway application calls any remote Web Service. It checks whether the call is acceptable from privacy perspective.

4.6 Case Study

The presented solution has been tested in the Angel privacy demonstrator. The objective was to demonstrate privacy management in the context of a realistic scenario of Angel system application. The privacy demonstrator scenario was as follows.

"Tom has subscribed to Angel. He already installed sensors to monitor his home environment (light and temperature sensors were used in this demonstrator). He acquired some personal devices (a step-counter was assumed in the demonstrator) to support him while exercising. Tom is happy with the system, but he is also very concerned with his privacy and want to have control over his private data disclosure. This in particular involves his body related parameters and the home environment parameters"

The demonstrator consisted of Service Centre, a fixed gateway (NXP STB810 [7]), wireless temperature sensors, wireless light sensors and wirelessly controlled colour lamp. The sensors were installed in Tom's bedroom and in the living room. The measurements were collected by an application deployed on the gateway and, if the temperature exceeded the predefined level, the application signalled an alarm by a red flashing light. The step-counter measurements and an outside temperature were also fed to the system. The application software used Angel middleware library to control data disclosure. Different application software deployed on the gateway displayed received measurements on the attached TV monitor. A similar application for data display was included in the service terminals deployed on a PDA device and on a desktop computer.

The following receiver categories were distinguished in Tom's privacy policy: Friends, Family, Trainer, Doctor and By-Stander (anybody near the TV set who can see the screen). The demonstrator considered various privacy related scenarios involving Tom and a related group of people, e.g. his wife, his friends, his trainer and his physician and visitors of his house. The demonstrator was tested and positively assessed during Angel consortium and evaluation meetings involving representatives of users (hospitals), technology providers (telecom industry, sensor producers), academic researchers, project officer and independent reviewers.

5 Related Work

There have been numerous proposals related to the privacy management in distributed environments and some of them address the issue of context dependence.

In PeCAN [8], context is a set of user beliefs (represented as atomic assertion and rules) applicable at a current state. The context is determined in relation to the visited web site, the role assumed by a user (father, researcher, etc.) and a transaction the user is involved in (browsing, buying, etc.). In DPM [9] context is determined by sensor measurements. Privacy preferences and policies are stored in the P3P format. TLC-PP [10, 11] assumes a predefined set of privacy contexts (called situations) and additionally a predefined set of 'rewards' (possible gratification for disclosing private data). In PRIME [12] access to private data is influenced by context, defined as information about entities of interest, as well as any ambient parameters concerning the environment, where a transaction takes place. Similar approach is chosen by Prime Life [13]. In MUPPS [14] context is understood as a characterisation of user's privacy situation (which includes transaction type, time, user location etc.) when accessing a particular website. In PERSIST [15, 16] user context is taken into account and is understood as a collection of attributes describing the user (including location, time, but also services being used by user).

Most of the above solutions are focusing on Internet users in various e-commerce scenarios or similar applications. Our solution is more focusing on the situations where the users are embedded in intelligent ambients equipped with wireless devices with sometimes highly limited resources. Therefore our priority was to find an effective mechanism applicable in the environment subjected to severe efficiency constraints.

The DPM solution [9] also focused on enforcing privacy on disclosure of WSN-gathered data, but it operates in a system where privacy related decisions are centralized. In our case, however, the privacy related decisions are distributed.

PERSIST [15, 16] covers a broad scope, including privacy, trust and identity management. Privacy related decisions are based on basic variables' values (the values of all these variables determine the current context) and Semantic Web techniques are used to support these decisions. This approach is general but may result in a considerable load related to application of reasoning engines. In our approach, the solution is more specific but the gain is in potential efficiency increase.

6 Conclusion and Future Work

Our approach was developed within the broader context of the approach addressing trustworthiness of the Angel system and platform [17]. In the presented solution we abstract from the way the user contexts were determined. In this sense our solution can be interfaced with any mechanism of context determination. In the demonstrator described in the paper, the decision about contexts selection was left to a user. We also assume that users' privacy policies refer to contexts explicitly while defining restrictions on private data.

Users' privacy policies refer to (user defined) contexts and set restrictions on private data disclosure to different receiver categories. The policies remain unchanged as long as the set of receiver categories is not changed. And again, we abstract from the way of determining such policies which means that the proposed solution can be interfaced to any method which results in a similar way of privacy policy representation. In the implementation presented in this paper, the policies were specified by the users by means of a dedicated graphical interface.

Privacy policies and the information of the current context of users forms the base for the mechanism controlling private data disclosure. The mechanism takes into account system configuration, and in particular its distribution into autonomous computing nodes. Each node is capable of disclosing data through its interfaces, and the mechanism installs a sort of a 'valve' on each interface. Closing and opening this valve is used to control private data release in accordance with the users' privacy policies. An important feature is that these decisions can be localized (to the computing nodes) with the possibility to keep at a given node only this information which is needed to make a decision. This provides for efficiency in terms of resources consumption which is highly relevant for mobile devices. A decision on private data release at a given gateway can be made based on locally stored data, without additional communication with remote nodes. And the amount of locally stored data needed to facilitate such decisions is limited. The locally stored information needs to be updated only if the system configuration or users' privacy policies change.

The proposed mechanism is highly transparent to the applications running on the nodes. It is hidden in the middleware (the platform) and the only what is required from an application is to call a proper middleware function before releasing data through an interface. As the platform is deployed on each node the mechanism is available on every node.

The distinguishing features of the presented solution can be summarised as follows:

- it is neutral to the context determination method; the only restriction is that the contexts are known and used as the parameter for the proposed mechanism,
- it assumes that users' privacy policies explicitly set restrictions on private data disclosure to different receiver categories in a context dependent way,
- it assumes that at any system state the current context of each user is determined,
- it provides a distributed mechanism which, for each node, implements a private data disclosure controlling function which enforces consistency with the privacy policies of data owners,
- the mechanism is resource efficient in the sense that on each node only the information necessary to support local decisions is maintained,
- the mechanism is hidden in the platform which makes it transparent to the applications running on the nodes.

In terms of scalability, our mechanism depends mainly on:

- number of data receivers *nr*,
- number of interfaces deployed on a gateway *ni*,
- number of contexts *nc*,

in the sense that the amount of information stored on a gateway is determined by the above factors (the required storage size is proportional to $nr*ni*nc$). The number of users and the number of gateways are not significant, as they influence the storage requirement of Service Centre (SC), which is not resource limited.

In reality however, *nr* and *ni* will not be a meaningful barrier for scalability, as these numbers are related to the number of applications deployed on a gateway. And it is reasonable to assume that the gateways with more applications deployed will be equipped with more resources at system configuration time.

In our implementation, context detection and switching was left to the users. In such case the number of different contexts managed by a user can not be too large and (which is even more important) the contexts have to be well understood by the users. In case of using an automated context management scheme that offers more support for the user, the number of contexts could grow. This could present a problem for scalability, if the number of contexts is very large (even though the amount of required data grows linearly with *nc*).

The mechanism presented in the paper can adapt to configuration changes (adding/removing applications deployed on a gateway, adding/removing gateways, changes in the set of receivers, etc.). However, the changes first need to be adequately represented in the configuration data. This poses a limit on applicability of the mechanism in a fully dynamic environment.

The next steps considered for further development of the proposed approach include:

- Investigating suitability of the mechanism for different context management approaches. In particular it is planned to investigate the consequences of removing the assumption that contexts are mutually exclusive.
- Extending the mechanism to Smart Node level. In Angel project, providing the privacy control mechanism on Smart Node level was initially considered, but following the decision that Smart Nodes will not disclose data, it wasn't further investigated.
- More flexibility in privacy policy definition scheme. The scheme for defining privacy policies worked well in the demonstrator scenario. However, in case of large numbers of receiver categories and data types, it could be unmanageable. A solution to this problem might introduce taxonomies of data receiver categories and private data types. This would help users to express the policies in more concise way.

Acknowledgments. The work presented in the paper was partially supported by the 6th FR STREP *Advanced Networked embedded platform as a Gateway to Enhance quality of Life* (ANGEL), Contract number IST-033506.

References

1. ZigBee Alliance, `http://www.zigbee.org/`
2. European Commission: Directive 95/46/EC of the European Parliament and of the Council on the protection of individuals with regard to the processing of personal data and on the free movement of such data. Offic. J. of the Euro. Communities L 281, 31–50 (1995)
3. Directive 2002/58/EC of the European Parliament and of the Council of 12 July 2002 concerning the processing of personal data and the protection of privacy in the electronic communications sector (Directive on privacy and electronic communications). Offic. J. L 201, 37–47 (2002)
4. OECD Guidelines on the Protection of Privacy and Transborder Flows of Personal Data (1980)

5. Health Insurance Portability and Accountability Act, Privacy/Security/Enforcement Regulation Text, 45 CFR Parts 160 and 164, U.S. Congress Act, with amendments (2003)
6. Bruynen, J., et al.: Deliverable D1.2: Angel System Specification. Technical report, Angel Consortium (2008)
7. Advanced IP STB reference platform STB810, `http://www.nxp.com/applications/set_top_box/ip_stb/stb810/`
8. Jutla, D.N., Bodorik, P., Zhang, Y.: PeCAN: An architecture for users' privacy-aware electronic commerce contexts on the semantic web. Infor. Syst. 31, 295–320 (2006)
9. Hong, D., Yuan, M., Shen, V.Y.: Dynamic Privacy Management: a Plugin Service for the Middleware in Pervasive Computing. In: 7th international conference on Human computer interaction with mobile devices & services, pp. 1–8. ACM, New York (2005)
10. Skinner, G.: The TLC-PP framework for delivering a Privacy Augmented Collaborative Environment (PACE). In: International Conference on Collaborative Computing: Networking, Applications and Worksharing, pp. 289–293. IEEE Computer Society, Washington (2007)
11. Skinner, G., Han, S., Chang, E.: Integration of Situational and Reward Elements for Fair Privacy Principles and Preferences (F3P). In: IEEE International Conference on Industrial Technology, pp. 3078–3082. IEEE Computer Society Press, Los Alamitos (2006)
12. Ardagna, C.A., Cremonini, M., De Capitani di Vimercati, S., Samarami, P.: A Privacy-Aware Access Control System. J. of Comp. Sec. 16, 369–392 (2008)
13. Ardagna, C.A., De Capitani di Vimercati, S., Paraboschi, S., Pedrini, E., Samarati, P.: An XACML-Based Privacy-Centered Access Control System. In: The 1st ACM Workshop on Information Security Governance, pp. 49–58. ACM, New York (2009)
14. Saleh, R., Jutla, D., Bodorik, P.: Management of Users' Privacy Preferences in Context. In: IEEE International Conference on Information Reuse and Integration, pp. 91–97. IEEE Computer Society, Washington (2007)
15. Liampotis, N., Roussaki, I., Papadopoulou, E., Abu-Shaaban, Y., Williams, M.H., Taylor, N.K., McBurney, S.M., Dolinar, K.: A Privacy Framework for Personal Self-Improving Smart Spaces. In: International Conference on Computational Science and Engineering, vol. 3, pp. 444–449. IEEE Computer Society, Los Alamitos (2009)
16. Venezia, C., Taylor, N., Williams, H., Doolin, K., Roussaki, I.: Novel Pervasive Computing Services Experienced through Personal Smart Spaces. In: Tenth International Conference on Mobile Data Management: Systems, Services and Middleware, pp. 484–489 (2009)
17. Górski, J., Gołaszewski, G., Miler, J., Piechówka, M., Baldus, H.: Trustworthiness: safety, security and privacy issues. In: 14th IEEE International Conference on Electronics, Circuits and Systems, ICECS 2007, Morocco, pp. 641–644 (2007)

Semantic Attestation of Node Integrity in Overlays

Fabrizio Baiardi[1] and Daniele Sgandurra[2]

[1] Polo G. Marconi, La Spezia
Università di Pisa, Italy
baiardi@di.unipi.it

[2] Dipartimento di Informatica
Università di Pisa, Italy
daniele@di.unipi.it

Abstract. Attestation of node integrity increases the security of overlay networks by detecting and removing nodes affected by malware. This is fundamental because in an overlay even a single node running some malware can greatly decrease the overlay security. Virtual Integrity Measurement System (VIMS) is a semantic attestation-based framework that determines whether a node can join an overlay according to both its configuration and its current behavior. VIMS fully exploits virtualization by running two virtual machines (VMs) on every overlay node: the Monitored VM (Mon-VM), which runs the overlay application, and the Assurance VM (A-VM), which checks the integrity of the Mon-VM. Before a node is allowed to join an overlay, some overlay nodes interact with the node A-VM to attest the integrity of the applications and of the OS of the node Mon-VM. After this start-up attestation, and as long as the node belongs to the overlay, the A-VM continuously checks the integrity of the Mon-VM to discover anomalies due to attacks. As soon as any check fails, the node is disconnected from the overlay. The security policy of the overlay defines the complexity and the execution frequency of the checks. The complexity ranges from integrity checks on the code of the application and of the OS to a detailed monitoring of the application behavior that exploits introspection. VIMS supports mutual trust because any node of an overlay can assess the integrity of any other node.

The paper presents the architecture of VIMS, its application to P2P and VPN overlays and a preliminary evaluation of the corresponding overhead.

1 Introduction

An overlay network, or simply overlay, is a logical and dynamic connection among logical or physical nodes belonging to a pool, which may either be well known and strictly ruled, e.g. a corporate network, or fully unconstrained, e.g. a peer-to-peer (P2P) network. Overlays are widely adopted because they can offer highly robust services to the nodes they interconnect. As an example, virtual private networks (VPNs) offer confidential communications while P2P networks implement a highly available, distributed data repository. On the other hand, any

R. Meersman et al. (Eds.): OTM 2010, Part I, LNCS 6426, pp. 656–671, 2010.

overlay property is at risk even if few overlay nodes run some malware because of an erroneous, or malicious, configuration or as a result of a successful attack. Hence, node integrity is a precondition of any overlay security policy and this integrity should be attested not only when a node joins an overlay but also as long as the node belongs to the overlay. At first, an initial attestation computes a set of measurements, i.e. functions, on a node and on the software it runs. Then, the attestation evaluates some assertion on the results of these functions: if the assertion does not hold, then the configuration of the node or of the software components that it runs differs from the expected one. A well-known example is the computation of a hash function of the code of a process and an assertion that compares the result against a known "good" value.

Virtual Integrity Measurement System (VIMS) is an architecture to continuously attest the integrity of overlay nodes by applying alternative measurements according to the security requirements of the overlay. To discover both erroneous configuration of a node and attacks against its integrity, VIMS applies a semantic attestation as it considers the behavior of some components of the node. To this end, VIMS defines both a start-up attestation and a continuous monitoring that are applied, respectively, before a node is allowed to join the overlay and as long as the node belongs to the overlay. To implement the corresponding measurements, VIMS applies static and run-time tools: the static tools return a description of the expected behavior of the overlay application running on the node, while the run-time ones monitor the application's run-time behavior and compare it against the one extracted by the static tools. VIMS supports alternative strategies to describe the expected behavior with distinct complexities and attack detection capabilities.

VIMS architecture strongly separates the attestation subsystem from the one to be attested by running a virtual machine monitor (VMM) and two virtual machines (VMs) on each physical node that may be connected to the overlay. These two VMs are the *Monitored VM* (Mon-VM) and the *Assurance VM* (A-VM). The Mon-VM is the target of the attestation and it runs the overlay application *OvApp*. The integrity of this application is monitored by the run-time tools on the A-VM. This VM cooperates with the A-VMs in other overlay nodes to apply integrity measurements according to the security policy of the overlay, by accessing the live state of the Mon-VM in its node through virtual machine introspection, which is the main implementation mechanism of the run-time tools. Anytime an A-VM detects a loss of integrity on its node, it kills the Mon-VM on its node and informs the other A-VMs. Trust in the measurements requires the correct configuration of both the A-VM and the underlying VMM and it is guaranteed by measurements and controls of a Trusted Platform Module (TPM) subsystem [1] [2] that acts as the root-of-trust for the chain of measurements.

The main contributions of VIMS described in the paper are:

1. with respect to solutions that exploit TPM-based measurements only, the integration of static and dynamic tools results in *more granular* and *more powerful* checks. In fact, TPM-based attestations neglect the behavior of a component because they only apply hashing assertions, i.e. they compare the result of a hash function of some memory areas against a constant value;

2. a sharp distinction between two types of attestation: a *start-up attestation*, which occurs when the node joins an overlay, and a *continuous monitoring* that is applied as long as the node belongs to the overlay. Each attestation can apply distinct measurements at distinct abstraction levels. Furthermore, the kind of measurements applied during the continuous monitoring can be updated as a result of modifications to the overlay security policy;
3. *mutual attestation*: any peer can be assured of the integrity of any other peer;
4. *scalability*: the attestation overhead is a function of the security policy (i.e., of the measurements to be applied) and it can be fairly low.

The rest of the paper is structured as follows. Section 2 presents the architecture of VIMS. Section 3 and 4 discuss, respectively, the current prototype and its performance. Section 5 discusses some related works. Finally, in Sect. 6 we draw some conclusions and outline future developments.

2 VIMS Architecture

After introducing the strategies supported by VIMS to measure the integrity of a component, this section describes its run-time architecture, its implementation and the handling of anomalous behaviors of a node.

VIMS defines a general framework that offers *alternative measurements* to attest the integrity of a node. It supports a *semantic attestation* that integrates static tools and dynamic tools that, respectively, extract the *expected behavior* of a software component at several abstraction levels and monitor the current behavior of the component to compare it against the expected one. VIMS static and run-time tools extend those presented in [3] [4] that also prove their effectiveness to detect anomalous behavior due to malware. Currently, static tools may return a description of the program to be attested that ranges from assertions on program variables that hold when a given system call is invoked to a context-free grammar that describes a superset of the sequences of system calls produced by a normal program execution and where each call may be coupled with an assertion on some program variables.

To strongly separate the system to be attested from the attesting one, VIMS runs a virtual machine monitor (VMM) and two virtual machines (VMs) on each node. The Monitored VM (Mon-VM) runs the system to be attested while the Assurance VM (A-VM) runs the attestation subsystem, i.e. the run-time tools to check the integrity of the Mon-VM. VIMS defines a protocol that rules both the messages exchanged among the components on the two VMs and the format of these messages. A *Remote Attestation Module* runs on the A-VM to:

1. coordinate the computation on the two VMs;
2. reply to attestation requests;
3. implement the start-up attestation.

VIMS exploits the TPM and vTPM [5] to apply the integrity measurements on a Mon-VM starting from a tamper-proof root-of-trust. However, VIMS not

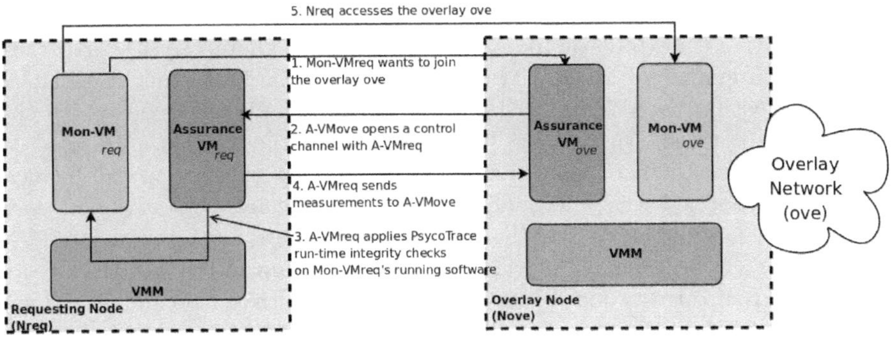

Fig. 1. Example Scenario

only applies the TPM mechanisms to check at boot-time the integrity of application binaries loaded by the Mon-VM but it also implements the continuous monitoring of the Mon-VM to detect attacks against the applications running on this VM. This results in a semantic-based attestation of the integrity of the components that applies measurements that consider the expected behavior of the component. Each measurement that the A-VM can apply results in an alternative strategy to describe the expected behavior of an application and in a distinct granularity and execution frequency of the controls. As an example, these features are a function of the number of system calls that are controlled and of the complexity of the assertions paired with each call.

Example. In the general case (see Fig. 1), an overlay application $OvApp_{req}$ running on Mon-VM$_{req}$ on a node N$_{req}$ contacts the Remote Attestation Module of an A-VM$_{ove}$ of a node N$_{ove}$ to connect to the overlay *ove*. Before allowing $OvApp_{req}$ to connect to *ove* and access any of its services, the Remote Attestation Module on A-VM$_{ove}$ establishes an out-of-band control channel with A-VM$_{req}$. A-VM$_{req}$ measures the current configuration of $OvApp_{req}$ and communicates the results to A-VM$_{ove}$. Then, as long as Mon-VM$_{req}$ belongs to *ove*, A-VM$_{req}$ implements the continuous monitoring by observing the current behavior of Mon-VM$_{req}$ and of $OvApp_{req}$ and by comparing it against the expected one. This VM can also exchange information with the Remote Attestation Module on A-VM$_{ove}$ through the control channel about (i) the checks to be applied in the continuous monitoring, (ii) the results of the measurements on Mon-VM$_{req}$. The protocol exploits the control channel also to alert the Remote Attestation Module on A-VM$_{ove}$ anytime Mon-VM$_{req}$ has been compromised.

2.1 Integrity Measurements

VIMS attestation and monitoring are fully transparent because virtual machine introspection enables the measurement systems on the A-VM to access the running status of off-the-shelf software on the Mon-VM that, therefore, has not to be aware of the integrity measurements. Attestation of a node requires the attestation of the run-time tools on the A-VM that, in turn, guarantee the correctness of the measurements of the A-VM on the Mon-VM, so that other A-VMs can establish trust on the node integrity based upon these measurements. To this purpose, at first the TrustedBoot [6] is loaded and the TPM applies a set of measurements on the boot-loader, so that from now on all the steps can be measured, from boot to kernel and modules loading. To securely attest the integrity of the VMM and of the A-VM, the hash of their code is signed with the TPM private key to create a chain-of-trust, from the BIOS up to the A-VM.

In the start-up attestation, VIMS measures the integrity of both Mon-VM and A-VM through hash functions of the kernel, e.g. critical data structures, code and kernel modules. Then, in the continuous monitoring, the A-VM periodically measures the integrity of the overlay application *OvApp* running on the Mon-VM and of the Mon-VM kernel according to the overlay security policy that is communicated when the node joins the overlay. A-VM may dynamically choose the assurance level that, in turn, determines the description of the expected behavior of *OvApp* and that results in distinct trade-offs between the assurance level and the corresponding overhead.

The integrity measurements may require the computation of one or more hash values on some modules, e.g. of kernel modules, or the evaluations of invariants on variables of the process executing *OvApp* or parsing the sequence of system calls produced by this process. Anytime the hash of some critical components of the Mon-VM or the behavior of *OvApp* differs from the expected ones, the Mon-VM cannot be trusted and it is killed by the A-VM that also tears down the connection. Since the behavior extracted by the static tools over approximate the run-time one of *OvApp*, no false positives can occur.

2.2 Start-Up Attestation and Continuous Monitoring

We describe now in more details the implementation of the integrity measurements. When a node N_{req} tries to join an overlay *ove*, A-VM_{ove} acts as an *appraiser* [7] that implements, on behalf of *ove*, the start-up attestation of N_{req}. A-VM_{ove} intercepts the request from Mon-VM_{req} and it deduces the IP address of A-VM_{req} from the one of Mon-VM_{req}.

The run-time tools on A-VM_{req} apply any measurements requested by the appraiser by directly accessing and examining the run-time status of Mon-VM_{req} through virtual machine introspection. The appraiser always applies hashing assertions to check the integrity of A-VM_{req}. After attesting the integrity of A-VM_{req}, A-VM_{ove} can trust this VM and delegate to it the attestation of Mon-VM_{req}. If the start-up attestation confirms the correct configuration of Mon-VM_{req}, A-VM_{req} starts the continuous monitoring by applying the strategy requested by A-VM_{ove}. A database in A-VM_{req} records the measurements that the appraiser can request in the start-up attestation and in the continuous monitoring.

To describe the start-up attestation, we consider the steps of the communication protocol among the VMs involved in the start-up attestation:

1. Mon-VM$_{req}$ contacts Mon-VM$_{ove}$ to join *ove*;
2. A-VM$_{ove}$ intercepts the request and transmits to A-VM$_{req}$ the measurements of the start-up attestation.
3. the run-time tools on A-VM$_{req}$ compute the requested measurements;
4. A-VM$_{req}$ returns the measurements to A-VM$_{ove}$;
5. if the attestation is successful, A-VM$_{ove}$ communicates to A-VM$_{req}$ the measurements that the continuous monitoring should apply and enables Mon-VM$_{req}$ to join *ove*.

Further features of the protocol are:

- the control channel between the A-VMs exists as long as N$_{req}$ belongs to *ove*;
- A-VM$_{req}$ can apply consistency checks on Mon-VM$_{req}$ on request from A-VM$_{ove}$;
- A-VM$_{ove}$ can request that some measurements are computed after a timeout.

An A-VM kills the Mon-VM on its node anytime the attestation of the Mon-VM fails or the behavior of *OvApp* differs from the expected one. The A-VM may also communicate this event to other A-VMs so that they update a blacklist of IP addresses that cannot belong to the overlay. Instead, if an A-VM detects that another A-VM cannot be attested or the configuration of another node has been updated, it communicates this information to other A-VMs that can either inform the Mon-VM on their nodes or simply destroy the connection to the removed node. It is useless to inform the A-VM of the disconnected node because it is untrusted.

2.3 Threat Model

To define the threat model of interest, we focus on the integrity of the measurement system because VIMS should detect rather than prevent attacks. As a consequence, the integrity of the overall measurement system depends upon that of the A-VM only since the Mon-VM may be completely controlled by an attacker. To detect updates to the configuration of the A-VM, a critical issue is the root-of-trust of the measurement system. VIMS exploits the TPM to measure the integrity of an A-VM through a hash chain that includes the authenticated boot of the VMM and of the kernel of A-VM from the BIOS and boot-loader. If the VMM is correctly configured and is safely started, then it can initialize the local A-VM to assure that also this VM is started in a safe state. A-VM$_{req}$ enables an appraiser A-VM$_{ove}$ to retrieve the values in the hash chain that it protects from accesses by Mon-VM$_{req}$. To preserve the integrity of the node hash chain, A-VM$_{req}$ sends to the appraiser the authenticated hash chain signed with the node key protected by the TPM and returned by a *quote* operation. In this way, the appraiser and the overlay can establish trust at first into A-VM$_{req}$ and its measurements and then into the applications on Mon-VM$_{req}$.

After its safe initialization, A-VM$_{req}$ can monitor the integrity of Mon-VM$_{req}$ and of $OvApp_{req}$ but it cannot prevent modifications of the configuration of N$_{req}$. VIMS can discover these updates through a *seal-plugin* module that exploits the TPM functions *seal* and *unseal*. During the start-up attestation of N$_{req}$, as soon as the appraiser A-VM$_{ove}$ has attested the integrity of A-VM$_{req}$, it asks this A-VM to seal a value K by listing all the TPM registers. From now on, the appraiser can discover updates to the configurations of N$_{req}$ by a challenge/response protocol that sends a nonce n encrypted with K. A-VM$_{req}$ has to unseal K, decrypt the received value and return n to the appraiser. Obviously, A-VM$_{req}$ can reply to the challenge only if the configuration of N$_{req}$ is stable, i.e. if the value of the TPM registers has not been changed. A-VM$_{ove}$ can distribute K to other A-VMs both at the end of the start-up attestation and before N$_{ove}$ leaves the overlay. In this way, each A-VM holds a set of keys, each for a distinct A-VM, and it may randomly choose one of them to control the configuration of the corresponding node. Two consecutive controls are separated by an interval T that depends upon the overlay security policy. The handling of the seal-plugin module shows how A-VMs can cooperate to create an overlay-wide appraiser.

The proposed solution may be ineffective against *intermittent configuration attacks* where a node oscillates between a malicious configuration and a correct one with a frequency that depends upon $1/T$ so that its configuration is correct anytime it is controlled. To detect these attacks, the time in-between two consecutive controls may be randomly chosen from a distribution with an average equal to T. However, since the configuration of an A-VM may be controlled by several other ones and the clocks of these A-VMs are not tightly synchronized, the complexity of foreseeing the timing of configuration controls is rather high even if the time in-between two controls is fixed. Hence, under the assumption that a node includes a TPM, the measurements of the components on the node Mon-VM can be trusted provided that the measurements implemented through the TPM prove that the configurations of the VMM and of the A-VM are trusted and that the seal-plugin module can prevent configuration updates. This is often the case if the nodes are in controlled environment, such as a corporate network. If physical attacks against the memory of a node, or other hardware components, cannot be avoided, then increasing the security of the overlay is very hard. However, robustness with respect to physical attacks can be improved by adopting code obfuscation techniques.

3 Prototype Implementation

Xen [8] 3.1.0 is the adopted technology to create the VMs, which are based on Debian Etch 4.0 with Linux kernel 2.6.18. We adopted the tools described in [3] [4] to define the semantic checks on critical Mon-VM processes and the Introspection Library to compute the assertion on the Mon-VM memory. The modules on A-VM that have been implemented are:

- Remote Attestation Module: an A-VM module that implements the start-up attestation and the attestation protocol;

– a database with the measurements that can be applied;
– a vTPM module interface;
– an interface for the low-level introspection function;
– an OpenVPN plugin [9] used to connect the node to a VPN;
– an extension to a Gnutella code [10].

The last two modules act as interfaces to join, respectively, a VPN and a Gnutella network. The attestation protocol has been implemented in Java. The attestation library consists of 4 Java classes of about 1500 lines of code, whereas the monitoring requires 1000 lines of Java code, including a small wrapper to interface with the introspection functions. The update of the Gnutella code to support the attestation consists of about 1500 lines of code.

In the first experiments, the overlay implements a VPN where the Mon-VM runs a VPN client to join a remote Intranet and Remote Attestation Module acts as a VPN server on N_{ove}. This covers those cases where an Intranet hosts critical resources such as SCADA devices that are remotely accessed and monitored. To protect the integrity of the VPN client, continuous monitoring evaluates assertions returned by the static tools. The VPN server has been modified to handle the remote attestation protocol. Java SSL libraries and TPM/J [11] are used to access the TPM values and to create a VPN connection. Finally, OpenVPN has been extended with plugins to enable remote attestation. The second experiment extends a Gnutella network with attestation. In both experiments, we assume that no measurement violates the user's privacy.

3.1 Remote Attestation Module

The Remote Attestation Module is at the core of the attestation protocol as it initializes the protocol and implements the communications between N_{ove}, an overlay node, and A-VM_{req}, the A-VM on the node that is trying to connect to the overlay. The protocol is triggered each time Mon-VM_{req} opens a connection to N_{ove} to join an overlay *ove*. The Remote Attestation Module on A-VM_{ove} acts as daemon service waiting for connections and it starts the handshaking phase. In a VPN overlay, this module is an OpenVPN plugin, whereas, in the P2P testbed scenario, it is a module on the A-VM that cooperates with a new thread in the Gnutella code to manage the control channel between the A-VMs. Once activated, the Remote Attestation Module maps the IP address of Mon-VM_{req} into the one of A-VM_{req} and it opens a connection to this A-VM.

The handshaking between the Remote Attestation Module on A-VM_{ove} and A-VM_{req} includes the mutual authentication and the initial parameters exchange. At the end of the handshake, A-VM_{req} applies the initial set of measurements to Mon-VM_{req} and it transmits their results and the hash chain computed by the TrustedBoot to the Remote Attestation Module on A-VM_{ove}. To attest the integrity of A-VM_{req} and discover the current configuration of Mon-VM_{req}, the Remote Attestation Module on A-VM_{ove} compares the hashes against those in the database. Then, A-VM_{ove} defines an assurance level that then communicates to A-VM_{req}. Finally, A-VM_{req} stores this level in its database and it implements the continuous monitoring by applying the corresponding measurements.

Currently, the Remote Attestation Module can apply further measurements besides those previously described. In fact, the Remote Attestation Module may apply either an *on-demand* or a *frequency* policy, based on a XML-encoded policy. On-demand policies includes all those previously described to detect attacks against a node. Furthermore, as long as a node belongs to an overlay, the Remote Attestation Module may request specific measurements to an A-VM anytime the Mon-VM has invoked a predefined number of system calls. Instead, in frequency-based policies, the Remote Attestation Module on the appraiser A-VM requires that the A-VM computes the hash values of some memory areas with a given frequency and return these values to the module. These values are computed concurrently with the computations on the Mon-VM.

The steps of the protocol between A-VM$_{req}$ and the Remote Attestation Module on A-VM$_{ove}$ are:

1. Mon-VM$_{req}$ opens a connection to the Remote Attestation Module on A-VM$_{ove}$;
2. the Remote Attestation Module on A-VM$_{ove}$ checks the user's credentials;
3. if Mon-VM$_{req}$ has been authenticated, the Remote Attestation Module on A-VM$_{ove}$ invokes a function to query the database;
4. the Remote Attestation Module on A-VM$_{ove}$ retrieves the IP address of A-VM$_{req}$ either though a function or by mapping Mon-VM$_{req}$ address;
5. the Remote Attestation Module on A-VM$_{ove}$ sets up a control channel with A-VM$_{req}$;
6. the Remote Attestation Module on A-VM$_{ove}$ sends the handshake message with some parameters;
7. A-VM$_{req}$ computes the hash values of *OvApp* and sends them to the Remote Attestation Module on A-VM$_{ove}$ chained with the hash chain of the underlying system computed by the TPM;
8. the Remote Attestation Module on A-VM$_{ove}$ compares the values from A-VM$_{req}$ against the expected ones;
9. the Remote Attestation Module on A-VM$_{ove}$ sends to A-VM$_{req}$ an XML configuration file with the measurements that it should apply. The function parameters are (i) *level*, an ID paired with a strategy in A-VM$_{req}$ database; (ii) *measurement*, whose value can either be *frequency* or *on demand*;
10. in a *frequency* policy, the Remote Attestation Module on A-VM$_{ove}$ sends a timeout value for the session. A-VM$_{req}$ computes the measurements when the timeout elapses and sends the results to the Remote Attestation Module on A-VM$_{ove}$;
11. from this moment on, A-VM$_{req}$ measures the integrity of the processes implementing *OvApp* and of the kernel and it returns the measurements to the Remote Attestation Module on A-VM$_{ove}$.

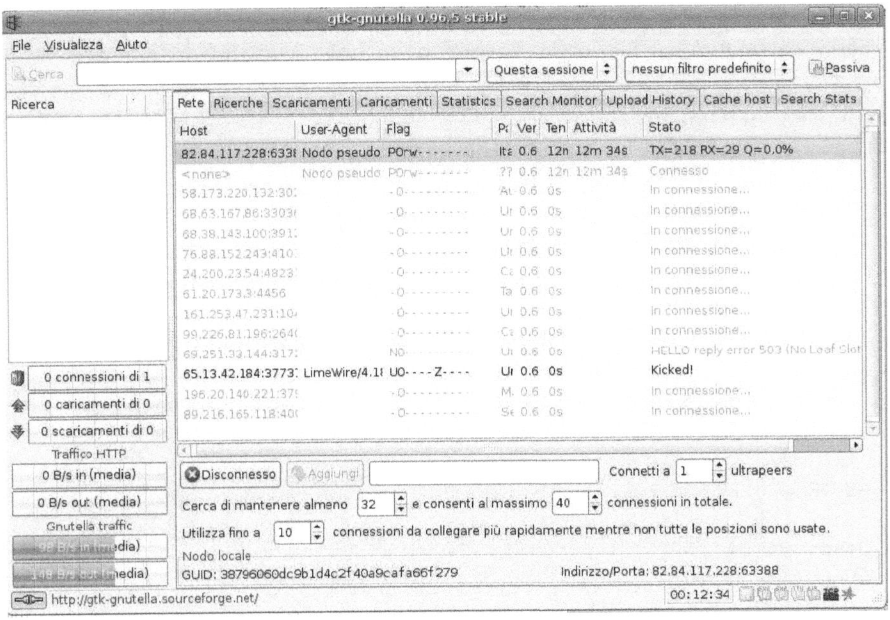

Fig. 2. Kicked Node in the Gnutella Implementation

3.2 Integrity Measurements in a P2P Overlay

The adoption of VIMS to protect a P2P overlay is not fully transparent because, to compute the integrity measurements, we have modified three distinct components in the Gnutella code [10] that implement, respectively, the handshake, the download and the exchange of Ping messages. Moreover, a further thread in the Gnutella code implements the message exchange between the Appraiser and *OvApp*, i.e. the Gnutella application. As an example, if the new thread receives an alert from an A-VM stating that a node has been compromised, it forces *OvApp* to "kick" the compromised node out of the overlay (see Fig. 2). Anytime a node attempts to connect to the Gnutella overlay, the new thread receives the request and informs the A-VM on its node to act as an appraiser and to interact with the A-VM on the requesting node. As soon as this node has been successfully attested, it can join the overlay. From now on the standard Gnutella protocol is executed. If required, also the requesting node can attest the Gnutella peer.

The handshake component has been modified to implement a revised version of the original Gnutella protocol where:

1. Mon-VM_{req} opens a TCP connections with Mon-VM_{ove};
2. Mon-VM_{req} sends the string "GNUTELLA CONNECT/0.6" to Mon-VM_{ove};
3. Mon-VM_{req} sends a header with its specifications containing new fields for the attestation to Mon-VM_{ove};

4. Mon-VM$_{ove}$ contacts A-VM$_{ove}$ to inform that Mon-VM$_{req}$ is willing to join the Gnutella Overlay;
5. A-VM$_{ove}$ contacts A-VM$_{req}$ using UDP to request the integrity measurements for Mon-VM$_{req}$;
6. A-VM$_{req}$ applies the initial integrity measurements, i.e. the hashing measurements on Mon-VM$_{req}$, and sends the results to A-VM$_{ove}$;
7. A-VM$_{ove}$ communicates the response to Mon-VM$_{ove}$;
8. if the response is positive, Mon-VM$_{ove}$ sends the string "GNUTELLA/0.6 200 OK" to Mon-VM$_{req}$, otherwise it closes the connections.

Then, steps 4 to 8 are repeated but this time the roles of Mon-VM$_{ove}$ and Mon-VM$_{req}$ are reversed, i.e. Mon-VM$_{req}$ requires A-VM$_{ove}$ to attest Mon-VM$_{ove}$.

The following is an example of the handshake messages exchanged between two nodes:

```
1)GNUTELLA CONNECT/0.6
  Node: 123.123.123.123:1234
  Pong-Caching: 0.1
  GGEP: 0.5
  Ip-Att: 123.123.123.123
  Port-Att: 6666
  AttEveryXPing: 5
  Dom-Name: Mon-VMreq

2)ATTESTATION MESSAGE
  Code-Message: ATTESTATION_ON_HANDSHAKE
  Ip-Node: 123.123.123.123
  Port-Node: 1234
  Ip-Att: 123.123.123.123
  Port-Att: 6666
  AttEveryXPing: 5
  Dom-Name: Mon-VMreq

3)ATTESTATION MESSAGE
  Code-Message: REQUEST_ATTESTATION
  Dom-Name:  Mon-VMreq

4-5)Integrity measurements on Mon-VMreq

6)ATTESTATION MESSAGE
  Code-Message: ATTESTATION_ON_HANDSHAKE
  Attestation: OK

7)ATTESTATION MESSAGE
  Code-Message: ATTESTATION_ON_HANDSHAKE
  Attestation: OK
```

```
8)GNUTELLA/0.6 200 OK
  User-Agent: gtk-gnutella/0.95
  Pong-Caching: 0.1ss
  GGEP: 0.5
  Ip-Att: 234.234.234.234
  Port-Att: 8888
  AttEveryXPing: 5
  Dom-Name: Bar
  Private-Data: 5ef89a
```

As soon as Mon-VM receives the "OK" string, steps 2-8 are repeated to attest the integrity of Mon-VM_{ove}. We do not detail here the update of the components implementing the downloads and Ping messages, since it recalls that of the handshake. It suffices to say that the original protocol has been modified to include integrity measurements as well. Anytime a file download is started, the A-VMs of the nodes involved in the download cooperate to attest the integrity of both Mon-VMs. Attestations may be fired by Ping messages as well. Furthermore, since A-VM continuously monitors the behavior of *OvApp*, Ping messages also include integrity results based upon measurements on *OvApp* and hashing assertions. As soon as Mon-VM receives a Ping message from another Mon-VM it replies with a Pong and then, if the number of Ping messages exceeds a threshold, it starts the mutual attestation of both Mon-VMs. As soon as the attestation of a peer Mon-VM fails, the appraiser A-VM informs the local Mon-VM and all its neighbor A-VMs that, in turn, inform the Gnutella application on the corresponding Mon-VMs to close the connection with the kicked Mon-VM.

4 Assessment Overhead

In the following, we discuss at first the overhead of start-up attestation and then the one of continuous monitoring. The system to run the prototype included a Pentium Centrino Duo T2250 1.7GHz. In all the tests, the A-VM Linux kernel version was 2.6.18-xen, 128MB of physical memory were allocated to the Mon-VM, running a Linux Debian distribution, and 874 MB to the A-VM.

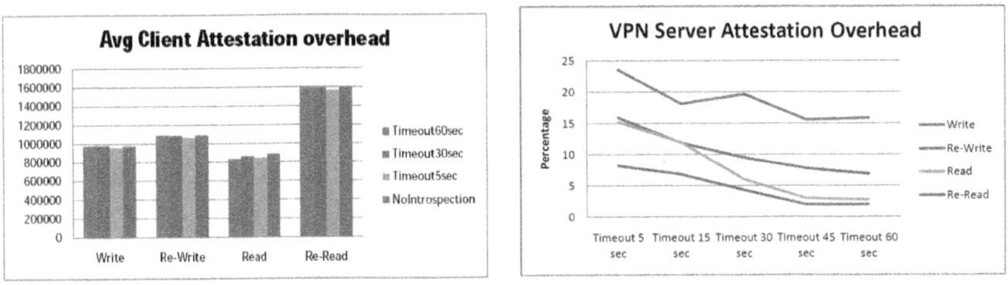

(a) (b)

Fig. 3. Average Client Attestation Overhead(a); VPN Server Attestation Overhead(b)

Figure 3(a) shows the throughput (KB/sec) of the IOzone [12] benchmark on a Mon-VM in the testbed VPN overlay when the integrity measurements are sent every 5 to 60 secs: the figure shows that network latency masks the protocol overhead and, for this reason, the overhead due to the attestation is negligible. Figure 3(b) shows the attestation overhead computed by IOzone on the Mon-VM when 3 nodes try to connect to the VPN overlay simultaneously. The figure shows the additional overhead (in percentage) as a function of timeout, i.e. the time interval in-between two consecutive attestations, with respect to a solution where no attestation is performed. In this scenario, the overhead is almost negligible if the measurement results are sent every 60 sec: we believe that this value for a timeout is a reasonable one since it allows VIMS to check the integrity of all the nodes without introducing a noticeable overhead.

To evaluate the overhead of the attestations of the Mon-VM kernel and of *OvApp* in the testbed Gnutella overlay, we recall that the integrity of a node is attested anytime it joins a Gnutella overlay, downloads a file or has exchanged a predefined number of Ping messages. The attestation overhead is low because the execution time increases at most of 10 percent if the Mon-VM runs the Gnutella application only. If it runs further applications, the slow-down of the download due to the attestation may be neglected provided that at most one attestation for minute occurs. As far as concerns the communication overhead, the number of exchanged messages increases from 4 in the original protocol to, at most, 8 to implement the attestation. However, 2 of these messages are exchanged between VMs on the same node.

5 Related Works

The adoption of [3] [4] to remotely attest the integrity of a node before connecting it to an overlay has been discussed in [13], which is focused on TPM-based measurements only and on client/server architectures. *Attestation-based Remote Policy Enforcement* [14] is an access control architecture to verify client integrity properties using a TPM, and to establish trust upon the capability of the client to enforce the policy before enabling the client to access a corporate Intranet. [15] proposes a trusted computing architecture to enforce access control policies in P2P applications. This architecture is based upon an abstract layer of trusted hardware that may be implemented through emerging trusted computing technologies. A trusted reference monitor verifies the integrity and other properties of running applications through the trusted computing's functions. It can also enforce various policies on behalf of object owners. [16] defines an attestation framework that integrates virtualization and TPM but only considers hashing measurements. *Pioneer* [17] is a software-based platform addressing the problem of verifiable code execution on legacy computing hosts without relying on secure co-processors or CPU virtualization extensions. Pioneer is based on a challenge-response protocol between an external trusted entity (the dispatcher) and an untrusted computing platform. *Prima* [18] is an extension of the Linux IMA system to measure information flow integrity that can be verified by remote parties. *Semantic integrity* [19] is a measurement approach targeting the dynamic state of the software during execution and, therefore, providing fresh measurement results. [20] improves software-based attestation protocols by using the time stamping functionality of a TPM so that the execution time of the fingerprint computation can be measured locally. This solution can be further strengthen with a trusted boot-loader to identify the processor's specification of the untrusted platform and provide accurate timing information about the checksum function. [21] describes three practical techniques to authenticate the code and other execution state of an OS using the services of the TPM and a hypervisor. These techniques are specialized OS images, authentication of OS images with persistent state and VM policy attestation. The techniques trade off detailed reporting of the OS code and configuration with the manageability and comprehensibility of reported configurations. [22] extends behavior-based attestation to a *model-driven remote attestation* to prove that a remote system is trusted as defined by TCG. The model-driven remote attestation verifies two compliance requirements to prove the trustworthiness of a remote system, i.e. expected and enforced behavior's compliance. Finally, [23] presents a non invasive method that respects a node privacy, but it only guarantees the integrity of anti-virus tools. *Trusted Network Connect* (TNC) [24] is an open architecture for network access control (NAC) developed by the Trusted Network Connect Work Group. TNC makes network access to a device dependent on its state and provides interoperability among multi-vendor network endpoints. TNC is limited to closed environments, such as local area networks and virtual private networks, i.e. it works up to network-level protocol. To this purpose, [25] proposes a protocol stack that enables the use of TNC in web-based environments. The resulting architecture uses security tokens to encapsulate TNC integrity check results to provide privacy protections to clients. In this way, the TNC can be implemented as a part of the authentication process of web-based applications.

6 Future Works and Conclusions

The integrity of the services of an overlay and of the information it manages, requires an initial attestation and a continuous monitoring of integrity to detect nodes affected by malware or rootkits. In turn, this requires that a node computes proper integrity measurements on the current status of another node. Virtual Integrity Measurement System is an architecture to support mutual and semantic attestation among nodes trying to join an overlay and the overlay itself. VIMS exploits virtualization and introspection to check the integrity of software components on a node and to attest it to other nodes, by running a shadow VM that applies the integrity measurements in a transparent way for the software stack of the node.

Future research will consider user-based security policies where the integrity measurements on a node determines the services that it can access after joining an overlay. Finally, the feasibility of monitoring information flowing to/from Mon-VMs is being evaluated to increase the efficacy of the run-monitoring [26].

References

1. Bajikar, S.: Trusted Platform Module (TPM) based Security on Notebook PCs-White Paper. Mobile Platforms Group, Intel Corporation (June 20, 2002)
2. Pearson, S.: Trusted Computing Platforms, the Next Security Solution. Trusted Computing Group Administration, Beaverton (2002)
3. Tamberi, F., Maggiari, D., Sgandurra, D., Baiardi, F.: Semantics-Driven Introspection in a Virtual Environment. In: IAS 2008: Proceedings of the 2008 The Fourth International Conference on Information Assurance and Security, Washington, DC, USA, pp. 299–302. IEEE Computer Society, Los Alamitos (2008)
4. Baiardi, F., Maggiari, D., Sgandurra, D., Tamberi, F.: Transparent Process Monitoring in a Virtual Environment. Electronic Notes in Theoretical Computer Science 236, 85–100 (2009); Proceedings of the 3rd International Workshop on Views On Designing Complex Architectures, VODCA 2008 (2008)
5. Berger, S., Cáceres, R., Goldman, K.A., Perez, R., Sailer, R., van Doorn, L.: vTPM: virtualizing the trusted platform module. In: USENIX-SS 2006: Proceedings of the 15th conference on USENIX Security Symposium. USENIX Association, Berkeley (2006)
6. SourceForge.net: Trusted Boot, `http://sourceforge.net/projects/tboot`
7. Coker, G., Guttman, J., Loscocco, P., Sheehy, J., Sniffen, B.T.: Attestation: Evidence and trust. In: Chen, L., Ryan, M.D., Wang, G. (eds.) ICICS 2008. LNCS, vol. 5308, pp. 1–18. Springer, Heidelberg (2008)
8. Barham, P., Dragovic, B., Fraser, K., Hand, S., Harris, T., Ho, A., Neugebauer, R., Pratt, I., Warfield, A.: Xen and the art of virtualization. In: SOSP 2003: Proceedings of the nineteenth ACM Symposium on Operating Systems Principles, pp. 164–177. ACM, New York (2003)
9. OpenVPN: An Open Source SSL VPN Solution, `http://openvpn.net/`
10. SourceForge.net: gtk-gnutella: The Graphical Unix Gnutella Client, `http://gtk-gnutella.sourceforge.net/`
11. TPM/J: Java-based API for the Trusted Platform Module (TPM), `http://projects.csail.mit.edu/tc/tpmj/`
12. IOzone: Filesystem Benchmark, `http://www.iozone.org/`
13. Baiardi, F., Cilea, D., Sgandurra, D., Ceccarelli, F.: Measuring Semantic Integrity for Remote Attestation. In: Chen, L., Mitchell, C.J., Martin, A. (eds.) Trust 2009. LNCS, vol. 5471, pp. 81–100. Springer, Heidelberg (2009)
14. Sailer, R., Jaeger, T., Zhang, X., van Doorn, L.: Attestation-based policy enforcement for remote access. In: CCS 2004: Proceedings of the 11th ACM conference on Computer and Communications Security, pp. 308–317. ACM, New York (2004)
15. Sandhu, R., Zhang, X.: Peer-to-peer access control architecture using trusted computing technology. In: SACMAT 2005: Proceedings of the tenth ACM Symposium on Access Control Models and Technologies, pp. 147–158. ACM, New York (2005)
16. Lioy, A., Ramunno, G., Vernizzi, D.: Trusted-Computing Technologies for the Protection of Critical Information Systems. Journal of Information Assurance and Security 4, 449–457 (2009)
17. Seshadri, A., Luk, M., Shi, E., Perrig, A., van Doorn, L., Khosla, P.: Pioneer: verifying code integrity and enforcing untampered code execution on legacy systems. In: SOSP 2005: Proceedings of the twentieth ACM symposium on Operating systems principles, pp. 1–16. ACM, New York (2005)
18. Jaeger, T., Sailer, R., Shankar, U.: PRIMA: policy-reduced integrity measurement architecture. In: Proceedings of the eleventh ACM symposium on Access control models and technologies, pp. 19–28. ACM, New York (2006)

19. Petroni Jr., N.L., Fraser, T., Walters, A., Arbaugh, W.A.: An architecture for specification-based detection of semantic integrity violations in kernel dynamic data. In: USENIX-SS 2006: Proceedings of the 15th conference on USENIX Security Symposium, pp. 289–304. USENIX Association, Berkeley (2006)
20. Schellekens, D., Wyseur, B., Preneel, B.: Remote attestation on legacy operating systems with trusted platform modules. Sci. Comput. Program. 74(1-2), 13–22 (2008)
21. England, P.: Practical Techniques for Operating System Attestation. In: Lipp, P., Sadeghi, A.-R., Koch, K.-M. (eds.) Trust 2008. LNCS, vol. 4968, pp. 1–13. Springer, Heidelberg (2008)
22. Gu, L., Ding, X., Deng, R.H., Zou, Y., Xie, B., Shao, W., Mei, H.: Model-driven remote attestation: Attesting remote system from behavioral aspect. In: ICYCS 2008: Proceedings of the 2008 The 9th International Conference for Young Computer Scientists, Washington, DC, USA, pp. 2347–2353. IEEE Computer Society, Los Alamitos (2008)
23. Traynor, P., Chien, M., Weaver, S., Hicks, B., Mc Daniel, P.: Non Invasive Methods for Host Certification. ACM Trans. on Information and System Security 11(3), 1–23 (2008)
24. Trusted Computing Group: TCG Trusted Network Connect TNC Architecture for Interoperability. Specification Version 1.3 Revision 6 (April 2008)
25. Rehbock, S., Hunt, R.: Trustworthy clients: Extending tnc to web-based environments. Comput. Commun. 32(5), 1006–1013 (2009)
26. Greenhalgh, A., Huici, F., Hoerdt, M., Papadimitriou, P., Handley, M., Mathy, L.: Flow processing and the rise of commodity network hardware. SIGCOMM Comput. Commun. Rev. 39(2), 20–26 (2009)

Applicability of Security Patterns

Roberto Ortiz[1], Santiago Moral-García[2], Santiago Moral-Rubio[3], Belén Vela[2], Javier Garzás[2,4], and Eduardo Fernández-Medina[5]

[1] S21SecLabs-SOC. Group S21Sec Gestión S.A., Valgrande, 10, 28108, Madrid, Spain
r.ortizpl@gmail.com
[2] Kybele Group. Dep. of Computer Languages and Systems II, University Rey Juan Carlos, Tulipán, s/n, 28933, Madrid, Spain
{santiago.moral,belen.vela,javier.garzas}@urjc.es
[3] Dep. Logical Security, BBVA, Batanes 3, 28760, Madrid, Spain
santiago.moral@grupobbva.es
[4] Kybele Consulting, Oliva, Las Rozas, Madrid
javier.garzas@kybeleconsulting.com
[5] GSyA Research Group, Dep. of Information Technologies and Systems, University of Castilla-La Mancha, Paseo de la Universidad, 4, Ciudad Real, Spain
Eduardo.FdezMedina@uclm.es

Abstract. Information Security has become one of the fundamental mainstays in organizations owing to the ever-increasing cyber attacks against them in recent years. Both the designers of security mechanisms and the security engineers therefore need reliable security solutions to minimize the impact of the attacks on an organization's systems. Good mechanisms for solving these deficiencies are security patterns, which present a reliable and tested scheme to deal with recurring security problems. In this paper, we perform an analysis of some of the most important works that describe security patterns. Our main objective is to verify their applicability for the analysis and design of secure architectures in real and complex environments. Finally, and after presenting the detected shortcomings of the existing security patterns, we show which features should be incorporated into the patterns to be applicable in the field of information security engineering related to the development of secure architectures.

Keywords: Security patterns, information security engineering, real environments.

1 Introduction

Technological advances are currently improving many aspects related to the development and design of information systems, thus entailing an increase in the complexity of systems, which in turn augments the number of computer attacks, since attackers have more possibilities of finding new vulnerabilities in systems, such as susceptibility to Cross Site Scripting, injection flaws, malicious file execution, man-in-the-middle, etc. [1].

Information Security is therefore one of the main concerns that organizations have had to deal with in recent years. On the one hand, companies wish to prevent their

R. Meersman et al. (Eds.): OTM 2010, Part I, LNCS 6426, pp. 672–684, 2010.

information from becoming endangered, and on the other hand, there is a growing number of attacks as a result of the great benefits that attackers may obtain with the information plundered from organizations. All this signifies that information systems engineers must include security requirements in their systems, i.e., they must ensure the confidentiality, integrity and availability of data, besides auditing, privacy/anonymity, authentication/authorization, non-repudiation, usability, etc., while safeguarding the organization's information assets. The importance of system security is growing, since most attacks on software systems are based on vulnerabilities caused by software that has been poorly designed and developed [2]. That's the reason why information systems engineers need reliable solutions to problems related to security in order to be able to reduce the number of successful attacks against these systems.

Patterns are a good means of satisfying this need, since they describe a problem which occurs time and again in our environment, thus providing a trustworthy solution that can be used on multiple occasions [3]. One of the main advantages of patterns is that they combine experience and good practices in the development of models [4], thus increasing efficiency in the design of systems. Therefore, information security engineers can use security patterns to obtain reliable solutions related to this field, since patterns are a good mechanism through which to systematize the process of solving a recurring security problem. Another advantage of security patterns is that they include extensive accumulated and structured knowledge about security, thus providing guidelines for the construction and evaluation of secure systems [5]. The use of security patterns as a guide for developing a secure system is an extremely widespread practice [6, 7]. In fact, the number of published security patterns has increased considerably in recent years [8, 9, 10, 11, 12, 13, 14, 15], and there is a great heterogeneity between the descriptions of each of the proposals [16, 17, 18, 19, 20]. Different patterns have even been defined to provide an answer to the same set of security problems or requirements [21, 22]. For this reason, in some works [23, 5, 24], authors affirm that security patterns do not satisfy their needs when applying them to real problems, since it is more difficult to select the most suitable patterns with which to solve a specific problem from among the great variety of patterns that exist to solve the same problem.

Numerous patterns currently exist for the construction of security mechanisms. Security mechanisms are artifacts that are designed to detect problems, prevent risks or perform immediate corrections and avoid undesirable events that jeopardize security. Examples of such mechanisms are a secure access system [25] or a secure authentication system [10]. These types of patterns are very useful for the security engineers who perform this work. After these mechanisms have been created, they are used by organizations' security engineers to analyze and design the security architectures of real systems.

The main goal of this paper is, therefore, to verify whether the security patterns that have been proposed to build security mechanisms are applicable to the analysis and design of security architectures in real and complex information systems. We understand a real and complex environment or an information system to be all the elements involved in an organization, i.e., human resources, business processes, systems and technologies. Moreover, the concept of security architecture can be defined as the practice of applying a structured, coordinated, and rigorous method with the intention of discovering an organization's structure, bearing in mind human resources, business processes and technologies, i.e., all the elements that are involved in the organization to provide its systems with security and thus ensure the safety of its assets. Ensuring the safety of assets implies the necessity to establish a set of technological infrastructure controls with which to identify the security mechanisms that are needed to define the system's security.

For this purpose, we have performed a systematic review [26] in the context of existing security patterns in the literature at an earlier date, up to March 2010, which is in period of validation for its publication. For this work, we have used digital libraries (Springer Link, Science@Direct, ACM digital library, IEEE digital library, etc.), book chapters and conferences (Pattern Languages of Programs (PLOP), Software Patterns and Quality (SPAQu), etc.) as sources. We will only focus on the works analyzed in this systematic review that describe security patterns, trying to cover the most important areas and aspects of information systems security. After synthesizing these works, a study on the applicability of the selected patterns will be carried out to find out to what extent these patterns can be applied to a particular environment, i.e., information security engineering that is focused on the analysis and design of security architectures.

The remainder of the paper is organized as follows: in Section 2, we shall present a synthesis of the analyzed proposals. In Section 3, we shall study the applicability of security patterns to specific environments, that is, in the field of information security engineering related to the development of security architectures. In section 4, we shall perform an analysis of the works that describe security patterns, presenting the results, and then discussing them. Finally, in Section 5 we shall set out our main conclusions and future work.

2 Synthesis of the Proposals

In this section, we shall sum up some of the proposals for the definition of new security patterns. In this set of works, extracted from a systematic review previously conducted in the field of security patterns, different means of creating security patterns are presented. Here, we have grouped these proposals according to the problem area for which they provide solutions: communications, privacy, access control, etc.

2.1 Description of Security Patterns for Secure Communications

This group includes those proposals related to security solutions for communication between several systems and for their sending and receiving of messages. Fernandez et al. [27] present four security patterns that could be used to design secure VoIP systems, describing mechanisms that can control many of the possible attacks. This approach also provides a framework for applying security. Chavhan and Chhabria [28] propose three design patterns for VoIP implementations related to specific security problems. The IPsec module for VoIP is deployed in the Client/Server environment. Fernandez and Ortega-Arjona [29] present the secure pipes and filters pattern, which is a secure version of the original pattern. The secure pipes and filters pattern may help us to add security controls during the processing stage, thus ensuring that only predefined operations are applied to data streams.

2.2 Description of Security Patterns for Secure Access Control and Identity

This group comprises the proposals regarding security patterns for building secure systems, focusing on building effective authorization, authentication and access control mechanisms. Delessy et al. [30] propose a pattern language for an identity management system based on trust relationships between different security domains. Cuevas et al. [31] describe a solution that ensures end-to-end access control for data generated by wireless sensors. They use security patterns for the definition of an abstract model for encryption-based access control to sensor data. Fernandez et al. [32] propose a security pattern for use in distributed systems. This pattern describes the identification of information which provides authentication and access control elements. Fernandez et al. [33] also describe several patterns for showing the effect of sessions on an access control model.

2.3 Description of Security Patterns for Securing Privacy

This group includes the proposals related to those security patterns defined to solve problems related to privacy. They consider this concept to be highly relevant in the exchange of personal information between users and systems. These works show several security solutions that reinforce the security policies of web sites, e-mails, web applications, and other systems, to preserve the user's identity. Lobato et al. [34] present a set of patterns for the standardization of the development of privacy policies for use on websites. These patterns mostly consider aspects related to security, integrity, and privacy, since in order to access these sites users need to provide personal information and expect that these issues will be born in mind. Schumacher [16] shows two security patterns for protecting the identity of users when they access a website or wish to use a mail service without revealing their identity. Romanosky et al. [35] describe patterns for web-based activity. These new patterns may help those security engineers associated with the development of information systems to solve the problem of maintaining privacy.

2.4 Description of Attack/ Misuse Patterns

This group includes the proposals for describing a new concept of security patterns. Fernandez et al. denominate them as attack patterns or misuse patterns. In this kind of patterns, authors put themselves on the side of the attacker, and describe all the elements of the attack step by step. Then, they set out the security patterns which neutralize this attack, and provide a description of how to trace the attack once it has occurred. In [19] a misuse pattern is proposed. A model that characterizes the structure of this type of pattern is also presented. Similarly, in [36] an attack pattern which provides a specific description of the attack objectives and the steps that the attack follows as it proceeds is presented. In addition, an attack of Denial-of-Service on VoIP networks is presented to demonstrate the value of the pattern.

2.5 Description of Security Patterns to Build Trust Relationships

This group includes those proposals for security patterns which are used to secure the trust relationships between user and systems or between two users when attempting to enforce security requirements such as integrity, confidentiality, and availability. Fischer et al. [37] present a security pattern, denominated as the secure GUI system. This pattern may help us to ensure the security of graphical user interface systems and evaluate their use in different systems. Sorniotti et al. [38] describe an untraceable secret handshake, a protocol that allows two users to mutually verify the other's properties without disclosing their identity.

2.6 Other Description of Security Patterns to Build Secure Systems

This group includes the proposals for security patterns which are used to build secure systems using patterns from both architectural security and security design. Fernandez et al. [39] propose the Secure Three-Tier Architecture pattern, which extends the Three-Tier Architecture pattern. Its authors have reviewed this pattern in order to separate and analyze its security aspects. Fernandez et al. [40] also describe security patterns for the representation of processes and threads of Operating Systems. Spanoudakis et al. [41] introduce patterns with which to express basic Security Monitoring Properties that can be checked during runtime using a general runtime requirements monitoring framework.

An analysis of the applicability of security patterns to support analysis and design of secure architectures in real and complex environments will be shown in the following section.

3 Analysis of the Applicability of Security Patterns to the Development of Security Architectures

According to the pattern definitions [10], their contribution is to provide a proven and documented solution for similar context problems. In order to identify whether security patterns can be applied to the analysis and design of security architectures in real and complex environments, it is essential to find out whether the existing security patterns satisfy these requirements.

On the basis of certain security experts' experience in the field of security patterns [42, 25, 43], security patterns should serve to attain at least the following goals:

- Simplification of the analysis process for information security engineers who have to design the security of a new information system, in order to reduce the time needed to complete the analysis;
- Reliable identification of good and bad practices to reduce the time and cost required in security analysis; and finally;
- Provision of a uniform security guide to allow different information security engineers to develop equivalent solutions.

Similarly, in some cases, security patterns should not be implemented in the development of a secure system if their use would cause the situations stated below and, in addition, a negative report of the analysis of risks of the system opposite to business requirements has been obtained:

a. The impact that the deployment of the solution will have on the rest of the components in the system will cause a decrease in performance;
b. The business processes, the architecture, and the number of physical and logical elements of which the information system is composed are not compatible with security patterns;
c. They do not consider the complexity and difficulties that a security engineer may encounter when implementing the solution;

d. They do not consider the complexity of use that the solution will have for the final user;
e. They do not consider how the management and maintenance tasks are performed.

In the following section, the proposals synthesized in Section 2 will be analyzed in an effort to verify whether the security patterns currently available in the literature can be applied to the development of security architectures. The results of this analysis will then be presented and discussed. Finally, the features that should be incorporated into the security patterns to help security engineers to develop security architecture will be shown.

4 Results and Discussion

Having carried out the synthesis of the proposals that describe security patterns and after analyzing the applicability of security patterns to the development of security architectures, in this section we shall conduct an analysis to verify whether these proposed patterns are really useful for those security engineers who have to analyze or design secure architectures in the field of systems engineering. Once this has been completed, we shall present a discussion of the obtained results

In order to analyze the applicability of the security patterns defined in the proposals synthesized in section 2, we shall now present the features (*Considerations*) (partially based on the considerations exposed in [44, 45, 46], which should be incorporated into the security patterns template to achieve more usable, robust and complete patterns) that have been considered to carry out our applicability study of security patterns. These features are the considerations (following items) that a security engineer should take into account when applying a security pattern within a real and complex system, because they reflect questions related to parameters as important as cost, performance, usability and manageability.

- *Impact on the other components* of the system (Performance, Cost): it should be checked whether the deployment of the proposed solution is compatible with other components of the system.
- *Complexity in the deployment* of a security pattern (Performance, Cost): it should be checked whether the deployment of the solution has a complexity that the organization may assume.
- *Complexity of use* of a security pattern (Usability): it should be checked whether the use of the solution for final user is the desired one.
- *Complexity of the maintenance* of the solution (Manageability): it should be checked whether the maintenance of the solution may be realizable by security engineers of the organization.

When a security engineer has to design a secure architecture, it is virtually impossible that he has not considered some of the features listed previously. In the case of not analyzing these considerations, the deployment and maintenance cost of the solution may increase dramatically, causing, in this way, the failure of the solution.

We shall carry out an analysis in relation to the aforementioned features. For each of the patterns studied, we shall verify whether it completely satisfies the features raised (F), whether it refers only briefly to these features (P) or whether it neither mentions nor considers them (N).

In Table 1, the vertical columns show the references for the analyzed proposals. These proposals are grouped into several contexts, according to the classification of the studied works of patterns carried out in Section 2. The horizontal rows show the features set out above. In Addition, Figure 1 shows a graphical representation of the analysis performed in Table 1. The following results are related to considerations that should be taken into account when applying security patterns:

Most proposals do not take the impact on the system's other components into account, because they do not consider aspects related to the system's performance after implementing the solution. One proposal makes a slight reference to this consideration [27], but it does not analyze it in depth, that is to say, it speaks about the possible impact on the systems involved, but it does not specify the possible impact on the system's components. Only one proposal fully considers this feature [31].

Table 1. Analysis of Results

		Considerations			
Context of patterns	References	Impact on the other components	Complexity in the deployment	Complexity of use	Complexity of the maintenance
Communications	[27]	P	N	P	P
	[28]	N	N	P	P
	[29]	N	N	P	N
Identity management	[30]	N	N	P	N
	[31]	F	N	N	F
	[32]	N	N	P	N
	[33]	N	N	P	P
Privacy	[34]	N	N	F	N
	[16]	N	N	F	N
	[35]	N	N	F	N
Attacker standpoint	[19]	N	N	N	N
	[36]	N	N	N	N
Trust relationships	[37]	N	N	P	P
	[38]	N	N	N	N
Others	[39]	N	N	P	N
	[40]	N	N	N	P
	[41]	N	N	N	N

None of the proposals consider the complexity that the deployment of the security patterns might entail for the engineers in charge of this work.

With regard to the considerations related to the complexity of security pattern usage, it is possible to observe that a significant amount of the proposals analyzed do not take this consideration into account [41, 31, 19]. A further significant amount of them only make a slight reference to this issue [39, 28, 37], that is to say, they briefly state that the application of the security patterns may have consequences for the people who use them, but they do not provide details on how this increases complexity. Only a few proposals take this consideration fully into account [16, 35, 34].

Finally, in relation to the considerations of complexity in the maintenance of the security pattern when it is applied, it is necessary to emphasize that most proposals ignore this consideration, for example [16, 35, 39, 19]. Some proposals state the need for maintenance of the solution but they do not explain the complexity that this task may imply for the engineers in charge [33, 40, 28]. Only one proposal [31] clearly states the consequences of security pattern implementation at the moment of carrying out maintenance tasks.

The following figure shows a graphical summary of these results.

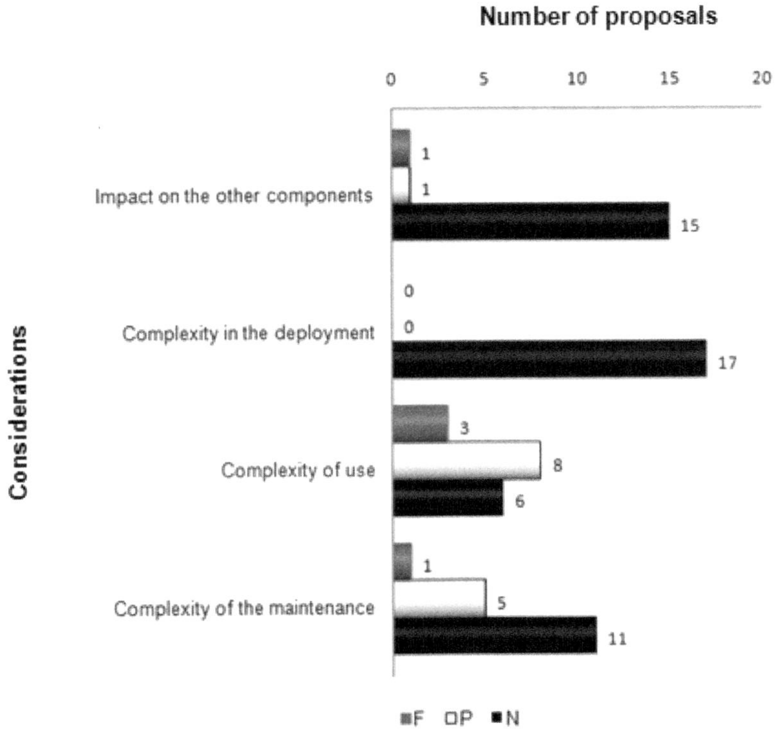

Fig. 1. Graph of the Results

As we have already stated, the main objective of this work is to verify whether the security patterns that exist in the literature can be used for the analysis and design of secure architectures in the field of security engineering in real and complex systems.

As it can be seen from the results, most of the currently described security patterns do not take into account the most important aspects related to the system into which they are introduced. Although these patterns, in their description, include a section called "uses known" which shows that they have been proven, it is not exposed in any section how to implement this solution methodologically within a real and complex system. This section is essential for the development of secure architectures in the field of security engineering, since it provides a clear vision of how to use patterns to add security to an organization's systems. In relation to this, after carrying out this analysis, we have detected a clear differentiation between two types of security patterns particularly concentrating on the security environment to which they can be applied. On the one hand, there are those security patterns which are orientated towards the development of security mechanisms [38]. On the other hand, we can find those security patterns which are orientated towards analyzing and designing secure architectures using the mechanisms previously developed [39]. Once this clear differentiation in the type of pattern had been detected, in this analysis we also detected that the majority of current security patterns are designed to support the development of security mechanisms, such as a secure access system [25] or a secure authentication system [10]. This type of security patterns may be very useful for those security engineers who work to develop this type of mechanisms for large companies (Oracle, Microsoft, IBM, Google, Cisco, etc.) and also for other small and medium enterprises, but they are not applicable to other security engineering sectors, which analyze and design secure architectures within the organizations in which they work. This is due to the fact that the security mechanisms which are incorporated into the architecture of real systems are developed by organizations that are specialized in the development of this kind of artifacts. These mechanisms are then purchased by other companies. For this reason, security patterns should be evolved in order to improve the deployment of these security mechanisms in organizations' technological architectures.

In order to complete current security patterns and make them more applicable to security architectures design, this type of patterns should overcome a set of shortcomings which involve:

- Specifying in the solution how they should be integrated within a real and complex system.
- Detailing the impact that the implementation of the solution will have on the other components in the system.
- Detailing the business processes, the architecture and the number of physical and logical elements of which the information system is comprised.
- Considering the complexity and difficulties that a security engineer may encounter when deploying the solution.
- Considering the complexity of use that the solution will have for the final user.
- Considering how the management and maintenance tasks are performed.

If these shortcomings were to be included in security patterns, these patterns could be improved in order to facilitate the implementation of security mechanisms to support the analysis and design of security architectures in real and complex environments.

5 Conclusions and Future Work

In this work, an analysis has been carried out to verify the applicability of security patterns in the analysis and design of secure architectures in real complex systems. To do this, we have first synthesized a set of proposals that describe security patterns extracted from a systematic review that we performed previously. We have then analyzed their applicability in the field of information security engineering to develop secure architectures. A number of shortcomings in the description of current patterns have subsequently been observed. Finally, a discussion has been presented in which we have attempted to refine the current patterns so that they can be used by information security engineers to design security within real systems. The main shortcoming that we have found is that security patterns, presented as useful guidelines for information security engineers, do not currently satisfy the engineers' actual needs when creating secure architectures. We have detected that this is because most of these patterns do not reflect the potential impact of the deployment of the solution on the various components involved in a system; they do not consider the complexity of the implementation of the pattern for the engineers in charge of this task; they ignore the complexity of using the system when the patterns are applied; and, they do not consider the complexity of maintaining the solution, implemented in the form of a pattern, by the engineers in charge of security in the systems. Therefore, and after stating the detected shortcomings, we have shown the features that should be incorporated into security patterns to make them useful for the analysis and design of secure architectures in real and complex systems.

At present, we are working on the definition of security patterns to enable them to be used in the analysis and design of secure architectures in real environments. These security patterns will be based on real cases obtained from our own experience together with that of some security experts in the field of information security engineering. We are also working on the development of a methodology with which to solve security issues in the field of information security engineering, and we are additionally working on the development of a methodology to guide both experts and non-experts in the analysis and design of security architectures.

Acknowledgements

This research has been carried out within the framework of the following projects: MODEL-CAOS (TIN2008-03582/TIN), ESPIA (TIN2007-67078) financed by the Spanish Ministry of Education and Science, QUASIMODO (PAC08-0157-0668), SISTEMAS (PII2I09-0150-3135) and SEGMENT (HITO-09-138) financed by the "Viceconsejería de Ciencia y Tecnología de la Junta de Comunidades de Castilla-La Mancha" and the FEDER and BUSINESS (PET2008-0136) financed by the "Ministerio de Ciencia e Innovación (CDTI)" (Spain), and IDONEO (PAC08-0160-6141), financed by the "Consejería de Ciencia y Tecnología de la Junta de Comunidades de Castilla-La Mancha".

References

1. The Open Web Application Security Project, OWASP (2010), `http://www.owasp.org`
2. Halkidis, S.T., Tsantalis, N., Chatzigeorgiou, A., Stephanides, G.: Architectural Risk Analysis of Software Systems Based on Security Patterns. IEEE Transactions on Dependable and Secure Computing, 129–142 (2008)
3. Alexander, C., Ishikawa, S., Silverstein, M.: A Pattern Language: Towns, Buildings, Constructions. Oxford University Press, Oxford (1977)
4. Fernández, E.B.: Security patterns and secure systems design. In: ACM Southeast Regional Conference (2007)
5. Fernandez, E., Washizaki, H., Yoshioka, N., Kubo, A., Fukazawa, Y.: Classifying Security Patterns. In: Progress in WWW Research and Development, pp. 342–347 (2008)
6. Fernandez, E.B., Wu, J., Larrondo-Petrie, M.M., Shao, Y.: On building secure SCADA systems using security patterns. In: Proceedings of the 5th Annual Workshop on Cyber Security and Information Intelligence Research: Cyber Security and Information Intelligence Challenges and Strategies, Oak Ridge, Tennessee (2009)
7. Maña, A., Serrano, D., Ruiz, J.F., Armenteros, A., Crespo, B.G.N., Muñoz, A.: Development of Applications Based on Security Patterns. In: Second International Conference on Dependability, DEPEND 2009, pp. 111–116 (2009)
8. Kienzle, D.M., Elder, M.C., Tyree, D., Edwards-Hewitt, J.: Security patterns repository, version 1.0 (2006)
9. Rosado, D.G., Gutiérrez, C., Fernández-Medina, E., Piattini, M.: Security patterns and requirements for internet-based applications. Internet Research: Electronic Networking Applications and Policy (2006)
10. Schumacher, M., Fernandez-Buglioni, E., Hybertson, D., Buschmann, F., Sommerlad, P.: Security Patterns: Integrating Security and Systems Engineering. Wiley, Chichester (2006)
11. Yskout, K., Heyman, T., Scandariato, R., Joosen, W.: An inventory of security patterns. Technical Report CW-469, Katholieke Universiteit Leuven, Department of Computer Science (2006)
12. Fernandez, E.B., Washizaki, H., Yoshioka, N.: Abstract security patterns. In: Proceedings of the 15th Conference on Pattern Languages of Programs, Nashville, Tennessee (2008)
13. Okubo, T., Tanaka, H.: Web security patterns for analysis and design. In: Proceedings of the 15th Conference on Pattern Languages of Programs, Nashville, Tennessee (2008)
14. Ortega-Arjona, J. L., Fernandez, E. B.: The secure blackboard pattern. In: Proceedings of the 15th Conference on Pattern Languages of Programs, Nashville, Tennessee (2008)
15. Serenity Project - System Engineering for Security & Dependability (2010), `http://www.serenity-project.org`
16. Schumacher, M.: B. Example Security Patterns and Annotations. In: Schumacher, M. (ed.) Security Engineering with Patterns. LNCS, vol. 2754, pp. 171–178. Springer, Heidelberg (2003)
17. Garzás, J., Piattini, M.: Object Oriented Microarchitectural Design Knowledge. IEEE Software, 28–33 (2005)

18. Anwar, Z., Yurcik, W., Johnson, R.E., Hafiz, M., Campbell, R.H.: Multiple design patterns for voice over IP (VoIP) security. In: 25th IEEE International Performance, Computing, and Communications Conference, IPCCC 2006 (2006)
19. Fernandez, E. B., Yoshioka, N., Washizaki, H.: Modeling Misuse Patterns. In International Conference on Availability, Reliability and Security, ARES 2009, pp. 566–571 (2009)
20. Moral-Garcia, S., Ortiz, R., Vela, B., Garzás, J., Fernández-Medina, E.: Patrones de Seguridad: ?'Homogéneos, validados y útiles. In: RECSI XI, Tarragona, Spain (submit accepted)
21. Fernandez, E.B., Pernul, G., Larrondo-Petrie, M.M.: Patterns and Pattern Diagrams for Access Control. In: Furnell, S.M., Katsikas, S.K., Lioy, A. (eds.) TrustBus 2008. LNCS, vol. 5185, pp. 38–47. Springer, Heidelberg (2008)
22. Sarmah, A., Hazarika, S.M., Sinha, S.K.: Security Pattern Lattice: A Formal Model to Organize Security Patterns. In: Bhowmick, S.S., Küng, J., Wagner, R. (eds.) DEXA 2008. LNCS, vol. 5181, pp. 292–296. Springer, Heidelberg (2008)
23. Heyman, T., Yskout, K., Scandariato, R., Joosen, W.: An Analysis of the Security Patterns Landscape. In: Proceedings of the Third International Workshop on Software Engineering for Secure Systems (2007)
24. Washizaki, H., Fernandez, E.B., Maruyama, K., Kubo, A., Yoshioka, N.: Improving the Classification of Security Patterns. In: 20th International Workshop on Database and Expert Systems Application, DEXA 2009, pp. 165–170 (2009)
25. Fernandez, E.: Security Patterns and Secure Systems Design. In: Dependable Computing, pp. 233–234 (2007)
26. Kitchenham, B.: Guideline for performing Systematic Literature Reviews in Software Engineering. Version 2.3. University of Keele (Software Engineering Group, School of Computer Science and Mathematics) and Durham (Department of Conputer Science) (2007)
27. Fernandez, E.B., Pelaez, J.C., Larrondo-Petrie, M.M.: Security Patterns for Voice over IP Networks. In: International Multi-Conference on Computing in the Global Information Technology, ICCGI 2007, pp. 33–33 (2007)
28. Chavhan, N.A., Chhabria, S.A.: Multiple design patterns for voice over IP security. In: Proceedings of the International Conference on Advances in Computing, Communication and Control, Mumbai, India (2009)
29. Fernandez, E.B., Ortega-Arjona, J.L.: The Secure Pipes and Filters Pattern. In: 20th International Workshop on Database and Expert Systems Application, DEXA 2009, pp. 181–185 (2009)
30. Delessy, N., Fernandez, E.B., Larrondo-Petrie, M.M.: A Pattern Language for Identity Management. In: International Multi-Conference on Computing in the Global Information Technology, ICCGI 2007, p. 31 (2007)
31. Cuevas, A., El Khoury, P., Gomez, L., Laube, A.: Security Patterns for Capturing Encryption-Based Access Control to Sensor Data. In: Second International Conference on Emerging Security Information, Systems and Technologies, SECURWARE 2008, pp. 62–67 (2008)
32. Morrison, P., Fernandez, E.B.: The credentials pattern. In: Proceedings of the 2006 conference on Pattern languages of programs, Portland, Oregon (2006)
33. Fernandez, E.B., Pernul, G.: Patterns for session-based access control. In: Proceedings of the 2006 conference on Pattern languages of programs, Portland, Oregon (2006)
34. Lobato, L.L., Fernandez, E.B., Zorzo, S.D.: Patterns to Support the Development of Privacy Policies. In: International Conference on Availability, Reliability and Security, ARES 2009, pp. 744–749 (2009)

35. Romanosky, S., Acquisti, A., Hong, J., Cranor, L.F., Friedman, B.: Privacy patterns for online interactions. In: Proceedings of the 2006 conference on Pattern languages of programs, Portland, Oregon (2006)
36. Fernandez, E., Pelaez, J., Larrondo-Petrie, M.: Attack Patterns: A New Forensic and Design Tool. In: Advances in Digital Forensics III, pp. 345–357 (2007)
37. Fischer, T., Sadeghi, A.R., Winandy, M.: A Pattern for Secure Graphical User Interface Systems. In: 20th International Workshop on Database and Expert Systems Application, DEXA 2009, pp. 186–190 (2009)
38. Sorniotti, A., El Khoury, P., Gomez, L., Cuevas, A., Laube, A.: A Security Pattern for Untraceable Secret Handshakes. In: SECURWARE 2009. Third International Conference on Emerging Security Information, Systems and Technologies, pp. 8–14 (2009)
39. Fernandez, E.B., Fonoage, M., VanHilst, M., Marta, M.: The Secure Three-Tier Architecture Pattern. In: International Conference on Complex, Intelligent and Software Intensive Systems, CISIS 2008, pp. 555–560 (2008)
40. Fernandez, E.B., Sorgente, T., Larrondo-Petrie, M.M.: Even more patterns for secure operating systems. In: Proceedings of the 2006 conference on Pattern languages of programs, Portland, Oregon (2006)
41. Spanoudakis, G., Kloukinas, C., Androutsopoulos, K.: Towards security monitoring patterns. In: Proceedings of the 2007 ACM symposium on Applied computing, Seoul, Korea (2007)
42. Schumacher, M.: Security Patterns - Security Patterns - Just another Way to Share Best Practices (2003), https://www.sdn.sap.com
43. Dougherty, C., Sayre, K., Seacord, R.C., Svoboda, D., Togashi, K.: Secure Design Patterns. Technical Report, CMU/SEI-2009-TR-010, ESC-TR-2009-010 (2009)
44. Kienzle, D.M., Elder, M.C., Tyree, D.S., Edwards-Hewitt, J.: Security patterns template and tutorial (2002)
45. The Open Group, Guide to Security Patterns - Arquitectural Patterns (2010), http://www.opengroup.org/architecture/togaf7-doc/arch/p4/patterns/patterns.htm
46. Moral-García, S., Ortiz, R., Moral-Rubio, S., Vela, B., Garzás, J., Fernández-Medina, E.: A New Pattern Template to Support the Design of Security Architectures. In: The Second International Conferences of Pervasive Patterns and Applications (submit-accepted, 2010)

Leakage Quantification of Cryptographic Operations*

Michael Wibmer[1], Debmalya Biswas[2], and Florian Kerschbaum[2]

[1] Interdisciplinary Center for Scientific Computing, Heidelberg University, Im Neuenheimer Feld 368, Heidelberg, Germany 69120
wibmer@uni-heidelberg.de
[2] SAP Research, Vincenz-Priessnitz-Strasse 1, Karlsruhe, Germany 76131
firstname.lastname@sap.com

Abstract. Perfectly secure protocols are often too inefficient performance wise to be used in a practical setting. On the other hand, an insecure (but faster) protocol might be deemed secure for a particular setting. Recent research has thus focused on precise leakage quantification of a security protocol. In this context, we first give precise leakage quantification of a basic cryptographic primitive, that of multiplicative hiding. We then show how the approach can be extended to compute worst case leakage bounds of arbitrary compositions of cryptographic operations. The composition results make our bounds applicable to a wide range of general security protocols.

1 Introduction

A fundamental question in analyzing the security of cryptographic protocols is to quantify the "strength of security". The problem is that even secure protocols leak some information however small, e.g. each unsuccessful run of a password checking program leaks information that the entered password was wrong. Basically, in the absence of perfect security, the all-or-nothing semantics (a protocol is either secure or insecure) does not work. Properties like non-interference [1] appear too strict in this context as "a single bit of compromised information is flagged as a security violation, even if one bit is all that is lost". This results in far too many protocols being characterized as insecure. In a practical setting, a protocol with some leakage can also be deemed secure after considering external factors such as the protocol control flow, execution stage at which leakage occurred, computational power of the attacker, criticality of the application, etc. The emphasis in this paper is thus on quantifying leakage, so that informed and practical decisions can be taken with respect to the security of a given protocol. Such quantifications are essential for complex cryptographic protocols to be usable in high performance settings.

The motivation for leakage quantification comes from our work in the domain of secure multiparty computation for the EU project SecureSCM [2]. SecureSCM

* This work is partly funded by the European Commission through the ICT program under Framework 7 grant 213531 to the SecureSCM project.

R. Meersman et al. (Eds.): OTM 2010, Part I, LNCS 6426, pp. 685–700, 2010.

deals with the problem of optimal planning in a supply chain network. Supply chain planning can be modeled as a linear program. The objective then is to solve linear equations in the framework of secure multiparty computation. The partners in the supply chain network correspond to parties in the multiparty framework. A secure multiparty version of the simplex algorithm that can be used to solve large linear programs is given in [10]. However, on actual implementation, we found the performance of the secure simplex protocol to be absolutely unfit for practical usage (the runtime of a computation with 5-6 parties was in the range of days). We drilled down the performance bottleneck to the secure comparison protocol that is invoked multiple times in a run of the simplex algorithm. In theory, it is well known that any multiparty function can be securely computed using generic circuit based protocols [4]. However, the general protocols tend to be very inefficient for practical usage, as also experienced by us in our experiments. We consequently proposed a fast[1] but not perfectly secure comparison protocol in [6]. The need then was for a statistical framework to be able to perform precise leakage quantification of such protocols.

We model the information flow in a security protocol as a discrete noisy channel and the desired measure is the leakage of this channel. Intuitively the leakage measures how much observing the output of the channel increases the ability of an adversary to guess the input of the channel. More precisely it is defined as the ratio of the ability of the adversary to guess the input of the channel before observing the output and after observing the output. See [5,8].

We first give a concrete application of the statistical measure to perform leakage quantification of "multiplicative hiding". Multiplicative hiding is a basic cryptographic primitive that consists of hiding a value x by multiplying it with a much larger random number r. In order to prevent factoring [9], a smaller random number $r' < r$ is further added. The leakage then depends on how effectively the channel "$y = rx + r'$" hides the input value x. We give precise upper and lower leakage bounds of this channel in Section 3.

Composition is a very powerful mechanism in security that allows us to reason about the leakage of a cryptographic protocol based on the leakages of its primitive operations. To the best of our knowledge, very few works have considered leakage composition in security literature. We give initial results to reason about the worst case leakage or leakage supremum of certain compositions in Section 4. The composition theorems lead to some interesting observations, e.g. the leakage supremum of a composite channel is less than or equal to that of the primitive channel having the least leakage supremum (See Theorem 2).

Section 5 discusses related works and Section 6 concludes the paper.

2 Notations and Preliminaries

We fix once and for all a universal probability space (Ω, Σ, p). All random variables will be discrete and defined on Ω (or measurable subsets of Ω). If

[1] The protocol is significantly faster than the state-of-the-art perfectly secure comparison protocol [7].

$\mathcal{X} = \{x_1, \ldots, x_n\}$ is a finite set then $\mathrm{Var}(\mathcal{X})$ denotes the set of random variables defined on Ω taking values in $\mathcal{X}$. If $X \in \mathrm{Var}(\mathcal{X})$ then $\overrightarrow{X} = (p(X = x_1), \ldots, p(X = x_n))$ denotes the distribution of X.

Definition 1 (Channel). *A channel (discrete, noisy, memoryless) C is given by the following data.*

- *A finite set $\mathcal{X} = \{x_1, \ldots, x_n\}$ called the* input alphabet,
- *a finite set $\mathcal{Y} = \{y_1, \ldots, y_m\}$ called the* output alphabet *and*
- *for each $x \in X$ a random variable $C|x$ that takes values in $\mathcal{Y}$.*

We use the notation $\mathcal{X} \xrightarrow{C} \mathcal{Y}$ to express that C is a channel with input alphabet $\mathcal{X}$ and output alphabet $\mathcal{Y}$. For each $x \in \mathcal{X}$ and $y \in \mathcal{Y}$

$$p(y|x) := p(C|x = y)$$

is the probability that the output of the channel is y when the input is x. The $n \times m$ matrix

$$M(C) := (p(y_j|x_i))_{1 \leq i \leq n, 1 \leq j \leq m}$$

is called the *channel matrix*. The channel determines a map $\mathrm{Var}(\mathcal{X}) \to \mathrm{Var}(\mathcal{Y})$, $X \mapsto C(X)$ by

$$C(X)(\omega) = (C|X(\omega))(\omega)$$

for every ω in Ω.

We say that a random variable is *independent from the channel C* if it is independent from $C|x$ for every $x \in \mathcal{X}$. If $X \in \mathrm{Var}(\mathcal{X})$ is independent from the channel then for $x_i \in \mathcal{X}$ and $y_j \in \mathcal{Y}$ we have

$$p(C(X) = y_j|X = x_i) = p(C|x_i = y_j|X = x_i) = p(C|x_i = y_j)$$

and so

$$\begin{aligned} p(C(X) = y_j) &= \sum_{i=1}^{n} p(X = x_i) p(C(X) = y_j|X = x_i) \\ &= \sum_{i=1}^{n} p(X = x_i) p(C|x_i = y_j). \end{aligned}$$

This means that if X is independent from C then

$$\overrightarrow{C(X)} = \overrightarrow{X} M(C).$$

Definition 2 (Independent Channels). *We say that two channels $\mathcal{X} \xrightarrow{C} \mathcal{Y}$ and $\mathcal{X}' \xrightarrow{C'} \mathcal{Y}'$ are* independent *if $C|x$ is independent from $C'|x'$ for every $x \in \mathcal{X}$ and $x' \in \mathcal{X}'$.*

In practice a channel is a protocol that has as input an integer (in a certain range) and then performs certain arithmetic operations on this integer possibly involving random numbers. To say that two such programs are independent means that the random numbers used in the first program are independent from the random numbers used in the second program (and this is the case by definition, more or less).

To model the leakage of a channel or security protocol, we consider the following scenario: The adversary knows the channel C and the distribution of the input variable X which is assumed to be independent from the channel. He is observing the output variable $Y = C(X)$ and then tries to guess the input of the channel. Intuitively, the leakage $\mathcal{L}_X(C)$ of C with respect to X measures how much observing the output of C increases the ability of the adversary to guess the input. It is defined as the ratio between the ability of the adversary to guess the input before observing the channel and after observing the channel. If the adversary has to guess the input without access to the channel the best strategy for him is to guess a $x \in \mathcal{X}$ such that the probability of $X = x$ is maximal. So the probability that the adversary can guess the right input without observing the channel (the a priori probability of a right guess) is

$$\mathrm{PR}_{priori}(X) = \max_{x \in \mathcal{X}} p(X = x).$$

When observing a given output $y \in \mathcal{Y}$, the best strategy for the adversary is to guess an input $x \in \mathcal{X}$ that maximizes the probability that the input is x under the assumption that the output is y. I.e. he wants to maximize

$$p(x|y) = p(X = x|C(X) = y).$$

This strategy is also referred to as the Maximum A Posteriori probability (MAP) rule. The overall probability then that the adversary can guess the correct input after observing the channel is

$$\begin{aligned}\mathrm{PR}_{posteriori}(X) &= \sum_{y \in \mathcal{Y}} p(C(X) = y) \max_{x \in \mathcal{X}} p(x|y) = \sum_{y \in \mathcal{Y}} \max_{x \in \mathcal{X}} p(X = x, C(X) = y) \\ &= \sum_{y \in \mathcal{Y}} \max_{x \in \mathcal{X}} p(X = x, C|x = y) = \sum_{y \in \mathcal{Y}} \max_{x \in \mathcal{X}} (p(X = x)p(y|x)).\end{aligned}$$

Then the leakage of C with respect to X is defined as

$$\mathcal{L}_X(C) = \frac{\mathrm{PR}_{posteriori}(X)}{\mathrm{PR}_{priori}(X)}.$$

This is referred to as the multiplicative leakage in [5].

Because $\max_{x \in \mathcal{X}} p(X = x) \leq \mathrm{PR}_{posteriori}(X) \leq 1$ and $\max_{x \in \mathcal{X}} p(X = x) \geq \frac{1}{|\mathcal{X}|}$ we see that $\mathcal{L}_X(C)$ takes values between 1 and $|\mathcal{X}|$, the cardinality of the input alphabet.

We define the leakage $\mathcal{L}(C)$ of the channel C as the supremum of the leakages with respect to X, where $X \in \mathrm{Var}(\mathcal{X})$ runs over all random variables independent from the channel.

$$\mathcal{L}(C) = \sup_X \mathcal{L}_X(C).$$

As it was already observed in [5] one has

$$\mathcal{L}(C) = \mathcal{L}_U(C) = \sum_{y \in \mathcal{Y}} \max_{x \in \mathcal{X}} p(y|x) \tag{1}$$

where $U \in \mathrm{Var}(\mathcal{X})$ is a uniformly distributed.

We collect the basic properties of leakage in the following proposition.

Proposition 1. *Let $\mathcal{X} \xrightarrow{C} \mathcal{Y}$ be a channel. Then the leakage $\mathcal{L}(C)$ is a real value between 1 and $|\mathcal{X}|$, the cardinality of the input alphabet. The leakage assumes the minimal value 1 iff the output of C does not depend on the input, i.e. for $x, x' \in \mathcal{X}$ the distributions of $C|x$ and $C|x'$ are identical. The leakage assumes the maximal value $|\mathcal{X}|$ iff the output reveals the input, i.e. for every $y \in \mathcal{Y}$ there exists at most one $x \in \mathcal{X}$ with $p(y|x) > 0$.*

Proof. We already observed above that $1 \leq \mathcal{L}_X(C) \leq |\mathcal{X}|$. Thus also $1 \leq \mathcal{L}(C) \leq |X|$. Assume that the leakage is 1 and fix $x' \in \mathcal{X}$. Then

$$1 = \sum_{y \in \mathcal{Y}} \max_{x \in \mathcal{X}} p(y|x) \geq \sum_{y \in \mathcal{Y}} p(y|x') = 1$$

shows that $p(y|x') = \max_{x \in \mathcal{X}} p(y|x)$. As $x' \in \mathcal{X}$ was arbitrary this shows that $p(y|x)$ does not depend on x.

Now assume that $\sum_{y \in \mathcal{Y}} \max_{x \in \mathcal{X}} p(y|x) = |\mathcal{X}|$. The sum of all entries in the channel matrix equals $|\mathcal{X}|$. So if the sum of the maxima of each column also equals $|\mathcal{X}|$, this means that each column has at most one non-zero entry. □

3 Leakage Quantification of Multiplicative Hiding

In this section, we provide leakage quantification of the multiplicative hiding primitive. Let $x_m \geq 0$ and $r_m \geq 1$ be integers. We define a channel "$y = rx + r'$" as follows: The input alphabet is $\mathcal{X} = \{0, \ldots, x_m\}$. The output alphabet is $\mathcal{Y} = \{0, \ldots, r_m x_m + r_m - 1\}$. For input $x \in \mathcal{X}$ the channel outputs $y = rx + r' \in \mathcal{Y}$ where r is a random number chosen uniformly from $\{1, \ldots, r_m\}$ and r' is a random number chosen uniformly from $\{0, \ldots, r - 1\}$. (So $0 \leq r' < r \leq r_m$.)

For $x \in \mathcal{X}$ and $y \in \mathcal{Y}$, let $N(x, y)$ denote the number of pairs (r, r') with $0 \leq r' < r \leq r_m$ and $y = rx + r'$. The number of all pairs (with $0 \leq r' < r \leq r_m$) equals $\frac{1}{2}((r_m + 1)^2 - (r_m + 1)) = \frac{r_m^2 + r_m}{2}$. Thus the probability that the channel outputs y when the input is x equals

$$p(y|x) = \frac{2N(x,y)}{r_m^2 + r_m}.$$

Next we will show that for $x \in \mathcal{X},\ x \geq 1$ and $y \in \mathcal{Y}$:

$$N(x,y) = \min\left\{r_m, \left\lfloor\frac{y}{x}\right\rfloor\right\} - \left\lceil\frac{y+1}{x+1}\right\rceil + 1 \tag{2}$$

We have

$$\begin{aligned} N(x,y) &= \#\left\{(r,r');\ 0 \leq r' < r \leq r_m,\ y = rx + r'\right\} \\ &= \#\{r;\ 1 \leq r \leq r_m,\ 0 \leq y - rx \leq r - 1\} \end{aligned}$$

The statement $0 \leq y - rx$ is equivalent to $r \leq \frac{y}{x}$ and $y - rx \leq r - 1$ is equivalent to $r \geq \frac{y+1}{x+1}$ and implies $r \geq 1$. Therefore $N(x,y)$ equals the number of integers r between $\frac{y+1}{x+1}$ and $\min\{r_m, \frac{y}{x}\}$. In other words, $N(x,y) = \min\left\{r_m, \left\lfloor\frac{y}{x}\right\rfloor\right\} - \left\lceil\frac{y+1}{x+1}\right\rceil + 1$.

As the next step we will show that

$$\max_{x \in \mathcal{X}} N(x,y) \leq \frac{y + r_m^2}{y + r_m} \tag{3}$$

We first treat the case $x \geq 1$. We consider the function $f(x) = \min\left\{r_m, \frac{y}{x}\right\} - \frac{y+1}{x+1} + 1$ as a real function of a real $x \geq 1$. We want to show that f assumes its maximum at $x = \frac{y}{r_m}$. If $1 \leq x \leq \frac{y}{r_m}$ then $f(x) = r_m - \frac{y+1}{x+1} + 1$ and the maximal value $r_m - \frac{y+1}{\frac{y}{r_m}+1} + 1 = \frac{y+r_m^2}{y+r_m}$ is assumed at $x = \frac{y}{r_m}$. If $x \geq \frac{y}{r_m}$,

$$f(x) = \frac{y}{x} - \frac{y+1}{x+1} + 1 = \frac{y-x}{x(x+1)} + 1$$

is decreasing as a function of x at least as long as $x \leq y$ and if $x > y$ then $f(x) < 1 \leq \frac{y+r_m^2}{y+r_m}$. Thus the maximal value assumed by f on $[1, +\infty)$ equals $\frac{y+r_m^2}{y+r_m}$. We have

$$\begin{aligned} \max_{x \in \mathcal{X}, x \geq 1} N(x,y) &= \max_{x \in \mathcal{X},\ x \geq 1} \left(\min\left\{r_m, \left\lfloor\frac{y}{x}\right\rfloor\right\} - \left\lceil\frac{y+1}{x+1}\right\rceil + 1\right) \\ &\leq \max_{x \in \mathcal{X}, x \geq 1} f(x) \leq \frac{y + r_m^2}{y + r_m} \end{aligned}$$

Now we treat the case $x = 0$. We have

$$N(0,y) = \#\{(r,r');\ 0 \leq r' < r \leq r_m,\ y = r'\} = \begin{cases} r_m - y & \text{if } y \leq r_m - 1 \\ 0 & \text{otherwise} \end{cases} \tag{4}$$

Because $r_m - y \leq \frac{y+r_m^2}{y+r_m}$, inequality 3) is proved. We are now in a position to give the leakage bounds of $y = rx + r'$.

3.1 Upper Bound

We first compute the upper bound for the leakage of $y = rx + r'$

$$\mathcal{L}(y = xr + r') = \sum_{y \in \mathcal{Y}} \max_{x \in \mathcal{X}} p(y|x) = \sum_{y \in \mathcal{Y}} \frac{2}{r_m^2 + r_m} \max_{x \in \mathcal{X}} N(x,y)$$
$$\leq \frac{2}{r_m^2 + r_m} \sum_{y=0}^{y_m} \frac{y + r_m^2}{y + r_m}$$

where $y_m = r_m x_m + r_m - 1$. Let $g(y) = \frac{y+r_m^2}{y+r_m}$. Because $g'(y) = \frac{r_m - r_m^2}{(y+r_m)^2} \leq 0$ we see that g is decreasing in y and so

$$\sum_{y=0}^{y_m} \frac{y + r_m^2}{y + r_m} \leq \int_{-1}^{y_m} \frac{y + r_m^2}{y + r_m}\, dy = \int_{r_m - 1}^{y_m + r_m} \frac{y - r_m + r_m^2}{y}\, dy$$
$$= \int_{r_m - 1}^{y_m + r_m} 1\, dy + (r_m^2 - r_m) \int_{r_m - 1}^{y_m + r_m} \frac{1}{y}\, dy$$
$$= y_m + r_m - (r_m - 1) + (r_m^2 - r_m)(\log(y_m + r_m) - \log(r_m - 1))$$
$$= r_m(x_m + 1) + (r_m^2 - r_m) \log\left(\frac{r_m(x_m + 2) - 1}{r_m - 1}\right).$$

Summarily we obtain

$$\mathcal{L}(y = rx + r') \leq \frac{2\left(x_m + 1 + (r_m - 1)\log\left(\frac{r_m(x_m+2)-1}{r_m-1}\right)\right)}{r_m + 1} \tag{5}$$

3.2 Lower Bound

Now we will establish a lower bound for the leakage of $y = rx + r'$. For $y \in \mathcal{Y}$ we have $\left\lfloor \frac{y}{r_m} \right\rfloor \leq \frac{y}{r_m}$ and so $r_m \leq \frac{y}{\left\lfloor \frac{y}{r_m} \right\rfloor}$ if $\left\lfloor \frac{y}{r_m} \right\rfloor \geq 1$. Thus it follows from equations (2) and (4) that

$$\max_{x \in \mathcal{X}} N(x,y) \geq N\left(\left\lfloor \frac{y}{r_m} \right\rfloor, y\right) = r_m - \left\lceil \frac{y+1}{\left\lfloor \frac{y}{r_m} \right\rfloor + 1} \right\rceil + 1.$$

We have

$$\begin{aligned}
\sum_{y\in\mathcal{Y}} \left\lceil \frac{y+1}{\left\lfloor \frac{y}{r_m} \right\rfloor + 1} \right\rceil &= \sum_{x=0}^{x_m} \sum_{k=0}^{r_m-1} \left\lceil \frac{r_m x + k + 1}{\left\lfloor \frac{r_m x + k}{r_m} \right\rfloor + 1} \right\rceil \\
&= \sum_{x=0}^{x_m} \sum_{k=0}^{r_m-1} \left\lceil \frac{r_m x + k + 1}{x+1} \right\rceil \\
&\leq \sum_{x=0}^{x_m} \sum_{k=0}^{r_m-1} \left(\frac{r_m x + k + 1}{x+1} + 1 \right) \\
&= \sum_{x=0}^{x_m} \sum_{k=0}^{r_m-1} \frac{(r_m+1)x + k + 2}{x+1} \\
&= \sum_{x=0}^{x_m} \frac{1}{x+1} \left(r_m((r_m+1)x+2) + \sum_{k=0}^{r_m-1} k \right) \\
&= \sum_{x=0}^{x_m} \frac{1}{x+1} \left(r_m((r_m+1)x+2) + \frac{1}{2}(r_m-1)r_m \right) \\
&= \frac{1}{2} \sum_{x=0}^{x_m} \frac{2(r_m^2+r_m)x + r_m^2 + 3r_m}{x+1}
\end{aligned}$$

We consider $f(x) = \frac{2(r_m^2+r_m)x+r_m^2+3r_m}{x+1}$ as a continuous function of $x \geq 0$. Then

$$f'(x) = \frac{r_m^2 - r_m}{(x+1)^2} \geq 0$$

and we see that $f(x)$ is increasing in x. Therefore

$$\sum_{x=0}^{x_m} f(x) \leq \int_0^{x_m+1} f(x)\, dx = 2(r_m^2+r_m)(x_m+1) - (r_m^2 - r_m)\log(x_m+2)$$

as one computes easily. Summarily we obtain

$$\sum_{y\in\mathcal{Y}} \left\lceil \frac{y+1}{\left\lfloor \frac{y}{r_m} \right\rfloor + 1} \right\rceil \leq (r_m^2+r_m)(x_m+1) - \frac{1}{2}(r_m^2 - r_m)\log(x_m+2)$$

and

$$\sum_{y\in\mathcal{Y}} \max_{x\in\mathcal{X}} N(x,y) \geq \sum_{y\in\mathcal{Y}} \left(r_m + 1 - \left\lceil \frac{y+1}{\left\lfloor \frac{y}{r_m} \right\rfloor + 1} \right\rceil \right)$$
$$\geq (r_m x_m + r_m)(r_m+1) - \left((r_m^2 + r_m)(x_m+1) - \frac{1}{2}(r_m^2 - r_m)\log(x_m+2) \right)$$
$$= \frac{1}{2}(r_m^2 - r_m)\log(x_m+2).$$

Finally we see that

$$\sum_{y\in\mathcal{Y}} \max_{x\in\mathcal{X}} p(y|x) = \sum_{y\in\mathcal{Y}} \max_{x\in\mathcal{X}} \frac{2N(x,y)}{r_m^2 + r_m} \geq \frac{(r_m^2 - r_m)\log(x_m+2)}{r_m^2 + r_m}.$$

Therefore

$$\mathcal{L}(y = rx + r') \geq \frac{(r_m - 1)\log(x_m+2)}{r_m + 1}. \tag{6}$$

3.3 Leakage Bounds

Making r_m large in equations (5) and (6) we obtain the following theorem.

Theorem 1. *In the limit $r_m \to +\infty$ we have the following bounds for the leakage of the channel $y = rx + r'$*

$$\log(x_m + 2) \;\leq\; \mathcal{L}(y = rx + r') \;\leq\; 2\log(x_m + 2).$$

The leakage of a channel is a value between 1 and the input size of the channel. In our case the input size is $x_m + 1$. Because $2\log(x_m + 2)$ is small compared to $x_m + 1$ we can conclude that that the operation $y = rx + r'$ is well-suited for hiding the value of x (when r_m is chosen sufficiently large enough). For example if $x_m = 1000000$ and $r_m = 2000000$ then it follows from the bound in equation (5) that the leakage of $y = rx + r'$ is lesser equal to 28.7. If $r_m = 10000$ we still obtain a bound of 227.7.

4 Composition of Channels and Their Leakages

If one is interested in computing (or bounding) the leakage of fairly sophisticated channels as they appear in real-life applications, it is important to be able to compute the overall leakage of a composite channel based on the leakages of its component channels. Therefore we present in this section some formulas and bounds for the leakage of certain compositions of channels.

4.1 Composition of Channels

Definition 3 (Composition of Channels). *Let* $\mathcal{X} \xrightarrow{C_1} \mathcal{Y}$ *and* $\mathcal{Y} \xrightarrow{C_2} \mathcal{Z}$ *be two channels. Then we can define the composition channel* $\mathcal{X} \xrightarrow{C_2 \circ C_1} \mathcal{Z}$ *by*

$$(C_2 \circ C_1|x)(\omega) = (C_2|(C_1|x)(\omega))(\omega)$$

for every $x \in \mathcal{X}$ *and* $\omega \in \Omega$.

Theorem 2. *Let* $\mathcal{X} \xrightarrow{C_1} \mathcal{Y}$ *and* $\mathcal{Y} \xrightarrow{C_2} \mathcal{Z}$ *be two independent channels. Then,* $M(C_2 \circ C_1) = M(C_1)M(C_2)$ *and* $\mathcal{L}(C_2 \circ C_1) \leq \min\{\mathcal{L}(C_1), \mathcal{L}(C_2)\}$.

Proof. Because C_1 and C_2 are independent we have

$$p\left((C_2 \circ C_1)|x = z \middle| \, C_1|x = y\right) = p\left(C_2|y = z \middle| \, C_1|x = y\right) = p(C_2|y = z)$$

and so

$$\begin{aligned} p((C_2 \circ C_1)|x = z) &= \sum_y p(C_1|x = y)p((C_2 \circ C_1)|x = z \middle| \, C_1|x = y) \\ &= \sum_y p(C_1|x = y)p(C_2|y = z). \end{aligned}$$

This shows that $M(C_2 \circ C_1) = M(C_1)M(C_2)$. We have

$$\begin{aligned} \max_x p((C_2 \circ C_1)|x = z) &= \max_x \sum_y p(C_1|x = y)p(C_2|y = z) \\ &\leq \sum_y \max_x p(C_1|x = y)p(C_2|y = z) \end{aligned}$$

and so

$$\begin{aligned} \mathcal{L}(C_2 \circ C_1) &= \sum_z \max_x p((C_2 \circ C_1)|x = z) \leq \sum_z \sum_y \max_x p(C_1|x = y)p(C_2|y = z) \\ &= \sum_y \max_x p(C_1|x = y) \sum_z p(C_2|y = z) = \sum_y \max_x p(C_1|x = y) \cdot 1 \\ &= \mathcal{L}(C_1). \end{aligned}$$

On the other hand because $\sum_y p(C_1|x = y) = 1$ it follows that

$$\begin{aligned} \max_x p((C_2 \circ C_1)|x = z) &= \max_x \sum_y p(C_1|x = y)p(C_2|y = z) \\ &\leq \max_x \sum_y p(C_1|x = y) \max_y p(C_2|y = z) \\ &= \max_y p(C_2|y = z). \end{aligned}$$

Therefore

$$\mathcal{L}(C_2 \circ C_1) = \sum_z \max_x p((C_2 \circ C_1)|x = z)$$
$$\leq \sum_z \max_y p(C_2|y = z) = \mathcal{L}(C_2).$$

□

In practice one often encounters independent channels. For example in round based protocols party P_{i+1} is operating independently from party P_i. We give sample protocols below to illustrate our leakage bounds.

Example 1. Let $\mathcal{X} = \{x_1, x_2, x_3\}, \mathcal{Y} = \{y_1, y_2, y_3\}$ and $\mathcal{Z} = \{z_1, z_2, z_3\}$. Let $\mathcal{X} \xrightarrow{C_1} \mathcal{Y}$ and $\mathcal{Y} \xrightarrow{C_2} \mathcal{Z}$ be two independent channels with channel matrices

C_1	y_1	y_2	y_3
x_1	1/2	1/4	1/4
x_2	1/4	1/2	1/4
x_3	1/4	1/4	1/2

C_2	z_1	z_2	z_3
y_1	1/2	1/4	1/4
y_2	1/4	1/2	1/4
y_3	1/4	1/4	1/2

We have $\mathcal{L}(C_1) = \mathcal{L}(C_2) = \frac{1}{2} + \frac{1}{2} + \frac{1}{2} = \frac{3}{2}$. The channel matrix $M(C_2 \circ C_1) = M(C_1)M(C_2)$ of $C_2 \circ C_1$ is

	z_1	z_2	z_3
x_1	3/8	5/16	5/16
x_2	5/16	3/8	5/16
x_3	5/16	5/16	3/8

So $\mathcal{L}(C_2 \circ C_1) = \frac{9}{8}$. As predicted by Theorem 2, we have $\frac{9}{8} \leq \frac{3}{2}$. □

Example 2. Let $\mathcal{X} = \mathcal{Y} = \{x_1, \ldots, x_n\}$ and R a random variable taking values in $\{0, 1\}$ with $p(R = 0) = p$ and $p(R = 1) = q$. Define a channel $\mathcal{X} \xrightarrow{C} \mathcal{Y}$ as follows: If $R = 0$, output a uniformly random $x \in \mathcal{X}$, if $R = 1$, output the input. The resulting channel matrix is

	x_1	x_2	$\ldots$	x_n
x_1	$q + p/n$	p/n	$\ldots$	p/n
x_2	p/n	$q + p/n$	$\ldots$	p/n
$\vdots$	$\vdots$	$\vdots$	$\vdots$	$\vdots$
x_n	p/n	p/n	$\ldots$	$q + p/n$

and so $\mathcal{L}(C) = qn + p$. In particular for $p = 0$ the leakage is maximal and for $p = 1$ minimal. □

The bound of Theorem 2 clearly does not hold in general without the assumption that C_1 and C_2 are independent. For example, let $\mathcal{X} = \mathcal{Y} = \mathcal{Z} = \{0, 1\}$ and R

a uniformly distributed random variable on $\{0,1\}$. Let C_1 be the channel that adds r (mod two) to the input and let C_2 be the channel that adds the *same* value r as C_1 to the input. (So in fact $C_1 = C_2$ and C_1, C_2 are not independent.) The channel matrix of C_1 is

	0	1
0	1/2	1/2
1	1/2	1/2

and the leakage of C_1 is the minimal value 1 (cf. Proposition 1). However, because we are computing modulo 2, the composition $C_2 \circ C_1$ simply outputs the input, i.e. the channel matrix of $C_2 \circ C_1$ equals

	0	1
0	1	0
1	0	1

and the leakage of $C_2 \circ C_1$ is the maximal value 2. This shows that without the assumption of independence, the composition of two channels can have maximal leakage even if the individual channels have minimal leakage.

4.2 Product of Channels

Definition 4 (Product of Channels). *Let $\mathcal{X} \xrightarrow{C} \mathcal{Y}$ and $\mathcal{X} \xrightarrow{C'} \mathcal{Y}'$ be two channels. Then we can define the product channel $\mathcal{X} \xrightarrow{C \cdot C'} \mathcal{Y} \times \mathcal{Y}'$ by*

$$C \cdot C'|x = (C|x, C'|x)$$

for $x \in \mathcal{X}$.

Theorem 3. *Let $\mathcal{X} \xrightarrow{C} \mathcal{Y}$ and $\mathcal{X} \xrightarrow{C'} \mathcal{Y}'$ be two independent channels. Then* $\max\{\mathcal{L}(C), \mathcal{L}(C')\} \leq \mathcal{L}(C \cdot C') \leq \mathcal{L}(C)\mathcal{L}(C')$.

Proof. We have

$$p(C \cdot C'|x = (y, y')) = p(C|x = y, C'|x = y') = p(C|x = y)p(C'|x = y)$$

and so

$$\begin{aligned}\mathcal{L}(C \cdot C') &= \sum_{y,y'} \max_x (p(C|x = y)p(C'|x = y')) \\ &\leq \sum_{y,y'} \max_x p(C|x = y) \max_x p(C'|x = y')) \\ &= \mathcal{L}(C)\mathcal{L}(C').\end{aligned}$$

If we fix $y \in \mathcal{Y}$ and and choose $x_0 \in \mathcal{X}$ such that $\max_x p(C|x = y) = p(C|x_0 = y)$ then

$$\sum_{y'} \max_x p(C|x = y)p(C'|x = y') \geq \sum_{y'} p(C|x_0 = y)p(C'|x_0 = y')$$
$$= p(C|x_0 = y) = \max_x p(C|x = y).$$

Consequently

$$\mathcal{L}(C \cdot C') = \sum_{y,y'} \max_x (p(C|x = y)p(C'|x = y'))$$
$$\geq \sum_y \max_x p(C|x = y) = \mathcal{L}(C).$$

The proof that $\mathcal{L}(C \cdot C') \geq \mathcal{L}(C')$ is similar. □

Definition 5 (Direct Product of Channels). *Let $\mathcal{X} \xrightarrow{C} \mathcal{Y}$ and $\mathcal{X}' \xrightarrow{C'} \mathcal{Y}'$ be two channels. Then we can define the direct product channel $\mathcal{X} \times \mathcal{X}' \xrightarrow{C \times C'} \mathcal{Y} \times \mathcal{Y}'$ by*

$$(C \times C')|(x, x') = (C|x, C'|x')$$

for $x \in \mathcal{X}$ and $x' \in \mathcal{X}'$.

Theorem 4. *Let $\mathcal{X} \xrightarrow{C} \mathcal{Y}$ and $\mathcal{X}' \xrightarrow{C'} \mathcal{Y}'$ be two independent channels. Then, $M(C \times C') = M(C) \otimes M(C')$ and $\mathcal{L}(C \times C') = \mathcal{L}(C) \cdot \mathcal{L}(C')$.*

Proof. Because C and C' are independent we have

$$p((C \times C')|(x, x') = (y, y')) = p(C|x = y, C'|x' = y') = p(C|x = y)p(C'|x' = y').$$

Thus $M(C \times C') = M(C) \otimes M(C')$ and

$$\max_{x,x'} p((C \times C')|(x, x') = (y, y')) = \max_x p(C|x = y) \cdot \max_{x'} p(C'|x' = y').$$

Therefore

$$\mathcal{L}(C \times C') = \sum_{y,y'} \max_{x,x'} p((C \times C')|(x, x') = (y, y'))$$
$$= \sum_y \max_x p(C|x = y) \cdot \sum_{y'} \max_{x'} p(C'|x' = y') = \mathcal{L}(C) \cdot \mathcal{L}(C').$$

□

Example 3. Let $\mathcal{X} = \{x_1, x_2, x_3\}, \mathcal{Y} = \{y_1, y_2, y_3\}$, $\mathcal{X}' = \{x'_1, x'_2, x'_3\}, \mathcal{Y}' = \{y'_1, y'_2, y'_3\}$. Let $\mathcal{X} \xrightarrow{C_1} \mathcal{Y}$ and $\mathcal{X}' \xrightarrow{C_2} \mathcal{Y}'$ be two independent channels with channel matrices

C_1	y_1	y_2	y_3
x_1	1/2	1/4	1/4
x_2	1/4	1/2	1/4
x_3	1/4	1/4	1/2

C_2	y'_1	y'_2	y'_3
x'_1	1/2	1/4	1/4
x'_2	1/4	1/2	1/4
x'_3	1/4	1/4	1/2

We have $\mathcal{L}(C_1) = \mathcal{L}(C_2) = \frac{1}{2} + \frac{1}{2} + \frac{1}{2} = \frac{3}{2}$. The direct product channel matrix $M(C_1 \times C_2) = M(C_1) \otimes M(C_2)$ is

	(y_1, y'_1)	(y_1, y'_2)	(y_1, y'_3)	(y_2, y'_1)	(y_2, y'_2)	(y_2, y'_3)	(y_3, y'_1)	(y_3, y'_2)	(y_3, y'_3)
(x_1, x'_1)	1/4	1/8	1/8	1/8	1/16	1/16	1/8	1/16	1/16
(x_1, x'_2)	1/8	1/4	1/8	1/16	1/8	1/16	1/16	1/8	1/16
(x_1, x'_3)	1/8	1/8	1/4	1/16	1/16	1/8	1/16	1/16	1/8
(x_2, x'_1)	1/8	1/16	1/16	1/4	1/8	1/8	1/8	1/16	1/16
(x_2, x'_2)	1/16	1/8	1/16	1/8	1/4	1/8	1/16	1/8	1/16
(x_2, x'_3)	1/16	1/16	1/8	1/8	1/8	1/4	1/16	1/16	1/8
(x_3, x'_1)	1/8	1/16	1/16	1/8	1/16	1/16	1/4	1/8	1/8
(x_3, x'_2)	1/16	1/8	1/16	1/16	1/8	1/16	1/8	1/4	1/8
(x_3, x'_3)	1/16	1/16	1/8	1/16	1/16	1/8	1/8	1/8	1/4

So $\mathcal{L}(C_1 \times C_2) = \frac{1}{4} + \frac{1}{4} + \frac{1}{4} + \frac{1}{4} + \frac{1}{4} + \frac{1}{4} + \frac{1}{4} + \frac{1}{4} + \frac{1}{4} = \frac{9}{4} = \mathcal{L}(C_1) \cdot \mathcal{L}(C_2)$. □

4.3 Iterative Composition of Channels

Finally, we consider the specific scenario of leakage in loops [11]. A looping construct can be decomposed into n iterations. For an initial value x, we consider the scenario where a protocol leaks the intermediate function value y at the end of iteration $i < n$. Let the final value at the end of iteration n be z. Because further iterations ($i+1$ onwards) only use y and not the initial value x to compute z, it is clear that an adversary who already knows y does not learn anything more about x by observing z. This is formalized in the following theorem.

Theorem 5. *Let $\mathcal{X} \xrightarrow{C_1} \mathcal{Y}$ and $\mathcal{Y} \xrightarrow{C_2} \mathcal{Z}$ be independent channels and $\mathcal{X} \xrightarrow{C} \mathcal{Y} \times \mathcal{Z}$ defined by $C = C_1 \cdot (C_2 \circ C_1)$. Then, $\mathcal{L}(C) = \mathcal{L}(C_1)$.*

Proof. We have

$$p(C|x = (y, z)) = p(C_1|x = y, C_2 \circ C_1|x = z) = p(C_1|x = y, C_2|y = z)$$
$$= p(C_1|x = y)p(C_2|y = z).$$

Therefore

$$\mathcal{L}(C) = \sum_{y,z} \max_x p(C|x = (y, z)) = \sum_y \max_x p(C_1|x = y) = \mathcal{L}(C_1).$$

□

5 Related Works

Statistical measures have long been used to quantify leakage of security protocols. The commonly used statistical measure for quantification is the notion of Shannon entropy [12]. To the best of our knowledge, [13] is the most recent and most related work in this direction. [13] gives leakage quantifications with respect to absolute leakage and rate of leakage of security protocols, and also presents compositionality results for both notions. Shannon entropy based measures have in the past been shown to be not so suitable for leakage quantification (See [14]). Recently, [8] also showed that Shannon entropy based measures are not suitable when the attacker attempts to guess the input value in one try. With respect to the compositionality results, the types of composition considered in both works are complementary. While [12] considers composition with respect to program semantics (e.g. sequential, parallel composition), our composition results are more tailored towards arithmetic functions on input/random variables.

With respect to studying leakage based on conditional entropy and the MAP rule, [5,15,16] are the most related to this work. While [15] studies approximating the MAP rule independent of the a priori distribution, [16] provides bounds for the same as a function of the input distribution. [5] proposes two statistical measures (additive and multiplicative) and compares their properties. We actually use the multiplicative statistical measure for leakage quantification in this work. This measure has the nice property that the leakage supremum coincides with leakage at the point of uniform distribution(See equation 1). This allows us to inherently take into account the a priori distribution as well while arguing about the leakage supremum of a protocol. None of the above works however give any compositionality results, which is one of the main contributions of this work.

6 Conclusion

This work addressed the need for precise leakage quantification of cryptographic operations. Recently, there has been a lot of emphasis in this area as people realize that perfectly secure protocols are more often than not inefficient performance wise to be usable in real-life scenarios. In this context, we first showed how statistical leakage quantification can be applied in practice for a concrete cryptographic operation. We worked out in detail the upper and lower leakage bounds of the multiplicative hiding primitive. The bounds allow assessing the suitability of the primitive based on the given application's characteristics. We then extended the leakage bounds to arbitrary compositions of channels. We believe that the ability to reason about leakages of compositions of channels has wide scale implications with respect to analyzing the security of complex cryptographic protocols.

Acknowledgement

We would like to thank Berry Schoenmakers for his helpful suggestions which helped to improve the work in this paper considerably.

References

1. Ryan, P.Y.A., McLean, J., Millen, J., Gilgor, V.: Noninterference, who needs it? In: Proceedings of the IEEE Computer Security Foundations Workshop, pp. 237–238 (2001)
2. SecureSCM project, http://www.securescm.org/
3. Shamir, A.: How to share a Secret. Communications of the ACM 22(11), 612–613 (1979)
4. Ben-Or, M., Goldwasser, S., Wigderson, A.: Completeness theorems for non-cryptographic fault-tolerant distributed computations. In: Proceedings of the Annual Symposium on Theory of Computing (STOC), pp. 1–10 (1988)
5. Braun, C., Chatzikokolakis, K., Palamidessi, C.: Quantitative notions of leakage for one-try attacks. In: Proceedings of the Conference on Mathematical Foundations of Programming Semantics (MFPS), pp. 75–91 (2009)
6. Kerschbaum, F., Biswas, D., de Hoogh, S.: Performance comparison of secure comparison protocols. In: Proceedings of the International Workshop on Business Processes Security (BPS), pp. 133–136 (2009)
7. Nishide, T., Ohta, K.: Multiparty computation for interval, equality, and comparison without bit-decomposition protocol. In: Okamoto, T., Wang, X. (eds.) PKC 2007. LNCS, vol. 4450, pp. 343–360. Springer, Heidelberg (2007)
8. Smith, G.: Adversaries and information leaks (Tutorial). In: Barthe, G., Fournet, C. (eds.) TGC 2007 and FODO 2008. LNCS, vol. 4912, pp. 383–400. Springer, Heidelberg (2008)
9. Kiltz, E., Leander, G., Malone-Lee, J.: Secure Computation of the Mean and Related Statistics. In: Kilian, J. (ed.) TCC 2005. LNCS, vol. 3378, pp. 283–302. Springer, Heidelberg (2005)
10. Toft, T.: Solving Linear Programs Using Multiparty Computation. In: Dingledine, R., Golle, P. (eds.) FC 2009. LNCS, vol. 5628, pp. 90–107. Springer, Heidelberg (2009)
11. Malacaria, P.: Assessing security threats of looping constructs. In: Proceedings of the Annual ACM SIGPLAN-SIGACT symposium on Principles of Programming Languages (POPL), pp. 225–235 (2007)
12. Shannon, C.E.: Communication theory of secrecy systems. Bell System Technical Journal 27, 379–423 (1948)
13. Boreale, M.: Quantifying information leakage in process calculi. Information and Computation 207(6), 699–725 (2009)
14. Pliam, J.O.: On the incomparability of entropy and marginal guesswork in Brute-force attacks. In: Roy, B., Okamoto, E. (eds.) INDOCRYPT 2000. LNCS, vol. 1977, pp. 67–79. Springer, Heidelberg (2000)
15. Chatzikokolakis, K., Palamidessi, C., Panangaden, P.: Anonymity protocols as noisy channels. In: Montanari, U., Sannella, D., Bruni, R. (eds.) TGC 2006. LNCS, vol. 4661, pp. 281–300. Springer, Heidelberg (2007)
16. Chatzikokolakis, K., Palamidessi, C., Panangaden, P.: Probability of error in information-hiding protocols. In: Proceedings of the IEEE Computer Security Foundations Symposium (CSF), pp. 341–354 (2007)

Author Index

GPSR Compliance

The European Union's (EU) General Product Safety Regulation (GPSR) is a set of rules that requires consumer products to be safe and our obligations to ensure this.

If you have any concerns about our products, you can contact us on ProductSafety@springernature.com

In case Publisher is established outside the EU, the EU authorized representative is:

Springer Nature Customer Service Center GmbH
Europaplatz 3
69115 Heidelberg, Germany

Batch number: 10844611

Printed by Printforce, the Netherlands